THE FILM BUFF'S CHECKLIST OF MOTION PICTURES
(first edition)

Manufactured in the United States of America
First Printing, July 1979

For additional copies and information, write to:
HOLLYWOOD FILM ARCHIVE
8344 Melrose Avenue
Hollywood, Calif. 90069

Library of Congress Cataloging in Publication Data
Main entry under title:

The Film buff's checklist of motion pictures (1912-1979).

   Includes index.
   1. Moving-pictures--Catalogs. I. Baer, D. Richard.
PN1998.F52   791.43'0291'6   79-14820
ISBN 0-913616-03-6
ISBN 0-913616-04-4 lib bdg.

0 9 8 7 6 5 4 3 2

CONTENTS

ACKNOWLEDGEMENTS

Photos, information and press materials supplied courtesy of ABC-TV, Allied Artists, American International, Avco-Embassy, CBS-TV, Columbia Pictures, Crown International, M-G-M, Monarch, NBC-TV, New World, Paramount, rbc films, RKO, Sanrio, Twentieth Century-Fox, United Artists, Universal Pictures, Walt Disney Productions, Warner Bros., and others.

To list the names of some of the many people who have helped us presents the possibility that we may forget someone important, but if we have, please forgive us. Although it's virtually impossible to acknowledge all of the assistance we've received in the compiling of information in this book, our special thanks is extended to Dennis Bade, Alexander H. Chorney, George Crittenden, Carol Cullen, Bob Epstein, Filmex, Todd French, Sam Gill, John Hall, Vernon Harbin, Walter E. Hurst, Marvin Jones, Arthur Knight, Walt Lee, Felice Nelson, Buddy Pepper, Rodney Recore, Sidney Shrager, John W. Slater, Tony Slide, David R. Smith, Mark Wanamaker, John V. Watson, Adrian Weiss, Steve Weiss, Murray Weissman, Tim Wohlgemuth,

and

The Academy of Motion Picture Arts and Sciences

FOREWORD

Welcome to **THE FILM BUFF'S CHECKLIST.** At long last we've finally published a revised and expanded version of the 1972 book **THE FILM BUFF'S BIBLE.** To readers and users of that book who have been imploring us for years to put out an updated edition, we can only promise to do so more often in the future.

The new book contains information compiled through June, 1979, and includes titles of a number of major films to be released through the end of 1979 (though a few of these may be delayed until 1980); naturally, there are no running times or ratings on many of the unreleased films as this book goes to press, and some of the yet-to-be released films may still undergo title changes (for example, had this book been published earlier, **Walk Proud** would have been listed as "Gang!").

We now list some 19,000 alphabetized titles, and that includes many pre-1972 films we had missed in the old edition. This book has more alternate titles (and these are now listed alphabetically along with the primary titles, instead of in a separate appendix as before), and lists many more original titles of foreign films, including a significant number not given in other reference sources.

As a practical matter, no popular film reference can list **all** of the movies made in the world in the past six decades; such a reference would have to contain hundreds of thousands of titles, most of which would be of little use to our readers. So we've had to be a bit selective, but 19,000 is a large number, and hopefully it covers virtually every popular feature available in the U.S. It also covers many movies made for TV, foreign films, shorts and silent films.

A number of readers wrote and gave us the titles of films they though we should list, and we accepted most of their suggestions. There may still be a few significant films we should include, so write to us if you feel there's something important we've left out.

By the way, it's not that we dislike our former title "The Film Buff's Bible" or that we've changed the book's content so much that we felt we had to retitle it. We simply decided that this book is much more of a checklist by comparison to a much larger reference we're now compiling. It won't be able to contain quite as many titles — it'll probably have some 6,000 to 8,000 of the most highly regarded and significant movies — but each entry will include a detailed cast list (with who played what role), production credits, plot, literary source, production and historical notes, and most of the vital statistics found in **THE FILM BUFF'S CHECKLIST.** How soon? There's still quite a bit of work to be done, with checking and re-checking for mistakes, but it's progressing steadily. The finished volume will be called *The Film Buff's Bible.*

NOTES

Okay, you got the book in order to look up information about movies, not to read these notes first, so go ahead and enjoy yourself with the movies section. Still, the front of the book is the most logical place to put explanations about what's in it, and almost every user eventually needs to know some things that are not obvious about information in the main text of the book, so please read these notes before you write to us saying that there's something you don't understand about the book's content. We do answer most legitimate questions of that nature (if accompanied by a self-addressed stamped envelope), but we'd rather not have to send back our form letter which says, "Please read the NOTES section on page _____ at the front of the book."

TITLES. Titles are alphabetized word by word rather than letter by letter; thus **I Walk the Line** comes before **I'd Rather Be Rich,** which comes ahead of **Idaho Transfer.** Abbreviated words are treated as if they were spelled out (e.g., **Dr. No** is alphabetized as "Doctor No"). Initials are usually treated as one-letter words, so **T.R. Baskin** comes at the beginning of the titles starting with "t," but initials which never take periods (such as **FM** or **WUSA**) are treated as a whole word. Groups of initials which are understood to spell a word (like **M*A*S*H** and **F.I.S.T.**) are treated as a whole word. Since the abbreviation for Federal Bureau of Investigation is not used consistently in movie titles (sometimes it's "F.B.I." — other times "FBI"), we have arbitrarily treated all occurrences of it as a whole word. The abbreviation "Mrs." is always alphabetized immediately after entries beginning with "Mr." (or "Mister"), and when movies are made with "Ms." as the first word of the title, they will come immediately after the "Mrs." titles.

Occasionally we find a reason to place a title slightly out of alphabetical order. Dates as the last word of a title are arranged with the lower numbers first, so **Hit Parade of 1947** precedes **Hit Parade of 1951.** However, dates at the beginning of a title are treated as if they were spelled out, so **1984** comes before **1900.** Where we otherwise arbitrarily place a title other than alphabetically, we normally leave a note to that effect, as in the case of **'Til We Meet Again** being alphabetized as **Till We Meet Again.**

English articles (a, an, the) preceding a title are placed last following a comma, and are disregarded for purposes of alphabetizing. The same is done with foreign language articles, although when the French *un* and the Italian or Spanish *uno* are used as the number "1" at the beginning of a title, they would be alphabetized by those words; another exception is the Spanish *EL*, which is often an integral part of a name such as **El Cid**, which would be alphabetized by the first word.

Our normal policy is to list the primary title of a film as it appears on the screen. **Birdman of Alcatraz** is the correct title of the film sometimes known as "Bird Man of Alcatraz." However, when a movie is extremely well known by its publicity title, we sometimes list that title as our primary title, with a note that a different title was shown on screen. Apparently **Ruby Gentry** (1953) was originally titled **Ruby,** but almost everyone knows it by the two-word title, and the movie **The Secret of Dorian Gray** was so widely publicized as **Dorian Gray** that virtually all reference sources, including ours, list it by the latter title.

Once a theatrical film comes to television, it may be given a different title; such films are seldom shown theatrically again — even so, our policy is to make the primary listing under the original theatrical title, with the appropriate cross reference.

There's not much we can do about mistakes made in newspaper TV logs; sometimes a local station gives the paper the wrong information, so you may not even know whom to blame. It's common to see a two-word title like **Horse Feathers** contracted to read "Horsefeathers" and vice-versa. There's little problem when **Atlantis, the Lost Continent** is listed as "Atlantis" but if the title **The D.A. — Conspiracy to Kill** is shortened to "Conspiracy to Kill," that puts it in a different place alphabetically. Not much confusion is caused when **Lady Without Passport** is mistakenly listed as "Lady Without A Passport," but we've also seen cases in which it takes an extensive knowledge of movie titles to know a mistake has been made in the listed title — we've seen **Meet Dr. Christian** listed as "Meet Mr. Christian," and **Father Goose** is sometimes given as "Mother Goose." If we've made any errors ourselves, we'd certainly appreciate being notified about them.

ALTERNATE TITLES. We sometimes wish there was a mandatory minimum fine of $150,000 assessed against anyone who changes a movie title (except for translating from one language to another).

Since a film's title can often be a major liability in marketing it, distributors frequently experiment with different titles in hope that audiences will be attracted by a more appealing title.

A "primary title" is one under which we list all of the basic information for a film — distributor, running time, cast, rating, etc. Many of these have alternate titles listed at the bottom of the entry. English language alternate titles are cross referenced throughout the book, and each cross reference carries the primary title to which it applies. Following are brief explanations of some of the major categories of alternate titles:

- Original title means that the primary title is not the one under which the film was originally shown. British films often have their titles changed when brought to the

U.S., as do most foreign language films; in most of these cases, we have used the U.S. title as the primary title. If the original title is a foreign language title, it is generally not alphabetically cross referenced unless it is famous or otherwise very significant.

- **British title** almost invariably means that the film was not of British origin (except in cases of British/U.S. co-productions), but that it was shown in Great Britain under the title so listed. Many such older films of U.S. origin are now known in Britain by their original titles.

- **TV title** is one used for television showings; for example, **11 Harrowhouse** (1974) was called **Anything for Love** when first shown on U.S. television.

- **Screen title** means that the title actually seen on the screen is different from the primary title we have given. We generally try to make the primary title listing the same as the screen title, but occasionally we think that we have a good reason not to do so. For example, the movie known to almost everyone as **Dr. Strangelove** has a much longer screen title.

- **Publicity title** means that to the best of our knowledge it has never been the on-screen title in theatrical showings in the U.S. For example, the British film **The Drum** (1938) was widely publicized as "Drums" in the U.S., but "Drums" has probably never appeared as the title on any print.

- **Title translation** can indicate that the title so listed is a title under which it was actually shown in the U.S., but only if the title is shown in ALL CAPITALS; otherwise, it's simply the English translation of the foreign primary title of the entry. Translations are also sometimes given in italics within parentheses following foreign language alternate titles; we believe the vast majority of these translations to be accurate, but would appreciate being advised of any errors or significant omissions.

- **Alternate title** is perhaps the least explanatory of the title types, but it means that, for whatever reason, we did not classify it in one of the more specific categories.

- **Common title error** means that the title is erroneously listed that way often enough for us point out that it's wrong. For example, the movie **The Phenix City Story** is often incorrectly spelled "The Phoenix City Story."

YEAR. The year shown is the one in which the film was released, not necessarily the year the film was completed. For foreign films, we have tried to give the year released in the country of origin rather than the year of first showing in the U.S., but occasionally only the latter information is available.

It's sometimes difficult to tell just when a film was released. Film festival showings count as a release. So do Academy Award qualifying runs (this means exhibition for a week in Los Angeles, even though the film is not shown anywhere else until the next year). Films are sometimes test marketed or sneak previewed well before publicized release takes place. Occasionally, American movies are released first in Great Britain or other countries before they are publicly shown here. Even the copyright records don't always give the correct year of release. And we've been known to make mistakes ourselves — we appreciate these being called to our attention.

DISTRIBUTORS (see also the Selected Companies Guide at the back of the book). Ideally, we have given the original American theatrical distributor for feature films listed. For TV movies, we should give the television distributor, but sometimes only the name of the network that first telecast it is available (or sometimes just the production company).

Of course, the original distributor is frequently not the current one. Sometimes a film is handled by more than one distributor simultaneously. Films are often handled by the original distributor only on a temporary basis, with rights reverting to the production company after a certain period of time; this is the case with virtually all pre-1951 United Artists films. Distributors have been known to sell large numbers of their films (the usual reason is that they need the money); this happened with most of Paramount's pre-1949 sound films (which are now owned by MCA/Universal) and Warner Bros.' pre-1950 films (which are now owned by United Artists). Companies sometimes merge, as in the case of Warner Bros. and Seven Arts. Companies sometimes go out of the film distribution business or out of business altogether; this is not too great a problem when most or all of their rights are sold to the same successor in interest, but can be an enormous headache for someone trying to determine a film's ownership when a bankrupt company's films are scattered to the winds, so to speak. There are companies which changed their names, sometimes for purposes of reorganization, but in other cases perhaps just to change their image; for example, Allied Artists was once known as Monogram Pictures. And finally there are those companies which operated subsidiary releasing companies, mainly for "semi-legitimate" films in the mid-1960s before R-rated films became generally acceptable; for M-G-M, it was Premier Pictures; for 20th Century-Fox, it was International Classics; and for Columbia, it was Royal Films International. (However, you should not assume that all films released by those subsidiary companies were of the "semi-legitimate" type.)

Throughout the main text of this book, where we know a listed distributor to have a successor in interest, we have put the successor's name in brackets [ ] following the original company's name. However, this does not necessarily mean that the bracketed name currently distributes that film. For example, First National merged with Warner Bros. in the late 1930s, but most or all those films were later sold to United Artists.

Foreign films tend to compound most of the above problems since the actual "original" distributors are usually foreign companies which lease rights to American companies for a few years, or the foreign company sometimes tries to do the American distribution itself. Sometimes there is no theatrical distributor for the U.S.; a film may simply be brought directly to American TV.

Film rights can be "fragmented," with one company owning theatrical rights, another owning TV rights, and yet another owning non-theatrical rights. New technologies are bringing about new classes of rights, such as cable TV rights and home-use rights. And all of these can be restricted to certain territories and limited time periods. Needless to say, the rights situation for any particular film can become extremely complicated.

It would be extremely helpful if someone would maintain and constantly update a directory of movie rights. We might even do it ourselves someday, but for the time being, we've prepared a Selected Companies Guide (at the back of this book) which hopefully will be of some value to people trying to locate current rights to movies.

COLOR/B&W.

We have chosen to designate all films as either **Color** or **B&W** (for black & white). That's the least complicated way of doing it, but you should be aware that there are other possibilities.

In the silent days and early sound era, many films were tinted, sometimes in different colors to convey a certain mood to the scene being shown, but all these are listed here as **B&W**.

There are also films which are mostly black & white which have color sequences. One such case is **Putney Swope** (1969), which has several brief color scenes (representing TV commercials). Another is **The Secret Garden** (1949), which has some slightly longer color scenes. However, in both cases, color constitutes only a small fraction of the film's footage, and films of this nature are designated as **B&W**.

For a movie to be listed as **Color,** it must have *substantial* color footage; we haven't decided upon an exact percentage of the running time, but it's probably somewhere between 20% and 40%.

Sometimes a movie is available both in color and black & white; these cases are listed as **Color.** However, if a film was shot in color but released only in black & white, it is listed as **B&W**. There are probably films which were once available in color but exist now only in black & white; we don't know of any for certain (and contrary to general belief, the 1935 Technicolor film **Becky Sharp** still exists in the vastly inferior Cinecolor process), but even if we did, we would still list them as **Color** for historical purposes.

RUNNING TIME.

In most cases, this is the running time in minutes of the most popular version; occasionally the number of reels is given for silent films. Determining the most popular running time can often be a problem for various reasons:

- Overlong films are sometimes cut after the initial release when the degree of audience boredom has been determined; we try to give the general release length.

- Foreign films are often drastically trimmed when brought to the U.S., sometimes for no clear-cut reason. Even so, we try to give the U.S. running time. In the 1930s and 1940s, many British films brought to the U.S. were cut by 10-20%; for most of these films, the U.S. time is shown. In the case of a few more popular British films that were cut, the original versions are now available, and our policy in such cases is to list the original time, but we have not been able to be entirely consistent in doing this.

- There are a few films for which no complete version exists. This is especially true of silent films, which were generally woefully neglected in the early days of sound films, and the nitrate negatives of many films hopelessly deteriorated, but eventually some such films were restored by assembling them from parts of existing prints. Erich Von Stroheim's **Foolish Wives** (1922) is one example of this having been done. Other classic cases of partially lost films are **Intolerance** (1916) and **Metropolis** (1926).

- Television? Most people who watch movies on TV know what can happen to movies left to the mercy of an editor who has to put a 110 minute (or longer) film into a 90 minute time slot with commercials. It's much easier to cut off the first 20 or 30 or 40 minutes of a film than to worry about whether viewers might appreciate it if more selective editing were done. And if it's a matter of showing a key scene or getting in an extra used car commercial, we don't have to tell anyone which one they'll be likely to see. Some independent stations frequently break into the middle of a heavy scene or a line of dialog for commercials, and a few are notorious for even leaving the film running during the commercials (!) so you wonder why there's been a strange shift in the action when the station returns to the movie.

There are also those strange cases of television actually *adding* footage to films, sometimes shooting new opening sequences for the story. Also, a network may sell so many commercial spots for a major motion picture's first run on TV that it's necessary to pad it with new scenes or outtakes from the original filming. This was done with both **King Kong** (1976) and **Airport '77** (1977).

We see more and more of the practice of showing parts of a picture on two or even three different days. Don't you appreciate the network's concern for keeping the public informed about events of momentous importance when they omit a half-hour of the second day to show the

President making a speech which can be seen on the other channels? And surely no right-minded citizen could fault the censors for blipping all of those shocking words and cutting the indecent scenes which would undoubtedly corrupt the moral fiber of every eight-year-old child watching the movies telecast after midnight.

COUNTRY.

Determination of a film's country was once a very simple matter. Italian films, for example, were made in Italy by Italian production companies and Italian production personnel, with Italian actors speaking the Italian language. Nowadays, the country in which a film is made, the nationality of the production company, the filmmakers, and the actors may all be different; movie soundtracks may have dialog in more than one language, and there may be different language versions of the same film. What to do?

The almost universal practice among film references is to regard a film's nationality as the nationality of its production company. Or companies — sometimes there are several, and this means that the country of each production company should be listed in the approximate order of importance (to the film), so as a general rule, the first country listed usually indicates the primary language of dialog in the film.

It may seem odd for pictures like **The Three Musketeers** (1974) and **The Four Musketeers** (1975) to be called Panamanian, but that designation is correct. In cases such as those, where a foreign nationality is shown for an English-language film, we try to clarify matters a bit by the notations "English language" or "English version" (the latter meaning that there is also a version in another language). These notations mean that the actors actually *speak* English in the film; if the movie is merely dubbed in English, we usually make no indication of that fact.

CAST.

If given the choice of having just one piece of information about a film, most people will want to know the leading actors, so that's what we've put on almost every film. Usually we've given the two or three most important names; occasionally more or less are appropriate. For certain kinds of films — cartoons, documentaries, compilations, etc. — there are no actors, or actors are unimportant, so we've given the director's name on those films (or producer, if there is no director).

There are cases of father and son actors using the same name (e.g., Tyrone Power, Lon Chaney, Jason Robards); we usually use "Sr." and "Jr." to distinguish between them. There are also a number of cases in which two unrelated actors have the same name — William Holden, Robert Shaw and Roger Moore, to mention a few. This seldom presents a problem because in most of such cases, one actor was (or is) a minor player whose name would never appear among leading players; however, on

very rare occasions (like Tom Baker in **Angels Die Hard!**) it does happen, and in those cases, we put an asterisk (*) following the name if it is the one who is *less* well-known.

There are also actors and actresses who have used more than one name in films, so we've sometimes put a bit of additional information in parentheses (   ) with the name. For example, if you see the name **Charles Buchinsky (Bronson),** you can easily guess that the person billed as **Charles Buchinsky** in the movie was the one now called **Charles Bronson.**

ENTERTAINMENT RATINGS.

We rate all films we have seen on a 1 to 10 scale, 10 is highest. Since these, unlike all the other information, are a matter of value judgement, they naturally cause a certain amount of controversy — and confusion. Only by not printing the ratings could we avoid the controversy, and since a significant proportion of our readers find them valuable, to do so would deprive them of information they are seeking. Perhaps, however, by explaining what the ratings are and are **not**, we can avoid some of the confusion.

Boldface numerical ratings followed by an asterisk (*) represent the opinions of the executive and senior editors as to the *entertainment* value of each movie seen and rated by them. The ratings in parentheses represent the editors' estimates of ratings for films not yet seen. These estimates are variously based on reviews, reputation, popularity, intuition and other factors; naturally they tend to be less accurate than asterisked ratings in reflecting our judgement, but we find that when a film with an estimated rating is eventually assigned an asterisked rating, it usually is within one point of the estimate.

It's no sin for a film to make a profound sociological comment, expose government injustice or corruption, promote racial tolerance and/or international brotherhood, etc., but none of those qualities will necessarily make a film qualify for a high rating; neither do we necessarily assign negative ratings for expressing opposite points of view. Some people can reasonably argue that it's impossible to adequately evaluate a film's direction, casting, acting, production values, cinematography, script and story, etc. in a single number, but all the rating actually attempts to do is answer the basic question, "How was it?"

Between ratings 1 and 8, a film rated a whole number above another means it's about twice as good as the lower-rated film. Even a half-point, then, represents more than just a subtle difference in quality, and there can be substantial differences within a half-point range. There are no ratings of 8½ or 9½, and the 9 and 10 ratings do not indicate 100% quality increases as in the 1 to 8 range; rather, the ratings of 8, 9 and 10 are all varying degrees of excellence. The ratings have the following approximate meanings:

10 - Superb (perhaps not flawless).

9 - Outstanding.

8 - Excellent. Recommended for all movie watchers.

7 - Very Good. Definitely worth watching.

6 - Good. Worth going to see in a theatre, or at least worth watching on TV.

5 - Passable. Maybe worth watching on TV, or perhaps even worth staying to see in a theatre if you have some better reason to be there (like you already paid to see the other feature).

4 - Mediocre. Probably not worth watching.

3 - Inferior. Not worth watching.

2 - Poor. Definitely not worth watching.

1 - Terrible. Reserved for the thoroughly miserable, witless, stupefying garbage that is painful to watch.

There is no zero rating, but if there were, the prime candidates would be **Wind From the East, Cat's Play, The Creeping Terror** and **Blackenstein.**

Here's a list of films rated 7½ or higher (the first five in order of preference):

Rated 10:
CABARET (1972)
ELMER GANTRY (1960)

Rated 9:
MY FAIR LADY (1964)
MIDNIGHT COWBOY (1969)
WEST SIDE STORY (1961)

Rated 8:
ALFIE (1966)
CASABLANCA (1942)
DELIVERANCE (1972)
THE EXORCIST (1973)
THE GRADUATE (1967)
THE GODFATHER (1972)
JAWS (1975)
ONE, TWO, THREE (1961)
ROOM AT THE TOP (1958)
STAR WARS (1977)
TOM JONES (1963)
WHO'S AFRAID OF VIRGINIA WOOLF? (1966)

Rated 7½:
AMERICAN GRAFFITI (1973)
THE APPRENTICESHIP OF DUDDY KRAVITZ (1974)
BEN-HUR (1959)
BUTCH CASSIDY AND THE SUNDANCE KID (1969)
CLOSE ENCOUNTERS OF THE THIRD KIND (1977)
DR. STRANGELOVE (1964)
FIVE EASY PIECES (1970)
FRENCH CONNECTION II (1975)
LITTLE BIG MAN (1970)
MORGAN! (1966)
THE MUSIC MAN (1962)
PATHS OF GLORY (1957)
PILLOW TALK (1959)
PLANET OF THE APES (1968)
THE QUIET MAN (1952)
SOME LIKE IT HOT (1959)
THE TREASURE OF THE SIERRA MADRE (1948)
TWO FOR THE ROAD (1967)

We are aware that the preceding list has only one film each for John Ford and William Wyler, and no films of Charlie Chaplin, Howard Hawks, Laurence Olivier, D. W. Griffith, Orson Welles or Alfred Hitchcock. We can recognize praiseworthy achievements by all of these individuals, but we have no sacred cows or demi-gods. The list contains no foreign language films, but they're eligible, of course, we have several rated at 7 in the book. We also hear objections that our highest rated movies are too heavily represented by films released from 1960 to present. Film critics and scholars may cry "blasphemy," but we suspect there is far more agreement among most contemporary general filmgoing audiences with our philosophy of film entertainment ratings, which can be summed up in two brief sentences: *Each film must stand on its own merits in comparison to the films of all other periods and nationalities. The best movies of all time have been made since the late-1950s in the U.S. and Great Britain.* Filmmakers of the past may have had minds as good as those of today, but they certainly didn't have the same equipment, artistic freedom or creative environment. Foreign filmmakers may someday make films as good or better than what we now consider excellent, but very few of them have thus far demonstrated the capability of doing so.

Since we recognize that there are other significant schools of thought about film evaluation, let us briefly describe them, and concede that people with any of these points of view will have substantial disagreements with many of our ratings:

- The Classics School. These people would argue that films of the 1915-1950 period ought to be evaluated in relation to the era in which they were made, and that **The Birth of a Nation, The Gold Rush, Grand Hotel, Stagecoach** and **The Magnificent Ambersons** were some of the best films of their own time (and of all time). Some people would even ask us to consider as a mitigating factor the fact that moral taboos severly restricted all movies' language and subject matter to acceptability for viewing by children, but these circumstances are of little more than curious interest to modern filmwatchers.

-The Art House School. From our point of view, those of this philosophy seem to believe that the very best films are understandable only to those who have a higher level of awareness and the ability to derive profound meaning from abstract, esoteric concepts. The films they give the highest praise seem to be those exhibiting an involvement with human psychology and a deep-rooted concern for social justice (whatever that means). We have actually heard the argument that the reason we sometimes see only paralyzingly boring, hopelessly muddled plotless nonsense in foreign language films is because the best foreign directors (particularly those of the western European "new wave") are so far ahead of the best American directors in filmmaking ability that we can't realize how much better they are. The "art house" critics may not hate all boxoffice champions like **the Godfather, Jaws** and **Star Wars**, but they generally discount them as common entertainment for *hoi polloi* while hailing the likes of **Cries and Whispers, 8½** and **L'Avventura** as being among the truly great films. Perhaps those of us who prefer films with a beginning, a middle and an end will never really understand why.

- The Cinematic School. Cinema scholars might argue that the highest ratings should go to the movies that had the most significant, long-lasting effect upon future filmmaking. **Intolerance, Potemkin** and **Citizen Kane** are representative of films highly regarded in this category, though most of such films were indifferently received at the time of their original release, and are of little more than academic interest today.

- The Boxoffice Watchers. A statistical analysis (we haven't made one) would undoubtedly show some sort of positive relationship between our ratings and reported boxoffice receipts. This generally makes our ratings more useful than the opinions of most professional critics (especially the "art house" type) to exhibitors and TV programmers, but we still inevitably get questions like, "How can you possibly give the same rating to _____ and_____when one was seen by ten times as many people." Our best answer is that the ratings attempt more to reflect how people will feel about a movie *after* they see it than to attempt to predict *whether* people will see it; this means that the ratings presume (rightly or wrongly) that the potential viewer will not be persuaded to see or dissuaded from seeing a movie because of when it was made, the appeal of its cast names, its subject matter, its title, the amount of promotion given it, or any number of similar factors. Also, the type of audience must be considered; our ratings will usually be valued more highly by those who attend revival theatres near college campuses than, say, those who patronize southern drive-in theatres. (Then again, a film like **Smokey and the Bandit,** rated 5½, has far more appeal to the latter type of audience than **Women In Love,** rated 3½, a film with more college audience appeal.)

We realize that we can't always satisfy even the majority of users of this book. Hopefully, those who lament our giving a low rating to their favorite film will understand that the ratings are more for the benefit of those who have **not** seen a particular film than for those who have seen the same film and have an established opinion about it. Although we usually give considerable thought to each rating we assign, we sometimes realize that we were wrong or that a movie is not as good as (or is better than) we once thought it was. Since the 1972 *FILM BUFF'S BIBLE* was published, we have re-rated many films (usually downward, occasionally upward), and will continue to do so in the future as we watch new ones and re-watch old ones.

PHOTOS. Some film reference books print a photo of a scene for every movie listed in them. You can imagine how big this book would have to be if we tried to do that, so we've had to be a bit selective about the stills included here. We tried to choose scenes indicative of the nature of the films, and naturally the illustrated movies tend to be among the more well-known, popular and cinematically significent. Availability of good photos is a very important factor; some studios were more cooperative than others, and there are some highly significant movies for which either there are no quality stills or such stills are very rare. Even the alphabetical position of a film sometimes determines whether or not a still can be used; for example, we could have printed stills from both **Island of Lost Souls** and **The Island of Dr. Moreau,** but those titles appear too close together alphabetically (not to mention being based on the same literary work).

RESEARCH. Our main function at Hollywood Film Archive is to compile and publish widely useable movie reference information. However, people sometimes need specialized research done on subjects not adequately covered in any reference books. Among the projects we've undertaken at the request of various people or companies in the past:

- Determining films' rights and ownership status.
- Locating feature films on specified subject matters or films with certain types of scenes.
- Researching actors, actresses and production personnel about whom little or nothing has been published. However, it is our policy not to give out addresses and phone numbers of movie stars, and we don't forward fan mail.
- Researching the history of particular films, before, during and after production.
- Determining the historical, factual or technical accuracy of proposed story material for a film in production.

If you make a research request, please be specific as to what is wanted, what you already have (or know), what is *not* wanted and how thorough (or superficial) a job is desired.

There is no charge for us to consider a request, and if we decide we can undertake a research project, we'll let you know what the approximate charges will be. We often have a heavy workload, so it sometimes takes three to four weeks before we can begin to work on a research job; if it has to be done on an urgent (next working day) basis, a premium must be charged. All such requests should be sent (accompanied by a self-addressed stamped envelope) to the following address:

Research Service
Hollywood Film Archive
8344 Melrose Avenue
Hollywood, CA 90069

list of illustrations

-A-

A.B.C. MURDERS, THE (1966) see ALPHABET MURDERS, THE

A-HAUNTING WE WILL GO (1942) 20th Century-Fox. **B&W-68min.** Stan Laurel, Oliver Hardy ....(3)

a.k.a. CASSIUS CLAY (1970) United Artists. **Color-79min.** *(Documentary). Director:* William Cayton ....(5)

A NOUS LA LIBERTÉ (1932) Tobis. **B&W-95min.** *(French).* Raymond Cordy, Henri Marchand..3*

AARON LOVES ANGELA (1975) Columbia. **Color-99min.** Kevin Hooks, Irene Cara ....(4)

AARON SLICK FROM PUNKIN CRICK (1952) Paramount. **Color-95min.** Alan Young, Dinah Shore 3½*
British title: MARSHMALLOW MOON

ABANDON SHIP! (1957) Columbia. **B&W-95min.** *(British).* Tyrone Power, Mai Zetterling 5½*
Original title: SEVEN WAVES AWAY

ABANDONED (1949) Universal. **B&W-79min.** Dennis O'Keefe, Gale Storm 3½*

ABBA -- THE MOVIE (1979) Warner Bros. **Color-   min.** ABBA..............

ABBOTT & COSTELLO GO TO MARS (1953) Universal. **B&W-77min.** Bud Abbott, Lou Costello 3*

ABBOTT & COSTELLO IN HOLLYWOOD (1945) M-G-M. **B&W-84min.** Bud Abbott, Lou Costello 4*

ABBOTT & COSTELLO IN THE FOREIGN LEGION (1950) Universal. **B&W-79min.** Bud Abbott, Lou Costello..........................3*

ABBOTT & COSTELLO IN THE NAVY (1941) see IN THE NAVY

ABBOTT & COSTELLO LOST IN ALASKA (1952) see LOST IN ALASKA

ABBOTT & COSTELLO MEET CAPTAIN KIDD (1952) Warner Bros. **Color-70min.** Bud Abbott, Lou Costello, Charles Laughton 3*

ABBOTT & COSTELLO MEET DR. JEKYLL AND MR. HYDE (1953) Universal. **B&W-77min.** Bud Abbott, Lou Costello, Boris Karloff 4*

ABBOTT & COSTELLO MEET FRANKENSTEIN (1948) Universal. **B&W-82min.** Bud Abbott, Lou Costello, Lon Chaney, Jr. 4½*
British title: MEET THE GHOSTS
Alternate British Title: ABBOTT AND COSTELLO MEET THE GHOSTS

ABBOTT & COSTELLO MEET THE INVISIBLE MAN (1951) Universal. **B&W-82min.** Bud Abbott, Lou Costello....................................4*

ABBOTT & COSTELLO MEET THE KEYSTONE KOPS (1955) Universal. **B&W-79min.** Bud Abbott, Lou Costello................................3½*

ABBOTT & COSTELLO MEET THE KILLER, BORIS KARLOFF (1949) Universal. **B&W-84min.** Bud Abbott, Lou Costello, Boris Karloff 4*

ABBOTT & COSTELLO MEET THE MUMMY (1955) Universal. **B&W-79min.** Bud Abbott, Lou Costello 3½*

ABBY (1974) American-International. **Color-89min.** William Marshall, Carol Speed ....(4)

ABDICATION, THE (1974) Warner Bros. **Color-103min.** *(U.S.-British).* Liv Ullmann, Peter Finch ....(4)

ABDUCTION (1975) Venture Distribution Co. **Color-100min.** Judith-Marie Bergan, David Pendleton ....(3)

ABDUCTION OF ST. ANNE, THE (1975) Quinn Martin Productions. **Color-75min.** *(Made for TV).* Robert Wagner, Kathleen Quinlan, William Windom 3*
Alternate title: THEY'VE KIDNAPPED ANNE BENEDICT

ABDUCTORS, THE (1957) 20th Century-Fox. **B&W-80min.** Victor McLaglen, George Macready..3*

ABDUCTORS, THE (1972) Joseph Brenner. **Color-95min.** Cheri Caffaro, William Grannel ....(1)

ABE LINCOLN IN ILLINOIS (1940) RKO. **B&W-110min.** Raymond Massey, Ruth Gordon 5*
British title: SPIRIT OF THE PEOPLE

ABIE'S IRISH ROSE (1928) Paramount. **B&W-116min.** *(Part-talking).* Charles Rogers, Nancy Carroll ....(3)

ABIE'S IRISH ROSE (1946) United Artists. **B&W-96min.** Joanne Dru, Richard Norris..(4)

ABILENE TOWN (1946) United Artists. **B&W-89min.** Randolph Scott, Ann Dvorak 3½*

ABOMINABLE DR. PHIBES, THE (1971) American-International. **Color-93min.** *(U.S.-British).* Vincent Price, Joseph Cotten 5*
Publicity title: DR. PHIBES

ABOMINABLE SNOWMAN OF THE HIMALAYAS, THE (1957) 20th Century-Fox. **B&W-83min.** *(British).* Peter Cushing, Forrest Tucker ..(4)
Original title: ABOMINABLE SNOWMAN, THE
TV title: ABOMINABLE SNOWMAN

ABOUT FACE (1952) Warner Bros. **Color-94min.** Gordon MacRae, Eddie Bracken..(3)

ABOUT MRS. LESLIE (1954) Paramount. **B&W-104min.** Shirley Booth, Robert Ryan 4*

ABOVE ALL LAWS (1948) see ADVENTURES IN SILVERADO

ABOVE ALL THINGS (1957) see FLOOD TIDE

ABOVE AND BEYOND (1952) M-G-M. **B&W-122min.** Robert Taylor, Eleanor Parker 5*

ABOVE SUSPICION (1943) M-G-M. **B&W-90min.** Joan Crawford, Fred MacMurray 5*

ABOVE US THE WAVES (1955) Republic. **B&W-99min.** *(British).* John Mills, John Gregson..(5)

ABRAHAM LINCOLN (1930) United Artists. **B&W-80min.** Walter Huston, Una Merkel 3*

ABROAD WITH TWO YANKS (1944) United Artists. **B&W-80min.** William Bendix, Helen Walker ....(4)

ABSENT-MINDED PROFESSOR, THE (1961) Buena Vista. **B&W-97min.** Fred MacMurray, Nancy Olson 5*

ABSINTHE (1929) see MADAME X

ACCATTONE! (1961) Brandon. **B&W-120min.** *(Italian).* Franco Citti, Franca Pasut 2½*
Translation title: The Sponger

ACCENT ON YOUTH (1935) Paramount. **B&W-77min.** Sylvia Sidney, Herbert Marshall..(5)

ACCIDENT (1967) Cinema 5. **Color-105min.** *(British).* Dirk Bogarde, Stanley Baker 3*

ACCIDENTAL DEATH (1963) Avco-Embassy. **B&W-57min.** *(British).* John Carson, Jacqueline Ellis ....(4)

ACCOMPLICES, THE (1959) Archway *(Brit.).* **B&W-93min.** *(Italian).* Sandro Luporini, Sandro Fizzotro ....(3)
Original title: INFERNO ADDOSSO, L'

ACCORDING TO MRS. HOYLE (1951) Monogram [Allied Artists]. **B&W-60min.** Spring Byington, Anthony Caruso ....(2)

ACCOUNT RENDERED (1957) J. Arthur Rank. **B&W-61min.** *(British).* Griffith Jones, Ursula Howells..(3)

ACCURSED, THE (1958) Allied Artists. **B&W-78min.** *(British).* Donald Wolfit, Robert Bray 4*
Original title: TRAITOR, THE

ACCUSED, THE (1948) Paramount. **B&W-101min.** Loretta Young, Robert Cummings..5½*

ACCUSED OF MURDER (1956) Republic. **Color-74min.** David Brian, Vera (Hruba) Ralston..(3)

ACE ELI AND RODGER OF THE SKIES (1973) 20th Century-Fox. **Color-92min.** Cliff Robertson, Pamela Franklin ....(4)

THE ACCUSED (1948). Detective Wendell Corey uses a model of the victim, Douglas Dick, to confront suspect Loretta Young.

ACE HIGH (1968) Paramount. **Color-122min.** (*Italian*). Eli Wallach, Terence Hill .... (3)
Original title: QUATTRO DELL'AVE MARIA, I
ACE IN THE HOLE (1951) Paramount. **B&W-112min.** Kirk Douglas, Jan Sterling **5½***
Alternate title: BIG CARNIVAL, THE
ACE UP YOUR SLEEVE (1975) *see* CRIME AND PASSION
ACES HIGH (1976) Cine Artists. **Color-114min.** (*British*). Malcolm McDowell, Christopher Plummer .... (5)
ACROSS 110th STREET (1972) United Artists. **Color-102min.** Anthony Quinn, Yaphet Kotto .... (4)
ACROSS THE BRIDGE (1957) J. Arthur Rank. **B&W-103min.** (*British*). Rod Steiger, David Knight **3***
Alternate title: ACROSS THE FORBIDDEN BRIDGE TO MEXICO
ACROSS THE GREAT DIVIDE (1977) Pacific International Enterprises. **Color-100min.** Robert Logan, Heather Rattray **4***
ACROSS THE PACIFIC (1942) Warner Bros. **B&W-97min.** Humphrey Bogart, Mary Astor **5***
ACROSS THE RIVER (1965) Debema Production. **B&W-85min.** Lou Gilbert, Kay Doubleday .... (4)
ACROSS THE WIDE MISSOURI (1951) M-G-M. **Color-78min.** Clark Gable, Ricardo Montalban .... (4)
ACT OF LOVE (1953) United Artists. **B&W-108min.** (*French-U.S., English language*). Kirk Douglas, Dany Robin **4***
ACT OF MURDER, AN (1948) Universal. **B&W-91min.** Fredric March, Florence Eldridge **5***
Original title: LIVE TODAY FOR TOMORROW
ACT OF THE HEART (1970) Universal. **Color-103min.** (*Canadian*). Genevieve Bujold, Donald Sutherland .... (5)
ACT OF VENGEANCE (1974) American-International. **Color-90min.** Jo Ann Harris, Peter Brown .... (3)
British title: VIOLATOR, THE
ACT OF VIOLENCE (1949) M-G-M. **B&W-82min.** Van Heflin, Robert Ryan **4***
ACT ONE (1963) Warner Bros. **B&W-110min.** George Hamilton, Jason Robards, Jr. **4***
ACTION FOR SLANDER (1938) United Artists. **B&W-83min.** (*British*). Clive Brook, Ann Todd .... (4)
ACTION IN ARABIA (1944) RKO. **B&W-75min.** George Sanders, Virginia Bruce **4***
ACTION IN THE NORTH ATLANTIC (1943) Warner Bros. **B&W-127min.** Humphrey Bogart, Raymond Massey **4***
ACTION MAN, THE (1967) H.K. Film Dist. **Color-95min.** (*French-Italian*). Jean Gabin, Robert Stack **4***
Original French title: SOLEIL DES VOYOUS, LE
ACTION OF THE TIGER (1957) M-G-M. **Color-93min.** (*British*). Van Johnson, Martine Carol .... (3)
ACTIVIST, THE (1969) Regional. **Color-86min.** Michael Smith, Leslie Gilbrum .... (3)
ACTORS AND SIN (1952) United Artists. **B&W-85min.** Edward G. Robinson, Marsha Hunt .... (5)
Screen title: ACTOR'S AND SIN
ACTRESS, THE (1953) M-G-M. **B&W-90min.** Spencer Tracy, Jean Simmons **4***
ADA (1961) M-G-M. **Color-108min.** Susan Hayward, Dean Martin **3½***
ADALEN '31 (1969) Paramount. **Color-115min.** (*Swedish*). Peter Schildt, Kerstin Tidelius .... (5)
ADAM AND EVALYN (1949) Universal. **B&W-92min.** (*British*). Stewart Granger, Jean Simmons .... (4)
Original title: ADAM AND EVELYNE
ADAM AND EVE (1956) William M. Horne. **Color-76min.** (*Mexican*). Carlos Baena, Christiane Martel .... (3)
Original title: ADAN Y EVA
ADAM AT SIX A.M. (1970) Nat'l General (for Cinema Center). **Color-100min.** Michael Douglas, Lee Purcell **4***
ADAM HAD FOUR SONS (1941) Columbia. **B&W-81min.** Ingrid Bergman, Warner Baxter **4½***
ADAM'S RIB (1923) Paramount. **B&W-106min.** (*Silent*). Milton Sills, Theodore Kosloff, Anna Q. Nilsson .... (4)
ADAM'S RIB (1949) M-G-M. **B&W-101min.** Spencer Tracy, Katharine Hepburn **5½***
ADAM'S WOMAN (1970) Warner Bros. **Color-115min.** (*Australian-U.S.*). Beau Bridges, Jane Merrow, James Booth, John Mills .... (3)
Alternate title: RETURN OF THE BOOMERANG

ADDING MACHINE, THE (1969) Regional. **Color-100min.** (*British-U.S.*). Milo O'Shea, Phyllis Diller **4***
ADDRESS UNKNOWN (1944) Columbia. **B&W-72min.** Paul Lukas, Carl Esmond .... (4)
ADELAIDE (1968) Sigma III. **Color-86min.** (*French*). Ingrid Thulin, Jean Sorel .... (3)
ADIOS AMIGO (1976) Atlas Films. **Color-87min.** Fred Williamson, Richard Pryor .... (4)
ADIOS, GRINGO (1965) Trans-Lux Distributing. **Color-95min.** (*Italian*). Montgomery Wood, Evelyn Stewart .... (1)
ADIOS, SABATA (1971) United Artists. **Color-106min.** (*Italian*). Yul Brynner, Dean Reed .... (2)
Original title: INDIO BLACK
ADMIRABLE CRICHTON, THE (1957) *see* PARADISE LAGOON
ADMIRAL WAS A LADY, THE (1950) United Artists. **B&W-87min.** Wanda Hendrix, Edmond O'Brien .... (3)
ADOPTED FATHER, THE (1933) *see* WORKING MAN, THE
ADORABLE CREATURES (1952) Continental [Walter Reade]. **B&W-106min.** (*French*). Daniel Gélin, Antonella Lualdi .... (4)
Original title: ADORABLES CREATURES
ADORABLE JULIA (1962) See-Art Films. **B&W-94min.** (*Austrian*). Lilli Palmer, Charles Boyer **4***
ADORABLE MENTEUSE (1962) Warner Bros. **B&W-110min.** (*French*). Marina Vlady, Macha Meril .... (3)
Translation title: Adorable Liar
ADRIFT (1970) MPO Films. **Color-108min.** (*Czechoslovakian-U.S.*). Rade Markovic, Milena Dravic .... (5)
Original title: TOUHA ZVANA ANADA (*A Longing Called Anada*)
ADULTERESS, THE (1958) Times Film Corp. **B&W-106min.** (*French*). Simone Signoret, Raf Vallone, Jacques Duby .... (4)
Original title: THERESE RAQUIN
ADVANCE TO THE REAR (1964) M-G-M. **B&W-97min.** Glenn Ford, Stella Stevens .... (4)
British title: COMPANY OF COWARDS?
ADVENTURE (1945) M-G-M. **B&W-126min.** Clark Gable, Greer Garson **4***
ADVENTURE IN BALTIMORE (1949) RKO. **B&W-89min.** Robert Young, Shirley Temple .... (4)
British title: BACHELOR BAIT
ADVENTURE IN CAPRI (1962) *see* PHONE RINGS EVERY NIGHT, THE
ADVENTURE IN DIAMONDS (1940) Paramount. **B&W-76min.** George Brent, Isa Miranda .... (4)
ADVENTURE IN MANHATTAN (1936) Columbia. **B&W-75min.** Jean Arthur, Joel McCrea .... (4)
British title: MANHATTAN MADNESS
ADVENTURE IN WASHINGTON (1941) Columbia. **B&W-85min.** Herbert Marshall, Virginia Bruce .... (3)
British title: FEMALE CORRESPONDENT
ADVENTURE ISLAND (1947) Paramount. **Color-67min.** Rory Calhoun, Paul Kelly .... (3)
ADVENTURE OF SHERLOCK HOLMES' SMARTER BROTHER, THE (1975) 20th Century-Fox. **Color-91min.** Gene Wilder, Madeline Kahn **4½***
Publicity title: SHERLOCK HOLMES' SMARTER BROTHER
ADVENTURER OF SEVILLE, THE (1954) **Color-90min.** (*Spanish*). Luis Mariano, Lolita Sevilla .... (3)
ADVENTURERS, THE (1951) *see* GREAT ADVENTURE, THE
ADVENTURERS, THE (1970) Paramount. **Color-191min.** Bekim Fehmiu, Candice Bergen, Leigh Taylor-Young **3***
ADVENTURES AT RUGBY (1940) *see* TOM BROWN'S SCHOOL DAYS
ADVENTURES IN INDO-CHINA (1961) American-International. **Color-85min.** (*French*). Jean Gaven, Dominique Wilms .... (2)
ADVENTURES IN SILVERADO (1948) Columbia. **B&W-75min.** William Bishop, Gloria Henry .... (4)
British title: ABOVE ALL LAWS
ADVENTURES OF A NOBLEMAN (1965) *see* SARAGOSSA MANUSCRIPT, THE
ADVENTURES OF A ROOKIE (1943) RKO. **B&W-64min.** Wally Brown, Alan Carney .... (4)
ADVENTURES OF A YOUNG MAN (1962) *see* HEMINGWAY'S ADVENTURES OF A YOUNG MAN
ADVENTURES OF ARSENE LUPIN, THE (1956) RKO. **Color-103min.** (*French*). Robert Lamoureux, O. E. Hasse .... (3)
ADVENTURES OF BULLWHIP GRIFFIN, THE (1967) Buena Vista. **Color-110min.** Roddy McDowall, Suzanne Pleshette .... (5)

Films are rated on a 1 to 10 scale, 10 is highest. **Boldface** ratings followed by an asterisk (*) are for films actually seen and rated by the executive and senior editors. All other ratings are estimates. (See Notes on Entertainment Ratings in the front section.)

ADVENTURES OF CAPTAIN FABIAN (1951) Republic. B&W-100min. Errol Flynn, Micheline Prelle (Presle)............................3½*

ADVENTURES OF CASANOVA (1948) Eagle Lion. B&W-83min. Arturo de Cordova, Turhan Bey..(3)

ADVENTURES OF CHICO (1938) Monogram [Allied Artists]. B&W-60min. (Documentary). Director: Stacy Woodward...................(4)

ADVENTURES OF DAVID GRAY (1932) see VAMPYR

ADVENTURES OF DON JUAN (1948) Warner Bros. Color-110min. Errol Flynn, Viveca Lindfors 4*
British title: NEW ADVENTURES OF DON JUAN, THE

ADVENTURES OF GALLANT BESS (1948) Eagle Lion. Color-73min. Cameron Mitchell, Audrey Long ....(3)

ADVENTURES OF GIL BLAS, THE (1955) Trans-America. Color-95min. (French). George Marchal, Susana Canales.....................(2)

ADVENTURES OF HAJJI BABA, THE (1954) 20th Century-Fox. Color-93min. John Derek, Elaine Stewart 3*

ADVENTURES OF HUCKLEBERRY FINN, THE (1939) M-G-M. B&W-90min. Mickey Rooney, Rex Ingram 4*
Alternate title: HUCKLEBERRY FINN

ADVENTURES OF HUCKLEBERRY FINN, THE (1960) M-G-M. Color-107min. Eddie Hodges, Archie Moore ....(5)
Alternate title: HUCKLEBERRY FINN

ADVENTURES OF ICHABOD AND MR. TOAD (1949) RKO (for Disney). Color-67min. (Cartoon). Director: Jack Kinney.....................5*
Publicity title: ICHABOD AND MR. TOAD
Alternate title: LEGEND OF SLEEPY HOLLOW, THE
Alternate title: MADCAP ADVENTURES OF MR. TOAD, THE

ADVENTURES OF JACK LONDON (1943) see JACK LONDON

ADVENTURES OF MANDERIN, THE (1949) Republic. B&W-82min. (Italian-French). Raf Vallone, Michele Philippe.................(3)
Original title: AVVENTURE DI MANDERIN, LE
British title: AFFAIR OF MADAME POMPADOUR, THE
Alternate title: CAPTAIN ADVENTURE

ADVENTURES OF MARCO POLO, THE (1938) United Artists. B&W-100min. Gary Cooper, Sigrid Gurie 4½*

ADVENTURES OF MARK TWAIN, THE (1944) Warner Bros. B&W-130min. Fredric March, Alexis Smith 5*

ADVENTURES OF MARTIN EDEN, THE (1942) Columbia. B&W-87min. Glenn Ford, Claire Trevor ....(5)
Alternate title: MARTIN EDEN

ADVENTURES OF MICHAEL STROGOFF (1937) see SOLDIER AND THE LADY

ADVENTURES OF MR. WONDERBIRD (1959) Lippert Productions. Color-70min. (French, Cartoon). Director: Pierre Grimault...(5)
Alternate title: CURIOUS ADVENTURES OF MR. WONDERBIRD

ADVENTURES OF NICK CARTER, THE (1972) MCA-TV. Color-73min. (Made for TV). Robert Conrad, Shelley Winters, Brooke Bundy, Broderick Crawford ....(4)

ADVENTURES OF QUENTIN DURWARD (1955) see QUENTIN DURWARD

ADVENTURES OF ROBIN HOOD, THE (1938) Warner Bros. Color-105min. Errol Flynn, Olivia de Havilland 5*

ADVENTURES OF ROBINSON CRUSOE (1954) United Artists. Color-90min. (Mexican, English language). Dan O'Herlihy, Jaime Fernandez..............................(6)
Alternate title: ROBINSON CRUSOE

ADVENTURES OF SADIE, THE (1954) 20th Century-Fox. Color-88min. (British). Joan Collins, Kenneth More ....(5)
Original title: OUR GIRL FRIDAY

ADVENTURES OF SCARAMOUCHE, THE (1963) Avco-Embassy. Color-98min. (French-Italian-Spanish). Gerard Barray, Michele Girardon ...(3)
French title: SCARAMOUCHE
Italian title: AVVENTURE DI SCARAMOUCHE
Spanish title: MASCARA DE SCARAMOUCHE, LA (Mask of Scaramouche)

ADVENTURES OF SHERLOCK HOLMES, THE (1939) 20th Century-Fox. B&W-85min. Basil Rathbone, Nigel Bruce 5*
British title: SHERLOCK HOLMES

ADVENTURES OF TARTU, THE (1943) M-G-M. B&W-103min. (British). Robert Donat, Valerie Hobson ....(4)
Alternate title: TARTU

ADVENTURES OF THE WILDERNESS FAMILY, THE (1976) Pacific International Enterprises. Color-94min. Robert F. Logan, Susan Damante Shaw ....(4)
British title: WILDERNESS FAMILY, THE

ADVENTURES OF TOM SAWYER, THE (1938) United Artists. Color-93min. Tommy Kelly, May Robson 4½*

ADVENTURES OF YOUNG DINK STOVER, THE (1950) see HAPPY YEARS, THE

ADVENTURESS, THE (1947) Eagle Lion. B&W-98min. (British). Deborah Kerr, Trevor Howard..............................5½*
Original title: I SEE A DARK STRANGER

ADVICE TO THE LOVELORN (1933) 20th Century-Fox. B&W-62min. Lee Tracy, Sally Blaine ....(4)

ADVISE AND CONSENT (1962) Columbia. B&W-139min. Henry Fonda, Walter Pidgeon 5*

AFFAIR, THE (1972) see THERE'S ALWAYS VANILLA

AFFAIR, THE (1972) Independent TV Corp (ITC). Color-92min. (Made for TV). Natalie Wood, Robert Wagner 2*

AFFAIR BLUM, THE (1949) Central Cinema Corp. B&W-90min. (German). Hans Christian Blech, Gisela Trowe ....(5)
Original title: AFFAIRE BLUM
British title: BLUM AFFAIR, THE

AFFAIR IN HAVANA (1957) Allied Artists. B&W-71min. John Cassavetes, Raymond Burr..............................(3)

AFFAIR IN MONTE CARLO (1952) Allied Artists. Color-75min. (British). Merle Oberon, Richard Todd ....(3)
Original title: 24 HOURS IN A WOMAN'S LIFE

AFFAIR IN RENO (1957) Republic. B&W-75min. John Lund, Doris Singleton ....(3)

AFFAIR IN TRINIDAD (1952) Columbia. B&W-98min. Rita Hayworth, Glenn Ford 3*

AFFAIR OF MADAME POMPADOUR, THE (1949) see ADVENTURES OF MANDERIN, THE

AFFAIR OF STATES, AN (1966) Teleworld. Color-94min. (W. German-French). Curt Jurgens, Lilli Palmer ....(3)
Original German title: ZWEI GIRLS VOM ROTEN STERN

AFFAIR OF SUSAN, THE (1935) Universal. B&W-70min. ZaSu Pitts, Hugh O'Connell ....(3)

AFFAIR OF THE SKIN, AN (1963) Zenith International. B&W-102min. Viveca Lindfors, Kevin McCarthy ....(4)

AFFAIR OF VILLA FIORITA, THE (1965) see BATTLE OF THE VILLA FIORITA, THE

AFFAIR TO REMEMBER, AN (1957) 20th Century-Fox. Color-119min. Cary Grant, Deborah Kerr 4*

AFFAIR WITH A KILLER (1967) International Classics [20th]. Color-90min. (Canadian). Stephen Young, Austin Willis.................(3)

AFFAIR WITH A STRANGER (1953) RKO. B&W-89min. Jean Simmons, Victor Mature..............................4*

AFFAIRS IN VERSAILLES (1954) see ROYAL AFFAIRS IN VERSAILLES

AFFAIRS OF CELLINI (1934) United Artists. B&W-80min. Fredric March, Constance Bennett.............................(5)

AFFAIRS OF DOBIE GILLIS, THE (1953) M-G-M. Color-74min. Bobby Van, Debbie Reynolds ....(4)

AFFAIRS OF DR. HOLL (1952) Associated British-Pathé [EMI]. B&W-88min. (German). Maria Schell, Dieter Borsche ....(3)
Original title: DOKTOR HOLL
Alternate title: DR. HOLL

AFFAIRS OF GERALDINE (1946) Republic. B&W-68min. Jane Withers, Jimmy Lydon..............................(3)

AFFAIRS OF JIMMY VALENTINE (1942) Republic. B&W-72min. Dennis O'Keefe, Ruth Terry..............................(4)
Alternate title: UNFORGOTTEN CRIME

AFFAIRS OF JULIE, THE (1957) Bakros-International. B&W-88min. (German). Lilo Pulver, Paul Hubschmid........................(3)
Original title(?): ZURCHER VERLOBUNG, DIE

AFFAIRS OF MARTHA, THE (1942) M-G-M. B&W-66min. Marsha Hunt, Richard Carlson..............................(4)
British title: ONCE UPON A THURSDAY

AFFAIRS OF MESSALINA (1952) Columbia. B&W-108min. (Italian). Memo Benassi, Maria Felix ....(4)
Alternate title: MESSALINA

AFFAIRS OF SALLY, THE (1950) see FULLER BRUSH GIRL, THE

AFFAIRS OF SUSAN, THE (1945) Paramount. B&W-110min. Joan Fontaine, George Brent ....(4)

AFFECTIONATELY YOURS (1941) Warner Bros. B&W-90min. Merle Oberon, Dennis Morgan ....(3)

AFRICA ADDIO (1966) Rizzoli Film. Color-120min. (Italian, Documentary). Director: Gualtiero Jacopetti......................(4)

AFRICA ADVENTURE (1954) RKO. Color-64min. (Documentary). Robert C. Ruark..............................(4)

Films are rated on a 1 to 10 scale, 10 is highest. **Boldface** ratings followed by an asterisk (*) are for films actually seen and rated by the executive and senior editors. All other ratings are estimates. (See Notes on Entertainment Ratings in the front section.)

AFRICA SCREAMS (1949) United Artists. **B&W-79min.** Bud Abbott, Lou Costello .... (3)

AFRICA - TEXAS STYLE! (1967) Paramount. **Color-109min.** *(British).* Hugh O'Brian, John Mills 4*

AFRICAN ADVENTURE (1971) Gold Key Entertainment. **Color-93min.** *(Documentary).* Producer: Marty Stouffer 4*

AFRICAN ELEPHANT, THE (1971) Nat'l General (for Cinema Center). **Color-92min.** *(Documentary).* Director: Simon Trevor 5*
British title: KING ELEPHANT

AFRICAN FURY (1951) see CRY, THE BELOVED COUNTRY

AFRICAN LION, THE (1955) Buena Vista. **Color-75min.** *(Documentary).* Director: James Algar .... (5)

AFRICAN MANHUNT (1955) Republic. **B&W-65min.** Myron Healy, Karen Booth .... (3)

AFRICAN QUEEN, THE (1951) United Artists. **Color-105min.** Humphrey Bogart, Katharine Hepburn 5½*

AFRICAN SAFARI (1969) Crown International. **Color-98min.** *(Documentary).* Director: Ron Shanin .... (5)
Original title: RIVERS OF FIRE AND ICE

AFRICAN TREASURE (1952) Monogram [Allied Artists]. **B&W-70min.** Johnny Sheffield, Laurette Luez .... (3)
British title: BOMBA AND THE AFRICAN TREASURE

AFTER MIDNIGHT (1950) see CAPTAIN CAREY, U.S.A.

AFTER MIDNIGHT WITH BOSTON BLACKIE (1943) Columbia. **B&W-64min.** Chester Morris, Richard Lane .... (3)
Alternate title: AFTER MIDNIGHT

AFTER OFFICE HOURS (1935) M-G-M. **B&W-75min.** Clark Gable, Constance Bennett .... (4)

AFTER THE BALL (1957) Romulus Films. **Color-89min.** *(British).* Laurence Harvey, Patricia Kirkwood .... (3)

AFTER THE DANCE (1935) Columbia. **B&W-61min.** Nancy Carroll, George Murphy .... (4)

AFTER THE FOX (1966) United Artists. **Color-103min.** *(Italian-U.S.-British).* Peter Sellers, Victor Mature 3*
Foreign title: CACCIA ALLA VOLPE

AFTER THE THIN MAN (1936) M-G-M. **B&W-110min.** William Powell, Myrna Loy, James Stewart 4*

AFTER TONIGHT (1933) RKO. **B&W-71min.** Constance Bennett, Gilbert Roland .... (3)
British title: SEALED LIPS

AFTER YOU, COMRADE (1966) Continental [Walter Reade]. **Color-84min.** *(South African).* Jamie Uys, Bob Courtney .... (3)
Original title: ALL THE WAY TO PARIS

AGAINST A CROOKED SKY (1975) Doty-Dayton. **Color-89min.** Richard Boone, Stewart Petersen .... (4)

AGAINST ALL FLAGS (1952) Universal. **Color-83min.** Errol Flynn, Maureen O'Hara 4*

AGAINST THE WIND (1948) Eagle Lion. **B&W-95min.** *(British).* Robert Beatty, Simone Signoret .... (5)

AGATHA (1979) Warner Bros. **Color-98min.** Dustin Hoffman, Vanessa Redgrave 4½*

AGE OF CONSENT (1970) Columbia. **Color-98min.** *(Australian).* James Mason, Helen Mirren .... (4)

AGE OF ILLUSIONS (1965) Brandon. **B&W-97min.** *(Hungarian).* Andras Balint, Ilona Béres .... (3)

AGE OF INFIDELITY (1955) Janus Films. **B&W-84min.** *(Spanish-Italian).* Lucia Bose, Alberta Closas .... (4)
Alternate title: DEATH OF A CYCLIST

AGE OF THE MEDICI (1973) Brandon. **Color-252min.** *(Italian, English language).* Marcello Di Falco, Virgilio Gazzolo .... (4)

AGENT FOR H.A.R.M. (1966) Universal. **Color-84min.** Mark Richmond, Wendell Corey .... (3)

AGENT FOR PANIC (1964) T.A.F.C. **B&W-86min.** *(Foreign).* Brad Newman, Eric Douglas .... (3)

AGENT FOR THE PLAINTIFF, AN (1968) MCA-TV. **Color-74min.** *(Made for TV).* Gene Barry, Susan Saint James, Maurice Evans .... (4)

AGENT 8 3/4 (1964) Continental [Walter Reade]. **Color-98min.** *(British).* Dirk Bogarde, Sylva Koscina .... (5)
Original title: HOT ENOUGH FOR JUNE
Publicity title: AGENT 008 3/4

AGENT OF DOOM (1963) G.R.K. Films. **B&W-90min.** *(French).* Annette Stroyberg, Michel Le Royer .... (4)
Original title: UN SOIR . . . PAR HASARD *(One Night . . . By Accident)*

AGENT 3S3/PASSPORT TO HELL (1965) Four Star. **Color-101min.** *(Italian-French-Spanish).* George Ardisson, Georges Riviere .... (3)
Original Italian title: AGENTE 3S3, PASSAPORTO PER L'INFERNO
Spanish title: AGENTE 3S3 - PASAPORTE PARA EL INFIERNO
Alternate title: PASSPORT TO HELL

AGENT 38-24-36 (THE WARMBLOODED SPY) (1964) Seven Arts [W.B.]. **B&W-105min.** *(French).* Brigitte Bardot, Anthony Perkins ..... (2)
Alternate title: RAVISHING IDIOT, A

AGENT 36-24-36 (1967) see COME SPY WITH ME

AGENT Z55 (1964) see DESPERATE MISSION

AGONY AND THE ECSTASY, THE (1965) 20th Century-Fox. **Color-140min.** *(U.S.-Italian).* Charlton Heston, Rex Harrison 5*

AGUIRRE, THE WRATH OF GOD (1972) New Yorker Films. **Color-90min.** *(W. Germany-Mexican-Peruvian).* Klaus Kinski, Helena Rojo, Ruy Guerra 4*
Original title: AGUIRRE, DER ZORN GOTTES

AH, WILDERNESS! (1935) M-G-M. **B&W-101min.** Wallace Beery, Aline MacMahon 5*

AIDA (1953) Italian Films Export. **Color-95min.** *(Italian).* Sophia Loren, Lois Maxwell .... (4)

AIN'T MISBEHAVIN' (1955) Universal. **Color-82min.** Rory Calhoun, Piper Laurie .... (4)

AIN'T NO TIME FOR GLORY (1957) Screen Gems. **B&W-75min.** Barry Sullivan, Gene Barry .... (3)

AIR CADET (1951) Universal. **B&W-94min.** Stephen McNally, Rock Hudson .... (3)
British title: JET MEN OF THE AIR

AIR FORCE (1943) Warner Bros. **B&W-124min.** John Ridgely, Gig Young 3*

AIR MAIL (1932) Universal. **B&W-83min.** Ralph Bellamy, Gloria Stuart (5)

AIR PATROL (1962) 20th Century-Fox. **B&W-70min.** Willard Parker, Merry Anders .... (3)

AIR RAID WARDENS (1943) M-G-M. **B&W-67min.** Stanley Laurel, Oliver Hardy 4*

AIR STRIKE (1955) Lippert Productions. **B&W-67min.** Richard Denning, Gloria Jean .... (3)

AIRBORNE (1962) Gillman Film Distributors. **B&W-80min.** Bobby Diamond, Carolyn Bird .... (3)

AIRPORT (1970) Universal. **Color-137min.** Burt Lancaster, Dean Martin 6*

AIRPORT - 1975 (1974) Universal. **Color-106min.** Charlton Heston, Karen Black 5½*

AIRPORT '77 (1977) Universal. **Color-113min.** Jack Lemmon, Lee Grant 5*

AKU AKU (1961) Continental [Walter Reade]. **Color-86min.** *(Documentary).* Thor Heyerdahl .... (4)

AIRPORT (1970). Pilot Dean Martin is at odds with airport manager Burt Lancaster over which runway to use during a severe snowstorm.

AL CAPONE (1959) Allied Artists. **B&W-105min.** Rod Steiger, Fay Spain 5*

AL JENNINGS OF OKLAHOMA (1951) Columbia. **Color-79min.** Dan Duryea, Gale Storm .... (3)

ALADDIN AND HIS LAMP (1952) Monogram [Allied Artists]. **Color-67min.** Patricia Medina, John Sands .... (3)

ALAKAZAM THE GREAT (1960) American-International. **Color-84min.** *(Japanese, Cartoon). Director:* Taiji Yabushita .... (4)
Original title: SAIYU-KI *(The Enchanted Monkey)*

ALAMO, THE (1960) United Artists. **Color-192min.** John Wayne, Richard Widmark 4*

ALARM ON 83RD STREET (1965) Teleworld. **B&W-91min.** *(Foreign).* George Nader, Sylvia Pascal .... (3)

ALASKA PASSAGE (1959) 20th Century-Fox. **B&W-71min.** Bill Williams, Nora Hayden .... (3)

ALASKA SEAS (1954) Paramount. **Color-78min.** Robert Ryan, Jan Sterling 3½*

ALASKAN ESKIMO (1953) RKO. **Color-26min.** *(Documentary). Director:* James Algar .... (5)

ALASKAN SAFARI (1968) American National Enterprises. **Color-93min.** 4*

ALBERT RN (1953) *see* BREAK TO FREEDOM

ALBERT SCHWEITZER (1957) De Rochemont. **Color-80min.** *(Documentary). Director:* Jerome Hill .... (5)

ALBUQUERQUE (1948) Paramount. **Color-89min.** Randolph Scott, Barbara Britton .... (3)
British title: SILVER CITY

ALCATRAZ EXPRESS (1962) Desilu. **B&W-90min.** *(Telefeature).* Robert Stack, Neville Brand 5*

ALEX & THE GYPSY (1976) 20th Century-Fox. **Color-99min.** Jack Lemmon, Genevieve Bujold 4*

ALEX IN WONDERLAND (1970) M-G-M. **Color-109min.** Donald Sutherland, Jeanne Moreau .... (3)

ALEXANDER (1968) Cinema 5. **Color-94min.** *(French).* Philippe Noiret, Francoise Brion .... (5)
Original title: ALEXANDRE LE BIENHEUREUX *(Alexander the Happiest)*
Alternate title: VERY HAPPY ALEXANDER

ALEXANDER GRAHAM BELL (1939) *see* STORY OF ALEXANDER GRAHAM BELL, THE

ALEXANDER HAMILTON (1931) Warner Bros. **B&W-73min.** George Arliss, Doris Kenyon .... (4)

ALEXANDER NEVSKY (1938) Amkino. **B&W-109min.** *(U.S.S.R.).* Nikolai Cherkassov, N. P. Okhlopkov 4*

ALEXANDER THE GREAT (1956) United Artists. **Color-141min.** Richard Burton, Fredric March 5*

ALEXANDER THE GREAT (1964) ABC-TV. **Color-60min.** *(Telefeature).* William Shatner, John Cassavetes, Joseph Cotten .... (3)

ALEXANDER'S RAGTIME BAND (1938) 20th Century-Fox. **B&W-105min.** Tyrone Power, Alice Faye .... (5)

ALF 'N' FAMILY (1968) Sherpix. **Color-100min.** *(British).* Warren Mitchell, Randy Nichols .... (4)

ALFIE (1966) Paramount. **Color-114min.** *(British).* Michael Caine, Shelley Winters 8*

ALFIE DARLING (1975) **Color-102min.** *(British).* Alan Price, Jill Townsend .... (4)
Alternate title: OH! ALFIE

ALFRED NOBEL STORY, THE (1952) Teledynamics. **B&W-91min.** *(German).* Hilda Krahl, Dieter Borsche .... (4)
Alternate title: NO GREATER LOVE
Original title: HERZ DER WELT *(Heart of the World)*

ALFRED THE GREAT (1969) M-G-M. **Color-122min.** *(British).* David Hemmings, Michael York 5*

ALFREDO, ALFREDO (1972) Paramount. **Color-97min.** *(Italian).* Dustin Hoffman, Stefania Sandrelli 5*

ALGIERS (1938) United Artists. **B&W-95min.** Charles Boyer, Hedy Lamarr 3*

ALI BABA AND THE FORTY THIEVES (1944) Universal. **Color-87min.** Jon Hall, Maria Montez .... (4)

ALI BABA AND THE FORTY THIEVES (1954) Republic. **Color-90min.** *(French).* Fernandel, Sarnia Gamal .... (3)
Original title: ALI-BABA

ALI BABA AND THE SACRED CROWN (1960) *see* SEVEN TASKS OF ALI BABA

ALI BABA AND THE SEVEN SARACENS (1964) American-International. **Color-83min.** *(Italian).* Gordon Mitchell, Dan Harrison (1)

ALI BABA GOES TO TOWN (1937) 20th Century-Fox. **B&W-80min.** Eddie Cantor, Tony Martin .... (4)

ALI THE MAN/ALI THE FIGHTER (1975) CinAmerica. **Color-142min.** *(Documentary). Director:* Rick Baxter 4*

ALIAS A GENTLEMAN (1948) M-G-M. **B&W-76min.** Wallace Beery, Tom Drake .... (3)

ALIAS BULLDOG DRUMMOND (1935) Gaumont-British [Rank]. **B&W-62min.** *(British).* Jack Hulbert, Fay Wray .... (4)
Original title: BULLDOG JACK

ALIAS FRENCH GERTIE (1930) RKO. **B&W-71min.** Bebe Daniels, Ben Lyon .... (3)

ALIAS JESSE JAMES (1959) United Artists. **Color-92min.** Bob Hope, Rhonda Fleming .... (5)

ALIAS JOHN PRESTON (1955) Associated Artists. **B&W-66min.** *(British).* Alexander Knox, Christopher Lee .... (3)

ALIAS MR. TWILIGHT (1946) Columbia. **B&W-69min.** Michael Duane, Trudy Marshall .... (3)

ALIAS NICK BEAL (1949) Paramount. **B&W-93min.** Ray Milland, Thomas Mitchell 5*
British title: CONTACT MAN, THE

ALIAS SMITH AND JONES (1971) Universal. **Color-74min.** *(Made for TV).* Peter Duel, Ben Murphy 4*

ALIAS THE CHAMP (1949) Republic. **B&W-60min.** Robert Rockwell, Barbara Fuller .... (4)

ALIBI (1929) United Artists. **B&W-90min.** Chester Morris, Regis Toomey .... (4)
British title: PERFECT ALIBI, THE

ALIBI FOR DEATH, AN (1964) Teleworld. **B&W-97min.** *(German).* Peter Van Eyck, Ruth Leuwerik .... (3)

ALIBI IKE (1935) Warner Bros. **B&W-73min.** Joe E. Brown, Olivia de Havilland 4*

ALICE ADAMS (1935) RKO. **B&W-99min.** Katharine Hepburn, Fred MacMurray 5*

ALICE DOESN'T LIVE HERE ANYMORE (1974) Warner Bros. **Color-112min.** Ellen Burstyn, Kris Kristofferson 5*

ALICE IN THE CITIES (1974) Bauer International. **B&W-110min.** *(German).* Yetta Rottlander, Rudiger Vogler ....
Original title: ALICE IN DEN STADTEN

ALICE IN THE NAVY (1963) Warner Bros. **Color-90min.** *(Greek).* Aliki Vouyouclaki, Dimitri Papamichael .... (3)

ALICE IN WONDERLAND (1933) Paramount. **B&W-90min.** Charlotte Henry, Cary Grant, W. C. Fields, Gary Cooper 3*

ALICE IN WONDERLAND (1949) Souvaine Selective. **Color-83min.** *(British).* Carol Marsh, Pamela Brown .... (4)

ALICE IN WONDERLAND (1951) RKO (for Disney). **Color-75min.** *(Cartoon). Director:* Clyde Geronimi 6½*

ALICE IN WONDERLAND (1976) General National Enterprises. **Color-88min.** Kristine DeBell, Larry Gelman 4*

ALICE OR THE LAST ESCAPADE (1976) Filmal. **Color-93min.** *(French).* Sylvia Kristel, Charles Vanel ....
Original title: ALICE OU LA DERNIERE FUGUE

ALICE, SWEET ALICE (1977) Allied Artists. **Color-108min.** Linda Miller, Paula Sheppard 4*
British title: COMMUNION

ALICE'S ADVENTURES IN WONDERLAND (1972) American National Enterprises. **Color-96min.** *(British).* Fiona Fullerton, Michael Crawford, Peter Sellers .... (3)

ALICE'S RESTAURANT (1969) United Artists. **Color-111min.** Arlo Guthrie, Pat Quinn 5½*

ALIEN (1979) 20th Century-Fox. **Color-124min.** *(U.S.-British).* Tom Skerritt, Yaphet Kotto, Veronica Cartwright 6½*

ALIEN SABOTAGE (1940) *see* PASSPORT TO ALCATRAZ

ALIEN THUNDER (1975) Cinerama Releasing. **Color-90min.** *(Canadian).* Donald Sutherland, Chief Dan George, Kevin McCarthy ....
Alternate title: DAN CADY'S LAW

ALIMONY (1949) Eagle Lion. **B&W-71min.** John Beal, Martha Vickers (3)

ALIVE ALIVE O (1972) *see* . . . AND NO ONE COULD SAVE HER

ALIVE AND KICKING (1958) Associated British-Pathé [EMI]. **B&W-95min.** *(British).* Stanley Holloway, Sybil Thorndike .... (5)

ALL ABOUT EVE (1950) 20th Century-Fox. **B&W-138min.** Bette Davis, Anne Baxter 7*

Films are rated on a 1 to 10 scale, 10 is highest. **Boldface** ratings followed by an asterisk (*) are for films actually seen and rated by the executive and senior editors. All other ratings are estimates. (See Notes on Entertainment Ratings in the front section.)

ALL AMERICAN, THE (1953) Universal. **B&W-83min.** Tony Curtis, Lori Nelson .... (3)
British title: WINNING WAY, THE

ALL-AMERICAN BOY, THE (1973) Warner Bros. **Color-118min.** Jon Voight, Carol Androsky .... (4)

ALL ASHORE (1953) Columbia. **Color-80min.** Mickey Rooney, Dick Haymes .... (3)

ALL AT SEA (1958) M-G-M. **B&W-87min.** (*British*). Alec Guinness, Irene Browne .... (5)
Original title: BARNACLE BILL

ALL AT SEA (1970) Children's Film Foundation. **Color-60min.** (*British*). Early Smith, Steven Mallett .... (3)

ALL BY MYSELF (1943) Universal. **B&W-62min.** Rosemary Lane, Patric Knowles .... (4)

ALL CREATURES GREAT AND SMALL (1975) Scotia American. **Color-90min.** (*British*). Simon Ward, Anthony Hopkins, Lisa Harrow ....

ALL FALL DOWN (1962) M-G-M. **B&W-110min.** Eva Marie Saint, Warren Beatty 5*

ALL FOR MARY (1956) Paul Soskin. **Color-82min.** (*British*). Nigel Patrick, Kathleen Harrison .... (3)

ALL HANDS ON DECK (1961) 20th Century-Fox. **Color-98min.** Pat Boone, Buddy Hackett 3*

ALL I DESIRE (1953) Universal. **B&W-70min.** Barbara Stanwyck, Richard Carlson .... (4)

ALL IN A NIGHT'S WORK (1961) Paramount. **Color-94min.** Dean Martin, Shirley MacLaine 4*

ALL MINE TO GIVE (1957) Universal. **Color-102min.** Glynis Johns, Cameron Mitchell .... (4)
British title: DAY THEY GAVE BABIES AWAY, THE

ALL MY DARLING DAUGHTERS (1972) MCA-TV. **Color-74min.** (*Made for TV*). Robert Young, Darleen Carr, Judy Strangis 4*

ALL MY SONS (1948) Universal. **B&W-94min.** Edward G. Robinson, Burt Lancaster 4*

ALL NEAT IN BLACK STOCKINGS (1969) National General. **Color-99min.** (*British*). Victor Henry, Susan George .... (3)

ALL NIGHT LONG (1961) Continental [Walter Reade]. **B&W-91min.** (*British*). Patrick McGoohan, Betsy Blair, Richard Attenborough .... (4)

ALL NUDITY WILL BE PUNISHED (1973) **Color-102min.** (*Brazilian*). Paulo Porto, Darlene Gloria .... (5)
Original title: TODA NUDEZ SERA CASTIGADA

ALL OF ME (1934) Paramount. **B&W-75min.** Fredric March, Miriam Hopkins .... (3)

ALL OVER THE TOWN (1948) Universal. **B&W-87min.** (*British*). Norman Wooland, Sarah Churchill .... (5)

ALL QUIET ON THE WESTERN FRONT (1930) Universal. **B&W-105min.** Lew Ayres, Louis Wolheim 4½*

ALL SCREWED UP (1974) New Line Cinema. **Color-105min.** (*Italian*). Luigi Diberti, Lina Polito ....
Original title: TUTTO A POSTE E NIENTE IN ORDINE (*All in Place, Nothing in Order*)

ALL THAT HEAVEN ALLOWS (1956) Universal. **Color-89min.** Jane Wyman, Rock Hudson 4*

ALL THAT JAZZ (1979) 20th Century-Fox. **Color-   min.** Roy Scheider, Ann Reinking ....

ALL THAT MONEY CAN BUY (1941) *see* DEVIL AND DANIEL WEBSTER, THE

ALL THE BROTHERS WERE VALIANT (1953) M-G-M. **Color-101min.** Robert Taylor, Stewart Granger 4*

ALL THE FINE YOUNG CANNIBALS (1960) M-G-M. **Color-112min.** Robert Wagner, Natalie Wood .... (3)

ALL THE KING'S HORSES (1935) Paramount. **B&W-87min.** Mary Ellis, Carl Brisson .... (3)

ALL THE KING'S MEN (1949) Columbia. **B&W-109min.** Broderick Crawford, John Ireland 6*

ALL THE LOVING COUPLES (1969) U-M Prods. **Color-85min.** Gloria Manon, Norman Alden .... (2)

ALL THE OTHER GIRLS DO (1964) Harlequin International. **B&W-90min.** (*Italian*). Rosemarie Dexter, Jacques Perrin .... (3)
Original title: TUTTE LE ALTRE RAGAZZE LO FANNO
Alternate Italian title: OLTRAGGIO AL PUDORE (*The Outrage and the Shame*)

ALL THE PRESIDENT'S MEN (1976) Warner Bros. **Color-138min.** Dustin Hoffman, Robert Redford 7*

ALL THE RIGHT NOISES (1971) 20th Century-Fox. **Color-92min.** (*British*). Tom Bell, Olivia Hussey, Judy Carne ....

ALL THE WAY (1957) *see* JOKER IS WILD, THE

ALL THE WAY HOME (1963) Paramount. **B&W-103min.** Jean Simmons, Robert Preston 5*

ALL THE WAY TO PARIS (1966) *see* AFTER YOU COMRADE

ALL THE YOUNG MEN (1960) Columbia. **B&W-87min.** Alan Ladd, Sidney Poitier 3*

ALL THESE WOMEN (1964) Janus Films. **Color-80min.** (*Swedish*). Jarl Kulle, Bibi Andersson .... (3)
Original title: FOR ATT INTE TALA OM ALLA DESSA KVINNOR (*Now About These Women*)

ALL THIS AND HEAVEN TOO (1940) Warner Bros. **B&W-143min.** Bette Davis, Charles Boyer 4*

ALL THIS AND MONEY TOO (1962) *see* LOVE IS A BALL

ALL THIS AND WORLD WAR II (1976) 20th Century-Fox. **B&W-88min.** .... (5)

ALL THROUGH THE NIGHT (1942) Warner Bros. **B&W-107min.** Humphrey Bogart, Conrad Veidt 3½*

ALL WEEKEND LOVERS (1967) *see* KILLING GAME, THE

ALL WOMEN HAVE SECRETS (1940) Paramount. **B&W-74min.** Jeanne Cagney, Joyce Matthews .... (3)

ALL YOU NEED IS CASH (1978) NBC-TV. **Color-74min.** (*British, Made for TV*). Eric Idle, Neil Innes, Rikki Fataar, John Halsey 5*

ALLEGHENY UPRISING (1939) RKO. **B&W-81min.** John Wayne, Claire Trevor 4*
British title: FIRST REBEL, THE

ALLEGRO NON TROPPO (1976) Specialty Films. **Color-85min.** (*Italian, Cartoon*). *Director:* Bruno Bozzetto 6½*
Translation title: Fast But Not Too Fast

ALLEZ FRANCE (1964) *see* COUNTERFEIT CONSTABLE, THE

ALLIGATOR NAMED DAISY, AN (1955) J. Arthur Rank. **Color-88min.** (*British*). Donald Sinden, Diana Dors .... (4)

ALLIGATOR PEOPLE, THE (1959) 20th Century-Fox. **B&W-74min.** Beverly Garland, George Macready 2*

ALLOTMENT WIVES (1945) Monogram [Allied Artists]. **B&W-83min.** Kay Francis, Paul Kelly .... (3)
British title: WOMAN IN THE CASE

ALMOST A BRIDE (1949) *see* KISS FOR CORLISS, A

ALMOST ANGELS (1962) Buena Vista. **Color-93min.** Vincent Winter, Sean Scully 5*

ALMOST PERFECT AFFAIR, AN (1979) Paramount. **Color-93min.** Monica Vitti, Keith Carradine, Raf Vallone ....

ALMOST SUMMER (1978) Universal. **Color-88min.** Bruno Kirby, Lee Purcell 6*

ALOHA, BOBBY AND ROSE (1975) Columbia. **Color-88min.** Paul Le Mat, Dianne Hull 3*

ALOMA OF THE SOUTH SEAS (1941) Paramount. **Color-77min.** Dorothy Lamour, Jon Hall .... (3)

ALONE AGAINST ROME (1962) Medallion. **Color-100min.** (*Italian*). Jeffrey Lang, Rosanna Podesta .... (3)
Original title: SOLO CONTRO ROMA

ALONG CAME A SPIDER (1970) 20th Century-Fox. **Color-75min.** (*Made for TV*). Ed Nelson, Suzanne Pleshette 4½*

ALONG CAME JONES (1945) RKO. **B&W-90min.** Gary Cooper, Loretta Young 4*

ALONG CAME YOUTH (1931) Paramount. **B&W-48min.** Charles Rogers, Stuart Erwin .... (2)

ALONG THE GREAT DIVIDE (1951) Warner Bros. **B&W-88min.** Kirk Douglas, Virginia Mayo 4*

ALONG THE MOHAWK TRAIL (1956) Sigmund Neufeld. **B&W-89min.** (*Telefeature*). Jon Hart, Lon Chaney (Jr.) .... (3)

ALPHA BETA (1973) Cine III Distributors. **Color-67min.** (*British*). Albert Finney, Rachel Roberts .... (5)

ALPHA CAPER, THE (1973) MCA-TV. **Color-75min.** (*Made for TV*). Henry Fonda, Larry Hagman 4½*

ALPHABET MURDERS, THE (1966) M-G-M. **B&W-85min.** (*British*). Tony Randall, Anita Ekberg .... (4)
Original title: A.B.C. MURDERS, THE

ALPHAVILLE (1965) Pathé Contemporary. **B&W-100min.** (*French*). Eddie Constantine, Anna Karina .... (4)

ALRAUNE (1928) UFA (*Ger.*). **B&W-122min.** (*German*). Brigitte Helm, Ivan Petrovitch .... (4)
Alternate title: DAUGHTER OF DESTINY
Alternate title: MANDRAGORE

ALTARS OF THE WORLD (1976) All State Prods., Inc. Color-150min. *(Documentary). Director:* Lew Ayres .... (5)

ALTERED STATES (1980) Warner Bros. Color-   min. William Hurt, Blair Brown..

ALVAREZ KELLY (1966) Columbia. Color-116min. William Holden, Richard Widmark 5*

ALWAYS A BRIDE (1953) Universal. B&W-83min. *(British).* Peggy Cummins, Terence Morgan.. (4)

ALWAYS A NEW BEGINNING (1973) Goodell Motion Pictures. Color-90min. *(Documentary). Director:* John D. Goodell.................... 5*

ALWAYS GOODBYE (1938) 20th Century-Fox. B&W-75min. Barbara Stanwyck, Herbert Marshall .... (4)

ALWAYS IN MY HEART (1942) Warner Bros. B&W-92min. Walter Huston, Kay Francis .... (3)

ALWAYS LEAVE THEM LAUGHING (1949) Warner Bros. B&W-116min. Milton Berle, Bert Lahr.. (4)

ALWAYS ON SUNDAY (1961) Avco-Embassy. B&W-95min. *(French-Italian).* Eddie Bracken, Jean-Pierre Aumont, Ugo Tognazzi 3*
Original French title: DIMANCHE D'ÉTÉ, UN
Italian title: DOMENICA D'ESTATE, UNA *(Summer Sunday)*

ALWAYS TOGETHER (1948) Warner Bros. B&W-78min. Robert Hutton, Joyce Reynolds, Cecil Kellaway .... (4)

AMANTI (1968) *see* PLACE FOR LOVERS, A

AMARCORD (1974) Warner Bros. Color-123min. *(Italian).* Magali Noel, Bruno Zanin 3*
Publicity title: FELLINI'S AMARCORD

AMAZING COLOSSAL MAN, THE (1956) American-International. B&W-80min. Glenn Langan, Cathy Downs............................... 3*

AMAZING DOBERMANS, THE (1976) Golden Films. Color-96min. Fred Astaire, James Franciscus .... (4)

AMAZING DR. CLITTERHOUSE, THE (1938) Warner Bros. B&W-95min. Edward G. Robinson, Humphrey Bogart 4½*

AMAZING DR. G., THE (1965) American-International. Color-85min. *(Italian).* Franco Franchi, Ciccio Ingrassia .... (3)
Original title: DUE MAFIOSI CONTRO GOLDGINGER *(Two Mafiosi vs. Goldginger)*

AMAZING GRACE (1974) United Artists. Color-97min. Moms Mabley, Slappy White, Stepin Fetchit... (4)

AMAZING HOWARD HUGHES, THE (1977) CBS-TV. Color-200min. *(Made for TV).* Tommy Lee Jones, Ed Flanders 5*

AMAZING MR. BEECHAM, THE (1949) Eagle Lion. B&W-85min. *(British).* Cecil Parker, A. E. Matthews, David Tomlinson .... (5)
Original title: CHILTERN HUNDREDS, THE

AMAZING MR. BLUNDEN, THE (1972) Goldstone Film Enterprises. Color-99min. *(British).* Laurence Naismith, Lynne Frederick, Garry Miller .... (4)

AMAZING MR. FORREST, THE (1939) Producers Rel. Corp. [Eagle Lion] B&W-78min. *(British).* Jack Buchanan, Syd Walker .... (4)
Original title: GANG'S ALL HERE, THE

AMAZING MR. WILLIAMS, THE (1939) Columbia. B&W-80min. Melvyn Douglas, Joan Blondell .... (4)

AMAZING MR. X, THE (1948) *see* SPIRITUALIST, THE

AMAZING MRS. HOLLIDAY, THE (1943) Universal. B&W-96min. Deanna Durbin, Edmond O'Brien .... (4)

AMAZING MONSIEUR FABRE, THE (1951) Distinguished Films. B&W-90min. *(French, English version).* Pierre Fresnay, Elina La Bourdette .... (5)
Alternate title: MONSIEUR FABRE

AMAZING QUEST OF ERNEST BLISS, THE (1936) *see* ROMANCE AND RICHES

AMAZING TRANSPARENT MAN, THE (1960) American-International. B&W-60min. Marguerite Chapman, Douglas Kennedy.......................... 3*

AMAZONS OF ROME (1960) Carlo Bragaglia. Color-93min. *(Italian-French-Yugoslavian).* Louis Jourdan, Sylvia Syms.................... (2)
Original Italian title: VERGINI DI ROMA, LE *(The Virgins of Rome)*

AMBASSADOR'S DAUGHTER, THE (1956) United Artists. Color-102min. Olivia de Havilland, John Forsythe............................ (4)

AMBUSH (1950) M-G-M. B&W-89min. Robert Taylor, John Hodiak ...... (4)

AMBUSH AT CIMARRON PASS (1958) 20th Century-Fox. B&W-73min. Scott Brady, Margia Dean .... (3)

AMBUSH AT TOMAHAWK GAP (1953) Columbia. Color-73min. John Hodiak, John Derek .... (3)

AMBUSH BAY (1966) United Artists. Color-109min. Hugh O'Brian, Mickey Rooney... 4*

AMBUSH IN LEOPARD STREET (1961) Columbia. B&W-60min. *(British).* James Kenney, Michael Brennan .... (3)

AMBUSHERS, THE (1967) Columbia. Color-102min. Dean Martin, Senta Berger 3*

AMELIA EARHART (1976) NBC-TV. Color-156min. *(Made for TV).* Susan Clark, Stephen Macht, John Forsythe ....

AMÉLIE (1961) United Motion Pic. Org. (UMPO). B&W-111min. *(French).* Marie-Jose Nat, Jean Sorel .... (3)
Original title: AMÉLIE OU LE TEMPS D'AIMER *(Amélie or the Time to Love)*

AMERICA (1924) United Artists. B&W-135min. Neil Hamilton, Erville Alderson 4*
Alternate title: AMERICA: 1776
British title: LOVE AND SACRIFICE

AMERICA AMERICA (1963) Warner Bros. B&W-174min. Stathis Giallelis .... (6)
British title: ANATOLIAN SMILE, THE

AMERICA AT THE MOVIES (1976) American Film Institute. B&W-116min. *(Compilation). Producer:* George Stevens, Jr........................

AMERICAN DREAM, AN (1966) Warner Bros. Color-103min. Stuart Whitman, Janet Leigh 3*
British title: SEE YOU IN HELL, DARLING

AMERICAN EMPIRE (1942) United Artists. B&W-82min. Richard Dix, Leo Carillo 4*
British title: MY SON ALONE

AMERICAN FRIEND, THE (1977) New Yorker Films. Color-127min. *(W. German-French).* Dennis Hopper, Bruno Ganz...................... (4)
German title: AMERIKANISCHE FREUND, DER

AMERICAN GAME, THE (1979) World Northal. Color-85min...................

AMERICAN GIGOLO (1979) Paramount. Color-   min. Richard Gere.......

AMERICAN GRAFFITI (1973) Universal. Color-112min. Richard Dreyfuss, Ronny Howard 7½*

AMERICAN GUERRILLA IN THE PHILIPPINES (1950) 20th Century-Fox. Color-105min. Tyrone Power, Micheline Prelle (Presle)............. 3*
British title: I SHALL RETURN

AMERICAN HOT WAX (1978) Paramount. Color-91min. Tim McIntire, Laraine Newman, John Lehne 5½*

AMERICAN IN PARIS, AN (1951) M-G-M. Color-113min. Gene Kelly, Leslie Caron.. 5*

AMERICAN REVOLUTION 2 (1969) Cannon Releasing. B&W-80min. ...(5)

AMERICAN ROMANCE, AN (1944) M-G-M. Color-122min. Brian Donlevy, Ann Richards... (4)

AMERICAN TRAGEDY, AN (1931) Paramount. B&W-95min. Phillips Holmes, Sylvia Sidney 4*

AMERICANIZATION OF EMILY, THE (1964) M-G-M. B&W-117min. James Garner, Julie Andrews.................................... 6*

AMERICAN GRAFFITI (1973). Candy Clark and Charlie Martin Smith have a bit of difficulty explaining to Ronny Howard why they don't have the car he lent them.

AMERICANO, THE (1955) RKO. **Color-85min.** Glenn Ford, Frank Lovejoy 3*

AMERICATHON (1979) United Artists. **Color-** min. Harvey Korman, John Ritter ....

AMITYVILLE HORROR, THE (1979) American-International. **Color-** min. James Brolin, Margot Kidder, Rod Steiger ....

AMMIE, COME HOME (1970) *see* HOUSE THAT WOULDN'T DIE, THE

AMONG THE HEADHUNTERS (1955) J. Arthur Rank. **Color-92min.** *(British, Travelog).* Armand Dennis, Michaela Dennis .... (5)

AMONG THE LIVING (1941) Paramount. **B&W-68min.** Albert Dekker, Susan Hayward .... (4)

AMONG VULTURES (1964) *see* FRONTIER HELLCAT

AMOROUS ADVENTURES OF DON QUIXOTE & SANCHO PANZA, THE (1976) Burbank International Pictures Corp. **Color-127min.** Corey John Fischer, Hy Pyke .... (4)
British title: WHEN SEX WAS A KNIGHTLY AFFAIR

AMOROUS ADVENTURES OF MOLL FLANDERS, THE (1965) Paramount. **Color-122min.** *(British).* Kim Novak, Richard Johnson 4*

AMOROUS GENERAL, THE (1962) *see* WALTZ OF THE TOREADORS

AMOROUS MR. PRAWN, THE (1962) Union Films. **B&W-89min.** *(British).* Ian Carmichael, Joan Greenwood .... (4)
Original title: AMOROUS PRAWN, THE
Alternate title: PLAYGIRL AND THE WAR MINISTER, THE

AMPHIBIAN MAN, THE (1964) NTA Pictures. **Color-86min.** *(U.S.S.R.).* Vladimir Korenev, Anastasia Vertinskaya .... (2)
Original title: CHELOVIEK AMPHIBIA

AMSTERDAM KILL, THE (1977) Columbia. **Color-89min.** *(Hong Kong, English language).* Robert Mitchum, Bradford Dillman, Richard Egan 4*

ANASTASIA (1956) 20th Century-Fox. **Color-105min.** Ingrid Bergman, Yul Brynner 6*

ANASTASIA, THE CZAR'S LAST DAUGHTER (1956) Gala *(Brit.).* **B&W-90min.** *(German).* Lilli Palmer, Ivan Desny .... (4)
Original title: ANASTASIA - DIE LETZTE ZARENTOCHTER
TV title: ANASTASIA
British title: IS ANNA ANDERSON ANASTASIA?

ANATOLIAN SMILE, THE (1963) *see* AMERICA, AMERICA

ANATOMIST, THE (1961) David Bader. **B&W-73min.** *(British).* Alastair Sim, George Cole .... (4)

ANATOMY OF A MARRIAGE (1963) Janus Films. **B&W-196min.** *(French-Italian).* Marie-Jose Nat, Jacques Charrier .... (4)
Original French title of first film: VIE CONJUGAL: JEAN-MARC, LA *(The Married Life: Jean-Marc)*
Original French title of second film: VIE CONJUGAL: FRANCOISE, LA *(The Married Life: Francoise)*
Alternate title of one film: MY NIGHTS WITH FRANCOISE
Alternate title of the other: MY DAYS WITH JEAN-MARC

ANATOMY OF A MURDER (1964) Columbia. **B&W-160min.** James Stewart, Lee Remick, Ben Gazzara 6½*

ANATOMY OF A PSYCHO (1961) Brooke L. Peters. **B&W-75min.** Darrell Howe, Ronnie Burns .... (2)

ANATOMY OF A SYNDICATE (1959) *see* BIG OPERATOR, THE

ANATOMY OF LOVE, THE (1953) Kassler Films. **B&W-97min.** *(Italian-French).* .... (5)
Original title: TEMPI NOSTRI *(Our Times)*
British title: SLICE OF LIFE, A

ANCHORS AWEIGH (1945) M-G-M. **Color-143min.** Gene Kelly, Frank Sinatra 4*

AND BABY MAKES THREE (1949) Columbia. **B&W-84min.** Robert Young, Barbara Hale 4*

AND GOD CREATED WOMAN (1957) Kingsley International. **Color-90min.** *(French).* Brigitte Bardot, Curt Jurgens .... (5)
Original title: ET DIEU . . . CRÉA LA FEMME
British title: AND WOMAN . . . WAS CREATED

. . . AND HOPE TO DIE (1972) 20th Century-Fox. **Color-99min.** *(French-U.S., English language).* Robert Ryan, Jean-Louis Trintignant............ (4)
Original French title: LA COURSE DU LIEVRE A TRAVERS LES CHAMPS *(The Race of the Hare Across the Fields)*

AND JUSTICE FOR ALL (1979) Columbia. **Color-** min. Al Pacino, Jack Warden ....

. . . AND NO ONE COULD SAVE HER (1972) Associated London Films. **Color-73min.** *(British, Made for TV).* Lee Remick, Milo O'Shea, Frank Grimes.. (4)
Alternate title: ALIVE ALIVE O

AND NOW FOR SOMETHING COMPLETELY DIFFERENT (1971) Columbia. **Color-89min.** *(British).* Graham Chapman, John Cleese..... 4½*

. . . AND NOW MIGUEL (1966) Universal. **Color-95min.** Pat Cardi, Michael Ansara 4*

AND NOW MY LOVE (1974) Avco-Embassy. **Color-121min.** *(French-Italian).* Marthe Keller 5*
Original French title: TOUTE UNE VIE *(A Lifetime)*

AND NOW THE SCREAMING STARTS (1973) Cinerama Releasing. **Color-87min.** *(British).* Peter Cushing, Stephanie Beacham .... (4)

AND NOW TOMORROW (1944) Paramount. **B&W-85min.** Alan Ladd, Loretta Young .... (4)

AND QUIET FLOWS THE DON (1957) United Artists. **Color-107min.** *(U.S.S.R.).* Ellina Bystritskaya, Pyotr Glebov .... (5)

AND SO THEY WERE MARRIED (1936) Columbia. **B&W-74min.** Melvyn Douglas, Mary Astor.. (4)

AND SO THEY WERE MARRIED (1944) *see* JOHNNY DOESN'T LIVE HERE ANYMORE

AND SOON THE DARKNESS (1970) Levitt-Pickman. **Color-100min.** *(British).* Pamela Franklin, Michele Dotrice...................... 3*

AND SUDDEN DEATH (1936) Paramount. **B&W-68min.** Randolph Scott, Frances Drake .... (3)

. . . AND SUDDENLY IT'S MURDER! (1960) Royal Films Int'l [Columbia]. **B&W-90min.** *(Italian-French).* Alberto Sordi, Vittorio Gassman .... (4)
Original Italian title: CRIMEN
French title: CHACUN SON ALIBI

AND SUDDENLY YOU RUN (1956) *see* TERROR AT MIDNIGHT

AND THE ANGELS SING (1944) Paramount. **B&W-96min.** Fred MacMurray, Dorothy Lamour .... (4)

AND THE SAME TO YOU (1960) Eros Films *(Brit.).* **B&W-70min.** *(British).* Brian Rix, Leo Franklyn ....

. . . AND THE WILD, WILD WOMEN (1958) Rima Films. **B&W-85min.** *(Italian-French).* Anna Magnani, Giulietta Masina .... (5)
Original Italian title: NELLA CITTA L'INFERNO *(Hell in the City)*
Original French title: ENFER DANS LA VILLE, L'
Alternate title: WILD, WILD WOMEN, THE

AND THEN THERE WERE NONE (1945) 20th Century-Fox. **B&W-98min.** Walter Huston, Barry Fitzgerald.................................... 5*
British title: TEN LITTLE NIGGERS

AND THEN THERE WERE NONE (1975) *see* TEN LITTLE INDIANS

AND THERE CAME A MAN (1965) Brandon. **Color-90min.** *(Italian).* .... (3)
Alternate title: MAN NAMED JOHN, A

AND WOMAN . . . WAS CREATED (1956) *see* AND GOD CREATED WOMAN

ANDALUSIAN DOG, THE (1929) **B&W-17min.** *(French, Silent).* Pierre Batcheff, Simone Mareuil... 3*
Original title: CHIEN ANDALOU, UN

ANDERSON PLATOON, THE (1967) Pathé Contemporary. **B&W-65min.** *(French, Documentary). Director:* Pierre Schoendorffer .... (4)
Original title: PATROUILLE ANDERSON, LA

ANDERSON TAPES, THE (1971) Columbia. **Color-98min.** Sean Connery, Dyan Cannon, Alan King.. 4½*

ANDREA CHENIER (1956) Archway *(Brit.).* **Color-110min.** *(Italian).* Raf Vallone .... (3)

ANDREI RUBLOV (1967) Mosfilm. **B&W-165min.** *(U.S.S.R.).* A. Solonitzine, N. Sergeev .... (5)

ANDROCLES AND THE LION (1953) RKO. **B&W-98min.** Alan Young, Jean Simmons.. 4*

ANDROMEDA STRAIN, THE (1971) Universal. **Color-131min.** Arthur Hill, David Wayne.. 5½*

ANDY (1965) Universal. **B&W-86min.** Norman Alden, Tamara Daykarhonova .... (5)

ANDY HARDY COMES HOME (1958) M-G-M. **B&W-80min.** Mickey Rooney, Patricia Breslin .... (4)

ANDY HARDY GETS SPRING FEVER (1939) M-G-M. **B&W-85min.** Mickey Rooney, Lewis Stone .... (4)

ANDY HARDY MEETS DEBUTANTE (1940) M-G-M. **B&W-86min.** Mickey Rooney, Lewis Stone .... (4)

ANDY HARDY'S BLONDE TROUBLE (1944) M-G-M. **B&W-107min.** Mickey Rooney, Lewis Stone .... (3)

ANDY HARDY'S DOUBLE LIFE (1942) M-G-M. **B&W-92min.** Mickey Rooney, Esther Williams... (3)

ANDY HARDY'S PRIVATE SECRETARY (1941) M-G-M. **B&W-101min.** Mickey Rooney, Kathryn Grayson .... (4)

ANDY WARHOL'S BAD (1977) New World. **Color-105min.** Carroll Baker, Perry King 4*
Alternate title: BAD

Films are rated on a 1 to 10 scale, 10 is highest. **Boldface** ratings followed by an asterisk (*) are for films actually seen and rated by the executive and senior editors. All other ratings are estimates. (See Notes on Entertainment Ratings in the front section.)

ANDY WARHOL'S DRACULA (1974) Bryanston. **Color-106min.** *(Italian-French, English language).* Udo Kier, Joe Dallesandro 4*
Alternate title: DRACULA
Original Italian title: DRACULA VUOLE VIVERE: CERCA SANGUE DI VERGINE!
British title: BLOOD FOR DRACULA

ANDY WARHOL'S FRANKENSTEIN (1974) Bryanston. **Color-95min.** Udo Kier, Joe Dallesandro 4*
British title: FLESH FOR FRANKENSTEIN
Italian title: CARNE PER FRANKENSTEIN
French title: DE LA CHAIR POUR FRANKENSTEIN
U.S. prerelease title: FRANKENSTEIN EXPERIMENT, THE

ANGEL (1937) Paramount. **B&W-98min.** Marlene Dietrich, Herbert Marshall, Melvyn Douglas.........................(3)

ANGEL AND SINNER (1945) AFE Corp. *(French).* **B&W-85min.** *(French).* Micheline Presle, Louis Salou.........................(4)
Original title: BOULE DE SUIF

ANGEL AND THE BADMAN (1946) Republic. **B&W-100min.** John Wayne, Gail Russell 4*

ANGEL, ANGEL, DOWN WE GO (1969) American-International. **Color-93min.** Jennifer Jones, Jordan Christopher.........................(3)
Alternate title: CULT OF THE DAMNED

ANGEL BABY (1961) Allied Artists. **B&W-97min.** Salome Jens, George Hamilton.........................4*

ANGEL FACE (1953) RKO. **B&W-90min.** Robert Mitchum, Jean Simmons.........................4*

ANGEL FROM TEXAS, AN (1940) Warner Bros. **B&W-69min.** Eddie Albert, Jane Wyman.........................(4)

ANGEL IN EXILE (1948) Republic. **B&W-90min.** John Carrol, Adele Mara.........................(5)

ANGEL IN MY POCKET (1968) Universal. **Color-105min.** Andy Griffith, Lee Meriwether.........................4*

ANGEL LEVINE, THE (1970) United Artists. **Color-104min.** Zero Mostel, Harry Belafonte.........................(5)

ANGEL ON EARTH (1961) NTA Pictures. **Color-88min.** *(German).* Romy Schneider, Jean-Paul Belmondo.........................(3)
Original title: ENGEL AUF ERDEN, EIN
Alternate title: ANGEL ON WHEELS, AN

ANGEL ON MY SHOULDER (1946) United Artists. **B&W-101min.** Paul Muni, Claude Rains.........................5*

ANGEL ON THE AMAZON (1948) Republic. **B&W-86min.** George Brent, Vera (Hruba) Ralston.........................3*
British title: DRUMS ALONG THE AMAZON

ANGEL STREET (1940) Anglo-American. **B&W-88min.** *(British-U.S.).* Anton Walbrook, Diana Wynyard.........................(4)
Original title: GASLIGHT
Alternate U.S. title(?): STRANGE CASE OF MURDER, A

ANGEL UNCHAINED (1970) American-International. **Color-90min.** Don Stroud, Luke Askew.........................(3)

ANGEL WHO PAWNED HER HARP, THE (1956) Associated Artists. **B&W-73min.** *(British).* Diane Cilento, Felix Aylmer.........................(5)

ANGEL WITH THE TRUMPET, THE (1949) Korda. **B&W-99min.** *(British).* Eileen Herlie, Norman Wooland.........................(4)
TV title: ANGEL WITH A TRUMPET

ANGEL WORE RED, THE (1960) M-G-M. **B&W-99min.** *(Italian-U.S.).* Ava Gardner, Dirk Bogarde.........................(4)
Italian title: SPOSA BELLA, LA *(The Fair Bride)*

ANGELA (1955) 20th Century-Fox. **B&W-81min.** Dennis O'Keefe, Rosanno Brazzi.........................(3)

ANGELA DAVIS - PORTRAIT OF A REVOLUTIONARY (1972) New Yorker Films. **B&W-60min.** *(Documentary). Director:* Yolande Du Luart.........................(5)

ANGELS (1976) Jape Productions. **Color-90min.** Vincent Schiavelli, Keith Berger.........................(3)

ANGEL'S ALLEY (1948) Monogram [Allied Artists]. **B&W-67min.** The Bowery Boys.........................(3)

ANGELS AND THE PIRATES, THE (1951) *see* ANGELS IN THE OUTFIELD

ANGELS DIE HARD! (1971) New World. **Color-87min.** Tom Baker*, William Smith.........................(2)

ANGELS HARD AS THEY COME (1971) New World. **Color-90min.** Scott Glenn, Charles Dierkop.........................(2)

ANGELS IN DISGUISE (1949) Monogram [Allied Artists]. **B&W-63min.** The Bowery Boys.........................(3)

ANGELS IN THE OUTFIELD (1951) M-G-M. **B&W-102min.** Paul Douglas, Janet Leigh.........................4½*
British title: ANGELS AND THE PIRATES, THE

ANGELS OF DARKNESS (1953) Excelsior. **B&W-84min.** *(Italian).* Linda Darnell, Giulietta Masina, Anthony Quinn.........................(3)
Original title: DONNE PROIBITE *(Forbidden Women)*

ANGELS ONE FIVE (1952) Stratford Pictures. **B&W-98min.** *(British).* Jack Hawkins, John Gregson.........................(4)

ANGELS OVER BROADWAY (1940) Columbia. **B&W-80min.** Douglas Fairbanks, Jr., Rita Hayworth.........................4½*

ANGELS WASH THEIR FACES (1939) Warner Bros. **B&W-76min.** Ann Sheridan, Ronald Reagan.........................4*

ANGELS WITH BROKEN WINGS (1941) Republic. **B&W-72min.** Binnie Barnes, Gilbert Roland.........................(4)

ANGELS WITH DIRTY FACES (1938) Warner Bros. **B&W-97min.** James Cagney, Pat O'Brien.........................4*

ANGRY BREED, THE (1968) Commonwealth United. **Color-89min.** Jan Sterling, James MacArthur.........................1*

ANGRY HILLS, THE (1959) M-G-M. **B&W-105min.** *(British).* Robert Mitchum, Elisabeth Mueller.........................3*

ANGRY RED PLANET, THE (1960) American-International. **Color-83min.** Gerald Mohr, Les Tremayne.........................2½*

ANGRY SILENCE, THE (1960) Valiant. **B&W-95min.** *(British).* Richard Attenborough, Pier Angeli.........................4*

ANIMAL CRACKERS (1930) Paramount. **B&W-100min.** Groucho Marx, Harpo Marx.........................4*

ANIMAL FARM (1954) De Rochemont. **Color-72min.** *(British, Cartoon). Director:* John Halas.........................6*

ANIMAL KINGDOM, THE (1932) RKO. **B&W-90min.** Ann Harding, Leslie Howard.........................(5)
British title: WOMAN IN HIS HOUSE, THE

ANIMAL WORLD, THE (1956) Warner Bros. **Color-82min.** *(Documentary). Director:* Irwin Allen.........................(5)

ANIMALS, THE (1959) Four Star. **B&W-87min.** *(French, Documentary). Director:* Frederic Rossif.........................6*
Original title: ANIMAUX, LES

ANIMALS, THE (1971) Levitt-Pickman. **Color-86min.** Henry Silva, Keenan Wynn.........................(3)
British title: FIVE SAVAGE MEN

ANN AND EVE (1970) Chevron. **Color-89min.** *(Swedish, English language).* Gio Petre, Marie Lijedhal.........................(3)

ANNA (1952) Italian Films Export. **B&W-100min.** *(Italian).* Silvano Mangano, Raf Vallone.........................(4)

ANNA AND THE KING OF SIAM (1946) 20th Century-Fox. **B&W-128min.** Irene Dunne, Rex Harrison.........................6*

ANNA CHRISTIE (1930) M-G-M. **B&W-86min.** Greta Garbo, Charles Bickford.........................5*

ANNA KARENINA (1928) *see* LOVE

ANNA KARENINA (1935) M-G-M. **B&W-95min.** Greta Garbo, Fredric March.........................5½*

ANNA KARENINA (1947) 20th Century-Fox. **B&W-123min.** *(British).* Vivien Leigh, Ralph Richardson.........................(5)

ANNA KARENINA (1975) Sovexportfilm. **Color-85min.** *(U.S.S.R.).* Maya Plisetskaya, Alexander Godounov.........................(4)

ANNA LUCASTA (1949) Columbia. **B&W-86min.** Paulette Goddard, William Bishop.........................(5)

ANNA LUCASTA (1958) United Artists. **B&W-97min.** Eartha Kitt, Sammy Davis, Jr..........................(4)

ANNAPOLIS STORY, AN (1955) Allied Artists. **Color-81min.** John Derek, Diana Lynn.........................3*
British title: BLUE AND THE GOLD, THE

ANNAPURNA (1953) Kingsley International. **Color-60min.** *(British, Documentary)*.........................(5)

ANNE AND MURIEL (1971) *see* TWO ENGLISH GIRLS

ANNE OF GREEN GABLES (1934) RKO. **B&W-79min.** *(British).* Anne Shirley, Tom Brown.........................(5)

ANNE OF THE INDIES (1951) 20th Century-Fox. **Color-81min.** Jean Peters, Louis Jourdan.........................3½*

ANNE OF THE THOUSAND DAYS (1969) Universal. **Color-143min.** *(British).* Richard Burton, Genevieve Bujold.........................6*

ANNE OF WINDY POPLARS (1940) RKO. **B&W-88min.** Anne Shirley, James Ellison.........................(4)
British title: ANNE OF WINDY WILLOWS

ANNIE GET YOUR GUN (1950) M-G-M. **Color-107min.** Betty Hutton, Howard Keel.........................4*

ANNIE HALL (1977) United Artists. **Color-93min.** Woody Allen, Diane Keaton.........................5½*

Films are rated on a 1 to 10 scale, 10 is highest. **Boldface** ratings followed by an asterisk (*) are for films actually seen and rated by the executive and senior editors. All other ratings are estimates. (See Notes on Entertainment Ratings in the front section.)

ANNE OF THE THOUSAND DAYS (1969). To marry Genevieve Bujold and divorce his first wife, Richard Burton (as King Henry VIII) has plunged England's relations between church and state into turmoil.

ANNIE OAKLEY (1935) RKO. **B&W-90min.** Barbara Stanwyck, Preston Foster.. 4*

ANNIVERSARY, THE (1968) 20th Century-Fox. **Color-95min.** *(British).* Bette Davis, Sheila Hancock .... (3)

ANONYMOUS VENETIAN, THE (1970) Allied Artists. **Color-91min.** *(Italian).* Tony Musante, Florinda Bolkan .... (2)
Original title: ANONIMO VENEZIANO
Alternate title: VENETIAN ANONYMOUS, THE

ANOTHER CHANCE (1952) *see* TWILIGHT WOMEN

ANOTHER DAWN (1937) Warner Bros. **B&W-73min.** Errol Flynn, Kay Francis.. 3*

ANOTHER MAN, ANOTHER CHANCE (1977) United Artists. **Color-132min.** *(U.S.-French, English language).* James Caan, Genevieve Bujold 4½*
French title: AUTRE HOMME, UNE AUTRE CHANCE, UN
British title: ANOTHER MAN, ANOTHER WOMAN

ANOTHER MAN'S POISON (1951) United Artists. **B&W-89min.** *(British).* Bette Davis, Anthony Steele.. (4)

ANOTHER PART OF THE FOREST (1948) Universal. **B&W-107min.** Fredric March, Florence Eldridge, Dan Duryea 6*

ANOTHER SHORE (1948) J. Arthur Rank. **B&W-77min.** *(British).* Robert Beatty, Moira Lister.. (4)

ANOTHER THIN MAN (1939) M-G-M. **B&W-105min.** William Powell, Myrna Loy .... (4)

ANOTHER TIME, ANOTHER PLACE (1958) Paramount. **B&W-98min.** *(British).* Lana Turner, Barry Sullivan..................................... 3½*

ANTARCTIC CROSSING (1958) Lester A. Schoenfeld Films. **Color-50min.** *(British).* .... (3)

ANTHONY ADVERSE (1936) Warner Bros. **B&W-120min.** Fredric March, Olivia de Havilland 5*

ANTIGONE (1961) Ellis Films. **B&W-88min.** *(Greek-U.S.).* Irene Papas, Manos Katrakis... (5)

ANTONIA: A PORTRAIT OF THE WOMAN (1974) Rocky Mountain Productions. **Color-58min.** *(Documentary). Director:* Judy Collins 4*

ANTONY AND CLEOPATRA (1972) J. Arthur Rank. **Color-160min.** *(Swiss-Spanish-British).* Charlton Heston, Hildegard Neil....................

ANXIOUS YEARS, THE (1937) *see* DARK JOURNEY

ANY GUN CAN PLAY (1967) Golden Eagle. **Color-103min.** *(Italian, English language).* Gilbert Roland, Edd Byrnes..................... 3*
Original title: VADO . . . L'AMMAZZO E TORNO *(I'll Go . . . I'll Kill Him and Come Back)*

ANY MAN'S WOMAN (1958) *see* NO ESCAPE

ANY NUMBER CAN PLAY (1949) M-G-M. **B&W-112min.** Clark Gable, Alexis Smith... 4*

Films are rated on a 1 to 10 scale, 10 is highest. **Boldface** ratings followed by an asterisk (*) are for films actually seen and rated by the executive and senior editors. All other ratings are estimates. (See Notes on Entertainment Ratings in the front section.)

ANY NUMBER CAN WIN (1963) M-G-M. **B&W-110min.** *(French).* Jean Gabin, Alain Delon 4*
Original title: MELODIE EN SOUS-SOL *(Basement Melody)*
British title: BIG SNATCH, THE

ANY SECOND NOW (1969) MCA-TV. **Color-97min.** *(Made for TV).* Stewart Granger, Lois Nettleton, Joseph Campanella .... (4)

ANY WEDNESDAY (1966) Warner Bros. **Color-109min.** Jane Fonda, Jason Robards 5*
British title: BACHELOR GIRL APARTMENT

ANYONE CAN PLAY (1967) Paramount. **Color-88min.** *(Italian).* Ursula Andress, Marisa Mell .... (3)
Original title: DOLCI SIGNORE, LE *(The Sweet Ladies)*

ANYTHING CAN HAPPEN (1952) Paramount. **B&W-107min.** José Ferrer, Kim Hunter .... (5)

ANYTHING FOR LOVE (1974) *see* 11 HARROWHOUSE

ANYTHING GOES (1936) Paramount. **B&W-92min.** Bing Crosby, Ethel Merman.. (4)
Alternate title: TOPS IS THE LIMIT

ANYTHING GOES (1956) Paramount. **Color-106min.** Bing Crosby, Donald O'Connor .... (4)

ANZIO (1968) Columbia. **Color-117min.** *(Italian, English version).* Robert Mitchum, Peter Falk 4*
Original title: SBARCO DI ANZIO, LO
British title: BATTLE FOR ANZIO, THE

APACHE (1954) United Artists. **Color-91min.** Burt Lancaster, Jean Peters, Charles Buchinsky (Bronson) 3*

APACHE AMBUSH (1955) Columbia. **B&W-68min.** Bill Williams, Richard Jaeckel .... (3)

APACHE COUNTRY (1952) Columbia. **B&W-62min.** Gene Autry, Pat Buttram .... (4)

APACHE DRUMS (1951) Universal. **Color-75min.** Stephen McNally, Coleen Gray .... (3)

APACHE FURY (1965) American-International. **Color-84min.** *(Spanish).* Frank Latimore, George Gordon .... (3)

APACHE GOLD (1963) Columbia. **Color-91min.** *(French-Italian-West German-Yugoslavian).* Lex Barker, Pierre Brice............ (3)
Original French title: RÉVOLTE DES INDIENS APACHES, LA *(The Revolt of the Apache Indians)*
Original Italian title: VALLE DEI LUNGHI COLTELLI, LA
Original German title: WINNETOU-I. TEIL
Original Yugoslavian title: VINETU

APACHE RIFLES (1964) 20th Century-Fox. **Color-92min.** Audie Murphy, Michael Danton 3*

APACHE TERRITORY (1958) Columbia. **Color-75min.** Rory Calhoun, Barbara Bates 2½*

APACHE TRAIL (1943) M-G-M. **B&W-66min.** Lloyd Nolan, Donna Reed .... (3)

APACHE UPRISING (1966) Paramount. **Color-90min.** Rory Calhoun, Corinne Calvet, Arthur Hunnicutt............................ (3)

APACHE WAR SMOKE (1952) M-G-M. **B&W-67min.** Gilbert Roland, Glenda Farrell .... (8)

APACHE WARRIOR (1957) 20th Century-Fox. **B&W-74min.** Keith Larsen, Jim Davis .... (3)

APACHE WOMAN (1955) American-International. **Color-83min.** Lloyd Bridges, Joan Taylor 2*

APARAJITO (1956) Harrison Pictures. **B&W-113min.** *(Indian).* Pinaki Sen Gupta, Smaran Ghosal 3*
Alternate title: UNVANQUISHED, THE

APARTMENT, THE (1960) United Artists. **B&W-125min.** Jack Lemmon, Shirley MacLaine 6*

APARTMENT FOR PEGGY (1948) 20th Century-Fox. **Color-98min.** Jeanne Crain, William Holden............................ 4*

APE, THE (1940) Monogram [Allied Artists]. **B&W-62min.** Boris Karloff, Henry Hall.. (3)

A*P*E (1976) Worldwide Entertainment/Jack H. Harris. **Color-87min.** *(Korean-U.S.).* Rod Arrants, Joanne De Verona, Alex Nicol .... (3)
Alternate title: APE
Alternate title: APE (NOT TO BE CONFUSED WITH KING KONG)

APE MAN, THE (1943) Monogram [Allied Artists]. **B&W-64min.** Bela Lugosi, Wallace Ford 3*
British title: LOCK YOUR DOORS!

APE MAN OF THE JUNGLE (1964) American-International. **Color-80min.** *(Italian).* Ralph Hudson, John Chevron, Archie Savage .... (1)
Original title: TARZAK CONTRO GLI UOMINI LEOPARDO *(Tarzak Against the Leopard Men)*

APE WOMAN, THE (1964) Avco-Embassy. **B&W-92min.** *(Italian).* Ugo Tognazzi, Annie Girardot .... (4)
Original title: DONNA SCIMMIA, LA
Alternate title: MONKEY WOMAN, THE
Alternate title: MOST UNUSUAL WOMAN, A

APHRODITE, GODDESS OF LOVE (1962) Avco-Embassy. **Color-86min.** *(Italian).* Isabel Corey, Antonio de Teffe .... (3)

APOCALYPSE NOW (1979) United Artists. **Color- min.** Marlon Brando, Martin Sheen, Robert Duvall ....

APPALOOSA, THE (1966) Universal. **Color-98min.** Marlon Brando, Anjanette Comer 4½*
British title: SOUTHWEST TO SONORA

APPLAUSE (1929) Paramount. **B&W-87min.** Helen Morgan, Joan Peers 3*

APPLE DUMPLING GANG, THE (1975) Buena Vista. **Color-100min.** Bill Bixby, Susan Clark 4*

APPLE DUMPLING GANG RIDES AGAIN, THE (1979) Buena Vista. **Color-88min.** Tim Conway, Don Knotts............................

APPLE WAR, THE (1973) Specialty. **Color-103min.** *(Swedish).* Hans Alfredson, Monica Zetterlund, Max Von Sydow ....
Original title: APPELKRIGET

APPOINTMENT, THE (1969) M-G-M. **Color-100min.** Omar Sharif, Anouk Aimee.. (3)

APPOINTMENT FOR LOVE (1941) Universal. **B&W-89min.** Charles Boyer, Margaret Sullavan .... (4)

APPOINTMENT IN BERLIN (1943) Columbia. **B&W-77min.** George Sanders, Marguerite Chapman.. (4)

APPOINTMENT IN HONDURAS (1953) RKO. **Color-79min.** Glenn Ford, Ann Sheridan.. 3*

APPOINTMENT IN LONDON (1953) Associated Artists. **B&W-96min.** *(British).* Dirk Bogarde, Ian Hunter 3*

APPOINTMENT WITH A SHADOW (1957) *see* MIDNIGHT STORY, THE

APPOINTMENT WITH A SHADOW (1958) Universal. **B&W-73min.** George Nader, Joanna Moore .... (3)
British title: BIG STORY, THE

APPOINTMENT WITH DANGER (1951) Paramount. **B&W-89min.** Alan Ladd, Phyllis Calvert 4*

APPOINTMENT WITH MURDER (1948) Film Classics [U.A.]. **B&W-67min.** John Calvert, Catherine Craig .... (4)

APPOINTMENT WITH VENUS (1951) *see* ISLAND RESCUE

APPRENTICESHIP OF DUDDY KRAVITZ, THE (1974) Paramount. **Color-121min.** *(Canadian).* Richard Dreyfuss, Micheline Lanctot....... 7½*

APRIL FOOLS, THE (1969) Nat'l General (for Cinema Center). **Color-95min.** Jack Lemmon, Catherine Deneuve, Charles Boyer 5½*

APRIL IN PARIS (1953) Warner Bros. **Color-101min.** Doris Day, Ray Bolger 4*

APRIL LOVE (1957) 20th Century-Fox. **Color-97min.** Pat Boone, Shirley Jones .... (4)

APRIL SHOWERS (1948) Warner Bros. **B&W-94min.** Ann Sothern, Jack Carson .... (4)

AQUA SEX, THE (1962) *see* MERMAIDS OF TIBURON, THE

AQUARIANS, THE (1970) Universal. **Color-100min.** *(Made for TV).* José Ferrer, Ricardo Montalban.. 3*

ARABELLA (1967) Universal. **Color-91min.** Virna Lisi, James Fox, Terry-Thomas 4*

ARABESQUE (1966) Universal. **Color-105min.** *(British-U.S.).* Gregory Peck, Sophia Loren 5*

ARABIAN ADVENTURE, AN (1979) EMI. **Color-98min.** Christopher Lee, Oliver Tobias, Peter Cushing ....

ARABIAN NIGHTS (1942) Universal. **Color-86min.** Jon Hall, Maria Montez.. 4½*

ARABIAN NIGHTS, THE (1974) United Artists. **Color-155min.** *(Italian-French).* Ninetto Davoli, Franco Merli .... (4)
Original Italian title: FIORE DELL MILLE E UNA NOTTE, IL *(Tales of a Thousand and One Nights)*
Alternate title: THOUSAND AND ONE NIGHTS, A

ARCH, THE (1967) Cinema 5. **B&W-94min.** *(Taiwan).* Lisa Lu, Roy Chiao Hung .... (4)

ARCH OF TRIUMPH (1948) United Artists. **B&W-120min.** Ingrid Bergman, Charles Boyer.. 3*

ARCHANGELS, THE (1963) Avco-Embassy. **B&W-102min.** *(Italian).* Roberto Bisacco, Paolo Graziosi .... (3)
Original title: ARCANGELI, GLI

archy and mehitabel (1971) *see* SHINBONE ALLEY

Films are rated on a 1 to 10 scale, 10 is highest. **Boldface** ratings followed by an asterisk (*) are for films actually seen and rated by the executive and senior editors. All other ratings are estimates. (See Notes on Entertainment Ratings in the front section.)

ARCTIC FLIGHT (1952) Monogram [Allied Artists]. **B&W-78min.** Wayne Morris, Lola Albright .... (4)

ARCTIC MANHUNT (1949) Universal. **B&W-69min.** Mikel Conrad, Carol Thurston .... (3)

ARE HUSBANDS NECESSARY? (1942) Paramount. **B&W-79min.** Ray Milland, Patricia Morison .... (3)

ARE PARENTS PEOPLE? (1925) Paramount. **B&W-73min.** *(Silent).* Betty Bronson, Florence Vidor .... (4)

ARE WE ALL MURDERERS? (1952) *see* WE ARE ALL MURDERERS

ARE YOU THERE? (1930) Fox Film Co. [20th]. **B&W-60min.** Beatrice Lillie, John Garrick .... (5)
Alternate title: EXIT LAUGHING

ARE YOU WITH IT? (1948) Universal. **B&W-90min.** Donald O'Connor, Olga San Juan .... (4)

ARENA (1953) M-G-M. **Color-83min.** Gig Young, Jean Hagen **4***

ARGONAUTS, THE (1960) *see* GIANTS OF THESSALY, THE

ARISE, MY LOVE (1940) Paramount. **B&W-113min.** Ray Milland, Claudette Colbert .... (4)

ARISTOCATS, THE (1970) Buena Vista. **Color-78min.** *(Cartoon). Director:* Wolfgang Reitherman **3½***

ARIZONA (1940) Columbia. **B&W-127min.** William Holden, Jean Arthur .... (4)

ARIZONA BUSHWACKERS (1968) Paramount. **Color-86min.** Howard Keel, Scott Brady .... (3)

ARIZONA COLT (1966) *see* MAN FROM NOWHERE, THE

ARIZONA MISSION (1956) *see* GUN THE MAN DOWN

ARIZONA RAIDERS (1965) Columbia. **Color-88min.** Audie Murphy, Michael Dante .... (3)

ARKANSAS JUDGE (1941) Republic. **B&W-72min.** The Weaver Brothers and Elviry, Roy Rogers .... (3)
British title: FALSE WITNESS

ARKANSAS TRAVELER, THE (1938) Paramount. **B&W-83min.** Bob Burns, Fay Bainter .... (4)

ARMORED ATTACK (1943) *see* NORTH STAR, THE

ARMORED CAR ROBBERY (1950) RKO. **B&W-68min.** Charles McGraw, Robert Sterling .... (4)

ARMORED COMMAND (1961) Allied Artists. **B&W-99min.** Howard Keel, Tina Louise .... (3)

ARMS AND THE WOMAN (1944) *see* MR. WINKLE GOES TO WAR

ARMY BOUND (1952) Monogram [Allied Artists]. **B&W-61min.** Stanley Clements, Karen Sharpe .... (2)

ARMY CAPERS (1952) *see* WAC FROM WALLA WALLA, THE

ARMY SURGEON (1942) RKO. **B&W-63min.** James Ellison, Jane Wyatt .... (3)

ARNELO AFFAIR, THE (1947) M-G-M. **B&W-86min.** John Hodiak, George Murphy **3***

ARNOLD (1973) Cinerama Releasing. **Color-94min.** Stella Stevens, Roddy McDowell, Elsa Lanchester **3***

AROUND THE WORLD (1943) RKO. **B&W-43min.** Kay Kyser, Joan Davis .... (4)

AROUND THE WORLD IN 80 DAYS (1956) United Artists. **Color-168min.** David Niven, Cantinflas **5½***

AROUND THE WORLD UNDER THE SEA (1966) M-G-M. **Color-117min.** Lloyd Bridges, Shirley Eaton .... (3)

AROUSE AND BEWARE (1940) *see* MAN FROM DAKOTA, THE

AROUSED (1966) Cambist. **B&W-82min.** Janine Lenon, Steve Hollister (3)

ARRANGEMENT, THE (1969) Warner Bros. **Color-127min.** Kirk Douglas, Faye Dunaway **3***

ARREST BULLDOG DRUMMOND (1939) Paramount. **B&W-57min.** John Howard, Heather Angel .... (4)

ARRIVEDERCI, BABY! (1966) Paramount. **Color-100min.** *(British).* Tony Curtis, Rosanna Schiaffino **3***
Original title: DROP DEAD, DARLING

ARROW IN THE DUST (1954) Allied Artists. **Color-80min.** Sterling Hayden, Colleen Gray .... (3)

ARROW OF THE AVENGER (1963) *see* GOLIATH AND THE REBEL SLAVE

ARROWHEAD (1953) Paramount. **Color-105min.** Charlton Heston, Jack Palance **3***

ARROWSMITH (1931) United Artists. **B&W-108min.** Ronald Colman, Helen Hayes .... (5)

ARRUZA (1972) Avco-Embassy. **Color-73min.** *(Documentary). Director:* Budd Boetticher .... (4)

AROUND THE WORLD IN 80 DAYS (1956) is a feat David Niven (far right) and his servant Cantinflas (second from right) are trying to accomplish, but detective Robert Newton (far left) is certain they have an ulterior motive, and also wonders why they picked up Shirley MacLaine in India.

ARSENE LUPIN (1932) M-G-M. **B&W-84min.** John Barrymore, Lionel Barrymore .... (5)

ARSENE LUPIN RETURNS (1938) M-G-M. **B&W-81min.** Melvyn Douglas, Virginia Bruce .... (4)

ARSENIC AND OLD LACE (1944) Warner Bros. **B&W-118min.** Cary Grant, Priscilla Lane **7***

ARSON FOR HIRE (1959) Allied Artists. **B&W-67min.** Steve Brodie, Lyn Thomas .... (2)

ART OF LOVE, THE (1965) Universal. **Color-99min.** James Garner, Dick Van Dyke **4***

ARTFUL PENETRATION, THE (1969) *see* BLACK ON WHITE

ARTFUL PENETRATION OF BARBARA, THE (1969) *see* BLACK ON WHITE

ARTISTS AND MODELS (1937) Paramount. **B&W-97min.** Jack Benny, Ida Lupino .... (4)

ARTISTS AND MODELS (1955) Paramount. **Color-108min.** Dean Martin, Jerry Lewis **4***

ARTISTS AND MODELS ABROAD (1938) Paramount. **B&W-90min.** Jack Benny, Joan Bennett .... (5)
British title: STRANDED IN PARIS

ARTURO'S ISLAND (1962) M-G-M. **B&W-90min.** *(Italian).* Vanni De Maigret, Reginald Kernan **4***
Original title: ISOLA DI ARTURO, L'

AS IF IT WERE RAINING (1963) Paramount. **B&W-88min.** *(French-Spanish).* Eddie Constantine, Elisa Montes .... (3)
Original French title: COMME S'IL EN PLEUVAIT

AS LONG AS THEY'RE HAPPY (1955) J. Arthur Rank. **Color-91min.** *(British).* Diana Dors, Jack Buchanan .... (3)

AS LONG AS YOU LIVE (1964) International Classics [20th]. **B&W-92min.** *(German).* Marianne Koch, Karin Dor **3***

AS LONG AS YOU'RE NEAR ME (1955) Warner Bros. **B&W-101min.** *(German).* Maria Schell, O. W. Fisher .... (3)

AS THE EARTH TURNS (1934) Warner Bros. **B&W-73min.** Jean Muir, Donald Woods .... (5)

AS THE SEA RAGES (1959) Columbia. **B&W-74min.** *(German, English language).* Maria Schell, Cliff Robertson .... (3)
Original title: RAUBFISCHER IN HELLAS *(Robber Fisherman in Greece)*

AS USUAL, UNKNOWN (1958) *see* BIG DEAL ON MADONNA STREET

AS YOU DESIRE ME (1932) M-G-M. **B&W-71min.** Greta Garbo, Melvyn Douglas **4***

AS YOUNG AS WE ARE (1959) Paramount. **B&W-76min.** Robert Harland, Pippa Scott .... (3)

AS YOUNG AS YOU FEEL (1951) 20th Century-Fox. **B&W-77min.** Monty Woolley, Thelma Ritter **5½***

ASH WEDNESDAY (1973) Paramount. **Color-99min.** Elizabeth Taylor, Henry Fonda **3***

Films are rated on a 1 to 10 scale, 10 is highest. **Boldface** ratings followed by an asterisk (*) are for films actually seen and rated by the executive and senior editors. All other ratings are estimates. (See Notes on Entertainment Ratings in the front section.)

AT THE CIRCUS (1939). Harpo, Groucho and Chico Marx try to help the young owner save his circus from a villain who holds the mortgage.

ASHANTI (1979) Warner Bros. **Color-117min.** *(Swiss-U.S.).* Michael Caine, Beverly Johnson, Peter Ustinov...

ASHES AND DIAMONDS (1959) Janus Films. **B&W-109min.** *(Polish).* Zbigniew Cybulski, Eva Krzyzewska **3***
Original title: POPIOL I DIAMENT

ASK ANY GIRL (1959) M-G-M. **Color-101min.** David Niven, Shirley MacLaine **3½***

ASPHALT JUNGLE, THE (1950) M-G-M. **B&W-112min.** Sterling Hayden, Louis Calhern.................................. **5½***

ASPHYX, THE (1972) Paragon Pictures. **Color-98min.** *(British).* Robert Stephens, Robert Powell .... **(4)**

ASSASSIN, THE (1947) *see* GUNFIGHTERS

ASSASSIN, THE (1952) United Artists. **B&W-90min.** *(British).* Richard Todd, Eva Bartok .... **(4)**
Original title: VENETIAN BIRD, THE

ASSASSIN, THE (1961) Manson Distributing Corp. **B&W-83min.** *(French-Italian).* Marcello Mastroianni, Micheline Presle.................................... **(4)**
Alternate title: LADY KILLER OF ROME, THE
Original French title: ASSASSIN, L'
Italian title: ASSASSINO, L'

ASSASSINATION BUREAU, THE (1969) Paramount. **Color-110min.** *(British).* Oliver Reed, Diana Rigg **5***

ASSASSINATION OF TROTSKY, THE (1972) Cinerama Releasing. **Color-103min.** *(French-Italian-British, English language).* Richard Burton, Alain Delon **2***

ASSAULT (1970) *see* IN THE DEVIL'S GARDEN

ASSAULT ON A QUEEN (1966) Paramount. **Color-106min.** Frank Sinatra, Virna Lisi **3***

ASSAULT ON PARADISE (1977) *see* MANIAC

ASSAULT ON PRECINCT 13 (1976) Turtle Releasing. **Color-91min.** Austin Stoker, Darwin Joston, Laurie Zimmer .... **(4)**

ASSAULT ON THE WAYNE (1971) Paramount. **Color-74min.** *(Made for TV).* Joseph Cotten, Leonard Nimoy **3***

ASSIGNMENT ABROAD (1955) Triangle. **B&W-73min.** *(Telefeature).* Robert Alda, Lois Hensen, Kay Callard.............................. **(2)**

ASSIGNMENT CHILDREN (1955) Paramount. **Color-19min.** *(Documentary).* Danny Kaye... **(5)**

ASSIGNMENT IN BRITTANY (1943) M-G-M. **B&W-96min.** Jean-Pierre Aumont, Susan Peters............................. **(3)**

ASSIGNMENT IN CHINA (1949) *see* STATE DEPARTMENT - FILE 649

ASSIGNMENT ISTANBUL (1968) *see* CASTLE OF FU MANCHU, THE

ASSIGNMENT K (1968) Columbia. **Color-97min.** *(British).* Stephen Boyd, Camilla Sparv .... **(3)**

ASSIGNMENT: MUNICH (1972) M-G-M. **Color-100min.** *(Made for TV).* Richard Basehart, Roy Scheider, Lesley Warren **4***

ASSIGNMENT - OUTER SPACE (1960) American-International. **Color-79min.** Rik von Nutter, Gabriella Fairnon .... **(2)**
Original title: SPACE MEN

ASSIGNMENT - PARIS (1952) Columbia. **B&W-85min.** Dana Andrews, George Sanders................................. **4***

ASSIGNMENT REDHEAD (1956) United Artists. **B&W-79min.** *(British).* Paul Carpenter, Kay Callard .... **(3)**
Alternate title: UNDERCOVER GIRL

ASSIGNMENT TO KILL (1969) Warner Bros. **Color-102min.** Patrick O'Neal, John Gielgud **3***

Films are rated on a 1 to 10 scale, 10 is highest. **Boldface** ratings followed by an asterisk (*) are for films actually seen and rated by the executive and senior editors. All other ratings are estimates. (See Notes on Entertainment Ratings in the front section.)

ASSOCIATION, THE (1975) Producers Golden Harvest-Golden Farm. Color-81min. *(Chinese-Korean).* Byong Yu, Tien Nei, Angela Mao .... (2)

ASTONISHED HEART, THE (1949) Universal. **B&W-92min.** *(British).* Noel Coward, Celia Johnson 3*

ASTOUNDING SHE MONSTER, THE (1957) American-International. **B&W-60min.** Robert Clarke, Shirley Kilpatrick 2*
British title: MYSTERIOUS INVADER, THE

ASTRONAUT, THE (1971) MCA-TV. Color-73min. *(Made for TV).* Monte Markham, Susan Clark, Jackie Cooper .... (4)

ASTRO-ZOMBIES, THE (1969) Gemeni Films. Color-90min. John Carradine, Wendell Corey.................... (2)

ASTROLOGER, THE (1975) Republic Arts. Color-96min. Craig Denney, Darrien Earle .... (3)

ASYLUM (1972) Robinson-Frelinghuysen-Rosenthal Productions. B&W-95min. *(British).* .... (5)

ASYLUM (1972) Cinerama Releasing. Color-88min. *(British).* Patrick Magee, Robert Powell 5*

ASYLUM FOR A SPY (1967) MCA-TV. Color-90min. *(Made for TV).* Robert Stack, Felicia Farr .... (4)

ASYLUM OF SATAN (1972) Bil-Ko Films. Color-87min. Charles Kissinger, Carla Borelli.................... (3)

AT ANY PRICE (1969) *see* VATICAN AFFAIR, THE

AT GUNPOINT (1955) Allied Artists. Color-81min. Fred MacMurray, Dorothy Malone 3½*
Alternate title: GUN POINT
British title: GUNPOINT!

AT LONG LAST LOVE (1975) 20th Century-Fox. Color-118min. Burt Reynolds, Cybill Shepherd.................... 4*

AT SWORD'S POINT (1952) RKO. Color-81min. Cornel Wilde, Maureen O'Hara 4*
British title: SONS OF THE MUSKETEERS

AT THE CIRCUS (1939) M-G-M. **B&W-87min.** Groucho Marx, Chico Marx 3*
Publicity title: MARX BROTHERS AT THE CIRCUS, THE

AT THE EARTH'S CORE (1976) American-International. Color-89min. *(British).* Doug McClure, Peter Cushing .... (4)

AT THE STROKE OF NINE (1957) Grand National *(Brit.).* **B&W-71min.** *(British).* Patricia Dainton, Stephen Murray .... (3)

AT WAR WITH THE ARMY (1950) Paramount. **B&W-93min.** Dean Martin, Jerry Lewis.................... 3*

ATHENA (1954) M-G-M. Color-96min. Jane Powell, Edmund Purdom.... (4)

ATLANTIC ADVENTURE (1935) Columbia. **B&W-70min.** Lloyd Nolan, Nancy Carroll .... (4)

ATLANTIC CITY (1944) Republic. **B&W-86min.** Constance Moore, Brad Taylor.................... (3)

ATLANTIC CONVOY (1942) Columbia. **B&W-66min.** Bruce Bennett, Virginia Field.................... (4)

ATLANTIS, THE LOST CONTINENT (1961) M-G-M. Color-90min. Anthony Hall, Joyce Taylor.................... 3*

ATLAS (1960) Allied Artists. Color-80min. Michael Forest, Frank Wolff (3)

ATLAS AGAINST THE CYCLOPS (1961) Medallion. Color-100min. *(Italian).* Mitchell Gordon, Chelo Alonso .... (1)
Original title: MACISTE NELLA TERRA DEI CICLOPI *(Maciste in the Land of the Cyclops)*
British title: MONSTER FROM THE UNKNOWN WORLD
Alternate title: ATLAS IN THE LAND OF THE CYCLOPS

ATLAS AGAINST THE CZAR (1964) Telewide Systems. Color-91min. *(Italian).* Kirk Morris, Gloria Milland.................... (1)

ATOLL K (1952) *see* UTOPIA

ATOM AGE VAMPIRE (1960) Topaz Film Corp. **B&W-87min.** *(Italian).* Alberto Lupo, Susanne Loret.................... 2*
Original title: SEDDOK, L'EREDE DI SATANA

ATOMIC AGENT (1959) American-International. **B&W-85min.** *(French).* Martine Carol, Felix Marten.................... (3)
Original title: NATHALIE SECRET AGENT

ATOMIC BRAIN, THE (1970) *see* MONSTROSITY

ATOMIC CITY, THE (1952) Paramount. **B&W-85min.** Gene Barry, Lydia Clarke.................... (5)

ATOMIC KID, THE (1954) Republic. **B&W-86min.** Mickey Rooney, Robert Strauss .... (3)

ATOMIC MAN, THE (1955) Allied Artists. **B&W-78min.** *(British).* Gene Nelson, Faith Domergue.................... (3)
Original title: TIMESLIP

ATOMIC MONSTER (1941) *see* MAN-MADE MONSTER

ATOMIC RULERS OF THE WORLD (1964) Teleworld. **B&W-80min.** *(Japanese).* Ken Utsui, Minako Yamada.................... (1)
Original title of first part: KOTETSU NO KYOJIN-KAISEIJIN NO MAJYO *(Invaders from the Planets)*
Original title of second part: KOTETSU NO KYOJIN-CHIKYU METZUBO SUNZEN *(The Earth in Danger)*
Alternate title: SUPER GIANT 3
Alternate title: SUPER GIANT 4
Alternate title: ATTACK OF THE FLYING SAUCERS
Alternate title: INVINCIBLE SPACEMAN
Alternate title: EARTH IN DANGER, THE
Alternate title: INVADERS FROM SPACE

ATOMIC SUBMARINE, THE (1960) Allied Artists. **B&W-72min.** Arthur Franz, Dick Foran 2*

ATOMIC WAR BRIDE (1966) Medallion. **B&W-77min.** *(Foreign).* Anton Vodak, Eva Krewskan .... (2)

ATRAGON (1964) American-International. Color-88min. *(Japanese).* Tadao Takashima, Yu Fujiki 2*
Alternate title: ATRAGON THE FLYING SUB

ATTACK! (1956) United Artists. **B&W-107min.** Jack Palance, Eddie Albert.................... 5*

ATTACK AND RETREAT (1963) *see* ITALIANO BRAVE GENTE

ATTACK OF THE CRAB MONSTERS (1957) Allied Artists. **B&W-64min.** Richard Garland, Pamela Duncan 3*

ATTACK OF THE 50 FOOT WOMAN (1958) Allied Artists. **B&W-66min.** Allison Hayes, William Hudson.................... 3*

ATTACK OF THE FLYING SAUCERS (1964) *see* ATOMIC RULERS OF THE WORLD

ATTACK OF THE GIANT LEECHES (1959) American-International. **B&W-62min.** Ken Clark, Yvette Vickers 3*
British title: DEMONS OF THE SWAMP
Publicity title: GIANT LEECHES, THE

ATTACK OF THE KILLER TOMATOES! (1978) NAI Entertainment. Color-87min. David Miller, George Wilson 3½*

ATTACK OF THE MAYAN MUMMY (1963) Medallion. **B&W-74min.** *(Mexican-U.S.).* Nina Knight, Richard Webb.................... 1*

ATTACK OF THE MOORS (1960) American-International. Color-80min. *(Italian).* Chelo Alonso, Rik Battaglia.................... (1)

ATTACK OF THE MUSHROOM PEOPLE (1964) American-International. Color-89min. *(Japanese).* Akiro Kubo, Yoshio Tsuchiya 3*
Original title: MATANGO

ATTACK OF THE NORMANS (1961) American-International. Color-79min. *(Italian).* Cameron Mitchell, Genevieve Grad.................... (3)

ATTACK OF THE PUPPET PEOPLE (1958) American-International. **B&W-78min.** John Agar, John Hoyt.................... 3*
British title: SIX INCHES TALL

ATTACK OF THE ROBOTS (1967) American-International. **B&W-85min.** *(French-Spanish).* Eddie Constantine, Fernando Rey .... (2)
Original French title: CARTES SUR TABLE *(Cards on the Table)*
Spanish title: CARTAS BOCA ARRIBA *(Cards Face Up)*

ATTACK ON TERROR (1975) Warner Bros. Color-194min. *(Made for TV).* Wayne Rogers, Rip Torn, L. Q. Jones, Ned Beatty.................... 5½*

ATTACK ON THE IRON COAST (1968) United Artists. Color-89min. *(U.S.-British).* Lloyd Bridges, Andrew Keir .... (3)

ATTACK SQUADRON (1963) Paramount. Color-102min. *(Japanese).* Toshiro Mifune .... (3)

ATTEMPT TO KILL (1961) Anglo Amalgamated [EMI]. **B&W-57min.** *(British).* Derek Farr, Tom Wright.................... (2)

ATTICA (1974) The Other Cinema. **B&W-80min.** *(Documentary).* Director: Cinda Firestone.................... (4)

ATTILA (1955) Attila Associates. Color-79min. *(Italian).* Anthony Quinn, Sophia Loren.................... (3)

ATTRACTION (1969) *see* BLACK ON WHITE

AU HAZARD BALTHAZAR (1966) New Yorker Films. **B&W-95min.** *(French-Swedish).* Anne Wiazemsky, Francois Lafarge.................... 3*

AUDREY ROSE (1977) United Artists. Color-112min. Marsha Mason, Anthony Hopkins.................... 4½*

AUGUSTINE OF HIPPO (1972) Color-120min. *(Italian, Made for TV).* Deri Berkani .... (4)
Original title: AGOSTINA DI IPPONA

AUNT CLARA (1954) Showcorporation. **B&W-84min.** *(British).* Margaret Rutherford, Ronald Shiner 4½*

AUNT TULA (1964) *see* TIA TULA, LA

AUNTIE MAME (1958) Warner Bros. Color-143min. Rosalind Russell, Forrest Tucker.................... 5*

AUSTERLITZ (1960) *see* BATTLE OF AUSTERLITZ, THE

AUTOBIOGRAPHY OF A FLEA, THE (1976) Mitchell Bros. **Color-90min.** Jean Jennings, Paul Thomas 1½*

AUTOBIOGRAPHY OF A PRINCESS (1975) Cinema 5. **Color-60min.** *(British).* James Mason, Madhur Jaffrey .... (4)

AUTOBIOGRAPHY OF MISS JANE PITTMAN, THE (1973) Viacom. **Color-100min.** *(Made for TV).* Cicely Tyson, Odetta 5*

AUTOPSY (1978) Joseph Brenner. **Color-125min.** *(Italian).* Mimsy Farmer, Barry Primus .... (3)

AUTOPSY OF A CRIMINAL (1964) Paramount. **B&W-92min.** *(Spanish).* Danielle Godet, Francisco Rabal .... (3)

AUTUMN LEAVES (1956) Columbia. **B&W-108min.** Joan Crawford, Cliff Robertson 4*

AUTUMN SONATA (1978) New World. **Color-97min.** *(German).* Ingrid Bergman, Liv Ullmann 3*
Original title: HERBSTSONATE
Swedish title: HOESTSONAT

AVALANCHE (1946) Producers Rel. Corp. [Eagle Lion]. **B&W-70min.** Bruce Cabot, Veda Ann Borg .... (3)

AVALANCHE (1978) New World. **Color-91min.** Rock Hudson, Mia Farrow 4*

AVALANCHE EXPRESS (1979) 20th Century-Fox. **Color-   min.** Lee Marvin, Robert Shaw

AVANTI! (1972) United Artists. **Color-144min.** *(U.S.-Italian).* Jack Lemmon, Juliet Mills 4*

AVENGER, THE (1960) UCC Films. **B&W-102min.** *(German).* Heinz Drache, Ingrid Von Bergen .... (3)
Original title: RAECHER, DER

AVENGER, THE (1962) Medallion. **Color-108min.** *(Italian-French).* Steve Reeves, Carla Marlier .... (1)
Original Italian title: LEGGENDA DI ENEA, LA
French title: CONQUÉRANTS HÉROIQUES
TV title: LAST GLORY OF TROY, THE

AVENGER OF THE SEVEN SEAS (1960) American-International. **Color-94min.** *(Italian).* Richard Harrison, Walter Barnes .... (1)

AVENGER OF VENICE (1963) Four Star. **Color-91min.** *(Italian-Spanish).* Brett Halsey, Gianna Maria Canale .... (1)
Original Italian title: PONTE DEI SOSPIRI, IL

AVENGERS, THE (1950) Republic. **B&W-90min.** John Carroll, Adele Mara .... (3)

AVVENTURA, L' (1960) Janus Films. **B&W-145min.** *(Italian).* Monica Vitti, Gabriele Ferzetti 3*
Translation title: The Adventure

AWAKENING, THE (1956) Kingsley International. **B&W-97min.** *(Italian).* Anna Magnani, Eleonora Rossi-Drago .... (5)
Original title: SUOR LETIZIA

AWAKENING GIANT - CHINA, THE (1973) Nordisk Film. **Color-93min.** *(Danish, Documentary).* Director: Jens Bjerre .... (5)

AWAY ALL BOATS (1956) Universal. **Color-114min.** Jeff Chandler, George Nader 4*

AWFUL DR. ORLOFF, THE (1962) Sigma III. **B&W-90min.** *(Spanish-French).* Howard Vernon, Conrado San Martin 2*
Original Spanish title: GRITOS EN LA NOCHE *(Screams in the Night)*
British title: DEMON DOCTOR, THE
Original French title: HORRIBLE DR. ORLOFF, L' *(The Horrible Dr. Orloff)*

AWFUL TRUTH, THE (1937) Columbia. **B&W-92min.** Irene Dunne, Cary Grant 4*

-B-

B.F.'S DAUGHTER (1948) M-G-M. **B&W-108min.** Barbara Stanwyck, Van Heflin .... (3)
British title: POLLY FULTON

B. G. REMEMBERS (1974) *see* BEN-GURION REMEMBERS

B.J. LANG PRESENTS (1971) Maron Films, Ltd. **Color-85min.** Mickey Rooney .... (2)

B.S. I LOVE YOU (1971) 20th Century-Fox. **Color-99min.** Peter Kastner, Joanna Barnes .... (3)

BABBITT (1934) First National [W.B.]. **B&W-74min.** Guy Kibbee, Aline MacMahon .... (5)

BABE (1975) M-G-M. **Color-100min.** *(Made for TV).* Susan Clark, Alex Karras 4½*

BABE RUTH STORY, THE (1948) Allied Artists. **B&W-106min.** William Bendix, Claire Trevor 3*

BABES IN ARMS (1939) M-G-M. **B&W-97min.** Mickey Rooney, Judy Garland 4½*

BABES IN BAGDAD (1952) United Artists. **Color-79min.** Paulette Goddard, John Boles .... (2)

BABES IN TOYLAND (1934) M-G-M. **B&W-73min.** Stan Laurel, Oliver Hardy 4*
Alternate title: MARCH OF THE WOODEN SOLDIERS
Alternate title: REVENGE IS SWEET
Alternate title: MARCH OF THE TOYS

BABES IN TOYLAND (1961) Buena Vista. **Color-105min.** Annette Funicello, Ray Bolger, Tommy Sands 3*

BABES ON BROADWAY (1941) M-G-M. **B&W-118min.** Mickey Rooney, Judy Garland .... (4)

BABETTE GOES TO WAR (1959) Columbia. **Color-100min.** *(French).* Brigitte Bardot, Jacques Charrier .... (4)
Original title: BABETTE S'EN VA-T-EN GUERRE

BABY, THE (1973) Scotia International *(Brit.).* **Color-85min.** Anjanette Comer, Ruth Roman, David Manzy 2½*

BABY AND THE BATTLESHIP, THE (1956) Distributors Corp. of America. **Color-96min.** *(British).* John Mills, Richard Attenborough ... (4)

BABY BE GOOD (1940) *see* BROTHER RAT AND A BABY

BABY BLUE MARINE (1976) Columbia. **Color-90min.** Jan-Michael Vincent, Glynnis O'Connor 4½*

BABY DOLL (1956) Warner Bros. **B&W-114min.** Karl Malden, Carroll Baker, Eli Wallach 5½*

BABY FACE NELSON (1957) United Artists. **B&W-85min.** Mickey Rooney, Carolyn Jones .... (4)

BABY LOVE (1969) Avco-Embassy. **Color-93min.** *(British).* Linda Hayden, Ann Lynn, Keith Barron .... (3)

BABY MAKER, THE (1970) National General. **Color-109min.** Barbara Hershey, Collin Wilcox-Horne .... (5)

BABY, THE RAIN MUST FALL (1965) Columbia. **B&W-100min.** Steve McQueen, Lee Remick 3½*

BABYSITTER, THE (1969) Crown International. **B&W-90min.** Patricia Wymer, George E. Carey .... (3)

BACCHANTES, THE (1961) Medallion. **Color-102min.** *(Italian-French).* Taina Elg, Pierre Brice .... (3)
Original Italian title: BACCANTI, LE

BACHELOR AND THE BOBBY-SOXER, THE (1947) RKO. **B&W-95min.** Cary Grant, Myrna Loy 5*
British title: BACHELOR KNIGHT

BACHELOR APARTMENT (1931) RKO. **B&W-83min.** Irene Dunne, Lowell Sherman .... (4)

BACHELOR BAIT (1949) *see* ADVENTURE IN BALTIMORE

BACHELOR FATHER (1931) RKO. **B&W-90min.** Marion Davies, Ralph Forbes .... (4)

BACHELOR FLAT (1962) 20th Century-Fox. **Color-91min.** Tuesday Weld, Richard Beymer 3*

BABY DOLL (1956). Child bride Carroll Baker is apprehensive about the motives of Eli Wallach, the vengeful Sicilian whose cotton gin was burned by an arsonist; the wronged man pressures her to reveal evidence that her husband is responsible, and is clearly intent upon seducing her in the process.

Films are rated on a 1 to 10 scale, 10 is highest. **Boldface** ratings followed by an asterisk (*) are for films actually seen and rated by the executive and senior editors. All other ratings are estimates. (See Notes on Entertainment Ratings in the front section.)

BACHELOR GIRL APARTMENT (1966) *see* ANY WEDNESDAY

BACHELOR GIRLS (1946) *see* BACHELOR'S DAUGHTERS, THE

BACHELOR IN PARADISE (1961) M-G-M. **Color-109min.** Bob Hope, Lana Turner..3*

BACHELOR KNIGHT (1947) *see* BACHELOR AND THE BOBBY-SOXER, THE

BACHELOR MOTHER (1939) RKO. **B&W-81min.** Ginger Rogers, David Niven..6½*

BACHELOR OF HEARTS (1958) Continental [Walter Reade]. **Color-97min.** *(British).* Hardy Kruger, Sylvia Sims.................(4)

BACHELOR PARTY, THE (1957) United Artists. **B&W-93min.** Don Murray, E. G. Marshall 5*

BACHELOR'S DAUGHTERS, THE (1946) United Artists. **B&W-88min.** Adolphe Menjou, Ann Dvorak ....(4)
British title: BACHELOR GIRLS

BACK AT THE FRONT (1953) Universal. **B&W-87min.** Tom Ewell, David Wayne ....(4)
Original title: WILLIE AND JOE BACK AT THE FRONT
British title: WILLIE AND JOE IN TOKYO

BACK DOOR TO HEAVEN (1939) Paramount. **B&W-85min.** Van Heflin, Wallace Ford ....(3)

BACK DOOR TO HELL (1964) 20th Century-Fox. **B&W-68min.** Jimmie Rodgers, Jack Nicholson ....(2)

BACK FROM ETERNITY (1956) RKO. **B&W-97min.** Robert Ryan, Anita Ekberg..(4)

BACK FROM THE DEAD (1957) 20th Century-Fox. **B&W-79min.** Peggie Castle, Arthur Franz ....(2)

BACK STREET (1932) Universal. **B&W-93min.** Irene Dunne, John Boles ....(5)

BACK STREET (1941) Universal. **B&W-89min.** Margaret Sullavan, Charles Boyer 4*

BACK STREET (1961) Universal. **Color-107min.** Susan Hayward, John Gavin ....(4)

BACK TO BATAAN (1945) RKO. **B&W-95min.** John Wayne, Anthony Quinn 3*

BACK TO GOD'S COUNTRY (1953) Universal. **Color-78min.** Rock Hudson, Marcia Henderson ....(3)

BACK TO THE WALL (1958) Ellis Films. **B&W-94min.** *(French).* Gerard Oury, Jeanne Moreau ....(5)
Original title: DOS AU MUR, LE

BACKFIRE (1950) Warner Bros. **B&W-91min.** Virginia Mayo, Gordon MacRae ....(3)

BACKFIRE (1961) Anglo Amalgamated [EMI]. **B&W-59min.** *(British).* Alfred Burke, Zena Marshall..(3)

BACKFIRE (1964) Royal Films Int'l [Columbia]. **B&W-97min.** *(French-Italian-Spanish).* Jean-Paul Belmondo, Jean Seberg..............(4)
Original French title: ÉCHAPPEMENT LIBRE *(Free Escape)*
Original Italian title: SCAPPAMENTO APERTO
Original Spanish title: ESCAPE LIBRE

BACKGROUND TO DANGER (1943) Warner Bros. **B&W-80min.** George Raft, Brenda Marshall ....(4)

BACKLASH (1947) 20th Century-Fox. **B&W-66min.** Richard Travis, Jean Rogers ....(3)

BACKLASH (1956) Universal. **Color-84min.** Richard Widmark, Donna Reed 4*

BACKTRACK (1969) Universal. **Color-97min.** *(Made for TV).* Neville Brand, James Drury 3*

BAD (1977) *see* ANDY WARHOL'S BAD

BAD AND THE BEAUTIFUL, THE (1952) M-G-M. **B&W-118min.** Kirk Douglas, Lana Turner 5½*

BAD BASCOMB (1946) M-G-M. **B&W-110min.** Wallace Beery, Margaret O'Brien ....(3)

BAD BLONDE (1953) Lippert Productions. **B&W-80min.** *(British).* Barbara Payton, Tony Wright ....(2)
Original title: FLANAGAN BOY, THE

BAD BOY (1949) Allied Artists. **B&W-86min.** Audie Murphy, Lloyd Nolan ....(5)

BAD CHARLESTON CHARLIE (1973) International Cinema Corp. **Color-91min.** Ross Hagen, Kelly Thordsen ....(4)

BAD COMPANY (1972) Paramount. **Color-91min.** Barry Brown, Jeff Bridges 5*

BAD DAY AT BLACK ROCK (1955) M-G-M. **Color-81min.** Spencer Tracy, Robert Ryan 5½*

BAD FOR EACH OTHER (1954) Columbia. **B&W-83min.** Charlton Heston, Lizabeth Scott..4*

BAD GIRL (1931) Fox Film Co. [20th]. **B&W-88min.** James Dunn, Sally Eilers..(4)

BAD GIRL (1956) *see* TEENAGE BAD GIRL

BAD GIRLS DON'T CRY (1959) *see* NOTTE BRAVA, LA

BAD LORD BYRON, THE (1949) J. Arthur Rank. **B&W-85min.** *(British).* Dennis Price, Joan Greenwood ....(3)

BAD MAN, THE (1941) M-G-M. **B&W-70min.** Wallace Beery, Lionel Barrymore ....(4)
British title: TWO-GUN CUPID

BAD MAN OF BRIMSTONE (1937) M-G-M. **B&W-90min.** Wallace Beery, Dennis O'Keefe 3*

BAD MAN OF WYOMING (1940) *see* WYOMING

BAD MEN OF MISSOURI (1941) Warner Bros. **B&W-74min.** Barry Sullivan, Broderick Crawford ....(5)

BAD MEN OF TOMBSTONE (1949) Allied Artists. **B&W-75min.** 3*

BAD NEWS BEARS, THE (1976) Paramount. **Color-102min.** Walter Matthau, Tatum O'Neal 6½*

BAD NEWS BEARS GO TO JAPAN, THE (1978) Paramount. **Color-91min.** Tony Curtis, Jackie Earle Haley 5*

BAD NEWS BEARS IN BREAKING TRAINING, THE (1977) Paramount. **Color-99min.** William Devane, Jackie Earle Haley 5½*

BAD ONE, THE (1957) *see* SORORITY GIRL

BAD SEED, THE (1956) Warner Bros. **B&W-129min.** Nancy Kelly, Patty McCormack 5½*

BAD SISTER (1947) Universal. **B&W-90min.** *(British).* Margaret Lockwood, Joan Greenwood ....(3)
Original title: WHITE UNICORN, THE

BADGE OF MARSHAL BRENNAN, THE (1957) Allied Artists. **B&W-76min.** Jim Davis, Arleen Whelan ....(3)

BADGE OR THE CROSS, THE (1971) *see* SARGE - THE BADGE OR THE CROSS

BADGE 373 (1973) Paramount. **Color-116min.** Robert Duvall, Verna Bloom ....(4)

BADLANDERS, THE (1958) M-G-M. **Color-83min.** Alan Ladd, Ernest Borgnine ....(5)

BADLANDS (1973) Warner Bros. **Color-95min.** Martin Sheen, Sissy Spacek 4*

BADLANDS OF DAKOTA (1941) Universal. **B&W-74min.** Broderick Crawford, Robert Stack ....(4)

BADLANDS OF MONTANA (1957) 20th Century-Fox. **B&W-75min.** Rex Reason, Margie Dean ....(3)

BADMAN'S COUNTRY (1958) Warner Bros. **B&W-68min.** George Montgomery, Neville Brand ....(3)

BADMAN'S TERRITORY (1946) RKO. **B&W-97min.** Randolph Scott, George "Gabby" Hayes..4*

BAFFLED! (1972) ABC-TV. **Color-73min.** *(Made for TV).* Leonard Nimoy, Susan Hampshire, Vera Miles ....(4)

BAGDAD (1949) Universal. **Color-82min.** Maureen O'Hara, Paul Christian ....(3)

BAHAMA PASSAGE (1941) Paramount. **Color-83min.** Madeleine Carroll, Sterling Hayden ....(3)

BAILOUT AT 43,000 (1957) United Artists. **B&W-78min.** John Payne, Karen Steele 3*
British title: BALE OUT AT 43,000

BAIT (1954) Columbia. **B&W-79min.** Cleo Moore, Hugo Haas, Cedric Hardwicke 3*

BAIT, THE (1973) Worldvision. **Color-74min.** *(Made for TV).* Donna Mills, Michael Constantine, William Devane ....(4)

BAITED TRAP, THE (1959) *see* TRAP, THE

BAKER'S HAWK (1976) Doty-Dayton. **Color-98min.** Clint Walker, Burl Ives 4*

BAKER'S WIFE, THE (1938) The Baker's Wife, Inc. **B&W-98min.** *(French).* Raimu, Ginette Leclerc, Charles Moulin ....(5)
Original title: FEMME DU BOULANGER, LA

BAKHITARI MIGRATION, THE (1975) *see* PEOPLE OF THE WIND

BAL TABARIN (1952) Republic. **B&W-84min.** William Ching, Muriel Lawrence ....(3)

BALALAIKA (1939) M-G-M. **B&W-102min.** Nelson Eddy, Ilona Massey..(3)

BALCONY, THE (1963) Continental [Walter Reade]. **B&W-84min.** Shelley Winters, Peter Falk 4*

BALE OUT AT 43,000 (1957) *see* BAILOUT AT 43,000

Films are rated on a 1 to 10 scale, 10 is highest. **Boldface** ratings followed by an asterisk (*) are for films actually seen and rated by the executive and senior editors. All other ratings are estimates. (See Notes on Entertainment Ratings in the front section.)

BALL OF FIRE (1941) RKO. **B&W-111min.** Gary Cooper, Barbara Stanwyck..5*

BALLAD OF A GUNFIGHTER (1964) Paramount. **Color-84min.** Marty Robbins, Bob Barron.......................................2*

BALLAD OF A SOLDIER (1960) Artkino. **B&W-89min.** *(U.S.S.R.).* Vladimir Ivashov, Shanna Prokhorenko.....................5½*
Original title: BALLADA O SOLDATYE

BALLAD OF ANDY CROCKER, THE (1969) ABC Films. **Color-80min.** *(Made for TV).* Lee Majors, Agnes Moorehead 4*

BALLAD OF CABLE HOGUE, THE (1970) Warner Bros. **Color-120min.** Jason Robards, Stella Stevens...............................6½*

BALLAD OF CROWFOOT, THE (1968) Nat'l Film Board of Canada. **B&W-10min.** *(Canadian, Documentary).* Director: Willie Dunn 5½*

BALLAD OF JOE HILL, THE (1971) *see* JOE HILL

BALLAD OF JOSIE, THE (1968) Universal. **Color-102min.** Doris Day, Peter Graves...............................4*

BALLAD OF LOVE, A (1965) Artkino. **B&W-45min.** *(U.S.S.R.).* Victoria Fyodorova, Valentin Smirnitsky ....(5)
Original title: DVOYE *(The Two)*

BALLAD OF NARAYAMA, THE (1958) Films Around The World. **Color-98min.** *(Japanese).* Kinuyo Tanaka, Teiji Takahashi ....(5)
Original title: NARAYAMA-BUSHI-KO

BALLERINA (1951) *see* DREAM BALLERINA

BALLERINA (1956) Sam Baker Associates. **B&W-91min.** *(German).* Elisabeth Mueller, Ivan Desny, Willy Birgel ....(3)
Original title: ROSEN FUER BETTINA

BALLON ROUGE, LE (1956) *see* RED BALLOON, THE

BALTIC EXPRESS (1959) *see* NIGHT TRAIN

BAMBI (1942) RKO (for Disney). **Color-70min.** *(Cartoon).* Director: Perce Pearce 5*

BAMBOLE! (1965) Royal Films Int'l [Columbia]. **B&W-111min.** *(Italian).* Gina Lollobrigida, Monica Vitti, Virna Lisi...........................(4)
Original title: BAMBOLE, LE
Alternate title: FOUR KINDS OF LOVE
Alternate title: DOLLS, THE

BAMBOO GODS AND IRON MEN (1974) American-International. **Color-96min.** *(Philippines).* James Iglehart, Shirley Washington.........(2)

BAMBOO PRISON, THE (1955) Columbia. **B&W-80min.** Robert Francis, Brian Keith 3*

BAMBOO SAUCER (1968) World Entertainment. **Color-100min.** Dan Duryea, John Ericson 2½*
Alternate title: COLLISION COURSE

BAMSE (1969) Chevron. **B&W-110min.** *(Swedish).* Grynet Molvig, Folke Sundquist, Bjorn Thambert ....(3)
Alternate title: TEDDY BEAR, THE

BANACEK (1972) MCA-TV. **Color-100min.** *(Made for TV).* George Peppard, Christine Belford 4*
Alternate title: DETOUR TO NOWHERE

BANANA PEEL (1963) Pathé Contemporary. **B&W-97min.** *(French-Italian).* Jeanne Moreau, Jean-Paul Belmondo...................(4)
Original French title: PEAU DE BANANE

BANANAS (1971) United Artists. **Color-82min.** Woody Allen, Louise Lasser 6*

BAND OF ANGELS (1957) Warner Bros. **Color-127min.** Clark Gable, Yvonne De Carlo 4½*

BAND OF OUTSIDERS (1964) Royal Films Int'l [Columbia]. **B&W-95min.** *(French).* Anna Karina, Sami Frey ....(5)
Original title: BANDE A PART

BAND WAGON, THE (1953) M-G-M. **Color-112min.** Fred Astaire, Cyd Charisse 4*

BANDIDO (1956) United Artists. **Color-92min.** Robert Mitchum, Ursula Thiess ....(4)

BANDIT AND THE PRINCESS, THE (1964) Screen Gems. **Color-91min.** *(German).* Helmut Lohner, Peter Weck ....(3)

BANDIT GENERAL (1951) *see* TORCH, THE

BANDIT OF SHERWOOD FOREST, THE (1946) Columbia. **Color-86min.** Cornel Wilde, Anita Louise 4*

BANDIT OF ZHOBE, THE (1959) Columbia. **Color-80min.** *(British).* Victor Mature, Anthony Newley.....................(3)

BANDITS OF CORSICA, THE (1953) United Artists. **B&W-81min.** Richard Greene, Paula Raymond ....(3)
British title: RETURN OF THE CORSICAN BROTHERS

BANDITS OF ORGOSOLO (1963) Pathé Contemporary. **B&W-98min.** *(Italian).* Michele Cossu, Peppeddu Cuccu 3*
Original title: BANDITI A ORGOSOLO

BANDOLERO! (1968) 20th Century-Fox. **Color-106min.** James Stewart, Dean Martin ....(3)

BANG BANG KID, THE (1968) Ajay Films. **Color-90min.** *(U.S.-Spanish-Italian).* Guy Madison, Sandra Milo.....................3*
Foreign title: BANG BANG

BANG, BANG, YOU'RE DEAD! (1966) American-International. **Color-92min.** *(British).* Tony Randall, Senta Berger 4*
British title: OUR MAN IN MARRAKESH
Alternate title: I SPY, YOU SPY

BANG THE DRUM SLOWLY (1973) Paramount. **Color-96min.** Michael Moriarty, Robert De Niro 4*

BANG! YOU'RE DEAD (1954) *see* GAME OF DANGER

BANISHED (1978) Toho. **Color-109min.** *(Japanese).* Shima Iwashita, Yoshiho Harada ....
Original title: HANARE GOZE ORIN

BANJO (1947) RKO. **B&W-68min.** Sharyn Moffett, Jacqueline White ....(2)

BANJO ON MY KNEE (1936) 20th Century-Fox. **B&W-80min.** Barbara Stanwyck, Joel McCrea ....(5)

BANJOMAN (1975) Atlantic Releasing Corp. **Color-105min.** *(Documentary).* Director: Richard G. Abramson.....................(4)

BANK DICK, THE (1940) Universal. **B&W-74min.** W. C. Fields, Franklin Pangborn 5½*
British title: BANK DETECTIVE, THE

BANK HOLIDAY (1938) *see* THREE ON A WEEK-END

BANK RAIDERS, THE (1958) J. Arthur Rank. **B&W-61min.** *(British).* Honor Blackman, Patrick Holt.....................(4)

BANK SHOT (1974) United Artists. **Color-83min.** George C. Scott, Joanna Cassidy ....(5)

BANNER IN THE SKY (1959) *see* THIRD MAN ON THE MOUNTAIN, THE

BANNERLINE (1951) M-G-M. **B&W-88min.** Sally Forrest, Keefe Brasselle.....................(3)

BANNING (1967) Universal. **Color-102min.** Robert Wagner, Anjanette Comer 4*

BANYON (1971) Warner Bros. **Color-100min.** *(Made for TV).* Robert Forster, Darren McGavin 5½*
Alternate title: WALK UP AND DIE

BAR SINISTER, THE (1955) *see* IT'S A DOG'S LIFE

BARABBAS (1961) Columbia. **Color-144min.** *(Italian, English language).* Anthony Quinn, Silvana Mangano 5*

BARBADOS QUEST (1955) *see* MURDER ON APPROVAL

BARBARA (1970) Olympia. **B&W-91min.** Jack Rader, Nancy Boyle, Barbara.....................(3)

BARBARELLA (1968) Paramount. **Color-98min.** *(French-Italian, English version).* Jane Fonda, John Phillip Law.....................3*

THE BANK DICK (1940). Grady Sutton has good reason to look worried — at the suggestion of W.C. Fields (with badge), he's temporarily "borrowed" $500, and bank examiner Franklin Pangborn has shown up unexpectedly.

Films are rated on a 1 to 10 scale, 10 is highest. **Boldface** ratings followed by an asterisk (*) are for films actually seen and rated by the executive and senior editors. All other ratings are estimates. (See Notes on Entertainment Ratings in the front section.)

BARBARIAN AND THE GEISHA, THE (1958) 20th Century-Fox. **Color-105min.** John Wayne, Eiko Ando...**4***

BARBARIAN KING, THE (1964) Four Star. **Color-89min.** (Bulgarian). Victor Stoichev, Ginka Stancheva..(3)

BARBARIANS, THE (1952) see PAGANS, THE

BARBARY COAST (1935) United Artists. **B&W-97min.** Joel McCrea, Miriam Hopkins...**3***

BARBARY COAST (1975) Paramount. **Color-100min.** (Made for TV). William Shatner, Dennis Cole..**4½***

BARBARY COAST GENT (1944) M-G-M. **B&W-87min.** Wallace Beery, John Carradine...(3)

BARBARY PIRATE (1949) Columbia. **B&W-65min.** Donald Woods, Trudy Marshall...(3)

BARBER OF SEVILLE (1945) Excelsior. **B&W-92min.** (Italian). Ferruccio Tagliavini, Tito Gobbi...(5)

BARBER OF SEVILLE (1956) Citation. **Color-100min.** (Italian). Tito Gobbi, Irene Genna...(3)

BARBER OF SEVILLE, THE (1973) Beta Film. **Color-141min.** (German-French). Bermann Prey, Teresa Berganza, Stefania Malagu..............(4)

BARE KNUCKLES (1978) Intercontinental Releasing Corp. **Color-90min.** Robert Viharo, Sherry Jackson...

BAREFOOT BATTALION (1954) 20th Century-Fox. **B&W-89min.** (Greek). Maria Costi, Nicos Fermas.......................................(3)

BAREFOOT CONTESSA, THE (1954) United Artists. **Color-128min.** (U.S.-Italian). Humphrey Bogart, Ava Gardner.....................**5½***

BAREFOOT EXECUTIVE, THE (1971) Buena Vista. **Color-95min.** Kurt Russell, Joe Flynn..**5***

BAREFOOT IN THE PARK (1967) Paramount. **Color-106min.** Robert Redford, Jane Fonda...**5***

BAREFOOT MAILMAN, THE (1951) Columbia. **Color-83min.** Robert Cummings, Terry Moore...(4)

BAREFOOT SAVAGE, THE (1954) see SENSUALITA

BARGAIN, THE (1931) First National [W.B.]. **B&W-70min.** Lewis Stone, Doris Kenyon...(4)

BARKLEYS OF BROADWAY, THE (1949) M-G-M. **Color-109min.** Fred Astaire, Ginger Rogers...**4***

BARNACLE BILL (1941) M-G-M. **B&W-98min.** Wallace Beery, Leo Carillo...**3½***

BARNACLE BILL (1958) see ALL AT SEA

BARNEY (1976) Columbia. **Color-87min.** (Australian-U.S.). Brett Maxworthy, Sean Kramer...

BARON BLOOD (1972) American-International. **Color-90min.** (Italian-West German). Joseph Cotten, Elke Sommer......................**2½***

BARON MUNCHAUSEN (1961) see FABULOUS BARON MUNCHAUSEN, THE

BARON OF ARIZONA, THE (1950) Lippert Productions. **B&W-90min.** Vincent Price, Ellen Drew...**4***

BARONESS AND THE BUTLER, THE (1938) 20th Century-Fox. **B&W-75min.** William Powell, Annabella.......................................(3)

BARON'S AFRICAN WAR, THE (1943) Republic. **B&W-100min.** (Re-edited Serial). Joan Marsh...(4)
Original title: SECRET SERVICE IN DARKEST AFRICA
Alternate title: MANHUNT IN THE AFRICAN JUNGLE

BARQUERO (1970) United Artists. **Color-108min.** Lee Van Cleef, Warren Oates...(4)

BARREN LIVES (1963) Pathé Contemporary. **B&W-100min.** (Brazilian). Atila Iorio, Maria Riberio...(5)
Original title: VIDAS SECAS

BARRETTS OF WIMPOLE STREET, THE (1934) M-G-M. **B&W-110min.** Norma Shearer, Fredric March..**5***
TV title: FORBIDDEN ALLIANCE

BARRETTS OF WIMPOLE STREET, THE (1957) M-G-M. **Color-105min.** Jennifer Jones, John Gielgud..**5***

BARRICADE (1939) 20th Century-Fox. **B&W-71min.** Alice Faye, Warner Baxter..(3)

BARRICADE (1950) Warner Bros. **Color-75min.** Dane Clark, Raymond Massey..(3)

BARRIER (1966) Janus Films. **B&W-83min.** (Polish). Joanna Szczerbic, Jan Nowicki...**2***
Original title: BARIERA

BARRIER OF THE LAW (1950) Italian Films Export. **B&W-81min.** (Italian). Rossano Brazzi, Jacques Sernas...........................(3)

BARRY LYNDON (1975) Warner Bros. **Color-184min.** (U.S.-British). Ryan O'Neal, Marisa Berenson..**5½***

BARTLEBY (1971) Maron Films, Ltd. **Color-79min.** (British). Paul Scofield, John McEnery...(3)

BASHFUL ELEPHANT, THE (1962) Allied Artists. **B&W-82min.** (German). Molly Mack, Helmut Schmid...(2)

BASKETBALL FIX, THE (1951) Realart. **B&W-68min.** John Ireland, Vanessa Brown..(4)
British title: BIG DECISION, THE

BAT, THE (1959) Allied Artists. **B&W-80min.** Agnes Moorehead, Vincent Price..(3)

BAT PEOPLE, THE (1974) American-International. **Color-94min.** Stewart Moss, Marianne McAndrew, Michael Pataki..........................(4)
Original title: IT LIVES BY NIGHT

BATAAN (1943) M-G-M. **B&W-114min.** Robert Taylor, George Murphy..**3***

BATAILLE, LE (1934) see BATTLE, THE

BATHING BEAUTY (1944) M-G-M. **Color-101min.** Esther Williams, Red Skelton...(4)

BATMAN (1966) 20th Century-Fox. **Color-105min.** Adam West, Burt Ward...**3***

BATMEN OF AFRICA (1936) Republic. **B&W-100min.** (Re-edited Serial). Clyde Beatty, Manuel King..(3)
Original title: DARKEST AFRICA
Alternate title: KING OF THE JUNGLELAND
British title: HIDDEN CITY

BATTERED (1977) see INTIMATE STRANGERS

BATTLE, THE (1934) United Artists. **B&W-79min.** (British-French). Charles Boyer, John Loder...(4)
Alternate title: THUNDER IN THE EAST
Alternate title: HARA-KIRI
French title: BATAILLE, LA

BATTLE AT APACHE PASS (1952) Universal. **Color-85min.** Jeff Chandler, John Lund...**3***

BATTLE AT BLOODY BEACH (1961) 20th Century-Fox. **B&W-83min.** Audie Murphy, Gary Crosby...**3***
British title: BATTLE ON THE BEACH

BATTLE BENEATH THE EARTH (1968) M-G-M. **Color-92min.** (U.S.-British). Kerwin Mathews, Viviane Ventura...........................(2)

BATTLE BEYOND THE SUN (1959) American-International. **Color-75min.** (U.S.S.R.). Ivan Pereverzev (Edd Perry), A. Popova (Arla Powell)..**2***
Original title: NEBO ZOVYOT (The Heavens Call)
Alternate transliteration: NEBO ZOWET

BATTLE CIRCUS (1953) M-G-M. **B&W-90min.** Humphrey Bogart, June Allyson...**3***

BATTLE CRY (1955) Warner Bros. **Color-149min.** Van Heflin, Aldo Ray...**4***

BATTLE FLAME (1959) Allied Artists. **B&W-78min.** Scott Brady, Elaine Edwards...(3)

BATTLE FOR ANZIO, THE (1968) see ANZIO

BATTLE FOR THE PLANET OF THE APES (1973) 20th Century-Fox. **Color-86min.** Roddy McDowall, Paul Williams.................**3½***

BATTLE HELL (1957) Distributors Corp. of America. **B&W-112min.** Richard Todd, William Hartnell.......................................(5)
British title: YANGTSE INCIDENT

BATTLE HYMN (1957) Universal. **Color-108min.** Rock Hudson, Dan Duryea..**3***

BATTLE IN OUTER SPACE (1959) Columbia. **Color-90min.** (Japanese). Ryo Ikebe, Kyoko Anzai...(2)
Original title: UCHU DAI SENSO

BATTLE OF ALGIERS (1966) Rizzoli Film. **B&W-125min.** (Italian-Algerian). Jean Martin, Yacef Saadi..................................**5½***
Original Italian title: BATTAGLIA DI ALGERI, LA
Original Algerian title: MAARAKAT ALGER

BATTLE OF AUSTERLITZ, THE (1960) 20th Century-Fox. **Color-123min.** (French). Leslie Caron, Vittorio De Sica, Jack Palance................(3)
Alternate title: AUSTERLITZ

BATTLE OF BERLIN, THE (1973) **B&W-83min.** (Documentary). Director: Franz Baske...**5½***
Original title: SCHLACHT UM BERLIN

BATTLE OF BLOOD ISLAND (1960) Filmgroup. **B&W-64min.** Richard Devon, Ron Kennedy...(4)

BATTLE OF BRITAIN (1969) United Artists. **Color-132min.** (British). Laurence Olivier, Robert Shaw..**5***

BATTLE OF MIDWAY (1976) see MIDWAY

BATTLE OF NERETVA (1969) American-International. Color-112min. (*Yugoslavian-U.S.-Italian-West German*). Yul Brynner, Orson Welles, Sergei Bondarchuk 3½*
Original Yugoslavian title: BITKA NA NERETVI
Alternate title: BATTLE ON THE RIVER NERETVA, THE

BATTLE OF POWDER RIVER (1951) *see* TOMAHAWK

BATTLE OF ROGUE RIVER (1954) Columbia. Color-71min. Martha Hyer, George Montgomery .... (3)

BATTLE OF SAN PIETRO, THE (1944) U.S. Government. B&W-33min. (*Documentary*). *Director:* John Huston 4½*
Alternate title: SAN PIETRO

BATTLE OF THE ASTROS (1970) *see* MONSTER ZERO

BATTLE OF THE BULGE (1965) Warner Bros. Color-163min. Henry Fonda, Robert Shaw 4*

BATTLE OF THE CORAL SEA, THE (1959) Columbia. B&W-80min. Cliff Robertson, Gia Scala .... (4)

BATTLE OF THE GIANTS (1940) *see* ONE MILLION B.C.

BATTLE OF THE RAILS (1947) Mayer-Burstyn. B&W-87min. (*French, Documentary*). *Director:* René Clement .... (5)
Original title: BATAILLE DU RAIL

BATTLE OF THE RIVER PLATE, THE (1956) *see* PURSUIT OF THE GRAF SPEE

BATTLE OF THE SEXES, THE (1959) Continental [Walter Reade]. B&W-88min. (*British*). Peter Sellers, Robert Morley 5½*

BATTLE OF THE SPARTANS (1963) *see* BRENNUS, ENEMY OF ROME

BATTLE OF THE VILLA FIORITA, THE (1965) Warner Bros. Color-105min. (*British-U.S.*). Maureen O'Hara, Rossano Brazzi 3*
Alternate title: AFFAIR OF VILLA FIORITA, THE

BATTLE OF THE WORLDS (1961) Topaz Film Corp./Manson Distributing Corp. B&W-84min. (*Italian*). Claude Rains, Bill Carter.... 2*
Original title: PIANETA DEGLI UOMINI SPENTI, IL (*The Planet of Extinguished Men*)

BATTLE ON THE BEACH (1961) *see* BATTLE AT BLOODY BEACH

BATTLE ON THE RIVER NERETVA, THE (1969) *see* BATTLE OF NERETVA

BATTLE SHOCK (1956) *see* WOMAN'S DEVOTION, A

BATTLE STATIONS (1956) Columbia. B&W-81min. John Lund, Keefe Brasselle .... (3)

BATTLE STRIPE (1950) *see* MEN, THE

BATTLE TAXI (1955) United Artists. B&W-82min. Sterling Hayden, Arthur Franz .... (3)

BATTLE ZONE (1952) Allied Artists. B&W-82min. John Hodiak, Linda Christian .... (3)

BATTLEAXE, THE (1961) Paramount. B&W-66min. (*British*). Jill Ireland, Francis Matthews .... (3)

BATTLEGROUND (1949) M-G-M. B&W-118min. Van Johnson, John Hodiak 4*

BATTLES OF CHIEF PONTIAC, THE (1952) Realart. B&W-75min. Lon Chaney (Jr.), Lex Barker 4*

BATTLESHIP POTEMKIN (1925) *see* POTEMKIN

BATTLESTAR GALACTICA (1978) Universal. Color-122min. Richard Hatch, Dirk Benedict, Lorne Greene 5*

BATTLING BELLHOP (1937) *see* KID GALAHAD

BATTLING BUTLER (1926) M-G-M. B&W-74min. (*Silent*). Buster Keaton, Sally O'Neil .... (5)

BAWDY ADVENTURES OF TOM JONES, THE (1975) Universal. Color-94min. (*British*). Nicky Henson, Madeline Smith, Trevor Howard....... 5*

BAXTER! (1973) National General. Color-105min. (*British*). Patricia Neal, Scott Jacoby 3½*

BAXTER MILLIONS, THE (1946) *see* LITTLE MISS BIG

BAY OF SAINT MICHEL, THE (1963) *see* OPERATION MERMAID

BAY OF THE ANGELS (1963) Pathé Contemporary. B&W-85min. (*French*). Jeanne Moreau, Claude Mann .... (4)
Original title: BAIE DES ANGES

BAYOU (1957) *see* POOR WHITE TRASH

BE BEAUTIFUL BUT SHUT UP (1957) B&W-94min. (*French*). Mylene Demongeot, Henri Vidal .... (3)

BE MY GUEST (1965) Columbia. B&W-82min. (*British*). David Hemmings, Avril Angers, Joyce Blair, Jerry Lee Lewis ....

BE YOURSELF! (1930) United Artists. B&W-77min. Fanny Brice, Robert Armstrong .... (4)

BEACH BALL (1965) Paramount. Color-83min. Edd Byrnes, Chris Noel (3)

BEACH BLANKET BINGO (1965) American-International. Color-98min. Frankie Avalon, Annette Funicello, Buster Keaton 3*

BEACH CASANOVA (1962) American-International. Color-85min. (*Italian*). Curt Jurgens, Capucine .... (4)
Original title: DON GIOVANNI DELLA COSTA AZZURRA, I (*Don Juan of the Cote d'Azure*)

BEACH GIRLS AND THE MONSTER, THE (1965) U.S. Films. B&W-70min. Jon Hall, Sue Casey 1*
TV title: MONSTER FROM THE SURF

BEACH PARTY (1963) American-International. Color-101min. Bob Cummings, Dorothy Malone 3*

BEACH PARTY - ITALIAN STYLE (1962) *see* EIGHTEEN IN THE SUN

BEACH RED (1967) United Artists. Color-105min. Cornel Wilde, Rip Torn .... (5)

BEACHCOMBER, THE (1938) Paramount. B&W-86min. (*British*). Charles Laughton, Elsa Lanchester 5½*
Original title: VESSEL OF WRATH

BEACHCOMBER, THE (1954) United Artists. Color-90min. (*British*). Robert Newton, Glynis Johns .... (5)

BEACHHEAD (1954) United Artists. Color-89min. Tony Curtis, Frank Lovejoy .... (4)

BEAR, THE (1963) Avco-Embassy. Color-86min. (*French-Italian*). Renato Rascel, Francis Blanche .... (5)
Original French title: OURS, L'

BEAR AND THE DOLL, THE (1971) Paramount. Color-89min. (*French*). Brigitte Bardot, Jean-Pierre Cassel .... (2)
Original title: OURS ET LA POUPÉE, L'

BEAR COUNTRY (1953) RKO (for Disney). Color-33min. (*Documentary*). *Director:* James Algar 5*

BEARS AND I, THE (1974) Buena Vista. Color-89min. Patrick Wayne, Chief Dan George .... (4)

BEAST FROM HAUNTED CAVE (1959) Allied Artists. B&W-75min. Michael Forest, Sheila Carol 2*

BEAST FROM 20,000 FATHOMS, THE (1953) Warner Bros. B&W-80min. Paul Christian, Paula Raymond 3*

BEAST IN THE CELLAR, THE (1971) Cannon Releasing. Color-87min. (*British*). Beryl Reid, Flora Robson 4*

BEAST MUST DIE, THE (1974) Cinerama Releasing. Color-93min. (*British*). Calvin Lockhart, Peter Cushing 4*

BEAST OF BABYLON AGAINST THE SON OF HERCULES, THE (1963) Avco-Embassy. Color-98min. (*Italian-French*). Gordon Scott, Genevieve Gard 3*
Original title: EROE DI BABILONIA, L'
Alternate title: HERO OF BABYLON, THE

BEAST OF BLOOD (1970) Hemisphere. Color-90min. (*U.S.-Philippine*). John Ashley, Celeste Yarnall, Eddie Garcia 1*
British title: BLOOD DEVILS
TV title: BEAST OF THE DEAD

BEAST OF BUDAPEST, THE (1958) Allied Artists. B&W-72min. Michael Mills, Greta Thyssen .... (3)

BEAST OF HOLLOW MOUNTAIN, THE (1956) United Artists. Color-77min. (*U.S.-Mexican*). Guy Madison, Patricia Medina 3*
Original Mexican title: MONSTRUO DE LA MONTANA HUECA, EL

BEAST OF MORROCO, THE (1968) American-International. Color-86min. (*British-Spanish*). William Sylvester, Diane Clare, Terence de Marney 2*
British title: HAND OF NIGHT

BEAST OF PARADISE ISLE (1953) *see* PORT SINISTER

BEAST OF THE CITY (1932) M-G-M. B&W-87min. Walter Huston, Jean Harlow 4*

BEAST OF THE DEAD (1970) *see* BEAST OF BLOOD

BEAST OF THE YELLOW NIGHT (1971) New World. Color-87min. (*Philippine-U.S.*). Eddie Garcia, John Ashley .... (2)

BEAST WITH A MILLION EYES (1956) American Releasing [A.I.P.]. B&W-71min. Paul Birch, Lorna Thayer .... (3)

BEAST WITH FIVE FINGERS, THE (1946) Warner Bros. B&W-88min. Peter Lorre, Andrea King .... (3)

BEASTS OF MARSEILLES (1957) Lopert [U.A.]. B&W-70min. (*British*). Stephen Boyd, Anna Gaylor .... (5)
Original title: SEVEN THUNDERS, THE

BEAT GENERATION, THE (1959) M-G-M. B&W-95min. Mamie Van Doren, Steve Cochran, Louis Armstrong .... (2)
Alternate title: THIS REBEL AGE

BEAT GIRL (1960) *see* WILD FOR KICKS

BEAT THE BAND (1947) RKO. B&W-67min. Frances Langford, Ralph Edwards .... (3)

Films are rated on a 1 to 10 scale, 10 is highest. **Boldface** ratings followed by an asterisk (*) are for films actually seen and rated by the executive and senior editors. All other ratings are estimates. (See Notes on Entertainment Ratings in the front section.)

BEAT THE DEVIL (1954) United Artists. **B&W-92min.** *(British-U.S.).* Humphrey Bogart, Jennifer Jones......................................4½*

BEATNIKS, THE (1959) Bajul International. **B&W-78min.** Tony Travis, Peter Breck ....(3)

BEAU BRUMMELL (1924) Warner Bros. **B&W-132min.** *(Silent).* John Barrymore, Mary Astor, Willard Louis ....(4)
Alternate title: BEAU BRUMMEL

BEAU BRUMMELL (1954) M-G-M. **Color-111min.** *(British-U.S.).* Stewart Granger, Elizabeth Taylor 5*

BEAU GESTE (1926) Paramount. **B&W-105min.** *(Silent).* Ronald Colman, Neil Hamilton, Ralph Forbes......................................5*

BEAU GESTE (1939) Paramount. **B&W-120min.** Gary Cooper, Ray Milland 5½*

BEAU GESTE (1966) Universal. **Color-103min.** Guy Stockwell, Doug McClure......................................3½*

BEAU JAMES (1957) Paramount. **Color-105min.** Bob Hope, Vera Miles 4*

BEAU SERGE, LE (1958) United Motion Pic. Org. (UMPO). **B&W-97min.** *(French).* Gerard Blain, Jean-Claude Brialy ....(4)

BEAUTE DU DIABLE, LA (1950) *see* BEAUTY AND THE DEVIL, THE

BEAUTIES OF THE NIGHT (1952) United Artists. **B&W-87min.** *(French-British-Italian).* Gerard Philipe, Martine Carol ....(5)
Original title: BELLES DE NUIT, LES

BEAUTIFUL BLONDE FROM BASHFUL BEND, THE (1949) 20th Century-Fox. **Color-77min.** Betty Grable, Cesar Romero 3*

BEAUTIFUL BUT DANGEROUS (1953) *see* SHE COULDN'T SAY NO

BEAUTIFUL BUT DANGEROUS (1955) 20th Century-Fox. **Color-103min.** *(Italian).* Gina Lollobrigida, Vittorio Gassman......................................(4)
Original title: DONNA PIU BELLA DEL MONDO, LA *(The Most Beautiful Woman in the World)*

BEAUTIFUL BUT DEADLY (1974) *see* DON IS DEAD, THE

BEAUTIFUL CHEAT, THE (1943) *see* WHAT A WOMAN!

BEAUTIFUL CHEAT, THE (1945) Universal. **B&W-59min.** Bonita Granville, Noah Beery, Jr......................................
British title: WHAT A WOMAN!

BEAUTIFUL PEOPLE (1974) Warner Bros. **Color-92min.** *(Documentary).* Director: Jamie Uys 5*

BEAUTIFUL STRANGER (1954) *see* TWIST OF FATE

BEAUTY AND THE BEAST (1946) Lopert [U.A.]. **B&W-90min.** *(French).* Josette Day, Jean Marais 4*
Original title: BELLE ET LA BETE, LA

BEAUTY AND THE BEAST (1963) United Artists. **Color-77min.** Joyce Taylor, Mark Damon ....(4)

BEAUTY AND THE BEAST (1976) NBC-TV. **Color-74min.** *(Made for TV).* Trish Van Devere, George C. Scott......................................

BEAUTY AND THE BULLFIGHTER (1954) *see* LOVE IN A HOT CLIMATE

BECKET (1964). The King, Peter O'Toole, and his friend Richard Burton (in the title role), who's to become Chancellor of England and eventually Archbishop of Canterbury, lead a triumphant procession through a captured French town.

BEAUTY AND THE DEVIL (1952) Arthur Davis Assoc. **B&W-95min.** *(French-British).* Michel Simon, Gerard Philipe......................................(5)
Original title: BEAUTÉ DU DIABLE, LA *(The Beauty of the Devil)*

BEAUTY AND THE ROBOT (1960) *see* SEX KITTENS GO TO COLLEGE

BEAUTY JUNGLE, THE (1954) *see* CONTEST GIRL

BEAUTY ON PARADE (1950) Columbia. **B&W-66min.** Robert Hutton, Lola Albright ....(3)

BEAVER VALLEY (1951) RKO (for Disney). **Color-32min.** *(Documentary).* Director: James Algar......................................5*

BEBO'S GIRL (1963) Continental [Walter Reade]. **B&W-106min.** *(Italian-French).* Claudia Cardinale, George Chakiris......................................(4)
Original title: RAGAZZA DI BUBE, LA

BECAUSE OF HIM (1946) Universal. **B&W-88min.** Deanna Durbin, Franchot Tone ....(5)

BECAUSE OF YOU (1952) Universal. **B&W-95min.** Loretta Young, Jeff Chandler 3½*

BECAUSE THEY'RE YOUNG (1960) Columbia. **B&W-102min.** Dick Clark, Tuesday Weld ....(4)

BECAUSE YOU'RE MINE (1952) M-G-M. **Color-103min.** Mario Lanza, Doretta Morrow 4*

BECKET (1964) Paramount. **Color-148min.** *(British).* Richard Burton, Peter O'Toole 7*

BECKET AFFAIR, THE (1966) Official Industries. **Color-95min.** *(Italian-French).* Lang Jeffries, Doris Kristianell ....(1)
Original Italian title: AFFARE BECKETT, L'

BECKY SHARP (1935) RKO. **Color-83min.** Miriam Hopkins, Frances Dee 3½*

BED, THE (1955) Getz-Kingsley. **B&W-101min.** *(French-Italian).* Richard Todd, Jeanne Moreau ....(5)
Original French title: SECRETS D'ALCOVE *(Secrets of the Alcove)*
Original Italian title: LETTO, IL

BED AND BOARD (1971) Columbia. **Color-95min.** *(French).* Jean-Pierre Leaud, Claude Jade ....(5)
Original title: DOMICILE CONJUGAL *(The Marital Home)*

BED OF FIRE (1964) *see* GLASS CAGE, THE

BED OF GRASS (1957) Trans-Lux Distributing. **B&W-92min.** *(Greek).* Anna Brazzou, Mike Nichols......................................(5)

BED SITTING ROOM, THE (1969) United Artists. **Color-90min.** *(British).* Ralph Richardson, Rita Tushingham......................................3*

BEDAZZLED (1967) 20th Century-Fox. **Color-103min.** *(British).* Peter Cook, Dudley Moore......................................5½*

BEDELIA (1946) Eagle Lion. **B&W-83min.** *(British).* Margaret Lockwood, Ian Hunter ....

BEDEVILLED (1955) M-G-M. **Color-85min.** Anne Baxter, Steve Forrest (3)

BEDFORD INCIDENT, THE (1965) Columbia. **B&W-102min.** *(U.S.-British).* Richard Widmark, Sidney Poitier......................................5½*

BEDKNOBS AND BROOMSTICKS (1971) Buena Vista. **Color-117min.** Angela Lansbury, David Tomlinson......................................5½*

BEDLAM (1946) RKO. **B&W-79min.** Boris Karloff, Anna Lee................4½*

BEDROOM VENDETTA (1959) *see* GREEN MARE, THE

BEDS AND BROADS (1962) *see* TALES OF PARIS

BEDSIDE MANNER (1945) United Artists. **B&W-70min.** Ruth Hussey, John Carroll ....(3)
TV title: HER FAVORITE PATIENT

BEDTIME FOR BONZO (1951) Universal. **B&W-82min.** Ronald Reagan, Diana Lynn ....(4)

BEDTIME STORY, A (1933) Paramount. **B&W-87min.** Maurice Chevalier, Helen Twelvetrees......................................(4)

BEDTIME STORY (1941) Columbia. **B&W-85min.** Fredric March, Loretta Young......................................6½*

BEDTIME STORY (1964) Universal. **Color- min.** Marlon Brando, David Niven......................................5½*

BEEN DOWN SO LONG IT LOOKS LIKE UP TO ME (1971) Paramount. **Color-92min.** Barry Primus, Linda De Coff ....(3)

BEES, THE (1978) New World. **Color-83min.** *(U.S.-Mexican).* John Saxon, Angel Tompkins, John Carradine......................................(4)

BEFORE I HANG (1940) Columbia. **B&W-71min.** Boris Karloff, Evelyn Keyes 4*

BEFORE I WAKE (1955) *see* SHADOW OF FEAR

BEFORE THE REVOLUTION (1964) New Yorker Films. **B&W-112min.** *(Italian).* Adriana Asti, Francesco Barilli......................................(4)
Original title: PRIMA DELLA RIVOLUZIONE

BEFORE WINTER COMES (1969) Columbia. **Color-103min.** *(British).* David Niven, Topol 4*

BEG, BORROW OR STEAL (1973) MCA-TV. Color-74min. *(Made for TV).* Mike Connors, Kent McCord, Michael Cole ....(4)

BEGGAR STUDENT, THE (1956) Sam Baker Associates. Color-97min. *(German).* Gerhard Riedmann, Waltraut Haas ....(3)
Original title: BETTELSTUDENT, DER

BEGGAR'S OPERA, THE (1953) Warner Bros. Color-94min. *(British).* Laurence Olivier, Yvonne Furneaux.....................5*

BEGINNER'S LUCK (1951) *see* TWO DOLLAR BETTOR

BEGINNING OF THE END (1957) Republic. B&W-73min. Peter Graves, Peggie Castle ....(3)

BEGINNING OR THE END, THE (1947) M-G-M. B&W-112min. Brian Donlevy, Robert Walker 4*

BEGUILED, THE (1971) Universal. Color-109min. Clint Eastwood, Geraldine Page 5*

BEHAVE YOURSELF (1951) RKO. B&W-81min. Farley Granger, Shelley Winters ....(4)

BEHEMOTH THE SEA MONSTER (1959) *see* GIANT BEHEMOTH, THE

BEHIND CLOSED DOORS (1944) *see* ONE MYSTERIOUS NIGHT

BEHIND GREEN LIGHTS (1946) 20th Century-Fox. B&W-64min. Carole Landis, John Ireland ....(4)

BEHIND LOCKED DOORS (1948) Eagle Lion. B&W-62min. Richard Carlson, Lucille Bremer ....(4)

BEHIND THAT CURTAIN (1929) Fox Film Co. [20th]. B&W-92min. Warner Baxter, Lois Moran ....(4)

BEHIND THE DOOR (1940) *see* MAN WITH NINE LIVES, THE

BEHIND THE FRONT (1926) Paramount. B&W-62min. *(Silent).* Wallace Beery, Raymond Hatton ....(4)

BEHIND THE HIGH WALL (1956) Universal. B&W-85min. Tom Tully, Sylvia Sidney ....(3)

BEHIND THE IRON CURTAIN (1948) *see* IRON CURTAIN, THE

BEHIND THE MASK (1932) Columbia. B&W-70min. Jack Holt, Boris Karloff...............................4*

BEHIND THE MASK (1958) Showcorporation. B&W-99min. *(British).* Michael Redgrave, Carl Mohner.....................3*

BEHIND THE MASK OF ZORRO (1965) NTA Pictures. Color-85min. *(Spanish-Italian).* Tony Russell, Maria José Alfonso, Jesus Puente .....(3)
Original Spanish title: ZORRO CABALGA OTRA VEZ, EL *(Zorro Rides Again)*

BEHIND THE RISING SUN (1943) RKO. B&W-89min. Margo, Tom Neal.............................(4)

BEHIND THE WALL (1971) Film Polski. B&W-70min. *(Polish, Made for TV).* Maja Komorowska, Zbigniew Zapasiewicz ....(5)
Original title: ZA SCIANA

BEHOLD A PALE HORSE (1964) Columbia. B&W-118min. Gregory Peck, Anthony Quinn 5*

BEHOLD MY WIFE (1935) Paramount. B&W-78min. Sylvia Sidney, Gene Raymond...............................(3)

BELATED FLOWERS (1972) Artkino. Color-100min. *(U.S.S.R.).* Iga Zhizneva, Irina Lavrentyeva, Alexander Lazarev ....(4)
Original title: CHVETI ZAPOZDALIE

BELIEVE IN ME (1971) M-G-M. Color-86min. Michael Sarrazin, Jacqueline Bisset ....(3)

BELL' ANTONIO (1960) Avco-Embassy. B&W-101min. *(Italian-French).* Marcello Mastroianni, Claudia Cardinale...............(4)
Translation title: Handsome Antonio

BELL, BOOK AND CANDLE (1958) Columbia. Color-103min. James Stewart, Kim Novak 5*

BELL FOR ADANO, A (1945) 20th Century-Fox. B&W-103min. Gene Tierney, John Hodiak 5*

BELL JAR, THE (1979) Avco-Embassy. Color-118min. Marilyn Hassett, Julie Harris, Anne Jackson 4*

BELLBOY, THE (1918) Paramount Famous Players-Lasky. B&W-22min. *(Silent).* Fatty Arbuckle, Buster Keaton 5*

BELLBOY, THE (1960) Paramount. B&W-72min. Jerry Lewis, Alex Gerry 3½*

BELLE AMERICAINE, LA (1961) Continental [Walter Reade]. B&W-100min. *(French).* Robert Dhéry, Colette Brosset ....(5)

BELLE DE JOUR (1967) Allied Artists. Color-100min. *(French-Italian).* Catherine Deneuve, Jean Sorel...................(5)
Translation title: Beauty of the Day

BELLE ET LA BETE, LA (1946) *see* BEAUTY AND THE BEAST

BELLE LE GRAND (1951) Republic. B&W-90min. John Carroll, Vera (Hruba) Ralston 3*

BELLE OF NEW YORK, THE (1952) M-G-M. Color-82min. Fred Astaire, Vera-Ellen 4*

BELLE OF OLD MEXICO (1949) Republic. B&W-70min. Estrelita, Robert Rockwell...............................(3)

BELLE OF THE NINETIES (1934) Paramount. B&W-75min. Mae West, Roger Pryor 4*

BELLE OF THE YUKON (1944) RKO. Color-84min. Dinah Shore, Gypsy Rose Lee ....(4)

BELLE SOMMERS (1962) Columbia. B&W-62min. Polly Bergen, David Janssen ....(3)

BELLE STARR (1941) 20th Century-Fox. Color-87min. Gene Tierney, Randolph Scott 4*

BELLE STARR'S DAUGHTER (1948) 20th Century-Fox. B&W-86min. Rod Cameron, Ruth Roman ....(3)

BELLES AND BALLETS (1960) Excelsior. Color-92min. *(French).* Maurice Bejart, Michele Seigneuret ....(4)

BELLES DE NUIT, LES (1952) *see* BEAUTIES OF THE NIGHT

BELLES OF ST. TRINIAN'S, THE (1954) Continental [Walter Reade]. B&W-90min. *(British).* Alastair Sim................4*

BELLES ON THEIR TOES (1952) 20th Century-Fox. Color-89min. Myrna Loy, Jeanne Crain 4½*

BELLISSIMA (1951) Italian Films Export. B&W-100min. *(Italian).* Anna Magnani, Walter Chiari..................(5)

BELLS ARE RINGING (1960) M-G-M. Color-127min. Judy Holliday, Dean Martin...............................4*

BELLS OF ST. MARY'S, THE (1945) Republic. B&W-126min. Bing Crosby, Ingrid Bergman.......................4½*

BELOVED ENEMY (1936) United Artists. B&W-90min. Merle Oberon, Brian Aherne 4*

BELOVED INFIDEL (1959) 20th Century-Fox. Color-123min. Gregory Peck, Deborah Kerr ....(4)

BELOVED ROGUE, THE (1926) United Artists. B&W-103min. *(Silent).* John Barrymore, Conrad Veidt 6*

BELOW THE BELT (1971) Boxoffice International. Color-90min. John Tull, (George?) Buck Flower ....(2)

BELOW THE SAHARA (1953) RKO. Color-65min. *(Travelog). Director:* Armand Denis ....(5)

BELSTONE FOX, THE (1973) 20th Century-Fox. Color-103min. *(British).* Eric Porter, Rachel Roberts, Bill Travers...........(4)

BEN (1972) Cinerama Releasing. Color-93min. Lee Hartcourt Montgomery, Joseph Campanella.....................4½*

BEN-GURION REMEMBERS (1972) Israfilm Ltd. Color-90min. *(Israeli, Documentary). Director:* Simon Hesera..............4*
British title: B. G. REMEMBERS

BEN-GURION STORY, THE (1970) *see* 42:6

BEN-HUR (1926) M-G-M. B&W-133min. *(Silent).* Ramon Novarro, Francis X. Bushman 4½*

BEN-HUR (1959) M-G-M. Color-217min. Charlton Heston, Jack Hawkins 7½*

BEND OF THE RIVER (1952) Universal. Color-91min. James Stewart, J. Arthur Kennedy 5*
British title: WHERE THE RIVER BENDS

BENEATH THE PLANET OF THE APES (1970) 20th Century-Fox. Color-95min. James Franciscus, Kim Hunter 3*

BENEATH THE 12-MILE REEF (1953) 20th Century-Fox. Color-102min. Robert Wagner, Terry Moore 4*

BENEFIT OF THE DOUBT, THE (1967) Color-70min. *(British).* Eric Allen, Mary Allen ....(3)

BENGAL BRIGADE (1954) Universal. Color-87min. Rock Hudson, Arlene Dahl 3*
British title: BENGAL RIFLES

BENGAL TIGER, THE (1972) Globe International Pictures. Color-83min. *(Documentary). Director:* Richard Martin 4½*

BENGAZI (1955) RKO. B&W-78min. Richard Carlson, Victor McLaglen (3)

BENJAMIN (1968) Paramount. Color-100min. *(French).* Pierre Clementi, Catherine Deneuve ....(4)
Original title: BENJAMIN OU LES MEMOIRES D'UN PUCEAU *(Benjamin or the Memoirs of a Virgin Boy)*

BENJI (1974) Mulberry Square. Color-85min. Higgins, Peter Breck.......(5)

BENNY AND BARNEY: LAS VEGAS UNDERCOVER (1977) MCA-TV. Color-74min. *(Made for TV).* Terry Kiser, Timothy Thomerson, Jane Seymour, George Gobel.......................4*

BENNY GOODMAN STORY, THE (1956) Universal. Color-116min. Steve Allen, Donna Reed...........................4*

Films are rated on a 1 to 10 scale, 10 is highest. **Boldface** ratings followed by an asterisk (*) are for films actually seen and rated by the executive and senior editors. All other ratings are estimates. (See Notes on Entertainment Ratings in the front section.)

As **BEN-HUR** (1959), Charlton Heston is implored by his beloved Haya Harareet to listen to the teachings of Jesus so that he might forget his hatred toward those who have brought misery to him and his family.

BEQUEST TO THE NATION (1973) *see* NELSON AFFAIR, THE

BERKELEY SQUARE (1933) Fox Film Co. [20th]. B&W-87min. Leslie Howard, Heather Angel.................................(5)

BERLIN AFFAIR (1970) Universal. Color-100min. *(Made for TV)*. Darren McGavin, Fritz Weaver.............................(4)

BERLIN CORRESPONDENT (1942) 20th Century-Fox. B&W-70min. Dana Andrews, Virginia Gilmore.......................(4)

BERLIN EXPRESS (1948) RKO. B&W-86min. Merle Oberon, Robert Ryan 5*

BERLIN: SYMPHONY OF A GREAT CITY (1927) 20th Century-Fox. B&W-75min. *(German, Silent, Documentary)*. *Director:* Walter Ruttmann..1*
Original title: BERLIN - DIE SYMPHONIE EINER GROSSSTADT

BERMUDA AFFAIR (1956) Distributors Corp. of America. B&W-77min. *(British)*. Kim Hunter, Gary Merrill ....(4)

BERMUDA MYSTERY (1944) 20th Century-Fox. B&W-65min. Preston Foster, Ann Rutherford.............................(3)

BERMUDA TRIANGLE, THE (1978) Sunn Classic. Color-93min. *(Documentary)*. *Director:* Richard Friedenberg ....(4)

BERNADETTE OF LOURDES (1960) Janus Films. B&W-105min. *(French-Italian)*. Daniele Ajoret, Nadine Alari ....(4)
Original title: IL SUFFIT D'AIMER *(It Is Enough to Love)*

BERNARDINE (1957) 20th Century-Fox. Color-95min. Richard Sargent, Pat Boone......................................3*

BERSERK (1967) Columbia. Color-96min. *(British-U.S.)*. Joan Crawford, Ty Hardin..3*

BESPOKE OVERCOAT, THE (1955) George K. Arthur. B&W-33min. *(British)*. Alfie Bass, David Kossoff ....(5)

BEST FOOT FORWARD (1943) M-G-M. Color-95min. Lucille Ball, June Allyson......................................4*

BEST FRIENDS (1975) Crown International. Color-83min. Richard Hatch, Susanne Benton....................(3)

BEST HOUSE IN LONDON, THE (1969) M-G-M. Color-96min. *(British)*. David Hemmings, Joanna Pettet ....(3)

BEST MAN, THE (1964) United Artists. B&W-102min. Henry Fonda, Cliff Robertson..................................6½*

BEST OF ENEMIES, THE (1961) Columbia. Color-104min. *(Italian-British, English language)*. David Niven, Alberto Sordi 6½*
Original Italian title: DUE NEMICI, I *(The Two Enemies)*

BEST OF EVERYTHING, THE (1959) 20th Century-Fox. Color-127min. Hope Lange, Stephen Boyd...........................4½*

BEST OF THE BADMEN (1951) RKO. Color-84min. Robert Ryan, Claire Trevor..3½*

BEST OF WALT DISNEY'S TRUE-LIFE ADVENTURES (1975) Buena Vista. Color-88min. *(Compilation)*. *Director:* James Algar 5½*

BEST THINGS IN LIFE ARE FREE, THE (1956) 20th Century-Fox. Color-104min. Gordon MacRae, Ernest Borgnine ....(4)

BEST YEARS OF OUR LIVES, THE (1946) RKO. B&W-172min. Myrna Loy, Fredric March 6*

BETRAYAL, THE (1956) United Artists. B&W-82min. *(British)*. Philip Friend, Diana Decker...................................(4)

BETRAYAL FROM THE EAST (1945) RKO. B&W-82min. Lee Tracy, Nancy Kelly ....(3)

BETRAYED (1944) *see* WHEN STRANGERS MARRY

BETRAYED (1954) M-G-M. Color-108min. Clark Gable, Lana Turner ....(4)

BETRAYED WOMEN (1955) Allied Artists. B&W-70min. Tom Drake, Carole Matthews.....................................(3)

BETSY, THE (1978) Allied Artists. Color-125min. Laurence Olivier, Katharine Ross.....................................5*

BETTER A WIDOW (1968) Universal. Color-101min. *(Italian-French)*. Virna Lisi, Peter McEnery ....(3)
Original Italian title: MEGLIO VEDOVA

BETWEEN HEAVEN AND HELL (1956) 20th Century-Fox. Color-94min. Robert Wagner, Terry Moore 4*

BETWEEN MIDNIGHT AND DAWN (1950) Columbia. B&W-89min. Mark Stevens, Edmond O'Brien.............................3*

BETWEEN THE LINES (1977) Midwest Films. Color-101min. John Heard, Lindsay Crouse, Jeff Goldblum..............................4*

BETWEEN TIME AND ETERNITY (1956) Universal. Color-84min. *(W. German-Spanish)*. Lilli Palmer, Carlos Thompson ....(4)
Original West German title: ZWISCHEN ZEIT UND EWIGKEIT
Original Spanish title: ENTRE HOY Y LA ETERNIDAD

BETWEEN TWO WOMEN (1944) M-G-M. B&W-83min. Lionel Barrymore, Van Johnson, Gloria De Haven ....(3)

BETWEEN TWO WORLDS (1944) Warner Bros. B&W-112min. John Garfield, Eleanor Parker....................................(4)

BETWEEN US GIRLS (1942) Universal. B&W-89min. Kay Francis, Diana Barrymore...(3)

BETWEEN WORLDS (1921) *see* DESTINY

BEWARE MY BRETHREN (1972) Cinerama Releasing. Color-90min. *(British)*. Patrick Magee, Ann Todd.............................
Original title: FIEND, THE
Publicity title: BEWARE OF THE BRETHREN

BEWARE, MY LOVELY (1952) RKO. B&W-77min. Ida Lupino, Robert Ryan..

BEWARE OF BLONDIE (1950) Columbia. B&W-66min. Arthur Lake, Penny Singleton...................................(3)

BEWARE OF CHILDREN (1960) American-International. B&W-80min. *(British)*. Leslie Phillips, Julia Lockwood......................(3)
Original title: NO KIDDING

BEWARE OF PITY (1946) Two Cities. B&W-103min. *(British)*. Lilli Palmer, Gladys Cooper ....(4)

BEWARE OF THE BRETHREN (1972) *see* BEWARE MY BRETHREN

BEWARE SPOOKS! (1939) Columbia. B&W-68min. Joe E. Brown, Mary Carlisle ....(3)

BEWARE! THE BLOB (1972) Jack H. Harris. Color-87min. Robert Walker (Jr.), Godfrey Cambridge, Carol Lynley.....................1*
Alternate title: SON OF BLOB

BEWITCHED (1945) M-G-M. B&W-65min. Phyllis Thaxter, Edmund Gwenn..(4)

BEYOND A REASONABLE DOUBT (1956) RKO. B&W-80min. Dana Andrews, Joan Fontaine....................................(4)

BEYOND ALL LIMITS (1957) Sutton Pictures-Omat Films. Color-115min. *(Mexican)*. Jack Palance, Pedro Armendariz ....(3)
Original title: FLOR DE MAYO *(Flower of May)*

BEYOND AND BACK (1978) Sunn Classic. Color-93min. *(Documentary)*. *Director:* James L. Conway.............................4*

BEYOND CONTROL (1968) William Mishkin. Color-89min. *(W. German-Italian)*. William Berger, Anthony Baker (Helmut Fornbacher) ....(2)
Original German title: SOMMERSPROSSEN *(Freckles)*
Alternate title: WHAT A WAY TO DIE!

BEYOND GLORY (1948) Paramount. B&W-82min. Alan Ladd, Donna Reed 3½*

BEYOND GOOD AND EVIL (1977) United Artists. Color-127min. *(Italian)*. Dominique Sanda, Erland Josephson ....(4)

BEYOND LOVE AND EVIL (1971) Allied Artists. Color-90min. *(French)*. Souchka, Lucas De Chabanieux ....(2)
Original title: PHILOSOPHIE DANS LE BOUDOIR, LA *(The Philosophy of the Bedroom)*
Alternate title: PHILOSOPHY OF THE BEDROOM

BEYOND MOMBASA (1956) Columbia. **Color-90min.** *(British).* Cornel Wilde, Donna Reed..3½*

BEYOND SING THE WOODS (1960) *see* DUEL WITH DEATH

BEYOND THE BERMUDA TRIANGLE (1975) Worldvision. **Color-74min.** *(Made for TV).* Fred MacMurray, Sam Groom, Donna Mills ....(3)

BEYOND THE BLUE HORIZON (1942) Paramount. **Color-76min.** Dorothy Lamour, Richard Denning ....(3)

BEYOND THE CURTAIN (1960) J. Arthur Rank. **B&W-88min.** *(British).* Richard Greene, Eva Bartok ....(4)

BEYOND THE DARKNESS (1976) Mid-Broadway. **Color-83min.** *(German).* Dagmar Hedrich, Werner Bruhns ....(3)

BEYOND THE DOOR (1974) Film Ventures International. **Color-100min.** *(Italian-U.S.).* Juliet Mills, Richard Johnson......................4*
Italian title: CHI SEI? *(Who Are You?)*
British title: DEVIL WITHIN HER

BEYOND THE DOOR II (1978) Film Ventures International. **Color-90min.** *(Italian).* John Steiner, Daria Nicolodi...................4½*

BEYOND THE FOREST (1949) Warner Bros. **B&W-96min.** Bette Davis, Joseph Cotten 3*

BEYOND THE LAW (1968) Grove Press. **B&W-110min.** Norman Mailer, Mickey Knox ....(5)

BEYOND THE POSEIDON ADVENTURE (1979) Warner Bros. **Color-122min.** Michael Caine, Sally Field, Telly Savalas, Peter Boyle ....

BEYOND THE RIVER (1956) *see* BOTTOM OF THE BOTTLE, THE

BEYOND THE TIME BARRIER (1960) American-International. **B&W-75min.** Robert Clarke, Darlene Thompson...............................(3)

BEYOND THE VALLEY OF THE DOLLS (1970) 20th Century-Fox. **Color-109min.** Dolly Reed, Cynthia Myers....................................3*

BEYOND THE WALL (1921) *see* DESTINY

BEYOND THIS PLACE (1959) *see* WEB OF EVIDENCE

BEYOND TOMORROW (1940) RKO. **B&W-84min.** Richard Carlson, Jean Parker ....(4)

BHOWANI JUNCTION (1956) M-G-M. **Color-110min.** *(British).* Ava Gardner, Stewart Granger 5*

BIBLE! (1974) Poolemar. **Color-84min.** Bo White, Caprice Couselle, Georgina Spelvin ....(3)
Alternate title: IN THE BEGINNING

BIBLE . . . IN THE BEGINNING, THE (1966) 20th Century-Fox. **Color-174min.** *(Italian-U.S.).* Michael Parks, Ulla Bergryd 6*
Foreign title: BIBBIA, LA

BICHES, LES (1968) Jack H. Harris. **Color-104min.** *(French-Italian).* Stéphane Audran, Jacqueline Sassard ....(4)
Translation title: The Does
Alternate title: GIRLFRIENDS, THE
Alternate title: HETEROSEXUAL, THE

BICYCLE THIEF, THE (1949) Mayer-Burstyn. **B&W-90min.** *(Italian).* Lamberto Maggiorani, Lianella Carell 4½*
Original title: LADRI DI BICICLETTE
British title: BICYCLE THIEVES

BIDONE, IL (1955) Astor. **B&W-92min.** *(Italian).* Broderick Crawford, Giulietta Masina 4*
Alternate title: SWINDLE, THE
Translation title: The Petty Swindler

BIG BAD MAMA (1974) New World. **Color-83min.** Angie Dickinson, William Shatner ....(4)

BIG BANKROLL, THE (1961) *see* KING OF THE ROARING 20s

BIG BEAT, THE (1958) Universal. **Color-82min.** William Reynolds, Gogi Grant..(3)

BIG BIRD CAGE, THE (1972) New World. **Color-92min.** Pam Grier, Sid Haig..(1)

BIG BLUFF, THE (1955) Tower. **B&W-73min.** John Bromfield, Martha Vickers..(2)

BIG BOODLE, THE (1957) United Artists. **B&W-83min.** Errol Flynn, Pedro Armendariz..(3)
British title: NIGHT IN HAVANA

BIG BOSS, THE (1973) *see* FISTS OF FURY

BIG BOUNCE, THE (1969) Warner Bros. **Color-102min.** Ryan O'Neal, Leigh Taylor-Young...2*

BIG BROADCAST, THE (1932) Paramount. **B&W-78min.** Bing Crosby, Stuart Erwin 4*

BIG BROADCAST OF 1936, THE (1935) Paramount. **B&W-97min.** Jack Oakie, George Burns, Gracie Allen ....(4)

BIG BROADCAST OF 1937, THE (1936) Paramount. **B&W-100min.** Jack Benny, George Burns..(5)

BIG BROADCAST OF 1938, THE (1938) Paramount. **B&W-90min.** W. C. Fields 3*

BIG BROWN EYES (1936) Paramount. **B&W-77min.** Cary Grant, Joan Bennett 3½*

BIG BUS, THE (1976) Paramount. **Color-88min.** Joseph Bologna, Stockard Channing..5*

BIG CAGE, THE (1933) Universal. **B&W-76min.** Clyde Beatty, Mickey Rooney..(4)

BIG CAPER, THE (1957) United Artists. **B&W-84min.** Rory Calhoun, Mary Costa ....(4)

BIG CARNIVAL, THE (1951) *see* ACE IN THE HOLE

BIG CAT, THE (1949) Eagle Lion. **Color-75min.** Lon McCallister, Peggy Ann Garner ....(4)

BIG CHANCE, THE (1957) J. Arthur Rank. **B&W-61min.** *(British).* Adrienne Corri, William Russell ....(3)

BIG CIRCUS, THE (1959) Allied Artists. **Color-108min.** Victor Mature, Red Buttons 5*

BIG CITY, THE (1937) M-G-M. **B&W-80min.** Luise Rainer, Spencer Tracy..(4)
Alternate title: SKYSCRAPER WILDERNESS

BIG CITY, THE (1948) M-G-M. **Color-103min.** Margaret O'Brien, Danny Thomas..(4)

BIG CITY, THE (1964) Harrison Pictures. **B&W-125min.** *(Indian).* Madhabi Mukherjee, Anil Chatterjee 3*
Original title: MAHANAGAR

BIG CITY BLUES (1932) Warner Bros. **B&W-65min.** Joan Blondell, Eric Linden ....(4)

BIG CLOCK, THE (1948) Paramount. **B&W-95min.** Ray Milland, Charles Laughton 6*

BIG COMBO, THE (1955) Allied Artists. **B&W-89min.** Cornel Wilde, Jean Wallace 4*

BIG COUNTRY, THE (1958) United Artists. **Color-165min.** Gregory Peck, Jean Simmons 5½*

BIG CUBE, THE (1969) Warner Bros. **Color-98min.** Lana Turner, George Chakiris ....(3)

BIG DAY, THE (1949) *see* JOUR DE FETE

BIG DEAL, THE (1949) *see* BLONDIE'S BIG DEAL

BIG DEAL AT DODGE CITY (1966) *see* BIG HAND FOR THE LITTLE LADY, A

BIG DEAL ON MADONNA STREET, THE (1958) United Motion Pic. Org. (UMPO). **B&W-91min.** *(Italian).* Vittorio Gassman, Marcello Mastroianni ....(5)
Original title: SOLITI IGNOTTI, I *(The Usual Unknown Persons)*
British title: PERSONS UNKNOWN
Alternate title: USUAL UNIDENTIFIED THIEVES, THE
Alternate title: BIG DEAL, THE
TV title: AS USUAL, UNKNOWN

THE BIG COUNTRY (1958). Ranch owner Jean Simmons tells newcomer Gregory Peck why the two feuding land barons want her property.

Films are rated on a 1 to 10 scale, 10 is highest. **Boldface** ratings followed by an asterisk (*) are for films actually seen and rated by the executive and senior editors. All other ratings are estimates. (See Notes on Entertainment Ratings in the front section.)

BIG DECISION, THE (1951) *see* BASKETBALL FIX, THE

BIG DOLL HOUSE, THE (1971) New World. **Color-93min.** Judy Brown, Pam Grier ....(2)

BIG FISHERMAN, THE (1959) Buena Vista. **Color-180min.** Howard Keel, Susan Kohner 4½*

BIG FIX, THE (1978) Universal. **Color-108min.** Richard Dreyfuss, Susan Anspach, Bonnie Bedelia..6*

BIG FRAME, THE (1952) RKO. **B&W-67min.** *(British).* Mark Stevens, Jean Kent ....(3)
Original title: LOST HOURS, THE

BIG FREEZE, THE (1961) *see* ON THIN ICE

BIG GAMBLE, THE (1961) Pathé-RKO. **Color-100min.** Stephen Boyd, Juliette Greco 3½*

BIG GUNDOWN, THE (1968) Columbia. **Color-90min.** *(Italian-Spanish).* Lee Van Cleef, Tomas Milian ....(3)
Original Italian title: RESA DE CONTI, LA *(Account Rendered)*
Spanish title: HALCON Y LA PRESA, EL

BIG GUNS (1973) *see* NO WAY OUT

BIG GUSHER, THE (1951) Columbia. **B&W-68min.** Wayne Morris, Preston Foster ....(3)

BIG GUY, THE (1940) Universal. **B&W-78min.** Victor McLaglen, Jackie Cooper ....(3)

BIG HAND FOR THE LITTLE LADY, A (1966) Warner Bros. **Color-95min.** Henry Fonda, Joanne Woodward 5*
British title: BIG DEAL AT DODGE CITY

BIG HANGOVER, THE (1950) M-G-M. **B&W-82min.** Van Johnson, Elizabeth Taylor 4*

BIG HEART, THE (1947) *see* MIRACLE ON 34th STREET

BIG HEAT, THE (1953) Columbia. **B&W-90min.** Glenn Ford, Gloria Grahame 4*

BIG HOUSE, THE (1930) M-G-M. **Color-88min.** Chester Morris, Wallace Beery ....(5)

BIG HOUSE, U.S.A. (1955) United Artists. **B&W-82min.** Broderick Crawford, Ralph Meeker ....(4)

BIG JACK (1949) M-G-M. **B&W-85min.** Wallace Beery, Richard Conte ..(4)

BIG JAKE (1971) National General. **Color-110min.** John Wayne, Richard Boone 4*

BIG JIM McLAIN (1952) Warner Bros. **B&W-90min.** John Wayne, Nancy Olson 3*

BIG JOHN (1973) *see* ELECTRA GLIDE IN BLUE

BIG KNIFE, THE (1955) United Artists. **B&W-111min.** Jack Palance, Ida Lupino 4*

BIG LAND, THE (1957) Warner Bros. **Color-92min.** Alan Ladd, Virginia Mayo 4*
British title: STAMPEDED

BIG LEAGUER, THE (1953) M-G-M. **B&W-70min.** Edward G. Robinson, Vera-Ellen ....(3)

BIG LIFT, THE (1950) 20th Century-Fox. **B&W-120min.** Montgomery Clift, Paul Douglas 4½*

BIG MO (1972) *see* MAURIE

BIG MONEY, THE (1958) J. Arthur Rank. **Color-86min.** *(British).* Ian Carmichael, Belinda Lee ....(3)

BIG MOUTH, THE (1967) Columbia. **Color-107min.** Jerry Lewis, Harold J. Stone 3*

BIG NIGHT, THE (1951) United Artists. **B&W-75min.** John Barrymore, Jr., Preston Foster ....(3)

BIG NIGHT, THE (1960) Paramount. **B&W-74min.** Randy Sparks, Dick Foran ....(3)

BIG NOISE, THE (1944) 20th Century-Fox. **B&W-74min.** Stanley Laurel, Oliver Hardy ....(3)

BIG OPERATOR, THE (1959) M-G-M. **B&W-91min.** Mickey Rooney, Steve Cochran 3*
Alternate title: ANATOMY OF A SYNDICATE

BIG PARADE, THE (1925) M-G-M. **B&W-128min.** *(Silent).* John Gilbert, Renée Adorée 3*

BIG PARADE OF COMEDY, THE (1964) *see* MGM'S BIG PARADE OF COMEDY

BIG POND, THE (1930) Paramount. **B&W-75min.** *(English language).* Maurice Chevalier, Claudette Colbert 3*
Foreign title: GRANDE MERE, LA

BIG PUNCH, THE (1948) Warner Bros. **B&W-80min.** Wayne Morris, Gordon MacRae ....(3)

BIG RED (1962) Buena Vista. **Color-93min.** Walter Pidgeon, Gilles Payant 4*

BIG RED ONE, THE (1979) U.A. (for Lorimar). **Color- min.** Lee Marvin, Kelly Ward, Mark Hamill ....

BIG RIPOFF, THE (1975) MCA-TV. **Color-100min.** *(Made for TV).* Tony Curtis, Barbara Feldon, Larry Hagman 4½*

BIG RISK, THE (1960) United Artists. **B&W-111min.** *(French-Italian).* Lino Ventura, Sandra Milo, Jean-Paul Belmondo ....(3)
Original French title: CLASSE TOUS RISQUES

BIG ROSE (1974) 20th Century-Fox. **Color-75min.** *(Made for TV).* Shelley Winters, Barry Primus 4*

BIG SEARCH, THE (1957) *see* EAST OF KILIMANJARO

BIG SHAKEDOWN, THE (1934) First National [W.B.]. **B&W-64min.** Bette Davis, Charles Farrell ....(4)

BIG SHOT, THE (1942) Warner Bros. **B&W-82min.** Humphrey Bogart, Irene Manning ....

BIG SHOW, THE (1936) Republic. **B&W-70min.** Gene Autry, Smiley Burnette 3*

BIG SHOW, THE (1961) 20th Century-Fox. **Color-113min.** Esther Williams, Cliff Robertson 3*

BIG SKY, THE (1952) RKO. **B&W-140min.** Kirk Douglas, Dewey Martin 4½*

BIG SLEEP, THE (1946) Warner Bros. **B&W-114min.** Humphrey Bogart, Lauren Bacall 5*

BIG SLEEP, THE (1978) United Artists. **Color-99min.** *(British-U.S.).* Robert Mitchum, Sarah Miles, James Stewart 3*

BIG SNATCH, THE (1963) *see* ANY NUMBER CAN WIN

BIG STEAL, THE (1949) RKO. **B&W-71min.** Robert Mitchum, Jane Greer 4*

BIG STORE, THE (1941) M-G-M. **B&W-80min.** The Marx Brothers.........3*

BIG STORY, THE (1958) *see* APPOINTMENT WITH A SHADOW

BIG STREET, THE (1942) RKO. **B&W-88min.** Henry Fonda, Lucille Ball ....(4)

BIG T.N.T. SHOW, THE (1966) American-International. **B&W-93min.** *(Documentary). Director:* Larry Peerce ....(3)

BIG TIMBER (1950) Monogram [Allied Artists]. **B&W-73min.** Roddy McDowall, Jeff Donnell...(3)

BIG TIP-OFF, THE (1955) Allied Artists. **B&W-78min.** Constance Smith, Richard Conte...(3)

BIG TOWN (1947) Paramount. **B&W-60min.** Philip Reed, Hillary Brooke ....(2)
TV title: GUILTY ASSIGNMENT

BIG TOWN AFTER DARK (1947) Paramount. **B&W-69min.** Philip Reed, Hillary Brooke ....(4)
TV title: UNDERWORLD AFTER DARK

BIG TOWN SCANDAL (1948) Paramount. **B&W-62min.** Philip Reed, Hillary Brooke ....(3)
TV title: UNDERWORLD SCANDAL

BIG TRAIL, THE (1930) Fox Film Co. [20th]. **B&W-126min.** John Wayne, Marguerite Churchill..2½*

BIG TREES, THE (1952) Warner Bros. **Color-89min.** Kirk Douglas, Eve Miller 4*

BIG WAVE, THE (1962) Allied Artists. **B&W-73min.** *(Japanese).* Sessue Hayakawa, Mickey Curtis ....(3)

BIG WEDNESDAY (1978) Warner Bros. **Color-126min.** Jan-Michael Vincent, William Katt, Gary Busey...........................5½*

BIG WHEEL, THE (1949) United Artists. **B&W-92min.** Mickey Rooney, Thomas Mitchell 3*

BIGAMIST, THE (1953) Filmmakers. **B&W-80min.** Edmond O'Brien, Joan Fontaine 4*

BIGAMIST, THE (1956) Distributors Corp. of America. **B&W-97min.** *(Italian).* Vittorio De Sica, Marcello Mastroianni ....(3)
Original title: BIGAMO, IL

BIGFOOT (1971) Ellman Enterprises. **Color-95min.** Chris Mitchum, John Carradine..(3)

BIGGER THAN LIFE (1956) 20th Century-Fox. **Color-95min.** James Mason, Barbara Rush 4*

BIGGEST BUNDLE OF THEM ALL, THE (1967) M-G-M. **Color-110min.** *(U.S.-Italian).* Vittorio De Sica, Raquel Welch..............4*

BIKINI BEACH (1964) American-International. **Color-100min.** Annette Funicello, Frankie Avalon, Boris Karloff.................(3)

BILITIS (1977) Topar. **Color-95min.** *(French).* Patti D'Arbanville, Bernard Giraudeau ....(3)

BILL AND COO (1947) Republic. **Color-61min.** Ken Murray 3*

BILL OF DIVORCEMENT, A (1932) RKO. **B&W-76min.** John Barrymore, Katharine Hepburn 4*

BILL OF DIVORCEMENT, A (1940) RKO. **B&W-74min.** Maureen O'Hara, Adolphe Menjou...(4)
Alternate title: NEVER TO LOVE
Alternate title: NOT FOR EACH OTHER

BILLIE (1965) United Artists. **Color-87min.** Patty Duke, Warren Berlinger **4***

BILLION DOLLAR BRAIN (1967) United Artists. **Color-108min.** *(British-U.S.).* Michael Caine, Karl Malden...........................(4)

BILLION DOLLAR HOBO, THE (1978) **Color-96min.** Tim Conway, Will Geer, Eric Weston..(4)

BILLY BUDD (1962) Allied Artists. **B&W-123min.** *(British-U.S.).* Terence Stamp, Robert Ryan....................................6½*

BILLY JACK (1971) Warner Bros. **Color-112min.** Tom Laughlin, Delores Taylor...**5***

BILLY JACK GOES TO WASHINGTON (1977) Taylor-Laughlin. **Color-155min.** Tom Laughlin, E. G. Marshall, Lucie Arnaz ....(5)

BILLY LIAR (1963) Continental [Walter Reade]. **B&W-96min.** *(British).* Tom Courtenay, Julie Christie...........................**5***

BILLY ROSE'S DIAMOND HORSESHOE (1945) 20th Century-Fox. **Color-104min.** Dick Haymes, Betty Grable **5***
Alternate title: DIAMOND HORSESHOE

BILLY ROSE'S JUMBO (1962) M-G-M. **Color-125min.** Doris Day, Stephen Boyd...**5***
Alternate title: JUMBO

BILLY THE KID (1930) M-G-M. **B&W-98min.** Johnny Mack Brown, Wallace Beery..**3***
TV title: HIGHWAYMAN RIDES, THE

BILLY THE KID (1941) M-G-M. **Color-95min.** Robert Taylor, Brian Donlevy...**3***

BILLY THE KID VS. DRACULA (1966) Avco-Embassy. **Color-84min.** John Carradine, Chuck Courtney..............................(2)

BILLY TWO HATS (1973) United Artists. **Color-80min.** *(British).* Gregory Peck, Desi Arnaz, Jr. ....**...**

BIMBO THE GREAT (1958) Warner Bros. **Color-96min.** *(German).* Klaus Holm, Elma Karlowa..(3)
Original title: RIVALEN DER MANEGE

BINGO LONG TRAVELING ALL-STARS AND MOTOR KINGS, THE (1976) Universal. **Color-110min.** Billy Dee Williams, James Earl Jones...**5***

BIOGRAPHY OF A BACHELOR GIRL (1935) M-G-M. **B&W-82min.** Ann Harding, Robert Montgomery................................(4)

BIRCH INTERVAL (1976) Gamma III. **Color-103min.** Susan McClung, Eddie Albert, Rip Torn...............................(5)

BIRD OF PARADISE (1932) RKO. **B&W-80min.** Dolores Del Rio, Joel McCrea...**4***

BIRD OF PARADISE (1951) 20th Century-Fox. **Color-100min.** Louis Jourdan, Debra Paget...............................(3)

BIRD WITH THE CRYSTAL PLUMAGE, THE (1970) UMC Pictures. **Color-98min.** Tony Musante, Suzy Kendall **4***

BIRDMAN OF ALCATRAZ (1962) United Artists. **B&W-147min.** Burt Lancaster, Karl Malden...**6***

BIRDMEN, THE (1971) MCA-TV. **Color-96min.** *(Made for TV).* Doug McClure, Chuck Connors, Richard Basehart **4***
Alternate title: ESCAPE OF THE BIRDMEN

BIRDS, THE (1963) Universal. **Color-120min.** Rod Taylor, Tippi Hedren..**5***

BIRDS AND THE BEES, THE (1948) *see* THREE DARING DAUGHTERS

BIRDS AND THE BEES, THE (1956) Paramount. **Color-94min.** George Gobel, Mitzi Gaynor...............................**4***

BIRDS DO IT (1966) Columbia. **Color-95min.** Soupy Sales, Beverly Adams...(3)

BIRDS DO IT . . . BEES DO IT . . . (1974) Columbia. **Color-89min.** *(Documentary). Director:* Nicolas Noxon ....(5)

BIRDS IN PERU (1968) Regional. **Color-95min.** *(French).* Jean Seberg, Maurice Ronet..(2)
Original title: OISEAUX VON MOURIR AU PEROU, LES *(The Birds Come to Die in Peru)*

BIRDS OF PREY (1972) Viacom. **Color-81min.** *(Made for TV).* David Janssen, Ralph Meeker......................................**4***

BIRDS, THE BEES AND THE ITALIANS, THE (1966) Claridge. **B&W-115min.** *(Italian).* Virna Lisi, Gastone Moschin..............(5)
Original title: SIGNORE E SIGNORI *(Ladies and Gentlemen)*

BIRDMAN OF ALCATRAZ (1962). Guard Neville Brand takes a sympathetic interest in life-term convict Burt Lancaster's work with birds.

BIRTH OF A NATION, THE (1915) United Artists. **B&W-157min.** *(Silent).* Henry B. Walthall, Lillian Gish, Mae Marsh **5***
Original title: CLANSMAN, THE
Unauthorized condensation: IN THE CLUTCHES OF THE KU KLUX KLAN

BIRTH OF THE BLUES (1941) Paramount. **B&W-85min.** Bing Crosby, Mary Martin...(5)

BIRTHDAY PARTY, THE (1968) Continental [Walter Reade]. **Color-123min.** *(British).* Robert Shaw, Patrick Magee ....(6)

BIRTHDAY PRESENT (1957) Showcorporation. **B&W-100min.** *(British).* Tony Britton, Sylvia Syms ....(5)

BIRTHPLACE OF THE HOOTENANNY (1963) *see* GREENWICH VILLAGE STORY

BISCUIT EATER, THE (1940) Paramount. **B&W-80min.** Billy Lee, Cordell Hickman...(4)
British title: GOD GAVE HIM A DOG

BISCUIT EATER, THE (1972) Buena Vista. **Color-92min.** Johnny Whitaker, George Spell....................................**5***

BISHOP MISBEHAVES, THE (1935) M-G-M. **B&W-86min.** Edmund Gwenn, Maureen O'Sullivan...............................(5)
British title: BISHOP'S MISADVENTURES, THE

BISHOP'S WIFE, THE (1947) RKO. **B&W-108min.** Cary Grant, Loretta Young...**5***

BITE THE BULLET (1975) Columbia. **Color-131min.** Gene Hackman, Candice Bergen...5½*

BITTER CREEK (1954) Allied Artists. **B&W-74min.** Wild Bill Elliott, Beverly Garland..(3)

BITTER HARVEST (1963) Continental [Walter Reade]. **Color-96min.** *(British).* Janet Munro, John Stride...................(3)

BITTER REUNION (1958) *see* BEAU SERGE, LE

BITTER RICE (1949) Lux Film America. **B&W-107min.** *(Italian).* Vittorio Gassman, Silvana Mangano **4***
Original title: RISO AMARO

BITTER SPRINGS (1950) J. Arthur Rank. **B&W-86min.** *(Australian).* Chips Rafferty, Tommy Trinder..............................(5)

BITTER SWEET (1940) M-G-M. **Color-92min.** Jeanette MacDonald, Nelson Eddy...(4)
Common title error: BITTERSWEET

BITTER TEA OF GENERAL YEN, THE (1933) Columbia. **B&W-89min.** Barbara Stanwyck, Nils Asther............................(4)

BITTER TEARS OF PETRA VON KANT, THE (1972) New Yorker Films. **Color-124min.** *(German).* Margit Carstensen, Irm Hermann ....
Original title: BITTERN TRAENEN DER PETRA VON KANT

BITTER VICTORY (1957) Columbia. **B&W-90min.** *(U.S.-French).* Curt Jurgens, Richard Burton.................................(4)
Original title: AMERE VICTORIE

Films are rated on a 1 to 10 scale, 10 is highest. **Boldface** ratings followed by an asterisk (*) are for films actually seen and rated by the executive and senior editors. All other ratings are estimates. (See Notes on Entertainment Ratings in the front section.)

BITTERSWEET LOVE (1976) Avco-Embassy. **Color-90min.** Meredith Baxter Birney, Scott Hylands, Lana Turner **4***

BLACK ABBOT, THE (1963) UCC Films. **B&W-95min.** *(German).* Joachim Fuchsberger, Grit Bottcher.................................. (3)
Original title: SCHWARZE ABT, DER

BLACK AND WHITE IN COLOR (1976) Allied Artists. **Color-90min.** *(Ivory Coast-French-Swiss).* Jean Carmet, Jacques Dufilho **3***
Original title: VICTOIRE EN CHANTANT, LA *(Singing Victory)*
Alternate Original Title: NOIR ET BLANCS EN COULEUR
Alternate title: BLACK VICTORY

BLACK ANGEL (1946) Universal. **B&W-80min.** Dan Duryea, Peter Lorre .... (4)

BLACK ANGELS (1970) Merrick International Pictures. **Color-92min.** Des Roberts, Linda Jackson.................................. (2)

BLACK ARROW, THE (1948) Columbia. **B&W-76min.** Louis Hayward, Janet Blair.................................. (5)
British title: BLACK ARROW STRIKES, THE

BLACK BART (1948) Universal. **Color-80min.** Dan Duryea, Yvonne DeCarlo.................................. (3)
British title: BLACK BART, HIGHWAYMAN

BLACK BEAUTY (1946) 20th Century-Fox. **B&W-74min.** Mona Freeman, Richard Denning.................................. (4)

BLACK BEAUTY (1971) Paramount. **Color-108min.** *(British-German-Spanish).* Mark Lester, Walter Slezak.................................. (4)

BLACK BELLY OF THE TARANTULA, THE (1972) M-G-M. **Color-88min.** *(Italian-French).* Giancarlo Giannini, Claudine Auger, Stefania Sandrelli ....
Original Italian title: TARANTOLA DAL VENTRE NERO, LA

BLACK BELT JONES (1974) Warner Bros. **Color-85min.** Jim Kelly, Gloria Hendry.................................. (3)

BLACK BIRD, THE (1975) Columbia. **Color-98min.** George Segal, Stéphane Audran.................................. **5***

BLACK BOOK, THE (1949) *see* REIGN OF TERROR

BLACK BOUNTY HUNTER, THE (1975) *see* BOSS NIGGER

BLACK CAESAR (1973) American-International. **Color-94min.** Fred Williamson, D'Urville Martin.................................. (3)
British title: GODFATHER OF HARLEM

BLACK CAMEL (1931) Fox Film Co. [20th]. **B&W-71min.** Warner Oland, Bela Lugosi

BLACK CASTLE, THE (1952) Universal. **B&W-81min.** Stephen McNally, Richard Greene, Boris Karloff.................................. (3)

BLACK CAT, THE (1934) Universal. **B&W-65min.** Boris Karloff, Bela Lugosi.................................. **4***
British title: HOUSE OF DOOM, THE

BLACK CAT, THE (1941) Universal. **B&W-70min.** Broderick Crawford, Basil Rathbone, Bela Lugosi.................................. **3***

BLACK CHAPEL, THE (1959) Screen Gems. **B&W-88min.** *(W. German-Italian).* Peter Van Eyck, Dawn Addams.................................. (3)
Original German title: GEHEIMAKTION SCHWARZE KAPELLE
Italian title: SICARI DI HITLER, I

BLACK CHRISTMAS (1975) Warner Bros. **Color-99min.** *(Canadian).* Olivia Hussey, Keir Dullea.................................. **4½***
Alternate title: SILENT NIGHT, EVIL NIGHT
TV title: STRANGER IN THE HOUSE

BLACK COBRA, THE (1961) UCC Films. **B&W-95min.** *(German).* Adrian Hoven, Ann Smyrner.................................. (3)

BLACK CROSS (1960) **Color-175min.** *(Polish).* Urszula Modrzynska, Grazyna Staniszewska.................................. (3)

BLACK DAKOTAS, THE (1954) Columbia. **Color-65min.** Gary Merrill, Wanda Hendrix.................................. (3)

BLACK DEVILS OF KALI, THE (1955) *see* MYSTERY OF THE BLACK JUNGLE

BLACK DRAGON OF MANZANAR (1943) Republic. **B&W-100min.** *(Re-edited Serial).* Rod Cameron, Constance Worth.................................. (4)
Original title: G-MEN VS. THE BLACK DRAGON

BLACK DUKE, THE (1963) Producers Releasing Org. **Color-90min.** *(Italian-Spanish).* Cameron Mitchell, Gloria Milland.................................. (3)
Original Italian title: DUCA NERO, IL
Spanish title: DUQUE NEGRO, EL

BLACK EYE (1974) Warner Bros. **Color-98min.** Fred Williamson, Rosemary Forsyth.................................. (4)

BLACK FLOWERS FOR THE BRIDE (1970) *see* SOMETHING FOR EVERYONE

BLACK FOX (1962) Capri Films. **B&W-89min.** *(Documentary).* Director: Louis Clyde Stoumen.................................. **6***

BLACK FRANKENSTEIN, THE (1973) *see* BLACKENSTEIN

BLACK FRIDAY (1940) Universal. **B&W-70min.** Boris Karloff, Stanley Ridges.................................. **3***

BLACK FURY (1935) First National [W.B.]. **B&W-92min.** Paul Muni, Karen Morley.................................. **5***

BLACK GESTAPO (1975) Bryanston. **Color-88min.** Rod Perry, Charles P. Robinson.................................. (3)

BLACK GIRL (1967) New Yorker Films. **B&W-60min.** *(French).* Mbissine Therese Diop, Robert Fontaine.................................. (5)

BLACK GIRL (1972) Cinerama Releasing. **Color-97min.** Brock Peters, Peggy Pettitt.................................. (4)

BLACK GLOVE, THE (1954) Lippert Productions. **B&W-84min.** *(British).* Alex Nicol, Eleanor Summerfield.................................. (4)
Original title: FACE THE MUSIC

BLACK GOLD (1947) Allied Artists. **Color-92min.** Anthony Quinn, Katherine DeMille.................................. **3½***

BLACK GOLD (1963) Warner Bros. **Color-98min.** Philip Carey, Diane McBain.................................. (3)

BLACK GUNN (1972) Columbia. **Color-94min.** Jim Brown, Martin Landau.................................. (3)

BLACK HAND (1950) M-G-M. **B&W-93min.** Gene Kelly, J. Carrol Naish **3***

BLACK HOLE, THE (1979) Buena Vista. **Color-   min.** Maximilian Schell, Anthony Perkins.................................

BLACK HORSE CANYON (1954) Universal. **Color-81min.** Joel McCrea, Mari Blanchard.................................. **4***

BLACK ICE, THE (1957) Parkside Prods. **B&W-62min.** *(British).* Paul Carpenter, Kim Parker.................................. (3)

BLACK INVADERS, THE (1960) American-International. **Color-90min.** *(Italian).* Danielle De Metz, Amedeo Nazzari.................................. (1)

BLACK JACK (1951) *see* CAPTAIN BLACKJACK

BLACK JACK (1973) *see* WILD IN THE SKY

BLACK JESUS (1971) Plaza Pictures. **Color-90min.** Woody Strode, Jean Servais.................................. (3)
Original title: SEDUTO ALLA SUA DESTRA
British title: OUT OF THE DARKNESS
Alternate title: SEATED AT HIS RIGHT

BLACK JOY (1977) Elliott Kastner-Arnon Milchan. **Color-110min.** *(British).* Norman Beaton, Trevor Thomas, Dawn Hope.................................

BLACK KNIGHT, THE (1954) Columbia. **Color-85min.** *(British).* Alan Ladd, Peter Cushing.................................. (3)

BLACK LANCERS, THE (1962) *see* CHARGE OF THE BLACK LANCERS

BLACK LEGION (1936) Warner Bros. **B&W-83min.** Humphrey Bogart, Richard (Dick) Foran.................................. **4***

BLACK LIKE ME (1964) Continental [Walter Reade]. **B&W-107min.** James Whitmore, Clifton James.................................. (4)

BLACK LOVE, WHITE LOVE (1967) *see* SWEET LOVE, BITTER

BLACK MAGIC (1944) Monogram [Allied Artists]. **B&W-67min.** Sidney Toler, Mantan Moreland.................................. (4)
Alternate title: MEETING AT MIDNIGHT
Alternate title: CHARLIE CHAN IN BLACK MAGIC

BLACK MAGIC (1949) United Artists. **B&W-105min.** Orson Welles, Nancy Guild.................................. **4***

BLACK MONOCLE, THE (1961) Orex Films. **B&W-85min.** *(French).* Paul Meurisse, Elga Andersen.................................. (3)
Original title: MONOCLE NOIR, LE

BLACK MOON (1975) 20th Century-Fox. **Color-92min.** *(French).* Catrhyn Harrison, Therese Giehse, Alexandra Stewart, Joe Dallesandro.......... (4)

BLACK NARCISSUS (1947) Universal. **Color-100min.** *(British).* Deborah Kerr, David Farrar.................................. **4***

BLACK OAK CONSPIRACY (1977) New World. **Color-92min.** Jesse Vint, Karen Carlson, Albert Salmi.................................. (4)

BLACK ON WHITE (1969) Audubon. **Color-80min.** *(Italian).* Anita Sanders, Nino Segurino.................................. (1)
Original title: NERO SU BIANCO
Alternate title: ARTFUL PENETRATION, THE
Alternate title: ARTFUL PENETRATION OF BARBARA, THE
Alternate title: SHAMEFUL
Alternate title: ATTRACTION

BLACK ORCHID, THE (1959) Paramount. **B&W-96min.** Sophia Loren, Anthony Quinn.................................. **4***

BLACK ORPHEUS (1959) Lopert [U.A.]. **Color-98min.** *(Brazilian).* Breno Mello, Marpessa Dawn.................................. **4***
Original title: ORFEU NEGRO

BLACK PANTHER, THE (1977) Alpha *(British).* **Color-102min.** *(British).* Donald Neilson, Debbie Farrington.................................

BLACK PANTHER OF RATANA, THE (1962) UCC Films. Color-94min. *(W. German/Italian/Thai).* Marianne Koche, Heinz Drache................(2)
Original German title: SCHWARZE PANTHER VON RATANA, DER

BLACK PARACHUTE, THE (1944) Columbia. B&W-65min. Larry Parks, John Carradine..(3)

BLACK PATCH (1958) Warner Bros. B&W-83min. George Montgomery, Diane Brewster..(3)

BLACK PETER (1964) Altura Films. B&W-85min. *(Czech).* Ladislav Jakim, Pavla Martinkova ....(5)
Original title: CERNY PETR

BLACK PIRATE, THE (1926) United Artists. Color-85min. *(Silent).* Douglas Fairbanks, Billie Dove ....(5)

BLACK PIRATES, THE (1954) Lippert Productions. Color-72min. Anthony Dexter, Lon Chaney (Jr.)............................(4)

BLACK PIT OF DR. M (1959) Azteca. B&W-72min. *(Mexican).* Rafael Bertrand, Gaston Santos 1*
Original title: MISTERIOS DE ULTRATUMBA *(Mysteries from Beyond the Tomb)*

BLACK RODEO (1972) Cinerama Releasing. Color-87min. *(Documentary).* Director: Jeff Kanew ....(4)

BLACK ROOM, THE (1935) Columbia. B&W-67min. Boris Karloff 4½*
British title: BLACK ROOM MYSTERY, THE

BLACK ROSE, THE (1950) 20th Century-Fox. Color-121min. *(British).* Tyrone Power, Orson Welles 5*

BLACK SABBATH (1963) American-International. Color-99min. *(U.S.-French-Italian).* Boris Karloff, Mark Damon 4½*
Original Italian title: TRE VOLTI DELLA PAURA, I *(The Three Faces of Fear)*
Original French title: TROIS VISAGES DE LA PEUR, LES *(same as Italian)*

BLACK SAMSON (1974) Warner Bros. Color-87min. Rockne Tarkington, William Smith ....

BLACK SCORPION, THE (1957) Warner Bros. B&W-88min. Richard Denning, Mara Corday 2*

BLACK SHAMPOO (1976) Dimension Pictures. Color-83min. John Daniels, Tanya Boyd ....(3)

BLACK SHIELD OF FALWORTH, THE (1954) Universal. Color-99min. Tony Curtis, Janet Leigh 5*

BLACK SIX, THE (1974) Cinemation. Color-90min. Gene Washington, Carl Eller ....

BLACK SLEEP, THE (1956) United Artists. B&W-81min. Basil Rathbone, Akim Tamiroff, Bela Lugosi ....(3)
Alternate title: DR. CADMAN'S SECRET

BLACK SPURS (1965) Paramount. Color-81min. Rory Calhoun, Linda Darnell ....(3)

BLACK STALLION, THE (1979) United Artists. Color- min. Kelly Reno, Mickey Rooney ....

BLACK SUNDAY (1960) American-International. B&W-83min. *(Italian).* Barbara Steele, John Richardson ....(3)
Original title: MASCHERA DE DOMONIO, LA *(The Mask of the Demon)*
British title: REVENGE OF THE VAMPIRE
U.S. Pre-release title: HOUSE OF FRIGHT

BLACK SUNDAY (1977) Paramount. Color-143min. Robert Shaw, Bruce Dern 6½*

BLACK SWAN, THE (1942) 20th Century-Fox. Color-85min. Tyrone Power, Maureen O'Hara....................................5½*

BLACK TENT, THE (1956) J. Arthur Rank. Color-93min. *(British).* Anthony Steel, Donald Sinden ....(3)

BLACK TIDE (1956) Astor. B&W-79min. *(British).* John Ireland, Derek Bond ....(3)

BLACK TIGHTS (1960) Magna Pictures. Color-120min. *(French).* Maurice Chevalier, Zizi Jeanmaire ....(5)
Original title: UN, DEUX, TROIS, QUATRE *(One, Two, Three, Four)*

BLACK TORMENT, THE (1964) Governor. Color-85min. *(British).* Heather Sears, John Turner ....(4)

BLACK TUESDAY (1955) United Artists. B&W-80min. Edward G. Robinson, Peter Graves ....(5)

BLACK VEIL FOR LISA, A (1968) Commonwealth United. Color-88min. *(Italian-German).* John Mills, Luciana Paluzzi ....(3)
Original Italian title: MORTE NON HA SESSO, LA
Original German title: GEHEIMNIS DER JUNGEN WITWE, DAS

BLACK VICTORY (1976) *see* BLACK AND WHITE IN COLOR

BLACK WATER GOLD (1970) ABC Films. Color-75min. *(Made for TV).* Aron Kincaid, Bradford Dillman, Keir Dullea.............3*

BLACK WHIP, THE (1956) 20th Century-Fox. B&W-77min. Hugh Marlowe, Coleen Gray......................................3*

BLACK WIDOW, THE (1947) *see* SOMBRA, THE SPIDER WOMAN

BLACK WIDOW (1954) 20th Century-Fox. Color-95min. Ginger Rogers, Van Heflin...4*

BLACK WINDMILL, THE (1974) Universal. Color-106min. *(U.S.-British).* Michael Caine, Joseph O'Conor 4*

BLACK ZOO (1963) Allied Artists. Color-88min. Michael Gough, Rod Lauren ....(2)

BLACKBEARD, THE PIRATE (1952) RKO. Color-99min. Robert Newton, Linda Darnell 3½*

BLACKBEARD'S GHOST (1968) Buena Vista. Color-107min. Peter Ustinov, Dean Jones...(4)

BLACKBOARD JUNGLE, THE (1955) M-G-M. B&W-101min. Glenn Ford, Anne Francis...5*

BLACKBOARD MASSACRE (1976) *see* MASSACRE AT CENTRAL HIGH

BLACKENSTEIN (1973) L. F. G. Films. Color-92min. Ivory Stone, Joe Desue, James Cousar ....(1)
Alternate title: BLACK FRANKENSTEIN, THE

BLACKIE AND THE LAW (1946) *see* BOSTON BLACKIE AND THE LAW

BLACKIE GOES TO HOLLYWOOD (1942) *see* BOSTON BLACKIE GOES TO HOLLYWOOD

BLACKIE'S RENDEZVOUS (1945) *see* BOSTON BLACKIE'S RENDEZVOUS

BLACKJACK KETCHUM, DESPERADO (1956) Columbia. Color-76min. Howard Duff, Victor Jory ....(3)

BLACKMAIL (1929) World Wide (Sono Art). B&W-75min. *(British).* Anny Ondra (silent), Joan Barry (sound), John Longden 3*

BLACKMAIL (1939) M-G-M. B&W-81min. Edward G. Robinson, Ruth Hussey 4*

BLACKMAIL (1947) Republic. B&W-67min. William Marshall*, Adele Mara ....(3)

BLACKMAILED (1950) Bell Pictures. B&W-85min. *(British).* Dirk Bogarde, Mai Zetterling.....................................(3)

BLACKMAILERS, THE (1960) Commonwealth United. Color-105min. *(Spanish).* Manuel Benitz, Alberto De Mendoza ....(3)

BLACKOUT (1940) *see* CONTRABAND

BLACKOUT (1955) Lippert Productions. B&W-87min. *(British).* Dane Clark, Belinda Lee ....(3)
Original title: MURDER BY PROXY

BLACKOUT (1978) New World. Color-90min. Jim Mitchum, Robert Carradine 3½*

BLACKSNAKE (1973) *see* SWEET SUZY

BLACKWELL STORY, THE (1957) CPT (TV). B&W-74min. *(Made for TV).* Joanne Dru, Dan O'Herlihy ....(5)

BLACKWELL'S ISLAND (1939) Warner Bros. B&W-71min. John Garfield, Rosemary Lane 3*

BLACULA (1972) American-International. Color-92min. William Marshall, Vonetta McGee ....(4)

BLADE (1973) Joseph Green. Color-92min. John Marley, Jon Cypher.....(3)

BLAISE PASCAL (1975) Audio Brandon. Color-131min. *(Italian).* Pierre Arditi, Mario Bardella..............................(4)

BLANCHE FURY (1948) Eagle Lion. Color-93min. *(British).* Valerie Hobson, Stewart Granger................................4*

BLANCHEVILLE MONSTER (1960) American-International. B&W-88min. *(Spanish-Italian).* Gérard Tichy, Joan Hills 3*
Alternate title: HORROR

BLAST (1972) *see* FINAL COMEDOWN, THE

BLAST OF SILENCE (1961) Universal. B&W-77min. Allen Baron, Molly McCarthy ....(3)

BLAST-OFF (1967) *see* THOSE FANTASTIC FLYING FOOLS

BLAZE OF GLORY (1950) *see* BOY FROM INDIANA

BLAZE OF NOON (1947) Paramount. B&W-91min. William Holden, Sterling Hayden, Anne Baxter 3*

BLAZING FOREST, THE (1952) Paramount. Color-90min. John Payne, Agnes Moorehead...3*

BLAZING MAGNUMS (1977) *see* STRANGE SHADOWS IN AN EMPTY ROOM

BLAZING SADDLES (1974) Warner Bros. Color-93min. Cleavon Little, Gene Wilder...5½*

BLAZING SAND (1960) Avco-Embassy. Color-98min. *(Israeli).* Daliah Lavi, Gert Gunther...(3)

BLESS THE BEASTS AND CHILDREN (1971) Columbia. Color-109min. Bill Mumy, Barry Robins.....................4*

Films are rated on a 1 to 10 scale, 10 is highest. **Boldface** ratings followed by an asterisk (*) are for films actually seen and rated by the executive and senior editors. All other ratings are estimates. (See Notes on Entertainment Ratings in the front section.)

BLESSED EVENT (1932) Warner Bros. **B&W-84min.** Lee Tracy, Dick Powell..(4)

BLIND ALIBI (1938) RKO. **B&W-62min.** Richard Dix, Whitney Bourne (4)

BLIND ALLEY (1939) Columbia. **B&W-70min.** Chester Morris, Ralph Bellamy..(5)

BLIND BARGAIN, A (1922) Goldwyn. **B&W-60min.** *(Silent).* Lon Chaney, Raymond McKee..(4)
Alternate title: OCTAVE OF CLAUDIUS, THE

BLIND CORNER (1964) *see* MAN IN THE DARK

BLIND DATE (1959) *see* CHANCE MEETING

BLIND DEAD, THE (1972) Hallmark. **Color-82min.** *(Spanish-Portugese).* Cesar Burner, Lone Fleming, Helen Harp (Hays)..............(2)
Original Spanish title: NOCHE DEL TERROR CIEGO, LA *(The Night of the Blind Terror)*
Alternate title: NIGHT OF THE BLIND DEAD, THE

BLIND GODDESS (1949) Universal. **B&W-88min.** *(British).* Eric Portman, Ann Crawford...(4)

BLIND HUSBANDS (1919) Universal. **B&W-8reels** *(Silent).* Erich von Stroheim, Sam de Grasse, Francela Billington..................(4)

BLIND JUSTICE (1961) Paramount. **B&W-97min.** *(German).* Peter Van Eyck..(4)
Alternate title: WHOLE TRUTH, THE

BLIND MAN'S BLUFF (1968) *see* CAULDRON OF BLOOD

BLIND SPOT (1947) Columbia. **B&W-73min.** Chester Morris, Constance Dowling..**4***

BLIND SPOT (1958) UCC Films. **B&W-72min.** *(British).* Robert Mackenzie, Delphi Lawrence...(3)

BLIND TERROR (1971) *see* SEE NO EVIL

BLINDFOLD (1966) Universal. **Color-102min.** Rock Hudson, Claudia Cardinale..**5***

BLINDMAN (1972) 20th Century-Fox. **Color-105min.** *(Italian).* Ringo Starr, Tony Anthony..(1)

BLISS OF MRS. BLOSSOM, THE (1968) Paramount. **Color-93min.** *(British).* Shirley MacLaine, Richard Attenborough.............**3½***

BLITHE SPIRIT (1945) United Artists. **Color-94min.** *(British).* Rex Harrison, Constance Cummings.................................**6***

BLITZ ON BRITAIN (1960) Anglo-Continental. **B&W-71min.** *(British, Documentary). Director:* Harry Booth.....................(4)

BLITZKRIEG - THE WAR FOR RUSSIA (1958) Continental [Walter Reade]. **B&W-93min.** *(German, Documentary).* Brian Horrocks..........(4)

BLOB, THE (1958) Paramount. **Color-86min.** Steven (Steve) McQueen, Aneta Corseaut..**3***

BLOCK BUSTERS (1944) Monogram [Allied Artists]. **B&W-60min.** The East Side Kids, Minerva Urecal, Harry Langdon.............(3)

BLOCK-HEADS (1938) M-G-M. **B&W-55min.** Stan Laurel, Oliver Hardy **4***

BLOCKADE (1938) United Artists. **B&W-85min.** Madeleine Carroll, Henry Fonda...(5)

BLOND WIFE, THE (1968) *see* KISS THE OTHER SHEIK

BLONDE BAIT (1956) M & A Alexander. **B&W-71min.** *(British).* Beverly Michaels, Jim Davis...(3)
Original title: WOMEN WITHOUT MEN

BLONDE BLACKMAILER (1958) Allied Artists. **B&W-58min.** *(British).* Richard Arlen, Susan Shaw..(2)

BLONDE BOMBSHELL (1933) *see* BOMBSHELL

BLONDE CRAZY (1931) Warner Bros. **B&W-73min.** James Cagney, Joan Blondell..(4)
British title: LARCENY LANE

BLONDE DYNAMITE (1950) Monogram [Allied Artists]. **B&W-66min.** The Bowery Boys, Adele Jergens...............................(3)

BLONDE FEVER (1944) M-G-M. **B&W-69min.** Mary Astor, Philip Dorn (3)

BLONDE FROM BROOKLYN (1945) Columbia. **B&W-65min.** Lynn Merrick, Robert Stanton..(3)

BLONDE IN A WHITE CAR (1958) *see* NUDE IN A WHITE CAR

BLONDE INSPIRATION (1941) M-G-M. **B&W-72min.** John Shelton, Virginia Grey..(4)

BLONDE RANSOM (1946) Universal. **B&W-68min.** Virginia Grey, Donald Cook...(3)

BLONDE VENUS (1932) Paramount. **B&W-80min.** Marlene Dietrich, Cary Grant...**4***

BLONDIE (1938) Columbia. **B&W-69min.** Penny Singleton, Arthur Lake..**4***

BLONDIE BRINGS UP BABY (1939) Columbia. **B&W-67min.** Arthur Lake, Penny Singleton, Larry Simms.......................(4)

BLONDIE FOR VICTORY (1942) Columbia. **B&W-70min.** Arthur Lake, Penny Singleton...(3)
British title: TROUBLES THROUGH BILLETS

BLONDIE GOES LATIN (1941) Columbia. **B&W-69min.** Arthur Lake, Penny Singleton...(4)
British title: CONGA SWING

BLONDIE GOES TO COLLEGE (1942) Columbia. **B&W-74min.** Arthur Lake, Penny Singleton, Larry Parks....................(3)
British title: BOSS SAID "NO", THE

BLONDIE HAS SERVANT TROUBLE (1940) Columbia. **B&W-70min.** Arthur Lake, Penny Singleton....................................(4)

BLONDIE HITS THE JACKPOT (1949) Columbia. **B&W-66min.** Arthur Lake, Penny Singleton.....................................(3)
British title: HITTING THE JACKPOT

BLONDIE IN SOCIETY (1941) Columbia. **B&W-75min.** Arthur Lake, Penny Singleton...(5)
British title: HENPECKED

BLONDIE IN THE DOUGH (1947) Columbia. **B&W-69min.** Arthur Lake, Penny Singleton, Hugh Herbert....................(3)

BLONDIE JOHNSON (1933) First National [W.B.]. **B&W-69min.** Joan Blondell, Chester Morris.....................................(4)

BLONDIE KNOWS BEST (1946) Columbia. **B&W-69min.** Arthur Lake, Penny Singleton, Shemp Howard........................(4)

BLONDIE MEETS THE BOSS (1939) Columbia. **B&W-58min.** Arthur Lake, Penny Singleton.....................................(4)

BLONDIE OF THE FOLLIES (1932) M-G-M. **B&W-90min.** Marion Davies, Robert Montgomery...................................(3)

BLONDIE ON A BUDGET (1940) Columbia. **B&W-73min.** Arthur Lake, Penny Singleton, Rita Hayworth.......................(4)

BLONDIE PLAYS CUPID (1940) Columbia. **B&W-68min.** Arthur Lake, Penny Singleton, Glenn Ford.............................(4)

BLONDIE TAKES A VACATION (1939) Columbia. **B&W-61min.** Arthur Lake, Penny Singleton.......................................(4)

BLONDIE'S ANNIVERSARY (1947) Columbia. **B&W-75min.** Arthur Lake, Penny Singleton, Adele Jergens...................(3)

BLONDIE'S BIG DEAL (1949) Columbia. **B&W-66min.** Arthur Lake, Penny Singleton..(3)
British title: BIG DEAL, THE

BLONDIE'S BIG MOMENT (1947) Columbia. **B&W-69min.** Arthur Lake, Penny Singleton, Anita Louise.......................(3)

BLONDIE'S BLESSED EVENT (1942) Columbia. **B&W-69min.** Arthur Lake, Penny Singleton, Hans Conried................(4)
British title: BUNDLE OF TROUBLE, A

BLONDIE'S HERO (1949) Columbia. **B&W-67min.** Arthur Lake, Penny Singleton..(3)

BLONDIE'S HOLIDAY (1947) Columbia. **B&W-67min.** Arthur Lake, Penny Singleton..(3)

BLONDIE'S LUCKY DAY (1946) Columbia. **B&W-75min.** Arthur Lake, Penny Singleton..(3)

BLONDIE'S REWARD (1948) Columbia. **B&W-67min.** Arthur Lake, Penny Singleton...(3)

BLONDIE'S SECRET (1948) Columbia. **B&W-68min.** Arthur Lake, Penny Singleton..(3)

BLOOD! (1973) Bryanston. **Color-69min.** Hope Stansbury, Allan Berendt..(3)

BLOOD ALLEY (1955) Warner Bros. **Color-115min.** John Wayne, Lauren Bacall...**4***

BLOOD AND BLACK LACE (1964) Allied Artists. **Color-88min.** *(Italian/ French/Monacan).* Eva Bartok, Cameron Mitchell..................**3***
Original Italian title: SEI DONNE PER L'ASSASSINO *(Six Women for the Assassin)*
Original French title: SIX FEMMES POUR L'ASSASSIN
British title?: FASHION HOUSE OF DEATH

BLOOD AND DEFIANCE (1966) Avco-Embassy. **Color-92min.** *(Italian).* Gerard Landry, José Greci......................................(1)

BLOOD AND GUTS (1978) Ambassador Films *(Canadian).* **Color-92min.** *(Canadian).* William Smith, Micheline Lanctot...................

BLOOD AND LACE (1971) American-International. **Color-87min.** Gloria Grahame, Melody Patterson........................**2***

BLOOD AND ROSES (1960) Paramount. **Color-74min.** *(Italian).* Annette Vadim, Elsa Martinelli...**3***
Original French title: ET MOURIR DE PLAISIR *(And Die of Pleasure)*

BLOOD AND SAND (1922) Paramount. **B&W-101min.** *(Silent).* Rudolph Valentino, Lila Lee, Nita Naldi................................**3***

BLOOD AND SAND (1941) 20th Century-Fox. **Color-123min.** Tyrone Power, Linda Darnell.....................................**4½***

Films are rated on a 1 to 10 scale, 10 is highest. **Boldface** ratings followed by an asterisk (*) are for films actually seen and rated by the executive and senior editors. All other ratings are estimates. (See Notes on Entertainment Ratings in the front section.)

BLOOD AND STEEL (1959) 20th Century-Fox. B&W-63min. John Lupton, Ziva Rodann .... (3)

BLOOD ARROW (1958) 20th Century-Fox. B&W-75min. Scott Brady, Paul Richards .... (2)

BLOOD BATH (1966) American-International. B&W-69min. William Campbell, Marissa Mathes .... (2)
TV title: TRACK OF THE VAMPIRE

BLOOD BATH (1975) Cannon Releasing. Color-81min. Harve Presnell (3)

BLOOD BEAST FROM OUTER SPACE (1965) World Entertainment. B&W-84min. *(British).* John Saxon, Maurice Denham .... (3)
Original title: NIGHT CALLER, THE

BLOOD BEAST TERROR, THE (1967) *see* VAMPIRE-BEAST CRAVES BLOOD, THE

BLOOD BRIDES (1968) *see* BRIDES OF BLOOD

BLOOD CEREMONY (1974) *see* LEGEND OF BLOOD CASTLE

BLOOD COUPLE (1973) Kelly-Jordan Enterprises. Color-110min. Duane Jones, Marlene Clark, Bill Gunn .... (3)
Original title: GANJA AND HESS
Alternate title: DOUBLE POSSESSION

BLOOD CREATURE (1959) *see* TERROR IS A MAN

BLOOD CROWD, THE (1970) *see* McMASTERS, THE

BLOOD DEMON, THE (1969) Hemisphere. Color-73min. *(German).* Christopher Lee, Lex Barker, Karin Dor.................... 2*
Original title: SCHLANGENGRUBE UND DAS PENDEL, DIE *(The Snake Pit and the Pendulum)*
TV title: TORTURE CHAMBER OF DOCTOR SADISM, THE

BLOOD DEVILS (1970) *see* BEAST OF BLOOD

BLOOD FEAST (1963) Box Office Spectaculars. Color-75min. Thomas Wood, Connie Mason .... (2)

BLOOD FIEND (1967) Hemisphere. Color-88min. *(British).* Christopher Lee, Lelia Goldoni, Julian Glover.................... (4)
Original title: THEATRE OF DEATH

BLOOD FOR DRACULA (1973) *see* ANDY WARHOL'S DRACULA

BLOOD FROM THE MUMMY'S TOMB (1972) American-International. Color-94min. Andrew Keir, Valerie Leon.................... (3)
TV title: CURSE OF THE MUMMY

BLOOD IN THE STREETS (1973) Independent International. Color-111min. *(Italian-French-German, English language).* Oliver Reed, Agostina Belli, Fabio Testi .... (3)

BLOOD IS MY HERITAGE (1957) *see* BLOOD OF DRACULA

BLOOD MANIA (1971) Crown International. Color-88min. Peter Carpenter, Maria De Aragon.................... 1*

BLOOD MONEY (1933) Fox Film Co. [20th]. B&W-65min. George Bancroft, Judith Anderson .... (4)

BLOOD MONEY (1962) *see* REQUIEM FOR A HEAVYWEIGHT

BLOOD MONEY (1975) *see* STRANGER AND THE GUNFIGHTER

BLOOD OF A POET, THE (1930) Brandon. B&W-60min. *(French).* Lee Miller, Enrique Rivero .... (3)
Original title: SANG D'UN POETE, LE

BLOOD OF DRACULA (1957) American-International. B&W-68min. Sandra Harrison, Louise Lewis 2*
Canadian title: BLOOD OF THE DEMON
British title: BLOOD IS MY HERITAGE

BLOOD OF DRACULA'S CASTLE (1969) Crown International. Color-84min. Alex D'Arcy, John Carradine.................... 2*
TV title: DRACULA'S CASTLE

BLOOD OF FRANKENSTEIN (1971) *see* DRACULA VS. FRANKENSTEIN

BLOOD OF FU MANCHU, THE (1968) *see* KISS AND KILL

BLOOD OF NOSTRADAMUS, THE (1960) Azteca. B&W-98min. *(Mexican).* German Robles, Julio Aleman 1*
Original title: SANGRE DE NOSTRADAMUS, LA

BLOOD OF THE CONDOR, THE (1969) B&W-74min. *(Bolivian).* Marcelino, Vincent Salinas .... (4)
Original title: YAWAR MALLKU *(Blood Condor)*

BLOOD OF THE DEMON (1957) *see* BLOOD OF DRACULA

BLOOD OF THE VAMPIRE (1958) Universal. Color-87min. *(British).* Donald Wolfit, Barbara Shelley .... (3)

BLOOD ON HIS LIPS (1955) *see* HIDEOUS SUN DEMON

BLOOD ON HIS SWORD (1961) Avco-Embassy. Color-126min. *(French-Italian).* Jean Marais, Rosanna Schiaffino, Jean-Louis Barrault .... (3)
Original French title: MIRACLE DES LOUPS, LE *(The Miracle of the Wolves)*

BLOOD ON MY HANDS (1948) *see* KISS THE BLOOD OFF MY HANDS

BLOOD ON SATAN'S CLAW, THE (1971) Cannon Releasing. Color-100min. Patrick Wymark, Linda Hayden.................... 3*
Original title: SATAN'S SKIN

BLOOD ON THE ARROW (1964) Allied Artists. Color-91min. Dale Robertson, Martha Hyer.................... 3*

BLOOD ON THE MOON (1948) RKO. B&W-88min. Robert Mitchum, Barbara Bel Geddes 4*

BLOOD ON THE SUN (1945) United Artists. B&W-98min. James Cagney, Sylvia Sidney 4*

BLOOD ORGY OF THE SHE-DEVILS (1973) Genini. Color-73min. Linda Zaborin, Tom Pace, William Bagdad.................... (2)

BLOOD ROSE, THE (1970) Allied Artists. Color-92min. Philippe Lemaire, Annie Duperey .... (2)
Original title: ROSE ECORCHÉE, LA *(The Flayed Rose)*
British title?: RAVAGED

BLOOD SISTERS (1973) *see* SISTERS

BLOOD SPATTERED BRIDE, THE (1972) Europix International. Color-83min. *(Spanish).* Alexandra Bastedo, Simon Andrew, Maribel Martin .... (3)
Original title: NOVIA ENSANGRENTADA, LA *(The Bloody Bride)*

BLOOD SUCKERS, THE (1967) *see* DR. TERROR'S GALLERY OF HORRORS

BLOOD WATERS OF DR. Z (1972) *see* ZAAT

BLOODBROTHERS (1978) Warner Bros. Color-112min. Paul Sorvino, Tony Lo Bianco, Richard Gere.................... 4½*
Common title error: BLOOD BROTHERS

BLOODHOUNDS OF BROADWAY (1952) 20th Century-Fox. Color-90min. Mitzi Gaynor, Scott Brady .... (4)

BLOODLINE (1979) *see* SIDNEY SHELDON'S BLOODLINE

BLOODLUST (1961) Crown International. B&W-68min. Wilton Graff, Lilyan Chauvin .... (2)

BLOODSPORT (1973) Worldvision. Color-74min. *(Made for TV).* Ben Johnson, Gary Busey, Larry Hagman 5*

BLOODY JUDGE, THE (1970) *see* NIGHT OF THE BLOOD MONSTER

BLOODY MAMA (1970) American-International. Color-92min. Shelley Winters, Don Stroud, Diane Varsi.................... (3)

BLOODY PIT OF HORROR (1965) Pacemaker Pictures. Color-74min. *(Italian-U.S.).* Mickey Hargitay, Walter Brandi.................... (1)
Original Italian title: BOIA SCARLATTO, IL *(The Scarlet Executioner)*
Alternate Italian title: CASTELLO DI ARTENA, IL *(The Castle of Artena)*
Alternate title: CRIMSON EXECUTIONER, THE
Publicity title: RED HANGMAN, THE
French title: DES VIERGES POUR LE BOURREAU *(Some Virgins for the Executioner)*

BLOW UP (1966). Vanessa Redgrave is nervously anxious to obtain the film of pictures photographer David Hemmings has taken of her and her lover in a London park.

BLOODY VAMPIRE, THE (1962) K. Gordon Murray. B&W-98min. *(Mexican)*. Carlos Agosti, Begona Palacios..........................(1)
Original title: VAMPIRO SANGRIENTO, EL
Publicity title: COUNT FRANKENHAUSEN

BLOOMFIELD (1972) *see* HERO, THE

BLOSSOMS IN THE DUST (1941) M-G-M. Color-100min. Greer Garson, Walter Pidgeon..........................4½*

BLOW OUT (1973) *see* GRAND BOUFFE, THE

BLOW UP (1966) Premier Pictures [MGM]. Color-111min. *(British-Italian)*. David Hemmings, Vanessa Redgrave..........................5*

BLOWING WILD (1953) Warner Bros. B&W-90min. Gary Cooper, Barbara Stanwyck..........................4*

BLUE (1968) Paramount. Color-113min. Terence Stamp, Joanna Pettet (2)

BLUE AND THE GOLD, THE (1955) *see* ANNAPOLIS STORY, AN

BLUE ANGEL, THE (1930) Paramount. B&W-100min. *(German, English version)*. Emil Jannings, Marlene Dietrich..........................5½*
Original title: BLAUE ENGEL, DER

BLUE ANGEL, THE (1959) 20th Century-Fox. Color-107min. Curt Jurgens, May Britt..........................(4)

BLUE BEAST, THE (1961) Toho. B&W-95min. *(Japanese)*. Tatsuya Nakadai, Yoko Tsukasa..........................(4)
Original title: AOI YAJU

BLUE BIRD, THE (1940) 20th Century-Fox. Color-88min. Shirley Temple, Johnny Russell..........................4*

BLUE BIRD, THE (1976) 20th Century-Fox. Color-100min. *(U.S.S.R.-U.S.)*. Patsy Kensit, Todd Lookinland, Elizabeth Taylor, Cicely Tyson..........4*

BLUE BLOOD (1951) Monogram [Allied Artists]. Color-72min. Bill Williams, Jane Nigh..........................(3)

BLUE COLLAR (1978) Universal. Color-114min. Richard Pryor, Harvey Keitel..........................5*

BLUE CONTINENT (1954) Galatea Prods. Color-95min. *(Italian, Documentary)*..........................(3)

BLUE DAHLIA, THE (1946) Paramount. B&W-96min. Alan Ladd, Veronica Lake..........................4*

BLUE DENIM (1959) 20th Century-Fox. B&W-89min. Brandon De Wilde, Carol Lynley..........................4*
British title: BLUE JEANS

BLUE GARDENIA, THE (1953) Warner Bros. B&W-90min. Anne Baxter, Richard Conte..........................(4)

BLUE GRASS OF KENTUCKY (1950) Monogram [Allied Artists]. Color-71min. Bill Williams, Jane Nigh..........................(4)

BLUE HAWAII (1961) Paramount. Color-101min. Elvis Presley, Joan Blackman..........................4*

BLUE JEANS (1959) *see* BLUE DENIM

BLUE KNIGHT, THE (1974) Viacom. Color-200min. *(Made for TV)*. William Holden, Lee Remick, Sam Elliott..........................5*

BLUE KNIGHT, THE (1975) Lorimar Productions. Color-75min. *(Made for TV)*. George Kennedy, Alex Rocco, Verna Bloom..........................3*

BLUE LAGOON, THE (1949) Universal. Color-101min. *(British)*. Susan Stranks, Jean Simmons, Donald Houston..........................5*

BLUE LIGHT, THE (1932) Du World. B&W-77min. *(German)*. Leni Riefenstahl, Mathias Wieman..........................3*
Original title: BLAUE LICHT, DAS

BLUE LAMP, THE (1950) Eagle Lion. B&W-84min. *(British)*. Jack Warner, Jimmy Hanley..........................(5)

BLUE MAX, THE (1966) 20th Century-Fox. Color-156min. *(British-U.S.)*. George Peppard, James Mason..........................6*

BLUE MURDER AT ST. TRINIAN'S (1957) Continental [Walter Reade]. B&W-86min. *(British)*. Joyce Grenfell, Terry-Thomas..........................4½*

BLUE PETER, THE (1955) *see* NAVY HEROES

BLUE SEXTET (1972) Unisphere Releasing Corp. Color-90min. John Damon, Peter Clune..........................(3)

BLUE SKIES (1946) Paramount. Color-104min. Bing Crosby, Fred Astaire..........................3½*

BLUE SURFARI (1967) *see* SURFARI

BLUE VEIL, THE (1951) RKO. B&W-113min. Jane Wyman, Charles Laughton..........................3½*

BLUE WATER, WHITE DEATH (1971) Nat'l General (for Cinema Center). Color-100min. *(Documentary)*. Director: Peter Gimbel..........3*

BLUE, WHITE AND PERFECT (1942) 20th Century-Fox. B&W-78min. Lloyd Nolan, Mary Beth Hughes..........................(4)

BLUEBEARD (1944) Producers Rel. Corp. [Eagle Lion]. B&W-73min. John Carradine, Jean Parker..........................3*

BLUEBEARD (1963) *see* LANDRU

BLUEBEARD (1972) Cinerama Releasing. Color-123min. *(Italian-French-West German)*. Richard Burton, Joey Heatherton..........................(4)

BLUEBEARD'S EIGHTH WIFE (1938) Paramount. B&W-87min. Gary Cooper, Claudette Colbert..........................5½*

BLUEBEARD'S TEN HONEYMOONS (1960) Allied Artists. B&W-92min. *(British)*. George Sanders, Corinne Calvet..........................4*

BLUEPRINT FOR MURDER, A (1953) 20th Century-Fox. B&W-76min. Joseph Cotten, Jean Peters..........................(4)

BLUEPRINT FOR ROBBERY (1961) Paramount. B&W-87min. Jay Barney, J. Pat O'Malley..........................(4)

BLUES BUSTERS (1950) Monogram [Allied Artists]. B&W-67min. The Bowery Boys, Craig Stevens..........................(3)

BLUES IN THE NIGHT (1941) Warner Bros. B&W-88min. Richard Whorf, Priscilla Lane..........................4*

BLUM AFFAIR, THE (1949) *see* AFFAIR BLUM

BLUME IN LOVE (1973) Warner Bros. Color-115min. George Segal, Susan Anspach..........................6*

BOATNIKS, THE (1970) Buena Vista. Color-100min. Robert Morse, Stefanie Powers..........................4½*

BOB AND CAROL AND TED AND ALICE (1969) Columbia. Color-104min. Robert Culp, Natalie Wood..........................5½*

BOB MATHIAS STORY, THE (1954) Allied Artists. B&W-80min. Bob Mathias, Melba Mathias..........................4*
British title: FLAMING TORCH, THE

BOB, SON OF BATTLE (1947) *see* THUNDER IN THE VALLEY

BOBBIE JO AND THE OUTLAW (1976) American-International. Color-88min. Marjoe Gortner, Lynda Carter..........................(4)

BOBBIKINS (1959) 20th Century-Fox. B&W-90min. *(British)*. Max Bygraves, Shirley Jones..........................(4)

BOBBY DEERFIELD (1977) Columbia. Color-124min. Al Pacino, Marthe Keller..........................4½*

BOBBY WARE IS MISSING (1955) Allied Artists. B&W-67min. Neville Brand, Arthur Franz..........................(3)

BOBO, THE (1967) Warner Bros. Color-105min. *(British)*. Peter Sellers, Britt Ekland..........................3*

BOCCACCIO '70 (1962) Avco-Embassy. Color-165min. *(Italian)*. Anita Ekberg, Peppino De Filippo..........................4½*

BODY, THE (1970) M-G-M. Color-112min. *(British, Documentary)*. *Director:* Roy Battersby..........................(4)

BODY AND SOUL (1945) *see* PRIDE OF THE MARINES

BODY AND SOUL (1947) United Artists. B&W-104min. John Garfield, Lilli Palmer..........................4*

BODY BENEATH, THE (1970) Nova International. Color-85min. Gavin Reed, Jackie Skarvellis..........................(2)

BODY DISAPPEARS, THE (1941) Warner Bros. B&W-72min. Jeffrey Lynn, Jane Wyman..........................(3)

BODY IS MISSING, THE (1962) *see* WHO STOLE THE BODY?

BODY SNATCHER, THE (1945) RKO. B&W-77min. Boris Karloff, Henry Daniell..........................4½*

BODY STEALERS, THE (1969) *see* INVASION OF THE BODY STEALERS

BODYGUARD (1948) Columbia. B&W-62min. Lawrence Tierney, Priscilla Lane..........................(3)

BODYHOLD (1949) Columbia. B&W-63min. Willard Parker, Lola Albright..........................(3)

BOEING BOEING (1965) Paramount. Color-102min. Tony Curtis, Jerry Lewis..........................(4)

BOFORS GUN, THE (1968) Regional. Color-106min. *(British)*. Nicol Williamson, David Warner..........................4*

BOGUS BANDITS (1933) *see* DEVIL'S BROTHER, THE

BOHEME, LA (1965) Warner Bros. Color-107min. *(Swiss)*. Gianni Raimondo, Mirella Freni..........................(5)

BOHEMIAN GIRL, THE (1936) M-G-M. B&W-70min. Stan Laurel, Oliver Hardy..........................4*

BOLD ADVENTURE, THE (1956) United Artists. Color-87min. *(French)*. Gerard Philipe, Jean Villar..........................(3)
Original title: THYL L'ESPIEGLE
Alternate title: TILL EULENSPIEGEL

BOLD AND THE BRAVE, THE (1956) RKO. B&W-87min. Wendell Corey, Mickey Rooney..........................(5)

BOLERO (1934) Paramount. B&W-83min. George Raft, Carole Lombard..........................(4)

Films are rated on a 1 to 10 scale, 10 is highest. **Boldface** ratings followed by an asterisk (*) are for films actually seen and rated by the executive and senior editors. All other ratings are estimates. (See Notes on Entertainment Ratings in the front section.)

BOLSHOI BALLET '67 (1966) Paramount. **Color-75min.** *(U.S.S.R.).* Natalya Bessmertnova, Mikhail Lavrovskiy.............................(4)
Original title: SEKRET USPEKHA

BOMB AT 10:10 (1966) Walter Reade. **B&W-86min.** George Montgomery, Branko Flesa ....(3)

BOMB FOR A DICTATOR, A (1957) Medallion. **B&W-73min.** *(French).* Pierre Fresnay, Grégoire Aslan ....(3)
Original title: FANATIQUES, LES *(The Fantatics)*
Alternate title: FANTATICS, THE

BOMB IN THE HIGH STREET (1963) Hemisphere. **B&W-60min.** *(British).* Ronald Howard, Terry Palmer......................(3)

BOMBA AND THE AFRICAN TREASURE (1952) *see* AFRICAN TREASURE

BOMBA AND THE ELEPHANT STAMPEDE (1951) *see* ELEPHANT STAMPEDE

BOMBA AND THE HIDDEN CITY (1950) Monogram [Allied Artists]. **B&W-71min.** Johnny Sheffield, Sue England ....(3)

BOMBA AND THE JUNGLE GIRL (1952) Monogram [Allied Artists]. **B&W-70min.** Johnny Sheffield, Karen Sharpe ....(3)
Alternate title: JUNGLE GIRL

BOMBA AND THE LION HUNTERS (1951) *see* LION HUNTERS, THE

BOMBA AND THE SAFARI DRUMS (1953) *see* SAFARI DRUMS

BOMBA ON PANTHER ISLAND (1949) Monogram [Allied Artists]. **B&W-76min.** Johnny Sheffield, Allene Roberts ....(3)
Alternate title: PANTHER ISLAND

BOMBA, THE JUNGLE BOY (1949) Monogram [Allied Artists]. **B&W-70min.** Johnny Sheffield, Peggy Ann Garner..........(3)

BOMBARDIER (1943) RKO. **B&W-99min.** Pat O'Brien, Randolph Scott (4)

BOMBAY TALKIE (1970) Dia Films. **Color-110min.** *(Indian).* Shashi Kapoor, Jennifer Kendal, Zia Mohyeddin, Aparna Sen......................(3)

BOMBERS B-52 (1957) Warner Bros. **Color-106min.** Karl Malden, Natalie Wood 3*
British title: NO SLEEP TILL DAWN

BOMBER'S MOON (1943) 20th Century-Fox. **B&W-70min.** George Montgomery, Annabella ....(3)

BOMBS OVER BURMA (1942) Producers Rel. Corp. [Eagle Lion]. **B&W-62min.** Anna May Wong, Noel Madison......................(3)

BOMBSHELL (1933) M-G-M. **B&W-91min.** Jean Harlow, Lee Tracy 4*
Alternate title: BLONDE BOMBSHELL, THE

BOMBSIGHT STOLEN (1941) *see* COTTAGE TO LET

BON VOYAGE (1962) Buena Vista. **Color-133min.** Fred MacMurray, Jane Wyman...(4)

BON VOYAGE, CHARLIE BROWN (1979) Paramount. **Color- min.** *(Cartoon).* Director: Bill Melendez...............................

BONAVENTURE (1951) *see* THUNDER ON THE HILL

BONHEUR, LE (1965) Clover Films. **B&W-87min.** *(French).* Jean-Claude Drouot, Claire Drouot ....(4)

BONJOUR TRISTESSE (1958) Columbia. **Color-94min.** *(British).* Deborah Kerr, David Niven.............................4½*

BONNE SOUPE, LA (1964) International Classics [20th]. **B&W-97min.** *(French).* Annie Girardot, Marie Bell....................4*
Translation title: The Good Soup

BONNES FEMMES, LES (1960) Robert Hakim. **B&W-95min.** *(French-Italian).* Bernadette Lafont, Lucile Saint-Simon 3*

BONNIE AND CLYDE (1967) Warner Bros. **Color-111min.** Warren Beatty, Faye Dunaway 6*

BONNIE PARKER STORY, THE (1958) American-International. **B&W-81min.** Dorothy Provine, Jack Hogan.....................3*

BONNIE PRINCE CHARLIE (1948) British Lion [EMI]. **Color-136min.** *(British).* David Niven, Margaret Leighton....................(4)

BONNIE SCOTLAND (1935) M-G-M. **B&W-80min.** Stan Laurel, Oliver Hardy ....(4)
Alternate title: HEROES OF THE REGIMENT

BONZO GOES TO COLLEGE (1952) Universal. **B&W-80min.** Maureen O'Sullivan, Edmund Gwenn, Bonzo...........................(3)

BOOBY TRAP, THE (1957) Eros Films *(Brit.).* **B&W-72min.** *(British).* Sydney Tafler, Patti Morgan...........................(4)

BOOK OF NUMBERS (1973) Avco-Embassy. **Color-81min.** Raymond St. Jacques, Philip Thomas, Freda Payne.......................(4)

BOOKED ON SUSPICION (1945) *see* BOSTON BLACKIE BOOKED ON SUSPICION

BOOM! (1968) Universal. **Color-113min.** *(U.S.-British).* Elizabeth Taylor, Richard Burton..............................2*

BOOM TOWN (1940) M-G-M. **B&W-116min.** Clark Gable, Spencer Tracy...5½*

BOOMERANG! (1947) 20th Century-Fox. **B&W-88min.** Dana Andrews, Jane Wyatt..4*

BOOT POLISH (1954) Hoffberg. **B&W-90min.** *(Indian).* Rattan Kumar, Baby Naaz..(4)
Alternate title: 1¢ (one cent)

BOOTLEGGERS (1974) Howco International. **Color-110min.** Paul Koslo, Dennis Fimple, Slim Pickens..........................3*

BOOTS MALONE (1952) Columbia. **B&W-103min.** William Holden, Johnny Stewart.......................................4*

BORA BORA (1970) American-International. **Color-90min.** *(Italian).* Haydee Politoff, Corrado Pani......................(1)

BORDER INCIDENT (1949) M-G-M. **B&W-92min.** Ricardo Montalban, George Murphy 3*

BORDER RIVER (1954) Universal. **Color-80min.** Joel McCrea, Yvonne De Carlo...4*

BORDERLINE (1950) Universal. **B&W-88min.** Claire Trevor, Fred MacMurray ....(4)

BORDERLINES (1963) *see* CARETAKERS, THE

BORDERTOWN (1935) Warner Bros. **B&W-90min.** Paul Muni, Bette Davis 4½*

BORGIA STICK, THE (1967) Universal. **Color-100min.** *(Made for TV).* Don Murray, Inger Stevens................................5*,

BORN AGAIN (1978) Avco-Embassy. **Color-110min.** Dean Jones, Anne Francis, Raymond St. Jacques.........................3½*

BORN FOR TROUBLE (1942) *see* MURDER IN THE BIG HOUSE

BORN FREE (1966) Columbia. **Color-95min.** *(British).* Virginia McKenna, Bill Travers.....................................6*

BORN INNOCENT (1974) Tomorrow Entertainment. **Color-94min.** *(Made for TV).* Linda Blair, Joanna Miles, Kim Hunter 4½*

BORN LOSERS (1967) American-International. **Color-112min.** Tom Laughlin, Elizabeth James............................3*

BORN RECKLESS (1959) Warner Bros. **B&W-79min.** Mamie Van Doren, Jeff Richards.....................................(3)

BORN TO BE BAD (1934) United Artists. **B&W-61min.** Loretta Young, Cary Grant...(3)

BORN TO BE BAD (1950) RKO. **B&W-94min.** Joan Fontaine, Robert Ryan...3½*

BORN TO BE LOVED (1959) Universal. **B&W-82min.** Carol Morris, Hugo Haas...(3)

BORN TO BOOGIE (1972) EMI. **Color-67min.** *(British, Documentary).* Director: Ringo Starr.......................................(4)

BORN TO DANCE (1936) M-G-M. **B&W-108min.** Eleanor Powell, James Stewart...(5)

BORN TO KILL (1947) RKO. **B&W-92min.** Lawrence Tierney, Claire Trevor...(3)
British title: LADY OF DECEIT

BORN TO KILL (1975) New World. **Color-83min.** Warren Oates, Richard B. Shull, Harry Dean Stanton.......................(4)
Original title: COCKFIGHTER

BORN TO SING (1942) M-G-M. **B&W-82min.** Virginia Weidler, Ray McDonald..(3)

BORN TO WIN (1971) United Artists. **Color-90min.** George Segal, Paula Prentiss, Karen Black................................(4)

BORN WILD (1968) American-International. **Color-100min.** Tom Nardini, Patty McCormack.......................................(3)

BORN YESTERDAY (1950) Columbia. **B&W-103min.** Judy Holliday, Broderick Crawford, William Holden 5½*

BORSALINO (1970) Paramount. **Color-123min.** *(French-Italian).* Jean-Paul Belmondo, Alain Delon......................5½*

BOSS, THE (1956) United Artists. **B&W-89min.** John Payne, Doe Avedon..4*

BOSS NIGGER (1975) Dimension Pictures. **Color-87min.** Fred Williamson, D'Urville Martin.............................
British title: BLACK BOUNTY KILLER

BOSS SAID "NO," THE (1942) *see* BLONDIE GOES TO COLLEGE

BOSTON BLACKIE AND THE LAW (1946) Columbia. **B&W-69min.** Chester Morris, Trudy Marshall ....(4)
British title: BLACKIE AND THE LAW

BOSTON BLACKIE BOOKED ON SUSPICION (1945) Columbia. **B&W-66min.** Chester Morris, Steve Cochran ....(4)
British title: BOOKED ON SUSPICION

BORN YESTERDAY (1950). Learning how to do anything besides play gin rummy is at first very difficult for Judy Holliday, even with a teacher as good as William Holden, whom crooked contractor Broderick Crawford has hired to teach her some social graces.

BOSTON BLACKIE GOES HOLLYWOOD (1942) Columbia. **B&W-68min.** Chester Morris, George E. Stone .... (4)
British title: BLACKIE GOES HOLLYWOOD

BOSTON BLACKIE'S CHINESE VENTURE (1948) Columbia. **B&W-59min.** Chester Morris, Philip Ahn........................... (4)
British title: CHINESE ADVENTURE

BOSTON BLACKIE'S RENDEZVOUS (1945) Columbia. **B&W-64min.** Chester Morris, Nina Foch .... (4)
British title: BLACKIE'S RENDEZVOUS

BOSTON STRANGLER, THE (1968) 20th Century-Fox. **Color-116min.** Tony Curtis, Henry Fonda........................ 5½*

BOTANY BAY (1953) Paramount. **Color-94min.** Alan Ladd, James Mason.. 3½*

BOTH ENDS OF THE CANDLE (1957) *see* HELEN MORGAN STORY, THE

BOTH SIDES OF THE LAW (1954) Universal. **B&W-94min.** *(British).* Anne Crawford, Peggy Cummins...................... (5)
Original title: STREET CORNER

BOTTOM OF THE BOTTLE, THE (1956) 20th Century-Fox. **Color-88min.** Van Johnson, Joseph Cotten....................... 3*
British title: BEYOND THE RIVER

BOTTOMS UP (1960) Associated British-Pathé [EMI]. **B&W-86min.** *(British).* Jimmy Edwards, Arthur Howard .... (3)

BOUCHEUR, LE (1970) *see* BUTCHER, THE

BOUDU SAVED FROM DROWNING (1932) Pathé Contemporary. **B&W-87min.** *(French).* Michel Simon, Charles Granval 4*
Original title: BOUDU SAUVÉ DES EAUX *(Boudu Saved from the Water)*

BOULEVARD NIGHTS (1979) Warner Bros. **Color-102min.** Richard Yniguez, Danny De La Paz......................... 4½*

BOUND FOR GLORY (1976) United Artists. **Color-147min.** David Carradine, Ronny Cox............................. 5½*

BOUNTY HUNTER, THE (1954) Warner Bros. **Color-79min.** Randolph Scott, Ernest Borgnine........................... (4)

BOUNTY KILLER, THE (1965) Avco-Embassy. **Color-92min.** Dan Duryea, Rod Cameron, Buster Crabbe................... 3½*

BOUNTY MAN (1972) Worldvision. **Color-73min.** *(Made for TV).* Clint Walker, Richard Basehart, Margot Kidder............. (4)

BOURBON ST. SHADOWS (1958) *see* INVISIBLE AVENGER

BOWERY, THE (1933) United Artists. **B&W-90min.** Wallace Beery, George Raft.. 5*

BOWERY AT MIDNIGHT (1942) Monogram [Allied Artists]. **B&W-63min.** Bela Lugosi, John Archer .... (3)

BOWERY BATALLION (1951) Monogram [Allied Artists]. **B&W-69min.** The Bowery Boys, Virginia Hewitt .... (3)

BOWERY BLITZKRIEG (1941) Monogram [Allied Artists]. **B&W-62min.** The East Side Kids, Warren Hull............... 3*
British title: STAND AND DELIVER

BOWERY BOMBSHELL (1946) Monogram [Allied Artists]. **B&W-65min.** The Bowery Boys, Sheldon Leonard............ (3)

BOWERY BOYS MEET THE MONSTERS, THE (1954) Allied Artists. **B&W-66min.** The Bowery Boys, Lloyd Corrigan .... (3)

BOWERY BUCKAROOS (1947) Monogram [Allied Artists]. **B&W-66min.** The Bowery Boys, Julie Briggs............... (3)

BOWERY CHAMPS (1944) Monogram [Allied Artists]. **B&W-62min.** The East Side Kids, Anne Sterling.................. (3)

BOWERY TO BAGDAD (1955) Allied Artists. **B&W-64min.** The Bowery Boys, Joan Shawlee, Eric Blore .... (3)

BOWERY TO BROADWAY (1944) Universal. **B&W-94min.** Maria Montez, Jack Oakie................................ (4)

BOXCAR BERTHA (1972) American-International. **Color-92min.** Barbara Hershey, David Carradine..................... (4)

BOXER, THE (1963) **B&W-120min.** *(Polish).* Stefan Kvietik, Manfred Krug 4½*
Alternate title: BOXER AND THE DEATH, THE

BOY (1969) Grove Press. **Color-96min.** *(Japanese).* Tetsuo Abe, Fumio Watanabe.. (4)
Original title: SHONEN

BOY AND HIS DOG, A (1975) Pacific Film Enterprises. **Color-87min.** Don Johnson, Susanne Benton................. 5*

BOY AND THE LAUGHING DOG, THE (1956) *see* GOODBYE, MY LADY

BOY AND THE PIRATES, THE (1960) United Artists. **Color-82min.** Murvyn Vye, Charles Herbert, Susan Gordon .... (4)

BOY CALLED CHARLIE BROWN, A (1970) *see* BOY NAMED CHARLIE BROWN, A

BOY CRIED MURDER, THE (1966) Universal. **Color-86min.** *(British).* Veronica Hurst, Phil Brown .... (3)

BOY, DID I GET A WRONG NUMBER! (1966) United Artists. **Color-99min.** Bob Hope, Phyllis Diller, Elke Sommer 2*

BOY FRIEND (1939) 20th Century-Fox. **B&W-72min.** Jane Withers, Richard Bond.............................. (3)

BOY FRIEND, THE (1971) M-G-M. **Color-108min.** *(British).* Twiggy, Christopher Gable.......................... 6*

BOY FROM BARNARDO'S, THE (1938) *see* LORD JEFF

BOY FROM INDIANA (1950) Eagle Lion. **B&W-66min.** Lois Butler, Lon McCallister................................ (3)
British title: BLAZE OF GLORY

BOY FROM OKLAHOMA, THE (1954) Warner Bros. **Color-88min.** Will Rogers, Jr., Nancy Olson........................ 5*

BOY FROM STALINGRAD (1943) Columbia. **B&W-70min.** Bobby Samarzich, Conrad Vinyon .... (3)

BOY IN THE PLASTIC BUBBLE, THE (1976) MPC (TV). **Color-100min.** *(Made for TV).* John Travolta, Glynis O'Connor 4*

BOY MEETS GIRL (1938) Warner Bros. **B&W-80min.** James Cagney, Pat O'Brien 2*

BOY NAMED CHARLIE BROWN, A (1970) Nat'l General (for Cinema Center). **Color-85min.** *(Cartoon).* Director: Bill Melendez 4½*
British title: BOY CALLED CHARLIE BROWN, A

BOY NEXT DOOR, THE (1972) *see* TO FIND A MAN

BOY OF THE STREETS (1937) Monogram [Allied Artists]. **B&W-76min.** Jackie Cooper, Maureen O'Connor .... (4)

BOY ON A DOLPHIN (1957) 20th Century-Fox. **Color-111min.** Alan Ladd, Clifton Webb.......................... 4½*

BOY SLAVES (1939) RKO. **B&W-72min.** Anne Shirley, Roger Daniel.... (5)

BOY TEN FEET TALL, A (1963) Paramount. **Color-128min.** *(British).* Fergus McClelland, Edward G. Robinson............. 5*
British title: SAMMY GOING SOUTH

BOY WHO CAUGHT A CROOK, THE (1961) United Artists. **B&W-72min.** Wanda Hendrix, Roger Mobley............... (3)

BOY WHO CRIED WEREWOLF, THE (1973) Universal. **Color-93min.** Scott Sealey, Kerwin Mathews 2½*

BOY WHO STOLE A MILLION, THE (1960) Paramount. **B&W-84min.** *(British).* Maurice Reyna, Virgilio Texera.......... (4)

BOY WITH GREEN HAIR, THE (1948) RKO. **Color-82min.** Dean Stockwell, Pat O'Brien 4*

BOYKO (1975) *see* SANDAKAN NO. 8

BOYS, THE (1961) Gala *(Brit.).* **B&W-123min.** *(British).* Richard Todd, Robert Morley............................... 5*

BOYS FROM BRAZIL, THE (1978) 20th Century-Fox. **Color-123min.** *(British).* Laurence Olivier, Gregory Peck 6½*

BOYS FROM SYRACUSE, THE (1940) Universal. **B&W-73min.** Martha Raye, Allan Jones.................................. (5)

BOYS IN COMPANY C, THE (1978) Columbia. **Color-126min.** *(Hong Kong-U.S., English language).* Stan Shaw, Andrew Stevens 5*

BOYS IN THE BAND, THE (1970) Nat'l General (for Cinema Center). **Color-120min.** Kenneth Nelson, Frederick Combs 6*

BOYS' NIGHT OUT (1962) M-G-M. **Color-115min.** Kim Novak, James Garner 4*

BOYS OF PAUL STREET, THE (1968) 20th Century-Fox. **Color-104min.** *(U.S.-Hungarian, English language).* Anthony Kemp, William Burleigh 5*
Foreign title: PAL UTCAI FIUK

BOYS OF THE CITY (1940) Monogram [Allied Artists]. **B&W-65min.** The East Side Kids, Dave O'Brien .... (4)
Alternate title: GHOST CREEPS, THE

BOY'S RANCH (1946) M-G-M. **B&W-97min.** Butch Jenkins, Skip Homeier 4*

BOYS TOWN (1938) M-G-M. **B&W-90min.** Spencer Tracy, Mickey Rooney 4*

BRAIN, THE (1962) Governor. **B&W-83min.** *(British-W. German).* Peter Van Eyck, Anne Heywood .... (4)
Original W. German title: TOTER SUCHT SEINER MORDER, EIN *(A Dead Man Seeks His Murderer)*
British title: VENGEANCE

BRAIN, THE (1969) Paramount. **Color-100min.** *(French-Italian).* David Niven, Jean-Paul Belmondo 4½*
Original French title: CERVEAU, LE
Italian title: CERVELLO, IL

BRAIN EATERS, THE (1958) American-International. **B&W-60min.** Edwin Nelson, Alan Frost .... (3)

BRAIN FROM PLANET AROUS (1958) Howco International. **B&W-70min.** John Agar, Joyce Meadows 2*

BRAIN MACHINE, THE (1954) RKO. **B&W-83min.** *(British).* Patrick Barr, Elizabeth Allan 3*

BRAIN OF BLOOD (1971) Hemisphere. **Color-88min.** Grant Williams, Kent Taylor .... (2)
TV title: CREATURE'S REVENGE, THE

BRAIN THAT WOULDN'T DIE, THE (1962) American-International. **B&W-81min.** Virginia Leith, Herb Evers 2*

BRAINIAC, THE (1961) Transcontinental. **B&W-77min.** *(Mexican).* Abel Salazar, Ariadna Welter 1*
Original title: BARON DEL TERROR, EL *(The Baron of Terror)*

BRAINSNATCHER, THE (1936) *see* MAN WHO LIVED AGAIN, THE

BRAINSTORM (1965) Warner Bros. **B&W-114min.** Jeffrey Hunter, Anne Francis, Dana Andrews .... (4)

BRAINWASHED (1960) Allied Artists. **B&W-102min.** *(German).* Curt Jurgens, Claire Bloom .... (3)
Alternate title: ROYAL GAME, THE

BRAMBLE BUSH, THE (1960) Warner Bros. **Color-105min.** Richard Burton, Barbara Rush .... (4)

BRAND NEW LIFE, A (1973) Tomorrow Entertainment. **Color-75min.** *(Made for TV).* Cloris Leachman, Martin Balsam 4*

BRAND X (1970) CMB Films. **Color-87min.** Taylor Mead .... (2)

BRANDED (1951) Paramount. **Color-104min.** Alan Ladd, Mona Freeman 4*

BRANDY ASHORE (1951) *see* GREEN GROW THE RUSHES

BRANDY FOR THE PARSON (1952) Mayer-Kingsley. **B&W-78min.** *(British).* James Donald, Kenneth More 4*

BRANNIGAN (1975) United Artists. **Color-111min.** *(British-U.S.).* John Wayne, Richard Attenborough 4*

BRASHER DOUBLOON, THE (1947) 20th Century-Fox. **B&W-74min.** George Montgomery, Nancy Guild 4*
British title: HIGH WINDOW, THE

BRASS BOTTLE, THE (1964) Universal. **Color-89min.** Tony Randall, Burl Ives 3½*

BRASS LEGEND, THE (1956) United Artists. **B&W-79min.** Hugh O'Brian, Nancy Gates .... (3)

BRASS TARGET (1978) U.A. (for M-G-M). **Color-111min.** George Kennedy, Sophia Loren, Max Von Sydow, John Cassavetes 5*

BRAVADOS, THE (1958) 20th Century-Fox. **Color-98min.** Gregory Peck, Joan Collins 4½*

BRAVE AND THE BEAUTIFUL, THE (1955) *see* MAGNIFICENT MATADOR, THE

BRAVE BULLS, THE (1951) Columbia. **B&W-108min.** Mel Ferrer, Miroslava 4*

BRAVE DON'T CRY, THE (1952) Mayer-Kingsley. **B&W-91min.** *(British).* John Gregson, Meg Buchanan .... (5)

BRAVE ONE, THE (1956) Universal. **Color-100min.** Michel Ray, Rodolfo Hoyos 4½*

BRAVE WARRIOR (1952) Columbia. **Color-73min.** Jon Hall, Christine Larson .... (3)

BRAVOS, THE (1971) MCA-TV. **Color-100min.** *(Made for TV).* George Peppard, Pernell Roberts 4*

BRAZEN WOMEN OF BALZAC (1969) Globe Pictures. **Color-80min.** *(German).* Joachim Hansen, Edwige Fenech .... (2)
Original title: KOMM, LIEBE MAID UND MACHE. . . *(Come, Dear Girl and Let's. . .)*
Alternate German title: TOLLDREISTEN GESCHICHTEN DES HONORÉ DE BALZAC, DIE *(The Most Daring Stories of Honoré de Balzac)*

BRAZIL (1944) Republic. **B&W-91min.** Tito Guizar, Virginia Bruce .... (4)

BREAD AND CHOCOLATE (1974) CIC. **Color-112min.** *(Italian).* Nino Manfredi, Anna Karina 4½*
Original title: PANE E CIOCCOLATA

BREAD, LOVE AND . . . (1955) *see* SCANDAL IN SORRENTO

BREAD, LOVE AND DREAMS (1953) Italian Films Export. **B&W-90min.** *(Italian).* Vittorio De Sica, Gina Lollobrigida .... (5)
Original title: PANE, AMORE, E FANTASIA *(Bread, Love and Imagination)*

BREAD, LOVE AND JEALOUSY (1954) *see* FRISKY

BREAD PEDDLER, THE (1963) Emery Pictures. **Color-122min.** *(French-Italian).* Suzanne Flon, Philippe Noiret .... (3)
Original French title: PORTEUSE DE PAIN, LA

BREAK, THE (1963) British Lion [EMI]. **B&W-75min.** *(British).* Tony Britton, William Lucas .... (3)

BREAK IN THE CIRCLE (1955) 20th Century-Fox. **B&W-71min.** *(British).* Forrest Tucker, Eva Bartok, Marius Goring 3*

BREAK LOOSE (1972) *see* PARADES

BREAK OF DAY (1976) GUO (Australian). **Color-106min.** *(Australian).* Sara Kestelman, Andrew McFarlane, Ingrid Mason ....

BREAK OF HEARTS (1935) RKO. **B&W-80min.** Katharine Hepburn, Charles Boyer .... (4)

BREAK TO FREEDOM (1953) United Artists. **B&W-88min.** *(British).* Anthony Steel, Jack Warner .... (4)
Original title: ALBERT RN

BREAKAWAY (1956) Associated Artists. **B&W-72min.** *(British).* Tom Conway, Honor Blackman .... (3)

BREAKDOWN (1952) Realart. **B&W-77min.** Ann Richards, William Bishop .... (3)

BREAKER BREAKER (1977) American-International. **Color-86min.** Chuck Norris, Terry O'Connor, George Murdock .... (3)

BREAKFAST AT TIFFANY'S (1961) Paramount. **Color-115min.** Audrey Hepburn, George Peppard 7*

BREAKFAST FOR TWO (1937) RKO. **B&W-65min.** Barbara Stanwyck, Herbert Marshall .... (4)

BREAKFAST AT TIFFANY'S (1961). Tiffany's salesman John McGiver, apprised of the fact that amoral playgirl Audrey Hepburn and struggling writer George Peppard have distinct financial limitations, offers them a sterling silver telephone dialer for $6.75.

Films are rated on a 1 to 10 scale, 10 is highest. **Boldface** ratings followed by an asterisk (*) are for films actually seen and rated by the executive and senior editors. All other ratings are estimates. (See Notes on Entertainment Ratings in the front section.)

BREAKFAST IN BED (1963) Screen Gems. **B&W-99min.** *(German).* Lex Barker, Lilo (Liselotte) Pulver, Ann Smyrner .... (3)
Original title: FRUEHSTUECK IM DOPPELBETT

BREAKFAST IN BED (1977) **Color-56min.** Jenny Sullivan, John Ritter, V. Phipps-Wilson

BREAKFAST IN HOLLYWOOD (1946) United Artists. **B&W-100min.** Bonita Granville, Billie Burke .... (3)
British title: MAD HATTER, THE

BREAKHEART PASS (1976) United Artists. **Color-95min.** Charles Bronson, Ben Johnson, Jill Ireland 4*

BREAKING AWAY (1979) 20th Century-Fox. **Color-100min.** Dennis Christopher, Dennis Quaid 5½*

BREAKING OF BUMBO, THE (1969) J. Arthur Rank. **Color-102min.** *(British).* Richard Warwyck, Joanna Lumley .... (3)

BREAKING POINT, THE (1950) Warner Bros. **B&W-97min.** John Garfield, Patricia Neal .... (5)

BREAKING POINT (1976) 20th Century-Fox. **Color-92min.** *(Canadian).* Bo Svenson, Robert Culp, John Colicos .... (4)

BREAKING THE SOUND BARRIER (1952) United Artists. **B&W-109min.** *(British).* Ralph Richardson, Ann Todd 5*
British title: SOUND BARRIER, THE
Publicity title: BREAKING THROUGH THE SOUND BARRIER

BREAKOUT (1959) Continental [Walter Reade]. **B&W-99min.** *(British).* Richard Todd, Richard Attenborough .... (4)
Original title: DANGER WITHIN

BREAKOUT (1959) Anglo Amalgamated [EMI]. **B&W-62min.** *(British).* Lee Patterson, Hazel Court .... (3)

BREAKOUT (1967) Universal. **Color-100min.** *(Made for TV).* James Drury, Woody Strode 4*

BREAKOUT (1975) Columbia. **Color-96min.** Charles Bronson, Robert Duvall 4½*

BREAKTHROUGH (1950) Warner Bros. **B&W-91min.** David Brian, John Agar 4*

BREAKTHROUGH (1978) **Color-115min.** *(German).* Richard Burton, Robert Mitchum, Rod Steiger ....
Alternate title: SERGEANT STEINER

BREATH OF SCANDAL, A (1960) Paramount. **Color-98min.** Sophia Loren, John Gavin 4*
Original Italian title: OLYMPIA

BREATHLESS (1960) Films Around The World. **B&W-90min.** *(French).* Jean Seberg, Jean-Paul Belmondo .... (5)
Original title: A BOUT DE SOUFFLE

BREEZY (1973) Universal. **Color-106min.** William Holden, Kay Lenz 5*

BRENNUS, ENEMY OF ROME (1963) American-International. **Color-93min.** *(Italian).* Gordon Mitchell, Tony Kendall .... (1)
Alternate title: BATTLE OF THE SPARTANS
Original title: BRENNO IL NEMICO DI ROMA

BREWSTER McCLOUD (1970) M-G-M. **Color-101min.** Bud Cort, Sally Kellerman 3½*

BREWSTER'S MILLIONS (1945) United Artists. **B&W-79min.** Dennis O'Keefe, Helen Walker 4½*

BRIAN'S SONG (1971) Screen Gems. **Color-75min.** *(Made for TV).* James Caan, Billy Dee Williams 5½*

BRIBE, THE (1949) M-G-M. **B&W-98min.** Robert Taylor, Ava Gardner, Charles Laughton .... (3)

BRIDAL PATH, THE (1959) Kingsley International. **Color-95min.** *(British).* Bill Travers, Bernadette O'Farrell .... (4)

BRIDE, THE (1973) Unisphere Releasing Corp. **Color-85min.** Robin Strasser, Arthur Roberts, John Beal .... (3)
Alternate title: HOUSE THAT CRIED MURDER, THE

BRIDE AND THE BEAST, THE (1958) Allied Artists. **B&W-78min.** Charlotte Austin, Lance Fuller .... (2)

BRIDE BY MISTAKE (1944) RKO. **B&W-80min.** Alan Marshall, Laraine Day .... (4)

BRIDE CAME C.O.D., THE (1941) Warner Bros. **B&W-92min.** James Cagney, Bette Davis .... (4)

BRIDE COMES HOME, THE (1935) Paramount. **B&W-82min.** Claudette Colbert, Fred MacMurray .... (4)

BRIDE FOR FRANK, A (1958) **B&W-90min.** *(Italian).* Walter Chiari ..... (3)

BRIDE FOR SALE (1949) RKO. **B&W-87min.** Claudette Colbert, Robert Young .... (4)

BRIDE GOES WILD, THE (1948) M-G-M. **B&W-98min.** Van Johnson, June Allyson ....

BRIDE IS MUCH TOO BEAUTIFUL, THE (1956) Ellis Films. **B&W-93min.** *(French).* Brigitte Bardot, Louis Jourdan .... (4)
Original title: MARIÉE EST TROP BELLA, LA

BRIDE OF FRANKENSTEIN, THE (1935) Universal. **B&W-80min.** Boris Karloff, Colin Clive 4*

BRIDE OF THE GORILLA (1951) Realart. **B&W-76min.** Lon Chaney, Jr., Barbara Peyton, Raymond Burr .... (2)

BRIDE OF THE MONSTER (1956) Banner. **B&W-67min.** Bela Lugosi, Tor Johnson 2*
Alternate title: BRIDE OF THE ATOM

BRIDE OF VENGEANCE (1949) Paramount. **B&W-91min.** Paulette Goddard, John Lund .... (3)

BRIDE WALKS OUT, THE (1936) RKO. **B&W-75min.** Barbara Stanwyck, Gene Raymond .... (3)

BRIDE WORE BLACK, THE (1968) Lopert [U.A.]. **Color-107min.** *(French-Italian).* Jeanne Moreau, Jean-Claude Brialy .... (5)
Original title: MARIÉE ETAIT EN NOIR, LA

BRIDE WORE BOOTS, THE (1946) Paramount. **B&W-86min.** Barbara Stanwyck, Robert Cummings .... (3)

BRIDE WORE RED, THE (1937) M-G-M. **B&W-103min.** Joan Crawford, Franchot Tone .... (3)

BRIDES OF BLOOD (1968) Hemisphere. **Color-92min.** *(U.S.-Philippine).* John Ashley, Kent Taylor, Mario Montenegro, Beverly Hills 1*
TV title: ISLAND OF LIVING HORROR
Alternate title: BLOOD BRIDES
Alternate title: BRIDES OF DEATH

BRIDES OF DRACULA, THE (1960) Universal. **Color-85min.** *(British).* Peter Cushing, David Peel .... (4)

BRIDES OF FU MANCHU, THE (1966) Seven Arts [W.B.]. **Color-91min.** *(British).* Christopher Lee, Marie Versini .... (3)

BRIDGE, THE (1959) Allied Artists. **B&W-102min.** *(German).* Volker Bohnet, Fritz Wepper 5½*
Original title: BRUCKE, DIE

BRIDGE AT REMAGEN, THE (1969) United Artists. **Color-115min.** George Segal, Robert Vaughn .... (4)

BRIDGE OF SAN LUIS REY, THE (1929) M-G-M. **B&W-88min.** *(Silent).* Ernest Torrence, Raquel Torres, Duncan Renaldo .... (4)

BRIDGE OF SAN LUIS REY, THE (1944) United Artists. **B&W-85min.** Lynn Bari, Francis Lederer .... (3)

BRIDGE ON THE RIVER KWAI, THE (1957) Columbia. **Color-161min.** William Holden, Alec Guinness 6½*

BRIDGE TO THE SUN (1961) M-G-M. **B&W-113min.** *(U.S.-French).* Carroll Baker, James Shigeta 4½*
French title: PONT VERS LE SOLEIL

BRIDGE TOO FAR, A (1977) United Artists. **Color-175min.** James Caan, Sean Connery, Laurence Olivier, Robert Redford 4½*

BRIDGER (1975) MCA-TV. **Color-100min.** *(Made for TV).* James Wainwright, Dirk Blocker, Sally Field .... (4)

BRIDGES AT TOKO-RI, THE (1955) Paramount. **Color-103min.** William Holden, Grace Kelly 4*

BRIEF ENCOUNTER (1945) Universal. **B&W-86min.** *(British).* Celia Johnson, Trevor Howard 5*

BRIEF ENCOUNTER (1974) NBC-TV. **Color-103min.** *(British, Made for TV).* Richard Burton, Sophia Loren ....

BRIEF VACATION, A (1974) Allied Artists. **Color-106min.** *(Italian-Spanish).* Florinda Bolkan, Renato Salvatori 4½*
Original Italian title: BREVE VACANZA, UNA

BRIGADOON (1954) M-G-M. **Color-108min.** Gene Kelly, Van Johnson ... 5*

BRIGAND, THE (1952) Columbia. **Color-94min.** Anthony Dexter, Anthony Quinn .... (3)

BRIGAND OF KANDAHAR, THE (1965) Columbia. **Color-81min.** *(British).* Ronald Lewis, Oliver Reed .... (4)

BRIGHAM YOUNG, FRONTIERSMAN (1940) 20th Century-Fox. **B&W-114min.** Dean Jagger, Tyrone Power 4*
British title: BRIGHAM YOUNG

BRIGHT EYES (1934) Fox Film Co. [20th]. **B&W-83min.** Shirley Temple, James Dunn 4*

BRIGHT LEAF (1950) Warner Bros. **B&W-110min.** Gary Cooper, Lauren Bacall 5*

BRIGHT LIGHTS (1935) First National [W.B.]. **B&W-83min.** Joe E. Brown, Ann Dvorak .... (3)
British title: FUNNY FACE

BRIGHT ROAD (1953) M-G-M. **B&W-68min.** Dorothy Dandridge, Philip Hepburn .... (4)
Alternate title: SEE HOW THEY RUN

Films are rated on a 1 to 10 scale, 10 is highest. **Boldface** ratings followed by an asterisk (*) are for films actually seen and rated by the executive and senior editors. All other ratings are estimates. (See Notes on Entertainment Ratings in the front section.)

BRIGHT VICTORY (1951) Universal. **B&W-97min.** Arthur Kennedy, Peggy Dow..4½*
British title: LIGHTS OUT

BRIGHTHAVEN EXPRESS (1950) **B&W-75min.** *(British).* John Bentley, Carol Marsh ....(3)

BRIGHTON ROCK (1947) Mayer-Kingsley. **B&W-91min.** *(British).* Richard Attenborough, Hermione Baddeley, William Hartnell, Carol Marsh...(5)
Alternate title: YOUNG SCARFACE

BRIGHTON STRANGLER, THE (1945) RKO. **B&W-67min.** John Loder, June Duprez 4*

BRIGHTY OF GRAND CANYON (1967) Feature Film Corp. **Color-89min.** Joseph Cotten, Pat Conway ....(3)

BRIMSTONE (1949) Republic. **Color-90min.** Rod Cameron, Walter Brennan...3*

BRING 'EM BACK ALIVE (1932) RKO. **B&W-70min.** *(Documentary).* Frank Buck ....(5)

BRING ME THE HEAD OF ALFREDO GARCIA (1974) United Artists. **Color-112min.** *(U.S.-Mexican).* Warren Oates, Isela Vega......................2*

BRING ME THE VAMPIRE (1964) Trans-International. **B&W-80min.** *(Mexican).* Maria Eugenia San Martin, Hector Godoy ....(1)
Original title: ECHENME AL VAMPIRO *(Throw Me to the Vampire)*

BRING ON THE GIRLS (1945) Paramount. **Color-92min.** Veronica Lake, Sonny Tufts ....(4)

BRING YOUR SMILE ALONG (1955) Columbia. **Color-83min.** Frankie Laine, Keefe Brasselle ....(4)

BRINGING UP BABY (1938) RKO. **B&W-102min.** Cary Grant, Katharine Hepburn...6½*

BRINK OF HELL (1956) *see* TOWARD THE UNKNOWN

BRINK OF LIFE (1958) Ajay Films. **B&W-82min.** *(Swedish).* Eva Dahlbeck, Ingrid Thulin 4*
Original title: NARA LIVET
British title: SO CLOSE TO LIFE

BRINK'S JOB, THE (1978) Universal. **Color-103min.** Peter Falk, Peter Boyle, Warren Oates 5½*

BRINK'S: THE GREAT ROBBERY (1976) Warner Bros. **Color-100min.** *(Made for TV).* Carl Betz, Darren McGavin, Leslie Nielsen 4*

BRITANIA MEWS (1949) *see* FORBIDDEN STREET, THE

BRITISH AGENT (1934) First National [W.B.]. **B&W-81min.** Leslie Howard, Kay Francis ....(4)

BRITISH INTELLIGENCE (1940) Warner Bros. **B&W-62min.** Boris Karloff, Margaret Lindsay..(3)
British title: ENEMY AGENT

BROAD COALITION, THE (1972) August Films. **Color-90min.** William C. Reilly, Anita Morris ....(3)

BROAD-MINDED (1931) First National [W.B.]. **B&W-72min.** Joe E. Brown, Ona Munson..(4)

BROADWAY (1942) Universal. **B&W-91min.** George Raft, Pat O'Brien (5)

BROADWAY BAD (1933) Fox Film Co. [20th]. **B&W-61min.** Joan Blondell, Ricardo Cortez, Ginger Rogers ....(4)
British title: HER REPUTATION

BROADWAY BILL (1934) Columbia. **B&W-101min.** Warner Baxter, Myrna Loy...
British title: STRICTLY CONFIDENTIAL

BROADWAY GONDOLIER (1935) Warner Bros. **B&W-98min.** Dick Powell, Joan Blondell ....(4)

BROADWAY LIMITED (1941) United Artists. **B&W-74min.** Dennis O'Keefe, Victor McLaglen...(3)

BROADWAY MELODY, THE (1929) M-G-M. **B&W-110min.** Bessie Love, Anita Page 4*

BROADWAY MELODY OF 1936 (1935) M-G-M. **B&W-103min.** Jack Benny, Robert Taylor 4½*

BROADWAY MELODY OF 1938 (1937) M-G-M. **B&W-110min.** Eleanor Powell, Robert Taylor ....(4)

BROADWAY MELODY OF 1940 (1940) M-G-M. **B&W-102min.** Fred Astaire, Eleanor Powell..(5)

BROADWAY MUSKETEERS (1938) First National [W.B.]. **B&W-62min.** Ann Sheridan, Marie Wilson, Margaret Lindsay ....(3)

BROADWAY RHYTHM (1944) M-G-M. **Color-114min.** George Murphy, Ginny Simms...(4)

BROADWAY SERENADE (1939) M-G-M. **B&W-114min.** Jeanette MacDonald, Lew Ayres ....(3)

BROADWAY THRU A KEYHOLE (1933) United Artists. **B&W-85min.** Constance Cummings, Russ Columbo ....(3)

BROCK'S LAST CASE (1972) MCA-TV. **Color-100min.** *(Made for TV).* Richard Widmark, Henry Darrow, Beth Bickell.....................4*

BROKEN ARROW (1950) 20th Century-Fox. **Color-93min.** James Stewart, Jeff Chandler 4½*

BROKEN BLOSSOMS (1919) D.W. Griffith Productions. **B&W-87min.** *(Silent).* Lillian Gish, Richard Barthelmess 4*

BROKEN HORSESHOE, THE (1953) Video Artists. **B&W-80min.** *(British).* Robert Beatty, Elizabeth Sellars ....(5)

BROKEN JOURNEY (1948) Eagle Lion. **B&W-89min.** *(British).* Phyllis Calvert, Margot Grahame 4*

BROKEN LANCE (1954) 20th Century-Fox. **Color-96min.** Spencer Tracy, Robert Wagner...5*

BROKEN LAND, THE (1962) 20th Century-Fox. **Color-60min.** Kent Taylor, Dianna Darin ....(3)

BROKEN LULLABY (1932) Paramount. **B&W-94min.** Lionel Barrymore, Nancy Carroll 4*
British and alternate U.S. title: MAN I KILLED, THE

BROKEN STAR, THE (1956) United Artists. **B&W-82min.** Howard Duff, Lita Baron, Bill Williams 3*

BROKEN WINGS, THE (1964) Continental [Walter Reade]. **B&W-90min.** *(Lebanese).* Pierre Bordey, Saladin Nader...................(4)
Original title: AGHNIHAT ELMOUTAKASRA, LAL

BRONCO BULLFROG (1970) British Lion [EMI]. **B&W-86min.** *(British).* Del Walker, Anne Gooding, Sam Shepherd ....(4)

BRONCO BUSTER (1952) Universal. **Color-81min.** John Lund, Scott Brady ....(3)

BROOD, THE (1979) New World. **Color-91min.** *(Canadian).* Oliver Reed, Samantha Eggar...3*

BROTH OF A BOY (1959) Kingsley International. **B&W-77min.** *(Irish).* Barry Fitzgerald, Tony Wright ....(4)

BROTHEL NO. 8 (1975) *see* SANDAKAN NO. 8

BROTHER, CAN YOU SPARE A DIME? (1975) Dimension Pictures. **B&W-106min.** *(British, Compilation). Director:* Philippe Mora 5½*

BROTHER JOHN (1971) Columbia. **Color-94min.** Sidney Poitier, Will Geer 3*

BROTHER OF THE WIND (1972) Sunn Classic. **Color-87min.** *(U.S.-Canada).* Dick Robinson..4½*

BROTHER ORCHID (1940) Warner Bros. **B&W-91min.** Edward G. Robinson, Ann Sothern 5*

BROTHER RAT (1938) Warner Bros. **B&W-90min.** Wayne Morris, Priscilla Lane 3*

BROTHER RAT AND A BABY (1940) Warner Bros. **B&W-87min.** Ronald Reagan, Eddie Albert ....(3)
British title: BABY BE GOOD

BROTHER SUN, SISTER MOON (1973) Paramount. **Color-121min.** *(Italian-British).* Graham Faulkner, Judi Bowker 4*
Original title: FRATELLO SOLE, SORELLA LUNA

BROTHERHOOD, THE (1968) Paramount. **Color-98min.** Kirk Douglas, Alex Cord 3*

BROTHERHOOD OF SATAN, THE (1971) Columbia. **Color-92min.** Strother Martin, L. Q. Jones 3*

BROTHERHOOD OF THE BELL, THE (1970) Cinema Center 100. **Color-100min.** *(Made for TV).* Glenn Ford, Rosemary Forsyth 5½*

BROTHERLY LOVE (1970) M-G-M. **Color-112min.** Peter O'Toole, Susannah York, Michael Craig 3*
Alternate title: SAME SKIN, THE

BROTHERS, THE (1947) Universal. **B&W-90min.** *(British).* Will Fyffe, Patricia Roc, Finlay Currie ....(3)

BROTHERS (1977) Warner Bros. **Color-105min.** Bernie Casey 4*

BROTHERS IN LAW (1957) Continental [Walter Reade]. **B&W-94min.** *(British).* Richard Attenborough, Ian Carmichael ....(5)

BROTHERS IN THE SADDLE (1949) RKO. **B&W-60min.** Tim Holt, Richard Martin...(4)

BROTHERS KARAMAZOV, THE (1958) M-G-M. **Color-146min.** Yul Brynner, Maria Schell..5*

BROTHERS O'TOOLE, THE (1972) CVD. **Color-94min.** John Astin, Steve Carlson...3*

BROTHERS RICO, THE (1957) Columbia. **B&W-92min.** Richard Conte, Dianne Foster, James Darren 3*

BROWNING VERSION, THE (1951) Universal. **B&W-90min.** *(British).* Michael Redgrave, Jean Kent 5½*

BRUBAKER (1980) 20th Century-Fox. **Color- min.** Robert Redford .....

BRUCE LEE AND I (1976) Pacific Grove Films. **Color-106min.** *(Chinese).* Betty Ting Pei, Li Hsiu Hsien...(2)

Films are rated on a 1 to 10 scale, 10 is highest. **Boldface** ratings followed by an asterisk (*) are for films actually seen and rated by the executive and senior editors. All other ratings are estimates. (See Notes on Entertainment Ratings in the front section.)

BRUSHFIRE (1962) Paramount. **B&W-80min.** John Ireland, Everett Sloane..(2)

BRUTE CORPS (1972) General Film Corp. **Color-90min.** Paul Carr, Joseph Kaufmann ....(3)

BRUTE FORCE (1947) Universal. **B&W-98min.** Burt Lancaster, Hume Cronyn 3½*

BRUTE MAN, THE (1946) Producers Rel. Corp. [Eagle Lion]. **B&W-60min.** Rondo Hatton, Tom Neal ....(3)

BUBBLE, THE (1967) Arch Oboler. **Color-112min.** Michael Cole, Deborah Walley, Johnny Desmond ....(3)
Alternate title: FANTASTIC INVASION OF PLANET EARTH

BUCCANEER, THE (1938) Paramount. **B&W-90min.** Fredric March, Franciska Gaal ....(5)

BUCCANEER, THE (1958) Paramount. **Color-121min.** Yul Brynner, Charlton Heston 4*

BUCCANEER'S GIRL (1950) Universal. **Color-77min.** Yvonne De Carlo, Philip Friend 3*

BUCHANAN RIDES ALONE (1958) Columbia. **Color-78min.** Randolph Scott, Craig Stevens ....(4)

BUCK AND THE PREACHER (1972) Columbia. **Color-102min.** Sidney Poitier, Harry Belafonte 4½*

BUCK BENNY RIDES AGAIN (1940) Paramount. **B&W-82min.** Jack Benny, Eddie "Rochester" Anderson, Phil Harris.............3*

BUCK PRIVATES (1941) Universal. **B&W-84min.** Bud Abbott, Lou Costello...4*
British title: ROOKIES

BUCK PRIVATES COME HOME (1947) Universal. **B&W-77min.** Bud Abbott, Lou Costello, Nat Pendleton 4*
British title: ROOKIES COME HOME

BUCK ROGERS (1939) *see* DESTINATION SATURN

BUCK ROGERS IN THE 25TH CENTURY (1979) Universal. **Color-89min.** Gil Gerard, Henry Silva.................................5*
Publicity title: BUCK ROGERS

BUCKET OF BLOOD, A (1959) American-International. **B&W-66min.** Dick Miller, Antony Carbone................................3½*

BUCKSKIN (1968) Paramount. **Color-97min.** Barry Sullivan, Wendell Corey ....(3)

BUCKSKIN LADY, THE (1957) United Artists. **B&W-66min.** Patricia Medina, Richard Denning ....(2)

BUCKTOWN (1975) American-International. **Color-94min.** Fred Williamson, Pam Grier ....(3)

BUD AND LOU (1978) NBC-TV. **Color-98min.** *(Made for TV).* Harvey Korman, Buddy Hackett ....(3)

BUDDENBROOKS (1959) Casino Films. **B&W-199min.** *(German).* Liselotte Pulver, Hansjorg Felmy ....(4)

THE BUCCANEER (1938). Hugh Sothern, as General Andrew Jackson, tries to enlist the aid of pirate chief Fredric March, as Jean Lafitte, in resisting a British attack on New Orleans in the War of 1812.

BUDDY HOLLY STORY, THE (1978) Columbia. **Color-113min.** Gary Busey, Don Stroud, Charles Martin Smith 5½*

BUFFALO BILL (1944) 20th Century-Fox. **Color-90min.** Joel McCrea, Maureen O'Hara 4*

BUFFALO BILL AND THE INDIANS, OR SITTING BULL'S HISTORY LESSON (1976) United Artists. **Color-123min.** Paul Newman, Joel Grey 5*

BUFFALO GUN (1962) Allied Artists. **B&W-72min.** Wayne Morris, Marty Robbins ....(2)

BUG (1975) Paramount. **Color-99min.** Bradford Dillman, Joanna Miles..3*

BUGLE SOUNDS, THE (1941) M-G-M. **B&W-110min.** Wallace Beery, Marjorie Main 3½*

BUGLES IN THE AFTERNOON (1952) Warner Bros. **Color-85min.** Ray Milland, Helena Carter 3*

BUGS BUNNY SUPERSTAR (1975) Hare Raising Films [Cate Enterprises]. **Color-90min.** *(Part-animated, Compilation). Director:* Bob Clampett 4½*

BUGSY MALONE (1976) Paramount. **Color-93min.** *(British).* Scott Baio, Florrie Dugger 5*

BUILD MY GALLOWS HIGH (1947) *see* OUT OF THE PAST

BULLDOG DRUMMOND (1929) United Artists. **B&W-90min.** Ronald Colman, Joan Bennett..(4)

BULLDOG DRUMMOND AT BAY (1937) Republic. **B&W-62min.** *(British).* John Lodge, Dorothy Mackaill..........................(4)

BULLDOG DRUMMOND AT BAY (1947) Columbia. **B&W-70min.** Ron Randell, Anita Louise ....(4)

BULLDOG DRUMMOND COMES BACK (1937) Paramount. **B&W-64min.** John Howard, John Barrymore ....(4)

BULLDOG DRUMMOND ESCAPES (1937) Paramount. **B&W-65min.** Ray Milland, Heather Angel ....(4)

BULLDOG DRUMMOND IN AFRICA (1938) Paramount. **B&W-60min.** John Howard, Heather Angel ....(4)

BULLDOG DRUMMOND STRIKES BACK (1934) United Artists. **B&W-83min.** Ronald Colman, Loretta Young.................(5)

BULLDOG DRUMMOND STRIKES BACK (1947) Columbia. **B&W-65min.** Ron Randell, Gloria Henry.......................(4)

BULLDOG DRUMMOND'S BRIDE (1939) Paramount. **B&W-55min.** John Howard, Heather Angel.............................(4)

BULLDOG DRUMMOND'S PERIL (1938) Paramount. **B&W-66min.** John Howard, Louise Campbell ....(4)

BULLDOG DRUMMOND'S REVENGE (1937) Paramount. **B&W-60min.** John Howard, John Barrymore ....(4)

BULLDOG DRUMMOND'S SECRET POLICE (1939) Paramount. **B&W-56min.** John Howard, Heather Angel ....(4)

BULLDOG JACK (1935) *see* ALIAS BULLDOG DRUMMOND

BULLET FOR A BADMAN (1964) Universal. **Color-80min.** Audie Murphy, Darren McGavin...(3)

BULLET FOR JOEY, A (1955) United Artists. **B&W-85min.** George Raft, Edward G. Robinson ....(3)

BULLET FOR PRETTY BOY, A (1970) American-International. **Color-91min.** Fabian Forte, Jocelyn Lang ....(3)

BULLET FOR SANDOVAL (1970) UMC Pictures. **Color-91min.** *(Italian-Spanish).* Ernest Borgnine, George Hilton 3*
Original Italian title: QUI DISPERATI CHE PAZZANO DI SUDORE E DI MORTI *(Those Desperate Men Who Smell of Sweat and Death)*
Spanish title: DESESPERADOS, LOS *(The Desperados)*

BULLET FOR STEFANO (1950) Lux Film America. **B&W-96min.** *(Italian).* Rossano Brazzi, Valentine Cortese ....(3)
Original title: PASSATORE, IL

BULLET FOR THE GENERAL, A (1967) Avco-Embassy. **Color-115min.** *(Italian).* Gian Maria Volonte, Klaus Kinski, Martine Beswick ....(3)
Alternate title: VIVA BANDITO
Original Italian title (in Spanish): QUIEN SABE? *(Who Knows?)*

BULLET IS WAITING, A (1954) Columbia. **Color-82min.** Rory Calhoun, Jean Simmons 4*

BULLETS OR BALLOTS (1936) First National [W.B.]. **B&W-77min.** Edward G. Robinson, Joan Blondell.....................4*

BULLFIGHT (1956) Janus Films. **B&W-76min.** *(French, Documentary). Director:* Pierre Braunberger ....(5)

BULLFIGHTER AND THE LADY, THE (1951) Republic. **B&W-87min.** Robert Stack, Joy Page..............................4*

BULLFIGHTERS, THE (1945) 20th Century-Fox. **B&W-61min.** Stan Laurel, Oliver Hardy ....(3)

BULLITT (1968) Warner Bros. **Color-113min.** Steve McQueen, Robert Vaughn 5*

BULLWHIP (1958) Allied Artists. **Color-80min.** Guy Madison, Rhonda Fleming .... (4)

BULLY (1978) Maturo, Image Corp. **Color-120min.** James Whitmore ...... (5)

BUNCO SQUAD (1950) RKO. **B&W-67min.** Robert Sterling, Joan Dixon .... (4)

BUNDLE OF JOY (1956) RKO. **Color-98min.** Eddie Fisher, Debbie Reynolds .... (4)

BUNDLE OF TROUBLE, A (1942) *see* BLONDIE'S BLESSED EVENT

BUNNY LAKE IS MISSING (1965) Columbia. **B&W-107min.** *(British).* Laurence Olivier, Carol Lynley, Keir Dullea 4*

BUNNY O'HARE (1971) American-International. **Color-92min.** Bette Davis, Ernest Borgnine 4*

BUONA SERA, MRS. CAMPBELL (1969) United Artists. **Color-111min.** Gina Lollobrigida, Shelley Winters, Peter Lawford 5*

BUREAU OF MISSING PERSONS (1933) First National [W.B.]. **B&W-79min.** Bette Davis, Pat O'Brien 4*

BURGLAR, THE (1957) Columbia. **B&W-90min.** Dan Duryea, Jayne Mansfield .... (3)

BURGLARS, THE (1971) Columbia. **Color-120min.** *(French-Italian).* Jean-Paul Belmondo, Omar Sharif 5*
Foreign title: CASSE, LE

BURMA CONVOY (1941) Universal. **B&W-72min.** Charles Bickford, Evelyn Ankers .... (4)

BURMESE HARP, THE (1956) Brandon. **B&W-116min.** *(Japanese).* Rentaro Mikuni, Shoji Yasui .... (5)
Original title: BIRUMA NO TATEGOTO *(The Harp of Burma)*
Alternate title: HARP OF BURMA

BURN! (1970) United Artists. **Color-112min.** *(Italian).* Marlon Brando, Evaristo Marquez 4½*
Foreign title: QUEIMADA!

BURN 'EM UP O'CONNOR (1939) M-G-M. **B&W-70min.** Dennis O'Keefe, Cecelia Parker .... (3)

BURN, WITCH, BURN (1962) American-International. **B&W-90min.** *(British).* Janet Blair, Peter Wyngarde 4*
British title: NIGHT OF THE EAGLE

BURNING ARROWS (1953) *see* CAPTAIN JOHN SMITH AND POCAHONTAS

BURNING HILLS, THE (1956) Warner Bros. **B&W-94min.** Tab Hunter, Natalie Wood 3*

BURNING QUESTION, THE (1939) *see* REEFER MADNESS

BURNOUT (1979) Crown International. **Color-90min.** Mark Schneider, Robert Louden ....

BURNT OFFERINGS (1976) United Artists. **Color-116min.** Karen Black, Oliver Reed 4½*

BURY ME AN ANGEL (1971) New World. **Color-86min.** Dixie Peabody, Terry Mace, Clyde Ventura .... (2)

BURY ME DEAD (1947) Eagle Lion. **B&W-71min.** Cathy O'Donnell, June Lockhart .... (4)

BUS, THE (1965) Harrison Pictures. **B&W-62min.** *(Documentary).* *Director:* Haskell Wexler .... (5)

BUS IS COMING, THE (1971) William Thompson International. **Color-101min.** Mike Sims, Stephanie Faulkner .... (4)

BUS RILEY'S BACK IN TOWN (1965) Universal. **Color-93min.** Michael Parks, Ann-Margret 4*

BUS STOP (1956) 20th Century-Fox. **Color-96min.** Marilyn Monroe, Don Murray 5*
Alternate title: WRONG KIND OF GIRL, THE

BUSH CHRISTMAS (1947) Universal. **B&W-76min.** *(Australian).* Chips Rafferty, John Fernside .... (5)

BUSHBABY, THE (1970) M-G-M. **Color-101min.** *(British).* Margaret Brooks, Lou Gossett .... (3)

BUSHIDO (1963) Toho. **B&W-123min.** *(Japanese).* Kinnosuke Nakamura, Masayuki Mori .... (5)
Original title: BUSHIDO ZANKOKU MONOGATARI

BUSHWHACKERS, THE (1951) Realart. **B&W-70min.** John Ireland, Wayne Morris .... (2)
British title: REBEL, THE

BUSMAN'S HONEYMOON (1940) *see* HAUNTED HONEYMOON

BUSSES ROAR (1942) Warner Bros. **B&W-61min.** Richard Travis, Julie Bishop .... (3)

BUSTER AND BILLIE (1974) Columbia. **Color-98min.** Jan-Michael Vincent, Joan Goodfellow 4½*

BUSTER KEATON STORY, THE (1957) Paramount. **B&W-91min.** Donald O'Connor, Ann Blyth 4*

BUSTIN' OUT (1975) *see* COONSKIN

BUSTING (1974) United Artists. **Color-91min.** Elliott Gould, Robert Blake .... (4)

BUSY BODY, THE (1967) Paramount. **Color-90min.** Sid Caesar, Robert Ryan .... (4)

BUT I DON'T WANT TO GET MARRIED (1970) ABC Films. **Color-75min.** *(Made for TV).* Herschel Bernardi, Kay Medford, Shirley Jones 4*

BUT NOT FOR ME (1959) Paramount. **B&W-105min.** Clark Gable, Carroll Baker .... (5)

BUT WHERE IS DANIEL VAX? (1972) **Color-95min.** *(Israeli).* Lior Yaeni, Michael Lipkin, Esther Zebko ....
Original title: LE'AM NE'ELAN DANIEL WAKS

BUTCH AND SUNDANCE: THE EARLY DAYS (1979) 20th Century-Fox. **Color-111min.** Tom Berenger, William Katt, Jill Eikenberry 5½*

BUTCH CASSIDY AND THE SUNDANCE KID (1969) 20th Century-Fox. **Color-110min.** Paul Newman, Robert Redford 7½*

BUTCH MINDS THE BABY (1942) Universal. **B&W-76min.** Broderick Crawford, Virginia Bruce .... (4)

BUTCHER, THE (1970) Cinerama Releasing. **Color-93min.** *(French-Italian).* Stéphane Audran, Jean Yanne 6*
Original title: BOUCHER, LE

BUTCHER BOY, THE (1917) Paramount Famous Players-Lasky. **B&W-2reels** *(Silent).* Fatty Arbuckle, Buster Keaton, Al St. John .... (4)

BUTLEY (1974) American Film Theatre. **Color-129min.** *(British).* Alan Bates, Jessica Tandy ....

BUTTERCUP CHAIN, THE (1970) Columbia. **Color-95min.** *(British).* Hywel Bennett, Leigh Taylor-Young .... (3)

BUTTERFIELD 8 (1960) M-G-M. **Color-109min.** Elizabeth Taylor, Laurence Harvey 5*

BUTTERFLIES ARE FREE (1972) Columbia. **Color-93min.** Goldie Hawn, Edward Albert 7*

BUY ME THAT TOWN (1941) Paramount. **B&W-70min.** Lloyd Nolan, Constance Moore 3½*

BWANA DEVIL (1952) United Artists. **Color-79min.** Robert Stack, Barbara Britton .... (3)

BY HOOK OR BY CROOK (1943) *see* I DOOD IT

BY LOVE POSSESSED (1961) United Artists. **Color-115min.** Lana Turner, Efrem Zimbalist, Jr. 3*

BY ROCKET TO THE MOON (1929) *see* WOMAN IN THE MOON

BY THE LIGHT OF THE SILVERY MOON (1953) Warner Bros. **Color-102min.** Doris Day, Gordon MacRae 5*

BYE BYE BIRDIE (1963) Columbia. **Color-111min.** Dick Van Dyke, Ann-Margret 5*

BYE BYE BRAVERMAN (1968) Warner Bros. **Color-94min.** George Segal, Jack Warden 4*

-C-

C.C. AND COMPANY (1970) Avco-Embassy. **Color-94min.** Joe Namath, Ann-Margret 2*

C-MAN (1949) Four Continents. **B&W-75min.** Dean Jagger, John Carradine .... (3)

CABARET (1954) Sam Baker Associates. **B&W-104min.** *(German).* Paul Henreid, Eva Kerbler .... (4)

CABARET (1972) Allied Artists. **Color-120min.** Liza Minnelli, Michael York, Joel Grey 10*

CABIN IN THE COTTON (1932) First National [W.B.]. **B&W-77min.** Bette Davis, Richard Barthelmess .... (4)

CABIN IN THE SKY (1943) M-G-M. **B&W-98min.** Ethel Waters, Eddie "Rochester" Anderson 5*

CABINET OF CALIGARI, THE (1962) 20th Century-Fox. **B&W-104min.** Dan O'Herlihy .... (3)

CABINET OF DR. CALIGARI, THE (1919) Samuel Goldwyn. **B&W-81min.** *(German, Silent).* Werner Krauss, Conrad Veidt 2*

CABIRIA (1957) *see* NIGHTS OF CABIRIA

CACTUS FLOWER (1969) Columbia. **Color-103min.** Walter Matthau, Ingrid Bergman, Goldie Hawn 6½*

CACTUS IN THE SNOW (1972) General Film Corp. **Color-90min.** Richard Thomas, Mary Layne .... (5)

CADDY, THE (1953) Paramount. **B&W-95min.** Dean Martin, Jerry Lewis, Donna Reed .... (4)

Films are rated on a 1 to 10 scale, 10 is highest. **Boldface** ratings followed by an asterisk (*) are for films actually seen and rated by the executive and senior editors. All other ratings are estimates. (See Notes on Entertainment Ratings in the front section.)

CACTUS FLOWER (1969). Goldie Hawn has been assured by her dentist lover Walter Matthau that she's not really breaking up a happy marriage; Jack Weston poses as the boyfriend of the dentist's "wife" Ingrid Bergman.

CADET GIRL (1941) 20th Century-Fox. B&W-69min. Carole Landis, George Montgomery..(2)

CADETS ON PARADE (1942) Columbia. B&W-63min. Freddie Bartholomew, Jimmy Lydon.................................(3)

CAESAR AND CLEOPATRA (1945) United Artists. Color-128min. (British). Claude Rains, Vivien Leigh...........................4*

CAESAR THE CONQUERER (1962) Telewide Systems. Color-103min. (Italian). Cameron Mitchell.......................(3)
Alternate title: JULIUS CAESAR, CONQUEROR OF GAUL

CAFE METROPOLE (1937) 20th Century-Fox. B&W-80min. Adolphe Menjou, Loretta Young.................................(5)

CAFE SOCIETY (1939) Paramount. B&W-83min. Madeleine Carroll, Fred MacMurray, Shirley Ross.........................(4)

CAGE OF DOOM (1958) see TERROR FROM THE YEAR 5000

CAGE OF EVIL (1960) United Artists. B&W-70min. Ron Foster, Pat Blair..(3)

CAGE OF GOLD (1950) Ellis Films. B&W-83min. (British). Jean Simmons, David Farrar.................................(4)

CAGED (1950) Warner Bros. B&W-96min. Eleanor Parker, Agnes Moorehead..(5)

CAGED FURY (1948) Paramount. B&W-60min. Buster Crabbe, Sheila Ryan...(4)

CAGED HEAT! (1974) New World. Color-83min. Juanita Brown, Erica Gavin, Barbara Steele.................................

CAGED VIRGINS (1972) Boxoffice International. Color-80min. (French). Marie Castel, Mirielle D'Argent, Philippe Gaste.............(3)
Original title: VIERGES ET VAMPIRES
Alternate title: CRAZED VAMPIRE, THE
Alternate title: VIRGINS AND THE VAMPIRES

CAHILL, UNITED STATES MARSHALL (1973) Warner Bros. Color-103min. John Wayne, George Kennedy.........................3*
British title: CAHILL

CAIN AND MABEL (1936) Warner Bros. B&W-90min. Clark Gable, Marion Davies.......................................(3)

CAINE MUTINY, THE (1954) Columbia. Color-125min. Humphrey Bogart, José Ferrer.......................................6*

CAIN'S WAY (1971) Fanfare. Color-95min. Scott Brady, John Carradine
Alternate title: CAIN'S CUT-THROATS

CAIRO (1942) M-G-M. B&W-101min. Jeanette MacDonald, Robert Young...(3)

CAIRO (1963) M-G-M. B&W-91min. George Sanders, Richard Johnson (3)

CAIRO ROAD (1950) Continental [Walter Reade]. B&W-90min. (British). Eric Portman, Laurence Harvey.........................(3)

CALAMITY JANE (1953) Warner Bros. Color-101min. Doris Day, Howard Keel..(5)

CALAMITY JANE AND SAM BASS (1949) Universal. Color-85min. Yvonne De Carlo, Howard Duff...........................4*

CALCUTTA (1947) Paramount. B&W-83min. Alan Ladd, Gail Russell, William Bendix.......................................3*

CALENDAR GIRL (1947) Republic. B&W-88min. Jane Frazee, Kenny Baker..(3)

CALIFORNIA (1947) Paramount. Color-97min. Ray Milland, Barbara Stanwyck..3*

CALIFORNIA (1963) American-International. B&W-77min. Jock Mahoney, Faith Domergue..................................(3)

CALIFORNIA CONQUEST (1952) Columbia. Color-79min. Cornel Wilde, Teresa Wright.......................................(3)

CALIFORNIA DREAMING (1979) American-International. Color-92min. Glynnis O'Connor, Seymour Cassell.....................5*

CALIFORNIA HOLIDAY (1966) see SPINOUT

CALIFORNIA KID, THE (1974) MCA-TV. Color-75min. (Made for TV). Martin Sheen, Vic Morrow.........................4*

CALIFORNIA PASSAGE (1950) Republic. B&W-90min. Forrest Tucker, Adele Mara.......................................(4)

CALIFORNIA REICH, THE (1976) Intercontinental Films. Color-58min. (Documentary). Director: Walter Parkes...............5*

CALIFORNIA SPLIT (1974) Columbia. Color-108min. Elliott Gould, George Segal.......................................4*

CALIFORNIA STRAIGHT AHEAD (1937) Universal. B&W-67min. John Wayne, Louise Lattimer.............................(3)

CALIFORNIA SUITE (1978) Columbia. Color-103min. Alan Alda, Jane Fonda..6*

CALL A MESSENGER (1939) Universal. B&W-65min. The Little Tough Guys, Robert Armstrong...........................

CALL DETROIT 9000 (1973) see DETROIT 9000

CALL HER MOM (1972) CPT (TV). Color-74min. (Made for TV). Connie Stevens, Jim Hutton, Van Johnson.................3*

CALL HER SAVAGE (1932) 20th Century-Fox. B&W-88min. Clara Bow, Monroe Owsley, Thelma Todd, Gilbert Roland.........4*

CALL HIM MR. SHATTER (1976) Avco-Embassy. Color-90min. (Chinese). Stuart Whitman, Ti Lung, Peter Cushing...........3*
Alternate title: SHATTER

CALL IT A DAY (1937) Warner Bros. B&W-89min. Olivia de Havilland, Ian Hunter.......................................(4)

CALL ME BWANA (1963) United Artists. Color-103min. (British). Bob Hope, Anita Ekberg...............................3*

CALL ME GENIUS (1961) Continental [Walter Reade]. Color-105min. (British). Tony Hancock, George Sanders, Irne Handl.......3½*
Original title: REBEL, THE

CALL ME MADAM (1953) 20th Century-Fox. Color-117min. Ethel Merman, Donald O'Connor............................4*

CALL ME MISTER (1951) 20th Century-Fox. Color-95min. Dan Dailey, Betty Grable.......................................4*

CALL NORTHSIDE 777 (1948) 20th Century-Fox. B&W-111min. James Stewart, Richard Conte............................5*
Alternate title: CALLING NORTHSIDE 777

CALL OF THE SOUTH SEAS (1944) Republic. B&W-55min. Janet Martin, Allan Lane.......................................(2)

CALL OF THE WILD (1935) United Artists. B&W-95min. Clark Gable, Loretta Young.......................................4*

CALL OF THE WILD, THE (1973) Intercontinental Films. Color-100min. (W. German-Spanish). Charlton Heston, Raimund Harmsdorf.........3½*
German title: RUF DE WILDNIS

CALL OF THE YUKON (1938) Republic. B&W-79min. Richard Arlen, Lyle Talbot, Beverly Roberts.............................(4)

CALL OUT THE MARINES (1942) RKO. B&W-67min. Victor McLaglen, Edmund Lowe.......................................(4)

CALL TO DANGER (1972) Paramount. Color-75min. (Made for TV). Peter Graves, Clu Gulager.............................4*

CALLAWAY WENT THATAWAY (1951) M-G-M. B&W-81min. Fred MacMurray, Dorothy McGuire......................(5)
British title: STAR SAID NO, THE

CALLING ALL HUSBANDS (1940) Warner Bros. B&W-64min. Ernest Truex, Florence Bates..............................(3)

CALLING BULLDOG DRUMMOND (1951) M-G-M. B&W-80min. (British). Walter Pidgeon, Margaret Leighton...........4*

CALLING DR. DEATH (1943) Universal. B&W-63min. Lon Chaney, Jr., J. Carrol Naish.......................................(4)

CALLING DR. GILLESPIE (1942) M-G-M. **B&W-82min.** Lionel Barrymore, Donna Reed.................................(3)

CALLING DR. KILDARE (1939) M-G-M. **B&W-86min.** Lionel Barrymore, Lew Ayres, Lana Turner.................................(4)

CALLING HOMICIDE (1956) Allied Artists. **B&W-61min.** Bill Elliott, Don Haggerty.................................(3)

CALLING NORTHSIDE 777 (1948) *see* CALL NORTHSIDE 777

CALLING PHILO VANCE (1940) Warner Bros. **B&W-62min.** James Stephenson, Margot Stevenson.................................(4)

CALTIKI, THE IMMORTAL MONSTER (1959) Allied Artists. **B&W-76min.** *(Italian-U.S.)*. John Merivale, Didi Sullivan (Perego).................(3)
Original Italian title: CALTIKI, IL MOSTRO IMMORTALE
Common title error: IMMORTAL MONSTER, THE

CALYPSO (1956) *see* MANFISH

CALYPSO HEAT WAVE (1957) Columbia. **B&W-86min.** Johnny Desmond, Merry Anders.................................(3)

CALYPSO JOE (1957) Allied Artists. **B&W-76min.** Herb Jeffries, Angie Dickinson.................................(3)

CALZONZIN INSPECTOR (1974) Azteca. **Color-90min.** *(Mexican)*. Alfonso Arau, Pancho Cordoba.................................(4)

CAMELOT (1967) Warner Bros. **Color-179min.** Richard Harris, Vanessa Redgrave, Franco Nero.................................**6***

CAMELS WEST (1954) *see* SOUTHWEST PASSAGE

CAMERAMAN, THE (1928) M-G-M. **B&W-78min.** *(Silent)*. Buster Keaton, Marceline Day.................................**4***

CAMILLE (1936) M-G-M. **B&W-108min.** Greta Garbo, Robert Taylor......**4***

CAMILLE 2000 (1969) Audubon. **Color-115min.** Daniele Gaubert, Nino Castelnuovo.................................(3)

CAMP ON BLOOD ISLAND, THE (1958) Columbia. **B&W-81min.** *(British)*. Carl Mohner, André Morell.................................**4***

CAMPBELL'S KINGDOM (1957) J. Arthur Rank. **Color-100min.** *(British)*. Dirk Bogarde, Stanley Baker.................................**4***

CAN-CAN (1960) 20th Century-Fox. **Color-131min.** Frank Sinatra, Shirley MacLaine.................................**4***

CAN HEIRONYMUS MERKIN EVER FORGET MERCY HUMPPE AND FIND TRUE HAPPINESS? (1969) Regional. **Color-104min.** *(British)*. Anthony Newley, Joan Collins, Milton Berle, George Jessel.................(3)

CAN I DO IT 'TIL I NEED GLASSES? (1977) National-American Entertainment. **Color-80min.** Moe Baker, Roger Behr, Conrad Brooks.................................(4)

CANADIAN MOUNTIES VS. ATOMIC INVADERS (1953) *see* MISSILE BASE AT TANIAK

CANADIAN PACIFIC (1949) 20th Century-Fox. **Color-95min.** Randolph Scott, Jane Wyatt.................................(4)

CANADIANS, THE (1961) 20th Century-Fox. **Color-85min.** Robert Ryan, John Dehner.................................**3***

CANAL ZONE (1942) Columbia. **B&W-78min.** Chester Morris, Harriet Hilliard (Nelson).................................(3)

CANARIS (1954) *see* DEADLY DECISION

CANARY MURDER CASE (1929) Paramount. **B&W-82min.** William Powell, Louise Brooks.................................(4)

CANCEL MY RESERVATION (1972) Warner Bros. **Color-99min.** Bob Hope, Eva Marie Saint, Ralph Bellamy.................................**3***

CANDIDATE, THE (1964) *see* PARTY GIRLS FOR THE CANDIDATE

CANDIDATE, THE (1972) Warner Bros. **Color-110min.** Robert Redford, Don Porter.................................**6½***

CANDIDATE FOR A KILLING (1969) GGP. **Color- min.** *(Italian-U.S.(-Spanish?))*. John Richardson, Anita Ekberg, Fernando Ray ....

CANDIDATE FOR MURDER (1962) Schoenfeld Film Distributing. **B&W-60min.** *(British)*. Michael Gough, Erika Remberg.................................(4)

CANDIDE (1961) Union Films. **B&W-90min.** *(French)*. Jean-Pierre Cassel, Dahlia Lavi.................................(4)
Original title: CANDIDE, OU L'OPTIMISME AU XXème SIECLE

CANDLESHOE (1977) Buena Vista. **Color-101min.** Jodie Foster, David Niven, Helen Hayes.................................**5***

CANDY (1968) Cinerama Releasing. **Color-119min.** *(U.S.-French-Italian)*. Ewa Aulin, John Astin.................................**2½***
Original Italian titlte: CANDY E IL SUL PAZZO MONDO

CANDY MAN, THE (1969) Allied Artists. **Color-97min.** George Sanders, Leslie Parrish, Manolo Fabregas.................................**3***

CANGACIERO - THE STORY OF AN OUTLAW (1953) Columbia. **B&W-91min.** *(Brazilian)*. Alberto Ruschel, Marisa Prado.................................(4)
Original title: CANGACIEROS, O

CANNIBAL ATTACK (1954) Columbia. **B&W-69min.** Johnny Weissmuller, Judy Walsh, David Bruce.................................(3)

CANNIBAL GIRLS (1973) American-International. **Color-83min.** *(Canadian)*. Eugene Levy, Andrea Martin.................................(2)

CANNON (1971) Quinn Martin Productions. **Color-100min.** *(Made for TV)*. William Conrad, Vera Miles.................................**4***

CANNON FOR CORDOBA (1970) United Artists. **Color-104min.** George Peppard, Giovanni Ralli.................................**3***

CANNONBALL (1976) New World. **Color-93min.** *(U.S.-Hong Kong)*. David Carradine, Bill McKinney.................................(4)
British title: CARQUAKE

CANON CITY (1948) Eagle Lion. **B&W-82min.** Scott Brady, Jeff Corey (5)
Alternate title: CANYON CITY

CAN'T HELP SINGING (1944) Universal. **Color-89min.** Deanna Durbin, David Bruce.................................(4)

CANTERBURY TALES (1974) United Artists. **Color-111min.** *(Italian)*. Hugh Griffith, Ninetto Davoli, Franco Citti.................................
Original title: RACCONTI DI CANTERBURY, I

CANTERVILLE GHOST, THE (1944) M-G-M. **B&W-96min.** Charles Laughton, Robert Young.................................**3***

CANYON CITY (1943) Republic. **B&W-56min.** Don "Red" Barry, Wally Vernon.................................

CANYON CITY (1948) *see* CANON CITY

CANYON CROSSROADS (1955) United Artists. **B&W-83min.** Phyllis Kirk, Richard Basehart.................................(4)

CANYON PASS (1951) *see* RATON PASS

CANYON PASSAGE (1946) Universal. **Color-90min.** Dana Andrews, Brian Donlevy.................................**4***

CANYON RIVER (1956) Allied Artists. **Color-80min.** George Montgomery, Marcia Henderson.................................(3)

CAPE CANAVERAL MONSTERS, THE (1960) M & A Alexander. **B&W-71min.** Scott Peters, Linda Connell.................................(2)

CAPE FEAR (1962) Universal. **B&W-105min.** Gregory Peck, Robert Mitchum.................................**4***

CAPER OF THE GOLDEN BULLS, THE (1967) Avco-Embassy. **Color-103min.** Stephen Boyd, Yvette Mimieux.................................(4)
British title: CARNIVAL OF THIEVES

CAPONE (1975) 20th Century-Fox. **Color-101min.** Ben Gazzara, Susan Blakely.................................**5***

CAPRICE (1967) 20th Century-Fox. **Color-98min.** Doris Day, Richard Harris.................................**3***

CAPRICE OF "DEAR CAROLINE" (1952) Gala-Cameo-Poly. **B&W-85min.** *(French)*. Martine Carol, Jacques Daqumine.................................(3)
Original title: CAPRICE DE CAROLINE CHÉRIE, UN

CAPRICIOUS SUMMER (1968) Sigma III. **Color-75min.** *(Czech)*. Rudolf Hrusinsky, Vlastimil Brodsky.................................(5)
Original title: ROZMARNE LETO

CAPRICORN ONE (1978) Warner Bros. **Color-127min.** Elliott Gould, James Brolin, Brenda Vaccaro.................................**5½***

CAPTAIN ADVENTURE (1949) *see* ADVENTURES OF MANDERIN

CAPTAIN APACHE (1971) Scotia International *(Brit.)*. **Color-94min.** *(British)*. Lee Van Cleef, Carroll Baker, Stuart Whitman.................(2)

CAPTAIN AVENGER (1979) U.A. (for M-G-M). **Color- min.** John Ritter, Anne Archer.................................

CAPTAIN BLACK JACK (1951) United Artists. **B&W-90min.** George Sanders, Patricia Roc.................................**3***
British title: BLACK JACK

CAPTAIN BLOOD (1935) First National [W.B.]. **B&W-119min.** Errol Flynn, Olivia de Havilland.................................**5***

CAPTAIN BLOOD (1960) E.J. Fancey *(Brit.)*. **Color-95min.** *(French-Italian)*. Jean Marais, Elsa Martinelli, Bourvil.................................(3)
French title: CAPITAINE, LE
Italian title: CAPITANO DE RE, IL

CAPTAIN BLOOD, FUGITIVE (1952) *see* CAPTAIN PIRATE

CAPTAIN BOYCOTT (1947) Universal. **B&W-93min.** *(British)*. Stewart Granger, Cecil Parker.................................**5***

CAPTAIN CAREY, U.S.A. (1950) Paramount. **B&W-83min.** Alan Ladd, Wanda Hendrix.................................**4***
British title: AFTER MIDNIGHT

CAPTAIN CAUTION (1940) United Artists. **B&W-85min.** Victor Mature, Louise Platt.................................(3)

CAPTAIN CHINA (1950) Paramount. **B&W-97min.** John Payne, Gail Russell.................................**3***

CAPTAIN CLEGG (1962) *see* NIGHT CREATURES

Films are rated on a 1 to 10 scale, 10 is highest. **Boldface** ratings followed by an asterisk (*) are for films actually seen and rated by the executive and senior editors. All other ratings are estimates. (See Notes on Entertainment Ratings in the front section.)

CAPTAIN BLOOD (1935). The pirate crew of escaped convicts hails their new leader, Errol Flynn, who proclaims the buccaneers' code the crew will be bound to follow.

CAPTAIN EDDIE (1945) 20th Century-Fox. **B&W-107min.** Fred MacMurray, Lynn Bari **4***

CAPTAIN FALCON (1959) Avco-Embassy. **Color-97min.** *(Italian).* Lex Barker, Rossana Rory .... (3)
Original title: CAPITAN FUOCO

CAPTAIN FROM CASTILE (1947) 20th Century-Fox. **Color-140min.** Tyrone Power, Jean Peters............................... **4***

CAPTAIN FROM KOEPENICK (1956) Hal Roach. **Color-93min.** *(German).* Heinz Ruhmann, Hannelore Schroth .... (6)
Original title: HAUPTMANN VON KOEPENICK, DER

CAPTAIN FURY (1939) United Artists. **B&W-91min.** Brian Aherne, Victor McLaglen **4***

CAPTAIN HATES THE SEA, THE (1934) Columbia. **B&W-92min.** John Gilbert, Victor McLaglen, Helen Vinson .... (3)

CAPTAIN HORATIO HORNBLOWER (1951) Warner Bros. **Color-117min.** Gregory Peck, Virginia Mayo **5***
British title: CAPTAIN HORATIO HORNBLOWER, R. N.
Alternate title: HORATIO HORNBLOWER

CAPTAIN IS A LADY, THE (1940) M-G-M. **B&W-63min.** Charles Coburn, Beulah Bondi .... (3)

CAPTAIN JANUARY (1936) 20th Century-Fox. **B&W-75min.** Shirley Temple, Guy Kibbee .... (4)

CAPTAIN JOHN SMITH AND POCAHONTAS (1953) United Artists. **Color-75min.** Anthony Dexter, Jody Lawrence .... (3)
British title: BURNING ARROWS

CAPTAIN KIDD (1945) United Artists. **B&W-89min.** Charles Laughton, John Carradine .... (3)

CAPTAIN KIDD AND THE SLAVE GIRL (1954) United Artists. **Color-83min.** Anthony Dexter, Eva Gabor........................ (2)
Alternate title: SLAVE GIRL, THE

CAPTAIN KRONOS: VAMPIRE HUNTER (1974) Paramount. **Color-91min.** *(British).* Horst Janson, John Carson................ (4)

CAPTAIN LIGHTFOOT (1955) Universal. **Color-91min.** Rock Hudson, Barbara Rush **4***

CAPTAIN MEPHISTO AND THE TRANSFORMATION MACHINE (1945) Republic. **B&W-100min.** *(Re-edited Serial).* Richard Bailey, Linda Stirling, Roy Barcroft .... (4)
Original title: MANHUNT OF MYSTERY ISLAND

CAPTAIN MILKSHAKE (1970) Twi National. **Color-100min.** Geoff Gage, Andrea Cagan .... (3)

CAPTAIN NEMO AND THE UNDERWATER CITY (1969) M-G-M. **Color-106min.** *(British).* Robert Ryan, Chuck Connors **4***

CAPTAIN NEWMAN, M.D. (1964) Universal. **Color-126min.** Gregory Peck, Tony Curtis.. **5***

CAPTAIN PIRATE (1952) Columbia. **Color-85min.** Louis Hayward, Patricia Medina **4***
British title: CAPTAIN BLOOD, FUGITIVE

CAPTAIN SCARLETT (1953) United Artists. **Color-75min.** Richard Greene, Leonara Amar .... (3)

CAPTAIN SINDBAD (1963) M-G-M. **Color-85min.** Guy Williams, Heidi Bruhl, Pedro Armendariz .... (3)

CAPTAIN SIROCCO (1949) *see* PIRATES OF CAPRI, THE

CAPTAIN TUGBOAT ANNIE (1945) Republic. **B&W-60min.** Jane Darwell, Edgar Kennedy .... (3)

CAPTAINS COURAGEOUS (1937) M-G-M. **B&W-116min.** Freddie Bartholomew, Spencer Tracy **5½***

CAPTAINS COURAGEOUS (1977) **Color-100min.** *(Made for TV).* Karl Malden, Jonathan Kahn

CAPTAINS OF THE CLOUDS (1942) Warner Bros. **Color-113min.** James Cagney, Dennis Morgan............................. **4***

CAPTAIN'S PARADISE, THE (1953) United Artists. **B&W-93min.** *(British).* Alec Guinness, Yvonne De Carlo **6***

CAPTAIN'S TABLE, THE (1959) 20th Century-Fox. **Color-90min.** *(British).* John Gregson, Peggy Cummins............ **4***

CAPTIVE CITY, THE (1952) United Artists. **B&W-91min.** John Forsythe, Joan Camden **4***

CAPTIVE GIRL (1950) Columbia. **B&W-73min.** Johnny Weissmuller, Buster Crabbe .... (3)

CAPTIVE HEART, THE (1946) Universal. **B&W-86min.** *(British).* Michael Redgrave, Rachel Kempson **4***

CAPTIVE WILD WOMAN (1943) Universal. **B&W-60min.** John Carradine, Evelyn Ankers, Acquanetta **3***

CAPTIVE WOMEN (1952) RKO. **B&W-65min.** Robert Clarke, Margaret Field .... (2)
British title: 3000 A.D.
Publicity title: 1000 YEARS FROM NOW

CAPTURE, THE (1950) RKO. **B&W-81min.** Lew Ayres, Teresa Wright (4)

CAPTURE THAT CAPSULE! (1962) *see* SPY SQUAD

CAPTURED (1933) Warner Bros. **B&W-72min.** Leslie Howard, Douglas Fairbanks, Jr... (4)

CAR, THE (1977) Universal. **Color-98min.** James Brolin, Ronny Cox...... **4***

CAR 99 (1935) Paramount. **B&W-68min.** Fred MacMurray, Ann Sheridan **4***

CAR WASH (1976) Universal. **Color-97min.** Ivan Dixon, Sully Boyar..... **5***

CARABINIERS, LES (1963) West End Films. **B&W-80min.** *(French-Italian).* Marino Mase, Albert Juross .... (5)

CARAVAN (1934) Fox Film Co. [20th]. **B&W-101min.** Charles Boyer, Loretta Young .... (4)

CARAVAN (1946) Eagle Lion. **B&W-80min.** *(British).* Stewart Granger, Jean Kent .... (4)

CARAVAN TO VACCARES (1974) Bryanston. **Color-98min.** *(British-French).* Charlotte Rampling, David Birney........... (4)

CARAVANS (1978) Universal. **Color-127min.** *(U.S.-Iranian).* Michael Sarrazin, Anthony Quinn, Jennifer O'Neill................ **5***

CARBINE WILLIAMS (1952) M-G-M. **B&W-91min.** James Stewart, Jean Hagen **4***

CARD, THE (1952) *see* PROMOTER, THE

CARDIGAN'S LAST CASE (1932) *see* STATE'S ATTORNEY

CARDINAL, THE (1963) Columbia. **Color-175min.** Tom Tryon, Romy Schneider **5½***

CARDINAL RICHELIEU (1935) United Artists. **B&W-83min.** George Arliss, Edward Arnold .... (4)

CAREER (1959) Paramount. **B&W-105min.** Dean Martin, Anthony Franciosa **5***

CAREER GIRL (1960) Astor. **Color-61min.** June Wilkinson, Charles Robert Keane .... (2)

CAREFREE (1938) RKO. **B&W-80min.** Fred Astaire, Ginger Rogers **5***

CAREFUL · SOFT SHOULDER (1942) 20th Century-Fox. **B&W-69min.** James Ellison, Virginia Bruce .... (4)

CARELESS YEARS, THE (1957) United Artists. **B&W-70min.** Dean Stockwell, Natalie Trundy .... (5)

CARESSED (1965) Joseph Brenner. **B&W-81min.** Robert Howay, Angela Gann .... (2)

CARETAKER, THE (1964) *see* GUEST, THE

CARETAKERS, THE (1963) United Artists. **B&W-97min.** Robert Stack, Polly Bergen **4***
British title: BORDERLINES

CAREY TREATMENT, THE (1972) M-G-M. **Color-100min.** James Coburn, Jennifer O'Neill.................................. **5½***

CARGO OF INNOCENTS (1942) *see* STAND BY FOR ACTION

Films are rated on a 1 to 10 scale. 10 is highest. **Boldface** ratings followed by an asterisk (*) are for films actually seen and rated by the executive and senior editors. All other ratings are estimates. (See Notes on Entertainment Ratings in the front section.)

CARGO TO CAPETOWN (1950) Columbia. **B&W-80min.** John Ireland, Ellen Drew .... (4)

CARIB GOLD (1957) Premier Pictures [MGM]. **B&W-71min.** Ethel Waters, Coley Wallace, Geoffrey Holder .... (3)

CARIBBEAN (1952) Paramount. **Color-97min.** John Payne, Arlene Dahl 4*
British title: CARIBBEAN GOLD

CARIBBEAN HAWK (1964) Telewide Systems. **Color-115min.** *(Spanish).* Johnny Desmond, Yvonne Molbur .... (3)

CARIBBEAN MYSTERY (1945) 20th Century-Fox. **B&W-65min.** James Dunn, Sheila Ryan .... (3)

CARIBOO TRAIL, THE (1950) 20th Century-Fox. **B&W-81min.** Randolph Scott, Bill Williams .... (4)

CARLTON-BROWNE OF THE F.O. (1959) *see* MAN IN A COCKED HAT

CARMEN, BABY (1967) Audubon. **Color-90min.** *(U.S.-Yugoslavian-W. German).* Uta Levka, Claude Ringer .... (2)

CARMEN JONES (1954) 20th Century-Fox. **Color-105min.** Dorothy Dandridge, Harry Belafonte 5*

CARNABY, M.D. (1966) Continental [Walter Reade]. **Color-101min.** *(British).* Leslie Phillips, James Robertson Justice, Shirley Ann Field 3*
Original title: DOCTOR IN CLOVER

CARNAL KNOWLEDGE (1971) Avco-Embassy. **Color-96min.** Jack Nicholson, Candice Bergen.. 6*

CARNATION FRANK (1961) **Color-85min.** *(German).* Chris Howland, Dagmar Hanks .... (2)

CARNEGIE HALL (1947) United Artists. **B&W-154min.** Marsha Hunt, William Prince.. (4)

CARNETS DU MAJOR THOMPSON, LES (1957) *see* FRENCH THEY ARE A FUNNY RACE, THE

CARNIVAL (1946) J. Arthur Rank. **B&W-93min.** *(British).* Sally Gray, Michael Wilding .... (5)

CARNIVAL IN COSTA RICA (1947) 20th Century-Fox. **Color-95min.** Dick Haymes, Vera-Ellen .... (3)

CARNIVAL IN FLANDERS (1935) American Tobis. **B&W-95min.** *(French).* Francoise Rosay, Alerme.. 2*
Original title: KERMESSE HEROIQUE, LA
German title: KLUGEN FRAVEN, DIE

CARNIVAL OF HERETICS (1968) *see* CREMATOR, THE

CARNIVAL OF SOULS (1962) Herts-Lion International. **B&W-80min.** Candace Hilligoss, Herk Harvey.................................... (4)

CARNIVAL OF THIEVES (1967) *see* CAPER OF THE GOLDEN BULLS, THE

CARNIVAL STORY (1954) RKO. **Color-95min.** Anne Baxter, Steve Cochran.. 3*

CAROLINA BLUES (1944) Columbia. **B&W-81min.** Kay Kyser, Ann Miller.. (3)

CAROLINA CANNONBALL (1955) Republic. **B&W-74min.** Judy Canova, Andy Clyde .... (3)

CAROSSE D'OR (1952) *see* GOLDEN COACH, THE

CAROUSEL (1956) 20th Century-Fox. **Color-128min.** Gordon MacRae, Shirley Jones 6*

CARPET OF HORROR, THE (1962) UCC Films. **B&W-93min.** *(German).* Joachim Fuchsberger, Eleanor Rossi-Drago .... (3)

CARPETBAGGERS, THE (1964) Paramount. **Color-150min.** George Peppard, Carroll Baker.. 5*

CARQUAKE (1976) *see* CANNONBALL

CARRIE (1952) Paramount. **B&W-118min.** Laurence Olivier, Jennifer Jones.. 5*

CARRIE (1976) United Artists. **Color-97min.** Sissy Spacek, Piper Laurie... 6*

CARRY IT ON (1970) Maron Films, Ltd. **B&W-80min.** *(Documentary).* Director: James Coyne .... (5)
British title: JOAN

CARRY ON ADMIRAL (1957) *see* SHIP WAS LOADED, THE

CARRY ON CABBY (1963) Governor. **B&W-91min.** *(British).* Sidney James, Hattie Jacques... (3)

CARRY ON CAMPING (1969) American-International. **Color-88min.** *(British).* Sidney James, Kenneth Williams .... (4)

CARRY ON CLEO (1964) Governor. **Color-92min.** *(British).* Sidney James, Kenneth Williams, Amanda Barrie........................ (4)

CARRY ON CONSTABLE (1960) Governor. **B&W-86min.** *(British).* Sidney James, Eric Barker .... (3)

CARRY ON CRUISING (1962) Governor. **Color-87min.** *(British).* Sidney James, Kenneth Williams, Kenneth Connor.................... (3)

CARRY ON DOCTOR (1968) American-International. **Color-95min.** *(British).* Frankie Howerd, Sidney James, Joan Sims, Kenneth Williams .... (3)

CARRY ON EMMANNUELLE (1978) **Color-88min.** *(British).* Suzanne Danielle, Kenneth Williams, Kenneth Connor............................

CARRY ON ENGLAND (1976) Fox-Rank *(Brit.).* **Color-89min.** *(British).* Kenneth Connor, Windsor Davies, Judy Geeson .... (4)

CARRY ON HENRY VIII (1970) American-International. **Color-90min.** *(British).* Sidney James, Kenneth Williams, Joan Sims.......... (3)
Original title: CARRY ON HENRY

CARRY ON NURSE (1959) Governor. **B&W-90min.** *(British).* Kenneth Connor, Kenneth Williams .... (5)

CARRY ON REGARDLESS (1961) Governor. **B&W-87min.** *(British).* Sidney James, Kenneth Connor .... (3)

CARRY ON SERGEANT (1958) Governor. **B&W-83min.** *(British).* William Hartnell, Bob Monkhouse, Shirley Eaton .... (4)

CARRY ON SPYING (1964) Governor. **B&W-83min.** *(British).* Kenneth Williams, Bernard Cribbins.. (4)

CARRY ON T.V. (1961) *see* GET ON WITH IT

CARRY ON TEACHER (1959) Governor. **B&W-86min.** *(British).* Kenneth Connor, Kenneth Williams, Joan Sims......................... (4)

CARRY ON VENUS (1964) Governor. **Color-87min.** *(British).* Juliet Mills, Kenneth Williams, Donald Houston .... (4)
Alternate title: CARRY ON JACK

CARSON CITY (1952) Warner Bros. **Color-87min.** Randolph Scott, Raymond Massey.. (4)

CARTER'S ARMY (1969) ABC-TV. **Color-80min.** *(Made for TV).* Stephen Boyd, Robert Hooks 5*

CARTHAGE IN FLAMES (1960) Columbia. **Color-93min.** *(French-Italian).* Anne Heywood, José Suarez .... (3)
Original French title: CARTHAGE EN FLAMMES
Original Italian title: CARTAGINE IN FIAMME

CARTOUCHE (1954) RKO. **B&W-73min.** *(Italian).* Richard Basehart, Patricia Roc, Akim Tamiroff .... (3)

CARTOUCHE (1962) Avco-Embassy. **Color-115min.** *(French-Italian).* Jean-Paul Belmondo, Claudia Cardinale........................... (5)

CARVE HER NAME WITH PRIDE (1958) Lopert [U.A.]. **B&W-116min.** *(British).* Virginia McKenna, Paul Scofield 5*

CASA RICORDI (1954) *see* HOUSE OF RICORDI

CASABLANCA (1942) Warner Bros. **B&W-102min.** Humphrey Bogart, Ingrid Bergman... 8*

CASANOVA (1955) ABC Films. **Color-90min.** *(Italian).* Gabriele Ferzetti, Corinne Calvet, Nadia Grey................................. (3)

CASANOVA (1976) *see* FELLINI'S CASANOVA

CASANOVA BROWN (1944) RKO. **Color-94min.** Gary Cooper, Teresa Wright 4*

In a flashback scene from **CASABLANCA** (1942), Dooley Wilson sings "As Time Goes By" while Humphrey Bogart pours champagne for girl-friend Ingrid Bergman; the Germans are marching into Paris, and the three are making ready to flee the city.

CASANOVA IN BURLESQUE (1944) Republic. **B&W-74min.** Joe E. Brown, June Havoc .... (3)

CASANOVA '70 (1965) Avco-Embassy. **Color-113min.** *(Italian-French).* Marcello Mastroianni, Virna Lisi 4½*

CASANOVA'S BIG NIGHT (1954) Paramount. **Color-86min.** Bob Hope, Joan Fontaine 4*

CASBAH (1948) Universal. **B&W-94min.** Tony Martin, Marta Toren, Peter Lorre 3*

CASE AGAINST BROOKLYN, THE (1958) Columbia. **B&W-82min.** Darren McGavin, Maggie Hayes .... (3)

CASE AGAINST MRS. AMES, THE (1936) Paramount. **B&W-85min.** George Brent, Madeleine Carroll .... (4)

CASE AGAINST PAUL RYKER, THE (1968) *see* SERGEANT RYKER

CASE OF DR. LAURENT, THE (1957) Trans-Lux Distributing. **B&W-110min.** *(French).* Jean Gabin, Nicole Courcel .... (5)
Original title: CAS DU DR. LAURENT, LE

CASE OF LENA SMITH, THE (1929) Paramount. **B&W-80min.** *(Silent).* Esther Ralston, James Hall ....

CASE OF MRS. LORING, THE (1958) *see* QUESTION OF ADULTERY, A

CASE OF MRS. PEMBROOK, THE (1936) *see* TWO AGAINST THE WORLD

CASE OF RAPE, A (1974) MCA-TV. **Color-75min.** *(Made for TV).* Elizabeth Montgomery, Ronny Cox 5*

CASE OF THE CURIOUS BRIDE, THE (1935) First National [W.B.]. **B&W-68min.** Warren William, Margaret Lindsay....................

CASE OF THE MISSING BLONDE, THE (1938) *see* LADY IN THE MORGUE

CASE OF THE MISSING BRIDES, THE (1942) *see* CORPSE VANISHES, THE

CASE OF THE MISSING SWITCHBOARD OPERATOR, THE (1967) *see* LOVE AFFAIR

CASE OF THE MUKKINESE BATTLEHORN, THE (1955) Union Films. **B&W-30min.** *(British).* Peter Sellers, Spike Milligan, Dick Emery 4*

CASE OF THE RED MONKEY (1955) Allied Artists. **B&W-73min.** *(British).* Richard Conte, Rona Anderson.................... (3)
Original title: LITTLE RED MONKEY

CASE 33: ANTWERP (1965) Parkside Prods. **B&W-85min.** *(German).* Adrian Hoven, Constance Collins.................... (3)

CASEY'S SHADOW (1978) Columbia. **Color-116min.** Walter Matthau, Michael Hershewe 5½*

C.A.S.H. (1975) *see* WHIFFS

CASH AND CARRY (1941) *see* RINGSIDE MAISIE

CASH McCALL (1960) Warner Bros. **Color-102min.** James Garner, Natalie Wood 4*

CASH ON DELIVERY (1954) RKO. **B&W-82min.** *(British).* Shelley Winters, John Gregson .... (3)
Original title: TO DOROTHY A SON

CASH ON DEMAND (1962) Columbia. **B&W-84min.** *(British).* Peter Cushing, André Morell.................... (4)

CASINO DE PAREE (1935) *see* GO INTO YOUR DANCE

CASINO DE PARIS (1957) Rizzoli Film. **Color-85min.** *(French-Italian).* Caterina Valente, Vittorio De Sica.................... (3)

CASINO MURDER CASE (1935) M-G-M. **B&W-85min.** Paul Lukas, Rosalind Russell, Alison Skipworth.................... (4)

CASINO ROYALE (1967) Columbia. **Color-131min.** *(British).* David Niven, Peter Sellers.................... 2½*

CASQUE D'OR (1952) Discina International. **B&W-96min.** *(French).* Simone Signoret, Serge Reggiani .... (5)
Alternate title: GIRL WITH GOLDEN HAIR, THE
Alternate title: GOLDEN MARIE
Translation title: Golden Helmet, The

CASS TIMBERLANE (1948) M-G-M. **Color-119min.** Spencer Tracy, Lana Turner .... (4)

CASSANDRA CROSSING, THE (1977) Avco-Embassy. **Color-126min.** *(British-Italian-W. German).* Sophia Loren, Richard Harris............. 5½*

CAST A DARK SHADOW (1955) Distributors Corp. of America. **B&W-82min.** *(British).* Dirk Bogarde, Margaret Lockwood.................... 4*

CAST A GIANT SHADOW (1966) United Artists. **Color-142min.** Kirk Douglas, Senta Berger ....

CAST A LONG SHADOW (1959) United Artists. **Color-82min.** Audie Murphy, Terry Moore.................... (3)

CAST IRON (1930) *see* VIRTUOUS SIN, THE

CASTA DIVA (1954) Continental [Walter Reade]. **Color-100min.** Maurice Ronet, Antanella Lualdi.................... (3)

CASTAWAY, THE (1945) *see* CHEATERS, THE

CASTAWAY COWBOY, THE (1974) Buena Vista. **Color-91min.** James Garner, Vera Miles.................... (4)

CASTILIAN, THE (1963) Warner Bros. **Color-129min.** *(U.S.-Spanish).* Spartaco Santoni, Cesar Romero.................... 3*
Original Spanish title: VALLE DE LAS ESPADAS, EL

CASTILLO DE LA PUREZA, EL (1974) *see* CASTLE OF PURITY

CASTLE, THE (1968) Continental [Walter Reade]. **Color-93min.** *(Swiss-W. German, English language).* Maximilian Schell, Cordula Trantow 2*
Original title: SCHLOSS, DAS

CASTLE IN THE AIR (1952) *see* RAINBOW 'ROUND MY SHOULDER

CASTLE IN THE AIR (1952) Stratford Pictures. **B&W-92min.** *(British).* David Tomlinson, Helen Cherry.................... (4)

CASTLE IN THE DESERT (1942) 20th Century-Fox. **B&W-63min.** Sidney Toler, Arleen Whelan.................... 4*

CASTLE KEEP (1969) Columbia. **Color-105min.** Burt Lancaster, Peter Falk 4*

CASTLE OF BLOOD (1964) *see* CASTLE OF TERROR

CASTLE OF FU MANCHU, THE (1968) **Color-92min.** *(W. German-Spanish-Italian-British).* Christopher Lee, Richard Greene, Maria Perschy .... (3)
German title: FOLTERKAMMER DES DOKTOR FU MAN CHU, DIE *(The Torture Chamber of Dr. Fu Manchu)*
Spanish title: CASTILLO DE FU MANCHU, EL
Alternate title: ASSIGNMENT ISTANBUL

CASTLE OF PURITY (1974) Azteca. **Color-116min.** *(Mexican).* Claudio Brook, Rita Macedo .... (4)
Original title: CASTILLO DE LA PUERZA, EL

CASTLE OF TERROR, THE (1964) Woolner Brothers. **B&W-85min.** *(Italian).* Barbara Steele, Georges Riviere 3*
Alternate title: CASTLE OF BLOOD

CASTLE OF TERROR, THE (1963) *see* HORROR CASTLE

CASTLE OF THE LIVING DEAD (1964) American-International. **B&W-90min.** *(Italian-French).* Christopher Lee, Gaia Germani, Donald Sutherland .... (3)
Original Italian title: CASTELLO DEI MORTI VIVI, IL
French title: CHATEAU DES MORTS VIVANTS, LE

CASTLE ON THE HUDSON (1940) Warner Bros. **B&W-77min.** John Garfield, Ann Sheridan.................... 3*
British title: YEARS WITHOUT DAYS

CASTLES IN SPAIN (1954) Victory Films. **Color-90min.** *(French-Spanish).* Danielle Darrieux, Pepin Martin Valezquez.................... (3)
Original French title: CHATEAUX EN ESPAGNE

CASUAL RELATIONS (1974) Mark Rappaport. **Color-80min.** Sis Smith, Mel Austin.................... (3)

CAT, THE (1958) Ellis Films. **B&W-108min.** *(French).* Francoise Arnoul, Bernard Blier.................... (5)

CAT, THE (1966) Avco-Embassy. **Color-87min.** Peggy Ann Garner, Roger Perry.................... 2*

CAT AND MOUSE (1958) Eros Films *(Brit.).* **B&W-79min.** *(British).* Lee Patterson, Ann Sears.................... 3*

CAT AND MOUSE (1970) Grove Press. **B&W-92min.** *(German).* Lars Brandt, Peter Brandt, Wolfgang Neuss.................... (3)
Original title: KATZ UND MAUS

CAT AND MOUSE (1975) Quartet Films. **Color-107min.** *(French).* Michele Morgan.................... 3½*
Original title: CHAT ET LA SOURIS, LE

CAT AND THE CANARY, THE (1927) Universal. **B&W-86min.** *(Silent).* Laura La Plante, Creighton Hale, Forrest Stanley .... (5)

CAT AND THE CANARY, THE (1939) Paramount. **B&W-74min.** Bob Hope, Paulette Goddard.................... 5*

CAT AND THE FIDDLE, THE (1934) M-G-M. **B&W-92min.** Ramon Novarro, Jeanette MacDonald .... (4)

CAT BALLOU (1965) Columbia. **Color-96min.** Jane Fonda, Lee Marvin.. 6*

CAT BURGLAR, THE (1961) United Artists. **B&W-65min.** Jack Hogan, June Kenney.................... (3)

CAT CREATURE, THE (1973) CPT (TV). **Color-74min.** *(Made for TV).* Meredith Baxter, Stuart Whitman, Gale Sondergaard, John Carradine 4*

CAT CREEPS, THE (1946) Universal. **B&W-58min.** June Collier, Paul Kelly.................... 3*

CAT FROM OUTER SPACE, THE (1978) Buena Vista. **Color-103min.** Ken Berry, Sandy Duncan.................... 4½*

CAT GIRL (1957) American-International. **B&W-69min.** *(British).* Barbara Shelley, Kay Callard.................... 3*

CAT MURKIL AND THE SILKS (1976) Gamma III. Color-102min. David Kyle, Steve Bond, Kelly Yaegermann .... (3)

CAT O' NINE TAILS, THE (1971) National General. Color-104min. *(Italian-W. German-French)*. Karl Malden, James Franciscus 4*
Original Italian title: GATTO A NOVE CODE, IL
German title: NEUNSCHWANZIGE KATZE, DER

CAT ON A HOT TIN ROOF (1958) M-G-M. Color-108min. Elizabeth Taylor, Paul Newman 6½*

CAT ON A HOT TIN ROOF (1976) NBC-TV. Color-100min. *(Made for TV)*. Laurence Olivier, Natalie Wood, Robert Wagner 5½*

CAT PEOPLE (1942) RKO. B&W-73min. Simone Simon, Kent Smith 4*

CAT WOMEN OF THE MOON (1953) Astor. B&W-64min. Sonny Tufts, Victor Jory, Marie Windsor .... (2)

CATACOMBS (1964) *see* WOMAN WHO WOULDN'T DIE, THE

CATCH MY SOUL (1974) Cinerama Releasing. Color-97min. Richie Havens, Lance Le Gault, Season Hubley ....

CATCH-22 (1970) Paramount. Color-121min. Alan Arkin, Martin Balsam 5*

CATCH US IF YOU CAN (1965) *see* HAVING A WILD WEEKEND

CATCHER, THE (1971) CPT (TV). Color-100min. *(Made for TV)*. Michael Witney, Jan-Michael Vincent, Tony Franciosa, Catherine Burns .... (4)

CATERED AFFAIR, THE (1956) M-G-M. B&W-93min. Bette Davis, Ernest Borgnine 6½*
British title: WEDDING BREAKFAST, THE

CATHERINE OF RUSSIA (1962) NTA Pictures. Color-105min. *(German)*. Hildegarde Neff, Sergio Fantoni .... (3)

CATHERINE THE GREAT (1934) United Artists. B&W-92min. *(British)*. Elizabeth Bergner, Douglas Fairbanks, Jr. 4*

CATHOLICS (1973) CBS-TV. Color-75min. *(Made for TV)*. Trevor Howard, Martin Sheen 5½*

CATHY TIPPEL (1976) *see* KEETJE TIPPEL

CATLOW (1971) M-G-M. Color-103min. Yul Brynner, Richard Crenna 4½*

CATS, THE (1964) Nat'l Showmanship Films. B&W-93min. *(Swedish)*. Eva Dahlbeck, Isa Quensel .... (2)

CAT'S PLAY (1974) Hungarofilm. Color-109min. *(Hungarian)*. Margit Dayka, Elma Bulla, Margit Makay 1*
Original title: MACSKAJATEK

CATTLE DRIVE (1951) Universal. Color-77min. Joel McCrea, Dean Stockwell .... (4)

CATTLE EMPIRE (1958) 20th Century-Fox. Color-83min. Joel McCrea, Gloria Talbot 3½*

CATTLE KING (1963) M-G-M. Color-88min. Robert Taylor, Joan Caulfield, Robert Middleton .... (3)
Alternate title: GUNS OF WYOMING

CATTLE QUEEN OF MONTANA (1954) RKO. Color-88min. Barbara Stanwyck, Ronald Reagan 3½*

CATTLE TOWN (1952) Warner Bros. B&W-71min. Dennis Morgan, Philip Carey .... (3)

CAUGHT (1949) M-G-M. B&W-88min. James Mason, Barbara Bel Geddes 4*

CAUGHT IN THE ACT (1966) William Mishkin. Color-82min. Brigitte Evans, Steve Hollister .... (4)

CAUGHT IN THE DRAFT (1941) Paramount. B&W-82min. Bob Hope, Dorothy Lamour .... (5)

CAULDRON OF BLOOD (1968) Cannon Releasing. Color-101min. *(Spanish-U.S.)*. Boris Karloff, Viveca Lindfors 3*
Original title: COLECCIONISTA DE CADAVERES, EL *(The Collector of Cadavers, The Corpse Collector)*
Alternate title: BLIND MAN'S BLUFF
Publicity title: MORTE VIENE DEL BUIO, LA *(Death Comes from the Dark)*

CAUSE FOR ALARM (1951) M-G-M. B&W-74min. Loretta Young, Barry Sullivan .... (4)

CAVALCADE (1933) Fox Film Co. [20th]. B&W-109min. Clive Brook, Diana Wynyard 4*

CAVALCADE OF THE WEST (1934) Diversion. B&W-62min. Hoot Gibson 4*

CAVALIER IN DEVIL'S CASTLE (1962) Telewide Systems. Color-87min. *(Italian)*. Massimo Serato, Irene Tunc .... (3)

CAVALLERIA RUSTICANA (1952) Astor. Color-53min. *(Italian)*. Mario Del Monaco, Rina Telli .... (3)

CAVALRY COMMAND (1964) Paramount. Color-81min. *(U.S.-Philippine)*. John Agar, Richard Arlen 3*
Original Philippine title: CAVALLERIA COMMANDOS

CAVALRY SCOUT (1951) Monogram [Allied Artists]. Color-78min. Rod Cameron, Audrey Long 3*

CAVE IN, THE (1936) *see* DRAEGERMAN COURAGE

CAVE MAN (1940) *see* ONE MILLION B.C.

CAVE OF OUTLAWS (1951) Universal. Color-75min. Macdonald Carey, Alexis Smith, Edgar Buchanan .... (3)

CAVERN, THE (1965) 20th Century-Fox. B&W-83min. Rosanna Schiffino, John Saxon .... (2)

CEASE FIRE (1954) Paramount. B&W-75min. Capt. Roy Thompson, Jr., Cpl. Henry Goszkowski, Albert Bernard Cook .... (5)

CEILING ZERO (1935) Warner Bros. B&W-95min. James Cagney, Pat O'Brien .... (5)

CELEBRATION AT BIG SUR (1971) 20th Century-Fox. Color-82min. *(Documentary)*. *Director:* Baird Bryant .... (4)
Alternate title: CELEBRATION

CELL 2455, DEATH ROW (1955) Columbia. B&W-77min. William Campbell, Robert Campbell .... (4)

CENSORSHIP IN DENMARK (1969) Sherpix. Color-75min. *(Documentary)*. *Director:* Alex DeRenzy .... (3)
Original title: PORNOGRAPHY IN DENMARK: A NEW APPROACH

CENTENNIAL SUMMER (1946) 20th Century-Fox. Color-102min. Jeanne Crain, Cornel Wilde .... (4)

CENTURION, THE (1962) Producers International. Color-78min. *(Italian-French)*. Jacques Sernas, John Drew Barrymore .... (2)
Original Italian title: CONQUISTATORE DI CORINTO, IL *(The Conqueror of Corinth)*
Original French title: BATAILLE DE CORINTHE, LA *(The Battle of Corinth)*

CENTURY TURNS, THE (1971) MCA-TV. Color-100min. *(Made for TV)*. Richard Boone, Sharon Acker, Harry Morgan 5*
Alternate title: HEC

CEREMONY, THE (1963) United Artists. B&W-106min. *(U.S.-Spanish)*. Laurence Harvey, Sarah Miles .... (3)

CERTAIN SMILE, A (1958) 20th Century-Fox. Color-106min. Rossano Brazzi, Christine Carere 4*

CERVANTES (1968) *see* YOUNG REBEL

CÉSAR (1936) Pathé Contemporary. B&W-170min. Raimu, Pierre Fresnay .... (5)

CÉSAR AND ROSALIE (1972) Cinema 5. Color-110min. *(French-Italian-W. German)*. Yves Montand, Romy Schneider .... (4)
Original French title: CÉSAR ET ROSALIE

CET OBSCURE OBJET DU DESIR (1977) *see* THAT OBSCURE OBJECT OF DESIRE

CHAC (1974) Libra Films. Color-95min. *(Mexican)*. Native Cast 2½*

CHAD HANNA (1940) 20th Century-Fox. Color-86min. Henry Fonda, Dorothy Lamour 4*

CHADWICK FAMILY, THE (1974) MCA-TV. Color-74min. *(Made for TV)*. Fred MacMurray, Kathleen Maguire, Darleen Carr .... (4)

CHAFED ELBOWS (1967) Impact Films. B&W-63min. George Morgan, Elsie Downey .... (5)

CHAIN LIGHTNING (1950) Warner Bros. B&W-94min. Humphrey Bogart, Eleanor Parker 4*

CHAIN OF EVIDENCE (1957) Allied Artists. B&W-64min. Bill Elliott, James Lydon .... (3)

CHAINED (1934) M-G-M. B&W-71min. Joan Crawford, Clark Gable ..... (4)

CHAIRMAN, THE (1969) 20th Century-Fox. Color-102min. *(U.S.-British)*. Gregory Peck, Anne Heywood 4*
British title: MOST DANGEROUS MAN IN THE WORLD, THE

CHALK GARDEN, THE (1964) Universal. Color-106min. *(British)*. Deborah Kerr, Hayley Mills 6*

CHALLENGE, THE (1948) 20th Century-Fox. B&W-68min. Tom Conway, June Vincent .... (3)

CHALLENGE, THE (1960) *see* IT TAKES A THIEF

CHALLENGE, THE (1970) 20th Century-Fox. Color-74min. *(Made for TV)*. Darren McGavin, Mako, James Whitmore 4*
Alternate title: SURROGATE, THE

CHALLENGE . . . A TRIBUTE TO MODERN ART, THE (1974) New Line Cinema. Color-104min. *(Documentary)*. *Director:* Herbert Kline .. 4*

CHALLENGE FOR ROBIN HOOD, A (1967) 20th Century-Fox. Color-85min. *(British)*. Barrie Ingham, James Hayter .... (4)

CHALLENGE OF THE GLADIATOR (1964) American-International. Color-90min. *(Italian)*. Rock Stevens, Gloria Milland .... (3)

CHALLENGE TO BE FREE (1975) Pacific International Enterprises. Color-88min. Mike Mazurki, Jimmy Kane, John McIntire .... (4)

Films are rated on a 1 to 10 scale, 10 is highest. **Boldface** ratings followed by an asterisk (*) are for films actually seen and rated by the executive and senior editors. All other ratings are estimates. (See Notes on Entertainment Ratings in the front section.)

CHALLENGE TO LASSIE (1949) M-G-M. **Color-76min.** Lassie, Edmund Gwenn, Geraldine Brooks..(4)

CHALLENGERS, THE (1969) Universal. **Color-100min.** *(Made for TV).* Darren McGavin, Sean Garrison, Anne Baxter **3***

CHAMADE, LA (1968) Lopert [U.A.]. **Color-102min.** *(French).* Catherine Deneuve, Michel Piccoli.......................................(4)

CHAMBER OF HORRORS (1940) Monogram [Allied Artists]. **B&W-80min.** *(British).* Leslie Banks, Lilli Palmer ....(4)
Original title: DOOR WITH SEVEN LOCKS, THE

CHAMBER OF HORRORS (1966) Warner Bros. **Color-99min.** *(Telefeature).* Patrick O'Neal, Cesare Danova, Wilfrid Hyde-White.....**4***

CHAMP, THE (1931) M-G-M. **B&W-86min.** Wallace Beery, Jackie Cooper **4½***

CHAMP, THE (1979) U.A. (for M-G-M). **Color-121min.** Jon Voight, Faye Dunaway, Ricky Schroder.............................**5½***

CHAMP FOR A DAY (1953) Republic. **B&W-90min.** Alex Nicol, Audrey Totter...(4)

CHAMPAGNE FOR CAESAR (1950) Universal. **B&W-99min.** Ronald Colman, Vincent Price...................................**6½***

CHAMPAGNE MURDERS, THE (1967) Universal. **Color-98min.** *(French, English language).* Anthony Perkins, Yvonne Furneaux ......(3)

CHAMPAGNE WALTZ (1937) Paramount. **B&W-85min.** Gladys Swarthout, Fred MacMurray ....(4)

CHAMPION (1949) United Artists. **B&W-99min.** Kirk Douglas, Marilyn Maxwell **6***

CHANCE MEETING (1954) Pacemaker Pictures. **B&W-96min.** *(British).* Odile Versois, David Knight.........................(5)
Original title: YOUNG LOVERS, THE

CHANCE MEETING (1959) Paramount. **B&W-96min.** *(British).* Hardy Kruger, Stanley Baker ....(4)
Original title: BLIND DATE

CHANDLER (1971) M-G-M. **Color-88min.** Warren Oates, Leslie Caron...(3)

CHANDU THE MAGICIAN (1932) Fox Film Co. [20th]. **B&W-74min.** Edmund Lowe, Bela Lugosi.........................**2***

CHANG (1927) Paramount Famous Lasky. **B&W-87min.** *(Silent, Documentary). Director:* Merian C. Cooper ....(4)

CHANGE OF HABIT (1969) Universal. **Color-93min.** Elvis Presley, Mary Tyler Moore.......................................(3)

CHANGE OF HEART (1934) Fox Film Co. [20th]. **B&W-76min.** Janet Gaynor, Charles Farrell ....(4)

CHANGE OF HEART (1938) 20th Century-Fox. **B&W-66min.** Gloria Stuart, Michael Whalen ....(4)

CHANGE OF HEART (1943) see HIT PARADE OF 1943

CHANGE OF MIND (1969) Cinerama Releasing. **Color-96min.** Raymond St. Jacques, Susan Oliver **3***

CHANGE PARTNERS (1966) Governor. **B&W-61min.** *(British).* Zena Walker, Kenneth Cope..................................(3)

CHANGES (1969) Cinerama Releasing. **Color-93min.** Kent Lane, Michele Carey...(5)

CHAPMAN REPORT, THE (1963) Warner Bros. **Color-125min.** Efrem Zimbalist, Jr., Shelley Winters **4***

CHAPPAQUA (1967) Regional. **Color-92min.** Jean-Louis Barrault, Conrad Rooks...(5)

CHARADE (1952) **B&W-86min.** James Mason, Pamela Kellino................(3)

CHARADE (1963) Universal. **Color-114min.** Cary Grant, Audrey Hepburn...**6½***

CHARGE AT FEATHER RIVER, THE (1953) Warner Bros. **Color-96min.** Guy Madison, Frank Lovejoy **3***

CHARGE IS MURDER, THE (1963) see TWILIGHT OF HONOR

CHARGE OF THE BLACK LANCERS (1961) Paramount. **Color-97min.** *(Italian-French).* Giacomo Gentilomo, Yvonne Furneaux, Mel Ferrer (4)
Original Italian title: LANCIERI NERI, I

CHARGE OF THE LANCERS (1954) Columbia. **Color-74min.** Jean Pierre Aumont, Paulette Goddard ....(3)

CHARGE OF THE LIGHT BRIGADE, THE (1936) Warner Bros. **B&W-116min.** Errol Flynn, Olivia de Havilland **5***

CHARGE OF THE LIGHT BRIGADE, THE (1968) United Artists. **Color-128min.** David Hemmings, Trevor Howard **5***

CHARIOTS OF THE GODS? (1969) Sunn Classic. **Color-97min.** *(German, Documentary). Director:* Harald Reinl **5***
Original title: ERINNERUNGEN AN DIE ZUKUNFT *(Memories of the Future)*

CHARLES, DEAD OR ALIVE (1969) New Yorker Films. **B&W-93min.** *(Swiss-French).* Francois Simon, Marie-Claire Dufour......................(4)
Original title: CHARLES MORT OU VIE

CHARLESTON (1979) NBC-TV. **Color-98min.** *(Made for TV).* Delta Burke, Jordan Clarke, Mandy Patinkin.............................

CHARLEY AND THE ANGEL (1973) Buena Vista. **Color-93min.** Fred MacMurray, Cloris Leachman, Harry Morgan ....(4)

CHARLEY ONE-EYE (1973) Paramount. **Color-107min.** Richard Roundtree, Roy Thinnes, Nigel Davenport ....(4)

CHARLEY VARRICK (1973) Universal. **Color-111min.** Walter Matthau, Joe Don Baker **5½***

CHARLEY'S AUNT (1941) 20th Century-Fox. **B&W-81min.** Jack Benny, Kay Francis **4***
British title: CHARLEY'S AMERICAN AUNT

CHARLIE BUBBLES (1968) Universal. **Color-89min.** *(British).* Albert Finney, Colin Blakely **3***

CHARLIE CHAN AND THE SCARLET CLUE (1945) see SCARLET CLUE, THE

CHARLIE CHAN AT MONTE CARLO (1937) 20th Century-Fox. **B&W-71min.** Warner Oland, Keye Luke, Virginia Field..................(4)

CHARLIE CHAN AT THE CIRCUS (1936) 20th Century-Fox. **B&W-72min.** Warner Oland, Keye Luke, Francis Ford ....(4)

CHARLIE CHAN AT THE OLYMPICS (1937) 20th Century-Fox. **B&W-71min.** Warner Oland, Keye Luke, Katherine DeMille..................(4)

CHARLIE CHAN AT THE OPERA (1936) 20th Century-Fox. **B&W-66min.** Warner Oland, Boris Karloff ....(4)

CHARLIE CHAN AT THE RACE TRACK (1936) 20th Century-Fox. **B&W-70min.** Warner Oland, Keye Luke, Helen Wood..................(4)

CHARLIE CHAN AT THE WAX MUSEUM (1940) 20th Century-Fox. **B&W-63min.** Sidney Toler, Sen Yung, C. Henry Gordon ....(4)

CHARLIE CHAN AT TREASURE ISLAND (1939) 20th Century-Fox. **B&W-59min.** Sidney Toler, Cesar Romero ....(4)

CHARLIE CHAN CARRIES ON (1931) Fox Film Co. [20th]. **B&W-76min.** Warner Oland, John Garrick ....(4)

CHARLIE CHAN IN BLACK MAGIC (1944) see BLACK MAGIC

CHARLIE CHAN IN CITY IN DARKNESS (1939) 20th Century-Fox. **B&W-75min.** Sidney Toler, Lynn Bari ....(4)
Alternate title: CITY IN DARKNESS

CHARLIE CHAN: HAPPINESS IS A WARM CLUE (1971) MCA-TV. **Color-96min.** *(Made for TV).* Ross Martin, Rocky Gunn, Virginia Ann Lee...(3)
Alternate title: RETURN OF CHARLIE CHAN

CHARLIE CHAN IN EGYPT (1935) 20th Century-Fox. **B&W-65min.** Warner Oland, Pat Paterson, Rita Cansino (Hayworth).................(4)

CHARLIE CHAN IN HONOLULU (1938) 20th Century-Fox. **B&W-65min.** Sidney Toler, Phyllis Brooks.................................(4)

CHARLIE CHAN IN LONDON (1934) Fox Film Co. [20th]. **B&W-79min.** Warner Oland, Ray Milland ....(4)

CHARLIE CHAN IN MURDER OVER NEW YORK (1940) see MURDER OVER NEW YORK

CHARLIE CHAN IN PANAMA (1940) 20th Century-Fox. **B&W-67min.** Sidney Toler, Jean Rogers....................................**4***

CHARLIE CHAN IN PARIS (1935) 20th Century-Fox. **B&W-70min.** Warner Oland, Mary Brian...................................(4)

CHARLIE CHAN IN RENO (1939) 20th Century-Fox. **B&W-70min.** Sidney Toler, Ricardo Cortez...............................(4)

CHARLIE CHAN IN RIO (1941) 20th Century-Fox. **B&W-60min.** Sidney Toler, Mary Beth Hughes.............................(4)

CHARLIE CHAN IN SHANGHAI (1935) 20th Century-Fox. **B&W-70min.** Warner Oland, Irene Hervey..................................(4)

CHARLIE CHAN IN THE CHINESE CAT (1944) see CHINESE CAT, THE

CHARLIE CHAN IN THE JADE MASK (1945) see JADE MASK, THE

CHARLIE CHAN IN THE SECRET SERVICE (1944) Monogram [Allied Artists]. **B&W-63min.** Sidney Toler, Mantan Moreland..................(4)

CHARLIE CHAN IN THE SHANGHAI COBRA (1945) see SHANGHAI COBRA, THE

CHARLIE CHAN ON BROADWAY (1937) 20th Century-Fox. **B&W-68min.** Warner Oland, Keye Luke, Joan Marsh ....(4)

CHARLIE CHAN'S CHANCE (1932) Fox Film Co. [20th]. **B&W-73min.** Warner Oland, Linda Watkins.................................(4)

CHARLIE CHAN'S COURAGE (1934) Fox Film Co. [20th]. **B&W-72min.** Warner Oland, Donald Woods...................................(4)

CHARLIE CHAN'S GREATEST CASE (1933) Fox Film Co. [20th]. **B&W-71min.** Warner Oland, Heather Angel...................................(4)

CHARLIE CHAN'S MURDER CRUISE (1940) 20th Century-Fox. **B&W-75min.** Sidney Toler, Sen Yung, Marjorie Weaver .... (4)

CHARLIE CHAN'S SECRET (1936) 20th Century-Fox. **B&W-71min.** Warner Oland, Rosina Lawrence .... (4)

CHARLIE CHAPLIN CARNIVAL (1938) RKO. **B&W-84min.** *(Compilation).* Charlie Chaplin 4*

CHARLIE CHAPLIN CAVALCADE (1938) RKO. **B&W-81min.** *(Compilation).* Charlie Chaplin 4*

CHARLIE CHAPLIN FESTIVAL (1938) RKO. **B&W-82min.** *(Compilation).* Charlie Chaplin 3*

CHARLIE McCARTHY, DETECTIVE (1939) Universal. **B&W-77min.** Edgar Bergen, Robert Cummings .... (4)

CHARLIE, THE LONESOME COUGAR (1967) Buena Vista. **Color-75min.** Ron Brown, Brian Russell .... (5)

CHARLOTTE'S WEB (1973) Paramount. **Color-93min.** *(Cartoon).* Director: Charles Nichols 5*
Publicity title: E. B. WHITE'S CHARLOTTE'S WEB

CHARLY (1968) Cinerama Releasing. **Color-106min.** Cliff Robertson, Claire Bloom 6*

CHARRINGTON, V.C. (1954) *see* COURT MARTIAL

CHARRO! (1969) Nat'l General (for Cinema Center). **Color-98min.** Elvis Presley, Ina Balin 3*

CHARTER PILOT (1940) 20th Century-Fox. **B&W-70min.** Lloyd Nolan, Lynn Bari .... (3)

CHARTROOSE CABOOSE (1960) Universal. **Color-75min.** Molly Bee, Ben Cooper, Edgar Buchanan .... (3)

CHARULATA (1964) R. D. Bansal Productions. **B&W-112min.** *(Indian).* Madhabi Mukherjee, Sailen Mukherjee, Soumitra Chatterjee 2*
Alternate title: LONELY WIFE, THE

CHASE, THE (1946) United Artists. **B&W-86min.** Robert Cummings, Michele Morgan .... (3)

CHASE, THE (1966) Columbia. **Color-135min.** Marlon Brando, Jane Fonda 4½*

CHASE A CROOKED SHADOW (1958) Warner Bros. **B&W-87min.** *(British).* Richard Todd, Anne Baxter .... (4)

CHASE ME CHARLIE (1932) Citation. **B&W-61min.** *(Compilation).* Charlie Chaplin, Chester Conklin, Edna Purviance .... (4)

As **CHARLY** (1968), Cliff Robertson plays a formerly mentally retarded man who has undergone an experimental treatment resulting in an amazing expansion of his capabilities and interests, which now include Claire Bloom. The setting is Boston.

CHASTITY (1969) American-International. **Color-85min.** Cher (Bono), Barbara London .... (2)

CHATO'S LAND (1972) United Artists. **Color-110min.** Charles Bronson, Jack Palance 4*

CHATTER-BOX (1977) American-International. **Color-73min.** Candice Rialson, Larry Gelman .... (3)

CHATTERBOX (1943) Republic. **B&W-76min.** Judy Canova, Joe E. Brown .... (4)

CHE! (1969) 20th Century-Fox. **Color-96min.** Omar Sharif, Jack Palance 3*

CHE? (1972) *see* WHAT?

CHEAP DETECTIVE, THE (1978) Columbia. **Color-92min.** Peter Falk, Stockard Channing 5½*

CHEAPER BY THE DOZEN (1950) 20th Century-Fox. **Color-85min.** Clifton Webb, Jeanne Crain 5*

CHEAT, THE (1915) Famous Players-Lasky-Paramount. **B&W-42min.** *(Silent).* Fannie Ward, Jack Dean, Sessue Hayakawa 3*

CHEATERS, THE (1945) Republic. **B&W-87min.** Joseph Schildkraut, Eugene Pallette .... (5)
Alternate title: CASTAWAY, THE

CHEATERS, THE (1958) Continental [Walter Reade]. **B&W-120min.** *(French-Italian).* Jacques Charrier, Pascale Petit .... (3)
Original French title: TRICHEURS, LES
Italian title: PECCATORI IN BLUE-JEANS

CHECK AND DOUBLE CHECK (1930) RKO. **B&W-71min.** Freeman F. Gosden, Charles V. Correll .... (4)

CHECKERED FLAG OR CRASH (1977) Universal. **Color-98min.** Joe Don Baker, Susan Sarandon ....

CHECKPOINT (1956) J. Arthur Rank. **B&W-84min.** *(British).* Anthony Steel, Odile Versois, Stanley Baker .... (4)

CHEERLEADERS, THE (1973) Cinemation. **Color-84min.** Stephanie Fondue, Denise Dillaway .... (3)
British title: 18 YEAR OLD SCHOOLGIRLS, THE

CHEERS FOR MISS BISHOP (1941) United Artists. **B&W-95min.** Martha Scott, William Gargan 4*

CHELSEA GIRLS, THE (1966) Filmmakers. **B&W-210min.** Ondine, Ingrid Superstar, Edie Sedgwick, Mary Might .... (3)

CHEROKEE STRIP (1940) Paramount. **B&W-84min.** Richard Dix, Florence Rice .... (3)
British title: FIGHTING MARSHAL

CHERRY, HARRY AND RAQUEL (1969) Eve Releasing Corp. **Color-71min.** Linda Ashton, Charles Napier, Larissa Ely .... (2)

CHETNIKS! (1943) 20th Century-Fox. **B&W-73min.** Philip Dorn, Anna Sten .... (4)

CHEYENNE (1947) Warner Bros. **B&W-100min.** Dennis Morgan, Jane Wyman 4*
Alternate title: WYOMING KID, THE

CHEYENNE AUTUMN (1964) Warner Bros. **Color-156min.** Richard Widmark, Carroll Baker 5*

CHEYENNE SOCIAL CLUB, THE (1970) National General. **Color-103min.** James Stewart, Henry Fonda 4½*

CHICAGO CALLING (1952) United Artists. **B&W-74min.** Dan Duryea, Mary Anderson .... (3)

CHICAGO, CHICAGO (1969) *see* GAILY, GAILY

CHICAGO CONFIDENTIAL (1957) United Artists. **B&W-73min.** Brian Keith, Beverly Garland .... (4)

CHICAGO DEADLINE (1949) Paramount. **B&W-87min.** Alan Ladd, Donna Reed 4*

CHICAGO KID, THE (1945) Republic. **B&W-68min.** Don "Red" Barry, Otto Kruger .... (5)

CHICAGO MASQUERADE (1951) *see* LITTLE EGYPT

CHICAGO SYNDICATE (1955) Columbia. **B&W-83min.** Dennis O'Keefe, Abbe Lane .... (3)

CHICKEN CHRONICLES, THE (1977) Avco-Embassy. **Color-92min.** *(Canadian).* Steven Guttenberg, Phil Silvers 5½*

CHICKEN EVERY SUNDAY (1949) 20th Century-Fox. **B&W-91min.** Dan Dailey, Celeste Holm .... (5)

CHIEF CRAZY HORSE (1955) Universal. **Color-86min.** Victor Mature, Suzan Ball .... (4)
British title: VALLEY OF FURY

CHIEN ANDALOU, UN (1929) *see* ANDALUSIAN DOG, THE

CHILD AND THE KILLER (1959) Lopert [U.A.]. **B&W-64min.** *(British).* Pat Driscoll, Robert Arden .... (3)

CHILD IN THE HOUSE (1956) Eros Films *(Brit.)*. B&W-88min. *(British)*. Eric Portman, Mandy Miller...(5)

CHILD IS BORN, A (1940) Warner Bros. B&W-79min. Nanette Fabray, Gladys George, Gloria Holden ....(5)

CHILD IS WAITING, A (1963) United Artists. B&W-102min. Burt Lancaster, Judy Garland......................................4½*

CHILD OF MANHATTAN (1933) Columbia. B&W-71min. Nancy Carroll, John Boles ....

CHILD UNDER A LEAF (1974) Cinema National Corp. Color-90min. Dyan Cannon, Donald Pilon, Joseph Campanella............................3*
British title: LOVE CHILD

CHILDISH THINGS (1967) *see* TALE OF THE COCK

CHILDREN OF PARADISE (1945) Tricolore. B&W-188min. *(French)*. Arletty, Jean-Louis Barrault 4*
Original title: ENFANTS DU PARADIS, LES

CHILDREN OF RAGE (1975) Coliseum Films Ltd. Color-106min. *(Palestinian-Israeli-British)*. Helmunt Griem, Olga Georges-Picot, Simon Ward..(4)

CHILDREN OF SANCHEZ, THE (1978) Lone Star International. Color-126min. *(U.S.-Mexican)*. Anthony Quinn, Lupita Ferrer.......................4*

CHILDREN OF THE DAMNED (1964) M-G-M. B&W-90min. *(British)*. Ian Hendry, Alan Badel...4*

CHILDREN OF THE LOTUS EATERS (1970) *see* PSYCHIATRIST: GOD BLESS THE CHILDREN, THE

CHILDREN OF THEATRE STREET, THE (1977) Peppercorn-Wormser. Color-90min. *(Documentary)*. Director: Robert Dornhelm...............

CHILDREN SHOULDN'T PLAY WITH DEAD THINGS (1972) Geneni Film Co. Color-101min. Alan Ormsby, Valerie Mamches.................2*

CHILDREN'S HOUR, THE (1962) United Artists. B&W-107min. Audrey Hepburn, Shirley MacLaine 6*
British title: LOUDEST WHISPER, THE

CHILD'S PLAY (1957) Distributors Corp. of America. B&W-68min. *(British)*. Peter Martyn, Mona Washbourne ....(3)

CHILD'S PLAY (1972) Paramount. Color-100min. James Mason, Robert Preston ....(5)

CHILL FACTOR, THE (1973) *see* COLD NIGHT'S DEATH, A

CHILLY SCENES OF WINTER (1980) United Artists. Color- min. John Heard, Mary Beth Hurt...

CHILTERN HUNDREDS, THE (1949) *see* AMAZING MR. BEECHAM, THE

CHIMES AT MIDNIGHT (1966) *see* FALSTAFF

CHINA (1943) Paramount. B&W-79min. Alan Ladd, Loretta Young ......(3)

CHINA! (1965) Janus Films. Color-65min. *(British, Travelog)*. Producer: Felix Greene..(6)

CHINA CARAVAN (1942) *see* YANK ON THE BURMA ROAD, THE

CHINA CLIPPER (1936) First National [W.B.]. B&W-85min. Pat O'Brien, Beverly Roberts...4*

CHINA CORSAIR (1951) Columbia. B&W-67min. Jon Hall, Lisa Ferraday ....(2)

CHINA DOLL (1958) United Artists. B&W-88min. Victor Mature, Lili Hua..(3)

CHINA GATE (1957) 20th Century-Fox. B&W-97min. Gene Barry, Angie Dickinson 3*

CHINA GIRL (1942) 20th Century-Fox. B&W-95min. Gene Tierney, George Montgomery......................................(4)

CHINA IS NEAR (1967) Royal Films Int'l [Columbia]. B&W-108min. *(Italian)*. Glauco Mauri, Elda Tattoli ....(5)
Original title: CINA E VICINA, LA

CHINA SEAS (1935) M-G-M. B&W-90min. Clark Gable, Jean Harlow 4½*

CHINA SKY (1945) RKO. B&W-78min. Ellen Drew, Ruth Warrick, Randolph Scott...(3)

CHINA SYNDROME (1979) Columbia. Color-122min. Jack Lemmon, Jane Fonda..5½*

CHINA VENTURE (1953) Columbia. B&W-83min. Edmond O'Brien, Barry Sullivan ....(3)

CHINA'S LITTLE DEVILS (1945) Monogram [Allied Artists]. B&W-74min. Paul Kelly, Harry Carey ....(3)

CHINATOWN (1974) Paramount. Color-130min. Jack Nicholson, Faye Dunaway 6½*

CHINATOWN AT MIDNIGHT (1949) Columbia. B&W-67min. Hurd Hatfield, Jean Willes...(4)

CHINATOWN NIGHTS (1929) Paramount. B&W-83min. Wallace Beery, Florence Vidor, Warner Oland.................................4*

CHINESE ADVENTURE (1949) *see* BOSTON BLACKIE'S CHINESE VENTURE

CHINESE CAT, THE (1944) Monogram [Allied Artists]. B&W-65min. Sidney Toler, Joan Woodbury....................................(4)
Alternate title: CHARLIE CHAN IN THE CHINESE CAT

CHINESE RING, THE (1947) Monogram [Allied Artists]. B&W-67min. Roland Winters, Louis Currie...................................(4)

CHINESE ROULETTE (1976) New Yorker Films. Color-96min. *(German)*. Margit Carstensen, Anna Karina...............................
Original title: CHINESISCHES ROULETT

CHINMOKU (1971) Toho. Color-126min. *(Japanese)*. Shima Iwashita, Eiji Okada ....
Translation title: Silence

CHINO (1973) Intercontinental Films. Color-93min. *(Ital.-Span.-Fren., Eng. version)*. Charles Bronson, Jill Ireland 4*
British title: VALDEZ, THE HALFBREED

CHINOISE, LA (1967) Leacock-Pennebaker. Color-95min. *(French)*. Anne Wiazemsky, Jean-Pierre Léaud...............................(4)
Translation title: The Chinese Girl

CHIP OFF THE OLD BLOCK (1944) Universal. B&W-82min. Donald O'Connor, Peggy Ryan...(4)

CHISUM (1970) Warner Bros. Color-111min. John Wayne, Forrest Tucker..4*

CHITTY CHITTY, BANG BANG (1968) United Artists. Color-156min. *(British)*. Dick Van Dyke, Sally Ann Howes........................4*

CHLOE IN THE AFTERNOON (1972) Columbia. Color-97min. *(French)*. Bernard Verly, Zouzou...(4)

CHOCOLATE SOLDIER, THE (1941) M-G-M. B&W-102min. Nelson Eddy, Rise Stevens..(4)

CHOICE OF WEAPONS, A (1976) *see* DIRTY KNIGHTS' WORK

CHOIRBOYS, THE (1977) Universal. Color-119min. Charles Durning, Perry King, Louis Gossett, Jr...........................4*

C.H.O.M.P.S. (1979) American-International. Color-90min. Valerie Bertinelli, Wesley Eure..

CHOOSE YOUR PARTNER (1940) *see* TWO GIRLS ON BROADWAY

CHOPPERS, THE (1962) Fairway International. B&W-70min. Arch Hall, Jr., Marianne Gaba ....(3)

CHOSEN SURVIVORS (1974) Columbia. Color-99min. *(U.S.-Mexican)*. Jackie Cooper, Alex Cord, Richard Jaeckel, Bradford Dillman ....

CHRISTA (1971) *see* SWEDISH FLY GIRLS

CHRISTIAN LICORICE STORE, THE (1971) Nat'l General (for Cinema Center). Color-90min. Beau Bridges, Maud Adams, Gilbert Roland .....(3)

CHRISTIAN THE LION (1976) Scotia American. Color-89min. *(British)*. Bill Travers, Virginia McKenna, George Adamson............................

CHRISTINE (1959) Color-100min. *(French)*. Romy Schneider, Alain Delon, Micheline Presle...(4)

CHRISTINE JORGENSEN STORY, THE (1970) United Artists. Color-89min. John Hansen, Quinn Redeker....................................(3)

CHRISTMAS CAROL, A (1938) M-G-M. B&W-69min. Reginald Owen, Gene Lockhart...5*

CHRISTMAS CAROL, A (1951) United Artists. B&W-86min. *(British)*. Alastair Sim, Mervyn Johns......................................5*
Original title: SCROOGE

CHRISTMAS EVE (1947) United Artists. B&W-90min. George Raft, Ann Harding..(2)
Alternate title: SINNER'S HOLIDAY

CHRISTMAS HOLIDAY (1944) Universal. B&W-92min. Gene Kelly, Deanna Durbin..(5)

CHRISTMAS IN CONNECTICUT (1945) Warner Bros. B&W-101min. Barbara Stanwyck, Dennis Morgan................................4½*
British title: INDISCRETION

CICADA IS NOT AN INSECT, THE (1963) *see* GAMES MEN PLAY, THE

CHRISTMAS IN JULY (1940) Paramount. B&W-70min. Dick Powell, Ellen Drew..6*

CHRISTMAS KID, THE (1966) Producers Releasing Org. Color-90min. *(U.S.-Spanish)*. Jeffrey Hunter, Louis Hayward ....(3)
Original Spanish title: JOE NAVIDAD

CHRISTMAS THAT ALMOST WASN'T, THE (1966) Childhood Productions. Color-95min. *(Italian-U.S.)*. Rossano Brazzi, Alberto Rabagliati, Paul Tripp...(3)
Italian title: NATALE CHE QUASI NON FU, IL

CHRISTMAS TREE, THE (1969) Continental [Walter Reade]. Color-110min. *(French-Italian, English version)*. William Holden, Brook Fuller 4*
Original title: ARBE DE NOEL, L'

CHRISTOPHER COLUMBUS (1949) Universal. **Color-104min.** *(British).* Fredric March, Florence Eldridge **4***

CHRISTOPHER STRONG (1933) RKO. **B&W-77min.** Katharine Hepburn, Colin Clive **4***

CHROME AND HOT LEATHER (1971) American-International. **Color-91min.** William Smith, Tony Young ...... (3)

CHRONICLE OF ANNA MAGDALENA BACH (1968) New Yorker Films. **B&W-93min.** *(Italian-W. German).* Christiane Lang, Gustav Leonhardt ...... (4)
Original Italian title: CRONACA DI ANNA MAGDALENA BACH
Original W. German title: CHRONIK DER ANNA MAGDALENA BACH

CHUBASCO (1968) Warner Bros. **Color-100min.** Christopher Jones, Susan Strasberg, Richard Egan ...... (3)

CHUKA (1967) Paramount. **Color-105min.** Rod Taylor, Ernest Borgnine ...... (4)

CHUMP AT OXFORD, A (1940) United Artists. **B&W-63min.** Stan Laurel, Oliver Hardy ...... (4)

CHUSHINGURA (1962) Toho. **Color-180min.** *(Japanese).* Koushiro Matsumoto, Yuzo Kayama ...... (5)
Alternate title: 47 RONIN
Alternate title: 47 SAMURAI
Alternate title: LOYAL 47 RONIN, THE
Alternate title: FAITHFUL 47, THE

CID, EL (1961) *see* EL CID

CIGARETTES, WHISKEY AND WILD WOMEN (1958) **B&W-90min.** *(French).* Nadine Tillier, Annie Cordy ...... (3)
Original title: CIGARETTES, WHISKY ET P'TITES PÉPÉES

CIMARRON (1931) RKO. **B&W-130min.** Richard Dix, Irene Dunne **5½***

CIMARRON (1960) M-G-M. **Color-147min.** Glenn Ford, Maria Schell..... (4)

CIMARRON KID, THE (1952) Universal. **Color-84min.** Audie Murphy, Yvette Dugay ...... (3)

CINCINNATI KID, THE (1965) M-G-M. **Color-113min.** Steve McQueen, Edward G. Robinson **5***

CINDERELLA (1949) RKO (for Disney). **Color-74min.** *(Cartoon).* Director: Wilfred Jackson ...... (6)

CINDERELLA (1961) Janus Films. **Color-84min.** *(U.S.S.R.).* Raisa Struchkova, Gennadiy Ledyakh ...... (5)
Original title: KHRUSTALNYY BASHMACHOK

CINDERELLA - ITALIAN STYLE (1966) *see* MORE THAN A MIRACLE

CINDERELLA JONES (1946) Warner Bros. **B&W-92min.** Joan Leslie, Robert Alda ...... (3)

CINDERELLA LIBERTY (1973) 20th Century-Fox. **Color-117min.** James Caan, Marsha Mason **6***

CINDERFELLA (1960) Paramount. **Color-91min.** Jerry Lewis, Ed Wynn ...... (4)

CINERAMA'S RUSSIAN ADVENTURE (1966) United Roadshow. **Color-140min.** *(U.S.S.R./U.S., Travelog).* Director: Leonid Kristi ...... (4)
Alternate title: RUSSIAN ADVENTURE

CIRCLE, THE (1957) Kassler Films. **B&W-84min.** *(British).* John Mills, Noelle Middleton ...... (5)
Original title: VICIOUS CIRCLE, THE

CIRCLE OF CHILDREN, A (1977) CBS-TV. **Color-100min.** *(Made for TV).* Jane Alexander, Rachel Roberts ...... (3)

CIRCLE OF DANGER (1951) Eagle Lion. **B&W-86min.** *(British).* Ray Milland, Marius Goring, Patricia Roc ...... (4)

CIRCLE OF DEATH (1960) **B&W-79min.** *(Mexican).* Sarita Montiel, Raul Ramirez ...... (3)

CIRCLE OF DECEPTION (1960) 20th Century-Fox. **B&W-100min.** *(British).* Bradford Dillman, Suzy Parker **4***

CIRCLE OF IRON (1978) New World. **Color-102min.** Jeff Cooper, David Carradine **4½***

CIRCLE OF LOVE (1964) Columbia. **Color-105min.** *(French).* Jean-Claude Brialy, Jane Fonda, Maurice Ronet ...... (3)
Original title: RONDE, LA *(The Round)*

CIRCULAR TRIANGLE, THE (1964) Paramount. **B&W-112min.** *(W. German-French-Italian).* Lilli Palmer, Sylva Koscina ...... (3)
Original German title: UNMORALISCHEN, DIE
French title: GRAIN DE SABLE, LE
Italian title: TRIANGOLO CIRCOLARE, IL

CIRCUMSTANTIAL EVIDENCE (1945) 20th Century-Fox. **B&W-68min.** Michael O'Shea, Lloyd Nolan ...... (3)

CIRCUMSTANTIAL EVIDENCE (1952) Phil Brandon, **B&W-61min.** *(British).* Rona Anderson, Patrick Holt ...... (3)

CIRCUS, THE (1928) United Artists. **B&W-71min.** *(Silent).* Charlie Chaplin, Merna Kennedy **5½***

CIRCUS CLOWN (1934) First National [W.B.]. **B&W-63min.** Joe E. Brown, Patricia Ellis ...... (3)

CIRCUS OF FEAR (1967) *see* PSYCHO-CIRCUS

CIRCUS OF HORRORS (1960) American-International. **Color-89min.** *(British).* Anton Diffring, Yvonne Monlaur **3½***

CIRCUS OF LOVE (1954) Distributors Corp. of America. **Color-93min.** *(German).* Eva Bartok, Curt Jurgens ...... (3)

CIRCUS STARS (1958) Paramount. **Color-61min.** *(U.S.S.R., Documentary).* Director: L. Kristy ...... (5)

CIRCUS WORLD (1964) Paramount. **Color-135min.** John Wayne, Claudia Cardinale **5***
British title: MAGNIFICENT SHOWMAN, THE

CISCO KID AND THE LADY, THE (1939) 20th Century-Fox. **B&W-73min.** Cesar Romero, Marjorie Weaver ...... (4)

CISCO PIKE (1971) Columbia. **Color-94min.** Kris Kristofferson, Karen Black **3***

CITADEL, THE (1938) M-G-M. **B&W-110min.** Robert Donat, Rosalind Russell **5***

CITADEL OF CRIME (1941) *see* MAN BETRAYED, A

CITIZEN KANE (1941) RKO. **B&W-119min.** Orson Welles, Joseph Cotten **6***

CITIZEN REBELS, THE (1974) Cineriz. **Color-98min.** *(Italian).* Franco Nero, Giancarlo Prete ...... (4)
Original title: CITTADINO SI RIBELLA, IL

CITIZEN'S BAND (1977) Paramount. **Color-98min.** Paul Le Mat, Candy Clark **5½***
Alternate title: HANDLE WITH CARE

CITTA APERTA (1945) *see* OPEN CITY

CITY, THE (1939) Civic Films. **B&W-32min.** *(Documentary).* Director: Ralph Steiner **5***

CITY, THE (1971) Universal. **Color-100min.** *(Made for TV).* Anthony Quinn, E. G. Marshall, Robert Reed **3***

CITY ACROSS THE RIVER (1949) Universal. **B&W-90min.** Stephen McNally, Thelma Ritter ...... (4)

CITY AFTER MIDNIGHT (1957) RKO. **B&W-84min.** *(British).* Phyllis Kirk, Dan O'Herlihy, Wilfrid Hyde-White ...... (3)
Original title: THAT WOMAN OPPOSITE

CITY BENEATH THE SEA (1953) Universal. **Color-87min.** Robert Ryan, Mala Powers, Anthony Quinn **4***

CITY BENEATH THE SEA (1971) 20th Century-Fox. **Color-100min.** *(Made for TV).* Robert Wagner, Stuart Whitman, Rosemary Forsyth **4***
British title: ONE HOUR TO DOOMSDAY

CITY FOR CONQUEST (1940) Warner Bros. **B&W-101min.** James Cagney, Ann Sheridan **5½***

CITY IN DARKNESS (1939) *see* CHARLIE CHAN IN CITY IN DARKNESS

CITY IN TERROR (1939) *see* MAN WHO DARED, THE

CITY IS DARK, THE (1954) *see* CRIME WAVE

CITY JUNGLE, THE (1959) *see* YOUNG PHILADELPHIANS, THE

CITY LIGHTS (1931) United Artists. **B&W-87min.** *(Silent).* Charlie Chaplin, Virginia Cherrill **6***

CITY OF BAD MEN (1953) 20th Century-Fox. **Color-82min.** Dale Robertson, Jeanne Crain ...... (4)

CITY OF FEAR (1959) Columbia. **B&W-81min.** Vince Edwards, John Archer ...... (3)

CITY OF FEAR (1965) Allied Artists. **B&W-75min.** *(British).* Paul Maxwell, Terry Moore **3***

CITY OF GOLD (1957) Nat'l Film Board of Canada. **B&W-23min.** *(Canadian, Documentary).* Director: Colin Low **5***

CITY OF SHADOWS (1955) Republic. **B&W-70min.** Victor McLaglen, Kathleen Crowley ...... (3)

CITY OF THE DEAD, THE (1960) *see* HORROR HOTEL

CITY ON A HUNT (1953) *see* NO ESCAPE

CITY STANDS TRIAL, THE (1954) I.F.E. Releasing Corp. **B&W-95min.** *(Italian).* Amedeo Nazzari, Paolo Stoppa, Franco Interlenghi ...... (4)

CITY STREETS (1931) Paramount. **B&W-82min.** Gary Cooper, Sylvia Sidney ...... (4)

CITY THAT NEVER SLEEPS, THE (1953) Republic. **B&W-90min.** Gig Young, Mala Powers ...... (4)

CITY UNDER THE SEA, THE (1965) *see* WAR GODS OF THE DEEP

CIVILIZATION (1916) Triangle. **B&W-121min.** *(Silent).* J. Barney Sherry, Enid Markey ...... (4)

Films are rated on a 1 to 10 scale, 10 is highest. **Boldface** ratings followed by an asterisk (*) are for films actually seen and rated by the executive and senior editors. All other ratings are estimates. (See Notes on Entertainment Ratings in the front section.)

CITY LIGHTS (1931). Blind flower girl Virginia Cherrill is grateful for the many kindnesses shown her by hobo Charlie Chaplin.

CLAIRE'S KNEE (1971) Columbia. **Color-103min.** *(French).* Jean-Claude Brialy, Laurence De Monaghan 3*
Original title: GENOU DE CLAIRE, LE

CLAMBAKE (1967) United Artists. **Color-99min.** Elvis Presley, Shelley Fabares.................................. 3*

CLANCY STREET BOYS (1943) Monogram [Allied Artists]. **B&W-66min.** The East Side Kids, Noah Beery, Jr. .... (3)

CLANSMAN, THE (1915) *see* BIRTH OF A NATION, THE

CLANSMAN, THE (1974) *see* KLANSMAN, THE

CLARENCE, THE CROSS-EYED LION (1965) M-G-M. **Color-98min.** Marshall Thompson, Betsy Drake .... (4)

CLASH BY NIGHT (1952) RKO. **B&W-105min.** Barbara Stanwick, Paul Douglas, Robert Ryan, Marilyn Monroe 4*

CLASH BY NIGHT (1964) *see* ESCAPE BY NIGHT

CLASH OF STEEL (1962) Screen Gems. **Color-79min.** *(French).* Gerard Barray, Giana Maria Canale.................. (3)

CLASS OF MISS MacMICHAEL, THE (1978) Brut Productions. **Color-90min.** *(British).* Glenda Jackson, Oliver Reed, Michael Murphy 4½*

CLASS OF '44 (1973) Warner Bros. **Color-95min.** Gary Grimes, Deborah Winters.................. 4*

CLASS OF '63 (1973) MPC (TV). **Color-75min.** *(Made for TV).* James Brolin, Joan Hackett.................. 5*

CLASS OF '74 (1972) General Film Corp. **Color-82min.** Pat Woodell, Marki Bey.................. (2)
British title: GIRLS MOST LIKELY TO, THE

CLAUDELLE INGLISH (1961) Warner Bros. **B&W-99min.** Diane McBain, Arthur Kennedy.................. (3)
Alternate title: YOUNG AND EAGER

CLAUDIA (1943) 20th Century-Fox. **B&W-91min.** Dorothy McGuire, Robert Young.................. 4*

CLAUDIA AND DAVID (1946) 20th Century-Fox. **B&W-78min.** Dorothy McGuire, Robert Young.................. 4*

CLAUDINE (1974) 20th Century-Fox. **Color-92min.** Diahann Carroll, James Earl Jones.................. 4½*

CLAW MONSTERS, THE (1955) Republic. **B&W-100min.** *(Re-edited Serial).* Phyllis Coates, Myron Healy.................. (3)
Original title: PANTHER GIRL OF THE KONGO

CLAY PIGEON, THE (1949) RKO. **B&W-63min.** Bill Williams, Barbara Hale.................. (3)

CLAY PIGEON (1971) M-G-M. **Color-96min.** Tom Stern, Telly Savalas, Robert Vaughn.................. (2)
British title: TRIP TO KILL

CLEAR AND PRESENT DANGER, A (1970) Universal. **Color-100min.** *(Made for TV).* Hal Holbrook, E. G. Marshall, Jack Albertson .... (4)

CLEO FROM 5 TO 7 (1961) Zenith International. **B&W-90min.** *(French-Italian).* Corinne Marchand, Antoine Bourseiller 3*
Original title: CLÉO DE CINQ A SEPT

CLEOPATRA (1934) Paramount. **B&W-101min.** Claudette Colbert, Warren William 3*

CLEOPATRA (1963) 20th Century-Fox. **Color-243min.** Elizabeth Taylor, Richard Burton 4*

CLEOPATRA JONES (1973) Warner Bros. **Color-89min.** Tamara Dobson, Shelley Winters 3*

CLEOPATRA JONES AND THE CASINO OF GOLD (1975) Warner Bros. **Color-94min.** Tamara Dobson, Stella Stevens.................. (3)

CLEOPATRA'S DAUGHTER (1961) Medallion. **Color-102min.** *(French-Italian).* Debra Paget, Ettore Manni, Erno Crisa.................. (3)
Original French title: VALLÉE DES PHARONS, LA *(The Valley of the Pharaoes)*
Original Italian title: SEPOLCRO DEI RE, IL *(The Tomb of the Kings)*
Alternate title: DAUGHTER OF CLEOPATRA

CLIMATS (1962) J. Arthur Rank. **B&W-100min.** *(French).* Marina Vlady, Michel Piccoli .... (4)

CLIMAX, THE (1944) Universal. **Color-86min.** Boris Karloff, Susanna Foster 4½*

CLIMAX, THE (1967) Lopert [U.A.]. **B&W-97min.** *(Italian-French).* Ugo Tognazzi, Stefania Sandrelli 4*
Original title: IMMORALE, L' *(The Immoralist)*

CLIMB AN ANGRY MOUNTAIN (1972) Warner Bros. **Color-97min.** *(Made for TV).* Fess Parker, Arthur Hunnicutt, Marj Dusay .... (4)

CLIMBERS, THE (1964) Paramount. **Color-85min.** Edmond O'Brien, Richard Basehart.................. (2)

CLIMBING HIGH (1939) Gaumont-British [Rank]. **B&W-79min.** *(British).* Jessie Matthews, Michael Redgrave.................. (4)

CLIPPED WINGS (1953) Allied Artists. **B&W-65min.** The Bowery Boys, June Vincent..................

CLIVE OF INDIA (1935) United Artists. **B&W-90min.** Ronald Colman, Loretta Young 4½*

CLOAK AND DAGGER (1946) Warner Bros. **B&W-106min.** Gary Cooper, Lilli Palmer.................. 3*

CLOAK WITHOUT DAGGER (1957) *see* OPERATION CONSPIRACY

CLOCK, THE (1945) M-G-M. **B&W-90min.** Judy Garland, Robert Walker 4*
British title: UNDER THE CLOCK

CLOCKMAKER OF ST. PAUL, THE (1973) Joseph Green. **Color-105min.** *(French).* Philippe Noiret, Jean Rochefort 4½*
Original title: HORLOGER DE ST. PAUL, L'
British title: WATCHMAKER OF SAINT-PAUL, THE

CLOCKWORK ORANGE, A (1971) Warner Bros. **Color-137min.** *(British).* Malcolm McDowell, Patrick Magee 7*

CLONES, THE (1973) Filmmakers International. **Color-93min.** Michael Greene, Gregory Sierra, Otis Young .... (3)

CLOPORTES (1965) International Classics [20th]. **B&W-102min.** *(French-Italian).* Lino Ventura, Charles Aznavour, Irina Demick.................. (5)
Original Italian title: SOTTO IL TALLONE
Original French title: MÉTAMORPHOSE DES CLOPORTES, LA *(The Metamorphosis of the Cloportes)*

CLOSE CALL FOR BOSTON BLACKIE, A (1946) Columbia. **B&W-60min.** Chester Morris, Lynn Merrick.................. (3)
British title: LADY OF MYSTERY

CLOSE CALL FOR ELLERY QUEEN, A (1942) Columbia. **B&W-67min.** William Gargan, Margaret Lindsay.................. (3)
British title: CLOSE CALL, A

CLOSE ENCOUNTERS OF THE THIRD KIND (1977) Columbia. **Color-135min.** Richard Dreyfuss, Francois Truffaut 7½*

CLOSE TO MY HEART (1951) Warner Bros. **B&W-90min.** Ray Milland, Gene Tierney.................. (4)

CLOSE-UP (1948) Eagle Lion. **B&W-76min.** Alan Baxter, Virginia Gilmore .... (4)

CLOSELY WATCHED TRAINS (1966) Sigma III. **B&W-89min.** *(Czech).* Vaclav Neckar, Jitka Bendova.................. 4*
Original title: OSTRE SLEDOVANE VLAKY
Publicity title: DIFFICULT LOVE, A

CLOUDBURST (1951) United Artists. **Color-92min.** *(British).* Robert Preston, Elizabeth Sellars .... (4)

CLOUDBURST, THE (1967) *see* WINGS OF FIRE

CLOUDED YELLOW, THE (1950) Columbia. **B&W-96min.** *(British).* Jean Simmons, Trevor Howard .... (5)

CLOUDS OVER EUROPE (1939) Columbia. **B&W-82min.** *(British).* Laurence Olivier, Valerie Hobson 4*
Original title: Q PLANES

CLOUDS OVER ISRAEL (1962) Hemisphere. **B&W-85min.** *(Israeli).* Yiftah Spector, Ehud Banai .... (5)
Original title: SINAIA

CLOWN, THE (1953) M-G-M. **B&W-92min.** Red Skelton, Tim Considine .... (4)

CLOWN, THE (1976) Constantin Film. **Color-120min.** *(German).* Helmut Griem, Hanna Schygulla, Gustav Rudolf Sellner .... (4)
Original title: ANSICHTEN EINES CLOWNS *(Views of a Clown)*

CLOWN AND THE KID, THE (1961) United Artists. **B&W-65min.** John Lupton, Mike McGreevey .... (3)

CLOWNS, THE (1971) Levitt-Pickman. **Color-90min.** *(Italian-French-German, Documentary). Director:* Federico Fellini 3*

CLUB HAVANA (1945) Producers Rel. Corp. [Eagle Lion]. **B&W-62min.** Tom Neal, Margaret Lindsay .... (3)

CLUE OF THE NEW PIN, THE (1960) Anglo Amalgamated [EMI]. **B&W-60min.** *(British).* Paul Daneman, Bernard Archard .... (4)

CLUE OF THE SILVER KEY, THE (1961) Anglo Amalgamated [EMI]. **B&W-59min.** *(British).* Bernard Lee, Finlay Currie .... (4)

CLUE OF THE TWISTED CANDLE, THE (1960) Schoenfeld Film Distributing. **B&W-61min.** *(British).* Bernard Lee, David Knight .... (3)

CLUNY BROWN (1946) 20th Century-Fox. **B&W-100min.** Jennifer Jones, Charles Boyer 5½*

C'MON, LET'S LIVE A LITTLE (1967) Paramount. **Color-85min.** Bobby Vee, Jackie DeShannon, Eddie Hodges .... (2)

COACH (1978) Crown International. **Color-100min.** Cathy Lee Crosby, Michael Biehn, Keenan Wynn 5*

COAL MINER'S DAUGHTER (1980) Universal. **Color- min.** Sissy Spacek, Tommy Jee Jones ....

COAST OF SKELETONS (1965) Seven Arts [W.B.]. **Color-90min.** *(British).* Richard Todd, Dale Robertson, Marianne Koch .... (3)

COBRA, THE (1967) American-International. **Color-93min.** *(Italian-Spanish).* Peter Martell, Jesus Puente, Dana Andrews .... (3)
Original Italian title: COBRA, IL
Original Spanish title: COBRA, EL

COBRA STRIKES, THE (1948) Eagle Lion. **B&W-62min.** Sheila Ryan, Leslie Brooks .... (3)

COBRA WOMAN (1944) Universal. **Color-70min.** Maria Montez, Sabu, Jon Hall .... (3)

COBWEB, THE (1955) M-G-M. **Color-124min.** Richard Widmark, Lauren Bacall 4½*

COCAINE FIENDS, THE (1937) New Line Cinema. **B&W-65min.** .... (3)

COCK-EYED WORLD, THE (1929) Fox Film Co. [20th]. **B&W-115min.** Victor McLaglen, Edmund Lowe .... (4)

COCKEYED COWBOYS OF CALICO COUNTY, THE (1970) Universal. **Color-99min.** Dan Blocker, Nanette Fabray, Jack Cassidy 4*

COCKEYED MIRACLE, THE (1946) M-G-M. **B&W-81min.** Frank Morgan, Keenan Wynn .... (4)
British title: MR. GRIGGS RETURNS

COCKFIGHTER (1975) *see* BORN TO KILL

COCKLESHELL HEROES, THE (1955) Columbia. **B&W-98min.** *(British).* José Ferrer, Trevor Howard 4½*

COCOANUT GROVE (1938) Paramount. **B&W-85min.** Fred MacMurray, Harriet Hilliard (Nelson) .... (3)

COCOANUTS, THE (1929) Paramount. **B&W-96min.** Groucho Marx, Harpo Marx 3*

CODE NAME: DIAMOND HEAD (1977) Quinn Martin Productions. **Color-74min.** *(Made for TV).* Roy Thinnes, France Nuyen .... (4)

CODE NAME: TIGER (1964) Four Star. **B&W-80min.** *(French).* Roger Hanin, Maria Hauban .... (3)

CODE NAME: TRIXIE (1973) *see* CRAZIES, THE

CODE OF SCOTLAND YARD (1947) Republic. **B&W-60min.** *(British).* Oscar Homolka, Muriela Pavlow .... (3)
Original title: HOUSE AT SLY CORNER, THE

CODE OF SILENCE (1958) Sterling World Distributors. **B&W-78min.** Terry Becker, Elisa Loti .... (3)
British title: KILLER'S CAGE

CODE 7, VICTIM 5 (1965) Columbia. **Color-88min.** Lex Barker, Ronald Fraser, Ann Smyrner .... (3)
Original title: VICTIM FIVE

CODE 645 (1947) Republic. **B&W-100min.** *(Re-edited Serial).* Clayton Moore, Ramsay Ames .... (3)
Original title: G-MEN NEVER FORGET

CODE TWO (1953) M-G-M. **B&W-69min.** Ralph Meeker, Robert Horton, Jeff Richards .... (3)

COFFEE, TEA OR ME? (1973) CBS-TV. **Color-74min.** *(Made for TV).* Karen Valentine, John Davidson, Michael Anderson, Jr. 4*

COFFIN, THE (1971) *see* FROM EAR TO EAR

COFFIN FROM HONG KONG, A (1964) UCC Films. **Color-93min.** *(German).* Heinz Drache, Rolf Walter .... (3)

COFFY (1973) American-International. **Color-91min.** Pam Grier, Booker Bradshaw .... (3)

COLD NIGHT'S DEATH, A (1973) Official Films. **Color-73min.** *(Made for TV).* Robert Culp, Eli Wallach, Michael C. Gwynne .... (5)
Alternate title: CHILL FACTOR, THE

COLD SUN, THE (1953) Official Industries. **B&W-78min.** *(Telefeature).* Richard Crane, Sally Mansfield .... (2)

COLD TURKEY (1971) United Artists. **Color-102min.** Dick Van Dyke, Pippa Scott 5*

COLD WIND IN AUGUST, A (1961) Lopert [U.A.]. **B&W-80min.** Lola Albright, Scott Marlowe .... (4)

COLDITZ STORY, THE (1954) Republic. **B&W-97min.** *(British).* John Mills, Eric Portman .... (5)

COLE YOUNGER, GUNFIGHTER (1958) Allied Artists. **Color-78min.** Frank Lovejoy, Abby Dalton .... (3)

COLLECTIONEUSE, LA (1967) Pathé Contemporary. **Color-88min.** *(French).* Patrick Bauchau, Haydee Politoff .... (3)
Translation title: The Collector

COLLECTOR, THE (1965) Columbia. **Color-119min.** Terence Stamp, Samantha Eggar 7*

COLLECTOR, THE (1967) *see* COLLECTIONEUSE, LA

COLLEEN (1936) Warner Bros. **B&W-89min.** Ruby Keeler, Dick Powell (4)

COLLEGE (1927) United Artists. **B&W-75min.** *(Silent).* Buster Keaton, Anne Cornwall 5½*

COLLEGE COACH (1933) Warner Bros. **B&W-75min.** Pat O'Brien, Dick Powell, Ann Dvorak .... (4)
British title: FOOTBALL COACH

COLLEGE CONFIDENTIAL (1960) Universal. **B&W-91min.** Steve Allen, Mamie Van Doren, Jayne Meadows .... (3)

COLLEGE DAYS (1925) *see* FRESHMAN, THE

COLLEGE HOLIDAY (1936) Paramount. **B&W-88min.** Jack Benny, George Burns .... (4)

COLLEGE HUMOR (1933) Paramount. **B&W-80min.** Bing Crosby, George Burns, Gracie Allen .... (5)

COLLEGE SWING (1938) Paramount. **B&W-86min.** Martha Raye, Bob Hope, George Burns, Gracie Allen .... (4)
British title: SWING, TEACHER, SWING

COLLISION COURSE (1968) *see* BAMBOO SAUCER, THE

COLONEL BLIMP (1943) *see* LIFE AND DEATH OF COLONEL BLIMP, THE

COLONEL EFFINGHAM'S RAID (1945) 20th Century-Fox. **B&W-70min.** Joan Bennett, Charles Coburn 4½*
British title: MAN OF THE HOUR

COLONEL WOLODYJOWSKI (1968) Film Polski. **Color-160min.** *(Polish).* Tadeusz Lomnicki, Magda Zawaska .... (5)
Original title: PAN WOLODYJOWSKI

COLOR ME DEAD (1969) Commonwealth United. **Color-97min.** *(Australian).* Tom Tryon, Carolyn Jones, Tony Ward 3*

COLOR OF HER SKIN, THE (1959) *see* NIGHT OF THE QUARTER MOON

COLORADO TERRITORY (1949) Warner Bros. **B&W-94min.** Joel McCrea, Virginia Mayo .... (4)

COLOSSUS AND THE AMAZON QUEEN (1960) American-International. **Color-96min.** *(Italian).* Fianna Maria Canale, Ed Fury, Rod Taylor .... (1)
Original title: REGINA DELLE AMAZZONI, LA *(The Queen of the Amazons)*
Alternate title: COLOSSUS AND THE AMAZONS

COLOSSUS AND THE HEADHUNTERS (1962) American-International. **Color-79min.** *(Italian).* Kirk Morris, Laura Brown .... (1)
Original title: MACISTE CONTRO I CACCIATORI DI TESTE *(Maciste Against the Headhunters)*

Films are rated on a 1 to 10 scale, 10 is highest. **Boldface** ratings followed by an asterisk (*) are for films actually seen and rated by the executive and senior editors. All other ratings are estimates. (See Notes on Entertainment Ratings in the front section.)

COLOSSUS AND THE HUNS (1960) American-International. Color-90min. *(Italian)*. Jerome Courtland, Lisa Gastoni .... (3)

COLOSSUS OF NEW YORK, THE (1958) Paramount. B&W-70min. John Baragrey, Charles Herbert, Mala Powers 4*

COLOSSUS OF RHODES, THE (1960) M-G-M. Color-129min. *(Italian-French-Spanish)*. Rory Calhoun, Lea Massari, Conrado San Martin .... (3)
Original Italian title: COLOSSO DI RODA, IL
Original French title: COLOSSE DE RHODES, LE
Original Spanish title: COLOSO DE RODAS, EL

COLOSSUS OF THE ARENA (1960) American-International. Color-99min. *(Italian)*. Mark Forest, Scilla Gabel .... (3)
Alternate title: DEATH IN THE ARENA
Original title: MACISTE, IL GLADIATORE PIU FORTE DEL MONDO *(Maciste, the Strongest Gladiator in the World)*

COLOSSUS, THE FORBIN PROJECT (1970) Universal. Color-100min. Eric Braeden, Susan Clark 5*
Alternate title: FORBIN PROJECT, THE

COLT .45 (1950) Warner Bros. **Color-74min.** Randolph Scott, Ruth Roman .... (4)
Alternate title: THUNDERCLOUD

COLUMBUS OF SEX (1971) *see* MY SECRET LIFE

COLUMN SOUTH (1953) Universal. **Color-85min.** Audie Murphy, Joan Evans .... (3)

COMA (1978) U.A. (for M-G-M). **Color-113min.** Genevieve Bujold, Michael Douglas 6*

COMANCHE (1956) United Artists. **Color-87min.** Dana Andrews, Linda Cristal 3*

COMANCHE STATION (1960) Columbia. **Color-74min.** Randolph Scott, Nancy Gates .... (4)

COMANCHE TERRITORY (1950) Universal. **Color-76min.** Maureen O'Hara, Macdonald Carey .... (3)

COMANCHEROS, THE (1961) 20th Century-Fox. **Color-107min.** John Wayne, Stuart Whitman 5*

COMBAT SQUAD (1953) Columbia. B&W-72min. John Ireland, Hal March .... (3)

COME AND GET IT (1936) United Artists. B&W-99min. Edward Arnold, Joel McCrea 6*
Alternate title: ROARING TIMBER

COME BACK, AFRICA (1959) Lionel Rogosin. B&W-95min. *(Documentary)*. *Director:* Lionel Rogosin .... (5)

COME BACK CHARLESTON BLUE (1972) Warner Bros. Color-100min. Godfrey Cambridge, Raymond St. Jacques .... (4)

COME BACK, LITTLE SHEBA (1952) Paramount. B&W-99min. Burt Lancaster, Shirley Booth 5*

COME BACK TO ME (1945) *see* DOLL FACE

COME BLOW YOUR HORN (1963) Paramount. **Color-112min.** Frank Sinatra, Tony Bill 3*

COME AND GET IT (1936). Walter Brennan (convincingly portraying a Swede) and lumber boss Edward Arnold both take a strong fancy to gambling hall hostess Frances Farmer.

COME DANCE WITH ME (1959) Kingsley International. **Color-91min.** *(French-Italian)*. Brigitte Bardot, Henri Vidal .... (4)
Original title: VOULEZ-VOUS DANSER AVEC MOI?

COME FILL THE CUP (1951) Warner Bros. B&W-113min. James Cagney, Phyllis Thaxter 4½*

COME FLY WITH ME (1963) M-G-M. **Color-109min.** *(British)*. Dolores Hart, Hugh O'Brian 4*

COME LIVE WITH ME (1941) M-G-M. B&W-86min. Hedy Lamarr, James Stewart .... (3)

COME NEXT SPRING (1956) Republic. **Color-92min.** Ann Sheridan, Steve Cochran .... (5)

COME-ON, THE (1956) Allied Artists. B&W-83min. Anne Baxter, Sterling Hayden .... (3)

COME OUT FIGHTING (1945) Monogram [Allied Artists]. B&W-62min. The East Side Kids, June Carlson ....

COME PLAY WITH ME (1968) *see* GRAZIE, ZIA

COME SEPTEMBER (1961) Universal. **Color-112min.** Rock Hudson, Gina Lollobrigida 5*

COME SPY WITH ME (1967) 20th Century-Fox. **Color-85min.** Troy Donahue, Andrea Dromm, Albert Dekker .... (2)
Alternate title: AGENT 36-24-36
Alternate title: RED OVER RED

COME TO THE STABLE (1949) 20th Century-Fox. B&W-94min. Loretta Young, Celeste Holm 4*

COMEDIANS, THE (1967) M-G-M. **Color-160min.** *(U.S.-Bermudan-French)*. Richard Burton, Elizabeth Taylor 4*
French title: COMÉDIENS, LES

COMEDY MAN, THE (1964) Continental [Walter Reade]. B&W-82min. *(British)*. Kenneth More, Cecil Parker .... (5)

COMEDY OF TERRORS, THE (1964) American-International. **Color-88min.** Vincent Price, Peter Lorre .... (4)
Alternate title: GRAVESIDE STORY, THE

COMES A HORSEMAN (1978) United Artists. **Color-118min.** Jane Fonda, James Caan 4*

COMETOGETHER (1971) Allied Artists. **Color-90min.** *(U.S.-Italian)*. Tony Anthony, Luciana Paluzzi .... (3)

COMIC, THE (1969) Columbia. **Color-94min.** Dick Van Dyke, Michele Lee 5*

COMIN' ROUND THE MOUNTAIN (1940) Paramount. B&W-63min. Bob Burns, Una Merkel .... (3)

COMIN' ROUND THE MOUNTAIN (1951) Paramount. B&W-107min. Bud Abbott, Lou Costello, Dorothy Shay 3*

COMING APART (1969) Kaleidoscope. B&W-110min. Rip Torn, Sally Kirkland, Viveca Lindfors .... (3)

COMING HOME (1978) United Artists. **Color-126min.** Jane Fonda, Jon Voight, Bruce Dern 4½*

COMING OUT PARTY (1934) Fox Film Co. [20th]. B&W-79min. Frances Dee, Gene Raymond .... (3)

COMING OUT PARTY, A (1961) Union Films. B&W-98min. *(British)*. James Robertson Justice, Leslie Phillips 4*
Original title: VERY IMPORTANT PERSON

COMMAND, THE (1954) Warner Bros. **Color-88min.** Guy Madison, Joan Weldon .... (4)

COMMAND DECISION (1948) M-G-M. B&W-112min. Clark Gable, Walter Pidgeon 4½*

COMMANDO (1962) American-International. B&W-95min. *(Italian-Belgian-Spanish-W. German)*. Stewart Granger, Dorian Gray 3*
Original Italian title: MARCIA O CREPA *(March or Die)*
British title: LEGION'S LAST PATROL, THE
Original German title: MARSCHIER ODER KREPIER
Original Spanish title: MARCHA O MUERE
Original Belgian title: HÉROS SANS RETOUR

COMMANDOS STRIKE AT DAWN (1943) Columbia. B&W-98min. Paul Muni, Anna Lee 4*

COMMITMENT, THE (1976) Commitment Co. **Color-88min.** Richard Grand, Barbara Graham .... (3)

COMMITTEE, THE (1969) Commonwealth United. **Color-90min.** Peter Bonerz, Barbara Bosson .... (5)
Alternate title: SESSION WITH THE COMMITTEE, A

COMMUNION (1977) *see* ALICE, SWEET ALICE

COMPANERO (1975) New Yorker Films. **Color-60min.** *(British, Documentary)*. *Director:* Martin Smith .... (4)

COMPANEROS (1972) Cinerama Releasing. **Color-107min.** Jack Palance, Franco Nero ....

COMPANIONS IN NIGHTMARE (1968) Universal. Color-100min. (Made for TV). Melvyn Douglas, Anne Baxter, Gig Young 5*

COMPANY OF COWARDS? (1964) see ADVANCE TO THE REAR

COMPANY OF KILLERS (1971) Universal. Color-84min. Van Johnson, Ray Milland, John Saxon 3*
Alternate title: PROTECTORS, THE

COMPANY SHE KEEPS, THE (1951) RKO. B&W-81min. Lizabeth Scott, Jane Greer, Dennis O'Keefe ....(4)

COMPULSION (1959) 20th Century-Fox. B&W-103min. Orson Welles, Dean Stockwell, Bradford Dillman 6*

COMPUTER KILLERS (1973) Hallmark. Color-91min. (British). Michael Gough, Robin Askwith 2*
Original title: HORROR HOSPITAL

COMPUTER WORE TENNIS SHOES, THE (1970) Buena Vista. Color-90min. Kurt Russell, Cesar Romero 4*

COMRADE X (1940) M-G-M. B&W-90min. Clark Gable, Hedy Lamarr .. 5*

CONCEALMENT (1934) see SECRET BRIDE, THE

CONCERT FOR BANGLADESH, THE (1972) 20th Century-Fox. Color-100min. (Documentary). Director: Saul Swimmer .... (5)

CONCERT OF INTRIGUE (1954) Howco International. B&W-93min. (Italian). Brigitte Bardot, Pierre Cressoy .... (3)
Original title: TRADITA (Treachery)
Alternate title: NIGHT OF LOVE

CONCERTO (1946) see I'VE ALWAYS LOVED YOU

CONCORDE - AIRPORT '79, THE (1979) Universal. Color-123min. Alain Delon, Susan Blakely ....

CONCRETE JUNGLE, THE (1960) Fanfare. B&W-86min. (British). Stanley Baker, Margit Saad ....(3)
Original title: CRIMINAL, THE

CONDEMNED (1929) United Artists. B&W-86min. Ronald Colman, Ann Harding, Dudley Digges................ 4*

CONDEMNED OF ALTONA, THE (1963) 20th Century-Fox. B&W-114min. (Italian-French, English language). Fredric March, Sophia Loren 4½*
Original title: SEQUESTRATI DI ALTONA, I

CONDEMNED WOMEN (1938) RKO. B&W-77min. Louis Hayward, Ann Shirley ....

CONDUCT UNBECOMING (1975) Allied Artists. Color-104min. (British). Michael York, Richard Attenborough.............. 5½*

CONE OF SILENCE (1960) see TROUBLE IN THE SKY

CONEY ISLAND (1943) 20th Century-Fox. Color-96min. Betty Grable, George Montgomery.............. (5)

CONFESS, DR. CORDA (1958) President Films. B&W-101min. (German). Hardy Kruger, Elisabeth Mueller.............. (3)
Original title: GESTEHEN SIE DR. CORDA!

CONFESSION (1937) Warner Bros. B&W-86min. Kay Francis, Basil Rathbone.............. (4)

CONFESSION (1955) see DEADLIEST SIN, THE

CONFESSION (1957) Screen Gems. B&W-74min. (Telefeature). Dennis O'Keefe, June Lockhart 4½*
Alternate title: GRAFT AND CORRUPTION

CONFESSION, THE (1970) Paramount. Color-142min. (French). Yves Montand, Simone Signoret 5½*
Original title: AVEU, L'

CONFESSIONS (1942) see CONFESSIONS OF BOSTON BLACKIE

CONFESSIONS FROM A HOLIDAY CAMP (1977) Columbia. Color-88min. (British). Robin Askwith, Anthony Booth ....

CONFESSIONS OF A COUNTERSPY (1960) see MAN ON A STRING

CONFESSIONS OF A NAZI SPY (1939) Warner Bros. B&W-102min. Edward G. Robinson, Francis Lederer 4*

CONFESSIONS OF A POP PERFORMER (1975) Columbia. Color-91min. (British). Robin Askwith, Anthony Booth .... (3)

CONFESSIONS OF A WINDOW CLEANER (1974) Columbia. Color-90min. (British). Robin Askwith, Anthony Booth.............. (3)

CONFESSIONS OF AN OPIUM EATER (1962) Allied Artists. B&W-85min. Vincent Price, Linda Ho.............. (2)
Alternate title: EVILS OF CHINATOWN

CONFESSIONS OF BOSTON BLACKIE (1941) Columbia. B&W-65min. Chester Morris, Harriet Hilliard (Nelson).............. (3)
British title: CONFESSIONS

CONFESSIONS OF FELIX KRULL (1958) Distributors Corp. of America. B&W-107min. (German). Henry Bookholt (Horst Buchholz), Lisa (Liselotte) Pulver .... (5)
Original title: BEKENNTNISSE DES HOCHSTAPLERS FELIX KRULL, DIE

CONFIDENCE GIRL (1952) United Artists. B&W-81min. Hillary Brooke, Tom Conway ....(3)

CONFIDENTIAL AGENT (1945) Warner Bros. B&W-118min. Charles Boyer, Lauren Bacall..............4½*

CONFIDENTIAL REPORT (1955) see MR. ARKADIN

CONFIDENTIALLY CONNIE (1953) M-G-M. B&W-74min. Van Johnson, Janet Leigh..............(4)

CONFIRM OR DENY (1941) 20th Century-Fox. B&W-73min. Don Ameche, Joan Bennett ....(4)

CONFLICT (1945) Warner Bros. B&W-86min. Humphrey Bogart, Alexis Smith..............4*

CONFLICT OF WINGS (1954) United Artists. Color-84min. (British). Kieron Moore, John Gregson ....(4)
Alternate title: FUSS OVER FEATHERS

CONFORMIST, THE (1971) Paramount. Color-116min. (Italian-French-German). Jean-Louis Trintignant, Stefania Sandrelli 4½*
Original title: CONFORMISTA, IL

CONFRONTATION, THE (1968) Color-86min. (Hungarian). Lajos Balazsovits, Andrea Drahota ....(3)
Original title: FÉNYES SZELEK

CONGA SWING (1941) see BLONDIE GOES LATIN

CONGO CROSSING (1956) Universal. Color-87min. George Nader, Virginia Mayo, Peter Lorre 4*

CONGO MAISIE (1940) M-G-M. B&W-70min. Ann Sothern, John Carroll ....(3)

CONGRATULATIONS, IT'S A BOY! (1971) Paramount. Color-73min. (Made for TV). Bill Bixby, Diane Baxter, Jack Albertson..............4*

CONJUGAL BED, THE (1963) Avco-Embassy. B&W-90min. (Italian-French). Ugo Tognazzi, Marina Vlady..............(5)
Original Italian title: STORIA MODERNA: L'APE REGINA, UNA (A Modern Story: The Queen Bee)

CONNECTICUT YANKEE, A (1931) Fox Film Co. [20th]. B&W-91min. Will Rogers, William Farnum ....
British title: YANKEE AT KING ARTHUR'S COURT, THE

CONNECTICUT YANKEE IN KING ARTHUR'S COURT, A (1949) Paramount. Color-107min. Bing Crosby, William Bendix..............5*
British title: YANKEE IN KING ARTHUR'S COURT, A

CONNECTION, THE (1962) Films Around The World. B&W-103min. Warren Finnerty, William Redfield ....(4)

CONNECTION (1973) MPC (TV). Color-75min. (Made for TV). Charles Durning, Ronnie Cox..............3*

CONQUERED CITY (1962) American-International. B&W-91min. (Italian). David Niven, Ben Gazzara, Michael Craig 3*
Original title: CITTA PRIGIONIERA, LA (The Imprisoned City)

CONQUEROR, THE (1956) RKO. Color-111min. John Wayne, Susan Hayward..............(5)

CONQUEROR OF ATLANTIS (1963) ABC Films. Color-93min. (Italian-Egyptian). Kirk Morris, Luciana Gilli ....(1)
Original Italian title: CONQUISTATORE DELL'ATLANTIDA, IL
British title: KINGDOM IN THE SAND

CONQUEROR OF MARACAIBO (1960) Telewide Systems. Color-101min. (Italian-Spanish). Hans Barsody, Brigit Corey ....(3)
Original Italian title: CONQUISTATORE DI MARACAIBO, IL

CONQUEROR OF THE DESERT (1958) Four Star. Color-110min. (Italian). Pedro Armendariz, Anna-Maria Sandri ....(3)

CONQUEROR OF THE ORIENT (1962) Avco-Embassy. Color-86min. (Italian). Gianna Maria Canale, Rik Battaglia ....(3)

CONQUEROR WORM, THE (1968) American-International. Color-87min. (British-U.S.). Vincent Price, Ian Ogilvy..............4*
British title: WITCHFINDER GENERAL

CONQUEST (1937) M-G-M. B&W-112min. Greta Garbo, Charles Boyer 4*
British title: MARIE WALEWSKA

CONQUEST OF COCHISE (1953) Columbia. Color-70min. John Hodiak, Robert Stack..............3*

CONQUEST OF EVEREST, THE (1954) United Artists. Color-78min. (British, Documentary). Producer: John Taylor 5½*

CONQUEST OF MYCENE (1963) Avco-Embassy. Color-102min. (Italian-French). Gordon Scott, Rosalba Neri, Alessandra Panaro..............(3)
Original Italian title: ERCOLE CONTRO MOLOCK (Hercules Against Moloch)
Original French title: HERCULE CONTRE MOLOCH

CONQUEST OF SPACE (1955) Paramount. Color-80min. Walter Brooke, Eric Fleming 3*

CONQUEST OF THE AIR (1940) United Artists. B&W-71min. (British, Documentary). Director: Zoltan Korda ....(3)

Films are rated on a 1 to 10 scale, 10 is highest. **Boldface** ratings followed by an asterisk (*) are for films actually seen and rated by the executive and senior editors. All other ratings are estimates. (See Notes on Entertainment Ratings in the front section.)

CONQUEST OF THE PLANET OF THE APES (1972) 20th Century-Fox. Color-86min. Roddy McDowall, Don Murray......................4*

CONRACK (1974) 20th Century-Fox. Color-107min. Jon Voight, Paul Winfield......................5½*

CONSPIRACY OF HEARTS (1960) Paramount. B&W-111min. *(British)*. Lilli Palmer, Sylvia Syms......................(5)
Alternate title: ITALY 1943

CONSPIRACY OF THE BORGIAS (1965) Screen Gems. Color-93min. *(Italian)*. Frank Latimore, Constance Smith......................(3)

CONSPIRATOR (1949) M-G-M. B&W-87min. *(British)*. Robert Taylor, Elizabeth Taylor......................4*

CONSPIRATORS, THE (1944) Warner Bros. B&W-101min. Hedy Lamarr, Paul Henreid, Peter Lorre, Sydney Greenstreet......................3*

CONSTANT HUSBAND, THE (1955) Showcorporation. Color-84min. *(British)*. Rex Harrison, Margaret Leighton......................5*

CONSTANT NYMPH, THE (1943) Warner Bros. B&W-112min. Charles Boyer, Joan Fontaine......................(5)

CONSTANTINE AND THE CROSS (1961) Avco-Embassy. Color-120min. *(Italian)*. Cornel Wilde, Christine Kaufmann......................(3)
Primary Italian title: COSTANTINO IL GRANDE *(Constantine the Great)*
Alternate Italian title: COSTANTINO IL GRANDE - IN HOC SIGNO VINCES

CONTACT MAN, THE (1949) *see* ALIAS NICK BEAL

CONTEMPT (1963) Avco-Embassy. Color-103min. *(French-Italian)*. Brigitte Bardot, Jack Palance, Michel Piccoli, Fritz Lang......................3*
Original French title: MÉPRIS, LE
Original Italian title: DISPREZZO, IL

CONTEST GIRL (1954) Continental [Walter Reade]. Color-82min. *(British)*. Janette Scott, Ian Hendry......................(4)
Original title: BEAUTY JUNGLE, THE

CONTRABAND (1940) Anglo-American. B&W-91min. *(British)*. Conrad Veidt, Valerie Hobson......................
Alternate title: BLACKOUT

CONTRABAND SPAIN (1955) Stratford Pictures. B&W-81min. *(British)*. Richard Greene, Anouk Aimee......................(4)

CONVERSATION, THE (1974) Paramount. Color-113min. Gene Hackman, John Cazale......................3½*

CONVERSATION PIECE (1975) New Line Cinema. Color-122min. *(Italian-French)*. Burt Lancaster, Silvana Mangano, Helmut Berger....
Original Italian title: GRUPPO DI FAMIGLIA IN UN INTERNO

CONVICTED (1950) Columbia. B&W-91min. Glenn Ford, Broderick Crawford......................3½*

CONVICTS FOUR (1962) Allied Artists. B&W-105min. Ben Gazzara, Stuart Whitman......................(5)
Original title: REPRIEVE

CONVOY (1978) United Artists. Color-110min. Kris Kristofferson, Ali MacGraw, Burt Young......................5*

COOGAN'S BLUFF (1968) Universal. Color-94min. Clint Eastwood, Lee J. Cobb......................4*

COOL AND THE CRAZY, THE (1958) American-International. B&W-78min. Scott Marlowe, Gigi Perreau......................(2)

COOL BREEZE (1972) M-G-M. Color-101min. Thalmus Rasulala, Judy Pace......................(2)

COOL HAND LUKE (1967) Warner Bros. Color-129min. Paul Newman, George Kennedy......................5½*

COOL MILLION (1972) MCA-TV. Color-100min. *(Made for TV)*. James Farentino, Christine Belford, Patrick O'Neal......................4*
Alternate title: MASK OF MARCELLA

COOL ONES, THE (1967) Warner Bros. Color-95min. Roddy McDowall, Debbie Watson......................(2)

COOL WORLD, THE (1964) Cinema 5. B&W-105min. Hampton Clanton, Yolanda Rodriguez......................(5)

COOLEY HIGH (1975) American-International. Color-107min. Glynn Turman, Lawrence-Hilton Jacobs......................3*

COONSKIN (1975) Bryanston. Color-82min. *(Part-animated)*. Barry White, Charles Gordone......................(5)
Alternate title: BUSTIN' OUT

COP, THE (1970) Audubon. Color-100min. *(French-Italian)*. Michel Bouquet, Francoise Fabian......................(5)
Original French title: CONDE, UN *(A Cop)*
Alternate title: MURDER GO ROUND
Prerelease American title: PRISON, THE
Prerelease American title: CONFESSIONS OF A BLOOD COP

COP HATER (1958) United Artists. B&W-75min. Robert Loggia, Gerald O'Loughlin......................(3)

COP-OUT (1967) Cinerama Releasing. Color-95min. *(British)*. James Mason, Geraldine Chaplin......................(3)
British title: STRANGER IN THE HOUSE

COPACABANA (1947) United Artists. B&W-92min. Groucho Marx, Carmen Miranda......................(3)

COPPER CANYON (1950) Paramount. Color-83min. Ray Milland, Hedy Lamarr......................4*

COPPER SKY (1957) 20th Century-Fox. B&W-77min. Jeff Morrow, Coleen Gray......................(2)

COPS AND ROBBERS (1973) United Artists. Color-89min. Cliff Gorman, Joe Bologna......................5½*

CORKY (1973) M-G-M. Color-88min. Robert Blake, Charlotte Rampling 3*
Alternate title: GOING ALL OUT
Alternate title: LOOKIN' GOOD

CORKY (1979) United Artists. Color-   min. Joseph Cortese, Talia Shire

CORN IS GREEN, THE (1945) Warner Bros. B&W-114min. Bette Davis, John Dall......................5*

CORNBREAD, EARL AND ME (1975) American-International. Color-94min. Keith (Jamall) Wilkes, Tierre Turner......................4*

CORNERED (1945) RKO. B&W-102min. Dick Powell, Walter Slezak......4*

CORONER CREEK (1948) Columbia. Color-93min. Randolph Scott, Marguerite Chapman......................(4)

CORPORAL DOLAN GOES A.W.O.L. (1951) *see* RENDEZVOUS WITH ANNIE

CORPSE CAME C.O.D., THE (1947) Columbia. B&W-87min. Joan Blondell, George Brent......................(3)

CORPSE VANISHED, THE (1943) *see* REVENGE OF THE ZOMBIES

CORPSE VANISHES, THE (1942) Monogram [Allied Artists]. B&W-64min. Bela Lugosi, Luana Walters......................(3)
British title: CASE OF THE MISSING BRIDES, THE

CORREGIDOR (1943) Producers Rel. Corp. [Eagle Lion]. B&W-73min. Otto Kruger, Elissa Landi......................(3)

CORRIDOR OF MIRRORS (1948) Universal. B&W-96min. *(British)*. Eric Portman, Edna Romney......................(5)

CORRIDORS OF BLOOD (1962) M-G-M. B&W-85min. *(British)*. Boris Karloff, Betta St. John......................(3)

CORRUPT ONES, THE (1966) Warner Bros. Color-92min. *(German-French-Italian, English language)*. Robert Stack, Elke Sommer......(3)
Original title: HOELLE VON MACAO, DIE
Alternate title: PEKING MEDALLION, THE

CORRUPTION (1968) Columbia. Color-91min. *(British)*. Peter Cushing, Sue Lloyd......................(2)

CORSICAN BROTHERS, THE (1941) United Artists. B&W-112min. Douglas Fairbanks, Jr.......................4*

CORSICAN BROTHERS, THE (1961) NTA Pictures. Color-85min. *(French-Italian)*. Geoffrey Horne, Jean Servais......................(3)
Original French title: FRERES CORSES, LES

CORVETTE K-225 (1943) Universal. B&W-99min. Randolph Scott, Ella Raines......................3*
British title: NELSON TOUCH, THE

CORVETTE SUMMER (1978) U.A. (for M-G-M). Color-105min. Mark Hamill, Annie Potts......................5½*

COSMIC MAN, THE (1959) Allied Artists. B&W-72min. John Carradine, Bruce Bennett......................(2)

COSMIC MONSTER, THE (1958) Warner Bros. B&W-75min. *(British)*. Forrest Tucker, Gaby André......................(3)
Original title: STRANGE WORLD OF PLANET X, THE
Publicity title: CREATURES FROM ANOTHER WORLD
Publicity title: COSMIC MONSTERS

COSSACKS, THE (1959) Universal. Color-113min. *(Italian-French)*. Edmund Purdom, John Drew Barrymore......................2*
Original Italian title: COSACCHI, I

COTTAGE TO LET (1941) J. Arthur Rank. B&W-90min. *(British)*. Leslie Banks, Alastair Sim, John Mills......................
Alternate title: BOMBSIGHT STOLEN

COTTER (1973) Gold Key Entertainment. Color-94min. *(Made for TV)*. Don Murray, Carol Lynley, Rip Torn......................(4)

COTTON COMES TO HARLEM (1970) United Artists. Color-97min. Godfrey Cambridge, Raymond St. Jacques......................4*

COUCH, THE (1962) Warner Bros. B&W-100min. Grant Williams, Shirley Knight......................(3)

COUGAR COUNTRY (1970) American National Enterprises. Color-106min. *(Documentary)*.......................(5)

COUNSELLOR-AT-LAW (1933) Universal. B&W-78min. *(British)*. John Barrymore, Bebe Daniels......................5*

Films are rated on a 1 to 10 scale, 10 is highest. **Boldface** ratings followed by an asterisk (*) are for films actually seen and rated by the executive and senior editors. All other ratings are estimates. (See Notes on Entertainment Ratings in the front section.)

COUNT DRACULA (1970) Crystal Pictures. **Color-99min.** *(Spanish-Italian-W. German-British).* Christopher Lee, Herbert Lom **2***
Original Spanish title: CONDE DRACULA, EL

COUNT DRACULA (1978) PBS. **Color-180min.** *(British, Made for TV).* Louis Jourdan, Frank Finlay.................... **5½***

COUNT DRACULA AND HIS VAMPIRE BRIDE (1974) *see* SATANIC RITES OF DRACULA, THE

COUNT DRACULA'S GREAT LOVE (1972) *see* DRACULA'S GREAT LOVE

COUNT FIVE AND DIE (1958) 20th Century-Fox. **B&W-92min.** *(British).* Jeffrey Hunter, Nigel Patrick .... (4)

COUNT FRANKENHAUSEN (1962) *see* BLOODY VAMPIRE, THE

COUNT OF BRAGELONNE, THE (1954) *see* LAST MUSKETEER, THE

COUNT OF MONTE CRISTO, THE (1934) United Artists. **B&W-113min.** Robert Donat, Elissa Landi **5½***

COUNT OF MONTE CRISTO, THE (1954) Sirius. **Color-183min.** *(French-Italian).* Jean Marais, Lia Amanda .... (4)
Original French title: COMTE DE MONTE-CRISTO, LE

COUNT OF MONTE CRISTO, THE (1955) Warner Bros. **B&W-180min.** *(French).* Pierre-Richard Wilm, Michele Alfa.................... (3)

COUNT OF MONTE CRISTO, THE (1962) *see* STORY OF THE COUNT OF MONTE CRISTO, THE

COUNT OF MONTE CRISTO, THE (1975) Independent TV Corp (ITC). **Color-103min.** *(British, Made for TV).* Richard Chamberlain, Tony Curtis, Trevor Howard.................... **6***

COUNT THE HOURS (1953) RKO. **Color-74min.** Macdonald Carey, Teresa Wright .... (3)
British title: EVERY MINUTE COUNTS

COUNT THREE AND PRAY (1955) Columbia. **Color-102min.** Van Heflin, Joanne Woodward **4***

COUNT YORGA, VAMPIRE (1970) American-International. **Color-91min.** Robert Quarry, Roger Perry.................... **3***

COUNT YOUR BLESSINGS (1959) M-G-M. **Color-102min.** Deborah Kerr, Rossano Brazzi.................... (4)

COUNTDOWN (1968) Warner Bros. **Color-101min.** James Caan, Joanna Moore **5***

THE COUNT OF MONTE CRISTO (1934). Elissa Landi is astonished at how much Robert Donat resembles the man she loved long, long ago, but she is far from certain he's the same man, and he isn't yet ready to reveal his identity.

COUNTDOWN AT KUSINI (1976) Columbia. **Color-99min.** *(U.S.-Nigerian).* Ruby Dee, Greg Morris **3½***

COUNTER-ATTACK (1945) Columbia. **B&W-90min.** Paul Muni, Larry Parks.................... (4)
British title: ONE AGAINST SEVEN

COUNTERBLAST (1948) British National. **B&W-99min.** *(British).* Mervyn Johns, Robert Beatty .... (3)

COUNTERFEIT CONSTABLE, THE (1964) Seven Arts [W.B.]. **Color-86min.** *(French).* Robert Dhéry, Colette Brosset .... (3)
Original title: ALLEZ FRANCE!

COUNTERFEIT KILLER, THE (1968) Universal. **Color-95min.** Jack Lord, Shirley Knight.................... **3½***

COUNTERFEIT PLAN, THE (1957) Warner Bros. **B&W-87min.** *(British).* Zachary Scott, Peggie Castle .... (3)

COUNTERFEIT TRAITOR, THE (1962) Paramount. **Color-140min.** William Holden, Lilli Palmer **5½***

COUNTERPLOT (1959) United Artists. **B&W-76min.** Forrest Tucker, Allison Hayes.................... (3)

COUNTERPOINT (1968) Universal. **Color-107min.** Charlton Heston, Maximilian Schell.................... **5***

COUNTESS DRACULA (1971) 20th Century-Fox. **Color-94min.** *(British).* Ingrid Pitt, Nigel Green .... (3)

COUNTESS FROM HONG KONG, A (1967) Universal. **Color-108min.** *(British).* Marlon Brando, Sophia Loren **3***

COUNTESS OF MONTE CRISTO, THE (1948) Universal. **B&W-77min.** Sonja Henie, Olga San Juan .... (3)

COUNTRY CUZZINS (1972) Boxoffice International. **Color-90min.** Rene Bond, John Tull, Pamela Princess .... (3)

COUNTRY DOCTOR, THE (1936) 20th Century-Fox. **B&W-110min.** Jean Hersholt, June Lang.................... (4)

COUNTRY GIRL, THE (1954) Paramount. **B&W-104min.** Bing Crosby, Grace Kelly **5½***

COUNTRY MUSIC HOLIDAY (1958) Paramount. **B&W-81min.** Ferlin Husky, Zsa Zsa Gabor, Rocky Graziano.................... (2)
Alternate title: COUNTRY MUSIC BOY

COUNTY FAIR (1950) Monogram [Allied Artists]. **Color-76min.** Rory Calhoun, Jane Nigh.................... (4)

COUPLE, THE (1965) *see* THERE WAS AN OLD COUPLE

COUPLE TAKES A WIFE, THE (1972) MCA-TV. **Color-73min.** *(Made for TV).* Bill Bixby, Paula Prentiss, Myrna Loy **4***

COURAGE OF BLACK BEAUTY (1957) 20th Century-Fox. **Color-77min.** John Crawford, Mimi Gibson .... (3)

COURAGE OF LASSIE (1946) M-G-M. **Color-92min.** Elizabeth Taylor, Frank Morgan.................... (4)

COURAGEOUS DR. CHRISTIAN, THE (1940) RKO. **B&W-67min.** Jean Hersholt, Dorothy Lovett .... (3)

COURAGEOUS MR. PENN (1941) Hoffberg. **B&W-78min.** *(British).* Clifford Evans, Deborah Kerr.................... **4***
Original title: PENN OF PENNSYLVANIA

COURT JESTER, THE (1956) Paramount. **Color-101min.** Danny Kaye, Glynis Johns.................... **5½***

COURT MARTIAL (1955) Kingsley International. **B&W-105min.** *(British).* David Niven, Margaret Leighton.................... (5)
Original title: CHARRINGTON, V.C.

COURT MARTIAL (1959) United Artists. **B&W-82min.** *(German).* Karlheinz (Karl) Boehm, Christian Wolff .... (4)
Original title: KRIEGSGERICHT

COURT MARTIAL OF BILLY MITCHELL, THE (1955) Warner Bros. **Color-100min.** Gary Cooper, Charles Bickford **5***
British title: ONE MAN MUTINY

COURT MARTIAL OF GENERAL GEORGE ARMSTRONG CUSTER, THE (1978) Warner Bros. **Color-100min.** *(Made for TV).* Brian Keith, Ken Howard, Stephen Elliott ....

COURT MARTIAL OF MAJOR KELLER, THE (1963) Warner Bros. **B&W-69min.** *(British).* Laurence Payne, Susan Stephen .... (4)

COURTNEY AFFAIR, THE (1947) Continental [Walter Reade]. **B&W-112min.** *(British).* Anna Neagle, Michael Wilding .... (4)
Original title: COURTNEYS OF CURZON STREET, THE

COURTNEYS OF CURZON STREET, THE (1947) *see* COURTNEY AFFAIR, THE

COURTSHIP OF ANDY HARDY, THE (1942) M-G-M. **B&W-93min.** Mickey Rooney, Donna Reed.................... (3)

COURTSHIP OF EDDIE'S FATHER, THE (1963) M-G-M. **Color-117min.** Glenn Ford, Ronny Howard.................... **4***

COUSIN ANGELICA (1974) Elias Querejeta. **Color-100min.** *(Spanish).* José Luis Lopez Vazquez, Lina Canalejas .... (4)
Original title: PRIMA ANGELICA, LA

COUSIN COUSINE (1976) Libra. **Color-95min.** *(French).* Marie-Christine Barrault, Victor Lanoux **4***
Translation title: Male Cousin, Female Cousin

COUSINS, THE (1958) Films Around The World. **B&W-103min.** *(French).* Jean-Claude Brialy, Gerard Blain **3***
Original title: COUSINS, LES

COUTURIER DE CES DAMES, LE (1956) *see* FERNANDEL THE DRESSMAKER

COVENANT WITH DEATH, A (1967) Warner Bros. **Color-97min.** George Maharis, Laura Devon **4***

COVER GIRL (1944) Columbia. **Color-107min.** Rita Hayworth, Gene Kelly **4½***

COVER ME BABE (1970) 20th Century-Fox. **Color-89min.** Robert Forster, Sondra Locke .... (3)

COVER UP (1949) United Artists. **B&W-85min.** William Bendix, Dennis O'Keefe .... (4)

COVERED WAGON, THE (1923) Paramount. **B&W-105min.** *(Silent).* Lois Wilson, J. Warren Kerrigan, Ernest Torrence .... (4)

COW AND I, THE (1959) Zenith International. **B&W-98min.** *(French-Italian-W. German, English version).* Fernandel, Rene Havard .... (5)
Original French title: VACHE ET LE PRISONNIER, LA *(The Cow and the Prisoner)*
Original Italian title: VACCA E IL PRIGIONIERO, LA

COW COUNTRY (1953) Allied Artists. **B&W-82min.** Edmond O'Brien, Helen Westcott .... (3)

COWARDS (1970) Jaylo International. **Color-89min.** John Ross, Susan Sparling .... (3)

COWBOY, THE (1954) Lippert Productions. **Color-54min.** *(Documentary).* Director: Elmo Williams **4***

COWBOY (1958) Columbia. **Color-92min.** Glenn Ford, Jack Lemmon..... **5***

COWBOY AND THE BLONDE, THE (1941) 20th Century-Fox. **B&W-68min.** Mary Beth Hughes, George Montgomery .... (3)

COWBOY AND THE LADY, THE (1938) United Artists. **B&W-91min.** Gary Cooper, Merle Oberon **4***

COWBOY FROM BROOKLYN (1938) Warner Bros. **B&W-80min.** Dick Powell, Pat O'Brien .... (4)
British title: ROMANCE AND RHYTHM

COWBOY IN MANHATTAN (1943) Universal. **B&W-60min.** Robert Paige, Frances Langford .... (3)

COWBOYS, THE (1972) Warner Bros. **Color-128min.** John Wayne, Roscoe Lee Browne **4***

CRACK IN THE MIRROR (1960) 20th Century-Fox. **B&W-97min.** Orson Welles, Juliette Greco, Bradford Dillman **4***

CRACK IN THE WORLD (1965) Paramount. **Color-96min.** Dana Andrews, Janette Scott .... (4)

CRACK-UP (1946) 20th Century-Fox. **B&W-93min.** Pat O'Brien, Claire Trevor **4***

CRACKED NUTS (1941) Universal. **B&W-61min.** Bert Wheeler, Robert Woolsey, Edna May Oliver .... (3)

CRACKSMAN, THE (1963) Warner Bros. **Color-112min.** *(British).* Charles Drake, George Sanders **3***

CRAIG'S WIFE (1936) Columbia. **B&W-75min.** Rosalind Russell, John Boles .... (4)

CRANES ARE FLYING, THE (1958) Artkino. **B&W-94min.** *(U.S.S.R.).* Tatyana Samoilova, Alexei Batalov **4½***
Original title: LETIAT JOURAVLY

CRASH! (1977) Group 1. **Color-85min.** Sue Lyon, José Ferrer, John Ericson, John Carradine .... (4)

CRASH DIVE (1943) 20th Century-Fox. **Color-105min.** Tyrone Power, Anne Baxter **4***

CRASH LANDING (1958) Columbia. **B&W-76min.** Gary Merrill, Nancy Davis .... (3)

CRASH OF SILENCE (1953) Universal. **B&W-93min.** *(British).* Mandy Miller, Phyllis Calvert **5***
Original title: MANDY
Alternate title: STORY OF MANDY, THE

CRASHING LAS VEGAS (1956) Allied Artists. **B&W-62min.** The Bowery Boys, Mary Castle .... (4)

CRASHOUT (1955) Filmmakers. **B&W-90min.** William Bendix, Gene Evans **3***

CRATER LAKE MONSTER, THE (1977) Crown International. **Color-89min.** Richard Cardella, Glenn Roberts, Mark Siegel **2***

CRAWLING EYE, THE (1958) UCC Films. **B&W-85min.** *(British).* Forrest Tucker, Laurence Payne 3½*
Original title: TROLLENBERG TERROR, THE

CRAWLING HAND, THE (1963) Medallion. **B&W-89min.** Rod Lauren, Peter Breck **2***
Alternate title: STRIKE ME DEADLY

CRAWLING MONSTER, THE (1964) *see* CREEPING TERROR, THE

CRAWLSPACE (1971) Viacom. **Color-74min.** *(Made for TV).* Teresa Wright, Arthur Kennedy, Tom Harper .... (4)

CRAZE (1974) Warner Bros. **Color-96min.** *(British).* Jack Palance, Diana Dors, Edith Evans, Trevor Howard .... (3)

CRAZED VAMPIRE, THE (1972) *see* CAGED VIRGINS

CRAZIES, THE (1973) Cambist. **Color-103min.** Lane Carroll, W. G. McMillan .... (3)
Alternate title: CODE NAME: TRIXIE

CRAZY DAY, A (1960) *see* FROM A ROMAN BALCONY

CRAZY DESIRE (1962) Avco-Embassy. **B&W-108min.** *(Italian).* Ugo Tognazzi, Catherine Sappak .... (5)
Original title: VOGLIA MATTA, LA *(That Certain Urge)*

CRAZY FOR LOVE (1951) Ellis Films. **B&W-84min.** *(French).* Bourvil, Brigitte Bardot .... (3)
Original title: TOUR NORMAND, LE *(The Norman Hole)*
Alternate title: TI TA TO

CRAZY HORSE (1977) SNC. **Color-90min.** *(French).* John Lennox .... (3)

CRAZY HOUSE (1943) Universal. **B&W-80min.** Ole Olsen, Chic Johnson, Allan Jones .... (5)

CRAZY JACK AND THE BOY (1974) *see* SILENCE

CRAZY JOE (1974) Columbia. **Color-100min.** *(U.S.-Italian).* Peter Boyle, Paula Prentiss 3*

CRAZY MAMA (1975) New World. **Color-82min.** Cloris Leachman, Stuart Whitman **4***

CRAZY OVER HORSES (1951) Monogram [Allied Artists]. **B&W-65min.** The Bowery Boys, Gloria Saunders .... (3)

CRAZY PARADISE (1962) Sherpix. **Color-95min.** *(Danish).* Dirch Passer, Hans W. Petersen .... (3)
Original title: TOSSEDE PARADIS, DET

CRAZY QUILT (1966) Continental [Walter Reade]. **B&W-75min.** Tom Rosquie, Ina Mela .... (5)

CRAZY RIDICULOUS AMERICAN PEOPLE (1977) *see* JABBERWALK

CRAZY TO KILL (1943) *see* DR. GILLESPIE'S CRIMINAL CASE

CRAZY WORLD (1964) *see* MONDO PAZZO

CRAZY WORLD OF JULIUS VROODER, THE (1974) 20th Century-Fox. **Color-98min.** Timothy Bottoms, Barbara Seagull .... (3)

CRAZY WORLD OF LAUREL AND HARDY, THE (1967) Joseph Brenner. **B&W-83min.** *(Compilation).* Producer: Hal Roach .... (5)

CRAZYLEGS (1954) Republic. **B&W-87min.** Elroy "Crazylegs" Hirsch, Lloyd Nolan .... (4)

CREATION OF THE HUMANOIDS, THE (1962) Emerson Films. **Color-75min.** Don Megowan, Erica Elliot .... (2)

CREATURE FROM BLACK LAKE (1976) Howco International. **Color-95min.** Jack Elam, Dub Taylor, John David Carson .... (3)

CREATURE FROM THE BLACK LAGOON (1954) Universal. **B&W-79min.** Richard Carlson, Julia (Julie) Adams **3***

CREATURE FROM THE HAUNTED SEA (1960) Filmgroup. **B&W-60min.** Antony Carbone, Betsy Jones-Moreland, Edward Wain (Robert Towne) .... (4)

CREATURE OF DESTRUCTION (1967) American-International. **Color-80min.** Les Tremayne, Aron Kincaid, Pat Delaney **1***
Common title error: CREATURES OF DESTRUCTION

CREATURE OF THE WALKING DEAD (1960) Medallion. **B&W-74min.** *(Mexican).* Fernando Casanova, Sonia Furio, Rock Madison (U.S. prints) **2***
Original title: MARCA DEL MUERTO, LA

CREATURE WALKS AMONG US, THE (1956) Universal. **B&W-78min.** Jeff Morrow, Rex Reason **2***

CREATURE WITH THE ATOM BRAIN (1955) Columbia. **B&W-70min.** Richard Denning, Angela Stevens .... (3)

CREATURE WITH THE BLUE HAND (1971) New World. **Color-72min.** *(German).* Klaus Kinski, Diana Kerner (Korner), Harald Leipnitz ..... (3)
Original title: BLAUE HAND, DIE

CREATURES OF THE PREHISTORIC PLANET (1970) *see* HORROR OF THE BLOOD MONSTERS

CREATURE'S REVENGE, THE (1971) *see* BRAIN OF BLOOD

Films are rated on a 1 to 10 scale, 10 is highest. **Boldface** ratings followed by an asterisk (*) are for films actually seen and rated by the executive and senior editors. All other ratings are estimates. (See Notes on Entertainment Ratings in the front section.)

CREATURES THE WORLD FORGOT (1971) Columbia. Color-95min. *(British)*. Julie Ege, Tony Bonner .... (3)

CREEPER, THE (1948) 20th Century-Fox. B&W-64min. Eduardo Ciannelli, Onslow Stevens .... (3)

CREEPING FLESH, THE (1973) Columbia. Color-89min. *(British)*. Christopher Lee, Peter Cushing 4*

CREEPING TERROR, THE (1964) Teledynamics. B&W-75min. Vic Savage, Shannon O'Neil, William Thourlby 1*
Alternate title: CRAWLING MONSTER, THE

CREEPING UNKNOWN, THE (1955) United Artists. B&W-78min. *(British)*. Brian Donlevy, Richard Wordsworth .... (3)
Original title: QUATERMASS XPERIMENT, THE

CREMATOR, THE (1968) Aquarius Releasing, Inc. B&W-92min. *(Czech)*. Rudolf Hrusinsky, Milos Vognic, Jana Stehnova .... (5)
Original title: SPALOVAC MRTVOL
Alternate title: CARNIVAL OF HERETICS

CRESCENDO (1969) Warner Bros. Color-83min. *(British)*. Stephanie Powers, James Olson .... (4)

CREST OF THE WAVE (1954) M-G-M. B&W-90min. *(British-U.S.)*. Gene Kelly, John Justin .... (4)
Alternate title: SEAGULLS OVER SORRENTO

CRIA! (1976) Jason Allen. Color-97min. *(Spanish)*. Ana Torrent, Geraldine Chaplin 2½*
Original title: CRIA CUERVOS *(Idiomatic; Raise Ravens, Bring Up Crows)*
Alternate title: RAISE RAVENS

CRIES AND WHISPERS (1972) New World. Color-94min. *(Swedish)*. Harriet Andersson, Kari Sylwan, Liv Ullmann 3*
Original title: VISKNINGAR OCH ROP *(Whispers and Cries)*

CRIME AGAINST JOE (1956) United Artists. B&W-69min. Julie London, John Bromfield .... (4)

CRIME AND PASSION (1975) American-International. Color-92min. Omar Sharif, Karen Black .... (4)
Original title: ACE UP YOUR SLEEVE

CRIME AND PUNISHMENT (1935) Columbia. B&W-88min. Peter Lorre, Edward Arnold .... (5)

CRIME AND PUNISHMENT (1956) Kingsley International. B&W-111min. *(French)*. Jean Gabin, Robert Hossein .... (5)
Original title: CRIME ET CHATIMENT
Alternate title: MOST DANGEROUS SIN, THE

CRIME AND PUNISHMENT (1970) Artkino. B&W-200min. *(U.S.S.R.)*. Georgi Taratorkin, Innokenti Smoktunovsky 4*

CRIME AND PUNISHMENT, U.S.A. (1959) Allied Artists. B&W-78min. George Hamilton, Frank Silvera 3*

CRIME BY NIGHT (1944) Warner Bros. B&W-72min. Jane Wyman, Jerome Cowan .... (4)

CRIME CLUB (1974) Charles Larson. Color-75min. *(Made for TV)*. Lloyd Bridges, Barbara Rush, William Devane, Cloris Leachman 4*

CRIME DOCTOR (1943) Columbia. B&W-66min. Warner Baxter, Margaret Lindsay .... (3)

CRIME DOCTOR'S COURAGE, THE (1945) Columbia. B&W-70min. Warner Baxter, Hillary Brooke .... (3)
British title: DOCTOR'S COURAGE, THE

CRIME DOCTOR'S DIARY, THE (1949) Columbia. B&W-61min. Warner Baxter, Stephen Dunne .... (3)

CRIME DOCTOR'S GAMBLE, THE (1947) Columbia. B&W-66min. Warner Baxter, Micheline Cheriel .... (3)
British title: DOCTOR'S GAMBLE, THE

CRIME DOCTOR'S MANHUNT (1946) Columbia. B&W-61min. Warner Baxter, Ellen Drew .... (3)

CRIME DOCTOR'S STRANGEST CASE, THE (1943) Columbia. B&W-68min. Warner Baxter, Lloyd Bridges .... (3)
British title: STRANGEST CASE, THE

CRIME DOCTOR'S WARNING, THE (1945) Columbia. B&W-69min. Warner Baxter, Dusty Anderson .... (3)
British title: DOCTOR'S WARNING, THE

CRIME DOES NOT PAY (1962) Avco-Embassy. B&W-159min. *(French-Italian)*. Edwige Feuilliere, Gabriele Ferzetti .... (5)
Original French title: CRIME NE PAIE PAS, LE
British title: GENTLE ART OF MURDER, THE
Original Italian title: DELITTO NON PAGA, IL

CRIME IN THE STREETS (1956) Allied Artists. B&W-91min. James Whitmore, John Cassavetes 3*

CRIME OF DR. CRESPI, THE (1935) Republic. B&W-63min. Erich von Stroheim, Dwight Frye .... (3)

CRIME OF DR. FORBES, THE (1936) 20th Century-Fox. B&W-75min. Gloria Stuart, Robert Kent .... (4)

CRIME OF DR. HALLET, THE (1938) Universal. B&W-68min. Ralph Bellamy, Josephine Hutchinson .... (3)

CRIME OF MONSIEUR LANGE, THE (1936) Brandon. B&W-90min. *(French)*. René Lefevre, Florelle, Henri Guisol 4*
Original title: CRIME DE MONSIEUR LANGE, LE

CRIME OF PASSION (1957) United Artists. B&W-84min. Barbara Stanwyck, Sterling Hayden .... (4)

CRIME OF THE CENTURY, THE (1952) *see* WALK EAST ON BEACON

CRIME SCHOOL (1938) Warner Bros. B&W-86min. Humphrey Bogart, The Dead End Kids 4*

CRIME WAVE (1954) Warner Bros. B&W-74min. Sterling Hayden, Gene Nelson .... (3)
British title: CITY IS DARK, THE

CRIME WITHOUT PASSION (1934) Paramount. B&W-80min. Claude Rains, Margo 5½*

CRIMES OF DR. MABUSE (1933) *see* TESTAMENT OF DR. MABUSE, THE

CRIMINAL, THE (1960) *see* CONCRETE JUNGLE, THE

CRIMINAL CODE, THE (1931) Columbia. B&W-100min. Walter Huston, Phillips Holmes, Boris Karloff 3*

CRIMINAL LAWYER (1951) Columbia. B&W-74min. Pat O'Brien, Jane Wyatt 3½*

CRIMINAL LIFE OF ARCHIBALDO DE LA CRUZ, THE (1955) Dan Talbot. B&W-91min. *(Mexican)*. Ernesto Alonso, Miroslava (Stern) ...... (4)
Original title: ENSAYO DE UN CRIMEN *(Rehearsal for Crime)*
Alternate Mexican title: VIDA CRIMINAL DE ARCHIBALDO de la CRUZ, LA

CRIMSON ALTAR, THE (1968) *see* CRIMSON CULT, THE

CRIMSON BLADE, THE (1963) Columbia. Color-81min. Lionel Jeffries, Oliver Reed, Jack Hedley, June Thorburn .... (3)
Original title: SCARLET BLADE, THE

CRIMSON CANARY (1945) Universal. B&W-64min. Noah Beery, Jr., Lois Collier .... (4)

CRIMSON CIRCLE, THE (1960) *see* RED CIRCLE, THE

CRIMSON CULT, THE (1968) American-International. Color-87min. *(British-U.S.)*. Boris Karloff, Christopher Lee, Barbara Steele .... (3)
Original title: CURSE OF THE CRIMSON ALTAR
Alternate title: CRIMSON ALTAR, THE

CRIMSON GHOST, THE (1946) *see* CYCLOTRODE "X"

CRIMSON KIMONO, THE (1959) Columbia. B&W-84min. Victoria Shaw, Glenn Corbett .... (3)

CRIMSON PIRATE, THE (1952) Warner Bros. Color-104min. Burt Lancaster, Nick Cravat 5*

CRIPPLE CREEK (1952) Columbia. Color-78min. George Montgomery, Karin Booth .... (4)

CRISIS (1950) M-G-M. B&W-95min. Cary Grant, José Ferrer 3*

CRISS CROSS (1949) Universal. B&W-87min. Burt Lancaster, Yvonne De Carlo 4*

CRITIC'S CHOICE (1963) Warner Bros. Color-100min. Bob Hope, Lucille Ball 3½*

CROMWELL (1970) Columbia. Color-139min. *(British)*. Richard Harris, Alec Guinness 6*

CROOK, THE (1971) United Artists. Color-120min. *(French)*. Jean-Louis Trintignant, Daniele Delorme .... (5)
Original title: VOYOU, LE *(The Hoodlum)*
British title: SIMON THE SWISS

CROOKED CIRCLE, THE (1957) Republic. B&W-72min. John Smith, Fay Spain .... (2)

CROOKED HEARTS, THE (1972) Worldvision. Color-74min. *(Made for TV)*. Douglas Fairbanks, Jr., Rosalind Russell, Maureen O'Sullivan .... (4)

CROOKED RING (1955) *see* DOUBLE JEOPARDY

CROOKED ROAD, THE (1964) Seven Arts [W.B.]. B&W-90min. *(British)*. Robert Ryan, Stewart Granger .... (2)

CROOKED SKY, THE (1957) United Artists. B&W-77min. *(British)*. Wayne Morris, Karin Booth .... (3)

CROOKED WAY, THE (1949) United Artists. B&W-90min. John Payne, Ellen Drew .... (3)

CROOKED WEB, THE (1955) Columbia. B&W-77min. Frank Lovejoy, Mari Blanchard .... (3)

CROOKS AND CORONETS (1969) *see* SOPHIE'S PLACE

CROOKS ANONYMOUS (1962) Janus Films. B&W-87min. *(British)*. Leslie Phillips, Stanley Baxter .... (4)

Films are rated on a 1 to 10 scale, 10 is highest. **Boldface** ratings followed by an asterisk (*) are for films actually seen and rated by the executive and senior editors. All other ratings are estimates. (See Notes on Entertainment Ratings in the front section.)

Richard Harris is **CROMWELL** (1970), whose successful revolution has left the defeated King Charles I (played by Alec Guinness) little choice but to listen to his demands.

CROSBY CASE, THE (1934) Universal. **B&W-60min.** Wynne Gibson, Alan Dinehart .... (4)
British title: CROSBY MURDER CASE, THE

CROSS AND THE SWITCHBLADE, THE (1970) Dick Ross & Associates. **Color-106min.** Pat Boone, Erik Estrada .... (4)

CROSS-COUNTRY ROMANCE (1940) RKO. **B&W-68min.** Gene Raymond, Wendy Barrie .... (3)

CROSS EXAMINATION (1932) Artclass. **B&W-61min.** H. B. Warner, Sally Blane 3*

CROSS MY HEART (1946) Paramount. **B&W-83min.** Betty Hutton, Sonny Tufts .... (3)

CROSS OF IRON (1977) Avco-Embassy. **Color-119min.** (*British-W. German*). James Coburn, Maximilian Schell, James Mason 4*

CROSS OF LORRAINE, THE (1943) M-G-M. **B&W-90min.** Jean-Pierre Aumont, Gene Kelly 4*

CROSS UP (1955) United Artists. **B&W-83min.** Larry Parks, Constance Smith .... (3)
Original title: TIGER BY THE TAIL

CROSSCURRENT (1971) Warner Bros. **Color-96min.** (*Made for TV*). Robert Hooks, Jeremy Slate, Robert Wagner, Carol Lynley ...... (4)
Alternate title: CABLE CAR MURDER, THE

CROSSED SWORDS (1954) United Artists. **Color-86min.** (*Italian*). Errol Flynn, Gina Lollobrigida .... (2)
Original title: MAESTRO DI DON GIOVANNI, IL (*The Master of Don Juan*)

CROSSED SWORDS (1977) Warner Bros. **Color-121min.** (*Panama, English language*). Mark Lester, Oliver Reed, Raquel Welch 6*
British title: PRINCE AND THE PAUPER, THE

CROSSFIRE (1947) RKO. **B&W-86min.** Robert Young, Robert Mitchum 5*

CROSSROADS (1942) M-G-M. **B&W-84min.** William Powell, Hedy Lamarr 4*

CROSSROADS TO CRIME (1960) Anglo Amalgamated [EMI]. **B&W-57min.** (*British*). Anthony Oliver, Patricia Henegan .... (3)

CROSSTRAP (1961) Unifilms. **B&W-62min.** (*British*). Laurence Payne, Jill Adams .... (3)

CROSSWINDS (1951) Paramount. **Color-93min.** John Payne, Rhonda Fleming 3*

CROWD, THE (1928) M-G-M. **B&W-95min.** Eleanor Boardman, James Murray (*Silent*). 3*

CROWD FOR LISETTE, A (1961) *see* LISETTE

CROWD ROARS, THE (1932) Warner Bros. **B&W-85min.** James Cagney, Joan Blondell, Ann Dvorak .... (4)

CROWD ROARS, THE (1938) M-G-M. **B&W-92min.** Robert Taylor, Frank Morgan, Jane Wyman 3½*

CROWDED PARADISE (1955) Tudor Pictures. **B&W-94min.** Hume Cronyn, Nancy Kelly .... (4)

CROWDED SKY, THE (1960) Warner Bros. **Color-105min.** Dana Andrews, Rhonda Fleming 4*

CROWHAVEN FARM (1970) Worldvision. **Color-72min.** (*Made for TV*). Hope Lange, Lloyd Bochner, John Carradine 4*

CROWNING EXPERIENCE, THE (1960) Moral Rearmament. **Color-100min.** Muriel Smith, Ann Buckles .... (4)

CRUCIBLE, THE (1957) Kingsley International. **B&W-140min.** (*French-E. German*). Simone Signoret, Yves Montand .... (5)
Original title: SORCIERES DE SALEM, LES (*The Witches of Salem*)
Alternate title: WITCHES OF SALEM, THE

CRUCIBLE OF HORROR (1971) Cannon Releasing. **Color-91min.** (*British*). Michael Gough, Yvonne Mitchell 1*
Original title: VELVET HOUSE

CRUCIBLE OF TERROR (1972) Scotia-Barber (*Brit.*). **Color-91min.** (*British*). Mike Raven, Mary Maude .... (3)

CRUEL SEA, THE (1952) Universal. **B&W-126min.** (*British*). Jack Hawkins, Donald Sinden .... (5)

CRUEL SWAMP (1955) *see* SWAMP WOMEN

CRUEL TOWER, THE (1957) Allied Artists. **B&W-80min.** John Ericson, Mari Blanchard .... (5)

CRUISIN' DOWN THE RIVER (1953) Columbia. **Color-81min.** Dick Haymes, Audrey Totter .... (3)

CRUISING CASANOVAS (1952) *see* GOBS AND GALS

CRUSADES, THE (1935) Paramount. **B&W-123min.** Loretta Young, Henry Wilcoxon .... (5)

CRY BABY KILLER, THE (1958) Allied Artists. **B&W-62min.** Jack Nicholson, Carolyn Mitchell .... (4)

CRY BLOOD, APACHE (1970) Golden Eagle International. **Color-82min.** Jody McCrea, Dan Kemp, Joel McCrea .... (2)

CRY DANGER (1951) RKO. **B&W-79min.** Dick Powell, Rhonda Fleming 4*

CRY FOR HAPPY (1961) Columbia. **Color-110min.** Glenn Ford, Donald O'Connor 4*

CRY FROM THE STREETS, A (1958) Tudor Pictures. **B&W-99min.** (*British*). Max Bygraves, Dana Wilson .... (5)

CRY HAVOC (1943) M-G-M. **B&W-97min.** Margaret Sullavan, Ann Sothern, Joan Blondell 3*

CRY IN THE NIGHT, A (1956) Warner Bros. **B&W-75min.** Edmond O'Brien, Brian Donlevy, Natalie Wood 3½*

CRY IN THE WILDERNESS (1974) MCA-TV. **Color-74min.** (*Made for TV*). George Kennedy, Lee H. Montgomery, Joanna Pettet ..... (3)

CRY OF BATTLE (1963) Allied Artists. **B&W-99min.** Van Heflin, James MacArthur .... (4)

CRY OF THE BANSHEE (1970) American-International. **Color-87min.** (*U.S.-British*). Vincent Price, Elisabeth Bergner 3*

CRY OF THE BEWITCHED (1956) Futuramic. **Color-80min.** (*Mexican*). Nonon Sevilla, Ramon Gay .... (3)
Alternate title: YOUNG AND EVIL
Original title: YAMBAO

CRY OF THE CITY (1948) 20th Century-Fox. **B&W-95min.** Victor Mature, Richard Conte 4*

CRY OF THE HUNTED (1953) M-G-M. **B&W-80min.** Barry Sullivan, Polly Bergen .... (4)

CRY OF THE PENGUINS (1971) Cinema Shares. **Color-101min.** (*British*). John Hurt, Dudley Sutton, Hayley Mills 4*
Original title: MR. FORBUSH AND THE PENGUINS

CRY OF THE WEREWOLF (1944) Columbia. **B&W-63min.** Nina Foch, Stephen Crane .... (3)

CRY OF THE WILD (1972) Gold Key Entertainment. **Color-91min.** (*Canadian, Documentary*). Director: Bill Mason 4*

CRY PANIC (1974) MPC (TV). **Color-74min.** (*Made for TV*). John Forsythe, Anne Francis .... (5)

CRY RAPE (1973) Warner Bros. **Color-75min.** (*Made for TV*). Peter Coffield, Andrea Marcovicci 5*

CRY SILENCE (1974) *see* SILENCE

CRY TERROR (1958) M-G-M. **B&W-96min.** James Mason, Rod Steiger, Inger Stevens 4*

CRY, THE BELOVED COUNTRY (1951) United Artists. **B&W-103min.** (*British*). Canada Lee, Charles Carson 4½*
Alternate title: AFRICAN FURY

CRY TOUGH (1959) United Artists. **B&W-83min.** John Saxon, Linda Cristal .... (4)

Films are rated on a 1 to 10 scale, 10 is highest. **Boldface** ratings followed by an asterisk (*) are for films actually seen and rated by the executive and senior editors. All other ratings are estimates. (See Notes on Entertainment Ratings in the front section.)

CRY UNCLE (1971) Cambist. **Color-87min.** Allen Garfield, Madeline le Roux ....(4)
British title: SUPER DICK

CRY VENGEANCE (1954) Allied Artists. **B&W-83min.** Mark Stevens, Joan Vohs 3*

CRY WOLF (1947) Warner Bros. **B&W-83min.** Errol Flynn, Barbara Stanwyck ....(3)

CRYPT OF DARK SECRETS (1976) Majestic International. **Color-71min.** Maureen Ridley, Chan ....(2)

CRYPT OF HORROR (1958) *see* TERROR IN THE CRYPT

CRYPT OF THE LIVING DEAD (1973) Atlas Films. **Color-93min.** Andrew Prine, Mark Damon, Patty Sheppard ....(3)
Alternate title: YOUNG HANNAH, QUEEN OF THE VAMPIRES
Alternate title: HANNAH, QUEEN OF THE VAMPIRES
British title: VAMPIRE WOMAN

CRYSTAL BALL, THE (1943) United Artists. **B&W-81min.** Ray Milland, Paulette Goddard ....(3)

CUBA (1979) United Artists. **Color- min.** Sean Connery, Brooke Adams ....

CUBAN FIREBALL (1951) Republic. **B&W-78min.** Estrelita Rodriguez, Warren Douglas ....(3)

CUL-DE-SAC (1966) Sigma III. **B&W-110min.** *(British).* Donald Pleasance, Francoise Dorleac 3*

CULPEPPER CATTLE COMPANY, THE (1972) 20th Century-Fox. **Color-92min.** Gary Grimes, Billy "Green" Bush 5*

CULT OF THE COBRA (1955) Universal. **B&W-82min.** Faith Domergue, Richard Long ....(4)

CULT OF THE DAMNED (1969) *see* ANGEL, ANGEL, DOWN WE GO

CUP GLORY (1972) Hemdale *(British).* **Color-84min.** *(British, Documentary).* Director: Tony Maylam ....

CURE FOR LOVE, THE (1949) Associated Artists. **B&W-97min.** *(British).* Robert Donat, Renée Asherson ....(4)

CURIOUS ADVENTURES OF MR. WONDERBIRD (1959) *see* ADVENTURES OF MR. WONDERBIRD

CURLEY (1947) United Artists. **Color-53min.** Larry Olsen, Frances Rafferty ....(3)
Part I of HAL ROACH COMEDY CARNIVAL, THE

CURLY TOP (1935) 20th Century-Fox. **B&W-75min.** Shirley Temple, John Boles ....(4)

CURSE OF DRACULA, THE (1958) *see* RETURN OF DRACULA, THE

CURSE OF FRANKENSTEIN, THE (1957) Warner Bros. **Color-83min.** *(British).* Peter Cushing, Christopher Lee 4*

CURSE OF NOSTRADAMUS, THE (1960) Azteca. **B&W-77min.** *(Mexican).* German Robles, Julio Aleman 1*
Original title: MALDICION DE NOSTRADAMUS, LA

CURSE OF SIMBA (1965) *see* CURSE OF THE VOODOO

CURSE OF THE ALLENBYS (1946) *see* SHE WOLF OF LONDON

CURSE OF THE AZTEC MUMMY, THE (1959) Azteca. **B&W-65min.** *(Mexican).* Ramon Gay, Rosita Arenas 1*
Original title: MALDICION DE LA MOMIA AZTECA, LA

CURSE OF THE BLOOD-GHOULS (1962) *see* SLAUGHTER OF THE VAMPIRES

CURSE OF THE CAT PEOPLE, THE (1944) RKO. **B&W-70min.** Simone Simon, Kent Smith 4*

CURSE OF THE CRIMSON ALTAR, THE (1968) *see* CRIMSON CULT, THE

CURSE OF THE CRYING WOMAN, THE (1961) Azteca. **B&W-74min.** *(Mexican).* Rosita Arenas, Abel Salazar ....(1)
Original title: MALDICION DE LA LLORONA, LA
Alternate Mexican title: CASA EMBRUJADA, LA *(The Bewitched House)*

CURSE OF THE DEAD (1966) *see* KILL BABY KILL

CURSE OF THE DEMON (1957) Columbia. **B&W-82min.** *(British).* Dana Andrews, Peggy Cummins 4*
British title: NIGHT OF THE DEMON

CURSE OF THE DOLL PEOPLE (1960) Trans-International. **B&W-81min.** *(Mexican).* Elvira Quintana, Ramon Gay 1*
Original title: MUNECOS INFERNALES

CURSE OF THE FACELESS MAN (1958) United Artists. **B&W-66min.** Richard Anderson, Elaine Edwards ....(2)

CURSE OF THE FLY, THE (1965) 20th Century-Fox. **B&W-86min.** *(British).* Brian Donlevy, Carole Gray 3*

CURSE OF THE HIDDEN VAULT, THE (1963) UCC Films. **B&W-95min.** *(German).* Judith Dornys, Harold Lieb (Harald Leipnitz) ....(3)
Original title: GRUFT MIT DEM RAETSELSCHLOSS, DIE

CURSE OF THE LIVING CORPSE, THE (1964) 20th Century-Fox. **B&W-84min.** Helen Waren, Roy Scheider ....(2)

CURSE OF THE LIVING DEAD (1966) *see* KILL BABY KILL

CURSE OF THE MUMMY (1972) *see* BLOOD FROM THE MUMMY'S TOMB

CURSE OF THE MUMMY'S TOMB, THE (1964) Columbia. **Color-80min.** *(British).* Ronald Howard, Terence Morgan, Fred Clark ....(3)

CURSE OF THE STONE HAND (1959) Medallion. **B&W-72min.** John Carradine, Ernest Walch ....(2)

CURSE OF THE UNDEAD (1959) Universal. **B&W-79min.** Eric Fleming, Michael Pate ....(3)
16mm title: MARK OF THE WEST

CURSE OF THE VAMPIRES (1970) Hemisphere. **Color-90min.** *(U.S.-Philippine).* Amalia Fuentes, Eddie Garcia ....(2)

CURSE OF THE VOODOO (1965) Allied Artists. **B&W-77min.** *(British-U.S.).* Bryant Halliday, Dennis Price ....(2)
Original title: CURSE OF SIMBA

CURSE OF THE WEREWOLF, THE (1961) Universal. **Color-91min.** *(British).* Oliver Reed, Clifford Evans ....(4)

CURSE OF THE YELLOW SNAKE, THE (1963) UCC Films. **B&W-100min.** *(German).* Joachim Berger (Fuchsberger), Pinkas Braun ......(3)

CURTAIN CALL (1940) RKO. **B&W-63min.** Barbara Read, Alan Mowbray ....(4)

CURTAIN CALL AT CACTUS CREEK (1950) Universal. **Color-86min.** Donald O'Connor, Gale Storm ....(4)
British title: TAKE THE STAGE

CURTAIN UP (1952) J. Arthur Rank. **B&W-81min.** *(British).* Robert Morley, Margaret Rutherford, Kay Kendall ....(4)

CURUCU, BEAST OF THE AMAZON (1956) Universal. **Color-76min.** John Bromfield, Beverly Garland 2*

CUSTER OF THE WEST (1967) Cinerama Releasing. **Color-120min.** *(U.S.-Spanish).* Robert Shaw, Mary Ure 5*
Alternate title: GOOD DAY FOR FIGHTING, A

CUSTOMS AGENT (1950) Columbia. **B&W-72min.** William Eythe, Jim Backus ....(3)

CUTTER (1972) MCA-TV. **Color-74min.** *(Made for TV).* Peter De Anda, Cameron Mitchell, Barbara Rush ....(4)

CUTTER'S TRAIL (1969) Viacom. **Color-100min.** *(Made for TV).* John Gavin, Marisa Pavan, Joseph Cotten ....(4)

CYBORG (1973) *see* SIX MILLION DOLLAR MAN, THE

CYBORG 2087 (1966) Feature Film Corp. **Color-90min.** Michael Rennie, Karen Steele, Warren Stevens ....(3)

CYCLE SAVAGES, THE (1970) American-International. **Color-82min.** Bruce Dern, Chris Robinson ....(2)

CYCLOPS, THE (1957) Allied Artists. **B&W-75min.** James Craig, Lon Chaney, Jr. ....(3)

CYCLOTRODE "X" (1946) Republic. **B&W-100min.** *(Re-edited Serial).* Rex Reese, Linda Stirling ....(4)
Original title: CRIMSON GHOST, THE

CYNARA (1932) United Artists. **B&W-75min.** Ronald Colman, Kay Francis ....(4)

CYNTHIA (1947) M-G-M. **B&W-98min.** Elizabeth Taylor, Mary Astor, George Murphy 3½*
British title: RICH, FULL LIFE, THE

CYNTHIA'S SECRET (1947) *see* DARK DELUSION

CYRANO DE BERGERAC (1950) United Artists. **B&W-112min.** Jose Ferrer, Mala Powers 6½*

CZARINA (1945) *see* ROYAL SCANDAL, A

-D-

D.A. - CONSPIRACY TO KILL, THE (1970) Universal. **Color-100min.** *(Made for TV).* Robert Conrad, Belinda Montgomery, William Conrad 4*

D.A. DRAWS A CIRCLE, THE (1971) *see* THEY CALL IT MURDER

D.A.: MURDER ONE, THE (1969) Universal. **Color-100min.** *(Made for TV).* Robert Conrad, Howard Duff 4*

D-DAY ON MARS (1945) Republic. **B&W-100min.** *(Re-edited Serial).* Dennis Moore, Linda Stirling, Roy Barcroft ....(3)
Original title: PURPLE MONSTER STRIKES, THE

D-DAY, THE SIXTH OF JUNE (1956) 20th Century-Fox. **Color-106min.** Robert Taylor, Richard Todd ....(5)

D.I., THE (1957) Warner Bros. **B&W-106min.** Jack Webb, Don Dubbins 4*

D.O.A. (1949) United Artists. **B&W-83min.** Edmond O'Brien, Pamela Britton 4½*

José Ferrer is **CYRANO DE BERGERAC** (1950), the film's long-nosed hero of 17th-century Paris whose caustic poetic wit is as sharp as his lightning sword; admiring the brash boldness of handsome William Prince, he decides to help him win the hand of the woman they both love.

D. W. GRIFFITH'S "THAT ROYLE GIRL" (1926) *see* "THAT ROYLE GIRL"

DADDY, I DON'T LIKE IT LIKE THIS (1978) CBS-TV. Color-100min. *(Made for TV).* Talia Shire, Burt Young.......................3*

DADDY LONG LEGS (1931) Fox Film Co. [20th]. B&W-73min. Janet Gaynor, Warner Baxter ....(4)

DADDY LONG LEGS (1955) 20th Century-Fox. Color-126min. Fred Astaire, Leslie Caron......................................4½*

DADDY-O (1959) American-International. B&W-74min. Dick Contino, Sandra Giles ....(2)
Alternate title: OUT ON PROBATION
British title: DOWNBEAT

DADDY'S GONE A-HUNTING (1969) National General. Color-108min. Carol White, Scott Hylands, Paul Burke ....(4)

DAFFODIL KILLER (1962) *see* DEVIL'S DAFFODIL, THE

DAGGERS DRAWN (1964) Paramount. B&W-85min. *(French).* Petula Clark, Francoise Arnoul....................................(3)

DAGGERS OF BLOOD (1962) *see* INVASION 1700

DAGMAR'S HOT PANTS, INC. (1971) American-International. Color-94min. *(Danish).* Diana Kjaer, Robert Strauss, Anne Grete..............(2)

DAGORA, THE SPACE MONSTER (1965) Toho. Color-81min. *(Japanese).* Yosuke Natsuki, Yoko Fujiyama...........................(1)
Original title: UCHU DAIKAIJU DOGORA *(Space Monster Dogora)*
Publicity title: DOGORA

DAISIES (1966) Sigma III. B&W-74min. *(Czech).* Jitka Crhova, Ivana Karbanova ....(3)
Original title: SEDMIKRASKY

DAISY KENYON (1947) 20th Century-Fox. B&W-99min. Joan Crawford, Dana Andrews 4*

DAISY MILLER (1974) Paramount. Color-90min. Cybill Shepherd, Barry Brown 4*

DAKOTA (1945) Republic. B&W-82min. John Wayne, Vera Hruba Ralston ....(3)

DAKOTA INCIDENT (1956) Republic. Color-88min. Linda Darnell, Dale Robertson 3½*

DAKOTA LIL (1950) 20th Century-Fox. Color-88min. George Montgomery, Marie Windsor...................................(4)

DALEKS - INVASION EARTH 2150 A.D. (1966) Continental [Walter Reade]. Color-84min. *(British).* Peter Cushing, Bernard Cribbins.......(4)
Alternate title: INVASION EARTH 2150 A.D.

DALLAS (1950) Warner Bros. Color-94min. Gary Cooper, Ruth Roman ..4*

DALLAS COWBOY CHEERLEADERS, THE (1979) ABC-TV. Color-98min. *(Made for TV).* Jane Seymour, Laraine Stephens, Bert Convy...........4½*

DALTON GIRLS, THE (1957) United Artists. B&W-71min. Merry Anders, Lisa Davis ....(2)

DAM BUSTERS, THE (1955) Warner Bros. B&W-102min. *(British).* Michael Redgrave, Richard Todd...............................5*

DAMES (1934) Warner Bros. B&W-90min. Joan Blondell, Dick Powell ..(5)

DAMIEN - OMEN II (1978) 20th Century-Fox. Color-109min. William Holden, Lee Grant, Jonathan Scott-Taylor............................4*

DAMN CITIZEN! (1958) Universal. B&W-88min. Keith Andes, Maggie Hayes ....(4)

DAMN THE DEFIANT! (1962) Columbia. Color-101min. *(British).* Alec Guinness, Dirk Bogarde 5*
Original title: H.M.S. DEFIANT

DAMN YANKEES (1958) Warner Bros. Color-110min. Ray Walston, Gwen Verdon, Tab Hunter 5*
British title: WHAT LOLA WANTS

DAMNATION ALLEY (1977) 20th Century-Fox. Color-95min. George Peppard, Jan-Michael Vincent, Dominique Sanda.....................4½*

DAMNED, THE (1962) *see* THESE ARE THE DAMNED

DAMNED, THE (1969) Warner Bros. Color-153min. *(Italian-W. German, English language).* Dirk Bogarde, Ingrid Thulin 4*
Original Italian title: CADUTA DEGLI DEI, LA (GOTTERDAM-MERUNG)
Alternate title: TWILIGHT OF THE GODS

DAMNED DON'T CRY, THE (1950) Warner Bros. B&W-103min. Joan Crawford, David Brian...4*

DAMON AND PYTHIAS (1962) M-G-M. Color-99min. *(Italian-U.S.).* Guy Williams, Don Burnett..3*
Original Italian title: TIRANNO DI SIRACUSA, IL *(The Tyrant of Syracuse)*

DAMSEL IN DISTRESS, A (1937) RKO. B&W-98min. Fred Astaire, George Burns, Joan Fontaine 4*

DAN CADY'S LAW (1975) *see* ALIEN THUNDER

DANCE, FOOLS, DANCE (1931) M-G-M. B&W-81min. Joan Crawford, Lester Vail, Clark Gable..(4)

DANCE, GIRL, DANCE (1940) RKO. B&W-90min. Maureen O'Hara, Louis Hayward..4*

DANCE HALL (1941) 20th Century-Fox. B&W-74min. Cesar Romero, Carole Landis...(3)

DANCE HALL (1950) J. Arthur Rank. B&W-80min. *(British).* Donald Houston, Diana Dors, Petula Clark............................(4)

DANCE, LITTLE LADY (1954) Trans-Lux Distributing. Color-87min. *(British).* Terence Morgan, Mai Zetterling.....................(4)

DANCE OF DEATH, THE (1960) Paramount. B&W-86min. *(French).* Michele Mercier, Felix Marten ....(3)
Original title: SAINT MENE LA DANSE, LE

DANCE OF DEATH, THE (1968) Paramount. Color-149min. *(British).* Laurence Olivier, Geraldine McEwan, Robert Lang.................(5)

DANCE OF THE VAMPIRES (1967) *see* FEARLESS VAMPIRE KILLERS

DANCE WITH ME, HENRY (1956) United Artists. B&W-80min. Lou Costello, Bud Abbott..(3)

DANCERS IN THE DARK (1932) Paramount. B&W-60min. Miriam Hopkins, Jack Oakie...(4)

DANCING CO-ED (1939) M-G-M. B&W-84min. Lana Turner, Richard Carlson ....(3)
British title: EVERY OTHER INCH A LADY

DANCING HEART, THE (1953) Sam Baker Associates. Color-91min. *(German).* Gertrud Kueckelmann, Gunnar Moeller...................(3)
Original title: TANZENDE HERZ, DAS

DANCING IN MANHATTAN (1944) Columbia. B&W-60min. Jeff Donnell, Fred Brady..(4)

DANCING IN THE DARK (1949) 20th Century-Fox. Color-92min. William Powell, Betsy Drake...(5)

DANCING LADIES (1945) *see* TEN CENTS A DANCE

DANCING LADY (1933) M-G-M. B&W-82min. Joan Crawford, Clark Gable..3*

DANCING MASTERS, THE (1943) 20th Century-Fox. B&W-63min. Stan Laurel, Oliver Hardy, Trudy Marshall..........................(3)

DANCING MOTHERS (1926) Paramount. B&W-80min. *(Silent).* Alice Joyce, Conway Tearle...(4)

DANCING ON A DIME (1941) Paramount. B&W-74min. Robert Paige, Grace McDonald ....(4)

DANDY IN ASPIC, A (1968) Columbia. Color-107min. *(British-U.S.).* Laurence Harvey, Tom Courtenay ....(3)

DANDY, THE ALL AMERICAN GIRL (1976) U.A. (for M-G-M). Color-89min. Stockard Channing, Sam Waterston.......................4*
Alternate title: SWEET REVENGE

DANGER BY MY SIDE (1962) Butcher's *(Brit.).* **B&W-63min.** *(British).* Anthony Oliver, Maureen Connell.........................(3)

DANGER: DIABOLIK (1967) Paramount. **Color-99min.** *(Italian-French).* John Phillip Law, Marisa Mell, Michel Piccoli, Terry-Thomas ....(3)
Original Italian title: DIABOLIK!

DANGER GROWS WILD (1966) *see* POPPY IS ALSO A FLOWER, THE

DANGER IN THE MIDDLE EAST (1959) Lutetia Films. **B&W-88min.** *(French).* Michel Piccoli, Francis Patrice.........................(3)

DANGER - LOVE AT WORK (1937) 20th Century-Fox. **B&W-81min.** Ann Sothern, Jack Haley.........................**4***

DANGER ON THE RIVER (1942) *see* MISSISSIPPI GAMBLER

DANGER ROUTE (1968) United Artists. **Color-91min.** *(British).* Richard Johnson, Carol Lynley.........................(3)

DANGER SIGNAL (1945) Warner Bros. **B&W-78min.** Jane Withers, Robert Lowery.........................(3)

DANGER TOMORROW (1960) Anglo Amalgamated [EMI]. **B&W-61min.** *(British).* Zena Walker, Robert Urquhart.........................(3)

DANGER WITHIN (1959) *see* BREAKOUT

DANGEROUS (1935) Warner Bros. **B&W-78min.** Bette Davis, Franchot Tone.........................**5***

DANGEROUS AGE, A (1957) Ajay Films. **B&W-70min.** *(Canadian).* Ben Piazza, Anne Pearson.........................(3)

DANGEROUS AGENT (1954) Lutetia Films. **B&W-88min.** *(French).* Eddie Constantine, Colette Dereal.........................(3)

DANGEROUS ASSIGNMENT (1950) **B&W-58min.** *(British).* Lionel Murton, Pamela Deeming.........................(3)

DANGEROUS BLONDES (1943) Columbia. **B&W-80min.** Allyn Joslyn, Evelyn Keyes.........................(5)

DANGEROUS CARGO (1954) Modern Sound Pictures. **B&W-61min.** *(British).* Jack Watling, Susan Stephen.........................(3)

DANGEROUS CHARTER (1962) Crown International. **Color-76min.** Chris Warfield, Sally Fraser.........................**3***

DANGEROUS CROSSING (1953) 20th Century-Fox. **B&W-75min.** Jeanne Crain, Michael Rennie.........................(4)

DANGEROUS DAYS OF KIOWA JONES, THE (1966) M-G-M. **Color-100min.** *(Telefeature).* Robert Horton, Diane Baker, Sal Mineo.........**3½***

DANGEROUS EXILE (1957) J. Arthur Rank. **Color-90min.** *(British).* Louis Jourdan, Belinda Lee.........................(4)

DANGEROUS FEMALE (1931) *see* MALTESE FALCON, THE

DANGEROUS GAME, A (1941) Universal. **B&W-60min.** Richard Arlen, Andy Devine.........................(3)

DANGEROUS GAMES (1958) Warner Bros. **B&W-93min.** *(French-Italian).* Jean Servais, Pascale Audret.........................(3)
Original title: JEUX DANGEREUX

DANGEROUS INHERITANCE (1950) *see* GIRLS' SCHOOL

DANGEROUS JOURNEY (1944) 20th Century-Fox. **B&W-73min.**...........(4)

DANGEROUS LOVE AFFAIRS (1959) *see* LIAISONS DANGEREUSES, LES

DANGEROUS MISSION (1954) RKO. **Color-75min.** Victor Mature, Piper Laurie, Vincent Price.........................(3)

DANGEROUS MISTS (1944) *see* U-BOAT PRISONER

DANGEROUS MONEY (1946) Monogram [Allied Artists]. **B&W-64min.** Sidney Toler, Gloria Warren.........................

DANGEROUS MOONLIGHT (1941) *see* SUICIDE SQUADRON

DANGEROUS PARTNERS (1945) M-G-M. **B&W-74min.** James Craig, Signe Hasso.........................(4)

DANGEROUS PASSAGE (1944) Paramount. **B&W-62min.** Robert Lowery, Phillis Brooks.........................(3)

DANGEROUS PROFESSION, A (1949) RKO. **B&W-79min.** Pat O'Brien, George Raft, Ella Raines.........................**3***

DANGEROUS TO KNOW (1938) Paramount. **B&W-70min.** Anna May Wong, Akim Tamiroff.........................(3)

DANGEROUS WHEN WET (1953) M-G-M. **Color-95min.** Esther Williams, Fernando Lamas, Jack Carson.........................(3)

DANGEROUS YEARS (1947) 20th Century-Fox. **B&W-62min.** William (Billy) Halop, Ann E. Todd.........................(3)

DANGEROUS YOUTH (1957) Warner Bros. **B&W-98min.** Frankie Vaughan, George Baker.........................(2)
Original title: THESE DANGEROUS YEARS

DANGEROUSLY THEY LIVE (1941) Warner Bros. **B&W-71min.** John Garfield, Nancy Coleman.........................**4***

DANGERS OF THE CANADIAN MOUNTED (1948) *see* R.C.M.P. AND THE TREASURE OF GHENGHIS KHAN

DANIEL BOONE, TRAIL BLAZER (1956) Republic. **Color-76min.** Bruce Bennett, Lon Chaney (Jr.).........................(3)

DANTE'S INFERNO (1935) 20th Century-Fox. **B&W-88min.** Spencer Tracy, Claire Trevor.........................**4***

DANUBE, THE (1961) Buena Vista. **Color-30min.** *(Documentary).* *Producer:* Walt Disney.........................**5***

DARBY O'GILL AND THE LITTLE PEOPLE (1959) Buena Vista. **Color-93min.** Albert Sharpe, ...**5½***

DARBY'S RANGERS (1958) Warner Bros. **B&W-121min.** James Garner, Etchika Choureau.........................(4)
British title: YOUNG INVADERS, THE

DAREDEVILS OF THE CLOUDS (1948) Republic. **B&W-60min.** Robert Livingston, Mae Clark.........................(3)

DARING DOBERMANS, THE (1973) Dimension Pictures. **Color-90min.** Charles Knox Robinson, Tim Considine, Claudio Martinez.........................

DARING GAME (1968) Paramount. **Color-100min.** Lloyd Bridges, Michael Ansara.........................(3)

DARING YOUNG MAN, THE (1942) Columbia. **B&W-73min.** Neil Hamilton, James Dunn.........................(3)

DARK, THE (1979) Film Ventures International. **Color-92min.** William Devane, Cathy Lee Crosby.........................**4½***

DARK ALIBI (1946) Monogram [Allied Artists]. **B&W-61min.** Sidney Toler, Benson Fong.........................(4)

DARK ANGEL, THE (1935) United Artists. **B&W-110min.** Fredric March, Merle Oberon, Herbert Marshall.........................**6***

DARK AT THE TOP OF THE STAIRS, THE (1960) Warner Bros. **Color-123min.** Robert Preston, Dorothy McGuire.........................**6***

DARK AVENGER, THE (1955) *see* WARRIORS, THE

DARK CITY (1950) Paramount. **B&W-88min.** Charlton Heston, Lizabeth Scott.........................(4)

DARK COMMAND (1940) Republic. **B&W-94min.** Walter Pidgeon, John Wayne.........................**3½***

DARK CORNER, THE (1946) 20th Century-Fox. **B&W-99min.** Lucille Ball, Clifton Webb.........................**4***

DARK DELUSION (1947) M-G-M. **B&W-90min.** Lionel Barrymore, James Craig.........................(4)
British title: CYNTHIA'S SECRET

DARK EYES OF LONDON (1939) *see* HUMAN MONSTER, THE

DARK HAZARD (1934) First National [W.B.]. **B&W-72min.** Edward G. Robinson, Genevieve Tobin.........................(4)

DARK HORSE (1932) First National [W.B.]. **B&W-75min.** Warren William, Guy Kibbee.........................**4½***

DARK HORSE, THE (1946) Universal. **B&W-80min.** Philip Terry, Ann Savage.........................(4)

DARK INTRUDER (1965) Universal. **B&W-59min.** Mark Richman, Leslie Nielsen.........................(3)

DARBY O'GILL AND THE LITTLE PEOPLE (1959). Having become a prisoner of the Leprechauns, wily old Albert Sharpe fiddles up a tune which will enable him to escape from the jolly King, Jimmy O'Dea, and his followers.

Films are rated on a 1 to 10 scale, 10 is highest. **Boldface** ratings followed by an asterisk (*****) are for films actually seen and rated by the executive and senior editors. All other ratings are estimates. (See Notes on Entertainment Ratings in the front section.)

DARK JOURNEY (1937) United Artists. B&W-82min. *(British).* Conrad Veidt, Vivien Leigh 4*
Alternate title: ANXIOUS YEARS, THE

DARK MAN, THE (1951) J. Arthur Rank. B&W-73min. *(British).* Edward Underdown, Maxwell Reed .... (4)

DARK MIRROR, THE (1946) Universal. B&W-85min. Olivia de Havilland 5*

DARK OF THE SUN (1968) M-G-M. Color-101min. *(British).* Rod Taylor, Yvette Mimieux, Kenneth More 5*
Original title: MERCENARIES, THE

DARK PAGE, THE (1952) *see* SCANDAL SHEET

DARK PASSAGE (1947) Warner Bros. B&W-106min. Humphrey Bogart, Lauren Bacall 5*

DARK PAST, THE (1949) Columbia. B&W-75min. William Holden, Nina Foch .... (5)

DARK PLACES (1974) Cinerama Releasing. Color-91min. *(British).* Christopher Lee, Robert Hardy, Joan Collins, Herbert Lom .... (3)

DARK PURPOSE (1964) Universal. Color-97min. *(Italian-French-U.S., English language).* Shirley Jones, Rossano Brazzi, George Sanders ..... (2)
Original Italian title: INTRIGO, L' *(The Intrigue)*

DARK STAR (1974) Bryanston. Color-83min. Brian Narelle, Dre Pahich 3½*

DARK VENTURE (1956) Allied Artists. Color-84min. John Calvert, John Carradine .... (2)

DARK VICTORY (1939) Warner Bros. B&W-106min. Bette Davis, George Brent 5*

DARK VICTORY (1976) MCA-TV. Color-150min. *(Made for TV).* Elizabeth Montgomery, Anthony Hopkins .... (4)

DARK WATERS (1944) United Artists. B&W-90min. Merle Oberon, Franchot Tone .... (4)

DARKER THAN AMBER (1970) Nat'l General (for Cinema Center). Color-97min. Rod Taylor, Suzy Kendall, Theodore Bikel 4*

DARKEST AFRICA (1936) *see* BATMEN OF AFRICA

DARKTOWN STRUTTERS (1975) *see* GET DOWN AND BOOGIE

DARLING (1965) Avco-Embassy. B&W-127min. *(British).* Julie Christie, Laurence Harvey, Dirk Bogarde 7*

DARLING, HOW COULD YOU! (1951) Paramount. B&W-96min. Joan Fontaine, John Lund .... (4)
British title: RENDEZVOUS

DARLING LILI (1970) Paramount. Color-130min. Julie Andrews, Rock Hudson 4½*

DARWIN ADVENTURE, THE (1972) 20th Century-Fox. Color-91min. Nicholas Clay, Ian Richardson .... (4)

DATE AT MIDNIGHT (1959) Warner Bros. B&W-57min. *(British).* Paul Carpenter, Jean Aubrey .... (3)

DATE BAIT (1960) Filmgroup. B&W-71min. Gary Clark, Marlo Ryan .... (2)

DATE WITH A LONELY GIRL, A (1971) *see* T. R. BASKIN

DATE WITH DEATH, A (1959) Pacific International. B&W-81min. Gerald Mohr, Liz Renay .... (2)

DATE WITH DESTINY, A (1940) *see* MAD DOCTOR, THE

DATE WITH DESTINY (1948) *see* RETURN OF OCTOBER, THE

DATE WITH DISASTER (1957) Astor. B&W-61min. *(British).* Tom Drake, Shirley Eaton .... (3)

DATE WITH JUDY, A (1948) M-G-M. Color-113min. Jane Powell, Wallace Beery 4½*

DATE WITH THE FALCON, A (1941) RKO. B&W-63min. George Sanders, Wendy Barrie .... (3)

DAUGHTER, THE (1970) *see* I, A WOMAN, PART III

DAUGHTER OF CLEOPATRA (1961) *see* CLEOPATRA'S DAUGHTER

DAUGHTER OF DARKNESS (1947) Screencraft. B&W-92min. *(British).* Anne Crawford, Siobhan McKenna .... (5)

DAUGHTER OF DECEIT (1951) Bauer International. B&W-80min. *(Mexican).* Fernando Soler, Alicia Caro ....
Original title: HIJA DEL ENGANO, LA

DAUGHTER OF DESTINY (1928) *see* ALRAUNE

DAUGHTER OF DR. JEKYLL (1957) Allied Artists. B&W-71min. Gloria Talbot, John Agar, Arthur Shields 2*

DAUGHTER OF MATA HARI (1954) *see* MATA HARI'S DAUGHTER

DAUGHTER OF ROSIE O'GRADY, THE (1950) Warner Bros. Color-104min. June Haver, Gordon MacRae, Debbie Reynolds 4*

DAUGHTER OF SHANGHAI (1937) Paramount. B&W-63min. Anna May Wong, Larry "Buster" Crabbe .... (3)
British title: DAUGHTER OF THE ORIENT

DAUGHTER OF THE JUNGLE (1949) Republic. B&W-69min. Lois Hall, James Cardwell .... (2)

DAUGHTER OF THE MIND (1969) 20th Century-Fox. Color-74min. *(Made for TV).* Ray Milland, Gene Tierney, Don Murray 5*

DAUGHTERS COURAGEOUS (1939) Warner Bros. B&W-103min. John Garfield, Priscilla Lane 4*

DAUGHTERS OF DARKNESS (1971) Maron Films, Ltd. Color-87min. *(Belgian-French-W. German-Italian, English version).* Delphine Seyrig, Daniele Ouimet, John Karlen .... (2)
Original French title: ROUGE AUX LEVRES, LE *(The Redness of the Lips)*
Alternate title: PROMISE OF RED LIPS, THE

DAUGHTERS OF DESTINY (1952) Arlan Pictures. B&W-54min. *(French-Italian).* Claudette Colbert, Michel Morgan, Martine Carol .... (4)
Oeiginal French title: DESTINEES *(The Destined Women)*

DAUGHTERS OF DRACULA (1974) *see* VAMPYRES

DAUGHTERS OF JOSHUA CABE, THE (1972) Worldvision. Color-73min. *(Made for TV).* Buddy Ebsen, Sandra Dee, Karen Valentine, Lesley Warren 4*

DAUGHTERS OF JOSHUA CABE RETURN, THE (1975) ABC-TV. Color-74min. *(Made for TV).* Dan Dailey, Christine Hart ....

DAUGHTERS OF SATAN (1972) United Artists. Color-90min. *(U.S.-Philippine).* Tom Selleck, Barra Grant .... (3)

DAVID AND BATHSHEBA (1952) 20th Century-Fox. Color-116min. Gregory Peck, Susan Hayward 5*

DAVID AND GOLIATH (1960) Allied Artists. Color-95min. *(Italian).* Orson Welles, Ivo Payer 4*
Original title: DAVID E GOLIA

DAVID AND LISA (1962) Continental [Walter Reade]. B&W-94min. Keir Dullea, Janet Margolin 6*

DAVID COPPERFIELD (1935) M-G-M. B&W-133min. W. C. Fields, Freddie Bartholomew 5*
Screen title: PERSONAL HISTORY, ADVENTURES, EXPERIENCE, AND OBSERVATIONS OF DAVID COPPERFIELD, THE YOUNGER, THE

DAVID COPPERFIELD (1970) 20th Century-Fox. Color-118min. *(British, Made for TV).* Robin Phillips, Susan Hampshire 5½*

DAVID HARDING, COUNTERSPY (1950) Columbia. B&W-71min. Howard St. John, Willard Parker, Audrey Long .... (4)

DAVID HARUM (1934) Fox Film Co. [20th]. B&W-83min. Will Rogers, Evelyn Venable .... (4)

DAVID THE OUTLAW (1960) *see* STORY OF DAVID, A

DAVY CROCKETT AND THE RIVER PIRATES (1956) Buena Vista. Color-85min. *(Telefeature).* Fess Parker, Buddy Ebsen 5*

DAVY CROCKETT, INDIAN SCOUT (1950) United Artists. B&W-71min. George Montgomery, Ellen Drew .... (3)
British title: INDIAN SCOUT

DAVY CROCKETT, KING OF THE WILD FRONTIER (1955) Buena Vista. Color-95min. *(Telefeature).* Fess Parker, Buddy Ebsen 5*

DAWN AT SOCORRO (1954) Universal. Color-80min. Rory Calhoun, Piper Laurie 3*

DAWN OF LIFE, THE (1932) *see* LIFE BEGINS

DAWN OF THE DEAD (1978) United Film Distribution. Color-125min. Ken Foree, David Emge 5*

DAWN PATROL, THE (1930) First National [W.B.]. B&W-112min. Richard Barthelmess, Douglas Fairbanks, Jr. .... (4)
TV title: FLIGHT COMMANDER

DAWN PATROL, THE (1938) Warner Bros. B&W-103min. Errol Flynn, David Niven 5*

DAWNS HERE ARE QUIET, THE (1972) Sovexportfilm. B&W-180min. *(U.S.S.R.).* Andrei Martinov, Irina Scevciuk, Irina Dolganova 5*
Original title: A SORI SDESI TIBJE *(That Dawn Should Be Peaceful)*
Alternate title: AT DAWN IT'S QUIET HERE

DAY AFTER TOMORROW, THE (1946) *see* STRANGE HOLIDAY

DAY AND THE HOUR, THE (1962) M-G-M. B&W-115min. *(French-Italian).* Simone Signoret, Stuart Whitman 4*
Original French title: JOUR ET L'HEURE, LE

DAY AT THE RACES, A (1937) M-G-M. B&W-111min. Groucho Marx, Chico Marx 4*

DAY FOR NIGHT (1973) Warner Bros. Color-120min. *(French-Italian).* Jacqueline Bisset, Valentina Cortese 5*
Original title: NUIT AMERICAINE, LA *(The American Night)*

DAY IN THE COUNTRY, A (1936) *(French).* B&W-37min. Georges Saint-Saens (Georges Darnoux), Jacques Borel (Jacques Brunius), Jeanne Marken, Sylvia Bataille .... (4)
Original title: PARTIE DE CAMPAGNE, UNE

DAY IN THE DEATH OF JOE EGG (1972) Columbia. Color-100min. *(British).* Alan Bates, Janet Suzman 4*

Films are rated on a 1 to 10 scale, 10 is highest. **Boldface** ratings followed by an asterisk (*) are for films actually seen and rated by the executive and senior editors. All other ratings are estimates. (See Notes on Entertainment Ratings in the front section.)

DAY IT RAINED, THE (1959) Paramount. **B&W-85min.** *(German).* Elke Sommer, Corny Collins ....(2)
Original title: AM TAG ALS DER REGEN KAM, AM

DAY MARS INVADED EARTH, THE (1963) 20th Century-Fox. **B&W-70min.** Kent Taylor, Marie Windsor....................................(3)

DAY OF ANGER (1967) National General. **Color-109min.** *(Italian-W. German).* Giuliano Gemma, Lee Van Cleef............................(3)
Original Italian title: GIORNI DELL'IRA, I
Original German title: TOD RITT DIENSTAGS, DER

DAY OF FEAR (1957) Martin Gosch. **B&W-83min.** *(Spanish, English language).* Ruben Rojo, Elena Barrios, Fernando Rey ....(3)

DAY OF FURY, A (1956) Universal. **Color-78min.** Dale Robertson, Mara Corday ....(4)

DAY OF THE ANIMALS (1977) Film Ventures International. **Color-95min.** Christopher George, Lynda Day George, Leslie Nielsen, Richard Jaeckel 4*

DAY OF THE BAD MAN, THE (1958) Universal. **Color-81min.** Fred MacMurray, Joan Weldon......................................3*

DAY OF THE DOLPHIN, THE (1973) Avco-Embassy. **Color-104min.** George C. Scott, Trish Van Devere 4*

DAY OF THE EVIL GUN (1968) M-G-M. **Color-95min.** Glenn Ford, Arthur Kennedy 4*

DAY OF THE JACKAL, THE (1973) Universal. **Color-141min.** *(British-French).* Edward Fox, Michel Lonsdale 7*

DAY OF THE LOCUST, THE (1975) Paramount. **Color-144min.** Donald Sutherland, Karen Black 4*

DAY OF THE OUTLAW (1959) United Artists. **B&W-90min.** Robert Ryan, Burl Ives ....(3)

DAY OF THE TRIFFIDS, THE (1963) Allied Artists. **Color-93min.** Howard Keel, Nicole Maurey 4*

DAY OF THE WOLVES (1973) Gold Key Entertainment. **Color-95min.** *(Made for TV).* Richard Egan, Rick Jason, Martha Hyer 3*

DAY OF TRIUMPH (1954) George J. Schaefer. **Color-110min.** Robert Wilson, Lee J. Cobb 4*
Foreign title: GREAT BETRAYAL, THE

DAY OF WRATH (1943) George Schaefer. **B&W-96min.** *(Danish).* Thorkild Roose, Lisbeth Movin..4*
Original title: VREDEN'S DAG
Alternate title: DIES IRAE

DAY THAT SHOOK THE WORLD, THE (1976) American-International. **Color-111min.** *(Yugoslavian-Czech).* Christopher Plummer, Florinda Bolkan 3*
Original Yugoslavian title: ATENTAT U SARAJEVU *(Assassination in Sarajevo)*

DAY THE EARTH CAUGHT FIRE, THE (1961) Universal. **B&W-90min.** *(British).* Janet Munro, Leo McKern 5*

THE DAY OF THE JACKAL (1973). Aged gunsmith Cyril Cusack has precision crafted a deadly instrument of destruction which assassin Edward Fox will attempt to use against French President De Gaulle.

DAY THE EARTH FROZE, THE (1959) American-International. **Color-69min.** *(Finland-U.S.S.R.).* Andris Oshin, A. Orochko, I. Voronov, Eve Kivi ....(3)
Original title: SAMPO

DAY THE EARTH MOVED, THE (1974) Worldvision. **Color-75min.** *(Made for TV).* Jackie Cooper, Stella Stevens 4*

DAY THE EARTH STOOD STILL, THE (1951) 20th Century-Fox. **B&W-92min.** Michael Rennie, Patricia Neal 5*

DAY THE FISH CAME OUT, THE (1967) International Classics [20th]. **Color-109min.** *(British-Greek-U.S.)* Tom Courtenay, Sam Wanamaker 2*

DAY THE HOT LINE GOT HOT, THE (1969) American-International. **Color-100min.** *(Spanish-French).* George Chakiris, Marie Dubois, Charles Boyer, Robert Taylor 3*
Original Spanish title: RUBLO DE LAS DOS CARAS, EL
French title: ROUBLE A DEUX FACES, LE
Alternate title(?): HOT LINE, THE

DAY THE SKY EXPLODED, THE (1958) Excelsior. **B&W-80min.** *(Italian-French).* Paul Hubschmid, Madeleine Fischer 3½*
Original Italian title: MORTE VIENE DALLO SPAZIO, LA *(Death Comes from Space)*
Original French title: DANGER VIENT DE L'ESPACE, LE *(Danger Comes from Space)*

DAY THE WORLD ENDED (1956) American Releasing [A.I.P.]. **B&W-80min.** Richard Denning, Adele Jergens 2*

DAY THE WORLD ENDED, THE (1979) Warner Bros. **Color-   min.** Paul Newman, William Holden, Jacqueline Bisset............................

DAY THEY GAVE BABIES AWAY, THE (1958) *see* ALL MINE TO GIVE

DAY THEY ROBBED THE BANK OF ENGLAND, THE (1960) M-G-M. **B&W-85min.** *(British).* Aldo Ray, Peter O'Toole 3*

DAY TO REMEMBER, A (1953) Republic. **B&W-92min.** *(British).* Stanley Holloway, Donald Sinden................................(4)

DAYBREAK (1938) Vog. **B&W-95min.** *(French).* Jean Gabin, Jacqueline Laurent, Arletty ....(4)
Original title: JOUR SE LEVE, LE

DAYBREAK (1947) J. Arthur Rank. **B&W-88min.** *(British).* Eric Portman, Ann Todd..(3)

DAYDREAMER, THE (1966) Avco-Embassy. **Color-101min.** *(Puppets).* Director: Jules Bass..5*

DAYS AND NIGHTS IN THE FOREST (1969) Pathé Contemporary. **B&W-115min.** *(Indian).* Soumitra Chatterjee, Subhendu Chatterjee, Samit Bhanja ....
Original title: ARANYER DIN RATRI

DAYS OF GLORY (1944) RKO. **B&W-86min.** Tamara Tournanova, Gregory Peck 3*

DAYS OF HEAVEN (1978) Paramount. **Color-95min.** Richard Gere, Brooke Adams..6*

DAYS OF '36 (1972) Finos Film *(Greek).* **Color-110min.** *(Greek).* Thanos Grammenos, George Kyritsis................................(3)
Original title(?): IMERES TOU '36
Original title(?): MERES TOU 1936

DAYS OF THRILLS AND LAUGHTER (1961) 20th Century-Fox. **B&W-93min.** *(Compilation).* Producer: Robert Youngson 4*

DAYS OF WINE AND ROSES (1962) Warner Bros. **B&W-117min.** Jack Lemmon, Lee Remick 6½*

DAYTIME WIFE (1939) 20th Century-Fox. **B&W-71min.** Tyrone Power, Linda Darnell..(4)

DAYTON'S DEVILS (1968) Commonwealth United. **Color-101min.** Rory Calhoun, Leslie Nielsen..(3)

DE SADE (1969) American-International. **Color-113min.** *(U.S.-W. German).* Keir Dullea, John Huston, Senta Berger ....(3)
Original German title: AUSSCHWEIFENDE LEBEN DES MARQUIS DE SADE, DAS

DEAD ARE ALIVE, THE (1972) National General. **Color-104min.** *(Italian-Yugoslavian-W. German).* Samantha Eggar, Alex Cord ....(3)
Original Italian title: ETRUSCO UCCIDI ENCORE, L'

DEAD DON'T DIE, THE (1975) NBC-TV. **Color-74min.** *(Made for TV).* George Hamilton, Ray Milland, Linda Cristal 3*

DEAD END (1937) United Artists. **B&W-93min.** Sylvia Sidney, Joel McCrea..4*

DEAD EYES OF LONDON (1961) Magna Pictures. **B&W-104min.** *(German).* Joachim Fuchsberger, Karin Baal, Dieter Borsche.............(2)
Original title: TOTEN AUGEN VON LONDON, DIE

DEAD HEAT ON A MERRY-GO-ROUND (1966) Columbia. **Color-104min.** James Coburn, Camilla Sparv................................5½*

DEAD IMAGE (1964) *see* DEAD RINGER

DEAD MAN'S CHEST (1965) Avco-Embassy. B&W-59min. (British). John Thaw, Ann Firbank, John Meillon .... (3)

DEAD MAN'S EYES (1944) Universal. B&W-64min. Lon Chaney, Jr., Jean Parker .... (3)

DEAD MEN TELL NO TALES (1971) 20th Century-Fox. Color-75min. (Made for TV). Christopher George, Judy Carne, Richard Anderson 4*
Alternate title: TO SAVE HIS LIFE

DEAD OF NIGHT (1945) Universal. B&W-104min. (British). Mervyn Johns, Roland Culver 5½*

DEAD OF NIGHT (1977) NBC-TV. Color-74min. (Made for TV). Joan Hackett, Patrick Macnee, Anjanette Comer .... (4)

DEAD OF SUMMER (1970) Plaza Pictures. Color-89min. (Italian-French). Jean Seberg, Luigi Pistilli .... (3)
Original Italian title: ONDATA DI CALORE

DEAD OR ALIVE (1967) see MINUTE TO PRAY, A SECOND TO DIE, A

DEAD RECKONING (1947) Columbia. B&W-100min. Humphrey Bogart, Lizabeth Scott 5*

DEAD RINGER (1964) Warner Bros. B&W-115min. Bette Davis............ (4)
British title: DEAD IMAGE

DEAD THAT WALK, THE (1957) see ZOMBIES OF MORA-TAU

DEAD TO THE WORLD (1961) United Artists. B&W-87min. Reedy Talton, Jana Pearce .... (2)

DEADFALL (1968) 20th Century-Fox. Color-120min. (British-U.S.). Michael Caine, Giovanna Ralli 3½*

DEADLIER THAN THE MALE (1955) Continental [Walter Reade]. B&W-104min. (French). Jean Gabin, Daniele Delorme.......................... (4)
Original title: VOICI LE TEMPS DES ASSASSIN

DEADLIER THAN THE MALE (1967) Universal. Color-98min. (British). Richard Johnson, Elke Sommer .... (4)

DEADLIEST SIN, THE (1955) Allied Artists. B&W-77min. (British). Sydney Chaplin, Audrey Dalton.. (3)
Original title: CONFESSION

DEADLINE AT DAWN (1946) RKO. B&W-83min. Susan Hayward, Bill Williams 4½*

DEADLINE MIDNIGHT (1959) see -30-

DEADLINE U.S.A. (1952) 20th Century-Fox. B&W-87min. Humphrey Bogart, Ethel Barrymore 5*
British title: DEADLINE

DEADLOCK (1969) Universal. Color-100min. (Made for TV). Leslie Nielsen, Aldo Ray, Hari Rhodes .... (5)

DEADLY AFFAIR, THE (1967) Columbia. Color-107min. (British). James Mason, Simone Signoret 4*

DEADLY BEES, THE (1967) Paramount. Color-83min. (British). Suzanna Leigh, Frank Finlay 3*

DEADLY COMPANIONS, THE (1961) Pathé-America. Color-90min. Maureen O'Hara, Brian Keith 5*

DEADLY DECISION (1954) Dominant Pictures. B&W-92min. (German). O. E. Hasse, Adrian Hoven .... (4)
Original title: CANARIS
British title: CANARIS MASTER SPY

DEADLY DECOY, THE (1962) Four Star. B&W-90min. (French). Roger Hanin, Roger Dumas .... (3)
Original title: GORILLE A MORDU L'ARCHEVEQUE, LE

DEADLY DREAM, THE (1971) MCA-TV. Color-73min. (Made for TV). Lloyd Bridges, Janet Leigh .... (4)

DEADLY DUO (1962) United Artists. B&W-70min. Craig Hill, Marcia Henderson .... (3)

DEADLY HERO (1976) Avco-Embassy. Color-99min. Don Murray, Diahn Williams, James Earl Jones 4*

DEADLY HONEYMOON (1973) see NIGHTMARE HONEYMOON

DEADLY HUNT, THE (1971) Viacom. Color-74min. (Made for TV). Tony Franciosa, Peter Lawford, Jim Hutton, Anjanette Comer 4*

DEADLY INVENTION, THE (1958) see FABULOUS WORLD OF JULES VERNE, THE

DEADLY IS THE FEMALE (1949) United Artists. B&W-87min. Peggy Cummins, John Dall .... (4)
Alternate title: GUN CRAZY

DEADLY MANTIS, THE (1957) Universal. B&W-78min. Craig Stevens, William Hopper 3*

DEADLY RAY FROM MARS, THE (1938) Universal. B&W-99min. (Re-edited Serial). Buster Crabbe, Jean Rogers, Charles Middleton .... (3)
Original title: FLASH GORDON'S TRIP TO MARS
Title of alternate 82-minute condensation: MARS ATTACKS THE WORLD

DEADLY RECORD (1959) Anglo Amalgamated [EMI]. B&W-59min. (British). Lee Patterson, Barbara Shelley.. (3)

DEADLY SILENCE (1970) see TARZAN AND THE DEADLY SILENCE

DEADLY TOWER, THE (1975) M-G-M. Color-100min. (Made for TV). Kurt Russell, Richard Yniguez, Ned Beatty 4½*

DEADLY TRACKERS, THE (1973) Warner Bros. Color-104min. Richard Harris, Rod Taylor 4*

DEADLY TRAP, THE (1971) National General. Color-91min. (French-Italian, English language). Faye Dunaway, Frank Langella 4*
Original French title: MAISON SOUS LES ARBRES, LA (The House Under the Trees)

DEADLY TRIANGLE, THE (1977) CPT (TV). Color-75min. (Made for TV). Dale Robinette, Taylor Archer 4*

DEADWOOD '76 (1964) Filmway International. Color-110min. Arch Hall, Jr., Jack Lester.. (2)

DEAF SMITH AND JOHNNY EARS (1972) M-G-M. Color-91min. (Italian). Anthony Quinn, Franco Nero .... (4)
Original title: AMIGOS, LOS (The Friends)

DEAFULA (1975) Signscope. B&W-95min. Peter Wechsberg, James Randall, Gary Holstrom .... (2)

DEALING: OR THE BERKELEY-TO-BOSTON FORTY-BRICK LOST-BAG BLUES (1972) Warner Bros. Color-88min. Barbara Hershey, Robert F. Lyons .... (4)

DEAR BRAT (1951) Paramount. B&W-82min. Mona Freeman, Edward Arnold .... (4)

DEAR BRIGITTE (1965) 20th Century-Fox. Color-100min. James Stewart, Billy Mumy 4*

DEAR CAROLINE (1951) Color-90min. (French). Martine Carol, Jacques Dacqmine .... (3)
Original title: CAROLINE CHÉRIE

DEAR, DEAD DELILAH (1972) Southern Star. Color-95min. Agnes Moorehead, Patricia Carmichael, Robert Gentry, Will Geer.................. 2*

DEAR HEART (1965) Warner Bros. B&W-114min. Glenn Ford, Geraldine Page 3½*

DEAR INSPECTOR (1977) Cinema 5. Color-105min. (French). Annie Girardot, Philippe Noiret 4½*
Original title: TENDRE POULET
Alternate title: DEAR DETECTIVE

DEAR JOHN (1964) Sigma III. B&W-115min. (Swedish). Jarl Kulle, Christina Schollin .... (5)
Original title: KARE JOHN

DEAR MR. PROHACK (1941) J. Arthur Rank. B&W-91min. (British). Cecil Parker, Glynis Johns, Hermione Baddeley, Dirk Bogarde............

DEAR MURDERER (1947) Universal. B&W-94min. (British). Eric Portman, Greta Gynt .... (3)

DEAR RUTH (1947) Paramount. B&W-95min. Joan Caulfield, William Holden.. (5)

DEAR WIFE (1950) Paramount. B&W-88min. William Holden, Joan Caulfield .... (5)

DEAREST LOVE (1971) see MURMUR OF THE HEART

DEATH AND THE SKY ABOVE (1959) B&W-60min. (British). Peter Williams, Petra Davies... (3)

DEATH AT LOVE HOUSE (1975) MPC (TV). Color-74min. (Made for TV). Robert Wagner, Kate Jackson, Sylvia Sidney, John Carradine.......... 3*

DEATH BE NOT PROUD (1975) Dan Goodman. Color-100min. (Made for TV). Arthur Hill, Jane Alexander, Robby Benson 4*

DEATH COLLECTOR (1977) Epoh. Color-85min. Joseph Cortese, Lou Criscuola ....

DEATH CORPS (1977) see SHOCK WAVES

DEATH CRUISE (1974) MPC (TV). Color-75min. (Made for TV). Edward Albert, Jr., Kate Jackson, Polly Bergen.. 4*

DEATH DANCE AT MADELIA (1967) see INTRUDERS, THE

DEATH DRUMS ALONG THE RIVER (1964) see SANDERS

DEATH GAME (1977) Levitt-Pickman. Color-89min. Sondra Locke, Colleen Camp, Seymour Cassel ....

DEATH HEAD VIRGIN, THE (1974) see DEATHHEAD VIRGIN

DEATH IN CANAAN, A (1978) CBS-TV. Color-125min. (Made for TV). Paul Clemens, Stefanie Powers, Tom Atkins...................................

DEATH IN SMALL DOSES (1957) Allied Artists. B&W-79min. Peter Graves, Mala Powers .... (3)

DEATH IN THE ARENA (1960) see COLOSSUS OF THE ARENA

DEATH IN THE GARDEN (1956) Bauer International. Color-97min. (French-Mexican). Simone Signoret, Georges Marchal, Michel Piccoli....
Original French title: MORT EN CE JARDIN, LA

Films are rated on a 1 to 10 scale, 10 is highest. **Boldface** ratings followed by an asterisk (*) are for films actually seen and rated by the executive and senior editors. All other ratings are estimates. (See Notes on Entertainment Ratings in the front section.)

DEATH IN VENICE (1971) Warner Bros. Color-121min. *(Italian-French, English language)*. Dirk Bogarde, Bjorn Andresen..................................2*
Original title: MORTE A VENEZIA

DEATH IS A WOMAN (1966) American-International. Color-80min. *(British)*. Patsy Ann Noble, Mark Burns..................................(3)
Alternate title: LOVE IS A WOMAN
Alternate title: SEX IS A WOMAN

DEATH IS MY TRADE (1977) WDR-Iduna (German). Color-139min. *(German)*. Goetz George, Elisabeth Schwarz..................................

DEATH LINE (1973) *see* RAW MEAT

DEATH MACHINES (1976) Crown International. Color-93min. John Lowe, Ron Marchini, Joshua Johnson, Michael Chong..................................(3)

DEATH MOON (1978) CBS-TV. Color-96min. *(Made for TV)*. Robert Foxworth, Barbara Trentham..................................3*

DEATH OF A CHAMPION (1939) Paramount. B&W-67min. Lynne Overman, Virginia Dale..................................(3)

DEATH OF A CYCLIST (1955) *see* AGE OF INFIDELITY

DEATH OF A GUNFIGHTER (1969) Universal. Color-94min. Richard Widmark, Lena Horne..................................4*

DEATH OF A JEW (1972) H.K. Film Dist. Color-90min. Assaf Dayan, Akim Tamiroff..................................
Alternate title: SABRA

DEATH OF A SALESMAN (1951) Columbia. B&W-115min. Fredric March, Mildred Dunnock..................................(6)

DEATH OF A SCOUNDREL (1956) RKO. B&W-119min. George Sanders, Yvonne De Carlo..................................(4)

DEATH OF HER INNOCENCE, THE (1974) *see* OUR TIME

DEATH OF INNOCENCE, A (1971) Mark Carliner Productions. Color-73min. *(Made for TV)*. Shelley Winters, Arthur Kennedy, Tisha Sterling..................................(4)

DEATH OF ME YET, THE (1971) Worldvision. Color-73min. *(Made for TV)*. Doug McClure, Darren McGavin, Richard Basehart..................................4*

DEATH OF SIEGFRIED (1923) *see* NIBELUNGEN, DIE

DEATH OF TARZAN, THE (1962) Brandon. B&W-72min. *(Czech)*. Rudolf Hrusinsky, Jana Stepankova..................................(4)
Original title: TARZANA SMRT
Alternate title: DEATH OF THE APE-MAN

DEATH ON THE NILE (1978) Paramount. Color-140min. Peter Ustinov, Mia Farrow, Bette Davis..................................6*

DEATH PLAY (1976) New Line Cinema. Color-86min. Karen Leslie, Michael Higgins, James Keach..................................(4)

DEATH RACE (1973) MCA TV. Color-75min. *(Made for TV)*. Lloyd Bridges, Roy Thinnes, Eric Braeden..................................4*

DEATH RACE 2000 (1975) New World. Color-78min. David Carradine, Simone Griffeth, Sylvester Stallone..................................(4)

DEATH RIDES A HORSE (1967) United Artists. Color-115min. *(Italian)*. John Phillip Law, Lee Van Cleef..................................3*
Original title: DA UOMO A UOMO

DEATH SCREAM (1975) ABC-TV. Color-96min. *(Made for TV)*. Raul Julia, Lucie Arnaz, Art Carney, Cloris Leachman..................................
Alternate title: WOMAN WHO CRIED MURDER

DEATH SENTENCE (1975) MPC (TV). Color-74min. *(Made for TV)*. Cloris Leachman, Laurence Luckinbill..................................4*

DEATH SMILES ON A MURDERER (1973) Avco-Embassy. Color-85min. *(Foreign)*. Ewa Aulin, Klaus Kinski..................................1*
Original title: MORTE SORRIDE ALL'ASSASSINO, LA

DEATH SQUAD, THE (1974) MPC (TV). Color-75min. *(Made for TV)*. Robert Forster, Melvyn Douglas, Claude Akins..................................4*

DEATH TAKES A HOLIDAY (1934) Paramount. B&W-78min. Fredric March, Evelyn Venable..................................5½*

DEATH TAKES A HOLIDAY (1971) Universal. Color-90min. *(Made for TV)*. Yvette Mimieux, Monte Markham..................................4*

DEATH TRAP (1962) Anglo Amalgamated [EMI]. B&W-56min. *(British)*. Albert Lieven, Barbara Shelley..................................(3)

DEATH TRAP (1976) *see* EATEN ALIVE

DEATH WHEELERS (1973) Scotia International *(Brit.)*. Color-89min. *(British)*. George Sanders, Beryl Reid, Nicky Henson..................................(3)
Original title: PSYCHOMANIA

DEATH WISH (1974) Paramount. Color-92min. Charles Bronson, Vincent Gardenia..................................5½*

DEATHHEAD VIRGIN (1974) Wargay. Color- min. Jock Gaynor, Larry Ward, Diane McBain..................................(2)
Alternate title: DEATH HEAD VIRGIN, THE

DEATHMASTER, THE (1972) American-International. Color-88min. Robert Quarry, Bill Ewing..................................(3)

DEATHRAY MIRROR OF DR. MABUSE (1961) *see* SECRET OF DR. MABUSE

DEATHSPORT (1978) New World. Color-83min. David Carradine.......2½*

DEATHWATCH (1967) Altura Films. B&W-88min. Leonard Nimoy, Michael Forest..................................(4)

DEBORAH (1974) Allied Artists. Color-107min. *(Italian)*. Gig Young, Bradford Dillman, Marina Malfatti..................................2*

DECAMERON, THE (1971) United Artists. Color-114min. *(Italian-French-W. German)*. Franco Citti, Ninetto Davoli..................................(3)
Original Italian title: DECAMERONE, IL

DECAMERON NIGHTS (1953) RKO. Color-94min. *(British)*. Joan Fontaine, Louis Jourdan..................................(5)

DECEIVERS, THE (1966) *see* INTIMACY

DECEPTION (1946) Warner Bros. B&W-112min. Bette Davis, Paul Henreid..................................4½*

DECISION AGAINST TIME (1957) M-G-M. B&W-87min. *(British)*. Jack Hawkins, Elizabeth Sellars..................................(4)
Original title: MAN IN THE SKY, THE

DECISION AT SUNDOWN (1957) Columbia. Color-95min. Randolph Scott, John Carroll..................................(4)

DECISION BEFORE DAWN (1951) 20th Century-Fox. B&W-119min. Richard Basehart, Gary Merrill, Oskar Werner..................................5*

DECISION OF CHRISTOPHER BLAKE, THE (1948) Warner Bros. B&W-75min. Alexis Smith, Robert Douglas..................................(4)

DECKS RAN RED, THE (1958) M-G-M. B&W-84min. James Mason, Dorothy Dandridge..................................4*

DECLINE AND FALL . . . OF A BIRD WATCHER (1968) 20th Century-Fox. Color-113min. *(British)*. Robin Phillips, Donald Wolfit, Genevieve Page..................................3½*

DECOY (1946) Monogram [Allied Artists]. B&W-76min. Jean Gillie, Edward Norris..................................(4)

DECOY (1962) *see* MYSTERY SUBMARINE

DECOY FOR TERROR (1970) Group IV. Color-90min. *(Canadian)*..........2*

DEEP, THE (1977) Columbia. Color-124min. Nick Nolte, Jacqueline Bisset, Robert Shaw..................................6½*

DEEP ADVENTURE (1957) Warner Bros. Color-46min. Ross Allen, Dottie Lee Phillips, William Fuller..................................(3)

DEEP BLUE SEA, THE (1955) 20th Century-Fox. Color-99min. *(British)*. Vivien Leigh, Kenneth More..................................4*

DEEP END (1971) Paramount. Color-87min. *(W. German-U.S.)*. Jane Asher, John Moulder-Brown..................................(4)

DEEP IN MY HEART (1954) M-G-M. Color-132min. José Ferrer, Merle Oberon..................................(5)

DEEP SIX, THE (1958) Warner Bros. Color-105min. Alan Ladd, William Bendix..................................(4)

DEEP THROAT (1972) Aquarius Releasing. Color-62min. Linda Lovelace, Harry Reems..................................2*

DEEP THROAT - PART II (1974) Bryanston. Color-87min. Linda Lovelace, Harry Reams..................................(1)
Publicity title: DEEP THROAT II

DEEP THRUST - THE HAND OF DEATH (1973) American-International. Color-88min. *(Chinese)*. Angela Mao, Chang Yi..................................1*

DEEP VALLEY (1947) Warner Bros. B&W-104min. Ida Lupino, Dane Clark..................................3*

DEEP WATERS (1948) 20th Century-Fox. B&W-85min. Dana Andrews, Jean Peters, Dean Stockwell..................................(4)

DEER HUNTER, THE (1978) Universal. Color-183min. Robert De Niro, John Cazale..................................5½*

DEERSLAYER, THE (1957) 20th Century-Fox. Color-78min. Lex Barker, Rita Moreno..................................(3)

DEFEAT OF HANNIBAL, THE (1937) *see* SCIPIO AFRICANUS

DEFEAT OF THE BARBARIANS, THE (1962) Trans-America. Color-85min. *(Italian)*. Ken Clark, Gerard Laudry..................................(1)

DEFECTION OF SIMAS KUDIRKA, THE (1978) CBS-TV. Color-100min. *(Made for TV)*. Alan Arkin, Richard Jordan, Shirley Knight..................................

DEFECTOR, THE (1966) Seven Arts [W.B.]. Color-106min. *(French-German)*. Montgomery Clift, Hardy Kruger..................................4*
Original French title: ESPION, L' *(The Spy)*
German title: LAUTLOSE WAFFEN

DEFIANCE (1979) American-International. Color-103min. Jan-Michael Vincent, Theresa Saldana..................................

DEFIANT DAUGHTERS (1961) *see* SHADOWS GROW LONGER

DEFIANT ONES, THE (1958) United Artists. B&W-97min. Tony Curtis, Sidney Poitier..................................5½*

DELICATE BALANCE, A (1973) American Film Theatre. **Color-132min.** Katharine Hepburn, Paul Scofield 4*

DELICATE DELINQUENT, THE (1957) Paramount. **B&W-100min.** Jerry Lewis, Darren McGavin................ 4*

DELICIOUS (1931) Fox Film Co. [20th]. **B&W-106min.** Janet Gaynor, Charles Farrell .... (4)

DELIGHTFULLY DANGEROUS (1945) United Artists. **B&W-93min.** Ralph Bellamy, Jane Powell, Constance Moore .... (3)

DELINQUENTS (1950) Official Industries. **B&W-55min.** Gloria Marlen, Charles Thornbridge .... (2)

DELIVER US FROM EVIL (1973) Warner Bros. **Color-75min.** *(Made for TV).* George Kennedy, Jan-Michael Vincent, Bradford Dillman 4*

DELIVERANCE (1972) Warner Bros. **Color-109min.** Jon Voight, Burt Reynolds 8*

DELPHI BUREAU, THE (1972) Warner Bros. **Color-99min.** *(Made for TV).* Laurence Luckinbill, Joanna Petet, Bradford Dillman .... (4)

DELTA FACTOR, THE (1971) American Continental. **Color-91min.** Yvette Mimieux, Christopher George .... (3)

DELUGE, THE (1974) Polish Corporation for Film Production & Bielorusfilm. **Color-300min.** *(Polish).* Daniel Olbrychski, Malgorzata Braunek 5*
Original title: POTOP

DEMENTIA 13 (1963) American-International. **B&W-81min.** William Campbell, Luana Anders 3*
British title: HAUNTED AND THE HUNTED, THE

DEMETRIUS AND THE GLADIATORS (1954) 20th Century-Fox. **Color-101min.** Victor Mature, Susan Hayward 5*

DEMON, THE (1964) *see* ONIBABA

DEMON (1976) New World. **Color-87min.** Tony Lo Bianco, Sandy Dennis 3*
Original title: GOD TOLD ME TO

DEMON DOCTOR, THE (1962) *see* AWFUL DR. ORLOFF, THE

DEMON LOVER, THE (1976) Wolf Lore Cinema. **Color-80min.** Gunnar Hansen, Val Mayerik .... (3)

DEMON PLANET, THE (1965) *see* PLANET OF THE VAMPIRES

DEMON SEED (1977) United Artists. **Color-94min.** Julie Christie, Fritz Weaver 5*

DEMONIAQUE (1957) United Motion Pic. Org. (UMPO). **B&W-97min.** *(French).* Francois Perier, Micheline Presle, Jeanne Moreau .... (5)

DEMONS (1972) Film Images. **B&W-135min.** *(Japanese).* Katsuo Nakamura, Yasuko Sanjo .... (4)
Original title: SHURA
Alternate title: PANDEMONIUM

DEMONS OF THE MIND (1973) **Color-89min.** *(British).* .... (2)

DEMONS OF THE SWAMP (1959) *see* ATTACK OF THE GIANT LEECHES

DELIVERANCE (1972). Ned Beatty, Burt Reynolds, Jon Voight and Ronny Cox are the not-so-intrepid adventurers who set out on a canoe trip down a wild river in the Georgia wilderness.

DEN OF DOOM (1964) *see* GLASS CAGE, THE

DENTIST IN THE CHAIR (1960) Ajay Films. **B&W-84min.** *(British).* Bob Monkhouse, Peggy Cummins, Ronnie Stevens................ (3)

DENTIST ON THE JOB (1961) *see* GET ON WITH IT!

DENVER AND RIO GRANDE, THE (1952) Paramount. **Color-89min.** Edmond O'Brien, Sterling Hayden................ 4*

DEPART, LE (1967) Pathé Contemporary. **B&W-90min.** *(Belgian).* Jean-Pierre Léaud, Catherine Duport................ (4)
Translation title: The Departure

DEPORTED (1950) Universal. **B&W-80min.** Jeff Chandler, Marta Toren 4*

DERANGED (1974) American-International. **Color-82min.** Roberts Blossom, Cosette Lee .... (3)

DERBY (1971) Cinerama Releasing. **Color-91min.** *(Documentary).*
Director: Robert Kaylor .... (5)
British title: ROLLER DERBY

DERBY DAY (1952) Continental [Walter Reade]. **B&W-84min.** *(British).* Anna Neagle, Michael Wilding .... (4)
Alternate title: FOUR AGAINST FATE

DERNIER TOURNANT, LE (1940) **B&W-93min.** *(French).* Ferdnand Gravet, Corinne Luchaire, Michel Simon ....
Translation title: The Last Time Around [*colloquial*]

DERSU UZALA (1975) New World. **Color-137min.** *(U.S.S.R.-Japanese).* Maksim Munzuk, Yuri Solomin 4½*

DESERT ATTACK (1958) 20th Century-Fox. **B&W-129min.** *(British).* John Mills, Sylvia Syms 4½*
Original title: ICE COLD IN ALEX

DESERT DESPERADOES (1959) RKO. **B&W-81min.** *(U.S.-Italian).* Ruth Roman, Akim Tamiroff .... (2)
Alternate title: SINNER, THE
British and alternate U.S. title: SINNER, THE

DESERT FIGHTERS (1960) American-International. **B&W-85min.** *(French).* Michel Auclair, Marcel Dalio................ (3)

DESERT FOX, THE (1951) 20th Century-Fox. **B&W-88min.** James Mason, Cedric Hardwicke 5*
British title: ROMMEL - DESERT FOX

DESERT FURY (1947) Paramount. **Color-95min.** Lizabeth Scott, Burt Lancaster 3*

DESERT HAWK, THE (1950) Universal. **Color-77min.** Richard Greene, Yvonne De Carlo, Jackie Gleason 4*

DESERT HELL (1958) 20th Century-Fox. **B&W-82min.** Brian Keith, Barbara Hale 2½*

DESERT LEGION (1953) Universal. **Color-86min.** Alan Ladd, Arlene Dahl................ (3)

DESERT PATROL (1953) *see* EL ALAMEIN

DESERT PATROL (1958) Universal. **B&W-78min.** *(British).* Richard Attenborough, John Gregson................ (5)
Original title: SEA OF SAND

DESERT PURSUIT (1952) Monogram [Allied Artists]. **B&W-71min.** Wayne Morris, Virginia Grey................ (2)

DESERT RAIDERS (1963) **Color-87min.** *(Italian).* Kirk Morris, Rosalba Neri .... (1)

DESERT RATS, THE (1953) 20th Century-Fox. **B&W-88min.** Richard Burton, James Mason................ 5*

DESERT SANDS (1955) United Artists. **Color-87min.** Ralph Meeker, Marla English................ (3)

DESERT SONG, THE (1944) Warner Bros. **B&W-96min.** Dennis Morgan, Irene Manning .... (4)

DESERT SONG, THE (1953) Warner Bros. **Color-110min.** Kathryn Grayson, Gordon MacRae................ 4½*

DESERT WAR (1960) American-International. **B&W-83min.** *(Italian).* Peter Baldwin, Chelo Alonso .... (3)

DESERT WARRIOR (1958) Medallion. **Color-87min.** *(Spanish-Italian).* Ricardo Montalban, Carmen Sevilla................ (3)
Original Spanish title: AMANTES DEL DESIERTO, LOS *(The Lovers of the Desert)*
Original Italian title: AMANTI DEL DESERTO
Alternate Italian title(?): FIGLIO DELLO SCEICCO, LA

DESERTER, THE (1971) Paramount. **Color-99min.** *(Italian-Yugoslavian-U.S.).* Bekim Fehmiu, John Huston, Richard Crenna................ (3)
Original Italian title: SPINA DORSALE DEL DIAVOLO, LA *(The Devil's Backbone)*

DESIGN FOR LIVING (1933) Paramount. **B&W-90min.** Fredric March, Gary Cooper, Miriam Hopkins 5*

DESIGN FOR LOVING (1960) Columbia. **B&W-68min.** *(British).* June Thorburn, Peter Murray .... (3)

Films are rated on a 1 to 10 scale, 10 is highest. **Boldface** ratings followed by an asterisk (*) are for films actually seen and rated by the executive and senior editors. All other ratings are estimates. (See Notes on Entertainment Ratings in the front section.)

DESIGN FOR SCANDAL (1941) M-G-M. **B&W-85min.** Walter Pidgeon, Rosalind Russell 4*

DESIGNING WOMAN (1957) M-G-M. Color-118min. Gregory Peck, Lauren Bacall 5*

DESIRABLE (1934) Warner Bros. **B&W-68min.** George Brent, Jean Muir..................(4)

DESIRE (1936) Paramount. **B&W-89min.** Marlene Dietrich, Gary Cooper 5*

DESIRE IN THE DUST (1960) 20th Century-Fox. **B&W-102min.** Ken Scott, Martha Hyer 3*

DESIRE ME (1947) M-G-M. **B&W-91min.** Greer Garson, Richard Hart, Robert Mitchum 4*

DESIRE UNDER THE ELMS (1958) Paramount. **B&W-111min.** Sophia Loren, Anthony Perkins, Burl Ives 4½*

DÉSIRÉE (1954) 20th Century-Fox. Color-110min. Marlon Brando, Jean Simmons 5*

DESK SET (1957) 20th Century-Fox. Color-103min. Spencer Tracy, Katharine Hepburn 5*
British title: HIS OTHER WOMAN

DESPERADO, THE (1954) Allied Artists. **B&W-81min.** Wayne Morris, Beverly Garland ....(3)

DESPERADOES, THE (1942) Columbia. Color-85min. Randolph Scott, Glenn Ford 4*

DESPERADOS, THE (1969) Columbia. Color-90min. Vince Edwards, Jack Palance..................3*

DESPERADOS ARE IN TOWN, THE (1956) 20th Century-Fox. **B&W-73min.** Rex Reason, Robert Arthur..................(3)

DESPERATE (1947) RKO. **B&W-73min.** Steve Brodie, Audrey Long......(4)

DESPERATE CHARACTERS (1971) Paramount. Color-88min. Shirley MacLaine, Kenneth Mars 2½*

DESPERATE HOURS, THE (1955) Paramount. **B&W-112min.** Humphrey Bogart, Fredric March 5*

DESPERATE JOURNEY (1942) Warner Bros. **B&W-107min.** Errol Flynn, Ronald Reagan..................4*

DESPERATE LIVING (1977) New Line Cinema. Color-90min. Mink Stole, Jean Hill ....(3)

DESPERATE MAN, THE (1959) Anglo Amalgamated [EMI]. **B&W-57min.** *(British).* Conrad Phillips, Jill Ireland ....(3)

DESPERATE MISSION (1964) Warner Bros. Color-112min. *(Italian).* Jerry (German) Cobbs, Yoko Tani ....(2)
Alternate title: AGENT Z55
Alternate title: AGENT Z55: DESPERATE MISSION

DESPERATE MISSION (1971) 20th Century-Fox. Color-100min. *(Made for TV).* Ricardo Montalban, Slim Pickens ....(4)
Alternate title: MURIETTA

DESPERATE MOMENT (1953) Universal. **B&W-88min.** *(British).* Dirk Bogarde, Mai Zetterling 5*

DESPERATE ONES, THE (1967) American-International. Color-104min. *(Spanish-U.S.).* Maximilian Schell, Raf Vallone, Theodore Bikel..........(4)
Original Spanish title: MAS ALLA DE LAS MONTANAS

DESPERATE SEARCH (1953) M-G-M. **B&W-73min.** Howard Keel, Jane Greer ....(4)

DESPERATE SIEGE (1952) *see* RAWHIDE

DESTINATION BIG HOUSE (1950) Republic. **B&W-60min.** Dorothy Patrick, Robert Rockwell ....(3)

DESTINATION DEATH (1961) Allied Artists. **B&W-93min.** *(German).* Hannes Messemer, Armin Dahlen ....(3)
Original title: TRANSPORT, DER

DESTINATION FURY (1961) American-International. **B&W-88min.** *(Italian-French).* Eddie Constantine, Renato Rascel..................(3)
Original Italian title: MANI I ALTO

DESTINATION GOBI (1953) 20th Century-Fox. Color-89min. Richard Widmark, Don Taylor ....(4)

DESTINATION INNER SPACE (1966) Magna Pictures. Color-83min. Scott Brady, Sheree North ....(3)
8mm title: TERROR OF THE DEEP

DESTINATION MIAMI (1966) Color-90min. *(Italian).* Claudio Gora, Bella Cortez..................3*

DESTINATION MOON (1950) Eagle Lion. Color-90min. Warner Anderson, John Archer ....(5)

DESTINATION SATURN (1939) Universal. **B&W-101min.** *(Re-edited Serial).* Buster Crabbe, Constance Moore 3*
Original title: BUCK ROGERS

DESTINATION 60,000 (1957) Allied Artists. **B&W-65min.** Preston Foster, Pat Conway ....(2)

DESTINATION TOKYO (1943) Warner Bros. **B&W-135min.** Cary Grant, John Garfield 3*

DESTINATION UNKNOWN (1942) Universal. **B&W-61min.** William Gargan, Irene Hervey ....(3)

DESTINY (1921) Artclass Pictures (Weiss Bros.). **B&W-100min.** *(German, Silent).* Lil Dagover, Walter Janssen ....(4)
Original title: MUEDE TOD, DER *(The Weary Death)*
Alternate title: THREE LIGHTS, THE
Alternate title: BETWEEN WORLDS
Alternate title: BEYOND THE WALL

DESTINY (1944) Universal. **B&W-65min.** Gloria Jean, Alan Curtis ....(3)

DESTINY OF A SPY (1969) Universal. Color-100min. *(Made for TV).* Harry Andrews, Anthony Quayle, Lorne Greene 4*

DESTROY ALL MONSTERS (1968) American-International. Color-88min. *(Japanese).* Akira Kubo, Jun Tazaki, Godzilla, Rodan 1*
Original title: KAIJU SOSHINGEKI *(Attack of the Marching Monsters)*

DESTROY ALL PLANETS (1968) American-International. Color-75min. *(Japanese).* Gamera, Kojiro Hongo, Toru Takatsuka 1*
Original title: GAMERA TAI UCHI KAIJU BAIRUSU *(Gamera Vs. Outer Space Monster Viras)*
Alternate Japanese title: GAMERA TAI VIRAS

DESTROYER (1943) Columbia. **B&W-99min.** Edward G. Robinson, Glenn Ford 3*

DESTRUCTORS, THE (1968) Feature Film Corp. Color-97min. Richard Egan, John Ericson ....(3)

DESTRUCTORS, THE (1974) American-International. Color-89min. *(U.S.-British-French).* Michael Caine, Anthony Quinn 4*
British title: MARSEILLES CONTRACT, THE

DESTRY (1955) Universal. Color-95min. Audie Murphy, Mari Blanchard 4*

DESTRY RIDES AGAIN (1939) Universal. **B&W-94min.** James Stewart, Marlene Dietrich 5*

DETECTIVE, THE (1955) Columbia. **B&W-91min.** *(British).* Alec Guinness, Joan Greenwood 5½*
Original title: FATHER BROWN

DETECTIVE, THE (1968) 20th Century-Fox. Color-114min. Frank Sinatra, Lee Remick 4*

DETECTIVE BELLI (1969) Plaza Pictures. Color-103min. *(Italian).* Franco Nero, Florinda Bolkan ....(3)
Original title: DETECTIVE, UN *(A Detective)*

DETECTIVE KITTY O'DAY (1944) Monogram [Allied Artists]. **B&W-63min.** Jean Parker, Peter Cookson ....(3)

DETECTIVE STORY (1951) Paramount. **B&W-103min.** Kirk Douglas, Eleanor Parker 5½*

DETOUR (1945) Producers Rel. Corp. [Eagle Lion]. **B&W-69min.** Tom Neal, Ann Savage..................(5)

DETOUR (1967) Brandon. **B&W-90min.** *(Bulgarian).* Nevena Kokanova, Ivan Andonov ....(4)
Original title: OTKLONENIE

DETOUR TO NOWHERE (1972) *see* BANACEK

DETROIT 9000 (1973) General Film Corp. Color-92min. Alex Rocco, Hari Rhodes 3*
Original title: MOTOWN 9000
British title: CALL DETROIT 9000

DEVI (1961) Harrison Pictures. **B&W-96min.** *(Indian).* Chhabi Biswas, Soumitra Chatterjee ....(4)
Alternate title: GODDESS, THE

DEVIL, THE (1963) *see* TO BED OR NOT TO BED

DEVIL AND DANIEL WEBSTER, THE (1941) RKO. **B&W-112min.** Walter Huston, Edward Arnold, James Craig 6*
Alternate title: ALL THAT MONEY CAN BUY

DEVIL AND MISS JONES, THE (1941) RKO. **B&W-90min.** Jean Arthur, Charles Coburn 5*

DEVIL AND MISS SARAH, THE (1971) MCA-TV. Color-73min. *(Made for TV).* Gene Barry, Janice Rule, James Drury ....(3)

DEVIL AND THE DEEP (1932) Paramount. **B&W-78min.** Tallulah Bankhead, Gary Cooper, Charles Laughton 3*

DEVIL AND THE TEN COMMANDMENTS, THE (1962) Union Films. **B&W-143min.** *(French-Italian).* Michel Simon, Dany Saval, Charles Aznavour, Fernandel, Alain Delon..................(4)
Original French title: DIABLE ET LES DIX COMMANDEMENTS, LE
Original Italian title: TENTAZIONI QUOTIDIANE, LE
Alternate Italian title: DIAVOLO E I DIECI COMANDAMENTI, IL

DEVIL AT 4 O'CLOCK, THE (1961) Columbia. Color-126min. Spencer Tracy, Frank Sinatra 4*

Films are rated on a 1 to 10 scale, 10 is highest. **Boldface** ratings followed by an asterisk (*) are for films actually seen and rated by the executive and senior editors. All other ratings are estimates. (See Notes on Entertainment Ratings in the front section.)

DEVIL AT MY HEELS (1966) Official Industries. **Color-88min.** *(French).* Sami Frey, Francoise Hardy .... (3)

DEVIL BAT (1941) Producers Rel. Corp. [Eagle Lion]. **B&W-69min.** Bela Lugosi, Suzanne Kaaren .... (3)

DEVIL BAT'S DAUGHTER (1946) Producers Rel. Corp. [Eagle Lion]. **B&W-66min.** Eddie Kane, Rosemary La Planche .... (3)

DEVIL BY THE TAIL, THE (1968) Lopert [U.A.]. **Color-93min.** *(French-Italian).* Yves Montand, Maria Schell .... (5)
Original title: DIABLE PAR LA QUEUE, LA

DEVIL CAT (1978) Dimension Pictures. **Color-84min.** Donald Pleasence, Nancy Kwan.. 3½*

DEVIL COMMANDS, THE (1941) Columbia. **B&W-65min.** Boris Karloff, Amanda Duff .... (3)
Common title error: WHEN THE DEVIL COMMANDS

DEVIL DOGS OF THE AIR (1935) Warner Bros. **B&W-86min.** James Cagney, Pat O'Brien 4*

DEVIL-DOLL, THE (1936) M-G-M. **B&W-79min.** Lionel Barrymore, Maureen O'Sullivan.. 5*

DEVIL DOLL (1964) Associated Film Dists. **B&W-70min.** *(British-U.S.).* Bryant Halliday, William Sylvester .... (4)

DEVIL GIRL FROM MARS (1955) Distributors Corp. of America. **B&W-76min.** *(British).* Patricia Laffen, Hazel Court, Hugh McDermott .... (2)

DEVIL GODDESS (1955) Columbia. **B&W-70min.** Johnny Weissmuller, Angela Stevens .... (3)

DEVIL IN LOVE, THE (1966) Warner Bros. **Color-97min.** *(Italian).* Vittorio Gassman, Claudine Auger, Mickey Rooney .... (1)
Original title: ARCIDIAVOLO, L' *(The Archdevil)*
Alternate Italian title: DIAVOLO INNAMORATO, IL

DEVIL IN MISS JONES, THE (1973) Marvin Films. **Color-74min.** Georgina Spelvin, John Clemens, Harry Reams 2½*

DEVIL IN THE FLESH (1947) A.F.E. Corp. **B&W-110min.** *(French-U.S.).* Micheline Presle, Gerard Philipe .... (5)
Original title: DIABLE AU CORPS, LE

DEVIL IS A SISSY (1936) M-G-M. **B&W-92min.** Freddie Bartholomew, Jackie Cooper.. (4)
British title: DEVIL TAKES THE COUNT, THE

DEVIL IS A WOMAN, THE (1935) Paramount. **B&W-85min.** Marlene Dietrich, Lionel Atwill, Cesar Romero .... (4)

DEVIL IS A WOMAN, THE (1974) 20th Century-Fox. **Color-105min.** *(Italian-British).* Glenda Jackson, Claudio Casinelli 3*
British title: TEMPTER, THE

DEVIL MADE A WOMAN, THE (1959) Medallion. **Color-87min.** *(Spanish).* Sarita (Sara) Montiel, George (Jorge) Mistral .... (3)
Original title: CARMEN, LA DE RONDA
Alternate title: GIRL AGAINST NAPOLEON, A

DEVIL MAKES THREE, THE (1952) M-G-M. **B&W-96min.** Gene Kelly, Pier Angeli .... (4)

DEVIL NEVER SLEEPS, THE (1962) *see* SATAN NEVER SLEEPS

DEVIL OF THE DESERT AGAINST THE SON OF HERCULES (1964) Avco-Embassy. **Color-93min.** *(Italian-Spanish-French).* Kirk Morris, Michele Giradon .... (3)

DEVIL ON HORSEBACK (1954) British Lion [EMI]. **B&W-88min.** *(British).* Googie Withers, John McCallum .... (3)

DEVIL PAYS OFF, THE (1941) Republic. **B&W-56min.** J. Edward Bromberg, Osa Massen.. (4)

DEVIL RIDER (1971) Goldstone Film Enterprises. **Color-75min.** Ross Kananza, Sharon Mahon.. (2)

DEVIL RIDES OUT, THE (1968) *see* DEVIL'S BRIDE, THE

DEVIL-SHIP PIRATES (1964) Columbia. **Color-86min.** *(British).* Christopher Lee, Andrew Keir .... (4)

DEVIL STRIKES AT NIGHT, THE (1958) Zenith International. **B&W-97min.** *(German).* Claus Holm, Mario Adorf, Hannes Messemer.......... (5)
Original title: NACHTS, WENN DER TEUFEL KAM *(Nights, When the Devil Comes)*
Alternate title: NAZI TERROR AT NIGHT

DEVIL THUMBS A RIDE, THE (1947) RKO. **B&W-65min.** Lawrence Tierney, Nan Leslie.. (3)

DEVIL TO PAY, THE (1931) United Artists. **B&W-65min.** Ronald Colman, Loretta Young .... (4)

DEVIL WITHIN HER (1974) *see* BEYOND THE DOOR

DEVIL WITHIN HER, THE (1975) American-International. **Color-90min.** *(British).* Joan Collins, Donald Pleasence 4*
Original title: I DON'T WANT TO BE BORN

DEVILS, THE (1971) Warner Bros. **Color-109min.** *(British).* Oliver Reed, Vanessa Redgrave 4*

DEVIL'S AGENT, THE (1962) British Lion [EMI]. **B&W-77min.** *(British).* Peter Van Eyck, Macdonald Carey, Marianne Koch, Christopher Lee (3)

DEVIL'S ANGELS (1967) American-International. **Color-84min.** John Cassavetes, Beverly Adams.. 3*

DEVIL'S BAIT (1959) **B&W-58min.** *(British).* Geoffrey Keen, Jane Hylton .... (3)

DEVIL'S BEDROOM, THE (1963) Allied Artists. **B&W-72min.** John Lupton, Valerie Allen.. (2)

DEVIL'S BRIDE, THE (1968) 20th Century-Fox. **Color-95min.** *(British).* Christopher Lee, Charles Gray .... (3)
Original title: DEVIL RIDES OUT, THE

DEVIL'S BRIGADE, THE (1968) United Artists. **Color-130min.** William Holden, Cliff Robertson 4½*

DEVIL'S BROTHER, THE (1933) M-G-M. **B&W-88min.** Stan Laurel, Oliver Hardy.. (5)
British title: FRA DIAVOLO
Alternate title: BOGUS BANDITS
Alternate title: VIRTUOUS TRAMPS, THE

DEVIL'S CANYON (1953) RKO. **Color-92min.** Virginia Mayo, Dale Robertson 3*

DEVIL'S CARGO (1948) Film Classics [U.A.]. **B&W-61min.** John Calvert, Lyle Talbot.. (3)

DEVIL'S CAVALIERS, THE (1958) Trans-America. **Color-92min.** *(Italian).* Frank Latimore, Emma Daniela................................ (3)

DEVIL'S DAFFODIL, THE (1961) Goldstone Film Enterprises. **B&W-86min.** *(British-W. German).* William Lucas, Christopher Lee, Penelope Horner.. (2)
Original German title: GEHEIMNIS DER GELBEN NARZISSEN, DAS
Alternate title: DAFFODIL KILLER

DEVIL'S DAUGHTER, THE (1972) Paramount. **Color-74min.** *(Made for TV).* Belinda Montgomery, Robert Foxworth, Shelley Winters, Joseph Cotten 3*

DEVIL'S DISCIPLE, THE (1959) United Artists. **B&W-82min.** *(British).* Burt Lancaster, Kirk Douglas.. 6*

DEVIL'S DOORWAY (1950) M-G-M. **B&W-84min.** Louis Calhern, Robert Taylor .... (5)

DEVIL'S 8, THE (1969) American-International. **Color-97min.** Christopher George, Ralph Meeker, Fabian........................ 3*

DEVIL'S EYE, THE (1960) Janus Films. **B&W-90min.** *(Swedish).* Jarl Kulle, Bibi Andersson.. 3*
Original title: DJAVULENS OGA

DEVIL'S GENERAL, THE (1955) Distributors Corp. of America. **B&W-120min.** *(German).* Curt Jurgens, Victor de Kowa .... (5)
Original title: TEUFELS GENERAL, DAS

DEVIL'S HAIRPIN, THE (1957) Paramount. **Color-82min.** Cornel Wilde, Jean Wallace.. (4)

THE DEVIL'S DISCIPLE (1959). As a British general, Laurence Olivier observes amusedly, but parson's wife Janette Scott is apprehensive as a colonial court-martial tries disreputable scoundrel Kirk Douglas, whom they think is the parson.

Films are rated on a 1 to 10 scale, 10 is highest. **Boldface** ratings followed by an asterisk (*) are for films actually seen and rated by the executive and senior editors. All other ratings are estimates. (See Notes on Entertainment Ratings in the front section.)

DEVIL'S HAND, THE (1961) Crown International. B&W-71min. Robert Alda, Linda Christian 2*
Alternate title: LIVE TO LOVE

DEVIL'S HENCHMAN, THE (1949) Columbia. B&W-69min. Warner Baxter, Mary Beth Hughes .... (3)

DEVIL'S HOLIDAY, THE (1930) Paramount. B&W-75min. Nancy Carroll, Phillips Holmes 3*

DEVIL'S IMPOSTOR, THE (1972) *see* POPE JOAN

DEVIL'S IN LOVE, THE (1933) Fox Film Co. [20th]. B&W-71min. Loretta Young, Victor Jory .... (4)

DEVIL'S ISLAND (1939) Warner Bros. B&W-62min. Boris Karloff, James Stephenson .... (4)

DEVIL'S MASK, THE (1946) Columbia. B&W-66min. Anita Louise, Jim Bannon .... (3)

DEVIL'S MEN, THE (1976) *see* LAND OF THE MINOTAUR

DEVIL'S MESSENGER, THE (1961) Herts-Lion International. B&W-72min. (U.S.-Swedish). Lon Chaney (Jr.), Karen Kadler, Michael Hinn .... (3)

DEVIL'S NIGHTMARE, THE (1972) Hemisphere. Color-87min. *(Italian-Belgian).* Erika Blanc, Jean Servais .... (3)
Original Italian title: NOTTE PIU LUNGA DEL DIAVOLO, LA *(The Longest Night of the Devil)*
Belgian title: PLUS LONGUE NUIT DU DIABLE, LA

DEVILS OF DARKNESS (1965) 20th Century-Fox. Color-88min. *(British).* William Sylvester, Hubert Noel 1*

DEVIL'S OWN, THE (1966) 20th Century-Fox. Color-90min. *(British).* Joan Fontaine, Kay Walsh 4*
Original title: WITCHES, THE

DEVIL'S PARTNER, THE (1960) Filmgroup. B&W-61min. Ed Nelson, Edgar Buchanan .... (3)

DEVIL'S PIPELINE, THE (1940) Universal. B&W-65min. Richard Arlen, Andy Devine .... (4)

DEVIL'S PLAYGROUND (1937) Columbia. B&W-74min. Richard Dix, Dolores Del Rio .... (4)

DEVIL'S RAIN, THE (1975) Bryanston. Color-85min. (U.S.-Mexican). Ernest Borgnine, William Shatner 3*

DEVIL'S TRAP (1962) Edward Salisbury. B&W-85min. (Czech). Vitezslav Vejrazka, Miroslav Machacek .... (5)
Original title: DABLOVA PAST

DEVIL'S WANTON, THE (1949) Avco-Embassy. B&W-80min. (Swedish). Doris Svedlund, Birger Malsten .... (4)
Original title: FANGELSE (Prison)

DEVIL'S WEDDING NIGHT, THE (1973) Dimension Pictures. Color-85min. (Italian). Mark Damon, Sarah Bay, Rosalba Neri .... (3)
PLENILUNIO DELLE VERGINI, IL (The Full Moon of the Virgins)

DEVIL'S WIDOW, THE (1971) *see* TAM LIN

DEVOTION (1946) Warner Bros. B&W-107min. Olivia de Havilland, Ida Lupino .... (4)

DIABOLIC INVENTION, THE (1958) *see* FABULOUS WORLD OF JULES VERNE, THE

DIABOLIK! (1967) *see* DANGER: DIABOLIK

DIABOLIQUE (1955) United Motion Pic. Org. (UMPO). B&W-107min. (French). Simone Signoret, Vera Clouzot 5½*
Original title: DIABOLIQUES, LES
British title: FIENDS, THE

DIAL HOT LINE (1969) MCA-TV. Color-98min. (Made for TV). Vince Edwards, Chelsea Brown, Kim Hunter .... (4)

DIAL M FOR MURDER (1954) Warner Bros. Color-105min. Ray Milland, Grace Kelly 6*

DIAL 999 (1955) *see* WAY OUT, THE

DIAL 1119 (1950) M-G-M. B&W-75min. Marshall Thompson, Virginia Field .... (4)
British title: VIOLENT HOUR, THE

DIAL RED O (1955) Allied Artists. B&W-63min. Bill Elliott, Keith Larsen .... (3)

DIAMOND, THE (1954) *see* DIAMOND WIZARD, THE

DIAMOND EARRINGS, THE (1953) *see* EARRINGS OF MADAME DE . . .

DIAMOND HEAD (1963) Columbia. Color-107min. Charlton Heston, Yvette Mimieux 4*

DIAMOND HORSESHOE (1945) *see* BILLY ROSE'S DIAMOND HORSESHOE

DIAMOND JIM (1935) Universal. B&W-93min. Edward Arnold, Binnie Barnes .... (5)

DIAMOND MERCENARIES, THE (1975) *see* KILLER FORCE

DIAMOND QUEEN, THE (1953) Warner Bros. Color-80min. Fernando Lamas, Gilbert Roland 3*

DIAMOND SAFARI (1958) 20th Century-Fox. B&W-67min. Kevin McCarthy, André Morell .... (3)

DIAMOND WIZARD, THE (1954) United Artists. B&W-83min. (British). Dennis O'Keefe, Margaret Sheridan .... (4)
Original title: DIAMOND, THE

DIAMONDS (1975) Avco-Embassy. Color-106min. (U.S.-Israeli). Robert Shaw 4½*

DIAMONDS AND CRIME (1943) *see* HI DIDDLE DIDDLE

DIAMONDS ARE FOREVER (1971) United Artists. Color-119min. (British). Sean Connery, Jill St. John 5*

DIAMONDS OF THE NIGHT (1964) Impact Films. B&W-75min. (Czech). Ladislav Jansky, Antonin Kumbera .... (4)
Original title: DEMANTY NOCI

DIANE (1956) M-G-M. Color-110min. Lana Turner, Pedro Armendariz..(4)

DIARY OF A BACHELOR (1964) American-International. B&W-88min. William Traylor, Dagne Crane .... (3)

DIARY OF A BAD GIRL (1958) Films Around The World. B&W-87min. (French). Anne Vernon, Danik Patisson, Francois Guerin .... (3)
Original title: LONG DES TROITTOIRS, LE (Along the Sidewalks)

DIARY OF A BRIDE (1948) *see* I, JANE DOE

DIARY OF A CHAMBERMAID, THE (1946) United Artists. B&W-86min. Paulette Goddard, Burgess Meredith .... (4)

DIARY OF A CHAMBERMAID, THE (1964) International Classics [20th]. B&W-97min. (French). Jeanne Moreau, Georges Geret .... (4)
Original title: JOURNAL D'UNE FEMME DE CHAMBRE

DIARY OF A COUNTRY PRIEST, THE (1950) Brandon. B&W-120min. (French). Claude Laydu, Nicole Maurey, Nicole Ladmiral .... (4)
Original title: JOURNAL D'UN CURÉ DE CAMPAGNE, LE

DIARY OF A HIGH SCHOOL BRIDE (1959) American-International. B&W-80min. Anita Sands, Ronald Foster .... (3)

DIARY OF A MAD HOUSEWIFE (1970) Universal. Color-94min. Carrie Snodgress, Richard Benjamin 4*

DIARY OF A MADMAN (1963) United Artists. Color-96min. Vincent Price, Nancy Kovack 4*

DIARY OF A SCHIZOPHRENIC GIRL (1968) Allied Artists. Color-108min. (Italian). Ghislaine d'Orsay, Umberto Raho .... (5)
Original title: DIARIO DI UNA SCHIZOFRENICA

DIARY OF A TEACHER (1972) B&W-272min. (Italian, Made for TV). Bruno Cirino, Marisa Fabbri, Mico Cundari .... (4)

DIARY OF ANNE FRANK, THE (1959) 20th Century-Fox. B&W-170min. Millie Perkins, Joseph Schildkraut 5½*

DIARY OF FORBIDDEN DREAMS (1972) *see* WHAT?

DIARY OF MAJOR THOMPSON, THE (1957) *see* FRENCH THEY ARE A FUNNY RACE, THE

DICK DEADEYE, OR DUTY DONE (1975) Intercontinental Releasing. Color-79min. (British-U.S., Cartoon). Director: Bill Melendez 5*
Alternate title: DICK DEADEYE

DICK TRACY (1945) RKO. B&W-62min. Morgan Conway, Anne Jeffreys .... (3)
Alternate title: DICK TRACY, DETECTIVE
British title: SPLITFACE

DICK TRACY MEETS GRUESOME (1947) RKO. B&W-65min. Ralph Byrd, Boris Karloff .... (4)
British title: DICK TRACY'S AMAZING ADVENTURE

DICK TRACY VERSUS CUEBALL (1946) RKO. B&W-62min. Morgan Conway, Dick Wessel .... (3)

DICK TRACY'S DILEMMA (1947) RKO. B&W-60min. Ralph Byrd, Jack Lambert .... (3)
British title: MARK OF THE CLAW

DICK TURPIN (1925) Fox Film Co. [20th]. B&W-70min. (Silent). Tom Mix, Kathleen Myers ....

DICK TURPIN'S RIDE (1951) *see* LADY AND THE BANDIT, THE

DICTATOR'S GUNS, THE (1964) Paramount. B&W-105min. (French-Spanish-Italian). Sylva Koscina, Leo Gordon, Lino Ventura .... (3)
Original French title: ARME A GAUCHE, L'

DID YOU HEAR THE ONE ABOUT THE TRAVELING SALESLADY? (1968) Universal. Color-97min. Phyllis Diller, Bob Denver 2*

DIE! DIE! MY DARLING! (1965) Columbia. Color-97min. (British). Tallulah Bankhead, Stefanie Powers 3*
Original title: FANATIC

DIE, MONSTER, DIE! (1965) American-International. Color-81min. *(U.S.-British)*. Boris Karloff, Nick Adams... (3)
British title: MONSTER OF TERROR

DIES IRAE (1943) *see* DAY OF WRATH

DIFFERENT STORY, A (1978) Avco-Embassy. Color-106min. Peter Donat, Perry King, Meg Foster...5½*

DIFFICULT LOVE, A (1966) *see* CLOSELY WATCHED TRAINS

DIG THAT JULIET (1961) *see* ROMANOFF AND JULIET

DIG THAT URANIUM (1956) Allied Artists. B&W-61min. The Bowery Boys, Mary Beth Hughes .... (3)

DIGBY, THE BIGGEST DOG IN THE WORLD (1973) Cinerama Releasing. Color-88min. *(British)*. Jim Dale, Spike Milligan, Angela Douglas .... (4)

DILLINGER (1945) Monogram [Allied Artists]. B&W-70min. Lawrence Tierney, Anne Jeffreys 4*

DILLINGER (1973) American-International. Color-107min. Warren Oates, Ben Johnson 5½*

DIME WITH A HALO (1963) M-G-M. B&W-94min. Barbara Luna, Roger Mobley 3*

DIMENSION 5 (1966) Feature Film Corp. Color-92min. Jeffrey Hunter, France Nuyen, Harold Sakata 3*

DIMPLES (1936) 20th Century-Fox. B&W-78min. Shirley Temple, Frank Morgan .... (4)

DINAH EAST (1970) Emerson Films. Color-87min. Jeremy Stockwell, Reid Smith .... (3)
Alternate title: STORY OF DINAH EAST, THE

DING DONG WILLIAMS (1946) RKO. B&W-62min. Glenn Vernon, Marcia Maguire .... (3)
British title: MELODY MAKER

DINGAKA (1965) Avco-Embassy. Color-97min. *(South African)*. Stanley Baker, Juliet Prowse 4*

DINKY (1935) Warner Bros. B&W-65min. Jackie Cooper, Mary Astor....(3)

DINNER AT EIGHT (1933) M-G-M. B&W-113min. Marie Dressler, John Barrymore 4*

DINNER AT THE RITZ (1937) 20th Century-Fox. B&W-77min. *(British)*. Annabella, David Niven .... (4)

DINO (1957) Allied Artists. B&W-94min. Sal Mineo, Brian Keith...........(4)
British title: KILLER DINO

DINOSAURUS! (1960) Universal. Color-85min. Ward Ramsey, Kristina Hanson 3½*

DION BROTHERS, THE (1974) Columbia. Color-94min. Stacy Keach, Frederic Forrest 5*
Original title: GRAVY TRAIN, THE

DIONYSUS IN '69 (1969) Sigma III. B&W-90min. William Finley, William Shephard.. (3)

DIPLOMATIC CORPSE (1957) J. Arthur Rank. B&W-65min. *(British)*. Liam Redmond, Susan Shaw .... (3)

DIPLOMATIC COURIER (1952) 20th Century-Fox. B&W-97min. Tyrone Power, Patricia Neal .... (5)

DIRIGIBLE (1931) Columbia. B&W-93min. Jack Holt, Ralph Graves.......4*

DIRT GANG, THE (1972) American-International. Color-89min. Paul Carr, Michael Forest .... (3)

DIRTY DINGUS MAGEE (1970) M-G-M. Color-91min. Frank Sinatra, George Kennedy 4*

DIRTY DOZEN, THE (1967) M-G-M. Color-149min. *(U.S.-British)*. Lee Marvin, Ernest Borgnine 5*

DIRTY GAME, THE (1965) American-International. Color-87min. *(French-Italian-W. German)*. Robert Ryan, Vittorio Gassman, Bourvil, Henry Fonda .... (3)
Alternate title: SECRET AGENTS, THE
Original French title: GUERRE SECRETE *(Secret War)*
Original Italian title: GUERRA SEGRETA, LA
W. German title: SPIONE UNTER SICH

DIRTY HANDS (1951) MacDonald. B&W-103min. *(French)*. Pierre Brasseur, Daniel Gélin .... (5)
Original title: MAINS SALES, LES *(Soiled Hands)*

DIRTY HANDS (1975) New Line Cinema. Color-102min. *(French-Italian-W. German)*. Rod Steiger, Romy Schneider, Paolo Giusti ....

DIRTY HARRY (1971) Warner Bros. Color-103min. Clint Eastwood, Andy Robinson 6*

DIRTY KNIGHTS' WORK (1976) Gamma III. Color-88min. *(British)*. John Mills, Donald Pleasence, David Birney, Peter Cushing ....
Original title: CHOICE OF WEAPONS, A

DIRTY LITTLE BILLY (1972) Columbia. Color-93min. Michael J. Pollard, Lee Purcell .... (3)

DIRTY MARY CRAZY LARRY (1974) 20th Century-Fox. Color-93min. Susan George, Peter Fonda 4*

DIRTY MONEY (1972) Allied Artists. Color-98min. *(French)*. Alain Delon, Catherine Deneuve, Richard Crenna...2*
Original title: FLIC, UN

DIRTY OUTLAWS, THE (1967) Transvue Pictures. Color-103min. *(Italian)*. Chip Corman (Andrea Giordana), Rosemarie Dexter .... (3)
Original title: DESPERADO, EL *(The Desperado)*

DIRTYMOUTH (1970) Chevron. Color-102min. Bernie Travis, Courtney Sherman .... (4)
Alternate title: STORY OF LENNY BRUCE - DIRTYMOUTH, THE

DISAPPEARANCE (1977) Color-100min. *(Canadian)*. Donald Sutherland, Francine Racette, David Hemmings, Christopher Plummer ....

DISAPPEARANCE OF AIMEE, THE (1976) NBC-TV. Color-100min. *(Made for TV)*. Faye Dunaway, Bette Davis.......................................

DISAPPEARANCE OF FLIGHT 412, THE (1973) Viacom. Color-74min. *(Made for TV)*. Glenn Ford, Bradford Dillman, Guy Stockwell...........3½*

DISASTER (1948) Paramount. B&W-60min. Richard Denning, Trudy Marshall .... (3)

DISC JOCKEY (1951) Allied Artists. B&W-77min. Tom Drake, Michael O'Shea .... (3)

DISC JOCKEY JAMBOREE (1957) *see* JAMBOREE

DISCIPLE OF DEATH (1972) Heritage Enterprises. Color-84min. *(British)*. Mike Raven, Stephen Bradley, Marguerite Hardiman 2*

DISCREET CHARM OF THE BOURGEOISIE, THE (1972) 20th Century-Fox. Color-102min. *(French)*. Fernando Rey, Delphine Seyrig 5½*
Original title: CHARME DISCRET DE LA BOURGEOISIE, LE

DISEMBODIED, THE (1957) Allied Artists. B&W-65min. Paul Burke, Allison Hayes.. (2)

DISHONORABLE DISCHARGE (1958) Paramount. B&W-105min. *(French-Italian)*. Eddie Constantine, Lino Ventura.............................(3)
Original French title: CES DAMES PREFERENT LE MAMBO

DISHONORED (1931) Paramount. B&W-91min. Marlene Dietrich, Victor McLaglen .... (4)

DISHONORED LADY (1947) United Artists. B&W-85min. Hedy Lamarr, Dennis O'Keefe .... (3)

DISOBEDIENT (1953) Carroll Pictures. B&W-85min. *(British)*. Marian Spencer, Russell Enoch .... (3)
Original title: INTIMATE RELATIONS

DISORDER (1962) Pathé Contemporary. B&W-105min. *(Italian-French)*. Louis Jourdan, Susan Strasberg, Curt Jurgens .... (3)
Original Italian title: DISORDINE, IL
Original French title: DÉSORDRE, LE

DISORDERLY ORDERLY, THE (1964) Paramount. Color-90min. Jerry Lewis, Glenda Farrell 4*

DISPATCH FROM REUTERS, A (1940) Warner Bros. B&W-89min. Edward G. Robinson, Edna Best .... (4)
British title: THIS MAN REUTER

DISPUTED PASSAGE (1939) Paramount. B&W-87min. Dorothy Lamour, John Howard .... (4)

DISRAELI (1929) Warner Bros. B&W-89min. George Arliss, Joan Bennett...5*

DISTANT DRUMS (1951) Warner Bros. Color-101min. Gary Cooper, Mari Aldon 4*

DISTANT THUNDER (1973) Cinema 5. Color-100min. *(Indian)*. Soumitra Chatterji, Babita ....
Original title: ASHANI SANKET

DISTANT TRUMPET, A (1964) Warner Bros. Color-117min. Troy Donahue, Suzanne Pleshette.. (4)

DIVE BOMBER (1941) Warner Bros. Color-133min. Errol Flynn, Fred MacMurray 3½*

DIVIDED HEART, THE (1954) Republic. B&W-81min. *(British)*. Cornell Borchers, Armin Dahlen, Yvonne Mitchell .... (5)

DIVIDING LINE, THE (1950) *see* LAWLESS, THE

DIVINE LADY, THE (1929) First National [W.B.]. B&W-110min. *(Part-talking)*. Corinne Griffith, Victor Varconi.................................... (4)

DIVINE LOVE (1932) *see* NO GREATER LOVE

DIVINE WOMAN, THE (1928) M-G-M. B&W-81min. *(Silent)*. G. Garbo (4)

DIVISION HEADQUARTERS (1972) *see* FIREBALL FORWARD

DIVORCE (1945) Monogram [Allied Artists]. B&W-71min. Kay Francis, Bruce Cabot .... (3)

Films are rated on a 1 to 10 scale, 10 is highest. **Boldface** ratings followed by an asterisk (*) are for films actually seen and rated by the executive and senior editors. All other ratings are estimates. (See Notes on Entertainment Ratings in the front section.)

DIVORCE, AMERICAN STYLE (1967) Columbia. **Color-109min.** Dick Van Dyke, Debbie Reynolds..6*

DIVORCE HIS, DIVORCE HERS (1972) Viacom. **Color-150min.** *(Made for TV).* Elizabeth Taylor, Richard Burton 2*

DIVORCE - ITALIAN STYLE (1961) Avco-Embassy. **B&W-104min.** *(Italian).* Marcello Mastroianni, Daniela Rocca 7*
Original title: DIVORZIO ALL' ITALIANA

DIVORCE OF LADY X, THE (1938) United Artists. **Color-90min.** *(British).* Merle Oberon, Laurence Olivier 5½*

DIVORCEE, THE (1930) M-G-M. **B&W-80min.** Norma Shearer, Chester Morris...(4)

DIXIE (1943) Paramount. **Color-89min.** Bing Crosby, Dorothy Lamour ..(5)

DO NOT DISTURB (1965) 20th Century-Fox. **Color-102min.** Doris Day, Rod Taylor..4*

DO NOT FOLD, SPINDLE OR MUTILATE (1971) Worldvision. **Color-73min.** *(Made for TV).* Helen Hayes, Vince Edwards, Myrna Loy 4*

DO YOU KNOW THIS VOICE? (1964) Screen Gems. **B&W-80min.** *(British).* Dan Duryea, Isa Miranda ....(4)

DO YOU LOVE ME? (1946) 20th Century-Fox. **Color-91min.** Maureen O'Hara, Dick Haymes ....(4)

DO YOU TAKE THIS STRANGER? (1970) MCA-TV. **Color-100min.** *(Made for TV).* Gene Barry, Lloyd Bridges ....(3)

DOBERMAN GANG, THE (1972) Dimension Pictures. **Color-87min.** Byron Mabe, Hal Freed 4*

DOBERMAN PATROL, THE (1973) *see* TRAPPED

DOC (1971) United Artists. **Color-96min.** Stacy Keach, Faye Dunaway (4)

DOC SAVAGE . . . THE MAN OF BRONZE (1975) Warner Bros. **Color-100min.** Ron Ely, Paul Wexler....................................(4)

DOCK BRIEF, THE (1962) *see* TRIAL AND ERROR

DOCKS OF NEW ORLEANS (1948) Monogram [Allied Artists]. **B&W-64min.** Roland Winters, Mantan Moreland............................

DOCKS OF NEW YORK, THE (1928) Paramount Famous Lasky. **B&W-80min.** *(Silent).* George Bancroft, Betty Compson ....(4)

DOCKS OF NEW YORK (1945) Monogram [Allied Artists]. **B&W-61min.** The East Side Kids, Gloria Pope 3½*

DOCTOR AND THE DEBUTANTE, THE (1941) *see* DR. KILDARE'S VICTORY

DOCTOR AND THE GIRL, THE (1949) M-G-M. **B&W-98min.** Glenn Ford, Charles Coburn...4*

DOCTOR AT LARGE (1957) Universal. **Color-104min.** *(British).* Dirk Bogarde, Muriel Pavlow ....(4)

DOCTOR AT SEA (1955) Republic. **Color-93min.** *(British).* Dirk Bogarde, Brigitte Bardot 4*

DR. BLACK MR. HYDE (1976) Dimension Pictures. **Color-87min.** Bernie Casey, Rosalind Cash, Ji-Tu Cumbuka..............................(3)

DR. BLOOD'S COFFIN (1961) United Artists. **Color-92min.** *(British).* Kieron Moore, Hazel Court ....(3)

DR. BROADWAY (1942) Paramount. **B&W-67min.** Macdonald Carey, Jean Phillips ....(5)

DOCTOR BULL (1933) Fox Film Co. [20th]. **B&W-75min.** Will Rogers, Louise Dresser, Marian Nixon ....(5)

DR. CADMAN'S SECRET (1956) *see* BLACK SLEEP, THE

DR. CHRISTIAN MEETS THE WOMEN (1940) RKO. **B&W-68min.** Jean Hersholt, Dorothy Lovett ....(3)

DR. COOK'S GARDEN (1971) Paramount. **Color-75min.** *(Made for TV).* Bing Crosby, Frank Converse......................................4*

DOCTOR COPPELIUS (1966) Childhood Productions. **Color-97min.** *(U.S.-Spanish).* Walter Slezak, Claudia Corday ....(4)
Original Spanish title: FANTASTICO MUNDO DEL DR. COPPELIUS, EL *(The Fantastic World of Dr. Coppelius)*
Alternate title: MYSTERIOUS HOUSE OF DR. C, THE
Alternate title: DR.?? COPPELIUS!!

DR. CRIPPEN (1963) Warner Bros. **B&W-97min.** *(British).* Donald Pleasance, Samantha Eggar.......................................(3)

DR. CYCLOPS (1940) Paramount. **Color-77min.** Albert Dekker, Janice Logan..4*

DOCTOR DEATH: SEEKER OF SOULS (1973) Cinerama Releasing. **Color-87min.** John Considine, Barry Coe ....(3)

DOCTOR DOLITTLE (1967) 20th Century-Fox. **Color-138min.** Rex Harrison, Samantha Eggar..4*

DR. EHRLICH'S MAGIC BULLET (1940) Warner Bros. **B&W-103min.** Edward G. Robinson, Ruth Gordon 4½*
British title: STORY OF DR. EHRLICH'S MAGIC BULLET, THE

DOCTOR FAUSTUS (1967) Columbia. **Color-93min.** *(British-Italian).* Richard Burton, Andreas Teuber ....(3)

DR. FRANKENSTEIN ON CAMPUS (1970) Medford. **Color-83min.** *(Canadian).* Robin Ward, Kathleen Sawyer......................(2)
Original title: FLICK

DR. GILLESPIE'S CRIMINAL CASE (1943) M-G-M. **B&W-89min.** Lionel Barrymore, Van Johnson ....(3)
British title: CRAZY TO KILL

DR. GILLESPIE'S NEW ASSISTANT (1942) M-G-M. **B&W-87min.** Lionel Barrymore, Van Johnson ....(3)

DR. GLAS (1968) 20th Century-Fox. **B&W-83min.** *(Danish).* Per Oscarsson, Ulf Palme ....(5)
Original title: DOKTOR GLAS

DR. GOLDFOOT AND THE BIKINI MACHINE (1965) American-International. **Color-90min.** Vincent Price, Frankie Avalon, Susan Hart, Dwayne Hickman 2*
British title: DR. G. AND THE BIKINI MACHINE

DR. GOLDFOOT AND THE GIRL BOMBS (1966) American-International. **Color-85min.** *(U.S.-Italian, English language).* Vincent Price, Fabian, Franco Franchi, Ciccio Ingrassia...................2*
Original Italian title: SPIE VENGONO DAL SEMIFREDDO, LE *(The Spy Came in from the Semi-Cold)*
Alternate Italian title: DUE MAFIOSI DELL'FBI, I (The Two Mafiosi from the FBI)

DR. HOLL (1952) *see* AFFAIRS OF DR. HOLL

DOCTOR IN CLOVER (1966) *see* CARNABY, M.D.

DOCTOR IN DISTRESS (1963) Governor. **Color-103min.** *(British).* Dirk Bogarde, James Robertson Justice 4½*

DOCTOR IN LOVE (1960) Governor. **Color-93min.** *(British).* Michael Craig, Virginia Maskell...(4)

DOCTOR IN THE HOUSE (1954) Republic. **Color-91min.** *(British).* Dirk Bogarde, Kenneth More...4½*

DOCTOR IN TROUBLE (1970) J. Arthur Rank. **Color-90min.** *(British).* Leslie Phillips, Harry Secombe, James Robertson Justice ....(3)

DR. JEKYLL AND MR. HYDE (1912) Thanhouser. **B&W-1reel.** *(Silent).* James Cruze, Marguerite Snow...................................3*

DR. JEKYLL AND MR. HYDE (1920) Paramount. **B&W-7reels** *(Silent).* John Barrymore, Martha Mansfield 4*

DR. JEKYLL AND MR. HYDE (1932) Paramount. **B&W-90min.** Fredric March, Miriam Hopkins 5*

DR. JEKYLL AND MR. HYDE (1941) M-G-M. **B&W-123min.** Spencer Tracy, Ingrid Bergman 5½*

DR. JEKYLL AND MR. HYDE (1968) *see* STRANGE CASE OF DR. JEKYLL AND MR. HYDE, THE

DR. JEKYLL AND SISTER HYDE (1971) American-International. **Color-97min.** *(British).* Ralph Bates, Martine Beswick 3½*

DR. KILDARE GOES HOME (1940) M-G-M. **B&W-78min.** Lew Ayres, Lionel Barrymore, Laraine Day ....(3)

DR. KILDARE'S CRISIS (1940) M-G-M. **B&W-75min.** Lew Ayres, Lionel Barrymore, Robert Young ....(3)

DR. KILDARE'S STRANGE CASE (1940) M-G-M. **B&W-76min.** Lew Ayres, Lionel Barrymore, Shepperd Strudwick ....(3)

DR. KILDARE'S VICTORY (1941) M-G-M. **B&W-92min.** Lew Ayres, Lionel Barrymore, Ann Ayars ....(3)
British title: DOCTOR AND THE DEBUTANTE, THE

DR. KILDARE'S WEDDING DAY (1941) M-G-M. **B&W-82min.** Lew Ayres, Lionel Barrymore, Laraine Day, Red Skelton ....(3)
British title: MARY NAMES THE DAY

DR. LOVE (1969) *see* TEENIE TULIP

DR. MABUSE, KING OF CRIME (1922) Janus Films. **B&W-93min.** *(German, Silent).* Rudolf Klein-Rogge, Paul Richter 3*

DR. MABUSE, THE GAMBLER (1922) Janus Films. **B&W-120min.** *(German, Silent).* Rudolf Klein-Rogge, Aud Egede Nissen 3*

DR. MABUSE VS. SCOTLAND YARD (1964) Screen Gems. **B&W-90min.** *(German).* Peter Van Eyck, Walter Rilla ....(3)
Original title: SCHARLACHROTE DSCHUNKE, DIE *(The Scarlet Jungle)*
Alternate German title: SCOTLAND YARD JAGT DOKTOR MABUSE *(Scotland Yard in Pursuit of Dr. Mabuse)*

DR. MANIAC (1936) *see* MAN WHO LIVED AGAIN, THE

DR. MAX (1974) CBS-TV. **Color-74min.** *(Made for TV).* Lee J. Cobb, Janet Ward ....(4)

DR. MORELLE (1949) Eros Films *(Brit.).* **B&W-73min.** *(British).* Valentine Dyall, Julia Lang...(3)
Original title: DR. MORELLE - THE CASE OF THE MISSING HEIRESS

DR. NO (1962) United Artists. **Color-105min.** *(British).* Sean Connery, Ursula Andress 5*

Films are rated on a 1 to 10 scale, 10 is highest. **Boldface** ratings followed by an asterisk (*) are for films actually seen and rated by the executive and senior editors. All other ratings are estimates. (See Notes on Entertainment Ratings in the front section.)

DR. STRANGELOVE (1964). The fate of civilization hinges on events in the war room, as America's top civilian and military leaders cope with the situation of a nuclear bomber squadron irretrievably dispatched toward the Soviet Union by an insane general. (Arrows indicate George C. Scott playing another general who avidly insists that the best course of action is an immediate all-out attack, and Peter Sellers as the President, who wants to avoid a catastrophic war, if possible.)

DOCTOR OF DOOM (1962) Trans-International. B&W-77min. *(Mexican)*. Lorena Velazquez, Roberto Canedo ....(1)
Original title: LUCHADORAS CONTRA EL MÉDICO ASESINO, LAS *(The Wrestling Women vs. the Murdering Doctor)*

DOCTOR PAUL JOSEPH GOEBBELS (1944) *see* ENEMY OF WOMEN

DR. PHIBES (1971) *see* ABOMINABLE DR. PHIBES, THE

DR. PHIBES RISES AGAIN! (1972) American-International. Color-89min. Vincent Price, Robert Quarry 4*

DR. RENAULT'S SECRET (1942) 20th Century-Fox. B&W-58min. George Zucco, J. Carrol Naish..(3)

DR. RHYTHM (1938) Paramount. B&W-80min. Bing Crosby, Beatrice Lillie ....(4)

DOCTOR SATAN'S ROBOT (1940) Republic. B&W-100min. *(Re-edited Serial)*. Eduardo Ciannelli, Robert Wilcox ....(4)
Original title: MYSTERIOUS DR. SATAN, THE

DR. SOCRATES (1935) Warner Bros. B&W-70min. Paul Muni, Ann Dvorak ....(5)

DR. STRANGELOVE (1964) Columbia. B&W-93min. *(British)*. Peter Sellers..7½*
Screen title: DR. STRANGELOVE: OR HOW I LEARNED TO STOP WORRYING AND LOVE THE BOMB

DR. SYN (1937) Gaumont-British [Rank]. B&W-80min. *(British)*. George Arliss, John Loder ....(4)

DR. SYN, ALIAS THE SCARECROW (1964) Buena Vista. Color-98min. *(British-U.S.)*. Patrick McGoohan, George Cole 4½*
TV title: SCARECROW OF ROMNEY MARSH, THE

DOCTOR TAKES A WIFE, THE (1940) Columbia. B&W-89min. Ray Milland, Loretta Young......................................5½*

DR. TARR'S TORTURE DUNGEON (1972) Group 1. Color-88min. *(Mexican)*. Claudio Brook, Ellen Sherman............................(3)

DR. TERROR'S GALLERY OF HORRORS (1967) American General. Color-84min. John Carradine, Lon Chaney (Jr.), Vic McGee 1*
Alternate title: BLOOD SUCKERS, THE
TV title: RETURN FROM THE PAST

DR. TERROR'S HOUSE OF HORRORS (1965) Paramount. Color-98min. *(British)*. Peter Cushing, Christopher Lee 4½*

DR. WHO AND THE DALEKS (1965) Continental [Walter Reade]. Color-83min. *(British)*. Peter Cushing, Roy Castle 3*

DOCTOR WITHOUT SCRUPLES (1960) Emery Pictures. B&W-96min. *(French)*. Barbara Rutting...(3)

DOCTOR X (1932) First National [W.B.]. Color-80min. Lionel Atwill, Fay Wray ....(5)

DOCTOR, YOU'VE GOT TO BE KIDDING (1967) M-G-M. Color-94min. Sandra Dee, George Hamilton..(3)

DOCTOR ZHIVAGO (1965) M-G-M. Color-197min. Omar Sharif, Julie Christie 6*

DOCTORS, THE (1956) Kingsley International. B&W-92min. *(French)*. Jeanne Moreau, Raymond Pellegrin ....(5)
Original title: HOMMES EN BLANC, LES *(The Men in White)*

DOCTOR'S COURAGE, THE (1945) *see* CRIME DOCTOR'S COURAGE, THE

DOCTOR'S DILEMMA, THE (1958) M-G-M. Color-99min. *(British)*. Leslie Caron, Dirk Bogarde...(5)

DOCTOR'S GAMBLE, THE (1947) *see* CRIME DOCTOR'S GAMBLE, THE

Films are rated on a 1 to 10 scale, 10 is highest. **Boldface** ratings followed by an asterisk (*) are for films actually seen and rated by the executive and senior editors. All other ratings are estimates. (See Notes on Entertainment Ratings in the front section.)

DOCTOR'S WARNING, THE (1945) *see* CRIME DOCTOR'S WARNING, THE

DOCTORS' WIVES (1971) Columbia. Color-100min. Richard Crenna, Janice Rule 3*

DODES'KA-DEN (1970) Toho. Color-140min. *(Japanese)*. Zuchi Yoshitaka, Kin Sugai 1*
Translation title: Clickety-Clack
Translation title: Sound of Street Cars

DODGE CITY (1939) Warner Bros. Color-105min. Errol Flynn, Olivia de Havilland 5*

DODSWORTH (1936) United Artists. B&W-90min. Walter Huston, Ruth Chatterton 5*

DOES, THE (1968) *see* BICHES, LES

DOG, A MOUSE AND A SPUTNIK, A (1958) *see* SPUTNIK

DOG AND CAT (1977) Paramount. Color-74min. *(Made for TV)*. Lou Antonio 4*

DOG DAY AFTERNOON (1975) Warner Bros. Color-130min. Al Pacino, John Cazale 7*

DOG OF FLANDERS, A (1935) RKO. B&W-72min. Frankie Thomas, Helen Parish .... (4)

DOG OF FLANDERS, A (1960) 20th Century-Fox. Color-96min. David Ladd, Donald Crisp 4½*

DOG SOLDIERS (1978) *see* WHO'LL STOP THE RAIN

DOGS (1977) R. C. Riddell & Associates. Color-90min. David McCallum, Fred Hice, Linda Gray .... (4)

DOG'S BEST FRIEND, A (1960) United Artists. B&W-70min. Bill Williams, Marcia Henderson .... (3)

DOG'S LIFE, A (1918) First National [W.B.]. B&W-40min. *(Silent)*. Charles Chaplin, Albert Austin, Sydney Chaplin, Edna Purviance 4*

DOG'S LIFE, A (1961) *see* MONDO CANE

DOLCE VITA, LA (1960) Astor. B&W-180min. *(Italian-French)*. Marcello Mastroianni, Anita Ekberg 4½*
French title: DOUCEUR DE VIVRE, LA
Translation title: The Sweet Life *or* The Good Life

DOLL, THE (1962) Kanawha Films Ltd. B&W-96min. *(Swedish)*. Per Oscarsson, Gio Petre .... (5)
Original title: VAXDOCKAN

DOLL FACE (1945) 20th Century-Fox. B&W-80min. Vivian Blaine, Dennis O'Keefe .... (4)
British title: COME BACK TO ME

DOLL THAT TOOK THE TOWN, THE (1957) Telewide Systems. B&W-81min. *(Foreign)*. Virna Lisi, Haya Harareet .... (3)
Original title: DONNA DEL GIORNO, LA *(The Woman of the Day)*

DOLLARS (1971) Columbia. Color-120min. Warren Beatty, Goldie Hawn 5½*
Screen title: $
British title: HEIST, THE

DOLLS, THE (1965) *see* BAMBOLE!

DOLL'S HOUSE, A (1973) Paramount. Color-95min. *(Canadian-U.S.)*. Claire Bloom, Anthony Hopkins 4*

DOLL'S HOUSE, A (1973) World Film Services. Color-106min. *(British-French)*. Jane Fonda, David Warner 4*

DOLLY SISTERS, THE (1945) 20th Century-Fox. Color-114min. Betty Grable, John Payne .... (4)

DOLWYN (1949) *see* WOMAN OF DOLWYN

DOMINO KID (1957) Columbia. B&W-73min. Rory Calhoun, Kristine Miller .... (3)

DOMINO PRINCIPLE, THE (1977) Avco-Embassy. Color-97min. *(British-U.S.)*. Gene Hackman, Candice Bergen 4*
British title: DOMINO KILLINGS, THE

DON GIOVANNI (1954) Distributors Corp. of America. Color-170min. *(British)*. Cesare Stepi, Elizabeth Grummer .... (5)

DON IS DEAD, THE (1973) Universal. Color-115min. Anthony Quinn, Frederic Forrest .... (4)
TV title: BEAUTIFUL BUT DEADLY

DON JUAN (1926) Warner Bros. B&W-111min. *(Silent)*. John Barrymore, Mary Astor 4½*

DON JUAN (1954) Times Film Corp. Color-89min. *(Austrian)*. Cesare Danova, Josef Neinrad .... (4)

DON JUAN QUILLIGAN (1945) 20th Century-Fox. B&W-75min. William Bendix, Joan Blondell .... (4)

DON Q, SON OF ZORRO (1925) United Artists. B&W-137min. *(Silent)*. Douglas Fairbanks, Mary Astor .... (4)

DON QUIXOTE (1933) United Artists. B&W-80min. *(British-French)*. Feodor Chaliapin, George Robey .... (4)

DON QUIXOTE (1957) M-G-M. Color-106min. *(U.S.S.R.)*. Nikolai Cherkasov, Yuri Tolubeyev 6*

DON QUIXOTE (1973) Continental [Walter Reade]. Color-107min. Robert Helpmann, Ray Powell, Rudolf Nureyev .... (4)

DONA FLOR AND HER TWO HUSBANDS (1977) New Yorker Films. Color-106min. *(Brazilian)*. Sonia Braga 4*

DONDI (1961) Allied Artists. B&W-100min. David Kory, David Janssen 2*

DONOVAN'S BRAIN (1953) United Artists. B&W-83min. Lew Ayres, Gene Evans 4*

DONOVAN'S REEF (1963) Paramount. Color-109min. John Wayne, Lee Marvin 4*

DON'T BE AFRAID OF THE DARK (1973) Viacom. Color-74min. *(Made for TV)*. Kim Darby, Jim Hutton .... (4)

DON'T BET ON BLONDES (1935) Warner Bros. B&W-60min. Warren William, Claire Dodd .... (4)

DON'T BLAME THE STORK (1953) B&W-80min. *(British)*. Ian Hunter, Veronica Hurst .... (3)

DON'T BOTHER TO KNOCK (1952) 20th Century-Fox. B&W-76min. Richard Widmark, Marilyn Monroe 4*

DON'T BOTHER TO KNOCK (1961) *see* WHY BOTHER TO KNOCK

DON'T DRINK THE WATER (1969) Avco-Embassy. Color-98min. Jackie Gleason, Estelle Parsons 4*

DON'T FENCE ME IN (1946) Republic. B&W-54min. Roy Rogers, Dale Evans 4*

DON'T GET PERSONAL (1942) Universal. B&W-60min. James Dunn, Sally Eilers .... (3)

DON'T GIVE UP THE SHIP (1959) Paramount. B&W-89min. Jerry Lewis, Dina Merrill 3*

DON'T GO NEAR THE WATER (1957) M-G-M. Color-107min. Glenn Ford, Gia Scala 4*

DON'T JUST STAND THERE (1968) Universal. Color-100min. Robert Wagner, Mary Tyler Moore .... (4)

DON'T KNOCK THE ROCK (1957) Columbia. B&W-84min. Alan Dale, Alan Freed, Bill Haley .... (4)

DON'T KNOCK THE TWIST (1962) Columbia. B&W-87min. Lang Jeffries, Georgine Darcy, Chubby Checker .... (3)

DON'T LOOK BACK (1967) Leacock-Pennebaker. B&W-96min. *(Documentary)*. *Director:* D. A. Pennebaker .... (5)

DON'T LOOK IN THE BASEMENT (1973) Hallmark. Color-95min. Rosie Holotik, Annie McAdams, William Bill McGhee 2*

DON'T LOOK NOW (1973) Paramount. Color-110min. *(British-Italian)*. Julie Christie, Donald Sutherland 3*

DON'T LOOK NOW . . . WE'RE BEING SHOT AT (1966) Cinepix. Color-105min. *(French-British)*. Terry-Thomas, Bourvil, Louis de Funes .... (4)
Original French title: GRANDE VADROUILLE, LA

DON'T MAKE WAVES (1967) M-G-M. Color-97min. Tony Curtis, Claudia Cardinale 3*

DON'T OPEN THE WINDOW (1974) Hallmark. Color-93min. *(Spanish-Italian)*. Ray Lovelock, Christine Galbo, Arthur Kennedy .... (3)
Original Spanish title: FIN DE SEMANA PARA LOS MUERTOS *(Weekend with the Dead)*
British title: LIVING DEAD AT THE MANCHESTER MORGUE, THE

DON'T PULL YOUR PUNCHES (1937) *see* KID COMES BACK, THE

DON'T PUSH, I'LL CHARGE WHEN I'M READY (1969) MCA-TV. Color-97min. *(Made for TV)*. Enzo Cerusico, Sue Lyon, Cesar Romero .... (4)

DON'T RAISE THE BRIDGE, LOWER THE RIVER (1968) Columbia. Color-99min. *(British)*. Jerry Lewis, Terry-Thomas, Jacqueline Pearce 3*

DON'T TAKE IT TO HEART (1944) Eagle Lion. B&W-90min. *(British)*. Richard Greene, Richard Bird 3*

DON'T TEMPT THE DEVIL (1963) United Motion Pic. Org. (UMPO). B&W-106min. *(French-Italian)*. Marina Vlady, Bourvil .... (5)
Original title: BONNES CAUSES, LES *(The Good Causes)*

DON'T TOUCH MY SISTER (1964) *see* GLASS CAGE, THE

DON'T TOUCH THE LOOT (1954) *see* GRISBI

DON'T TRUST YOUR HUSBAND (1948) United Artists. B&W-90min. Madeleine Carroll, Fred MacMurray .... (4)
Original title: INNOCENT AFFAIR, AN

DON'T TURN 'EM LOOSE (1936) RKO. B&W-65min. Lewis Stone, Bruce Cabot .... (4)

Films are rated on a 1 to 10 scale, 10 is highest. **Boldface** ratings followed by an asterisk (*) are for films actually seen and rated by the executive and senior editors. All other ratings are estimates. (See Notes on Entertainment Ratings in the front section.)

DON'T WORRY, WE'LL THINK OF A TITLE (1966) United Artists. B&W-83min. Morey Amsterdam, Rose Marie........................(2)

DOOLINS OF OKLAHOMA, THE (1949) Columbia. B&W-90min. Randolph Scott, George Macready 4*
British title: GREAT MANHUNT, THE

DOOMSDAY FLIGHT, THE (1966) Universal. Color-100min. *(Made for TV).* Jack Lord, Van Johnson, Edmond O'Brien 5*

DOOMWATCH (1972) Avco-Embassy. Color-89min. *(British).* Ian Bannen, Judy Geeson, George Sanders 4*

DOOR-TO-DOOR MANIAC (1961) Sutton Pictures. B&W-80min. Johnny Cash, Donald Woods ....(2)
Alternate title: FIVE MINUTES TO LIVE

DOOR WITH SEVEN LOCKS, THE (1940) *see* CHAMBER OF HORRORS

DOOR WITH SEVEN LOCKS, THE (1962) UCC Films. B&W-96min. *(German).* Heinz Drache, Sabrina Sesselmann ....(3)
Original title: TUR MIT DEN SIEBEN SCHLOSSERN, DIE

DOPPELGANGER (1969) *see* JOURNEY TO THE FAR SIDE OF THE SUN

DORIAN GRAY (1970) American-International. Color-95min. *(Italian-Leichtenstein-W. German).* Helmut Berger, Richard Todd, Herbert Lom ....(2)
Screen title: SECRET OF DORIAN GRAY, THE
Original German title: BILDNIS DES DORIAN GRAY, DAS
Italian title: DIO CHIAMATO DORIAN, IL *(The God Called Dorian)*

DOUBLE, THE (1963) Anglo Amalgamated [EMI]. B&W-56min. *(British).* Jeanette Sterke, Alan MacNaughtan ....(3)

DOUBLE AFFAIR, THE (1964) *see* SPY WITH MY FACE, THE

DOUBLE AGENTS, THE (1962) Allied Artists. B&W-80min. *(French).* Marina Vlady, Robert Hossein ....(3)
Alternate title: NIGHT ENCOUNTER

DOUBLE ALIBI (1940) Universal. B&W-60min. Wayne Morris, William Lindsay ....(3)

DOUBLE BUNK (1961) Showcorporation. B&W-92min. *(British).* Ian Carmichael, Janette Scott ....(3)

DOUBLE CON, THE (1972) *see* TRICK BABY

DOUBLE CONFESSION (1950) Stratford Pictures. B&W-85min. *(British).* Derek Farr, Joan Hopkins, Peter Lorre ....(3)

DOUBLE CROSS (1941) Producers Rel. Corp. [Eagle Lion]. B&W-66min. Kane Richmond, Pauline Moore ....(3)

DOUBLE CROSS (1949) Italian Films Export. B&W-77min. *(Italian).* Vittorio Gassman, Amedeo Nazzari ....(4)

DOUBLE CROSS (1956) Eros Films *(Brit.).* B&W-71min. *(British).* Donald Houston, Anton Difring ....(3)

DOUBLE CROSSBONES (1951) Universal. Color-75min. Donald O'Connor, Helena Carter ....(3)

DOUBLE DANGER (1938) RKO. B&W-62min. Preston Foster, Whitney Bourne ....(3)

DOUBLE DARING (1939) *see* FIXER DUGAN

DOUBLE DEAL (1950) RKO. B&W-65min. Marie Windsor, Richard Denning ....(3)

DOUBLE DECEPTION (1960) United Motion Pic. Org. (UMPO). B&W-101min. *(French).* Jacques Riberolles, Alice Kessler ....(3)
Original title: MAGICIENNES, LES *(The Magicians)*

DOUBLE DOOR (1934) Paramount. B&W-75min. Mary Morris, Evelyn Venable........................3*

DOUBLE DYNAMITE (1951) RKO. B&W-80min. Jane Russell, Groucho Marx, Frank Sinatra........................3½*

DOUBLE EXPOSURE (1944) Paramount. B&W-63min. Chester Morris, Nancy Kelly ....(4)

DOUBLE EXPOSURE (1954) J. Arthur Rank. B&W-63min. *(British).* John Bentley, Rona Anderson ....(4)

DOUBLE IDENTITY (1940) *see* RIVER'S END

DOUBLE IDENTITY (1941) *see* HURRICANE SMITH

DOUBLE INDEMNITY (1944) Paramount. B&W-106min. Fred MacMurray, Barbara Stanwyck 6*

DOUBLE INDEMNITY (1973) MCA-TV. Color-75min. *(Made for TV).* Richard Crenna, Samantha Eggar, Lee J. Cobb 5*

DOUBLE JEOPARDY (1955) Republic. B&W-70min. Rod Cameron, Gale Robbins ....(3)
British title: CROOKED RING

DOUBLE LIFE, A (1947) Universal. B&W-104min. Ronald Colman, Signe Hasso 5½*

DOUBLE MAN, THE (1967) Warner Bros. Color-105min. *(British).* Yul Brynner, Britt Ekland........................4*

DOUBLE INDEMNITY (1944). Insurance salesman Fred MacMurray listens as alluring Barbara Stanwyck suggests how they might murder her husband and collect his insurance.

DOUBLE McGUFFIN, THE (1979) Mulberry Square. Color-101min. Ernest Borgnine, George Kennedy, Elke Sommer ....

DOUBLE NICKELS (1977) Smokey Productions. Color-89min. Jack Vacek, Ed Abrams........................

DOUBLE OR NOTHING (1937) Paramount. B&W-95min. Bing Crosby, Mary Carlisle ....(4)

DOUBLE POSSESSION (1973) *see* BLOOD COUPLE

DOUBLE TROUBLE (1967) M-G-M. Color-90min. Elvis Presley, Annette Day ....(3)

DOUBLE VERDICT (1961) Paramount. B&W-102min. *(French).* Serge Sauvion, Paul Frankeur........................(3)

DOUBLE WEDDING (1937) M-G-M. B&W-87min. William Powell, Myrna Loy ....(5)

DOUGHBOYS (1930) M-G-M. B&W-65min. Buster Keaton, Sally Eilers (3)
British title: FORWARD MARCH

DOUGHGIRLS, THE (1944) Warner Bros. B&W-102min. Ann Sheridan, Jane Wyman........................(4)

DOVE, THE (1968) Coe/Davis Ltd. B&W-14min. David Zirlin, Madeline Kahn, Sidney Davis 5½*

DOVE, THE (1974) EMI. Color-105min. *(British).* Joseph Bottoms, Deborah Raffin 5*

DOWN AMONG THE SHELTERING PALMS (1953) 20th Century-Fox. Color-87min. Mitzi Gaynor, William Lundigan........................3½*

DOWN ARGENTINE WAY (1940) 20th Century-Fox. Color-94min. Betty Grable, Don Ameche ....(4)

DOWN IN SAN DIEGO (1941) M-G-M. B&W-70min. Leo Gorcey, Bonita Granville ....(4)

DOWN MEMORY LANE (1949) Eagle Lion. B&W-72min. *(Compilation).* Mack Sennett, Steve Allen, Bing Crosby, W. C. Fields........................(3)

DOWN THREE DARK STREETS (1954) United Artists. B&W-85min. Broderick Crawford, Ruth Roman ....(5)

DOWN TO EARTH (1932) Fox Film Co. [20th]. B&W-73min. Will Rogers, Irene Rich ....(4)

DOWN TO EARTH (1947) Columbia. Color-101min. Rita Hayworth, Larry Parks........................(5)

DOWN TO THE SEA IN SHIPS (1922) W. W. Hodkinson. B&W-83min. *(Silent).* Marguerite Courtot, J. Thornton Baston, Raymond McKee 4*

DOWN TO THE SEA IN SHIPS (1949) 20th Century-Fox. B&W-120min. Richard Widmark, Lionel Barrymore........................5*

DOWN WENT McGINTY (1940) *see* GREAT McGINTY, THE

DOWNBEAT (1959) *see* DADDY-O

DOWNFALL (1963) Avco-Embassy. B&W-58min. *(British).* Maurice Denham, Nadja Regin ....(3)

DOWNHILL RACER (1969) Paramount. Color-102min. Robert Redford, Gene Hackman........................5*

Films are rated on a 1 to 10 scale, 10 is highest. **Boldface** ratings followed by an asterisk (*) are for films actually seen and rated by the executive and senior editors. All other ratings are estimates. (See Notes on Entertainment Ratings in the front section.)

DOWNPOUR (1972) B&W-126min. (Iranian). Parviz Fannizadeh, Parvaneh Masoumi ....

DRACULA (1931) Universal. B&W-84min. Bela Lugosi, Edward Van Sloan 3*

DRACULA (1958) see HORROR OF DRACULA

DRACULA (1973) see ANDY WARHOL'S DRACULA

DRACULA (1974) Dan Curtis Prods. Color-100min. (Made for TV). Jack Palance, Simon Ward 4*

DRACULA (1979) Universal. Color-115min. Frank Langella, Laurence Olivier 5*

DRACULA A.D. 1972 (1972) Warner Bros. Color-100min. (British). Christopher Lee, Peter Cushing ....(4)

DRACULA HAS RISEN FROM THE GRAVE (1968) Warner Bros. Color-92min. (British). Christopher Lee, Veronica Carlson 4*

DRACULA - PRINCE OF DARKNESS (1966) 20th Century-Fox. Color-90min. (British). Christopher Lee, Barbara Shelley 3½*

DRACULA VS. FRANKENSTEIN (1971) Independent International. Color-90min. J. Carrol Naish, Lon Chaney (Jr.), Russ Tamblyn 1½*
Alternate title: BLOOD OF FRANKENSTEIN

DRACULA'S CASTLE (1969) see BLOOD OF DRACULA'S CASTLE

DRACULA'S DAUGHTER (1936) Universal. B&W-72min. Gloria Holden, Otto Kruger 3*

DRACULA'S DOG (1977) Crown International. Color-90min. Michael Pataki, Reggie Nalder, José Ferrer ....
British title: ZOLTAN . . . HOUND OF DRACULA

DRACULA'S GREAT LOVE (1972) International Amusements. Color-85min. (Spanish). Paul Naschy, Rossana Yanni ....(3)
Original title: GRAN AMOR DEL CONDE DRACULA, EL (The Great Love of Count Dracula)
Screen title: COUNT DRACULA'S GREAT LOVE

DRAEGERMAN COURAGE (1936) Warner Bros. B&W-58min. Barton MacLane, Jean Muir ....(4)
British title: CAVE IN, THE

DRAGNET (1954) Warner Bros. Color-89min. Jack Webb, Ben Alexander 4½*

DRAGNET (1969) Universal. Color-100min. (Made for TV). Jack Webb, Harry Morgan 4*

DRAGON FLIES, THE (1975) 20th Century-Fox. Color-103min. (Australian-Hong Kong). Jimmy Wang Yu, George Lazenby ....(2)

DRAGON LIVES, THE (1978) Film Ventures International. Color-90min. (Hong Kong). Bruce Li, Caryn White ....

DRAGON MURDER CASE, THE (1934) First National [W.B.]. B&W-68min. Warren William, Margaret Lindsay ....(3)

DRAGON SEED (1944) M-G-M. B&W-145min. Katharine Hepburn, Walter Huston 4*

DRAGONFLY (1976) American-International. Color-95min. Beau Bridges, Susan Sarandon ....(4)
Alternate title: ONE SUMMER LOVE

DRAGONFLY SQUADRON (1954) Allied Artists. B&W-82min. Barbara Britton, John Hodiak ....(3)

DRAGON'S BLOOD, THE (1957) Trans-America. Color-97min. (Italian). Katherina Mayberg, Rolf Tasna, Giorgio Constantini ....(3)
Original title: SIGFRIDO (Siegfried)

DRAGON'S GOLD (1953) United Artists. B&W-70min. John Archer, Hillary Brooks ....(2)

DRAGONWYCK (1946) 20th Century-Fox. B&W-103min. Gene Tierney, Walter Huston 4*

DRAGOON WELLS MASSACRE (1957) Allied Artists. Color-88min. Barry Sullivan, Mona Freeman ....(5)

DRAGSTRIP GIRL (1957) American-International. B&W-69min. Fay Spain, Steve Terrell ....(3)

DRAGSTRIP RIOT (1958) American-International. B&W-68min. Gary Clarke, Fay Wray, Yvonne Lime ....(3)
British title: RECKLESS AGE, THE

DRAMA OF JEALOUSY AND OTHER THINGS, A (1970) see PIZZA TRIANGLE, THE

DRAMATIC SCHOOL (1938) M-G-M. B&W-80min. Luise Rainer, Paulette Goddard ....(4)

DRANGO (1957) United Artists. B&W-92min. Jeff Chandler, John Lupton 3*

DREAM BALLERINA (1951) A.F.E. Films. B&W-78min. (French). Violette Verdy, Romney Brent, Henri Guisol ....(3)
TV title: BALLERINA

DREAM CITY (1976) Peppercorn-Wormser. Color-96min. (W. German-Czech). Per Oscarsson, Rosemarie Fendel ....

DREAM GIRL (1948) Paramount. B&W-85min. Betty Hutton, Macdonald Carey ....(4)

DREAM MAKER, THE (1963) Universal. Color-86min. (British). Tommy Steele, Michael Medwin ....(3)
Original title: IT'S ALL HAPPENING

DREAM OF KINGS, A (1969) National General. Color-107min. Anthony Quinn, Irene Papas ....(5)

DREAM OF PASSION, A (1978) SNC, Coline. Color-110min. (Greek). Melina Mercouri, Ellen Burstyn 2½*

DREAM WIFE (1953) M-G-M. B&W-101min. Cary Grant, Deborah Kerr 4*

DREAMBOAT (1952) 20th Century-Fox. B&W-83min. Clifton Webb, Ginger Rogers ....(5)

DREAMER, THE (1970) Cannon Releasing. Color-86min. (Israeli-U.S.). Tuvia Tavi, Leora Rivlin ....(4)
Original Israeli title: HA'TIMHONI

DREAMER (1979) 20th Century-Fox. Color-91min. Tim Matheson, Susan Blakely 5*

DREAMING LIPS (1937) United Artists. B&W-94min. (British). Elizabeth Bergner, Raymond Massey, Romney Brent ....(4)

DREAMS (1955) Janus Films. B&W-86min. (Swedish). Eva Dahlbeck, Harriet Andersson, Gunnar Bjornstrand 3*
Original title: KVINNODROM
British title: JOURNEY INTO AUTUMN

DREAMS DIE FIRST (1979) American-International. Color- min. ....

DREAMS OF GLASS (1970) Universal. Color-83min. John Denos, Caroline Barrett ....(5)

DRESSED TO KILL (1941) 20th Century-Fox. B&W-74min. Lloyd Nolan, Mary Beth Hughes ....(4)

DRESSED TO KILL (1946) Universal. B&W-72min. Basil Rathbone, Nigel Bruce 4*
British title: SHERLOCK HOLMES AND THE SECRET CODE

DRIFTER, THE (1966) Film-Makers' Distribution Center. B&W-74min. John Tracy, Sadja Marr ....(5)

DRIFTING WEEDS (1959) see FLOATING WEEDS

DRIFTWOOD (1948) Republic. B&W-88min. Ruth Warrick, Walter Brennan 4*

DRIVE A CROOKED ROAD (1954) Columbia. B&W-82min. Mickey Rooney, Dianne Foster ....(4)

DRIVE HARD, DRIVE FAST (1969) MCA-TV. Color-95min. (Made for TV). Brian Kelly, Joan Collins, Henry Silva ....(4)

DRIVE, HE SAID (1971) Columbia. Color-90min. William Tepper, Karen Black 2½*

DRIVE-IN (1976) Columbia. Color-96min. Lisa Lemole, Glenn Morshower 5*

DRIVER, THE (1978) 20th Century-Fox. Color-88min. Ryan O'Neal, Bruce Dern, Isabelle Adjani 5*

DROP DEAD, DARLING (1966) see ARRIVEDERCI, BABY

DROPS OF BLOOD (1960) see MILL OF THE STONE WOMEN

DROWNING POOL, THE (1975) Warner Bros. Color-108min. Paul Newman, Joanne Woodward 4*

DRUM, THE (1938) United Artists. Color-99min. (British). Sabu, Raymond Massey 5*
Publicity title: DRUMS

DRUM (1976) United Artists. Color-100min. Warren Oates, Ken Norton, Isela Vega 5*

DRUM BEAT (1954) Warner Bros. Color-111min. Alan Ladd, Audrey Dalton 4½*

DRUM CRAZY (1959) see GENE KRUPA STORY, THE

DRUMS (1938) see DRUM, THE

DRUMS ACROSS THE RIVER (1954) Universal. Color-78min. Audie Murphy, Walter Brennan ....(3)

DRUMS ALONG THE AMAZON (1948) see ANGEL ON THE AMAZON

DRUMS ALONG THE MOHAWK (1939) 20th Century-Fox. Color-103min. Claudette Clobert, Henry Fonda 3*

DRUMS IN THE DEEP SOUTH (1951) RKO. Color-87min. James Craig, Guy Madison ....(3)

DRUMS OF AFRICA (1963) M-G-M. Color-92min. Frankie Avalon, Mariette Hartley ....(3)

DRUMS OF TAHITI (1954) Columbia. Color-73min. Dennis O'Keefe, Patricia Medina ....(2)

DUAL ALIBI (1947) NTA Pictures. B&W-81min. (British). Herbert Lom, Phyllis Dixey, Terence de Marney ....(4)

DUBARRY WAS A LADY (1943) M-G-M. Color-101min. Lucille Ball ....(5)

DUBLIN NIGHTMARE (1958) J. Arthur Rank. **B&W-64min.** *(British).* William Sylvester, Marla LanpI .... (3)

DUCHESS AND THE DIRTWATER FOX, THE (1976) 20th Century-Fox. **Color-104min.** George Segal, Goldie Hawn **5½***

DUCHESS OF IDAHO (1950) M-G-M. **Color-98min.** Esther Williams, Van Johnson .... (4)

DUCHIN STORY, THE (1956) *see* EDDY DUCHIN STORY, THE

DUCK IN ORANGE SAUCE (1976) Cineriz. **Color-105min.** *(Italian).* Monica Vitti, Ugo Tognazzi ....
Original title: ANATRA ALL'ARANCIA, L'

DUCK SOUP (1933) Paramount. **B&W-70min.** Groucho Marx, Harpo Marx **3***

DUCK, YOU SUCKER (1971) United Artists. **Color-138min.** *(Italian-U.S., English language).* Rod Steiger, James Coburn **5***
Original title: GIU LA TESTA *(Down With Your Head)*
Alternate title: FISTFUL OF DYNAMITE, A

DUDE GOES WEST, THE (1948) Allied Artists. **B&W-87min.** Eddie Albert, Gale Storm **3***

DUEL (1971) Universal. **Color-95min.** *(Made for TV).* Dennis Weaver... **4½***

DUEL AT APACHE WELLS (1957) Republic. **B&W-70min.** Ben Cooper, Anna Maria Alberghetti .... (3)

DUEL AT DIABLO (1966) United Artists. **Color-103min.** James Garner, Sidney Poitier **4½***

DUEL AT SILVER CREEK, THE (1952) Universal. **Color-77min.** Audie Murphy, Faith Domergue **3***

DUEL AT THE RIO GRANDE (1962) Teleworld. **Color-91min.** *(Italian).* Sean Flynn, Danielle de Metz .... (3)

DUEL IN DURANGO (1957) *see* GUN DUEL IN DURANGO

DUEL IN THE FOREST (1958) **Color-112min.** *(German).* Curt Jurgens, Maria Schell .... (4)
Original title: SCHINDERHANNES, DER

DUEL IN THE JUNGLE (1954) Warner Bros. **Color-102min.** *(British).* Dana Andrews, Jeanne Crain .... (3)

DUEL IN THE SUN (1946) Selznick Releasing. **Color-138min.** Jennifer Jones, Joseph Cotten, Gregory Peck **5***

DUEL OF CHAMPIONS (1961) Medallion. **Color-105min.** *(Italian-Spanish).* Alan Ladd, Franca Bettoja .... (3)
Original Italian title: ORAZI E CURIAZI

DUEL OF FIRE (1960) American-International. **Color-85min.** *(Italian).* Fernando Lamas, Liana Orfe .... (3)

DUEL OF THE SPACE MONSTERS (1965) *see* FRANKENSTEIN MEETS THE SPACE MONSTER

DUEL OF THE TITANS (1961) Paramount. **Color-90min.** *(Italian).* Steve Reeves, Gordon Scott **3***
Original title: ROMOLO E REMO *(Romulus and Remus)*

DUEL ON THE MISSISSIPPI (1955) Columbia. **Color-72min.** Lex Barker, Patricia Medina .... (3)

DUEL WITH DEATH (1959) Emery Pictures. **Color-103min.** *(Austrian).* Gert Frobe, Mai-Britt Nilsson .... (3)
Original title: UND EWIG SINGEN DIE WAELDER
Alternate title: BEYOND SING THE WOODS
Alternate title: VENGEANCE IN TIMBER VALLEY

DUELLISTS, THE (1977) Paramount. **Color-95min.** *(British).* Keith Carradine, Harvey Keitel **5½***

DUET FOR CANNIBALS (1969) Grove Press. **B&W-105min.** *(Swedish).* Adriana Asti, Lars Ekborg, Gosta Ekman, Jr., Agneta Ekmanner .... (4)
Original title: DUETT FOR KANNIBALER

DUFFY (1968) Columbia. **Color-101min.** *(British).* James Coburn, James Mason, James Fox **4***

DUFFY OF SAN QUENTIN (1954) Warner Bros. **B&W-78min.** Paul Kelly, Maureen O'Sullivan .... (4)
British title: MEN BEHIND BARS

DUFFY'S TAVERN (1945) Paramount. **B&W-98min.** Ed Gardner, Victor Moore .... (4)

DUKE OF CHICAGO (1949) Republic. **B&W-59min.** Tom Brown, Audrey Long .... (3)

DUKE OF WEST POINT, THE (1938) United Artists. **B&W-96min.** Louis Hayward, Joan Fontaine .... (4)

DULCIMA (1971) Cinevision Films. **Color-93min.** *(British).* John Mills, Carol White .... (4)

DULCIMER STREET (1948) Universal. **B&W-110min.** *(British).* Richard Attenborough, Alastair Sim .... (5)
Original title: LONDON BELONGS TO ME

DULCY (1940) M-G-M. **B&W-64min.** Ann Sothern, Billie Burke .... (3)

DUMBO (1941) RKO (for Disney). **Color-64min.** *(Cartoon).* *Director:* Vladimir Tytla **5½***

DUNGEONS OF HORROR (1962) Herts-Lion International. **B&W-80min.** Russ Harvey, Helen Hogan .... (2)
Alternate title: DUNGEON OF HORROR

DUNKIRK (1958) M-G-M. **B&W-113min.** *(British).* John Mills, Robert Urquhart **4***

DUNWICH HORROR, THE (1970) American-International. **Color-90min.** Sandra Dee, Dean Stockwell, Ed Begley **3***

DURANT AFFAIR, THE (1962) Paramount. **B&W-73min.** *(British).* Jane Griffiths, Conrad Phillips, Nigel Green .... (3)

DUST BE MY DESTINY (1939) Warner Bros. **B&W-88min.** John Garfield, Priscilla Lane **4***

DUSTY AND SWEETS McGEE (1971) Warner Bros. **Color-90min.** *(Documentary).* *Director:* Floyd Mutrux .... (3)

DUTCHMAN (1966) Continental [Walter Reade]. **B&W-55min.** *(British).* Shirley Knight, Al Freeman, Jr. .... (5)

DYING (1976) PBS. **Color-97min.** *(Made for TV, Documentary).* **4½***

DYING ROOM ONLY (1973) Viacom. **Color-73min.** *(Made for TV).* Cloris Leachman, Ross Martin **3***

DYNAMITE (1929) Pathé. **B&W-129min.** Conrad Nagel, Kay Johnson ... (4)

DYNAMITE (1949) Paramount. **B&W-69min.** William Gargan, Virginia Welles .... (2)

DYNAMITE MAN FROM GLORY JAIL (1971) *see* FOOLS' PARADE

DYNAMITERS, THE (1956) Astor. **B&W-74min.** *(British).* Wayne Morris, James Kenney .... (3)

DYNASTY (1976) Cinema Shares. **Color-94min.** *(Hong Kong).* Bobby Ming, Pai Ying, Lin Tashing ....

-E-

E. B. WHITE'S CHARLOTTE'S WEB (1973) *see* CHARLOTTE'S WEB

EACH DAWN I DIE (1939) Warner Bros. **B&W-92min.** James Cagney, George Raft **4***

EAGLE, THE (1925) United Artists. **B&W-72min.** *(Silent).* Rudolph Valentino, Vilma Banky **4***

EAGLE AND THE HAWK, THE (1933) Paramount. **B&W-68min.** Fredric March, Cary Grant **4***

EAGLE AND THE HAWK, THE (1950) Paramount. **Color-104min.** John Payne, Rhonda Fleming **3***

EAGLE HAS LANDED, THE (1976) Columbia. **Color-134min.** *(British).* Michael Caine, Donald Sutherland **4½***

EAGLE IN A CAGE (1972) National General. **Color-98min.** *(U.S./Yugoslavian).* Kenneth Haigh, John Gielgud .... (3)

EAGLE SQUADRON (1942) Universal. **B&W-109min.** Robert Stack, Diana Barrymore .... (4)

EAGLES OF THE FLEET (1952) *see* FLAT TOP

EARL CARROLL SKETCHBOOK (1946) Republic. **B&W-90min.** Constance Moore, William Marshall* .... (3)
British title: HATS OFF TO RHYTHM

EARL CARROLL VANITIES (1945) Republic. **B&W-91min.** Dennis O'Keefe, Eve Arden .... (4)

EARL OF CHICAGO, THE (1940) M-G-M. **B&W-85min.** Robert Montgomery, Edward Arnold **3½***

EARLY BIRD, THE (1965) Alan Enterprises. **Color-98min.** *(British).* Norman Wisdom, Edward Chapman **3***

EARLY SPRING (1956) New Yorker Films. **B&W-144min.** *(Japanese).* Ryo Ikebe, Chikage Awashima ....
Original title: SOSHUN

EARLY TO BED (1936) Paramount. **B&W-75min.** Charles Ruggles, Mary Boland .... (4)

EARRINGS OF MADAME DE . . ., THE (1953) Arlan Pictures. **B&W-102min.** *(French).* Danielle Darrieux, Charles Boyer .... (4)
Original title: MADAME DE . . .
Alternate title: DIAMOND EARRINGS

EARTH (1930) Vufku. **B&W-90min.** *(U.S.S.R., Silent).* Semyon Svashenko, Stepan Shkurat **2***
Original title: ZEMLYA

EARTH CRIES OUT, THE (1949) Premier Pictures [MGM]. **B&W-79min.** *(Italian).* Andrea Checcki, Luigi Tosi, Peter Trent .... (3)
Original title: GRIDE DELLA TERRA, IL

EARTH DIES SCREAMING, THE (1965) 20th Century-Fox. **B&W-62min.** *(British).* Willard Parker, Dennis Price .... (3)

EARTH IN DANGER, THE (1964) *see* ATOMIC RULERS OF THE WORLD

Films are rated on a 1 to 10 scale, 10 is highest. **Boldface** ratings followed by an asterisk (*) are for films actually seen and rated by the executive and senior editors. All other ratings are estimates. (See Notes on Entertainment Ratings in the front section.)

EARTH IS A SINFUL SONG, THE (1973) Seaberg. **Color-108min.** *(Finnish).* Maritta Viitamaki, Pauli Juahojarvi, Aimo Saukko **3***
Original title: MAA ON SYNTINEN LAULAU
Alternate title: EARTH IS OUR SINFUL SONG

EARTH II (1971) M-G-M. **Color-100min.** *(Made for TV).* Tony Franciosa, Gary Lockwood, Mariette Hartley **3***

EARTH VS. THE FLYING SAUCERS (1956) Columbia. **B&W-83min.** Hugh Marlowe, Joan Taylor **3***

EARTH VS. THE SPIDER (1958) American-International. **B&W-75min.** Ed Kemmer, June Kenney .... (2)
Publicity title: SPIDER, THE

EARTHBOUND (1940) 20th Century-Fox. **B&W-67min.** Warner Baxter, Andrea Leeds .... (3)

EARTHQUAKE (1974) Universal. **Color-122min.** Charlton Heston, Ava Gardner **6***

EARTHWORM TRACTORS (1936) First National [W.B.]. **B&W-63min.** Joe E. Brown, June Travis .... (4)
British title: NATURAL BORN SALESMAN, A

EAST END CHANT (1934) *see* LIMEHOUSE BLUES

EAST LYNNE (1931) Fox Film Co. [20th]. **B&W-102min.** Ann Harding, Clive Brook .... (4)

EAST MEETS WEST (1936) Gaumont-British [Rank]. **B&W-74min.** *(British).* George Arliss, Lucie Mannheim, Godfrey Tearle .... (4)

EAST OF EDEN (1955) Warner Bros. **Color-115min.** James Dean, Julie Harris **5***

EAST OF JAVA (1950) *see* SOUTH SEA SINNER

EAST OF KILIMANJARO (1957) Paramount. **Color-75min.** *(U.S.-British-Italian).* Marshall Thompson, Gaby André **2***
British title: BIG SEARCH, THE
Original Italian title: GRANDE CACCIA, LA

EAST OF SHANGHAI (1932) *see* RICH AND STRANGE

EAST OF SUDAN (1964) Columbia. **Color-84min.** *(British).* Anthony Quayle, Sylvia Syms .... (3)

EAST OF SUMATRA (1953) Universal. **Color-82min.** Jeff Chandler, Anthony Quinn **4***

EAST OF THE RISING SUN (1950) *see* MALAYA

EAST OF THE RIVER (1940) Warner Bros. **B&W-73min.** John Garfield, William Lundigan **3***

EAST SIDE OF HEAVEN (1939) Universal. **B&W-90min.** Bing Crosby, Joan Blondell .... (4)

EAST SIDE, WEST SIDE (1950) M-G-M. **B&W-108min.** Barbara Stanwyck, James Mason **4***

EAST WIND (1969) *see* WIND FROM THE EAST

EASTER PARADE (1948) M-G-M. **Color-103min.** Fred Astaire, Judy Garland **5***

EARTHQUAKE (1974). The devastation of Los Angeles.

EASY COME, EASY GO (1947) Paramount. **B&W-77min.** Barry Fitzgerald, Diana Lynn .... (4)

EASY COME, EASY GO (1967) Paramount. **Color-95min.** Elvis Presley, Dodie Marshall .... (4)

EASY GO (1930) *see* FREE AND EASY

EASY LIFE, THE (1962) Avco-Embassy. **B&W-105min.** *(Italian).* Vittorio Gassman, Jean-Louis Trintignant .... (5)
Original title: SORPASSO, IL *(Overtaken on the Road)*

EASY LIVING (1937) Paramount. **B&W-90min.** Jean Arthur, Edward Arnold **4***

EASY LIVING (1949) RKO. **B&W-77min.** Victor Mature, Lucille Ball ..... (4)

EASY MONEY (1948) Eagle Lion. **B&W-94min.** *(British).* Greta Gynt, Dennis Price .... (4)

EASY RIDER (1969) Columbia. **Color-94min.** Peter Fonda, Dennis Hopper **6½***

EASY TO LOOK AT (1945) Universal. **B&W-65min.** Gloria Jean, Kirby Grant .... (3)

EASY TO LOVE (1953) M-G-M. **Color-96min.** Esther Williams, Van Johnson .... (4)

EASY TO WED (1946) M-G-M. **Color-110min.** Van Johnson, Esther Williams **4***

EASY WAY, THE (1952) *see* ROOM FOR ONE MORE

EAT MY DUST (1976) New World. **Color-89min.** Ron Howard, Christopher Norris **4***

EATEN ALIVE (1976) Virgo International. **Color-90min.** .... (3)
Alternate title: DEATH TRAP
Alternate title: SLAUGHTER HOTEL
Alternate title: STARLIGHT SLAUGHTER

EBB TIDE (1937) Paramount. **Color-94min.** Oscar Homolka, Frances Farmer .... (4)

EBIRAH, HORROR OF THE DEEP (1966) *see* GODZILLA VS. THE SEA MONSTER

ECCO (1963) Cresa Roma. **Color-100min.** *(Italian, Documentary).* Director: Gianni Proia .... (3)
Original title: MONDO DI NOTTE *(World of Night)*

ECHOES OF A SUMMER (1976) Cine Artists. **Color-99min.** *(U.S.-Canadian).* Jodie Foster, Richard Harris .... (4)

ECHOES OF SILENCE (1967) Film-Makers' Distribution Center. **B&W-74min.** Miguel Chacour, Viraj Amonsin .... (4)

ECHOES - PINK FLOYD (1972) RM Productions. **Color-62min.** *(German-French, Documentary).* Director: D'Adriann Maben .... (4)

ECHOS OF THE ROAD (1972) *see* PICKUP ON 101

ECLIPSE (1962) Times Film Corp. **B&W-123min.** *(Italian-French).* Monica Vitti, Alain Delon **2***
Original Italian title: ECLISSE, L'
Original French title: ÉCLIPSE, L'

ECSTASY (1932) Eureka Productions. **B&W-82min.** *(Czech).* Hedy Keisler (Lamarr), Jaromir Rogoz ....
Original title: EXTASE
Alternate title: MY LIFE

EDDIE CANTOR STORY, THE (1954) Warner Bros. **Color-116min.** Keefe Brasselle, Marilyn Erskine .... (3)

EDDY DUCHIN STORY, THE (1956) Columbia. **Color-123min.** Tyrone Power, Kim Novak .... (4)
Alternate title: DUCHIN STORY, THE

EDGE, THE (1968) Filmmakers. **B&W-100min.** Jack Rader, Tom Griffin .... (5)

EDGE OF DARKNESS (1943) Warner Bros. **B&W-120min.** Errol Flynn, Ann Sheridan **4***

EDGE OF DOOM (1950) RKO. **B&W-99min.** Dana Andrews, Farley Granger **4***
British title: STRONGER THAN FEAR

EDGE OF ETERNITY (1959) Columbia. **Color-80min.** Cornel Wilde, Victoria Shaw **3***

EDGE OF FEAR (1964) Avco-Embassy. **B&W-90min.** *(Spanish).* May Heatherly, Virgilio Teixeira .... (3)
Alternate title: NIGHT OF FEAR

EDGE OF HELL (1956) Universal. **B&W-76min.** Hugo Haas, Francesca de Scaffa .... (2)

EDGE OF THE CITY (1957) M-G-M. **B&W-85min.** John Cassavetes, Sidney Poitier **5***
British title: MAN IS TEN FEET TALL, A

EDISON, THE MAN (1940) M-G-M. **B&W-107min.** Spencer Tracy, Rita Johnson **5***

EDUCATION OF SONNY CARSON, THE (1974) Paramount. Color-104min. Rony Clanton, Don Gordon......................................(5)

EDVARD MUNCH (1976) New Yorker Films. Color-215min. (Swedish-Norwegian). Geir Westby, Gro Fraas ....(4)

EDWARD, MY SON (1948) M-G-M. B&W-112min. (British). Spencer Tracy, Deborah Kerr 4*

EEGAH! (1963) Fairway International. Color-90min. Arch Hall, Jr., Marilyn Manning, Richard Kiel ....(2)

EFFECT OF GAMMA RAYS ON MAN-IN-THE-MOON MARIGOLDS, THE (1972) 20th Century-Fox. Color-100min. Pauline Woodward, Nell Potts..4*

EFFI BRIEST (1974) New Yorker Films. B&W-140min. (German). Hanna Schygulla, Wolfgang Schenck ....

EGG AND I, THE (1947) Universal. B&W-108min. Claudette Colbert, Fred MacMurray 4*

EGGHEAD ON HILL 656 (1971) see RELUCTANT HEROES, THE

EGYPTIAN, THE (1954) 20th Century-Fox. Color-140min. Edmund Purdom, Jean Simmons 5*

EIGER SANCTION, THE (1975) Universal. Color-125min. Clint Eastwood, George Kennedy 6*

8 1/2 (1963) Avco-Embassy. B&W-135min. (Italian). Marcello Mastroianni, Claudia Cardinale 3*

800 LEAGUES OVER THE AMAZON (1960) Clasa-Mohme. Color-78min. (Mexican). Carlos Moctezuma, Elvira Quintant ....(3)

EIGHT IRON MEN (1952) Columbia. B&W-80min. Bonar Colleano, Arthur Franz ....(4)

EIGHT O'CLOCK WALK (1954) Associated Artists. B&W-87min. (British). Richard Attenborough, Cathy O'Donnell 4*

EIGHT ON THE LAM (1967) United Artists. Color-106min. Bob Hope, Phyllis Diller, Jonathan Winters 3*
British title: EIGHT ON THE RUN

EIGHTEEN AND ANXIOUS (1957) Republic. B&W-93min. Martha Scott, Jim Backus, Mary Webster ....(3)

EIGHTEEN IN THE SUN (1962) Goldstone Film Enterprises. Color-85min. (Italian). Catherine Spaak, Lisa Gastoni ....(3)
Original title: DICIOTTENNI AL SOLE (Teenagers in the Sun)
TV title: BEACH PARTY -- ITALIAN STYLE

18 YEAR OLD SCHOOLGIRLS, THE (1973) see CHEERLEADERS, THE

8th DAY OF THE WEEK, THE (1958) Continental [Walter Reade]. B&W-84min. (Polish-W. German). Sonia Ziemann, Zbigniew Cybulski ....(5)
Original German title: ACHTE WOCHENTAG, DER

81st BLOW, THE (1975) B&W-115min. (Israeli, Documentary). Director: David Bergman 4½*

80 STEPS TO JONAH (1969) Warner Bros. Color-107min. Wayne Newton, Jo Van Fleet 4*

80,000 SUSPECTS (1963) Continental [Walter Reade]. B&W-113min. (British). Claire Bloom, Richard Johnson ....(4)

EL (1952) Ultramar Films. B&W-100min. (Mexican). Arturo de Cordova, Delia Garcés, Luis Beristain ....(4)
Alternate title: THIS STRANGE PASSION

EL ALAMEIN (1953) Columbia. B&W-67min. Scott Brady, Edward Ashley ....(3)
British title: DESERT PATROL

EL CID (1961) Allied Artists. Color-184min. Charlton Heston, Sophia Loren 6*

EL CONDOR (1970) National General. Color-102min. Jim Brown, Lee Van Cleef 4*

EL DORADO (1967) Paramount. Color-126min. John Wayne, Robert Mitchum..4*

EL GRECO (1964) 20th Century-Fox. Color-94min. (Italian-French). Mel Ferrer, Rosanna Schiaffino ....

EL PASO (1949) Paramount. Color-92min. John Payne, Gail Russell......(3)

EL TOPO (1971) Abkco Films. Color-123min. (Mexican). Alexandro Jodorowsky, Robert John..2*
Translation title: The Mole

ELEANOR ROOSEVELT STORY, THE (1966) Commonwealth United. B&W-91min. (Documentary). Director: Richard Kaplan 5½*

ELECTRA (1962) Lopert [U.A.]. B&W-110min. (Greek). Irene Papas, Aleka Catselli 4½*

ELECTRA GLIDE IN BLUE (1973) United Artists. Color-106min. Robert Blake, Billy Green Bush 4*
Alternate title: LEGEND OF BIG JOHN, THE
Alternate title: BIG JOHN

ELECTRIC HORSEMAN, THE (1979) Columbia/Universal. Color- min. Robert Redford, Jane Fonda.......................................

ELECTRIC MAN, THE (1941) see MAN-MADE MONSTER

ELECTRONIC MONSTER, THE (1958) Columbia. B&W-72min. (British). Rod Cameron, Mary Murphy ....(2)
Original title: ESCAPEMENT

ELEPHANT BOY (1937) United Artists. B&W-82min. (British). Sabu, Walter Hudd..4*

ELEPHANT CALLED SLOWLY, AN (1969) Continental [Walter Reade]. Color-91min. (British). Bill Travers, Virginia McKenna...............5*

ELEPHANT FURY (1955) Teledynamics. B&W-83min. (German). Harry Piel, Herbert Bohme..(3)

ELEPHANT GUN (1959) Lopert [U.A.]. Color-84min. (British). Belinda Lee, Michael Craig ....(4)
Original title: NOR THE MOON BY NIGHT

ELEPHANT STAMPEDE (1951) Monogram [Allied Artists]. B&W-71min. Johnny Sheffield, Donna Martell ....(3)
British and alternate U.S. title: BOMBA AND THE ELEPHANT STAMPEDE

ELEPHANT WALK (1954) Paramount. Color-103min. Elizabeth Taylor, Peter Finch..4*

ELEPHANTS NEVER FORGET (1939) see ZENOBIA

ELEVATOR, THE (1974) MCA-TV. Color-75min. (Made for TV). Myrna Loy, Teresa Wright, Carol Lynley 4*

ELEVATOR TO THE GALLOWS (1958) see FRANTIC

11 HARROWHOUSE (1974) 20th Century-Fox. Color-95min. (British). Charles Grodin, Candice Bergen 5½*
TV title: ANYTHING FOR LOVE

ELIZA FRASER (1976) Roadshow (Australian). Color-130min. (Australian). Susannah York, Noel Ferrier, Trevor Howard......................

ELIZABETH THE QUEEN (1939) see PRIVATE LIVES OF ELIZABETH AND ESSEX, THE

ELLA CINDERS (1926) First National [W.B.]. B&W-73min. (Silent). Colleen Moore, Lloyd Hughes 4½*

ELLEN (1950) see SECOND WOMAN, THE

ELLERY QUEEN (1975) MCA-TV. Color-100min. (Made for TV). Jim Hutton, David Wayne, Ray Milland.......................................5½*
Alternate title: TOO MANY SUSPECTS

ELLERY QUEEN AND THE MURDER RING (1941) Columbia. B&W-65min. Ralph Bellamy, Margaret Lindsay, Mona Barrie ....(3)
British title: MURDER RING, THE

ELLERY QUEEN AND THE PERFECT CRIME (1941) Columbia. B&W-68min. Ralph Bellamy, Margaret Lindsay, Spring Byington ....(3)
British title: PERFECT CRIME, THE

ELLERY QUEEN: DON'T LOOK BEHIND YOU (1971) MCA-TV. Color-95min. (Made for TV). Peter Lawford, Harry Morgan, Stefanie Powers...(4)

ELLERY QUEEN, MASTER DETECTIVE (1940) Columbia. B&W-66min. Ralph Bellamy, Margaret Lindsay, Michael Whalen ....(3)

ELLERY QUEEN'S PENTHOUSE MYSTERY (1941) Columbia. B&W-69min. Ralph Bellamy, Margaret Lindsay, Anna May Wong................(3)

ELMER GANTRY (1960) United Artists. Color-146min. Burt Lancaster, Jean Simmons 10*

ELMER THE GREAT (1933) First National [W.B.]. B&W-74min. Joe E. Brown, Patricia Ellis..4*

ELOPEMENT (1951) 20th Century-Fox. B&W-82min. Clifton Webb, Anne Francis ....(3)

ELUSIVE CORPORAL, THE (1962) Pathé Contemporary. B&W-108min. (French). Jean-Pierre Cassel, Claude Brasseur ....(5)
Original title: CAPORAL EPINGLE, LE (The Hard-Luck Corporal)
British title: VANISHING CORPORAL, THE

ELVIRA MADIGAN (1967) Cinema 5. Color-89min. (Swedish). Pia Degermark, Thommy Berggren 5*

ELVIS ON TOUR (1972) M-G-M. Color-92min. (Music Film). Director: Pierre Adidge: Robert Abel ....(4)

ELVIS - THAT'S THE WAY IT IS (1970) M-G-M. Color-108min. (Music Film). Director: Denis Sanders...4*

EMBALMER, THE (1965) Europix-Consolidated. B&W-83min. (Italian). Maureen Brown, Gin Mart..(1)
Original title: MOSTRO DI VENEZIA, IL (The Monster of Venice)

EMBEZZLED HEAVEN (1958) De Rochemont. Color-91min. (German). Annie Rosar, Hans Holt ....(4)
Original title: VERUNTREUTE HIMMEL, DER

EMBEZZLER, THE (1954) J. Arthur Rank. B&W-61min. (British). Charles Victor, Zena Marshall ....(3)

EMBRACEABLE YOU (1948) Warner Bros. B&W-80min. Dane Clark, Geraldine Brooks...(3)

EMBRYO (1976) Cine Artists. **Color-108min.** Rock Hudson, Barbara Carrera 4½*

EMERGENCY (1962) Butcher's *(Brit.).* **B&W-63min.** *(British).* Glyn Houston, Zena Walker ....(3)

EMERGENCY (1971) MCA-TV. **Color-100min.** *(Made for TV).* Robert Fuller, Julie London, Bobby Troup, Randolph Mantooth ....(4)

EMERGENCY CALL (1952) *see* HUNDRED HOUR HUNT

EMERGENCY WARD (1972) *see* CAREY TREATMENT, THE

EMERGENCY WEDDING (1950) Columbia. **B&W-78min.** Larry Parks, Barbara Hale ....(3)
British title: JEALOUSY

EMIGRANTS, THE (1971) Warner Bros. **Color-148min.** *(Swedish).* Max von Sydow, Liv Ullmann 5½*
Original title: UTVANDRARNA

EMIL AND THE DETECTIVES (1964) Buena Vista. **Color-99min.** *(U.S.-W. German).* Bryan Russell, Walter Slezak 5*

EMILY (1976) Emily Productions. **Color-84min.** *(British).* Koo Stark, Sarah Brackett ....(4)

EMMA (1932) M-G-M. **B&W-73min.** Marie Dressler, Richard Cromwell (4)

EMMA MAE (1976) PRO-International. **Color-100min.** Jerri Hayes, Ernest Williams Ii ....(3)

EMMANUELLE (1974) Columbia. **Color-92min.** *(French).* Sylvia Kristel, Alain Cuny 3*

EMMANUELLE THE JOYS OF A WOMAN (1975) Paramount. **Color-92min.** *(French).* Sylvia Kristel, Umberto Orsini 3*
British title: EMMANUELLE 2
Alternate title: EMMANUELLE L'ANTIVIERGE *(Emmanuelle the Antivirgin)*

EMPEROR JONES, THE (1933) United Artists. **B&W-80min.** Paul Robeson, Dudley Digges 3*

EMPEROR OF THE NORTH, THE (1973) 20th Century-Fox. **Color-118min.** Lee Marvin, Ernest Borgnine 5½*
Original title: EMPEROR OF THE NORTH POLE, THE

EMPEROR WALTZ, THE (1948) Paramount. **Color-106min.** Bing Crosby, Joan Fontaine.................................(5)

EMPEROR'S CANDLESTICKS, THE (1937) M-G-M. **B&W-89min.** William Powell, Luise Rainer ....(4)

EMPEROR'S NIGHTINGALE, THE (1949) Rembrandt. **Color-72min.** *(Czech).* ....(3)
Original title: CISARUV SLAVIK

EMPIRE IN THE SUN (1956) Commonwealth United TV. **Color-90min.** *(Italian, Documentary).* Enrico Paca, Dolores Primor ....(5)

EMPIRE OF THE ANTS (1977) American-International. **Color-89min.** Robert Lansing, Joan Collins ....(3)

EMPRESS MESSALINA MEETS THE SON OF HERCULES (1963) *see* MESSALINA AGAINST THE SON OF HERCULES

THE EMIGRANTS (1971). Having come from Sweden in 1850, Liv Ullmann and husband Max Von Sydow disembark from the ship which has brought them to America.

EMPTY CANVAS, THE (1963) Avco-Embassy. **B&W-118min.** *(Italian-French).* Horst Buchholz, Catherine Spaak.............................3*
Original Italian title: NOIA, LA
French title: ENNUI ET SA DIVERSION, L'ÉROTISME, L'

ENCHANTED APRIL (1935) RKO. **B&W-66min.** Ann Harding, Frank Morgan...(3)

ENCHANTED COTTAGE, THE (1945) RKO. **B&W-91min.** Dorothy McGuire, Robert Young.............................4*

ENCHANTED FOREST (1945) Producers Rel. Corp. [Eagle Lion]. **Color-78min.** Edmund Lowe, Harry Davenport....................(4)

ENCHANTED ISLAND (1958) Warner Bros. **Color-94min.** Dana Andrews, Jane Powell.......................................(3)

ENCHANTMENT (1948) RKO. **B&W-102min.** David Niven, Teresa Wright 4*

ENCORE (1951) Paramount. **B&W-89min.** *(British).* Nigel Patrick, Kay Walsh, Glynis Johns.........................5*

ENCOUNTER (1952) *see* STRANGER ON THE PROWL

END, THE (1978) United Artists. **Color-100min.** Burt Reynolds, Dom De Luise.......................................5½*

END AS A MAN (1957) *see* STRANGE ONE, THE

END OF DESIRE (1958) Continental [Walter Reade]. **Color-86min.** *(French-Italian).* Maria Schell, Christian Marquand.....................(4)
Original French title: UNE VIE *(One Life or A Life)*
Original Italian title: UNA VITA
Alternate title: ONE LIFE

END OF THE AFFAIR, THE (1955) Columbia. **B&W-106min.** *(British).* Deborah Kerr, Van Johnson ....(5)

END OF THE BELLE, THE (1961) *see* PASSION OF SLOW FIRE, THE

END OF THE DIALOGUE (1970) Contemporary *(British).* **B&W-50min.** *(South African, Documentary). Director:* Nana Mahomo....................(5)
Original title: PHELA NDABA

END OF THE GAME (1975) 20th Century-Fox. **Color-107min.** *(German-Italian, English language).* Jon Voight, Jacqueline Bisset, Martin Ritt, Robert Shaw ....(4)
Original German title: RICHTER UND SEIN HENKER, DER *(The Judge and His Hangman)*
Alternate title: MURDER ON THE BRIDGE

END OF THE LINE, THE (1957) Eros Films *(Brit.).* **B&W-66min.** *(British).* Barbara Shelley, Alan Baxter ....(3)

END OF THE RAINBOW (1947) *see* NORTHWEST OUTPOST

END OF THE RIVER, THE (1947) Universal. **B&W-83min.** *(British).* Sabu, Bibi Ferreira ....(3)

END OF THE ROAD, THE (1954) Distributors Corp. of America. **B&W-76min.** *(British).* Edward Chapman, George Merritt.....................(4)

END OF THE ROAD (1970) Allied Artists. **Color-110min.** Stacy Keach, Harris Yulan 1*

END OF THE WORLD (1962) *see* PANIC IN YEAR ZERO!

END OF THE WORLD (1977) Group 1. **Color-82min.** Christopher Lee, Sue Lyon, Kirk Scott....................................2½*

END OF THE WORLD IN OUR USUAL BED IN A NIGHT FULL OF RAIN, THE (1978) Warner Bros. **Color-104min.** Giancarlo Giannini, Candice Bergen............................(4)
Alternate title: NIGHT FULL OF RAIN

ENDLESS NIGHT (1972) British Lion [EMI]. **Color-99min.** *(British).* Hayley Mills, Hywel Bennett.........................4½*

ENDLESS SUMMER, THE (1966) Cinema 5. **Color-95min.** *(Documentary). Director:* Bruce Brown.............................7*

ENEMIES OF THE PUBLIC (1931) *see* PUBLIC ENEMY

ENEMY AGENT (1940) *see* BRITISH INTELLIGENCE

ENEMY AGENTS MEET ELLERY QUEEN (1942) Columbia. **B&W-65min.** William Gargan, Margaret Lindsay, Gale Sondergaard....................(3)
British title: LIDO MYSTERY, THE

ENEMY BELOW, THE (1957) 20th Century-Fox. **Color-98min.** Robert Mitchum, Curt Jurgens......................................5*

ENEMY FROM SPACE (1957) United Artists. **B&W-84min.** *(British).* Brian Donlevy, John Longden...........................(3)
Original title: QUATERMASS II

ENEMY GENERAL, THE (1960) Columbia. **B&W-74min.** Van Johnson, Jean-Pierre Aumont...............................(4)

ENEMY OF THE PEOPLE, AN (1978) Warner Bros. **Color-103min.** Steve McQueen, Charles Durning ....

ENEMY OF WOMEN (1944) Monogram [Allied Artists]. **B&W-86min.** Paul Andor, Claudia Drake, Donald Woods............(4)
Original title: LIFE AND LOVES OF DR. PAUL JOSEPH GOEBBELS, THE
Alternate title: DR. PAUL JOSEPH GOEBBELS
Alternate title: PRIVATE LIFE OF DR. PAUL JOSEPH GOEBBELS, THE
Alternate title: MAD LOVER
ENEMY WITHIN, THE (1949) *see* RED MENACE, THE
ENFANTS DU PARADIS, LES (1945) *see* CHILDREN OF PARADISE
ENFANTS TERRIBLES, LES (1950) *see* STRANGE ONES, THE
ENFORCER, THE (1951) Warner Bros. **B&W-87min.** Humphrey Bogart, Roy Roberts............5*
British title: MURDER, INC.
ENFORCER, THE (1976) Warner Bros. **Color-96min.** Clint Eastwood, Tyne Daly............5½*
ENGAGEMENT, THE (1963) *see* FIANCES, THE
ENGLAND MADE ME (1973) International Amusement Corp. **Color-100min.** *(British-U.S.-Yugoslavian).* Peter Finch, Michael York.........(4)
ENGLISH WITHOUT TEARS (1948) *see* HER MAN GILBEY
ENIGMA OF KASPAR HAUSER, THE (1974) *see* MYSTERY OF KASPAR HAUSER, THE
ENOUGH ROPE (1963) Artixo Prods. **B&W-104min.** *(French-Italian-W. German).* Marina Vlady, Robert Hossein, Maurice Ronet............(3)
Original French title: MEURTIER, LE *(The Murderer)*
Original Italian title: OMICIDA, L'
Original German title: MORDER, DER
Alternate title: MURDERER, THE
ENSIGN PULVER (1964) Warner Bros. **Color-104min.** Robert Walker, Burl Ives............4*
ENTER ARSENE LUPIN (1944) Universal. **B&W-72min.** Charles Korvin, Ella Raines............(3)
ENTER INSPECTOR MAIGRET (1967) Independent TV Corp (ITC). **Color-90min.** *(W. German-French).* Heinz Ruhmann, Eddi Arent............(4)
ENTER LAUGHING (1967) Columbia. **Color-112min.** Reni Santoni, José Ferrer............5*
ENTER MADAM (1935) Paramount. **B&W-83min.** Elissa Landi, Cary Grant............(4)
ENTER THE DEVIL (1975) Sunset International. **Color-87min.** Irene Kelly, Josh Bryant............3*
ENTER THE DRAGON (1973) Warner Bros. **Color-98min.** *(U.S.A./Hong Kong).* Bruce Lee, John Saxon............4½*
ENTERTAINER, THE (1960) Continental [Walter Reade]. **B&W-97min.** *(British).* Laurence Olivier, Brenda de Banzie............4½*
ENTERTAINER, THE (1976) RSO. **Color-90min.** *(Made for TV).* Jack Lemmon, Sada Thompson, Ray Bolger............5*
ENTERTAINING MR. SLOANE (1970) Continental [Walter Reade]. **Color-94min.** *(British).* Beryl Reid, Peter McEnery............(5)
ENTICEMENT (1954) *see* SENSUALITA
EPIC HERO AND THE BEAST, THE (1956) *see* SWORD AND THE DRAGON, THE
EQUESTRIAN ACROBATICS (1937) M-G-M. **B&W-8min.** *(Documentary).* *Director:* David Miller............6*
EQUINOX (1971) VIP Distributors. **Color-81min.** Edward Connell, Barbara Hewitt............(2)
EQUUS (1977) United Artists. **Color-137min.** Richard Burton, Peter Firth............4*
ERASERHEAD (1977) David Lynch/A.F.I. **B&W-89min.** Jack Nance, Charlotte Stewart............2½*
ERIC (1975) Viacom. **Color-94min.** *(Made for TV).* John Savage, Patricia Neal, Claude Akins............(5)
ERIC SOYA'S "17" (1965) Peppercorn-Wormser. **Color-87min.** *(Danish).* Ole Soltoft, Ghita Norby............(3)
Original title: SYTTEN
Alternate title: SEVENTEEN
ERIK THE CONQUEROR (1961) American-International. **Color-90min.** *(Italian-French).* Cameron Mitchell, Giorgio Ardisson............(2)
Original Italian title: GLI INVASORI INVASORI, GLI
Original French title: RUÉE DES VIKINGS, LA
Alternate title: FURY OF THE VIKINGS
EROTIC ADVENTURES OF SIEGFRIED, THE (1971) *see* LONG, SWIFT SWORD OF SIEGFRIED,
ERRAND BOY, THE (1962) Paramount. **B&W-92min.** Jerry Lewis, Brian Donlevy............2*
ESCADRILLE (1937) *see* WOMAN I LOVE, THE
ESCAPADE (1951) *see* UTOPIA

ESCAPADE (1955) Distributors Corp. of America. **B&W-87min.** *(British).* John Mills, Alastair Sim, Peter Asher............(3)
ESCAPADE IN JAPAN (1957) Universal. **Color-92min.** Jon Provost, Roger Nakagawa............4*
ESCAPE (1940) M-G-M. **B&W-104min.** Norma Shearer, Robert Taylor...4*
ESCAPE (1948) 20th Century-Fox. **B&W-79min.** *(British).* Rex Harrison, Peggy Cummins............5*
ESCAPE (1971) Paramount. **Color-75min.** *(Made for TV).* Christopher George, Marilyn Mason, Avery Schrieber............3*
ESCAPE BY NIGHT (1937) Republic. **B&W-64min.** William Hall, Anne Neagle............(3)
ESCAPE BY NIGHT (1954) Eros Films *(Brit.).* **B&W-78min.** *(British).* Bonar Colleano, Andrew Ray............(4)
ESCAPE BY NIGHT (1960) Lux Film America. **B&W-82min.** *(Italian).* Leo Genn, Peter Baldwin............(4)
Alternate title: WAIT FOR THE DAWN
ESCAPE BY NIGHT (1964) Allied Artists. **B&W-75min.** *(British).* Terence Longdon, Jennifer Jayne............(3)
Original title: CLASH BY NIGHT
ESCAPE FROM ALCATRAZ (1979) Paramount. **Color-112min.** Clint Eastwood, Patrick McGoohan............5½*
ESCAPE FROM CRIME (1942) Warner Bros. **B&W-60min.** Richard Travis, Julie Bishop............(3)
ESCAPE FROM EAST BERLIN (1962) M-G-M. **B&W-94min.** *(W. German-U.S., English version).* Don Murray, Christine Kaufmann............(4)
British title: TUNNEL 28
ESCAPE FROM FORT BRAVO (1953) M-G-M. **Color-98min.** William Holden, Eleanor Parker............4*
ESCAPE FROM HELL ISLAND (1963) Crown International. **B&W-80min.** Mark Stevens, Jack Donner............2*
Original title: MAN IN THE WATER, THE
ESCAPE FROM HONG KONG (1942) Universal. **B&W-60min.** Leo Carillo, Andy Devine, Marjorie Lord............(3)
ESCAPE FROM RED ROCK (1958) 20th Century-Fox. **B&W-75min.** Brian Donlevy, Ellene Janssen............(2)
ESCAPE FROM SAHARA (1963) Medallion. **B&W-95min.** *(German).* Hildegard Neff, Harry Meyer............(3)
ESCAPE FROM SAIGON (1960) American-International. **B&W-85min.** *(French).* Jean Chevrier, Fivos Rasi............(5)
ESCAPE FROM SAN QUENTIN (1957) Columbia. **B&W-81min.** Johnny Desmond, Merry Anders............(2)
ESCAPE FROM TERROR (1960) Coogan-Rogers. **B&W-81min.** Jackie Coogan, Mona Knox............(2)
ESCAPE FROM THE DARK (1976) *see* LITTLEST HORSE THIEVES, THE
ESCAPE FROM THE PLANET OF THE APES (1971) 20th Century-Fox. **Color-98min.** Roddy McDowall, Kim Hunter............5*
ESCAPE FROM YESTERDAY (1938) *see* RIDE A CROOKED MILE
ESCAPE FROM ZAHRAIN (1962) Paramount. **Color-93min.** Yul Brynner, Sal Mineo............3*
ESCAPE IN THE DESERT (1945) Warner Bros. **B&W-81min.** Philip Dorn, Helmut Dantine............(4)
ESCAPE IN THE FOG (1945) Columbia. **B&W-65min.** Otto Kruger, Nina Foch............(3)
ESCAPE ME NEVER (1947) Warner Bros. **B&W-104min.** Ida Lupino, Errol Flynn............4*
ESCAPE OF THE BIRDMEN (1971) *see* BIRDMEN, THE
ESCAPE ROUTE (1953) *see* I'LL GET YOU
ESCAPE TO ATHENA (1979) Associated Film Dists. **Color-101min.** *(British).* Roger Moore, David Niven, Telly Savalas............5½*
ESCAPE TO BURMA (1955) RKO. **Color-87min.** Barbara Stanwyck, Robert Ryan............(3)
ESCAPE TO GLORY (1940) Columbia. **B&W-74min.** Pat O'Brien, Constance Bennett............(4)
Alternate title: SUBMARINE ZONE
ESCAPE TO HAPPINESS (1939) *see* INTERMEZZO
ESCAPE TO MINDANAO (1968) Universal. **Color-100min.** *(Made for TV).* George Maharis, Willi Coopman............(4)
ESCAPE TO THE SUN (1972) Cinevision Films. **Color-105min.** *(Israeli-W. German-French, English language).* Yehuda Barkan, John Ireland, Laurence Harvey, Jack Hawkins............(4)
Original Israeli title: HABRICHA EL HASHEMESH
ESCAPE TO WITCH MOUNTAIN (1975) Buena Vista. **Color-97min.** Kim Richards, Ike Eisenmann, Eddie Albert, Ray Milland............(4)

ESCAPEMENT (1958) *see* ELECTRONIC MONSTER, THE

ESCORT FOR HIRE (1960) M-G-M. Color-66min. *(British).* June Thorburn, Peter Murray .... (3)

ESCORT WEST (1959) United Artists. B&W-75min. Victor Mature, Elaine Stewart.. (4)

ESKIMO (1934) M-G-M. B&W-117min. Mala, Lotus, W. S. Van Dyke..... (4)
British title: MALA THE MAGNIFICENT

ESPIONAGE AGENT (1939) Warner Bros. B&W-83min. Joel McCrea, Brenda Marshall.. 3*

ESTHER AND THE KING (1960) 20th Century-Fox. Color-109min. *(U.S.-Italian).* Joan Collins, Richard Egan.. (3)
Italian title: ESTHER E IL RE

ESTHER WATERS (1948) J. Arthur Rank. B&W-108min. *(British).* Kathleen Ryan, Dirk Bogarde.. (4)
Alternate title: SIN OF ESTHER WATERS, THE

ET DIEU CREA LA FEMME (1956) *see* AND GOD CREATED WOMAN

ETERNAL CHAIN, THE (1951) B&W-85min. *(Italian).* Marcello Mastroianni, Gianna Maria Canale.. (3)
Original title: ETERNA CATENA, L'

ETERNAL HUSBAND, THE (1946) Vog. B&W-91min. *(French).* Raimu, Aime Clariond, Gisele Casadesus .... (4)

ETERNAL SEA, THE (1955) Republic. B&W-103min. Sterling Hayden, Alexis Smith.. 4*

ETERNAL WALTZ, THE (1954) Bakros International. Color-99min. *(German).* Bernhard Wicki, Hilde Krahl.. (3)
Original title: EWIGER WALTZER

ETERNALLY YOURS (1939) United Artists. B&W-95min. Loretta Young, David Niven 4*

EUGENIE . . . THE STORY OF HER JOURNEY INTO PERVERSION (1970) Distinction Films. Color-91min. *(British-Spanish-W. German).* Marie Lijedahl, Maria Rohm, Christopher Lee .... (2)

EUREKA STOCKADE (1948) J. Arthur Rank. B&W-103min. *(Australian).* Chips Rafferty, Jane Barrett.. 5*
Alternate title: MASSACRE HILL

EUROPA '51 (1951) *see* GREATEST LOVE, THE

EVA (1962) Times Film Corp. B&W-111min. *(French, English language).* Jeanne Moreau, Stanley Baker.. (4)
British title: EVE

EVE (1968) Commonwealth United. Color-97min. *(U.S.-British-Spanish).* Robert Walker, Jr., Celeste Yarnall, Herbert Lom, Christopher Lee ... (2)
British title: FACE OF EVE, THE

EVE AND THE HANDYMAN (1961) Pad-Ram Enterprises. Color-64min. Anthony-James Ryan, Eve Meyer.. (3)

EVE KNEW HER APPLES (1945) Columbia. B&W-64min. Ann Miller, William Wright.. (4)

EVE OF ST. MARK, THE (1944) 20th Century-Fox. B&W-96min. Anne Baxter, William Eythe.. 2*

EVEL KNIEVEL (1971) Fanfare. Color-94min. George Hamilton, Sue Lyon.. 3*

EVELYN PENTICE (1934) M-G-M. B&W-80min. Myrna Loy, William Powell.. (5)

EVENING WITH THE ROYAL BALLET, AN (1964) Sigma III. Color-85min. *(British, Documentary).* Margot Fonteyn, Rudolf Nureyev...... (5)

EVENT, AN (1969) Continental [Walter Reade]. Color-88min. *(Yugoslavian).* Pavle Vujisic, Serdjo Mimica.. (5)
Original title: DOGADJAJ

EVER SINCE EVE (1937) Warner Bros. B&W-79min. Robert Montgomery, Marion Davies .... (4)

EVERGREEN (1934) Gaumont-British [Rank]. B&W-98min. *(British).* Jessie Matthews, Sonnie Hale 5*

EVERY BASTARD A KING (1968) Continental [Walter Reade]. Color-93min. *(Israeli).* Pier Angeli, William Berger .... (2)
Original title: KOL MAMZER MELECH

EVERY DAY IS A HOLIDAY (1966) Columbia. Color-76min. *(Spanish).* Marisol, Angel Peralta.. (3)
Original title: CABRIOLA

EVERY DAY'S A HOLIDAY (1937) Paramount. B&W-80min. Mae West, Edmund Lowe 4*

EVERY DAY'S A HOLIDAY (1964) *see* SEASIDE SWINGERS

EVERY GIRL SHOULD BE MARRIED (1948) RKO. B&W-85min. Cary Grant, Betsy Drake.. (4)

EVERY LITTLE CROOK AND NANNY (1972) M-G-M. Color-100min. Lynn Redgrave, Victor Mature.. 4*

EVERY MAN FOR HIMSELF AND GOD AGAINST ALL (1974) *see* MYSTERY OF KASPAR HAUSER, THE

EVERY MAN NEEDS ONE (1972) Worldvision. Color-74min. *(Made for TV).* Connie Stevens, Ken Berry .... (4)

EVERY MAN'S WOMAN (1966) *see* ROSE FOR EVERYONE, A

EVERY MINUTE COUNTS (1953) *see* COUNT THE HOURS

EVERY MINUTE COUNTS (1960) Unifilms. B&W-95min. *(French).* Dominique Wilms, Jean Lara .... (3)
Original title: CHAQUE MINUTE COMPTE

EVERY NIGHT AT EIGHT (1935) Paramount. B&W-80min. George Raft, Alice Faye .... (4)

EVERY OTHER INCH A LADY (1939) *see* DANCING CO-ED

EVERY WHICH WAY BUT LOOSE (1978) Warner Bros. Color-119min. Clint Eastwood, Sondra Locke.. 5*

EVERYBODY DOES IT (1949) 20th Century-Fox. B&W-98min. Paul Douglas, Linda Darnell.. 4*

EVERYBODY GO HOME! (1960) Royal Films Int'l [Columbia]. B&W-115min. *(Italian-French).* Alberto Sordi, Serge Reggiani.. (5)
Original title: TUTTI A CASA

EVERYBODY SING (1938) M-G-M. B&W-80min. Judy Garland, Fannie Brice .... (4)

EVERYBODY'S AT IT (1972) *see* FEMALE RESPONSE, THE

EVERYBODY'S BABY (1939) 20th Century-Fox. B&W-62min. Spring Byington, Jed Prouty .... (4)

EVERYBODY'S CHEERING (1949) *see* TAKE ME OUT TO THE BALL GAME

EVERYMAN'S WOMAN (1967) *see* ROSE FOR EVERYONE, A

EVERYTHING BUT THE TRUTH (1956) Universal. Color-83min. Maureen O'Hara, John Forsythe, Tim Hovey 4½*

EVERYTHING HAPPENS AT NIGHT (1939) 20th Century-Fox. B&W-77min. Sonja Henie, Ray Milland, Robert Cummings.. 4*

EVERYTHING HAPPENS TO US (1943) *see* HI YA, CHUM

EVERYTHING I HAVE IS YOURS (1952) M-G-M. Color-92min. Marge and Gower Champion, Dennis O'Keefe .... (4)

EVERYTHING YOU ALWAYS WANTED TO KNOW ABOUT SEX* *BUT WERE AFRAID TO ASK (1972) United Artists. Color-88min. Woody Allen, Lynn Redgrave.. 5½*

EVERYTHING'S DUCKY (1961) Columbia. B&W-81min. Mickey Rooney, Buddy Hackett .... (3)

EVERYWOMAN'S MAN (1933) *see* PRIZEFIGHTER AND THE LADY, THE

EVICTORS, THE (1979) Color-92min. Michael Parks, Jessica Harper.......

EVIL, THE (1978) New World. Color-89min. Richard Crenna, Joanna Pettet, Victor Buono.. 3½*

EVIL EYE (1963) American-International. B&W-92min. *(Italian).* Leticia Roman, John Saxon 3*
Original title: RAGAZZA CHE SAPEVA TROPPO, LA

EVIL FORCE, THE (1959) *see* 4-D MAN

EVIL OF DRACULA (1975) Toho. Color-   min. *(Japanese).* Mori Kishida, Toshio Kurosawa, Kunie Tanaka..
Original title: CHIO SU BARA

EVIL OF FRANKENSTEIN, THE (1964) Universal. Color-86min. *(British).* Peter Cushing, Peter Woodthorpe.. (3)

EVIL ROY SLADE (1971) MCA-TV. Color-100min. *(Made for TV).* John Astin, Edie Adams, Dick Shawn.. 4*

EVILS OF CHINATOWN (1967) *see* CONFESSIONS OF AN OPIUM EATER

EX-CHAMP (1939) Universal. B&W-64min. Victor McLaglen, Tom Brown.. (4)
British title: GOLDEN GLOVES

EX-LADY (1933) Warner Bros. B&W-65min. Bette Davis, Gene Raymond .... (3)

EX-MRS. BRADFORD, THE (1936) RKO. B&W-80min. William Powell, Jean Arthur.. 5*

EXCLUSIVE (1937) Paramount. B&W-85min. Fred MacMurray, Frances Farmer.. 4*

EXCLUSIVE STORY (1936) M-G-M. B&W-75min. Franchot Tone, Madge Evans .... (4)

EXCUSE MY DUST (1951) M-G-M. Color-82min. Red Skelton, Sally Forest.. (4)

EXECUTION OF PRIVATE SLOVIK, THE (1974) MCA-TV. Color-120min. *(Made for TV).* Martin Sheen, Ned Beatty 5½*

EXECUTIONER, THE (1970) Columbia. Color-107min. *(British).* George Peppard, Judy Collins.. 3½*

EXECUTIONERS, THE (1958) *see* HITLER'S EXECUTIONERS

Films are rated on a 1 to 10 scale, 10 is highest. **Boldface** ratings followed by an asterisk (*) are for films actually seen and rated by the executive and senior editors. All other ratings are estimates. (See Notes on Entertainment Ratings in the front section.)

EXECUTIVE ACTION (1973) National General. **Color-90min.** Burt Lancaster, Robert Ryan 5½*

EXECUTIVE SUITE (1954) M-G-M. **B&W-104min.** William Holden, June Allyson 5½*

EXHIBITION (1975) SND. **Color-110min.** *(French).* Claudine Beccarie ... (3)

EXILE, THE (1947) Universal. **B&W-95min.** Douglas Fairbanks, Jr., Maria Montez 4*

EXIT LAUGHING (1930) *see* ARE YOU THERE?

EXIT SMILING (1926) M-G-M. **B&W-72min.** *(Silent).* Beatrice Lillie, Jack Pickford 4*

EXODUS (1960) United Artists. **Color-213min.** Paul Newman, Eva Marie Saint 6½*

EXORCISM'S DAUGHTER (1974) Howard Mahler. **Color-93min.** *(Spanish).* Amelia Gade, Francisco Rabal, Espartaco Santoni ....(3)

EXORCIST, THE (1973) Warner Bros. **Color-122min.** Ellen Burstyn, Max Von Sydow 8*

EXORCIST II: THE HERETIC (1977) Warner Bros. **Color-117min.** Linda Blair, Richard Burton 4*

EXOTIC DREAMS OF CASANOVA, THE (1971) Boxoffice International. **Color-90min.** Johnny Rocco, Jane Louise ....(3)
Alternate title: YOUNG SWINGERS, THE

EXPERIMENT IN TERROR (1962) Columbia. **B&W-123min.** Lee Remick, Glenn Ford 4*
British title: GRIP OF FEAR, THE

EXPERIMENT PERILOUS (1944) RKO. **B&W-91min.** Hedy Lamarr, George Brent ....(4)

EXPLOSION (1972) *see* PURSUIT

EXPLOSIVE GENERATION, THE (1961) United Artists. **B&W-89min.** William Shatner, Patty McCormack ....(4)

EXPRESSO BONGO (1959) Continental [Walter Reade]. **B&W-111min.** *(British).* Laurence Harvey, Cliff Richard 5*

EXTERMINATING ANGEL, THE (1962) Altura Films. **B&W-91min.** *(Mexican).* Silvia Pinal, Enrique Rambal ....(5)
Original title: ANGEL EXTERMINADOR, EL

EXTRA DAY, THE (1956) United Artists. **Color-83min.** *(British).* Richard Basehart, Simone Simon, Laurence Naismith ....(5)
Alternate title: ONE EXTRA DAY
Alternate title: 12 DESPERATE HOURS

EXTRA GIRL, THE (1923) Pathé. **B&W-63min.** *(Silent).* Mabel Normand, Ralph Graves 3*

EXTRAORDINARY SEAMAN, THE (1969) M-G-M. **Color-80min.** David Niven, Faye Dunaway ....(3)

EXTREME CLOSE-UP (1973) National General. **Color-82min.** James McMullan, Kate Woodville, Bara Byrnes ....(3)

THE EXORCIST (1973). Scar-covered Linda Blair is levitated by the demon possessing her, as priests Max Von Sydow and Jason Miller try to break the evil spell.

EYE FOR AN EYE, AN (1957) Ajay Films. **Color-93min.** *(French-Italian).* Curt Jurgens, Folco Lulli ....(3)
French title: OEIL POUR OEIL

EYE FOR AN EYE, AN (1966) Avco-Embassy. **Color-92min.** Robert Lansing, Patrick Wayne, Slim Pickens ....(3)

EYE OF EVIL (1960) *see* 1000 EYES OF DR. MABUSE, THE

EYE OF THE CAT (1969) Universal. **Color-102min.** Michael Sarrazin, Gayle Hunnicutt 4*

EYE OF THE DEVIL (1967) M-G-M. **B&W-92min.** *(British).* David Niven, Deborah Kerr 3*

EYE OF THE MONOCLE, THE (1962) Parkside Prods. **B&W-102min.** *(French).* Paul Meurisse, Elga Anderson ....(3)
Original title: OEIL DU MONOCLE, L'

EYE WITNESS (1950) Eagle Lion. **B&W-104min.** *(British).* Robert Montgomery, Leslie Banks ....(5)
Original title: YOUR WITNESS

EYEBALL (1978) Joseph Brenner. **Color-91min.** *(Italian).* John Richardson, Martine Brochard ....(2)

EYES IN THE NIGHT (1942) M-G-M. **B&W-80min.** Edward Arnold, Ann Harding ....(3)

EYES OF ANNIE JONES, THE (1963) 20th Century-Fox. **B&W-71min.** *(British-U.S.).* Richard Conte, Francesca Annis ....(2)

EYES OF CHARLES SAND, THE (1972) Warner Bros. **Color-75min.** *(Made for TV).* Peter Haskell, Joan Bennett, Hugh Benson ....(4)

EYES OF HELL (1961) *see* MASK, THE

EYES OF LAURA MARS (1978) Columbia. **Color-104min.** Faye Dunaway, Tommy Lee Jones 4*

EYES OF THE SAHARA (1957) American-International. **B&W-79min.** *(French-Italian).* Curt Jurgens, Lea Padovani ....(3)
Original French title: OEIL POUR OEIL
Italian title: OCCHIO PER OCCHIO

EYES OF THE SKIES (1953) *see* MISSION OVER KOREA

EYES OF THE UNDERWORLD (1943) Universal. **B&W-61min.** Wendy Barrie, Richard Dix, Lon Chaney, Jr. ....(4)

EYES WITHOUT A FACE (1963) *see* HORROR CHAMBER OF DR. FAUSTUS, THE

EYEWITNESS (1970) *see* SUDDEN TERROR

-F-

F FOR FAKE (1974) Specialty Films. **Color-85min.** *(French-Iranian-German, English language).* Orson Welles, Elmyr de Hory, Clifford Irving ....(5)
Foreign title: VÉRITÉS ET MENSONGES *(Truths and Lies)*
Original title: FAKE!
Alternate title: ?
Alternate title: QUESTION MARK

F.I.S.T. (1978) *alphabetized as* FIST

F. SCOTT FITZGERALD AND THE LAST OF THE BELLES (1975) ABC-TV. **Color-98min.** *(Made for TV).* Richard Chamberlain, Blythe Danner, Susan Sarandon ....

F. SCOTT FITZGERALD IN HOLLYWOOD (1976) Dan Goodman Productions. **Color-100min.** *(Made for TV).* Jason Miller, Tuesday Weld, Julia Foster 4½*

F.T.A. (1972) American-International. **Color-94min.** *(Documentary).* Jane Fonda, Donald Sutherland, Peter Boyle ....(4)

FABIOLA (1949) 20th Century-Fox. **B&W-97min.** *(Italian).* Michele Morgan, Henri Vidal, Michel Simon ....(4)

FABULOUS BARON MUNCHAUSEN, THE (1961) Teleworld. **Color-83min.** *(Czech, Part-animated).* Milos Kopecky, Jana Brejchova 3*
Original title: BARON PRASIL
Alternate title: BARON MUNCHAUSEN

FABULOUS DORSEYS, THE (1947) United Artists. **B&W-88min.** Tommy Dorsey, Jimmy Dorsey, Janet Blair ....(3)

FABULOUS JOE, THE (1947) United Artists. **Color-60min.** Walter Abel, Marie Wilson ....(3)
Part II of HAL ROACH COMEDY CARNIVAL, THE

FABULOUS SENORITA, THE (1952) Republic. **B&W-80min.** Estelita Rodriguez, Robert Clarke ....(3)

FABULOUS SUZANNE, THE (1946) Republic. **B&W-71min.** Barbara Britton, Rudy Vallee ....(3)

FABULOUS TEXAN, THE (1947) Republic. **B&W-95min.** William (Wild Bill) Elliott, John Carroll ....(4)

FABULOUS WORLD OF JULES VERNE, THE (1958) Warner Bros. **B&W-83min.** *(Czech, Part-animated).* Lubor Tokos (Louis Tock), Arnost Navratil (Ernest Navara) .... (5)
Original title: VYNALEZ ZKAZY *(An Invention of Destruction)*
Alternate title: WEAPONS OF DESTRUCTION
Alternate title: DIABOLIC INVENTION, THE
Alternate title: DEADLY INVENTION, THE

FACE BEHIND THE MASK, THE (1941) Columbia. **B&W-69min.** Peter Lorre, Evelyn Keyes .... (4)

FACE IN THE CROWD, A (1957) Warner Bros. **B&W-125min.** Andy Griffith, Patricia Neal .... (6)

FACE IN THE NIGHT (1957) *see* MENACE IN THE NIGHT

FACE IN THE RAIN, A (1963) Avco-Embassy. **B&W-91min.** Rory Calhoun, Marina Berti .... (4)

FACE OF A FUGITIVE (1959) Columbia. **Color-81min.** Fred MacMurray, Lin McCarthy .... (4)

FACE OF EVE, THE (1968) *see* EVE

FACE OF FEAR, THE (1971) Quinn Martin Productions. **Color-72min.** *(Made for TV).* Ricardo Montalban, Elizabeth Ashley, Jack Warden ... (4)

FACE OF FIRE (1959) Allied Artists. **B&W-83min.** *(U.S.-Swedish).* Cameron Mitchell, James Whitmore .... (4)

FACE OF FU MANCHU, THE (1965) Seven Arts [W.B.]. **Color-94min.** *(British).* Christopher Lee, Nigel Green .... (5)

FACE OF MARBLE (1946) Monogram [Allied Artists]. **B&W-70min.** John Carradine, Claudia Drake .... (3)

FACE OF THE FROG (1959) UCC Films. **B&W-92min.** *(W. German-Danish).* Siegfried Lowitz, Joachim Fuchsberger .... (3)
Alternate title: FELLOWSHIP OF THE FROG

FACE OF WAR, A (1968) Commonwealth United. **B&W-72min.** *(Documentary).* Director: Eugene S. Jones 4*

FACE OF WAR, THE (1963) Janus Films. **B&W-105min.** *(Swedish-Japanese, Documentary).* Director: Tore Sjoberg .... (5)
Original Swedish title: KRIGETS VANVETT
Alternate Swedish title: KRIGETS ANSIKTE

FACE THAT LAUNCHED A THOUSAND SHIPS, THE (1954) *see* LOVE OF THREE QUEENS

FACE THE MUSIC (1954) *see* BLACK GLOVE, THE

FACE TO FACE (1952) RKO. **B&W-92min.** James Mason, Michael Pate (5)

FACE TO FACE (1976) Paramount. **Color-136min.** *(Swedish, Telefeature).* Liz Ullmann, Erland Josephson, Gunnar Bjornstrand 3½*
Original title: ANSIKTE MOT ANSIKTE

FACES (1968) Continental [Walter Reade]. **B&W-129min.** John Marley, Gena Rowlands 3*

FACTS OF LIFE, THE (1960) United Artists. **B&W-103min.** Bob Hope, Lucille Ball 3½*

FACTS OF MURDER, THE (1959) Seven Arts [W.B.]. **B&W-100min.** *(Italian).* Pietro Germi, Claudia Cardinale, Nino Castelnuovo .... (5)
Original title: MALEDETTO IMBROGLIO, UN

FADE IN (1968) Paramount. **Color-120min.** Burt Reynolds, Barbara Loden 4½*

FAHRENHEIT 451 (1966) Universal. **Color-112min.** *(British).* Oskar Werner, Julie Christie 5½*

FAIL-SAFE (1964) Columbia. **B&W-111min.** Dan O'Herlihy, Henry Fonda 6*

FAILING OF RAYMOND, THE (1971) Universal. **Color-75min.** *(Made for TV).* Jane Wyman, Dean Stockwell, Dana Andrews 4*

FAIR WIND TO JAVA (1953) Republic. **Color-92min.** Fred MacMurray, Vera Ralston 3½*

FAIRY TALE MURDER (1945) *see* RIVER GANG

FAITHFUL CITY (1952) RKO. **B&W-86min.** *(Israeli).* Jamie Smith, Rachel Markus .... (5)

FAITHFUL 47, THE (1962) *see* CHUSHINGURA

FAITHFUL IN MY FASHION (1946) M-G-M. **B&W-81min.** Donna Reed, Tom Drake .... (4)

FAITHLESS (1932) M-G-M. **B&W-76min.** Tallulah Bankhead, Robert Montgomery .... (3)

FAKE, THE (1953) United Artists. **B&W-80min.** *(British).* Dennis O'Keefe, Coleen Gray .... (4)

FAKE! (1974) *see* F FOR FAKE

FAKERS, THE (1970) *see* HELL'S BLOODY DEVILS

FALCON AND THE CO-EDS, THE (1943) RKO. **B&W-68min.** Tom Conway, Jean Brooks, Isabel Jewell .... (4)

FALCON IN DANGER, THE (1943) RKO. **B&W-73min.** Tom Conway, Jean Brooks, Elaine Shepard .... (4)

FALCON IN HOLLYWOOD, THE (1944) RKO. **B&W-67min.** Tom Conway, Barbara Hale, Veda Ann Borg .... (4)

FALCON IN MEXICO, THE (1944) RKO. **B&W-70min.** Tom Conway, Mona Maris .... (4)

FALCON IN SAN FRANCISCO, THE (1945) RKO. **B&W-66min.** Tom Conway, Rita Corday .... (4)

FALCON OUT WEST, THE (1944) RKO. **B&W-64min.** Tom Conway, Barbara Hale, Carole Gallagher .... (4)

FALCON STRIKES BACK, THE (1943) RKO. **B&W-66min.** Tom Conway, Harriet Hilliard (Nelson) .... (4)

FALCON TAKES OVER, THE (1942) RKO. **B&W-63min.** George Sanders, Lynn Bari 3½*

FALCON'S ADVENTURE, THE (1946) RKO. **B&W-61min.** Tom Conway, Madge Meredith .... (4)

FALCON'S ALIBI, THE (1946) RKO. **B&W-62min.** Tom Conway, Rita Corday .... (4)

FALCON'S BROTHER, THE (1942) RKO. **B&W-63min.** George Sanders, Tom Conway, Jane Randolph .... (4)

FALL GIRL (1961) *see* LISETTE

FALL OF ROME, THE (1962) Medallion. **Color-89min.** *(Italian).* Carl Mohner, Loredana Nusciak .... (3)
Original title: CROLLO DI ROMO, IL

FALL OF THE HOUSE OF USHER, THE (1948) Gibraltar. **B&W-70min.** *(British).* Gwendoline Watford, Kay Tendeter, Irving Steen .... (4)

FALL OF THE HOUSE OF USHER, THE (1960) *see* HOUSE OF USHER

FALL OF THE ROMAN EMPIRE (1964) Paramount. **Color-188min.** Sophia Loren, Stephen Boyd 3*

FALLEN ANGEL (1945) 20th Century-Fox. **B&W-97min.** Alice Faye, Dana Andrews 4*

FALLEN ANGEL (1964) *see* IMPERFECT ANGEL

FALLEN IDOL, THE (1948) Selznick Releasing. **B&W-94min.** *(British).* Ralph Richardson, Michele Morgan 5½*

FALLEN SPARROW, THE (1943) RKO. **B&W-94min.** John Garfield, Maureen O'Hara .... (5)

FALSE FACE (1977) *see* SCALPEL

FALSE WITNESS (1941) *see* ARKANSAS JUDGE

FALSE WITNESS (1970) *see* ZIGZAG

FALSTAFF (1966) Peppercorn-Wormser. **B&W-115min.** *(Spanish-Swiss).* Orson Welles, Jeanne Moreau, John Gielgud .... (5)
Alternate title: CHIMES AT MIDNIGHT
Original Spanish title: CAMPANADAS A MEDIANOCHE

FAME IS THE NAME OF THE GAME (1966) Universal. **Color-100min.** *(Made for TV).* Anthony Franciosa, Jill St. John 4*

FAME IS THE SPUR (1946) Oxford Films. **B&W-116min.** *(British).* Michael Redgrave, Rosamund John .... (5)

FAMILY, THE (1970) International Co-Productions. **Color-94min.** *(Italian-French).* Charles Bronson, Telly Savalas, Jill Ireland 4*
Original Italian title: CITTA VIOLENTA *(Violent City)*
Alternate title: VIOLENT CITY

FAMILY AFFAIR, A (1937) M-G-M. **B&W-69min.** Lionel Barrymore, Spring Byington, Mickey Rooney .... (4)

FAMILY AFFAIR (1954) Exclusive. **B&W-65min.** *(British).* Bebe Daniels, Ben Lyon .... (3)
Original title: LIFE WITH THE LYONS

FAMILY DIARY (1962) M-G-M. **Color-115min.** *(Italian).* Marcello Mastroianni, Jacques Perrin .... (5)
Original title: CRONACA FAMILIARE

FAMILY DOCTOR (1958) *see* Rx MURDER

FAMILY FLIGHT (1972) MCA-TV. **Color-73min.** *(Made for TV).* Rod Taylor, Dina Merrill, Kristoffer Tabori .... (4)

FAMILY HONEYMOON (1949) Universal. **B&W-80min.** Claudette Colbert, Fred MacMurray 3½*

FAMILY JEWELS, THE (1965) Paramount. **Color-100min.** Jerry Lewis, Sebastian Cabot, Donna Butterworth 2*

FAMILY LIFE (1971) *see* WEDNESDAY'S CHILD

FAMILY PLOT (1976) Universal. **Color-120min.** Barbara Harris, Bruce Dern 6½*

FAMILY RICO, THE (1972) CBS-TV. **Color-73min.** *(Made for TV).* Ben Gazzara, James Farentino, Sal Mineo .... (4)

FAMILY SECRET, THE (1951) Columbia. **B&W-85min.** John Derek, Lee J. Cobb .... (4)

FAMILY STORY, A (1944) *see* MOM AND DAD

Films are rated on a 1 to 10 scale, 10 is highest. **Boldface** ratings followed by an asterisk (*) are for films actually seen and rated by the executive and senior editors. All other ratings are estimates. (See Notes on Entertainment Ratings in the front section.)

FAMILY UPSIDE DOWN, A (1978) NBC-TV. Color-98min. *(Made for TV)*. Helen Hayes, Fred Astaire, Patty Duke Astin ....

FAMILY WAY, THE (1966) Warner Bros. Color-115min. *(British)*. Hayley Mills, Hywel Bennett 5½*

FAN, THE (1949) 20th Century-Fox. B&W-89min. Jeanne Crain, Madeleine Carroll 4*
British title: LADY WINDERMERE'S FAN

FAN-FAN THE TULIP (1952) *see* FANFAN THE TULIP

FANATIC (1965) *see* DIE! DIE! MY DARLING!

FANATICS, THE (1957) *see* BOMB FOR A DICTATOR, A

FANATICS, THE (1963) Transcontinental. B&W-87min. *(British)*. Craig Stevens, Eugene Deckers ....(3)

FANCY PANTS (1950) Paramount. Color-92min. Bob Hope, Lucille Ball 5*

FANDO AND LIS (1969) Cannon Releasing. B&W-82min. *(Mexican)*. Sergio Klainer, Diana Mariscal ....(1)
Original title: FANDO Y LIS

FANFAN THE TULIP (1952) United Artists. B&W-96min. *(French)*. Gérard Philippe, Gina Lollobrigida ....(5)
Alternate title: SOLDIER OF LOVE

FANG AND CLAW (1935) RKO. B&W-74min. *(Documentary)*. Frank Buck ....(5)

FANGS OF THE ARCTIC (1953) Allied Artists. B&W-63min. Kirby Grant, Lorna Hansen ....(2)

FANNY (1932) Pathé Contemporary. B&W-128min. *(French)*. Raimu, Charpin ....(5)

FANNY (1961) Warner Bros. Color-133min. Leslie Caron, Maurice Chevalier 7*

FANNY BY GASLIGHT (1944) *see* MAN OF EVIL

FANNY HILL: MEMOIRS OF A WOMAN OF PLEASURE (1964) Pan World. B&W-105min. *(U.S.-W. German)*. Leticia Roman, Miriam Hopkins ....(2)
Alternate title?: ROMP OF FANNY HILL

FANTASIA (1940) RKO (for Disney). Color-135min. *(Cartoon)*. Producer: Walt Disney 6*

FANTASTIC DISAPPEARING MAN, THE (1958) *see* RETURN OF DRACULA, THE

FANTASTIC INVASION OF PLANET EARTH, THE (1967) *see* BUBBLE, THE

FANTASTIC PLANET (1973) New World. Color-72min. *(French-Czech, Cartoon)*. Director: René Laloux 5*
Original French title: PLANETE SAUVAGE, LA *(The Savage Planet)*

FANTASTIC PLASTIC MACHINE, THE (1969) Crown International. Color-93min. *(Documentary)*. Director: Eric Blum ....(5)

FANTASTIC VOYAGE (1966) 20th Century-Fox. Color-100min. Stephen Boyd, Raquel Welch 5½*

FANTASY ISLAND (1976) ABC-TV. Color-100min. *(Made for TV)*. Bill Bixby, Sandra Dee, Peter Lawford, Carol Lynley 4½*

FANTOMAS (1964) Lopert [U.A.]. Color-105min. *(French-Italian)*. Jean Marais, Louis de Funes, Mylene Demongeot ....(4)
Original Italian title: FANTOMAS CONTRO SCOTLAND YARD
Alternate title: FANTOMAS AGAINST SCOTLAND YARD

FANTOME DE LA LIBERTÉ, LE (1974) *see* PHANTOM OF LIBERTÉ, THE

FAR COUNTRY, THE (1954) Universal. Color-97min. James Stewart, Ruth Roman 4*

FAR FROM THE MADDING CROWD (1967) M-G-M. Color-169min. *(British-U.S.)*. Julie Christie, Terence Stamp, Peter Finch, Alan Bates 5*

FAR FROM VIETNAM (1967) New Yorker Films. B&W-90min. *(French)* ....(5)
Original title: LOIN DU VIETNAM

FAR HORIZONS, THE (1955) Paramount. Color-108min. Fred MacMurray, Charlton Heston 4*

FAR OUT WEST, THE (1968) MCA-TV. Color-87min. *(Made for TV)*. Ann Sheridan, Ruth McDevitt, Douglas Fowley 3*

FAR SHORE, THE (1976) New Cinema. Color-104min. *(Canadian)*. Celine Lomez, Frank Moore ....(4)

FAREWELL AGAIN (1937) United Artists. B&W-81min. *(British)*. Leslie Banks, Flora Robson ....(4)
Alternate title: TROOPSHIP

FAREWELL CONCERT OF CREAM, THE (1969) Color-25min. *(Documentary)*. Eric Clapton, Jack Bruce, Ginger Baker ....(4)

FAREWELL FRIEND (1968) Paramount. Color-115min. *(French)*. Alain Delon, Charles Bronson, Olga Georges-Picot 4*
Original title: ADIEU L'AMI *(So Long, Pal)*

FAREWELL, MY LOVELY (1944) *see* MURDER, MY SWEET

FAREWELL, MY LOVELY (1975) Avco-Embassy. Color-97min. Robert Mitchum, Charlotte Rampling 5*

FAREWELL TO ARMS, A (1932) Paramount. B&W-78min. Helen Hayes, Gary Cooper 4*

FAREWELL TO ARMS, A (1957) 20th Century-Fox. Color-150min. Rock Hudson, Jennifer Jones ....(4)

FAREWELL TO MANZANAR (1976) MCA-TV. Color-100min. *(Made for TV)*. Yuki Simoda, Nobu McCarthy 5*

FARGO (1952) Monogram [Allied Artists]. B&W-69min. Wild Bill Elliott, Phyllis Coates ....(3)

FARMER, THE (1977) Columbia. Color-97min. Gary Conway, Angel Tompkins ....

FARMER TAKES A WIFE, THE (1935) 20th Century-Fox. B&W-91min. Janet Gaynor, Henry Fonda ....(4)

FARMER TAKES A WIFE, THE (1953) 20th Century-Fox. Color-81min. Betty Grable, Dale Robertson ....(3)

FARMER'S DAUGHTER, THE (1940) Paramount. B&W-60min. Martha Raye, Charlie Ruggles ....(3)

FARMER'S DAUGHTER, THE (1947) RKO. B&W-97min. Loretta Young, Joseph Cotten 6*

FASCIST, THE (1965) *see* FEDERALE, IL

FASHION HOUSE OF DEATH (1964) *see* BLOOD AND BLACK LACE

FASHIONS OF 1934 (1934) First National [W.B.]. B&W-78min. William Powell, Bette Davis ....(4)
TV title: FASHIONS

FAST AND FURIOUS (1939) M-G-M. B&W-73min. Franchot Tone, Ann Sothern ....(3)

FAST AND LOOSE (1930) Paramount. B&W-75min. Miriam Hopkins, Carole Lombard ....(3)

FAST AND LOOSE (1939) M-G-M. B&W-80min. Robert Montgomery, Rosalind Russell ....(4)

FAST AND LOOSE (1954) J. Arthur Rank. B&W-75min. *(British)*. Stanley Holloway, Kay Kendall ....(4)

FAST AND SEXY (1957) Columbia. Color-98min. *(Italian-French)*. Gina Lollobrigida, Vittorio De Sica 4*
Original title: ANNA DI BROOKLYN *(Anna of Brooklyn)*

FAST AND THE FURIOUS, THE (1954) American Releasing [A.I.P.]. B&W-73min. John Ireland, Dorothy Malone 3*

FAST BREAK (1979) Columbia. Color-107min. Gabriel Kaplan, Harold Sylvester 5½*

FAST CHARLIE . . . THE MOONBEAM RIDER (1979) Universal. Color-99min. David Carradine, Brenda Vaccaro 5*

FAST COMPANY (1938) M-G-M. B&W-74min. Melvyn Douglas, Florence Rice ....
TV title: RARE BOOK MURDER, THE
Alternate title?: KING OF SPORTS

FAST COMPANY (1953) M-G-M. B&W-68min. Howard Keel, Polly Bergen ....(3)

FASTEST GUITAR ALIVE, THE (1967) M-G-M. Color-85min. Roy Orbison, Joan Freeman 3*

FASTEST GUN ALIVE, THE (1956) M-G-M. B&W-92min. Glenn Ford, Jeanne Crain 4*

FAT CHANCE (1975) *see* PEEPER

FAT CITY (1972) Columbia. Color-96min. Stacy Keach, Jeff Bridges 4*

FAT MAN, THE (1951) Universal. B&W-77min. J. Scott Smart, Julie London, Rock Hudson ....(4)

FAT SPY, THE (1966) Magna Pictures. Color-75min. Jack E. Leonard, Brian Donlevy, Phyllis Diller ....(2)

FATAL DESIRE (1953) Ultra Pictures Corp. Color-80min. *(Italian)*. Anthony Quinn, Kerima, May Britt ....(3)
Original title: CAVALLERIA RUSTICANA

FATAL WITNESS, THE (1945) Republic. B&W-59min. Evelyn Ankers, Richard Fraser ....(3)

FATE IS THE HUNTER (1964) 20th Century-Fox. B&W-106min. Glenn Ford, Rod Taylor 4*

FATE OF A MAN (1959) Artkino. B&W-101min. *(U.S.S.R.)*. Sergei Bondarchuk, Pavlik Boriskin ....(5)
Original title: SUDBA CZELOVEKIA

FATE TAKES A HAND (1961) M-G-M. B&W-72min. *(British)*. Ronald Howard, Christine Gregg ....(3)

FATHER (1966) Continental [Walter Reade]. B&W-95min. *(Hungarian)*. Andras Balint, Miklos Gabor, Daniel Erdélyi ....(3)
Original title: APA

Films are rated on a 1 to 10 scale, 10 is highest. **Boldface** ratings followed by an asterisk (*) are for films actually seen and rated by the executive and senior editors. All other ratings are estimates. (See Notes on Entertainment Ratings in the front section.)

FATHER BROWN (1954) *see* DETECTIVE, THE

FATHER GOOSE (1965) Universal. **Color-115min.** Cary Grant, Leslie Caron 5*

FATHER IS A BACHELOR (1950) Columbia. **B&W-84min.** William Holden, Coleen Gray 3*

FATHER MAKES GOOD (1950) Monogram [Allied Artists]. **B&W-61min.** Raymond Walburn, Walter Catlett ....(3)

FATHER OF A SOLDIER (1965) Artkino. **B&W-83min.** *(U.S.S.R.).* Sergo Zakariadze, Vladimir Privaltsev ....(5)
Original title: ODETS SOLDATA

FATHER OF THE BRIDE (1950) M-G-M. **B&W-93min.** Spencer Tracy, Elizabeth Taylor, Joan Bennett 5½*

FATHER TAKES A WIFE (1941) RKO. **B&W-79min.** Gloria Swanson, Adolphe Menjou ....(4)

FATHER TAKES THE AIR (1951) Monogram [Allied Artists]. **B&W-61min.** Raymond Walburn, Walter Catlett ....(3)

FATHER WAS A FULLBACK (1949) 20th Century-Fox. **B&W-84min.** Fred MacMurray, Maureen O'Hara 4*

FATHER'S DILEMMA (1950) Davis Distribution Co. **B&W-88min.** *(Italian).* Aldo Fabrizi, Gaby Morlay ....(5)
Original title: PRIMA COMUNIONE *(First Communion)*

FATHER'S LITTLE DIVIDEND (1951) M-G-M. **B&W-82min.** Spencer Tracy, Joan Bennett, Elizabeth Taylor 5½*

FATHER'S WILD GAME (1950) Monogram [Allied Artists]. **B&W-61min.** Raymond Walburn, Walter Catlett ....(3)

FATHOM (1967) 20th Century-Fox. **Color-99min.** *(British).* Tony Franciosa, Raquel Welch 4*

FATSO (1980) 20th Century-Fox. **Color- min.** Dom DeLuise, Anne Bancroft ....

FAUST AND THE DEVIL (1950) Columbia. **B&W-87min.** *(Italian).* Italo Tajo, Nelly Corradi ....(5)

FAVORITA, LA (1952) Continental [Walter Reade]. **B&W-79min.** *(Italian).* Gino Sinemberghi, Paolo Silveri ....(3)

F.B.I. CODE 98 (1964) Warner Bros. **B&W-94min.** Ray Danton, Jack Kelly ....(3)

F.B.I. GIRL (1951) Lippert Productions. **B&W-74min.** Audrey Totter, George Brent ....(3)

FBI STORY, THE (1959) Warner Bros. **Color-149min.** James Stewart, Vera Miles 4*

FBI 99 (1945) Republic. **B&W-100min.** *(Re-edited Serial).* Martin Lamont, Helen Talbot ....(3)
Original title: FEDERAL OPERATOR 99

FEAR (1946) Monogram [Allied Artists]. **B&W-68min.** Peter Cookson, Warren William ....(3)

FATHER OF THE BRIDE (1950). Spencer Tracy listens uneasily as Taylor Holmes tells him and his wife, Joan Bennett, how much their daughter's wedding is likely to cost.

FEAR (1955) Astor. **B&W-84min.** *(German).* Ingrid Bergman, Mathia Wiemann, Kurt Kreuger, Renate Mannhardt ....(3)
Original title: ANGST

FEAR, THE (1966) Trans-Lux Distributing. **B&W-110min.** *(Greek).* Elli Fotiou, Elena Nathanael ....(3)
Original title: HO FOVOS

FEAR AND DESIRE (1953) Joseph Burstyn. **B&W-68min.** Frank Silvera, Kenneth Harp, Virginia Leith, Paul Mazursky ....(3)

FEAR IN THE NIGHT (1947) Paramount. **B&W-72min.** DeForest Kelley, Paul Kelly ....(4)

FEAR IS THE KEY (1973) EMI. **Color-105min.** *(British).* Barry Newman, Suzy Kendall ....(4)

FEAR NO EVIL (1969) Universal. **Color-100min.** *(Made for TV).* Louis Jourdan, Bradford Dillman, Wilfrid Hyde-White 4*

FEAR NO MORE (1961) Sutton Pictures. **B&W-87min.** Jacques Bergerac, Mala Powers ....(4)

FEAR ON TRIAL (1975) Worldvision. **Color-100min.** *(Made for TV).* William Devane, George C. Scott 5*

FEAR STRIKES OUT (1957) Paramount. **B&W-100min.** Anthony Perkins, Karl Malden 5*

FEARLESS FAGAN (1952) M-G-M. **B&W-79min.** Carleton Carpenter, Janet Leigh ....(4)

FEARLESS FRANK (1967) American-International. **Color-78min.** Jon Voight, Severn Darden 1*
Original title: FRANK'S GREATEST ADVENTURE

FEARLESS VAMPIRE KILLERS, THE (1967) M-G-M. **Color-98min.** *(British).* Jack MacGowran, Roman Polanski 3½*
British title: DANCE OF THE VAMPIRES

FEARMAKERS, THE (1958) United Artists. **B&W-83min.** Dana Andrews, Dick Foran ....(3)

FEATHERED SERPENT, THE (1948) Monogram [Allied Artists]. **B&W-61min.** Roland Winters, Keye Luke ....(4)

FEDERAL AGENTS VS. CRIME, INC. (1949) *see* GOLDEN HANDS OF KURIGAL

FEDERAL OPERATOR 99 (1945) *see* FBI 99

FEDORA (1978) United Artists. **Color-110min.** *(W. German-French, English language).* William Holden, Marthe Keller 5*

FEDRA, THE DEVIL'S DAUGHTER (1957) Times Film Corp. **B&W-102min.** *(Spanish).* Emma Penella, Enrique Diosdado ....(5)

FELLINI - A DIRECTOR'S NOTEBOOK (1968) NBC-TV. **Color-54min.** *(Documentary, Made for TV).* Director: Federico Fellini 1½*

FELLINI SATYRICON (1970) United Artists. **Color-127min.** *(Italian-French).* Martin Potter, Hiram Keller 1*
Alternate title: SATYRICON

FELLINI'S AMARCORD (1974) *see* AMARCORD

FELLINI'S CASANOVA (1976) Universal. **Color-166min.** *(U.S.-Italian).* Donald Sutherland, Peter Gonzales, Britta Barnes 3*
Alternate title: CASANOVA
Alternate title: CASANOVA DI FEDERICO FELLINI, IL

FELLINI'S ROMA (1972) United Artists. **Color-120min.** *(Italian-French).* Federico Fellini 3*
Alternate title: ROMA

FELLOWSHIP OF THE FROG (1959) *see* FACE OF THE FROG

FEMALE, THE (1958) *see* WOMAN LIKE SATAN, A

FEMALE, THE (1962) Cambist. **B&W-89min.** Isabel Sarli, Francisco Rabal ....(2)
Original title: SETENTA VECES SIETE
Alternate title: SEVENTY TIMES SEVEN

FEMALE AND THE FLESH (1955) *see* LIGHT ACROSS THE STREET

FEMALE ANIMAL, THE (1958) Universal. **B&W-84min.** Hedy Lamarr, Jane Powell 3*

FEMALE ANIMAL (1970) Cinemation. **Color-75min.** *(Italian-Spanish).* Arlene Tiger, Vassili Lambrinos ....(2)
Original Spanish title: MUJER DEL GATO, LA

FEMALE ARTILLERY (1973) MCA-TV. **Color-73min.** *(Made for TV).* Dennis Weaver, Ida Lupino, Sally Ann Howes ....(4)

FEMALE BUNCH, THE (1971) Dalia Productions. **Color-86min.** Russ Tamblyn, Jennifer Bishop ....(1)

FEMALE BUTCHER (1974) *see* LEGEND OF BLOOD CASTLE

FEMALE CORRESPONDENT (1941) *see* ADVENTURE IN WASHINGTON

FEMALE INSTINCT (1972) *see* SNOOP SISTERS, THE

FEMALE JUNGLE (1956) American-International. **B&W-56min.** Kathleen Crowley, Lawrence Tierney, John Carradine ....(3)

FEMALE ON THE BEACH (1955) Universal. B&W-97min. Joan Crawford, Jeff Chandler 4*

FEMALE RESPONSE, THE (1972) Trans-America. Color-88min. Jacque Lynn Colton, Michaela Hope .... (3)
British title: EVERYBODY'S AT IT

FEMALE TRAP, THE (1968) see NAME OF THE GAME IS KILL!, THE

FEMALE TROUBLE (1974) New Line Cinema. Color-95min. Divine, David Lochary 3*

FEMININE TOUCH, THE (1941) M-G-M. B&W-97min. Rosalind Russell, Don Ameche 4*

FEMININE TOUCH, THE (1956) see GENTLE TOUCH, THE

FEMINIST AND THE FUZZ, THE (1971) Screen Gems. Color-75min. *(Made for TV).* David Hartman, Barbara Eden 4*

FEMME INFIDELE, LA (1969) Allied Artists. Color-97min. *(French-Italian).* Stéphane Audran, Michel Bouquet, Maurice Ronet 4½*
Alternate title: UNFAITHFUL WIFE, THE

FERNANDEL THE DRESSMAKER (1956) Union Films. B&W-92min. *(French).* Fernandel, Suzy Delair .... (4)
Original title: COUTURIER DE CES DAMES, LE

FERRY CROSS THE MERSEY (1965) United Artists. B&W-86min. *(British).* Gerry Marsden, Fred Marsden .... (3)

FERRY TO HONG KONG (1959) 20th Century-Fox. Color-103min. *(British).* Curt Jurgens, Orson Welles 4*

FESTIVAL (1967) Peppercorn-Wormser. B&W-95min. *(Music Film).* Director: Murray Lerner .... (5)
Alternate title: NEWPORT FESTIVAL

FEU FOLLET, LE (1963) see FIRE WITHIN, THE

FEUDIN' FOOL (1952) Monogram [Allied Artists]. B&W-63min. The Bowery Boys, Dorothy Ford .... (3)

FEUDIN', FUSSIN', AND A-FIGHTIN' (1948) Universal. B&W-78min. Marjorie Main, Donald O'Connor .... (3)

FEVER HEAT (1956) William Mishkin. B&W-95min. *(French).* Roger Duchesne, Isabelle Corey ....
Original title: BOB LE FLAMBEUR

FEVER HEAT (1968) Paramount. Color-105min. Nick Adams, Jeannine Riley .... (2)

FEVER IN THE BLOOD, A (1961) Warner Bros. B&W-117min. Efrem Zimbalist, Jr., Angie Dickinson .... (4)

FIANCES, THE (1963) Janus Films. B&W-84min. *(Italian).* Carlo Cabrini, Anna Canzi .... (5)
Original title: FIDANZATI, I
British title: ENGAGEMENT, THE

FICKLE FINGER OF FATE, THE (1967) Producers Releasing Org. Color-91min. *(U.S.-Spanish).* Tab Hunter, Luis Prendes............ 2*
Original Spanish title: DEDO DEL DESTINO, EL

FIDDLER ON THE ROOF (1971) United Artists. Color-178min. Topol, Norma Crane 6*

FIDEL (1970) New Yorker Films. Color-96min. *(Documentary).* Director: Saul Landau .... (5)

FIEND, THE (1972) see BEWARE MY BRETHREN

FIEND WHO WALKED THE WEST, THE (1958) 20th Century-Fox. B&W-101min. Hugh O'Brien, Robert Evans .... (4)

FIEND WITHOUT A FACE (1958) M-G-M. B&W-74min. *(British).* Marshall Thompson, Terence Kilburn 2*

FIENDISH GHOULS, THE (1960) see MANIA

FIENDS, THE (1955) see DIABOLIQUE

FIERCEST HEART, THE (1961) 20th Century-Fox. Color-91min. Stuart Whitman, Juliet Prowse .... (4)

FIESTA (1947) M-G-M. Color-104min. Esther Williams, Ricardo Montalban 3½*

15 FROM ROME (1963) McAbee Pictures. B&W-87min. *(Italian-French).* Vittorio Gassman, Ugo Tognazzi .... (3)
Alternate title: OPIATE '67
Original Italian title: MOSTRI, I *(The Monsters)*
Original French title: MONSTRES, LES

15 MAIDEN LANE (1936) 20th Century-Fox. B&W-65min. Claire Trevor, Cesar Romero .... (3)

FIFTH AVENUE GIRL (1939) RKO. B&W-83min. Ginger Rogers, James Ellison .... (4)

FIFTH CHAIR, THE (1945) see IT'S IN THE BAG

FIFTH DAY OF PEACE, THE (1972) Scotia International *(Brit.).* Color-98min. *(Italian).* Richard Johnson, Franco Nero .... (3)

FIFTH HORSEMAN IS FEAR, THE (1965) Sigma III. B&W-100min. *(Czech).* Miroslav Machacek, Olga Scheinpflugova .... (5)
Original title: A PATY JEZDEC JE STRACH
British title: FIFTH RIDER IS FEAR, THE

FIFTH MUSKETEER, THE (1977) Columbia. Color-103min. *(Austrian, English language).* Sylvia Kristel, Beau Bridges 5*

55 DAYS AT PEKING (1963) Allied Artists. Color-154min. Charlton Heston, Ava Gardner 5½*

FIFTY MILLION FRENCHMEN (1931) Warner Bros. B&W-74min. Ole Olsen, Chic Johnson, William Gaxton .... (3)

FIFTY ROADS TO TOWN (1937) 20th Century-Fox. B&W-81min. Ann Sothern, Don Ameche .... (3)

FIFTY YEARS BEFORE YOUR EYES (1950) Warner Bros. B&W-73min. *(Compilation).* Director: Robert G. Youngson .... (5)

FIGHT FOR YOUR LIFE (1977) William Mishkin. Color-89min. William Sanderson, Robert Judd .... (2)

FIGHTER, THE (1952) United Artists. B&W-78min. Richard Conte, Vanessa Brown .... (5)

FIGHTER ATTACK (1953) Allied Artists. Color-80min. Sterling Hayden, Joy Page .... (4)

FIGHTER SQUADRON (1948) Warner Bros. Color-96min. Robert Stack, Edmond O'Brien 3*

FIGHTERS, THE (1974) Walter Reade. Color-114min. *(Documentary).* Director: William Greaves .... (4)

FIGHTING CHANCE, THE (1955) Republic. B&W-70min. Rod Cameron, Ben Cooper, Julie London .... (3)

FIGHTING COAST GUARD (1951) Republic. B&W-86min. Brian Donlevy, Forrest Tucker .... (3)

FIGHTING DEVIL DOGS (1938) see TORPEDO OF DOOM

FIGHTING FATHER DUNNE (1948) RKO. B&W-93min. Pat O'Brien, Darryl Hickman 4*

FIGHTING FOOLS (1949) Monogram [Allied Artists]. B&W-69min. The Bowery Boys, Lyle Talbot .... (3)

FIGHTING FOR OUR LIVES (1975) Color-59min. *(Documentary).* Director: Glen Pearcy 5*

FIGHTING GUARDSMAN (1945) Columbia. B&W-84min. Willard Parker, George Macready .... (3)

FIGHTING KENTUCKIAN, THE (1949) Republic. B&W-100min. John Wayne, Vera Ralston 4*

FIGHTING LAWMAN, THE (1953) Allied Artists. B&W-71min. Wayne Morris, Virginia Grey .... (2)

FIGHTING MAD (1948) Monogram [Allied Artists]. B&W-75min. Joe Kirkwood, Jr., Leon Errol, John Hubbard .... (3)
British and alternate U.S. title: JOE PALOOKA IN FIGHTING MAD

FIGHTING MAD (1976) 20th Century-Fox. Color-90min. Peter Fonda, Lynn Lowry 4*

FIGHTING MAN OF THE PLAINS (1949) 20th Century-Fox. Color-94min. Randolph Scott, Bill Williams .... (4)

FIGHTING MARSHAL (1940) see CHEROKEE STRIP

FIGHTING O'FLYNN, THE (1949) United Artists. B&W-94min. Douglas Fairbanks, Jr., Helena Carter .... (4)

FIGHTING PRINCE OF DONEGAL, THE (1966) Buena Vista. Color-112min. *(British-U.S.).* Peter McEnery, Susan Hampshire .... (4)

FIGHTING RATS OF TOBRUK (1945) Renown Pictures. B&W-71min. *(Australian).* Chips Rafferty, Grant Taylor .... (4)

FIGHTING SEABEES, THE (1944) Republic. B&W-100min. John Wayne, Dennis O'Keefe 3½*

FIGHTING 7th, THE (1951) see LITTLE BIG HORN

FIGHTING 69th, THE (1940) Warner Bros. B&W-89min. James Cagney, Pat O'Brien... 4*

FIGHTING SULLIVANS, THE (1944) see SULLIVANS, THE

FIGHTING TROUBLE (1956) Allied Artists. B&W-61min. The Bowery Boys, Adele Jergens .... (3)

FIGHTING WILDCATS, THE (1957) Republic. B&W-74min. *(British).* Keefe Brasselle, Kay Callard 3*
Original title: WEST OF SUEZ

FIGURES IN A LANDSCAPE (1971) Nat'l General (for Cinema Center). Color-111min. *(British).* Robert Shaw, Malcolm McDowall .... (5)

FILE OF THE GOLDEN GOOSE, THE (1969) United Artists. Color-105min. *(British).* Yul Brynner, Charles Gray 3*

FILE ON THELMA JORDON, THE (1949) Paramount. B&W-100min. Barbara Stanwyck, Wendell Corey 4*
Publicity title: THELMA JORDON

Films are rated on a 1 to 10 scale, 10 is highest. **Boldface** ratings followed by an asterisk (*) are for films actually seen and rated by the executive and senior editors. All other ratings are estimates. (See Notes on Entertainment Ratings in the front section.)

FILLMORE (1972) 20th Century-Fox. **Color-105min.** *(Documentary).* *Director:* Richard T. Heffron..(3)

FILM WITHOUT A NAME (1948) Oxford Films. **B&W-79min.** *(German).* Hildegarde Neff, Willy Fritsch, Hans Sohnker ....(4)
Original title: FILM OHNE TITEL

FINAL CHAPTER - WALKING TALL (1977) American-International. **Color-112min.** Bo Svenson, Margaret Blye, Morgan Woodward..........3½*

FINAL COMEDOWN, THE (1972) New World. **Color-85min.** Billy Dee Williams, D'Urville Martin ....(3)
Alternate title: BLAST

FINAL PROGRAMME, THE (1975) *see* LAST DAYS OF MAN ON EARTH, THE

FINAL TEST, THE (1953) J. Arthur Rank. **B&W-91min.** *(British).* Robert Morley, Jack Warner...(5)

FIND THE BLACKMAILER (1943) Warner Bros. **B&W-55min.** Gene Lockhart, Faye Emerson ....(3)

FIND THE LADY (1956) J. Arthur Rank. **B&W-56min.** *(British).* Donald Houston, Beverley Brooks......................................(3)

FINDERS KEEPERS (1966) United Artists. **Color-94min.** *(British).* Cliff Richard, Robert Morley..(3)

FINDERS KEEPERS, LOVERS WEEPERS (1968) Eve Releasing Corp. **Color-71min.** Anne Chapman, Paul Lockwood ....(3)

FINE AND DANDY (1950) *see* WEST POINT STORY

FINE MADNESS, A (1966) Warner Bros. **Color-104min.** Sean Connery, Joanne Woodward..3*

FINE PAIR, A (1968) Nat'l General (for Cinema Center). **Color-89min.** *(Italian, English language).* Rock Hudson, Claudia Cardinale..............(2)
Original title: RUBA AL PROSSIMO TUO

FINEST HOURS, THE (1964) Columbia. **B&W-116min.** *(British, Documentary).* *Director:* Peter Baylis............................(6)

FINGER MAN (1955) Allied Artists. **B&W-82min.** Frank Lovejoy, Forrest Tucker...(4)

FINGER OF GUILT (1956) RKO. **B&W-95min.** *(British).* Richard Basehart, Mary Murphy..(3)
Original title: INTIMATE STRANGER, THE

FINGER ON THE TRIGGER (1965) Allied Artists. **Color-87min.** *(U.S.-Spanish).* Rory Calhoun, James Philbrook ....(2)
Original Spanish title: DEDO EN EL GATILLO, EL

FINGER POINTS, THE (1931) First National [W.B.]. **B&W-90min.** Richard Barthelmess, Fay Wray ....(5)

FINGERS (1978) Brut Productions. **Color-90min.** Harvey Keitel, Jim Brown...2½*

FINGERS AT THE WINDOW (1942) M-G-M. **B&W-80min.** Lew Ayres, Basil Rathbone ....(3)

FINIAN'S RAINBOW (1968) Warner Bros. **Color-145min.** Fred Astaire, Petula Clark...4*

FINNEGAN'S WAKE (1967) *see* PASSAGES FROM "FINNEGAN'S WAKE"

FINNEY (1969) Gold Coast. **B&W-72min.** Robert Kilcullen, Bill Levinson ....(2)

FIRE! (1977) Warner Bros. **Color-100min.** *(Made for TV).* Fred MacMurray, Alex Cord, Lloyd Nolan, Vera Miles...............4½*
Alternate title: IRWIN ALLEN'S PRODUCTION OF FIRE!

FIRE AND ICE (1961) Paramount. **B&W-105min.** *(French).* Romy Schneider, Jean-Louis Trintignant ....(5)
Original title: COMBAT DANS L'ILE, LE

FIRE AND SWORD (1962) *see* INVASION 1700

FIRE DOWN BELOW (1957) Columbia. **Color-116min.** Rita Hayworth, Robert Mitchum..4½*

FIRE IN THE SKY, A (1978) NBC-TV. **Color-150min.** *(Made for TV).* Richard Crenna, Elizabeth Ashley.............................4½*

FIRE OVER AFRICA (1954) Columbia. **Color-84min.** Maureen O'Hara, Macdonald Carey...3*
Original title: MALAGA

FIRE OVER ENGLAND (1937) United Artists. **B&W-89min.** *(British).* Flora Robson, Laurence Olivier 4½*

FIRE SALE (1977) 20th Century-Fox. **Color-88min.** Alan Arkin, Rob Reiner..4*

FIRE WITHIN, THE (1963) Governor. **B&W-110min.** *(French).* Maurice Ronet, Lena Skerla ....(5)
Original title: FEU FOLLET, LE *(The Maddening Flame, or Fox Fire, or Will-o'-the-Wisp)*
British title: TIME TO LIVE AND A TIME TO DIE, A

FIREBALL, THE (1950) 20th Century-Fox. **B&W-84min.** Mickey Rooney, Pat O'Brien ....(4)

FIREBALL (1965) *see* SECRET AGENT FIREBALL

FIREBALL 500 (1966) American-International. **Color-92min.** Frankie Avalon, Annette Funicello, Fabian.............................3*

FIREBALL FORWARD (1972) 20th Century-Fox. **Color-98min.** *(Made for TV).* Ben Gazzara, Eddie Albert, Ricardo Montalban ....(4)
Alternate title: DIVISION HEADQUARTERS

FIREBRAND, THE (1962) 20th Century-Fox. **B&W-63min.** Kent Taylor, Lisa Montell ....(3)

FIRECHASERS, THE (1970) Independent TV Corp (ITC). **Color-73min.** *(Made for TV).* Chad Everett, Anjanette Comer 4*

FIRECREEK (1968) Warner Bros. **Color-104min.** James Stewart, Henry Fonda...3*

FIREFLY, THE (1937) M-G-M. **B&W-138min.** Jeanette MacDonald, Allan Jones...(4)

FIREHOUSE (1973) MPC (TV). **Color-75min.** *(Made for TV).* Vince Edwards, Richard Roundtree 4*

FIREMAN, SAVE MY CHILD (1932) First National [W.B.]. **B&W-67min.** Joe E. Brown, Guy Kibbee ....(4)

FIREMAN, SAVE MY CHILD (1954) Universal. **B&W-80min.** Spike Jones, The City Slickers..3*

FIREMAN'S BALL, THE (1967) Cinema 5. **Color-73min.** *(Czech).* Vaclav Stockel, Josef Svet..(5)
Original title: HORI, MA PANENKO
Translation title?: SONG OF THE FIREMEN

FIREPOWER (1979) Associated Film Dists. **Color-104min.** James Coburn, Sophia Loren, O. J. Simpson 4½*

FIRST A GIRL (1935) Gaumont-British [Rank]. **B&W-94min.** Jessie Matthews, Sonnie Hale, Anna Lee ....

FIRST AMERICAN TEENAGER, THE (1975) *see* JAMES DEAN, THE FIRST AMERICAN TEENAGER

FIRST AND THE LAST, THE (1939) *see* 21 DAYS TOGETHER

FIRST CIRCLE, THE (1973) Paramount. **Color-95min.** *(Danish-W. German-U.S.).* Gunther Malzacher, Elizbieta Czyzewska 4½*

FIRST COMES COURAGE (1943) Columbia. **B&W-88min.** Brian Aherne, Merle Oberon ....(4)

FIRST GREAT TRAIN ROBBERY, THE (1979) *see* GREAT TRAIN ROBBERY, THE

FIRST HUNDRED YEARS, THE (1938) M-G-M. **B&W-73min.** Robert Montgomery, Virginia Bruce ....

FIRST LADY (1937) Warner Bros. **B&W-82min.** Kay Francis, Preston Foster...(5)

FIRST LEGION, THE (1951) United Artists. **B&W-86min.** Charles Boyer, William Demarest...(5)

FIRST LOVE (1939) Universal. **B&W-84min.** Deanna Durbin, Robert Stack ....(5)

FIRST LOVE (1958) Gala *(Brit.).* **B&W-103min.** *(Italian).* Carla Gravina, Geronimo Meynier..(3)
Original title: PRIMO AMORE

FIRST LOVE (1970) UMC Pictures. **Color-90min.** *(Swiss-W. German).* John Moulder-Brown, Dominique Sanda, Maximilian Schell........................(4)
Original title: ERSTE LIEBE

FIRST LOVE (1977) Paramount. **Color-91min.** William Katt, Susan Dey...5½*

FIRST MAN INTO SPACE (1959) M-G-M. **B&W-77min.** *(British).* Marshall Thompson, Bill Edwards...................................(2)

FIRST MEN IN THE MOON (1964) Columbia. **Color-103min.** *(British-U.S.).* Lionel Jeffries, Edward Judd, Martha Hyer 5*

FIRST NUDIE MUSICAL, THE (1976) Paramount. **Color-97min.** Stephen Nathan, Cindy Williams..(4)

FIRST OF THE FEW (1942) *see* SPITFIRE

FIRST POSITION (1972) Gerald E. Seltzer. **Color-91min.** *(Documentary).* *Director:* William Richert..(4)

FIRST REBEL (1939) *see* ALLEGHENY UPRISING

FIRST SPACESHIP ON VENUS (1960) Crown International. **Color-78min.** *(E. German-Polish).* Yoko Tani, Oldrich Lukes 2*
Original East German title: SCHWEIGENDE STERN, DER *(The Silent Star)*
Original Polish title: MILCZACA GWIAZDA

FIRST STEP, THE (1975) Sovexportfilm. **Color-80min.** *(U.S.S.R.).* Dodo Abachidze, Wasil Nadaraya................................(4)

FIRST TEXAN, THE (1956) Allied Artists. **Color-82min.** Joel McCrea, Felicia Farr..(4)

FIRST TIME, THE (1952) Columbia. **B&W-89min.** Robert Cummings, Barbara Hale...3*

FIRST TIME, THE (1969) United Artists. **Color-90min.** Jacqueline Bisset, Wes Stern ....(4)
British title: YOU DON'T NEED PAJAMAS AT ROSIE'S

FIRST TIME, THE (1976) EDP Films, Inc. **Color-85min.** *(French).* Alain Cohen, Charles Denner ....(4)
Original title: PREMIERE FOIS, LA

FIRST TO FIGHT (1967) Warner Bros. **Color-97min.** Chad Everett, Marilyn Devin ....(3)

FIRST TRAVELING SALESLADY, THE (1956) RKO. **Color-92min.** Ginger Rogers, Barry Nelson ....(3)

FIRST YANK INTO TOKYO (1945) RKO. **B&W-82min.** Tom Neal, Barbara Hale ....(3)
British title: MASK OF FURY

FIRST YOU CRY (1978) **Color-100min.** *(Made for TV).* Mary Tyler Moore, Anthony Perkins ....

FISH THAT SAVED PITTSBURGH, THE (1979) U.A. (for Lorimar). **Color-** min. Julius Irving, Meadowlark Lemon ....

F.I.S.T. (1978) United Artists. **Color-145min.** Sylvester Stallone, Rod Steiger..5½*

FIST IN HIS POCKET (1966) Peppercorn-Wormser. **B&W-105min.** *(Italian).* Lou Castel, Paola Pitagora ....(5)
Original title: PUGNI IN TASCA, I

FISTFUL OF DOLLARS, A (1964) United Artists. **Color-96min.** *(Italian-Spanish-W. German).* Clint Eastwood, Marianne Koch 4½*
Original Italian title: PER UN PUGNO DI DOLLARI *(For a Handful of Dollars)*
Original Spanish title: POR UN PUNADO DE DOLARES
Original German title: FUR EINE HANDVOLL DOLLARS
Publicity title: FOR A FISTFUL OF DOLLARS

FISTFUL OF DYNAMITE (1971) *see* DUCK, YOU SUCKER

FISTS OF FURY (1973) National General. **Color-103min.** *(Hong Kong).* Bruce Lee, Maria Yi ....(2)
Original title: BIG BOSS, THE

FITZWILLY (1967) United Artists. **Color-102min.** Dick Van Dyke, Barbara Feldon 5½*
British title: FITZWILLY STRIKES BACK

FIVE (1951) Columbia. **B&W-93min.** William Phipps, Susan Douglas.......4*

FIVE AGAINST THE HOUSE (1955) Columbia. **B&W-84min.** Guy Madison, Kim Novak 3*

FIVE ANGLES ON MURDER (1950) *see* WOMAN IN QUESTION, THE

FIVE AT THE FUNERAL, THE (1972) Gamalex. **Color-90min.** Jenifer Bishop, Jacqueline Hyde, Mitchell Gregg ....(3)
Alternate title: HOUSE OF TERROR

FIVE BLOODY GRAVES (1970) Independent International. **Color-88min.** Robert Dix, Scott Brady ....(3)

FIVE BOLD WOMEN (1959) Citation. **Color-82min.** Jeff Morrow, Merry Anders 2*

FIVE BRANDED WOMEN (1960) Paramount. **B&W-101min.** *(U.S.-Italian-Yugoslavian).* Van Heflin, Silvana Mangano..........................4½*
Italian title: JOVANKA E L'ALTRI *(Jovanka and the Others)*

FIVE CAME BACK (1939) RKO. **B&W-75min.** Chester Morris, Lucille Ball 3½*

5 CARD STUD (1968) Paramount. **Color-103min.** Dean Martin, Robert Mitchum..4*

FIVE DAY LOVER, THE (1961) Kingsley International. **B&W-86min.** *(French-Italian).* Jean Seberg, Jean-Pierre Cassel............................(5)
Original French title: AMANT DE CINQ JOURS, L'
Original Italian title: AMANTE DI CINQUE GIORNI, L'
British title: INFIDELITY

FIVE DAYS (1954) *see* PAID TO KILL

FIVE DAYS FROM HOME (1978) Universal. **Color-108min.** George Peppard, Neville Brand..4½*

FIVE DESPERATE WOMEN (1971) Worldvision. **Color-73min.** *(Made for TV).* Anjanette Comer, Robert Conrad, Joan Hackett, Stephanie Powers 4*

FIVE EASY PIECES (1970) Columbia. **Color-95min.** Jack Nicholson, Karen Black 7½*

FIVE FINGER EXERCISE (1962) Columbia. **B&W-109min.** Rosalind Russell, Jack Hawkins..(4)

FIVE FINGERS (1952) 20th Century-Fox. **B&W-108min.** James Mason, Danielle Darrieux..5*

5 FINGERS OF DEATH (1971) Warner Bros. **Color-98min.** *(Hong Kong).* Lo Lieh, Wang Ping..4*
Original title: KING BOXER

FIVE GATES TO HELL (1959) 20th Century-Fox. **B&W-98min.** Neville Brand, Ken Scott..3*

FIVE EASY PIECES (1970). Searching for a new direction in life, Jack Nicholson realizes he's just marking time at his job as an oil rigger in southern California.

FIVE GOLDEN DRAGONS (1967) Commonwealth United TV. **Color-70min.** *(British).* Robert Cummings, Brian Donlevy, Dan Duryea, Christopher Lee ....(3)

FIVE GOLDEN HOURS (1960) Columbia. **B&W-90min.** *(British-Italian).* Ernie Kovacs, Cyd Charisse, George Sanders..........................(4)
Original Italian title: CINQUE ORE IN CONTANTI

FIVE GRAVES TO CAIRO (1943) Paramount. **B&W-96min.** Franchot Tone, Anne Baxter..5*

FIVE GUNS TO TOMBSTONE (1961) United Artists. **B&W-71min.** James Brown, John Wilder..(2)

FIVE GUNS WEST (1955) American Releasing [A.I.P.]. **Color-78min.** John Lund, Dorothy Malone 2*

500 POUND JERK, THE (1973) Wolper Productions. **Color-75min.** *(Made for TV).* James Franciscus, Alex Karras, Hope Lange..........................4*

FIVE MAN ARMY, THE (1969) M-G-M. **Color-107min.** *(Italian).* Peter Graves, James Daly, Tetsuro Tamba ....(3)
Original title: ESERCITO DI 5 UOMINI, UN

FIVE MILES TO MIDNIGHT (1963) United Artists. **B&W-110min.** *(U.S.-French-Italian, English language).* Sophia Loren, Anthony Perkins ...(4)
Original French title: COUTEAU DANS LA PLAIE, LE
Alternate French title: TROISEME DIMENSION, LA *(The Third Dimension)*
Original Italian title: COLTELLO NELLA PIAGA, IL
Alternate Italian title: TERZA DIMENSIONE, LA

FIVE MILLION YEARS TO EARTH (1967) 20th Century-Fox. **Color-98min.** *(British).* Andrew Keir, James Donald..................................3*
Original title: QUATERMASS AND THE PIT

FIVE MINUTES TO LIVE (1962) *see* DOOR-TO-DOOR MANIAC

FIVE OF A KIND (1938) 20th Century-Fox. **B&W-85min.** The Dionne Quintuplets, Jean Hersholt ....(3)

FIVE ON THE BLACK HAND SIDE (1973) United Artists. **Color-96min.** Clarice Tayler, Leonard Jackson ....(4)

FIVE PENNIES, THE (1959) Paramount. **Color-117min.** Danny Kaye, Barbara Bel Geddes 4*

FIVE SAVAGE MEN (1971) *see* ANIMALS, THE

FIVE STAR FINAL (1931) First National [W.B.]. **B&W-89min.** Edward G. Robinson, H. B. Warner..4*

FIVE STEPS TO DANGER (1957) United Artists. **B&W-80min.** Ruth Roman, Sterling Hayden ....(3)

5,000 FINGERS OF DR. T, THE (1953) Columbia. **Color-88min.** Peter Lind Hayes, Mary Healy, Hans Conried, Tommy Rettig 4*

FIVE WEEKS IN A BALLOON (1962) 20th Century-Fox. **Color-101min.** Cedric Hardwicke, Red Buttons..3*

FIXED BAYONETS (1951) 20th Century-Fox. **B&W-92min.** Richard Basehart, Gene Evans ....(4)
Original title: OLD SOLDIERS NEVER DIE

FIXER, THE (1968) M-G-M. **Color-132min.** Alan Bates, Dirk Bogarde 5½*

Films are rated on a 1 to 10 scale, 10 is highest. **Boldface** ratings followed by an asterisk (*) are for films actually seen and rated by the executive and senior editors. All other ratings are estimates. (See Notes on Entertainment Ratings in the front section.)

FIXER DUGAN (1939) RKO. **B&W-68min.** Lee Tracy, Virginia Weidler (3)
British title: DOUBLE DARING

FLAME, THE (1947) Republic. **B&W-97min.** Vera Ralston, Broderick Crawford...(4)

FLAME (1975) VPS/Goodtimes *(British).* **Color-91min.** *(British).* Noddy Holder, Jim Lea ....

FLAME AND THE ARROW, THE (1950) Warner Bros. **Color-88min.** Burt Lancaster, Virginia Mayo...5*

FLAME AND THE FLESH, THE (1954) M-G-M. **Color-104min.** Lana Turner, Pier Angeli ....(3)

FLAME BARRIER, THE (1958) United Artists. **B&W-70min.** Arthur Franz, Kathleen Crowley ....(3)
Publicity title: IT FELL FROM THE FLAME BARRIER

FLAME IN THE STREETS (1961) Atlantic Pictures. **Color-93min.** *(British).* John Mills, Sylvia Syms ....(5)

FLAME OF ARABY (1952) Universal. **Color-77min.** Maureen O'Hara, Jeff Chandler ....(3)

FLAME OF CALCUTTA (1953) Columbia. **Color-70min.** Denise Darcel, Patric Knowles ....(2)

FLAME OF NEW ORLEANS, THE (1941) Universal. **B&W-78min.** Marlene Dietrich, Bruce Cabot...5*

FLAME OF STAMBOUL (1951) Columbia. **B&W-68min.** Richard Denning, Lisa Ferraday ....(3)

FLAME OF THE BARBARY COAST (1945) Republic. **B&W-91min.** John Wayne, Ann Dvorak 4½*

FLAME OF THE ISLANDS (1955) Republic. **Color-90min.** Yvonne De Carlo, Howard Duff 3*

FLAME OF YOUTH (1949) Republic. **B&W-60min.** Barbara Fuller, Ray McDonald ....(2)

FLAME OVER INDIA (1959) 20th Century-Fox. **Color-130min.** *(British-U.S.).* Lauren Bacall, Kenneth More 4*
British title: NORTH WEST FRONTIER

FLAME WITHIN, THE (1935) M-G-M. **B&W-71min.** Ann Harding, Herbert Marshall..(3)

FLAMING FEATHER (1952) Paramount. **Color-77min.** Sterling Hayden, Arleen Whelan 3*

FLAMING FRONTIER (1958) 20th Century-Fox. **B&W-70min.** Bruce Bennett, Jim Davis..(3)

FLAMING FRONTIER (1965) Warner Bros. **Color-93min.** *(W. German-Yugoslavian, English language).* Stewart Granger, Pierre Brice, Leticia Roman ....(3)
Original West German title: OLD SUREHAND, L. TEIL
Original Yugoslavian title: LAVIRINT SMRTI

FLAMING FURY (1949) Republic. **B&W-60min.** Roy Roberts, George Cooper ....(4)

FLAMING STAR (1960) 20th Century-Fox. **Color-101min.** Elvis Presley, Barbara Eden..4*

FLAMING TORCH, THE (1954) *see* BOB MATHIAS STORY, THE

FLAMINGO ROAD (1949) Warner Bros. **B&W-94min.** Joan Crawford, Zachary Scott..4*

FLANAGAN (1976) **Color-104min.** *(Netherlands).* Guido de Moor, Eric Schneider ....(3)

FLANAGAN BOY, THE (1953) *see* BAD BLONDE

F L A P (1970) Warner Bros. **Color-105min.** Anthony Quinn, Claude Akins...4*
British title: LAST WARRIOR, THE

FLAREUP (1969) M-G-M. **Color-100min.** Raquel Welch, Luke Askew 3*
Publicity title: FLARE-UP

FLASH GORDON (1936) *see* SPACESHIP TO THE UNKNOWN

FLASH GORDON CONQUERS THE UNIVERSE (1940) *see* PERIL FROM THE PLANET MONGO

FLASH GORDON CONQUERS THE UNIVERSE (1940) *see* PURPLE DEATH FROM OUTER SPACE

FLASH GORDON'S TRIP TO MARS (1938) *see* DEADLY RAY FROM MARS, THE

FLAT TOP (1952) Allied Artists. **Color-83min.** Sterling Hayden, Richard Carlson..(4)
British title: EAGLES OF THE FLEET

FLAVOR OF GREEN TEA OVER RICE, THE (1952) New Yorker Films. **B&W-115min.** *(Japanese).* Shin Saburi, Koji Tsuruta.............................
Original title: OCHAZUKE NO AJI

FLAXY MARTIN (1949) Warner Bros. **B&W-86min.** Virginia Mayo, Zachary Scott..3*

FLEA IN HER EAR, A (1968) 20th Century-Fox. **Color-94min.** *(U.S.-French).* Rex Harrison, Rosemary Harris.................................(3)
Original French title: PUCE A L'OREILLE, LA

FLEET'S IN, THE (1942) Paramount. **B&W-93min.** Dorothy Lamour, William Holden...(4)

FLESH (1932) M-G-M. **B&W-95min.** Wallace Beery, Karen Morley ....(5)

FLESH AND BLOOD (1949) Showcorporation. **B&W-102min.** *(British).* Richard Todd, Glynis Johns ....

FLESH AND DESIRE (1954) Ellis Films. **B&W-94min.** *(French-Italian).* Rossano Brazzi, Viviane Romance, Peter Van Eyck ....(3)
Original French title: CHAIR ET LE DIABLE, LA *(The Flesh and the Devil)*
Italian title: FUOCO NELLE VENE, IL

FLESH AND FANTASY (1943) Universal. **B&W-93min.** Robert Benchley, David Hoffman..4½*

FLESH AND FLAME (1959) *see* NIGHT OF THE QUARTER MOON

FLESH AND FURY (1952) Universal. **B&W-82min.** Tony Curtis, Jan Sterling...(4)

FLESH AND THE DEVIL (1927) M-G-M. **B&W-97min.** *(Silent).* John Gilbert, Greta Garbo 4½*

FLESH AND THE FIENDS, THE (1960) *see* MANIA

FLESH AND THE WOMAN (1954) Dominant Pictures. **Color-102min.** *(French-Italian).* Gina Lollobrigida, Arletty, Jean-Claude Pascal, Peter Van Eyck ....(3)
Original French title: GRAND JEU, LE *(The Big Game)*

FLESH EATERS (1964) Cinema Distributors of America. **B&W-87min.** Martin Kosleck, Rita Morley 3*

FLESH FOR FRANKENSTEIN (1974) *see* ANDY WARHOL'S FRANKENSTEIN

FLESH GORDON (1972) Mammoth Films. **Color-78min.** Jason Williams, Suzanne Fields 4*

FLICK (1970) *see* DR. FRANKENSTEIN ON CAMPUS

FLICKORNA (1968) *see* GIRLS, THE

FLIGHT (1929) Columbia. **B&W-119min.** Ralph Graves, Jack Holt...........4*

FLIGHT ANGELS (1940) Warner Bros. **B&W-74min.** Jane Wyman, Dennis Morgan...(3)

FLIGHT COMMAND (1940) M-G-M. **B&W-110min.** Robert Taylor, Ruth Hussey...4*

FLIGHT COMMANDER (1930) *see* DAWN PATROL, THE

FLIGHT FOR FREEDOM (1943) RKO. **B&W-99min.** Rosalind Russell, Fred MacMurray 3½*

FLIGHT FROM ASHIYA (1964) United Artists. **Color-100min.** *(U.S.-Japanese).* Yul Brynner, Richard Widmark 4*
Original Japanese title: ASHIYA KARA NO HIKO

FLIGHT FROM DESTINY (1941) Warner Bros. **B&W-73min.** Thomas Mitchell, Geraldine Fitzgerald...(5)

FLIGHT FROM SINGAPORE (1965) 20th Century-Fox. **B&W-74min.** *(British).* Patrick Allan, Patrick Holt, Jane Rogers............................(3)

FLIGHT FROM TERROR (1962) *see* SATAN NEVER SLEEPS

FLIGHT FROM TREASON (1960) **B&W-60min.** *(British).* John Gregson, Robert Brown ....(3)

FLIGHT FROM VIENNA (1955) E.J. Fancey *(Brit.).* **B&W-58min.** *(British).* John Bentley, Theodore Bikel ....(3)

FLIGHT LIEUTENANT (1942) Columbia. **B&W-80min.** Glenn Ford, Pat O'Brien ....(3)

FLIGHT NURSE (1954) Republic. **B&W-90min.** Joan Leslie, Forrest Tucker...(3)

FLIGHT OF THE DOVES (1971) Columbia. **Color-101min.** *(British).* Ron Moody, Jack Wild ....(5)

FLIGHT OF THE LOST BALLOON, THE (1961) Woolner Brothers. **Color-91min.** Mala Powers, Marshall Thompson ....(2)

FLIGHT OF THE PHOENIX, THE (1965) 20th Century-Fox. **Color-147min.** James Stewart, Richard Attenborough 6*

FLIGHT OF THE WHITE STALLIONS (1963) *see* MIRACLE OF THE WHITE STALLIONS, THE

FLIGHT THAT DISAPPEARED, THE (1961) United Artists. **B&W-71min.** Craig Hill, Paula Raymond..(2)

FLIGHT TO HONG KONG (1956) United Artists. **B&W-88min.** Rory Calhoun, Barbara Rush ....(3)

FLIGHT TO MARS (1951) Monogram [Allied Artists]. **Color-72min.** Arthur Franz, Marguerite Chapman...3*

FLIGHT TO NOWHERE (1946) Screen Guild [Lippert]. **B&W-75min.** Alan Curtis, Jack Holt ....(2)

Films are rated on a 1 to 10 scale, 10 is highest. **Boldface** ratings followed by an asterisk (*) are for films actually seen and rated by the executive and senior editors. All other ratings are estimates. (See Notes on Entertainment Ratings in the front section.)

FLIGHT TO TANGIER (1953) Paramount. **Color-90min.** Joan Fontaine, Jack Palance..(4)

FLIM-FLAM MAN, THE (1967) 20th Century-Fox. **Color-104min.** George C. Scott, Michael Sarrazin...6*
British title: ONE BORN EVERY MINUTE

FLIPPER (1963) M-G-M. **Color-90min.** Chuck Connors, Luke Halpin......(4)

FLIPPER'S NEW ADVENTURE (1964) M-G-M. **Color-103min.** Luke Halpin, Pamela Franklin...(4)
Alternate title: FLIPPER AND THE PIRATES

FLIRTATION WALK (1934) First National [W.B.]. **B&W-97min.** Dick Powell, Ruby Keeler...3*

FLIRTING WITH FATE (1938) M-G-M. **B&W-69min.** Joe E. Brown, Leo Carillo..(4)

FLOATING WEEDS (1959) Altura Films. **Color-119min.** *(Japanese).* Ganjiro Nakamura, Haruko Sugimura, Hiroshi Kawaguchi...........3*
Original title: UKIGUSA
Alternate title: DRIFTING WEEDS

FLOOD! (1976) NBC-TV. **Color-120min.** *(Made for TV).* Robert Culp, Carol Lynley, Barbara Hershey, Roddy McDowall............................

FLOOD TIDE (1958) Universal. **B&W-82min.** George Nader, Michel Ray...3*
British title: ABOVE ALL THINGS

FLOODS OF FEAR (1958) Universal. **B&W-82min.** *(British).* Howard Keel, Anne Heywood..(4)

FLORADORA GIRL, THE (1930) M-G-M. **B&W-80min.** Marion Davies, Lawrence Gray...(4)
British title: GAY NINETIES, THE

FLORIAN (1940) M-G-M. **B&W-91min.** Robert Young, Helen Gilbert.....3*

FLORIDA SPECIAL (1936) Paramount. **B&W-70min.** Jack Oakie, Sally Eilers...(3)

FLOWER DRUM SONG (1961) Universal. **Color-133min.** Myoshi Umeki, Nancy Kwan, James Shigeta.............................5*

FLOWING GOLD (1940) Warner Bros. **B&W-82min.** John Garfield, Pat O'Brien..(4)

FLUFFY (1965) Universal. **Color-92min.** Tony Randall, Shirley Jones......4*

FLUTE AND THE ARROW, THE (1958) Janus Films. **Color-78min.** *(Swedish).* Ginju, Riga...(5)
Original title: DJUNGELSAGA, EN *(A Jungle Saga)*

FLY, THE (1958) 20th Century-Fox. **Color-94min.** Al (David) Hedison, Patricia Owens..4½*

FLY BY NIGHT (1943) Paramount. **B&W-68min.** Richard Carlson, Nancy Kelly..(4)
British title: SECRET OF G.32

FLYING CADETS (1941) Universal. **B&W-60min.** William Gargan, Edmund Lowe...(4)

FLYING DEUCES, THE (1939) RKO. **B&W-65min.** Stan Laurel, Oliver Hardy, Jean Parker...4*

FLYING DISC MAN FROM MARS (1958) *see* MISSILE MONSTERS

FLYING DOWN TO RIO (1933) RKO. **B&W-89min.** Dolores Del Rio, Gene Raymond..5*

FLYING FONTAINES, THE (1959) Columbia. **Color-84min.** Michael Callan, Evy Norlund...(4)

FLYING FORTRESS (1942) Warner Bros. **B&W-68min.** *(British).* Richard Greene, Donald Stewart..........................(3)

FLYING HIGH (1931) M-G-M. **B&W-80min.** Bert Lahr, Charlotte Greenwood, Pat O'Brien...(4)
British title: HAPPY LANDING

FLYING IRISHMAN, THE (1939) RKO. **B&W-72min.** Paul Kelly, Douglas Corrigan..(4)

FLYING LEATHERNECKS (1951) RKO. **Color-102min.** John Wayne, Robert Ryan..3*

FLYING MATCHMAKER, THE (1965) Nat'l Showmanship Films. **Color-104min.** *(Israeli).* Mike Burstein, Germaine Unikovsky, Raphael Klatschkin..(3)
Original title: SHNEI KUNI LEMEL

FLYING MISSILE, THE (1951) Columbia. **B&W-93min.** Glenn Ford, Viveca Lindfors...3½*

FLYING SAUCER, THE (1950) Film Classics [U.A.]. **B&W-69min.** Mikel Conrad, Denver Pyle...(3)

FLYING SAUCER, THE (1965) Avco-Embassy. **Color-95min.** *(Italian).* Alberto Sordi, Monica Vitti, Silvana Mangano.............(3)
Original title: DISCO VOLANTE, IL *(The Flying Disc)*
Publicity title: MARTIANS, THE

FLYING SCOT, THE (1957) *see* MAILBAG ROBBERY

FLYING DEUCES, THE (1939). Stan Laurel and Oliver Hardy have joined the French Foreign Legion so the latter can forget his romantic woes, but it only increases their problems; they've been sentenced to be shot for desertion, but attempt here to escape.

FLYING SERPENT, THE (1946) Producers Rel. Corp. [Eagle Lion]. **B&W-59min.** George Zucco, Ralph Lewis..........................(3)

FLYING TIGERS (1942) Republic. **B&W-102min.** John Wayne, John Carroll...3*

FLYING WILD (1941) Monogram [Allied Artists]. **B&W-62min.** The East Side Kids, Dave O'Brien...

FM (1978) Universal. **Color-104min.** Michael Brandon, Eileen Brennan, Martin Mull, Linda Ronstadt....................................4½*

FOG, THE (1979) Avco-Embassy. **Color-   min.** Adrienne Barbeau, Hal Holbrook, Janet Leigh...

FOG ISLAND (1945) Producers Rel. Corp. [Eagle Lion]. **B&W-72min.** Veda Ann Borg, Lionel Atwill.............................(3)

FOG OVER FRISCO (1934) First National [W.B.]. **B&W-68min.** Bette Davis, Lyle Talbot...(3)

FOLIES BERGERE (1935) United Artists. **B&W-84min.** Maurice Chevalier...(4)
British title: MAN FROM THE FOLIES BERGERE, THE

FOLIES BERGERE (1958) Films Around The World. **Color-90min.** *(French).* Jeanmaire, Eddie Constantine................................(3)

FOLKS AT RED WOLF INN, THE (1972) Scope III, Inc. **Color-90min.** Linda Gillin, Arthur Space...2½*
Alternate title: TERROR HOUSE

FOLLOW A STAR (1959) Zenith International. **B&W-102min.** *(British).* Norman Wisdom, June Laverick..................................(3)

FOLLOW ME . . . (1968) *see* SIX DAYS TO ETERNITY

FOLLOW ME (1972) *see* PUBLIC EYE, THE

FOLLOW ME, BOYS! (1966) Buena Vista. **Color-131min.** Fred MacMurray, Vera Miles...(5)

FOLLOW ME QUIETLY (1949) RKO. **B&W-59min.** William Lundigan, Dorothy Patrick..(4)

FOLLOW THAT CAMEL (1967) Schoenfeld Film Distributing. **Color-95min.** *(British).* Phil Silvers, Jim Dale.............................4*

FOLLOW THAT DREAM (1962) United Artists. **Color-110min.** Elvis Presley, Arthur O'Connell...(4)

FOLLOW THAT GUY WITH THE ONE BLACK SHOE (1972) *see* TALL BLOND MAN WITH ONE BLACK SHOE, THE

FOLLOW THAT WOMAN (1945) Paramount. **B&W-69min.** William Gargan, Nancy Kelly...(3)

FOLLOW THE BOYS (1944) Universal. **B&W-122min.** George Raft, Vera Zorina...(5)

FOLLOW THE BOYS (1963) M-G-M. **Color-95min.** Connie Francis, Paula Prentiss, Russ Tamblyn 4*

FOLLOW THE FLEET (1936) RKO. **B&W-110min.** Fred Astaire, Ginger Rogers...4*

FOLLOW THE LEADER (1944) Monogram [Allied Artists]. **B&W-64min.** The East Side Kids, Joan Marsh 4*

FOLLOW THE SUN (1951) 20th Century-Fox. **B&W-93min.** Glenn Ford, Anne Baxter...4*

FOLLY TO BE WISE (1952) Fine Arts. **B&W-91min.** *(British).* Alastair Sim, Roland Culver 4*

FOOD OF THE GODS, THE (1976) American-International. **Color-88min.** Marjoe Gortner, Pamela Franklin 3*

FOOL KILLER, THE (1965) Allied Artists. **B&W-99min.** Anthony Perkins, Edward Albert, Jr., Henry Hull ....(4)
Alternate title: VIOLENT JOURNEY, A
Publicity title: LEGEND OF THE FOOL KILLER, THE

FOOLISH WIVES (1922) Universal. **B&W-100min.** *(Silent).* Erich von Stroheim, Mae Busch 4*

FOOLS (1970) Cinerama Releasing. **Color-93min.** Jason Robards, Jr., Katharine Ross...3*

FOOLS FOR LUCK (1928) Paramount. **B&W-64min.** W. C. Fields, Chester Conklin ....

FOOLS FOR SCANDAL (1938) Warner Bros. **B&W-81min.** Carole Lombard, Fernand Gravet ....(4)

FOOLS' PARADE (1971) Columbia. **Color-98min.** James Stewart, George Kennedy 4*
British title: DYNAMITE MAN FROM GLORY JAIL

FOOLS RUSH IN (1948) J. Arthur Rank. **B&W-82min.** *(British).* Sally Ann Howes, Guy Rolfe ....(3)

FOOTBALL COACH (1933) *see* COLLEGE COACH

FOOTLIGHT GLAMOUR (1943) Columbia. **B&W-75min.** Penny Singleton, Arthur Lake ....(3)

FOOTLIGHT PARADE (1933) Warner Bros. **B&W-102min.** James Cagney, Joan Blondell 5*

FOOTLIGHT SERENADE (1942) 20th Century-Fox. **B&W-80min.** John Payne, Betty Grable, Victor Mature.....................(4)

FOOTLIGHT VARITIES (1951) RKO. **B&W-61min.** Jack Paar, Liberace, Leon Errol ....(3)

FOOTSTEPS IN THE DARK (1941) Warner Bros. **B&W-96min.** Errol Flynn, Brenda Marshall.................................(4)

FOOTSTEPS IN THE FOG (1955) Columbia. **Color-90min.** *(British).* Jean Simmons, Stewart Granger ....(4)

FOOTSTEPS IN THE NIGHT (1957) Allied Artists. **B&W-62min.** Bill Elliott, Don Haggerty ....(3)

FOR A FEW DOLLARS MORE (1966) United Artists. **Color-130min.** *(Italian-German-Spanish).* Clint Eastwood, Lee Van Cleef...........4*
Italian title: PER QUALCHE DOLLARIO IN PIU
German title: FUR EIN PAR DOLLAR MEHR
Spanish title: MUERTE TENIA UN PRECIO, LA *(Death Has a Price)*

FOR A FISTFUL OF DOLLARS (1964) *see* FISTFUL OF DOLLARS, A

FOR BETTER FOR WORSE (1954) Stratford Pictures. **Color-81min.** *(British).* Dirk Bogarde, Susan Stephen ....(4)

FOR BETTER, FOR WORSE (1974) *see* ZANDY'S BRIDE

FOR HEAVEN'S SAKE (1950) 20th Century-Fox. **B&W-92min.** Clifton Webb, Joan Bennett...4*

FOR LOVE OF IVY (1968) Cinerama Releasing. **Color-101min.** Sidney Poitier, Abbey Lincoln.................................5*

FOR LOVE OR MONEY (1963) Universal. **Color-108min.** Kirk Douglas, Mitzi Gaynor ....(4)

FOR ME AND MY GAL (1942) M-G-M. **B&W-104min.** Judy Garland, Gene Kelly...4*
British title: FOR ME AND MY GIRL

FOR MEN ONLY (1952) Lippert Productions. **B&W-93min.** Paul Henreid, Kathleen Hughes ....(4)
Alternate title: TALL LIE, THE

FOR PETE'S SAKE! (1967) World Wide Pictures. **Color-90min.** Billy Graham, Robert Sampson, Sam Groom ....(4)

FOR PETE'S SAKE (1974) Columbia. **Color-90min.** Barbra Streisand, Michael Sarrazin 5½*

FOR SINGLES ONLY (1968) Columbia. **Color-91min.** John Saxon, Mary Ann Mobley...2*

FOR THE FIRST TIME (1959) M-G-M. **Color-97min.** *(U.S.-West German-Italian).* Mario Lanza, Johanna Von Koczian 4½*

FOR THE LOVE OF BENJI (1977) Mulberry Square. **Color-85min.** Benjine, Patsy Garrett 5*

FOR THE LOVE OF MARY (1948) Universal. **B&W-90min.** Deanna Durbin, Edmond O'Brien ....(4)

FOR THE LOVE OF MIKE (1960) 20th Century-Fox. **Color-84min.** Richard Basehart, Danny Bravo 4*
British title: NONE BUT THE BRAVE

FOR THOSE WHO THINK YOUNG (1964) United Artists. **Color-96min.** James Darren, Pamela Tiffin..........................3*

FOR WHOM THE BELL TOLLS (1943) Paramount. **Color-170min.** Gary Cooper, Ingrid Bergman...........................4½*

FOR YOU ALONE (1937) *see* WHEN YOU'RE ALONE

FORBIDDEN (1932) Columbia. **B&W-83min.** Barbara Stanwyck, Adolphe Menjou, Ralph Bellamy.................................

FORBIDDEN (1948) London Films *(Brit.).* **B&W-87min.** *(British).* Douglass Montgomery, Hazel Court ....

FORBIDDEN (1954) Universal. **B&W-85min.** Tony Curtis, Joanne Dru..(3)

FORBIDDEN (1956) Documento Films. **Color-90min.** *(Italian-French).* Mel Ferrer, Amedeo Nazzari, Eduardo Cianelli.............(3)
Original Italian title: PROBITO

FORBIDDEN ALLIANCE (1934) *see* BARRETTS OF WIMPOLE STREET, THE

FORBIDDEN CARGO (1954) Fine Arts. **B&W-85min.** *(British).* Nigel Patrick, Elizabeth Sellars.................................(4)

FORBIDDEN DESERT (1957) Warner Bros. **Color-45min.** Rafik Shammas, Abdallah Saleh...(5)

FORBIDDEN FRUIT (1952) Films Around The World. **B&W-97min.** *(French).* Fernandel, Francoise Arnoul.....................(4)
Original title: FRUIT DEFENDU, LE

FORBIDDEN GAMES (1951) Times Film Corp. **B&W-87min.** *(French).* Brigitte Fossey, Georges Poujouly...................4½*
Foreign title: JEUX INTERDITS

FORBIDDEN ISLAND (1959) Columbia. **Color-66min.** Jon Hall, Nan Adams...(3)

FORBIDDEN PLANET (1956) M-G-M. **Color-98min.** Walter Pidgeon, Anne Francis, Leslie Nielsen 4*

FORBIDDEN STREET, THE (1949) 20th Century-Fox. **B&W-91min.** *(British).* Maureen O'Hara, Dana Andrews, Sybil Thorndike...........4*
Original title: BRITANNIA MEWS

FORBIN PROJECT, THE (1970) *see* COLOSSUS, THE FORBIN PROJECT

FORCE OF ARMS (1951) Warner Bros. **B&W-100min.** William Holden, Nancy Olson ....(4)

FORCE OF EVIL (1948) M-G-M. **B&W-78min.** John Garfield, Beatrice Pearson...4*

FORCE 10 FROM NAVARONE (1978) American-International. **Color-118min.** Robert Shaw, Harrison Ford, Barbara Bach 5*

FOREIGN AFFAIR, A (1948) Paramount. **B&W-116min.** Jean Arthur, Marlene Dietrich, John Lund 5*

FOREIGN CORRESPONDENT (1940) United Artists. **B&W-119min.** Joel McCrea, Laraine Day 5*

FOREIGN EXCHANGE (1970) ABC Films. **Color-74min.** *(Made for TV).* Robert Horton, Sebastian Cabot, Jill St. John 4*

FOREIGN INTRIGUE (1956) United Artists. **Color-100min.** Robert Mitchum, Genevive Page ....(4)

FOREMAN WENT TO FRANCE, THE (1942) United Artists. **B&W-88min.** *(British).* Tommy Trinder, Constance Evans, Robert Morley...(5)
Alternate title: SOMEWHERE IN FRANCE

FOREPLAY (1975) Cinema National Corp. **Color-75min.** Zero Mostel, Estelle Parsons, Pat Paulsen, Jerry Orbach ....(4)
Alternate title: PRESIDENT'S WOMEN, THE

FOREST RANGERS, THE (1942) Paramount. **Color-87min.** Fred MacMurray, Paulette Goddard 3*

FOREVER AMBER (1947) 20th Century-Fox. **Color-140min.** Linda Darnell, Cornel Wilde 4*

FOREVER AND A DAY (1943) RKO. **B&W-104min.** Kent Smith, Ruth Warwick 4*

FOREVER DARLING (1956) M-G-M. **Color-96min.** Lucille Ball, Desi Arnaz, James Mason ....(4)

FOREVER FEMALE (1953) Paramount. **B&W-93min.** Ginger Rogers, William Holden .... (5)

FOREVER IN LOVE (1945) *see* PRIDE OF THE MARINES

FOREVER MY LOVE (1962) Paramount. **Color-167min.** *(Austrian).* Romy Schneider, Karl Boehm .... (4)
Titles of the three original films: SISSI *(1956)*; SISSI -- DIE JUNGE KAISERIN *(1957)*; SISSI -- SCHICKSALSJAHRE EINER KAISERIN *(1958)*.

FOREVER YOUNG, FOREVER FREE (1976) Universal. **Color-87min.** José Ferrer, Karen Valentine, Muntu Nbebele, Norman Knox .... (4)

FORGER OF LONDON (1961) UCC Films. **B&W-91min.** *(German).* Karin Dor, Helmut Lange .... (3)
Original title: FAELSCHER VON LONDON, DER

FORGERY (1950) *see* SOUTHSIDE 1-1000

FORGIVEN SINNER, THE (1961) **B&W-101min.** *(French-Italian).* Jean-Paul Belmondo, Emmanuele Riva .... (5)
Original French title: LÉON MORIN, PRETE *(Léon Morin, Priest)*

FORGOTTEN MAN, THE (1971) Worldvision. **Color-73min.** *(Made for TV).* Dennis Weaver, Anne Francis, Andrew Duggan 4*

FORGOTTEN WOMAN, THE (1939) Universal. **B&W-63min.** Sigrid Gurie, Eve Arden .... (4)

FORSAKING ALL OTHERS (1935) M-G-M. **B&W-84min.** Joan Crawford, Clark Gable .... (4)

FORSYTE SAGA, THE (1949) *see* THAT FORSYTE WOMAN

FORT ALGIERS (1953) United Artists. **B&W-78min.** Yvonne De Carlo, Carlos Thompson .... (2)

FORT APACHE (1948) RKO. **B&W-127min.** John Wayne, Henry Fonda 3½*

FORT BOWIE (1958) United Artists. **B&W-80min.** Ben Johnson, Jan Harrison .... (3)

FORT COURAGEOUS (1965) 20th Century-Fox. **B&W-72min.** Fred Beir, Donald Barry .... (3)

FORT DEFIANCE (1951) United Artists. **Color-81min.** Dane Clark, Ben Johnson .... (4)

FORT DOBBS (1958) Warner Bros. **B&W-90min.** Clint Walker, Brian Keith .... (3)

FORT MASSACRE (1958) United Artists. **Color-80min.** Joel McCrea, Forrest Tucker .... (3)

FORT OSAGE (1952) Monogram [Allied Artists]. **Color-72min.** Rod Cameron, Jane Nigh .... (2)

FORT TI (1953) Columbia. **Color-73min.** George Montgomery, Joan Vohs .... (3)

FORT UTAH (1967) Paramount. **Color-83min.** John Ireland, Robert Strauss, Scott Brady 3*

FORT VENGEANCE (1953) Allied Artists. **Color-75min.** James Craig, Rita Moreno .... (3)

FORT WORTH (1951) Warner Bros. **Color-80min.** Randolph Scott, David Brian .... (4)

FORT YUMA (1955) United Artists. **Color-78min.** Peter Graves, Joan Vohs .... (3)

FORTRESS OF THE DEAD (1965) Commonwealth United TV. **B&W-78min.** Joan Hackett, Conrad Parham .... (4)

FORTUNE, THE (1975) Columbia. **Color-88min.** Warren Beatty, Jack Nicholson, Stockard Channing 5½*

FORTUNE AND MEN'S EYES (1971) M-G-M. **Color-102min.** Wendell Burton, Zooey Hall, Michael Greer .... (5)

FORTUNE COOKIE, THE (1966) United Artists. **B&W-125min.** Jack Lemmon, Walter Matthau 5½*
British title: MEET WHIPLASH WILLIE

FORTUNE HUNTER, THE (1954) *see* OUTCAST, THE

FORTUNE IN DIAMONDS, A (1951) *see* GREAT ADVENTURE, THE

FORTUNE IS A WOMAN (1957) *see* SHE PLAYED WITH FIRE

FORTUNES OF CAPTAIN BLOOD (1950) Columbia. **B&W-91min.** Louis Hayward, Patricia Medina .... (4)

40 CARATS (1973) Columbia. **Color-108min.** Liv Ullmann, Edward Albert, Gene Kelly 4*

FORTY-EIGHT HOUR MILE, THE (1970) MCA-TV. **Color-97min.** *(Made for TV).* Darren McGavin, William Windom, Carrie Snodgress .... (4)

48 HOURS (1942) *see* WENT THE DAY WELL?

48 HOURS TO LIVE (1959) Medallion. **B&W-75min.** *(U.S.-Swedish).* Anthony Steel, Marlies Behrens, Ingemar Johansson .... (3)
Original title: MAN IN THE MIDDLE

FORTY GUNS (1957) 20th Century-Fox. **B&W-80min.** Barbara Stanwyck, Dean Jagger 3*

FORTY GUNS TO APACHE PASS (1967) Columbia. **Color-95min.** Audie Murphy, Michael Burns, Kenneth Tobey 3*

FORTY LITTLE MOTHERS (1940) M-G-M. **B&W-90min.** Eddie Cantor, Judith Anderson .... (4)

FORTY NAUGHTY GIRLS (1937) RKO. **B&W-63min.** James Gleason, Joan Woodbury .... (5)

FORTY-NINERS, THE (1954) Allied Artists. **B&W-71min.** Wild Bill Elliott, Virginia Grey 3*

49th MAN, THE (1953) Columbia. **B&W-73min.** John Ireland, Richard Denning .... (3)

FORTY-NINTH PARALLEL, THE (1941) Columbia. **B&W-105min.** *(British).* Eric Portman, Raymond Lovell 5*
Alternate title: INVADERS, THE

40 POUNDS OF TROUBLE (1963) Universal. **Color-106min.** Tony Curtis, Claire Wilcox 4*

FORTY-SECOND STREET (1933) Warner Bros. **B&W-98min.** Warner Baxter, Bebe Daniels 5*

47 RONIN (1962) *see* CHUSHINGURA

47 SAMURAI (1962) *see* CHUSHINGURA

FORTY THOUSAND HORSEMEN (1941) Sherman S. Krellberg. **B&W-89min.** *(Australian).* Grant Taylor, Betty Bryant, Chips Rafferty .... (5)

42:6 (BEN-GURION) (1970) **Color-103min.** *(Swiss, Documentary).* Director: Simon Hesera .... (3)
Alternate title: BEN-GURION STORY, THE

FORWARD MARCH (1930) *see* DOUGHBOYS

FOSTER AND LAURIE (1975) Worldvision. **Color-100min.** *(Made for TV).* Perry King, Dorian Harewood, Talia Shire 5*

FOUL PLAY (1978) Paramount. **Color-116min.** Goldie Hawn, Chevy Chase 6½*

FOUNTAIN, THE (1934) RKO. **B&W-83min.** Ann Harding, Paul Lukas (4)

FOUNTAIN OF LOVE, THE (1965) Crown International. **Color-83min.** *(Austrian).* Hans-Jurgen Baumler, Sieghardt Rupp .... (3)
Original title: LIEBESQUELLE, DIE

FOUNTAINHEAD, THE (1949) Warner Bros. **B&W-114min.** Gary Cooper, Patricia Neal 4½*

FOUR AGAINST FATE (1952) *see* DERBY DAY

FOUR BAGS FULL (1956) Trans-Lux Distributing. **B&W-84min.** *(French).* Jean Gabin, Bourvil, Louis de Funes .... (5)
Original title: TRAVERSÉE DE PARIS, LA

4 CLOWNS (1971) 20th Century-Fox. **B&W-97min.** *(Compilation).* Producer: Robert Youngson .... (5)

4D MAN, THE (1959) Universal. **Color-85min.** Robert Lansing, Lee Meriwether 3*
British title: EVIL FORCE, THE
Alternate title: MASTER OF HORROR

FOUL PLAY (1978). Romance between police detective Chevy Chase and fright victim Goldie Hawn is one of the more pleasant sidelights of the intrigue in which they encounter a bizarre group of villains.

Films are rated on a 1 to 10 scale, 10 is highest. **Boldface** ratings followed by an asterisk (*) are for films actually seen and rated by the executive and senior editors. All other ratings are estimates. (See Notes on Entertainment Ratings in the front section.)

FOUR DAUGHTERS (1938) Warner Bros. **B&W-90min.** Priscilla Lane, Rosemary Lane 4*

FOUR DAYS IN NOVEMBER (1964) United Artists. **B&W-120min.** (Documentary). Director: Mel Stuart .... (6)

FOUR DAYS IN PARIS (1955) **B&W-90min.** (French). Luis Mariano, Dary Cowl .... (3)

FOUR DAYS' LEAVE (1950) Film Classics [U.A.]. **B&W-98min.** (Swiss, English language). Cornel Wilde, Josette Day, Simone Signoret .... (4)
Original title: SWISS TOUR

FOUR DAYS OF NAPLES, THE (1962) M-G-M. **B&W-116min.** (Italian). Regina Bianchi, Aldo Giuffre 5*
Original title: QUATTRO GIORNATE DI NAPOLI, LE

FOUR DESPERATE MEN (1959) Continental [Walter Reade]. **B&W-105min.** (Australian-British). Aldo Ray, Heather Sears 4*
Original title: SIEGE OF PINCHGUT, THE

FOUR FACES WEST (1948) United Artists. **B&W-90min.** Joel McCrea, Frances Dee 4*
British title: THEY PASSED THIS WAY
Alternate title: NEW MEXICO
Alternate title: WANTED

FOUR FAST GUNS (1959) Universal. **B&W-72min.** James Craig, Paul Richards .... (2)

FOUR FEATHERS, THE (1939) United Artists. **Color-115min.** (British). Ralph Richardson, C. Aubrey Smith 5*

FOUR FEATHERS, THE (1978) NBC-TV. **Color-100min.** (Made for TV). Beau Bridges, Jane Seymour, Robert Powell 5½*

FOUR FLIES ON GREY VELVET (1972) Paramount. **Color-102min.** (Italian-French). Michael Brandon, Mimsy Farmer .... (2)
Original Italian title: QUATTRO MOSCHE DI VELLUTO GRIGIO

4 FOR TEXAS (1963) Warner Bros. **Color-124min.** Frank Sinatra, Dean Martin 3*

FOUR FRIGHTENED PEOPLE (1934) Paramount. **B&W-78min.** Herbert Marshall, Claudette Colbert 3½*

FOUR GIRLS IN TOWN (1957) Universal. **Color-85min.** Julie Adams, Marianne Cook 4*

FOUR GUNS TO THE BORDER (1954) Universal. **Color-82min.** Rory Calhoun, Colleen Miller 3*

FOUR HORSEMEN OF THE APOCALYPSE, THE (1962) M-G-M. **Color-153min.** Glenn Ford, Ingrid Thulin .... (4)

400 BLOWS, THE (1958) Zenith International. **B&W-94min.** (French). Jean-Pierre Léaud, Albert Rémy 4*
Original title: QUATRE-CENTS COUPS, LES

FOUR IN A JEEP (1951) United Artists. **B&W-96min.** (Swiss). Viveca Lindfors, Ralph Meeker .... (5)

FOUR JACKS AND A JILL (1942) RKO. **B&W-68min.** Ray Bolger, Desi Arnaz .... (3)

FOUR JILLS IN A JEEP (1944) 20th Century-Fox. **B&W-89min.** Carole Landis, Kay Francis .... (3)

FOUR KINDS OF LOVE (1965) see BAMBOLE!

FOUR MEN AND A PRAYER (1938) 20th Century-Fox. **B&W-85min.** Loretta Young, Richard Greene .... (5)

FOUR MOTHERS (1941) Warner Bros. **B&W-86min.** Priscilla Lane, Rosemary Lane 3*

FOUR MUSKETEERS, THE (1975) 20th Century-Fox. **Color-108min.** (Panamanian-Spanish, English language). Michael York, Oliver Reed 6½*
Alternate title: REVENGE OF MILADY, THE

FOUR NIGHTS OF A DREAMER (1971) New Yorker Films. **Color-91min.** (French). Isabelle Weingarten, Guillaume Des Forets, Maurice Monnayer .... (4)
Original title: QUATRE NUITS D'UN REVEUR

491 (1964) Peppercorn-Wormser. **B&W-110min.** (Swedish). Lars Lind, Leif Nymark .... (3)

FOUR POSTER, THE (1953) Columbia. **B&W-103min.** Rex Harrison, Lilli Palmer 5*

FOUR SKULLS OF JONATHAN DRAKE, THE (1959) United Artists. **B&W-70min.** Henry Daniell, Eduard Franz .... (2)

FOUR SONS (1940) 20th Century-Fox. **B&W-89min.** Don Ameche, Alan Curtis .... (4)

**** (four stars) (1967) see LOVES OF ONDINE

FOUR WAYS OUT (1954) Carroll Pictures. **B&W-77min.** (Italian). Gina Lollobrigida, Renato Baldini .... (4)

FOUR WIVES (1939) Warner Bros. **B&W-110min.** Claude Rains, Gale Page .... (4)

FOUR'S A CROWD (1938) Warner Bros. **B&W-91min.** Errol Flynn, Rosalind Russell .... (4)

14-18 (1963) see OVER THERE 1914-1918

FOURTEEN HOURS (1951) 20th Century-Fox. **B&W-92min.** Paul Douglas, Richard Basehart 5*

FOURTH FOR MARRIAGE, A (1964) see WHAT'S UP FRONT

FOURTH SQUARE, THE (1961) Anglo Amalgamated [EMI]. **B&W-58min.** (British). Conrad Phillips, Natasha Perry .... (3)

FOX, THE (1968) Claridge. **Color-110min.** Sandy Dennis, Keir Dullea, Anne Heywood 4*

FOX AND HIS FRIENDS (1975) New Yorker Films. **Color-123min.** (German). Rainer Werner Fassbinder, Peter Chatel ....
Original title: FAUSTRECHT DER FREIHEIT
British title: FOX

FOXES OF HARROW, THE (1947) 20th Century-Fox. **B&W-117min.** Rex Harrison, Maureen O'Hara 5*

FOXFIRE (1955) Universal. **Color-92min.** Jane Russell, Jeff Chandler 4*

FOXHOLE IN CAIRO (1960) Paramount. **B&W-79min.** (British). James Robertson Justice, Adrian Hoven .... (4)

FOXIEST GIRL IN PARIS, THE (1957) Times Film Corp. **B&W-96min.** (French). Martine Carol, Michel Piccoli .... (4)
Original title: NATHALIE

FOXTROT (1976) New World. **Color-91min.** (Mexican-Swiss). Peter O'Toole, Charlotte Rampling, Max von Sydow .... (4)
Alternate title: OTHER SIDE OF PARADISE, THE

FOXY BROWN (1974) American-International. **Color-91min.** Pam Grier, Antonio Fargas .... (3)

FRA DIAVOLO (1933) see DEVIL'S BROTHER, THE

FRAGMENT OF FEAR (1970) Columbia. **Color-95min.** (British). David Hemmings, Gayle Hunnicutt .... (3)

FRAMED (1947) Columbia. **B&W-82min.** Glenn Ford, Janis Carter .... (4)
British title: PAULA

FRAMED (1975) Paramount. **Color-106min.** Joe Don Baker, Conny Van Dyke .... (4)

FRANCIS (1950) Universal. **B&W-91min.** Donald O'Connor, Patricia Medina 4*

FRANCIS COVERS THE BIG TOWN (1953) Universal. **B&W-86min.** Donald O'Connor, Nancy Guild 4*

FRANCIS GARY POWERS: THE TRUE STORY OF THE U-2 SPY INCIDENT (1976) Worldvision. **Color-100min.** Lee Majors, Noah Beery, Jr., Nehemiah Persoff .... (4)

FRANCIS GOES TO THE RACES (1951) Universal. **B&W-88min.** Donald O'Connor, Piper Laurie 4*

FRANCIS GOES TO WEST POINT (1952) Universal. **B&W-81min.** Donald O'Connor, Lori Nelson 4*

FRANCIS IN THE HAUNTED HOUSE (1956) Universal. **B&W-80min.** Mickey Rooney, Virginia Welles 3*

FRANCIS IN THE NAVY (1955) Universal. **B&W-80min.** Donald O'Connor 3*

FRANCIS JOINS THE WACS (1954) Universal. **B&W-94min.** Donald O'Connor, Julia (Julie) Adams 4½*

FRANCIS OF ASSISI (1961) 20th Century-Fox. **Color-106min.** Bradford Dillman, Dolores Hart .... (4)

FRANK JAMES RIDES AGAIN (1950) see GUNFIRE

FRANKENSTEIN (1931) Universal. **B&W-71min.** Colin Clive, Boris Karloff 4*

FRANKENSTEIN AND THE MONSTER FROM HELL (1974) Paramount. **Color-93min.** (British). Peter Cushing, Shane Briant, David Prowse ...(3)

FRANKENSTEIN CONQUERS THE WORLD (1966) American-International. **Color-87min.** (Japanese-U.S.). Nick Adams, Tadao Takashima .... (2)
Original Japanese title: FURANKENSHUTAIN TAI BARAGON (Frankenstein vs. Baragon)

FRANKENSTEIN CREATED WOMAN (1967) 20th Century-Fox. **Color-86min.** (British). Peter Cushing, Susan Denberg 3½*

FRANKENSTEIN MEETS THE SPACE MONSTER (1965) Allied Artists. **B&W-78min.** James Karen, Robert Reilly .... (2)
British title: DUEL OF THE SPACE MONSTERS
Puerto Rican title: MARTE INVADE A PUERTO RICO (Mars Invades Puerto Rico)

FRANKENSTEIN MEETS THE WOLF MAN (1943) Universal. **B&W-72min.** Lon Chaney, Jr., Bela Lugosi 4*

FRANKENSTEIN MUST BE DESTROYED! (1970) Warner Bros. **Color-97min.** (British). Peter Cushing, Simon Ward, Freddie Jones 3*

Films are rated on a 1 to 10 scale, 10 is highest. **Boldface** ratings followed by an asterisk (*) are for films actually seen and rated by the executive and senior editors. All other ratings are estimates. (See Notes on Entertainment Ratings in the front section.)

FRANKENSTEIN - 1970 (1958) Allied Artists. **B&W-83min.** Boris Karloff, Tom Duggan 3*

FRANKENSTEIN: THE TRUE STORY (1973) MCA-TV. **Color-175min.** *(Made for TV)*. Leonard Whiting, Michael Sarrazin, David McCallum, James Mason 5*

FRANKENSTEIN'S BLOODY TERROR (1968) Independent International. **Color-83min.** *(Spanish)*. Paul Naschy, Dianik Zurakowska 1*
Original title: MARCA DEL HOMBRE LOBO, LA *(The Mark of the Wolf Man)*
Publicity title: HELL'S CREATURES
Publicity title: WOLFMAN OF COUNT DRACULA, THE

FRANKENSTEIN'S DAUGHTER (1958) Astor. **B&W-85min.** John Ashley, Sandra Knight 2*

FRANKIE AND JOHNNY (1966) United Artists. **Color-87min.** Elvis Presley, Donna Douglas, Nancy Kovak 4*

FRANK'S GREATEST ADVENTURE (1969) *see* FEARLESS FRANK

FRANTIC (1958) Times Film Corp. **B&W-90min.** *(French)*. Jeanne Moreau, Maurice Ronet .... (4)
Original title: ASCENSEUR POUR L'ÉCHAFAUD
British title: LIFT TO THE SCAFFOLD
Alternate title: ELEVATOR TO THE GALLOWS

FRASIER, THE SENSUOUS LION (1973) LCS Distributing. **Color-97min.** Michael Callan, Katherine Justice .... (4)

FRATERNALLY YOURS (1933) *see* SONS OF THE DESERT

FRATERNITY ROW (1977) Paramount. **Color-101min.** Peter Fox, Gregory Harrison 5*

FRAU IM MOND, DIE (1929) *see* WOMAN IN THE MOON

FRAULEIN (1958) 20th Century-Fox. **Color-98min.** Dana Wynter, Mel Ferrer 3*

FRAULEIN DOKTOR (1969) Paramount. **Color-102min.** *(Italian-Yugoslavian, English language)*. Suzy Kendall, Kenneth More, Capucine 2*
Yugoslavian title: GOSPODJICA DOKTOR - SPIJUNKA BEZ IMENA

FREAKS (1932) M-G-M. **B&W-64min.** Wallace Ford, Leila Hyams 5*

FREAKY FRIDAY (1976) Buena Vista. **Color-95min.** Barbara Harris, Jodie Foster 5*

FRECKLES (1960) 20th Century-Fox. **Color-84min.** Martin West, Carol Christensen .... (3)

FREE (1973) Indie Pix Releasing. **Color-80min.** *(Music Film)*. Director: Bert Tenzer .... (3)

FREE AND EASY (1930) M-G-M. **B&W-75min.** Buster Keaton, Anita Page .... (4)
Alternate title: EASY GO

FREE AND EASY (1941) M-G-M. **B&W-55min.** Robert Cummings, Ruth Hussey .... (4)

FREE, BLONDE AND TWENTY-ONE (1940) 20th Century-Fox. **B&W-67min.** Lynn Bari, Joan Davis .... (3)

FREE FOR ALL (1949) Universal. **B&W-83min.** Robert Cummings, Ann Blyth 3*

FREE SOUL, A (1931) M-G-M. **B&W-91min.** Norma Shearer, Lionel Barrymore .... (4)

FREE TO LIVE (1938) *see* HOLIDAY

FREE, WHITE AND 21 (1963) American-International. **B&W-102min.** Frederick O'Neal, Annalena Lund .... (3)

FREE WOMAN, A (1972) New Yorker Films. **Color-100min.** *(German)*. Margarethe von Trotta, Friedhelm Ptok, Martin Luttge 4*
Original title: STROHFEUER *(Summer Lightning)*

FREEBIE AND THE BEAN (1974) Warner Bros. **Color-112min.** James Caan, Alan Arkin 5*

FREEDOM RADIO (1940) *see* VOICE IN THE NIGHT, A

FREEDOM TO DIE (1961) Butcher's *(Brit.)*. **B&W-61min.** *(British)*. Paul Maxwell, Felicity Young .... (3)

FREEDOM TO LOVE (1970) Grove Press. **Color-96min.** *(German, Documentary)*. Kess Vanderwusten, Hugh Hefner, Billie Dixon, Eberhard Kronhausen .... (3)
Original title: FREIHEIT FUR DIE LIEBE

FREEWHEELIN' (1976) Turtle Releasing. **Color-80min.** Stacy Peralta, Camille Darrin .... (4)

FRENCH-CANCAN (1954) *see* ONLY THE FRENCH CAN

FRENCH CONNECTION, THE (1971) 20th Century-Fox. **Color-104min.** Gene Hackman, Fernando Rey 5½*

FRENCH CONNECTION II (1975) 20th Century-Fox. **Color-119min.** Gene Hackman, Fernando Rey 7½*
British title: FRENCH CONNECTION NUMBER 2

FRENCH COUSINS, THE (1971) *see* FROM EAR TO EAR

FRENCH KEY, THE (1946) Republic. **B&W-64min.** Albert Dekker, Mike Mazurki .... (4)

FRENCH LINE, THE (1953) RKO. **Color-102min.** Jane Russell, Gilbert Roland .... (3)

FRENCH MISTRESS, A (1960) Films Around The World. **B&W-98min.** *(British)*. Cecil Parker, James Robertson Justice, Agnes Laurent .... (4)

FRENCH PROVINCIAL (1975) New Yorker Films. **Color-95min.** *(French)*. Jeanne Moreau, Michel Auclair, Marie-France Pisier ....
Original title: SOUVENIRS D'EN FRANCE

FRENCH QUARTER (1978) Crown International. **Color-   min.** Virginia Mayo, Bruce Davison, Alisha Fontaine ....

FRENCH THEY ARE A FUNNY RACE, THE (1957) Continental [Walter Reade]. **B&W-83min.** *(French)*. Jack Buchanan, Martine Carol 3*
French title: CARNETS DU MAJOR THOMPSON, LES *(The Notebooks of Major Thompson)*
British title: DIARY OF MAJOR THOMPSON, THE

FRENCH WITHOUT TEARS (1940) Paramount. **B&W-67min.** *(British)*. Ray Milland, Ellen Drew .... (3)

FRENCH WOMAN, THE (1978) Monarch. **Color-97min.** *(French)*. Francoise Fabian, Dayle Haddon ....
Original title: MADAME CLAUDE

FRENCHIE (1950) Universal. **Color-81min.** Joel McCrea, Shelley Winters 3*

FRENCHMAN'S CREEK (1944) Paramount. **Color-113min.** Joan Fontaine, Arturo de Cordova 5*

FRENZY (1944) *see* TORMENT

FRENZY (1972) Universal. **Color-116min.** *(British-U.S.)*. Jon Finch, Barry Foster 6*

FRESH FROM PARIS (1955) 20th Century-Fox. **Color-70min.** Forrest Tucker, Margaret Whiting .... (3)
Original title: PARIS FOLLIES OF 1956

FRESHMAN, THE (1925) Pathé. **B&W-76min.** *(Silent)*. Harold Lloyd, Jobyna Ralston 5*
British title: COLLEGE DAYS

FREUD (1962) Universal. **B&W-139min.** Montgomery Clift, Susannah York 6*
Alternate title: SECRET PASSION, THE

FRIDAY FOSTER (1975) American-International. **Color-89min.** Pam Grier, Yaphet Kotto, Godfrey Cambridge .... (4)

FRIDAY THE RABBI SLEPT LATE (1976) *see* LANIGAN'S RABBI

FRIEDA (1947) Universal. **B&W-98min.** *(British)*. Mai Zetterling, David Farrar .... (5)

FRIEND OF THE FAMILY (1964) International Classics [20th]. **B&W-95min.** *(French-Italian)*. Jean Marais, Danielle Darrieux .... (5)
Original French title: PATATE

FRIENDLY ENEMIES (1942) United Artists. **B&W-95min.** Charles Winninger, Charles Ruggles 4*

THE FRESHMAN (1925). Although his enthusiasm far exceeds his athletic ability, Harold Lloyd is determined to impress pretty coed Jobyna Ralston by attempting to become a football hero.

FRIENDLY PERSUASION (1956) Allied Artists. **Color-139min.** Gary Cooper, Dorothy McGuire 6½*

FRIENDLY PERSUASION (1975) Allied Artists. **Color-100min.** *(Made for TV).* Richard Kiley, Shirley Knight 4½*

FRIENDS (1971) Paramount. **Color-102min.** *(British).* Sean Bury, Anicee Alvina .... (3)

FRIENDS AND LOVERS (1969) Stratford Pictures. **B&W-82min.** Anne Linden, Mary Kahn .... (3)
Original title: VIXENS, THE
Alternate title: WOMEN, THE

FRIENDS OF EDDIE COYLE, THE (1973) Paramount. **Color-100min.** Robert Mitchum, Peter Boyle 3½*

FRIGHT (1956) Allied Artists. **B&W-68min.** Nancy Malone, Eric Fleming .... (3)

FRIGHT (1971) Allied Artists. **Color-87min.** *(British).* Susan George, Honor Blackman, Ian Bannen 3*

FRIGHTENED BRIDE, THE (1952) Beverly. **B&W-75min.** *(British).* Mai Zetterling, Michael Denison, Flora Robson .... (4)
Original title: TALL HEADLINES

FRIGHTENED CITY (1950) *see* KILLER THAT STALKED NEW YORK, THE

FRIGHTENED CITY, THE (1961) Allied Artists. **B&W-97min.** *(British).* Herbert Lom, John Gregson, Sean Connery .... (3)

FRIGHTMARE (1974) Ellman. **Color-88min.** *(British).* Rupert Davies, Sheila Keith, Leo Genn ....

FRISCO KID (1935) Warner Bros. **B&W-77min.** James Cagney, Margaret Lindsay 3*

FRISCO SAL (1945) Universal. **B&W-63min.** Susanna Foster, Alan Curtis .... (4)

FRISKY (1954) Distributors Corp. of America. **B&W-98min.** *(Italian).* Gina Lollobrigida, Vittorio De Sica .... (4)
Original title: PANE, AMORE E GELOSIA
Alternate title: BREAD, LOVE AND JEALOUSY

FRITZ THE CAT (1972) Cinemation. **Color-78min.** *(Cartoon). Director:* Ralph Bakshi 5*

FROGMEN, THE (1951) 20th Century-Fox. **B&W-96min.** Richard Widmark, Dana Andrews 4*

FROGS (1972) American-International. **Color-91min.** Ray Milland, Sam Elliott 4*

FROM A ROMAN BALCONY (1960) Continental [Walter Reade]. **B&W-84min.** *(Italian-French).* Jean Sorel, Lea Massari .... (5)
Original Italian title: GIORNATA BALORDA, LA
Original French title: CA S'EST PASSÉ A ROME
Alternate title: CRAZY DAY, A
Alternate title: LOVE IS A DAY'S WORK
Alternate title: PICKUP IN ROME

FROM BEYOND THE GRAVE (1973) Warner Bros. **Color-98min.** *(British).* Peter Cushing, David Warner 4*

FROM CHINA WITH DEATH (1974) Howard Mahler. **Color-109min.** *(Hong Kong?).* Willie Ma, Carmen Yee 3*

FROM EAR TO EAR (1971) Cinemation. **Color-81min.** *(French).* Solange Pradel, Daniele Argence, Nicole Debonne .... (2)
Original title: COUSINES, LES *(The Cousins)*
Alternate title: FRENCH COUSINS, THE
Publicity title: COFFIN, THE

FROM HELL IT CAME (1957) Allied Artists. **B&W-71min.** Tod Andrews, Tina Carver 3*

FROM HELL TO BORNEO (1964) Commonwealth United TV. **Color-96min.** George Montgomery, Torin Thatcher .... (3)

FROM HELL TO TEXAS (1958) 20th Century-Fox. **Color-100min.** Don Murray, Diane Varsi .... (4)
British title: MANHUNT

FROM HERE TO ETERNITY (1953) Columbia. **B&W-118min.** Burt Lancaster, Montgomery Clift 5*

FROM ISTANBUL - ORDERS TO KILL (1965) Sigma III. **Color-82min.** *(European).* Christopher Logan, Geraldine Pearsall .... (3)

FROM NASHVILLE WITH MUSIC (1969) Craddock Films. **Color-87min.** Marilyn Maxwell, Leo G. Carroll, Marty Robbins, Charley Pride .... (3)

FROM NOON TILL THREE (1976) United Artists. **Color-98min.** Charles Bronson, Jill Ireland 6*

FROM RUSSIA WITH LOVE (1963) United Artists. **Color-118min.** *(British).* Sean Connery, Daniela Bianchi 5½*

FROM THE EARTH TO THE MOON (1958) Warner Bros. **Color-100min.** Joseph Cotten, George Sanders .... (4)

FROM THE MIXED-UP FILES OF MRS. BASIL E. FRANKWEILER (1973) Cinema 5. **Color-105min.** Ingrid Bergman, Sally Prager, Johnny Doran ....
Alternate title: HIDEAWAYS, THE

FROM THE TERRACE (1960) 20th Century-Fox. **Color-144min.** Paul Newman, Joanne Woodward 5½*

FROM THIS DAY FORWARD (1946) RKO. **B&W-95min.** Joan Fontaine, Mark Stevens .... (5)

FRONT, THE (1976) Columbia. **Color-93min.** Woody Allen, Zero Mostel 6*

FRONT PAGE, THE (1931) United Artists. **B&W-101min.** Adolphe Menjou, Pat O'Brien 5*

FRONT PAGE, THE (1974) Universal. **Color-105min.** Jack Lemmon, Walter Matthau 6½*

FRONT PAGE STORY (1954) Associated Artists. **B&W-95min.** *(British).* Jack Hawkins, Elizabeth Allan .... (4)

FRONT PAGE WOMAN (1935) Warner Bros. **B&W-82min.** Bette Davis, George Brent .... (4)

FRONTIER BADMEN (1943) Universal. **B&W-77min.** Robert Paige, Anne Gwynne, Lon Chaney (Jr.) .... (4)

FRONTIER GAL (1945) Universal. **Color-84min.** Yvonne De Carlo, Rod Cameron 4*
British title: BRIDE WASN'T WILLING, THE

FRONTIER GAMBLER (1956) Associated Film Dists. **B&W-76min.** John Bromfield, Jim Davis .... (3)

FRONTIER GUN (1958) 20th Century-Fox. **B&W-70min.** John Agar, Joyce Meadows .... (3)

FRONTIER HELLCAT (1964) Columbia. **Color-98min.** *(W. German-French-Italian-Yugoslavian).* Stewart Granger, Pierre Brice, Elke Sommer 2*
Original W. German title: UNTER GEIERN
Original French title: PARMI LES VATOURS
Original Yugoslavian title: MEDJU JASTREBOVIMA

FRONTIER SCOUT (1956) *see* QUINCANNON, FRONTIER SCOUT

FRONTIER UPRISING (1961) United Artists. **B&W-68min.** Jim Davis, Nancy Hadley .... (3)

FRONTIER WOLF (1950) Trans-America. **B&W-76min.** *(Italian).* Piero Lulli, Maria Frau .... (3)

FROU FROU (1938) *see* TOY WIFE, THE

FROZEN ALIVE (1964) Commonwealth United TV. **B&W-80min.** *(British-W. German, English version).* Mark Stevens, Marianne Koch .... (2)
Original W. German title: FALL X701, DER

FROZEN DEAD, THE (1967) Warner Bros. **Color-95min.** *(British).* Dana Andrews, Anna Palk .... (3)

FROZEN GHOST, THE (1945) Universal. **B&W-61min.** Lon Chaney, Jr., Evelyn Ankers .... (3)

FRUITS OF SUMMER, THE (1954) Ellis Films. **B&W-101min.** *(French).* Edwige Feuillere, Etchika Choureau .... (4)
Original title: FRUITS DE L'ÉTÉ, LES

FUEGO (1968) Haven International. **Color-81min.** *(Argentinian).* Isabel Sarli, Armando Bo .... (2)

FUGA, LA (1965) International Classics [20th]. **B&W-92min.** *(Italian).* Giovanna Ralli, Anouk Aimée .... (3)
Translation title: The Flight

FUGITIVE, THE (1947) RKO. **B&W-104min.** Henry Fonda, Dolores Del Rio 4*

FUGITIVE FROM A PRISON CAMP (1940) Columbia. **B&W-59min.** Jack Holt, Marian Marsh .... (3)

FUGITIVE FROM JUSTICE, A (1940) Warner Bros. **B&W-53min.** Roger Pryor, Don Douglas .... (3)

FUGITIVE IN SAIGON (1957) J. Arthur Rank. **B&W-100min.** *(French).* Daniel Gélin, Anh Mechard .... (3)
Alternate title: MORT EN FRAUDE

FUGITIVE KIND, THE (1960) United Artists. **B&W-135min.** Marlon Brando, Anna Magnani 4½*

FUGITIVE LADY (1951) Republic. **B&W-78min.** Janis Paige, Binnie Barnes .... (3)

FULL CIRCLE (1977) **Color-98min.** *(Canadian-British).* Mia Farrow, Keir Dullea ....

FULL CONFESSION (1939) RKO. **B&W-73min.** Victor McLaglen, Sally Ellers .... (4)

FULL HEARTS AND EMPTY POCKETS (1963) Screen Gems. **B&W-88min.** *(W. German-Italian).* Tomas Fritsch, Senta Berger .... (4)
Original German title: VOLLES HERZ UND LEERE TASCHEN

FULL HOUSE (1952) *see* O. HENRY'S FULL HOUSE

Films are rated on a 1 to 10 scale, 10 is highest. **Boldface** ratings followed by an asterisk (*) are for films actually seen and rated by the executive and senior editors. All other ratings are estimates. (See Notes on Entertainment Ratings in the front section.)

FULL OF LIFE (1957) Columbia. **B&W-91min.** Judy Holliday, Richard Conte.. 4*
Alternate title: LADY IS WAITING, THE

FULL TREATMENT, THE (1961) *see* STOP ME BEFORE I KILL!

FULLER BRUSH GIRL, THE (1950) Columbia. **B&W-85min.** Lucille Ball, Eddie Albert.. 4*
British title: AFFAIRS OF SALLY, THE

FULLER BRUSH MAN, THE (1948) Columbia. **B&W-93min.** Red Skelton, Janet Blair .... (4)
British title: THAT MAD MR. JONES

FUN AND FANCY FREE (1947) RKO (for Disney). **Color-73min.** (Cartoon). *Director:* Ward Kimball 5*

FUN IN ACAPULCO (1963) Paramount. **Color-97min.** Elvis Presley, Ursula Andress... 3½*

FUN ON A WEEKEND (1947) United Artists. **B&W-93min.** Priscilla Lane, Eddie Albert... (3)

FUN WITH DICK AND JANE (1977) Columbia. **Color-95min.** George Segal, Jane Fonda 5½*

FUNERAL IN BERLIN (1966) Paramount. **Color-102min.** *(British).* Michael Caine, Eva Renzi... 4*

FUNNY FACE (1935) *see* BRIGHT LIGHTS

FUNNY FACE (1957) Paramount. **Color-103min.** Audrey Hepburn, Fred Astaire 5*

FUNNY GIRL (1968) Columbia. **Color-151min.** Barbra Streisand, Omar Sharif 5½*

FUNNY LADY (1975) Columbia. **Color-136min.** Barbra Streisand, James Caan 5½*

FUNNY THING HAPPENED ON THE WAY TO THE FORUM, A (1966) United Artists. **Color-99min.** Zero Mostel, Phil Silvers 5½*

FUNNYMAN (1971) New Yorker Films. **B&W-102min.** Peter Bonerz, Sandra Archer .... (4)

FURIES, THE (1950) Paramount. **B&W-109min.** Barbara Stanwyck, Wendell Corey 4*

FURIOUS ENCOUNTER (1962) Commonwealth United TV. **B&W-74min.** *(Mexican).* Ofelia Montesco, Rodolfo De Anda .... (1)

FURTHER ADVENTURES OF THE WILDERNESS FAMILY, PART II (1978) Pacific International Enterprises. **Color-105min.** Robert Logan, Susan D. Shaw, Heather Rattray, Ham Larsen .... (4)
Publicity title: WILDERNESS FAMILY PART 2
Publicity title: ADVENTURES OF THE WILDERNESS FAMILY PART 2, THE

FURTHER PERILS OF LAUREL AND HARDY (1967) 20th Century-Fox. **B&W-99min.** .... (5)

FURY (1936) M-G-M. **B&W-90min.** Spencer Tracy, Sylvia Sidney 6*

FURY, THE (1978) 20th Century-Fox. **Color-117min.** Kirk Douglas, John Cassavetes 5*

FURY AT FURNACE CREEK (1948) 20th Century-Fox. **B&W-88min.** Victor Mature, Coleen Gray .... (4)

FURY AT GUNSIGHT PASS (1956) Columbia. **B&W-68min.** David Brian, Neville Brand .... (3)

FURY AT SHOWDOWN (1957) United Artists. **B&W-75min.** Nick Adams, John Derek .... (3)

FURY AT SMUGGLER'S BAY (1961) Avco-Embassy. **Color-92min.** *(British).* Peter Cushing, John Fraser .... (2)

FURY IN PARADISE (1955) Filmmakers. **Color-77min.** *(Mexican).* Peter Thompson, Rea Iturbide .... (1)

FURY OF ACHILLES (1962) American-International. **Color-116min.** *(Italian).* Jacques Bergerac, Gordon Mitchell .... (3)

FURY OF HERCULES, THE (1961) Telewide Systems. **Color-95min.** *(Italian-French).* Brad Harris, Brigitte Corey .... (3)
Original Italian title: FURIA DI ERCOLE, LA
Alternate TV title: FURY OF SAMSON, THE

FURY OF THE CONGO (1951) Columbia. **B&W-69min.** Johnny Weissmuller, Sherry Moreland .... (3)

FURY OF THE PAGANS (1960) Columbia. **Color-86min.** *(Italian).* Edmund Purdom, Rossana Podesta .... (2)
Original title: FURIA DEL BARBARI, LA

FURY OF THE VIKINGS (1961) *see* ERIK THE CONQUEROR

FURY UNLEASHED (1958) *see* HOT ROD GANG

FUSS OVER FEATHERS (1954) *see* CONFLICT OF WINGS

FUTURE COP (1976) Paramount. **Color-74min.** *(Made for TV).* Ernest Borgnine, Michael Shannon, John Amos .... (4)

FUTUREWORLD (1976) American-International. **Color-107min.** Peter Fonda, Blythe Danner... 6½*

FUTUREWORLD (1976). Stuart Margolin, a worker at the fantastic pleasure resort, discusses the recent sinister developments there as investigative reporter Peter Fonda listens; their friend offers no arguments.

FUTZ (1969) Commonwealth United. **Color-92min.** John Pakos, Victor Lipari .... (2)

FUZZ (1972) United Artists. **Color-92min.** Burt Reynolds, Jack Weston 4*

FUZZY PINK NIGHTGOWN, THE (1957) United Artists. **B&W-87min.** Jane Russell, Keenan Wynn .... (3)

FX 18, SECRET AGENT (1965) Paramount. **Color-95min.** *(Spanish-French).* Richard Wyler, Jany Clair .... (2)
Original Spanish title: ORDEN: FX 18 DEBE MORIR *(Order: FX 18 Must Die)*

-G-

G.I. BLUES (1960) Paramount. **Color-104min.** Elvis Presley, Juliet Prowse 4*

G.I. JOE (1945) *see* STORY OF G.I. JOE, THE

G-MEN (1935) Warner Bros. **B&W-85min.** James Cagney, Ann Dvorak 4*

G-MEN NEVER FORGET (1947) *see* CODE 645

G-MEN VS. THE BLACK DRAGON (1943) *see* BLACK DRAGON OF MANZANAR

GABLE AND LOMBARD (1976) Universal. **Color-131min.** James Brolin, Jill Clayburgh 5½*

GABRIEL OVER THE WHITE HOUSE (1933) M-G-M. **B&W-87min.** Walter Huston, Karen Morley 4*

GABY (1956) M-G-M. **Color-97min.** Leslie Caron, John Kerr 3*

GAILY, GAILY (1969) United Artists. **Color-106min.** Beau Bridges, Melina Mercouri 4*
British title: CHICAGO, CHICAGO

GAL WHO TOOK THE WEST, THE (1949) Universal. **Color-84min.** Yvonne De Carlo, Scott Brady 3½*

GALIA (1966) Zenith International. **B&W-105min.** *(French).* Mireille Darc, Venantino Venantini .... (4)
Alternate title: I, AND MY LOVERS
Alternate title: I AND MY LOVE

GALILEO (1975) American Film Theatre. **Color-145min.** *(British-Canadian).* Topol, Edward Fox.. 5*

GALLANT BESS (1946) M-G-M. **Color-101min.** Marshall Thompson, Clem Bevans .... (3)

GALLANT BLADE, THE (1948) Columbia. **Color-81min.** Larry Parks, Marguerite Chapman .... (4)

GALLANT HOURS, THE (1960) United Artists. **B&W-111min.** James Cagney, Dennis Weaver.. 3½*

GALLANT JOURNEY (1946) Columbia. **B&W-85min.** Glenn Ford, Janet Blair .... (4)

GALLANT LADY (1934) Fox Film Co. [20th]. **B&W-86min.** Ann Harding, Clive Brook, Dickie Moore .... (3)

GALLANT LEGION, THE (1948) Republic. **B&W-88min.** Bill Elliott, Bruce Cabot .... (5)

GALLANT SONS (1940) M-G-M. **B&W-70min.** Jackie Cooper, Leo Gorcey .... (3)

GALLOPING MAJOR, THE (1950) Souvaine Selective. **B&W-82min.** (British). Basil Radford, Jimmy Hanley............................ (4)

GAMBIT (1966) Universal. **Color-109min.** Shirley MacLaine, Michael Caine **6***

GAMBLER, THE (1974) Paramount. **Color-109min.** James Caan, Paul Sorvino **5***

GAMBLER AND THE LADY, THE (1952) Lippert Productions. **B&W-74min.** (British). Dane Clark, Naomi Chance...................... (3)

GAMBLER FROM NATCHEZ, THE (1954) 20th Century-Fox. **Color-88min.** Dale Robertson, Debra Paget **4***

GAMBLERS, THE (1949) see JUDGE, THE

GAMBLER'S CHOICE (1944) Paramount. **B&W-66min.** Chester Morris, Nancy Kelly .... (3)

GAMBLING HOUSE (1951) RKO. **B&W-80min.** Victor Mature, Terry Moore... (3)

GAMBLING LADY (1934) Warner Bros. **B&W-66min.** Barbara Stanwyck, Pat O'Brien .... (4)

GAMBLING ON THE HIGH SEAS (1940) Warner Bros. **B&W-56min.** Wayne Morris, Jane Wyman .... (3)

GAMBLING SHIP (1933) Paramount. **B&W-72min.** Cary Grant, Benita Hume **4***

GAME FOR THREE LOSERS (1964) Avco-Embassy. **B&W-56min.** (British). Michael Gough, Mark Eden .... (3)

GAME IS OVER, THE (1966) Royal Films Int'l [Columbia]. **Color-98min.** (French-Italian, English version). Jane Fonda, Peter McEnery, Michel Piccoli .... (4)
Original French title: CUREE, LA

GAME OF DANGER (1954) Associated Artists. **B&W-88min.** (British). Jack Warner, Derek Farr .... (4)
Original title: BANG! YOU'RE DEAD

GAME OF DEATH, A (1946) RKO. **B&W-72min.** John Loder, Audrey Long .... (3)

GAME OF LOVE, THE (1953) Times Film Corp. **B&W-108min.** (French). Nicole Berger, Pierre-Michel Beck .... (5)
Original title: BLÉ EN HERBE, LE

GAME PASS (1972) see JAIL BAIT

GAMERA VS. MONSTER X (1970) American-International. **Color-81min.** (Japanese). Gamera, Tsutomu Takakuwa, Kelly Varis **1***
Original title: GAMERA TAI DAIMAJU JAIGA (Gamera vs. Jiger)
Alternate title: MONSTERS INVADE EXPO '70

GAMES (1967) Universal. **Color-100min.** Simone Signoret, James Caan **5***

GAMES, THE (1970) 20th Century-Fox. **Color-95min.** (British). Michael Crawford, Stanley Baker **4***

GAMES MEN PLAY, THE (1963) Joseph Brenner. **B&W-92min.** Maria Antinea, Amelia Bence .... (2)
Original title: CIGARRA NO ES UN BICHO, LA (The Cicada Is Not an Insect)
Publicity title: CICADA IS NOT AN INSECT, THE
Alternate title(?): HOTEL, THE

GAMES OF DESIRE (1964) Times Film Corp. **B&W-90min.** (W. German-French). Ingrid Thulin, Paul Hubschmid, Claudine Auger .... (2)
Original W. German title: LADY, DIE

GAMES OF THE XXI OLYMPIAD MONTREAL 1976 (1977) Nat'l Film Board of Canada. **Color-119min.** (Canadian, Documentary). Director: Jean-Claude Labrecque ....

GAMMA PEOPLE, THE (1956) Columbia. **B&W-79min.** (British). Paul Douglas, Leslie Phillips **3***

GAMMERA THE INVINCIBLE (1965) World Entertainment. **B&W-86min.** (Japanese). Albert Dekker, Brian Donlevy, Eiji Funakoshi **1***
Original title: DAIKAIJU GAMERA

GANG MADE GOOD, THE (1941) see TUXEDO JUNCTION

GANG THAT COULDN'T SHOOT STRAIGHT, THE (1971) M-G-M. **Color-96min.** Jerry Orbach, Lionel Stander **4***

GANG WAR (1958) 20th Century-Fox. **B&W-75min.** Charles Bronson, Kent Taylor **3***

GANG WAR (1962) United Artists. **B&W-65min.** (British). Sean Kelly, Eira Heath .... (3)

GANGBUSTERS (1955) Visual Drama, Inc. **B&W-78min.** Myron Healey, Don C. Harvey .... (3)

GANG'S ALL HERE, THE (1939) see AMAZING MR. FORREST, THE

GANG'S ALL HERE, THE (1941) Monogram [Allied Artists]. **B&W-61min.** Frankie Darro, Marcia Mae Jones......................... (3)
British title: IN THE NIGHT

GANG'S ALL HERE, THE (1943) 20th Century-Fox. **Color-103min.** Alice Faye, Carmen Miranda 3½*
British title: GIRLS HE LEFT BEHIND, THE

GANGSTER, THE (1947) Allied Artists. **B&W-84min.** Barry Sullivan, Belita.. (4)

GANGSTER BOSS (1959) Emery Pictures. **B&W-100min.** (French). Fernandel .... (3)

GANGSTER STORY (1959) Republic. **B&W-65min.** Walter Matthau, Carol Grace .... (3)

GANGSTER'S REVENGE (1960) see GET OUTTA TOWN

GANGWAY (1937) Gaumont-British [Rank]. **B&W-89min.** (British). Jessie Matthews, Barry Mackay, Nat Pendleton .... (4)

GANGWAY FOR TOMORROW (1943) RKO. **B&W-69min.** Margo, John Carradine, Robert Ryan .... (3)

GANJA AND HESS (1973) see BLOOD COUPLE

GAOL BIRDS (1931) see PARDON US

GAOLBREAK (1962) see JAILBREAK

GAPPA - TRIPHIBIAN MONSTER (1963) see MONSTER FROM A PREHISTORIC PLANET

GARDEN OF ALLAH, THE (1936) United Artists. **Color-85min.** Marlene Dietrich, Charles Boyer .... (5)

GARDEN OF DELIGHTS (1970) Altura Films. **Color-95min.** (Spanish). José Luis Lopez Vazquez, Luchy Soto .... (4)
Original title: JARDIN DE LAS DELICIAS, EL

GARDEN OF EVIL (1954) 20th Century-Fox. **Color-100min.** Gary Cooper, Susan Hayward **4***

GARDEN OF THE FINZI-CONTINIS, THE (1971) Cinema 5. **Color-94min.** (Italian-W. German). Dominique Sanda, Lino Capolicchio **5***
Original Italian title: GIARDINO DEI FINZI CONTINI, IL

GARDEN OF THE MOON (1938) Warner Bros. **B&W-94min.** Pat O'Brien, John Payne .... (4)

GARDENER, THE (1974) Nolan Productions. **Color-95min.** Katharine Houghton, Joe Dallesandro, Rita Gam ....
Alternate title: SEEDS OF EVIL, THE

GARGON TERROR, THE (1959) see TEENAGERS FROM OUTER SPACE

GARGOYLES (1972) Warner Bros. **Color-74min.** (Made for TV). Cornel Wilde, Jennifer Salt, Bernie Casey 3*

GARIBALDI (1961) Trans-America. **Color-110min.** (Italian). Renzo Ricci, Paolo Stoppa 3*
Original title: VIVA L'ITALIA (Hurrah for Italy)

GARMENT JUNGLE, THE (1957) Columbia. **B&W-88min.** Lee J. Cobb, Kerwin Mathews .... (4)

GARU THE MAD MONK (1970) see GURU THE MAD MONK

GAS-OIL (1955) Intermondia Films. **B&W-95min.** (French). Jean Gabin, Jeanne Moreau .... (8)
Alternate title: HI-JACK HIGHWAY

GAS-S-S-S! (1970) American-International. **Color-80min.** Robert Corff, Bud Cort, Talia Coppola (Shire), Elaine Giftos .... (3)
Screen title: GAS-S-S-S . . . OR IT BECAME NECESSARY TO DESTROY THE WORLD IN ORDER TO SAVE IT!

GASLIGHT (1940) see ANGEL STREET

GASLIGHT (1944) M-G-M. **B&W-114min.** Charles Boyer, Ingrid Bergman **5***
British title: MURDER IN THORNTON SQUARE

GASLIGHT FOLLIES (1945) Embassy Pictures. **B&W-110min.** (Compilation). Producer: Joseph E. Levine .... (3)

GATE OF HELL (1953) Harrison Pictures. **Color-90min.** (Japanese). Kazuo Hasegawa, Machiko Kyo **5***
Original title: JIGOKUMEN
Alternate title: HELL'S GATE

GATES OF PARIS (1957) Lopert [U.A.]. **B&W-103min.** (French). Pierre Brasseur, Georges Brassens, Henri Vidal .... (5)
Original title: PORTE DES LILAS

GATEWAY (1938) 20th Century-Fox. **B&W-73min.** Don Ameche, Arleen Whelan .... (3)

GATHERING OF EAGLES, A (1963) Universal. **Color-115min.** Rock Hudson, Rod Taylor 4½*

GATOR (1976) United Artists. **Color-115min.** Burt Reynolds, Jack Weston 4½*

GAUNTLET, THE (1977) Warner Bros. **Color-114min.** Clint Eastwood, Sondra Locke 5½*

GAY ADVENTURE, THE (1953) United Artists. **B&W-87min.** (British). Yvonne Arnaud, Barry Jones .... (5)

Films are rated on a 1 to 10 scale, 10 is highest. **Boldface** ratings followed by an asterisk (*) are for films actually seen and rated by the executive and senior editors. All other ratings are estimates. (See Notes on Entertainment Ratings in the front section.)

GAY BLADES (1946) Republic. **B&W-67min.** Allan "Rocky" Lane, Jean Rogers .... (4)
Alternate title: TOURNAMENT TEMPO

GAY BRIDE, THE (1934) M-G-M. **B&W-80min.** Carole Lombard, Chester Morris .... (3)

GAY CABALLERO, THE (1940) 20th Century-Fox. **B&W-57min.** Cesar Romero, Sheila Ryan .... (4)

GAY CITY, THE (1941) *see* LAS VEGAS NIGHTS

GAY DECEIVERS, THE (1969) Fanfare. **Color-91min.** Kevin Coughlin, Lawrence Casey, Michael Greer .... (3)

GAY DECEPTION, THE (1935) 20th Century-Fox. **B&W-76min.** Francis Lederer, Frances Dee **3***

GAY DESPERADO, THE (1936) United Artists. **B&W-85min.** Nino Martini, Ida Lupino .... (5)

GAY DIVORCÉE, THE (1934) RKO. **B&W-107min.** Fred Astaire, Ginger Rogers **5***
British title: GAY DIVORCE, THE

GAY FALCON, THE (1941) RKO. **B&W-67min.** George Sanders, Wendy Barrie .... (4)

GAY IMPOSTORS, THE (1938) *see* GOLD DIGGERS IN PARIS

GAY LADY, THE (1949) Eagle Lion. **Color-91min.** *(British).* Jean Kent, James Donald .... (4)
Original title: TROTTIE TRUE

GAY MRS. TREXEL, THE (1940) *see* SUSAN AND GOD

GAY NINETIES, THE (1930) *see* FLORADORA GIRL, THE

GAY PURR-EE (1962) Warner Bros. **Color-86min.** *(Cartoon). Director:* Abe Levitow **4***

GAY SENORITA, THE (1946) Columbia. **B&W-69min.** Jinx Falkenburg, Jim Bannon .... (3)

GAY SISTERS, THE (1942) Warner Bros. **B&W-108min.** Barbara Stanwyck, George Brent .... (3)

GAY VAGABOND, THE (1941) Republic. **B&W-66min.** Roscoe Karns, Ruth Donnelly .... (3)

GAZEBO, THE (1960) M-G-M. **B&W-100min.** Glenn Ford, Debbie Reynolds **5½***

GEISHA BOY, THE (1958) Paramount. **Color-98min.** Jerry Lewis, Marie McDonald **4***

GEMINI MAN (1976) MCA-TV. **Color-100min.** *(Made for TV).* Ben Murphy, Katherine Crawford, Richard Dysart .... (4)

GENE KRUPA STORY, THE (1959) Columbia. **B&W-101min.** Sal Mineo, Susan Kohner **4***
British title: DRUM CRAZY

GENERAL, THE (1927) United Artists. **B&W-83min.** *(Silent).* Buster Keaton, Marion Mack **5½***

GENERAL DELLA ROVERE (1959) Continental [Walter Reade]. **B&W-139min.** *(Italian-French).* Vittorio De Sica, Hannes Messemer **4***

GENERAL DIED AT DAWN, THE (1936) Paramount. **B&W-97min.** Gary Cooper, Madeleine Carroll **4½***

GENERAL IDI AMIN DADA (1974) Tinc. **Color-90min.** *(French, Documentary). Director:* Barbet Schroeder .... (4)
Original title: IDI AMIN DADA
British title: GENERAL AMIN

GENERATION (1969) Avco-Embassy. **B&W-104min.** David Janssen, Kim Darby **4***
British title: TIME FOR GIVING, A

GENESIS II (1973) Warner Bros. **Color-74min.** *(Made for TV).* Alex Cord, Mariette Hartley, Harvey Jason **4***

GENEVIEVE (1953) Universal. **Color-86min.** *(British).* John Gregson, Dinah Sheridan **6***

GENGHIS KHAN (1952) United Artists. **B&W-88min.** *(Philippine).* Manuel Conde, Elvira Reyes .... (4)
Alternate title: GHENGIS KHAN

GENGHIS KHAN (1965) Columbia. **Color-124min.** *(U.S.-West German-Yugoslavian).* Omar Sharif, Stephen Boyd **3***
Alternate title: GHENGIS KHAN

GENGHIS KHAN AND HIS MONGOLS (1960) *see* KING OF THE MONGOLS

GENIUS AT WORK (1946) RKO. **B&W-61min.** Wally Brown, Alan Carney, Bela Lugosi, Lionel Atwill .... (2)

GENIUS IN THE FAMILY, A (1946) *see* SO GOES MY LOVE

GENIUS, TWO FRIENDS AND A FOOL, A (1976) *see* UN GENIO, DUE COMPARI, UN POLLO

GENTLE ANNIE (1944) M-G-M. **B&W-80min.** James Craig, Donna Reed .... (4)

GENTLE ART OF MURDER, THE (1962) *see* CRIME DOES NOT PAY

GENTLE GIANT (1967) Paramount. **Color-93min.** Dennis Weaver, Vera Miles .... (4)

GENTLE GUNMAN, THE (1952) Universal. **B&W-86min.** *(British).* John Mills, Dirk Bogarde **4***

GENTLE PEOPLE, THE (1972) Commercial Film Co. **Color-110min.** Patsy McBride, Reed Apaghian, Robert Counsel .... (4)

GENTLE RAIN, THE (1966) Comet Film. **Color-110min.** *(U.S.-Brazilian, English language).* Christopher George, Lynda Day, Fay Spain .... (4)

GENTLE SERGEANT, THE (1955) *see* THREE STRIPES IN THE SUN

GENTLE SEX, THE (1943) Two Cities. **B&W-89min.** *(British).* Lilli Palmer, John Gates .... (4)

GENTLE TOUCH, THE (1955) J. Arthur Rank. **Color-86min.** *(British).* George Baker, Belinda Lee .... (3)
Original title: FEMININE TOUCH, THE

GENTLEMAN AFTER DARK (1942) United Artists. **B&W-77min.** Brian Donlevy, Miriam Hopkins .... (3)

GENTLEMAN AT HEART, A (1942) 20th Century-Fox. **B&W-66min.** Cesar Romero, Carole Landis, Milton Berle .... (4)

GENTLEMAN FOR A DAY (1932) *see* UNION DEPOT

GENTLEMAN JIM (1942) Warner Bros. **B&W-104min.** Errol Flynn, Alexis Smith **5½***

GENTLEMAN OF PARIS, A (1927) Paramount. **B&W-65min.** *(Silent).* Adolphe Menjou, Shirley O'Hara **5***

GENTLEMAN TRAMP, THE (1975) RBC Films. **B&W-78min.** *(Documentary). Director:* Richard Patterson .... (5)

GENTLEMAN'S AGREEMENT (1947) 20th Century-Fox. **B&W-118min.** Gregory Peck, Dorothy McGuire **5½***

GENTLEMEN MARRY BRUNETTES (1955) United Artists. **Color-97min.** Jane Russell, Jeanne Crain .... (3)

GENTLEMEN OF THE NIGHT (1963) Paramount. **Color-98min.** *(Italian-French).* Guy Madison, Lisa Gastoni .... (3)
Original Italian title: PIOMBI DI VENEZIA, I *(The Dungeons of Venice)*

GENTLEMEN PREFER BLONDES (1928) Paramount. **B&W-76min.** *(Silent).* Ruth Taylor, Alice White ....

GENTLEMEN PREFER BLONDES (1953) 20th Century-Fox. **Color-91min.** Jane Russell, Marilyn Monroe **5***

GEORDIE (1955) *see* WEE GEORDIE

GEORGE RAFT STORY, THE (1961) Allied Artists. **B&W-106min.** Ray Danton, Jayne Mansfield **4***
British title: SPIN OF A COIN

GEORGE WASHINGTON SLEPT HERE (1942) Warner Bros. **B&W-93min.** Jack Benny, Ann Sheridan .... (4)

GEORGE WHITE'S 1935 SCANDALS (1935) Fox Film Co. [20th]. **B&W-83min.** James Dunn, Alice Faye, Eleanor Powell .... (4)

GEORGE WHITE'S SCANDALS (1934) Fox Film Co. [20th]. **B&W-78min.** Rudy Vallee, Jimmy Durante, Alice Faye .... (4)

GEORGE WHITE'S SCANDALS (1945) RKO. **B&W-95min.** Joan Davis, Jack Haley .... (3)

GEORGIA, GEORGIA (1972) Cinerama Releasing. **Color-91min.** *(U.S.-Swedish).* Diana Sands, Minnie Gentry .... (3)

GEORGY GIRL (1966) Columbia. **B&W-99min.** *(British).* Lynn Redgrave, James Mason **6***

GERALDINE (1954) Republic. **B&W-90min.** John Carroll, Mala Powers .. (3)

GERMANY YEAR ZERO (1947) Superfilm. **B&W-74min.** *(German-French).* Edmund Meschke .... (4)

GERONIMO (1939) Paramount. **B&W-89min.** Preston Foster, Ellen Drew .... (3)

GERONIMO (1962) United Artists. **Color-101min.** *(U.S.-Mexican).* Chuck Connors, Kamala Devi **4***

GERTIE WAS A LADY (1968) *see* STAR!

GERTRUD (1964) Pathé Contemporary. **B&W-120min.** *(Danish).* Nina Pens Rode, Bendt Rothe .... (3)

GERVAISE (1956) Continental [Walter Reade]. **B&W-116min.** *(French).* Maria Schell, Francis Perier .... (5)

GESTAPO (1940) *see* NIGHT TRAIN

GET-AWAY, THE (1941) M-G-M. **B&W-89min.** Robert Sterling, Donna Reed .... (3)

GET CARTER (1971) M-G-M. **Color-111min.** *(British).* Michael Caine, Ian Hendry .... (4)

GET CHARLIE TULLY (1976) T.B.S. Distributing. **Color-97min.** *(British).* Dick Emery, Darren Nesbitt .... (4)

Films are rated on a 1 to 10 scale, 10 is highest. **Boldface** ratings followed by an asterisk (*) are for films actually seen and rated by the executive and senior editors. All other ratings are estimates. (See Notes on Entertainment Ratings in the front section.)

GEORGY GIRL (1966). Plumpish, frumpy Lynn Redgrave is grateful for the generosity of her father's wealthy employer, James Mason, but isn't ready to accept his proposition that she become his mistress.

GET CHRISTIE LOVE! (1974) Wolper Productions. **Color-75min.** *(Made for TV).* Theresa Graves, Harry Guardino **4***

GET DOWN AND BOOGIE (1975) New World. **Color-93min.** Trina Parks, Roger E. Mosley... (3)
Original title: DARKTOWN STRUTTERS

GET HEP TO LOVE (1942) Universal. **B&W-71min.** Gloria Jean, Jane Frazee .... (3)
British title: SHE'S MY LOVELY

GET OFF MY BACK (1965) *see* SYNANON

GET ON WITH IT! (1961) Governor. **B&W-88min.** *(British).* Bob Monkhouse, Kenneth Connor, Shirley Eaton......................... (3)
Original title: DENTIST ON THE JOB
TV title: CARRY ON T.V.

GET OUT YOUR HANDKERCHIEFS (1978) New Line Cinema. **Color-108min.** *(French).* Gerard Depardieu, Carole Laure, Patrick Dewaere **5½***
Original title: PREPAREZ VOS MOUCHOIRS

GET OUTTA TOWN (1960) Sterling World Distributors. **B&W-65min.** Douglas Wilson, Jeanne Baird.. (3)
Alternate title: GANGSTER'S REVENGE

GET TO KNOW YOUR RABBIT (1972) Warner Bros. **Color-91min.** Tom Smothers, Katharine Ross, Orson Welles, John Astin .... (3)

GET YOURSELF A COLLEGE GIRL (1964) M-G-M. **Color-86min.** Mary Ann Mobley, Chad Everett.. **3***
British title: SWINGING SET, THE

GETAWAY, THE (1972) National General. **Color-122min.** Steve McQueen, Ali MacGraw.. **4½***

GETTING AWAY FROM IT ALL (1971) Viacom. **Color-74min.** *(Made for TV).* Barbara Feldon, Larry Hagman, Jim Backus............................ (4)

GETTING GERTIE'S GARTER (1945) United Artists. **B&W-72min.** Marie McDonald, Dennis O'Keefe.................................... **4***

GETTING STRAIGHT (1970) Columbia. **Color-124min.** Elliott Gould, Candice Bergen **5***

GETTING TOGETHER (1976) Total Impact. **Color-110min.** Malcolm Groome, Kathleen Seward .... (3)

GHENGIS KHAN *see* GENGHIS KHAN

GHIDRAH, THE THREE-HEADED MONSTER (1965) Continental [Walter Reade]. **Color-85min.** *(Japanese).* Godzilla, Rodan, Mothra, Ghidrah, Yosuke Natsuki... (2)
Original title: SANDAI KAIJU CHIKYU SAIDAI NO KESSEN
Publicity title: BIGGEST FIGHT ON EARTH, THE
Publicity title: GREATEST BATTLE ON EARTH, THE

GHOST, THE (1963) Magna Pictures. **Color-96min.** *(Italian).* Barbara Steele, Peter Baldwin, Leonard Elliott................................. (2)
Original title: SPETTRO DE DR. HICHCOCK, LO *(The Ghost of Dr. Hichcock)*
Alternate Italian title: SPETTRO, LO
British title(?): SPECTRE, THE

GHOST AND MR. CHICKEN, THE (1966) Universal. **Color-90min.** Don Knotts, Joan Staley.. **4***

GHOST AND MRS. MUIR, THE (1947) 20th Century-Fox. **B&W-104min.** Gene Tierney, Rex Harrison............................. **5***

GHOST BREAKERS, THE (1940) Paramount. **B&W-82min.** Bob Hope, Paulette Goddard.. **5***

GHOST CATCHERS (1944) Universal. **B&W-67min.** Ole Olsen, Chic Johnson, Gloria Jean.. (4)

GHOST CHASERS (1951) Monogram [Allied Artists]. **B&W-69min.** The Bowery Boys, Lloyd Corrigan.................................. **3***

GHOST COMES HOME, THE (1940) M-G-M. **B&W-79min.** Frank Morgan, Billie Burke... (3)

GHOST CREEPS, THE (1940) *see* BOYS OF THE CITY

GHOST DIVER (1957) 20th Century-Fox. **B&W-76min.** James Craig, Audrey Totter.. (3)

GHOST GOES WEST, THE (1935) United Artists. **B&W-78min.** *(British).* Robert Donat.. (5)

GHOST IN THE INVISIBLE BIKINI (1966) American-International. **Color-82min.** Tommy Kirk, Boris Karloff, Basil Rathbone, Susan Hart **2***

GHOST OF DRAGSTRIP HOLLOW, THE (1959) American-International. **B&W-65min.** Jody Fair, Martin Braddock **3***

GHOST OF FRANKENSTEIN, THE (1942) Universal. **B&W-68min.** Lon Chaney (Jr.), Cedric Hardwicke................................ (4)

GHOST OF THE CHINA SEA (1958) Columbia. **B&W-79min.** David Brian, Lynn Bernay.. (3)

GHOST OF ZORRO (1949) Republic. **B&W-69min.** *(Re-edited Serial).* Clayton Moore, Pamela Blake.................................... (3)

GHOST SHIP, THE (1943) RKO. **B&W-69min.** Richard Dix, Russell Wade .... (5)

GHOST SHIP (1952) Lippert Productions. **B&W-69min.** *(British).* Dermot Walsh, Hazel Court.. (3)

GHOST TOWN (1956) United Artists. **B&W-75min.** Kent Taylor, Marian Carr .... (3)

GHOST TRAIN, THE (1941) General Film *(British).* **B&W-85min.** *(British).* Arthur Askey, Richard Murdoch..............................

GHOSTS IN THE NIGHT (1943) *see* GHOSTS ON THE LOOSE

GHOSTS - ITALIAN STYLE (1967) M-G-M. **Color-92min.** *(Italian-French, English language).* Sophia Loren, Vittorio Gassman **3***
Original Italian title: QUESTI FANTASMI *(These Ghosts)*

GHOSTS OF BERKELEY SQUARE (1947) NTA Pictures. **B&W-90min.** *(British).* Robert Morley, Felix Aylmer.................... (4)

GHOSTS OF ROME (1960) Teleworld. **Color-105min.** *(Italian).* Marcello Mastroianni, Sandra Milo, Vittorio Gassman......................... **4***
Original title: FANTASMI A ROMA
British title: PHANTOM LOVERS
Screen title(?): GHOSTS IN ROME

GHOSTS ON THE LOOSE (1943) Monogram [Allied Artists]. **B&W-65min.** Bela Lugosi, Ava Gardner, The East Side Kids **3***
British title: GHOSTS IN THE NIGHT

GHOUL, THE (1933) Gaumont-British [Rank]. **B&W-85min.** *(British).* Boris Karloff, Cedric Hardwicke, Ernest Thesiger .... (4)

GHOUL, THE (1975) J. Arthur Rank. **Color-88min.** *(British).* Peter Cushing, John Hurt.. (3)

GHOUL IN SCHOOL, THE (1962) *see* WEREWOLF IN A GIRLS' DORMITORY

GIANT (1956) Warner Bros. **Color-198min.** Elizabeth Taylor, Rock Hudson.. **6***

GIANT BEHEMOTH, THE (1959) Allied Artists. **B&W-79min.** *(British).* Gene Evans, André Morell...................................... (3)
Original title: BEHEMOTH THE SEA MONSTER

GIANT CLAW, THE (1957) Columbia. **B&W-76min.** Jeff Morrow, Mara Corday **2***

GIANT FROM THE UNKNOWN (1958) Astor. **B&W-80min.** Ed Kemmer, Sally Fraser, Buddy Baer **2***

GIANT GILA MONSTER, THE (1959) McLendon. **B&W-74min.** Don Sullivan, Lisa Simone.. **2***

GIANT LEECHES, THE (1959) *see* ATTACK OF THE GIANT LEECHES

GIANT MONSTER (1960) *see* NIGHT THEY KILLED RASPUTIN, THE

GIANT OF MARATHON, THE (1959) M-G-M. **Color-92min.** *(Italian).* Steve Reeves, Mylene Demongeot.......................... (3)
Original Italian title: BATTAGLIA DI MARATONA, LA *(The Battle of Marathon)*

GIANT OF METROPOLIS, THE (1961) Warner Bros. **Color-92min.** (*Italian*). Gordon Mitchell, Roldano Lupi .... (2)
Original title: GIGANTE DI METROPOLIS, IL

GIANT OF THE EVIL ISLAND (1965) Romana Films. **Color-80min.** (*Italian*). Rock Stevens, Dina DeSantis.......................... (1)
Original title: MISTERO DELL' ISOLA MALETESTA, IL (*The Mystery of the Evil Island*)

GIANT SPIDER INVASION, THE (1975) Group 1. **Color-103min.** Steve Brodie, Barbara Hale, Robert Easton 3*

GIANTS OF THESSALY, THE (1960) Telewide Systems. **Color-86min.** (*Italian*). Roland Carey, Ziva Rodann .... (3)
Original Italian title: GIGANTI DELLA TESSAGLIA, I
French title: GÉANT DE THESSALIE, LE
Alternate title: ARGONAUTS, THE
Alternate title: JASON AND THE GOLDEN FLEECE

GIDEON OF SCOTLAND YARD (1958) Columbia. **Color-91min.** (*British*). Jack Hawkins, Anna Lee .... (4)
Original title: GIDEON'S DAY

GIDEON'S DAY (1958) *see* GIDEON OF SCOTLAND YARD

GIDGET (1959) Columbia. **Color-95min.** Sandra Dee, James Darren 3*

GIDGET GETS MARRIED (1972) CPT (TV). **Color-73min.** (*Made for TV*). Monie Ellis, Michael Burns, Paul Lynde, Macdonald Carey 3*

GIDGET GOES HAWAIIAN (1961) Columbia. **Color-102min.** Deborah Walley, James Darren 3*

GIDGET GOES TO ROME (1963) Columbia. **Color-101min.** Cindy Carol, James Darren .... (3)

GIDGET GROWS UP (1969) Screen Gems. **Color-75min.** (*Made for TV*). Karen Valentine, Paul Peterson, Robert Cummings 4*

GIFT (1966) *see* VENOM

GIFT FOR HEIDI, A (1958) RKO. **Color-71min.** Sandy Descher, Douglas Fowley.. (3)

GIFT HORSE, THE (1952) *see* GLORY AT SEA

GIFT OF LOVE, THE (1958) 20th Century-Fox. **Color-105min.** Lauren Bacall, Robert Stack .... (4)

GIFT OF LOVE, THE (1978) ABC-TV. **Color-98min.** (*Made for TV*). Marie Osmond, Timothy Bottoms ....

GIFT OF THE MAGI (1978) NBC-TV. **Color-74min.** (*Made for TV*). Debby Boone, John Rubinstein...................................

GIGANTIS, THE FIRE MONSTER (1955) Warner Bros. **B&W-78min.** (*Japanese*). Hiroshi Koizumi, Yuko Kasama, Godzilla, Angorus........... (3)
Original title: GOJIRA NO GYAKUSHU (*Godzilla's Counterattack*)
Publicity title: GODZILLA RAIDS AGAIN
Publicity title: COUNTER-ATTACK OF THE MONSTER

GIGI (1948) Spalter International. **B&W-85min.** (*French*). Daniele Delorme, Franck Villard .... (5)

GIGI (1958) M-G-M. **Color-116min.** Leslie Caron, Maurice Chevalier, Louis Jourdan.. 6*

GIGOT (1962) 20th Century-Fox. **Color-104min.** Jackie Gleason, Katherine Kath 6*

GILBERT AND SULLIVAN (1953) United Artists. **Color-109min.** (*British*). Robert Morley, Maurice Evans...................... (6)
Original title: STORY OF GILBERT AND SULLIVAN, THE
Alternate title: GREAT GILBERT AND SULLIVAN, THE

GILDA (1946) Columbia. **B&W-110min.** Rita Hayworth, Glenn Ford 4½*

GILDED LILY, THE (1935) Paramount. **B&W-80min.** Claudette Colbert, Fred MacMurray .... (5)

GILDERSLEEVE'S GHOST (1944) RKO. **B&W-64min.** Harold Peary, Marion Martin .... (3)

GIMME SHELTER (1971) Cinema 5. **Color-91min.** (*Documentary*). *Director:* David Maysles. 4*

GINA (1956) Sutton Pictures. **Color-90min.** (*French-Mexican*). Simone Signoret, Michel Piccoli, Georges Marchal .... (3)
Original French title: MORT EN CE JARDIN, LA (*Death in This Garden*)
Original Mexican title: MUERTE EN ESTE JARDIN, LA

GINGER (1971) Joseph Brenner. **Color-102min.** Cheri Caffaro, William Grannell .... (2)

GINGER IN THE MORNING (1973) National Film. **Color-92min.** Sissy Spacek, Monte Markham, Mark Miller, Susan Oliver 4*

GIRL, A GUY, AND A GOB, A (1941) RKO. **B&W-91min.** George Murphy, Lucille Ball .... (4)
British title: NAVY STEPS OUT, THE

GIRL AGAINST NAPOLEON, A (1959) *see* DEVIL MADE A WOMAN, THE

GIRL AND THE GENERAL, THE (1967) M-G-M. **Color-105min.** (*Italian-French*). Rod Steiger, Virna Lisi .... (4)
Original Italian title: RAGAZZE E IL GENERALE, LA

GIRL AND THE LEGEND, THE (1962) **Color-90min.** (*German*). Romy Schneider, Horst Buchholz.................................... (3)
Original title: ROBINSON SOLL NICHT STERBEN

GIRL AND THE RIVER, THE (1958) Continental [Walter Reade]. **B&W-98min.** (*French*). Pascale Audret, Andrée Desbar .... (3)

GIRL CAN'T HELP IT, THE (1956) 20th Century-Fox. **Color-99min.** Tom Ewell, Jayne Mansfield .... (4)

GIRL CRAZY (1943) M-G-M. **B&W-99min.** Mickey Rooney, Judy Garland... 4*

GIRL CRAZY (1965) *see* WHEN THE BOYS MEET THE GIRLS

GIRL FRIENDS (1978) Warner Bros. **Color-86min.** Melanie Mayron, Anita Skinner.. 4*

GIRL FROM AVENUE A (1940) 20th Century-Fox. **B&W-73min.** Jane Withers, Elyse Knox...................................... (3)

GIRL FROM FLANDERS, THE (1956) Screen Gems. **B&W-105min.** (*German*). Maximillian Schell, Nicole Berger..................... (3)
Original title: MAEDCHEN AUS FLANDERN, EIN

GIRL FROM HAVANA (1940) Republic. **B&W-69min.** Dennis O'Keefe, Claire Carleton .... (3)

GIRL FROM HONG KONG, THE (1961) NTA Pictures. **Color-95min.** (*German*). Akiko, Helmut Griem............................ (3)
Original title: BIS ZUM ENDE ALLER TAGE

GIRL FROM JONES BEACH, THE (1949) Warner Bros. **B&W-78min.** Ronald Reagan, Virginia Mayo.................................. (4)

GIRL FROM MANHATTAN, THE (1948) United Artists. **B&W-81min.** Dorothy Lamour, Charles Laughton.............................. (3)

GIRL FROM MISSOURI, THE (1934) M-G-M. **B&W-75min.** Jean Harlow, Franchot Tone... 4*
British title: 100 PER CENT PURE

GIRL FROM PETROVKA, THE (1974) Universal. **Color-103min.** Goldie Hawn, Hal Holbrook....................................... 4*

GIRL FROM 10th AVENUE, THE (1935) First National [W.B.]. **B&W-69min.** Bette Davis, Ian Hunter.................................. (4)
British title: MEN ON HER MIND

GIRL FROM TEXAS, THE (1948) *see* TEXAS, BROOKLYN AND HEAVEN

GIRL GETTERS, THE (1964) American-International. **B&W-93min.** (*British*). Oliver Reed, Jane Merrow .... (5)
Original title: SYSTEM, THE

GIRL HAPPY (1965) M-G-M. **Color-96min.** Elvis Presley, Shelley Fabares... (4)

GIRL HE LEFT BEHIND, THE (1956) Warner Bros. **B&W-103min.** Tab Hunter, Natalie Wood .... (4)

GIRL HUNTERS, THE (1963) Colorama Features. **B&W-97min.** (*British*). Mickey Spillane, Shirley Eaton, Lloyd Nolan .... (4)

GIRL IN A MILLION, A (1945) Distinguished Films. **B&W-81min.** (*British*). Hugh Williams, Joan Greenwood .... (3)

GIRL IN BLACK, A (1955) Kingsley International. **B&W-104min.** (*Greek*). Elle Lambetti, Dimitri Horn.................................. (5)
Original title: KORITSI ME TA MAVRO, TO

GIRL IN BLACK STOCKINGS, THE (1957) United Artists. **B&W-73min.** Lex Barker, Anne Bancroft.................................... (4)

GIRL IN BLUE, THE (1974) Cinerama Releasing. **Color-103min.** (*Canadian*). David Selby, Maud Adams .... (4)

GIRL IN EVERY PORT, A (1952) RKO. **B&W-86min.** Groucho Marx, Marie Wilson, William Bendix.............................. (3)

GIRL IN HIS POCKET (1957) Medeleine Films. **B&W-82min.** (*French*). Jean Marais, Agnes Laurent .... (4)
Original title: AMOUR DE POCHE, UN (*A Pocket Love*)
Alternate title: NUDE IN HIS POCKET

GIRL IN LOVER'S LANE, THE (1960) Futuramic. **B&W-80min.** Joyce Meadows, Brett Halsey .... (2)

GIRL IN OVERALLS, THE (1943) *see* SWING SHIFT MAISIE

GIRL IN PAWN (1934) *see* LITTLE MISS MARKER

GIRL IN ROOM 13, THE (1961) Astor. **B&W-97min.** Brian Donlevy, Andrea Bayard .... (2)

GIRL IN ROOM 17, THE (1953) *see* VICE SQUAD

GIRL IN THE BIKINI, THE (1952) Atlantis Films. **B&W-76min.** (*French*). Brigitte Bardot, Jean-Francois Calvé .... (3)
Original title: MANINA, LA FILLE SANS VOILE (*Manina, the Girl Without a Veil*)
British title: LIGHTHOUSE KEEPER'S DAUGHTER, THE

GIRL IN THE CASE (1944) Columbia. **B&W-64min.** Edmund Lowe, Janice Carter.. (3)
British title: SILVER KEY, THE

GIRL IN THE KREMLIN, THE (1957) Universal. **B&W-81min.** Zsa Zsa Gabor, Lex Barker............(3)

GIRL IN THE MIST, A (1955) Toho. **B&W-44min.** *(Japanese).* Yoku Tsukasa, Hitomi Nakahara............(4)

GIRL IN THE MOON (1929) *see* WOMAN IN THE MOON

GIRL IN THE NEWS (1940) 20th Century-Fox. **B&W-78min.** *(British).* Margaret Lockwood, Barry K. Barnes............(4)

GIRL IN THE PAINTING, THE (1948) *see* PORTRAIT FROM LIFE

GIRL IN THE RED VELVET SWING, THE (1955) 20th Century-Fox. **Color-109min.** Ray Milland, Joan Collins............(4)

GIRL IN THE WOODS (1958) Republic. **B&W-71min.** Forrest Tucker, Maggie Hayes............(3)

GIRL IN WHITE, THE (1952) M-G-M. **B&W-93min.** June Allyson, Arthur Kennedy............(4)
British title: SO BRIGHT THE FLAME

GIRL MOST LIKELY, THE (1958) Universal. **Color-98min.** Jane Powell, Cliff Robertson............**4½***

GIRL MOST LIKELY TO . . ., THE (1973) Worldvision. **Color-75min.** *(Made for TV).* Stockard Channing, Warren Berlinger, Edward Asner............**6***

GIRL NAMED TAMIKO, A (1963) Paramount. **Color-110min.** Laurence Harvey, France Nuyen............**4***

GIRL NEXT DOOR, THE (1953) 20th Century-Fox. **Color-92min.** June Haver, Dan Dailey............(4)

GIRL OF THE GOLDEN WEST, THE (1938) M-G-M. **B&W-120min.** Jeanette MacDonald, Nelson Eddy............(4)

GIRL OF THE LIMBERLOST (1945) Columbia. **B&W-60min.** Ruth Nelson, Dorinda Clifton............**3***

GIRL OF THE NIGHT (1960) Warner Bros. **B&W-93min.** Anne Francis, Lloyd Nolan............(3)

GIRL OF THE YEAR (1950) *see* PETTY GIRL, THE

GIRL ON A MOTORCYCLE, THE (1968) Claridge. **Color-91min.** *(British-French).* Alain Delon, Marianne Faithfull............(2)
Original French title: MOTOCYCLETTE, LA
Alternate title: NAKED UNDER LEATHER

GIRL ON APPROVAL (1962) Continental [Walter Reade]. **B&W-75min.** *(British).* Rachel Roberts, James Maxwell, Annette Whitely............(3)

GIRL ON THE BRIDGE, THE (1951) 20th Century-Fox. **B&W-77min.** Hugo Haas, Beverly Michaels............(2)

GIRL RUSH (1944) RKO. **B&W-65min.** Wally Brown, Alan Carney, Frances Langford............(3)

GIRL RUSH, THE (1955) Paramount. **Color-85min.** Rosalind Russell, Fernando Lamas............**3½***

GIRL SWAPPERS, THE (1962) *see* TWO AND TWO MAKE SIX

GIRL TROUBLE (1942) 20th Century-Fox. **B&W-82min.** Don Ameche, Joan Bennett............(3)

GIRL WAS YOUNG, THE (1937) *see* YOUNG AND INNOCENT

GIRL WHO CAME GIFT WRAPPED, THE (1974) MPC (TV). **Color-74min.** *(Made for TV).* Richard Long, Karen Valentine............**4***

GIRL WHO COULDN'T SAY NO, THE (1969) 20th Century-Fox. **Color-83min.** *(Italian, English version).* Virna Lisi, George Segal, Lila Kedrova, Akim Tamiroff............(2)
Original title: TENDERLY
Alternate Italian title: SUO MODO DI FARE, IL

GIRL WHO DARED, THE (1944) Republic. **B&W-56min.** Lorna Gray, Peter Cookson, Kirk Alyn............(3)

GIRL WHO HAD EVERYTHING, THE (1953) M-G-M. **B&W-69min.** Elizabeth Taylor, Fernando Lamas, William Powell............(3)

GIRL WHO KNEW TOO MUCH, THE (1969) Commonwealth United. **Color-96min.** Adam West, Nancy Kwan............(2)

GIRL WITH A SUITCASE, THE (1961) Ellis Films. **B&W-108min.** *(Italian).* Claudia Cardinale, Jacques Perrin............(5)
Original title: RAGAZZA CON LA VALIGIA, LA
Alternate title: PLEASURE GIRL

GIRL WITH GOLDEN HAIR, THE (1952) *see* CASQUE D'OR

GIRL WITH GREEN EYES (1964) Lopert [U.A.]. **B&W-91min.** *(British).* Rita Tushingham, Peter Finch............**4***

GIRL WITH THE GOLDEN EYES, THE (1961) Kingsley International. **B&W-90min.** *(French).* Marie Laforet, Paul Guers............(4)
Original title: FILLE AUX YEUX D'OR, LA

GIRL WITH THREE CAMELS, THE (1967) Continental [Walter Reade]. **B&W-98min.** *(Czech).* Zuzana Ondrouchova, Slavka Budinova............(5)
Original title: DIVKA S TREMI VELBLOUDY

GIRLFRIENDS, THE (1968) *see* BICHES, LES

GIRLS, LES (1957) *see* LES GIRLS

GIRLS, THE (1968) New Line Cinema. **B&W-100min.** *(Swedish).* Bibi Andersson, Harriet Andersson............**3***
Original title: FLICKORNA

GIRLS ARE FOR LOVING (1973) Continental Releasing. **Color-95min.** Cheri Caffaro, Timothy Brown............(3)

GIRLS AT SEA (1958) Warner Bros. **Color-80min.** *(British).* Guy Rolfe, Anne Kimbell, Mary Steele............(3)

GIRLS' DORMITORY (1936) 20th Century-Fox. **B&W-66min.** Herbert Marshall, Simone Simon............(4)

GIRLS! GIRLS! GIRLS! (1962) Paramount. **Color-106min.** Elvis Presley, Stella Stevens............**4***

GIRLS HE LEFT BEHIND, THE (1943) *see* GANG'S ALL HERE, THE

GIRLS IN ACTION (1958) *see* OPERATION DAMES

GIRLS IN PRISON (1956) American-International. **B&W-87min.** Richard Denning, Joan Taylor............(3)

GIRLS IN THE NIGHT (1953) Universal. **B&W-83min.** Joyce Holden, Glenda Farrell............(3)
British title: LIFE AFTER DARK

GIRLS IN UNIFORM (1931) *see* MAEDCHEN IN UNIFORM

GIRLS MOST LIKELY TO, THE (1972) *see* CLASS OF '74, THE

GIRLS NEVER TELL (1951) *see* HER FIRST ROMANCE

GIRLS OF HUNTINGTON HOUSE, THE (1973) Viacom. **Color-74min.** *(Made for TV).* Shirley Jones, Mercedes McCambridge, Sissy Spacek, William Windom............(4)

GIRLS OF PLEASURE ISLAND, THE (1953) Paramount. **Color-95min.** Leo Genn, Abby Dalton............**4***

GIRLS OF SPIDER ISLAND (1960) *see* IT'S HOT IN PARADISE

GIRLS OF THE NIGHT (1957) Continental [Walter Reade]. **B&W-114min.** *(French).* Georges Marchal, Nicole Berger............(3)
Original title: FILLES DE NUIT

GIRLS ON THE BEACH (1965) Paramount. **Color-80min.** Noreen Corcoran, Martin West, The Beach Boys............(2)

GIRLS ON THE LOOSE (1958) Universal. **B&W-78min.** Mara Corday, Mark Richmond............(3)

GIRLS' SCHOOL (1938) Columbia. **B&W-73min.** Ann Shirley, Ralph Bellamy............(4)

GIRLS' SCHOOL (1950) Columbia. **B&W-62min.** Joyce Reynolds, Ross Ford............(2)
British title: DANGEROUS INHERITANCE

GIRLS' TOWN (1959) M-G-M. **B&W-92min.** Mel Tormé, Mamie Van Doren............(2)

GIRLY (1970) Cinerama Releasing. **Color-101min.** *(British).* Ursula Howells, Pat Heywood, Michael Bryant............(3)
Original title: MUMSY, NANNY, SONNY AND GIRLY

GIT! (1965) Avco-Embassy. **Color-90min.** Jack Chaplian, Heather North, Seldom-Seen Sioux............**3***

GIUSEPPE VERDI (1953) Citation. **Color-105min.** *(Italian).* Pierre Cressoy, Anna Maria Ferraro............(3)

GIVE A GIRL A BREAK (1954) M-G-M. **Color-82min.** Marge and Gower Champion, Debbie Reynolds............(4)

GIVE 'EM HELL (1955) *see* THERE GOES BARDER

GIVE 'EM HELL, HARRY! (1975) Theatre Television Inc. **Color-102min.** James Whitmore............**6½***

GIVE HER THE MOON (1970) United Artists. **Color-92min.** *(French-Italian).* Marthe Keller, Bert Convy............(5)
Original French title: CAPRICES DE MARIE, LES *(The Caprices of Marie)*

GIVE ME A SAILOR (1938) Paramount. **B&W-80min.** Martha Raye, Bob Hope............(4)

GIVE ME YOUR HEART (1936) Warner Bros. **B&W-87min.** Kay Francis, George Brent............**3***
British title: SWEET ALOES
Alternate title: I GIVE MY HEART

GIVE MY REGARDS TO BROADWAY (1948) 20th Century-Fox. **Color-89min.** Dan Dailey, Charlie Winninger............**4***

GIVE US THIS DAY (1949) *see* SALT TO THE DEVIL

GIVE US WINGS (1940) Universal. **B&W-62min.** The Dead End Kids, Wallace Ford............(4)

GIVEN WORD, THE (1962) Lionex. **B&W-98min.** *(Brazilian).* Leonardo Vilar, Gloria Menezes............(5)
Original title: PAGADOR DE PROMESSAS, O

GIZMO (1977) New Line Cinema. **Color-79min.** *(Documentary).* Director: Howard Smith............(4)

Films are rated on a 1 to 10 scale, 10 is highest. **Boldface** ratings followed by an asterisk (*) are for films actually seen and rated by the executive and senior editors. All other ratings are estimates. (See Notes on Entertainment Ratings in the front section.)

GIVE 'EM HELL, HARRY (1975). James Whitmore is a lively one-man show as he portrays sharp-tongued, cantankerous President Harry S Truman.

GLACIER FOX, THE (1978) Sanrio. **Color-89min.** *(Japanese).* Arthur Hill 4½*

GLADIATOR, THE (1938) Columbia. **B&W-70min.** Joe E. Brown, June Travis .... (4)

GLADIATOR OF ROME (1962) Telewide Systems. **Color-100min.** *(Italian).* Gordon Scott, Wandisa Guida .... (3)
Original title: GLADIATORE DI ROMA, IL
Alternate title: BATTLES OF THE GLADIATORS

GLADIATORS SEVEN (1964) M-G-M. **Color-92min.** *(Italian-Spanish).* Richard Harrison, Loredana Nusciak .... (3)
Original Italian title: SETTE GLADIATORI, I
Original Spanish title: SIETE ESPARTANOS, LOS *(The Seven Spartans)*

GLAMOUR BOY (1940) *see* MILLIONAIRE PLAYBOY

GLAMOUR BOY (1941) Paramount. **B&W-80min.** Jackie Cooper, Walter Abel .... (4)
British title: HEARTS IN SPRINGTIME

GLAMOUR FOR SALE (1940) Columbia. **B&W-57min.** Anita Louise, Roger Pryor .... (3)

GLASS ALIBI, THE (1946) Republic. **B&W-70min.** Paul Kelly, Anne Gwynne .... (4)

GLASS BOTTOM BOAT, THE (1966) M-G-M. **Color-110min.** Doris Day, Rod Taylor 4*

GLASS CAGE, THE (1955) *see* GLASS TOMB, THE

GLASS CAGE, THE (1964) Futuramic. **B&W-78min.** Arline Sax, John Hoyt .... (3)
Alternate title: DEN OF DOOM
Alternate title(?): DON'T TOUCH MY SISTER
Alternate title(?): BED OF FIRE

GLASS HOUSE, THE (1972) Viacom. **Color-92min.** *(Made for TV).* Alan Alda, Clu Gulager, Vic Morrow .... (5)

GLASS HOUSES (1971) Columbia. **Color-90min.** Bernard Barrow, Jennifer O'Neill .... (2)

GLASS KEY, THE (1935) Paramount. **B&W-77min.** George Raft, Edward Arnold .... (5)

GLASS KEY, THE (1942) Paramount. **B&W-85min.** Brian Donlevy, Veronica Lake, Alan Ladd 4*

GLASS MENAGERIE, THE (1950) Warner Bros. **B&W-107min.** Jane Wyman, Kirk Douglas 5*

GLASS MENAGERIE, THE (1973) ABC-TV. **Color-100min.** *(British-U.S., Made for TV).* Katherine Hepburn, Sam Waterston, Joanna Miles, Michael Moriarty

GLASS MOUNTAIN, THE (1948) Eagle Lion. **B&W-94min.** *(British).* Valentina Cortesa, Michael Denison 4*

GLASS SLIPPER, THE (1955) M-G-M. **Color-94min.** Leslie Caron, Michael Wilding .... (5)

GLASS SPHINX, THE (1967) American-International. **Color-91min.** *(Spanish-Italian-Egyptian).* Robert Taylor, Anita Ekberg, Gianna Serra .... (3)
Original Spanish title: ESFINGE DE CRISTAL, LA *(The Crystal Sphinx)*
Italian title: SFINGE D'ORO, LA *(The Golden Sphinx)*
Alternate Italian title: SFINGE TUTTA D'ORO, UNA *(An All-Golden Sphinx)*

GLASS TOMB, THE (1955) Lippert Productions. **B&W-59min.** *(British).* John Ireland, Honor Blackman .... (4)
Original title: GLASS CAGE, THE

GLASS TOWER, THE (1957) Ellis Films. **B&W-104min.** *(German).* Lilli Palmer, O. E. Hasse, Peter Van Eyck .... (3)
Original title: GLAESERNE TURM, DER

GLASS WALL, THE (1953) Columbia. **B&W-82min.** Vittorio Gassman, Gloria Grahame .... (4)

GLASS WEB, THE (1953) Universal. **B&W-81min.** Edward G. Robinson, John Forsythe 4½*

GLEN AND RANDA (1971) UMC Pictures. **Color-94min.** Steven Curry, Shelley Plimpton .... (2)

GLENN MILLER STORY, THE (1954) Universal. **Color-116min.** James Stewart, June Allyson 4*

GLOBAL AFFAIR, A (1964) M-G-M. **B&W-84min.** Bob Hope, Lilo Pulver .... (3)

GLORIFYING THE AMERICAN GIRL (1929) Paramount. **B&W-86min.** Mary Eaton, Edward Crandall 2*

GLORIOUS AVENGER (1950) United Artists. **Color-105min.** *(Italian).* Armando Franicoli, Vittorio Sanipoli .... (3)

GLORY (1956) RKO. **Color-100min.** Walter Brennan, Margaret O'Brien 3½*

GLORY ALLEY (1952) M-G-M. **B&W-79min.** Leslie Caron, Ralph Meeker 4*

GLORY AT SEA (1952) M & A Alexander. **B&W-88min.** *(British).* Trevor Howard, Richard Attenborough, Sonny Tufts 3*
Original title: GIFT HORSE, THE

GLORY BOY (1971) Cinerama Releasing. **Color-93min.** Arthur Kennedy, Mitchell Ryan, William Devane, Michael Moriarty .... (4)
British title: MY OLD MAN'S PLACE

GLORY BRIGADE, THE (1953) 20th Century-Fox. **B&W-82min.** Victor Mature, Alexander Scourby .... (4)

GLORY GUYS, THE (1965) United Artists. **Color-112min.** Tom Tryon, Harve Presnell, James Caan .... (3)

GLORY STOMPERS, THE (1967) American-International. **Color-85min.** Dennis Hopper, Jody McCrea, Jock Mahoney .... (2)

GNOME-MOBILE, THE (1967) Buena Vista. **Color-90min.** Walter Brennan, Matthew Garber, Karen Dotrice .... (5)

GO ASK ALICE (1972) MPC (TV). **Color-74min.** *(Made for TV).* Jamie Smith Jackson, William Shatner, Andy Griffith 4*

GO-BETWEEN, THE (1971) Columbia. **Color-116min.** *(British).* Julie Christie, Alan Bates 4*

GO FOR BROKE (1951) M-G-M. **B&W-92min.** Van Johnson, Lane Nakano 4*

GO FOR IT (1976) World Entertainment. **Color-96min.** *(Documentary).* *Director:* Paul Rapp 4*

GO GETTER, THE (1937) Warner Bros. **B&W-92min.** George Brent, Anita Louise .... (4)

GO GO MANIA (1965) American-International. **Color-70min.** *(British, Music Film).* *Director:* Frederic Goode .... (3)
Original title: POP GEAR

Films are rated on a 1 to 10 scale, 10 is highest. **Boldface** ratings followed by an asterisk (*) are for films actually seen and rated by the executive and senior editors. All other ratings are estimates. (See Notes on Entertainment Ratings in the front section.)

GO INTO YOUR DANCE (1935) First National [W.B.]. **B&W-89min.** Al Jolson, Ruby Keeler .... (5)
British title: CASINO DE PAREE

GO, JOHNNY, GO! (1958) Valiant. **B&W-75min.** Jimmy Clanton, Sandy Stewart, Chuck Berry .... (3)

GO, MAN, GO! (1954) United Artists. **B&W-82min.** Dane Clark, Pat Breslin .... (4)

GO NAKED IN THE WORLD (1961) M-G-M. **Color-103min.** Gina Lollobrigida, Anthony Franciosa 4*

GO TELL THE SPARTANS (1978) Avco-Embassy. **Color-114min.** Burt Lancaster, Craig Wasson 4*

GO WEST (1925) M-G-M. **B&W-68min.** *(Silent).* Buster Keaton, Kathleen Myers 4½*

GO WEST (1940) M-G-M. **B&W-81min.** Groucho Marx, Chico Marx 4*
British title: MARX BROTHERS GO WEST, THE

GO WEST, YOUNG LADY (1941) Columbia. **B&W-70min.** Glenn Ford, Ann Miller .... (4)

GO WEST, YOUNG MAN (1936) Paramount. **B&W-82min.** Mae West, Warren William 4*

GOAL! (1966) Royal Films Int'l [Columbia]. **Color-107min.** *(British-Liechtensteinian, Documentary). Director:* Abidine Dino .... (5)
British title: GOAL! WORLD CUP 1966

GOALIE'S ANXIETY AT THE PENALTY KICK, THE (1971) Bauer International. **Color-101min.** *(German).* Arthur Brauss, Kai Fischer ......
Original title: ANGST DES TORMANNS BIEN ELFMETER
British title: GOALKEEPER'S FEAR OF THE PENALTY, THE

GOAT, THE (1921) Metro. **B&W-20min.** *(Silent).* Buster Keaton, Virginia Fox, Mal St. Clair 6*

GOAT HORN, THE (1972) Filmbulgaria. **B&W-105min.** *(Bulgarian).* Katia Paskaleva, Anton Gortchev, Milene Penev .... (5)
Original title: KOZUU POS
Alternate Bulgarian title: KOZIJAT ROG

GOBS AND GALS (1952) Republic. **B&W-86min.** George and Bert Bernard, Cathy Downs .... (3)
British title: CRUISING CASANOVAS

GOD BLESS THE CHILDREN (1970) *see* PSYCHIATRIST: GOD BLESS THE CHILDREN, THE

GOD FORGIVES - I DON'T (1967) American-International. **Color-97min.** *(Italian-Spanish).* Terence Hill, Frank Wolff .... (2)
Original Italian title: DIO PERDONA -- IO NO
Original Spanish title: TU PERDONAS -- YO NO

GOD GAVE HIM A DOG (1940) *see* BISCUIT EATER, THE

GOD IS MY CO PILOT (1945) Warner Bros. **B&W-90min.** Dennis Morgan, Dane Clark .... (4)

GOD IS MY PARTNER (1957) 20th Century-Fox. **B&W-80min.** Walter Brennan, John Hoyt 3*

GOD TOLD ME TO (1976) *see* DEMON

GODCHILD, THE (1974) ABC-TV. **Color-74min.** *(Made for TV).* Jack Palance, Jack Warden, Keith Carradine ....

GODDESS, THE (1958) Columbia. **B&W-105min.** Kim Stanley, Lloyd Bridges 4½*

GODDESS, THE (1960) *see* DEVI

GODDESS OF LOVE, THE (1957) 20th Century-Fox. **Color-68min.** *(Italian-French).* Belinda Lee, Jacques Sernas .... (2)
Original Italian title: VENERE DE CHERONEA, LA *(The Venus of Cheronea)*

GODFATHER, THE (1972) Paramount. **Color-177min.** Marlon Brando, Al Pacino 8*

GODFATHER OF HARLEM, THE (1973) *see* BLACK CAESAR

GODFATHER PART II, THE (1974) Paramount. **Color-200min.** Al Pacino, Robert De Niro 5½*

GOD'S COUNTRY (1946) Screen Guild [Lippert]. **Color-62min.** Robert Lowery, Helen Gilbert, Buster Keaton .... (3)

GOD'S COUNTRY AND THE WOMAN (1936) Warner Bros. **Color-80min.** George Brent, Beverly Roberts .... (4)

GOD'S LITTLE ACRE (1958) United Artists. **B&W-110min.** Robert Ryan, Aldo Ray 4*

GODSON, THE (1967) Boxoffice International. **Color-92min.** *(French-Italian, English language).* Alain Delon, Nathalie Delon .... (4)
Original title: SAMOURAI, LE *(The Samurai)*

GODSPELL (1973) Columbia. **Color-103min.** 3*

GODZILLA, KING OF THE MONSTERS (1955) Avco-Embassy. **B&W-80min.** *(Japanese).* Raymond Burr, Takashi Shimura 3*
Original title: GOJIRA
British title: GODZILLA

GODZILLA RAIDS AGAIN (1955) *see* GIGANTIS THE FIRE MONSTER

GODZILLA VS. MEGALON (1973) Cinema Shares. **Color-85min.** *(Japanese).* Godzilla, Katshuhiko Sasaki, Hiroyuki Kawase 1*
Original title: GOJIRA TAI MEGALON

GODZILLA VS. THE SEA MONSTER (1966) Toho. **Color-88min.** *(Japanese).* Godzilla, Mothra, Akira Takarada, Toru Watanabe 1*
Original title: NANKAI NO DAI KETTO *(Big Duel in the North Sea)*
British title: EBIRAH, HORROR OF THE DEEP

GODZILLA VS. THE SMOG MONSTER (1972) American-International. **Color-87min.** *(Japanese).* Godzilla, Akira Yamauchi, Toshie Kimura 1*
Original title: GOJIRA TAI HEDORAH *(Godzilla vs. Hedorah)*

GODZILLA VS. THE THING (1964) American-International. **Color-90min.** *(Japanese).* Godzilla, Mothra, Akira Takarada, Yuriko Hoshi 1*
Original title: GOJIRA TAI MOSURA *(Godzilla vs. Mothra)*

GODZILLA'S REVENGE (1969) UPA. **Color-92min.** *(Japanese).* Kenji Sahara, Tomonori Yazaki, Godzilla 1*
Original title: ORU KAIJU DAISHINGEKI

GOG (1954) United Artists. **Color-85min.** Richard Egan, Constance Dowling .... (3)

GOIN' COCONUTS (1978) **Color-93min.** Donny Osmond, Marie Osmond .... (4)

GOIN' DOWN THE ROAD (1970) Chevron. **Color-90min.** *(Canadian).* Doug McGrath, Paul Bradley .... (5)

GOIN' HOME (1976) Prentiss Prods. **Color-97min.** Todd Christiansen, Bernard Triche .... (4)

GOIN' SOUTH (1978) Paramount. **Color-101min.** Jack Nicholson, Mary Steenburgen 5½*

GOIN' TO TOWN (1935) Paramount. **B&W-74min.** Mae West, Paul Cavanaugh .... (4)

GOIN' TO TOWN (1944) RKO. **B&W-69min.** Lum (Chester Lauck), Abner (Norris Goff), Barbara Hale .... (4)

GOING ALL OUT (1973) *see* CORKY

GOING HOLLYWOOD (1933) M-G-M. **B&W-80min.** Bing Crosby, Marion Davies 4*

GOING HOME (1971) M-G-M. **Color-97min.** Robert Mitchum, Brenda Vaccaro, Jan-Michael Vincent .... (4)

GOING HOME (1972) **Color-61min.** *(Documentary). Director:* Adolfas Mekas .... (4)

GOING IN STYLE (1979) Warner Bros. **Color-   min.** George Burns, Art Carney ....

GOING MY WAY (1944) Paramount. **B&W-130min.** Bing Crosby, Barry Fitzgerald 5*

GOING PLACES (1938) Warner Bros. **B&W-84min.** Dick Powell, Anita Louise .... (4)

GOING PLACES (1974) Cinema 5. **Color-117min.** *(French).* Gerard Depardieu, Patrick Dewaere .... (5)
Original title: VALSEUSES, LES *(The Waltzers)*

GOING STEADY (1958) Columbia. **B&W-79min.** Molly Bee, Allan Reed, Jr. .... (3)

GOING TO TOWN (1950) *see* MA AND PA KETTLE GO TO TOWN

GOLD (1974) Allied Artists. **Color-118min.** Roger Moore, Susannah York 5*

GOLD DIGGERS IN PARIS (1938) Warner Bros. **B&W-95min.** Rudy Vallee, Rosemary Lane .... (4)
British title: GAY IMPOSTORS, THE

GOLD DIGGERS OF BROADWAY (1929) Warner Bros. **Color-98min.** Nancy Welford, Conway Tearle .... (4)

GOLD DIGGERS OF 1933 (1933) Warner Bros. **B&W-96min.** Warren William, Joan Blondell 5*

GOLD DIGGERS OF 1935 (1935) First National [W.B.]. **B&W-95min.** Dick Powell, Adolphe Menjou .... (5)

GOLD DIGGERS OF 1937 (1936) First National [W.B.]. **B&W-100min.** Dick Powell, Joan Blondell .... (4)

GOLD EXPRESS, THE (1955) J. Arthur Rank. **B&W-58min.** *(British).* Vernon Gray, Ann Walford .... (3)

GOLD FEVER (1953) Monogram [Allied Artists]. **B&W-63min.** John Calvert, Ralph Morgan .... (3)

GOLD FOR THE CAESARS (1963) M-G-M. **Color-86min.** *(Italian-French).* Jeffrey Hunter, Mylene Demongeot 2½*
Original Italian title: ORO PER I CESARI
Original french title: OR POUR LES CESARS

GOLD IS WHERE YOU FIND IT (1938) Warner Bros. **B&W-90min.** George Brent, Olivia de Havilland .... (4)

GOLD OF NAPLES (1955) Distributors Corp. of America. **B&W-107min.** *(Italian).* Toto, Sophia Loren, Vittorio De Sica, Silvana Mangano........(5)
Original title: ORO DI NAPOLI, L'

GOLD OF THE SEVEN SAINTS (1961) Warner Bros. **B&W-88min.** Clint Walker, Roger Moore .... (3)

GOLD RAIDERS (1951) United Artists. **B&W-56min.** George O'Brien, Sheila Ryan, The Three Stooges .... (3)
British title: STOOGES GO WEST

GOLD RUSH, THE (1925) United Artists. **B&W-95min.** *(Silent).* Charlie Chaplin, Georgia Hale.. 5½*

GOLD RUSH MAISIE (1940) M-G-M. **B&W-82min.** Ann Sothern, Lee Bowman .... (3)

GOLDBERGS, THE (1951) *see* MOLLY

GOLDEN AGE OF COMEDY, THE (1958) Distributors Corp. of America. **B&W-78min.** *(Compilation). Director:* Robert Youngson 4½*

GOLDEN ARROW, THE (1936) First National [W.B.]. **B&W-68min.** Bette Davis, George Brent .... (4)

GOLDEN ARROW, THE (1962) M-G-M. **Color-91min.** *(Italian).* Tab Hunter, Rossana Podesta .... (3)
Original title: FRECCIA D'ORO, LA

GOLDEN BLADE, THE (1953) Universal. **Color-81min.** Rock Hudson, Piper Laurie.. (3)

GOLDEN BOY (1939) Columbia. **B&W-99min.** Barbara Stanwyck, Adolphe Menjou, William Holden 4*

GOLDEN COACH, THE (1952) Italian Films Export. **Color-100min.** *(Italian-French, English language).* Anna Magnani, Duncan Lamont. (5)
Italian title: CAROZZO D'ORO, IL
French title: CAROSSE D'OR, LE
Original Italian title: CAROZZE D'ORO, IL
Publicity title: GOLDEN CARRIAGE, THE

GOLDEN DEMON (1956) Harrison Pictures. **Color-95min.** *(Japanese).* Fujiko Yamamoto, Jun Negami .... (4)
Original title: KONJIKI YASHA

GOLDEN DISC, THE (1958) *see* IN-BETWEEN AGE, THE

GOLDEN EARRINGS (1947) Paramount. **B&W-95min.** Ray Milland, Marlene Dietrich 4*

GOLDEN EYE, THE (1948) Monogram [Allied Artists]. **B&W-69min.** Roland Winters, Mantan Moreland .... (4)

.THE GOLD RUSH (1925). Starvation and bitter cold are among the hardships the Tramp, Charlie Chaplin, must endure as he seeks gold in Alaska, and his troubles have only just begun.

GOLDEN FISH, THE (1959) Columbia. **Color-19min.** *(French).* 5½*
Original title: HISTOIRE D'UN POISSON ROUGE *(Story of a Goldfish [literally: Red Fish])*

GOLDEN GIRL (1951) 20th Century-Fox. **Color-108min.** Mitzi Gaynor, Dale Robertson .... (4)

GOLDEN GLOVES (1939) *see* EX-CHAMP

GOLDEN GLOVES STORY, THE (1950) Eagle Lion. **B&W-76min.** James Dunn, Dewey Martin .... (3)

GOLDEN GODDESS OF RIO BENI (1964) Casino Films. **Color-93min.** *(German).* Pierre Brice, Harald Juhnke .... (3)

GOLDEN HANDS OF KURIGAL (1949) Republic. **B&W-100min.** *(Re-edited Serial).* Kirk Alyn, Rosemary La Planche.................... (3)
Original title: FEDERAL AGENTS VS. CRIME, INC.

GOLDEN HAWK, THE (1952) Columbia. **Color-83min.** Rhonda Fleming, Sterling Hayden .... (3)

GOLDEN HOOFS (1941) 20th Century-Fox. **B&W-67min.** Jane Withers, Charles "Buddy" Rogers .... (4)

GOLDEN HORDE, THE (1951) Universal. **Color-77min.** Ann Blyth, David Farrar .... (3)

GOLDEN HOUR, THE (1941) *see* POT O' GOLD

GOLDEN IDOL, THE (1954) Allied Artists. **B&W-71min.** Johnny Sheffield, Anne Kimbell ....

GOLDEN IVORY (1957) *see* WHITE HUNTRESS

GOLDEN LADY, THE (1979) Target International *(British).* **Color-96min.** *(British).* Christina World, Suzanne Danielle ....

GOLDEN MADONNA, THE (1949) Stratford Pictures. **B&W-88min.** *(British).* Phyllis Calvert, Michael Rennie .... (4)

GOLDEN MARIE (1952) *see* CASQUE D'OR

GOLDEN MASK, THE (1953) United Artists. **Color-88min.** *(British).* Van Heflin, Wanda Hendrix .... (4)
Original title: SOUTH OF ALGIERS

GOLDEN MISTRESS, THE (1954) United Artists. **Color-82min.** John Agar, Rosemarie Bowe.. (4)

GOLDEN NEEDLES (1974) American-International. **Color-93min.** Joe Don Baker, Elizabeth Ashley 4*

GOLDEN PATSY, THE (1962) **B&W-84min.** *(German).* Gert Frobe......... (3)

GOLDEN RENDEZVOUS (1977) J. Arthur Rank. **Color-103min.** Richard Harris, Ann Turkel .... (4)

GOLDEN SALAMANDER, THE (1950) Eagle Lion. **B&W-96min.** *(British).* Trevor Howard, Anouk (Aimée)............................ (5)

GOLDEN TWENTIES, THE (1950) RKO. **B&W-68min.** *(Compilation). Producer:* Richard de Rochemont .... (5)

GOLDEN VOYAGE OF SINBAD, THE (1973) Columbia. **Color-105min.** *(British).* John Phillip Law, Caroline Munro .... (4)

GOLDENGIRL (1979) Avco-Embassy. **Color-104min.** Susan Anton, James Coburn 5*

GOLDENROD (1977) CBS-TV. **Color-100min.** *(Made for TV).* Tony Lo Bianco, Gloria Carlin 4*

GOLDFINGER (1964) United Artists. **Color-109min.** *(British).* Sean Connery, Gert Frobe 5½*

GOLDSTEIN (1965) Altura Films. **B&W-82min.** Lou Gilbert, Ellen Madison.. (3)

GOLDWYN FOLLIES, THE (1938) United Artists. **Color-115min.** Adolphe Menjou, Andrea Leeds 3½*

GOLEM, THE (1914) Hawk. **B&W- min.** *(German, Silent).* Paul Wegener, Henrik Galeen .... (2)
Alternate title: MONSTER OF FATE, THE

GOLEM, THE (1920) UFA *(Ger.).* **B&W-97min.** *(German, Silent).* Paul Wegener, Albert Steinruck 2*
Original title: GOLEM, WIE ER IN DIE WELT KAM, DER *(The Golem, How He Came Into the World)*

GOLEM, THE (1936) United Artists. **B&W-91min.** *(French).* Harry Baur, Ferdinand Hart (the Golem) .... (4)
Original title: GOLEM, LE
British title: LEGEND OF PRAGUE, THE

GOLIATH AGAINST THE GIANTS (1961) Medallion. **Color-90min.** *(Italian-Spanish).* Brad Harris, Gloria Milland, Fernando Rey............ (2)
Original Italian title: GOLIATH CONTRO I GIGANTI
Original Spanish title: GOLIAT CONTRA LOS GIGANTES

GOLIATH AND THE BARBARIANS (1959) American-International. **Color-86min.** *(Italian).* Steve Reeves, Chelo Alonso, Bruce Cabot .... (2)
Original title: TERRORE DEI BARBARI, IL *(The Terror of the Barbarians)*

GOLIATH AND THE DRAGON (1960) American-International. Color-87min. *(Italian-French)*. Mark Forest, Broderick Crawford................(2)
Original Italian title: VENDETTA DE ERCOLE, LA *(The Revenge of Hercules)*

GOLIATH AND THE REBEL SLAVE (1963) Color-86min. *(Italian-French)*. Gordon Scott, Massimo Serrato.....................(3)
Original Italian title: GOLIATH E LA SCHIAVA RIBELLE *(Goliath and the Rebel Slave Girl)*
British title: ARROW OF THE AVENGER

GOLIATH AND THE SINS OF BABYLON (1963) American-International. Color-80min. *(Italian)*. Mark Forest, Eleanora Bianchi.....................(1)
Original Italian title: MACISTE, L'ERO PIU GRANDE DEL MONDO *(Maciste, the World's Greatest Hero)*
Alternate title: SINS OF BABYLON, THE

GOLIATH AND THE VAMPIRES (1961) American-International. Color-92min. *(Italian)*. Gordon Scott, Gianna Maria Canale, Jacques Sernas 2*
Original title: MACISTE CONTRO IL VAMPIRO

GOLIATH AT THE CONQUEST OF DAMASCUS (1964) American-International. Color-86min. *(Italian)*. Rock Stevens, Helga Line.........(1)
Original title: GOLIA ALL CONQUISTA DI BAGDAD *(Goliath at the Conquest of Bagdad)*

GONE ARE THE DAYS! (1963) Trans-Lux Distributing. B&W-97min. Ossie Davis, Ruby Dee..................................5½*
Alternate title: MAN FROM C.O.T.T.O.N., OR: HOW I STOPPED WORRYING AND LEARNED TO LOVE THE BOLL WEEVIL, THE

GONE IN 60 SECONDS (1974) H.B. Halicki International. Color-105min. H. B. Halicki, Marion Busia 4*

GONE TO EARTH (1950) *see* WILD HEART

GONE WITH THE WIND (1939) M-G-M. Color-219min. Vivien Leigh, Clark Gable 7*

GOOD AND THE BAD, THE (1977) Paramount. Color-123min. Marlene Jobert, Jacques Dutronc ....

GOOD COMPANIONS, THE (1933) Gaumont-British [Rank]. B&W-113min. *(British)*. Jessie Matthews, Edmund Gwenn, John Gieulgud (4)

GOOD DAME (1934) Paramount. B&W-74min. Sylvia Sidney, Fredric March..................(4)
British title: GOOD GIRL

GOOD DAY FOR A HANGING (1959) Columbia. Color-85min. Fred MacMurray, Robert Vaughn..................(4)

GOOD DAY FOR FIGHTING, A (1967) *see* CUSTER OF THE WEST

GOOD DIE YOUNG, THE (1954) United Artists. B&W-98min. *(British)*. Laurence Harvey, Gloria Grahame, Richard Basehart ....(4)

GOOD EARTH, THE (1937) M-G-M. B&W-138min. Paul Muni, Luise Rainer..................6*

GOOD FAIRY, THE (1935) Universal. B&W-90min. Margaret Sullavan, Herbert Marshall 4*

GOOD FELLOWS, THE (1943) Paramount. B&W-70min. Cecil Kellaway, Helen Walker ....(3)

GOOD GIRL (1934) *see* GOOD DAME

GOOD GIRLS GO TO PARIS (1939) Columbia. B&W-75min. Melvyn Douglas, Joan Blondell ....(4)

GOOD GUYS ALWAYS WIN, THE (1973) *see* OUTFIT, THE

GOOD GUYS AND THE BAD GUYS, THE (1969) Warner Bros. Color-91min. Robert Mitchum, George Kennedy 4½*

GOOD GUYS WEAR BLACK (1978) American Cinema Releasing, Inc. Color-96min. Chuck Norris, Anne Archer, James Franciscus.............3½*

GOOD HUMOR MAN, THE (1950) Columbia. B&W-79min. Jack Carson, Lola Albright..................4*

GOOD LUCK, MR. YATES (1943) Columbia. B&W-70min. Claire Trevor, Jess Barker..................(3)

GOOD LUCK, MISS WYCKOFF (1979) Bel Air/Gradison Prods. Color-105min. Anne Heywood, Donald Pleasance..................4*

GOOD MORNING, AND GOODBYE! (1968) Eve Releasing Corp. Color-80min. Alaina Capri, Stuart Lancaster, Pat Wright ....(2)
British title: LUST SEEKERS, THE

GOOD MORNING, BOYS (1936) *see* WHERE THERE'S A WILL

GOOD MORNING, DOCTOR (1941) *see* YOU BELONG TO ME

GOOD MORNING, MISS DOVE (1955) 20th Century-Fox. Color-107min. Jennifer Jones, Robert Stack 4*

GOOD NEIGHBOR SAM (1964) Columbia. Color-130min. Jack Lemmon, Romy Schneider ....(5)

GOOD NEWS (1947) M-G-M. Color-95min. June Allyson, Peter Lawford..................4*

GOOD OLD SCHOOL DAYS, THE (1940) *see* THOSE WERE THE DAYS

GOOD SAM (1948) RKO. B&W-113min. Gary Cooper, Ann Sheridan ..4½*

GOOD SOLDIER SCHWEIK, THE (1960) Lionex. B&W-98min. *(German)*. Heinz Ruhmann, Ernst Stankowski ....(5)
Original title: BRAVE SOLDAD SCHWEJK, DER

GOOD, THE BAD AND THE UGLY, THE (1966) United Artists. Color-161min. *(Italian, English language)*. Clint Eastwood, Eli Wallach, Lee Van Cleef 5½*
Original title: BUONO, IL BRUTTO E IL CATTIVE, IL

GOOD TIME GIRL (1948) Film Classics [U.A.]. B&W-81min. *(British)*. Jean Kent, Dennis Price ....(2)

GOOD TIMES (1967) Columbia. Color-91min. Sonny Bono, Cher (Bono) 4*

GOODBYE AGAIN (1961) United Artists. B&W-120min. *(U.S.-French)*. Ingrid Bergman, Yves Montand, Anthony Perkins 4½*
French title: AIMEZ-VOUS BRAHMS?

GOODBYE, CHARLIE (1964) 20th Century-Fox. Color-117min. Debbie Reynolds, Tony Curtis, Pat Boone..................3*

GOODBYE, COLUMBUS (1969) Paramount. Color-105min. Richard Benjamin, Ali MacGraw 5½*

GOODBYE GEMINI (1970) Cinerama Releasing. Color-80min. *(British)*. Judy Geeson, Martin Potter, Michael Redgrave ....(3)

GOODBYE GIRL, THE (1977) Warner Bros. Color-110min. Richard Dreyfuss, Marsha Mason, Quinn Cummings..................7*

GOODBYE, MR. CHIPS (1939) M-G-M. B&W-114min. Robert Donat, Greer Garson 6*

GOODBYE, MR. CHIPS (1969) M-G-M. Color-147min. *(U.S.-British)*. Peter O'Toole, Petula Clark..................5½*

GOODBYE, MY FANCY (1951) Warner Bros. B&W-107min. Joan Crawford, Robert Young 5½*

GOODBYE, MY LADY (1956) Warner Bros. B&W-95min. Walter Brennan, Brandon de Wilde..................(4)
Alternate title: BOY AND THE LAUGHING DOG, THE

GOODNIGHT, MY LOVE (1972) ABC Circle Films. Color-73min. *(Made for TV)*. Richard Boone, Michael Dunn, Barbara Bain..................(5)

GOODBYE, NORMA JEAN (1976) Filmways. Color-95min. *(U.S.-Australian)*. Misty Rowe, Terence Locke..................(4)

GOODBYE RAGGEDY ANN (1971) CBS-TV. Color-75min. *(Made for TV)*. Mia Farrow, Hal Holbrook 2*

GOODBYE TO THE HILL (1970) *see* PADDY

GOODNIGHT SWEETHEART (1944) Republic. B&W-67min. Robert Livingston, Ruth Terry..................(4)

GOOSE AND THE GANDER, THE (1935) Warner Bros. B&W-65min. George Brent, Kay Francis..................(3)

GORATH (1962) Brenco. Color-83min. *(Japanese)*. Ryo Ikebe, Akihiko Hirata 1*
Original title: YOSEI GORASU

GORDON'S WAR (1973) 20th Century-Fox. Color-89min. Paul Winfield, Carl Lee..................(4)

GOODBYE, MR. CHIPS (1939). It's a dismaying hello for "Mr. Chips," played by Robert Donat, on his first day at Brookfield School when headmaster Lyn Harding arrives as the schoolboys are ragging the newcomer.

Films are rated on a 1 to 10 scale, 10 is highest. **Boldface** ratings followed by an asterisk (*) are for films actually seen and rated by the executive and senior editors. All other ratings are estimates. (See Notes on Entertainment Ratings in the front section.)

GORGEOUS HUSSY, THE (1936) M-G-M. B&W-102min. Joan Crawford, Robert Taylor 4*

GORGO (1961) M-G-M. Color-76min. (British). Bill Travers, William Sylvester 3*

GORGON, THE (1964) Columbia. Color-83min. (British). Peter Cushing, Christopher Lee, Barbara Shelley 4½*

GORILLA, THE (1939) 20th Century-Fox. B&W-66min. The Ritz Brothers, Patsy Kelly, Bela Lugosi .... (4)

GORILLA (1944) see NABONGA

GORILLA AT LARGE (1954) 20th Century-Fox. Color-84min. Cameron Mitchell, Lee J. Cobb, Anne Bancroft 3*

GORILLA MAN, THE (1942) Warner Bros. B&W-64min. John Loder, Ruth Ford .... (3)

G.O.R.P.* (1979) American-International. Color- min. Michael Lembeck, Phillip Casnoff ....

GORY CREATURES, THE (1959) see TERROR IS A MAN

GOSPEL ACCORDING TO ST. MATTHEW, THE (1964) Continental [Walter Reade]. B&W-135min. (Italian). Enrique Irazoqui, Margherita Caruso 3*
Original title: VANGELO SECONDO MATTEO, IL

GOSPEL ROAD, THE (1973) 20th Century-Fox. Color-93min. Robert Elfstrom, June Carter Cash, Johnny Cash .... (4)

GOVERNMENT GIRL (1943) RKO. B&W-94min. Olivia de Havilland, Sonny Tufts .... (4)

GRACE MOORE STORY, THE (1953) see SO THIS IS LOVE

GRACIE ALLEN MURDER CASE, THE (1939) Paramount. B&W-74min. Gracie Allen, Warren William .... (4)

GRADUATE, THE (1967) Avco-Embassy. Color-105min. Dustin Hoffman, Anne Bancroft 8*

GRAF SPEE (1956) see PURSUIT OF THE GRAF SPEE

GRAFT AND CORRUPTION (1957) see CONFESSION

GRAND CANYON (1958) Buena Vista. Color-29min. (Travelog). Director: James Algar 5*
Alternate title: GRAND CANYON SUITE

GRAND CENTRAL MURDER (1942) M-G-M. B&W-72min. Van Heflin, Patricia Dane .... (5)

GRAND HOTEL (1932) M-G-M. B&W-115min. Greta Garbo, John Barrymore 5*

GRAND ILLUSION (1937) World Pictures. B&W-110min. (French). Jean Gabin, Pierre Fresnay, Erich Von Stroheim 4½*
Original title: GRANDE ILLUSION, LA

GRAND MANEUVER, THE (1955) United Motion Pic. Org. (UMPO). Color-106min. (French). Gérard Philipe, Michele Morgan, Brigitte Bardot .... (5)
Original title: GRANDES MANOEUVRES, LES (The Big Maneuvers)
British title: SUMMER MANOEUVRES

GRAND OLYMPICS, THE (1961) Times Film Corp. Color-120min. (Italian, Documentary). Director: Romolo Marcellini .... (5)
Original title: GRANDE OLIMPIADE, LA

GRAND PRIX (1966) M-G-M. Color-179min. James Garner, Eva Marie Saint 4*

GRAND SLAM (1967) Paramount. Color-121min. (Italian-Spanish-W. German, English version). Edward G. Robinson, Janet Leigh 4*
Original Italian title: AD OGNI COSTO (At Any Cost)
Original Spanish title: DIAMANTES A GO-GO
Original German title: TOP JOB

GRAND THEFT AUTO (1977) New World. Color-89min. Ron Howard, Nancy Morgan .... (4)

GRANDE BOUFFE, THE (1973) ABKCO Films. Color-125min. (French). Marcello Mastroianni, Ugo Tognazzi, Michel Piccoli, Philippe Noiret ..(4)
Original title: GRANDE BOUFFE, LA (The Big Feast)
British title: BLOW OUT

GRANDE BOURGEOISIE, LA (1975) Atlantic Releasing. Color-115min. (Italian-French). Giancarlo Giannini, Catherine Deneuve, Fernando Rey 4*
Original Italian title: FATTI DI GENTE PERBENE (Drama of the Rich)

GRANDMA'S BOY (1922) Associated Exhibitors. B&W-68min. (Silent). Harold Lloyd, Mildred Davis 4½*

GRANNY GET YOUR GUN (1940) Warner Bros. B&W-56min. May Robson, Margot Stevenson .... (3)

GRAPES OF WRATH, THE (1940) 20th Century-Fox. B&W-128min. Henry Fonda, Jane Darwell 5½*

GRASS (1925) Paramount. B&W-45min. (Silent, Documentary). Director: Merian C. Cooper 4*

GRASS IS ALWAYS GREENER OVER THE SEPTIC TANK, THE (1978) CBS-TV. Color-98min. (Made for TV). Carol Burnett, Charles Grodin ....

GRASS IS GREENER, THE (1960) Universal. Color-105min. Cary Grant, Deborah Kerr 5½*

GRASSHOPPER, THE (1970) National General. Color-95min. Jacqueline Bisset, Jim Brown, Joseph Cotten .... (4)

GRATEFUL DEAD, THE (1977) Monarch-Noteworthy. Color-131min. (Music Film). Director: Jerry Garcia .... (4)

GRAVE OF THE VAMPIRE (1973) Entertainment Pyramid. Color-95min. William Smith, Michael Pataki 2*

GRAVE ROBBERS FROM OUTER SPACE (1956) see PLAN 9 FROM OUTER SPACE

GRAVESIDE STORY, THE (1964) see COMEDY OF TERRORS, THE

GRAVEYARD OF HORROR (1971) American-International. Color-86min. (Mexican). Bill Curran, Yocasta Grey 1*

GRAVY TRAIN, THE (1974) see DION BROTHERS, THE

GRAY LADY DOWN (1977) Universal. Color-111min. Charlton Heston, David Carradine 5*

GRAYEAGLE (1977) American-International. Color-4min. Alex Cord, Lana Wood, Ben Johnson .... (4)

GRAZIE, ZIA (1968) Avco-Embassy. B&W-93min. (Italian). Lisa Gastoni, Lou Castel .... (4)
Alternate title: COME PLAY WITH ME

GREASE (1978) Paramount. Color-110min. John Travolta, Olivia Newton-John, Stockard Channing 5½*

GREASED LIGHTNING (1977) Warner Bros. Color-96min. Richard Pryor, Beau Bridges, Pam Grier 5*

GREASER'S PALACE (1972) Greaser's Palace, Ltd. Color-91min. Albert Henderson, Allan Arbus 1*

GREAT ADVENTURE, THE (1951) J. Arthur Rank. B&W-82min. (British). Jack Hawkins, Peter Hammond .... (4)
Original title: ADVENTURERS, THE
Alternate title: FORTUNE IN DIAMONDS

GREAT ADVENTURE, THE (1953) De Rochemont. B&W-73min. (Swedish). Anders Norborg, Kjell Sucksdorff 5*

GREAT AMERICAN BEAUTY CONTEST, THE (1973) Worldvision. Color-73min. (Made for TV). Eleanor Parker, Bob Cummings, Barbi Benson 4½*

GREAT AMERICAN BROADCAST, THE (1941) 20th Century-Fox. B&W-92min. Alice Faye, Jack Oakie .... (4)

GREAT AMERICAN COWBOY, THE (1974) Sunn Classic. Color-90min. (Documentary). Director: Kieth Merrill 4*

GREAT AMERICAN PASTIME, THE (1956) M-G-M. B&W-89min. Tom Ewell, Anne Francis .... (4)

GREAT AMERICAN TRAGEDY, THE (1972) MPC (TV). Color-75min. (Made for TV). George Kennedy, Vera Miles, William Windom 4*

GREAT BALOON ADVENTURE, THE (1978) see OLLY OLLY OXEN FREE

GREAT BANK HOAX, THE (1977) Warner Bros. Color-88min. Burgess Meredith, Richard Basehart, Ned Beatty .... (4)
Original title: SHENANIGANS
Alternate title: GREAT GEORGIA BANK HOAX, THE

GREAT BANK ROBBERY, THE (1969) Warner Bros. Color-97min. Zero Mostel, Kim Novak, Clint Walker 3*

GREAT BARRIER, THE (1937) Gaumont-British [Rank]. B&W-82min. (British). Richard Arlen, Antoinette Cellier .... (4)
Alternate title: SILENT BARRIERS

GREAT BETRAYAL, THE (1954) see DAY OF TRIUMPH

GREAT BRITISH TRAIN ROBBERY, THE (1965) Peppercorn-Wormser. B&W-104min. (German, English language, Telefeature). Horst Tappert, Hans Cossy .... (3)
Original title: GENTLEMEN BITTEN ZUR KASSE, DIE
Alternate German title(?): POSTZUG-UBERFALL, DER

GREAT CARUSO, THE (1951) M-G-M. Color-109min. Mario Lanza, Ann Blyth 5*

GREAT CATHERINE (1968) Warner Bros. Color-99min. (British). Peter O'Toole, Zero Mostel, Jeanne Moreau 3*

GREAT CHASE, THE (1962) Continental [Walter Reade]. B&W-77min. (Compilation). Producer: Harvey Cort 5*

GREAT DAN PATCH, THE (1949) United Artists. B&W-94min. Dennis O'Keefe, Gail Russell .... (4)

GREAT DAY (1945) RKO. B&W-80min. (British). Eric Portman, Flora Robson .... (4)

GREAT DAY IN THE MORNING (1956) RKO. Color-92min. Virginia Mayo, Robert Stack .... (4)

GREAT DIAMOND ROBBERY, THE (1954) M-G-M. B&W-69min. Red Skelton, Cara Williams .... (3)

GREAT DICTATOR, THE (1940) United Artists. B&W-126min. Charles Chaplin 5*

GREAT ESCAPE, THE (1963) United Artists. Color-168min. Steve McQueen, James Garner 6*

GREAT EXPECTATIONS (1934) Universal. B&W-100min. Phillips Holmes, Jane Wyatt .... (4)

GREAT EXPECTATIONS (1946) Universal. B&W-118min. (British). John Mills, Valerie Hobson 5*

GREAT EXPECTATIONS (1974) NBC-TV. Color-124min. (British-U.S., Made for TV). Michael York, Sarah Miles, James Mason .... (5)

GREAT FLAMARION, THE (1945) Republic. B&W-78min. Erich von Stroheim, Mary Beth Hughes .... (4)

GREAT GAMBINI, THE (1937) Paramount. B&W-70min. Akim Tamiroff, John Trent ....(4)

GREAT GARRICK, THE (1937) Warner Bros. B&W-89min. Brian Aherne, Olivia de Havilland 4½*

GREAT GATSBY, THE (1949) Paramount. B&W-92min. Alan Ladd, Betty Field.......................... 4*

GREAT GATSBY, THE (1974) Paramount. Color-144min. Robert Redford, Mia Farrow 5*

GREAT GEORGIA BANK HOAX, THE (1978) see GREAT BANK HOAX, THE

GREAT GILBERT AND SULLIVAN, THE (1953) see GILBERT AND SULLIVAN

GREAT GUNDOWN, THE (1977) Sun. Color-95min. Robert Padilla, Malila St. Duval..........................

GREAT GUNS (1941) 20th Century-Fox. B&W-74min. Stan Laurel, Oliver Hardy, Sheila Ryan .... (3)

GREAT GUY (1936) Grand National (American). B&W-75min. James Cagney, Mae Clarke 4*
British title: PLUCK OF THE IRISH

GREAT IMPERSONATION, THE (1935) Universal. B&W-67min. Edmund Lowe, Valerie Hobson .... (3)

GREAT IMPOSTOR, THE (1961) Universal. B&W-112min. Tony Curtis, Karl Malden 5*

GREAT JESSE JAMES RAID, THE (1953) Lippert Productions. Color-74min. Willard Parker, Barbara Payton .... (3)

GREAT JEWEL ROBBERY, THE (1950) Warner Bros. B&W-91min. David Brian, Marjorie Reynolds .... (3)

GREAT JOHN L., THE (1945) United Artists. B&W-96min. Greg McClure, Linda Darnell .... (4)
British title: MAN CALLED SULLIVAN, A

GREAT LIE, THE (1941) Warner Bros. B&W-107min. Bette Davis, George Brent.......................... 1*

GREAT LOCOMOTIVE CHASE, THE (1956) Buena Vista. Color-85min. Fess Parker, Jeffrey Hunter 5½*

GREAT LOVER, THE (1949) Paramount. B&W-80min. Bob Hope, Rhonda Fleming 5*

GREAT MADCAP, THE (1949) Bauer International. B&W-90min. (Mexican). Fernando Soler, Andres Soler ....
Original title: GRAN CALAVERA, EL
Alternate title: HAPPY SCOUNDREL, THE

GREAT MAN, THE (1956) Universal. B&W-92min. José Ferrer, Dean Jagger.......................... 5*

GREAT MAN VOTES, THE (1939) RKO. B&W-70min. John Barrymore, Peter Holden 5*

GREAT MANHUNT, THE (1949) see DOOLINS OF OKLAHOMA, THE

GREAT MANHUNT, THE (1950) see STATE SECRET

GREAT MAN'S LADY, THE (1942) Paramount. B&W-90min. Brian Donlevy, Barbara Stanwyck, Joel McCrea .... (4)

GREAT MAN'S WHISKERS, THE (1971) MCA-TV. Color-96min. (Made for TV). Dennis Weaver, Cindy Eilbacher, Dean Jones .... (4)

GREAT McGINTY, THE (1940) Paramount. B&W-81min. Brian Donlevy, Akim Tamiroff 6*
British title: DOWN WENT McGINTY

GREAT McGONAGALL, THE (1974) Color-98min. (British). Spike Milligan, Peter Sellers ....

GREAT MIKE, THE (1944) Producers Rel. Corp. [Eagle Lion]. B&W-70min. Stuart Erwin, Carl "Alfalfa" Switzer .... (3)

GREAT MISSOURI RAID, THE (1951) Paramount. Color-83min. Macdonald Carey, Ellen Drew, Wendell Corey.......................... 4*

GREAT MR. NOBODY, THE (1941) Warner Bros. B&W-70min. Eddie Albert, Joan Leslie .... (4)

GREAT MOMENT, THE (1944) Paramount. B&W-83min. Joel McCrea, Betty Field 3½*

GREAT NIAGARA, THE (1974) Worldvision. Color-75min. (Made for TV). Richard Boone, Michael Sacks, Randy Quaid 4*

GREAT NORTHFIELD, MINNESOTA RAID, THE (1972) Universal. Color-91min. Cliff Robertson, Robert Duvall.......................... 4*

GREAT O'MALLEY, THE (1937) Warner Bros. B&W-71min. Pat O'Brien, Sybil Jason 3*

GREAT PROFILE, THE (1940) 20th Century-Fox. B&W-82min. John Barrymore, Mary Beth Hughes .... (4)

GREAT RACE, THE (1965) Warner Bros. Color-150min. Jack Lemmon, Tony Curtis 5*

GREAT RUPERT, THE (1950) Eagle Lion. B&W-86min. Jimmy Durante, Tom Drake .... (4)

GREAT ST. LOUIS BANK ROBBERY, THE (1959) United Artists. B&W-86min. Steve McQueen, David Clarke .... (3)

GREAT SANTINI, THE (1979) Warner Bros. Color- min. Robert Duvall, Blythe Danner ....

GREAT SCHNOZZLE, THE (1934) see PALOOKA

GREAT SCOUT & CATHOUSE THURSDAY, THE (1976) American-International. Color-102min. Lee Marvin, Oliver Reed 4½*

GREAT SINNER, THE (1949) M-G-M. B&W-110min. Gregory Peck, Ava Gardner .... (4)

GREAT SIOUX MASSACRE, THE (1965) Columbia. Color-91min. Joseph Cotten, Darren McGavin, Philip Carey .... (4)

GREAT SIOUX UPRISING, THE (1953) Universal. Color-80min. Jeff Chandler, Faith Domergue .... (4)

GREAT SMOKEY ROADBLOCK, THE (1976) Dimension Pictures. Color-90min. Henry Fonda, Eileen Brennan, Robert Englund .... (4)
Original title: LAST OF THE COWBOYS, THE

GREAT SPY CHASE, THE (1964) American-International. B&W-87min. (French). Lino Ventura, Bernard Blier .... (2)
Original title: BARBOUZES, LES

GREAT SPY MISSION, THE (1965) see OPERATION CROSSBOW

GREAT STONE FACE, THE (1968) Funnyman, Inc. B&W-90min. (Compilation). Buster Keaton 5*

GREAT TEXAS DYNAMITE CHASE, THE (1976) New World. Color-90min. Claudia Jennings, Jocelyn Jones 4½*

GREAT TRAIN ROBBERY, THE (1903) The Edison Company. B&W-10min. "Bronco Billy" Anderson, A. C. Abadie, Marie Murray.............. 1*

GREAT TRAIN ROBBERY, THE (1940) Republic. B&W-61min. Bob Steele, Claire Carleton .... (3)

GREAT TRAIN ROBBERY, THE (1979) United Artists. Color-110min. (British). Sean Connery, Donald Sutherland, Lesley-Anne Down 5½*
Original title: FIRST GREAT TRAIN ROBBERY, THE

GREAT VAN ROBBERY, THE (1959) United Artists. B&W-73min. (British). Denis Shaw, Kay Callard.......................... (3)

GREAT VICTOR HERBERT, THE (1939) Paramount. B&W-84min. Walter Connolly, Allan Jones.......................... (4)

GREAT WALDO PEPPER, THE (1975) Universal. Color-108min. Robert Redford, Bo Svenson 6*

GREAT WALLENDAS, THE (1978) NBC-TV. Color-98min. (Made for TV). Lloyd Bridges, Britt Ekland .... (5)

GREAT WALTZ, THE (1938) M-G-M. B&W-102min. Fernand Gravet, Luise Rainer.......................... 4*

GREAT WALTZ, THE (1972) M-G-M. Color-135min. Horst Buchholz, Mary Costa 5*

GREAT WAR, THE (1959) United Artists. B&W-118min. (Italian). Vittorio Gassman, Silvana Mangano, Alberto Sordi .... (4)
Original title: GRANDE GUERRA, LA

GREAT WHITE HOPE, THE (1970) 20th Century-Fox. Color-106min. James Earl Jones, Jane Alexander 4*

GREAT ZIEGFELD, THE (1936) M-G-M. B&W-184min. William Powell, Luise Rainer, Myrna Loy 5½*

GREATEST, THE (1977) Columbia. Color-101min. (British). Muhammad Ali, Ernest Borgnine 5*

GREATEST LOVE, THE (1951) Italian Films Export. B&W-116min. (Italian, English language). Ingrid Bergman, Alexander Knox.......... (3)
Alternate title: EUROPA '51

GREATEST SHOW ON EARTH, THE (1952) Paramount. Color-153min. Charlton Heston, Cornel Wilde 6*

Films are rated on a 1 to 10 scale, 10 is highest. **Boldface** ratings followed by an asterisk (*) are for films actually seen and rated by the executive and senior editors. All other ratings are estimates. (See Notes on Entertainment Ratings in the front section.)

As **THE GREAT WALDO PEPPER** (1975), barnstormer Robert Redford prepares to rev up the engine of his biplane as he sells rides to curious thrill-seekers.

GREATEST STORY EVER TOLD, THE (1965) United Artists. Color-195min. Max Von Sydow, Dorothy McGuire......................3*

GREED (1925) Metro-Goldwyn. B&W-112min. (Silent). Gibson Gowland, ZaSu Pitts, Jean Hersholt, Chester Conklin 5*

GREEK TYCOON, THE (1978) Universal. Color-106min. Anthony Quinn, Jacqueline Bisset.....................5*

GREEKS HAD A WORD FOR THEM, THE (1932) United Artists. B&W-79min Madge Evans, Joan Blondell, Ina Claire ....(5)
Alternate title: THREE BROADWAY GIRLS

GREEN ARCHER, THE (1961) Casino Films. B&W-95min. (German). Gert Frobe, Karin Dor, Klausjurgen Wussow, Eddi Arent ....(3)
Original title: GRUNE BOGENSCHUTZE, DER

GREEN BERETS, THE (1968) Warner Bros. Color-141min. John Wayne, David Janssen.....................3*

GREEN CARNATION (1960) *see* TRIALS OF OSCAR WILDE, THE

GREEN DOLPHIN STREET (1947) M-G-M. B&W-141min. Lana Turner, Van Heflin 3½*

GREEN-EYED BLONDE, THE (1957) Warner Bros. B&W-76min. Susan Oliver, Linda Plowman ....(2)

GREEN-EYED WOMAN, THE (1942) *see* TAKE A LETTER, DARLING

GREEN EYES (1976) ABC-TV. Color-100min. (Made for TV). Paul Winfield, Rita Tushingham, Jonathan Lippe ....

GREEN FINGERS (1947) Anglo-American. B&W-83min. (British). Robert Beatty, Carol Raye ....(5)

GREEN FIRE (1955) M-G-M. Color-100min. Stewart Granger, Grace Kelly.....................(4)

GREEN FOR DANGER (1947) Eagle Lion. B&W-93min. (British). Alastair Sim, Trevor Howard 5½*

GREEN GLOVE, THE (1952) United Artists. B&W-88min. Glenn Ford, Geraldine Brooks.....................(4)

GREEN GODDESS, THE (1930) Warner Bros. B&W-80min. George Arliss, Alice Joyce.....................(3)

GREEN GRASS OF WYOMING (1948) 20th Century-Fox. Color-89min. Peggy Cummins, Charles Coburn 4*

GREEN GROW THE RUSHES (1951) British Lion [EMI]. B&W-77min. (British). Roger Livesey, Honor Blackman, Richard Burton.................(5)
Alternate title: BRANDY ASHORE

GREEN HELL (1940) Universal. B&W-87min. Douglas Fairbanks, Jr., Joan Bennett ....(4)

GREEN HELMET, THE (1961) M-G-M. B&W-88min. (British). Bill Travers, Ed Begley.....................(3)

GREEN LIGHT (1937) Warner Bros. B&W-85min. Errol Flynn, Anita Louise ....(4)

GREEN MAGIC (1955) Italian Films Export. Color-85min. (Italian, Documentary). Director: Gian Gaspare Napolitano ....(5)
Original title: MAGIA VERDE

GREEN MAN, THE (1956) Distributors Corp. of America. B&W-80min. (British). Alastair Sim, George Cole 6*

GREEN MANSIONS (1959) M-G-M. Color-101min. Audrey Hepburn, Anthony Perkins 4*

GREEN MARE, THE (1959) Zenith International. Color-93min. (French-Italian). Bourvil, Sandra Milo ....(5)
Original French title: JUMENT VERTE, LA
Original Italian title: GIUMENTA VERDE, LA
Alternate title: BEDROOM VENDETTA

GREEN PASTURES, THE (1936) Warner Bros. B&W-93min. Rex Ingram, Oscar Polk ....(5)

GREEN PROMISE, THE (1949) RKO. B&W-93min. Walter Brennan, Marguerite Chapman.....................(4)
British title: RAGING WATERS

GREEN ROOM, THE (1978) New World. Color-94min. (French). Francois Truffaut, Nathalie Baye ....
Original title: CHAMBRE VERT, LA

GREEN SCARF, THE (1954) Associated Artists. B&W-96min. (British). Michael Redgrave, Ann Todd.....................5*

GREEN SLIME, THE (1969) M-G-M. Color-90min. (U.S.-Japanese). Robert Horton, Richard Jaeckel, Luciana Paluzzi ....(3)
Japanese title: GAMMO SANGO UCHO DAISAKUSEN

GREEN WALL, THE (1969) Altura Films. Color-110min. (Peruvian). Julio Aleman, Sandra Riva.....................4*
Original title: MURALLA VERDE, LA

GREEN YEARS, THE (1946) M-G-M. B&W-127min. Charles Coburn, Dean Stockwell 5*

GREENE MURDER CASE, THE (1929) Paramount. B&W-69min. William Powell, Florence Eldridge ....(4)

GREENGAGE SUMMER, THE (1961) *see* LOSS OF INNOCENCE

GREENWICH VILLAGE (1944) 20th Century-Fox. Color-82min. Don Ameche, Carmen Miranda.....................(3)

GREENWICH VILLAGE STORY (1963) Shawn International. B&W-95min. Robert Hogan, Melinda Plank ....(5)
Alternate title: BIRTHPLACE OF THE HOOTENANNY
Alternate title: THEY LOVE AS THEY PLEASE

GREETINGS (1968) Sigma III. Color-88min. Jonathan Warden, Robert De Niro 3*

GREYFRIARS BOBBY (1961) Buena Vista. Color-90min. (U.S.-British). Donald Crisp, Laurence Naismith ....(5)

GRIDO, IL (1957) Astor. B&W-115min. (Italian-U.S.). Steve Cochran, Alida Valli, Betsy Blair ....(4)
Translation title: The Outcry

GRIFFIN AND PHOENIX: A LOVE STORY (1976) ABC-TV. Color-100min. (Made for TV). Peter Falk, Jill Clayburgh 5½*

GRIMM'S FAIRY TALES FOR ADULTS ONLY (1971) Cinemation. Color-76min. (German). Marie Liljedah, Eva V. Rueber-Staier, Walter Giller ....(3)
Original title: GRIMM'S MARCHEN -- FUR LUSTERNE PARCHEN (Grimm's Fairy Tales for Lusting Couples)

GRIP OF FEAR, THE (1962) *see* EXPERIMENT IN TERROR

GRIP OF THE STRANGLER (1958) *see* HAUNTED STRANGLER, THE

GRISBI (1954) United Motion Pic. Org. (UMPO). B&W-95min. (French). Jean Gabin, René Dary.....................(4)
Original title: TOUCHEZ PAS AU GRISBI (Don't Touch the Loot)
Alternate title: PARIS UNDERGROUND
Alternate title: DON'T TOUCH THE LOOT
Alternate title: HANDS OFF THE LOOT

GRISSLY'S MILLIONS (1945) Republic. B&W-54min. Robert H. Barrat, Virginia Grey ....(4)

GRISSOM GANG, THE (1971) Cinerama Releasing. Color-127min. Kim Darby, Tony Musante, Scott Wilson ....(3)

GRIZZLY (1976) Film Ventures International. Color-90min. Christopher George, Andrew Prine, Richard Jaeckel.....................3½*
TV title: KILLER GRIZZLY

GROOM WORE SPURS, THE (1951) Universal. B&W-80min. Ginger Rogers, Jack Carson.....................(2)

GROOVE TUBE, THE (1974) Levitt-Pickman. **Color-75min.** Ken Shapiro, Richard Belzer...**5***

GROUNDS FOR MARRIAGE (1950) M-G-M. **B&W-91min.** Van Johnson, Kathryn Grayson..(4)

GROUNDSTAR CONSPIRACY, THE (1972) Universal. **Color-96min.** *(U.S.-Canadian).* George Peppard, Michael Sarrazin...............**4½***

GROUP, THE (1966) United Artists. **Color-150min.** Candice Bergen, Joan Hackett..**4***

GROUPIES (1970) Maron Films, Ltd. **Color-92min.** *(Music Film).* Director: Ron Dorfman..(3)

GUADALCANAL DIARY (1943) 20th Century-Fox. **B&W-93min.** Preston Foster, Lloyd Nolan..**3***

GUARDIAN OF THE WILDERNESS (1977) Sunn Classic. **Color-112min.** Denver Pyle, John Dehner...(4)
TV title: MOUNTAIN MAN

GUARDSMAN, THE (1931) M-G-M. **B&W-83min.** Alfred Lunt, Lynn Fontanne...(5)

GUENDALINA (1956) Lopert [U.A.]. **B&W-95min.** *(Italian-French).* Jacqueline Sassard, Raf Mattioli, Sylva Koscina, Raf Vallone............(4)

GUERILLA GIRL (1953) United Artists. **B&W-81min.** Helmut Dantine, Marianna..(3)

GUERILLAS IN PINK LACE (1964) Commonwealth United TV. **Color-96min.** George Montgomery, Joan Shawlee.....................(3)

GUERRE EST FINIE, LA (1966) Brandon. **B&W-121min.** *(French-Swedish).* Yves Montand, Ingrid Thulin.................................**3***
Translation title: WAR IS OVER, THE
Swedish title: KRIGET AR SLUT

GUESS WHAT WE LEARNED IN SCHOOL TODAY? (1970) Cannon Releasing. **Color-96min.** Richard Carballo, Devin Goldenberg..............(4)
Alternate title: GUESS WHAT!?!
Alternate title: I AIN'T NO BUFFALO

GUESS WHO'S COMING TO DINNER (1967) Columbia. **Color-108min.** Spencer Tracy, Sidney Poitier.....................................**6***

GUESS WHO'S SLEEPING IN MY BED? (1973) ABC Circle Films. **Color-74min.** *(Made for TV).* Barbara Eden, Dean Jones................**4***

GUEST, THE (1964) Janus Films. **B&W-105min.** *(British).* Donald Pleasence, Alan Bates, Robert Shaw...............................**3***
Original title: CARETAKER, THE

GUEST IN THE HOUSE (1944) United Artists. **B&W-121min.** Anne Baxter, Ralph Bellamy...(4)

GUEST WIFE (1945) United Artists. **B&W-90min.** Claudette Colbert, Don Ameche...(4)

GUESTS ARE COMING (1962) Mitchell Kowal. **B&W-110min.** *(Polish).* Paul Glass, Mitchell Kowal, Zygmunt Zintel.......................(5)
Original title: JADA GOSCIE

GUIDE, THE (1965) Stratton International. **Color-120min.** *(U.S.-Indian).* Dev Anand, Waheeda Rehman...................................(5)
Alternate title: SURVIVAL

GUIDE FOR THE MARRIED MAN, A (1967) 20th Century-Fox. **Color-89min.** Walter Matthau, Robert Morse...................**5***

GUIDE FOR THE MARRIED WOMAN, A (1978) ABC-TV. **Color-98min.** *(Made for TV).* Cybill Shepherd, Charles Frank...........**3***

GUILT (1965) Crown International. **B&W-90min.** *(Swedish).* Sven Bertil Taube, Helena Brodin..(2)
Original title: TILLSAMMANS MED GUNILA MANDAG KVALL OCH TISDAG

GUILT IS MY SHADOW (1950) Stratford Pictures. **B&W-85min.** *(British).* Elizabeth Sellars, Patrick Holt...................(4)

GUILT OF JANET AMES, THE (1947) Columbia. **B&W-83min.** Rosalind Russell, Melvyn Douglas.................................**4***

GUILTY, THE (1947) Monogram [Allied Artists]. **B&W-70min.** Bonita Granville, Don Castle...(4)

GUILTY (1956) Showcorporation. **B&W-93min.** *(British).* John Justin, Barbara Laage, Donald Wolfit...........................(3)

GUILTY ASSIGNMENT (1947) *see* BIG TOWN

GUILTY BYSTANDER (1950) Film Classics [U.A.]. **B&W-92min.** Zachary Scott, Faye Emerson.......................................(4)

GUILTY HANDS (1931) M-G-M. **B&W-68min.** Lionel Barrymore, Madge Evans..(4)

GUILTY OF TREASON (1950) Eagle Lion. **B&W-86min.** Charles Bickford, Paul Kelly..(4)
British title: TREASON

GUILTY OR INNOCENT: THE SAM SHEPPARD MURDER CASE (1975) MCA-TV. **Color-156min.** *(Made for TV).* George Peppard, William Windom, Nina Van Pallandt..**5½***

GUINEA PIG, THE (1948) *see* OUTSIDER, THE

GUITARS OF LOVE (1954) Sam Baker Associates. **Color-90min.** *(German).* Vico Torriani, Annunzio Mantovani, Elma Karlowa...........(3)
Original title: GITARREN DER LIEBE

GULLIVER'S TRAVELS (1939) Paramount. **Color-74min.** *(Cartoon).* Director: Dave Fleischer...**5***

GULLIVER'S TRAVELS (1977) EMI. **Color-80min.** *(British-Belgian, Part-animated).* Richard Harris, Catherine Schell...............

GULLIVER'S TRAVELS BEYOND THE MOON (1965) Continental [Walter Reade]. **Color-85min.** *(Japanese, English language, Cartoon).* Director: Yoshio Kuroda..(4)

GUMBALL RALLY, THE (1976) Warner Bros. **Color-106min.** Michael Sarrazin, Normann Burton...**5***

GUMSHOE (1972) Columbia. **Color-84min.** *(British).* Albert Finney, Billie Whitelaw..**4***

GUN, THE (1974) MCA-TV. **Color-75min.** *(Made for TV).* Steven Elliott, Pep Serna, Edith Diaz...................................**4***

GUN AND THE PULPIT, THE (1974) Worldvision. **Color-74min.** *(Made for TV).* Marjoe Gortner, Estelle Parsons, Slim Pickens...............**5***

GUN BATTLE AT MONTEREY (1957) Allied Artists. **B&W-67min.** Sterling Hayden, Pamela Duncan....................................(3)

GUN BELT (1953) United Artists. **Color-77min.** George Montgomery, Tab Hunter..(3)

GUN BROTHERS (1956) United Artists. **B&W-79min.** Buster Crabbe, Neville Brand...(3)

GUN CRAZY (1949) *see* DEADLY IS THE FEMALE

GUN DUEL IN DURANGO (1957) United Artists. **B&W-73min.** George Montgomery, Ann Robinson.......................................(3)
Alternate title: DUEL IN DURANGO

GUN FEVER (1958) United Artists. **B&W-81min.** Mark Stevens, John Lupton..(3)

GUN FOR A COWARD (1957) Universal. **Color-73min.** Fred MacMurray, Jeffrey Hunter...**3***

GUN FURY (1953) Columbia. **Color-83min.** Rock Hudson, Donna Reed..**3***

GUN GLORY (1957) M-G-M. **Color-89min.** Stewart Granger, Rhonda Fleming..(3)

GUN HAWK, THE (1963) Allied Artists. **Color-92min.** Rory Calhoun, Rod Cameron..(3)

GUN MOLL (1949) *see* JIGSAW

GUN OF ZANGARA (1959) Desilu. **B&W-90min.** *(Telefeature).* Robert Stack, Robert Middleton..**5***

GUN POINT (1955) *see* AT GUNPOINT

GUN RUNNER, THE (1956) *see* SANTIAGO

GUN RUNNERS, THE (1958) United Artists. **B&W-83min.** Audie Murphy, Eddie Albert...(4)

GUN THAT WON THE WEST, THE (1955) Columbia. **Color-71min.** Dennis Morgan, Paula Raymond..(3)

GUN THE MAN DOWN (1956) United Artists. **B&W-78min.** James Arness, Angie Dickinson...(3)
Alternate title: ARIZONA MISSION

GUNFIGHT, A (1971) Paramount. **Color-90min.** Kirk Douglas, Johnny Cash..**4***

GUNFIGHT AT COMANCHE CREEK (1963) Allied Artists. **Color-90min.** Audie Murphy, Colleen Miller...................................(3)

GUNFIGHT AT DODGE CITY, THE (1959) United Artists. **Color-81min.** Joel McCrea, Julie Adams...................................**4***

GUNFIGHT AT RED SANDS (1965) Screen Gems. **Color-97min.** *(Spanish).* Richard Harrison, Mikaela, Giacomo Rossi-Stuart.............(3)

GUNFIGHT AT THE O.K. CORRAL (1957) Paramount. **Color-122min.** Burt Lancaster, Kirk Douglas.......................................**6½***

GUNFIGHT IN ABILENE (1967) Universal. **Color-86min.** Bobby Darin, Emily Banks, Leslie Nielsen.....................................(3)

GUNFIGHTER, THE (1950) 20th Century-Fox. **B&W-84min.** Gregory Peck, Helen Westcott..**4***

GUNFIGHTERS (1947) Columbia. **Color-87min.** Randolph Scott, Barbara Britton..(4)
British title: ASSASSIN, THE

GUNFIGHTERS OF ABILENE (1960) United Artists. **B&W-122min.** Buster Crabbe, Barton MacLane....................................(2)

GUNFIGHTERS OF CASA GRANDE (1964) M-G-M. **Color-92min.** *(Spanish-U.S.).* Alex Nicol, Jorge Mistral................................(2)
Original Spanish title: PISTOLEROS DE CASA GRANDE, LOS

GUNFIRE (1950) Lippert Productions. **B&W-60min.** Don "Red" Barry, Robert Lowery .... (3)
British title: FRANK JAMES RIDES AGAIN

GUNFIRE AT INDIAN GAP (1957) Republic. **B&W-70min.** Vera Ralston, Anthony George, George Macready .... (3)

GUNG HO! (1943) Universal. **B&W-88min.** Randolph Scott, Noah Beery, Jr. **3***

GUNGA DIN (1939) RKO. **B&W-117min.** Cary Grant, Victor McLaglen **5½***

GUNMAN IN THE STREETS (1950) *see* TIME RUNNING OUT

GUNMAN'S WALK (1958) Columbia. **Color-97min.** Van Heflin, Tab Hunter **3½***

GUNMEN FROM LAREDO (1959) Columbia. **Color-67min.** Robert Knapp, Jana Davi .... (2)

GUNMEN OF THE RIO GRANDE (1965) Allied Artists. **Color-86min.** *(Italian-Spanish-French).* Guy Madison, Madeleine Lebeau, Gérard Tichy **3½***
Original Italian title: SFIDA A RIO BRAVO
Spanish title: DESAFIO EN RIO BRAVO
Alternate Spanish title #1: JENNIE LEES A UNA NUOVA PISTOLA
Alternate Spanish title #2: SHERIFF DEL O.K. CORRAL, EL
French title: DUEL A RIO BRAVO

GUNN (1967) Paramount. **Color-95min.** Craig Stevens, Laura Devon, Edward Asner .... (3)

GUNPOINT! (1955) *see* AT GUNPOINT

GUNPOINT (1966) Universal. **Color-86min.** Audie Murphy, Joan Staley, Warren Stevens .... (3)

GUNS AT BATASI (1964) 20th Century-Fox. **B&W-103min.** *(British-U.S.).* Richard Attenborough, Jack Hawkins **4½***

GUNS FOR SAN SEBASTIAN (1967) M-G-M. **Color-111min.** *(U.S.-French-Italian-Mexican, English language).* Anthony Quinn, Anjanette Comer, Charles Bronson **3***
Original French title: BATAILLE DE SAN SEBASTIAN, LA *(The Battle of San Sebastian)*
Original Italian title: CANNONI DI SAN SEBASTIAN, I
Original Mexican title: CANONES DE SAN SEBASTIAN, LOS

GUNS, GIRLS AND GANGSTERS (1959) United Artists. **B&W-70min.** Mamie Van Doren, Gerald Mohr .... (3)

GUNS IN THE AFTERNOON (1962) *see* RIDE THE HIGH COUNTRY

GUNS OF AUGUST, THE (1964) Universal. **B&W-100min.** *(Documentary).* Director: Nathan Kroll **5½***

GUNS OF DARKNESS (1962) Warner Bros. **B&W-103min.** *(British).* Leslie Caron, David Niven .... (4)

GUNS OF DIABLO (1964) M-G-M. **B&W-56min.** *(Telefeature).* Charles Bronson, Susan Oliver, Kurt Russell .... (4)

GUNS OF FORT PETTICOAT, THE (1957) Columbia. **Color-82min.** Audie Murphy, Kathryn Grant .... (5)

GUNS OF HATE (1948) RKO. **B&W-62min.** Tim Holt, Richard Martin.. (2)
Alternate title: GUNS OF WRATH

GUNS OF JUANA GALLO, THE (1958) Azteca. **Color-91min.** *(Mexican).* Jorge Mistral, Maria Felix .... (3)
Alternate title: JUANA GALLO

GUNS OF NAVARONE, THE (1961) Columbia. **Color-159min.** *(U.S.-British).* Gregory Peck, David Niven, Anthony Quinn **6½***

GUNS OF THE BLACK WITCH (1961) American-International. **Color-81min.** *(Italian-French).* Don Megowan, Silvana Pampanini .... (2)
Original Italian title: TERRORE DEI MARE, IL *(The Terror of the Sea)*
Original French title: TERREUR DES MERS, LA

GUNS OF THE MAGNIFICENT SEVEN (1969) United Artists. **Color-106min.** George Kennedy, Monte Markham **3***

GUNS OF THE TIMBERLAND (1960) Warner Bros. **Color-91min.** Alan Ladd, Jeanne Crain .... (4)

GUNS OF WRATH (1948) *see* GUNS OF HATE

GUNS OF WYOMING (1963) *see* CATTLE KING

GUNSIGHT RIDGE (1957) United Artists. **B&W-85min.** Joel McCrea, Mark Stevens.. (3)

GUNSLINGER, THE (1956) American-International. **Color-83min.** John Ireland, Beverly Garland... **2***

GUNSMOKE (1953) Universal. **Color-75min.** Audie Murphy, Susan Cabot... **4***

GUNSMOKE IN TUCSON (1958) Allied Artists. **Color-80min.** Mark Stevens, Forrest Tucker .... (3)

GURU, THE (1969) 20th Century-Fox. **Color-112min.** Michael York, Rita Tushingham **3***

GURU THE MAD MONK (1970) Nova International. **Color-62min.** Neil Flanagan, Judy Israel .... (1)
Alternate title: GARU THE MAD MONK

GUS (1976) Buena Vista. **Color-96min.** Edward Asner, Don Knotts .... (4)

GUV'NOR, THE (1935) *see* MR. HOBO

GUY CALLED CAESAR, A (1962) Columbia. **B&W-62min.** *(British).* Conrad Phillips, George Moon .... (3)

GUY NAMED JOE, A (1943) M-G-M. **B&W-118min.** Spencer Tracy, Irene Dunne .... (4)

GUY WHO CAME BACK, THE (1951) 20th Century-Fox. **B&W-91min.** Paul Douglas, Joan Bennett .... (3)

GUYS AND DOLLS (1955) M-G-M. **Color-149min.** Marlon Brando, Jean Simmons **7***

GYPSY (1962) Warner Bros. **Color-149min.** Rosalind Russell, Natalie Wood **5***

GYPSY AND THE GENTLEMAN, THE (1958) J. Arthur Rank. **Color-89min.** *(British).* Melina Mercouri, Keith Michell, Flora Robson.......... (4)

GYPSY COLT (1954) M-G-M. **Color-72min.** Donna Corcoran, Ward Bond .... (5)

GYPSY FURY (1951) Monogram [Allied Artists]. **B&W-63min.** Viveca Lindfors, Christopher Kent .... (3)

GYPSY GIRL (1966) Continental [Walter Reade]. **Color-102min.** *(British).* Hayley Mills, Ian McShane.............................. **3***

GYPSY MOTHS, THE (1969) M-G-M. **Color-106min.** Burt Lancaster, Deborah Kerr **5***

GYPSY WILDCAT (1944) Universal. **Color-75min.** Maria Montez, Jon Hall.. (3)

-H-

H.M. PULHAM, ESQ. (1941) M-G-M. **B&W-120min.** Robert Young, Hedy Lamarr .... (5)

H.M.S. DEFIANT (1962) *see* DAMN THE DEFIANT!

H-MAN, THE (1958) Columbia. **Color-79min.** *(Japanese).* Yumi Shirakawa, Kenji Sahara.. (3)
Original title: BIYO TO EKITAININGEN *(Beautiful Women and the Hydrogen Man)*

HAGBARD AND SIGNE (1967) Prentoulis Films. **Color-92min.** *(Danish-Swedish-Icelandic).* Oleg Vidov, Gitte Haenning................... (5)
Original title: ROEDE KAPPE, DEN *(The Red Mantle)*
Alternate title: RED MANTLE, THE

HAIL, HERO! (1969) Nat'l General (for Cinema Center). **Color-100min.** Michael Douglas, Arthur Kennedy, Teresa Wright .... (4)

HAIL! MAFIA (1965) Goldstone Film Enterprises. **B&W-90min.** *(French-Italian).* Henry Silva, Jack Klugman, Eddie Constantine, Elsa Martinelli .... (2)
Original French title: JE VOUS SALUE, MAFFIA
Original Italian title: DA NEW YORK: MAFIA UCCIDE!

GUYS AND DOLLS (1956). Dapper professional gambler Marlon Brando offers mission sister Jean Simmons a sporting proposition — he'll supply the mission with a dozen genuine sinners in return for a small favor.

HAIL THE CONQUERING HERO (1944) Paramount. B&W-101min. Eddie Bracken, Ella Raines...............6½*

HAIR (1979) United Artists. Color-118min. John Savage, Treat Williams, Beverly D'Angelo 5½*

HAIRY APE, THE (1944) United Artists. B&W-90min. William Bendix, Susan Hayward ....(5)

HAL ROACH COMEDY CARNIVAL, THE (1947) see CURLEY

HAL ROACH COMEDY CARNIVAL, THE (1947) see FABULOUS JOE, THE

HALF A HERO (1953) M-G-M. B&W-71min. Red Skelton, Jean Hagen..(4)

HALF A HOUSE (1976) Rampart Releasing. Color-95min. Anthony Eisley, Pat Delaney, Francine York 4*

HALF A SIXPENCE (1967) Paramount. Color-148min. (British-U.S.). Tommy Steele, Julia Foster ....(5)

HALF ANGEL (1951) 20th Century-Fox. Color-77min. Loretta Young, Joseph Cotten 4*

HALF-BREED, THE (1952) RKO. Color-81min. Robert Young, Janis Carter 3*

HALF HUMAN (1955) Distributors Corp. of America. B&W-70min. (Japanese). Akira Takarada, Kenji Kasahara, John Carradine ....(3)
Original title: JUJIN YUKIOTOKO *(Monster Snowman)*
Publicity title: SNOWMAN

HALF WAY TO SHANGHAI (1942) Universal. B&W-62min. Irene Hervey, Kent Taylor ....(3)

HALFWAY HOUSE, THE (1944) A.F.E. Corp. B&W-95min. (British). Francoise Rosay, Mervyn Johns, Glynis Johns ....(4)

HALLELUJAH! (1929) M-G-M. B&W-109min. Daniel L. Haynes, Nina Mae McKinney 2½*

HALLELUJAH I'M A BUM! (1933) United Artists. B&W-82min. Al Jolson, Madge Evans 4½*
British title: HALLELUJAH, I'M A TRAMP
TV title: HEART OF NEW YORK

HALLELUJAH THE HILLS (1963) New York Cinema Co. B&W-82min. Peter H. Beard, Marty Greenbaum ....(2)

HALLELUJAH TRAIL, THE (1965) United Artists. Color-165min. Burt Lancaster, Lee Remick 4*

HALLIDAY BRAND, THE (1957) United Artists. B&W-77min. Joseph Cotten, Viveca Lindfors...............(4)

HALLOWEEN (1978) Compass International. Color-93min. Donald Pleasence, Jamie Lee Curtis...............4*

HALLS OF ANGER (1970) United Artists. Color-98min. Calvin Lockhart, James A. Watson, Jr., Rob Reiner...............4*

HALLS OF MONTEZUMA, THE (1951) 20th Century-Fox. Color-113min. Richard Widmark, Walter (Jack) Palance ....(5)

HALLUCINATION GENERATION (1967) Trans-America. B&W-90min. George Montgomery, Danny Stone ....(2)

HALLUCINATORS, THE (1970) see NAKED ZOO, THE

HAMLET (1948) Universal. B&W-153min. (British). Laurence Olivier, Jean Simmons...............5½*

HAMLET (1960) Emerson Film Enterprises. B&W-120min. (German, Made for TV). Maximilian Schell, Dunja Movar...............

HAMLET (1964) Warner Bros. B&W-186min. Richard Burton, Linda Marsh...............

HAMLET (1964) United Artists. B&W-148min. (U.S.S.R.). Innokentiy Smoktunovskiy, Anastasiya Vertinskaya...............(5)
Original title: GAMLET

HAMLET (1969) Columbia. Color-114min. (British). Nicol Williamson, Marianne Faithfull...............4*

HAMMER (1972) United Artists. Color-91min. Fred Williamson, Bernie Casey...............(3)

HAMMERHEAD (1968) Columbia. Color-99min. (British). Vince Edwards, Judy Geeson...............(2)

HAMMERSMITH IS OUT (1972) J. Cornelius Crean. Color-108min. Elizabeth Taylor, Richard Burton...............(4)

HAMMOND MYSTERY, THE (1942) see UNDYING MONSTER, THE

HAMSTER OF HAPPINESS (1979) U.A. (for Lorimar). Color- min. Robert Blake, Barbara Harris...............

HAND, THE (1960) American-International. B&W-60min. (British). Derek Bond, Reed De Rouen...............(3)

HAND IN HAND (1960) Columbia. B&W-80min. (British). Loretta Parry, Philip Needs...............4*

HAND OF DEATH (1962) 20th Century-Fox. B&W-60min. John Agar, Paula Raymond...............(2)

HAND OF NIGHT (1968) see BEAST OF MOROCCO, THE

HAND OF THE GALLOWS (1960) see TERRIBLE PEOPLE, THE

HANDLE WITH CARE (1958) M-G-M. B&W-82min. Dean Jones, Joan O'Brien...............(3)

HANDLE WITH CARE (1972) H.K. Film Dist. Color-90min. (Foreign). Robert Mark, Luisa Rivelli...............

HANDLE WITH CARE (1977) see CITIZEN'S BAND

HANDS ACROSS THE TABLE (1935) Paramount. B&W-80min. Carole Lombard, Fred MacMurray...............4*

HANDS OF A KILLER (1961) see PLANETS AGAINST US

HANDS OF A STRANGER (1962) Allied Artists. B&W-86min. Paul Lukather, Joan Harvey...............(4)

HANDS OF ORLAC, THE (1924) B&W- min. (Austrian, Silent). Conrad Veidt, Fritz Kortner, Carmen Cartellieri ....(4)
Original title: UNHEIMLICHEN HANDE DES DR. ORLAK, DIE (The Sinister Hands of Dr. Orlak)
Alternate Austrian title: ORLAC HAENDE

HANDS OF ORLAC, THE (1935) see MAD LOVE

HANDS OF ORLAC, THE (1961) Continental [Walter Reade]. B&W-77min. (French-British). Mel Ferrer, Christopher Lee...............(3)
Original French title: MAINS D'ORLAC, LES
Alternate title: HANDS OF A STRANGER

HANDS OF THE RIPPER (1971) Universal. Color-85min. (British). Eric Porter, Angharad Rees...............(4)

HANDS OFF THE LOOT (1954) see GRISBI

HANDS UP! (1926) Paramount. B&W-70min. (Silent). Raymond Griffith, Marian Nixon...............4*

HANG 'EM HIGH (1968) United Artists. Color-114min. Clint Eastwood, Inger Stevens...............4½*

HANGED MAN, THE (1964) Universal. Color-110min. (Made for TV). Robert Culp, Vera Miles, Edmond O'Brien...............(4)

HANGED MAN, THE (1974) MCA-TV. Color-74min. (Made for TV). Steve Forrest, Cameron Mitchell, Sharon Acker...............4*

HANGING TREE, THE (1959) Warner Bros. Color-106min. Gary Cooper, Maria Schell...............5*

HANGMAN, THE (1959) Paramount. B&W-86min. Robert Taylor, Tina Louise, Fess Parker...............(3)

HANGMAN'S HOUSE (1928) Fox Film Co. [20th]. B&W-87min. (Silent). June Collyer, Larry Kent, Earle Foxe...............(4)

HANGMAN'S KNOT (1952) Columbia. Color-81min. Randolph Scott, Donna Reed...............3*

HANGMAN'S NOOSE (1947) see OCTOBER MAN, THE

HANGMEN ALSO DIE (1943) United Artists. B&W-131min. Brian Donlevy, Walter Brennan...............(4)

HANGOVER SQUARE (1945) 20th Century-Fox. B&W-77min. Laird Cregar, Linda Darnell...............(4)

HANNAH LEE (1954) see OUTLAW TERRITORY

HANNIBAL (1960) Warner Bros. Color-103min. (Italian). Victor Mature, Rita Gam...............4*
Original title: ANNIBALE

HANNIBAL BROOKS (1969) United Artists. Color-101min. (British). Oliver Reed, Michael J. Pollard...............(4)

HANNIE CAULDER (1971) Paramount. Color-85min. (British). Raquel Welch, Robert Culp, Ernest Borgnine, Christopher Lee...............4*

HANOVER STREET (1979) Columbia. Color-109min. Harrison Ford, Lesley-Anne Down, Christopher Plummer...............5½*

HANS CHRISTIAN ANDERSEN (1952) RKO. Color-120min. Danny Kaye, Farley Granger...............5*

HANSEL AND GRETEL (1954) RKO. Color-75min. (Puppets). Director: John Paul...............(5)

HAPPENING, THE (1967) Columbia. Color-92min. Anthony Quinn, George Maharis...............(3)

HAPPIEST DAYS OF YOUR LIFE, THE (1950) London Films (Brit.). B&W-81min. (British). Alastair Sim, Margaret Rutherford...............5*

HAPPIEST MILLIONAIRE, THE (1967) Buena Vista. Color-159min. Fred MacMurray, Tommy Steele...............(5)

HAPPINESS AHEAD (1934) First National [W.B.]. B&W-86min. Dick Powell, Frank McHugh...............(4)

HAPPINESS CAGE, THE (1972) see MIND SNATCHERS, THE

HAPPINESS OF 3 WOMEN, THE (1954) see WISHING WELL, THE

HAPPINESS OF US ALONE (1961) Toho. B&W-114min. (Japanese). Hideko Takamine, Keiju Kobayashi...............(5)
Original title: NAMONAKU MAZUSHIKU UTSUKUSHIKU

Films are rated on a 1 to 10 scale, 10 is highest. **Boldface** ratings followed by an asterisk (*) are for films actually seen and rated by the executive and senior editors. All other ratings are estimates. (See Notes on Entertainment Ratings in the front section.)

HAPPY ANNIVERSARY (1959) United Artists. B&W-81min. David Niven, Mitzi Gaynor...(5)

HAPPY AS THE GRASS WAS GREEN (1973) Gateway Films. Color-105min. Geraldine Page, Pat Hingle ....(4)
Alternate title: HAZEL'S PEOPLE

HAPPY BIRTHDAY, WANDA JUNE (1971) Columbia. Color-105min. Rod Steiger, Susannah York..................... 4*

HAPPY END (1967) Continental [Walter Reade]. B&W-73min. *(Czech).* Vladimir Mensik, Jaroslava Obermayerova....................(5)
Made under English title; alternate Czech title: STASTNY KONEC

HAPPY ENDING, THE (1969) United Artists. Color-112min. Jean Simmons, John Forsythe.................................4½*

HAPPY EVER AFTER (1954) *see* TONIGHT'S THE NIGHT

HAPPY FAMILY, THE (1952) *see* MR. LORD SAYS NO

HAPPY GO LOVELY (1951) RKO. Color-88min. *(British).* David Niven, Vera-Ellen...(4)

HAPPY GO LUCKY (1943) Paramount. Color-81min. Mary Martin, Dick Powell ....(4)

HAPPY HOOKER, THE (1975) Cannon Releasing. Color-96min. Lynn Redgrave, Jean-Pierre Aumont..............(3)

HAPPY HOOKER GOES TO WASHINGTON, THE (1977) Cannon Releasing. Color-89min. Joey Heatherton, George Hamilton..............1½*

HAPPY IS THE BRIDE (1958) Kassler Films. B&W-84min. *(British).* Ian Carmichael, Janette Scott, Terry-Thomas....................(4)

HAPPY LAND, THE (1943) 20th Century-Fox. B&W-73min. Don Ameche, Frances Dee.......................................(4)

HAPPY LANDING (1931) *see* FLYING HIGH

HAPPY LANDING (1938) 20th Century-Fox. B&W-102min. Sonja Henie, Don Ameche ....(4)

HAPPY MOTHER'S DAY . . . LOVE, GEORGE (1973) Cinema 5. Color-90min. Patrica Neal, Cloris Leachman.................. 3*
TV title: RUN, STRANGER, RUN

HAPPY NEW YEAR (1973) Avco-Embassy. Color-112min. *(French-Italian).* Lino Ventura, Francoise Fabian 5½*
Original French title: BONNE ANNÉE, LA *(The Good Year)*
Publicity title: HAPPY NEW YEAR CAPER, THE

HAPPY ROAD, THE (1957) M-G-M. B&W-100min. Gene Kelly, Barbara Laage.. 4*

HAPPY THIEVES, THE (1962) United Artists. B&W-88min. Rita Hayworth, Rex Harrison............................... 4*

HAPPY TIME, THE (1952) Columbia. B&W-94min. Charles Boyer, Bobby Driscoll.. 5*

HAPPY YEARS, THE (1950) M-G-M. Color-110min. Dean Stockwell, Darryl Hickman ....(5)
Alternate title: ADVENTURES OF YOUNG DINK STOVER, THE

HARA-KIRI (1934) *see* BATTLE, THE

HARAKIRI (1962) Toho. B&W-135min. *(Japanese).* Tatsuya Nakadai, Shima Iwashita 4*
Original title: SEPPUKU

HARBOR LIGHTS (1963) 20th Century-Fox. B&W-68min. Kent Taylor, Jeff Morrow...(2)

HARBOR OF MISSING MEN (1950) Republic. B&W-60min. Richard Denning, Barbara Fuller..........................(3)

HARD-BOILED CANARY, THE (1941) *see* THERE'S MAGIC IN MUSIC

HARD-BOILED MAHONEY (1947) Monogram [Allied Artists]. B&W-63min. The Bowery Boys, Betty Compson....................(3)

HARD CONTRACT (1969) 20th Century-Fox. Color-106min. James Coburn, Lee Remick 4*

HARD DAY'S NIGHT, A (1964) United Artists. B&W-85min. *(British).* The Beatles................................... 3*

HARD DRIVER (1973) *see* LAST AMERICAN HERO, THE

HARD, FAST AND BEAUTIFUL (1951) RKO. B&W-79min. Claire Trevor, Sally Forrest.. 3*

HARD MAN, THE (1957) Columbia. Color-80min. Guy Madison, Valerie French..(4)

HARD RIDE, THE (1971) American-International. Color-93min. Robert Fuller, Sherry Bain................................ 2*

HARD TIMES (1975) Columbia. Color-92min. James Coburn, Charles Bronson... 5½*
British title: STREETFIGHTER, THE

HARD TIMES FOR DRACULA (1959) *see* UNCLE WAS A VAMPIRE

HARD TO GET (1938) Warner Bros. B&W-80min. Olivia de Havilland, Dick Powell...(4)

HARD TO HANDLE (1933) Warner Bros. B&W-75min. James Cagney, Mary Brian....................................3*

HARD WAY, THE (1942) Warner Bros. B&W-109min. Ida Lupino, Dennis Morgan...(5)

HARDCASE (1971) Viacom. Color-74min. *(Made for TV).* Clint Walker, Stefanie Powers, Alex Karras ....(4)

HARDCORE (1979) Columbia. Color-105min. George C. Scott, Peter Boyle, Season Hubley....................................5*

HARDER THEY COME, THE (1972) New World. Color-100min. *(Jamaican).* Jimmy Cliff, Janet Barkley.................... 4*

HARDER THEY FALL, THE (1956) Columbia. B&W-109min. Humphrey Bogart, Rod Steiger 5*

HARDYS RIDE HIGH, THE (1939) M-G-M. B&W-80min. Lewis Stone, Mickey Rooney ....(4)

HAREM GIRL (1952) Columbia. B&W-70min. Joan Davis, Peggy Castle (3)

HAREM HOLIDAY (1965) *see* HARUM SCARUM

HAREM KEEPER OF THE OIL SHEIKS (1976) *see* ILSA, HAREM KEEPER OF THE OIL SHEIKS

HARLAN COUNTY, U.S.A. (1976) Cabin Creek Films. Color-103min. *(Documentary). Director:* Barbara Kopple...............4½*

HARLEM GLOBETROTTERS, THE (1951) Columbia. B&W-80min. Thomas Gomez, Dorothy Dandridge 4*

HARLEM ROCK 'N' ROLL (1956) *see* ROCK 'N' ROLL REVUE

HARLOW (1965) Paramount. Color-125min. Carroll Baker, Martin Balsam... 3*

HARLOW (1965) Magna Pictures. B&W-108min. Carol Lynley, Efrem Zimbalist, Jr. 2*

HARMONY PARADE, THE (1936) *see* PIGSKIN PARADE

HARNESS, THE (1971) Universal. Color-100min. *(Made for TV).* Lorne Greene, Julie Sommars 4*

HAROLD AND MAUDE (1971) Paramount. Color-90min. Bud Cort, Ruth Gordon 6½*

HAROLD LLOYD'S WORLD OF COMEDY (1962) Columbia. B&W-94min. *(Compilation). Producer:* Harold Lloyd....................(5)

HARP OF BURMA (1956) *see* BURMESE HARP, THE

HARPER (1966) Warner Bros. Color-121min. Paul Newman, Lauren Bacall 4*
British title: MOVING TARGET, THE

HARPER VALLEY P.T.A. (1978) April Fools Productions. Color-107min. Barbara Eden, Susan Swift, Ronny Cox, Nanette Fabray ....(4)

HARPY (1971) Cinema Center 100. Color-100min. *(Made for TV).* Hugh O'Brien, Elizabeth Ashley, Marlyn Mason.................. 3*

HARRAD EXPERIMENT, THE (1973) Cinerama Releasing. Color-96min. James Whitmore, Tippi Hedren 5½*

HAROLD AND MAUDE (1971). With his obnoxious mother arranging computer dates for him, Bud Cort stages another of his fake suicides to scare off the latest selection, Ellen Geer, but he doesn't count on her being an actress who's ready to do him one better at his own game.

HARRAD SUMMER (1974) Cinerama Releasing. **Color-105min.** Robert Reiser, Laurie Walters 5*

HARRIET CRAIG (1950) Columbia. **B&W-94min.** Joan Crawford, Wendell Corey 4½*

HARRIGAN'S KID (1943) M-G-M. **B&W-80min.** William Gargan, Bobby Readick .... (3)

HARRY AND TONTO (1974) 20th Century-Fox. **Color-115min.** Art Carney, Tonto 5½*

HARRY AND WALTER GO TO NEW YORK (1976) Columbia. **Color-105min.** James Caan, Elliott Gould 5*

HARRY BLACK AND THE TIGER (1958) 20th Century-Fox. **Color-107min.** (British). Stewart Granger, Barbara Rush 3*
Alternate title: HARRY BLACK

HARRY IN YOUR POCKET (1973) United Artists. **Color-102min.** James Coburn, Michael Sarrazin 5*
Alternate title: HARRY NEVER HOLDS

HARUM SCARUM (1965) M-G-M. **Color-95min.** Elvis Presley, Mary Ann Mobley 3*
British and alternate U.S. title: HAREM HOLIDAY

HARVEST (1937) French Cinema Center. **B&W-80min.** (French). Gabriel Gabrio, Fernandel, Edouard Delmont ....
Original title: REGAIN

HARVEY (1950) Universal. **B&W-104min.** James Stewart, Josephine Hull 6*

HARVEY GIRLS, THE (1946) M-G-M. **Color-104min.** Judy Garland, John Hodiak 4*

HARVEY MIDDLEMAN, FIREMAN (1965) Columbia. **Color-75min.** Gene Troobnick, Hermione Gingold .... (4)

HAS ANYBODY SEEN MY GAL (1952) Universal. **Color-89min.** Piper Laurie, Rock Hudson 4½*

HASTY HEART, THE (1949) Warner Bros. **B&W-99min.** Ronald Reagan, Patricia Neal, Richard Todd 4½*

HATARI (1962) Paramount. **Color-159min.** John Wayne, Hardy Kruger 4*

HATCHET FOR THE HONEYMOON (1969) G.G.P. **Color-83min.** (Italian-Spanish). Stephen Forsyth, Dagmar Lassander, Laura Betti 2*
Original Italian title: ROSSO SEGNO DELLA FOLLIA, IL (*The Red Mark of Madness*)
Spanish title: HACHA PARA LA LUNA DE MIEL, UNA
British title: BLOOD BRIDES

HATCHET MAN, THE (1932) First National [W.B.]. **B&W-74min.** Edward G. Robinson, Loretta Young 3*
British title: HONOURABLE MR. WONG, THE

HATFUL OF RAIN, A (1957) 20th Century-Fox. **B&W-109min.** Eva Marie Saint, Don Murray 5½*

HATS OFF TO RHYTHM (1946) *see* EARL CARROLL SKETCHBOOK

HATTER'S CASTLE (1941) Paramount. **B&W-105min.** (British). Robert Newton, Deborah Kerr .... (4)

HAUNTED AND THE HUNTED, THE (1963) *see* DEMENTIA 13

HAUNTED HONEYMOON (1940) M-G-M. **B&W-83min.** (British). Robert Montgomery, Constance Cummings .... (4)
Original title: BUSMAN'S HONEYMOON

HAUNTED HOUSE, THE (1921) Metro. **B&W-20min.** (Silent). Buster Keaton, Virginia Fox 5*

HAUNTED HOUSE OF HORROR, THE (1970) *see* HORROR HOUSE

HAUNTED PALACE, THE (1964) American-International. **Color-85min.** Vincent Price, Debra Paget, Lon Chaney (Jr.) 3½*

HAUNTED PLANET (1965) *see* PLANET OF THE VAMPIRES

HAUNTED STRANGLER, THE (1958) M-G-M. **B&W-81min.** (British). Boris Karloff, Jean Kent .... (3)
Original title: GRIP OF THE STRANGLER

HAUNTING, THE (1963) M-G-M. **B&W-112min.** (U.S.-British). Julie Harris, Claire Bloom 3*

HAUNTS (1977) Intercontinental Films. **Color-98min.** May Britt, Aldo Ray, Cameron Mitchell 3*
Alternate title: VEIL, THE

HAUNTS OF THE VERY RICH (1972) Worldvision. **Color-75min.** (Made for TV). Lloyd Bridges, Cloris Leachman, Anne Francis, Edward Asner 4*

HAUSER'S MEMORY (1970) Universal. **Color-100min.** (Made for TV). David McCallum, Susan Strasberg, Lilli Palmer, Robert Webber 4*

HAVANA ROSE (1951) Republic. **B&W-77min.** Estrelita Rodriguez, Bill Williams .... (3)

HAVE ROCKET, WILL TRAVEL (1959) Columbia. **B&W-76min.** The Three Stooges, Jerome Cowan .... (2)

HAVE YOU HEARD OF THE SAN FRANCISCO MIME TROUPE? (1968) Filmmakers. **Color-60min.** .... (4)

HAVING A WILD WEEKEND (1965) Warner Bros. **B&W-91min.** The Dave Clark Five, Barbara Ferris .... (3)
Original title: CATCH US IF YOU CAN

HAVING BABIES (1976) Jozak Company. **Color-100min.** (Made for TV). Desi Arnaz, Jr., Adrienne Barbeau, Ronny Cox, Jan Sterling 2½*

HAVING BABIES II (1977) ABC-TV. **Color-100min.** (Made for TV). Tony Bill, Carol Lynley, Paula Prentiss, Wayne Rogers ....

HAVING BABIES III (1978) ABC-TV. **Color-100min.** (Made for TV). Susan Sullivan, Patty Duke Astin, Jamie Smith Jackson, Rue McClanahan....

HAVING WONDERFUL CRIME (1945) RKO. **B&W-70min.** Pat O'Brien, George Murphy .... (5)

HAVING WONDERFUL TIME (1938) RKO. **B&W-71min.** Ginger Rogers, Douglas Fairbanks, Jr. .... (4)

HAWAII (1966) United Artists. **Color-186min.** Julie Andrews, Max Von Sydow 5*

HAWAII FIVE-O (1968) Viacom. **Color-73min.** (Made for TV). Jack Lord, Nancy Kwan, Leslie Nielsen 4*

HAWAIIANS, THE (1970) United Artists. **Color-134min.** Charlton Heston, Geraldine Chaplin 5*
British title: MASTER OF THE ISLANDS

HAWK OF THE WILDERNESS (1938) *see* LOST ISLAND OF KIOGA

HAWKINS ON MURDER (1973) M-G-M. **Color-74min.** (Made for TV). James Stewart, Bonnie Bedelia, Strother Martin .... (4)

HAWKS AND THE SPARROWS, THE (1966) Brandon. **B&W-91min.** (Italian). Toto, Ninetto Davoli .... (5)
Original title: UCCELLACCI E UCCELLINI

HAWMPS (1976) Mulberry Square. **Color-126min.** James Hampton, Christopher Connelly 4*

HAZARD (1948) Paramount. **B&W-95min.** Macdonald Carey, Paulette Goddard .... (3)

HAZEL'S PEOPLE (1973) *see* HAPPY AS THE GRASS WAS GREEN

HAZING, THE (1978) Miraleste Company. **Color-90min.** Jeff East, Brad David ....

HE LAUGHED LAST (1956) Columbia. **Color-77min.** Frankie Laine, Lucy Marlow .... (4)

HE MARRIED HIS WIFE (1940) 20th Century-Fox. **B&W-83min.** Joel McCrea, Nancy Kelly .... (3)

HE RAN ALL THE WAY (1951) United Artists. **B&W-77min.** John Garfield, Shelley Winters .... (4)

HE RIDES TALL (1964) Universal. **B&W-84min.** Tony Young, Dan Duryea .... (3)

HE STAYED FOR BREAKFAST (1940) Columbia. **B&W-89min.** Loretta Young, Melvyn Douglas .... (3)

HE WALKED BY NIGHT (1948) Eagle Lion. **B&W-79min.** Richard Basehart, Scott Brady 4*

HE WAS HER MAN (1934) Warner Bros. **B&W-70min.** James Cagney, Joan Blondell .... (4)

HE WHO GETS SLAPPED (1924) M-G-M. **B&W-76min.** (Silent). Lon Chaney, Norma Shearer, John Gilbert 3*

HE WHO MUST DIE (1957) Lopert [U.A.]. **B&W-129min.** (French). Pierre Vaneck, Melina Mercouri 6*
Foreign title: CELUI QUI DOIT MOURIER

HE WHO RIDES A TIGER (1966) Sigma III. **B&W-103min.** (British). Tom Bell, Judi Dench .... (5)

HEAD, THE (1959) Trans-Lux Distributing. **B&W-92min.** (German). Horst Frank, Michel Simon, Karin Kernke .... (2)
Original title: NACKTE UND DER SATAN, DIE
Alternate title: HEAD FOR THE DEVIL, A
Alternate title: SCREAMING HEAD, THE

HEAD (1968) Columbia. **Color-86min.** The Monkees, Victor Mature, Timothy Carey 3½*

HEAD OF A TYRANT (1959) Universal. **Color-94min.** (Italian-French). Isabelle Corey, Massimo Girotti .... (3)
Original Italian title: GIUDETTA E OLOFERNE
Alternate title: JUDITH AND HOLOPHERNES

HEADIN' FOR HEAVEN (1947) Eagle Lion. **B&W-71min.** Stuart Erwin, Glenda Farrell .... (3)

HEADLESS GHOST, THE (1959) American-International. **B&W-63min.** (British). Richard Lyon, Clive Revill .... (2)

HEADLINE HUNTERS (1955) Republic. **B&W-70min.** Rod Cameron, Julie Bishop .... (3)

HEADLINES OF DESTRUCTION (1955) American-International. **B&W-85min.** (French-Italian). Eddie Constantine, Bella Darvi .... (3)

HEADQUARTERS STATE SECRET (1962) Telewide Systems. **B&W-103min.** *(German).* Gert Frobe, Peter Carsten.................................(3)

HEALERS, THE (1974) Warner Bros. **Color-100min.** *(Made for TV).* John Forsythe, Pat Harrington, Beverly Garland.................(4)

HEALTH (1979) 20th Century-Fox. **Color-   min.** Carol Burnett, Lauren Bacall, James Garner, Glenda Jackson

HEAR ME GOOD (1957) Paramount. **B&W-80min.** Hal March, Merry Anders ....(3)

HEART BEAT (1979) Warner Bros. (for Orion). **Color-   min.** Nick Nolte, Sissy Spacek, John Heard ....

HEART IS A LONELY HUNTER, THE (1968) Warner Bros. **Color-124min.** Alan Arkin, Sondra Locke...................................**5½***

HEART OF A CHILD (1958) United Artists. **B&W-76min.** *(British).* Jean Anderson, Donald Pleasance............................(5)

HEART OF A MAN (1959) Continental [Walter Reade]. **B&W-92min.** *(British).* Frankie Vaughan, Anne Heywood....................(3)

HEART OF GLASS (1976) New Yorker Films. **Color-93min.** *(German).* Josef Bierbieler, Stefan Guttler...........................
Original title: HERZ AUS GLAS

HEART OF NEW YORK (1933) *see* HALLELUJAH, I'M A BUM

HEART OF THE MATTER, THE (1953) Associated Artists. **B&W-105min.** *(British).* Trevor Howard, Elizabeth Allan **3***

HEART OF VIRGINIA (1948) Republic. **B&W-55min.** Janet Martin, Robert Lowery...(3)

HEART WITHIN, THE (1957) J. Arthur Rank. **B&W-61min.** *(British).* James Hayter, Earl Cameron ....(3)

HEARTBEAT (1946) RKO. **B&W-102min.** Ginger Rogers, Jean-Pierre Aumont ....(4)

HEARTBREAK KID, THE (1972) 20th Century-Fox. **Color-104min.** Charles Grodin, Cybill Shepherd, Jeannie Berlin **6***

HEARTS AND MINDS (1974) Columbia. **Color-110min.** *(Documentary).* Director: Peter Davis **4***

HEARTS DIVIDED (1936) First National [W.B.]. **B&W-87min.** Dick Powell, Marion Davies..................................(4)

HEARTS IN SPRINGTIME (1941) *see* GLAMOUR BOY

HEARTS OF THE WEST (1975) U.A. (for M-G-M). **Color-102min.** Jeff Bridges, Andy Griffith **5½***
British title: HOLLYWOOD COWBOY

HEARTS OF THE WORLD (1918) D. W. Griffith. **B&W-117min.** *(Silent).* Robert Harron, Lillian Gish **3***

HEAT (1972) Levitt-Pickman. **Color-100min.** Joe Dallesandro, Sylvia Miles...**2***

HEAT OF ANGER (1971) MPC (TV). **Color-74min.** *(Made for TV).* Susan Hayward, James Stacy, Lee J. Cobb...................(4)

HEAT WAVE (1954) Lippert Productions. **B&W-68min.** *(British).* Alex Nicol, Hillary Brooke ....(3)
Original title: HOUSE ACROSS THE LAKE, THE

HEAT WAVE (1974) MCA-TV. **Color-74min.** *(Made for TV).* Ben Murphy, Bonnie Bedelia, Lew Ayres.........................(4)

HEAT'S ON, THE (1943) Columbia. **B&W-80min.** Mae West, Victor Moore **4***
British title: TROPICANA

HEAVEN CAN WAIT (1943) 20th Century-Fox. **Color-113min.** Don Ameche, Gene Tierney..................................**6½***

HEAVEN CAN WAIT (1978) Paramount. **Color-100min.** Warren Beatty, Julie Christie, James Mason **6***

HEAVEN FELL THAT NIGHT (1958) *see* NIGHT HEAVEN FELL, THE

HEAVEN KNOWS, MR. ALLISON (1957) 20th Century-Fox. **Color-107min.** Deborah Kerr, Robert Mitchum...............**5***

HEAVEN ON EARTH (1960) JB Film Enterprises. **Color-84min.** *(U.S.-Italian).* Barbara Florian, Charles Fawcett, Arnoldo Foa...........(3)

HEAVEN ONLY KNOWS (1947) United Artists. **B&W-95min.** Robert Cummings, Brian Donlevy...........................(4)
Alternate title: MONTANA MIKE

HEAVEN WITH A BARBED WIRE FENCE (1939) 20th Century-Fox. **B&W-62min.** Glenn Ford, Jean Rogers.................(4)

HEAVEN WITH A GUN (1969) M-G-M. **Color-101min.** Glenn Ford, Carolyn Jones.......................................**3½***

HEAVENLY BODY, THE (1943) M-G-M. **B&W-95min.** Hedy Lamarr, William Powell...................................(3)

HEAVENLY DAYS (1944) RKO. **B&W-71min.** Fibber McGee and Molly, Barbara Hale..(3)

HEAVENS ABOVE! (1963) Janus Films. **B&W-105min.** *(British).* Peter Sellers, Cecil Parker ....(5)

HEAVEN CAN WAIT (1943). Amorous Don Ameche impulsively poses as a sales clerk and tries to dissuade bride-to-be Gene Tierney from her wedding plans. (This movie has no connection with the 1978 film of the same title, but see note on the next photo, page 115).

HEAVEN'S GATE (1980) United Artists. **Color-   min.** Kris Kristofferson, Christopher Walken...........................

HEAVY TRAFFIC (1973) American-International. **Color-76min.** *(Cartoon).* Director: Ralph Bakshi **5***

HEC (1971) *see* CENTURY TURNS, THE

HEDDA (1975) Brut Productions. **Color-104min.** *(British).* Glenda Jackson, Peter Eyre **4***

HEIDI (1937) 20th Century-Fox. **B&W-88min.** Shirley Temple, Jean Hersholt **5***

HEIDI (1952) United Artists. **B&W-85min.** *(Swiss).* Elspeth Sigmund, Heinrich Gretler...............................(5)

HEIDI AND PETER (1955) United Artists. **Color-89min.** *(Swiss).* Elspeth Sigmund, Heinrich Gretler, Thomas Klameth............(4)

HEIRESS, THE (1949) Paramount. **B&W-115min.** Olivia de Havilland, Montgomery Clift..................................**6½***

HEIST, THE (1971) *see* DOLLARS

HEIST, THE (1972) Paramount. **Color-74min.** *(Made for TV).* Christopher George, Elizabeth Ashley......................(4)

HELEN MORGAN STORY, THE (1957) Warner Bros. **B&W-118min.** Ann Blyth, Paul Newman.....................**4½***
British title: BOTH ENDS OF THE CANDLE

HELEN OF TROY (1956) Warner Bros. **Color-118min.** Rossana Podesta, Jacques Sernas ....(4)

HELEN OF TROY (1964) *see* LION OF THEBES, THE

HELGA (1967) American-International. **Color-76min.** *(German).* Ruth Gassmann, Eberhard Mondry ....(3)
Original title: VOM WERDEN DES MENSCHLICHEN LEBENS

HELGA UND MICHAEL (1968) *see* MICHAEL AND HELGA

HELL AND HIGH WATER (1954) 20th Century-Fox. **Color-103min.** Richard Widmark, Bella Darvi........................(4)

HELL BELOW (1933) M-G-M. **B&W-105min.** Robert Montgomery, Walter Huston...(4)

HELL BELOW ZERO (1954) M-G-M. **Color-91min.** *(British).* Alan Ladd, Joan Tetzel..(3)

HELL BENT FOR GLORY (1957) *see* LAFAYETTE ESCADRILLE

HELL BENT FOR LEATHER (1960) Universal. **Color-82min.** Audie Murphy, Felicia Farr...............................(4)

HELL BOATS (1970) United Artists. **Color-95min.** *(British).* James Franciscus, Elizabeth Shepherd **4***

HELL CANYON OUTLAWS (1957) Republic. **B&W-72min.** Dale Robertson, Brian Keith ....(4)
British title: TALL TROUBLE, THE

HELL DIVERS (1931) M-G-M. **B&W-113min.** Wallace Beery, Clark Gable..**4***

HELL DRIVERS (1957) J. Arthur Rank. **B&W-91min.** *(British).* Stanley Baker, Herbert Lom.................................(4)

HELL IN KOREA (1956) Distributors Corp. of America. B&W-82min. *(British)*. George Baker, Stanley Baker, Harry Andrews 4*
Original title: HILL IN KOREA, A

HELL IN THE PACIFIC (1969) Cinerama Releasing. Color-103min. Lee Marvin, Toshiro Mifune .... (4)

HELL IS A CITY (1960) Columbia. B&W-96min. *(British)*. Stanley Baker, Donald Pleasence .... (4)

HELL IS FOR HEROES (1962) Paramount. B&W-90min. Steve McQueen, Bobby Darin .... (5)

HELL OF LOST PILOTS, THE (1948) B&W-90min. *(French)*. Daniel Gélin, Henri Vidal .... (3)
Original title: PARADIS DES PILOTES PERDUS, LE *(The Paradise of Lost Pilots)*

HELL ON DEVIL'S ISLAND (1957) 20th Century-Fox. B&W-74min. Helmut Dantine, William Talman .... (3)

HELL ON FRISCO BAY (1956) Warner Bros. Color-98min. Alan Ladd, Edward G. Robinson .... (3)

HELL ON WHEELS (1967) Crown International. Color-96min. Marty Robbins, John Ashley, Gigi Perreau .... (2)

HELL RAIDERS (1968) American-International. Color-80min. *(Made for TV)*. John Agar, Richard Webb 2*

HELL RAIDERS OF THE DEEP (1954) Italian Films Export. B&W-93min. *(Italian)*. Eleonora Rossi-Drago, Pierre Cressoy .... (5)
Original title: SETTE DELL' ORSA MAGGIORE, I

HELL SHIP MUTINY (1957) Republic. B&W-66min. Jon Hall, John Carradine, Peter Lorre .... (3)

HELL SQUAD (1958) American-International. B&W-64min. Wally Campo, Brandon Carroll .... (3)

HELL TO ETERNITY (1960) Allied Artists. B&W-132min. Jeffrey Hunter, David Janssen .... (5)

HELL UP IN HARLEM (1973) American-International. Color-96min. Fred Williamson, Julius W. Harris .... (3)

HELL WITH HEROES, THE (1968) Universal. Color-102min. Rod Taylor, Claudia Cardinale 3½*

HELLBENDERS, THE (1966) Avco-Embassy. Color-92min. *(Italian-Spanish)*. Joseph Cotten, Norma Bengell .... (3)
Original Italian title: CRUDELI, I
Original Spanish title: DESPIADADOS, LOS

HELLCATS, THE (1968) Crown International. Color-90min. Ross Hagen, Dee Duffy .... (3)

HELLCATS OF THE NAVY (1957) Columbia. B&W-82min. Ronald Reagan, Nancy Davis .... (4)

HELLER IN PINK TIGHTS (1960) Paramount. Color-100min. Sophia Loren, Anthony Quinn 4*

HELLFIGHTERS (1968) Universal. Color-121min. John Wayne, Katharine Ross, Jim Hutton 3*

HELLFIRE (1949) Republic. B&W-90min. William Elliott, Marie Windsor 4*

HELLFIRE CLUB, THE (1961) Avco-Embassy. Color-93min. *(British)*. Keith Michell, Kai Fischer, Peter Cushing .... (3)

HELLGATE (1952) Lippert Productions. B&W-87min. Sterling Hayden, Joan Leslie .... (4)

HELLIONS, THE (1961) Columbia. Color-80min. *(British)*. Richard Todd, Anne Aubrey .... (3)

HELLO! BEAUTIFUL (1942) *see* POWERS GIRL, THE

HELLO, DOLLY! (1969) 20th Century-Fox. Color-148min. Barbra Streisand, Walter Matthau 5½*

HELLO DOWN THERE (1969) Paramount. Color-98min. Tony Randall, Janet Leigh 3*

HELLO ELEPHANT (1952) Arlan Pictures. B&W-83min. *(Italian)*. Vittorio De Sica, Sabu, Maria Mercader .... (3)
Original title: BUONGIORNO, ELEFANTE! *(Good Morning, Elephant!)*
Alternate title: PARDON MY TRUNK

HELLO FRISCO, HELLO (1943) 20th Century-Fox. Color-98min. Alice Faye, John Payne 4*

HELLO - GOODBYE (1970) 20th Century-Fox. Color-107min. Michael Crawford, Genevieve Gilles .... (3)

HELLO, SISTER (1933) Fox Film Co. [20th]. B&W-62min. James Dunn, Boots Mallory .... (4)
Alternate title(?): WALKING DOWN BROADWAY

HELLO SUCKER (1941) Universal. B&W-60min. Hugh Herbert, Peggy Moran, Tom Brown .... (3)

HELL'S ANGELS (1930) United Artists. B&W-135min. Ben Lyon, James Hall 3*

HELL'S ANGELS ON WHEELS (1967) U.S. Films. Color-95min. Jack Nicholson, Adam Roarke 3*

HELL'S ANGELS '69 (1969) American-International. Color-97min. Tom Stern, Jeremy Slate .... (2)

HELL'S BELLES (1969) American-International. Color-98min. Jeremy Slate, Adam Roarke, Jocelyn Lane .... (3)

HELL'S BLOODY DEVILS (1970) Independent International. Color-92min. Kent Taylor, John Gabriel, Broderick Crawford, Robert Dix ... (2)
British title: SMASHING THE CRIME SYNDICATE
TV title: FAKERS, THE

HELL'S CREATURES (1968) *see* FRANKENSTEIN'S BLOODY TERROR

HELL'S CROSSROADS (1957) Republic. B&W-73min. Stephen McNally, Peggie Castle .... (3)

HELL'S FIVE HOURS (1958) Allied Artists. B&W-73min. Stephen McNally, Vic Morrow .... (3)

HELL'S GATE (1953) *see* GATE OF HELL

HELL'S HALF ACRE (1954) Republic. B&W-91min. Wendell Corey, Evelyn Keyes .... (3)

HELL'S HEROES (1930) Universal. B&W-65min. *(Silent)*. Charles Bickford, Raymond Hatton 4*

HELL'S HIGHWAY (1932) RKO. B&W-80min. Richard Dix, Tom Brown 4*

HELL'S HINGES (1916) Triangle. B&W-39min. *(Silent)*. William S. Hart, Clara Williams 3*

HELL'S HORIZON (1955) Columbia. B&W-80min. John Ireland, Marla English .... (3)

HELL'S ISLAND (1955) Paramount. Color-84min. John Payne, Mary Murphy 3*

HELL'S KITCHEN (1939) Warner Bros. B&W-81min. Billy Halop, Bobby Jordan 3*

HELL'S LONG ROAD (1963) Color-89min. *(Italian)*. Elena Brazzi, Kay Nolandi, Berto Frankis .... (4)

HELL'S OUTPOST (1954) Republic. B&W-90min. Rod Cameron, Joan Leslie .... (3)

HELLSTROM CHRONICLE, THE (1971) Cinema 5. Color-90min. *(Documentary)*. *Director:* Walon Green 6*

HELLZAPOPPIN! (1941) Universal. B&W-84min. Ole Olsen, Chic Johnson 3*

HELP! (1965) United Artists. Color-92min. *(British)*. The Beatles, Victor Spinetti 2½*

HELTER SKELTER (1976) Lorimar Productions. Color-200min. *(Made for TV)*. George DiCenzo, Steven Railsback 5½*

HEMINGWAY'S ADVENTURES OF A YOUNG MAN (1962) 20th Century-Fox. Color-145min. Richard Beymer, Arthur Kennedy 4*
Alternate title: ADVENTURES OF A YOUNG MAN

HENNESSY (1975) American-International. Color-104min. *(British)*. Rod Steiger, Lee Remick, Trevor Howard .... (4)

HENPECKED (1941) *see* BLONDIE IN SOCIETY

HENRIETTE (1953) *see* HOLIDAY FOR HENRIETTA

HENRY ALDRICH, BOY SCOUT (1944) Paramount. B&W-66min. Jimmy Lydon, Charles Smith, Diana Lynn .... (4)
British title: HENRY -- BOY SCOUT

HENRY ALDRICH, EDITOR (1942) Paramount. B&W-72min. Jimmy Lydon, Charles Smith, Rita Quigley .... (3)

HENRY ALDRICH FOR PRESIDENT (1941) Paramount. B&W-70min. Jimmy Lydon, Charles Smith, June Preisser .... (3)

HENRY ALDRICH GETS GLAMOUR (1943) Paramount. B&W-72min. Jimmy Lydon, Charles Smith, Diana Lynn .... (3)
British title: HENRY GETS GLAMOUR

HENRY ALDRICH HAUNTS A HOUSE (1943) Paramount. B&W-73min. Jimmy Lydon, Charles Smith, Joan Mortimer .... (3)
British title: HENRY HAUNTS A HOUSE

HENRY ALDRICH PLAYS CUPID (1944) Paramount. B&W-65min. Jimmy Lydon, Charles Smith, Diana Lynn .... (3)
British title: HENRY PLAYS CUPID

HENRY ALDRICH SWINGS IT (1943) Paramount. B&W-65min. Jimmy Lydon, Charles Smith, Mimi Chandler .... (3)
British title: HENRY SWINGS IT

HENRY ALDRICH'S LITTLE SECRET (1944) Paramount. B&W-74min. Jimmy Lydon, Charles Smith, Joan Mortimer .... (3)
British title: HENRY'S LITTLE SECRET

HENRY AND DIZZY (1942) Paramount. B&W-71min. Jimmy Lydon, Mary Anderson, Charles Smith .... (3)

HENRY GOES ARIZONA (1939) M-G-M. B&W-67min. Frank Morgan, Guy Kibbee...(3)
British title: SPATS TO SPURS

HENRY MILLER ODYSSEY, THE (1974) Grove Press. Color-110min. *(Documentary). Director:* Robert Snyder..(3)

HENRY, THE RAINMAKER (1949) Monogram [Allied Artists]. B&W-64min. Raymond Walburn, Walter Catlett.......................................(3)

HENRY V (1944) J. Arthur Rank. Color-137min. *(British).* Laurence Olivier, Robert Newton...4*

HENRY VIII AND HIS SIX WIVES (1972) Levitt-Pickman. Color-125min. *(British).* Keith Michell, Donald Pleasence, Charlotte Rampling, Jane Asher..

HER ADVENTUROUS NIGHT (1946) Universal. B&W-76min. Dennis O'Keefe, Helen Walker...(4)

HER CARDBOARD LOVER (1942) M-G-M. B&W-93min. Norma Shearer, Robert Taylor...(3)

HER FAVORITE PATIENT (1945) *see* BEDSIDE MANNER

HER FIRST ROMANCE (1951) Columbia. B&W-73min. Margaret O'Brien, Allan Martin, Jr...(3)
British title: GIRLS NEVER TELL

HER HIGHNESS AND THE BELLBOY (1945) M-G-M. B&W-112min. Hedy Lamarr, Robert Walker...4*

HER HUSBAND'S AFFAIRS (1947) Columbia. B&W-82min. Franchot Tone, Lucille Ball...(3)

HER JUNGLE LOVE (1938) Paramount. Color-81min. Dorothy Lamour, Ray Milland...(3)

HER KIND OF MAN (1946) Warner Bros. B&W-78min. Dane Clark, Janis Paige...(3)

HER LUCKY NIGHT (1945) Universal. B&W-63min. The Andrews Sisters, Noah Beery, Jr...(3)

HER MAJESTY, LOVE (1931) First National [W.B.]. B&W-75min. Marilyn Miller, Ben Lyon, W. C. Fields.....................................(4)

HER MAN GILBEY (1948) Universal. B&W-89min. *(British).* Michael Wilding, Lilli Palmer...(4)
Alternate title: ENGLISH WITHOUT TEARS

HER PANELLED DOOR (1950) Souvaine Selective. B&W-84min. *(British).* Phyllis Calvert, Edward Underdown, Richard Burton....................(5)
Original title: WOMEN WITH NO NAME, THE

HER PRIMITIVE MAN (1944) Universal. B&W-79min. Robert Paige, Louise Allbritton, Robert Benchley..(3)

HER REPUTATION (1933) *see* BROADWAY BAD

HER SISTER'S SECRET (1946) Producers Rel. Corp. [Eagle Lion]. B&W-86min. Nancy Coleman, Philip Reed...(4)

HER TWELVE MEN (1954) M-G-M. Color-91min. Greer Garson, Robert Ryan..(4)

HERBIE GOES TO MONTE CARLO (1977) Buena Vista. Color-105min. Dean Jones, Don Knotts, Julie Sommars...................................(5)

HERBIE RIDES AGAIN (1974) Buena Vista. Color-88min. Helen Hayes, Ken Berry..(4)

HERCULE (1938) Pathé Consortium Films *(French).* B&W-90min. *(French).* Fernandel, Gaby Morlay..(3)

HERCULES (1957) Warner Bros. Color-107min. *(Italian).* Steve Reeves, Sylva Koscina...3½*
Original title: FATICHE DI ERCOLE, LE *(The Labors of Hercules)*

HERCULES AGAINST ROME (1964) American-International. Color-87min. *(Italian-French).* Alan Steel, Wandisa Guida....................(2)
Original Italian title: ERCOLE CONTRO ROMA
Original French title: HERCULE CONTRE ROME

HERCULES AGAINST THE BARBARIANS (1964) American-International. Color-91min. *(Italian).* Mark Forrest, José Greci.............(1)
Original title: MACISTE NELL' INFERNO DI GENGIS KHAN *(Maciste in Ghengis Khan's Hell)*

HERCULES AGAINST THE MONGOLS (1960) American-International. Color-90min. *(Italian).* Mark Forrest, Jose Gréci......................(1)

HERCULES AGAINST THE MOON MEN (1965) Governor. Color-88min. *(Italian-French).* Alan Steel, Jany Clair..............................(2)
Original Italian title: MACISTE E LA REGINA DI SAMAR *(Maciste and the Queen of Samar)*
Original French title: MACISTE CONTRE LES HOMMES DE PIERRE *(Maciste vs. the Stone Men)*
Alternate Italian title: MACISTE CONTRO GLI UOMINI DELLA LUNA *(Maciste vs. the Moon Men)*

HERCULES AGAINST THE SONS OF THE SUN (1964) Screen Gems. Color-89min. *(Italian-Spanish).* Mark Forest, Anna Maria Pace..........(2)
Original Italian title: ERCOLE CONTRO I FIGLI DEL SOLE
Original Spanish title: HERCULES CONTRA LOS HIJOS DEL SOL

HERCULES AND THE BLACK PIRATES (1962) American-International. Color-91min. *(Italian).* Alan Steel, Rosalba Neri.................(1)
Original title: SANSONE CONTRO IL CORSARO NERO *(Samson vs. the Black Pirate)*

HERCULES AND THE CAPTIVE WOMEN (1961) Woolner Brothers. Color-87min. *(Italian-French).* Reg Park, Fay Spain.............(3)
Original title: ERCOLE ALLA CONQUISTA DI ATLANTIDE *(Hercules and the Conquest of Atlantis)*
British title: HERCULES CONQUERS ATLANTIS

HERCULES AND THE MASKED RIDER (1963) American-International. Color-86min. *(Italian).* Alan Steel, Ettore Manni...............(1)
Original title: GOLIA E IL CAVALIERE MASCHERATO *(Goliath and the Masked Rider)*

HERCULES AND THE TEN AVENGERS (1964) *see* HERCULES VS. THE GIANT WARRIORS

HERCULES AND THE TREASURE OF THE INCAS (1965) American-International. Color-90min. *(Italian).* Alan Steel (Sergio Ciani), Mario Petri..(1)
Original title: SANSONE E IL TESORO DEGLI INCAS *(Samson and the Treasure of the Incas)*
Alternate title: LOST TREASURE OF THE AZTECS

HERCULES AND THE TYRANTS OF BABYLON (1964) American-International. Color-86min. *(Italian).* Rock Stevens, Helga Line.........(1)
Original title: ERCOLE CONTRO I TIRANNI DI BABILONIA

HERCULES CONQUERS ATLANTIS (1963) *see* HERCULES AND THE CAPTIVE WOMEN

HERCULES IN NEW YORK (1970) RAF Industries. Color-90min. Arnold Stang, Arnold Strong (Schwarzenegger)............................(3)

HERCULES IN THE HAUNTED WORLD (1961) Woolner Brothers. Color-91min. *(Italian).* Reg Park, Christopher Lee.................(3)
Original title: ERCOLE AL CENTRO DELLA TERRA *(Hercules at the Center of the Earth)*

HERCULES IN THE VALE OF WOE (1962) Avco-Embassy. Color-95min. *(Italian).* Kirk Morris, Bice Valori..............................(3)
Alternate title: MACISTE AGAINST HERCULES IN THE VALE OF WOE

HERCULES OF THE DESERT (1964) Color-80min. *(Italian).* Kirk Morris, Heléne Chanel...(1)
Original title: VALLE DELL' ECO TONANTE, LA *(The Valley of the Thundering Echo)*

HERCULES, PRISONER OF EVIL (1964) American-International. Color-90min. *(Italian).* Reg Park, Mireille Granelli..................(1)
Alternate title: TERROR OF THE KIRGHIZ

HERCULES, SAMSON AND ULYSSES (1964) M-G-M. Color-85min. *(Italian).* Kirk Morris, Richard Lloyd, Enzo Cerusico...........(2)
Original title: ERCOLE SFIDA SANSONE *(Hercules Challenges Samson)*

HERCULES, SAMPSON, MACISTE AND URSUS VS. THE UNIVERSE (1964) *see* SAMSON AND THE SEVEN CHALLENGES

HERCULES THE AVENGER (1965) Color-90min. *(Italian).* Reg Park, Gya Sandri...(3)

HERCULES UNCHAINED (1959) Warner Bros. Color-101min. *(Italian-French).* Steve Reeves, Sylva Koscina, Primo Carnera...............3*
Original Italian title: ERCOLE E LA REGINA DI LIDIA *(Hercules and the Queen of Lidia)*

HERCULES VS. THE GIANT WARRIORS (1964) Alexander. Color-94min. *(Italian-French).* Dan Vadis, Moira Orfei....................(1)
Original Italian title: TRIONFO DI ERCOLE, IL
British title: TRIUMPH OF HERCULES, THE
TV title: HERCULES AND THE TEN AVENGERS

HERCULES VS. ULYSSES (1961) *see* ULYSSES AGAINST THE SON OF HERCULES

HERE COME THE CO-EDS (1945) Universal. B&W-87min. Bud Abbott, Lou Costello...3½*

HERE COME THE GIRLS (1953) Paramount. Color-78min. Bob Hope, Tony Martin, Arlene Dahl...4*

HERE COME THE JETS (1959) 20th Century-Fox. B&W-71min. Steve Brodie, Lyn Thomas...(2)

HERE COME THE MARINES (1952) Monogram [Allied Artists]. B&W-66min. The Bowery Boys, Myrna Dell.....................................(4)

HERE COME THE NELSONS (1952) Universal. B&W-76min. Ozzie Nelson, Harriet Nelson...(4)
Alternate title: MEET THE NELSONS

HERE COME THE TIGERS (1978) American-International. Color-90min. Richard Lincoln, James Zvanut, Samantha Grey.....................5½*

HERE COME THE WAVES (1944) Paramount. B&W-99min. Bing Crosby, Betty Hutton...(5)

HERE COMES COOKIE (1935) Paramount. B&W-65min. George Burns, Gracie Allen, Betty Furness...(4)
British title: PLOT THICKENS, THE

HERE COMES EVERY BODY (1972) Artistic Lake Prods. **Color-100min.** *(British, Documentary).* Director: John Whitmore ....

HERE COMES MR. JORDAN (1941) Columbia. **B&W-93min.** Robert Montgomery, Evelyn Keyes, Claude Rains **5½***

HERE COMES THE GROOM (1951) Paramount. **B&W-113min.** Bing Crosby, Jane Wyman .... (5)

HERE COMES THE NAVY (1934) Warner Bros. **B&W-86min.** James Cagney, Pat O'Brien **3***

HERE IS MY HEART (1934) Paramount. **B&W-75min.** Bing Crosby, Kitty Carlisle .... (5)

HERE WE GO AGAIN (1941) *see* PRIDE OF THE BOWERY

HERE WE GO AGAIN (1942) RKO. **B&W-76min.** Edgar Bergen, Fibber McGee and Molly .... (3)

HERE WE GO ROUND THE MULBERRY BUSH (1968) Lopert [U.A.]. **Color-96min.** *(British).* Barry Evans, Judy Geeson .... (3)

HERE'S YOUR LIFE (1966) Brandon. **B&W-110min.** *(Swedish).* Eddie Axberg, Ulla Sjoblom, Gunnar Bjornstrand .... (5)
Original title: HAR HAR DU DITT LIV

HERO, THE (1972) Avco-Embassy. **Color-97min.** *(British-Israeli).* Richard Harris, Romy Schneider .... (4)
Original British title: BLOOMFIELD

HERO AIN'T NOTHIN' BUT A SANDWICH, A (1977) New World. **Color-107min.** Larry B. Scott, Paul Winfield, Cicely Tyson **3***

HERO OF BABYLON (1963) *see* BEAST OF BABYLON AGAINST THE SON OF HERCULES, THE

HERO OF ROME (1964) Avco-Embassy. **Color-90min.** *(Italian).* Gordon Scott, Massimo Serato .... (3)
Original title: COLOSSO DI ROMA, IL *(The Colossus of Rome)*
Alternate Italian title: MUZIO SCEVOLA *(Marcus Scavola)*

HEROD THE GREAT (1959) Allied Artists. **Color-93min.** *(Italian-French).* Edmund Purdom, Sylvia Lopez, Sandra Milo .... (2)
Original Italian title: ERODE IL GRANDE

HEROES (1977) Universal. **Color-113min.** Henry Winkler, Sally Field ... **4***

HEROES AND SINNERS (1955) Janus Films. **B&W-105min.** *(French).* Yves Montand, Maria Felix, Curt Jurgens, Gert Frobe .... (5)
Original title: HEROS SONT FATIGUES, LES *(The Heroes Are Tired)*

HEROES DIE YOUNG (1960) Allied Artists. **B&W-76min.** Erika Peters, Scott Borland .... (3)

HEROES FOR SALE (1933) First National [W.B.]. **B&W-73min.** Loretta Young, Richard Barthelmess .... (3)

HEROES OF TELEMARK, THE (1965) Columbia. **Color-131min.** *(British).* Kirk Douglas, Richard Harris **4½***

HEROES OF THE REGIMENT (1935) *see* BONNIE SCOTLAND

HEROIN GANG, THE (1968) *see* SOL MADRID

HERO'S ISLAND (1962) United Artists. **Color-94min.** James Mason, Neville Brand, Kate Manx **3***

HERE COMES MR. JORDAN (1941). Because of the bungling of heavenly messenger Edward Everett Horton, Claude Rains (in the title role) has to find boxer Robert Montgomery a new body. This was remade as *HEAVEN CAN WAIT* in 1978.

HEROSTRATUS (1967) Zanthus. **Color-140min.** *(British).* Michael Gothard, Gabriella Licudi 1*

HERS TO HOLD (1943) Universal. **B&W-94min.** Deanna Durbin, Joseph Cotten .... (3)

HE'S A COCKEYED WONDER (1950) Columbia. **B&W-77min.** Mickey Rooney, Terry Moore .... (3)

HESTER STREET (1975) Midwest Films. **B&W-90min.** Steven Keats, Carol Kane **5½***

HETEROSEXUAL, THE (1968) *see* BICHES, LES

HETS (1944) *see* TORMENT

HEX (1973) 20th Century-Fox. **Color-92min.** Tina Herazo, Keith Carradine .... (3)

HEY BOY! HEY GIRL! (1959) Columbia. **B&W-81min.** Louis Prima, Keely Smith .... (3)

HEY, I'M ALIVE (1975) Worldvision. **Color-75min.** *(Made for TV).* Edward Asner, Sally Struthers 5*

HEY, LET'S TWIST! (1961) Paramount. **B&W-80min.** Joey Dee, Teddy Randazzo, Zohra Lampert .... (2)

HEY, PINEAPPLE! (1960) Paramount. **Color-97min.** *(Japanese).* Naoki Sugiura, Mike Sano .... (3)
Original title: PINEAPPLE BUTAI

HEY, ROOKIE (1944) Columbia. **B&W-77min.** Larry Parks, Ann Miller (4)

HEY THERE, IT'S YOGI BEAR (1964) Columbia. **Color-89min.** *(Cartoon).* Director: William Hanna **3***

HI DIDDLE DIDDLE (1943) United Artists. **B&W-72min.** Dennis O'Keefe, Martha Scott, Adolphe Menjou .... (4)
Alternate title: DIAMONDS AND CRIME

HI-JACK HIGHWAY (1955) *see* GAS-OIL

HI, MOM! (1970) Sigma III. **Color-87min.** Robert De Niro, Jennifer Salt, Gerritt Graham .... (4)

HI, NELLIE! (1934) Warner Bros. **B&W-75min.** Paul Muni, Glenda Farrell .... (4)

HI-RIDERS (1978) Dimension Pictures. **Color-90min.** Steven McNally, Mel Ferrer ....

HI YA, CHUM (1943) Universal. **B&W-61min.** The Ritz Brothers, Jane Frazee, Robert Paige .... (3)
British title: EVERYTHING HAPPENS TO US

HI YA, SAILOR (1943) Universal. **B&W-63min.** Donald Woods, Elyse Knox .... (3)

HIAWATHA (1952) Allied Artists. **Color-80min.** Vincent Edwards, Yvette Dugay **3***

HICKEY AND BOGGS (1972) United Artists. **Color-111min.** Bill Cosby, Robert Culp **4½***

HIDDEN CITY (1936) *see* BATMEN OF AFRICA

HIDDEN EYE, THE (1945) M-G-M. **B&W-69min.** Edward Arnold, Frances Rafferty .... (4)

HIDDEN FEAR (1957) United Artists. **B&W-83min.** John Payne, Alexander Knox .... (3)

HIDDEN FORTRESS, THE (1958) Toho. **B&W-126min.** *(Japanese).* Toshiro Mifune, Misa Uehara 5*
Original title: KAKUSHI TORIDE NO SAN-AKUNIN *(Three Bad Men in a Hidden Fortress)*

HIDDEN GUNS (1956) Republic. **B&W-66min.** Bruce Bennett, Richard Arlen .... (2)

HIDDEN HOMICIDE (1959) Republic. **B&W-70min.** *(British).* Griffith Jones, Maya Koumani .... (2)

HIDDEN ROOM, THE (1949) Eagle Lion. **B&W-98min.** *(British).* Robert Newton, Sally Gray .... (5)
Original title: OBSESSION

HIDDEN ROOM OF 1,000 HORRORS (1962) *see* TELL-TALE HEART, THE

HIDDEN SECRET (1952) *see* YANK IN INDO-CHINA, A

HIDE AND SEEK (1964) Universal. **B&W-90min.** *(British).* Ian Carmichael, Janet Munro .... (4)

HIDE IN PLAIN SIGHT (1979) U.A. (for M-G-M). **Color- min.** James Caan, Jill Eikenberry, Robert Viharo ....

HIDEAWAYS, THE (1973) *see* FROM THE MIXED-UP FILES OF MRS. BASIL E. FRANKWEILER

HIDEOUS SUN DEMON (1959) Pacific International. **B&W-74min.** Robert Clarke, Patricia Manning .... (2)
British title: BLOOD ON HIS LIPS

HIDE-OUT (1934) M-G-M. **B&W-82min.** Robert Montgomery, Maureen O'Sullivan .... (4)

HIDEOUT (1948) *see* SMALL VOICE, THE

Films are rated on a 1 to 10 scale, 10 is highest. **Boldface** ratings followed by an asterisk (*) are for films actually seen and rated by the executive and senior editors. All other ratings are estimates. (See Notes on Entertainment Ratings in the front section.)

HIDEOUT, THE (1949) Republic. **B&W-59min.** Lloyd Bridges, Adrian Booth .... (4)

HIDEOUT, THE (1956) J. Arthur Rank. **B&W-57min.** *(British).* Dermot Walsh, Rona Anderson .... (3)

HIDEOUT, THE (1961) Miracle. **B&W-80min.** *(French).* Marcel Mouloudji, Yves Vincent .... (4)
Original title: PLANQUE, LA

HIDING PLACE, THE (1975) World Wide Pictures. **Color-150min.** Julie Harris, Eileen Heckart **5***

HIGH (1967) Joseph Brenner. **B&W-82min.** *(Canadian).* Astri Thorvik, Lanny Beckman .... (2)
Alternate title: "IN"

HIGH AND DRY (1954) Universal. **B&W-93min.** *(British).* Paul Douglas, Alex Mackenzie **5***
Original title: MAGGIE, THE

HIGH AND HAPPY (1947) *see* HIT PARADE OF 1947

HIGH AND LOW (1962) Continental [Walter Reade]. **B&W-142min.** *(Japanese).* Toshiro Mifune, Kyoko Kagawa **5***
Original title: TENGOKU TO JIGOKU *(Heaven and Hell)*
British title: RANSOM, THE

HIGH AND THE MIGHTY, THE (1954) Warner Bros. **Color-147min.** John Wayne, Claire Trevor **3½***

HIGH ANXIETY (1977) 20th Century-Fox. **Color-94min.** Mel Brooks, Harvey Korman, Madeline Kahn, Cloris Leachman **5½***

HIGH BALLIN' (1978) American-International. **Color-100min.** Peter Fonda, Jerry Reed, Helen Shaver **5***

HIGH BARBAREE (1947) M-G-M. **B&W-91min.** Van Johnson, June Allyson **3***

HIGH BRIGHT SUN, THE (1964) *see* McGUIRE GO HOME

HIGH COMMISSIONER, THE (1968) Cinerama Releasing. **Color-93min.** *(British-U.S.).* Rod Taylor, Christopher Plummer, Lilli Palmer .... (4)
Original title: NOBODY RUNS FOREVER

HIGH COST OF LOVING, THE (1958) M-G-M. **B&W-87min.** José Ferrer, Gena Rowlands .... (5)

HIGH FLIGHT (1957) Columbia. **B&W-89min.** *(British).* Ray Milland, Anthony Newley .... (3)

HIGH FURY (1948) United Artists. **B&W-71min.** *(British).* Madeleine Carroll, Ian Hunter .... (3)
Original title: WHITE CRADLE INN

HIGH HELL (1958) Paramount. **B&W-87min.** *(British).* John Derek, Elaine Stewart .... (3)

HIGH INFIDELITY (1965) Magna Pictures. **B&W-120min.** *(Italian-French).* Nino Manfredi, Charles Aznavour, Monica Vitti, Ugo Tognazzi .... (5)
Original Italian title: ALTA INFIDELTA
Original French title: HAUTE INFIDÉLITÉ

HIGH LONESOME (1950) Eagle Lion. **Color-81min.** John Barrymore, Jr., Chill Wills **3***

HIGH NOON (1952) United Artists. **B&W-85min.** Gary Cooper, Grace Kelly **5½***

HIGH PLAINS DRIFTER (1973) Universal. **Color-105min.** Clint Eastwood, Verna Bloom **4***

HIGH-POWERED RIFLE, THE (1960) 20th Century-Fox. **B&W-60min.** Willard Parker, Allison Hayes .... (2)

HIGH RISK (1976) M-G-M. **Color-74min.** *(Made for TV).* Victor Buono, Joseph Sirola .... (4)

HIGH SCHOOL (1940) 20th Century-Fox. **B&W-74min.** Jane Withers, Joe Brown, Jr. .... (3)

HIGH SCHOOL (1969) Osti Films. **B&W-75min.** *(Documentary). Director:* Frederick Wiseman .... (5)

HIGH SCHOOL BIG SHOT (1959) Sparta. **B&W-70min.** Tom Pittman, Virginia Aldridge .... (3)
British title: YOUNG SINNERS, THE

HIGH SCHOOL CAESAR (1960) Filmgroup. **B&W-63min.** John Ashley, Judy Nugent .... (2)

HIGH SCHOOL CONFIDENTIAL (1958) M-G-M. **B&W-85min.** Russ Tamblyn, Mamie Van Doren .... (2)
Alternate title: YOUNG HELLIONS
Alternate title(?): YOUNG KILLERS

HIGH SCHOOL HELLCATS (1958) American-International. **B&W-68min.** Yvonne Lime, Brett Halsey .... (3)
British title: SCHOOL FOR VIOLENCE

HIGH SIERRA (1941) Warner Bros. **B&W-100min.** Humphrey Bogart, Ida Lupino **4½***

HIGH SOCIETY (1955) Allied Artists. **B&W-61min.** The Bowery Boys, Amanda Blake .... (3)

HIGH SOCIETY (1956) M-G-M. **Color-107min.** Bing Crosby, Grace Kelly **5***

HIGH TERRACE (1956) Allied Artists. **B&W-82min.** *(British).* Dale Robertson, Lois Maxwell .... (3)

HIGH TIDE (1947) Monogram [Allied Artists]. **B&W-72min.** Lee Tracy, Don Castle .... (4)

HIGH TIME (1960) 20th Century-Fox. **Color-130min.** Bing Crosby, Fabian **4***

HIGH TREASON (1951) J. Arthur Rank. **B&W-93min.** *(British).* Liam Redmond, André Morell **4***

HIGH VELOCITY (1977) Turtle Releasing. **Color-106min.** Ben Gazzara, Britt Ekland, Paul Winfield, Keenan Wynn **4***

HIGH VENTURE (1951) *see* PASSAGE WEST

HIGH VERMILION (1951) *see* SILVER CITY

HIGH WALL (1948) M-G-M. **Color-99min.** Robert Taylor, Audrey Totter **4½***

HIGH, WIDE, AND HANDSOME (1937) Paramount. **B&W-112min.** Irene Dunne, Randolph Scott .... (4)

HIGH, WILD AND FREE (1968) American-International. **Color-105min.** *(Documentary). Producer:* Gordon Eastman .... (4)

HIGH WIND IN JAMAICA, A (1965) 20th Century-Fox. **Color-103min.** *(British).* Anthony Quinn, James Coburn, Deborah Baxter **4***

HIGH WINDOW, THE (1947) *see* BRASHER DOUBLOON, THE

HIGHER AND HIGHER (1943) RKO. **B&W-90min.** Michele Morgan, Leon Errol **4***

HIGHLY DANGEROUS (1951) Lippert Productions. **B&W-88min.** *(British).* Margaret Lockwood, Dane Clark **4***

HIGHWAY DRAGNET (1954) Allied Artists. **B&W-71min.** Richard Conte, Joan Bennett .... (3)

HIGHWAY GIRL (1975) *see* RETURN TO MACON COUNTY

HIGHWAY 301 (1951) Warner Bros. **B&W-83min.** Steve Cochran, Virginia Grey .... (3)

HIGHWAY TO BATTLE (1960) Paramount. **B&W-71min.** *(British).* Gerard Heinz, Margaret Tyzack .... (3)

HIGHWAY TO FREEDOM (1942) *see* JOE SMITH, AMERICAN

HIGHWAY WEST (1941) Warner Bros. **B&W-63min.** William Lundigan, Arthur Kennedy .... (4)

HIGHWAYMAN, THE (1951) Allied Artists. **Color-82min.** Philip Friend, Wanda Hendrix, Charles Coburn .... (4)

HIGHWAYS BY NIGHT (1942) RKO. **B&W-63min.** Richard Carlson, Jane Randolph .... (4)

HIJACK (1973) MPC (TV). **Color-74min.** *(Made for TV).* David Janssen, Keenan Wynn, Lee Purcell .... (4)

HILDA CRANE (1956) 20th Century-Fox. **Color-87min.** Jean Simmons, Guy Madison **3***

HILL, THE (1965) M-G-M. **B&W-123min.** *(British).* Sean Connery, Harry Andrews **3***

HILL IN KOREA, A (1956) *see* HELL IN KOREA

HILL 24 DOESN'T ANSWER (1955) Continental [Walter Reade]. **B&W-100min.** *(Israeli).* Michael Wager, Edward Mulhare **4***

HILLS HAVE EYES, THE (1977) Vanguard. **Color-90min.** Janus Blythe, Russ Grieve, James Whitworth ....

HILLS OF HOME (1948) M-G-M. **Color-97min.** Edmund Gwenn, Donald Crisp, Lassie **4***
British title: MASTER OF LASSIE

HILLS OF THE BRAVE (1950) *see* PALOMINO, THE

HILLS RUN RED, THE (1966) United Artists. **Color-89min.** *(Italian).* Thomas Hunter, Henry Silva, Dan Duryea .... (3)
Original title: FIUME DI DOLLARI, UN

HINDENBURG, THE (1975) Universal. **Color-125min.** George C. Scott, Anne Bancroft **5½***

HINDLE WAKES (1952) *see* HOLIDAY WEEK

HINDU, THE (1955) *see* SABAKA

HIPPODROME (1959) Continental [Walter Reade]. **Color-96min.** *(W. German-Austrian).* Gerhard Riedmann, Margit Nunke .... (4)
Original title: GELIEBTE BESTIE
Alternate German title #1: MANNER MUSSEN SO SEIN
Alternate German title #2: MADCHEN IM TIGERFELL, DAS

HIRED GUN, THE (1957) M-G-M. **Color-63min.** Rory Calhoun, Anne Francis .... (3)

HIRED HAND, THE (1971) Universal. **Color-93min.** Peter Fonda, Warren Oates **3***

Films are rated on a 1 to 10 scale, 10 is highest. **Boldface** ratings followed by an asterisk (*) are for films actually seen and rated by the executive and senior editors. All other ratings are estimates. (See Notes on Entertainment Ratings in the front section.)

HIRED KILLER, THE (1966) Paramount. **Color-95min.** *(Italian-French).* Robert Webber, Franco Nero................................(4)
Original Italian title: TECNICA DI UN OMICIDIO *(Technique of a Murderer)*
Original French title: TECHNIQUE D'UN MUERTRE

HIRED MAN, THE (1918) Ince. **B&W-66min.** *(Silent).* Charles Ray, Doris May ....(4)

HIRED WIFE (1940) Universal. **B&W-93min.** Rosalind Russell, Brian Aherne...**4***

HIRELING, THE (1973) Columbia. **Color-95min.** *(British).* Robert Shaw, Sarah Miles..(5)

HIROSHIMA, MON AMOUR (1959) Zenith International. **B&W-88min.** *(French).* Emmanuelle Riva, Eiji Okada **4***

HIS AFFAIR (1937) *see* THIS IS MY AFFAIR

HIS BROTHER'S WIFE (1936) M-G-M. **B&W-90min.** Robert Taylor, Barbara Stanwyck......................................3½*

HIS BUTLER'S SISTER (1943) Universal. **B&W-94min.** Deanna Durbin, Franchot Tone..(4)

HIS DOUBLE LIFE (1934) Paramount. **B&W-68min.** Lillian Gish, Roland Young...(4)

HIS GIRL FRIDAY (1940) Columbia. **B&W-92min.** Cary Grant, Rosalind Russell...**5***

HIS GREATEST ROLE (1957) *see* SENECHAL THE MAGNIFICENT

HIS KIND OF WOMAN (1951) RKO. **B&W-120min.** Robert Mitchum, Jane Russell...**4***

HIS LAST TWELVE HOURS (1951) IFE Releasing Corp. **B&W-89min.** *(Italian).* Jean Gabin, Mariella Lotti ....(4)
Original title: SUE ULTIME 12 ORE, LE
Alternate Italian title: E' PIU' FACILE CHE UN CAMMELLO

HIS LORDSHIP (1936) *see* MAN OF AFFAIRS

HIS MAJESTY O'KEEFE (1954) Warner Bros. **Color-90min.** Burt Lancaster, Joan Rice...**4***

HIS OTHER WOMAN (1957) *see* DESK SET

HIS WOMAN (1931) Paramount. **B&W-80min.** Gary Cooper, Claudette Colbert..(3)

HISTORY IS MADE AT NIGHT (1937) United Artists. **B&W-97min.** Charles Boyer, Jean Arthur.............................4½*

HISTORY OF MR. POLLY, THE (1949) International Releasing Organization. **B&W-96min.** *(British).* John Mills, Sally Ann Howes.....(5)

HIT (1973) Paramount. **Color-133min.** Billy Dee Williams, Richard Pryor...(4)

HIT AND RUN (1957) United Artists. **B&W-84min.** Hugo Haas, Cleo Moore...(2)

HIT MAN (1972) M-G-M. **Color-90min.** Bernie Casey, Pamela (Pam) Grier...(4)

HIT PARADE, THE (1937) Republic. **B&W-83min.** Frances Langford, Phil Regan...(3)
TV title: I'LL REACH FOR A STAR

HIT PARADE OF 1941, THE (1940) Republic. **B&W-88min.** Kenny Baker, Frances Langford ....(3)

HIT PARADE OF 1943 (1943) Republic. **B&W-82min.** John Carroll, Susan Hayward ....(4)
Alternate title: CHANGE OF HEART

HIT PARADE OF 1947 (1947) Republic. **B&W-90min.** Eddie Albert, Constance Moore ....(4)
TV title: HIGH AND HAPPY

HIT PARADE OF 1951 (1950) Republic. **B&W-85min.** John Carroll, Marie McDonald ....(3)

HIT THE DECK (1955) M-G-M. **Color-112min.** Jane Powell, Tony Martin ....(5)

HIT THE ICE (1943) Universal. **B&W-82min.** Bud Abbott, Lou Costello, Ginny Simms......................................3*

HIT THE ROAD (1941) Universal. **B&W-60min.** Billy Halop, Huntz Hall, Gabriel Dell, Gladys George ....

HITCH HIKE TO HAPPINESS (1945) Republic. **B&W-72min.** Al Pearce, Dale Evans...(3)

HITCH-HIKER, THE (1953) RKO. **B&W-71min.** Edmond O'Brien, Frank Lovejoy...(4)

HITCHED (1971) MCA-TV. **Color-73min.** *(Made for TV).* Sally Field, Tim Matheson, Neville Brand..........................(4)

HITCHHIKE! (1974) MCA-TV. **Color-74min.** *(Made for TV).* Cloris Leachman, Michael Brandon ....(4)

HITCHHIKERS, THE (1972) Entertainment Ventures. **Color-93min.** Misty Rowe, Norman Klar ....(3)

HITLER (1962) Allied Artists. **B&W-107min.** Richard Basehart, Maria Emo...3*
Alternate title: WOMEN OF NAZI GERMANY

HITLER, A CAREER (1977) Safar Films Ltd. *(British).* **B&W-150min.** *(German, Documentary).* Director: Joachim C. Fest..............(5)
Original title: HITLER, EINE KARRIERE

HITLER, A FILM FROM GERMANY (1977) **Color-400min.** *(W. German-British-French).* Heinz Schubert, Harry Baer, Peter Kern ....(4)

HITLER · DEAD OR ALIVE (1943) Ben Judell. **B&W-70min.** Ward Bond, Dorothy Tree, Warren Hymer ....(3)

HITLER GANG, THE (1944) Paramount. **B&W-101min.** Robert (Bobby) Watson, Roman Bohnen.................................4½*

HITLER: THE LAST TEN DAYS (1973) Paramount. **Color-106min.** *(British-Italian).* Alec Guinness, Doris Kunstmann **4***

HITLER'S CHILDREN (1943) RKO. **B&W-83min.** Tim Holt, Bonita Granville...(5)

HITLER'S EXECUTIONERS (1958) Vitalite. **B&W-78min.** *(German, Documentary).* Director: Felix von Podmanitzky ....(5)
Original title: NUERNBERGER PROZESS, DER *(The Nuremberg Trial)*
Alternate title: EXECUTIONERS, THE

HITLER'S MADMAN (1943) M-G-M. **B&W-84min.** Patricia Morison, John Carradine, Alan Curtis ....(4)
Alternate title: HITLER'S HANGMAN

HITTING A NEW HIGH (1937) RKO. **B&W-60min.** Lily Pons, Jack Oakie..(4)

HITTING THE HEADLINES (1942) *see* YOKEL BOY

HITTING THE JACKPOT (1949) *see* BLONDIE HITS THE JACKPOT

HOA BINH (1970) Transvue Pictures. **Color-93min.** *(French).* Phil Lan, Huynh Cazenas......................................(5)

HOAX, THE (1972) All-Scope International. **Color-85min.** Bill Ewing, Frank Bonner..(3)

HOAXTERS, THE (1953) M-G-M. **B&W-36min.** *(Documentary).* Producer: Dore Schary ....(4)

HOBSON'S CHOICE (1954) United Artists. **B&W-107min.** *(British).* Charles Laughton, Brenda de Banzie..................6½*

HOFFMAN (1970) Levitt-Pickman. **Color-111min.** *(British).* Peter Sellers, Sinead Cusack **4***

HOLD BACK THE DAWN (1941) Paramount. **B&W-115min.** Charles Boyer, Olivia de Havilland..............................5½*

HOLD BACK THE NIGHT (1956) Allied Artists. **B&W-80min.** John Payne, Mona Freeman......................................**4***

HOLD BACK TOMORROW (1955) Universal. **B&W-75min.** John Agar, Cleo Moore ....(2)

HOLD ON! (1966) M-G-M. **Color-85min.** Herman's Hermits, Shelley Fabares...(3)

HOBSON'S CHOICE (1954). Brenda de Banzie is firmly in control of the situation as her obstinate bootmaker father Charles Laughton and her sisters Prunella Scales and Daphne Anderson look to her husband John Mills for the sympathy they're not likely to get.

HOLD THAT BABY (1949) Monogram [Allied Artists]. **B&W-64min.** The Bowery Boys, Anabel Shaw .... (4)

HOLD THAT BLONDE (1945) Paramount. **B&W-76min.** Eddie Bracken, Veronica Lake ....

HOLD THAT CO-ED (1938) 20th Century-Fox. **B&W-80min.** John Barrymore, George Murphy .... (5)
British title: HOLD THAT GIRL

HOLD THAT GHOST (1941) Universal. **B&W-86min.** Bud Abbott, Lou Costello **4***

HOLD THAT HYPNOTIST (1957) Allied Artists. **B&W-61min.** The Bowery Boys, Jane Nigh .... (3)

HOLD THAT LINE (1952) Monogram [Allied Artists]. **B&W-64min.** The Bowery Boys, John Bromfield .... (3)

HOLD TIGHT FOR THE SATELLITE (1958) *see* SPUTNIK

HOLD YOUR MAN (1933) M-G-M. **B&W-89min.** Jean Harlow, Clark Gable **4½***

HOLE, THE (1965) *see* ONIBABA

HOLE IN THE HEAD, A (1959) United Artists. **Color-120min.** Frank Sinatra, Edward G. Robinson **4***

HOLIDAY (1930) Pathé-RKO. **B&W-89min.** Ann Harding, Mary Astor .. (5)

HOLIDAY (1938) Columbia. **B&W-93min.** Katharine Hepburn, Cary Grant **5***
British title: UNCONVENTIONAL LINDA
British title: FREE TO LIVE

HOLIDAY AFFAIR (1949) RKO. **B&W-87min.** Robert Mitchum, Janet Leigh .... (5)

HOLIDAY CAMP (1947) Universal. **B&W-97min.** *(British).* Flora Robson, Dennis Price .... (5)

HOLIDAY FOR HENRIETTA (1953) Ardee Films. **B&W-103min.** *(French).* Dany Robin, Michel Auclair .... (5)
Original title: FETE A HENRIETTE, LA
British title: HENRIETTE

HOLIDAY FOR LOVERS (1959) 20th Century-Fox. **Color-103min.** Clifton Webb, Jane Wyman **4***

HOLIDAY FOR SINNERS (1952) M-G-M. **B&W-72min.** Keenan Wynn, Janice Rule .... (4)

HOLIDAY IN HAVANA (1949) Columbia. **B&W-73min.** Dezi Arnaz, Mary Hatcher .... (3)

HOLIDAY IN MEXICO (1946) M-G-M. **Color-127min.** Walter Pidgeon, Jane Powell .... (5)

HOLIDAY INN (1942) Paramount. **B&W-101min.** Bing Crosby, Fred Astaire **4***

HOLIDAY RHYTHM (1950) Lippert Productions. **B&W-60min.** Mary Beth Hughes, David Street ....

HOLIDAY WEEK (1952) Monarch. **B&W-88min.** *(British).* Leslie Dwyer, Lisa Daniely .... (2)
Original title: HINDLE WAKES

HOLLOW TRIUMPH (1948) Eagle Lion. **B&W-83min.** Paul Henreid **4***
British and alternate U.S. title: SCAR, THE

HOLLY AND THE IVY, THE (1952) Pacemaker. **B&W-83min.** *(British).* Ralph Richardson, Celia Johnson **3***

HOLLYWOOD BOULEVARD (1976) New World. **Color-83min.** Candice Rialson, Dick Miller **4***

HOLLYWOOD CANTEEN (1944) Warner Bros. **B&W-124min.** Joan Leslie, Robert Hutton .... (4)

HOLLYWOOD CAVALCADE (1939) 20th Century-Fox. **Color-96min.** Alice Faye, Don Ameche .... (5)

HOLLYWOOD COWBOY (1975) *see* HEARTS OF THE WEST

HOLLYWOOD! HOLLYWOOD! (1976) *see* THAT'S ENTERTAINMENT, PART 2

HOLLYWOOD HOTEL (1937) Warner Bros. **B&W-109min.** Dick Powell, Rosemary Lane **4***

HOLLYWOOD OR BUST (1956) Paramount. **Color-95min.** Dean Martin, Jerry Lewis **4***

HOLLYWOOD PARTY (1934) M-G-M. **B&W-70min.** Jimmy Durante, Lupe Velez, Stanley Laurel, Oliver Hardy .... (4)

HOLLYWOOD REVUE, THE (1929) M-G-M. **B&W-116min.** Jack Benny, Conrad Nagel **3***
Alternate title: HOLLYWOOD REVUE OF 1929, THE

HOLLYWOOD STORY (1951) Universal. **B&W-77min.** Richard Conte, Julie Adams **4***

HOLY MATRIMONY (1943) 20th Century-Fox. **B&W-87min.** Monty Woolley, Gracie Fields .... (5)

HOLY MOUNTAIN, THE (1974) ABKCO. **Color-126min.** *(Mexican-U.S.).* Alexandro Jodorowsky, Horacio Salinas ....

HOMBRE (1967) 20th Century-Fox. **Color-111min.** Paul Newman, Fredric March 5½*

HOME AT SEVEN (1952) *see* MURDER ON MONDAY

HOME BEFORE DARK (1958) Warner Bros. **B&W-137min.** Jean Simmons, Rhonda Fleming **4***

HOME FOR THE HOLIDAYS (1972) Worldvision. **Color-74min.** *(Made for TV).* Sally Field, Julie Harris, Eleanor Parker, Walter Brennan .... (4)

HOME FROM THE HILL (1960) M-G-M. **Color-150min.** Robert Mitchum, Eleanor Parker 5½*

HOME IN INDIANA (1944) 20th Century-Fox. **Color-103min.** Walter Brennan, Lon McAllister **4***

HOME IS THE HERO (1959) Showcorporation. **B&W-83min.** Walter Macken, Arthur Kennedy .... (4)

HOME OF THE BRAVE (1949) United Artists. **B&W-85min.** James Edwards, Frank Lovejoy **4½***

HOME, SWEET HOMICIDE (1946) 20th Century-Fox. **B&W-90min.** Peggy Ann Garner, Randolph Scott, Lynn Bari, Dean Stockwell .... (3)

HOME TO STAY (1978) CBS-TV. **Color-74min.** *(Made for TV).* Henry Fonda, Kristen Vigard, Michael McGuire ....

HOMEBODIES (1974) Avco-Embassy. **Color-96min.** Ian Wolfe, Ruth McDevitt, Peter Brocco, Paula Trueman ....

HOMECOMING (1948) M-G-M. **B&W-113min.** Clark Gable, Lana Turner **3***

HOMECOMING: A CHRISTMAS STORY, THE (1971) Warner Bros. **Color-100min.** *(Made for TV).* Patricia Neal, Richard Thomas **3***

HOMECOMING, THE (1973) American Film Theatre. **Color-111min.** *(British).* Cyril Cusack, Ian Holm **5***

HOMER (1970) Nat'l General (for Cinema Center). **Color-91min.** Don Scardino, Alex Nicol, Tisa Farrow .... (3)

HOMESTEADERS, THE (1953) Allied Artists. **B&W-62min.** Wild Bill Elliott, Robert Lowery .... (3)

HOMESTRETCH, THE (1947) 20th Century-Fox. **Color-96min.** Cornel Wilde, Maureen O'Hara .... (4)

HOMICIDAL (1961) Columbia. **B&W-87min.** Jean Arless, Glenn Corbett, Patricia Breslin .... (4)

HOMO EROTICUS (1971) *see* MAN OF THE YEAR

HONDO (1953) Warner Bros. **Color-84min.** John Wayne, Geraldine Page 5½*

HONDO AND THE APACHES (1966) M-G-M. **Color-85min.** *(Telefeature).* Ralph Taeger, Kathie Browne .... (4)

HONEY POT, THE (1967) United Artists. **Color-131min.** *(British-U.S.-Italian).* Rex Harrison, Susan Hayward 5½*
Alternate title: IT COMES UP MURDER

HONEYCHILE (1951) Republic. **Color-90min.** Judy Canova, Eddie Foy, Jr. .... (3)

HONEYCOMB (1969) Cine Globe. **Color-90min.** *(Spanish, English language).* Geraldine Chaplin, Per Oscarsson 1*
Original title: MADRIGUERA, LA *(The Burrow)*

HONEYMOON (1947) RKO. **B&W-74min.** Shirley Temple, Franchot Tone .... (3)
British title: TWO MEN AND A GIRL

HONEYMOON (1959) RKO. **Color-90min.** *(Spanish, English language).* Anthony Steel, Ludmilla Tcherina .... (3)
Alternate title: Spanish title: LUNA DE MIEL

HONEYMOON AHEAD (1945) Universal. **B&W-60min.** Allan Jones, Grace McDonald .... (3)

HONEYMOON FOR THREE (1941) Warner Bros. **B&W-77min.** Ann Sheridan, George Brent .... (4)

HONEYMOON HOTEL (1964) M-G-M. **Color-89min.** Robert Goulet, Nancy Kwan, Robert Morse .... (3)

HONEYMOON IN BALI (1939) Paramount. **B&W-95min.** Fred MacMurray, Madeleine Carroll .... (5)
British title: HUSBANDS OR LOVERS

HONEYMOON KILLERS, THE (1970) Cinerama Releasing. **B&W-110min.** Shirley Stoler, Tony LoBianco .... (4)

HONEYMOON MACHINE, THE (1961) M-G-M. **Color-82min.** Steve McQueen, Brigid Bazlen 5*

HONEYMOON WITH A STRANGER (1969) 20th Century-Fox. **Color-74min.** *(Made for TV).* Janet Leigh, Rossano Brazzi, Cesare Danova ... (4)

HONEYMOONS WILL KILL YOU (1964) American-International. **Color-91min.** *(Italian).* Tony Russell .... (3)

Films are rated on a 1 to 10 scale, 10 is highest. **Boldface** ratings followed by an asterisk (*) are for films actually seen and rated by the executive and senior editors. All other ratings are estimates. (See Notes on Entertainment Ratings in the front section.)

HONG KONG (1951) Paramount. **Color-92min.** Ronald Reagan, Rhonda Fleming .... (3)

HONG KONG AFFAIR (1958) Allied Artists. **B&W-79min.** Jack Kelly, May Wynn .... (2)

HONG KONG CONFIDENTIAL (1958) United Artists. **B&W-67min.** Gene Barry, Beverly Tyler .... (3)

HONG KONG HOT HARBOR (1962) UCC Films. **Color-102min.** *(W. German-Italian).* Marian Cook, Klausjurgen Wussow .... (2)
Original German title: HEISSEN HAFEN HONGKONG

HONKERS, THE (1972) United Artists. **Color-103min.** James Coburn, Lois Nettleton, Slim Pickens 3*

HONKY (1971) Jack H. Harris. **Color-89min.** Brenda Sykes, John Neilson .... (2)

HONKY TONK (1941) M-G-M. **B&W-105min.** Clark Cable, Lana Turner 4*

HONOLULU (1939) M-G-M. **B&W-83min.** Eleanor Powell, George Burns, Gracie Allen, Robert Young... (4)

HONOLULU LU (1941) Columbia. **B&W-72min.** Lupe Velez, Forrest Tucker .... (3)

HONOR THY FATHER (1973) MPC (TV). **Color-100min.** *(Made for TV).* Raf Vallone, Richard Castellano, Brenda Vaccaro.............. 3*

HONOURABLE MR. WONG, THE (1932) *see* HATCHET MAN, THE

HONOURABLE MURDER, AN (1959) Warner Bros. **B&W-70min.** *(British).* Norman Wooland, Margaretta Scott .... (3)

HOODLUM, THE (1951) United Artists. **B&W-61min.** Lawrence Tierney, Allene Roberts... (3)

HOODLUM EMPIRE (1952) Republic. **B&W-98min.** Brian Donlevy, Claire Trevor.. (4)

HOODLUM PRIEST, THE (1961) United Artists. **B&W-101min.** Don Murray, Larry Gates.. 5*

HOODLUM SAINT, THE (1946) M-G-M. **B&W-91min.** William Powell, Esther Williams... 4*

HOOK, THE (1963) M-G-M. **B&W-98min.** Kirk Douglas, Robert Walker 4*

HOOK, LINE AND SINKER (1969) Columbia. **Color-92min.** Jerry Lewis, Peter Lawford 3*

HOOKED GENERATION (1968) Allied Artists. **Color-92min.** Jeremy Slate, Steve Alaimo .... (2)

HOOPER (1978) Warner Bros. **Color-99min.** Burt Reynolds, Jan-Michael Vincent, Sally Field 5*

HOOTENANNY HOOT (1963) M-G-M. **B&W-91min.** Peter Breck, Ruta Lee, Johnny Cash, The Brothers Four........................... (2)

HOPELESS ONES, THE (1966) *see* ROUND UP, THE

HOPPITY GOES TO TOWN (1941) *see* MR. BUG GOES TO TOWN

HORATIO HORNBLOWER (1951) *see* CAPTAIN HORATIO HORNBLOWER

HORIZONS WEST (1952) Universal. **Color-81min.** Robert Ryan, Rock Hudson.. 3*

HORIZONTAL LIEUTENANT, THE (1962) M-G-M. **Color-90min.** Jim Hutton, Paula Prentiss 4*

HORN (1979) Warner Bros. **Color-   min.** Steve McQueen, Linda Evans

HORN BLOWS AT MIDNIGHT, THE (1945) Warner Bros. **B&W-78min.** Jack Benny, Alexis Smith 5*

HORNET'S NEST (1970) United Artists. **Color-110min.** Rock Hudson, Sylva Koscina .... (3)

HORRIBLE DR. HICHCOCK, THE (1962) Sigma III. **Color-76min.** *(Italian).* Robert Flemyng, Barbara Steele........................... 2*
Original title: ORRIBLE SEGRETO DEL DR. HICHCOCK, L'
British title: TERROR OF DR. HICHCOCK, THE

HORRIBLE HOUSE ON THE HILL (1974) *see* PEOPLETOYS

HORRIBLE STONE WOMEN, THE (1960) *see* MILL OF THE STONE WOMEN

HORROR (1960) *see* BLANCHEVILLE MONSTER

HORROR AT 37,000 FEET (1972) Anthony Wilson. **Color-73min.** *(Made for TV).* William Shatner, Buddy Ebsen, Tammy Grimes 3*

HORROR CASTLE (1963) Zodiac Films. **Color-82min.** *(Italian).* Rossana Podesta, Georges Riviere.. 3*
Alternate title: CASTLE OF TERROR
Alternate title: TERROR CASTLE
Original title: VERGINE DI NORIMBERGA, LE *(The Virgin of Nuremberg)*
Alternate title: HORROR CASTLE (WHERE THE BLOOD FLOWS)

HORROR CHAMBER OF DR. FAUSTUS (1971) Lopert [U.A.]. **B&W-94min.** *(French-Italian).* Pierre Brasseur, Alida Valli, Edith Scob.......(3)
Original French title: YEUX SANS VISAGE, LES
Original Italian title: OCCHI SENZA VOLTO
British title: EYES WITHOUT A FACE

HORROR CREATURES OF THE PREHISTORIC PLANET (1970) *see* HORROR OF THE BLOOD MONST

HORROR EXPRESS (1972) Scotia International *(Brit.).* **Color-98min.** *(Spanish-British).* Peter Cushing, Christopher Lee, Telly Savalas........ 3*
Spanish title: PANICO EN EL TRANSIBERIANO *(Panic on the Trans-Siberian)*

HORROR HIGH (1973) Crown International. **Color-85min.** Pat Cardi, John Niland, Rosie Holotik.. 2*
TV title: TWISTED BRAIN

HORROR HOSPITAL (1973) *see* COMPUTER KILLERS

HORROR HOTEL (1960) Trans-Lux Distributing. **B&W-76min.** *(British).* Patricia Jessel, Betta St. John, Christopher Lee .... (4)
Original title: CITY OF THE DEAD, THE

HORROR HOUSE (1970) American-International. **Color-79min.** *(British-U.S.).* Frankie Avalon, Jill Haworth, Julian Barnes...................... (2)
British title: HAUNTED HOUSE OF HORROR, THE

HORROR ISLAND (1941) Universal. **B&W-60min.** Dick Foran, Leo Carrillo 3*

HORROR OF DRACULA (1958) Universal. **Color-82min.** *(British).* Peter Cushing, Christopher Lee 4*
British title: DRACULA

HORROR OF FRANKENSTEIN, THE (1970) Levitt-Pickman. **Color-95min.** *(British).* Ralph Bates, Kate O'Mara........................... (3)

HORROR OF IT ALL, THE (1964) 20th Century-Fox. **B&W-75min.** *(British).* Pat Boone, Erica Rogers, Dennis Price.................. (3)

HORROR OF PARTY BEACH, THE (1964) 20th Century-Fox. **B&W-82min.** John Scott, Alice Lyon .... (2)

HORROR OF THE BLOOD MONSTERS (1970) Independent International. **B&W-85min.** John Carradine, Robert Dix.................... (2)
Alternate title: CREATURES OF THE PREHISTORIC PLANET
Alternate title: HORROR CREATURES OF THE PREHISTORIC PLANET
TV title: VAMPIRE MEN OF THE LOST PLANET

HORROR OF THE STONE WOMEN (1960) *see* MILL OF THE STONE WOMEN

HORROR ON SNAPE ISLAND (1972) Fanfare. **Color-86min.** *(British).* Bryant Halliday, Jill Haworth.. (3)
Alternate title: TOWER OF EVIL

HORRORS OF SPIDER ISLAND (1960) *see* IT'S HOT IN PARADISE

HORRORS OF THE BLACK MUSEUM (1959) American-International. **Color-81min.** *(British).* Michael Gough, June Cunningham .... (3)

HORSE AND CARRIAGE (1957) Greek Motion Pictures. **B&W-104min.** *(Greek).* Orestes Makris, Antigone Valakou .... (3)
Original title: AMAXAKI, TO *(The Carriage)*

HORSE CALLED COMANCHE, A (1958) *see* TONKA

HORSE FEATHERS (1932) Paramount. **B&W-70min.** Groucho Marx, Harpo Marx 4½*

HORSE IN THE GRAY FLANNEL SUIT, THE (1968) Buena Vista. **Color-113min.** Dean Jones, Diane Baker .... (4)

HORSE SOLDIERS, THE (1959) United Artists. **Color-119min.** John Wayne, William Holden 5½*

HORSE WITH THE FLYING TAIL, THE (1961) Buena Vista. **Color-48min.** *(Documentary). Director:* Larry Lansburgh .... (5)

HORSEMEN, THE (1971) Columbia. **Color-110min.** Omar Sharif, Jack Palance 4*

HORSE'S MOUTH, THE (1953) *see* ORACLE, THE

HORSE'S MOUTH, THE (1958) United Artists. **Color-93min.** *(British).* Alec Guinness, Kay Walsh.. 7*

HOSPITAL (1970) Zipporah Films. **B&W-84min.** *(Documentary). Director:* Frederick Wiseman .... (5)

HOSPITAL, THE (1971) United Artists. **Color-104min.** George C. Scott, Diana Rigg 5*

HOSTAGE, THE (1966) Crown International. **Color-84min.** Danny Martins, Don O'Kelly, Dean Stanton, John Carradine.................... 3*

HOSTAGE HEART, THE (1977) CBS-TV. **Color-100min.** *(Made for TV).* Bradford Dillman, Vic Morrow .... (5)

HOSTAGES (1943) Paramount. **B&W-88min.** Luise Rainer, Arturo de Cordova .... (3)

HOSTILE GUNS (1967) Paramount. **Color-91min.** George Montgomery, Yvonne De Carlo, Tab Hunter, Brian Donlevy......................... (3)

Films are rated on a 1 to 10 scale, 10 is highest. **Boldface** ratings followed by an asterisk (*) are for films actually seen and rated by the executive and senior editors. All other ratings are estimates. (See Notes on Entertainment Ratings in the front section.)

HOT ANGEL, THE (1958) Paramount. **B&W-73min.** Jackie Loughery, Edward Kemmer .... (3)

HOT BLOOD (1956) Columbia. **Color-85min.** Jane Russell, Cornel Wilde .... (3)

HOT BOX, THE (1972) New World. **Color-87min.** Andrea Cagan, Rickey Richardson .... (3)

HOT CAR GIRL (1958) Allied Artists. **B&W-71min.** Jana Lund, Richard Bakalyan .... (3)

HOT CARS (1956) United Artists. **B&W-60min.** John Bromfield, Joi Lansing .... (3)

HOT ENOUGH FOR JUNE (1964) *see* AGENT 8 3/4

HOT HORSE (1963) *see* ONCE UPON A HORSE

HOT ICE (1952) Apex. **B&W-85min.** *(British).* Barbara Murray, John Justin .... (5)

HOT LEAD AND COLD FEET (1978) Buena Vista. **Color-90min.** Jim Dale, Karen Valentine, Don Knotts 4½*

HOT LINE, THE (1969) *see* DAY THE HOT LINE GOT HOT, THE

HOT MILLIONS (1968) M-G-M. **Color-105min.** *(British).* Peter Ustinov, Maggie Smith 5½*

HOT MONEY GIRL (1959) *see* TREASURE OF SAN TERESA, THE

HOT NEWS (1953) Allied Artists. **B&W-68min.** Stanley Clements, Gloria Henry .... (3)

HOT PEPPER (1933) Fox Film Co. [20th]. **B&W-76min.** Victor McLaglen, Edmund Lowe, Lupe Velez .... (4)

HOT POTATO (1976) Warner Bros. **Color-87min.** Jim Kelly, George Memmoli 3*

HOT ROCK, THE (1972) 20th Century-Fox. **Color-101min.** Robert Redford, George Segal 5½*
British title: HOW TO STEAL A DIAMOND IN FOUR UNEASY LESSONS

HOT ROD GANG (1958) American-International. **B&W-72min.** John Ashley, Jody Fair .... (2)
British title: FURY UNLEASHED

HOT ROD GIRL (1956) American-International. **B&W-75min.** Lori Nelson, John Smith, Chuck Connors .... (2)

HOT ROD RUMBLE (1957) Allied Artists. **B&W-79min.** Brett Halsey, Richard Bakalyan .... (3)

HOT RODS TO HELL (1967) M-G-M. **Color-92min.** Dana Andrews, Jeanne Crain 3*

HOT SATURDAY (1932) Paramount. **B&W-73min.** Cary Grant, Nancy Carroll .... (4)

HOT SHOTS (1956) Allied Artists. **B&W-61min.** The Bowery Boys, Joi Lansing .... (4)

HOT SPELL (1958) Paramount. **B&W-86min.** Shirley Booth, Anthony Quinn 4½*

HOT SPOT (1941) *see* I WAKE UP SCREAMING

HOT STUFF (1979) Columbia. **Color-103min.** Dom DeLuise, Suzanne Pleshette ....

HOT SUMMER NIGHT (1957) M-G-M. **B&W-86min.** Leslie Nielsen, Colleen Miller .... (3)

HOTEL, THE (1963) *see* GAMES MEN PLAY, THE

HOTEL (1967) Warner Bros. **Color-124min.** Rod Taylor, Catherine Spaak 5½*

HOTEL BERLIN (1945) Warner Bros. **B&W-98min.** Faye Emerson, Helmut Dantine .... (4)

HOTEL FOR WOMEN (1939) 20th Century-Fox. **B&W-83min.** Linda Darnell, Ann Sothern .... (3)

HOTEL IMPERIAL (1939) Paramount. **B&W-67min.** Isa Miranda, Ray Milland .... (3)

HOTEL PARADISO (1966) M-G-M. **Color-100min.** *(British-U.S.).* Gina Lollobrigida, Alec Guinness 4½*

HOTEL RESERVE (1944) RKO. **B&W-79min.** *(British).* James Mason, Lucie Mannheim .... (5)

HOTEL SAHARA (1951) United Artists. **B&W-96min.** *(British).* Yvonne De Carlo, Peter Ustinov .... (4)

HOUDINI (1953) Paramount. **Color-106min.** Tony Curtis, Janet Leigh ... 5*

HOUND-DOG MAN (1959) 20th Century-Fox. **Color-87min.** Stuart Whitman, Carol Lynley, Fabian .... (4)

HOUND OF THE BASKERVILLES, THE (1939) 20th Century-Fox. **B&W-80min.** Basil Rathbone, Richard Greene, Nigel Bruce 5*

HOUND OF THE BASKERVILLES, THE (1959) United Artists. **Color-84min.** *(British).* Peter Cushing, André Morell, Christopher Lee 5*

HOTEL (1967). House detective Richard Conte, in one of the film's many subplots, takes an extortion payoff from Merle Oberon, whose husband was the driver in a fatal hit-and-run accident.

HOUND OF THE BASKERVILLES, THE (1972) MCA-TV. **Color-73min.** *(Made for TV).* Stewart Granger, Bernard Fox, William Shatner .... (4)
Alternate title: SHERLOCK HOLMES: HOUND OF THE BASKERVILLES

HOUND OF THE BASKERVILLES, THE (1978) **Color-84min.** *(British).* Peter Cook, Dudley Moore, Kenneth Williams ....

HOUNDED (1949) *see* JOHNNY ALLEGRO

HOUNDS OF ZAROFF, THE (1932) *see* MOST DANGEROUS GAME, THE

HOUR BEFORE THE DAWN, THE (1944) Paramount. **B&W-75min.** Franchot Tone, Veronica Lake .... (3)

HOUR OF DECISION (1955) Astor. **B&W-74min.** *(British).* Jeff Morrow, Hazel Court .... (3)

HOUR OF GLORY (1948) *see* SMALL BACK ROOM

HOUR OF THE FURNACES, THE (1968) Third World Cinema Group. **B&W-250min.** *(Argentinian, Documentary). Director:* Octavio Getino..(4)
Original title: HORA DE LOS HORNOS, LA

HOUR OF THE GUN (1967) United Artists. **Color-100min.** James Garner, Jason Robards 3*

HOUR OF THE WOLF (1968) Lopert [U.A.]. **B&W-88min.** *(Swedish).* Liv Ullmann, Max von Sydow 2*
Original title: VARGTIMMEN

HOUR OF 13, THE (1952) M-G-M. **B&W-78min.** *(British).* Peter Lawford, Dawn Addams .... (4)

HOURS OF LOVE, THE (1963) Cinema 5. **B&W-89min.** *(Italian).* Ugo Tognazzi, Emmanuelle Riva, Barbara Steele .... (4)
Original title: ORE DELL'AMORE, LE

HOUSE ACROSS THE BAY, THE (1940) United Artists. **B&W-72min.** George Raft, Joan Bennett .... (4)

HOUSE ACROSS THE LAKE, THE (1954) *see* HEAT WAVE

HOUSE ACROSS THE STREET, THE (1949) Warner Bros. **B&W-69min.** Wayne Morris, Janis Paige .... (3)

HOUSE AT SLY CORNER, THE (1947) *see* CODE OF SCOTLAND YARD, THE

HOUSE BY THE LAKE, THE (1976) American-International. **Color-89min.** *(Canadian).* Brenda Vaccaro, Don Stroud, Chuck Shamata.... 4½*

HOUSE BY THE RIVER (1950) Republic. **B&W-88min.** Louis Hayward, Jane Wyatt .... (3)

HOUSE CALLS (1978) Universal. **Color-98min.** Walter Matthau, Glenda Jackson 6*

HOUSE DIVIDED, A (1932) Universal. **B&W-70min.** Walter Huston, Kent Douglass 4*

HOUSE IN THE SQUARE (1951) *see* I'LL NEVER FORGET YOU

HOUSE IS NOT A HOME, A (1964) Avco-Embassy. **B&W-90min.** Shelley Winters, Robert Taylor .... (3)

HOUSE OF A THOUSAND DOLLS (1967) American-International. Color-78min. *(W. German-Spanish).* Vincent Price, Martha Hyer, George Nader ....(2)
Original German title: HAUS DER TAUSEND FREUDEN, DAS
Original Spanish title: CASA DE LAS MIL MUNECAS, LA

HOUSE OF BAMBOO (1955) 20th Century-Fox. Color-102min. Robert Ryan, Robert Stack................................4*

HOUSE OF CARDS (1969) Universal. Color-105min. George Peppard, Inger Stevens, Orson Welles................................4*

HOUSE OF DARK SHADOWS (1970) M-G-M. Color-96min. Jonathan Frid, Joan Bennett, Grayson Hall.....................3½*

HOUSE OF DOOM (1934) *see* BLACK CAT, THE

HOUSE OF DRACULA (1945) Universal. B&W-67min. Lon Chaney (Jr.), Onslow Stevens, John Carradine.........................3*

HOUSE OF EXORCISM, THE (1975) Peppercorn-Wormser. Color-91min. *(Italian).* Telly Savalas, Elke Sommer, Sylva Koscina, Robert Alda.....(3)
Original title: CASA DELL' ESORCISMO, LA
Title of film prior to re-editing and addition of Robert Alda's scenes: LISA AND THE DEVIL

HOUSE OF FATE (1936) *see* MUSS 'EM UP

HOUSE OF FEAR (1939) Universal. B&W-66min. William Gargan, Irene Hervey 4*

HOUSE OF FEAR, THE (1945) Universal. B&W-69min. Basil Rathbone, Nigel Bruce......................5*

HOUSE OF FRANKENSTEIN (1945) Universal. B&W-71min. Boris Karloff, Lon Chaney, Jr., John Carradine.........................4*
8mm title: DOOM OF DRACULA

HOUSE OF FRIGHT (1960) American-International. Color-89min. *(British).* Paul Massie, Dawn Addams, Christopher Lee 4*
Original & TV title: TWO FACES OF DR. JEKYLL, THE

HOUSE OF HORRORS (1946) Universal. B&W-65min. Martin Kosleck, Rondo Hatton, Robert Lowery 3*
British title: JOAN MEDFORD IS MISSING

HOUSE OF INTRIGUE, THE (1957) Allied Artists. Color-94min. *(Italian).* Curt Jurgens, Dawn Addams, Folco Lulli ....(3)
Original title: LONDRA CHIAMA POLO NORD *(London Calling the North Pole)*

HOUSE OF LOVERS (1957) *see* POT BOUILLE

HOUSE OF MENACE (1935) *see* KIND LADY

HOUSE OF MYSTERY (1942) *see* NIGHT MONSTER, THE

HOUSE OF MYSTERY (1961) Anglo Amalgamated [EMI]. B&W-56min. *(British).* Jane Hylton, Peter Dyneley ....(4)

HOUSE OF NUMBERS (1957) M-G-M. B&W-92min. Jack Palance, Barbara Long......................(4)

HOUSE OF 1,000 WOMEN (1944) *see* TWO THOUSAND WOMEN

HOUSE OF RICORDI (1956) Manson. Color-117min. *(Italian).* Paolo Stoppa, Roland Alexandre ....(3)
Original title: CASA RICORDI

HOUSE OF ROTHSCHILD, THE (1934) United Artists. B&W-86min. George Arliss......................5½*

HOUSE OF SECRETS (1956) *see* TRIPLE DECEPTION

HOUSE OF SETTLEMENT (1949) *see* MR. SOFT TOUCH

HOUSE OF STRANGERS (1949) 20th Century-Fox. B&W-101min. Edward G. Robinson, Susan Hayward......................5*

HOUSE OF TERROR (1972) *see* FIVE AT THE FUNERAL

HOUSE OF THE BLACK DEATH (1965) Medallion. B&W-80min. Lon Chaney (Jr.), John Carradine, Andrea King, Tom Drake 2*

HOUSE OF THE DAMNED (1963) 20th Century-Fox. B&W-62min. Ron Foster, Merry Anders......................(3)

HOUSE OF THE SEVEN CORPSES, THE (1974) International Amusements. Color-90min. John Ireland, Faith Domergue, John Carradine......................(3)

HOUSE OF THE SEVEN GABLES, THE (1940) Universal. B&W-89min. Nan Grey, George Sanders, Vincent Price......................6*

HOUSE OF THE SEVEN HAWKS, THE (1959) M-G-M. B&W-92min. *(British).* Robert Taylor, Nicole Maurey......................(3)

HOUSE OF USHER (1960) American-International. Color-85min. Vincent Price, Mark Damon......................4*
Alternate title: FALL OF THE HOUSE OF USHER, THE

HOUSE OF WAX (1953) Warner Bros. Color-88min. Vincent Price, Frank Lovejoy......................4½*

HOUSE OF WOMEN (1962) Warner Bros. B&W-85min. Shirley Knight, Andrew Duggan......................(3)

HOUSE ON CHELOUCHE STREET, THE (1973) Productions Unlimited, Inc. Color-115min. *(Israeli).* Gila Almagor, Ophir Shalhin......................4*

HOUSE ON GREENAPPLE ROAD (1970) Quinn Martin Productions. Color-100min. *(Made for TV).* Christopher George, Janet Leigh, Julie Harris......................3*

HOUSE ON HAUNTED HILL (1959) Allied Artists. B&W-75min. Vincent Price, Carol Ohmart......................4½*

HOUSE ON MARSH ROAD, THE (1960) *see* INVISIBLE CREATURE, THE

HOUSE ON 92nd STREET, THE (1945) 20th Century-Fox. B&W-88min. William Eythe, Lloyd Nolan......................4*
Alternate title: NOW IT CAN BE TOLD

HOUSE ON SKULL MOUNTAIN, THE (1974) 20th Century-Fox. Color-89min. Victor French, Janee Michelle......................(4)

HOUSE ON TELEGRAPH HILL, THE (1951) 20th Century-Fox. B&W-93min. Richard Basehart, Valentina Cortesa......................4*

HOUSE ON THE WATERFRONT, THE (1955) Union Films. B&W-90min. *(French).* Jean Gabin, Andrée Debar, Henri Vidal......................(4)
Original title: PORT DE DESIR, LE *(Port of Desire)*

HOUSE THAT CRIED MURDER, THE (1973) *see* BRIDE, THE

HOUSE THAT DRIPPED BLOOD, THE (1971) Cinerama Releasing. Color-101min. *(British).* Christopher Lee, Peter Cushing, Denholm Elliott, Jon Pertwee......................5*

HOUSE THAT SCREAMED, THE (1970) American-International. Color-94min. *(Spanish, English language).* Lilli Palmer, John Moulder Brown......................3½*
Original title: RESIDENCIA, LA *(The Boarding School)*

HOUSE THAT VANISHED, THE (1973) Hallmark. Color-99min. *(British).* Andrea Allan, Karl Lanchbury, Joesph Larraz......................(3)
Original title: SCREAM . . . AND DIE!
U.S. pre-release title: DON'T GO INTO THE BEDROOM

HOUSE THAT WOULDN'T DIE, THE (1970) ABC Films. Color-74min. *(Made for TV).* Barbara Stanwyck, Richard Egan, Michael Anderson, Jr......................4*
Alternate title: AMMIE, COME HOME

HOUSEBOAT (1958) Paramount. Color-110min. Cary Grant, Sophia Loren 4*

HOUSEHOLDER, THE (1963) Royal Films Int'l [Columbia]. B&W-100min. *(Indian-U.S., English language).* Shashi Kapoor, Leela Naidu, Hariendernath Chattopadaya......................(5)
Original Indian title: GHARBAR

HOUSEKEEPER'S DAUGHTER, THE (1939) United Artists. B&W-79min. Joan Bennett, Adolphe Menjou......................(4)

HOUSEWIFE (1934) Warner Bros. B&W-69min. Bette Davis, George Brent......................(3)

HOUSTON STORY, THE (1956) Columbia. B&W-79min. Gene Barry, Barbara Hale, Edward Arnold......................(3)

HOUSTON, WE'VE GOT A PROBLEM (1974) MCA-TV. Color-74min. *(Made for TV).* Robert Culp, Clu Gulager......................(4)

HOW AWFUL ABOUT ALLEN (1970) ABC Films. Color-74min. *(Made for TV).* Anthony Perkins, Julie Harris, Joan Hackett......................4*

HOW DO I LOVE THEE? (1970) Cinerama Releasing. Color-98min. Jackie Gleason, Maureen O'Hara......................3*

HOW FUNNY CAN SEX BE (1973) In-Frame. B&W-97min. *(Italian).* Giancarlo Giannini, Laura Antonelli, Alberto Lionello......................4½*
Original title: SESSO MATTO *(Sex Madness)*

HOW GREEN WAS MY VALLEY (1941) 20th Century-Fox. B&W-118min. Walter Pidgeon, Maureen O'Hara......................6*

HOW I SPENT MY SUMMER VACATION (1967) Universal. Color-100min. *(Made for TV).* Rogert Wagner, Lola Albright, Peter Lawford......................3*

HOW I WON THE WAR (1967) United Artists. Color-109min. *(British).* Michael Crawford, John Lennon......................(4)

HOW NOT TO ROB A DEPARTMENT STORE (1965) Artixo Prods. B&W-95min. *(French-Italian).* Jean-Claude Brialy, Marie Laforét......(3)
Original French title: CENT BRIQUES ET DES TUILES
Original Italian title: COLPO GROSSO A PARIGI

HOW SWEET IT IS! (1968) National General. Color-99min. James Garner, Debbie Reynolds, Terry-Thomas......................4*

HOW THE WEST WAS WON (1963) M-G-M. Color-165min. Debbie Reynolds, James Stewart, George Peppard, Carroll Baker, Henry Fonda, Gregory Peck......................4½*

HOW TO BE VERY, VERY POPULAR (1955) 20th Century-Fox. Color-89min. Betty Grable, Sheree North......................4*

HOW TO COMMIT MARRIAGE (1969) Cinerama Releasing. Color-98min. Bob Hope, Jackie Gleason......................3*

Films are rated on a 1 to 10 scale, 10 is highest. **Boldface** ratings followed by an asterisk (*) are for films actually seen and rated by the executive and senior editors. All other ratings are estimates. (See Notes on Entertainment Ratings in the front section.)

HOW TO FRAME A FIGG (1971) Universal. Color-103min. Don Knotts, Joe Flynn .... (4)

HOW TO MAKE A MONSTER (1958) American-International. B&W-74min. Robert H. Harris, Gary Conway............................ (2)

HOW TO MARRY A MILLIONAIRE (1953) 20th Century-Fox. Color-95min. Betty Grable, Marilyn Monroe, Lauren Bacall 5*

HOW TO MURDER A RICH UNCLE (1957) Columbia. B&W-79min. (British). Charles Coburn, Nigel Patrick .... (4)

HOW TO MURDER YOUR WIFE (1965) United Artists. Color-118min. Jack Lemmon, Virna Lisi 3½*

HOW TO ROB A BANK (1958) see NICE LITTLE BANK THAT SHOULD BE ROBBED, A

HOW TO SAVE A MARRIAGE - AND RUIN YOUR LIFE (1968) Columbia. Color-102min. Dean Martin, Stella Stevens.................. 3*

HOW TO SEDUCE A PLAYBOY (1966) Chevron. Color-94min. (Austrian-French-Italian). Peter Alexander, Renato Salvatori, Antonella Lualdi .... (2)
Original Austrian title: BEL AMI 2000 ODER: WIE VERFUHRT MAN EINEN PLAYBOY?
Original Italian title: 100 RAGAZZE PER UN PLAYBOY

HOW TO SEDUCE A WOMAN (1974) Cinerama Releasing. Color-110min. Angus Duncan, Angel Tompkins, Heidi Bruhl ....

HOW TO STEAL A DIAMOND IN FOUR UNEASY LESSONS (1972) see HOT ROCK, THE

HOW TO STEAL A MILLION (1966) 20th Century-Fox. Color-127min. Audrey Hepburn, Peter O'Toole 6½*

HOW TO STEAL AN AIRPLANE (1971) MCA-TV. Color-100min. (Made for TV). Peter Duel, Clinton Greyn, Sal Mineo .... (4)
Alternate title: ONLY ONE DAY LEFT BEFORE TOMORROW
Alternate title: ONE DAY BEFORE TOMORROW

HOW TO STEAL THE WORLD (1968) M-G-M. Color-89min. (Telefeature). Robert Vaughn, David McCallum, Barry Sullivan, Eleanor Parker..... (4)

HOW TO STUFF A WILD BIKINI (1965) American-International. Color-90min. Annette Funicello, Dwayne Hickman, Brian Donlevy, Buster Keaton 2*

HOW TO SUCCEED IN BUSINESS WITHOUT REALLY TRYING (1967) United Artists. Color-119min. Robert Morse, Rudy Vallee 6*

HOW TO SUCCEED WITH SEX (1970) Medford Films. Color-77min. Zack Taylor, Mary Jane Carpenter .... (2)
Alternate title: HOW TO SUCCEED WITH THE OPPOSITE SEX

HOWARDS OF VIRGINIA, THE (1940) Columbia. B&W-122min. Cary Grant, Martha Scott.. 4*
British title: TREE OF LIBERTY, THE

HOWLING IN THE WOODS, A (1971) MCA-TV. Color-96min. (Made for TV). Larry Hagman, Barbara Eden, Vera Miles 3*

HOW'S ABOUT IT (1943) Universal. B&W-61min. The Andrews Sisters, Robert Paige, Grace McDonald............................. (3)

HOWZER (1972) URI Productions. Color-82min. Peter Desiante, Melissa Stocking, Royal Dano, William (Billy) Gray .... (3)

HUCKLEBERRY FINN (1931) Paramount. B&W-80min. Jackie Coogan, Junior Durkin... (4)

HUCKLEBERRY FINN (1939) see ADVENTURES OF HUCKLEBERRY FINN, THE

HUCKLEBERRY FINN (1960) see ADVENTURES OF HUCKLEBERRY FINN, THE

HUCKLEBERRY FINN (1974) United Artists. Color-117min. Jeff East, Paul Winfield .... (4)

HUCKSTERS, THE (1947) M-G-M. B&W-115min. Clark Gable, Deborah Kerr 5*

HUD (1963) Paramount. B&W-112min. Paul Newman, Melvyn Douglas, Patricial Neal 6*

HUDSON'S BAY (1940) 20th Century-Fox. B&W-95min. Paul Muni, Gene Tierney 4½*

HUE AND CRY (1947) Fine Arts. B&W-82min. (British). Alastair Sim, Jack Warner .... (5)

HUGGETTS ABROAD, THE (1949) J. Arthur Rank. B&W-87min. (British). Jack Warner, Kathleen Harrison ....

HUGO THE HIPPO (1976) 20th Century-Fox. Color-78min. (U.S.-Hungarian, Cartoon). Director: Bill Feigenbaum .... (4)

HUGS AND KISSES (1967) Avco-Embassy. B&W-93min. (Swedish). Agneta Ekmanner, Sven-Bertil Taube .... (3)
Original title: PUSS OCH KRAM

HUK (1956) United Artists. Color-84min. George Montgomery, Mona Freeman .... (4)

HULLABALOO (1940) M-G-M. B&W-77min. Frank Morgan, Billie Burke .... (3)

HUMAN CARGO (1936) 20th Century-Fox. B&W-66min. Claire Trevor, Brian Donlevy... (3)

HUMAN COMEDY, THE (1943) M-G-M. B&W-118min. Mickey Rooney, James Craig 4*

HUMAN CONDITION, THE (1961) Shochiku. B&W-579min. (Japanese). Tatsuya Nakadai, Michio Aratama .... (5)

HUMAN DESIRE (1954) Columbia. B&W-90min. Glenn Ford, Gloria Grahame, Broderick Crawford .... (4)

HUMAN DUPLICATORS, THE (1965) Allied Artists. Color-82min. George Nader, Barbara Nichols, Richard Kiel................. (3)

HUMAN FACTOR, THE (1975) Bryanston. Color-95min. (British). George Kennedy, John Mills..................................... 4½*

HUMAN JUNGLE, THE (1954) Allied Artists. B&W-82min. Gary Merrill, Regis Toomey .... (4)

HUMAN MONSTER, THE (1939) Monogram [Allied Artists]. B&W-73min. (British). Bela Lugosi, Hugh Williams................... (4)
Original title: DARK EYES OF LONDON

HUMAN VAPOR, THE (1960) Brenco Pictures. Color-79min. (Japanese). Yoshio Tsuchiya, Kaoru Yachigusa .... (4)
Original title: GASU NINGEN DAI ICHI-GO

HUMANOID, THE (1979) Color- min. (Italian-U.S.). Richard Kiel, Barbara Bach, Arthur Kennedy................................

HUMORESQUE (1920) Paramount. B&W-6reels (Silent). Vera Gordon, Dore Davidson .... (4)

HUMORESQUE (1947) Warner Bros. B&W-125min. Joan Crawford, John Garfield 4*

HUNCHBACK OF NOTRE DAME, THE (1923) Universal. B&W-122min. (Silent). Lon Chaney, Patsy Ruth Miller.................. 4*

HUNCHBACK OF NOTRE DAME, THE (1939) RKO. B&W-117min. Charles Laughton, Cedric Hardwicke, Maureen O'Hara 5½*

HUNCHBACK OF NOTRE DAME, THE (1957) RKO. Color-104min. (French). Anthony Quinn, Gina Lollobrigida 4*
Original title: NOTRE DAME DE PARIS

HUNCHBACK OF NOTRE DAME, THE (1977) NBC-TV. Color-100min. (British, Made for TV). Warren Clarke, Kenneth Haigh, Michelle Newell 5½*

HUNDRED HOUR HUNT (1952) Abner J. Greshler. B&W-88min. (British). Anthony Steel, Jack Warner .... (5)
Original title: EMERGENCY CALL

HUNGER (1966) Sigma III. B&W-115min. (Danish-Swedish-Norwegian). Per Oscarsson, Gunnel Lindblom 4*
Danish title: SULT
Swedish title: SVALT

HUNGRY HILL (1947) Universal. B&W-92min. (British). Margaret Lockwood, Dennis Price.................................... 4*

HUNGRY WIVES (1973) Jack H. Harris. Color-89min. Jan White, Ray Laine, Anne Muffly .... (3)

HUNS, THE (1960) Producers International. Color-85min. (Italian-French). Chelo Alonso, Jacques Sernas, Folco Lulli .... (2)
Original Italian title: REGINA DEI TARTARI, LA (The Queen of the Tartars)

HUNT, THE (1960) American-International. Color-86min. (Italian-French). Marina Vlady, Fausto Tozzi .... (3)

HUNT, THE (1966) Trans-Lux Distributing. B&W-93min. (Spanish). Ismael Merlo, Alfredo Mayo .... (4)
Original title: CAZA, LA

HUNT THE MAN DOWN (1950) RKO. B&W-68min. Gig Young, Lynn Roberts.. (4)

HUNTED, THE (1948) Allied Artists. B&W-67min. Belita, Preston Foster .... (4)

HUNTED (1952) see STRANGER IN BETWEEN, THE

HUNTED MEN (1938) Paramount. B&W-65min. Lloyd Nolan, Mary Carlisle .... (3)

HUNTER (1971) CBS-TV. Color-73min. (Made for TV). John Vernon, Steve Ihnat, Sabrina Scharf .... (4)

HUNTER, THE (1979) Paramount. Color- min. Steve McQueen ....

HUNTERS, THE (1958) 20th Century-Fox. Color-108min. Robert Mitchum, Robert Wagner 4½*

HUNTERS ARE FOR KILLING (1970) CBS-TV. Color-100min. (Made for TV). Burt Reynolds, Melvyn Douglas, Suzanne Pleshette 4*

HUNTERS OF THE DEEP (1955) Distributors Corp. of America. Color-64min. (Documentary). Producer: Tom Gries .... (5)

Films are rated on a 1 to 10 scale, 10 is highest. **Boldface** ratings followed by an asterisk (*) are for films actually seen and rated by the executive and senior editors. All other ratings are estimates. (See Notes on Entertainment Ratings in the front section.)

HUNTING PARTY, THE (1971) United Artists. **Color-108min.** *(British).* Oliver Reed, Candice Bergen, Gene Hackman......................(2)

HURRICANE, THE (1937) United Artists. **B&W-110min.** Dorothy Lamour, Jon Hall................4½*

HURRICANE (1975) MPC (TV). **Color-74min.** *(Made for TV).* Larry Hagman, Jessica Walter, Will Geer................3½*

HURRICANE (1979) Paramount. **Color-119min.** Mia Farrow, Max Von Sydow, Dayton Ka'Ne................5*

HURRICANE ISLAND (1951) Columbia. **Color-70min.** Jon Hall, Marie Windsor................(3)

HURRICANE SMITH (1941) Republic. **B&W-69min.** Ray Middleton, Jane Wyatt................(3)
Alternate title: DOUBLE IDENTITY

HURRICANE SMITH (1952) Paramount. **Color-90min.** John Ireland, Yvonne De Carlo................3*

HURRY, CHARLIE, HURRY (1941) RKO. **B&W-65min.** Leon Errol, Mildred Coles................(4)

HURRY SUNDOWN (1967) Paramount. **Color-146min.** Michael Caine, Jane Fonda................4*

HURRY TOMORROW (1975) Hound Dog Films. **B&W-80min.** *(Documentary). Director:* Richard Cohen................(3)

HURRY UP OR I'LL BE 30 (1973) Avco-Embassy. **Color-88min.** John Lefkowitz, Linda Decoff................(3)

HUSBANDS (1970) Columbia. **Color-138min.** Ben Gazzara, Peter Falk, John Cassavetes................2*

HUSBANDS OR LOVERS (1939) *see* HONEYMOON IN BALI

HUSH . . . HUSH, SWEET CHARLOTTE (1964) 20th Century-Fox. **B&W-133min.** Bette Davis, Olivia de Havilland................4*

HUSTLE (1975) Paramount. **Color-120min.** Burt Reynolds, Catherine Deneuve................4½*

HUSTLER, THE (1961) 20th Century-Fox. **B&W-135min.** Paul Newman, Piper Laurie, George C. Scott, Jackie Gleason................6*

HUSTLING (1975) Worldvision. **Color-96min.** *(Made for TV).* Lee Remick, Monte Markham, Jill Clayburgh................5*

HYPNOTIC EYE, THE (1960) Allied Artists. **B&W-79min.** Jacques Bergerac, Merry Anders, Allison Hayes................(3)

HYSTERIA (1965) M-G-M. **B&W-86min.** *(British).* Robert Webber, Anthony Newlands, Maurice Denham, Leila Goldoni................(3)

-I-

I, A LOVER (1966) Crown International. **B&W-90min.** *(Danish-Swedish).* Jorgen Ryg, Jessie Flaws................(3)
Original Danish title: JEG - EN ELSKER
Original Swedish title: JAG - EN ALSKARE

THE HURRICANE (1937). C. Aubrey Smith (standing), Thomas Mitchell and Mary Astor watch as Jerome Cowan is accused by island administrator Raymond Massey of having helped the native fugitive escape.

I, A WOMAN (1965) Audubon. **B&W-90min.** *(Danish-Swedish).* Essy Persson, Jorgen Reenberg................(4)
Original Danish title: JEG - EN KVINDE
Swedish title: JAG - EN KVINNA

I, A WOMAN, PART II (1968) Chevron. **Color-81min.** *(Danish-Swedish).* Gio Petré, Lars Lunae................(2)
Alternate title: '2'
Original Danish title: JEG - EN KVINDE II
Original Swedish title: JAG - EN KVINNA II

I, A WOMAN, PART III (1970) Chevron. **Color-85min.** *(Danish).* Inger Sundh, Tom Scott, Gun Falck................(2)
Alternate title: DAUGHTER, THE
Original title: TRE SLAGS KAERLIGHED
Alternate title: I, A WOMAN -- 3
Alternate title: I AM A WOMAN III

I ACCUSE (1958) M-G-M. **B&W-99min.** José Ferrer, Viveca Lindfors, Leo Genn................4½*

I AIM AT THE STARS (1960) Columbia. **B&W-107min.** Curt Jurgens, Victoria Shaw................4*

I AIN'T NO BUFFALO (1970) *see* GUESS WHAT WE LEARNED IN SCHOOL TODAY?

I AM A CAMERA (1955) Distributors Corp. of America. **B&W-98min.** *(British).* Julie Harris, Laurence Harvey................(5)

I AM A DANCER (1972) Cinevision. **Color-93min.** *(British, Documentary). Director:* Pierre Jourdan................(4)

I AM A FUGITIVE FROM A CHAIN GANG (1932) Warner Bros. **B&W-93min.** Paul Muni, Glenda Farrell................5½*

I AM A THIEF (1935) Warner Bros. **B&W-64min.** Ricardo Cortez, Mary Astor................(3)

I AM CURIOUS (BLUE) (1968) Grove Press. **B&W-103min.** *(Swedish).* Lena Nyman, Vilgot Sjoman, Borje Ahlstedt................(2)
Original title: JAR AR NYFIKEN - BLA

I AM CURIOUS (YELLOW) (1967) Grove Press. **B&W-120min.** *(Swedish).* Lena Nyman, Vilgot Sjoman................2*
Original title: JAG AR NYFIKEN (GUL)

I AM THE LAW (1938) Columbia. **B&W-83min.** Edward G. Robinson, Barbara O'Neil................(4)

I AND MY LOVE (1966) *see* GALIA

I, AND MY LOVERS (1966) *see* GALIA

I BECAME A CRIMINAL (1947) Warner Bros. **B&W-78min.** *(British).* Sally Gray, Trevor Howard................(4)
Original title: THEY MADE ME A FUGITIVE
Alternate title: THEY MADE ME A CRIMINAL

I BELIEVE IN YOU (1952) Universal. **B&W-95min.** *(British).* Cecil Parker, Celia Johnson................(5)

I BOMBED PEARL HARBOR (1960) Parade. **Color-98min.** *(Japanese).* Yosuke Natsuki, Toshiro Mifune................3*
Original title: TAIHEYO NO ARASHI
Alternate title: STORM OVER THE PACIFIC, THE

I BURY THE LIVING (1958) United Artists. **B&W-75min.** Richard Boone, Theodore Bikel................(4)

I CALL FIRST (1968) *see* WHO'S THAT KNOCKING AT MY DOOR

I CAN GET IT FOR YOU WHOLESALE (1951) 20th Century-Fox. **B&W-91min.** Susan Hayward, Dan Dailey................(5)
TV title: ONLY THE BEST
British title: THIS IS MY AFFAIR

I CAN'T . . . I CAN'T (1970) *see* WEDDING NIGHT

I CAN'T GIVE YOU ANYTHING BUT LOVE, BABY (1940) Universal. **B&W-60min.** Broderick Crawford, Peggy Moran................(4)

I CONFESS (1953) Warner Bros. **B&W-95min.** Montgomery Clift, Anne Baxter................4½*

I COULD GO ON SINGING (1963) United Artists. **Color-99min.** *(British).* Judy Garland, Dirk Bogarde................(4)

I COULD NEVER HAVE SEX WITH ANY MAN WHO HAS SO LITTLE REGARD FOR MY HUSBAND (1973) Cinema 5. **Color-90min.** Carmine Caridi, Andrew Duncan, Cynthia Harris, Lynne Lipton................(3)

I COVER BIG TOWN (1947) Paramount. **B&W-63min.** Phillip Reed, Hillary Brooke................(3)
Alternate title: I COVER THE UNDERWORLD

I COVER THE UNDERWORLD (1955) Republic. **B&W-70min.** Sean McClory, Joanne Jordan................(3)

I COVER THE WAR (1937) Universal. **B&W-68min.** John Wayne, Gwen Gaze................4*

I COVER THE WATERFRONT (1933) United Artists. **B&W-70min.** Claudette Colbert, Ben Lyon................4*

I DEAL IN DANGER (1966) 20th Century-Fox. **Color-89min.** *(Telefeature).* Robert Goulet, Christine Carere.................................(3)

I DIED A THOUSAND TIMES (1955) Warner Bros. **Color-109min.** Jack Palance, Shelley Winters.................................(4)

I DISMEMBER MAMA (1974) Europix International. **Color-81min.** Zooey Hall, Geri Reisch, Joanne Moore Jordan.................................(3)

I DON'T CARE GIRL, THE (1953) 20th Century-Fox. **Color-78min.** Mitzi Gaynor, David Wayne.................................(3)

I DON'T WANT TO BE BORN (1975) *see* DEVIL WITHIN HER, THE

I DOOD IT (1943) M-G-M. **B&W-102min.** Red Skelton, Eleanor Powell..(4)
British title: BY HOOK OR BY CROOK

I DREAM OF JEANIE (1952) Republic. **Color-90min.** Bill Shirley, Eileen Christy, Ray Middleton.................................(3)
Publicity title: I DREAM OF JEANIE WITH THE LIGHT BROWN HAIR

I DREAM TOO MUCH (1935) RKO. **B&W-95min.** Lily Pons, Henry Fonda.................................(4)

I DRINK YOUR BLOOD (1971) Cinemation. **Color-83min.** Bhaskar, Jadine Wong, Riley Mills.................................(2)

I EAT YOUR SKIN (1971) Cinemation. **B&W-81min.** William Joyce, Heather Hewitt.................................(2)
Publicity title: VOODOO BLOOD BATH

I ESCAPED FROM DEVIL'S ISLAND (1973) United Artists. **Color-87min.** Jim Brown, Christopher George, Rick Ely.................................(3)

I ESCAPED FROM THE GESTAPO (1943) Monogram [Allied Artists]. **B&W-75min.** Dean Jagger, John Carradine.................................(3)
Alternate title: NO ESCAPE

I EVEN MET HAPPY GYPSIES (1967) Prominent Films. **Color-90min.** *(Yugoslavian).* Bekim Fehmiu, Gordana Jovanovic, Bata Zivojinovic..(4)
Original title: SKUPLJACI PERJA
Alternate Yugoslavian title: STEO SAM CAK I SRECNE CIGANE

I.F. STONE'S WEEKLY (1973) I.F. Stone Project. **B&W-62min.** *(Documentary).* Director: Jerry Bruck, Jr. **4***

I FOUND STELLA PARISH (1935) First National [W.B.]. **B&W-84min.** Kay Francis, Ian Hunter.................................(3)

I GIVE MY HEART (1935) *see* LOVES OF MADAME DUBARRY, THE

I GIVE MY HEART (1936) *see* GIVE ME YOUR HEART

I GOT A NAME (1973) *see* LAST AMERICAN HERO, THE

I HAD SEVEN DAUGHTERS (1956) *see* MY SEVEN LITTLE SINS

I HATE YOUR GUTS (1962) *see* INTRUDER, THE

I, JANE DOE (1948) Republic. **B&W-85min.** Vera Ralston, John Carroll (3)
British title: DIARY OF A BRIDE

I KILLED GERONIMO (1950) United Artists. **B&W-63min.** James Ellison, Smith Ballew, Virginia Herrick.................................(3)

I KILLED RASPUTIN (1967) *see* RASPUTIN

I KILLED WILD BILL HICKOK (1956) Associated Artists. **Color-63min.** John Forbes, Helen Westcott, Tom Brown.................................(2)

I KNOW WHERE I'M GOING (1945) Universal. **B&W-91min.** *(British).* Wendy Hiller, Roger Livesey.................................(6)

I LIKE MONEY (1961) 20th Century-Fox. **Color-81min.** *(British).* Peter Sellers, Nadia Gray.................................(4)
Original title: MR. TOPAZE

I LIVE IN FEAR (1955) Brandon. **B&W-113min.** *(Japanese).* Toshiro Mifune, Takashi Shimura.................................(5)
Original title: IKIMONO NO KIROKU
Alternate title: RECORD OF A LIVING BEING
Alternate title: WHAT THE BIRDS KNEW

I LIVE IN GROSVENOR SQUARE (1945) *see* YANK IN LONDON, A

I LIVE MY LIFE (1935) M-G-M. **B&W-81min.** Joan Crawford, Brian Aherne.................................(4)

I LIVED A LIE (1960) *see* I PASSED FOR WHITE

I LOVE A BANDLEADER (1945) Columbia. **B&W-70min.** Phil Harris, Leslie Brooks.................................(3)
British title: MEMORY FOR TWO

I LOVE A MYSTERY (1945) Columbia. **B&W-70min.** Nina Foch, Jim Bannon.................................(3)

I LOVE A MYSTERY (1967) MCA-TV. **Color-98min.** *(Made for TV).* David Hartman, Les Crane, Ida Lupino.................................**3***

I LOVE A SOLDIER (1944) Paramount. **B&W-106min.** Paulette Goddard, Sonny Tufts.................................(3)

I LOVE MELVIN (1953) M-G-M. **Color-76min.** Debbie Reynolds, Donald O'Connor.................................(4)

I LOVE MY WIFE (1970) Universal. **Color-95min.** Elliott Gould, Brenda Vaccaro.................................**4***

I LOVE THAT MAN (1933) Paramount. **B&W-75min.** Nancy Carroll, Edmund Lowe, Robert Armstrong.................................(4)

I LOVE TROUBLE (1947) Columbia. **B&W-94min.** Franchot Tone, Janet Blair.................................(5)

I LOVE YOU AGAIN (1940) M-G-M. **B&W-99min.** William Powell, Myrna Loy.................................(5)

I LOVE YOU, ALICE B. TOKLAS! (1968) Warner Bros. **Color-94min.** Peter Sellers, Jo Van Fleet.................................**4***

I LOVE YOU . . . GOODBYE (1974) Viacom. **Color-77min.** *(Made for TV).* Hope Lange, Earl Holliman, Michael Murphy.................................(4)

I LOVE YOU, I DON'T (1976) *see* JE T'AIME MOI NON PLUS

I LOVE, YOU LOVE (1961) Royal Films Int'l [Columbia]. **Color-90min.** *(Italian-French, Documentary).* Director: Alessandro Blasetti.................................(4)
Original Italian title: IO AMO, TU AMI
Original French title: J'AIME, TU AIMES

I LOVE YOU, ROSA (1972) Leisure Media. **Color-100min.** *(Israeli).* Michal Bat-Adam, Gabi Otterman, Moishe Tal.................................**5***
Original title: ANI OBEV OTACH ROSA

I LOVED A WOMAN (1933) First National [W.B.]. **B&W-90min.** Edward G. Robinson, Kay Francis.................................(4)

I MARRIED A COMMUNIST (1949) RKO. **B&W-73min.** Robert Ryan, Laraine Day, John Agar, Janis Carter.................................(4)
Alternate title: WOMAN ON PIER 13, THE

I MARRIED A DOCTOR (1936) Warner Bros. **B&W-83min.** Pat O'Brien, Josephine Hutchinson.................................(4)

I MARRIED A MONSTER FROM OUTER SPACE (1958) Paramount. **B&W-78min.** Ton Tryon, Gloria Talbott.................................(3)

I MARRIED A WITCH (1942) United Artists. **B&W-76min.** Fredric March, Veronica Lake.................................**4½***

I MARRIED A WOMAN (1958) Universal. **B&W-84min.** George Gobel, Diana Dors, Adolphe Menjou.................................(4)

I MARRIED AN ANGEL (1942) M-G-M. **B&W-84min.** Nelson Eddy, Jeanette MacDonald.................................(3)

I MET A MURDERER (1939) York Pictures. **B&W-70min.** *(British).* James Mason, Pamela Kellino.................................**4***

I MET HIM IN PARIS (1937) Paramount. **B&W-86min.** Claudette Colbert, Melvyn Douglas.................................(5)

I MET MY LOVE AGAIN (1938) United Artists. **B&W-77min.** Joan Bennett, Henry Fonda.................................(4)

I, MOBSTER (1959) 20th Century-Fox. **B&W-80min.** Steve Cochran, Lita Milan.................................(4)

I, MONSTER (1972) Cannon Releasing. **Color-75min.** *(British).* Christopher Lee, Peter Cushing.................................**3***

I NEVER PROMISED YOU A ROSE GARDEN (1977) New World. **Color-96min.** Bibi Andersson, Kathleen Quinlan.................................**3***

I NEVER SANG FOR MY FATHER (1970) Columbia. **Color-90min.** Melvyn Douglas, Gene Hackman.................................**5***

I PASSED FOR WHITE (1960) Allied Artists. **B&W-93min.** Sonya Wilde, James Franciscus.................................(3)
Alternate title: I LIVED A LIE

I REMEMBER MAMA (1948) RKO. **B&W-134min.** Irene Dunne, Barbara Bel Geddes.................................**6***

I SAW WHAT YOU DID (1965) Universal. **B&W-82min.** Ann Garrett, Sarah Lane.................................(4)

I SAILED TO TAHITI WITH AN ALL-GIRL CREW (1969) United National-National Telefilm. **Color-95min.** Gardner McKay, Diane McBain, Pat Buttram, Edy Williams.................................(3)

I SEE A DARK STRANGER (1947) *see* ADVENTURESS, THE

I SHALL RETURN (1950) *see* AMERICAN GUERILLA IN THE PHILIPPINES, AN

I SHOT JESSE JAMES (1949) Lippert Productions. **B&W-81min.** John Ireland, Preston Foster, Reed Hadley.................................(4)

I SPIT ON YOUR GRAVE (1959) Audubon. **B&W-100min.** *(French).* Christian Marquand, Antonella Lualdi.................................(2)
Original title: J'IRAI CRACHER SUR VOS TOMBES

I SPY, YOU SPY (1966) *see* BANG! BANG! YOU'RE DEAD

I STAND CONDEMNED (1935) United Artists. **B&W-75min.** *(British).* Laurence Olivier, Harry Baur.................................**4½***
Original title: MOSCOW NIGHTS

I TAKE THIS WOMAN (1931) Paramount. **B&W-74min.** Gary Cooper, Carole Lombard.................................(4)

I TAKE THIS WOMAN (1940) M-G-M. **B&W-97min.** Spencer Tracy, Hedy Lamarr.................................**3***

Films are rated on a 1 to 10 scale, 10 is highest. **Boldface** ratings followed by an asterisk (*) are for films actually seen and rated by the executive and senior editors. All other ratings are estimates. (See Notes on Entertainment Ratings in the front section.)

I THANK A FOOL (1962) M-G-M. Color-100min. (British). Susan Hayward, Peter Finch 4*

I, THE JURY (1953) United Artists. B&W-87min. Biff Elliot, Preston Foster 3*

I WAKE UP SCREAMING (1941) 20th Century-Fox. B&W-81min. Betty Grable, Victor Mature, Laird Cregar 4*
British and alternate U.S. title: HOT SPOT

I WALK ALONE (1948) Paramount. B&W-98min. Burt Lancaster, Kirk Douglas .... (4)

I WALK THE LINE (1970) Columbia. Color-95min. Gregory Peck, Tuesday Weld 3*

I WALKED WITH A ZOMBIE (1943) RKO. B&W-69min. James Ellison, Frances Dee 3*

I WANNA HOLD YOUR HAND (1978) Universal. Color-104min. Nancy Allen, Bobby DiCicco, Susan Kendall Newman 5½*

I WANT A DIVORCE (1940) Paramount. B&W-75min. Dick Powell, Joan Blondell .... (3)

I WANT TO KEEP MY BABY! (1976) CBS-TV. Color-120min. (Made for TV). Mariel Hemingway, Susan Anspach, Jack Rader .... (4)

I WANT TO LIVE! (1958) United Artists. B&W-120min. Susan Hayward, Simon Oakland 5½*

I WANT WHAT I WANT (1972) Cinerama Releasing. Color-91min. (British). Anne Heywood, Harry Andrews 3*

I WANT YOU (1952) RKO. B&W-102min. Dana Andrews, Dorothy McGuire 4*

I WANTED WINGS (1941) Paramount. B&W-131min. Ray Milland, William Holden 3½*

I WAS A COMMUNIST FOR THE F.B.I. (1951) Warner Bros. B&W-83min. Frank Lovejoy, Dorothy Hart .... (4)

I WAS A MALE WAR BRIDE (1949) 20th Century-Fox. B&W-105min. Cary Grant, Ann Sheridan 3*
British title: YOU CAN'T SLEEP HERE

I WAS A PARISH PRIEST (1957) B&W-87min. (Spanish-French). Claude Laydu, Francisco Rabal .... (5)

I WAS A PRISONER ON DEVIL'S ISLAND (1941) Columbia. B&W-71min. Donald Woods, Eduardo Ciannelli .... (3)

I WAS A SHOPLIFTER (1950) Universal. B&W-82min. Scott Brady, Mona Freeman 3½*

I WAS A TEENAGE CAVEMAN (1958) see TEENAGE CAVEMAN

I WAS A TEENAGE FRANKENSTEIN (1957) American-International. B&W-72min. Whit Bissell, Gary Conway 3*
British title: TEENAGE FRANKENSTEIN

I WAS A TEENAGE WEREWOLF (1957) American-International. B&W-70min. Michael Landon, Yvonne Lime 3*

I WAS AN ADVENTURESS (1940) 20th Century-Fox. B&W-81min. Erich Von Stroheim, Vera Zorina, Peter Lorre .... (4)

I WAS AN AMERICAN SPY (1951) Allied Artists. B&W-85min. Gene Evans, Ann Dvorak .... (3)

I WAS HAPPY HERE (1966) see TIME LOST AND TIME REMEMBERED

I WAS MONTY'S DOUBLE (1958) NTA Pictures. B&W-101min. (British). John Mills, Cecil Parker, M. E. Clifton James 5*
Alternate title: MONTY'S DOUBLE

I WILL . . . I WILL . . . FOR NOW (1976) 20th Century-Fox. Color-107min. Elliott Gould, Diane Keaton 5*

I WONDER WHO'S KISSING HER NOW (1947) 20th Century-Fox. Color-108min. June Haver, Mark Stevens 4*

IBANEZ' TORRENT (1926) see TORRENT, THE

ICE (1970) New Yorker Films. B&W-132min. Robert Kramer, Tom Griffin .... (3)

ICE-CAPADES (1941) Republic. B&W-88min. Dorothy Lewis, James Ellison, Jerry Colonna .... (3)

ICE-CAPADES REVUE (1942) Republic. B&W-79min. Ellen Drew, Richard Denning, Jerry Colonna .... (3)
Alternate title: RHYTHM HITS THE ICE

ICE CASTLES (1978) Columbia. Color-113min. Robby Benson, Lynn-Holly Johnson 5½*

ICE COLD IN ALEX (1958) see DESERT ATTACK

ICE FOLLIES OF 1939, THE (1939) M-G-M. B&W-82min. Joan Crawford, James Stewart, Lew Ayres .... (3)

ICE PALACE (1960) Warner Bros. Color-113min. Richard Burton, Robert Ryan .... (4)

ICE STATION ZEBRA (1968) M-G-M. Color-148min. Rock Hudson, Ernest Borgnine 4*

IDIOT'S DELIGHT (1939). Clark Gable plays an uncharacteristic part as a song-and-dance man in a traveling act called "Harry Van and Les Blondes." Beside him are Virginia Grey, Paula Stone, Virginia Dale, Bernadene Hayes, Joan Marsh and Lorraine Krueger.

ICELAND (1942) 20th Century-Fox. B&W-79min. Sonja Henie, John Payne, Jack Oakie .... (4)
British title: KATINA

ICEMAN COMETH, THE (1973) American Film Theatre. Color-239min. Lee Marvin, Robert Ryan 5*

ICHABOD AND MR. TOAD (1949) see ADVENTURES OF ICHABOD AND MR. TOAD

I'D CLIMB THE HIGHEST MOUNTAIN (1951) 20th Century-Fox. Color-88min. Susan Hayward, William Lundigan 4*

I'D RATHER BE RICH (1964) Universal. Color-96min. Sandra Dee, Robert Goulet, Maurce Chevalier .... (4)

IDAHO TRANSFER (1973) Cinemation. Color-87min. Kelley Bohanan, Kevin Hearst, Keith Carradine 1*

IDEAL HUSBAND, AN (1947) 20th Century-Fox. Color-96min. (British). Paulette Goddard, Michael Wilding .... (4)

IDENTITY UNKNOWN (1945) Republic. B&W-71min. Richard Arlen, Cheryl Walker .... (3)

IDENTITY UNKNOWN (1960) Paramount. B&W-66min. (British). Richard Wyler, Pauline Yates .... (3)

IDI AMIN DADA (1974) see GENERAL IDI AMIN DADA

IDIOT, THE (1951) Shochiku. B&W-165min. (Japanese). Masayuki Mori, Toshiro Mifune, Setsuko Hara .... (3)
Original title: HAKUCHI

IDIOT, THE (1958) Artkino. Color-122min. (U.S.S.R.). Yuri Yakovlev, Yulia Borisova .... (5)

IDIOT'S DELIGHT (1939) M-G-M. B&W-105min. Norma Shearer, Clark Gable 4½*

IDLE CLASS, THE (1921) First National [W.B.]. B&W-24min. (Silent). Charles Chaplin, Henry Bergman, Edna Purviance 4*

IDOL, THE (1966) Avco-Embassy. B&W-107min. (British). Jennifer Jones, Michael Parks 3*

IDOLS IN THE DUST (1951) see SATURDAY'S HERO

IF . . . (1968) Paramount. Color-110min. (British). Malcolm McDowell, David Wood 4*

IF A MAN ANSWERS (1962) Universal. Color-102min. Sandra Dee, Bobby Darin 4*

IF ALL THE GUYS IN THE WORLD . . . (1956) Buena Vista. B&W-95min. (French). André Valmy, Jean Gaven, Marc Cassot .... (4)
Original title: SI TOUS LES GARS DU MONDE . . .
Alternate title: IF EVERY GUY IN THE WORLD . . .
British title: RACE FOR LIFE

IF EVER I SEE YOU AGAIN (1978) Columbia. Color-105min. Joe Brooks, Shelley Hack 4½*

IF EVERY GUY IN THE WORLD . . . (1956) see IF ALL THE GUYS IN THE WORLD . . .

Films are rated on a 1 to 10 scale, 10 is highest. **Boldface** ratings followed by an asterisk (*) are for films actually seen and rated by the executive and senior editors. All other ratings are estimates. (See Notes on Entertainment Ratings in the front section.)

IF HE HOLLERS, LET HIM GO! (1968) Cinerama Releasing. Color-106min. Dana Wynter, Raymond St. Jacques, Kevin McCarthy .... (3)

IF I HAD A MILLION (1932) Paramount. B&W-88min. Richard Bennett 5½*

IF I HAD A MILLION (1973) MCA-TV. Color-52min. (Made for TV). John Schuck, Joseph Wiseman, Ruth McDevitt, Kenneth Mars................... 3*

IF I HAD MY WAY (1940) Universal. B&W-94min. Bing Crosby, Gloria Jean.. (4)

IF I WERE KING (1938) Paramount. B&W-100min. Ronald Colman, Basil Rathbone 6*

IF I'M LUCKY (1946) 20th Century-Fox. B&W-79min. Vivian Blaine, Perry Como, Phil Silvers .... (3)

IF IT'S TUESDAY, THIS MUST BE BELGIUM (1969) United Artists. Color-99min. Suzanne Pleshette, Ian McShane 4*

IF THIS BE SIN (1950) United Artists. B&W-72min. (British). Myrna Loy, Roger Livesey....................................... (3)
Original title: THAT DANGEROUS AGE

IF TOMORROW COMES (1971) Worldvision. Color-73min. (Made for TV). Patty Duke, Frank Liu, James Whitmore.................... 4*

IF WINTER COMES (1948) M-G-M. B&W-97min. Walter Pidgeon, Deborah Kerr 3*

IF YOU COULD ONLY COOK (1935) Columbia. B&W-70min. Herbert Marshall, Jean Arthur...................................... (5)

IF YOU DON'T STOP IT YOU'LL GO BLIND (1975) Topar Films/SFD. Color-83min. Keefe Brasselle, Pat McCormick................... (4)

IF YOU FEEL LIKE SINGING (1950) see SUMMER STOCK

IF YOU KNEW SUSIE (1948) RKO. B&W-90min. Eddie Cantor, Joan Davis .... (4)

IKARIE XB 1 (1963) see VOYAGE TO THE ENDS OF THE UNIVERSE

IKIRU (1952) Brandon. B&W-140min. (Japanese). Takashi Shimura, Nobuo Kaneko... 4*
Translation title: To Live
Translation title: Living

I'LL BE SEEING YOU (1944) United Artists. B&W-85min. Ginger Rogers, Joseph Cotten .... (4)

I'LL BE YOURS (1947) Universal. B&W-93min. Deanna Durbin, Tom Drake .... (4)

I'LL CRY TOMORROW (1955) M-G-M. B&W-117min. Susan Hayward, Richard Conte 5*

I'LL GET BY (1950) 20th Century-Fox. Color-83min. June Haver, William Lundigan 4*

I'LL GET YOU (1953) Lippert Productions. B&W-79min. (British). George Raft, Sally Gray.. (3)
Original title: ESCAPE ROUTE

I'LL GET YOU FOR THIS (1951) see LUCKY NICK CAIN

I'LL GIVE A MILLION (1938) 20th Century-Fox. B&W-72min. Warner Baxter, Marjorie Weaver, Peter Lorre, John Carradine .... (4)

I'LL LOVE YOU ALWAYS (1935) Columbia. B&W-63min. Nancy Carroll, George Murphy ....

ILL MET BY MOONLIGHT (1957) see NIGHT AMBUSH

I'LL NEVER FORGET WHAT'S 'IS NAME (1967) Regional. Color-99min. (British). Orson Welles, Oliver Reed 4*

I'LL NEVER FORGET YOU (1951) 20th Century-Fox. Color-90min. (British). Tyrone Power, Ann Blyth......................... (4)
Original title: HOUSE IN THE SQUARE, THE

I'LL REACH FOR A STAR (1937) see HIT PARADE, THE

I'LL REMEMBER APRIL (1945) Universal. B&W-63min. Gloria Jean, Samuel S. Hinds, Kirby Grant........................... (3)

I'LL SEE YOU IN HELL (1963) Medallion. B&W-83min. (Italian). John Drew Barrymore, Eva Bartok......................... (4)

I'LL SEE YOU IN MY DREAMS (1951) Warner Bros. Color-110min. Danny Thomas, Doris Day............................... 4½*

I'LL TAKE ROMANCE (1937) Columbia. B&W-85min. Grace Moore, Melvyn Douglas .... (4)

I'LL TAKE SWEDEN (1965) United Artists. Color-96min. Bob Hope, Tuesday Weld 3*

I'LL TELL THE WORLD (1945) Universal. B&W-61min. Lee Tracy, Brenda Joyce .... (3)

I'LL WAIT FOR YOU (1941) M-G-M. B&W-75min. Robert Sterling, Marsha Hunt .... (3)

ILLEGAL (1955) Warner Bros. B&W-88min. Edward G. Robinson, Nina Foch 4*

ILLEGAL CARGO (1958) B&W-90min. (French). Francoise Arnoul, Jean-Claude Michel .... (3)

ILLEGAL ENTRY (1949) Universal. B&W-84min. Howard Duff, Marta Toren .... (4)

ILLEGAL TRAFFIC (1938) Paramount. B&W-67min. J. Carrol Naish, Mary Carlisle, Robert Preston......................... (4)

ILLICIT INTERLUDE (1951) Robert Hakim. B&W-90min. (Swedish). Maj-Britt Nilsson, Birger Malmsten, Alf Kjellin............... 4*
Original title: SOMMARLEK
British title: SUMMER INTERLUDE

ILLUSION TRAVELS BY STREETCAR, THE (1953) Bauer International. B&W-84min. (Mexican). Lilia Prado, Carlos Navarro ....
Original title: ILUSION VIAJA EN TRANVIA, LA

ILLUSTRATED MAN, THE (1969) Warner Bros. Color-103min. Rod Steiger, Claire Bloom 4½*

ILSA, HAREM KEEPER OF THE OIL SHEIKS (1976) Cambist. Color-93min. Dyanne Thorne, Michael Thayer............... (3)
Publicity title: HAREM KEEPER OF THE OIL SHEIKS

ILSA, SHE WOLF OF THE SS (1975) Cambist. Color-95min. Dyann Thorne, Greg Knoph..

ILYA MOUROMETZ (1956) see SWORD AND THE DRAGON, THE

I'M ALL RIGHT, JACK (1959) Columbia. B&W-104min. (British). Ian Carmichael, Peter Sellers................................ 5*

I'M FROM MISSOURI (1939) Paramount. B&W-80min. Bob Burns, Gladys George .... (5)

I'M NO ANGEL (1933) Paramount. B&W-87min. Mae West, Cary Grant 4*

I'M NOBODY'S SWEETHEART NOW (1940) Universal. B&W-63min. Dennis O'Keefe, Constance Moore.................... (4)

IMAGES (1972) Columbia. Color-100min. (Irish). Susannah York, René Auberjonois 3*

IMAGINARY SWEETHEART (1933) see PROFESSIONAL SWEETHEART

IMITATION GENERAL (1958) M-G-M. B&W-120min. Glenn Ford, Red Buttons 4*

IMITATION OF LIFE (1934) Universal. B&W-106min. Claudette Colbert, Warren William 5*

IMITATION OF LIFE (1959) Universal. Color-124min. Lana Turner, John Gavin 4*

IMMORTAL, THE (1969) Paramount. Color-75min. (Made for TV). Christopher George, Barry Sullivan, Jessica Walter, Ralph Bellamy.... 4*

IMMORTAL BATTALION, THE (1944) see WAY AHEAD, THE

IMMORTAL MONSTER, THE (1959) see CALTIKI, THE IMMORTAL MONSTER

IMMORTAL SERGEANT, THE (1943) 20th Century-Fox. B&W-91min. Henry Fonda, Thomas Mitchell...................... (4)

IMMORTAL STORY, THE (1968) Fleetwood Films. Color-63min. (French, English language). Orson Welles, Jeanne Moreau, Norman Eshley, Roger Coggio.. (5)
Original title: HISTOIRE IMMORTELLE, UNE

IMPACT (1949) United Artists. B&W-111min. Brian Donlevy, Ella Raines .... (3)

IMPASSE (1969) United Artists. Color-100min. Burt Reynolds, Anne Francis 3½*

IMPATIENT HEART, THE (1971) MCA-TV. Color-95min. (Made for TV). Carrie Snodgress, Michael Constantine, Michael Brandon............. (4)

IMPATIENT YEARS, THE (1944) Columbia. B&W-91min. Jean Arthur, Lee Bowman .... (4)

IMPERFECT ANGEL (1964) Paramount. B&W-98min. (German). Peter Van Eyck, Corny Collins........................... (3)
Alternate title: FALLEN ANGEL

IMPERFECT LADY, THE (1947) Paramount. B&W-97min. Ray Milland, Teresa Wright .... (4)
British title: MRS. LORING'S SECRET

IMPERSONATOR, THE (1961) Continental [Walter Reade]. B&W-64min. (British). John Crawford, Jane Griffiths................. (2)

IMPORTANCE OF BEING EARNEST, THE (1952) Universal. Color-95min. (British). Michael Redgrave, Joan Greenwood 7*

IMPOSSIBLE ON SATURDAY (1965) Magna Pictures. B&W-120min. (French-Israeli). Robert Hirsch, Dahlia Friedland............. (5)
Original French title: PAS QUESTION LE SAMEDI (No Questions on Saturday)
Original Israeli title: RAQ LO B'SHABBAT

IMPOSSIBLE YEARS, THE (1968) M-G-M. Color-92min. David Niven, Lola Albright, Ozzie Nelson................................ 2*

Films are rated on a 1 to 10 scale, 10 is highest. **Boldface** ratings followed by an asterisk (*) are for films actually seen and rated by the executive and senior editors. All other ratings are estimates. (See Notes on Entertainment Ratings in the front section.)

IMPOSTOR, THE (1944) Universal. **B&W-95min.** Jean Gabin, Richard Whorf, Ellen Drew .... (4)
Alternate title: STRANGE CONFESSION
Alternate title: IMPOSTER, THE

IMPRECATEUR, L' (1977) Parafrance *(French).* **Color-102min.** *(French).* Jean Yanne, Michel Piccoli, Jean-Claude Brialy ....
Translation title: The Accuser

IMPULSE (1975) Camelot Entertainment. **Color-89min.** William Shatner, Ruth Roman, Jennifer Bishop, Kim Nicholas...................... (3)

"IN" (1967) *see* HIGH

IN A LONELY PLACE (1950) Columbia. **B&W-91min.** Humphrey Bogart, Gloria Grahame 5½*

IN-BETWEEN AGE, THE (1958) Allied Artists. **B&W-76min.** *(British).* Lee Patterson, Mary Steele .... (3)
Original title: GOLDEN DISC, THE

IN BROAD DAYLIGHT (1971) ABC-TV. **Color-75min.** *(Made for TV).* Richard Boone, John Marley 4*

IN CALIENTE (1935) First National [W.B.]. **B&W-84min.** Dolores Del Rio, Pat O'Brien .... (4)

IN CELEBRATION (1974) American Film Theatre. **Color-131min.** *(British-Canadian).* Alan Bates, Bill Owen 4*

IN COLD BLOOD (1967) Columbia. **B&W-134min.** Robert Blake, Scott Wilson 6*

IN DARKNESS WAITING (1969) *see* STRATEGY OF TERROR

IN ENEMY COUNTRY (1968) Universal. **Color-107min.** Tony Franciosa, Anjanette Comer .... (4)

IN FAST COMPANY (1946) Monogram [Allied Artists]. **B&W-61min.** The Bowery Boys, Judy Clark .... (3)

IN HARM'S WAY (1965) Paramount. **B&W-165min.** John Wayne, Kirk Douglas 3½*

IN HOLLYWOOD (1939) *see* JONES FAMILY IN HOLLYWOOD, THE

IN-LAWS, THE (1979) Warner Bros. **Color-103min.** Peter Falk, Alan Arkin 5½*

IN LIKE FLINT (1967) 20th Century-Fox. **Color-114min.** James Coburn, Lee J. Cobb 4*

IN LOVE AND WAR (1958) 20th Century-Fox. **Color-111min.** Robert Wagner, Jeffrey Hunter...................................... 3½*

IN NAME ONLY (1939) RKO. **B&W-102min.** Cary Grant, Carole Lombard 4*

IN NAME ONLY (1969) Screen Gems. **Color-75min.** *(Made for TV).* Michael Callan, Ann Prentiss, Paul Ford, Eve Arden 4*

IN OLD ARIZONA (1929) Fox Film Co. [20th]. **B&W-97min.** Edmund Lowe, Warner Baxter.. (4)

IN OLD CALIFORNIA (1942) Republic. **B&W-88min.** John Wayne, Patsy Kelly .... (3)

IN OLD CHICAGO (1937) 20th Century-Fox. **B&W-110min.** Tyrone Power, Alice Faye 4*

IN OLD KENTUCKY (1935) 20th Century-Fox. **B&W-86min.** Will Rogers, Dorothy Wilson .... (4)

IN OLD OKLAHOMA (1943) Republic. **B&W-102min.** John Wayne, Martha Scott 4*
Alternate title: WAR OF THE WILDCATS

IN OLD SACRAMENTO (1946) Republic. **B&W-89min.** Wild Bill Elliott, Constance Moore .... (4)

IN OLD VIENNA (1956) Republic. **Color-69min.** *(U.S.-Austrian).* Heinz Roettinger, Robert Killick, Kurt Jaggberg .... (2)

IN OUR TIME (1944) Warner Bros. **B&W-110min.** Ida Lupino, Paul Henreid 4*

IN PERSON (1935) RKO. **B&W-87min.** Ginger Rogers, George Brent... (4)

IN PRAISE OF OLDER WOMEN (1978) Avco-Embassy. **Color-106min.** Tom Berenger, Karen Black, Susan Strasberg................ 5½*

IN SAIGON: SOME MAY LIVE (1967) *see* SOME MAY LIVE

IN SEARCH OF AMERICA (1971) Four Star. **Color-75min.** *(Made for TV).* Vera Miles, Carl Betz, Jeff Bridges, Kim Hunter 5*

IN SEARCH OF GREGORY (1970) Universal. **Color-90min.** *(British-Italian).* Julie Christie, Michael Sarrazin.......................... (4)
Original Italian title: ALLA RICERCA DI GREGORY

IN SEARCH OF NOAH'S ARK (1977) Sunn Classic. **Color-95min.** *(Documentary).* Producer: Charles E. Sellier, Jr.................... 4*

IN SEARCH OF THE CASTAWAYS (1962) Buena Vista. **Color-100min.** *(U.S.-British).* Hayley Mills, Maurice Chevalier 5*

IN SOCIETY (1944) Universal. **B&W-75min.** Bud Abbott, Lou Costello, Kirby Grant .... (3)

IN THE BEGINNING . . . (1974) *see* BIBLE!

IN THE CLUTCHES OF THE KU KLUX KLAN (1915) *see* BIRTH OF A NATION, THE

IN THE COOL OF THE DAY (1963) M-G-M. **Color-89min.** Jane Fonda, Peter Finch, Angela Lansbury.......................... (3)

IN THE DEVIL'S GARDEN (1970) Hemisphere. **Color-91min.** *(British).* Suzy Kendall, Frank Finlay.......................... 3*
Original title: ASSAULT
TV title: TOWER OF TERROR

IN THE DOGHOUSE (1961) Continental [Walter Reade]. **B&W-93min.** *(British).* Leslie Phillips, Peggy Cummins .... (5)

IN THE FRENCH STYLE (1963) Columbia. **B&W-106min.** *(U.S.-French).* Jean Seberg, Stanley Baker, Philippe Forquet 4*
Original French title: A LA FRANCAISE

IN THE GOOD OLD SUMMERTIME (1949) M-G-M. **Color-102min.** Judy Garland, Van Johnson 4*

IN THE HEAT OF THE NIGHT (1967) United Artists. **Color-109min.** Sidney Poitier, Rod Steiger.. 6*

IN THE MEANTIME, DARLING (1944) 20th Century-Fox. **B&W-72min.** Jeanne Crain, Frank Latimore .... (3)

IN THE MONEY (1958) Allied Artists. **B&W-61min.** The Bowery Boys, Patricia Donahue 3*

IN THE NAVY (1941) Universal. **B&W-85min.** Bud Abbott, Lou Costello, Dick Powell.. 4*
Alternate title: ABBOTT AND COSTELLO IN THE NAVY

IN THE NIGHT (1941) *see* GANG'S ALL HERE, THE

IN THE REALM OF THE SENSES (1976) **Color-105min.** *(Japanese-French).* Tatsuya Fuji, Eiko Matsuda 2*
Original Japanese title and British release title: AI NO CORRIDA
Original French title: EMPIRE DES SENS, L'

IN THE WAKE OF A STRANGER (1958) Paramount. **B&W-69min.** *(British).* Tony Wright, Shirley Eaton .... (3)

IN THE WAKE OF THE BOUNTY (1933) Expeditionary Films. **B&W-70min.** *(Australian).* Mayne Lynton, Errol Flynn.................. (3)

IN THE YEAR OF THE PIG (1969) Pathé Contemporary. **B&W-101min.** *(Documentary).* Director: Emile De Antonio .... (5)

IN THE YEAR 2889 (1968) *see* YEAR 2889

IN THIS OUR LIFE (1942) Warner Bros. **B&W-97min.** Bette Davis, Olivia de Havilland .... (5)

IN WHICH WE SERVE (1942) Universal. **B&W-114min.** *(British).* Noel Coward, Bernard Miles.. 4*

INADMISSIBLE EVIDENCE (1968) Paramount. **B&W-96min.** *(British).* Nicol Williamson, Eleanor Fazan .... (5)

INCENDIARY BLONDE (1945) Paramount. **Color-113min.** Betty Hutton, Arturo de Cordova.. 4*

IN COLD BLOOD (1967). Following their murdering a Kansas farm family, ex-convicts Robert Blake and Scott Wilson plan their next move as they travel across the southwestern desert.

INCIDENT, THE (1967) 20th Century-Fox. **B&W-107min.** Tony Musante, Martin Sheen, Beau Bridges, Thelma Ritter 5*

INCIDENT AT MIDNIGHT (1963) Schoenfeld Film Distributing. **B&W-58min.** *(British).* Anton Diffring, William Sylvester, Justine Lord......(3)

INCIDENT AT PHANTOM HILL (1966) Universal. **Color-88min.** Dan Duryea, Robert Fuller ....(4)

INCIDENT IN AN ALLEY (1962) United Artists. **B&W-83min.** Chris Warfield, Erin O'Donnell.................................(3)

INCIDENT IN SAIGON (1960) American-International. **B&W-85min.** *(French).* Odilie Versois, Pierre Massima.................................(3)

INCIDENT IN SAN FRANCISCO (1971) ABC Films. **Color-100min.** *(Made for TV).* Richard Kiley, Chris Connelly, Leslie Nielsen.................................4*

INCIDENT ON A DARK STREET (1972) 20th Century-Fox. **Color-75min.** *(Made for TV).* James Olson, William Shatner, Richard Castellano.................................(4)

INCREDIBLE JOURNEY, THE (1963) Buena Vista. **Color-80min.** *(U.S.-Canadian).* Emile Genest, John Drainie.................................(5)

INCREDIBLE JOURNEY OF DOCTOR MEG LAUREL, THE (1979) CBS-TV. **Color-148min.** *(Made for TV).* Lindsay Wagner, Jane Wyman.......

INCREDIBLE MACHINE, THE (1975) National Geographic & Wolper. **Color-45min.** 5*

INCREDIBLE MELTING MAN, THE (1977) American-International. **Color-86min.** Alex Rebar, Burr De Benning 2*

INCREDIBLE MR. LIMPET, THE (1964) Warner Bros. **Color-99min.** *(Part-animated).* Don Knotts, Carole Cook 4*

INCREDIBLE PETRIFIED WORLD, THE (1958) Governor. **B&W-70min.** John Carradine, Phyllis Coates, Robert Clarke ....(3)

INCREDIBLE SARAH, THE (1976) Readers' Digest Films. **Color-105min.** Glenda Jackson, Daniel Massey.................................5½*

INCREDIBLE SHRINKING MAN, THE (1957) Universal. **B&W-81min.** Grant Williams, Randy Stuart.................................4½*

INCREDIBLE 2-HEADED TRANSPLANT, THE (1971) American-International. **Color-88min.** Bruce Dern, Albert Cole, John Bloom 3*

INCREDIBLY STRANGE CREATURES WHO STOPPED LIVING AND BECAME MIXED-UP ZOMBIES, THE (1962) Fairway International. **Color-82min.** Cash Flagg (Ray Dennis Steckler), Brett O'Hara, Carolyn Brandt.................................(2)
Publicity title: INCREDIBLY STRANGE CREATURES, THE

INDESTRUCTIBLE MAN, THE (1956) Allied Artists. **B&W-70min.** Lon Chaney (Jr.), Casey Adams 3*

INDIAN FIGHTER, THE (1955) United Artists. **Color-88min.** Kirk Douglas, Elsa Martinelli 4*

INDIAN LOVE CALL (1936) *see* ROSE MARIE

INDIAN PAINT (1966) Crown International. **Color-91min.** Johnny Crawford, Jay Silverheels.................................(3)

INDIAN SCARF, THE (1963) UCC Films. **B&W-85min.** *(German).* Heinz Drache, Corny Collins, Klaus Kinski.................................(3)
Original title: INDISCHE TUCH, DAS

INDIAN SCOUT (1950) *see* DAVY CROCKETT, INDIAN SCOUT

INDIAN SUMMER (1948) *see* JUDGE STEPS OUT, THE

INDIAN UPRISING (1952) Columbia. **Color-75min.** George Montgomery, Audrey Long.................................(3)

INDICT AND CONVICT (1974) MCA-TV. **Color-100min.** *(Made for TV).* George Grizzard, Reni Santoni, William Shatner, Myrna Loy.................................4*

INDISCREET (1958) Warner Bros. **Color-100min.** *(British).* Cary Grant, Ingrid Bergman.................................5*

INDISCRETION (1945) *see* CHRISTMAS IN CONNECTICUT

INDISCRETION OF AN AMERICAN WIFE (1954) Columbia. **B&W-63min.** Jennifer Jones, Montgomery Clift.................................(4)
British title: INDISCRETION

INFERNO (1953) 20th Century-Fox. **Color-83min.** Robert Ryan, Rhonda Fleming.................................4*

INFIDELITY (1961) *see* FIVE DAY LOVER, THE

INFORMATION RECEIVED (1961) Universal. **B&W-77min.** *(British).* Sabina Sesselmann, William Sylvester ....(3)

INFORMER, THE (1935) RKO. **B&W-91min.** Victor McLaglen, Heather Angel.................................5*

INFORMERS, THE (1963) *see* UNDERWORLD INFORMERS

INFRA-MAN (1976) Joseph Brenner. **Color-92min.** *(Hong Kong).* Li Hsiu-Hsien, Wang Hsieh, Terry Liu, Lin Wen-Wei.................................(2)

INGA (1968) Cinemation. **Color-81min.** *(Swedish).* Marie Lijedahl, Monica Strommerstedt, Thomas Ungewitter.................................(2)
Original Swedish title: JAG - EN OSKULD

INGMAR BERGMAN (1972) Svensk Filminstitutet. **B&W-50min.** *(Swedish, Documentary). Director:* Stig Bjorkman ....(4)

INHERIT THE WIND (1960) United Artists. **B&W-127min.** Spencer Tracy, Fredric March.................................6½*

INHERITANCE, THE (1947) J. Arthur Rank. **B&W-98min.** *(British).* Jean Simmons, Derrick de Marney, Katina Paxinou 4*
Original title: UNCLE SILAS

INHERITANCE, THE (1962) Shochiku. **B&W-107min.** *(Japanese).* Keiko Kishi, Misako Watanabe ....(5)
Original title: KARAMI-AI

INHERITANCE, THE (1976) **Color-102min.** Anthony Quinn, Dominique Sanda *(Italian).* S.J. International Pictures. 4½*

INN OF THE FRIGHTENED PEOPLE (1971) Hemisphere. **Color-89min.** *(British).* Joan Collins, James Booth 3*
Alternate title: TERROR FROM UNDER THE HOUSE

INN OF THE SIXTH HAPPINESS, THE (1958) 20th Century-Fox. **Color-158min.** *(British).* Ingrid Bergman, Curt Jurgens 5*

INN ON DARTMOOR, THE (1964) UCC Films. **B&W-90min.** *(German).* Heinz Drache, Paul Klinger 2*
Original title: WIRTSHAUS VON DARTMOOR, DAS

INN ON THE RIVER, THE (1962) UCC Films. **B&W-95min.** *(German).* Klaus Kinski, Joachim Fuchsberger, Brigitte Grothum ....(3)
Original title: GASTHAUS AN DER THEMSE, DAS *(The Inn on the Thames)*

INNER SANCTUM (1948) Film Classics [U.A.]. **B&W-62min.** Mary Beth Hughes, Lee Patrick ....(3)

INNER SCAR (1972) Philippe Garrel. **Color-58min.** *(French).* Pierre Clementi, Nico ....(3)
Original title: CICATRICE INTERIEURE, LA

INNOCENCE IS BLISS (1949) *see* MISS GRANT TAKES RICHMOND

INNOCENT AFFAIR, AN (1948) *see* DON'T TRUST YOUR HUSBAND

INNOCENT BYSTANDERS (1973) Paramount. **Color-111min.** *(British).* Stanley Baker, Geraldine Chaplin, Donald Pleasence, Dana Andrews ..

INNOCENTS, THE (1961) 20th Century-Fox. **B&W-100min.** *(British-U.S.).* Deborah Kerr, Martin Stephens, Pamela Franklin 6½*

INNOCENTS IN PARIS (1953) Tudor Pictures. **B&W-103min.** *(British).* Alastair Sim, Ronald Shiner 4*

INSERTS (1975) United Artists. **Color-100min.** *(British).* Richard Dreyfuss, Jessica Harper 4½*

INSIDE A GIRLS' DORMITORY (1953) Ellis Films. **B&W-102min.** *(French).* Jean Marais, Francoise Arnoul, Jeanne Moreau ....(3)
Original title: DORTOIR DES GRANDES
Alternate title: GIRLS' DORMITORY

INSIDE DAISY CLOVER (1965) Warner Bros. **Color-128min.** Natalie Wood, Christopher Plummer 3*

INSIDE DETROIT (1956) Columbia. **B&W-82min.** Dennis O'Keefe, Pat O'Brien 3*

INSIDE JOB (1946) Universal. **B&W-65min.** Preston Foster, Ann Rutherford ....(3)

INSIDE MARILYN CHAMBERS (1976) Mitchell Bros. **Color-78min.** *(Documentary). Director:* Jim Mitchell ....(3)

INSIDE NORTH VIET NAM (1967) Impact Films. **Color-85min.** *(Documentary). Director:* Felix Greene ....(5)

INSIDE OUT (1975) Warner Bros. **Color-97min.** *(British).* Telly Savalas, Robert Culp, James Mason.................................(4)

INSIDE STORY, THE (1948) Republic. **B&W-87min.** Marsha Hunt, William Lundigan ....(3)

INSIDE STRAIGHT (1951) M-G-M. **B&W-89min.** David Brian, Arlene Dahl ....(4)

INSIDE THE MAFIA (1959) United Artists. **B&W-72min.** Cameron Mitchell, Elaine Edwards.................................(3)

INSIDE THE WALLS OF FOLSOM PRISON (1951) Warner Bros. **B&W-87min.** Steve Cochran, David Brian ....(3)

INSPECTOR, THE (1962) *see* LISA

INSPECTOR CALLS, AN (1954) Associated Artists. **B&W-79min.** *(British).* Alastair Sim, Jane Wenham 5*

INSPECTOR CALZONZIN (1973) Azteca. **Color-90min.** *(Mexican).* Alfonso Arau, Francisco Cordova ....

INSPECTOR CLOUSEAU (1968) United Artists. **Color-101min.** *(British).* Alan Arkin, Delia Boccardo 3*

INSPECTOR GENERAL, THE (1949) Warner Bros. **Color-102min.** Danny Kaye, Walter Slezak.................................4*

Films are rated on a 1 to 10 scale, 10 is highest. **Boldface** ratings followed by an asterisk (*) are for films actually seen and rated by the executive and senior editors. All other ratings are estimates. (See Notes on Entertainment Ratings in the front section.)

INSPECTOR MAIGRET (1958) Lopert [U.A.]. **B&W-110min.** *(French-Italian)*. Jean Gabin, Annie Girardot........................(4)
Original title: MAIGRET TEND UN PIEGE *(Maigret Sets a Trap)*
Alternate title: WOMAN BAIT

INSPIRATION (1931) M-G-M. **B&W-74min.** Greta Garbo, Lewis Stone, Robert Montgomery..(4)

INTENT TO KILL (1958) 20th Century-Fox. **B&W-89min.** *(British)*. Richard Todd, Herbert Lom.........................**3***

INTERIORS (1978) United Artists. **Color-93min.** Diane Keaton, Maureen Stapleton, Geraldine Page....................**4***

INTERLUDE (1957) Universal. **Color-90min.** June Allyson, Rossano Brazzi..**3½***

INTERLUDE (1968) Columbia. **Color-113min.** *(British)*. Oskar Werner, Barbara Ferris.................................**4½***

INTERMEZZO (1936) Svenskfilmindustri. **B&W-88min.** *(Swedish)*. Gosta Ekman, Inga Tidblad, Ingrid Bergman....................(5)

INTERMEZZO (1939) United Artists. **B&W-66min.** Leslie Howard, Ingrid Bergman.................................**5½***
Publicity title: INTERMEZZO, A LOVE STORY
British title: ESCAPE TO HAPPINESS

INTERNATIONAL COUNTERFEITERS (1957) Republic. **Color-70min.** *(German)*. Gordon Howard, Irina Garden....................(2)

INTERNATIONAL HOUSE (1933) Paramount. **B&W-70min.** Peggy Hopkins Joyce, W. C. Fields.........................**3***

INTERNATIONAL LADY (1941) United Artists. **B&W-102min.** Basil Rathbone, Ilona Massey, George Brent....................(4)

INTERNATIONAL SETTLEMENT (1938) 20th Century-Fox. **B&W-75min.** Dolores Del Rio, George Sanders.................**3***

INTERNATIONAL SQUADRON (1941) Warner Bros. **B&W-87min.** Ronald Reagan, James Stephenson....................(4)

INTERNATIONAL VELVET (1978) U.A. (for M-G-M). **Color-126min.** Tatum O'Neal, Anthony Hopkins, Christopher Plummer...........**5½***

INTERNECINE PROJECT, THE (1974) Allied Artists. **Color-89min.** *(British)*. James Coburn, Lee Grant, Harry Andrews.....................(4)

INTERNES CAN'T TAKE MONEY (1937) Paramount. **B&W-77min.** Joel McCrea, Barbara Stanwyck.........................**3***
British title: YOU CAN'T TAKE MONEY

INTERNS, THE (1962) Columbia. **B&W-120min.** Michael Callan, Cliff Robertson..**5***

INTERPLAY (1970) Times Film Corp. **Color-97min.** Zee Wilson, Ed Moore...(2)
British title: PART-TIME VIRGINS

INTERPOL (1957) *see* PICKUP ALLEY

INTERPOL CODE 8 (1965) Paramount. **Color-94min.** *(Japanese)*. Tatsuya Mihashi, Makoto Sato.........................(1)

INTERRUPTED JOURNEY, THE (1949) Continental [Walter Reade]. **B&W-80min.** *(British)*. Valerie Hobson, Richard Todd....................(4)

INTERMEZZO (1939). Talented pianist Ingrid Bergman greatly admires and finds herself falling in love with married concert violin virtuoso Leslie Howard.

INTERRUPTED MELODY (1955) M-G-M. **Color-106min.** Glenn Ford, Eleanor Parker..**3***

INTERVAL (1973) Avco-Embassy. **Color-84min.** *(U.S.-Mexican)*. Merle Oberon, Robert Wolders.........................(4)

INTIMACY (1966) Goldstone Film Enterprises. **B&W-87min.** Jack Ging, Joan Blackman, Barry Sullivan....................(3)
Alternate title: DECEIVERS, THE

INTIMATE LIGHTING (1966) Promenade. **B&W-71min.** *(Czech)*. Vera Kresadlova, Zdenek Bezusek....................**3***
Original title: INTIMMI OSVETLENI

INTIMATE RELATIONS (1953) *see* DISOBEDIENT

INTIMATE STRANGER, THE (1956) *see* FINGER OF GUILT

INTIMATE STRANGERS (1977) Worldvision. **Color-100min.** *(Made for TV)*. Dennis Weaver, Sally Struthers, Tyne Daly...................
Alternate title: BATTERED

INTOLERANCE (1916) Wark Producing Corp. **B&W-220min.** *(Silent)*. Lillian Gish, Constance Talmadge.........................**4***

INTRIGUE (1947) United Artists. **B&W-90min.** George Raft, June Havoc...**3***

INTRUDER, THE (1953) Associated Artists. **B&W-84min.** *(British)*. Jack Hawkins, Hugh Williams.........................(5)

INTRUDER, THE (1962) Pathé-America. **B&W-80min.** William Shatner, Frank Maxwell...(5)
Alternate title: I HATE YOUR GUTS
Alternate title: SHAME
British title: STRANGER, THE

INTRUDER IN THE DUST (1949) M-G-M. **B&W-89min.** David Brian, Claude Jarman, Jr.........................**4½***

INTRUDERS, THE (1967) Universal. **Color-100min.** *(Made for TV)*. Edmond O'Brien, Don Murray, Anne Francis, John Saxon...............(4)
Alternate title: DEATH DANCE AT MADELIA

INVADERS, THE (1941) *see* FORTY-NINTH PARALLEL, THE

INVADERS FROM MARS (1953) 20th Century-Fox. **Color-78min.** Jimmy Hunt, Helena Carter.........................**3***

INVADERS FROM SPACE (1964) *see* ATOMIC RULERS OF THE WORLD

INVASION (1966) American-International. **B&W-82min.** *(British)*. Edward Judd, Yoko Tani.........................(4)

INVASION EARTH 2150 A.D. (1966) *see* DALEKS - INVASION EARTH 2150 A.D.

INVASION OF ASTRO-MONSTERS (1970) *see* MONSTER ZERO

INVASION OF THE ANIMAL PEOPLE (1960) A. D. P. Productions. **B&W-73min.** *(U.S.-Swedish)*. Barbara Wilson, Stan Gester, John Carradine, Robert Burton.........................(3)
British title: TERROR IN THE MIDNIGHT SUN
Alternate title: SPACE INVASION OF LAPPLAND

INVASION OF THE BEE GIRLS (1973) Centaur. **Color-85min.** William Smith, Anitra Ford, Victoria Vetri...................

INVASION OF THE BLOOD FARMERS (1972) NMD. **Color- min.** Cynthia Fleming, Norman Kelly, Tanna Hunter....................(3)

INVASION OF THE BODY SNATCHERS (1956) Allied Artists. **B&W-80min.** Kevin McCarthy, Dana Wynter.........................**4***

INVASION OF THE BODY SNATCHERS (1978) United Artists. **Color-115min.** Donald Sutherland, Leonard Nimoy, Veronica Cartwright......**5***

INVASION OF THE BODY STEALERS (1969) Allied Artists. **Color-91min.** *(British-U.S.)*. George Sanders, Maurice Evans.........................(3)
Original title: THIN AIR
Alternate title: BODY STEALERS, THE

INVASION OF THE HELL CREATURES (1957) *see* INVASION OF THE SAUCER MEN

INVASION OF THE NEPTUNE MEN (1963) Teleworld. **B&W-82min.** *(Japanese)*. Shinichi Chiba, Kappei Matsumoto....................(1)
Original title: UCHU KAISOKU-SEN *(Invasion from a Planet)*
Publicity title: SPACE GREYHOUND

INVASION OF THE SAUCER MEN (1957) American-International. **B&W-69min.** Steve Terrell, Frank Gorshin, Lyn Osborne....................**2***
British title: INVASION OF THE HELL CREATURES
Publicity title: HELL CREATURES, THE

INVASION OF THE STAR CREATURES (1962) American-International. **B&W-70min.** Robert Ball, Frankie Ray.........................**3***

INVASION OF THE VAMPIRES, THE (1961) Azteca. **B&W-92min.** *(Mexican)*. Carlos Agosti, Rafael Etienne.........................**1***
Original title: INVASION DE LOS VAMPIROS, LA

INVASION QUARTET (1961) M-G-M. **B&W-87min.** *(British)*. Bill Travers, Spike Milligan, Grégoire Aslan.........................**3***

INVASION 1700 (1962) Medallion. **Color-112min.** *(Italian-French-Yugoslavian).* Jeanne Crain, John Drew Barrymore, Akim Tamiroff .. (3)
Original Italian title: COL FERRO E COL FUOCO *(By Steel and By Fire)*
Original French title: PAR LE FER ET PAR LE FEU
TV title: DAGGERS OF BLOOD
TV title: FIRE AND SWORD
TV title: WITH FIRE AND SWORD

INVASION, U.S.A. (1953) Columbia. **B&W-74min.** Dan O'Herlihy, Gerald Mohr, Peggie Castle .... (3)

INVESTIGATION OF A CITIZEN ABOVE SUSPICION (1970) Columbia. **Color-112min.** *(Italian).* Gian Maria Volonte, Florinda Bolkan 7*
Original title: INDAGINE SU UN CITTADINO AL DI SOPRA DI OGNI

INVESTIGATION OF MURDER, AN (1973) *see* LAUGHING POLICEMAN, THE

INVINCIBLE BROTHERS MACISTE, THE (1964) ABC Films. **Color-92min.** *(Italian).* Richard Lloyd, Claudie Lange .... (1)
Original title: INVINCIBILI FRATELLI MACISTE, GLI

INVINCIBLE GLADIATOR, THE (1961) Warner Bros. **Color-92min.** *(Italian-Spanish).* Richard Harrison, Isabelle Corey .... (3)
Original Italian title: GLADIATORE INVINCIBILE, IL
Original Spanish title: GLADIADOR INVENCIBLE, EL

INVINCIBLE SIX, THE (1970) Continental [Walter Reade]. **Color-94min.** *(U.S.-Iran).* Stuart Whitman, Elke Sommer, Curt Jurgens .... (3)

INVINCIBLE SPACEMAN (1964) *see* ATOMIC RULERS OF THE WORLD

INVISIBLE AGENT (1942) Universal. **B&W-81min.** Jon Hall, Ilona Massey .... (3)

INVISIBLE AVENGER (1958) Republic. **B&W-60min.** Richard Derr, Mark Daniels, Helen Westcott .... (4)
Alternate title: BOURBON ST. SHADOWS

INVISIBLE BOY, THE (1957) M-G-M. **B&W-85min.** Richard Eyer, Philip Abbott, Robby The Robot .... (4)

INVISIBLE CREATURE, THE (1960) American-International. **B&W-70min.** *(British).* Sandra Dorne, Tony Wright .... (3)
Original title: HOUSE ON MARSH ROAD, THE

INVISIBLE DR. MABUSE, THE (1962) Telewide Systems. **B&W-89min.** *(German).* Lex Barker, Karin Dor, Wolfgang Preiss .... (3)
Original title: UNSICHTBAREN KRALLEN DES DOKTOR MABUSE, DIE *(The Invisible Claws of Dr. Mabuse)*
Publicity title: INVISIBLE HORROR, THE

INVISIBLE GHOST, THE (1941) Monogram [Allied Artists]. **B&W-64min.** Bela Lugosi, Polly Ann Young .... (3)

INVISIBLE INVADERS (1959) United Artists. **B&W-67min.** John Agar, Robert Hutton, John Carradine .... (2)

INVISIBLE MAN, THE (1933) Universal. **B&W-71min.** Claude Rains, Gloria Stuart 5*

INVISIBLE MAN, THE (1975) MCA-TV. **Color-74min.** *(Made for TV).* David McCallum, Jackie Cooper 4*

INVISIBLE MAN RETURNS, THE (1940) Universal. **B&W-81min.** Vincent Price, Cedric Hardwicke 5*

INVISIBLE MAN'S REVENGE, THE (1944) Universal. **B&W-77min.** Jon Hall, Lester Matthews .... (4)

INVISIBLE MENACE (1938) Warner Bros. **B&W-55min.** Boris Karloff, Marie Wilson .... (4)

INVISIBLE MONSTER, THE (1950) *see* SLAVES OF THE INVISIBLE MONSTER

INVISIBLE RAY, THE (1936) Universal. **B&W-81min.** Boris Karloff, Bela Lugosi .... (4)

INVISIBLE STRIPES (1939) Warner Bros. **B&W-82min.** George Raft, William Holden 4*

INVISIBLE TERROR, THE (1963) UCC Films. **B&W-102min.** *(German).* Hanaes Hauser, Ellen Schwiers .... (3)
Original title: UNSICHTBARE, DER *(The Invisible Man)*

INVISIBLE WOMAN, THE (1941) Universal. **B&W-72min.** John Barrymore, Virginia Bruce 3½*

INVITATION (1952) M-G-M. **B&W-84min.** Van Johnson, Dorothy McGuire 3*

INVITATION, L' (1973) Janus Films. **Color-100min.** *(Swiss).* Michel Robin, Jean-Luc Bideau, Jean Champion 2*

INVITATION TO A GUNFIGHTER (1964) United Artists. **Color-92min.** Yul Brynner, George Segal 3*

INVITATION TO HAPPINESS (1939) Paramount. **B&W-95min.** Irene Dunne, Fred MacMurray .... (4)

INVITATION TO MURDER (1959) Atlantic Pictures. **B&W-55min.** *(British, Telefeature).* Robert Beatty, Lisa Daniely .... (3)

INVITATION TO THE DANCE (1956) M-G-M. **Color-92min.** *(U.S.-British, Part-animated).* Gene Kelly 4½*

IPCRESS FILE, THE (1965) Universal. **Color-107min.** *(British).* Michael Caine, Nigel Green, Guy Doleman 5*

IPHIGENIA (1977) Cinema 5. **Color-129min.** *(Greek).* Costa Kazakos, Tatiana Papamouskou, Irene Papas 4½*

IRENE (1940) RKO. **B&W-104min.** Anna Neagle, Ray Milland .... (5)

IRISH EYES ARE SMILING (1944) 20th Century-Fox. **Color-90min.** Dick Haymes, June Haver .... (4)

IRISH IN US, THE (1935) Warner Bros. **B&W-84min.** James Cagney, Olivia de Havilland, Pat O'Brien .... (3)

IRMA LA DOUCE (1963) United Artists. **Color-142min.** Jack Lemmon, Shirley MacLaine 5*

IRON CURTAIN, THE (1948) 20th Century-Fox. **B&W-87min.** Dana Andrews, Gene Tierney .... (5)
Alternate title: BEHIND THE IRON CURTAIN

IRON DUKE, THE (1934) Gaumont-British [Rank]. **B&W-90min.** *(British).* George Arliss, Ellaline Terriss 4*
Alternate title: WELLINGTON

IRON GLOVE, THE (1954) Columbia. **Color-77min.** Robert Stack, Ursula Thiess 3½*

IRON HORSE, THE (1924) Fox Film Co. [20th]. **B&W-119min.** *(Silent).* George O'Brien, Madge Bellamy .... (5)

IRON MAIDEN, THE (1962) *see* SWINGIN' MAIDEN, THE

IRON MAJOR, THE (1943) RKO. **B&W-85min.** Pat O'Brien, Ruth Warrick .... (4)

IRON MAN (1931) Universal. **B&W-73min.** Lew Ayres, Jean Harlow .... (3)

IRON MAN (1951) Universal. **B&W-82min.** Jeff Chandler, Evelyn Keyes 4*

IRON MASK, THE (1929) United Artists. **B&W-98min.** *(Part-talking).* Douglas Fairbanks, Marguerite De La Motte .... (5)

IRON MISTRESS, THE (1952) Warner Bros. **Color-110min.** Alan Ladd, Virginia Mayo .... (4)

IRON PETTICOAT, THE (1956) M-G-M. **Color-90min.** *(British-U.S.).* Bob Hope, Katharine Hepburn .... (4)

IRON SHERIFF, THE (1957) United Artists. **B&W-73min.** Sterling Hayden, Constance Ford .... (3)

IRONSIDE (1967) Universal. **Color-98min.** *(Made for TV).* Raymond Burr, Geraldine Brooks, Don Galloway 5*

IROQUOIS TRAIL (1950) United Artists. **B&W-85min.** George Montgomery, Dan O'Herlihy .... (4)
British title: TOMAHAWK TRAIL, THE

IRWIN ALLEN'S PRODUCTION OF FIRE! (1977) *see* FIRE!

IS ANNA ANDERSON ANASTASIA? (1956) *see* ANASTASIA, THE CZAR'S LAST DAUGHTER

IS EVERYBODY HAPPY? (1943) Columbia. **B&W-73min.** Ted Lewis, Larry Parks .... (4)

IS PARIS BURNING? (1966) Paramount. **B&W-135min.** *(French-U.S.).* Gert Froebe, Orson Welles 4*
Foreign title: PARIS BRULE-T-IL?
French title: PARIS BRULE-T-IL?

IS THERE SEX AFTER DEATH? (1971) Abel-Child. **Color-97min.** Alan Abel, Buck Henry, Jim Moran .... (4)

IS YOUR HONEYMOON REALLY NECESSARY? (1953) Associated Artists. **B&W-80min.** *(British).* David Tomlinson, Diana Dors, Bonar Colleano .... (3)

ISABEL (1968) Paramount. **Color-108min.** *(Canadian).* Genevieve Bujold, Marc Strange .... (5)

ISADORA (1968) Universal. **Color-131min.** *(British).* Vanessa Redgrave, James Fox 4½*
Publicity title: LOVES OF ISADORA, THE

ISLAND, THE (1961) Zenith International. **B&W-96min.** *(Japanese).* Nobuko Otowa, Taiji Tonoyama .... (5)
Original title: HADAKA NO SHIMA *(Naked Island)*

ISLAND AT THE TOP OF THE WORLD, THE (1974) Buena Vista. **Color-95min.** Donald Sinden, David Hartman 4½*

ISLAND ESCAPE (1962) *see* NO MAN IS AN ISLAND

ISLAND IN THE SKY (1953) Warner Bros. **B&W-109min.** John Wayne, Lloyd Nolan .... (5)

ISLAND IN THE SUN (1957) 20th Century-Fox. **Color-119min.** Harry Belafonte, Joan Fontaine 5*

ISLAND OF DESIRE (1952) United Artists. **Color-103min.** *(British).* Linda Darnell, Tab Hunter, Donald Gray .... (4)
Original title: SATURDAY ISLAND

ISLAND OF DR. MOREAU, THE (1977) American-International. **Color-98min.** Burt Lancaster, Michael York 5½*

ISLAND OF DOOMED MEN (1940) Columbia. **B&W-67min.** Rochelle Hudson, Peter Lorre .... (3)

ISLAND OF LIVING HORROR (1968) see BRIDES OF BLOOD

ISLAND OF LOST MEN (1939) Paramount. **B&W-63min.** Anna May Wong, J. Carroll Naish, Anthony Quinn .... (3)

ISLAND OF LOST SOULS (1933) Paramount. **B&W-70min.** Charles Laughton, Richard Arlen 4*

ISLAND OF LOST WOMEN (1959) Warner Bros. **B&W-71min.** Jeff Richards, Venetia Stevenson .... (2)

ISLAND OF LOVE (1963) Warner Bros. **Color-101min.** Robert Preston, Tony Randall 4*

ISLAND OF MONTE CRISTO (1953) see SWORD OF VENUS

ISLAND OF SHAME (1961) see YOUNG ONE, THE

ISLAND OF TERROR (1966) Universal. **Color-87min.** (British). Edward Judd, Peter Cushing .... (4)

ISLAND OF THE BLUE DOLPHINS (1964) Universal. **Color-93min.** Celia Kaye, Larry Domasin 4*

ISLAND OF THE BURNING DAMNED (1972) Maron Films, Ltd. **Color-94min.** (British). Christopher Lee, Peter Cushing, Patrick Allen 3*
Original title: NIGHT OF THE BIG HEAT
TV title: ISLAND OF THE BURNING DOOMED

ISLAND OF THE DAMNED (1976) American-International. **Color-100min.** (Spanish). Lewis Fiander, Prunella Ransome ....
Original title: QUIEN PUEDE MATAR A UN NINO? (Who Can Kill a Child?)

ISLAND PRINCESS, THE (1955) Trans-America. **Color-98min.** (Italian). Silvana Pampanini, Marcello Mastroianni .... (3)
Original title: PRINCESSA PESSA DEL A CANARIA
Alternate title: ISOLA

ISLAND RESCUE (1951) Universal. **B&W-87min.** (British). David Niven, Glynis Johns .... (4)
Original title: APPOINTMENT WITH VENUS

ISLANDS IN THE STREAM (1977) Paramount. **Color-105min.** George C. Scott, David Hemmings 4*

ISLAND OF LOST SOULS (1933). The more Charles Laughton shows him of the mysterious island, the more confused and amazed uninvited visitor Richard Arlen becomes.

ISLE OF FURY (1936) Warner Bros. **B&W-60min.** Margaret Lindsay, Humphrey Bogart .... (3)

ISLE OF LEVANT (1957) Films Around The World. **Color-71min.** (Swiss-Danish, Travelog). Producer: Werner Kunz .... (3)

ISLE OF SIN (1960) Manson. **B&W-63min.** (German). Christiane Nielsen, Erwin Strahl .... (3)
Original title: FLITTERWOCHEN IN DER HOLLE

ISLE OF THE DEAD (1945) RKO. **B&W-72min.** Boris Karloff, Ellen Drew 4*

ISLE OF THE SNAKE PEOPLE (1968) see SNAKE PEOPLE, THE

ISN'T IT ROMANTIC? (1948) Paramount. **B&W-87min.** Veronica Lake, Mona Freeman .... (3)

ISN'T IT SHOCKING? (1973) Worldvision. **Color-73min.** (Made for TV). Edmond O'Brien, Will Geer, Alan Alda 5*

ISN'T LIFE WONDERFUL (1924) United Artists. **B&W-105min.** Carol Dempster, Neil Hamilton 4*

ISRAEL WHY (1973) **B&W-185min.** (French, Documentary). Director: Claude Lanzmann .... (4)

ISTANBUL (1957) Universal. **Color-84min.** Errol Flynn, Cornell Borchers 3½*

ISTANBUL EXPRESS (1968) Universal. **Color-100min.** (Made for TV). Gene Barry, John Saxon, Senta Berger 4*

IT! (1967) Warner Bros. **Color-95min.** (British). Roddy McDowall, Jill Haworth 3*

IT AIN'T EASY (1972) Dandelion Prods. **Color-90min.** Lance Henriksen, Barra Grant .... (3)

IT AIN'T HAY (1943) Universal. **B&W-80min.** Bud Abbott, Lou Costello, Eugene Pallette 4*
British title: MONEY FOR JAM

IT ALL CAME TRUE (1940) Warner Bros. **B&W-97min.** Ann Sheridan, Humphrey Bogart .... (4)

IT ALWAYS RAINS ON SUNDAY (1947) Eagle Lion. **B&W-92min.** (British). Googie Withers, Jack Warner .... (4)

IT CAME FROM BENEATH THE SEA (1955) Columbia. **B&W-80min.** Kenneth Tobey, Faith Domergue 3*

IT CAME FROM OUTER SPACE (1953) Universal. **B&W-81min.** Richard Carlson, Barbara Rush 4*

IT COMES UP MURDER (1967) see HONEY POT, THE

IT CONQUERED THE WORLD (1956) American-International. **B&W-68min.** Peter Graves, Beverly Garland .... (3)

IT FELL FROM THE FLAME BARRIER (1958) see FLAME BARRIER, THE

IT GROWS ON TREES (1952) Universal. **B&W-84min.** Irene Dunne, Dean Jagger .... (4)

IT HAD TO BE YOU (1947) Columbia. **B&W-98min.** Ginger Rogers, Cornel Wilde .... (4)

IT HAD TO HAPPEN (1936) 20th Century-Fox. **B&W-79min.** George Raft, Rosalind Russell .... (4)

IT HAPPENED AT THE WORLD'S FAIR (1963) M-G-M. **Color-105min.** Elvis Presley, Joan O'Brien .... (4)

IT HAPPENED HERE (1966) Lopert [U.A.]. **B&W-95min.** (British). Pauline Murray, Sebastian Shaw .... (5)

IT HAPPENED IN ATHENS (1962) 20th Century-Fox. **Color-105min.** Jayne Mansfield, Trax Colton, Bob Mathias ..... (2)

IT HAPPENED IN BROAD DAYLIGHT (1958) Continental [Walter Reade]. **B&W-97min.** (Swiss-German). Heinz Ruhmann, Michel Simon .... (5)
Original title: ES GESCHAH AM HELLICHTEN TAG

IT HAPPENED IN BROOKLYN (1947) M-G-M. **B&W-105min.** Frank Sinatra, Jimmy Durante, Kathryn Grayson .... (3)

IT HAPPENED IN FLATBUSH (1942) 20th Century-Fox. **B&W-80min.** Lloyd Nolan, Carole Landis .... (4)

IT HAPPENED IN PARIS (1952) Films de France. **B&W-78min.** (French). Evelyn Keyes, Henri Vidal .... (3)
Original title: C'EST ARRIVE A PARIS

IT HAPPENED IN ROME (1957) J. Arthur Rank. **Color-105min.** (Italian). June Laverick, Ingeborg Schoener ..... (3)
Original title: SOUVENIR d'ITALIE (Souvenir of Italy)

IT HAPPENED IN THE PARK (1954) Ellis Films. **B&W-81min.** (Italian-French). Anna Maria Ferrero, Vittorio De Sica, Gerard Philipe, Micheline Presle .... (5)
Original Italian title: VILLA BORGHESE
French title: AMANTS DE VILLA BORGHESE, LES (The Lovers of the Villa Borghese)

IT HAPPENED ON FIFTH AVENUE (1947) Allied Artists. **B&W-115min.** Charles Ruggles, Gale Storm .... (4)

IT HAPPENED ONE CHRISTMAS (1977) ABC-TV. **Color-110min.** *(Made for TV).* Marlo Thomas, Orson Welles 5*

IT HAPPENED ONE NIGHT (1934) Columbia. **B&W-105min.** Claudette Colbert, Clark Gable 6*

IT HAPPENED ONE SUMMER (1945) *see* STATE FAIR

IT HAPPENED TO JANE (1959) Columbia. **Color-98min.** Doris Day, Jack Lemmon 5*
Alternate title: THAT JANE FROM MAINE
Alternate title: TWINKLE AND SHINE

IT HAPPENED TOMORROW (1944) United Artists. **B&W-84min.** Dick Powell, Linda Darnell.. (5)

IT HAPPENS EVERY SPRING (1949) 20th Century-Fox. **B&W-80min.** Ray Milland, Jean Peters .... (5)

IT HAPPENS EVERY THURSDAY (1953) Universal. **B&W-80min.** John Forsythe, Loretta Young... (5)

IT HAPPENS IN ROMA (1956) **B&W-92min.** *(Italian).* Vittorio de Sica, Linda Darnell, Rossano Brazzi .... (5)

IT LIVES AGAIN (1978) Warner Bros. **Color-91min.** Frederic Forrest, Kathleen Lloyd, John P. Ryan .... (4)
Alternate title: IT'S ALIVE 2

IT LIVES BY NIGHT (1974) *see* BAT PEOPLE, THE

IT MEANS THAT TO ME (1961) ABC Films. **B&W-88min.** *(French).* Eddie Constantine, Bernadette Lafont............................... (3)
Original title: ME FAIRE CA A MOI!

IT ONLY HAPPENS TO OTHERS (1971) GSF Productions. **Color-88min.** *(French-Italian).* Marcello Mastroianni, Catherine Deneuve............... (4)
Original French title: CA N'ARRIVE QU'AUX AUTRES

IT SHOULD HAPPEN TO YOU (1954) Columbia. **B&W-81min.** Judy Holliday, Jack Lemmon, Peter Lawford........................... 4*

IT SHOULDN'T HAPPEN TO A DOG (1946) 20th Century-Fox. **B&W-70min.** Carole Landis, Allyn Joslyn .... (4)

IT SHOULDN'T HAPPEN TO A VET (1976) EMI. **Color-94min.** *(British).* John Alderton, Colin Blakely, Lisa Harrow .... (4)

IT STARTED IN NAPLES (1960) Paramount. **Color-100min.** Clark Gable, Sophia Loren 4*

IT STARTED IN PARADISE (1953) Astor. **Color-88min.** *(British).* Martita Hunt, Jane Hylton .... (5)

IT STARTED IN TOKYO (1961) *see* TWENTY PLUS TWO

IT STARTED WITH A KISS (1959) M-G-M. **Color-104min.** Glenn Ford, Debbie Reynolds 4*

IT STARTED WITH EVE (1941) Universal. **B&W-90min.** Charles Laughton, Deanna Durbin, Robert Cummings .... (5)

IT TAKES A THIEF (1960) Valiant. **B&W-89min.** *(British).* Jayne Mansfield, Anthony Quayle .... (3)
Original title: CHALLENGE, THE

IT TAKES ALL KINDS (1969) Goldsworthy. **Color-97min.** *(Australian-U.S.).* Robert Lansing, Vera Miles, Barry Sullivan 3*

IT! THE TERROR FROM BEYOND SPACE (1958) United Artists. **B&W-69min.** Marshall Thompson, Shawn Smith .... (3)

IT WON'T RUB OFF, BABY! (1967) *see* SWEET LOVE, BITTER

ITALIAN CONNECTION, THE (1973) American-International. **Color-87min.** *(U.S.-Italian-W. German).* Henry Silva, Woody Strode, Mario Adorf, Adolfo Celi .... (3)
Original Italian title: MALA ORDINA, LA *(The Underworld Orders)*

ITALIAN JOB, THE (1969) Paramount. **Color-101min.** *(British).* Michael Caine, Noel Coward 5½*

ITALIAN STRAW HAT, THE (1927) Albatross. **B&W-76min.** *(French, Silent).* Alice Tissot, Albert Prejean............................. 3*
Original title: CHAPEAU DE PAILLE D'ITALIE, UN

ITALIANO BRAVA GENTE (1963) Avco-Embassy. **B&W-156min.** *(Italian-U.S.S.R.).* Arthur Kennedy, Peter Falk, Tatyana Samoylova, Raffaele Pisu .... (5)
Alternate title: ATTACK AND RETREAT
Original Italian title: ITALIANI BRAVA GENTE *(Italians, Good People)*
Original Soviet title: ONI SHLI NA VOSTOK

ITALY 1943 (1960) *see* CONSPIRACY OF HEARTS

IT'S A BIG COUNTRY (1952) M-G-M. **B&W-89min.** Ethel Barrymore, Gary Cooper, Gene Kelly, Fredric March................... (5)

IT'S A BIKINI WORLD (1967) Trans-America. **Color-86min.** Deborah Walley, Tommy Kirk .... (3)

IT'S A DOG'S LIFE (1955) M-G-M. **Color-88min.** Jeff Richards, Jarma Lewis .... (5)
Alternate title: BAR SINISTER, THE

IT'S A GIFT (1934) Paramount. **B&W-73min.** W. C. Fields, Jean Rouveral 4*

IT'S A GREAT FEELING (1949) Warner Bros. **Color-85min.** Jack Carson, Doris Day... 4*

IT'S A GREAT LIFE (1943) Columbia. **B&W-75min.** Arthur Lake, Penny Singleton, Hugh Herbert .... (4)

IT'S A GREAT LIFE (1962) *see* PHONY AMERICAN, THE

IT'S A JOKE, SON (1947) Eagle Lion. **B&W-63min.** Kenny Delmar, Una Merkel .... (3)

IT'S A MAD, MAD, MAD, MAD WORLD (1963) United Artists. **Color-162min.** Spencer Tracy, Milton Berle............................. 5*

IT'S A PLEASURE (1945) RKO. **Color-90min.** Sonja Henie, Michael O'Shea, Marie McDonald .... (3)

IT'S A WONDERFUL LIFE (1946) RKO. **B&W-129min.** James Stewart, Donna Reed... 5*

IT'S A WONDERFUL WORLD (1939) M-G-M. **B&W-86min.** James Stewart, Claudette Colbert 4*

"IT'S ALIVE!" (1968) American-International. **Color-80min.** *(Made for TV).* Tommy Kirk, Shirley Bonne, Billy Thurman............... 1*

IT'S ALIVE (1974) Warner Bros. **Color-90min.** John Ryan, Sharon Farrell 3*

IT'S ALIVE 2 (1978) *see* IT LIVES AGAIN

IT'S ALL HAPPENING (1963) *see* DREAM MAKER, THE

IT'S ALWAYS FAIR WEATHER (1955) M-G-M. **Color-102min.** Gene Kelly, Dan Dailey... 4*

IT'S GOOD TO BE ALIVE (1974) MPC (TV). **Color-100min.** *(Made for TV).* Paul Winfield, Ruby Dee, Lou Gossett 4½*

IT'S GREAT TO BE YOUNG (1946) Columbia. **B&W-68min.** Robert Stanton, Leslie Brooks .... (2)

IT'S GREAT TO BE YOUNG (1956) Fine Arts. **Color-92min.** *(British).* John Mills, Cecil Parker.. (5)

IT'S HOT IN PARADISE (1960) Pacemaker Pictures. **B&W-86min.** *(German).* Alex D'Arcy, Barbara Valentin .... (2)
Alternate title: HORRORS OF SPIDER ISLAND
Original title: TOTER HING IM NETZ, EIN *(Dead Body in the Web)*
Alternate title: SPIDER'S WEB, THE
Alternate title: GIRLS OF SPIDER ISLAND

IT'S IN THE AIR (1935) M-G-M. **B&W-80min.** Jack Benny, Una Merkel .... (4)

IT'S IN THE BAG (1945) United Artists. **B&W-87min.** Fred Allen, Binnie Barnes.. 4*
British title: FIFTH CHAIR, THE

IT'S LOVE AGAIN (1936) Gaumont-British [Rank]. **B&W-83min.** *(British).* Jessie Matthews, Robert Young......................... 5*

IT'S LOVE I'M AFTER (1937) First National [W.B.]. **B&W-90min.** Leslie Howard, Bette Davis.. 6½*

IT'S MAGIC (1948) *see* ROMANCE ON THE HIGH SEAS

IT'S NEVER TOO LATE (1956) Seven Arts [W.B.]. **Color-96min.** *(British).* Phyllis Calvert, Guy Rolfe............................... (4)

IT'S NOT CRICKET (1949) J. Arthur Rank. **B&W-78min.** *(British).* Maurice Denham, Basil Radford, Naunton Wayne .... (3)

IT'S NOT THE SIZE THAT COUNTS! (1974) Joseph Brenner. **Color-90min.** *(British).* Leigh Lawson, Elke Sommer, Vincent Price ....
Original title: PERCY'S PROGRESS

IT'S ONLY MONEY (1962) Paramount. **B&W-84min.** Jerry Lewis, Zachary Scott 3½*

IT'S SHOWTIME (1976) United Artists. **B&W-86min.** *(Documentary).* Producer: Fred Weintraub... (5)

IT'S THE OLD ARMY GAME (1926) Paramount. **B&W-70min.** *(Silent).* W. C. Fields, Louise Brooks... (4)

IT'S TOUGH TO BE FAMOUS (1932) First National [W.B.]. **B&W-79min.** Douglas Fairbanks, Jr., Mary Brian .... (5)

IT'S TRAD, DAD (1962) *see* RING-A-DING RHYTHM

IT'S YOUR MOVE (1968) American-International. **Color-93min.** *(Italian).* Edward G. Robinson, Adolfo Celi, Terry-Thomas .... (3)
Original Italian title: SCACCO TUTTO MATTO, UNO
Spanish title: ATRACO DE IDA Y VUELTA, UN *(Return Attack)*
Publicity title: MAD CHECKMATE

IT'S YOUR THING (1970) Medford Films. **Color-120min.** *(Music Film).* Director: Mike Gargiulo .... (4)

IVALLO THE GREAT (1963) Four Star. **Color-89min.** *(Bulgarian).* Bogomil Simenov, Lona Davidova................................ (3)

IT'S LOVE I'M AFTER (1937). Having agreed to teach her a lesson, stage star Leslie Howard pretends to respond romantically to Olivia de Havilland, who's smitten with him.

IVAN (1954) Distributors Corp. of America. **B&W-75min.** *(Foreign?).* Paul Campbell, Nadia Gray .... (3)
Alternate title: IVAN, SON OF THE WHITE DEVIL

IVAN THE TERRIBLE, PART I (1943) Artkino. **B&W-95min.** *(U.S.S.R.).* Nikolai Cherkasov, Ludmila Tselikovskaya 3*
Original title: IVAN GROZNY

IVAN THE TERRIBLE, PART II (1958) Artkino. **B&W-87min.** *(U.S.S.R.).* Nikolai Cherkassov, Serafima Birman .... (4)
Original title: IVAN GROZNY
Alternate title: REVOLT OF THE BOYARS, THE

IVANHOE (1952) M-G-M. **Color-106min.** Robert Taylor, Elizabeth Taylor.. 6*

IVAN'S CHILDHOOD (1962) *see* MY NAME IS IVAN

I'VE ALWAYS LOVED YOU (1946) Republic. **Color-117min.** Philip Dorn, Catherine McLeod 4*
British title: CONCERTO

I'VE LIVED BEFORE (1956) Universal. **B&W-82min.** Jock Mahoney, Leigh Snowden .... (4)

IVORY COAST ADVENTURE (1965) *see* MAN FROM COCODY

IVORY HUNTER (1951) Universal. **Color-97min.** *(British).* Anthony Steel, Dinah Sheridan .... (5)
Original title: WHERE NO VULTURES FLY

IVY (1947) Universal. **B&W-99min.** Joan Fontaine, Patric Knowles 4*

IVY LEAGUE KILLERS (1962) Paramount. **B&W-70min.** *(Canadian).* Don Borisenko, Barbara Bricker.. (3)

-J-

J.D.'s REVENGE (1976) American-International. **Color-95min.** Glynn Turman, Lou Gossett.. 4*

J.R. (1969) *see* WHO'S THAT KNOCKING AT MY DOOR

J.W. COOP (1972) Columbia. **Color-112min.** Cliff Robertson, Geraldine Page.. 4*
Screen title: JW COOP

JA, JA, MEIN GENERAL! BUT WHICH WAY TO THE FRONT? (1971) *see* WHICH WAY TO THE FRONT?

JABBERWALK (1977) I.T.M. **Color-98min.** *(Documentary). Director:* Romano Vanderbes .... (4)
Original title: THIS IS AMERICA
British title: CRAZY RIDICULOUS AMERICAN PEOPLE

JABBERWOCKY (1977) Cinema 5. **Color-100min.** *(British).* Michael Palin, Max Wall 5*

JACK AND THE BEANSTALK (1952) Warner Bros. **B&W-87min.** Bud Abbott, Lou Costello 3*

JACK FROST (1965) Avco-Embassy. **Color-79min.** *(U.S.S.R.).* Aleksandr Khvylya, Natasha Sedykh 3*
Original title: MOROZHKO *(Grandfather Frost)*

JACK JOHNSON (1971) Brandon. **B&W-90min.** *(Documentary). Director:* William Cayton .... (5)

JACK LONDON (1943) United Artists. **B&W-94min.** Michael O'Shea, Susan Hayward.. 4*
Alternate title: ADVENTURES OF JACK LONDON

JACK McCALL, DESPERADO (1953) Columbia. **Color-76min.** George Montgomery, Angela Stevens....................................... (3)

JACK OF DIAMONDS (1967) M-G-M. **Color-108min.** *(U.S.-W. German).* George Hamilton, Joseph Cotten, Marie Laforet.................... (3)

JACK SLADE (1953) Allied Artists. **B&W-90min.** Mark Stevens, Dorothy Malone .... (3)
British title: SLADE

JACK THE GIANT KILLER (1962) United Artists. **Color-94min.** Kerwin Mathews, Judi Meredith 5*

JACK THE RIPPER (1959) Paramount. **B&W-88min.** *(British).* Lee Patterson, Eddie Byrne 3*

JACKASS MAIL (1942) M-G-M. **B&W-80min.** Wallace Beery, Marjorie Main.. 3*

JACKIE ROBINSON STORY, THE (1950) Eagle Lion. **B&W-76min.** Jackie Robinson, Ruby Dee 4*

JACKPOT, THE (1950) 20th Century-Fox. **B&W-85min.** James Stewart, Barbara Hale.. 4*

JACKPOT (1960) Grand National *(Brit.).* **B&W-71min.** *(British).* William Hartnell, Betty McDowell .... (3)

JACKSON COUNTY JAIL (1976) New World. **Color-89min.** Yvette Mimieux, Tommy Lee Jones, Severn Darden 4*

JACQUELINE (1956) J. Arthur Rank. **Color-92min.** *(British).* Kathleen Ryan, John Gregson .... (4)

JACQUELINE SUSANN'S ONCE IS NOT ENOUGH (1975) Paramount. **Color-121min.** Kirk Douglas, Alexis Smith 5*
Alternate title: ONCE IS NOT ENOUGH

JACQUES BREL IS ALIVE AND WELL AND LIVING IN PARIS (1975) American Film Theatre. **Color-145min.** *(French-Canadian, English language).* Elly Stone, Mort Shuman, Joe Masiell 3*

JACOB THE LIAR (1975) Macmillan Films. **Color-95min.** *(East German).* Vlastimil Brodsky, Erwin Geschonneck, Manuela Simon............. (4)
Original title: JAKOB DER LUEGNER

JADE MASK, THE (1945) Monogram [Allied Artists]. **B&W-66min.** Sidney Toler, Mantan Moreland, Janet Warren .... (4)
Alternate title: CHARLIE CHAN IN THE JADE MASK

JAGUAR (1956) Republic. **B&W-66min.** Michael Connors, Barton MacLane, Sabu .... (4)

JAIL BAIT (1972) New Yorker Films. **Color-99min.** *(German).* Eva Mattes, Harry Baer .... (4)
Original title: WILDWECHSEL *(Game Pass)*
British title: WILD GAME
Alternate British title: GAME PASS

JAIL BUSTERS (1955) Allied Artists. **B&W-61min.** The Bowery Boys, Barton MacLane .... (3)

JAIL HOUSE BLUES (1941) Universal. **B&W-62min.** Robert Paige, Anne Gwynne .... (4)

JAILBREAK (1962) Butcher's *(Brit.).* **B&W-61min.** *(British).* Peter Reynolds, Avice Landone... (3)
Original title: GAOLBREAK

JAILBREAKERS, THE (1960) American-International. **B&W-64min.** Robert Hutton, Mary Castle .... (2)

JAILHOUSE ROCK (1957) M-G-M. **B&W-96min.** Elvis Presley, Judy Tyler 4*

JALOPY (1953) Allied Artists. **B&W-62min.** The Bowery Boys, Bob (Robert) Lowery .... (3)

JAM SESSION (1944) Columbia. **B&W-77min.** Ann Miller, Jess Barker, Louis Armstrong .... (3)

JAMAICA INN (1939) Paramount. **B&W-98min.** *(British).* Charles Laughton, Robert Newton 5*

JAMAICA RUN (1953) Paramount. **Color-92min.** Ray Milland, Arlene Dahl .... (3)

JAMBOREE (1957) Warner Bros. **B&W-86min.** Kay Medford, Fats Domino, Jerry Lee Lewis, Frankie Avalon .... (3)
British title: DISC JOCKEY JAMBOREE

JAMES AT 15 (1977) NBC-TV. **Color-100min.** *(Made for TV).* Lance Kerwin, Melissa Sue Martin, Kate Jackson .... (4)

JAMES BROTHERS, THE (1957) *see* TRUE STORY OF JESSE JAMES, THE

JAMES DEAN: PORTRAIT OF A FRIEND (1976) Viacom. **Color-100min.** *(Made for TV).* Stephen McHattie, Michael Brandon, Candy Clark 5*

JAMES DEAN STORY, THE (1957) Warner Bros. **B&W-82min.** *(Documentary). Director:* George W. George 4*

JAMES DEAN, THE FIRST AMERICAN TEENAGER (1975) Ziv International. **Color-80min.** *(British, Documentary). Director:* Ray Connolly .... (5)
Alternate title: FIRST AMERICAN TEENAGER, THE

JAMES JOYCE'S ULYSSES (1967) *see* ULYSSES

JAMILYA (1970) Artkino. **Color-78min.** *(U.S.S.R.).* Natalya Arinbasarova, Suimenkul Chkmorov, Nasredin Dubashev .... (5)

JAN HUS (1955) Contemporary. **Color-120min.** *(Czech).* Zdenek Stepanek, Karel Hoger .... (4)

JANE EYRE (1934) Monogram [Allied Artists]. **B&W-70min.** Virginia Bruce, Colin Clive .... (4)

JANE EYRE (1944) 20th Century-Fox. **B&W-96min.** Orson Welles, Joan Fontaine 5*

JANE EYRE (1971) British Lion [EMI]. **Color-100min.** *(British, Made for TV).* Susannah York, George C. Scott 5½*

JANICE MEREDITH (1924) Metro-Goldwyn. **B&W-118min.** *(Silent).* Marion Davies, Holbrook Binn .... (4)

JANIE (1944) Warner Bros. **B&W-106min.** Joyce Reynolds, Robert Hutton, Edward Arnold .... (4)

JANIE GETS MARRIED (1946) Warner Bros. **B&W-89min.** Joan Leslie, Robert Hutton, Edward Arnold .... (4)

JANIS (1974) Universal. **B&W-96min.** *(Music Film). Director:* Howard Alk .... (4)

JAPANESE WAR BRIDE (1952) 20th Century-Fox. **B&W-91min.** Don Taylor, Shirley Yamaguchi .... (4)

JASON AND THE ARGONAUTS (1963) Columbia. **Color-104min.** *(British).* Todd Armstrong, Nancy Kovack 4*

JASON AND THE GOLDEN FLEECE (1960) *see* GIANTS OF THESSALY, THE

JASSY (1944) Universal. **Color-96min.** *(British).* Margaret Lockwood, Basil Sydney 4*

JAVA HEAD (1934) First Division. **B&W-70min.** *(British).* Anna May Wong, Edmund Gwenn .... (3)

JAWS (1975) Universal. **Color-124min.** Roy Scheider, Robert Shaw, Richard Dreyfuss 8*

JAWS 2 (1978) Universal. **Color-117min.** Roy Scheider, Lorraine Gary ..5*

JAWS OF DEATH, THE (1976) Cannon Releasing. **Color-93min.** Richard Jaeckel, Jennifer Bishop 2*

JAYHAWKERS, THE (1959) Paramount. **Color-100min.** Jeff Chandler, Fess Parker 4*

JAZZ BALL (1956) Hal Roach. **B&W-60min.** Betty Hutton, Peggy Lee... (3)

JAZZ BOAT (1960) Columbia. **B&W-96min.** *(British).* Anthony Newley, Anne Aubrey .... (4)

JAZZ ON A SUMMER'S DAY (1960) Galaxy Attractions. **Color-85min.** *(Music Film). Director:* Bert Stern 3*

JAZZ SINGER, THE (1927) Warner Bros. **B&W-88min.** *(Part-talking).* Al Jolson, May McAvoy 3*

JAZZ SINGER, THE (1953) Warner Bros. **Color-107min.** Danny Thomas, Peggy Lee 4*

JE T'AIME, JE T'AIME (1968) New Yorker Films. **Color-94min.** *(French-Spanish).* Claude Rich, Olga Georges-Picot 1½*
Translation title: I Love You, I Love You

JEALOUSY (1934) Columbia. **B&W-60min.** Nancy Carroll, Donald Cook...

JEALOUSY (1945) Republic. **B&W-71min.** John Loder, Nils Asther, Jane Randolph .... (4)

JEALOUSY (1950) *see* EMERGENCY WEDDING

JEANNE EAGELS (1957) Columbia. **B&W-109min.** Kim Novak, Jeff Chandler 4*

JEANNIE (1941) English Films. **B&W-85min.** *(British).* Michael Redgrave, Barbara Mullen .... (4)

JENNIE (1948) *see* PORTRAIT OF JENNIE

JENNIE GERHARDT (1933) Paramount. **B&W-85min.** Sylvia Sidney, Mary Astor, Donald Cook .... (5)

JENNIFER (1953) Allied Artists. **B&W-73min.** Howard Duff, Ida Lupino .... (3)

JENNIFER (1978) Cinegate *(British).* **Color-90min.** Lisa Pelikan, Bert Convy, Nina Foch .... (3)

JENNIFER ON MY MIND (1971) United Artists. **Color-90min.** Tippy Walker, Michael Brandon .... (2)

JENNY (1970) Cinerama Releasing. **Color-88min.** Marlo Thomas, Alan Alda 4*

JENNY LIND (1930) *see* LADY'S MORALS, A

JEOPARDY (1953) M-G-M. **B&W-69min.** Barbara Stanwyck, Barry Sullivan .... (4)

JEREMIAH JOHNSON (1972) Warner Bros. **Color-107min.** Robert Redford, Will Geer 5½*

JEREMY (1973) United Artists. **Color-90min.** Robby Benson, Glynnis O'Connor 5*

JERK, THE (1979) Universal. **Color-   min.** Steve Martin, Bernadette Peters ....

JERRICO THE WONDER CLOWN (1955) *see* THREE RING CIRCUS

JERUSALEM FILE, THE (1972) M-G-M. **Color-96min.** *(U.S.-Israeli).* Bruce Davison, Daria Halprin, Nicol Williamson, Donald Pleasence 3*

JESSE JAMES (1939) 20th Century-Fox. **Color-105min.** Tyrone Power, Henry Fonda 4*

JESSE JAMES MEETS FRANKENSTEIN'S DAUGHTER (1966) Avco-Embassy. **Color-82min.** John Lupton, Narda Onyx, Cal Bolder .... (2)

JESSE JAMES VS. THE DALTONS (1954) Columbia. **Color-65min.** Brett King, Barbara Lawrence .... (3)

JESSE JAMES' WOMEN (1954) United Artists. **Color-83min.** Don "Red" Barry, Jack Beutel, Peggie Castle .... (3)

JESSICA (1962) United Artists. **Color-112min.** *(U.S.-Italian-French, English language).* Angie Dickinson, Maurice Chevalier 3½*
French title: SAGE FEMME, LE CURÉ ET LE BON DIEU, LA

JESUS CHRIST SUPERSTAR (1973) Universal. **Color-107min.** Ted Neeley, Carl Anderson 5½*

JESUS OF NAZARETH (1977) Independent TV Corp (ITC). **Color-300min.** *(Italian, Made for TV, English language).* 5*

JESUS TRIP, THE (1971) Emco Films. **Color-84min.** Tippy Walker, Robert Porter .... (3)
Alternate title: RAVAGED

JET ATTACK (1958) American-International. **B&W-68min.** John Agar, Audrey Totter .... (3)
British title: THROUGH HELL TO GLORY

JET JOB (1952) Monogram [Allied Artists]. **B&W-63min.** Stanley Clements, Elena Verdugo .... (2)

JET MEN OF THE AIR (1951) *see* AIR CADET

JET OVER THE ATLANTIC (1959) Intercontinental. **B&W-95min.** Virginia Mayo, Guy Madison, George Raft .... (3)

JET PILOT (1957) Universal. **Color-112min.** John Wayne, Janet Leigh (4)

JET STORM (1959) United Producers Org. **B&W-88min.** *(British).* Richard Attenborough, Stanley Baker, Sybil Thorndike, George Rose .... (5)

JETÉE, LA (1962) Arcturus Films. **B&W-29min.** *(French).* Hélene Chatelain, Jacques Ledoux .... (4)
Translation title: The Runway

JEW SUSS (1934) Gaumont-British [Rank]. **B&W-108min.** *(British).* Conrad Veidt, Frank Vosper ....
Alternate title: POWER

JEWEL ROBERY (1932) Warner Bros. **B&W-70min.** William Powell, Kay Francis .... (4)

JEZEBEL (1938) Warner Bros. **B&W-104min.** Bette Davis, Henry Fonda 5*

JIGSAW (1949) United Artists. **B&W-70min.** Franchot Tone, Jean Wallace .... (4)
Alternate title: GUN MOLL

JIGSAW (1962) Beverly. **B&W-107min.** *(British).* Jack Warner, Ronald Lewis .... (3)

JIGSAW (1968) Universal. **Color-97min.** Bradford Dillman, Harry Guardino, Pat Hingle 4*

Films are rated on a 1 to 10 scale, 10 is highest. **Boldface** ratings followed by an asterisk (*) are for films actually seen and rated by the executive and senior editors. All other ratings are estimates. (See Notes on Entertainment Ratings in the front section.)

JEZEBEL (1938). Wearing a scarlet dress to the lavish ball, where all unmarried women traditionally wear white, has proven to be more disrupting than Bette Davis had imagined; her escort Henry Fonda is embarrassed but prepared to defend her. Orchestra leader is Jac George.

JIM THE WORLD'S GREATEST (1976) Universal. Color-91min. Gregory Harrison, Robbie Wolcott 3*
Original title: STORY OF A TEENAGER

JIM THORPE - ALL AMERICAN (1951) Warner Bros. B&W-107min. Burt Lancaster, Charles Bickford 4*
British title: MAN OF BRONZE

JIMI HENDRIX (1973) Warner Bros. Color-102min. *(Music Film).* Producer: Joe Boyd .... (4)

JIMMY AND SALLY (1933) Fox Film Co. [20th]. B&W-68min. James Dunn, Claire Trevor .... (4)

JIMMY THE GENT (1934) Warner Bros. B&W-67min. James Cagney, Bette Davis .... (4)

JINX MONEY (1948) Monogram [Allied Artists]. B&W-68min. The Bowery Boys, Sheldon Leonard .... (3)

JITTERBUGS (1943) 20th Century-Fox. B&W-74min. Stanley Laurel, Oliver Hardy, Vivian Blaine 4*

JIVARO (1954) Paramount. Color-91min. Fernando Lamas, Rhonda Fleming .... (4)
British title: LOST TREASURE OF THE AMAZON

JOAN (1970) *see* CARRY IT ON

JOAN MEDFORD IS MISSING (1946) *see* HOUSE OF HORRORS

JOAN OF ARC (1948) RKO. Color-145min. Ingrid Bergman, José Ferrer 4*

JOAN OF OZARK (1942) Republic. B&W-80min. Judy Canova, Joe E. Brown .... (3)
British title: QUEEN OF SPIES

JOAN OF PARIS (1942) RKO. B&W-95min. Michele Morgan, Paul Henreid 4*

JOAN OF THE ANGELS? (1961) Telepix Corp. B&W-101min. *(Polish).* Lucyna Winnicka, Mieczyslaw Voit 2*
Original title: MATKA JOANNA OD ANIOLOW *(Mother Joan of the Angels)*

JOANNA (1968) 20th Century-Fox. Color-107min. *(British).* Genevieve Waite, Calvin Lockhart, Donald Sutherland ...... (4)

JOAQUIN MURIETTA (1965) *see* MURIETA

"JOCK" PETERSEN (1974) Avco-Embassy. Color-103min. *(Australian).* Jack Thompson, Jacki Weaver ....
Original title: PETERSEN

JOE (1970) Cannon Releasing. Color-107min. Peter Boyle, Dennis Patrick 7*

JOE AND ETHEL TURP CALL ON THE PRESIDENT (1939) M-G-M. B&W-70min. William Gargan, Ann Sothern .... (4)

JOE BUTTERFLY (1957) Universal. Color-90min. Burgess Meredith, Audie Murphy 4*

JOE COCKER/MAD DOGS AND ENGLISHMEN (1971) *see* MAD DOGS AND ENGLISHMEN

JOE DAKOTA (1957) Universal. Color-79min. Jock Mahoney, Luana Patten 4½*

JOE HILL (1971) Paramount. Color-113min. *(Swedish-U.S., English language).* Thommy Berggren, Anja Schmidt 4½*
Alternate title: BALLAD OF JOE HILL, THE

JOE KIDD (1972) Universal. Color-88min. Clint Eastwood, Robert Duvall 4*

JOE LOUIS STORY, THE (1953) United Artists. B&W-88min. Coley Wallace, Paul Stewart .... (4)

JOE MACBETH (1955) Columbia. B&W-90min. *(British-U.S.).* Paul Douglas, Ruth Roman .... (4)

JOE PALOOKA (1934) *see* PALOOKA

JOE PALOOKA IN FIGHTING MAD (1948) *see* FIGHTING MAD

JOE PALOOKA IN TRIPLE CROSS (1951) Monogram [Allied Artists]. B&W-60min. Joe Kirkwood, Jr., James Gleason, Cathy Downs .... (2)
British title: TRIPLE CROSS, THE

JOE PANTHER (1976) Artists Creation & Associates. Color-110min. Ray Tracey, Brian Keith, A Martinez, Ricardo Montalban .... (3)

JOE SMITH, AMERICAN (1942) M-G-M. B&W-63min. Robert Young, Marsha Hunt .... (4)
British title: HIGHWAY TO FREEDOM

JOFROI (1950) *see* WAYS OF LOVE

JOHN AND JULIE (1955) Distributors Corp. of America. Color-82min. *(British).* Colin Gibson, Lesley Dudley, Wilfrid Hyde-White, Moira Lister .... (4)

JOHN AND MARY (1969) 20th Century-Fox. Color-92min. Dustin Hoffman, Mia Farrow 5*

JOHN DOE, DYNAMITE (1941) *see* MEET JOHN DOE

JOHN F. KENNEDY: YEARS OF LIGHTNING, DAY OF DRUMS (1966) Avco-Embassy. Color-87min. *(Documentary). Director:* Bruce Herschenson 5½*

JOHN GOLDFARB, PLEASE COME HOME! (1965) 20th Century-Fox. Color-96min. Shirley MacLaine, Peter Ustinov, Richard Crenna 2½*

JOHN LOVES MARY (1949) Warner Bros. B&W-96min. Ronald Reagan, Jack Carson, Patricia Neal 4*

JOHN MEADE'S WOMAN (1937) Paramount. B&W-87min. Edward Arnold, Francine Larrimore, Gail Patrick .... (3)

JOHN PAUL JONES (1959) Warner Bros. Color-126min. Robert Stack, Marisa Pavan 4*

JOHNNY ALLEGRO (1949) Columbia. B&W-81min. George Raft, Nina Foch .... (4)
British title: HOUNDED

JOHNNY ANGEL (1945) RKO. B&W-79min. George Raft, Claire Trevor 4*

JOHNNY APOLLO (1940) 20th Century-Fox. B&W-93min. Tyrone Power, Dorothy Lamour 4*

JOHNNY BANCO (1967) Ben Barry and Associates. Color-90min. *(French-Italian-W. German).* Horst Buchholz, Sylva Koscina ...... (4)
Original German title: JONNY BANCO - GELIEBTER TAUGENICHTS

JOHNNY BELINDA (1948) Warner Bros. B&W-102min. Jane Wyman, Lew Ayres 6*

JOHNNY CASH! THE MAN, HIS WORLD, HIS MUSIC (1969) Continental [Walter Reade]. Color-94min. *(Documentary). Director:* Robert Elfstrom .... (5)
Alternate title: JOHNNY CASH!

JOHNNY COME LATELY (1943) United Artists. B&W-97min. James Cagney, Grace George .... (4)
British title: JOHNNY VAGABOND

JOHNNY CONCHO (1956) United Artists. B&W-84min. Frank Sinatra, Keenan Wynn 4½*

JOHNNY COOL (1963) United Artists. B&W-101min. Henry Silva, Elizabeth Montgomery 3*

JOHNNY DARK (1954) Universal. Color-85min. Tony Curtis, Piper Laurie .... (4)

JOHNNY DOESN'T LIVE HERE ANY MORE (1944) Monogram [Allied Artists]. B&W-79min. Simone Simon, James Ellison .... (4)
Alternate title: AND SO THEY WERE MARRIED

JOHNNY DOUGHBOY (1942) Republic. B&W-63min. Jane Withers, Henry Wilcoxon .... (3)

JOHNNY EAGER (1941) M-G-M. B&W-107min. Robert Taylor, Lana Turner 4*

JOHNNY FIRECLOUD (1975) Entertainment Ventures. Color-90min. Victor Mohica, Ralph Meeker, David Canary ....

JOHNNY GOT HIS GUN (1971) Cinemation. Color-112min. Timothy Bottoms, Jason Robards (Jr.), Donald Sutherland 4½*

Films are rated on a 1 to 10 scale, 10 is highest. **Boldface** ratings followed by an asterisk (*) are for films actually seen and rated by the executive and senior editors. All other ratings are estimates. (See Notes on Entertainment Ratings in the front section.)

JOHNNY GUITAR (1954) Republic. **Color-110min.** Joan Crawford, Sterling Hayden...5½*

JOHNNY GUNMAN (1957) Tudor Pictures. **B&W-70min.** Martin Brooks, Ann Donaldson.................................(2)

JOHNNY HAMLET (1972) Transvue Pictures. **Color-91min.** *(Italian)*. Chip Corman (Andrea Giordana), Gilbert Roland.................(3)
Original title: QUELLA SPORCA STORIA DEL WEST *(That Dirty Story of the West)*

JOHNNY HOLIDAY (1950) United Artists. **B&W-92min.** William Bendix, Allen Martin, Jr.................................4*

JOHNNY IN THE CLOUDS (1945) *see* WAY TO THE STARS

JOHNNY MINOTAUR (1971) Impact Films. **Color-80min.** Nikos Koulizakis, Yiannis Koutsis.................(2)

JOHNNY NOBODY (1961) Medallion. **B&W-88min.** *(British)*. Nigel Patrick, Yvonne Mitchell, Aldo Ray, William Bendix.................(4)

JOHNNY O'CLOCK (1947) Columbia. **B&W-95min.** Dick Powell, Lee J. Cobb.................................4*

JOHNNY ONE-EYE (1950) United Artists. **B&W-78min.** Pat O'Brien, Wayne Morris.................................(3)

JOHNNY RENO (1966) Paramount. **Color-83min.** Dana Andrews, Jane Russell, Lyle Bettger.................(3)

JOHNNY ROCCO (1958) Allied Artists. **B&W-84min.** Stephen McNally, Richard Eyer.................................(3)

JOHNNY SOKKO AND HIS GIANT ROBOT (1968) *see* VOYAGE INTO SPACE

JOHNNY STOOL PIGEON (1949) Universal. **B&W-76min.** Howard Duff, Shelley Winters, Dan Duryea.................4*

JOHNNY TIGER (1966) Universal. **Color-102min.** Robert Taylor, Geraldine Brooks, Chad Everett.................3*

JOHNNY TREMAIN (1957) Buena Vista. **Color-80min.** Hal Stalmaster, Luana Patten.................................(5)

JOHNNY TROUBLE (1957) Warner Bros. **B&W-80min.** Ethel Barrymore, Cecil Kellaway, Stuart Whitman.................3*

JOHNNY VAGABOND (1943) *see* JOHNNY COME LATELY

JOHNNY, WE HARDLY KNEW YE (1977) NBC-TV. **Color-100min.** *(Made for TV)*. Paul Rudd, William Prince, Burgess Meredith.................

JOHNNY, YOU'RE WANTED (1956) Eros Films *(Brit.)*. **B&W-72min.** *(British)*. John Slater, Alfred Marks.................(3)

JOHNNY YUMA (1966) Atlantic Pictures. **Color-99min.** *(Italian)*. Mark Damon, Lawrence Dobkin, Rosalba Neri.................(2)

JOKER, THE (1961) Lopert [U.A.]. **B&W-86min.** *(French)*. Anouk Aimée, Jean-Pierre Cassel.................(4)
Original title: FARCEUR, LE

JOKER IS WILD, THE (1957) Paramount. **B&W-126min.** Frank Sinatra, Mitzi Gaynor.................................5½*
Alternate title: ALL THE WAY

JOKERS, THE (1967) Universal. **Color-94min.** *(British)*. Michael Crawford, Oliver Reed.................6*

JOLLY BAD FELLOW, A (1964) *see* THEY ALL DIED LAUGHING

JOLSON SINGS AGAIN (1949) Columbia. **Color-96min.** Larry Parks, Barbara Hale.................................4*

JOLSON STORY, THE (1946) Columbia. **Color-128min.** Larry Parks, Evelyn Keyes.................................5½*

JONAH WHO WILL BE 25 IN THE YEAR 2000 (1976) New Yorker Films. **Color-110min.** *(Swiss)*. Jean-Luc Bideau, Myrian Meziere.........(4)
Original title: JONAS -- QUI AURA 25 ANS EN L'AN 2000

JONATHAN (1970) New Yorker Films. **Color-103min.** *(German)*. Jurgen Jung, Ilse Kunkele, Paul Albert Krumm.................(4)

JONATHAN LIVINGSTON SEAGULL (1973) Paramount. **Color-114min.** James Franciscus, Juliet Mills.................(4)

JONES FAMILY IN HOLLYWOOD (1939) 20th Century-Fox. **B&W-60min.** Jed Prouty, Spring Byington.................(3)
Alternate title: IN HOLLYWOOD

JORY (1973) Avco-Embassy. **Color-97min.** Robby Benson, John Marley.(3)

JOSEPH AND HIS BRETHREN (1960) *see* STORY OF JOSEPH AND HIS BRETHREN, THE

JOSEPH ANDREWS (1977) Paramount. **Color-103min.** *(British)*. Peter Firth, Ann-Margret.................................4½*

JOSEPH KILIAN (1966) Contemporary. **B&W-40min.** *(Czech)*. Karei Vasicek, Consuela Moravkova.................(5)

JOSEPHINE AND MEN (1955) Continental [Walter Reade]. **Color-97min.** *(British)*. Glynis Johns, Donald Sinden, Peter Finch.................(3)

JOSETTE (1938) 20th Century-Fox. **B&W-73min.** Simone Simon, Don Ameche, Bert Lahr.................................(4)

JOSHUA (1976) Po'boy. **Color-80min.** Fred Williamson, Isela Vega........(3)

JOUR DE FETE (1949) Mayer-Kingsley. **B&W-75min.** *(French)*. Jacques Tati, Paul Frankeur.................................3*
Alternate title: BIG DAY, THE

JOUR SE LEVE, LE (1938) *see* DAYBREAK

JOURNEY, THE (1959) M-G-M. **Color-125min.** Deborah Kerr, Yul Brynner.................................4*

JOURNEY, THE (1963) *see* LASSIE'S GREAT ADVENTURE

JOURNEY BACK TO OZ (1973) EBA Film Distributors. **Color-86min.** *(Cartoon)*. Director: Hal Sutherland.................(4)

JOURNEY BENEATH THE DESERT (1961) Avco-Embassy. **Color-105min.** *(Italian-French)*. Haya Harareet, Jean-Louis Trintignant.................(3)
Original Italian title: ANTINEA, L'AMANTE DELLA CITTA SEPOLTA
Original French title: ATLANTIDE, L'

JOURNEY FOR MARGARET (1942) M-G-M. **B&W-81min.** Robert Young, Laraine Day, Margaret O'Brien.................4*

JOURNEY FROM DARKNESS (1975) CPT (TV). **Color-74min.** *(Made for TV)*. Mark Singer, Kay Lenz, Wendell Burton.................4*

JOURNEY INTO FEAR (1942) RKO. **B&W-69min.** Joseph Cotten, Dolores del Rio.................................4*

JOURNEY INTO FEAR (1975) Stirling Gold. **Color-97min.** *(Canadian-U.S.)*. Sam Waterston, Vincent Price, Yvette Mimieux, Donald Pleasence.................................3*

JOURNEY INTO LIGHT (1951) 20th Century-Fox. **B&W-87min.** Sterling Hayden, Viveca Lindfors.................4*

JOURNEY INTO AUTUMN (1955) *see* DREAMS

JOURNEY INTO MIDNIGHT (1968) 20th Century-Fox. **Color-100min.** *(Telefeature)*. Chad Everett, Julie Harris, Edward Fox.................3*

JOURNEY INTO NOWHERE (1963) President Films. **B&W-67min.** *(British)*. Sonja Ziemann, Tony Wright, Helmut Schmid.................4½*
Alternate title: MURDER BY AGREEMENT

JOURNEY OF ROBERT F. KENNEDY, THE (1970) Wolper Productions. **Color-75min.** *(Documentary, Made for TV)*. Director: Mel Stuart..........(5)
Alternate title: UNFINISHED JOURNEY OF ROBERT F. KENNEDY, THE

JOURNEY THROUGH ROSEBUD (1972) GSF. **Color-93min.** Robert Forster, Kristoffer Tabori.................(4)

JOURNEY TO FREEDOM (1957) Republic. **B&W-60min.** Jacques Scott, Genevieve Aumont.................................(2)

JOURNEY TO ITALY (1954) *see* STRANGERS

JOURNEY TO JERUSALEM, A (1968) Sigma III. **Color-84min.** *(Documentary)*. Director: Michael Mindlin, Jr.................(5)

JOURNEY TO SHILOH (1968) Universal. **Color-101min.** James Caan, Michael Sarrazin.................................(3)

JOURNEY TO THE CENTER OF THE EARTH (1959) 20th Century-Fox. **Color-132min.** James Mason, Pat Boone.................5½*

JOURNEY TO THE CENTER OF TIME (1967) American General. **Color-82min.** Scott Brady, Anthony Eisley, Gigi Perreau.................(4)

JOURNEY TO THE FAR SIDE OF THE SUN (1969) Universal. **Color-99min.** *(British)*. Ian Hendry, Roy Thinnes.................4*
Original title: DOPPELGANGER

JOURNEY TO THE LOST CITY (1958) American-International. **Color-94min.** *(W. German-French-Italian)*. Debra Paget, Paul Christian (Hubschmid).................................(3)
British title: TIGER OF BENGAL

JOURNEY TO THE SEVENTH PLANET (1961) American-International. **Color-80min.** *(U.S.-Danish)*. John Agar, Greta Thyssen.................2*

JOURNEY TO THE UNKNOWN (1969) 20th Century-Fox. **Color-106min.** *(U.S.-British, Telefeature)*. Vera Miles, Patty Duke.................3*

JOURNEY TOGETHER (1945) English Films. **B&W-95min.** *(British)*. Richard Attenborough, Edward G. Robinson.................(3)

JOURNEY'S END (1930) Tiffany Productions. **B&W-130min.** Colin Clive, Ian MacLaren.................................(4)

JOY HOUSE (1964) M-G-M. **B&W-95min.** *(French, English language)*. Jane Fonda, Alain Delon, Lola Albright.................(4)
Original title: FELINS, LES *(The Felines)*
Alternate title: LOVE CAGE

JOY IN THE MORNING (1965) M-G-M. **Color-103min.** Richard Chamberlain, Yvette Mimieux.................4½*

JOY OF LIVING (1938) RKO. **B&W-90min.** Irene Dunne, Douglas Fairbanks, Jr.................................(5)

JOY PARADE, THE (1937) *see* LIFE BEGINS IN COLLEGE

JOY RIDE (1958) Allied Artists. **B&W-60min.** Rad Fulton, Ann Doran..(3)

JOYLESS STREET, THE (1925) *see* STREET OF SORROW

Films are rated on a 1 to 10 scale, 10 is highest. **Boldface** ratings followed by an asterisk (*) are for films actually seen and rated by the executive and senior editors. All other ratings are estimates. (See Notes on Entertainment Ratings in the front section.)

JOYRIDE (1977) American-International. **Color-92min.** Desi Arnaz, Jr., Robert Carradine 5*

JUANA GALLO (1958) see GUNS OF JUANA GALLO, THE

JUAREZ (1939) Warner Bros. **B&W-132min.** Paul Muni, Bette Davis...... 6*

JUBAL (1956) Columbia. **Color-101min.** Glenn Ford, Ernest Borgnine ... 5*

JUBILEE (1978) **Color-103min.** (British). Jenny Runacre, Jordan, Little Nell 5*

JUBILEE TRAIL (1954) Republic. **B&W-103min.** Vera Ralston, Pat O'Brien 3½*

JUDGE, THE (1949) East Coast. **B&W-69min.** Milburn Stone, Katherine DeMille .... (3)
British title: GAMBLERS, THE

JUDGE AND JAKE WYLER, THE (1972) MCA-TV. **Color-100min.** (Made for TV). Bette Davis, Doug McClure 4*

JUDGE DEE IN THE MONASTERY MURDERS (1974) ABC Circle Films. **Color-100min.** (Made for TV). Khigh Dhiegh, Mako, Soon-Taik Oh, Miiko Taka.. 3*
Original title: JUDGE DEE

JUDGE HARDY AND SON (1939) M-G-M. **B&W-87min.** Lewis Stone, Mickey Rooney .... (3)

JUDGE HARDY'S CHILDREN (1938) M-G-M. **B&W-78min.** Lewis Stone, Mickey Rooney .... (4)

JUDGE HORTON AND THE SCOTTSBORO BOYS (1976) Tomorrow Entertainment. **Color-100min.** (Made for TV). Arthur Hill, Vera Miles, Lewis J. Stadlen 5*

JUDGE PRIEST (1934) Fox Film Co. [20th]. **B&W-79min.** Will Rogers, Tom Brown, Anita Louise... 5*

JUDGE STEPS OUT, THE (1948) RKO. **B&W-91min.** Alexander Knox, Ann Sothern 4*
British title: INDIAN SUMMER

JUDGMENT AT NUREMBERG (1961) United Artists. **B&W-189min.** Spencer Tracy, Burt Lancaster 6½*

JUDITH (1966) Paramount. **Color-109min.** (U.S.-British-Israeli). Sophia Loren, Peter Finch 4½*

JUDITH AND HOLOPHERNES (1959) see HEAD OF A TYRANT

JUDITH OF BETHULIA (1913) American Biograph. **B&W-4reels** (Silent). Blanche Sweet, Henry B. Walthall .... (4)

JUGGERNAUT (1974) United Artists. **Color-109min.** Richard Harris, Omar Sharif 5½*
Publicity title: TERROR ON THE BRITTANIC

JUGGLER, THE (1953) Columbia. **B&W-86min.** Kirk Douglas, Milly Vitale 4*

JUKE BOX RHYTHM (1959) Columbia. **B&W-81min.** Jo Morrow, Brian Donlevy .... (2)

JUKE GIRL (1942) Warner Bros. **B&W-90min.** Ronald Reagan, Ann Sheridan... (4)

JULES AND JIM (1962) Janus Films. **B&W-105min.** (French). Oskar Werner, Jeanne Moreau, Henri Serre..................................... 5*
Original title: JULES ET JIM

JULES VERNE'S ROCKET TO THE MOON (1967) see THOSE FANTASTIC FLYING FOOLS

JULIA (1976) Cine-Media International. **Color-83min.** (German). Sylvia Kristel, Jean-Claude Bouillon .... (3)
Original title: LIEBERSCHULER, DER

JULIA (1977) 20th Century-Fox. **Color-116min.** Jane Fonda, Vanessa Redgrave, Jason Robards (Jr.) 4*

JULIA MISBEHAVES (1948) M-G-M. **B&W-99min.** Greer Garson, Walter Pidgeon 4*

JULIE (1956) M-G-M. **B&W-99min.** Doris Day, Louis Jourdan 3*

JULIE THE REDHEAD (1959) Shawn International. **B&W-100min.** (French). Daniel Gélin, Pascale Petit .... (4)
Original title: JULIE LA ROUSSE

JULIET OF THE SPIRITS (1965) Rizzoli Film. **Color-148min.** (Italian-French-W. German). Giulietta Masina, Sandra Milo, Mario Pisu 1½*
Original Italian title: GIULIETTA DEGLI SPIRITI
Original French title: JULIETTE DES ESPRITS
Original German title: JULIA UND DIE GEISTER

JULIETTA (1953) Kingsley International. **B&W-96min.** (French). Dany Robin, Jean Marais, Jeanne Moreau .... (4)

JULIETTE DE SADE (1970) Haven International. **Color-83min.** (Italian?). Maria Pia Conte, Lea Nanni .... (1)

JULIUS CAESAR (1953) M-G-M. **B&W-120min.** Marlon Brando, James Mason 4½*

JULIUS CAESAR (1970) American-International. **Color-117min.** (British). Charlton Heston, Jason Robards (Jr.), John Gielgud 4*

JULIUS CAESAR, CONQUEROR OF GAUL (1962) see CAESAR THE CONQUEROR

JUMBO (1962) see BILLY ROSE'S JUMBO

JUMP INTO HELL (1955) Warner Bros. **B&W-93min.** Jacques Sernas, Kurt Kasznar .... (3)

JUMPING JACKS (1952) Paramount. **B&W-96min.** Dean Martin, Jerry Lewis, Mona Freeman 4*

JUNE BRIDE (1948) Warner Bros. **B&W-97min.** Bette Davis, Robert Montgomery 5½*

JUNGLE, THE (1952) Lippert Productions. **B&W-74min.** Rod Cameron, Marie Windsor, Cesar Romero...................................... (2)

JUNGLE BOOK, THE (1942) United Artists. **Color-109min.** Sabu, Joseph Calleia 4½*

JUNGLE BOOK, THE (1967) Buena Vista. **Color-78min.** (Cartoon). Director: Wolfgang Reitherman 4½*

JUNGLE CAPTIVE (1945) Universal. **B&W-63min.** Otto Kruger, Rondo Hatton, Vicky Lane 3*
Alternate title: WILD JUNGLE CAPTIVE

JUNGLE CAT (1960) Buena Vista. **Color-70min.** (Documentary). Director: James Algar... (5)

JUNGLE DRUMS OF AFRICA, THE (1953) see U-238 AND THE WITCH DOCTOR

JUNGLE FIGHTERS (1961) Continental [Walter Reade]. **B&W-105min.** (British). Richard Todd, Laurence Harvey.......................... 3*
Original title: LONG AND THE SHORT AND THE TALL, THE

JUNGLE GENTS (1954) Allied Artists. **B&W-64min.** The Bowery Boys, Patrick O'Moore .... (3)

JUNGLE GIRL (1952) see BOMBA AND THE JUNGLE GIRL

JUNGLE GIRL AND THE SLAVER (1959) Medallion. **Color-70min.** (German). Marion Michael, Adrian Hoven................................ (2)

JUNGLE GODDESS (1948) Screen Guild [Lippert]. **B&W-65min.** George Reeves, Wanda McKay... (3)

JUNGLE GOLD (1944) Republic. **B&W-100min.** (Re-edited Serial). Allan "Rocky" Lane, Linda Sterling.................................. (4)
Original title: TIGER WOMAN, THE
Alternate title: PERILS OF THE DARKEST JUNGLE

JUNGLE HEADHUNTERS (1951) RKO. **Color-66min.** (Travelog). Producer: Julian Lesser.. (4)

JUNGLE HELL (1956) Medallion. **B&W-78min.** Sabu, K. T. Stevens, David Bruce... (2)

JUNGLE JIM (1948) Columbia. **B&W-73min.** Johnny Weissmuller, Virginia Grey .... (3)

JUNGLE JIM IN THE FORBIDDEN LAND (1952) Columbia. **B&W-65min.** Johnny Weissmuller, Angela Greene........................ (3)
Publicity title: FORBIDDEN LAND, THE

Paul Muni is **JUAREZ** (1939), the Mexican leader who headed the struggle to free his country from foreign domination in the 1860s.

Films are rated on a 1 to 10 scale, 10 is highest. **Boldface** ratings followed by an asterisk (*) are for films actually seen and rated by the executive and senior editors. All other ratings are estimates. (See Notes on Entertainment Ratings in the front section.)

JUNGLE MAN-EATERS (1954) Columbia. **B&W-68min.** Johnny Weissmuller, Karin Booth .... (3)

JUNGLE MANHUNT (1951) Columbia. **B&W-66min.** Johnny Weissmuller, Bob Waterfield .... (3)

JUNGLE MOON MEN (1955) Columbia. **B&W-70min.** Johnny Weissmuller, Jean Byron .... (3)

JUNGLE PATROL (1948) 20th Century-Fox. **B&W-70min.** Kristine Miller, Arthur Franz .... (4)

JUNGLE PRINCESS, THE (1936) Paramount. **B&W-85min.** Dorothy Lamour, Ray Milland .... (4)

JUNGLE RAMPAGE (1963) see RAMPAGE

JUNGLE STAMPEDE (1950) Republic. **B&W-60min.** (Travelog). Director: George Breakston .... (3)

JUNGLE WOMAN (1944) Universal. **B&W-54min.** Evelyn Ankers, J. Carroll Naish, Acquanetta .... (3)

JUNGLE WOMAN, THE (1944) see NABONGA

JUNIOR ARMY (1942) Columbia. **B&W-71min.** Freddie Bartholomew, Billy Halop .... (3)

JUNIOR BONNER (1972) Cinerama Releasing. **Color-100min.** Steve McQueen, Robert Preston **4***

JUNIOR MISS (1945) 20th Century-Fox. **B&W-94min.** Peggy Ann Garner, Allyn Joslyn .... (4)

JUPITER'S DARLING (1955) M-G-M. **Color-96min.** Esther Williams, Howard Keel .... (4)

JUST A GIGOLO (1979) **Color-105min.** (German). David Bowie, Sydne Rome, Kim Novak, Marlene Dietrich ....

JUST ACROSS THE STREET (1952) Universal. **B&W-78min.** Ann Sheridan, John Lund .... (4)

JUST AROUND THE CORNER (1938) 20th Century-Fox. **B&W-70min.** Shirley Temple, Joan Davis, Charles Farrell .... (3)

JUST BEFORE DAWN (1946) Columbia. **B&W-65min.** Warner Baxter, Adelle Roberts .... (4)

JUST BEFORE NIGHTFALL (1971) Libra. **Color-100min.** (French). Stephane Audran, Michel Bouquet ....
Original title: JUSTE AVANT LA NUIT

JUST CRAZY ABOUT HORSES (1978) Fred Baker Films. **Color-105min.** (Documentary). Director: Tim Lovejoy ....

JUST FOR FUN (1963) Columbia. **B&W-72min.** Mark Wynter, Cherry Roland .... (3)

JUST FOR YOU (1952) Paramount. **Color-104min.** Bing Crosby, Jane Wyman .... (5)

JUST IMAGINE (1930) Fox Film Co. [20th]. **B&W-102min.** Maureen O'Sullivan, John Garrick, El Brendel .... (3)

JUST OFF BROADWAY (1942) 20th Century-Fox. **B&W-66min.** Lloyd Nolan, Marjorie Weaver .... (3)

JUST TELL ME WHAT YOU WANT (1979) Warner Bros. **Color-   min.** Ali MacGraw, Alan King ....

JUST THIS ONCE (1952) M-G-M. **B&W-90min.** Peter Lawford, Janet Leigh .... (4)

JUST TO BE LOVED (1968) see NEW LIFE STYLE, THE

JUST YOU AND ME, KID (1979) Columbia. **Color-93 min.** George Burns, Brooke Shields ....

JUSTICE IS DONE (1950) Joseph Burstyn. **B&W-105min.** (French). Claude Nollier, Balpetre .... (5)
Subtitled: The Secret Lives and Loves of a French Jury
Original title: JUSTICE EST FAITE
British title: LET JUSTICE BE DONE

JUSTINE (1969) 20th Century-Fox. **Color-115min.** Anouk Aimee, Dirk Bogarde .... (4)

JUVENILE JUNGLE (1958) Republic. **B&W-69min.** Corey Allen, Rebecca Welles .... (3)

JW COOP (1972) see J.W. COOP

-K-

KAIDAN (1964) see KWAIDAN

KALEIDOSCOPE (1966) Warner Bros. **Color-103min.** (British). Warren Beatty, Susannah York 5½*

KAMERADSHAFT (1931) Associated Cinema. **B&W-75min.** (German). Ernst Busch, Elisabeth Wendt, Alexander Granach 3*
Translation title: Comradeship

KANAL (1956) Kingsley International. **B&W-96min.** (Polish). Teresa Izewska, Tadeusz Janczar 4*
Translation title: Sewer
Alternate title: THEY LOVED LIFE

KANGAROO (1952) 20th Century-Fox. **Color-84min.** Peter Lawford, Maureen O'Hara, Richard Boone 4*

KANSAN, THE (1943) United Artists. **B&W-79min.** Richard Dix, Victor Jory .... (4)

KANSAS CITY BOMBER (1972) M-G-M. **Color-99min.** Raquel Welch, Kevin McCarthy 4*

KANSAS CITY CONFIDENTIAL (1953) United Artists. **B&W-98min.** Preston Foster, John Payne .... (4)
British title: SECRET FOUR, THE

KANSAS CITY KITTY (1944) Columbia. **B&W-63min.** Joan Davis, Jane Frazee .... (4)

KANSAS PACIFIC (1953) Allied Artists. **Color-73min.** Sterling Hayden, Eve Miller .... (4)

KANSAS RAIDERS, THE (1950) Universal. **Color-80min.** Audie Murphy, Brian Donlevy .... (4)

KANSAS TERRITORY (1952) Monogram [Allied Artists]. **B&W-73min.** Wild Bill Elliott, Peggy Stewart .... (4)

KARAMOJA (1954) Hallmark Productions. **Color-60min.** (Travelog). Director: Dr. and Mrs. William B. Treutle .... (4)

KARATE (1961) Joseph Brenner. **B&W-80min.** Joel Holt, Frank Blaine, Akira Shiga .... (2)

KARATE KILLER, THE (1974) Howard Mahler. **Color-   min.** (Foreign). 1*

KASEKI (1975) New Yorker Films. **Color-210min.** (Japanese). Shin Saburi, Keiko Kishi ....
Translation title: Fossilized

KASPAR HAUSER (1974) see MYSTERY OF KASPAR HAUSER, THE

KATERINA IZMAILOVA (1967) Artkino. **Color-118min.** (U.S.S.R.). Galina Vishnevskaya, Artyom Inozemtsev, Nikolai Boyarski .... (4)

KATHERINE (1975) Viacom. **Color-98min.** (Made for TV). Sissy Spacek, Henry Winkler, Art Carney 5*

KATHLEEN (1941) M-G-M. **B&W-88min.** Shirley Temple, Herbert Marshall .... (3)

KATHY O' (1958) Universal. **Color-99min.** Patty McCormack, Dan Duryea 3*

KATIE DID IT (1951) Universal. **B&W-81min.** Ann Blyth, Mark Stevens .... (4)

KATIE: PORTRAIT OF A CENTERFOLD (1978) NBC-TV. **Color-98min.** (Made for TV). Kim Basinger, Melanie Mayron 5*

KATINA (1942) see ICELAND

KAZABLAN (1973) M-G-M. **Color-114min.** (Israeli, English language). Yohoram Gaon, Efrat Lavie 4*

KAZAN (1949) Columbia. **B&W-65min.** Stephen (Steve) Dunne, Lois Maxwell, Zoro .... (3)

KEEP 'EM FLYING (1941) Universal. **B&W-86min.** Bud Abbott, Lou Costello, Martha Raye 4*

KEEP 'EM SLUGGING (1943) Universal. **B&W-60min.** The Little Tough Guys, Frank Albertson ....

KEEP IT CLEAN (1955) UCC Films. **B&W-74min.** (British). Ronald Shiner, Diane Hart .... (3)

KEEP IT COOL (1958) see LET'S ROCK

KEEP OFF MY GRASS (1972) Capitol Productions. **Color-90min.** Gary Wood, Mickey Dolenz .... (3)

KEEP ON ROCKIN' (1972) see SWEET TORONTO

KEEP TALKING, BABY (1961) Paramount. **B&W-95min.** (French). Eddie Constantine, Mariella Lozzi .... (2)

KEEP YOUR POWDER DRY (1945) M-G-M. **B&W-93min.** Lana Turner, Laraine Day .... (3)

KEEPER OF THE BEES (1947) Columbia. **B&W-68min.** Michael Duane, Gloria Henry .... (3)

KEEPER OF THE FLAME (1942) M-G-M. **B&W-100min.** Spencer Tracy, Katharine Hepburn 4*

KEEPING COMPANY (1940) M-G-M. **B&W-80min.** Frank Morgan, Ann Rutherford .... (4)

KEETJE TIPPEL (1975) Cinema National. **Color-104min.** (Netherlands). Monique van de Ven, Andrea Domburg, Rutger Hauer 5*
Publicity title: CATHY TIPPEL

KELLY AND ME (1957) Universal. **Color-86min.** Van Johnson, Piper Laurie 3½*

KELLY'S HEROES (1970) M-G-M. **Color-145min.** (U.S.-Yugoslavian). Clint Eastwood, Telly Savalas 5*

KENNEL MURDER CASE (1933) Warner Bros. **B&W-73min.** William Powell, Mary Astor 4½*

Films are rated on a 1 to 10 scale, 10 is highest. **Boldface** ratings followed by an asterisk (*) are for films actually seen and rated by the executive and senior editors. All other ratings are estimates. (See Notes on Entertainment Ratings in the front section.)

KENNER (1969) M-G-M. Color-92min. Jim Brown, Madlyn Rhue...........(3)

KENNY & CO. (1976) 20th Century-Fox. Color-90min. Dan McCann, Mike Baldwin....................(4)

KENTUCKIAN, THE (1955) United Artists. Color-104min. Burt Lancaster, Donald MacDonald.....................5*

KENTUCKY (1938) 20th Century-Fox. Color-95min. Loretta Young, Richard Greene.....................4*

KENTUCKY FRIED MOVIE, THE (1977) United Film Distribution. Color-90min. Evan Kim, George Lazenby, Marilyn Joi.....................5½*

KENTUCKY MOONSHINE (1938) 20th Century-Fox. B&W-85min. The Ritz Brothers, Tony Martin.....................(4)
British title: THREE MEN AND A GIRL

KES (1970) United Artists. Color-113min. *(British).* David Bradley, Lynne Perrie.....................(5)

KETTLES IN THE OZARKS, THE (1956) Universal. B&W-81min. Marjorie Main, Arthur Hunnicutt.....................(3)

KETTLES ON OLD MACDONALD'S FARM, THE (1957) Universal. B&W-80min. Marjorie Main, Parker Fennelly.....................(3)

KEY, THE (1934) Warner Bros. B&W-71min. Edna Best, William Powell, Colin Clive.....................(5)

KEY, THE (1958) Columbia. B&W-125min. *(British).* William Holden, Sophia Loren, Trevor Howard.....................4*

KEY LARGO (1948) Warner Bros. B&W-101min. Humphrey Bogart, Edward G. Robinson.....................5*

KEY MAN (1954) *see* LIFE AT STAKE, A

KEY MAN, THE (1957) United Artists. B&W-63min. *(British).* Lee Patterson, Colin Gordon.....................(3)

KEY TO MURDER, THE (1956) Alexander Wilson. Color-71min. Lynn Dollar, Sam Kressen, John Zacherle.....................(2)

KEY TO THE CITY (1950) M-G-M. B&W-99min. Clark Gable, Loretta Young.....................4*

KEY WEST (1972) NBC-TV. Color-100min. *(Made for TV).* Stephen Boyd, Woody Strode, Sheree North.....................3*

KEY WITNESS (1960) M-G-M. B&W-82min. Jeffrey Hunter, Pat Crowley.....................(4)

KEYS OF THE KINGDOM, THE (1944) 20th Century-Fox. B&W-137min. Gregory Peck, Rosa Stradner.....................5*

KHARTOUM (1966) United Artists. Color-134min. *(British-U.S.).* Charlton Heston, Laurence Olivier.....................5*

KHYBER PATROL (1954) United Artists. Color-71min. Richard Egan, Dawn Addams.....................(3)

KID, THE (1920) First National [W.B.]. B&W-59min. *(Silent).* Charlie Chaplin, Jackie Coogan.....................5*

KID BLUE (1973) 20th Century-Fox. Color-100min. Dennis Hopper, Warren Oates, Ben Johnson.....................(4)

KID COMES BACK, THE (1937) Warner Bros. B&W-61min. Wayne Morris, Barton MacLane.....................(4)
British title: DON'T PULL YOUR PUNCHES

KID DYNAMITE (1943) Monogram [Allied Artists]. B&W-73min. The East Side Kids, Pamela Blake.....................(3)
Alternate title: QUEEN OF BROADWAY

KID FOR TWO FARTHINGS, A (1955) Lopert [U.A.]. Color-96min. *(British).* Jonathan Ashmore, Celia Johnson.....................(5)

KID FROM BROOKLYN, THE (1946) RKO. Color-114min. Danny Kaye, Virginia Mayo.....................4*

KID FROM CLEVELAND, THE (1949) Republic. B&W-89min. George Brent, Lynn Bari.....................(3)

KID FROM KANSAS, THE (1941) Universal. B&W-66min. Leo Carrillo, Andy Devine.....................(3)

KID FROM KOKOMO, THE (1939) Warner Bros. B&W-92min. Wayne Morris, Pat O'Brien, Joan Blondell.....................(3)
British title: ORPHAN OF THE RING, THE

KID FROM LEFT FIELD, THE (1953) 20th Century-Fox. B&W-80min. Dan Dailey, Anne Bancroft, Billy Chapin.....................(4)

KID FROM SPAIN, THE (1932) United Artists. B&W-90min. Eddie Cantor, Lyda Roberti.....................5*

KID FROM TEXAS, THE (1950) Universal. Color-78min. Audie Murphy, Gale Storm.....................(3)
British title: TEXAS KID, OUTLAW

KID GALAHAD (1937) Warner Bros. B&W-101min. Edward G. Robinson, Wayne Morris.....................4*
Alternate title: BATTLING BELLHOP

KID GALAHAD (1962) United Artists. Color-95min. Elvis Presley, Gig Young.....................4*

THE KID (1921). Charlie Chaplin and his "adopted" kid Jackie Coogan are constantly looking over their shoulders · · for the law.

KID GLOVE KILLER (1942) M-G-M. B&W-74min. Van Heflin, Marsha Hunt.....................(5)

KID MILLIONS (1934) United Artists. B&W-90min. Eddie Cantor, Ethel Merman.....................4*

KID NIGHTINGALE (1939) Warner Bros. B&W-57min. John Payne, Jane Wyman.....................(4)

KID RODELO (1966) Paramount. Color-91min. *(U.S.-Spanish).* Don Murray, Janet Leigh, Broderick Crawford, Richard Carlson.....................(3)

KIDNAPPED (1938) 20th Century-Fox. B&W-90min. Warner Baxter, Freddie Bartholomew.....................4*

KIDNAPPED (1948) Monogram [Allied Artists]. B&W-80min. Roddy McDowall, Sue England.....................3½*

KIDNAPPED (1960) Buena Vista. Color-97min. *(U.S.-British).* James MacArthur, Peter Finch.....................(4)

KIDNAPPED (1971) American-International. Color-100min. *(British).* Michael Caine, Lawrence Douglas.....................(4)

KIDNAPPERS, THE (1954) *see* LITTLE KIDNAPPERS, THE

KIDNAPPERS, THE (1964) B&W-73min. Burgess Meredith, William Phipps.....................(3)
Alternate title: MAN ON THE RUN

KIDS ARE ALRIGHT, THE (1979) New World. Color-107min. *(British).* The Who....................

KID'S LAST FIGHT, THE (1933) *see* LIFE OF JIMMY DOLAN, THE

KILL A DRAGON (1967) United Artists. Color-91min. Jack Palance, Fernando Lamas.....................3*

KILL BABY KILL (1966) Europix-Consolidated. Color-83min. *(Italian).* Erika Blanc, Giacomo Rossi-Stuart.....................(3)
Original title: OPERAZIONE PAURA *(Operation Fear)*
British title: CURSE OF THE DEAD
Alternate title: CURSE OF THE LIVING DEAD

KILL HER GENTLY (1958) Columbia. B&W-63min. *(British).* Griffith Jones, Maureen Connell, Marc Lawrence.....................(3)

KILL ME IF YOU CAN (1977) NBC-TV. Color-100min. *(Made for TV).* Alan Alda, Talia Shire, John Hillerman.....................5½*

KILL ME TOMORROW (1958) Tudor Pictures. B&W-80min. *(British).* Pat O'Brien, George Coulouris.....................(3)

Films are rated on a 1 to 10 scale, 10 is highest. **Boldface** ratings followed by an asterisk (*) are for films actually seen and rated by the executive and senior editors. All other ratings are estimates. (See Notes on Entertainment Ratings in the front section.)

THE FILM BUFF'S CHECKLIST

KILL OR BE KILLED (1950) Eagle Lion. B&W-67min. Lawrence Tierney, George Coulouris 3*

KILL OR CURE (1962) M-G-M. B&W-88min. (British). Terry-Thomas, Eric Sykes .... (3)

KILL THE UMPIRE (1950) Columbia. B&W-78min. William Bendix, Una Merkel 4*

KILL THEM ALL AND COME BACK ALONE (1968) Fanfare. Color-97min. (Italian-Spanish). Chuck Connors, Frank Wolff .... (1)
Original Italian title: AMMAZZALI TUTTI E TORNA SOLO
Original Spanish title: MATALOS Y VUELVE

KILLDOZER (1974) MCA-TV. Color-74min. (Made for TV). Clint Walker, James Wainwright, Neville Brand .... (4)

KILLER! (1969) *see* THIS MAN MUST DIE

KILLER, THE (1973) *see* SACRED KNIVES OF VENGEANCE, THE

KILLER APE (1953) Columbia. B&W-68min. Johnny Weissmuller, Carol Thurston .... (3)

KILLER BEES (1974) Worldvision. Color-74min. (Made for TV). Gloria Swanson, Edward Albert, Kate Jackson 3*

KILLER BY NIGHT (1971) Viacom. Color-100min. (Made for TV). Robert Wagner, Diane Baker, Robert Lansing .... (4)

KILLER DINO (1957) *see* DINO

KILLER ELITE, THE (1975) United Artists. Color-122min. James Caan, Robert Duvall 3*

KILLER FORCE (1975) American-International. Color-100min. (Swiss-Irish, English language). Telly Savalas, Peter Fonda 4½*
British title: DIAMOND MERCENARIES, THE

KILLER GRIZZLY (1976) *see* GRIZZLY

KILLER INSIDE ME, THE (1976) Warner Bros. Color-99min. Stacy Keach, Susan Tyrell .... (4)

KILLER IS LOOSE, THE (1956) United Artists. B&W-73min. Joseph Cotten, Rhonda Fleming .... (4)

KILLER LEOPARD (1954) Allied Artists. B&W-70min. Johnny Sheffield, Beverly Garland .... (3)

KILLER McCOY (1947) M-G-M. B&W-104min. Mickey Rooney, Brian Donlevy 4*

KILLER ON A HORSE (1967) *see* WELCOME TO HARD TIMES

KILLER SHARK (1950) Monogram [Allied Artists]. B&W-76min. Roddy McDowall, Laurette Luez .... (3)

KILLER SHREWS, THE (1959) McLendon. B&W-72min. James Best, Ingrid Goude 2*

KILLER SPY (1965) American-International. B&W-82min. (French-W. German). Jean Marais, Nadja Tiller .... (3)
Original French title: PLEINS FEUX SUR STANISLAS
German title: RENDEZVOUS DER KILLER

KILLER THAT STALKED NEW YORK, THE (1950) Columbia. B&W-79min. Evelyn Keyes, Charles Korvin 4*
British title: FRIGHTENED CITY

KILLER WHO WOULDN'T DIE, THE (1976) Paramount. Color-100min. (Made for TV). Mike Connors, Grégoire Aslan, Mariette Hartley, Clu Gulager 4*

KILLERS, THE (1946) Universal. B&W-105min. Burt Lancaster, Ava Gardner, Edmond O'Brien 5*

KILLERS, THE (1964) Universal. Color-95min. Lee Marvin, Angie Dickinson 4*
Publicity title: ERNEST HEMINGWAY'S THE KILLERS

KILLERS ARE CHALLENGED (1965) *see* SECRET AGENT FIREBALL

KILLERS' CAGE (1958) *see* CODE OF SILENCE

KILLER'S CARNIVAL (1966) Paramount. Color-94min. (W. German-Italian). Stewart Granger, Lex Barker, Karin Dor .... (4)
Original German title: GERN HAB' ICH DIE FRAUEN GEKILLT
Alternate title: REQUIEM FOR A SECRET AGENT

KILLERS FROM SPACE (1954) RKO. B&W-71min. Peter Graves, James Seay .... (3)

KILLER'S KISS (1955) United Artists. B&W-67min. Frank Silvera, Jamie Smith .... (3)

KILLERS OF KILIMANJARO (1959) Columbia. Color-91min. (British). Robert Taylor, Anthony Newley 3½*

KILLERS OF THE EAST (1958) Teledynamics. Color-75min. (Italian). Lex Barker, Florence Mari .... (1)

KILLERS THREE (1968) American-International. Color-88min. Robert Walker (Jr.), Diane Varsi, Dick Clark .... (2)

KILLING, THE (1956) United Artists. B&W-83min. Sterling Hayden, Jay C. Flippen 5*

KILLING GAME, THE (1967) Regional. Color-94min. (French). Jean-Pierre Cassel, Claudine Auger .... (4)
Original title: JEU DE MASSACRE
Alternate title: ALL WEEKEND LOVERS

KILLING KIND, THE (1973) Media Cinema. Color-95min. John Savage, Ann Sothern, Cindy Williams .... (3)

KILLING OF A CHINESE BOOKIE, THE (1976) Faces Distribution Co. Color-135min. Ben Gazzara, Soto Joe Hugh, Timothy Agoglia Carey... (2)

KILLING OF SISTER GEORGE, THE (1968) Cinerama Releasing. Color-137min. Susannah York, Beryl Reid, Coral Browne 5*

KILROY WAS HERE (1947) Monogram [Allied Artists]. B&W-68min. Jackie Cooper, Jackie Coogan .... (3)

KIM (1950) M-G-M. Color-113min. Dean Stockwell, Errol Flynn 5*

KIMBERLY JIM (1963) Avco-Embassy. Color-82min. (South African). Jim Reeves, Madeleine Usher .... (3)

KIND HEARTS AND CORONETS (1949) Eagle Lion. B&W-104min. (British). Dennis Price, Joan Greenwood, Alec Guinness 7*

KIND LADY (1935) M-G-M. B&W-78min. Aline MacMahon, Basil Rathbone .... (5)
Alternate title: HOUSE OF MENACE

KIND LADY (1951) M-G-M. B&W-78min. Ethel Barrymore, Maurice Evans .... (5)

KIND OF LOVING, A (1962) Governor. B&W-112min. (British). Alan Bates, June Ritchie 4½*

KINDAR THE INVULNERABLE (1965) ABC Films. Color-98min. (Italian). Mark Forrest, Mimmo Palmara, Rosalba Neri .... (1)
Original title: KINDAR, L'INVULNERABILE

KING (1978) NBC-TV. Color-300min. (Made for TV). Paul Winfield, Cicely Tyson .... (5)

KING: A FILMED RECORD . . . MONTGOMERY TO MEMPHIS (1970) Maron Films, Ltd. B&W-177min. Paul Newman, Burt Lancaster, Sidney Poitier, Charlton Heston .... (5)

KING AND COUNTRY (1964) Commonwealth United. B&W-86min. (British). Dirk Bogarde, Tom Courtenay 5½*

KING AND FOUR QUEENS, THE (1956) United Artists. Color-86min. Clark Gable, Eleanor Parker 3*

KING AND I, THE (1956) 20th Century-Fox. Color-133min. Deborah Kerr, Yul Brynner 7*

KING AND THE CHORUS GIRL, THE (1937) Warner Bros. B&W-94min. Ferdinand Gravet, Jane Wyman .... (5)
British title: ROMANCE IN PARIS

KING BOXER (1973) *see* FIVE FINGERS OF DEATH

KING CREOLE (1958) Paramount. B&W-116min. Elvis Presley, Carolyn Jones 4*

KING DINOSAUR (1955) Lippert Productions. B&W-63min. Bill Bryant, Wanda Curtis .... (2)

KING ELEPHANT (1971) *see* AFRICAN ELEPHANT, THE

KING IN NEW YORK, A (1957) Archway (Brit.). B&W-105min. (British). Charles Chaplin, Dawn Addams 4*

KING IN SHADOW (1956) Exclusive International. Color-78min. (German). O. W. Fischer, Horst Buchholz, Odile Versois .... (4)
Original title: HERRSCHER OHNE KRONE

KING KONG (1933) RKO. B&W-100min. Robert Armstrong, Fay Wray 5½*

KING KONG (1976) Paramount. Color-134min. Rick Baker, Jeff Bridges, Charles Grodin, Jessica Lange 5½*

KING KONG ESCAPES (1967) Universal. Color-96min. (Japan-U.S.). Rhodes Reason, Mie Hama, Eisei Amamoto 1*
Original Japanese title: KINGU KONGU NO GYAKUSHU

KING KONG VS. GODZILLA (1962) Universal. Color-90min. (Japanese). Tadao Takashima, Mie Hama, Godzilla 2*
Original title: KINGU KONGU TAI GOJIRA
Alternate Japanese title: KING KONG TAI GODZILLA

KING LEAR (1971) Altura Films. B&W-137min. (British-Danish). Paul Scofield, Irene Worth 3*

KING LEAR (1971) Artkino. B&W-136min. (U.S.S.R.). Yuri Jarvet, Elsa Radzins, Galina Volchek ....

KING, MURRAY (1969) Eyer Productions. B&W-86min. Murray Ramsey, Laura Kaye .... (4)

KING OF ALCATRAZ (1938) Paramount. B&W-56min. Lloyd Nolan, Gail Patrick .... (4)
British title: KING OF THE ALCATRAZ

KING OF BURLESQUE (1935) 20th Century-Fox. B&W-83min. Warner Baxter, Alice Faye 4½*

KING OF CHINATOWN (1939) Paramount. **B&W-60min.** Anna May Wong, Akim Tamiroff...(4)

KING OF HEARTS (1966) Lopert [U.A.]. **Color-102min.** *(French-Italian).* Alan Bates, Genevieve Bujold..............................5*
Original title: ROI DE COEUR, LE

KING OF JAZZ (1930) Universal. **Color-101min.** Paul Whiteman, John Boles, Bing Crosby..(4)

KING OF KINGS (1927) Pathé. **B&W-115min.** *(Silent).* H. B. Warner, Dorothy Cumming, Ernest Torrence..........................4*

KING OF KINGS (1961) M-G-M. **Color-168min.** Jeffrey Hunter, Robert Ryan...5*

KING OF MARVIN GARDENS, THE (1972) Columbia. **Color-103min.** Jack Nicholson, Bruce Dern.......................................(3)

KING OF SPORTS (1938) *see* FAST COMPANY

KING OF THE ALCATRAZ (1938) *see* KING OF ALCATRAZ

KING OF THE CORAL SEA (1954) Allied Artists. **B&W-86min.** *(Australian).* Chips Rafferty, Lloyd Berrell, Rod Taylor............(4)

KING OF THE GRIZZLIES (1970) Buena Vista. **Color-93min.** *(U.S.-Canadian).* John Yenso, Chris Wiggins.......................4*

KING OF THE GYPSIES (1978) Paramount. **Color-112min.** Sterling Hayden, Eric Roberts, Susan Sarandon, Brooke Shields.........5*

KING OF THE JUNGLE (1933) Paramount. **B&W-65min.** Buster Crabbe, Frances Dee...4*

KING OF THE JUNGLELAND (1936) *see* BATMEN OF AFRICA

KING OF THE KHYBER RIFLES (1954) 20th Century-Fox. **Color-100min.** Tyrone Power, Terry Moore.........................3*

KING OF THE LUMBERJACKS (1940) Warner Bros. **B&W-58min.** John Payne, Gloria Dixon..(3)

KING OF THE MONGOLS (1960) American-International. **Color-88min.** *(Japanese).* Hashizo Okawa, Yoshio Yoshida.............(3)
Alternate title: GENGHIS KHAN AND HIS MONGOLS

KING OF THE ROARING 20s - THE STORY OF ARNOLD ROTHSTEIN (1961) Allied Artists. **B&W-106min.** David Janssen, Dianne Foster ..5*
British title: BIG BANKROLL, THE

KING OF THE ROCKET MEN (1949) *see* LOST PLANET AIRMEN

KING OF THE UNDERWORLD (1939) Warner Bros. **B&W-69min.** Kay Francis, Humphrey Bogart.....................................3*

KING OF THE VIKINGS (1964) American-International. **Color-81min.** *(Spanish).* Antonio Vilar, Marie Mahor.................(2)

KING OF THE WILD HORSES (1947) Columbia. **B&W-79min.** Preston Foster, Gail Patrick...(3)

KING OF THE WILD STALLIONS (1959) Allied Artists. **Color-75min.** George Montgomery, Diane Brewster.....................3*

KING OF THE ZOMBIES (1941) Monogram [Allied Artists]. **B&W-67min.** Dick Purcell, Joan Woodbury, Mantan Moreland..........(3)

KING ON HORSEBACK (1958) United Motion Pic. Org. (UMPO). **Color-88min.** *(French).* Jean Marais, Nadja Tiller, Eleanora Rossi-Drago.....(3)

KING, QUEEN, KNAVE (1972) Avco-Embassy. **Color-92min.** *(W.German-U.S.).* David Niven, Gina Lollobrigida, John Moulder Brown..................
Original W. German title: HERZBUBE

KING RAT (1965) Columbia. **B&W-133min.** George Segal, Tom Courtenay...6*

KING RICHARD AND THE CRUSADERS (1954) Warner Bros. **Color-114min.** Rex Harrison, Virginia Mayo.....................5*

KING ROBOT (1952) *see* MY SON, THE VAMPIRE

KING SOLOMON'S MINES (1937) Gaumont-British [Rank]. **B&W-80min.** *(British).* Cedric Hardwicke, Paul Robeson, Roland Young.....(5)

KING SOLOMON'S MINES (1950) M-G-M. **Color-102min.** Stewart Granger, Deborah Kerr...5*

KING STEPS OUT, THE (1936) Columbia. **B&W-85min.** Franchot Tone, Grace Moore...(5)

KINGDOM IN THE CLOUDS (1971) Xerox Films. **Color-87min.** *(Rumanian).* Mircea Breazu, Ana Szeles, Carmen Stanescu........(4)
Original title: TINERETE FARA BATRINETE *(Youth Without Age)*

KINGDOM IN THE SAND (1963) *see* CONQUEROR OF ATLANTIS

KINGDOM OF THE SPIDERS (1977) Dimension Pictures. **Color-94min.** William Shatner, Tiffany Bolling..........................(3)

KINGS GO FORTH (1958) United Artists. **B&W-109min.** Frank Sinatra, Tony Curtis..4*

KINGS OF THE ROAD (1976) Bauer International. **B&W-165min.** *(German).* Rudiger Vogler, Hanns Zischler.......................
Original title: IM LAUF DER ZEIT

KINGS OF THE SUN (1963) United Artists. **Color-108min.** Yul Brynner, George Chakiris...4*

KING'S PIRATE, THE (1967) Universal. **Color-100min.** Doug McClure, Jill St. John, Guy Stockwell...........................4½*

KING'S RHAPSODY (1955) United Artists. **Color-93min.** *(British).* Errol Flynn, Anna Neagle..(3)

KING'S ROW (1942) Warner Bros. **B&W-127min.** Ann Sheridan, Robert Cummings, Ronald Reagan.................................5*

KING'S STORY, A (1965) Continental [Walter Reade]. **B&W-100min.** *(British, Documentary). Director:* Harry Booth..............5½*

KING'S THIEF, THE (1955) M-G-M. **Color-78min.** Ann Blyth, Edmund Purdom...(4)

KING'S VACATION, THE (1933) Warner Bros. **B&W-60min.** George Arliss, Marjorie Gateson...(4)

KIPPS (1941) *see* REMARKABLE MR. KIPPS, THE

KISMET (1931) First National [W.B.]. **B&W-92min.** Loretta Young, Otis Skinner...(4)

KISMET (1944) M-G-M. **Color-100min.** Ronald Colman, Marlene Dietrich..4*
Alternate title: ORIENTAL DREAMS

KISMET (1955) M-G-M. **Color-113min.** Howard Keel, Ann Blyth............5*

KISS, THE (1929) Universal. **B&W-50min.** *(Silent).* Greta Garbo, Conrad Nagel..(4)

KISS & KILL (1968) Commonwealth United. **Color-92min.** *(U.S.-British-Spanish-W. German).* Christopher Lee, Richard Greene, Tsai Chin.....(3)
British title: BLOOD OF FU MANCHU, THE
Spanish title: FU MANCHU Y EL BESO DE LA MUERTE *(Fu Manchu and the Kiss of Death)*
W. German title: TODESKUSS DES DOKTOR FU MAN CHU *(The Death-kiss of Dr. Fu Man Chu)*
British pre-release title: FU MANCHU AND THE KISS OF DEATH

KISS AND TELL (1945) Columbia. **B&W-90min.** Shirley Temple, Jerome Courtland...(4)

KISS BEFORE DYING, A (1956) United Artists. **Color-94min.** Robert Wagner, Jeffrey Hunter..(4)

KISS BEFORE THE MIRROR, THE (1933) Universal. **B&W-67min.** Nancy Carroll, Paul Lukas...(4)

KISS FOR CORLISS, A (1949) United Artists. **B&W-88min.** Shirley Temple, David Niven ....(3)
Alternate title: ALMOST A BRIDE

KISS IN THE DARK, A (1949) Warner Bros. **B&W-87min.** Jane Wyman, David Niven..4*

KISS KISS - BANG BANG (1966) Rizzoli Film. **Color-90min.** *(Italian-Spanish).* Giuliano Gemma, George Martin...................(4)

KISS ME AGAIN (1931) First National [W.B.]. **B&W-74min.** Walter Pidgeon, Bernice Claire..(5)
British title: TOAST OF THE LEGION

KISS ME DEADLY (1955) United Artists. **B&W-105min.** Ralph Meeker, Albert Dekker..(3)

Ginger Rogers (right) is **KITTY FOYLE** (1940), who recalls, in this flashback scene, the wise counsel of her Irish father Ernest Cossart in her girlhood days in Philadelphia.

Films are rated on a 1 to 10 scale, 10 is highest. **Boldface** ratings followed by an asterisk (*) are for films actually seen and rated by the executive and senior editors. All other ratings are estimates. (See Notes on Entertainment Ratings in the front section.)

KISS ME KATE (1953) M-G-M. **Color-109min.** Kathryn Grayson, Howard Keel 5*

KISS ME, KISS ME, KISS ME! (1968) William Mishkin. **B&W-80min.** Natalie Rogers, Don Williams .... (3)

KISS ME MONSTER (1968) Joseph Green. **Color-79min.** *(Spanish-W. German).* Janine Reynaud, Rossana Yanni, Adrian Hoven ....
Original Spanish title: BESAME, MONSTRUO

KISS ME, STUPID (1964) Lopert [U.A.]. **B&W-126min.** Dean Martin, Kim Novak 5*

KISS OF DEATH (1947) 20th Century-Fox. **B&W-98min.** Victor Mature, Brian Donlevy, Richard Widmark 5*

KISS OF EVIL (1963) *see* KISS OF THE VAMPIRE

KISS OF FIRE (1955) Universal. **Color-87min.** Jack Palance, Barbara Rush .... (3)

KISS OF THE VAMPIRE (1963) Universal. **Color-88min.** *(British).* Clifford Evans, Noel Willman .... (4)
TV title: KISS OF EVIL

KISS THE BLOOD OFF MY HANDS (1948) Universal. **B&W-79min.** Burt Lancaster, Joan Fontaine .... (3)
British title: BLOOD ON MY HANDS

KISS THE BOYS GOODBYE (1941) Paramount. **B&W-85min.** Don Ameche, Mary Martin .... (4)

KISS THE GIRLS AND MAKE THEM DIE (1967) Columbia. **Color-106min.** *(U.S.-Italian, English version).* Michael Connors, Dorothy Provine, Raf Vallone 3½*
Original Italian title: SE TUTTE LE DONNE DEL MONDO *(If All the Women in the World)*
Alternate Italian title: OPERAZIONE PARADISO *(Operation Paradise)*

KISS THE OTHER SHEIK (1968) M-G-M. **Color-85min.** *(Italian-French).* Marcello Mastroianni, Pamela Tiffin, Virna Lisi .... (2)
This is two of the three episodes from: OGGI, DOMANI E DOPODOMANI *(Today, Tomorrow and the Day After That)*
Alternate title: BLOND WIFE, THE
Pre-release U.S. title: PARANOIA

KISS THEM FOR ME (1957) 20th Century-Fox. **Color-105min.** Cary Grant, Jayne Mansfield 4*

KISS TOMORROW GOODBYE (1950) Warner Bros. **B&W-102min.** James Cagney, Barbara Payton 3½*

KISSES FOR BREAKFAST (1941) Warner Bros. **B&W-85min.** Dennis Morgan, Jane Wyatt .... (3)

KISSES FOR MY PRESIDENT (1964) Warner Bros. **B&W-113min.** Fred MacMurray, Polly Bergen 3*

KISSIN' COUSINS (1964) M-G-M. **Color-96min.** Elvis Presley, Arthur O'Connell, Pamela Austin 4*

KISSING BANDIT, THE (1949) M-G-M. **Color-102min.** Frank Sinatra, Kathryn Grayson .... (3)

KIT CARSON (1940) United Artists. **B&W-97min.** Jon Hall, Lynn Bari 4*

KITCHEN, THE (1961) Kingsley International. **B&W-74min.** *(British).* Carl Mohner, Mary Yeomans .... (5)

KITTEN WITH A WHIP (1964) Universal. **B&W-83min.** Ann-Margret, John Forsythe .... (3)

KITTY (1945) Paramount. **B&W-103min.** Paulette Goddard, Ray Milland 5*

KITTY FOYLE (1940) RKO. **B&W-108min.** Ginger Rogers, Dennis Morgan 5*

KLANSMAN, THE (1974) Paramount. **Color-112min.** Lee Marvin, Richard Burton .... (3)

KLONDIKE ANNIE (1936) Paramount. **B&W-80min.** Mae West, Victor McLaglen 3*

KLONDIKE KATE (1943) Columbia. **B&W-64min.** Ann Savage, Glenda Farrell .... (3)

KLUTE (1971) Warner Bros. **Color-114min.** Jane Fonda, Donald Sutherland 4*

KNACK . . . AND HOW TO GET IT, THE (1965) United Artists. **B&W-84min.** *(British).* Rita Tushingham, Ray Brooks, Michael Crawford.... 3*
Original title: KNACK, THE

KNAVE OF HEARTS (1954) *see* LOVERS, HAPPY LOVERS

KNICKERBOCKER HOLIDAY (1944) United Artists. **B&W-85min.** Nelson Eddy, Charles Coburn, Constance Dowling .... (3)

KNIFE IN THE WATER (1962) Kanawha Films Ltd. **B&W-94min.** *(Polish).* Leon Niemczyk, Jolanta Umecka, Zygmunt Malanowicz........ 4*
Original title: NOZ W WODZIE

KNIGHT WITHOUT ARMOR (1937) United Artists. **B&W-107min.** *(British).* Marlene Dietrich, Robert Donat........................ (5)
Original title: KNIGHT WITHOUT ARMOUR

KNIGHTS OF THE BLACK CROSS (1960) Telewide Systems. **Color-180min.** Urszula Modrzynska, Grazyna Staniszawska .... (4)
Original title: KRZYZACY
Alternate title: KNIGHTS OF THE TEUTONIC ORDER

KNIGHTS OF THE ROUND TABLE (1953) M-G-M. **Color-115min.** Robert Taylor, Ava Gardner.................................... 5*

KNOCK ON ANY DOOR (1949) Columbia. **B&W-100min.** Humphrey Bogart, John Derek.. 4*

KNOCK ON WOOD (1954) Paramount. **Color-103min.** Danny Kaye, Mai Zetterling 4*

KNOCKOUT (1941) Warner Bros. **B&W-73min.** Arthur Kennedy, Olympe Bradna .... (3)

KNOCKOUT (1977) Turn-of-the-Century Fights. **B&W-104min.** *(Compilation).* Director: Jim Jacobs .... (3)

KNUTE ROCKNE - ALL AMERICAN (1940) Warner Bros. **B&W-98min.** Pat O'Brien, Gale Page 4*
British title: MODERN HERO, A

KOJAK AND THE MARCUS-NELSON MURDERS (1973) *see* MARCUS-NELSON MURDERS, THE

KON-TIKI (1951) RKO. **B&W-73min.** *(Documentary).* Director: Thor Heyerdahl 5½*

KONA COAST (1968) Warner Bros. **Color-93min.** Richard Boone, Vera Miles.. 3*

KONGA (1961) American-International. **Color-90min.** *(British-U.S.).* Michael Gough, Margo Johns 3*

KONGO (1932) M-G-M. **B&W-85min.** Walter Huston, Lupe Velez........... (4)

KOROSHI (1966) Independent TV Corp (ITC). **Color-93min.** *(Telefeature).* Patrick McGoohan, Yoko Tani.................. (3)

KOTCH (1971) Cinerama Releasing. **Color-118min.** Walter Matthau, Deborah Winters 5*

KOUMIKO MYSTERY, THE (1966) New Yorker Films. **Color-47min.** *(French-Japanese)*.................................. (4)

KRAKATOA, EAST OF JAVA (1969) Cinerama Releasing. **Color-128min.** Maximilian Schell, Diane Baker 4*
TV title: VOLCANO

KRAMER VS. KRAMER (1979) Columbia. **Color- min.** Dustin Hoffman, Meryl Streep..

KREMLIN LETTER, THE (1970) 20th Century-Fox. **Color-113min.** Richard Boone, Patrick O'Neal......................... 4*

KRIEMHILD'S REVENGE (1923) *see* NIBELUNGEN, DIE

KRONOS (1957) 20th Century-Fox. **B&W-78min.** Jeff Morrow, Barbara Lawrence 3*

KUHLE WAMPE (1932) Kinematrade. **B&W-65min.** *(German).* Herta Thiele, Ernst Busch.................................. 2*
Alternate title: WHITHER GERMANY?

KUNG FU (1971) Warner Bros. **Color-75min.** *(Made for TV).* David Carradine, Barry Sullivan, Philip Ahn .... (4)

KWAIDAN (1964) Continental [Walter Reade]. **Color-125min.** *(Japanese).* Michiyo Aratama, Misako Watanabe................ 4*
Original title: KAIDAN
Alternate title: WEIRD TALES

-L-

L-SHAPED ROOM, THE (1962) Columbia. **B&W-124min.** *(British).* Leslie Caron, Tom Bell 5½*

LA DOLCE VITA (1960) *alphabetized as* DOLCE VITA, LA

LACEMAKER, THE (1977) New Yorker Films. **Color-108min.** *(Swiss-French).* Isabelle Huppert, Yves Beneyton....................
Original title: DENTELLIERE, LA

LACOMBE, LUCIEN (1974) CIC. **Color-136min.** *(French-Italian-W. German).* Pierre Blaise, Aurore Clément 4½*

LAD: A DOG (1962) Warner Bros. **Color-98min.** Peter Breck, Peggy McCay, Carroll O'Connor.......................... (4)

LADDIE (1940) RKO. **B&W-70min.** Tim Holt, Virginia Gilmore............. (4)

LADIES AND GENTLEMEN, THE ROLLING STONES (1974) Dragon Aire, Ltd. **Color-90min.** *(Music Film).* Director: Rollin Binzer............. (4)

LADIES COURAGEOUS (1944) Universal. **B&W-88min.** Loretta Young, Diana Barrymore.. (3)

LADIES' DAY (1943) RKO. **B&W-62min.** Lupe Velez, Eddie Albert........ (3)

LADIES FIRST (1963) Paramount. **B&W-90min.** *(French-Italian).* Eddie Constantine, Henri Cogan .... (3)
Original French title: A TOI DE FAIRE, MIGNONNE

LADIES IN LOVE (1936) 20th Century-Fox. **B&W-97min.** Janet Gaynor, Constance Bennett.................................... (4)

Films are rated on a 1 to 10 scale, 10 is highest. **Boldface** ratings followed by an asterisk (*) are for films actually seen and rated by the executive and senior editors. All other ratings are estimates. (See Notes on Entertainment Ratings in the front section.)

LADIES IN RETIREMENT (1941) Columbia. **B&W-92min.** Ida Lupino, Louis Hayward .... (5)

LADIES' MAN (1931) Paramount. **B&W-70min.** William Powell, Kay Francis .... (3)

LADIES' MAN (1947) Paramount. **B&W-91min.** Eddie Bracken, Cass Daley .... (3)

LADIES' MAN, THE (1961) Paramount. **Color-106min.** Jerry Lewis, Helen Traubel **3***

LADIES' MAN (1962) Paramount. **B&W-95min.** *(French).* Eddie Constantine, Francoise Brion .... (3)
Original title: LEMMY POUR LES DAMES

LADIES MUST LIVE (1940) Warner Bros. **B&W-58min.** Wayne Morris, Rosemary Lane .... (3)

LADIES OF THE BIG HOUSE (1932) Paramount. **B&W-76min.** Sylvia Sidney, Gene Raymond .... (4)

LADIES OF THE CHORUS (1948) Columbia. **B&W-61min.** Adele Jergens, Rand Brooks .... (3)

LADIES SHOULD LISTEN (1934) Paramount. **B&W-62min.** Cary Grant, Frances Drake .... (3)

LADIES WHO DO (1963) Continental [Walter Reade]. **B&W-85min.** *(British).* Peggy Mount, Robert Morley **4½***

LADY AND THE BANDIT, THE (1951) Columbia. **B&W-79min.** Patricia Medina, Louis Hayward .... (3)
British title: DICK TURPIN'S RIDE

LADY AND THE MOB, THE (1939) Columbia. **B&W-66min.** Fay Bainter, Lee Bowman .... (4)

LADY AND THE MONSTER, THE (1944) Republic. **B&W-86min.** Erich Von Stroheim, Richard Arlen, Vera Hruba Ralston .... (3)
British title: LADY AND THE DOCTOR, THE

LADY AND THE OUTLAW, THE (1974) *see* BILLY TWO HATS

LADY AND THE TRAMP (1955) Buena Vista. **Color-75min.** *(Cartoon).* *Director:* Hamilton Luske **5½***

LADY BE GOOD (1941) M-G-M. **B&W-111min.** Eleanor Powell, Robert Young .... (5)

LADY BODYGUARD (1943) Paramount. **B&W-70min.** Eddie Albert, Anne Shirley .... (3)

LADY BY CHOICE (1934) Columbia. **B&W-78min.** Carole Lombard, May Robson .... (4)

LADY CAROLINE LAMB (1972) U.A. (for M-G-M). **Color-122min.** *(British-Italian).* Sarah Miles, Jon Finch **4***

LADY CHATTERLEY'S LOVER (1955) Kingsley International. **B&W-102min.** *(French).* Danielle Darrieux, Leo Genn, Erno Crisa .... (4)
Original title: AMANT DE LADY CHATTERLEY, L'

LADY CONFESSES, THE (1945) Producers Rel. Corp. [Eagle Lion]. **B&W-66min.** Mary Beth Hughes, Hugh Beaumont .... (3)

LADY AND THE TRAMP (1955). Words of wisdom from Scotch terrier Jock go unheeded by the carefree mongrel known as The Tramp (without collar), but pedigreed cocker spaniel Lady and bloodhound Trusty listen attentively.

LADY CONSENTS, THE (1936) RKO. **B&W-75min.** Herbert Marshall, Ann Harding .... (4)

LADY DANCES, THE (1934) *see* MERRY WIDOW, THE

LADY DOCTOR, THE (1957) **B&W-103min.** *(Italian-French-Spanish).* Toto, Vittorio De Sica, Abbe Lane .... (4)
Original Italian title: TOTO, VITTORIO E LA DOTTORESSA *(Toto, Vittorio and the Lady Doctor)*
Original Spanish title: MI MUJER ES DOCTOR *(My Wife's a Doctor)*
Original French title: DITES 33

LADY EVE, THE (1941) Paramount. **B&W-97min.** Barbara Stanwyck, Henry Fonda **5***

LADY FOR A DAY (1933) Columbia. **B&W-95min.** Warren William, May Robson .... (5)

LADY FOR A NIGHT (1941) Republic. **B&W-87min.** Joan Blondell, John Wayne .... (3)

LADY FROM BOSTON, THE (1951) *see* PARDON MY FRENCH

LADY FROM CHEYENNE (1941) Universal. **B&W-87min.** Loretta Young, Robert Preston **4½***

LADY FROM CHUNGKING (1942) Producers Rel. Corp. [Eagle Lion]. **B&W-66min.** Anna May Wong, Harold Huber .... (3)

LADY FROM KENTUCKY, THE (1939) *see* LADY'S FROM KENTUCKY, THE

LADY FROM LOUISIANA (1941) Republic. **B&W-82min.** John Wayne, Ona Munson **4½***

LADY FROM SHANGHAI, THE (1948) Columbia. **B&W-87min.** Rita Hayworth, Orson Welles **4***

LADY FROM TEXAS, THE (1951) Universal. **Color-77min.** Howard Duff, Mona Freeman .... (4)

LADY GAMBLES, THE (1949) Universal. **B&W-99min.** Barbara Stanwyck, Robert Preston **4***

LADY GANGSTER (1942) Warner Bros. **B&W-62min.** Faye Emerson, Julie Bishop .... (3)

LADY GODIVA (1955) Universal. **Color-89min.** Maureen O'Hara, George Nader .... (4)
British title: LADY GODIVA OF COVENTRY

LADY HAMILTON (1941) *see* THAT HAMILTON WOMAN

LADY HAS PLANS, THE (1942) Paramount. **B&W-77min.** Ray Milland, Paulette Goddard **3***

LADY ICE (1973) National General. **Color-93min.** Donald Sutherland, Jennifer O'Neill, Robert Duvall **3***

LADY IN A CAGE (1964) Paramount. **B&W-93min.** Olivia de Havilland, James Caan, Ann Sothern **3***

LADY IN A JAM (1942) Universal. **B&W-78min.** Irene Dunne, Ralph Bellamy .... (4)

LADY IN CEMENT (1968) 20th Century-Fox. **Color-93min.** Frank Sinatra, Raquel Welch .... (3)

LADY IN DISTRESS (1939) Times Film Corp. **B&W-76min.** *(British).* Michael Redgrave, Sally Gray, Paul Lukas .... (4)
Original title: WINDOW IN LONDON, A

LADY IN QUESTION, THE (1940) Columbia. **B&W-81min.** Brian Aherne, Rita Hayworth .... (4)

LADY IN RED, THE (1979) New World. **Color- min.**

LADY IN THE CAR WITH GLASSES AND A GUN, THE (1970) Columbia. **Color-100min.** *(French-U.S., English version).* Samantha Eggar, Oliver Reed .... (3)
Original French title: DAME DANS L'AUTO AVEC DES LUNETTES ET UN FUSIL, LA

LADY IN THE DARK (1944) Paramount. **Color-100min.** Ginger Rogers, Ray Milland .... (5)

LADY IN THE FOG (1952) *see* SCOTLAND YARD INSPECTOR

LADY IN THE IRON MASK (1952) 20th Century-Fox. **Color-78min.** Patricia Medina, Louis Hayward .... (3)

LADY IN THE LAKE (1946) M-G-M. **B&W-103min.** Robert Montgomery, Audrey Totter **5***

LADY IN THE MORGUE (1938) Universal. **B&W-67min.** Preston Foster, Patricia Ellis .... (4)
British title: CASE OF THE MISSING BLONDE, THE

LADY IS WAITING, THE (1957) *see* FULL OF LIFE

LADY IS WILLING, THE (1942) Columbia. **B&W-92min.** Marlene Dietrich, Fred MacMurray **4***

LADY JANE GRAY (1936) *see* NINE DAYS A QUEEN

LADY KILLER (1933) Warner Bros. **B&W-76min.** James Cagney, Mae Clarke **5***

Films are rated on a 1 to 10 scale, 10 is highest. **Boldface** ratings followed by an asterisk (*) are for films actually seen and rated by the executive and senior editors. All other ratings are estimates. (See Notes on Entertainment Ratings in the front section.)

LADY KILLER OF ROME, THE (1961) *see* ASSASSIN, THE

LADY L (1965) M-G-M. **Color-107min.** *(U.S.-French-Italian).* Sophia Loren, Paul Newman **4***

LADY LIBERTY (1972) United Artists. **Color-95min.** *(Italian-French).* Sophia Loren, Luigi Proietti, William Devane **4***
Original Italian title: MORTADELLA, LA *(The Sausage)*

LADY LUCK (1946) RKO. **B&W-97min.** Robert Young, Barbara Hale..... **5***

LADY OF BURLESQUE (1943) United Artists. **B&W-96min.** Barbara Stanwyck, Michael O'Shea **4***
British title: STRIP-TEASE LADY

LADY OF DECEIT (1947) *see* BORN TO KILL

LADY OF MONZA, THE (1970) Tower. **Color-98min.** Anne Heywood, Antonio Sabato .... (2)
Original title: MONACA DI MONZA, LA
Alternate Italian title: STORIA LOMBARDA, UNA
Alternate title: NUN OF MONZA, THE

LADY OF MYSTERY (1946) *see* CLOSE CALL FOR BOSTON BLACKIE, A

LADY OF SECRETS (1936) Columbia. **B&W-73min.** Ruth Chatterton, Otto Kruger, Lionel Atwill .... (4)

LADY OF THE BOULEVARDS (1934) *see* NANA

LADY OF THE HOUSE (1978) NBC-TV. **Color-100min.** *(Made for TV).* Dyan Cannon, Armand Assante..

LADY OF THE TROPICS (1939) M-G-M. **B&W-92min.** Robert Taylor, Hedy Lamarr.. **4***

LADY OF VENGEANCE (1957) United Artists. **B&W-73min.** *(British).* Dennis O'Keefe, Ann Sears .... (3)

LADY ON A TRAIN (1945) Universal. **B&W-93min.** Deanna Durbin, David Bruce .... (5)

LADY ON THE TRACKS, THE (1966) Royal Films Int'l [Columbia]. **Color-83min.** *(Czech).* Jirina Bohdalova, Radoslav Brzobohaty .... (4)
Original title: DAMA NO KOLEJICH

LADY PAYS OFF, THE (1951) Universal. **B&W-80min.** Linda Darnell, Stephen McNally **4½***

LADY POSSESSED, A (1952) Republic. **B&W-87min.** James Mason, June Havoc .... (3)

LADY SAYS NO, THE (1951) United Artists. **B&W-80min.** David Niven, Joan Caulfield .... (3)

LADY SCARFACE (1941) RKO. **B&W-69min.** Judith Anderson, Dennis O'Keefe, Frances Neal .... (3)

LADY SINGS THE BLUES (1972) Paramount. **Color-144min.** Diana Ross, Billy Dee Williams... **4***

LADY SURRENDERS, A (1944) Universal. **B&W-113min.** *(British).* Margaret Lockwood, Stewart Granger .... (5)
Original title: LOVE STORY

LADY TAKES A CHANCE, A (1943) RKO. **B&W-86min.** Jean Arthur, John Wayne **4½***

LADY TAKES A FLYER, THE (1958) Universal. **Color-84min.** Lana Turner, Jeff Chandler **3***

LADY TAKES A SAILOR, THE (1949) Warner Bros. **B&W-99min.** Jane Wyman, Dennis Morgan.. **4***

LADY VANISHES, THE (1938) Gaumont-British [Rank]. **B&W-97min.** *(British).* Margaret Lockwood, Michael Redgrave **5***

LADY WANTS MINK, THE (1953) Republic. **Color-92min.** Ruth Hussey, Dennis O'Keefe **4***

LADY WINDERMERE'S FAN (1925) Warner Bros. **B&W-87min.** *(Silent).* Irene Rich, May McAvoy, Ronald Colman **4½***

LADY WINDERMERE'S FAN (1949) *see* FAN, THE

LADY WITH A LAMP, THE (1951) Continental [Walter Reade]. **B&W-110min.** *(British).* Anna Neagle, Michael Wilding **4***

LADY WITH RED HAIR (1940) Warner Bros. **B&W-81min.** Claude Rains, Miriam Hopkins .... (4)

LADY WITH THE DOG, THE (1960) Artkino. **B&W-86min.** *(U.S.S.R.).* Iya Savvina, Aleksey Batalov .... (4)
Original title: DAMA S SOBACHKOY

LADY WITHOUT PASSPORT, A (1950) M-G-M. **B&W-72min.** Hedy Lamarr, John Hodiak .... (4)

LADYBUG, LADYBUG (1963) United Artists. **B&W-81min.** William Daniels, Nancy Marchand... (5)

LADYKILLERS, THE (1955) Continental [Walter Reade]. **Color-97min.** *(British).* Alec Guinness, Katie Johnson **5½***

LADY'S FROM KENTUCKY, THE (1939) Paramount. **B&W-67min.** George Raft, Ellen Drew .... (4)

LADY'S MORALS, A (1930) M-G-M. **B&W-75min.** Grace Moore, Reginald Denny .... (3)
British title: JENNY LIND

LAFAYETTE (1962) Maco Film. **Color-112min.** *(French-Italian).* Michel Le Royer, Jack Hawkins, Orson Welles **3***
Original French title: La FAYETTE
Original Italian title: LAFAYETTE (UNA SPADA PER DUE BANDIERE)

LAFAYETTE ESCADRILLE (1958) William A. Wellman. **B&W-93min.** Tab Hunter, Etchika Choureau **4***
British title: HELL BENT FOR GLORY

LAKE OF DRACULA (1971) Toho. **Color-82min.** *(Japanese).* Mori Kishida, Midori Fujita, Choei Takahashi .... (3)
Original title: CHI O SUU ME *(Bloodthirsty Eyes)*
Publicity title: DRACULA'S LUST FOR BLOOD

LAKE PLACID SERENADE (1944) Republic. **B&W-85min.** Vera Vague, Vera Hruba Ralston .... (3)

LAMP STILL BURNS, THE (1943) General Film. **B&W-90min.** *(British).* Rosamund John, Stewart Granger, Godfrey Tearle ....

LANCELOT AND GUINEVERE (1963) *see* SWORD OF LANCELOT

LANCELOT OF THE LAKE (1974) New Yorker Films. **Color-85min.** *(French-Italian).* Luc Simon, Laura Duke Condominas, Vladimir Antolek-Oresek ....
Original title: LANCELOT DU LAC

LANCER SPY (1937) 20th Century-Fox. **B&W-84min.** George Sanders, Peter Loore, Dolores Del Rio .... (5)

LAND OF FURY (1954) Universal. **Color-82min.** *(British).* Jack Hawkins, Glynis Johns **4***
Original title: SEEKERS, THE

LAND OF THE MINOTAUR (1976) Crown International. **Color-88min.** *(British).* Peter Cushing, Donald Pleasence, Luan Peters ....

LAND OF THE PHARAOHS (1955) Warner Bros. **Color-106min.** Jack Hawkins, Joan Collins **5½***

LAND RAIDERS (1970) Columbia. **Color-101min.** Telly Savalas, George Maharis **3***

LAND THAT TIME FORGOT, THE (1975) American-International. **Color-91min.** *(British-U.S.).* Doug McClure, John McEnery, Susan Penhaligon .... (3)

LAND UNKNOWN, THE (1957) Universal. **B&W-78min.** Jock Mahoney, Shawn Smith .... (3)

LANDLORD, THE (1970) United Artists. **Color-113min.** Beau Bridges, Pearl Bailey **3***

LANDRU (1963) Avco-Embassy. **Color-114min.** *(French-Italian).* Charles Denner, Michele Morgan, Danielle Darrieux.............................. **3***
Alternate title: BLUEBEARD

LANIGAN'S RABBI (1976) MCA-TV. **Color-100min.** *(Made for TV).* Art Carney, Stuart Margolin, Janet Margolin.......................... **4½***
Alternate title: FRIDAY THE RABBI SLEPT LATE

LARCENY (1948) Universal. **B&W-89min.** John Payne, Joan Caulfield. **3½***

LARCENY, INC. (1942) Warner Bros. **B&W-95min.** Edward G. Robinson, Jane Wyman... **3½***

LARCENY LANE (1931) *see* BLONDE CRAZY

LARGE ROPE, THE (1953) *see* LONG ROPE, THE

LARRY (1974) CBS-TV. **Color-78min.** *(Made for TV).* Frederic Forrest, Tyne Daly ....

LAS VEGAS HILLBILLYS (1966) Woolner Brothers. **Color-90min.** Ferlin Husky, Mamie Van Doren .... (2)

LAS VEGAS LADY (1976) Crown International. **Color-87min.** Stella Stevens, Stuart Whitman .... (4)

LAS VEGAS NIGHTS (1941) Paramount. **B&W-89min.** Phil Regan, Constance Moore, Bert Wheeler...................................... (3)
British title: GAY CITY, THE

LAS VEGAS SHAKEDOWN (1955) Allied Artists. **B&W-79min.** Dennis O'Keefe, Coleen Gray .... (3)

LAS VEGAS STORY, THE (1952) RKO. **B&W-88min.** Jane Russell, Victor Mature **4***

LASERBLAST (1978) Irwin Yablans [Compass]. **Color-85min.** Kim Milford, Cheryl Smith **3***

LASSIE COME HOME (1943) M-G-M. **Color-88min.** Roddy McDowall, Donald Crisp.. **4***

LASSIE'S GREAT ADVENTURE (1963) 20th Century-Fox. **Color-103min.** *(Telefeature).* Lassie, June Lockhart, Jon Provost .... (4)
Original title: JOURNEY, THE

LAST ADVENTURE, THE (1967) Universal. **Color-102min.** *(Italian-French)*. Alain Delon, Lino Ventura, Joanna Shimkus .... (3)
Original Italian title: TRE AVVENTURIERI, I *(The Three Adventurers)*
Original French title: AVENTURIERS, LES *(The Adventurers)*

LAST AMERICAN HERO, THE (1973) 20th Century-Fox. **Color-95min.** Jeff Bridges, Valerine Perrine 4*
Alternate title: I GOT A NAME
TV title: HARD DRIVER

LAST ANGRY MAN, THE (1959) Columbia. **B&W-100min.** Paul Muni, David Wayne 5*

LAST ANGRY MAN, THE (1974) CPT (TV). **Color-100min.** *(Made for TV).* Pat Hingle, Lynn Carlin ....

LAST BANDIT, THE (1949) Republic. **Color-80min.** William Elliott, Adran Booth 3½*

LAST BLITZKRIEG, THE (1959) Columbia. **B&W-84min.** Van Johnson, Kerwin Mathews .... (3)

LAST BRIDGE, THE (1953) Union Films. **B&W-95min.** *(Austrian).* Maria Schell, Carl Moehner .... (5)
Original title: LETZTE BRUCKE, DIE

LAST CASTLE, THE (1976) *see* ECHOES OF A SUMMER

LAST CHALLENGE, THE (1967) M-G-M. **Color-96min.** Glenn Ford, Angie Dickinson, Chad Everett .... (3)
Alternate title: PISTOLERO OF RED RIVER, THE

LAST CHANCE, THE (1945) M-G-M. **B&W-105min.** *(Swiss).* E. G. Morrison, John Hoy .... (5)

LAST CHAPTER, THE (1966) Ben-Lar Productions. **B&W-90min.** *(Documentary). Director:* Benjamin Rothman .... (5)

LAST CHARGE, THE (1964) **Color-88min.** *(Italian).* Tony Russell, Haya Harareet .... (1)

LAST CHILD, THE (1971) Worldvision. **Color-73min.** *(Made for TV).* Van Heflin, Michael Cole, Janet Margolin 4½*

LAST COMMAND, THE (1928) Paramount. **B&W-91min.** *(Silent).* Emil Jannings, Evelyn Brent, William Powell .... (4)

LAST COMMAND, THE (1955) Republic. **Color-110min.** Sterling Hayden, Anna Maria Alberghetti 4½*

LAST CRY FOR HELP, A (1979) ABC-TV. **Color-98min.** *(Made for TV).* Linda Purl, Shirley Jones, Tony Lo Bianco ....

LAST DAYS OF DOLWYN, THE (1949) *see* WOMAN OF DOLWYN

LAST DAYS OF MAN ON EARTH, THE (1975) New World. **Color-81min.** *(British).* Jon Finch, Jenny Runacre, Sterling Hayden 2½*
Original title: FINAL PROGRAMME, THE

LAST DAYS OF POMPEII, THE (1935) RKO. **B&W-96min.** Preston Foster, Alan Hale 4½*

LAST DAYS OF POMPEII, THE (1959) RKO. **Color-105min.** *(Italian-Spanish).* Steve Reeves, Christine Kaufmann .... (3)
Original Italian title: ULTIMI GIORNI DI POMPEII

LAST DETAIL, THE (1973) Columbia. **Color-103min.** Jack Nicholson, Otis Young, Randy Quaid 5½*

LAST DINOSAUR, THE (1977) ABC-TV. **Color-100min.** *(U.S.-Japanese).* Richard Boone, Joan Van Ark, Luther Rackley, Steven Keats 3*

LAST EMBRACE (1979) United Artists. **Color-103min.** Roy Scheider, John Glover, Janet Margolin 4½*

LAST ESCAPE, THE (1970) United Artists. **Color-90min.** Stuart Whitman, John Collin .... (3)

LAST FLIGHT, THE (1931) First National [W.B.]. **B&W-77min.** Richard Barthelmess, Johnny Mack Brown, David Manners .... (4)

LAST FOUR DAYS, THE (1977) Group 1. **Color-98min.** *(Italian).* Rod Steiger, Lisa Gastoni, Henry Fonda, Franco Nero ....

LAST FRONTIER, THE (1956) Columbia. **Color-98min.** Victor Mature, Guy Madison 3*
Alternate title: SAVAGE WILDERNESS

LAST GANGSTER, THE (1937) M-G-M. **B&W-81min.** Edward G. Robinson, James Stewart 4*

LAST GANGSTER, THE (1944) *see* ROGER TOUHY, GANGSTER

LAST GENTLEMAN, THE (1934) Fox Film Co. [20th]. **B&W-80min.** George Arliss, Edna May Oliver .... (5)

LAST GLORY OF TROY, THE (1961) *see* AVENGER, THE

LAST GRENADE, THE (1970) Cinerama Releasing. **Color-94min.** *(British).* Stanley Baker, Alex Cord 3*

LAST GUN, THE (1964) Parkside Prods. **Color-88min.** *(Spanish).* Cameron Mitchell .... (2)

LAST GUNFIGHT, THE (1964) Commonwealth United TV. **Color-95min.** *(Japanese).* Toshiro Mifune, Yohko Tsukasa .... (5)
Original title: ANKOKUGAI NO TAIKETSU

LAST HARD MEN, THE (1976) 20th Century-Fox. **Color-103min.** Charlton Heston, James Coburn 4½*

LAST HOLIDAY (1950) Stratford Pictures. **B&W-88min.** *(British).* Alec Guinness, Beatrice Campbell 5*

LAST HOUSE ON THE LEFT, THE (1972) Hallmark. **Color-83min.** David Hess, Lucy Grantham, Sandra Cassel 1*

LAST HUNDRED DAYS OF NAPOLEON, THE (1971) *see* WATERLOO

LAST HUNT, THE (1956) M-G-M. **Color-108min.** Robert Taylor, Stewart Granger 3*

LAST HURRAH, THE (1958) Columbia. **B&W-121min.** Spencer Tracy, Jeffrey Hunter 5*

LAST HURRAH, THE (1978) CPT (TV). **Color-100min.** *(Made for TV).* Carroll O'Connor, Mariette Hartley 4½*

LAST LAUGH, THE (1924) Universal. **B&W-71min.** *(German, Silent).* Emil Jannings, Mary Delschaft 1*
Original title: LETZE MANN, DER *(The Last Man)*

LAST MAN ON EARTH, THE (1964) American-International. **B&W-86min.** *(Italian-U.S.).* Vincent Price, Franca Bettoja, Giacomo Rossi-Stuart .... (3)
Original Italian title: ULTIMO UOMO DELLA TERRA, L'

LAST MAN TO HANG, THE (1956) Columbia. **B&W-75min.** *(British).* Tom Conway, Eunice Gayson .... (3)

LAST MILE, THE (1932) World Wide (Sono Art). **B&W-74min.** Howard Phillips, Preston Foster 3*

LAST MILE, THE (1959) United Artists. **B&W-81min.** Mickey Rooney, Clifford David .... (4)

LAST MOVIE, THE (1971) Universal. **Color-108min.** Dennis Hopper, Stella Garcia .... (3)

LAST MUSKETEER, THE (1952) Republic. **B&W-67min.** Rex Allen, Mary Ellen Kay .... (4)

LAST MUSKETEER, THE (1954) **Color-95min.** *(French).* Georges Marchal, Dawn Addams .... (3)
Alternate title: COUNT OF BRAGELONNE, THE

LAST OF MRS. CHEYNEY, THE (1929) M-G-M. **B&W-94min.** Norma Shearer, Basil Rathbone .... (4)

LAST OF MRS. CHEYNEY, THE (1937) M-G-M. **B&W-98min.** Joan Crawford, William Powell .... (4)

LAST OF SHEILA, THE (1973) Warner Bros. **Color-120min.** James Coburn, Richard Benjamin, James Mason 6*

LAST OF THE BADMEN (1957) Allied Artists. **Color-79min.** George Montgomery, James Best 3*

LAST OF THE BELLES, THE (1974) *see* F. SCOTT FITZGERALD AND THE LAST OF THE BELLES

LAST OF THE BUCCANEERS (1950) Columbia. **Color-79min.** Paul Henreid, Jack Oakie, Karin Booth 3½*

LAST OF THE COMANCHES (1953) Columbia. **Color-85min.** Broderick Crawford, Barbara Hale, Lloyd Bridges 3*
British title: SABRE AND THE ARROW, THE

LAST OF THE COWBOYS, THE (1976) *see* GREAT SMOKEY ROADBLOCK, THE

LAST OF THE DESPERADOES (1955) Associated Film Dists. **B&W-71min.** James Craig, Jim Davis .... (3)

LAST OF THE FAST GUNS (1958) Universal. **Color-82min.** Jock Mahoney, Gilbert Roland 4*

LAST OF THE MOBILE HOTSHOTS, THE (1970) Warner Bros. **Color-108min.** James Coburn, Lynn Redgrave, Robert Hooks .... (3)

LAST OF THE MOHICANS, THE (1936) United Artists. **B&W-91min.** Randolph Scott, Binnie Barnes 4½*

LAST OF THE PAGANS (1935) M-G-M. **B&W-84min.** Ray Mala, Lotus Long .... (4)

LAST OF THE RED HOT LOVERS (1972) Paramount. **Color-98min.** Alan Arkin, Sally Kellerman 4*

LAST OF THE REDMEN (1947) Columbia. **Color-77min.** Jon Hall, Michael O'Shea, Evelyn Ankers .... (4)
British title: LAST OF THE REDSKINS

LAST OF THE SECRET AGENTS?, THE (1966) Paramount. **Color-92min.** Marty Allen, Steve Rossi 3½*

LAST OF THE SKI BUMS, THE (1969) U-M Prods. **Color-86min.** *(Documentary). Director:* Dick Barrymore 4½*

LAST OF THE VIKINGS (1960) Medallion. **Color-102min.** *(Italian-French).* Cameron Mitchell, Edmund Purdom, Isabelle Corey .... (3)
Original Italian title: ULTIMO DE VICHINGHI, L'
French title: DERNIER DES VIKINGS, LE

LAST OUTLAW, THE (1936) RKO. **B&W-62min.** Harry Carey, Hoot Gibson 4*

LAST OUTPOST, THE (1935) Paramount. **B&W-70min.** Cary Grant, Claude Rains 4*

LAST OUTPOST, THE (1951) Paramount. **Color-88min.** Ronald Reagan, Rhonda Fleming .... (4)

LAST PAGE, THE (1952) *see* MAN BAIT

LAST PARADISE, THE (1958) United Artists. **Color-83min.** *(Italian-French, Travelog). Director:* Folco Quilici .... (4)

LAST PICTURE SHOW, THE (1971) Columbia. **B&W-118min.** Timothy Bottoms, Jeff Bridges 6½*

LAST POSSE, THE (1953) Columbia. **B&W-73min.** Broderick Crawford, John Derek .... (4)

LAST REBEL, THE (1956) Sterling World Distributors. **Color-83min.** *(Mexican).* Carlos Thompson, Ariadne Welter, Rodolfo Acosta .... (3)
Original title: ULTIMO REBELDE, EL

LAST REBEL, THE (1971) Columbia. **Color-90min.** Joe Namath, Jack Elam .... (2)

LAST REMAKE OF BEAU GESTE, THE (1977) Universal. **Color-84min.** Marty Feldman, Michael York 4½*

LAST RIDE, THE (1944) Warner Bros. **B&W-56min.** Richard Travis, Eleanor Parker .... (3)

LAST RIDE TO SANTA CRUZ, THE (1964) Casino Films. **Color-99min.** *(German).* Edmund Purdom, Marianne Koch, Maria Adorf, Klaus Kinski .... (3)
Original title: LETZTE RITT NACH SANTE CRUZ, DER

LAST RUN, THE (1971) M-G-M. **Color-100min.** George C. Scott, Tony Musante 4*

LAST SAFARI, THE (1967) Paramount. **Color-115min.** *(British).* Kaz Garas, Stewart Granger, Gabriella Licudi .... (4)

LAST SHOT YOU HEAR, THE (1969) 20th Century-Fox. **B&W-91min.** *(British).* Hugh Marlowe, Zena Walker, Patricia Haines, William Dysart .... (3)

LAST STAGECOACH WEST (1957) Republic. **B&W-67min.** Jim Davis, Mary Castle .... (3)

LAST SUMMER (1969) Allied Artists. **Color-97min.** Barbara Hershey, Richard Thomas, Bruce Davison 5½*

LAST SUNSET, THE (1961) Universal. **Color-112min.** Rock Hudson, Kirk Douglas .... (4)

LAST SURVIVOR, THE (1972) American-International. **Color-83min.** *(Italian-Thailand).* Massimo Foschi, Me-Me Lai, Ivan Rassimov ....
Original Italian title: PAESE DEL SESSO SELVAGGIO, IL *(The Country of Wild Sex)*

LAST TANGO IN PARIS (1972) United Artists. **Color-130min.** *(Italian-French, English language).* Marlon Brando, Maria Schneider 3*
Original Italian title: ULTIMO TANGO A PARIGI, L'

THE LAST PICTURE SHOW (1971). Sheltered virgin Cybill Shepherd has some of her idealized notions about romance deflated as she's counseled by her cynical mother, Ellen Burstyn, about the realities of life in the dying Texas oil town.

LAST TEN DAYS, THE (1955) Columbia. **B&W-108min.** *(German).* Albin Skoda, Lotto Tobisch, Oskar Werner .... (5)
Original title: LETZTE AKT, DER *(The Last Act)*
Alternate title: LAST TEN DAYS OF ADOLF HITLER, THE

LAST TIME I SAW ARCHIE, THE (1961) United Artists. **B&W-98min.** Robert Mitchum, Jack Webb 4*

LAST TIME I SAW PARIS, THE (1954) M-G-M. **Color-116min.** Elizabeth Taylor, Van Johnson 4*

LAST TRAIN FROM BOMBAY (1952) Columbia. **B&W-72min.** Jon Hall, Christine Larson .... (3)

LAST TRAIN FROM GUN HILL, THE (1959) Paramount. **Color-94min.** Kirk Douglas, Anthony Quinn 5*

LAST TRAIN FROM MADRID, THE (1937) Paramount. **B&W-77min.** Dorothy Lamour, Lew Ayres, Gilbert Roland .... (3)

LAST TYCOON, THE (1976) Paramount. **Color-122min.** Robert DeNiro, Ingrid Boulting 3½*

LAST VALLEY, THE (1971) Cinerama Releasing. **Color-126min.** *(British).* Michael Caine, Omar Sharif .... (3)

LAST VOYAGE, THE (1960) M-G-M. **Color-91min.** Robert Stack, Dorothy Malone 5½*

LAST WAGON, THE (1956) 20th Century-Fox. **Color-99min.** Richard Widmark, Felicia Farr 4*

LAST WALTZ, THE (1978) United Artists. **Color-115min.** *(Music Film). Director:* Martin Scorsese 3½*

LAST WARNING, THE (1939) Universal. **B&W-63min.** Frances Robinson, Preston Foster .... (5)

LAST WARRIOR, THE (1970) *see* FLAP

LAST WAVE, THE (1977) World Northal. **Color-105min.** *(Australian).* Richard Chamberlain, (David) Gulpilil 2*

LAST WOMAN ON EARTH, THE (1960) Filmgroup. **Color-71min.** Antony Carbone, Betsy Jones-Morland 2*

LAST YEAR AT MARIENBAD (1961) Astor. **B&W-93min.** *(French).* Delphine Seyrig, Giorgio Albertazzi, Sacha Pitoeff 3½*
Original title: ANNEE DERNIERE A MARIENBAD, L'

LATE AUTUMN (1960) New Yorker Films. **Color-127min.** *(Japanese).* Setsuko Hara, Yoko Tsukasu ....
Original title: AKIBI YORI

LATE EDWINA BLACK, THE (1951) *see* OBSESSED

LATE GEORGE APLEY, THE (1947) 20th Century-Fox. **B&W-98min.** Ronald Colman, Peggy Cummins 6*

LATE GREAT PLANET EARTH, THE (1978) Pacific International Enterprises. **Color-90min.** *(Documentary). Director:* Robert Amran ....

LATE LIZ, THE (1971) Dick Ross & Associates. **Color-120min.** Anne Baxter, Steve Forrest .... (4)

LATE SHOW, THE (1977) Warner Bros. **Color-94min.** Art Carney, Lily Tomlin 4*

LATIN LOVERS (1953) M-G-M. **Color-104min.** Lana Turner, Ricardo Montalban .... (4)

LATIN LOVERS (1961) Gala *(Brit.).* **B&W-80min.** *(Italian-French).* Maria di Giuseppe, Mariella Zanetti, José Greci .... (3)
Original Italian title: ITALIANE E L'AMORE, LE *(Italian Women and Love)*

LATITUDE ZERO (1970) National General. **Color-99min.** *(Japanese-U.S.).* Joseph Cotten, Cesar Romero, Richard Jaeckel .... (2)
Original Japanese title: IDO ZERO DAISAKUSEN

LAUGH YOUR BLUES AWAY (1942) Columbia. **B&W-70min.** Jinx Falkenburg, Douglass Drake, Bert Gordon .... (3)

LAUGHING ANNE (1953) Republic. **Color-90min.** *(British).* Margaret Lockwood, Wendell Corey .... (3)

LAUGHING LADY, THE (1946) Four Continents. **Color-93min.** *(British).* Ann Ziegler, Webster Booth ....

LAUGHING POLICEMAN, THE (1973) 20th Century-Fox. **Color-111min.** Walter Matthau, Bruce Dern 3*
British title: INVESTIGATION OF MURDER, AN

LAUGHING WOMAN, THE (1969) Audubon. **Color-90min.** *(Italian).* Philippe Leroy, Dagmar Lassander .... (2)
Original title: FEMINA RIDENS

LAUGHTER (1930) Paramount. **B&W-81min.** Nancy Carroll, Fredric March .... (4)

LAUGHTER IN PARADISE (1951) Stratford Pictures. **B&W-93min.** *(British).* Alastair Sim, Fay Compton .... (5)

LAUGHTER IN THE DARK (1969) Lopert [U.A.]. **Color-101min.** *(British-French).* Nicol Williamson, Anna Karina, Jean-Claude Drouot .... (4)

LAURA (1944) 20th Century-Fox. **B&W-88min.** Dana Andrews, Gene Tierney, Clifton Webb 5½*

LAUREL AND HARDY'S LAUGHING 20'S (1965) M-G-M. B&W-90min. *(Compilation). Producer:* Robert Youngson.............................(5)

LAVENDER HILL MOB, THE (1951) Universal. B&W-78min. *(British).* Alec Guinness, Stanley Holloway 6½*

LAW, THE (1958) *see* WHERE THE HOT WIND BLOWS

LAW, THE (1974) MCA-TV. Color-120min. *(Made for TV).* Judd Hirsch, John Beck, Bonnie Franklin 5*

LAW AND DISORDER (1940) RKO. B&W-74min. *(British).* Barry K. Barnes, Diana Churchill, Alastair Sim ....(4)

LAW AND DISORDER (1958) Continental [Walter Reade]. B&W-76min. *(British).* Michael Redgrave, Robert Morley..............(4)

LAW AND DISORDER (1974) Columbia. Color-103min. Carroll O'Connor, Ernest Borgnine 5*

LAW AND JAKE WADE, THE (1958) M-G-M. Color-86min. Robert Taylor, Richard Widmark ....(5)

LAW AND ORDER (1932) Universal. B&W-70min. Walter Huston, Harry Carey.................................(5)

LAW AND ORDER (1953) Universal. Color-80min. Ronald Reagan, Dorothy Malone ....(4)

LAW AND ORDER (1976) Paramount. Color-150min. *(Made for TV).* Darren McGavin, Keir Dullea, Suzanne Pleshette, James Olson 5*

LAW AND THE LADY, THE (1951) M-G-M. B&W-105min. Greer Garson, Michael Wilding ....(4)

LAW IS THE LAW, THE (1957) Continental [Walter Reade]. B&W-103min. *(French-Italian).* Fernandel, Toto ....(4)
Original French title: LOI C'EST LA LOI, LA
Original Italian title: LEGGE E LEGGE, LA

LAW OF THE LAWLESS (1964) Paramount. Color-87min. Dale Robertson, Yvonne De Carlo, John Agar, Bruce Cabot 3*

LAW OF THE SEA (1932) Monogram. B&W-64min. William Farnum, Rex Bell, Sally Blane 3*

LAW OF THE STREETS (1956) Columbia. B&W-100min. *(French).* Silvana Pampanini, Raymond Pellegrin ....(3)

LAW OF THE TROPICS (1941) Warner Bros. B&W-76min. Jeffrey Lynn, Constance Bennett ....(3)

LAW OF THE UNDERWORLD (1938) RKO. B&W-61min. Chester Morris, Anne Shirley ....(3)

LAW VS. BILLY THE KID, THE (1954) Columbia. Color-73min. Scott Brady, Betta St. John ....(3)

LAW WEST OF TOMBSTONE, THE (1938) RKO. B&W-73min. Tim Holt, Harry Carey.................................(5)

LAWLESS, THE (1950) Paramount. B&W-83min. Macdonald Carey, Gail Russell ....(5)
British title: DIVIDING LINE, THE

LAWLESS BREED, THE (1953) Universal. Color-83min. Rock Hudson, Julia Adams................................3*

LAWLESS EIGHTIES, THE (1957) Republic. B&W-70min. Buster Crabbe, John Smith ....(3)

LAWLESS RIDER, THE (1954) United Artists. B&W-62min. Johnny Carpenter, Frankie Darro 2*

LAWLESS STREET, A (1955) Columbia. B&W-78min. Randolph Scott, Angela Lansbury ....(4)

LAWMAN (1971) United Artists. Color-98min. Burt Lancaster, Robert Ryan 3*

LAWRENCE OF ARABIA (1962) Columbia. Color-221min. *(British).* Peter O'Toole, Alec Guinness, Omar Sharif 6*

LAWYER, THE (1970) Paramount. Color-120min. Barry Newman, Robert Colbert 5*

LAWYER MAN (1932) Warner Bros. B&W-72min. William Powell, Joan Blondell ....(4)

LAXDALE HALL (1953) *see* SCOTCH ON THE ROCKS

LAY THAT RIFLE DOWN (1955) Republic. B&W-71min. Judy Canova, Robert Lowery ....(3)

LE MANS (1971) Nat'l General (for Cinema Center). Color-106min. Steve McQueen, Siegfried Rauch 3*

LEADBELLY (1976) Paramount. Color-126min. Roger E. Mosley, Art Evans...................................5*

LEAGUE OF GENTLEMEN, THE (1960) Kingsley International. B&W-114min. *(British).* Jack Hawkins, Nigel Patrick 4½*

LEARNING TREE, THE (1969) Warner Bros. Color-107min. Kyle Johnson, Alex Clarke 3*

LEASE OF LIFE (1954) Italian Films Export. Color-94min. *(British).* Robert Donat, Kay Walsh 5*

LEATHER BOYS, THE (1964) Allied Artists. B&W-108min. *(British).* Rita Tushingham, Dudley Sutton ....(5)

LEATHER GLOVES (1948) Columbia. B&W-75min. Cameron Mitchell, Jane Nigh ....(3)
British title: LOSER TAKE ALL

LEATHER SAINT, THE (1956) Paramount. B&W-86min. John Derek, Paul Douglas 3½*

LEATHERNECKS HAVE LANDED, THE (1936) Republic. B&W-67min. Lew Ayres, Isabel Jewell ....(3)
British title: MARINES HAVE LANDED, THE

LEAVE HER TO HEAVEN (1945) 20th Century-Fox. Color-111min. Gene Tierney, Cornel Wilde..................4*

LEAVE IT TO BLONDIE (1945) Columbia. B&W-75min. Arthur Lake, Penny Singleton ....(4)

LEAVE IT TO HENRY (1949) Monogram [Allied Artists]. B&W-57min. Raymond Walburn, Walter Catlett ....(3)

LEBANESE MISSION, THE (1956) B&W-90min. *(French-Italian).* Jean-Claude Fascal, Jean Servais...............(4)
Original French title: CHATELAINE DU LIBAN, LA

LEDA (1959) Times Film Corp. Color-110min. *(French-Italian).* Antonella Lualdi, Madeleine Robinson, Jean-Paul Belmondo, André Jocelyn......(4)
Original French title: A DOUBLE TOUR *(Double Twist)*
Italian title: A DOPPIA MANDATA
Alternate title: WEB OF PASSION

LEECH WOMAN, THE (1960) Universal. B&W-77min. Coleen Gray, Grant Williams.........................(2)

LEFT HAND OF GOD, THE (1955) 20th Century-Fox. Color-87min. Humphrey Bogart, Gene Tierney 4*

LEFT-HANDED GUN, THE (1958) Warner Bros. B&W-102min. Paul Newman, Lita Milan 4½*

LEFT, RIGHT AND CENTRE (1959) BCG Films. B&W-95min. *(British).* Ian Carmichael, Alastair Sim ....(4)

LEGACY (1976) Kino International. Color-90min. George McDaniel, Joan Hotchkis ....

LEGACY, THE (1979) Universal. Color- min. Katharine Ross, Sam Elliott, Roger Daltry ....

LEGACY OF SATAN (1973) Damiano. Color-68min. Lisa Cristian, John Francis, Paul Barry ....(3)

LEGEND OF BIG JOHN, THE (1973) *see* ELECTRA GLIDE IN BLUE

LEGEND OF BLACK CHARLEY, THE (1972) *see* LEGEND OF NIGGER CHARLEY, THE

LEGEND OF BLOOD CASTLE (1974) Film Ventures International. Color-85min. *(Foreign).* Ewa Aulin..................(3)
Alternate title: FEMALE BUTCHER
Alternate title: BLOOD CEREMONY

LEGEND OF BOGGY CREEK, THE (1972) Howco International. Color-90min. *(Documentary). Director:* Charles Pierce 3*

LEGEND OF CUSTER, THE (1968) 20th Century-Fox. Color-94min. *(Telefeature).* Wayne Maunder, Slim Pickens, Michael Danter ....(3)

LEGEND OF FRENCHIE KING, THE (1971) K-Tel. Color-95min. *(French-Spanish-Italian-British).* Brigitte Bardot, Claudia Cardinale, Michael J. Pollard 4*
Original title: PÉTROLEUSES, LES *(The Oil Girls)*

LEGEND OF HELL HOUSE, THE (1972) 20th Century-Fox. Color-94min. *(British-U.S.).* Pamela Franklin, Roddy McDowall 3*

LEGEND OF HILLBILLY JOHN, THE (1972) Jack H. Harris. Color-86min. Hedge Capers, Severn Darden, Sharon Henesy ....(3)
Original title: WHO FEARS THE DEVIL?

LEGEND OF LIZZIE BORDEN, THE (1975) Paramount. Color-100min. *(Made for TV).* Elizabeth Montgomery, Fritz Weaver............5*

LEGEND OF LOBO, THE (1962) Buena Vista. Color-67min. Rex Allen ..4*

LEGEND OF LYLAH CLARE, THE (1968) M-G-M. Color-130min. Kim Novak, Peter Finch, Ernest Borgnine.................4*

LEGEND OF MUSASHI, THE (1954) *see* SAMURAI

LEGEND OF NIGGER CHARLEY, THE (1972) Paramount. Color-99min. Fred Williamson, D'Urville Martin ....(3)
Publicity title: LEGEND OF BLACK CHARLEY, THE

LEGEND OF PRAGUE, THE (1936) *see* GOLEM, THE

LEGEND OF SLEEPY HOLLOW, THE (1949) *see* ADVENTURES OF ICHABOD AND MR. TOAD

LEGEND OF SPIDER FOREST (1974) New Line Cinema. Color-88min. *(British).* Simon Brent, Neda Arneric..................(3)
Original title: VENOM

LEGEND OF THE FOOL KILLER, THE (1965) *see* FOOL KILLER, THE

LEGEND OF THE LAWMAN (1975) *see* PART 2 WALKING TALL

SEND THIS CARD ⟶
FOR FREE INFORMATION

(Or if the card is missing, send us your name and address on a postcard or in a letter to the address below.)

If you didn't buy the book directly from Hollywood Film Archive, we won't be able to notify you by mail about future editions of this and other quality film reference books we offer in the future unless you send us your name and address.

You can even use the "comments" portion of the card to tell us what your particular interest in movies is — we may already have something that will help you.

Should you send us your home or business address? If you use the book regularly in your work, then you probably should give us your company name and address, and tell us what your position is; if you inform us as to the types of information you use most (or need most but can't find in the book), that will enable us (as it has in the past) to provide additional information users need. But if the book is for your personal use at home, then please send us your home address; the book was originally intended for use in the entertainment industry, but we hope that more and more people who just enjoy watching movies will use it in the future, so if you're a film buff, please tell us what you'd like to see most in the way of additional movie reference information — if we can't give it to you in future editions of this book, maybe we can supply it in another type of book.

And if you want to receive notices about our publications and other offerings, it's important for you to notify us when you change addresses — that's why we have provided a place on the tear-out card for change of address. If you're already on Hollywood Film Archive's mailing list (which everyone who buys a book directly from HFA is automatically put on), then there's no need to send the card unless you change addresses; we can then delete you old address from our file, and make sure that you receive announcements at your new address.

Our address: Hollywood Film Archive
8344 Melrose Avenue
Hollywood, California 90069

THIS IS
ONLY THE BEGINNING...

...of an amazing assortment of film reference publications which will eventually follow from *The Film Buff's Checklist* and the original *Film Buff's Bible*.

For many years, there has been the growing need for a popular, comprehensive reference book giving movie casts, credits, plots, literary sources, etc., and covering films of all types throughout movie history. Many attempts to produce books of this nature have resulted in works with various drawbacks — some contained only a few dozen or a few hundred films, some covered only limited time periods (like a year or ten years), some were confined to particular nationalities, genres or personalities, and those which dealt with large numbers of films had extremely limited information for each one; occasionally there comes a voluminous tome approaching the degree of thoroughness needed to make a really useful movie reference, but always the price puts it beyond the budget of the average person.

So film buffs still wait for a book that will give them all the basic information about the many thousands of popular movies available for viewing theatrically and on TV. Soon such a book will be published, because we're working on it right now, and when it's ready, we'll let everyone on our mailing list know about it. Some people worry that it won't be possible for us to offer it for less than several hundred dollars, but with any luck, the cost will be less than a day's take-home pay to the average film buff.

Even that will only be the start of a series of books of film information that will logically stem from the information in that basic volume. The world of computers is making it much easier and economical to select and sort information in ways that could only be dreamed about a decade or so ago. Naturally, the first step is a cross-reference book of acting and production credits. Then a listing of films by the companies which made and distributed them. And a book of films categorized by the genres into which they fall. The possibilities seem almost endless. Any additional suggestions, dear readers?

LEGEND OF THE LOST (1957) United Artists. **Color-109min.** John Wayne, Sophia Loren 4*

LEGEND OF TOM DOOLEY, THE (1959) Columbia. **B&W-79min.** Michael Landon, Jo Morrow .... (3)

LEGEND OF VALENTINO, THE (1975) MPC (TV). **Color-100min.** *(Made for TV).* Franco Nero, Suzanne Pleshette, Yvette Mimieux, Milton Berle 5*

LEGENDARY CHAMPIONS, THE (1968) Turn of the Century Fights. **B&W-77min.** *(Documentary). Director:* Harry Chapin .... (5)

LEGENDARY CURSE OF LEMORA, THE (1974) Media Cinema. **Color-90min.** William Witton, Lesley Glib, Cheryl Smith .... (3)
TV title: LEMORA, THE LADY DRACULA

LEGION OF THE DOOMED (1958) Allied Artists. **B&W-75min.** Bill Williams, Dawn Richard .... (2)

LEGION'S LAST PATROL, THE (1962) *see* COMMANDO

LEGIONS OF THE NILE (1959) 20th Century-Fox. **Color-91min.** *(Italian-French-Spanish).* Linda Cristal, Ettore Manni, Georges Marchal .... (1)
Original Italian title: LEGIONI DI CLEOPATRA, LE *(The Legions of Cleopatra)*

LEMON DROP KID, THE (1951) Paramount. **B&W-91min.** Bob Hope, Marilyn Maxwell 4*

LEMONADE JOE (1964) Allied Artists. **B&W-90min.** *(Czech).* Karel Fiala, Milos Kopecky, Olga Schoberova .... (5)
Original title: LIMONADOVY JOE
Alternate Czech title: KONSKA OPERA

LENNY (1974) United Artists. **B&W-111min.** Dustin Hoffman, Valerie Perrine 6*

LENNY BRUCE PERFORMANCE FILM (1974) Grove Press. **B&W-65min.** *(Documentary). Director:* John Magnuson .... (4)

LENNY BRUCE WITHOUT TEARS (1972) Fred Baker Films. **B&W-90min.** *(Documentary). Director:* Fred Baker .... (4)

LEO THE LAST (1970) United Artists. **Color-103min.** *(British).* Marcello Mastroianni, Billie Whitelaw .... (4)

LEONARDO DA VINCI (1952) Pictura Films. **Color-70min.** *(Italian, Documentary). Director:* Luciano Emmer .... (5)

LEOPARD, THE (1963) 20th Century-Fox. **Color-165min.** *(Italian-French).* Burt Lancaster, Alain Delon 3*
Original Italian title: GATTOPARDO, IL
French title: GUÉPARD, LE

LEOPARD MAN, THE (1943) RKO. **B&W-66min.** Dennis O'Keefe, Jean Brooks 4*

LEPKE (1975) Warner Bros. **Color-109min.** Tony Curtis, Anjanette Comer 4*

LES GAULOISES BLEUES (1968) *see* GAULOISES BLEUES, LES

LES GIRLS (1957) M-G-M. **Color-114min.** Gene Kelly, Mitzi Gaynor 4*

LES MISÉRABLES (1934) Franco-American. **B&W-162min.** *(French).* Harry Baur, Charles Vanel .... (5)

LES MISÉRABLES (1935) United Artists. **B&W-108min.** Fredric March, Charles Laughton 5½*

LES MISÉRABLES (1947) Lux Film America. **B&W-122min.** *(Italian).* Gino Cervi, John Hinrich .... (4)

LES MISÉRABLES (1952) 20th Century-Fox. **B&W-104min.** Michael Rennie, Robert Newton 5*

LES MISÉRABLES (1957) Continental [Walter Reade]. **Color-210min.** *(French-W. German).* Jean Gabin, Bernard Blier .... (5)

LES MISÉRABLES (1978) CBS-TV. **Color-140min.** *(Made for TV).* Richard Jordan, Anthony Perkins 5*

LESSON IN LOVE, A (1953) Janus Films. **B&W-95min.** *(Swedish).* Eva Dahlbeck, Gunnar Bjornstrand 4*
Original title: LEKTION I KARLEK, EN

LET FREEDOM RING (1939) M-G-M. **B&W-100min.** Nelson Eddy, Virginia Bruce .... (4)

LET IT ALL HANG OUT (1971) Atco Gibralter. **Color-75min.** *(W. German-Italian).* Edwige Fenech, Willi Colombini, Rainer Basedow .... (3)
Original Italian title: UOMO DAL PENNELLO D'ORO, L' *(The Man With the Golden Brush)*

LET IT BE (1970) United Artists. **Color-80min.** *(British, Documentary). Director:* Michael Lindsay-Hogg .... (4)

LET JOY REIGN SUPREME . . . (1975) Specialty Films. **Color-120min.** *(French).* Philippe Noiret, Jean Rochefort .... (4)
Original title: QUE LA FETE COMMENCE . . .

LET JUSTICE BE DONE (1950) *see* JUSTICE IS DONE

LET NO MAN WRITE MY EPITAPH (1960) Columbia. **B&W-106min.** James Darren, Shelley Winters 2½*

LET THE GOOD TIMES ROLL (1973) Columbia. **Color-99min.** *(Music Film). Director:* Robert Abel 4½*

LET US LIVE (1939) Columbia. **B&W-68min.** Maureen O'Sullivan, Henry Fonda .... (4)

LET'S BE HAPPY (1957) Allied Artists. **Color-106min.** *(British).* Tony Martin, Vera-Ellen .... (3)

LET'S DANCE (1950) Paramount. **Color-112min.** Betty Hutton, Fred Astaire, Robert Young .... (4)

LET'S DO IT AGAIN (1953) Columbia. **Color-95min.** Jane Wyman, Ray Milland 4*

LET'S DO IT AGAIN (1975) Warner Bros. **Color-112min.** Sidney Poitier, Bill Cosby 5½*

LET'S FACE IT (1943) Paramount. **B&W-76min.** Bob Hope, Betty Hutton... (3)

LET'S GET MARRIED (1937) Columbia. **B&W-69min.** Ralph Bellamy, Ida Lupino .... (4)

LET'S GET TOUGH! (1942) Monogram [Allied Artists]. **B&W-62min.** The East Side Kids, Florence Rice .... (3)

LET'S GO NAVY (1951) Monogram [Allied Artists]. **B&W-68min.** The Bowery Boys, Allen Jenkins .... (3)

LET'S GO STEADY (1945) Columbia. **B&W-60min.** Mel Torme, Arnold Stang... (3)

LET'S HAVE FUN (1943) Columbia. **B&W-65min.** Margaret Lindsay, John Beal .... (3)

LET'S KILL UNCLE (1966) Universal. **Color-92min.** Nigel Green, Mary Badham... (3)

LET'S LIVE A LITTLE (1948) 20th Century-Fox. **B&W-85min.** Hedy Lamarr, Robert Cummings.................................... (4)

LET'S LIVE AGAIN (1948) 20th Century-Fox. **B&W-67min.** John Emery, Diana Douglas .... (3)

LET'S MAKE IT LEGAL (1951) 20th Century-Fox. **B&W-77min.** Claudette Colbert, Macdonald Carey............................ 4*

LET'S MAKE LOVE (1960) 20th Century-Fox. **Color-118min.** Marilyn Monroe, Yves Montand .... (5)

LET'S MAKE MUSIC (1941) RKO. **B&W-85min.** Jean Rogers, Bob Crosby .... (3)

LET'S DO IT AGAIN (1975). Amateur wheeler-dealers Bill Cosby and Sidney Poitier go up against underworld gamblers and get involved more deeply than they had reckoned in a fixed boxing match.

Films are rated on a 1 to 10 scale, 10 is highest. **Boldface** ratings followed by an asterisk (*) are for films actually seen and rated by the executive and senior editors. All other ratings are estimates. (See Notes on Entertainment Ratings in the front section.)

LET'S MAKE UP (1954) United Artists. **Color-94min.** *(British).* Anna Neagle, Errol Flynn .... (3)
Original title: LILACS IN THE SPRING

LET'S ROCK (1958) Columbia. **B&W-79min.** Julius LaRosa, Phyllis Newman ....(3)
British title: KEEP IT COOL

LET'S SCARE JESSICA TO DEATH (1971) Paramount. **Color-89min.** Zohra Lampert, Barton Heyman.....................2*

LET'S TALK ABOUT MEN (1965) Allied Artists. **Color-93min.** *(Italian).* Nino Manfredi, Luciana Paluzzi ....
Original title: QUESTA VOLTA PARLIAMO DI UOMINI

LET'S TALK ABOUT WOMEN (1964) Avco-Embassy. **B&W-108min.** *(Italian-French).* Vittorio Gassman, Maria Fiore .... (5)
Original Italian title: SE PERMETTE, PARLIAMO DI DONNE *(If you Permit, We'll Talk of Women)*
Alternate Italian title: PARLIAMO DI DONNE

LETTER, THE (1929) Paramount. **B&W-72min.** Jeanne Eagels, Herbert Marshall ....(4)

LETTER, THE (1940) Warner Bros. **B&W-97min.** Bette Davis, Herbert Marshall 5*

LETTER FOR EVIE, A (1945) M-G-M. **B&W-89min.** Marsha Hunt, John Carroll, Hume Cronyn ....(4)

LETTER FROM AN UNKNOWN WOMAN (1948) Universal. **B&W-90min.** Joan Fontaine, Louis Jourdan....................4*

LETTER FROM KOREA (1951) *see* YANK IN KOREA, A

LETTER OF INTRODUCTION (1938) Universal. **B&W-104min.** Andrea Leeds, Adolphe Menjou ....(4)

LETTER TO THREE HUSBANDS (1950) *see* THREE HUSBANDS

LETTER TO THREE WIVES, A (1949) 20th Century-Fox. **B&W-103min.** Jeanne Crain, Linda Darnell 5½*

LETTERS, THE (1973) Time-Life Films. **Color-74min.** *(Made for TV).* John Forsythe, Ida Lupino, Barbara Stanwyck 4*

LETTERS FROM MY WINDMILL (1954) Tohan. **B&W-114min.** *(French).* Henri Velbert, Daxley, Rellys.................... (5)
Original title: LETTRES DE MON MOULIN, LES

LETTERS FROM THREE LOVERS (1973) MPC (TV). **Color-75min.** *(Made for TV).* Barry Sullivan, June Allyson, Juliet Mills 4*

LETTO, IL (1954) *see* BED, THE

LIAISONS DANGEREUSES, LES (1959) Astor. **B&W-106min.** *(Fren.-Ital.).* Gérard Philipe, Jeanne Moreau ....(4)
Original Italian title: RELAZIONI PERICOLOSE
Publicity title: DANGEROUS LOVE AFFAIRS

LIANE, JUNGLE GODDESS (1956) Distributors Corp. of America. **Color-85min.** *(German).* Marion Michael, Hardy Kruger ....(2)
Original title: LIANE - DAS MAEDCHEN AUS DEM URWALD

LIBEL (1959) M-G-M. **B&W-100min.** *(British).* Dirk Bogarde, Olivia de Havilland....................5*

LIBELED LADY (1936) M-G-M. **B&W-98min.** Jean Harlow, William Powell, Myrna Loy, Spencer Tracy....................5*

LIBERATION OF L. B. JONES, THE (1970) Columbia. **Color-101min.** Lee J. Cobb, Roscoe Lee Brown 4*

LIBERTINE, THE (1968) Audubon. **Color-90min.** *(Italian).* Catherine Spaak, Jean-Louis Trintignant ....(3)
Original title: MATRIARCA, LA

LICENSE TO KILL (1964) Four Star. **B&W-95min.** *(French).* Eddie Constantine, Yvonne Monlaur....................(3)
Original title: NICK CARTER VA TOUT CASSER

LICENSED TO KILL (1965) *see* SECOND BEST SECRET AGENT IN THE WHOLE WIDE WORLD, THE

LICKERISH QUARTET, THE (1970) Audubon. **Color-90min.** *(U.S.-Italian-W. German).* Silvana Venturelli, Frank Wolff, Erika Remberg, Paolo Turco ....(3)

LIDO MYSTERY, THE (1942) *see* ENEMY AGENTS MEET ELLERY QUEEN

LIE DETECTOR, THE (1946) *see* TRUTH ABOUT MURDER, THE

LIES MY FATHER TOLD ME (1975) Columbia. **Color-103min.** *(Canadian).* Yossi Yadin, Jeffrey Lynas 6½*

LT. ROBIN CRUSOE, U.S.N. (1966) Buena Vista. **Color-110min.** Dick Van Dyke, Nancy Kwan, Akim Tamiroff ....(3)

LIEUTENANT SCHUSTER'S WIFE (1972) MCA-TV. **Color-73min.** *(Made for TV).* Lee Grant, Jack Warden, Don Galloway....................(4)

LIEUTENANT WORE SKIRTS, THE (1956) 20th Century-Fox. **Color-99min.** Tom Ewell, Sheree North....................(4)

LIFE AFTER DARK (1953) *see* GIRLS IN THE NIGHT

LIFE AND ASSASSINATION OF THE KINGFISH, THE (1977) NBC-TV. **Color-100min.** *(Made for TV).* Edward Asner, Nicholas Pryor, Diane Kagan ....

LIFE AND DEATH OF COLONEL BLIMP, THE (1943) Archers-General. **Color-163min.** *(British).* Roger Livesey, Anton Walbrook....................5½*
Alternate title: COLONEL BLIMP

LIFE AND LOVES OF DR. PAUL JOSEPH GOEBBELS, THE (1944) *see* ENEMY OF WOMEN

LIFE AND LOVES OF MOZART, THE (1956) Bakros International. **B&W-87min.** *(German).* Oskar Werner, Anni Gottlieb ....(4)
Original title: REICH MIR DIE HAND MEIN LEBEN *(Give Me Your Hand My Love)*

LIFE AND TIMES OF GRIZZLY ADAMS, THE (1974) Sunn Classic. **Color-93min.** Dan Haggerty, Lisa Jones.....................4*

LIFE AND TIMES OF JUDGE ROY BEAN, THE (1972) National General. **Color-120min.** Paul Newman, Jacqueline Bisset....................5*

LIFE AND TIMES OF XAVIER HOLLANDER, THE (1974) Mature Pictures. **Color-76min.** Samantha McClearn, Rick Cassidy ....(3)
Alternate title: LIFE AND TIMES OF A HAPPY HOOKER, THE

LIFE AT STAKE, A (1954) Gibraltar Motion Picture Distributors. **B&W-78min.** Angela Lansbury, Keith Andes ....(4)
Alternate title: KEY MAN

LIFE AT THE TOP (1965) Royal Films Int'l [Columbia]. **B&W-117min.** *(British).* Laurence Harvey, Jean Simmons 4*

LIFE BEGINS (1932) First National [W.B.]. **B&W-71min.** Loretta Young, Preston Foster ....(5)
British title: DAWN OF LIFE, THE

LIFE BEGINS AT COLLEGE (1937) *see* LIFE BEGINS IN COLLEGE

LIFE BEGINS AT EIGHT-THIRTY (1942) 20th Century-Fox. **B&W-85min.** Monty Woolley, Ida Lupino....................(5)
British title: LIGHT OF HEART, THE

LIFE BEGINS AT FORTY (1935) 20th Century-Fox. **B&W-85min.** Will Rogers, Rochelle Hudson....................(5)

LIFE BEGINS AT 17 (1958) Columbia. **B&W-75min.** Mark Damon, Dorothy Johnson....................(2)

LIFE BEGINS FOR ANDY HARDY (1941) M-G-M. **B&W-100min.** Mickey Rooney, Lewis Stone ....(4)

LIFE BEGINS IN COLLEGE (1937) 20th Century-Fox. **B&W-94min.** Joan Davis, Tony Martin, The Ritz Brothers ....(4)
TV title: LIFE BEGINS AT COLLEGE
British title: JOY PARADE, THE

LIFE FOR RUTH (1962) *see* WALK IN THE SHADOW

LIFE IN EMERGENCY WARD 10 (1958) Eros Films *(Brit.).* **B&W-86min.** *(British).* Michael Craig, Dorothy Allison ....(3)

LIFE IN THE BALANCE, A (1955) 20th Century-Fox. **B&W-74min.** Ricardo Montalban, Anne Bancroft ....(3)

LIFE LOVE DEATH (1969) Lopert [U.A.]. **Color-115min.** *(French).* Amidou, Carolino Collier ....(5)
Original title: VIE, L'AMOUR, LA MORT, LA

LIFE OF DONIZETTI (1951) Lupa Film. **B&W-97min.** *(Italian).* Amedeo Nazzari, Mariella Lotti ....(3)
Original title: VITA DI DONIZETTI, LA

LIFE OF EMILE ZOLA, THE (1937) Warner Bros. **B&W-116min.** Paul Muni, Joseph Schildkraut 6*

LIFE OF HER OWN, A (1950) M-G-M. **B&W-108min.** Ray Milland, Lana Turner, Tom Ewell ....(4)

LIFE OF JIMMY DOLAN, THE (1933) Warner Bros. **B&W-70min.** Douglas Fairbanks, Jr., Loretta Young....................(4)
British title: KID'S LAST FIGHT, THE

LIFE OF RILEY, THE (1949) Universal. **B&W-87min.** William Bendix, James Gleason ....(4)

LIFE OF VERGIE WINTERS, THE (1934) RKO. **B&W-82min.** Ann Harding, John Boles ....(4)

LIFE STUDY (1973) Nebbco. **Color-99min.** Bartholomew Miro, Jr., Erika Peterson, Ziska ....(3)

LIFE UPSIDE DOWN (1965) Commonwealth United. **B&W-93min.** *(French).* Charles Denner, Anna Gaylor ....(5)
Original title: VIE A L'ENVERS, LA
Festival title: INSIDE OUT

LIFE WITH BLONDIE (1946) Columbia. **B&W-64min.** Penny Singleton, Arthur Lake, Marc Lawrence ....(4)

LIFE WITH FATHER (1947) Warner Bros. **Color-118min.** William Powell, Irene Dunne 6*

LIFE WITH HENRY (1941) Paramount. **B&W-81min.** Jackie Cooper, Eddie Bracken....................(4)

LIFE WITH THE LYONS (1954) *see* FAMILY AFFAIR

LIFEBOAT (1944) 20th Century-Fox. B&W-96min. Tallulah Bankhead, William Bendix..5½*

LIFEGUARD (1976) Paramount. Color-96min. Sam Elliott, Kathleen Quinlan...6*

LIFT TO THE SCAFFOLD (1958) *see* FRANTIC

LIGHT ACROSS THE STREET, THE (1955) United Motion Pic. Org. (UMPO). B&W-99min. *(French).* Brigitte Bardot, Raymond Pellegrin (4)
Original title: LUMIERE D'EN FACE, LA
Alternate title: FEMALE AND THE FLESH

LIGHT AT THE EDGE OF THE WORLD (1971) National General. Color-122min. *(U.S.-Spanish-Liechtenstein).* Kirk Douglas, Yul Brynner......(3)

LIGHT FANTASTIC, THE (1951) *see* LOVE IS BETTER THAN EVER

LIGHT FANTASTIC (1963) Avco-Embassy. B&W-85min. Dolores McDougal, Barry Bartle..(3)

LIGHT FINGERS (1957) Canfield Productions. B&W-86min. *(British).* Ronald Culver, Eunice Gayson.............................(3)

LIGHT IN THE FOREST, THE (1958) Buena Vista. Color-93min. James MacArthur, Carol Lynley.....................................(5)

LIGHT IN THE PIAZZA (1962) M-G-M. Color-101min. *(British).* Olivia de Havilland, Rossano Brazzi.............................4½*

LIGHT OF HEART, THE (1942) *see* LIFE BEGINS AT EIGHT-THIRTY

LIGHT THAT FAILED, THE (1939) Paramount. B&W-97min. Ronald Colman, Walter Huston...3*

LIGHT TOUCH, THE (1951) M-G-M. B&W-110min. Stewart Granger, Pier Angeli, George Sanders.............................(4)

LIGHT TOUCH, THE (1955) *see* TOUCH AND GO

LIGHT UP THE SKY (1960) *see* SKYWATCH

LIGHTHOUSE KEEPER'S DAUGHTER, THE (1952) *see* GIRL IN THE BIKINI, THE

LIGHTNING BOLT (1966) Woolner Brothers. Color-96min. *(Italian-Spanish).* Anthony Eisley, Wandisa Leigh.............(1)
Original Italian title: OPERAZIONE GOLDMAN *(Operation Goldman)*
Original Spanish title: OPERACION GOLDMAN

LIGHTNING STRIKES TWICE (1951) Warner Bros. B&W-91min. Ruth Roman, Richard Todd..(4)

LIGHTNING SWORDS OF DEATH (1973) Columbia. Color-83min. *(Japanese).* Tomisaburo Wakayama, Go Kato, Yuko Hama...............(3)
Original title: KOZURE OHKAMI
Alternate title: SWORD OF VENGEANCE III
Translation title: BABY CART IN HELL

LIGHTS OF NEW YORK, THE (1928) Warner Bros. B&W-57min. Helene Costello, Cullen Landis..(4)

LIGHTS OUT (1951) *see* BRIGHT VICTORY

LIKE FATHER, LIKE SON (1957) *see* TAILOR'S MAID, THE

LIKE FATHER, LIKE SON (1961) *see* YOUNG SINNER, THE

LIKELY STORY, A (1947) RKO. B&W-88min. Barbara Hale, Bill Williams..(5)

LI'L ABNER (1940) RKO. B&W-78min. Granville Owen, Martha O'Driscoll...(3)
British title: TROUBLE CHASER

LI'L ABNER (1959) Paramount. Color-114min. Peter Palmer, Leslie Parrish..(5)

LILACS IN THE SPRING (1954) *see* LET'S MAKE UP

LILI (1953) M-G-M. Color-81min. Leslie Caron, Mel Ferrer..................5½*

LILIES OF THE FIELD (1963) United Artists. B&W-94min. Sidney Poitier, Lilia Skala..5½*

LILIOM (1933) Fox-Europa (France). B&W-120min. *(French).* Charles Boyer, Madeline Ozeray.....................................(4)

LILITH (1964) Columbia. B&W-114min. Warren Beatty, Jean Seberg..4½*

LILLI MARLENE (1950) RKO. B&W-75min. *(British).* Lisa Daniely, Hugh McDermott..(3)

LILLIAN RUSSELL (1940) 20th Century-Fox. B&W-127min. Alice Faye, Don Ameche, Henry Fonda...4*

LIMBO (1972) *see* WOMEN IN LIMBO

LIMBO LINE, THE (1968) Group W. Color-99min. *(British).* Craig Stevens, Kate O'Mara, Vladek Sheybal...................(3)

LIMEHOUSE BLUES (1934) Paramount. B&W-65min. George Raft, Jean Parker..(3)
Alternate title: EAST END CHANT

LIMELIGHT (1952) United Artists. B&W-143min. Charles Chaplin, Claire Bloom..6*

LIMIT, THE (1972) Cannon Releasing. Color-90min. Yaphet Kotto, Quinn Redeker, Ted Cassidy....................................(3)

LIMPING MAN, THE (1953) Lippert Productions. B&W-76min. *(British).* Lloyd Bridges, Moira Lister.................................(3)

LINCOLN CONSPIRACY, THE (1977) Sunn Classic. Color-90min. Bradford Dillman, John Anderson............................3½*

LINDA (1973) MCA-TV. Color-74min. *(Made for TV).* Stella Stevens, Ed Nelson, John Saxon...(4)

LINDBERGH KIDNAPPING CASE, THE (1976) CPT (TV). Color-155min. *(Made for TV).* Cliff DeYoung, Anthony Hopkins, Joseph Cotten.........5*

LINEUP, THE (1958) Columbia. B&W-86min. Warner Anderson, Eli Wallach...4½*

LINKS OF JUSTICE (1958) J. Arthur Rank. B&W-68min. *(British).* Jack Watling, Sarah Lawson.....................................(3)

LION, THE (1962) 20th Century-Fox. Color-96min. *(British-U.S.).* William Holden, Trevor Howard.............................3*

LION AND THE HORSE, THE (1952) Warner Bros. Color-83min. Steve Cochran, Sherry Jackson......................................(4)

LION HUNTERS, THE (1951) Monogram [Allied Artists]. B&W-75min. Johnny Sheffield, Morris Ankrum..........................(3)
British title: BOMBA AND THE LION HUNTERS

LION IN WINTER, THE (1968) Avco-Embassy. Color-132min. *(British).* Peter O'Toole, Katharine Hepburn..........................5½*

LION IS IN THE STREETS, A (1953) Warner Bros. Color-88min. James Cagney, Barbara Hale..4*

LION OF ST. MARK, THE (1963) Avco-Embassy. Color-87min. *(Italian).* Gordon Scott, Gianna Maria Canale......................(3)
Original title: LEONE DI SAN MARCO, IL

LION OF THEBES, THE (1964) Avco-Embassy. Color-89min. *(Italian-French).* Mark Forest, Yvonne Furneaux.................(1)
Original Italian title: LEONE DI TEBE, IL
Original French title: LION DE THEBES, LE
Alternate title(?): HELEN OF TROY

LIONS ARE LOOSE, THE (1961) Franco-London. B&W-96min. *(French-Italian).* Claudia Cardinale, Jean-Claude Brialy.........(4)
Original French title: LIONS SONT LACHES, LAS
Italian title: LEONI SCATERRATI, I

LIONS LOVE (1969) Max L. Rabb. Color-115min. Viva, James Rado, Gerome Ragni, Peter Bogdanovich.....................(4)

LIPSTICK (1976) Paramount. Color-89min. Margaux Hemingway, Chris Sarandon...5*

LIQUIDATOR, THE (1966) M-G-M. Color-104min. *(British).* Rod Taylor, Trevor Howard, Jill St. John................................5*

LISA (1962) 20th Century-Fox. Color-112min. Stephen Boyd, Dolores Hart..4*
British title: INSPECTOR, THE

LISBON (1956) Republic. Color-90min. Ray Milland, Maureen O'Hara...4*

LISETTE (1961) Medallion. B&W-83min. Greta Chi, John Agar.............(3)
Alternate title: FALL GIRL
Alternate title: CROWD FOR LISETTE, A

LIST OF ADRIAN MESSENGER, THE (1963) Universal. B&W-98min. George C. Scott, Kirk Douglas......................................5½*

LISTEN DARLING (1938) M-G-M. B&W-70min. Judy Garland, Freddie Bartholomew, Mary Astor.......................................(4)

LISTEN, LET'S MAKE LOVE (1968) Lopert [U.A.]. Color-91min. *(Italian-French).* Pierre Clementi, Beba Loncar.................(1)
Original Italian title: SUSI, FACCIAMO L'AMORE *(Pardon Me, Do You Want to Make Love?)*
Original French title: ET SI ON FASAIT L'AMOUR? *(And If We Would Make Love?)*

LISZTOMANIA (1975) Warner Bros. Color-104min. *(British).* Roger Daltrey, Sara Kestelman.....................................4*

LITTLE ACCIDENT (1939) Universal. B&W-65min. Baby Sandy, Hugh Herbert, Richard Carlson..(3)

LITTLE AMERICA (1935) Paramount. B&W-52min. *(Documentary).* *Producer:* Dario Faralla...(4)

LITTLE ANNIE ROONEY (1925) United Artists. B&W-98min. *(Silent).* Mary Pickford, William Haines.............................(4)

LITTLE ARK, THE (1972) Nat'l General (for Cinema Center). Color-101min. Theodore Bikel, Philip Frame.........................(5)

LITTLE BIG HORN (1951) Lippert Productions. B&W-86min. Marie Windsor, Lloyd Bridges, John Ireland..........................3*
British and alternate U.S. title: FIGHTING 7th, THE

LITTLE BIG MAN (1970) Nat'l General (for Cinema Center). Color-139min. Dustin Hoffman, Faye Dunaway.......................7½*

LITTLE BIT OF HEAVEN, A (1940) Universal. B&W-87min. Gloria Jean, Robert Stack..(3)

Films are rated on a 1 to 10 scale, 10 is highest. **Boldface** ratings followed by an asterisk (*) are for films actually seen and rated by the executive and senior editors. All other ratings are estimates. (See Notes on Entertainment Ratings in the front section.)

LITTLE BOY LOST (1953) Paramount. **B&W-95min.** Bing Crosby, Claude Dauphin 4½*

LITTLE CAESAR (1930) First National [W.B.]. **B&W-77min.** Edward G. Robinson, Douglas Fairbanks, Jr.. 4½*

LITTLE CIGARS (1973) American-International. **Color-92min.** Angel Tompkins, Billy Curtis .... (4)

LITTLE COLONEL, THE (1935) 20th Century-Fox. **B&W-80min.** Shirley Temple, Lionel Barrymore .... (5)

LITTLE DARLINGS (1980) Paramount. **Color-** min. Tatum O'Neal, Kristy McNichol ....

LITTLE EGYPT (1951) Universal. **Color-82min.** Mark Stevens, Rhonda Fleming, Nancy Guild 4½*
British title: CHICAGO MASQUERADE

LITTLE FAUSS AND BIG HALSY (1970) Paramount. **Color-99min.** Robert Redford, Michael J. Pollard 4*

LITTLE FOXES, THE (1941) RKO. **B&W-116min.** Bette Davis, Herbert Marshall.. 6*

LITTLE FUGITIVE, THE (1953) Joseph Burstyn. **B&W-75min.** Richie Andrusco, Ricky Brewster 4*

LITTLE GAME, A (1971) MCA-TV. **Color-73min.** *(Made for TV).* Ed Nelson, Diane Baker .... (4)

LITTLE GIANT (1946) Universal. **B&W-91min.** Bud Abbott, Lou Costello, Brenda Joyce 4*
British title: ON THE CARPET

LITTLE GIANT, THE (1933) First National [W.B.]. **B&W-75min.** Edward G. Robinson, Mary Astor 4*

LITTLE GIRL WHO LIVES DOWN THE LANE, THE (1977) American-International. **Color-94min.** *(U.S.-Canadian-French).* Jodie Foster, Scott Jacoby 5½*

LITTLE HUT, THE (1957) M-G-M. **Color-78min.** Ava Gardner, Stewart Granger .... (4)

LITTLE KIDNAPPERS, THE (1954) United Artists. **B&W-93min.** *(British).* Duncan Macrae, Jean Anderson 5*
British title: KIDNAPPERS, THE

LITTLE LADIES OF THE NIGHT (1977) ABC-TV. **Color-100min.** *(Made for TV).* David Soul, Linda Purl, Lou Gossett, Clifton Davis............... 4½*

LITTLE LORD FAUNTLEROY (1921) United Artists. **B&W-111min.** *(Silent).* Mary Pickford, Claude Gillingwater ....

LITTLE LORD FAUNTLEROY (1936) United Artists. **B&W-98min.** Freddie Bartholomew, Dolores Costello.. 5½*

LITTLE MALCOLM (1974) Multicetera. **Color-112min.** *(British).* John Hurt, John McEnery .... (4)

LITTLE MAN, WHAT NOW? (1934) Universal. **B&W-91min.** Margaret Sullavan, Douglass Montgomery ....

LITTLE MEN (1940) RKO. **B&W-84min.** Frankie Darrow, Frank Morgan.. (3)

LITTLE MINISTER, THE (1934) RKO. **B&W-110min.** John Beal, Katharine Hepburn 5*

LITTLE MISS BIG (1946) Universal. **B&W-57min.** Fay Holden, Frank McHugh .... (3)
British title: BAXTER MILLIONS, THE

LITTLE MISS BROADWAY (1938) 20th Century-Fox. **B&W-70min.** Shirley Temple, George Murphy, Jimmy Durante 4*

LITTLE MISS BROADWAY (1947) Columbia. **B&W-69min.** Jean Porter, John Shelton .... (3)

LITTLE MISS MARKER (1934) Paramount. **B&W-80min.** Adolphe Menjou, Shirley Temple, Dorothy Dell............................. (5)
British title: GIRL IN PAWN

LITTLE MISS MARKER (1980) Universal. **Color-** min. Walter Matthau, Julie Andrews, Sara Stimson ....

LITTLE MISS THOROUGHBRED (1938) Warner Bros. **B&W-63min.** Ann Sheridan, John Litel .... (3)

LITTLE MISTER JIM (1947) M-G-M. **B&W-61min.** Jackie "Butch" Jenkins, James Craig .... (5)

LITTLE MO (1978) NBC-TV. **Color-150min.** *(Made for TV).* Glynnis O'Connor, Michael Learned, Anne Baxter ....

LITTLE MURDERS (1971) 20th Century-Fox. **Color-110min.** Elliott Gould, Marcia Rodd 5*

LITTLE NELLIE KELLY (1940) M-G-M. **B&W-100min.** Judy Garland...... (4)

LITTLE NIGHT MUSIC, A (1977) New World. **Color-124min.** Elizabeth Taylor, Diana Rigg 5*

LITTLE NUNS, THE (1963) Avco-Embassy. **B&W-101min.** *(Italian).* Catherine Spaak, Sylva Koscina.. (4)
Original title: MONACHINE, LE

LITTLE OLD NEW YORK (1923) Goldwyn-Cosmopolitan. **B&W-138min.** *(Silent).* Marion Davies, Stephen Carr........................... (4)

LITTLE OLD NEW YORK (1940) 20th Century-Fox. **B&W-100min.** Richard Greene, Alice Faye.. (4)

LITTLE ONES, THE (1965) Columbia. **B&W-81min.** *(British).* Carl Gonzales, Kim Smith.. (5)

LITTLE ORVIE (1940) RKO. **B&W-68min.** Johnny Sheffield, Ernest Truex.. (3)

LITTLE PRINCE, THE (1974) Paramount. **Color-88min.** *(British).* Steven Warner, Richard Kiley 5*

LITTLE PRINCESS, THE (1939) 20th Century-Fox. **B&W-91min.** Shirley Temple, Richard Greene.. 4*

LITTLE REBELS, THE (1955) **B&W-93min.** *(French).* Jean Gabin, Jacques Moulieres... (4)
Original title: CHIENS PERDUS SANS COLLIER *(Lost Dogs Without Collars)*

LITTLE RED MONKEY (1955) *see* CASE OF THE RED MONKEY

LITTLE ROMANCE, A (1979) Warner Bros. (for Orion). **Color-108min.** Laurence Olivier, Sally Kellerman, Arthur Hill 6*

LITTLE SAVAGE, THE (1959) 20th Century-Fox. **B&W-73min.** Terry Rangno, Pedro Armendariz, Robert Palmer............................ (3)

LITTLE SHEPHERD OF KINGDOM COME, THE (1961) 20th Century-Fox. **Color-108min.** Jimmie Rodgers, Luana Patten 3½*

LITTLE SHOP OF HORRORS, THE (1960) Filmgroup. **B&W-70min.** Jonathan Haze, Jackie Joseph.. 4*

LITTLE SOLDIER, THE (1962) *see* PETIT SOLDAT, LE

LITTLE THEATRE OF JEAN RENOIR, THE (1969) Phoenix Films. **Color-100min.** *(French-Italian-German, Telefeature).* Nini Formicola, Jeanne Moreau, Pierre Olaf, Fernand Sardou.. (4)
Original title: PETIT THEATRE DE JEAN RENOIR, LE

LITTLE TOKYO, U.S.A. (1942) 20th Century-Fox. **B&W-64min.** Preston Foster, Brenda Joyce.. (3)

LITTLE WOMEN (1933) RKO. **B&W-107min.** Katharine Hepburn, Joan Bennett... 4*

LITTLE WOMEN (1949) M-G-M. **Color-121min.** June Allyson, Margaret O'Brien 4*

LITTLE WORLD OF DON CAMILLO (1951) Italian Films Export. **B&W-96min.** *(French).* Fernandel, Giono Cervi .... (5)
Original title: PETIT MONDE DE DON CAMILLO, LE

LITTLEST HOBO, THE (1958) Allied Artists. **B&W-77min.** London, Fleecie 4*

LITTLEST HORSE THIEVES, THE (1976) Buena Vista. **Color-104min.** *(U.S.-British).* Andrew Harrison, Chloe Franks................. (5)
British title: ESCAPE FROM THE DARK

LITTLEST OUTLAW, THE (1955) Buena Vista. **Color-73min.** Andres Velasquez, Pedro Armendariz.. 5*

LITTLE LORD FAUNTLEROY (1936). Attended by servants, gruff nobleman C. Aubrey Smith dines with his grandson Freddie Bartholomew, though the boy's mother is still treated as an outcast.

LITTLEST REBEL, THE (1935) 20th Century-Fox. **B&W-70min.** Shirley Temple, John Boles 4*

LIVE A LITTLE, LOVE A LITTLE (1968) M-G-M. **Color-90min.** Elvis Presley, Michele Carey, Rudy Vallee .... (2)

LIVE A LITTLE, STEAL A LOT (1974) American-International. **Color-105min.** Robert Conrad, Don Stroud 4½*
Original title: MURPH THE SURF

LIVE AND LET DIE (1973) United Artists. **Color-121min.** Roger Moore, Yaphet Kotto 5½*

LIVE FAST, DIE YOUNG (1958) Universal. **B&W-82min.** Mary Murphy, Norma Eberhardt .... (3)

LIVE FOR LIFE (1967) United Artists. **Color-130min.** (French-Italian). Yves Montand, Candice Bergen .... (5)
Original French title: VIVRE POUR VIVRE
Italian title: VIVERE PER VIVERE

LIVE IT UP (1964) *see* SING AND SWING

LIVE, LOVE AND LEARN (1937) M-G-M. **B&W-78min.** Robert Montgomery, Rosalind Russell .... (4)

LIVE TO LOVE (1961) *see* DEVIL'S HAND, THE

LIVE TODAY FOR TOMORROW (1948) *see* ACT OF MURDER, AN

LIVE WIRES (1946) Monogram [Allied Artists]. **B&W-64min.** The Bowery Boys, Pamela Blake .... (3)

LIVELY SET, THE (1964) Universal. **Color-95min.** James Darren, Pamela Tiffin 4*

LIVES OF A BENGAL LANCER (1935) Paramount. **B&W-109min.** Gary Cooper, Franchot Tone 5*

LIVES OF JENNY DOLAN, THE (1975) Paramount. **Color-100min.** (Made for TV). Shirley Jones, Stephen Boyd, John Gavin 4*

LIVING COFFIN, THE (1958) Trans-International. **B&W-72min.** (Mexican). Gaston Santos, Maria Duval .... (1)
Original title: GRITO DE LA MUERTE, EL *(The Cry of Death)*
Publicity title: SCREAM OF DEATH

LIVING DEAD AT THE MANCHESTER MORGUE, THE (1974) *see* DON'T OPEN THE WINDOW

LIVING DESERT, THE (1953) Buena Vista. **Color-73min.** (Documentary). *Director:* James Algar .... (6)

LIVING FREE (1972) Columbia. **Color-92min.** (British). Susan Hampshire, Nigel Davenport 5*

LIVING HEAD, THE (1961) Azteca. **B&W-75min.** (Mexican). Mauricio Garcés, German Robles, Abel Salazar 1*
Original title: CABEZA VIVIENTE, LA

LIVING IDOL, THE (1957) M-G-M. **Color-101min.** Steve Forrest, Lilliane Montevecchi, James Robertson Justice .... (3)

LIVING IN A BIG WAY (1947) M-G-M. **B&W-103min.** Gene Kelly, Marie MacDonald .... (3)

LIVING IT UP (1954) Paramount. **Color-95min.** Dean Martin, Jerry Lewis 4*

LIVING ON VELVET (1935) First National [W.B.]. **B&W-80min.** Warren William, Kay Francis, George Brent .... (3)

LIZZIE (1957) M-G-M. **B&W-81min.** Eleanor Parker, Richard Boone ...... (4)

LLOYDS OF LONDON (1936) 20th Century-Fox. **B&W-115min.** Tyrone Power, Guy Standing 4*

LOAN SHARK (1952) Lippert Productions. **B&W-74min.** George Raft, Dorothy Hart .... (3)

LOCAL BOY MAKES GOOD (1931) First National [W.B.]. **B&W-67min.** Joe E. Brown, Dorothy Lee .... (4)

LOCK, STOCK AND BARREL (1970) MCA-TV. **Color-96min.** (Made for TV). Jack Albertson, Belinda Montgomery, Tim Matheson, Burgess Meredith 4*

LOCK UP YOUR DAUGHTERS! (1969) Columbia. **Color-102min.** Christopher Plummer, Susannah York, Glynis Johns .... (3)

LOCK YOUR DOORS (1943) *see* APE MAN, THE

LOCKER SIXTY-NINE (1962) Anglo Amalgamated [EMI]. **B&W-56min.** (British). Eddie Byrne, Paul Daneman .... (3)

LOCKET, THE (1946) RKO. **B&W-86min.** Laraine Day, Gene Raymond (4)

LOCUSTS (1974) ABC-TV. **Color-74min.** (Made for TV). Ben Johnson, Ron Howard .... (4)

LODGER, THE (1944) 20th Century-Fox. **B&W-84min.** Laird Cregar, Merle Oberon 4*

LOG OF THE BLACK PEARL, THE (1974) MCA-TV. **Color-100min.** (Made for TV). Ralph Bellamy, Jack Kruschen .... (4)

LOGAN'S RUN (1976) U.A. (for M-G-M). **Color-118min.** Michael York, Richard Jordan 5½*

LOLA (1970) American-International. **Color-88min.** (British-Italian). Charles Bronson, Susan George 3*
Original title: TWINKY

LOLA MONTES (1955) Brandon. **Color-90min.** (French-German). Martine Carol, Peter Ustinov 2*
Alternate title: SINS OF LOLA MONTES, THE

LOLITA (1962) M-G-M. **B&W-152min.** (U.S.-British). James Mason, Sue Lyon 5*

LOLLY-MADONNA XXX (1973) M-G-M. **Color-105min.** Season Hubley, Rod Steiger, Robert Ryan 5*
British title: LOLLY-MADONNA WAR, THE

LONDON AFTER MIDNIGHT (1927) M-G-M. **B&W-63min.** (Silent). Lon Chaney, Marceline Day, Henry B. Walthall .... (4)

LONDON BELONGS TO ME (1948) *see* DULCIMER STREET

LONDON TOWN (1946) Continental [Walter Reade]. **Color-100min.** (British). Sid Field, Greta Gynt, Tessie O'Shea .... (3)
Alternate title: MY HEART GOES CRAZY

LONE COWBOY (1933) Paramount. **B&W-68min.** Jackie Cooper, Lila Lee 4*

LONE GUN, THE (1954) United Artists. **Color-78min.** George Montgomery, Dorothy Malone .... (3)

LONE HAND, THE (1953) Universal. **Color-80min.** Joel McCrea, Barbara Hale 3*

LONE RANGER, THE (1956) Warner Bros. **Color-86min.** Clayton Moore, Jay Silverheels .... (4)

LONE RANGER AND LOST CITY OF GOLD, THE (1958) United Artists. **Color-80min.** Clayton Moore, Jay Silverheels, Douglas Kennedy .... (3)

LONE STAR (1952) M-G-M. **B&W-94min.** Clark Gable, Ava Gardner..... 4*

LONE TEXAN, THE (1959) 20th Century-Fox. **B&W-70min.** Willard Parker, Grant Williams .... (2)

LONE WOLF AND HIS LADY, THE (1949) Columbia. **B&W-60min.** Ron Randell, June Vincent, Alan Mowbray .... (4)

LONE WOLF IN LONDON, THE (1947) Columbia. **B&W-68min.** Gerald Mohr, Nancy Saunders, Eric Blore .... (4)

LONE WOLF IN MEXICO, THE (1947) Columbia. **B&W-69min.** Gerald Mohr, Sheila Ryan, Eric Blore .... (4)

LONE WOLF IN PARIS, THE (1938) Columbia. **B&W-66min.** Francis Lederer, Frances Drake .... (4)

LONE WOLF KEEPS A DATE, THE (1941) Columbia. **B&W-65min.** Warren William, Frances Robinson, Eric Blore .... (4)

LONE WOLF MEETS A LADY, THE (1940) Columbia. **B&W-71min.** Warren William, Jean Muir, Eric Blore .... (4)

LONE WOLF RETURNS, THE (1936) Columbia. **B&W-69min.** Melvyn Douglas, Gail Patrick .... (4)

LONE WOLF SPY HUNT, THE (1939) Columbia. **B&W-67min.** Warren William, Ida Lupino, Rita Hayworth .... (4)
British title: LONE WOLF'S DAUGHTER, THE

LONE WOLF STRIKES, THE (1940) Columbia. **B&W-57min.** Warren William, Joan Perry, Eric Blore .... (4)

LONE WOLF TAKES A CHANCE, THE (1941) Columbia. **B&W-76min.** Warren William, June Storey, Eric Blore .... (4)

LONELIEST RUNNER, THE (1977) NBC-TV. **Color-74min.** (Made for TV). Lance Kerwin, Brian Keith, Melissa Sue Anderson .... (4)

LONELINESS OF THE LONG DISTANCE RUNNER, THE (1962) Continental [Walter Reade]. **B&W-103min.** (British). Tom Courtenay, Michael Redgrave 5½*
Alternate title: REBEL WITH A CAUSE

LONELY ARE THE BRAVE (1962) Universal. **B&W-107min.** Kirk Douglas, Gena Rowlands 5½*

LONELY HEARTS BANDITS (1950) Republic. **B&W-60min.** Robert Rockwell, Dorothy Patrick .... (3)

LONELY MAN, THE (1957) Paramount. **B&W-87min.** Jack Palance, Anthony Perkins 3*

LONELY NIGHT, THE (1952) Mayer-Kingsley. **B&W-62min.** Marian Seldes, Charles W. Moffett .... (4)

LONELY PROFESSION, THE (1969) Universal. **Color-100min.** (Made for TV). Harry Guardino, Dina Merrill, Joseph Cotten .... (5)

LONELY WIFE, THE (1964) *see* CHARULATA

LONELY WOMAN, THE (1954) *see* STRANGERS

LONELYHEARTS (1958) United Artists. **B&W-102min.** Montgomery Clift, Robert Ryan .... (4)

LONERS, THE (1972) Fanfare. **Color-80min.** Dean Stockwell, Pat Stich, Todd Susman .... (3)

Films are rated on a 1 to 10 scale, 10 is highest. **Boldface** ratings followed by an asterisk (*) are for films actually seen and rated by the executive and senior editors. All other ratings are estimates. (See Notes on Entertainment Ratings in the front section.)

LONESOME TRAIL, THE (1955) Lippert Productions. **B&W-73min.** John Agar, Wayne Morris .... (3)

LONG ABSENCE, THE (1961) Commercial Pictures. **B&W-85min.** *(French-Italian).* Alida Valli, Georges Wilson .... (5)
Original French title: AUSSI LONGUE ABSENCE, UNE *(A Too-Long Absence)*
Original Italian title: INVERNO TI FARA TORNARE, L'

LONG AGO TOMORROW (1971) Cinema 5. **Color-111min.** Malcolm McDowell, Nanette Newman **6***
Original title: RAGING MOON, THE

LONG AND THE SHORT AND THE TALL, THE (1961) *see* JUNGLE FIGHTERS

LONG ARM, THE (1956) *see* THIRD KEY, THE

LONG DARK HALL, THE (1951) Eagle Lion. **B&W-86min.** *(British).* Rex Harrison, Lilli Palmer .... (4)

LONG DAY'S DYING, THE (1968) Paramount. **Color-93min.** *(British).* David Hemmings, Tom Bell, Tony Beckley, Alan Dobie .... (4)

LONG DAY'S JOURNEY INTO NIGHT (1962) Avco-Embassy. **B&W-136min.** Katharine Hepburn, Ralph Richardson **6***

LONG DUEL, THE (1967) Paramount. **Color-115min.** *(British).* Yul Brynner, Trevor Howard, Harry Andrews .... (4)

LONG GOODBYE, THE (1973) United Artists. **Color-111min.** Elliott Gould, Nina Van Pallandt **3***

LONG GRAY LINE, THE (1955) Columbia. **Color-138min.** Tyrone Power, Maureen O'Hara **5***

LONG HAUL, THE (1957) Columbia. **B&W-88min.** *(British).* Victor Mature, Diana Dors .... (3)

LONG, HOT SUMMER, THE (1958) 20th Century-Fox. **Color-115min.** Paul Newman, Joanne Woodward, Orson Welles **5***

LONG JOHN SILVER (1954) New Trends Associates. **Color-109min.** *(Australian).* Robert Newton, Kit Taylor, Connie Gilchrist .... (4)
Alternate title: LONG JOHN SILVER RETURNS TO TREASURE ISLAND

LONG, LONG TRAILER, THE (1954) M-G-M. **Color-96min.** Lucille Ball, Desi Arnaz **4***

LONG LOST FATHER (1934) RKO. **B&W-63min.** John Barrymore, Donald Cook, Helen Chandler .... (3)

LONG MEMORY, THE (1953) Astor. **B&W-96min.** *(British).* John Mills, John McCallum .... (3)

LONG NIGHT, THE (1947) RKO. **B&W-101min.** Henry Fonda, Barbara Bel Geddes .... (4)

LONG RIDE FROM HELL, A (1968) Cinerama Releasing. **Color-94min.** *(Italian).* Steve Reeves, Wayde Preston, Dick Palmer (Mimmo Palmara) .... (2)
Original title: VIVO PER LA TUA MORTE *(I Live for Your Death)*

LONG RIDE HOME, THE (1967) *see* TIME FOR KILLING, A

LONG RIFLE AND THE TOMAHAWK, THE (1956) Independent TV Corp (ITC) **B&W-88min.** *(Telefeature).* John Hart, Lon Chaney (Jr.), John Vernon .... (3)

LONG ROPE, THE (1953) Associated Artists. **B&W-72min.** *(British).* Donald Houston, Susan Shaw .... (4)
Original title: LARGE ROPE, THE

LONG ROPE, THE (1961) 20th Century-Fox. **B&W-61min.** Hugh Marlowe, Alan Hale (Jr.) .... (3)

LONG SEARCH, THE (1952) *see* MEMORY OF LOVE

LONG SHADOW, THE (1961) Screen Gems. **B&W-64min.** *(British).* John Crawford, Susan Hampshire .... (3)

LONG SHIPS, THE (1964) Columbia. **Color-125min.** *(British-Yugoslavian).* Richard Widmark, Sidney Poitier, Russ Tamblyn .... (4)
Original Yugoslavian title: DUGI BRODOVI

LONG, SWIFT SWORD OF SIEGFRIED, THE (1971) Entertainment Ventures. **Color-92min.** *(U.S.-W. German).* Lance Boyle (Raymond Harmstorf), Sybelle Denninger (Sybil Danning), Heidi Ho (Heidi Bohlen) .... (3)
Alternate title: SIEGFRIED UND DAS SAGENHAFTE LIEBESLEBEN DER NIBELUNGEN
British title: EROTIC ADVENTURES OF SIEGFRIED, THE

LONG VOYAGE HOME, THE (1940) United Artists. **B&W-104min.** John Wayne, Thomas Mitchell **4***

LONG WAIT, THE (1954) United Artists. **B&W-93min.** Anthony Quinn, Charles Coburn **4***

LONGEST DAY, THE (1962) 20th Century-Fox. **B&W-180min.** John Wayne, Robert Mitchum, Henry Fonda **5½***

LONGEST HUNDRED MILES, THE (1966) Universal. **Color-100min.** *(Made for TV).* Doug McClure, Katharine Ross, Ricardo Montalban **4***

LONGEST NIGHT, THE (1972) MCA-TV. **Color-74min.** *(Made for TV).* David Janssen, James Farentino, Skye Aubrey **4***

LONGEST YARD, THE (1974) Paramount. **Color-121min.** Burt Reynolds, Eddie Albert **5½***
British title: MEAN MACHINE, THE

LONGSTREET (1971) Paramount. **Color-90min.** *(Made for TV).* James Franciscus, Bradford Dillman **5***

LOOK AT LIV, A (1977) Win/Knap Prods. **Color-67min.** *(Documentary).* Director: Richard Kaplan .... (4)

LOOK BACK IN ANGER (1959) Warner Bros. **B&W-99min.** *(British).* Richard Burton, Claire Bloom, Mary Ure **3***

LOOK FOR THE SILVER LINING (1949) Warner Bros. **Color-100min.** June Haver, Gordon MacRae, Ray Bolger .... (4)

LOOK IN ANY WINDOW (1961) Allied Artists. **B&W-87min.** Paul Anka, Ruth Roman .... (3)

LOOK WHAT'S HAPPENED TO ROSEMARY'S BABY (1976) Paramount. **Color-100min.** *(Made for TV).* Stephen McHattie, Ruth Gordon, Ray Milland, Patty Duke Astin **3***

LOOK WHO'S LAUGHING (1941) RKO. **B&W-79min.** Charlie McCarthy, Lucille Ball, Fibber McGee .... (4)

LOOKIN' GOOD (1973) *see* CORKY

LOOKING FOR DANGER (1957) Allied Artists. **B&W-62min.** The Bowery Boys, Lili Kardell .... (3)

LOOKING FOR LOVE (1964) M-G-M. **Color-83min.** Connie Francis, Jim Hutton .... (2)

LOOKING FOR MR. GOODBAR (1977) Paramount. **Color-135min.** Diane Keaton, Tuesday Weld **4***

LOOKING FOR TROUBLE (1934) United Artists. **B&W-80min.** Spencer Tracy, Jack Oakie, Constance Cummings **3***

LOOKING GLASS WAR, THE (1970) Columbia. **Color-108min.** *(British).* Christopher Jones, Pia Degermark **2***

LOOKING UP (1977) Levitt-Pickman. **Color-94min.** Marilyn Chris, Dick Shawn ....

LOONIES ON BROADWAY (1945) *see* ZOMBIES ON BROADWAY

LOOPHOLE (1954) Allied Artists. **B&W-80min.** Barry Sullivan, Dorothy Malone .... (4)

LOOSE IN LONDON (1953) Allied Artists. **B&W-62min.** The Bowery Boys, Angela Greene .... (4)

LOOT (1972) British Lion [EMI]. **Color-101min.** *(British).* Richard Attenborough, Lee Remick, Hywel Bennett .... (4)

LOOTERS, THE (1955) Universal. **B&W-87min.** Rory Calhoun, Julie Adams .... (4)

LORD JEFF (1938) M-G-M. **B&W-78min.** Freddie Bartholomew, Charles Coburn, Mickey Rooney **4***
British title: BOY FROM BARNARDO'S, THE

LORD JIM (1965) Columbia. **Color-154min.** *(British).* Peter O'Toole, James Mason **3***

LOOKING FOR MR. GOODBAR (1977). Amoral schoolteacher Diane Keaton longingly looks up at the latest of her many lovers, oblivious as usual to the hazards of the swinging life.

Films are rated on a 1 to 10 scale, 10 is highest. **Boldface** ratings followed by an asterisk (*) are for films actually seen and rated by the executive and senior editors. All other ratings are estimates. (See Notes on Entertainment Ratings in the front section.)

LORD LOVE A DUCK (1966) United Artists. **B&W-95min.** Roddy McDowall, Tuesday Weld 5*

LORD OF THE FLIES (1963) Continental [Walter Reade]. **B&W-91min.** *(British).* James Aubrey, Tom Chapin 4½*

LORD OF THE JUNGLE (1955) Allied Artists. **B&W-69min.** Johnny Sheffield, Wayne Morris .... (3)

LORD OF THE RINGS, THE (1978) United Artists. **Color-134min.** *(Cartoon). Director:* Ralph Bakshi 5*

LORD SHANGO (1975) Bryanston. **Color-91min.** Lawrence Cook, Marlene Clark, Avis McCarthur ....
Publicity title: SOULMATES OF SHANGO

LORD'S OF FLATBUSH, THE (1974) Columbia. **Color-86min.** Perry King, Sylvester Stallone 3*

LORNA (1964) Eve Releasing Corp. **B&W-78min.** Lorna Maitland, Mark Bradley .... (2)

LORNA DOONE (1951) Columbia. **Color-88min.** Barbara Hale, Richard Greene 5*

LOSER TAKE ALL (1948) *see* LEATHER GLOVES

LOSER TAKES ALL (1956) Distributors Corp. of America. **Color-88min.** *(British).* Rossano Brazzi, Glynis Johns .... (4)

LOSERS, THE (1970) Fanfare. **Color-95min.** William Smith, Bernie Hamilton, Adam Roarke 2*

LOSS OF INNOCENCE (1961) Columbia. **Color-99min.** *(British).* Kenneth More, Susannah York 5½*
Original title: GREENGAGE SUMMER, THE

LOST (1955) *see* TEARS FOR SIMON

LOST AND FOUND (1979) Columbia. **Color-104min.** George Segal, Glenda Jackson 5½*

LOST ANGEL (1943) M-G-M. **B&W-91min.** Margaret O'Brien, James Craig .... (4)

LOST BATTALION, THE (1962) American-International. **B&W-83min.** *(U.S.-Philippine).* Leopoldo Salcedo, Diane Jergens .... (3)

LOST BOUNDARIES (1949) Four Continents. **B&W-99min.** Beatrice Pearson, Mel Ferrer .... (5)

LOST COMMAND (1966) Columbia. **Color-127min.** Anthony Quinn, Alain Delon .... (4)

LOST CONTINENT (1951) Lippert Productions. **B&W-86min.** Cesar Romero, Hillary Brooke, John Hoyt 3*

LOST CONTINENT (1955) Lopert [U.A.]. **Color-64min.** *(Italian, Travelog). Director:* Leonardo Bonzi .... (5)
Original title: CONTINENTE PERDUTO

LOST CONTINENT, THE (1968) 20th Century-Fox. **Color-98min.** *(British).* Eric Porter, Hildegard Knef, Suzanna Leigh .... (3)

LOST FLIGHT (1970) Universal. **Color-104min.** Lloyd Bridges, Anne Francis, Ralph Meeker 4*

LOST HONEYMOON (1947) Eagle Lion. **B&W-71min.** Franchot Tone, Ann Richards .... (3)

LOST HONOR OF KATHARINA BLUM, THE (1975) New World. **Color-97min.** *(German).* Angela Winkler, Mario Adorf, Dieter Laser .... (4)
Original title: VERLORENE EHRE DER KATHARINA BLUM, DIE

LOST HORIZON (1937) Columbia. **B&W-118min.** Ronald Colman, Jane Wyatt 6*
Screen title: LOST HORIZON OF SHANGRI-LA

LOST HORIZON (1973) Columbia. **Color-150min.** Peter Finch, Liv Ullmann 3*

LOST HOURS, THE (1952) *see* BIG FRAME, THE

LOST IN A HAREM (1944) M-G-M. **B&W-89min.** Bud Abbott, Lou Costello, Marilyn Maxwell 3*

LOST IN ALASKA (1952) Universal. **B&W-76min.** Bud Abbott, Lou Costello, Tom Ewell 3*
British and alternate U.S. title: ABBOTT AND COSTELLO LOST IN ALASKA

LOST IN THE STARS (1974) American Film Theatre. **Color-114min.** Brock Peters, Melba Moore 5*

LOST ISLAND OF KIOGA (1938) Republic. **B&W-100min.** *(Re-edited Serial).* Mala, Bruce Bennett .... (3)
Original title: HAWK OF THE WILDERNESS

LOST LAGOON (1958) United Artists. **B&W-79min.** Jeffrey Lynn, Peter Donat .... (3)

LOST MAN, THE (1969) Universal. **Color-113min.** Sidney Poitier, Joanna Shimkus 3*

LOST MISSILE, THE (1958) United Artists. **B&W-70min.** Robert Loggia, Ellen Parker .... (4)

LOST MOMENT, THE (1947) Universal. **B&W-88min.** Robert Cummings, Susan Hayward, Agnes Moorehead 4*

LOST ONE, THE (1948) Columbia. **B&W-82min.** *(Italian).* Nelly Corradi, Gino Mattera .... (5)
Original title: TRAVIATA, LA

LOST PATROL, THE (1934) RKO. **B&W-74min.** Victor McLaglen, Boris Karloff 4*

LOST PEOPLE, THE (1949) J. Arthur Rank. **B&W-89min.** *(British).* Dennis Price, Mai Zetterling .... (4)

LOST PLANET AIRMEN (1949) Republic. **B&W-65min.** *(Re-edited Serial).* Tristram Coffin, Mae Clarke .... (3)
Original title: KING OF THE ROCKET MEN

LOST SEX (1966) Chevron. **B&W-97min.** *(Japanese).* Hideo Kanze, Nobuko Otowa .... (4)
Original title: HONNO

LOST SQUADRON, THE (1932) RKO. **B&W-72min.** Richard Dix, Erich Von Stroheim .... (4)

LOST TREASURE OF THE AMAZON (1953) *see* JIVARO

LOST TREASURE OF THE AZTECS (1964) *see* HERCULES AND THE TREASURE OF THE INCAS

LOST TRIBE, THE (1949) Columbia. **B&W-72min.** Johnny Weissmuller, Myrna Dell .... (3)

LOST VOLCANO, THE (1950) Monogram [Allied Artists]. **B&W-75min.** Johnny Sheffield, Donald Woods .... (3)

LOST WEEKEND, THE (1945) Paramount. **B&W-101min.** Ray Milland, Jane Wyman 5½*

LOST WORLD, THE (1925) First National [W.B.]. **B&W-108min.** *(Silent).* Wallace Beery, Lewis Stone, Bessie Love 4*

LOST WORLD, THE (1960) 20th Century-Fox. **Color-98min.** Claude Rains, Michael Rennie 3*

LOST WORLD OF SINBAD, THE (1964) American-International. **Color-95min.** *(Japanese).* Toshiro Mifune, Makoto Sato .... (3)
Original title: DAITOZOKU
Alternate title: SAMURAI PIRATE

LOTTERY BRIDE, THE (1930) United Artists. **B&W-83min.** Jeanette MacDonald, John Garrick, Joe E. Brown .... (4)

LOTUS FOR MISS QUON, A (1967) Independent TV Corp (ITC). **Color-92min.** *(W. German-Italian-French).* Lang Jeffries, Francisca Tu 3*
German title: LOTOSBLUETEN FUER MISS QUON

LOU COSTELLO AND HIS 30-FOOT BRIDE (1959) *see* 30-FOOT BRIDE OF CANDY ROCK, THE

LOUDEST WHISPER, THE (1962) *see* CHILDREN'S HOUR, THE

LOUIS ARMSTRONG - CHICAGO STYLE (1976) Worldvision. **Color-75min.** *(Made for TV).* Ben Vereen, Red Buttons, Janet MacLachlan 4½*
Alternate title: LOUIS ARMSTRONG, 1931

LOUISA (1950) Universal. **B&W-90min.** Spring Byington, Charles Coburn .... (5)

LOUISIANA HAYRIDE (1944) Columbia. **B&W-67min.** Judy Canova, Lloyd Bridges .... (3)

LOUISIANA PURCHASE (1941) Paramount. **Color-98min.** Bob Hope, Vera Zorina, Victor Moore 4½*

LOUISIANA STORY (1948) Lopert [U.A.]. **B&W-77min.** Joseph Budreaux, Lionel LeBlanc 4*

LOUISIANA TERRITORY (1953) RKO. **Color-65min.** *(Travelog).* Val Winter, Leo Zinser .... (4)

LOVE (1927) M-G-M. **B&W-82min.** *(Silent).* Greta Garbo, John Gilbert ... 4*
British title: ANNA KARENINA

LOVE AFFAIR (1939) RKO. **B&W-87min.** Irene Dunne, Charles Boyer ... 4*

LOVE AFFAIR; OR THE CASE OF THE MISSING SWITCHBOARD OPERATOR (1967) Brandon. **B&W-70min.** *(Yugoslavian).* Eva Ras, Slobodan Aligrudic .... (5)
Original title: LJUBAVNI SLUCAJ ILI TRAGEDIJA SLUZBENICE P.T.T.
Festival title: AFFAIR OF THE HEART, AN
Alternate title: CASE OF THE MISSING SWITCHBOARD OPERATOR, THE

LOVE AMONG THE RUINS (1975) ABC Circle Films. **Color-100min.** *(Made for TV).* Laurence Olivier, Katharine Hepburn 5*

LOVE AND ANARCHY (1973) Peppercorn-Wormser. **Color-108min.** *(Italian).* Giancarlo Giannini, Mariangela Melato 4*
Original title: FILM D'AMORE E D'ANARCHIA *(Film of Love and of Anarchy)*
Alternate Italian title: AMORE E ANARCHIA
Publicity title: STORY OF LOVE AND ANARCHY

LOVE AND BULLETS (1979) Independent TV Corp (ITC). **Color-95min.** *(British).* Charles Bronson, Jill Ireland, Rod Steiger ....

LOVE AND DEATH (1975) United Artists. Color-85min. Woody Allen, Diane Keaton 6*

LOVE AND FAITH (1978) Toho. Color-150min. (Japanese). Takashi Shimura, Ryoko Nakano, Toshiro Mifune ....
Original title: OGINSAMA

LOVE AND KISSES (1965) Universal. Color-87min. Rick Nelson, Jack Kelly, Kristin Nelson .... (4)

LOVE AND LARCENY (1960) Major Film. B&W-94min. (Italian-French). Vittorio Gassman, Anna Maria Ferrero .... (5)
Original Italian title: MATTATORE, IL *(The Matador* [slang] *)*
Original French title: HOMME AUX CENT VISAGES, L' *(The Man with a Hundred Faces)*

LOVE AND LEARN (1947) Warner Bros. B&W-83min. Jack Carson, Robert Hutton .... (3)

LOVE AND MARRIAGE (1964) Avco-Embassy. B&W-106min. (Italian). Lando Buzzanca, Ingeborg Schoner, Eleonora Rossi-Drago, Sylva Koscina .... (3)
Original title: IDEA FISSA, L'

LOVE AND PAIN and the whole damn thing (1973) Columbia. Color-109min. Maggie Smith, Timothy Bottoms 4*

LOVE AND SACRIFICE (1924) *see* AMERICA

LOVE AND THE FRENCHWOMAN (1960) Kingsley International. B&W-135min. (French). Pierre-Jean Vaillard, Marie-José Nat, Jean-Paul Belmondo, Annie Girardot .... (5)
Original title: FRANCAISE ET L'AMOUR, LA *(The Frenchwoman and Love)*

LOVE AND THE MIDNIGHT AUTO SUPPLY (1978) Producers Capital Corporation. Color-93min. Michael Parks, Linda Cristal, Scott Jacoby (4)
Publicity title: MIDNIGHT AUTO SUPPLY, THE

LOVE AT FIRST BITE (1979) American-International. Color-96min. George Hamilton, Susan Saint James........................... 5*

LOVE AT TWENTY (1962) Avco-Embassy. B&W-110min. (French-Italian-Japanese-Polish-W. German). Henri Serre, Eleonora Rossi-Drago, Zbigniew Cybulski, Christian Doermer .... (5)
Original French title: AMOUR A VINGT ANS, L'
Original Italian title: AMORE A VENT'ANNI
Original Japanese title: HATACHI NO KOI
Original Polish title: MILOSC DWUDZIESTOLATKOW
Original W. German title: LIEBE MIT ZWANZIG

LOVE BEFORE BREAKFAST (1936) Universal. B&W-70min. Carole Lombard, Preston Foster .... (4)

LOVE BUG, THE (1969) Buena Vista. Color-110min. Dean Jones, Michele Lee.. 4½*

LOVE CAGE (1964) *see* JOY HOUSE

LOVE CHILD (1974) *see* CHILD UNDER A LEAF

LOVE CRAZY (1941) M-G-M. B&W-100min. William Powell, Myrna Loy 5*

LOVE CYCLES (1972) H.K. Film Dist. B&W-87min. (Greek). Elena Nathanael, Spyros Focas, Theo Roubanis .... (3)

LOVE DOCTORS, THE (1969) Sigma III. Color-90min. Ann Jannin, Ann Acres .... (2)

LOVE FACTOR (1974) Film Ventures International. Color-85min. (Foreign). Anna Gael .... (3)

LOVE FINDS ANDY HARDY (1938) M-G-M. B&W-90min. Lewis Stone, Mickey Rooney 4½*

LOVE FROM A STRANGER (1937) United Artists. B&W-83min. (British). Ann Harding, Basil Rathbone ....

LOVE FROM A STRANGER (1947) Eagle Lion. B&W-81min. Sylvia Sidney, John Hodiak... 4*
British title: STRANGER WALKED IN, A

LOVE FROM PARIS (1957) *see* MONPTI

LOVE GOD?, THE (1969) Universal. Color-101min. Don Knotts, Anne Francis, Edmond O'Brien 3*

LOVE GODDESSES, THE (1965) Continental [Walter Reade]. B&W-87min. (Compilation). Producer: Saul J. Turell............... (5)

LOVE HAPPY (1949) United Artists. B&W-91min. The Marx Brothers, Ilona Massey, Marilyn Monroe 3*

LOVE HAS MANY FACES (1965) Columbia. Color-105min. Lana Turner, Cliff Robertson, Hugh O'Brian .... (3)

LOVE HATE LOVE (1971) ABC Films. Color-74min. (Made for TV). Ryan O'Neal, Lesley Warren, Peter Haskell 4*

LOVE, HONOR AND BEHAVE (1938) Warner Bros. B&W-71min. Wayne Morris, Priscilla Lane .... (4)

LOVE, HONOR AND GOODBYE (1945) Republic. B&W-87min. Virginia Bruce, Nils Asther .... (3)

LOVE IN A FOUR-LETTER WORD (1970) Allied Artists. Color-93min. (Canadian). Michael Kane, Andre Lawrence................. (3)
Alternate Canadian French-language title: VIENS, MON AMOUR
British title: SEX ISN'T SIN

LOVE IN A GOLDFISH BOWL (1961) Paramount. Color-88min. Tommy Sands, Fabian, Toby Michaels.............................. 3*

LOVE IN A HOT CLIMATE (1954) Hoffberg. Color-70min. (French). Daniel Gélin, Zsa Zsa Gabor .... (3)
Original title: SANG ET LUMIERES *(Blood and Lights)*
Alternate title: BEAUTY AND THE BULLFIGHTER

LOVE IN BLOOM (1935) Paramount. B&W-75min. George Burns and Gracie Allen, Dixie Lee .... (4)

LOVE IN 4 DIMENSIONS (1963) Eldorado Pictures International. B&W-108min. (Italian-French). Sylva Koscina, Philippe Leroy, Michele Mercier .... (5)
Original Italian title: AMORE IN 4 DIMENSIONI
Original French title: AMOUR EN 4 DIMENSIONS, L'

LOVE IN JAMAICA (1957) B&W-90min. (French). Louise Mariano, Gisele Robert .... (3)

LOVE IN JERUSALEM (1971) *see* MARGO

LOVE-IN '72 (1971) William Mishkin. Color-86min. Linda Southern, Daniel Nugent .... (3)

LOVE IN THE AFTERNOON (1957) Allied Artists. B&W-130min. Gary Cooper, Audrey Hepburn 7*

LOVE IN THE CITY (1953) Italian Films Export. B&W-90min. (Italian, Documentary). Director: Dino Risi....................... (4)
Original title: AMORE IN CITTA

LOVE-INS, THE (1967) Columbia. Color-86min. Richard Todd, James MacArthur, Susan Oliver................................ 2*

LOVE IS A BALL (1963) United Artists. Color-111min. Glenn Ford, Hope Lange... 4*
British title: ALL THIS AND MONEY TOO

LOVE IS A DAY'S WORK (1960) *see* FROM A ROMAN BALCONY

LOVE IS A FUNNY THING (1969) United Artists. Color-110min. (French-Italian). Jean-Paul Belmondo, Annie Girardot, Farrah Fawcett (Majors).. (5)
Original French title: HOMME QUI ME PLAIT, UN
Original Italian title: TIPO CHE MI PIACE, UN

LOVE IS A MANY-SPLENDORED THING (1955) 20th Century-Fox. Color-102min. William Holden, Jennifer Jones............... 4*

LOVE IS A WOMAN (1966) *see* DEATH IS A WOMAN

LOVE IS BETTER THAN EVER (1952) M-G-M. B&W-81min. Elizabeth Taylor, Larry Parks................................... (4)
British title: LIGHT FANTASTIC, THE

LOVE IS MY PROFESSION (1958) Kingsley International. B&W-111min. (French). Jean Gabin, Brigitte Bardot................. (3)
Original title: EN CAS DE MALHEUR *(In Case of Emergency)*

LOVE IS NEWS (1937) 20th Century-Fox. B&W-78min. Tyrone Power, Loretta Young .... (3)

LOVE LAUGHS AT ANDY HARDY (1946) M-G-M. B&W-93min. Mickey Rooney, Lewis Stone, Bonita Granville .... (3)

LOVE LETTERS (1945) Paramount. B&W-101min. Jennifer Jones, Joseph Cotten... 3½*

LOVE LOTTERY, THE (1953) Continental [Walter Reade]. Color-89min. (British). David Niven, Peggy Cummins.............. (3)

LOVE MACHINE, THE (1971) Columbia. Color-108min. John Phillip Law, Dyan Cannon... 3*

LOVE MAKERS, THE (1960) *see* VIACCIA, LA

LOVE MATCH, THE (1955) British Lion [EMI]. B&W-85min. (British). Arthur Askey, Thora Hird............................... (3)

LOVE MATES (1961) Altura Films. Color-90min. (Swedish). Jarl Kulle, Christina Schollin .... (3)
Original title: ANGLAR, FINSS DOM?

LOVE ME FOREVER (1935) Columbia. B&W-90min. Grace Moore, Leo Carrillo .... (4)
British title: ON WINGS OF SONG

LOVE ME - LOVE ME NOT (1962) Transcontinental. B&W-86min. (British). Craig Stevens, Erica Rogers.................. (3)

LOVE ME OR LEAVE ME (1955) M-G-M. Color-122min. Doris Day, James Cagney... 4*

LOVE ME TENDER (1956) 20th Century-Fox. B&W-89min. Elvis Presley, Richard Egan.. 3*

LOVE ME TONIGHT (1932) Paramount. B&W-104min. Maurice Chevalier, Jeanette MacDonald......................... 4½*

LOVE, MELODY (1971) *see* MELODY

LOVE NEST (1951) 20th Century-Fox. **B&W-84min.** June Haver, William Lundigan .... (3)

LOVE NEVER DIES (1921) Associated Producers. **B&W-75min.** *(Silent).* Lloyd Hughes, Madge Bellamy.......................... 4*

LOVE OF THREE QUEENS (1954) Robert Patrick Productions. **Color-73min.** *(Italian).* Hedy Lamarr, Massimo Serato.................. 3*
Original title: AMANTE DI PARIDE, L'
British title: FACE THAT LAUNCHED A THOUSAND SHIPS, THE

LOVE ON A BUDGET (1938) 20th Century-Fox. **B&W-64min.** Jed Prouty, Spring Byington.. (3)

LOVE ON A PILLOW (1962) Royal Films Int'l [Columbia]. **Color-102min.** *(French-Italian).* Brigitte Bardot, Robert Hossein, James Robertson Justice .... (3)
Original French title: REPOS DU GUERRIER, LE
Original Italian title: RIPOSO DEL GUERRIERO, IL

LOVE ON THE DOLE (1941) United Artists. **B&W-100min.** *(British).* Deborah Kerr, Clifford Evans......................... (5)

LOVE ON THE RIVIERA (1958) Ultra Pictures Corp. **Color-88min.** *(Italian-French).* Alberto Sordi, Michele Morgan, Marcello Mastroianni .... (3)
Original Italian title: RACCONTI D'ESTATE
Original French title: FEMMES D'UN ÉTÉ *(Women of a Summer)*
Alternate title: SUMMER TALES

LOVE ON THE RUN (1936) M-G-M. **B&W-80min.** Joan Crawford, Clark Gable... (4)

LOVE ON THE RUN (1979) New World. **Color-94min.** *(French).* Jean-Pierre Léaud, Marie-France Pisier, Claude Jade .... (5)
Original title: AMOUR EN FUITE, L'

LOVE PARADE, THE (1929) Paramount. **B&W-110min.** Maurice Chevalier, Jeanette MacDonald.......................... 4½*

LOVE SLAVES OF THE AMAZON (1957) Universal. **Color-81min.** Don Taylor, Eduardo Ciannelli, Gianna Segale.................. (3)

LOVE SPECIALIST, THE (1958) Medallion. **Color-99min.** *(Italian).* Diana Dors, Vittorio Gassman........................... (3)
Original title: RAGAZZA DEL PALIO, LA *(The Girl of the Palio)*

LOVE STORY (1944) *see* LADY SURRENDERS, A

LOVE STORY (1970) Paramount. **Color-100min.** Ali MacGraw, Ryan O'Neal 7*

LOVE THAT BRUTE (1950) 20th Century-Fox. **B&W-85min.** Paul Douglas, Jean Peters.. (4)

LOVE, THE ITALIAN WAY (1960) Trans-Lux Distributing. **Color-90min.** *(Italian).* Ugo Tognazzi, Sylva Koscina, Elke Sommer......... (3)
Original title: FEMMINE DI LUSSO *(Luxurious Women)*
Alternate title: LOVE ITALIAN STYLE

LOVE THY NEIGHBOR (1940) Paramount. **B&W-82min.** Jack Benny, Fred Allen, Mary Martin.............................. (4)

LOVE UNDER FIRE (1937) 20th Century-Fox. **B&W-75min.** Loretta Young, Don Ameche.. (4)

LOVE STORY (1970). Despite opposition to their marriage by his snobbish, wealthy father, who refuses to aid them financially or otherwise, Ryan O'Neal and his wife Ali MacGraw occasionally find time for recreation.

LOVE WAR, THE (1970) Worldvision. **Color-74min.** *(Made for TV).* Lloyd Bridges, Angie Dickinson, Harry Basch 3*
Alternate title: SIXTH COLUMN

LOVE WITH THE PROPER STRANGER (1963) Paramount. **B&W-100min.** Natalie Wood, Steve McQueen.................... 5½*

LOVED ONE, THE (1965) M-G-M. **B&W-116min.** Robert Morse, Jonathan Winters, Rod Steiger.......................... 5½*

LOVEJOY'S NUCLEAR WAR (1975) Green Mountain Post Films. **Color-60min.** *(Documentary).* .... (4)

LOVELY TO LOOK AT (1937) *see* THIN ICE

LOVELY TO LOOK AT (1952) M-G-M. **Color-105min.** Kathryn Grayson, Red Skelton, Howard Keel......................... (4)

LOVELY WAY TO DIE, A (1968) Universal. **Color-104min.** Kirk Douglas, Sylva Koscina, Eli Wallach........................ 4*

LOVEMAKER, THE (1958) Trans-Lux Distributing. **B&W-98min.** *(Spanish-French).* Betsy Blair, José Suarez, Yves Massard........ (5)
Original Spanish title: CALLE MAJOR *(Main Street)*

LOVER BOY (1954) *see* LOVERS, HAPPY LOVERS

LOVER COME BACK (1946) Universal. **B&W-90min.** George Brent, Lucille Ball.. (4)

LOVER COME BACK (1962) Universal. **Color-107min.** Rock Hudson, Doris Day... 7*

LOVERS, THE (1958) Zenith International. **B&W-90min.** *(French).* Jeanne Moreau, Alain Cuny............................. (5)
Original title: AMANTS, LES

LOVERS AND LOLLIPOPS (1956) Trans-Lux Distributing. **B&W-80min.** Lori March, Gerald O'Loughlin 3*

LOVERS AND OTHER RELATIVES (1976) Seymour Borde. **Color-98min.** *(Italian).* Laura Antonelli, Alessandro Momo, Orazio Orlando ....

LOVERS AND OTHER STRANGERS (1970) Cinerama Releasing. **Color-106min.** Bonnie Bedelia, Michael Brandon.............. 4*

LOVERS AND THIEVES (1957) Zenith International. **B&W-81min.** *(French).* Jean Poiret, Michel Serrault, Magali Noel .... (5)
Original title: ASSASSINS ET VOLEURS *(Killers and Thieves)*

LOVERS, HAPPY LOVERS! (1954) 20th Century-Fox. **B&W-99min.** *(British).* Gerard Philipe, Valerie Hobson, Joan Greenwood .... (4)
Original title: KNAVE OF HEARTS
Alternate title: LOVER BOY

LOVERS OF MONTPARNASSE, THE (1958) *see* MODIGLIANI OF MONTPARNASSE

LOVERS OF PARIS (1957) *see* POT BOUILLE

LOVERS OF TERUEL, THE (1962) Continental [Walter Reade]. **Color-90min.** *(French).* Ludmilla Tcherina, René-Louis Lafforgue .... (5)
Original title: AMANTS DE TERUEL, LES

LOVERS ON A TIGHTROPE (1960) Interworld Film. **B&W-90min.** *(French).* Annie Girardot, Francois Périer, Gérard Buhr .... (3)
Original title: CORDE RAIDE, LA

LOVES AND TIMES OF SCARAMOUCHE, THE (1976) Avco-Embassy. **Color-91min.** *(Italian-Yugoslavian).* Michael Sarrazin, Ursula Andress 4½*

LOVES OF A BLONDE, THE (1965) Prominent Films. **B&W-88min.** *(Czech).* Hana Brejchova, Vladimir Pucholt..................... (5)
Original title: LASKY JEDNÉ PLAVOVLASKY

LOVES OF CARMEN, THE (1948) Columbia. **Color-99min.** Rita Hayworth, Glenn Ford.. 4*

LOVES OF EDGAR ALLEN POE, THE (1942) 20th Century-Fox. **B&W-67min.** Linda Darnell, John Shepperd (Shepperd Strudwick) .... (4)

LOVES OF HERCULES, THE (1960) Screen Gems. **Color-94min.** *(Italian-French).* Jayne Mansfield, Mickey Hargitay................ 1*
Italian title: AMORE DI ERCOLE, GLI

LOVES OF ISADORA, THE (1968) *see* ISADORA

LOVES OF JOANNA GODDEN, THE (1947) Associated British-Pathé [EMI]. **B&W-89min.** *(British).* Googie Withers, Jean Kent, John McCallum .... (4)

LOVES OF MADAME DUBARRY, THE (1935) Hoffberg. **B&W-90min.** *(British).* Gitta Alpar, Patrick Waddington, Owen Nares.............. (4)
Original title: I GIVE MY HEART

LOVES OF ONDINE, THE (1968) Filmmakers. **Color-86min.** Ondine, Viva, Joe Dallesandro............................. (2)
Original title: **** *(four stars)*

LOVES OF SALAMMBO, THE (1959) 20th Century-Fox. **Color-72min.** *(Italian-French).* Jeanne Valérie, Jacques Sernas, Edmund Purdom ..(3)
Original Italian title: SALAMBO
Original French title: SALAMMBO

LOVES OF THREE QUEENS (1954) *see* LOVE OF THREE QUEENS

LOVIN' MOLLY (1974) Columbia. Color-98min. Anthony Perkins, Beau Bridges, Blythe Danner ....(4)

LOVING (1970) Columbia. Color-90min. George Segal, Eva Marie Saint 4*

LOVING COUPLES (1964) Prominent Films. B&W-113min. (Swedish). Harriet Andersson, Gunnel Lindblom, Gio Petré..........................(5)
Original title: ALSKANDE PAR

LOVING COUSINS (1974) Independent International. Color-87min. (Italian). Susan Player, Hugh Griffith, Alfredo Pea ....
Original title: CUGINI CARNALI
British title: VISITOR, THE

LOVING YOU (1957) Paramount. Color-101min. Elvis Presley, Lizabeth Scott 4*

LOWER DEPTHS, THE (1957) Brandon. B&W-125min. (Japanese). Toshiro Mifune, Isuzu Yamada, Kamatari Fujiwara............................
Original title: DONZOKO

LOYAL 47 RONIN, THE (1962) see CHUSHINGURA

LUCAN (1977) ABC-TV. Color-74min. (Made for TV). Stockard Channing, Ned Beatty...(4)

LUCAS TANNER (1974) MCA-TV. Color-74min. (Made for TV). David Hartman, Rosemary Murphy 4*

LUCIA (1968) ICA. B&W-155min. (Cuban). Raquel Revuelta, Eslinda Nunez, Adela Legra 2½*

LUCK OF GINGER COFFEY, THE (1964) Continental [Walter Reade]. B&W-100min. (Canadian-U.S.). Robert Shaw, Mary Ure 5*

LUCK OF THE IRISH, THE (1948) 20th Century-Fox. B&W-99min. Tyrone Power, Anne Baxter, Cecil Kellaway..............................(4)

LUCKY CISCO KID (1940) 20th Century-Fox. B&W-68min. Cesar Romero, Evelyn Venable..(3)

LUCKY JIM (1957) Kingsley International. B&W-95min. (British). Ian Carmichael, Terry-Thomas ....(4)

LUCKY JORDAN (1942) Paramount. B&W-84min. Alan Ladd, Helen Walker 3*

LUCKY LADY (1975) 20th Century-Fox. Color-117min. Liza Minnelli, Burt Reynolds, Gene Hackman 5½*

LUCKY ME (1954) Warner Bros. Color-100min. Doris Day, Robert Cummings..(3)

LUCKY NICK CAIN (1951) 20th Century-Fox. B&W-87min. (British). George Raft, Coleen Gray ....(4)
Original title: I'LL GET YOU FOR THIS

LUCKY NIGHT (1939) M-G-M. B&W-90min. Myrna Loy, Robert Taylor (3)

LUCKY PARTNERS (1940) RKO. B&W-102min. Ronald Colman, Ginger Rogers...4*

LUCKY STIFF, THE (1949) United Artists. B&W-99min. Dorothy Lamour, Brian Donlevy...3½*

LUCKY TO BE A WOMAN (1955) Films Around The World. B&W-90min. (Italian-French). Sophia Loren, Charles Boyer, Marcello Mastroianni. (4)
Original Italian title: FORTUNA DI ESSERE DONNA, LA
Original French title: CHANCE D'ETRE FEMME, LA
Alternate title: WHAT A WOMAN!
Alternate title: MATING MODERN STYLE

LUCY GALLANT (1955) Paramount. Color-104min. Jane Wyman, Charlton Heston 4*

LUDWIG (1973) M-G-M. Color-173min. (Italian-French-W. German). Helmut Berger, Romy Schneider, Trevor Howard ....(3)

LULLABY (1931) see SIN OF MADELON CLAUDET, THE

LULLABY OF BROADWAY, THE (1951) Warner Bros. Color-92min. Doris Day, Gene Nelson..4*

LULU BELLE (1948) Columbia. B&W-87min. Dorothy Lamour, Otto Kruger ....(3)

LUMIERE (1976) New World. Color-95min. (French). Jeanne Moreau, Francine Racette...(3)

LUNA (1979) 20th Century-Fox. Color- min. (Italian-U.S.). Jill Clayburgh, Matthew Barry ....

LUPA, LA (1954) Republic. B&W-95min. (Italian). Kerima, Ettore Manni ....(4)
Translation title: The She Wolf

LUPO! (1970) Cannon Releasing. Color-100min. (Israeli). Yuda Barkan, Gabi Amrani...(5)

LURE OF THE SILA (1950) Italian Films Export. B&W-74min. (Italian). Silvana Mangano, Amedeo Nazzari, Vittorio Gassman ....(3)
Original title: LUPO DELLA SILA, IL
British title: WOLF OF THE SILA, THE

LURE OF THE SWAMP (1957) 20th Century-Fox. B&W-74min. Willard Parker, Joan Vohs ....(2)

LURE OF THE WILDERNESS (1952) 20th Century-Fox. Color-92min. Walter Brennan, Jean Peters, Jeffrey Hunter 4*

LURED (1947) Universal. B&W-102min. Lucille Ball, George Sanders, Boris Karloff...(4)
British and alternate U.S. title: PERSONAL COLUMN

LUST FOR A VAMPIRE (1971) Levitt-Pickman. Color-95min. (British). Ralph Bates, Suzanna Leigh, Yutte Stensgaard.....................(2)
TV title: TO LOVE A VAMPIRE

LUST FOR GOLD (1949) Columbia. B&W-90min. Glenn Ford, Ida Lupino 4*

LUST FOR LIFE (1956) M-G-M. Color-122min. Kirk Douglas, Anthony Quinn 7*

LUST SEEKERS, THE (1968) see GOOD MORNING, AND GOODBYE!

LUST TO KILL (1957) Barjul International. B&W-69min. Jim Davis, Don Megowan, Allison Hayes...(2)

LUSTY MEN, THE (1952) RKO. B&W-113min. Susan Hayward, Robert Mitchum..4*

LUTHER (1974) American Film Theatre. Color-112min. Stacy Keach, Patrick Magee 5½*

LUV (1967) Columbia. Color-95min. Jack Lemmon, Peter Falk, Elaine May, Nina Wayne 4*

LUXURY LINER (1948) M-G-M. Color-98min. George Brent, Jane Powell..(4)

LYCANTHROPUS (1962) see WEREWOLF IN A GIRLS' DORMITORY

LYDIA (1941) United Artists. B&W-100min. Merle Oberon, Joseph Cotten 4*

LYDIA BAILEY (1952) 20th Century-Fox. Color-89min. Anne Francis, Dale Robertson..4*

-M-

M (1930) Paramount. B&W-99min. (German). Peter Lorre, Otto Wernicke 5½*

M (1951) Columbia. B&W-88min. David Wayne, Howard da Silva..........(5)

M.M.M. 83 (1965) American-International. Color-78min. (Italian-French-Spanish). Fred Beir, Pier Angeli, Gerard Blain ....(3)
Original Italian title: M.M.M. 83 (MISSIONE MORTALE MOLO 83)
Alternate title: M.M.M. 83 - OPERATION, DEATH ON WHARF 83

MA & PA KETTLE (1949) Universal. B&W-75min. Marjorie Main, Percy Kilbride 4*

MA & PA KETTLE AT HOME (1954) Universal. B&W-81min. Marjorie Main, Percy Kilbride, Alice Kelley..............................3*

MA & PA KETTLE AT THE FAIR (1952) Universal. B&W-78min. Marjorie Main, Percy Kilbride, Lori Nelson.........................4*

MA & PA KETTLE AT WAIKIKI (1955) Universal. B&W-79min. Marjorie Main, Percy Kilbride 3*

MA & PA KETTLE BACK ON THE FARM (1951) Universal. B&W-80min. Marjorie Main, Percy Kilbride, Richard Long 4*

MA AND PA KETTLE GO TO PARIS (1953) see MA AND PA KETTLE ON VACATION

MA & PA KETTLE GO TO TOWN (1950) Universal. B&W-79min. Marjorie Main, Percy Kilbride, Richard Long.......................(4)
British title: GOING TO TOWN

MA & PA KETTLE ON VACATION (1953) Universal. B&W-75min. Marjorie Main, Percy Kilbride, Ray Collins.........................3*
British title: MA AND PA KETTLE GO TO PARIS

MA BARKER'S KILLER BROOD (1960) Filmservice. B&W-82min. Lurene Tuttle, Tris Coffin ....(3)

MACABRE (1958) Allied Artists. B&W-73min. Jim Backus, William Prince 3*

MACAO (1952) RKO. B&W-80min. Robert Mitchum, Jane Russell, William Bendix...4*

MACARIO (1960) Azteca. B&W-91min. (Mexican). Ignacio Lopez Tarso, Pina Pellicer..5*

MacARTHUR (1977) Universal. Color-128min. Gregory Peck, Ed Flanders...5½*

MACBETH (1948) Republic. B&W-105min. Orson Welles, Jeanette Nolan 4½*

MACBETH (1961) British Lion [EMI]. Color-108min. (British). Maurice Evans, Judith Anderson 6*

MACBETH (1971) Columbia. Color-140min. (British). Jon Finch, Francesca Annis 6*

MacDONALD OF THE CANADIAN MOUNTIES (1952) see PONY SOLDIER

MACHETE (1958) United Artists. B&W-75min. Mari Blanchard, Albert Dekker ....(2)

Films are rated on a 1 to 10 scale, 10 is highest. **Boldface** ratings followed by an asterisk (*) are for films actually seen and rated by the executive and senior editors. All other ratings are estimates. (See Notes on Entertainment Ratings in the front section.)

MACHINE GUN KELLY (1958) American-International. **B&W-80min.** Charles Bronson, Susan Cabot................................**3***

MACHINE GUN McCAIN (1968) Columbia. **Color-94min.** *(Italian, English language).* John Cassavetes, Britt Ekland ....(3) *Original title:* INTOCCABILI, GLI

MACHO CALLAHAN (1970) Avco-Embassy. **Color-99min.** David Janssen, Jean Seberg................................**3***

MACISTE AGAINST HERCULES IN THE VALE OF WOE (1964) *see* HERCULES IN THE VALE OF WOE

MACISTE IN KING SOLOMON'S MINES (1963) Avco-Embassy. **Color-92min.** *(Italian).* Reg Park, Wandisa Guida ....(1) *Original title:* MACISTE NELLE MINIERE DE RE SALOMONE *Alternate title:* SAMSON IN KING SOLOMON'S MINES

MACISTE THE MIGHTY (1960) *see* SON OF SAMSON

MACISTE, THE STRONGEST MAN IN THE WORLD (1963) *see* MOLE MEN VS. THE SON OF HERCULES

MACK, THE (1973) Cinerama Releasing. **Color-110min.** Max Julien, Don Gordon, Richard Pryor................................(4)

MACKENNA'S GOLD (1969) Columbia. **Color-128min.** Gregory Peck, Omar Sharif................................**2***

MACKINTOSH & T.J. (1976) Penland Prods. **Color-96min.** Roy Rogers, Clay O'Brien................................**4***

MACKINTOSH MAN, THE (1973) Warner Bros. **Color-98min.** *(British-U.S.).* Paul Newman, Dominique Sanda................**4***

MACOMBER AFFAIR, THE (1947) United Artists. **B&W-89min.** Gregory Peck, Joan Bennett, Robert Preston................**4***

MACON COUNTY LINE (1974) American-International. **Color-87min.** Alan Vint, Jesse Vint, Max Baer................**4***

MACUMBA LOVE (1960) United Artists. **Color-86min.** Walter Reed, Ziva Rodann................................(3)

MACUNAIMA (1969) New Line Cinema. **Color-95min.** *(Brazilian).* Grande Otelo, Paulo Jose................(3)

MAD ABOUT MEN (1955) General Film Distribs. *(Br.).* **Color-90min.** *(British).* Glynis Johns, Margaret Rutherford................(3)

MAD ABOUT MUSIC (1938) Universal. **B&W-98min.** Deanna Durbin, Herbert Marshall................(5)

MAD ADVENTURES OF "RABBI" JACOB, THE (1973) 20th Century-Fox. **Color-96min.** *(French-Italian).* Louis de Funes, Claude Giraud, Marcel Dalio................**6*** *Original French title:* AVENTURES DE RABBI JACOB, LES *Publicity title:* ADVENTURES OF RABBI JACOB, THE

MAD AT THE WORLD (1955) Filmmakers. **B&W-72min.** Keefe Brasselle, Frank Lovejoy................(3)

MAD BOMBER, THE (1973) Cinemation. **Color-91min.** Chuck Connors, Neville Brand, Vince Edwards................**3***

MAD DOCTOR, THE (1941) Paramount. **B&W-90min.** Basil Rathbone, Ellen Drew................(3) *British title:* DATE WITH DESTINY, A

MAD DOCTOR OF MARKET STREET, THE (1942) Universal. **B&W-61min.** Una Merkel, Lionel Atwill................(3)

MAD DOG (1976) Cinema Shares. **Color-102min.** *(Australian).* Dennis Hopper, Jack Thompson................**4*** *Publicity title:* MAD DOG MORGAN

MAD DOG COLL (1961) Columbia. **B&W-86min.** John Davis Chandler, Kay Doubleday................(3)

MAD DOGS AND ENGLISHMEN (1971) M-G-M. **Color-114min.** *(Music Film).* Director: Pierre Adidge................(5) *Alternate title:* JOE COCKER/MAD DOGS AND ENGLISHMEN

MAD EXECUTIONERS, THE (1963) Paramount. **B&W-92min.** *(German).* Hansjorg Felmy, Maria Perschy, Dieter Borsche................(3) *Original title:* HENKER VON LONDON, DER

MAD GENIUS, THE (1931) Warner Bros. **B&W-81min.** John Barrymore, Marion Marsh................**3***

MAD GHOUL, THE (1943) Universal. **B&W-65min.** George Zucco, David Bruce, Evelyn Ankers................**3***

MAD HATTER, THE (1946) *see* BREAKFAST IN HOLLYWOOD

MAD LITTLE ISLAND (1958) J. Arthur Rank. **Color-94min.** *(British).* Donald Sinden, Jeannie Carson................(4) *Original title:* ROCKETS GALORE

MAD LOVE (1935) M-G-M. **B&W-83min.** Peter Lorre, Frances Drake ....**4*** *British title:* HANDS OF ORLAC, THE

MAD LOVER (1944) *see* ENEMY OF WOMEN

MAD MAGICIAN, THE (1954) Columbia. **B&W-72min.** Vincent Price, Mary Murphy................(4)

MAD MARTINDALES, THE (1942) 20th Century-Fox. **B&W-65min.** Jane Withers, Marjorie Weaver................(3)

MAD MISS MANTON, THE (1938) RKO. **B&W-65min.** Barbara Stanwyck, Henry Fonda................(5)

MAD MONSTER, THE (1942) Producers Rel. Corp. [Eagle Lion]. **B&W-77min.** George Zucco, Anne Nagel, Glenn Strange ....

MAD MONSTER PARTY (1967) Avco-Embassy. **Color-94min.** *(Puppets).* Director: Jules Bass................**4***

MAD ROOM, THE (1969) Columbia. **Color-92min.** Stella Stevens, Shelley Winters................**4***

MAD WEDNESDAY (1947) RKO. **B&W-89min.** Harold Lloyd, Frances Ramsden................**4*** *Original title:* SIN OF HAROLD DIDDLEBOCK, THE

MADAM KITTY (1976) Trans-American Films [A.I.P.]. **Color-110min.** *(Italian-W. German-French).* Helmut Berger, Ingrid Thulin ....3½* *British title:* SALON KITTY

MADAM SATAN (1930) M-G-M. **B&W-80min.** Lillian Roth, Kay Johnson, Reginald Denny................(3)

MADAME (1962) Avco-Embassy. **Color-100min.** *(Italian-French-Spanish).* Sophia Loren, Robert Hossein, Julien Bertheau................(3) *Original European title:* MADAME SANS-GENE

MADAME BOVARY (1949) M-G-M. **B&W-115min.** Jennifer Jones, Van Heflin................(5)

MADAME BUTTERFLY (1932) Paramount. **B&W-86min.** Sylvia Sidney, Cary Grant................(4)

MADAME BUTTERFLY (1955) Italian Films Export. **Color-114min.** *(Italian-Japanese).* Kaoru Yaschigusa, Nicola Filacuridi................5*

MADAME CLAUDE (1978) *see* FRENCH WOMAN, THE

MADAME CURIE (1943) M-G-M. **B&W-124min.** Greer Garson, Walter Pidgeon................4½*

MADAME DE . . . (1953) *see* EARRINGS OF MADAME DE . . .

MADAME DU BARRY (1934) Warner Bros. **B&W-77min.** Dolores Del Rio, Reginald Owen, Victor Jory................(5)

MADAME PIMPERNEL (1945) *see* PARIS UNDERGROUND

MADAME ROSA (1977) Atlantic Releasing Corp. **Color-105min.** *(French).* Simone Signoret, Sammy Ben Youb................4½* *Original title:* VIE DEVANT SOI, LA *(The Life Ahead of You)*

MADAME SIN (1972) Scotia-Barber *(Brit.).* **Color-75min.** *(British, Made for TV).* Bette Davis, Robert Wagner................**4***

MADAME X (1929) M-G-M. **B&W-95min.** Lewis Stone, Ruth Chatterton................(3) *TV title:* ABSINTHE

MADAME X (1937) M-G-M. **B&W-71min.** Gladys George, John Beal, Warren William ....

MADAME X (1966) Universal. **Color-99min.** Lana Turner, John Forsythe, Constance Bennett................**3***

MADAME BUTTERFLY (1932). Cary Grant is the handsome American Naval officer who woos novice geisha girl Sylvia Sidney in 19th-century Japan.

Films are rated on a 1 to 10 scale, 10 is highest. **Boldface** ratings followed by an asterisk (*) are for films actually seen and rated by the executive and senior editors. All other ratings are estimates. (See Notes on Entertainment Ratings in the front section.)

MADCAP ADVENTURES OF MR. TOAD, THE (1949) see ADVENTURES OF ICHABOD AND MR. TOAD

MADCHEN IN UNIFORM see MAEDCHEN IN UNIFORM

MADDALENA (1971) International Co-Productions. Color-105min. (Italian). Lisa Gastoni, Eric Woofe, Ivo Garrani ....(4)

MADE FOR EACH OTHER (1939) United Artists. B&W-85min. Carole Lombard, James Stewart........4*

MADE FOR EACH OTHER (1971) 20th Century-Fox. Color-104min. Renée Taylor, Joseph Bologna........4*

MADE IN HEAVEN (1952) J. Arthur Rank. Color-80min. (British). Petula Clark, David Tomlinson, Sonja Ziemann ....(4)

MADE IN ITALY (1966) Royal Films Int'l [Columbia]. Color-101min. (Italian-French). Marina Berti, Claudio Gora.........(5)
Original French title: A L'ITALIENNE

MADE IN PARIS (1966) M-G-M. Color-103min. Ann-Margret, Louis Jourdan, Richard Crenna ....(3)

MADELEINE (1949) Universal. B&W-101min. (British). Ann Todd, Ivan Desny.........4*
Alternate title: STRANGE CASE OF MADELEINE, THE

MADELEINE (1958) B&W-86min. (German). Eva Bartok, Sabina Sesselmann ....(3)

MADEMOISELLE (1966) Lopert [U.A.]. B&W-103min. (French-British). Jeanne Moreau, Ettore Manni, Keith Skinner ....(3)

MADEMOISELLE FIFI (1944) RKO. B&W-69min. Simone Simon, John Emery ....(3)

MADEMOISELLE FROM PARIS (1955) Regent. Color-92min. (French, English version). Gisele Pascal, Jean-Pierre Aumont ....(3)
Original title: MADEMOISELLE DE PARIS

MADEMOISELLE STRIPTEASE (1957) see PLEASE, MR. BALZAC

MADHOUSE (1974) American-International. Color-89min. (U.S.-British). Vincent Price, Peter Cushing, Robert Quarry........4*

MADIGAN (1968) Universal. Color-101min. Richard Widmark, Henry Fonda........4*

MADIGAN'S MILLIONS (1969) American-International. Color-77min. (Spanish-Italian). Dustin Hoffman, Elsa Martinelli, Cesar Romero......3*
Original Spanish title: MILLON DE MADIGAN, EL
Alternate Spanish title: TESTAMENTO DE MADIGAN, EL (The Testament of Madigan)
Original Italian title: DOLLARO PER 7 VIGLIACCHI, UN

MADISON AVENUE (1962) 20th Century-Fox. B&W-94min. Dana Andrews, Eleanor Parker........4*

MADMEN OF MANDORAS (1964) Crown International. B&W-74min. Walter Stocker, Audrey Caire........2*
TV title: THEY SAVED HITLER'S BRAIN

MADNESS OF THE HEART (1949) Universal. B&W-74min. (British). Margaret Lockwood, Maxwell Reed ....(4)

MADONNA OF THE DESERT (1948) Republic. B&W-60min. Lynne Roberts, Donald Barry ....(3)

MADONNA OF THE SEVEN MOONS (1944) Universal. B&W-88min. (British). Phyllis Calvert, Stewart Granger........4*

MADONNA'S SECRET, THE (1946) Republic. B&W-79min. Francis Lederer, Gail Patrick ....(4)

MADRON (1970) Four Star-Excelsior. Color-93min. Richard Boone, Leslie Caron ....(2)

MADWOMAN OF CHAILLOT, THE (1969) Warner Bros. Color-145min. (British). Katharine Hepburn, Charles Boyer 4½*

MAEDCHEN IN UNIFORM (1931) Krimsky-Cochran. B&W-90min. (German). Emilia Unda, Dorothea Wieck 3*
Alternate title: GIRLS IN UNIFORM

MAEDCHEN IN UNIFORM (1958) Seven Arts [W.B.]. Color-91min. (W. German-French). Lilli Palmer, Romy Schneider, Christine Kaufmann ....(4)
Original French title: JEUNES FILLES EN UNIFORME

MAFIOSO (1962) Zenith International. B&W-100min. (Italian). Alberto Sordi, Norma Benguell ....(5)

MAFU CAGE, THE (1978) Clouds Production. Color-102min. Lee Grant, Carol Kane, Will Geer, James Olson ....(3)

MAGGIE, THE (1954) see HIGH AND DRY

MAGIC (1978) 20th Century-Fox. Color-106min. Anthony Hopkins, Ann-Margret, Burgess Meredith 6*

MAGIC BOW, THE (1946) Universal. B&W-105min. (British). Stewart Granger, Phyllis Calvert ....(4)

MAGIC BOX, THE (1951) J. Arthur Rank. Color-103min. (British). Robert Donat, Margaret Johnston 5*

MAGIC CARPET, THE (1951) Columbia. Color-84min. Lucille Ball, John Agar........3*

MAGIC CARPET (1971) MCA-TV. Color-97min. (Made for TV). Susan Saint James, Robert Pratt, Nanette Fabray ....(4)

MAGIC CHRISTIAN, THE (1970) American-International. Color-93min. (British). Peter Sellers, Ringo Starr 3*

MAGIC FACE, THE (1951) Columbia. B&W-89min. Luther Adler...........(4)

MAGIC FIRE (1956) Republic. Color-95min. Alan Badel, Yvonne De Carlo 3½*

MAGIC FLUTE, THE (1975) Surrogate Releasing. Color-134min. (Swedish, Telefeature). Josef Kostlinger, Irma Urrila, Ulrik Cold 3*
Original title: TROLLFLOJTEN

MAGIC FOUNTAIN, THE (1961) Classic World Films. Color-82min. Peter Nestler, Helmo Kindermann, Cedric Hardwicke ....(3)

MAGIC GARDEN, THE (1951) Mayer-Kingsley. B&W-63min. (British). Tommy Ramokgopa, Dolly Rathebe.........(5)
Alternate title: PENNYWHISTLE BLUES

MAGIC GARDEN OF STANLEY SWEETHEART, THE (1970) M-G-M. Color-113min. Don Johnson, Linda Gillin.........(4)

MAGIC OF LASSIE, THE (1978) International Picture Show. Color-99min. James Stewart, Mickey Rooney 4*

MAGIC SERPENT, THE (1966) American-International. Color-85min. (Japanese). Hiroki Matsukata, Tomoko Ogawa........1*
Original title: KAIRYU DAIKESSEN
Publicity title: GRAND DUEL IN MAGIC
Publicity title: FROGGO AND DROGGO

MAGIC SWORD, THE (1962) United Artists. Color-80min. Gary Lockwood, Basil Rathbone........4*

MAGIC TOWN (1947) RKO. B&W-103min. James Stewart, Jane Wyman 4*

MAGIC VOYAGE OF SINBAD, THE (1953) Filmgroup. Color-79min. (U.S.S.R.). Edward Stolar (Sergey Stolyarov), Anna Larion (Alla Larionova), Maurice Troyan (Mark Troyankovskiy).........(2)
Original title: SADKO

MAGIC WEAVER, THE (1960) Allied Artists. Color-87min. (U.S.S.R.). Mikhail Kuznetsov, Ninel Myshkova ....(5)
Original title: MARYA-ISKUSNITSA
Alternate title(?): MARIA, THE WONDERFUL WEAVER

MAGIC WORLD OF TOPO GIGIO (THE ITALIAN MOUSE), THE (1961) Columbia. Color-75min. (Italian, Puppets). Peppino Mazzulo, Ermanno Roveri ....(3)
Original title: AVVENTURE DI TOPO GIGIO, LE (The Adventure of Topo Gigio)

MAGICAL MYSTERY TOUR (1968) Carson Entertainment. Color-54min. (British, Made for TV). The Beatles, Jessie Robins, Victor Spinetti 1*

MAGICIAN, THE (1958) Janus Films. B&W-102min. (Swedish). Max Von Sydow, Ingrid Thulin........5*
Original title: ANSIKTET (The Face)

MAGNET, THE (1951) Universal. B&W-78min. (British). William Fox, Stephen Murray.........(5)

MAGNETIC MONSTER, THE (1953) United Artists. B&W-76min. Richard Carlson, King Donovan.........(4)

MAGNIFICENT AMBERSONS, THE (1942) RKO. B&W-88min. Joseph Cotten, Dolores Costello 4*

MAGNIFICENT BRUTE, THE (1936) Universal. B&W-80min. Victor McLaglen, Binnie Barnes, William Hall ....(4)

MAGNIFICENT CUCKOLD, THE (1964) Continental [Walter Reade]. B&W-117min. (Italian-French). Claudia Cardinale, Ugo Tognazzi.......(4)
Original title: MAGNIFICO CORNUTO, IL

MAGNIFICENT DOLL, THE (1946) Universal. B&W-95min. Ginger Rogers, David Niven 4*

MAGNIFICENT DOPE, THE (1942) 20th Century-Fox. B&W-83min. Henry Fonda, Lynn Bari........5*

MAGNIFICENT FRAUD, THE (1939) Paramount. B&W-78min. Akim Tamiroff, Lloyd Nolan ....(3)

MAGNIFICENT MATADOR, THE (1955) 20th Century-Fox. Color-94min. Anthony Quinn, Maureen O'Hara 4*
British title: BRAVE AND THE BEAUTIFUL, THE

MAGNIFICENT OBSESSION (1935) Universal. B&W-112min. Irene Dunne, Robert Taylor 4*

MAGNIFICENT OBSESSION (1954) Universal. Color-108min. Jane Wyman, Rock Hudson 4*

MAGNIFICENT ROGUE, THE (1946) Republic. B&W-74min. Lynn Roberts, Warren Douglas.........(4)

MAGNIFICENT ROUGHNECKS (1956) Allied Artists. B&W-73min. Jack Carson, Mickey Rooney.........(2)

Films are rated on a 1 to 10 scale, 10 is highest. **Boldface** ratings followed by an asterisk (*) are for films actually seen and rated by the executive and senior editors. All other ratings are estimates. (See Notes on Entertainment Ratings in the front section.)

MAGNIFICENT SEVEN, THE (1954) see SEVEN SAMURAI, THE

MAGNIFICENT SEVEN, THE (1960) United Artists. **Color-126min.** Yul Brynner, Steve McQueen......6*

MAGNIFICENT SEVEN RIDE!, THE (1972) United Artists. **Color-100min.** Lee Van Cleef, Michael Callan......4*

MAGNIFICENT SHOWMAN, THE (1964) see CIRCUS WORLD

MAGNIFICENT SINNER (1959) Film-Mart. **Color-95min.** (French). Romy Schneider, Curt Jurgens......(4)
Alternate French title: JEUNE FILLE, UN SEUL AMOUR, UNE

MAGNIFICENT TWO, THE (1967) see WHAT HAPPENED AT CAMPO GRANDE?

MAGNIFICENT YANKEE, THE (1950) M-G-M. **B&W-80min.** Louis Calhern, Ann Harding......5*
British title: MAN WITH THIRTY SONS, THE

MAGNIFIQUE, LE (1974) Cine III. **Color-86min.** (French). Jean-Paul Belmondo, Jacqueline Bisset, Vittorio Caprioli......(4)
Translation title: The Magnificent One

MAGNUM FORCE (1973) Warner Bros. **Color-122min.** Clint Eastwood, Hal Holbrook......5*

MAGUS, THE (1968) 20th Century-Fox. **Color-116min.** (British). Michael Caine, Anthony Quinn......4*

MAHANAGAR (1964) see BIG CITY, THE

MAHLER (1974) Specialty Films. **Color-115min.** (British). Robert Powell, Georgina Hale......(4)

MAHOGANY (1975) Paramount. **Color-109min.** Diana Ross, Billy Dee Williams......5*

MAID IN PARIS (1957) Continental [Walter Reade]. **B&W-84min.** (French). Dany Robin, Daniel Gélin......(4)

MAID IN SWEDEN (1971) Cannon Releasing. **Color-90min.** (U.S.-Swedish, English language). Kristina Lindberg, Monika Ekman, Krister Ekman......(3)

MAID OF SALEM (1937) Paramount. **B&W-86min.** Claudette Colbert, Fred MacMurray......(5)

MAIDEN FOR A PRINCE, A (1965) Royal Films Int'l [Columbia]. **Color-92min.** (Italian-French). Vittorio Gassman, Virna Lisi, Philippe Leroy......(3)
Original Italian title: VERGINE PER IL PRINCIPE, UNA (A Virgin for the Prince)
Original French title: VIERGE POUR LE PRINCE, UNE
Alternate title: MAIDEN FOR THE PRINCE, A

MAIDS, THE (1975) American Film Theatre. **Color-95min.** (British-Canadian). Glenda Jackson, Susannah York......3*

MAID'S NIGHT OUT (1938) RKO. **B&W-64min.** Joan Fontaine, Allan "Rocky" Lane......(3)

MAIDSTONE (1970) Supreme Mix. **Color-110min.** Norman Mailer, Rip Torn......(3)

MAIL ORDER BRIDE (1964) M-G-M. **Color-83min.** Buddy Ebsen, Keir Dullea......4*
British title: WEST OF MONTANA

MAILBAG ROBBERY (1957) Tudor Pictures. **B&W-70min.** (British). Lee Patterson, Kay Callard, Alan Gifford......(3)
Original title: FLYING SCOT, THE

MAIN ATTRACTION, THE (1962) M-G-M. **Color-85min.** (British). Pat Boone, Nancy Kwan......(3)

MAIN CHANCE, THE (1965) Avco-Embassy. **B&W-61min.** (British). Grégoire Aslan, Edward DeSouza, Tracy Reed......(4)

MAIN EVENT, THE (1979) Warner Bros. **Color-112min.** Barbra Streisand, Ryan O'Neal......5½*

MAIN STREET AFTER DARK (1944) M-G-M. **B&W-57min.** Edward Arnold, Dan Duryea, Audrey Totter......(3)

MAIN STREET KID, THE (1948) Republic. **B&W-64min.** Al Pearce, Alan Mowbray......(3)

MAIN STREET TO BROADWAY (1953) M-G-M. **B&W-102min.** Tom Morton, Mary Murphy, Tallulah Bankhead......(4)

MAINS SALES, LES (1951) see DIRTY HANDS

MAISIE (1939) M-G-M. **B&W-74min.** Ann Sothern, Robert Young......(4)

MAISIE GETS HER MAN (1942) M-G-M. **B&W-85min.** Ann Sothern, Red Skelton, Leo Gorcey......(3)
British title: SHE GOT HER MAN

MAISIE GOES TO RENO (1944) M-G-M. **B&W-90min.** Ann Sothern, John Hodiak, Ava Gardner......(3)

MAISIE WAS A LADY (1941) M-G-M. **B&W-79min.** Ann Sothern, Lew Ayres......(3)
British title: YOU CAN'T DO THAT TO ME

MAITRESSE (1976) Tinc Productions. **Color-112min.** (French). Gerard Depardieu, Bulle Ogier......
Translation title: Mistress

MAJIN (1966) American-International. **Color-82min.** (Japanese). Miwa Takada, Yoshihiko Aoyama, Ryutaro Gomi......2*
Original title: DAIMAJIN
Alternate title: MAJIN, THE MONSTER OF TERROR
Publicity title: MAJIN THE HIDEOUS IDOL
Publicity title: DEVIL GOT ANGRY, THE
Regional title: VENGEANCE OF THE MONSTER, THE

MAJOR AND THE MINOR, THE (1942) Paramount. **B&W-100min.** Ginger Rogers, Ray Milland......5½*

MAJOR BARBARA (1941) United Artists. **B&W-121min.** (British). Wendy Hiller, Rex Harrison......6*

MAJOR DUNDEE (1965) Columbia. **Color-134min.** Charlton Heston, Richard Harris......5*

MAJORITY OF ONE, A (1962) Warner Bros. **Color-153min.** Rosalind Russell, Alec Guinness......5*

MAKE A FACE (1971) Karen Sperling. **Color-90min.** Karen Sperling, Paolo Patti......(3)

MAKE BELIEVE BALLROOM (1949) Columbia. **B&W-79min.** Ruth Warrick, Ron Randell, Nat "King" Cole......(3)

MAKE HASTE TO LIVE (1954) Republic. **B&W-90min.** Dorothy McGuire, Stephen McNally......(4)

MAKE ME AN OFFER (1954) Dominant Pictures. **Color-88min.** (British). Adrienne Corri, Peter Finch......(4)

MAKE MINE LAUGHS (1949) RKO. **B&W-64min.** Frances Langford, Ray Bolger, Joan Davis......(3)

MAKE MINE MINK (1960) Continental [Walter Reade]. **B&W-101min.** (British). Terry-Thomas, Athene Seyler......5½*

MAKE MINE MUSIC! (1946) RKO (for Disney). **Color-75min.** (Cartoon). Producer: Walt Disney......(5)

MAKE WAY FOR A LADY (1936) RKO. **B&W-65min.** Anne Shirley, Herbert Marshall......(4)

MAKE WAY FOR LILA (1958) Paramount. **Color-90min.** (W. German-Swedish). Erika Remberg, Joachim Hansen......(4)
Original W. German title: LAILA - LIEBE UNTER DER MITTERNACHTSSONNE (Laila - Love under the Midnight Sun)
Original Swedish title: LAILA

MAKE WAY FOR TOMORROW (1937) Paramount. **B&W-92min.** Victor Moore, Beulah Bondi......4½*

MAKE YOUR OWN BED (1944) Warner Bros. **B&W-82min.** Jack Carson, Irene Manning......(3)

MAKING IT (1971) 20th Century-Fox. **Color-97min.** Kristoffer Tabori, Marlyn Mason......(4)

MALA THE MAGNIFICENT (1934) see ESKIMO

MALAGA (1954) see FIRE OVER AFRICA

MALAGA (1960) Warner Bros. **B&W-97min.** (British). Trevor Howard, Dorothy Dandridge, Edmund Purdom......(3)
Original title: MOMENT OF DANGER

MALAMONDO (1964) Magna Pictures. **Color-80min.** (Italian, Documentary). Director: Paolo Cavara......(3)

MALAYA (1950) M-G-M. **B&W-98min.** Spencer Tracy, James Stewart....3*
British title: EAST OF THE RISING SUN

MALCOLM X (1972) Warner Bros. **Color-92min.** (Documentary). Producer: Marvin Worth......(5)

MALE AND FEMALE (1919) Famous Players-Lasky. **B&W-9reels** (Silent). Gloria Swanson, Thomas Meighan......(4)

MALE ANIMAL, THE (1942) Warner Bros. **B&W-101min.** Henry Fonda, Olivia de Havilland......5*

MALE COMPANION (1964) International Classics [20th]. **Color-92min.** (French-Italian). Jean-Pierre Cassel, Catherine Deneuve......(4)
Original French title: MONSIEUR DE COMPAGNIE, UN
Original Italian title: PI TI SPOSERO

MALE HUNT (1964) Pathé Contemporary. **B&W-92min.** (French-Italian). Jean-Paul Belmondo, Jean-Claude Brialy, Catherine Deneuve, Francoise Dorleac......(5)
Original French title: CHASSE A L'HOMME, LA
Original Italian title: CACCIA AL MASCHIO

MALIBU BEACH (1978) Crown International. **Color-93min.** Kim Lankford, James Daughton......4½*
British title: SUNSET COVE

MALIBU HIGH (1979) Crown International. **Color-91min.** Jill Lansing, Stuart Taylor......4*

Films are rated on a 1 to 10 scale, 10 is highest. **Boldface** ratings followed by an asterisk (*) are for films actually seen and rated by the executive and senior editors. All other ratings are estimates. (See Notes on Entertainment Ratings in the front section.)

MALIZIA (1974) Paramount. **Color-98min.** *(Italian).* Laura Antonelli, Alessandro Momo **5***
Translation title: Malice

MALLORY: CIRCUMSTANTIAL EVIDENCE (1976) MCA-TV. **Color-100min.** *(Made for TV).* Raymond Burr, Robert Loggia, Mark Hamill **4½***
Original title: MALLORY

MALPAS MYSTERY, THE (1961) Schoenfeld Film Distributing. **B&W-60min.** *(British).* Maureen Swanson, Allan Cuthbertson .... (4)

MALTA STORY, THE (1953) Universal. **B&W-103min.** *(British).* Alec Guinness, Jack Hawkins .... (4)

MALTESE BIPPY, THE (1969) M-G-M. **Color-92min.** Dan Rowan, Dick Martin, Carol Lynley .... (3)

MALTESE FALCON, THE (1931) Warner Bros. **B&W-80min.** Ricardo Cortez, Bebe Daniels .... (4)
Alternate title: DANGEROUS FEMALE

MALTESE FALCON, THE (1941) Warner Bros. **B&W-100min.** Humphrey Bogart, Mary Astor **7***

MAMBO (1954) Paramount. **B&W-94min.** *(U.S.-Italian, English language).* Silvana Mangano, Michael Rennie .... (3)

MAME (1974) Warner Bros. **Color-132min.** Lucille Ball, Beatrice Arthur **4***

MAMMY (1930) Warner Bros. **B&W-84min.** Al Jolson, Louise Dresser ... (3)

MAM'SELLE STRIPTEASE (1956) *see* PLEASE MR. BALZAC

MAM'ZELLE PIGALLE (1955) Films Around The World. **Color-86min.** *(French).* Brigitte Bardot, Jean Bretonniere, Francoise Fabian .... (3)
Original title: CETTE SACREE GAMIN *(This Damned Gamin)*
Alternate title: NAUGHTY GIRL
Alternate title: THAT NAUGHTY GIRL

MAN, THE (1972) Paramount. **Color-93min.** James Earl Jones, Martin Balsam **5***

MAN ABOUT THE HOUSE, A (1947) 20th Century-Fox. **B&W-96min.** *(British).* Kieron Moore, Margaret Johnston .... (4)

MAN ABOUT TOWN (1939) Paramount. **B&W-85min.** Jack Benny, Dorothy Lamour .... (5)

MAN ABOUT TOWN (1947) RKO. **B&W-89min.** *(French).* Maurice Chevalier, Francois Perier .... (5)

MAN AFRAID (1957) Universal. **B&W-84min.** George Nader, Phyllis Thaxter, Tim Hovey .... (4)

MAN ALIVE (1945) RKO. **B&W-70min.** Pat O'Brien, Adolphe Menjou ...(4)

MAN ALONE, A (1955) Republic. **Color-96min.** Ray Milland, Mary Murphy **3***

MAN AND A WOMAN, A (1966) Allied Artists. **Color-102min.** *(French).* Anouk Aimée, Jean-Louis Trintignant **5½***
Original title: HOMME ET UNE FEMME, UN

MAN AND BOY (1971) Levitt-Pickman. **Color-98min.** Bill Cosby, George Spell, Gloria Foster .... (4)

THE MALTESE FALCON (1941). Detective Humphrey Bogart, crook Peter Lorre, mystery woman Mary Astor, and Sidney Greenstreet all have an intense interest in the seemingly insignificant black statuette.

MAN AND CHILD (1957) Paramount. **B&W-90min.** *(French).* Eddie Constantine, Juliette Greco .... (3)

MAN AND HIS MATE (1940) *see* ONE MILLION B.C.

MAN AND THE MONSTER, THE (1958) Trans-International. **B&W-78min.** *(Mexican).* Enrique Rambal, Martha Roth, Abel Salazar .... (1)
Original title: HOMBRE Y EL MONSTRUO, EL

MAN AT THE CARLTON TOWER (1961) Anglo Amalgamated [EMI]. **B&W-57min.** *(British).* Maxine Audley, Lee Montague .... (3)

MAN AT THE TOP (1973) EMI. **Color-87min.** *(British).* Kenneth Haigh, Nanette Newman, Harry Andrews .... (4)

MAN BAIT (1952) Lippert Productions. **B&W-77min.** *(British).* George Brent, Marguerite Chapman .... (4)
Original title: LAST PAGE, THE

MAN BEAST (1957) Medallion. **B&W-69min.** Rock Madison, Virginia Maynor .... (3)

MAN BEHIND THE GUN, THE (1953) Warner Bros. **Color-82min.** Randolph Scott, Patrice Wymore **3½***

MAN BETRAYED, A (1941) Republic. **B&W-83min.** John Wayne, Frances Dee **4***
Alternate title: WHEEL OF FORTUNE
British title: CITADEL OF CRIME

MAN BETWEEN, THE (1953) United Artists. **B&W-101min.** *(British).* James Mason, Claire Bloom **5***

MAN CALLED ADAM, A (1966) Avco-Embassy. **B&W-102min.** Sammy Davis, Jr., Ossie Davis, Cicely Tyson **4***

MAN CALLED DAGGER, A (1968) M-G-M. **Color-82min.** Paul Mantee, Terry Moore, Jan Murray .... (2)

MAN CALLED FLINTSTONE, THE (1966) Columbia. **Color-87min.** *(Cartoon). Director:* Joseph Barbera **4***

MAN CALLED GANNON, A (1969) Universal. **Color-105min.** Tony Franciosa, Michael Sarrazin, Judi West **3***

MAN CALLED HORSE, A (1970) Nat'l General (for Cinema Center). **Color-114min.** Richard Harris, Judith Anderson **4***

MAN CALLED NOON, THE (1973) National General. **Color-94min.** *(British).* Richard Crenna, Stephen Boyd, Rosanna Schiaffino .... (4)

MAN CALLED PETER, A (1955) 20th Century-Fox. **Color-119min.** Richard Todd, Jean Peters .... (5)

MAN CALLED SLEDGE, A (1971) Columbia. **Color-90min.** James Garner, Dennis Weaver **3***

MAN CALLED SULLIVAN, A (1945) *see* GREAT JOHN L., THE

MAN COULD GET KILLED, A (1966) Universal. **Color-99min.** James Garner, Melina Mercouri **4***

MAN CRAZY (1953) 20th Century-Fox. **B&W-79min.** Neville Brand, Christine White .... (3)

MAN DETAINED (1961) Anglo Amalgamated [EMI]. **B&W-59min.** *(British).* Bernard Archard, Elvi Hale .... (4)

MAN-EATER OF KUMAON (1948) Universal. **B&W-79min.** Sabu, Wendell Corey, Joanne Page .... (4)

MAN ESCAPED, A (1956) Continental [Walter Reade]. **B&W-102min.** *(French).* Francois Leterrier, Charles LeClainche .... (5)
Original French title: CONDAMNE A MORT S'EST ECHAPPE, UN *(A Condemned Man Escapes)*
Alternate French title: VENT SOUFFLE OU IL VEUT, LE *(The Wind Blows Where It Will)*

MAN FOR ALL SEASONS, A (1966) Columbia. **Color-120min.** *(British).* Paul Scofield, Wendy Hiller **7***

MAN FRIDAY (1975) Avco-Embassy. **Color-115min.** *(British).* Peter O'Toole, Richard Roundtree **5½***

MAN FROM ATLANTIS, THE (1977) NBC-TV. **Color-100min.** *(Made for TV).* Patrick Duffy, Belinda Montgomery, Victor Buono .... (4)

MAN FROM BITTER RIDGE, THE (1955) Universal. **Color-80min.** Lex Barker, Mara Corda, Stephen McNally **3***

MAN FROM BUTTON WILLOW (1965) United Screen Arts. **Color-84min.** *(Cartoon). Director:* David Detiege .... (3)

MAN FROM CAIRO (1953) Lippert Productions. **B&W-82min.** George Raft, Gianna Maria Canale .... (3)

MAN FROM COCODY (1965) American-International. **Color-84min.** *(French-Italian).* Jean Marais, Liselotte Pulver **3***
Original French title: GENTLEMAN DE COCODY, LE
Original Italian title: DONNE, MITRA E DIAMANTI
Alternate title: IVORY COAST ADVENTURE

MAN FROM COLORADO, THE (1948) Columbia. **Color-99min.** Glenn Ford, William Holden **5***

MAN FROM C.O.T.T.O.N. (1963) *see* GONE ARE THE DAYS!

MAN FROM DAKOTA, THE (1940) M-G-M. B&W-75min. Wallace Beery, John Howard 3½*
British title: AROUSE AND BEWARE

MAN FROM DEL RIO (1956) United Artists. B&W-82min. Anthony Quinn, Katy Jurado .... (3)

MAN FROM DOWN UNDER, THE (1943) M-G-M. B&W-103min. Charles Laughton, Donna Reed 3*

MAN FROM FRISCO (1944) Republic. B&W-91min. Michael O'Shea, Dan Duryea, Anne Shirley .... (4)

MAN FROM GALVESTON, THE (1964) Warner Bros. B&W-57min. Jeffrey Hunter, Preston Foster, James Coburn .... (2)

MAN FROM GOD'S COUNTRY (1958) Allied Artists. Color-72min. George Montgomery, Randy Stuart .... (3)

MAN FROM LARAMIE, THE (1955) Columbia. Color-104min. James Stewart, Arthur Kennedy 4*

MAN FROM NEVADA, THE (1950) *see* NEVADAN, THE

MAN FROM NOWHERE, THE (1966) G. G. Productions. Color-107min. *(Italian-French-Spanish).* Giuliano Gemma, Fernando Sancho .... (2)
Original title: ARIZONA COLT

MAN FROM O.R.G.Y., THE (1970) Cinemation. Color-72min. Robert Walker (Jr.), Steve Rossi, Louisa Moritz .... (2)
Alternate title: REAL GONE GIRLS, THE

MAN FROM OKLAHOMA, THE (1964) Parkside Prods. Color-85min. *(German).* Rick Horn, Sabine Bethman .... (2)

MAN FROM PLANET X, THE (1951) United Artists. B&W-70min. Robert Clarke, Margaret Field, William Schallert .... (2)

MAN FROM TANGIER (1957) *see* THUNDER OVER TANGIER

MAN FROM THE ALAMO, THE (1953) Universal. Color-79min. Glenn Ford, Julia (Julie) Adams 4*

MAN FROM THE DINERS' CLUB, THE (1963) Columbia. B&W-96min. Danny Kaye, Cara Williams 3*

MAN FROM THE FOLIES BERGERE, THE (1935) *see* FOLIES BERGERE

MAN FROM YESTERDAY, THE (1932) Paramount. B&W-71min. Charles Boyer, Claudette Colbert, Clive Brook 4*

MAN HE FOUND, THE (1951) *see* WHIP HAND, THE

MAN HUNT (1941) 20th Century-Fox. B&W-105min. Walter Pidgeon, George Sanders, Joan Bennett 5*

MAN HUNTER, THE (1969) MCA-TV. Color-98min. *(Made for TV).* Sandra Dee, Roy Thinnes, Al Hirt .... (4)

MAN I KILLED, THE (1932) *see* BROKEN LULLABY

MAN I LOVE, THE (1947) Warner Bros. B&W-96min. Ida Lupino, Robert Alda 3½*

MAN I MARRIED, THE (1940) 20th Century-Fox. B&W-77min. Joan Bennett, Francis Lederer .... (5)

MAN IN A COCKED HAT (1959) Showcorporation. B&W-88min. *(British).* Terry-Thomas, Peter Sellers .... (4)
Original title: CARLETON-BROWNE OF THE F. O.

MAN IN BLACK, THE (1950) Adrian Weiss. B&W-75min. *(British).* Valentine Dyall, Betty Anne Davies, Sidney James ....

MAN IN GREY, THE (1943) Universal. B&W-116min. *(British).* Margaret Lockwood, James Mason, Phyllis Calvert, Stewart Granger 4*

MAN IN HALF MOON STREET, THE (1944) Paramount. B&W-92min. Nils Asther, Helen Walker .... (3)

MAN IN HIDING (1953) United Artists. B&W-78min. *(British).* Paul Henreid, Lois Maxwell, Kieron Moore .... (3)
Original title: MANTRAP

MAN IN OUTER SPACE (1964) American-International. B&W-85min. *(Czech).* Milos Kopecky, Radovan Lukavsky 3*
Original title: MUZZ PRVNIHO STOLETI *(Man from the First Century)*

MAN IN POSSESSION, THE (1937) *see* PERSONAL PROPERTY

MAN IN THE ATTIC (1953) 20th Century-Fox. B&W-82min. Jack Palance, Constance Smith .... (4)

MAN IN THE BACK SEAT, THE (1961) Anglo Amalgamated [EMI]. B&W-57min. *(British).* Derren Nesbitt, Carol White, Keith Faulkner (4)

MAN IN THE DARK (1953) Columbia. B&W-70min. Edmond O'Brien, Audrey Totter .... (3)

MAN IN THE DARK (1964) Universal. B&W-80min. William Sylvester, Barbara Shelley .... (3)
Original title: BLIND CORNER

MAN IN THE GLASS BOOTH, THE (1975) American Film Theatre. Color-117min. Maximilian Schell, Lois Nettleton 5*

MAN IN THE GRAY FLANNEL SUIT, THE (1956) 20th Century-Fox. Color-153min. Gregory Peck, Jennifer Jones 5*

MAN IN THE IRON MASK, THE (1939) United Artists. B&W-110min. Louis Hayward 5*

MAN IN THE IRON MASK, THE (1977) Independent TV Corp (ITC). Color-100min. *(U.S.-British, Made for TV).* Richard Chamberlain, Jenny Agutter, Patrick McGoohan, Louis Jourdan 5½*

MAN IN THE MIDDLE (1959) *see* 48 HOURS TO LIVE

MAN IN THE MIDDLE, THE (1964) 20th Century-Fox. B&W-94min. *(U.S.-British).* Robert Mitchum, France Nuyen 4*

MAN IN THE MOON (1960) Trans-Lux Distributing. B&W-98min. *(British).* Kenneth More, Shirley Anne Field ...... (5)

MAN IN THE NET, THE (1959) United Artists. B&W-97min. Alan Ladd, Carolyn Jones .... (3)

MAN IN THE RAINCOAT, THE (1956) Kingsley International. B&W-87min. *(French-Italian).* Fernandel, Bernard Blier ...... (5)
Original French title: HOMME A L'IMPERMEABLE, L'

MAN IN THE ROAD, THE (1956) Republic. B&W-84min. *(British).* Derek Farr, Ella Raines .... (3)

MAN IN THE SADDLE (1951) Columbia. Color-87min. Randolph Scott, Joan Leslie 4*
British title: OUTCAST, THE

MAN IN THE SHADOW (1958) Universal. B&W-80min. Jeff Chandler, Orson Welles .... (4)
British title: PAY THE DEVIL

MAN IN THE SKY, THE (1957) *see* DECISION AGAINST TIME

MAN IN THE TRUNK, THE (1942) 20th Century-Fox. B&W-71min. Raymond Walburn, Lynne Roberts .... (2)

MAN IN THE VAULT (1956) RKO. B&W-73min. Anita Ekberg, William Campbell .... (3)

MAN IN THE WATER (1963) *see* ESCAPE FROM HELL ISLAND

MAN IN THE WHITE SUIT, THE (1951) Universal. B&W-84min. *(British).* Alec Guinness, Joan Greenwood 6½*

MAN IN THE WILDERNESS (1958) Warner Bros. Color-105min. Richard Harris, John Huston 5*

MAN INSIDE, THE (1958) Columbia. B&W-90min. *(British).* Jack Palance, Anita Ekberg .... (3)

MAN IS ARMED, THE (1956) Republic. B&W-70min. Dane Clark, May Wynn .... (3)

MAN IS TEN FEET TALL, A (1957) *see* EDGE OF THE CITY

MAN MAD (1958) *see* NO PLACE TO LAND

MAN-MADE MONSTER (1941) Universal. B&W-68min. Lon Chaney, Jr., Lionel Atwill, Anne Nagel .... (3)
British title: ELECTRIC MAN, THE
Alternate title: ATOMIC MONSTER

MAN NAMED JOHN, A (1965) *see* AND THERE CAME A MAN

MAN NAMED ROCCA, A (1961) Telewide Systems. B&W-106min. *(French).* Jean-Paul Belmondo, Christine Kaufmann ...... (3)
Original title: NOMMÉ LA ROCCA, UN

MAN OF A THOUSAND FACES (1957) Universal. B&W-122min. James Cagney, Dorothy Malone 5½*

MAN OF AFFAIRS (1936) Gaumont-British [Rank]. B&W-71min. *(British).* George Arliss, René Ray ....
Original title: HIS LORDSHIP

MAN OF ARAN (1934) Gaumont-British [Rank]. B&W-74min. *(Documentary).* Director: Robert Flaherty 4*

MAN OF BRONZE (1951) *see* JIM THORPE - ALL AMERICAN

MAN OF CONFLICT (1953) Atlas. B&W-72min. Edward Arnold, John Agar .... (3)

MAN OF CONQUEST (1939) Republic. B&W-105min. Richard Dix, Gail Patrick 4*

MAN OF EVIL (1944) United Artists. B&W-107min. *(British).* Phyllis Calvert, James Mason, Stewart Granger ...... (3)
Original title: FANNY BY GASLIGHT

MAN OF IRON (1956) *see* RAILROAD MAN, THE

MAN OF IRON (1973) Bardene International Films. Color-92min. *(Hong Kong).* Chen Kuan-Tai, Ching Li, Wang Chung .... (2)

MAN OF LA MANCHA (1972) United Artists. Color-130min. *(U.S.-Italian).* Peter O'Toole 4½*

MAN OF THE HOUR (1945) *see* COLONEL EFFINGHAM'S RAID

MAN OF THE WEST (1958) United Artists. Color-100min. Gary Cooper, Julie London 4*

MAN OF THE WORLD (1931) Paramount. B&W-71min. William Powell, Carole Lombard, Wynne Gibson .... (3)

Films are rated on a 1 to 10 scale, 10 is highest. **Boldface** ratings followed by an asterisk (*) are for films actually seen and rated by the executive and senior editors. All other ratings are estimates. (See Notes on Entertainment Ratings in the front section.)

MAN OF THE YEAR (1971) Universal. **Color-94min.** *(Italian).* Lando Buzzanca, Rossana Podesta ....
Alternate title: HOMO EROTICUS

MAN OF TWO WORLDS (1934) RKO. **B&W-97min.** Francis Lederer, Elissa Landi .... (4)

MAN ON A STRING (1960) Columbia. **B&W-92min.** Ernest Borgnine, Kerwin Mathews .... (5)
British title: CONFESSIONS OF A COUNTERSPY

MAN ON A STRING (1971) CPT (TV). **Color-75min.** *(Made for TV).* Christopher George, William Schallert, Joel Grey 4*

MAN ON A SWING (1974) Paramount. **Color-108min.** Cliff Robertson, Joel Grey 5½*

MAN ON A TIGHTROPE (1953) 20th Century-Fox. **B&W-105min.** Fredric March, Terry Moore.................... 4*

MAN ON AMERICA'S CONSCIENCE, THE (1942) *see* TENNESSEE JOHNSON

MAN ON FIRE (1957) M-G-M. **B&W-95min.** Bing Crosby, Inger Stevens......................... 3½*

MAN ON THE EIFFEL TOWER, THE (1948) RKO. **Color-82min.** Charles Laughton, Franchot Tone .... (5)

MAN ON THE FLYING TRAPEZE, THE (1935) Paramount. **B&W-65min.** W. C. Fields, Mary Brian 5½*
British title: MEMORY EXPERT, THE

MAN ON THE OUTSIDE (1973) MCA-TV. **Color-102min.** *(Made for TV).* Lorne Greene, James Olson, Lorraine Gary 4½*

MAN ON THE ROOF (1977) Cinema 5. **Color-110min.** *(Swedish).* Carl Gustaf Lindstedt, Sven Wollter............ 5*

MAN ON THE RUN (1949) Stratford Pictures. **B&W-82min.** *(British).* Derek Farr, Joan Hopkins, Edward Chapman .... (3)

MAN ON THE RUN (1964) *see* KIDNAPPERS, THE

MAN OR GUN (1958) Republic. **B&W-79min.** Macdonald Carey, Audrey Totter .... (3)

MAN OUTSIDE, THE (1968) Allied Artists. **Color-97min.** *(British).* Van Heflin, Heidelinde Weis 3*

MAN-PROOF (1938) M-G-M. **B&W-74min.** Myrna Loy, Franchot Tone, Rosalind Russell .... (4)

MAN THEY COULD NOT HANG, THE (1939) Columbia. **B&W-72min.** Boris Karloff, Lorna Gray 4*

MAN TO MAN TALK (1958) *see* PREMIER MAY

MAN TO REMEMBER, A (1938) RKO. **B&W-80min.** Edward Ellis, Anne Shirley .... (5)

MAN TO RESPECT, A (1974) *see* MASTER TOUCH, THE

MAN-TRAP (1961) Paramount. **B&W-93min.** Jeffrey Hunter, David Janssen, Stella Stevens .... (3)

MAN UPSTAIRS, THE (1958) Kingsley International. **B&W-88min.** *(British).* Richard Attenborough, Bernard Lee .... (5)

MAN WHO BROKE THE BANK AT MONTE CARLO, THE (1935) 20th Century-Fox. **B&W-70min.** Ronald Colman, Joan Bennett, Colin Clive .... (4)

MAN WHO CAME BACK, THE (1941) *see* SWAMP WATER

MAN WHO CAME TO DINNER, THE (1941) Warner Bros. **B&W-112min.** Monty Woolley, Bette Davis.................... 6½*

MAN WHO CHANGED HIS MIND, THE (1936) *see* MAN WHO LIVED AGAIN, THE

MAN WHO CHEATED HIMSELF, THE (1951) 20th Century-Fox. **B&W-81min.** Lee J. Cobb, Jane Wyatt .... (4)

MAN WHO CHEATED LIFE, THE (1926) Affiliated European Producers. **B&W-67min.** *(German, Silent).* Conrad Veidt, Werner Krauss .... (4)
Original title: STUDENT VON PRAG, DER
Alternate title: STUDENT OF PRAGUE, THE

MAN WHO COULD CHEAT DEATH, THE (1959) Paramount. **Color-83min.** *(British).* Anton Diffring, Hazel Court .... (3)

MAN WHO COULD TALK TO KIDS, THE (1973) Tomorrow Entertainment. **Color-75min.** *(Made for TV).* Peter Boyle, Robert Reed, Scott Jacoby 4*

MAN WHO COULD WORK MIRACLES, THE (1937) United Artists. **B&W-82min.** *(British).* Roland Young, Joan Gardner............ 6*

MAN WHO CRIED WOLF, THE (1937) Universal. **B&W-66min.** Lewis Stone, Tom Brown .... (4)

MAN WHO DARED, THE (1933) Fox Film Co. [20th]. **B&W-75min.** Preston Foster, Zita Johann .... (4)

MAN WHO DARED, THE (1939) Warner Bros. **B&W-60min.** Charley Grapewin, Jane Bryan .... (3)
TV title: CITY IN TERROR

MAN WHO DARED, THE (1946) Columbia. **B&W-65min.** Forrest Tucker, George Macready, Leslie Brooks .... (4)

MAN WHO DIED TWICE, THE (1958) Republic. **B&W-70min.** Rod Cameron, Vera Ralston .... (3)

MAN WHO DIED TWICE, THE (1970) CBS-TV. **Color-100min.** *(Made for TV).* Stuart Whitman, Brigitte Fossey .... (4)

MAN WHO FELL TO EARTH, THE (1976) British Lion [EMI]. **Color-118min.** *(British).* David Bowie, Rip Torn.................... 2*

MAN WHO FINALLY DIED, THE (1963) Goldstone Film Enterprises. **B&W-98min.** *(British).* Stanley Baker, Peter Cushing ....

MAN WHO FOUND HIMSELF (1937) RKO. **B&W-67min.** John Beal, Joan Fontaine .... (4)

MAN WHO HAD POWER OVER WOMEN, THE (1970) Warner Bros. **Color-89min.** *(British).* Rod Taylor, Carol White .... (3)

MAN WHO HAUNTED HIMSELF, THE (1970) Levitt-Pickman. **Color-94min.** *(British).* Roger Moore, Hildegarde Neil 4*

MAN WHO KNEW TOO MUCH, THE (1934) Gaumont-British [Rank]. **B&W-74min.** *(British).* Leslie Banks, Edna Best, Peter Lorre............ 3*

MAN WHO KNEW TOO MUCH, THE (1956) Paramount. **Color-120min.** James Stewart, Doris Day 6*

MAN WHO LIKED FUNERALS, THE (1959) J. Arthur Rank. **B&W-60min.** *(British).* Leslie Phillips, Susan Beaumont .... (3)

MAN WHO LIVED AGAIN, THE (1936) Gaumont-British [Rank]. **B&W-61min.** *(British).* Boris Karloff, Anna Lee .... (3)
Original title: MAN WHO CHANGED HIS MIND, THE
Alternate title: BRAINSNATCHER, THE
Alternate title: DR. MANIAC

MAN WHO LIVED TWICE, THE (1936) Columbia. **B&W-73min.** Ralph Bellamy, Marian Marsh .... (3)

MAN WHO LOVED CAT DANCING, THE (1973) M-G-M. **Color-114min.** Burt Reynolds, Sarah Miles 3*

MAN WHO LOVED REDHEADS, THE (1955) United Artists. **Color-89min.** *(British).* Moira Shearer, John Justin .... (5)

MAN WHO LOVED WOMEN, THE (1977) Cinema 5. **Color-119min.** *(French).* Charles Denner, Brigitte Fossey 5½*
Original title: HOMME QUI AIMAIT LES FEMMES, L'

MAN WHO NEVER WAS, THE (1956) 20th Century-Fox. **Color-103min.** Clifton Webb, Gloria Grahame.................... 5*

MAN WHO PLAYED GOD, THE (1932) Warner Bros. **B&W-81min.** George Arliss, Violet Heming 4½*
British title: SILENT VOICE, THE

MAN WHO RECLAIMED HIS HEAD, THE (1934) Universal. **B&W-82min.** Claude Rains, Joan Bennett, Lionel Atwill 4*

MAN WHO RETURNED TO LIFE (1942) Columbia. **B&W-60min.** John Howard, Ruth Ford .... (4)

MAN WHO SHOT LIBERTY VALANCE, THE (1962) Paramount. **B&W-122min.** John Wayne, James Stewart.................... 5*

MAN WHO SKIED DOWN EVEREST, THE (1975) Crawley Films, Ltd. **Color-86min.** *(Canadian-Japanese, Documentary). Director:* Isao Zeniya 5½*

MAN WHO TALKED TOO MUCH, THE (1940) Warner Bros. **B&W-75min.** George Brent, Virginia Bruce .... (4)

MAN WHO TURNED TO STONE, THE (1957) Columbia. **B&W-80min.** Victor Jory, Charlotte Austin .... (2)

MAN WHO UNDERSTOOD WOMEN, THE (1959) 20th Century-Fox. **Color-105min.** Leslie Caron, Henry Fonda.................... 4*

MAN WHO WAGGED HIS TAIL, THE (1957) Continental [Walter Reade]. **B&W-91min.** *(Spanish).* Peter Ustinov, Pablito Calfo .... (5)
Original title: ANGEL PASO SOBRE BROOKLYN, UN *(An Angel Passes Over Brooklyn)*

MAN WHO WANTED TO LIVE FOREVER, THE (1970) ABC-TV. **Color-75min.** *(Canadian-U.S., Made for TV).* Stuart Whitman, Sandy Dennis, Burl Ives 4½*
British title: ONLY WAY OUT IS DEAD, THE

MAN WHO WAS NOBODY, THE (1960) Anglo Amalgamated [EMI]. **B&W-58min.** *(British).* Hazel Court, John Crawford .... (3)

MAN WHO WATCHED TRAINS GO BY, THE (1953) *see* PARIS EXPRESS, THE

MAN WHO WOULD BE KING, THE (1975) Columbia. **Color-129min.** Sean Connery, Michael Caine.................... 6*

MAN WHO WOULD NOT DIE, THE (1975) Dandrea Releasing. **Color-83min.** Dorothy Malone, Keenan Wynn, Aldo Ray 2½*

MAN WHO WOULDN'T DIE, THE (1942) 20th Century-Fox. **B&W-65min.** Lloyd Nolan, Marjorie Weaver .... (3)

THE MAN WHO WOULD BE KING (1975) is Sean Connery. He and his comrade Michael Caine have realized wealth beyond their wildest dreams bestowed on them by the primitive people of Kafiristan.

MAN WHO WOULDN'T TALK, THE (1940) 20th Century-Fox. **B&W-**72min. Lloyd Nolan, Jean Rogers.................................... (3)

MAN WHO WOULDN'T TALK, THE (1958) Showcorporation. **B&W-**85min. *(British).* Anthony Quayle, Anna Neagle .... (4)

MAN WITH A CLOAK, THE (1951) M-G-M. **B&W-81min.** Joseph Cotten, Barbara Stanwyck .... (4)

MAN WITH A MILLION (1954) United Artists. **Color-90min.** *(British).* Gregory Peck, Jane Griffiths 5½*
British title: MILLION POUND NOTE, THE

MAN WITH CONNECTIONS, THE (1971) Columbia. **Color-91min.** *(French).* Guy Bedos, Yves Robert, Rosy Varte .... (5)
Original title: PISTONNÉ, LE

MAN WITH MY FACE, THE (1951) United Artists. **B&W-86min.** John Harvey, Barry Nelson .... (4)

MAN WITH NINE LIVES, THE (1940) Columbia. **B&W-73min.** Boris Karloff, Roger Pryor 3*
British title: BEHIND THE DOOR

MAN WITH THE BALLOONS, THE (1964) Sigma III. **B&W-85min.** *(French-Italian).* Marcello Mastroianni, Catherine Spaak, Ugo Tognazzi .... (4)
Original Italian title: UOMO DAI CINQUE PALLONI, L'
Alternate Italian title: UOMO DAI PALLONCINI, L'
Included in: OGGI, DOMANI E DOPODOMANI *(Today, Tomorrow and the Next Day)*

MAN WITH THE GOLDEN ARM, THE (1955) United Artists. **B&W-**119min. Frank Sinatra, Eleanor Parker................... 4½*

MAN WITH THE GOLDEN GUN, THE (1974) United Artists. **Color-**125min. *(British).* Roger Moore, Christopher Lee 5½*

MAN WITH THE GOLDEN KEYS (1956) **B&W-90min.** *(French).* Pierre Fresnay, Annie Girardot .... (3)

MAN WITH THE GREEN CARNATION, THE (1960) *see* TRIALS OF OSCAR WILDE, THE

MAN WITH THE GUN (1955) United Artists. **B&W-83min.** Robert Mitchum, Jan Sterling 3½*
British title: TROUBLE SHOOTER, THE

MAN WITH THE X-RAY EYES, THE (1963) *see* X - THE MAN WITH THE X-RAY EYES

MAN WITH THIRTY SONS, THE (1950) *see* MAGNIFICENT YANKEE, THE

MAN WITH TWO FACES, THE (1934) First National [W.B.]. **B&W-**72min. Edward G. Robinson, Mary Astor .... (4)

MAN WITH TWO FACES (1964) Commonwealth United TV. **B&W-**80min. Tab Hunter, Zina Walker................................ (3)

MAN WITH TWO HEADS, THE (1972) William Mishkin. **Color-80min.** Denis DeMarne, Julia Stratton.............................. (2)

MAN WITHIN, THE (1947) *see* SMUGGLERS, THE

MAN WITHOUT A BODY, THE (1957) Budd Rogers. **B&W-80min.** *(British).* Robert Hutton, George Coulouris, Michael Golden ....

MAN WITHOUT A STAR (1955) Universal. **Color-89min.** Kirk Douglas, Jeanne Crain... 5*

MANCHU EAGLE MURDER CAPER MYSTERY, THE (1975) United Artists. **Color-80min.** Gabriel Dell, Will Geer, Joyce Van Patten.......... (4)

MANCHURIAN CANDIDATE, THE (1962) United Artists. **B&W-126min.** Frank Sinatra, Laurence Harvey 7*

MANDALAY (1934) First National [W.B.]. **B&W-65min.** Ricardo Cortez, Kay Francis, Lyle Talbot .... (4)

MANDINGO (1975) Paramount. **Color-126min.** James Mason, Susan George, Perry King, Ken Norton 5*

MANDRAGOLA (1965) Europix-Consolidated. **B&W-98min.** *(Italian-French).* Rosanna Schiaffino, Philippe Leroy .... (4)
Translation title: The Mandrake *or* The Love Root

MANDRAGORE (1928) *see* ALRAUNE

MANDY (1952) *see* CRASH OF SILENCE

MANEATER (1973) MCA-TV. **Color-74min.** *(Made for TV).* Ben Gazzara, Sheree North, Richard Basehart 3*

MANFISH (1956) United Artists. **Color-76min.** John Bromfield, Lon Chaney (Jr.), Victor Jory................................... (3)
British title: CALYPSO

MANHANDLED (1949) Paramount. **B&W-97min.** Dorothy Lamour, Sterling Hayden, Dan Duryea .... (3)

MANHATTAN (1979) United Artists. **B&W-96min.** Woody Allen, Diane Keaton, Michael Murphy, Meryl Streep 6*

MANHATTAN ANGEL (1948) Columbia. **B&W-68min.** Gloria Jean, Ross Ford.. (3)

MANHATTAN HEARTBEAT (1940) 20th Century-Fox. **B&W-71min.** Virginia Gilmore, Joan Davis, Robert Sterling .... (3)

MANHATTAN MADNESS (1936) *see* ADVENTURE IN MANHATTAN

MANHATTAN MELODRAMA (1934) M-G-M. **B&W-93min.** Clark Gable, William Powell.. 3½*

MANHUNT (1958) *see* FROM HELL TO TEXAS

MANHUNT IN SPACE (1954) Official Industries. **B&W-78min.** *(Telefeature).* Richard Crane, Robert Lydon .... (2)

MANHUNT IN THE AFRICAN JUNGLE (1943) *see* BARON'S AFRICAN WAR, THE

MANHUNT IN THE JUNGLE (1958) Warner Bros. **Color-79min.** Robin Hughes, James Wilson .... (3)

MANHUNT OF MYSTERY ISLAND (1945) *see* CAPTAIN MEPHISTO AND THE TRANSFORMATION MACHINE

MANHUNTER (1974) Viacom. **Color-74min.** *(Made for TV).* Ken Howard, Gary Lockwood, Stefanie Powers........................ 4*

MANIA (1960) Valiant. **B&W-97min.** *(British).* Peter Cushing, George Rose, Donald Pleasence .... (4)
British title: FLESH AND THE FIENDS, THE
Alternate title: FIENDISH GHOULS, THE

MANIAC (1963) Columbia. **B&W-86min.** *(British).* Kerwin Mathews, Nadia Gray, Donald Houston.............................. (3)

MANIAC (1977) New World. **Color-90min.** Oliver Reed, Paul Koslo, Stuart Whitman ....
Original title: ASSAULT ON PARADISE
Alternate title: TOWN THAT CRIED TERROR, THE

MANILA CALLING (1942) 20th Century-Fox. **B&W-81min.** Lloyd Nolan, Carole Landis.. (3)

MANITOU, THE (1978) Avco-Embassy. **Color-104min.** Susan Strasberg, Tony Curtis.. 5*

MANNEQUIN (1937) M-G-M. **B&W-95min.** Joan Crawford, Spencer Tracy 3½*

MANON (1949) Discina International. **B&W-91min.** *(French).* Cecile Aubry, Michel Auclair .... (5)

MANPOWER (1941) Warner Bros. **B&W-105min.** Edward G. Robinson, Marlene Dietrich, George Raft.......................... 3*

MAN'S CASTLE, A (1933) Columbia. **B&W-75min.** Spencer Tracy, Loretta Young.. 4½*

MAN'S FAVORITE SPORT? (1964) Universal. **Color-120min.** Rock Hudson, Paula Prentiss................................... 4*

MAN'S HERITAGE (1939) *see* SPIRIT OF CULVER

MAN'S WORLD, A (1942) Columbia. **B&W-60min.** Marguerite Chapman, William Wright .... (3)

MANSION OF THE DOOMED (1975) Group 1. **Color-85min.** Richard Basehart, Gloria Grahame 4*
British title: TERROR OF DR. CHANEY, THE

MANSON (1972) Tobann International. **Color-93min.** *(Documentary).* *Director:* Robert Hendrickson 5½*
Alternate title: MANSON FAMILY, THE

MANSTER, THE (1962) Lopert [U.A.]. **B&W-72min.** *(U.S.-Japanese).* Peter Dyneley, Jane Hylton .... (2)

MANTRAP (1926) Paramount. **B&W-81min.** *(Silent).* Clara Bow, Ernest Torrence, Percy Marmount .... (4)

MANTRAP (1953) *see* MAN IN HIDING

MANUELA (1957) *see* STOWAWAY GIRL

MANUSCRIPT FOUND IN SARAGOSSA (1965) *see* SARAGOSSA MANUSCRIPT, THE

MANY HAPPY RETURNS (1934) Paramount. **B&W-60min.** George Burns, Gracie Allen .... (3)

MANY RIVERS TO CROSS (1955) M-G-M. **Color-92min.** Robert Taylor, Eleanor Parker .... (5)

MARA MARU (1952) Warner Bros. **B&W-98min.** Errol Flynn, Ruth Roman 4*

MARA OF THE WILDERNESS (1965) Allied Artists. **Color-90min.** Linda Saunders, Adam West 3*

MARACAIBO (1958) Paramount. **Color-88min.** Cornel Wilde, Francis Lederer, Abbe Lane 4*

MARAT/SADE (1967) United Artists. **Color-115min.** *(British).* Patrick Magee, Ian Richardson, Glenda Jackson 4*
Screen title: PERSECUTION AND ASSASSINATION OF JEAN-PAUL MARAT AS PERFORMED BY THE INMATES OF THE ASYLUM OF CHARENTON UNDER THE DIRECTION OF THE MARQUIS DE SADE, THE

MARATHON MAN (1976) Paramount. **Color-125min.** Dustin Hoffman, Laurence Olivier 6½*

MARAUDERS, THE (1955) M-G-M. **Color-81min.** Dan Duryea, Keenan Wynn, Jeff Richards 3*

MARAUDERS OF THE SEA (1962) **B&W-85min.** *(British, Telefeature).* Terence Morgan, Jean Kent .... (3)

MARCELINO (1955) United Motion Pic. Org. (UMPO). **B&W-90min.** Pablito Calvo, Rafael Rivelles .... (5)
Publicity title: MIRACLE OF MARCELINO, THE
Original title: MARCELINO PAN Y VINO *(Marcelino Bread and Wine)*

MARCH OF THE TOYS (1934) *see* BABES IN TOYLAND

MARCH OF THE WOODEN SOLDIERS (1934) *see* BABES IN TOYLAND

MARCH OR DIE (1977) Columbia. **Color-107min.** *(British).* Gene Hackman, Terence Hill 4*

MARCHING ALONG (1952) *see* STARS AND STRIPES FOREVER

MARCO (1973) Cinerama Releasing. **Color-109min.** Desi Arnaz, Jr., Zero Mostel 3*

MARCO POLO (1961) American-International. **Color-95min.** *(Italian-French, English version).* Rory Calhoun, Yoko Tani 3*

MARCO THE MAGNIFICENT (1966) M-G-M. **Color-100min.** *(French-Afghanistani-Egyptian-Italian-Yugoslavian).* Horst Buchholz, Anthony Quinn, Orson Welles 3*
Original French title: FABULEUSE AVENTURE DE MARCO POLO, LA
Original Italian title: MERAVIGLIOSE AVVENTURE DI MARCO POLO, LE
Original Yugoslav title: MARKO POLO

MARCUS-NELSON MURDERS, THE (1973) MCA-TV. **Color-125min.** *(Made for TV).* Telly Savalas, Marjoe Gortner, José Ferrer 5*
Alternate title: KOJAK AND THE MARCUS-NELSON MURDERS

MARCUS WELBY, M.D. (1969) Universal. **Color-100min.** *(Made for TV).* Robert Young, James Brolin, Anne Baxter 4*
Alternate title: MATTER OF HUMANITIES

MARDI GRAS (1958) 20th Century-Fox. **Color-107min.** Pat Boone, Tommy Sands, Christine Carere .... (4)

MARGIE (1946) 20th Century-Fox. **Color-94min.** Jeanne Crain, Glenn Langan 4*

MARGIN FOR ERROR (1943) 20th Century-Fox. **B&W-74min.** Joan Bennett, Milton Berle, Otto Preminger .... (4)

MARGO (1971) Cannon Releasing. **B&W-90min.** *(Israeli).* Levana Finklstein, Oded Teomi, Ayner Hizkyahu .... (5)
Original title: MARGO SHELI *(My Margo)*
Publicity title: LOVE IN JERUSALEM
Publicity title: MY LOVE IN JERUSALEM

MARIA, THE WONDERFUL WEAVER (1960) *see* MAGIC WEAVER, THE

MARIANNE (1929) M-G-M. **B&W-112min.** Marion Davies, George Baxter .... (4)

MARIANNE OF MY YOUTH (1955) United Motion Pic. Org. (UMPO). **B&W-105min.** *(French).* Marianne Hold, Pierre Vaneck .... (3)
Original title: MARIANNE DE MA JEUNESSE

MARIE ANTOINETTE (1938) M-G-M. **B&W-160min.** Norma Shearer, Tyrone Power 5*

MARIE ANTOINETTE (1956) Rizzoli Film. **Color-108min.** *(French-Italian).* Michele Morgan, Richard Todd, Jean Morel .... (4)

MARIE DU PORT, LA (1949) Bellon-Foulke. **B&W-95min.** *(French).* Jean Gabin, Blanchette Brunoy, Nicole Courcel .... (5)
Translation title: Marie of the Port

MARIE-OCTOBRE (1959) Lopert [U.A.]. **B&W-98min.** *(French).* Danielle Darrieux, Bernard Blier .... (5)
Alternate title: SECRET MEETING

MARIE OF THE ISLES (1961) Telewide Systems. **Color-111min.** *(Italian).* Belinda Lee, Alain Saury .... (3)

MARIE WALEWSKA (1937) *see* CONQUEST

MARIE'S MILLIONS (1928) *see* TILLIE'S PUNCTURED ROMANCE

MARILYN (1963) 20th Century-Fox. **B&W-83min.** *(Compilation).* Rock Hudson, Marilyn Monroe 5*

MARINE RAIDERS (1944) RKO. **B&W-91min.** Pat O'Brien, Robert Ryan .... (3)

MARINERS OF THE SKY (1936) *see* NAVY BORN

MARINES FLY HIGH (1940) RKO. **B&W-68min.** Chester Morris, Richard Dix, Lucille Ball .... (5)

MARINES HAVE LANDED, THE (1936) *see* LEATHERNECKS HAVE LANDED, THE

MARINES, LET'S GO! (1961) 20th Century-Fox. **Color-104min.** Tom Tryon, David Hedison, Tom Reese 3*

MARIUS (1931) Pathé Contemporary. **B&W-120min.** *(French).* Raimu, Orane Demazis .... (5)

MARIZINIA (1962) International Film/Diamond/Golden Eagle. **Color-82min.** *(U.S.-Brazilian).* John Sutton, Gina Albert, Zygmunt Sulistrowski 2*
Alternate title: MARIZINIA, THE WITCH BENEATH THE SEA
Alternate title: WITCH BENEATH THE SEA, THE

MARJOE (1972) Cinema 5. **Color-88min.** *(Documentary). Director:* Howard Smith 6*

MARJORIE MORNINGSTAR (1958) Warner Bros. **Color-123min.** Natalie Wood, Gene Kelly 3*

MARK, THE (1961) Continental [Walter Reade]. **B&W-127min.** *(British).* Stuart Whitman, Maria Schell, Rod Steiger 5½*

MARK OF CAIN (1948) J. Arthur Rank. **B&W-88min.** *(British).* Eric Portman, Sally Gray .... (4)

MARK OF THE CLAW (1947) *see* DICK TRACY'S DILEMMA

MARK OF THE DEVIL (1970) Hallmark. **Color-95min.** *(W. German-British).* Herbert Lom, Olivera Vuco, Udo Kier .... (1)
Original W. German title: BRENN: HEXE, BRENN *(Burn, Witch, Burn)*

MARK OF THE DEVIL, PART II (1972) Hallmark. **Color-90min.** *(German).* Erika Blanc, Anton Diffring .... (1)
Original title: HEXEN: GESCHANDET UND ZU TODE GEQUALT
Alternate title: WITCHES: VIOLATED AND TORTURED TO DEATH

MARK OF THE GORILLA (1950) Columbia. **B&W-68min.** Johnny Weissmuller, Trudy Marshall .... (3)

MARK OF THE HAWK, THE (1958) Universal. **Color-83min.** Sidney Poitier, Juano Hernandez 4*

MARK OF THE PHOENIX (1957) United Artists. **B&W-63min.** *(British).* Sheldon Lawrence, Julia Arnall .... (3)

MARK OF THE RENEGADE (1951) Universal. **Color-81min.** Ricardo Montalban, Cyd Charisse 4*

MARK OF THE VAMPIRE (1935) M-G-M. **B&W-85min.** Lionel Barrymore, Elizabeth Allan, Bela Lugosi 3*

MARK OF THE VAMPIRE, THE (1957) *see* VAMPIRE, THE

MARK OF THE WEST (1959) *see* CURSE OF THE UNDEAD

MARK OF THE WHISTLER, THE (1944) Columbia. **B&W-61min.** Richard Dix, Janis Carter .... (5)
British title: MARKED MAN, THE

MARK OF THE WITCH (1972) Favorite Films of California. **Color-77min.** Robert Elston, Anitra Walsh, Darryl Wells .... (2)

MARK OF ZORRO, THE (1920) United Artists. **B&W-80min.** *(Silent).* Douglas Fairbanks, Marguerite de la Motte, Noah Beery 5*

MARK OF ZORRO, THE (1940) 20th Century-Fox. **B&W-93min.** Tyrone Power, Linda Darnell 5½*

MARK OF ZORRO, THE (1974) ABC-TV. **Color-74min.** *(Made for TV).* Frank Langella, Ricardo Montalban ....

MARKED MAN, THE (1944) *see* MARK OF THE WHISTLER, THE

MARKED WOMAN (1937) Warner Bros. **B&W-96min.** Bette Davis, Humphrey Bogart 3*

Films are rated on a 1 to 10 scale, 10 is highest. **Boldface** ratings followed by an asterisk (*) are for films actually seen and rated by the executive and senior editors. All other ratings are estimates. (See Notes on Entertainment Ratings in the front section.)

MARKSMAN, THE (1953) Allied Artists. B&W-62min. Wayne Morris, Elena Verdugo..(3)

MARLOWE (1969) M-G-M. Color-100min. James Garner, Gayle Hunnicutt..4*

MARNIE (1964) Universal. Color-129min. 'Tippi' Hedren, Sean Connery..5*

MAROC 7 (1966) Paramount. Color-92min. (British). Gene Barry, Elsa Martinelli, Cyd Charisse................................3*

MAROONED (1969) Columbia. Color-133min. Gregory Peck, Richard Crenna..4*

MARQUISE OF O . . ., THE (1976) New Line Cinema. Color-102min. (French-W. German). Edith Clever, Bruno Ganz................
Original German title: MARQUISE VON O . . ., DIE

MARRIAGE CAME TUMBLING DOWN, THE (1968) Royal Films Int'l [Columbia]. Color-88min. (French). Michel Simon, Marie Dubois, Yves Lefebvre..(5)
Original title: CE SACRÉ GRAND-PERE *(That Damned Grandfather)*

MARRIAGE-GO-ROUND, THE (1961) 20th Century-Fox. Color-98min. Susan Hayward, James Mason................................3*

MARRIAGE IS A PRIVATE AFFAIR (1944) M-G-M. B&W-116min. Lana Turner, James Craig..(3)

MARRIAGE ITALIAN STYLE (1964) Avco-Embassy. Color-102min. (Italian-French). Sophia Loren, Marcello Mastroianni................5*
Original Italian title: MATRIMONIA ALL'ITALIANA
Original French title: MARIAGE A L'ITALIENNE

MARRIAGE OF A YOUNG STOCKBROKER, THE (1971) 20th Century-Fox. Color-95min. Richard Benjamin, Joanna Shimkus................3½*

MARRIAGE OF FIGARO, THE (1959) Pathé Contemporary. Color-105min. (French). Georges Descrieres, Yvonne Gaudeau................(5)
Original title: MARIAGE DE FIGARO, LE

MARRIAGE ON THE ROCKS (1965) Warner Bros. Color-109min. Frank Sinatra, Deborah Kerr..(4)

MARRIAGE: YEAR ONE (1971) MCA-TV. Color-97min. (Made for TV). Sally Field, Robert Pratt, Cicely Tyson, William Windom................4*
Alternate title: YEAR 1

MARRIED BACHELOR (1941) M-G-M. B&W-81min. Robert Young, Ruth Hussey..(4)

MARRIED BEFORE BREAKFAST (1937) M-G-M. B&W-70min. Robert Young, Florence Rice..(4)

MARRIED - BUT SINGLE (1941) see THIS THING CALLED LOVE

MARRIED COUPLE, A (1969) Aquarius. Color-97min. (Canadian, Documentary). Director: Allan King................................(4)

MARRIED WOMAN, THE (1964) Royal Films Int'l [Columbia]. B&W-94min. (French). Macha Méril, Bernard Noel, Philippe Leroy................(4)
Original title: FEMME MARIÉE, LA

MARRY ME! (1949) J. Arthur Rank. B&W-97min. (British). Derek Bond, Zena Marshall..(4)

MARRY ME AGAIN (1954) RKO. B&W-73min. Marie Wilson, Robert Cummings..(4)

MARRY ME! MARRY ME! (1968) Allied Artists. Color-87min. (French). Claude Berri, Elisabeth Winer................................4*
Original title: MAZEL TOV OU LE MARIAGE *(Mazel Tov or the Marriage)*

MARRY THE BOSS' DAUGHTER (1941) 20th Century-Fox. B&W-60min. Brenda Joyce, Bruce Edwards................................(2)

MARRYING KIND, THE (1952) Columbia. B&W-93min. Judy Holliday, Aldo Ray..3½*

MARS ATTACKS THE WORLD (1938) see DEADLY RAY FROM MARS, THE

MARS, GOD OF WAR (1962) see VENUS AGAINST THE SON OF HERCULES

MARS NEEDS WOMEN (1968) American-International. Color-82min. Tommy Kirk, Yvonne Craig..2*

MARSEILLES CONTRACT, THE (1974) see DESTRUCTORS, THE

MARSHAL'S DAUGHTER, THE (1953) United Artists. B&W-71min. Laurie Anders, Ken Murray, Hoot Gibson................................(2)

MARSHMALLOW MOON (1952) see AARON SLICK FROM PUNKIN CRICK

MARTIANS, THE (1965) see FLYING SAUCER, THE

MARTIN EDEN (1942) see ADVENTURES OF MARTIN EDEN, THE

MARTIN LUTHER (1953) De Rochemont. B&W-103min. Niall MacGinnis, John Ruddock..(5)

MARTY (1955) United Artists. B&W-99min. Ernest Borgnine, Betsy Blair..5½*

MARX BROTHERS AT THE CIRCUS (1939) see AT THE CIRCUS

MARX BROTHERS GO WEST, THE (1940) see GO WEST

MARY BURNS, FUGITIVE (1935) Paramount. B&W-84min. Sylvia Sidney, Melvyn Douglas..(5)

MARY LOU (1948) Columbia. B&W-66min. Joan Barton, Robert Lowery..(2)

MARY, MARY (1963) Warner Bros. Color-126min. Debbie Reynolds, Barry Nelson..5*

MARY NAMES THE DAY (1941) see DR. KILDARE'S WEDDING DAY

MARY OF SCOTLAND (1936) RKO. B&W-123min. Katharine Hepburn, Fredric March..5*

MARY POPPINS (1964) Buena Vista. Color-140min. Julie Andrews, Dick Van Dyke..6½*

MARY, QUEEN OF SCOTS (1971) Universal. Color-128min. (British-U.S.). Vanessa Redgrave, Glenda Jackson................6½*

MARY WHITE (1977) ABC-TV. Color-105min. (Made for TV). Kathleen Beller, Ed Flanders..4*

MARYJANE (1968) American-International. Color-95min. Fabian, Diane McBain, Kevin Coughlin..(2)

MARYLAND (1940) 20th Century-Fox. Color-92min. Walter Brennan, Fay Bainter..(4)

MASCULINE FEMININE (1966) Royal Films Int'l [Columbia]. B&W-103min. (French-Swedish). Jean-Pierre Leaud, Chantal Goya................(4)
Original French title: MASCULIN FÉMININ
Swedish title: MASKULINUM-FEMININUM

M*A*S*H (1969) 20th Century-Fox. Color-116min. Donald Sutherland, Elliott Gould..5*

MASK, THE (1961) Warner Bros. B&W-83min. (Canadian-U.S.). Paul Stevens, Claudette Nevins..(2)
Alternate title: EYES OF HELL

MASK OF DIIJON, THE (1946) Producers Rel. Corp. [Eagle Lion]. B&W-73min. Erich von Stroheim, Jeanne Bates................(3)

MASK OF DIMITRIOS, THE (1944) Warner Bros. B&W-95min. Peter Lorre, Sydney Greenstreet

MASK OF FU MANCHU, THE (1932) M-G-M. B&W-72min. Boris Karloff, Lewis Stone..3*

MASK OF FURY (1945) see FIRST YANK INTO TOKYO

MASK OF MARCELLA (1972) see COOL MILLION

MASK OF THE AVENGER (1951) Columbia. Color-83min. John Derek, Jody Lawrence, Anthony Quinn................................3½*

MASK OF THE MUSKETEERS (1960) American-International. Color-101min. (Italian). Gordon Scott, José Greco................(3)

MASKED CONQUERER, THE (1960) American-International. Color-94min. (Italian). Alberto Lupo, Giorgio Ardisson................(1)

MASKED MAN AGAINST THE PIRATES, THE (1962) ABC Films. Color-105min. (Spanish). George Hilton, Claude Dantes................(2)

As **MARY POPPINS** (1964), Julie Andrews rests on a cloud before she floats down to assume her new duties as a nanny to a pair of London children.

Films are rated on a 1 to 10 scale, 10 is highest. **Boldface** ratings followed by an asterisk (*) are for films actually seen and rated by the executive and senior editors. All other ratings are estimates. (See Notes on Entertainment Ratings in the front section.)

MASKED MARVEL, THE (1943) see SAKIMA AND THE MASKED MARVEL

MASKED PIRATE, THE (1949) see PIRATES OF CAPRI

MASQUE OF THE RED DEATH, THE (1964) American-International. Color-90min. (U.S.-British). Vincent Price, Hazel Court, Jane Asher.... 5*

MASQUERADE (1965) United Artists. Color-102min. (British). Cliff Robertson, Jack Hawkins................4*

MASQUERADE IN MEXICO (1945) Paramount. B&W-96min. Dorothy Lamour, Arturo De Cordova ....(3)

MASQUERADER, THE (1933) United Artists. B&W-78min. Ronald Colman, Elissa Landi.....................4*

MASSACRE (1956) 20th Century-Fox. Color-76min. Dane Clark, James Craig.....................3*

MASSACRE AT CENTRAL HIGH (1976) Brian Distributing. Color-85min. Derrel Maury, Andrew Stevens....................(3)
British title: BLACKBOARD MASSACRE

MASSACRE AT FORT PERDITION (1965) Avco-Embassy. Color-92min. (Spanish). Jerry Cobb (German Cobos), Martha May (Marta May), Hugh Pepper (Hugo Pimentel) ....(3)
Original title: FUERTE PERDIDO (Fort Perdition)

MASSACRE CANYON (1954) Columbia. B&W-66min. Philip Carey, Audrey Totter.....................(3)

MASSACRE HILL (1948) see EUREKA STOCKADE

MASSACRE IN ROME (1973) Champion Cinematografica. Color-103min. (Italian-French). Richard Burton, Marcello Mastroianni ....(4)
Original Italian title: RAPPRESAGLIA

MASSACRE IN THE BLACK FOREST (1965) Majestic Pictures. Color-95min. (Foreign). Cameron Mitchell, Antonella Lualdi....................2*

MASSACRE RIVER (1949) Allied Artists. B&W-75min. Guy Madison, Rory Calhoun, Carole Matthews ....(3)

MASTER GUNFIGHTER, THE (1975) Taylor-Laughlin. Color-121min. Tom Laughlin, Ron O'Neal ....(4)

MASTER MINDS (1949) Monogram [Allied Artists]. B&W-64min. The Bowery Boys, Alan Napier, Glenn Strange....................(3)

MASTER OF BALLANTRAE, THE (1953) Warner Bros. Color-89min. (British). Errol Flynn, Roger Livesey....................5*

MASTER OF HORROR (1959) see 4D MAN

MASTER OF LASSIE (1948) see HILLS OF HOME

MASTER OF THE ISLANDS (1970) see HAWAIIANS, THE

MASTER OF THE WORLD (1961) American-International. Color-104min. Vincent Price, Charles Bronson 5*

MASTER PLAN (1954) Astor. B&W-77min. (British). Wayne Morris, Tilda Thamar, Norman Wooland....................(3)

MASTER RACE, THE (1944) RKO. B&W-96min. George Couloris, Stanley Ridges.....................(5)

MASTER SPY (1963) Allied Artists. B&W-71min. (British). Stephen Murray, June Thorburon ....(3)

MASTER TOUCH, THE (1974) Warner Bros. Color-96min. (Italian-W. German). Kirk Douglas, Florinda Bolkan ....(4)
Original Italian title: UOMO DA RISPETTARE, UN (A Man to Be Respected)
British title: MAN TO RESPECT, A

MASTERS OF THE CONGO JUNGLE (1959) 20th Century-Fox. Color-88min. (Belgian, Documentary). Director: Heinz Sielmann 5*
Original title: SEIGNEURS DE LA FORET, LES (Masters of the Forest)

MASTERSON OF KANSAS (1955) Columbia. Color-73min. George Montgomery, Nancy Gates ....(3)

MATA HARI (1932) M-G-M. B&W-91min. Greta Garbo, Ramon Novarro ....(5)

MATA HARI, AGENT H-21 (1964) Magna Pictures. B&W-106min. (French-Italian). Jeanne Moreau, Jean-Louis Trintignant, Claude Rich ....(3)
Original French title: MATA-HARI AGENT H-21
Italian title: MATA HARI, AGENTE SEGRETO H-21

MATA HARI'S DAUGHTER (1954) Trans-America. Color-102min. (Italian). Ludmilla Tcherina, Frank Latimore ....(3)
Original title: FILLE DE MATI-HARI, LA (The Daughter of Mata Hari)
Alternate title: DAUGHTER OF MATA HARI

MATANGO (1964) see ATTACK OF THE MUSHROOM PEOPLE

MATCH KING, THE (1932) First National [W.B.]. B&W-79min. Warren William, Glenda Farrell ....

MATCHLESS (1966) United Artists. Color-104min. (Italian). Patrick O'Neal, Ira von Furstenberg, Donald Pleasence 3*

MATCHMAKER, THE (1958) Paramount. B&W-101min. Shirley Booth, Anthony Perkins, Shirley MacLaine....................5½*

MATERNELLE, LA (1932) Tapernoux-Metropolis. B&W-86min. (French). Madeleine Renaud, Alice Tissot....................(4)

MATILDA (1978) American-International. Color-105min. Elliott Gould, Robert Mitchum, Clive Revill 5*

MATING GAME, THE (1959) M-G-M. Color-96min. Debbie Reynolds, Tony Randall....................4*

MATING MODERN STYLE (1955) see LUCKY TO BE A WOMAN

MATING OF MILLIE, THE (1948) Columbia. B&W-87min. Evelyn Keyes, Glenn Ford 4½*

MATING SEASON, THE (1951) Paramount. B&W-101min. Thelma Ritter, Gene Tierney, John Lund ....(5)

MATING URGE, THE (1958) Citation. Color-116min. (Documentary). Producer: Howard C Brown ....(5)

MATT HELM (1975) CPT (TV). Color-74min. (Made for TV). Tony Franciosa, Patrick Macnee, Laraine Stephens....................4*

MATTEI AFFAIR, THE (1973) Paramount. Color-118min. (Italian). Gian Maria Volonté, Edda Ferronao ....(4)
Original title: CASO MATTEI, IL

MATTER OF DAYS, A (1969) Royal Films Int'l [Columbia]. Color-106min. (French-Czech). Thalie Fruges, Vit Olmer....................(4)
Original French title: A QUELQUES JOURS PRES

MATTER OF HUMANITIES (1969) see MARCUS WELBY, M.D.

MATTER OF INNOCENCE, A (1967) Universal. Color-102min. (British). Hayley Mills, Trevor Howard ....(4)
Original title: PRETTY POLLY

MATTER OF LIFE AND DEATH, A (1946) see STAIRWAY TO HEAVEN

MATTER OF MORALS, A (1960) United Artists. B&W-90min. (U.S.-Swedish). Patrick O'Neal, Maj-Britt Nilsson ....(4)
Original Swedish title: DE SISTA STEGEN

MATTER OF RESISTANCE, A (1966) see VIE DE CHATEAU, LA

MATTER OF TIME, A (1976) American-International. Color-99min. (U.S.-Italian). Liza Minnelli, Ingrid Bergman 4*
Alternate title: NINA

MATTER OF WHO, A (1961) Herts-Lion International. B&W-90min. (British). Terry-Thomas, Alex Nicol ....(5)

MATTER OF WIFE . . . AND DEATH, A (1975) CPT (TV). Color-74min. (Made for TV). Rod Taylor, Tom Drake, Anita Gillette....................4*

MAURIE (1973) National General. Color-112min. Bernie Casey, Bo Swenson, Janet MacLachlan....................(4)
TV title: BIG MO

MAURIZIUS CASE, THE (1953) B&W-110min. (French). Daniel Gélin, Eleanore Rossi-Drago, Anton Walbrook ....(4)

MAVERICK, THE (1952) Allied Artists. B&W-71min. Wild Bill Elliott, Phyllis Coates ....(4)

MAVERICK QUEEN, THE (1956) Republic. Color-92min. Barbara Stanwyck, Barry Sullivan....................3*

MAXIME (1958) Interworld Film Distributors. B&W-94min. (French). Charles Boyer, Michele Morgan....................3½*

MAYA (1966) M-G-M. Color-91min. Clint Walker, Jay North 3½*

MAYBE I'LL COME HOME IN THE SPRING (1971) ABC Films. Color-75min. (Made for TV). Eleanor Parker, Jackie Cooper, Sally Field....................3*

MAYDAY IN PARIS (1958) see PREMIER MAY

MAYERLING (1968) M-G-M. Color-140min. (French-British, English language). Omar Sharif, Catherine Deneuve 4*

MAYOR OF 44th STREET (1942) RKO. B&W-86min. George Murphy, Anne Shirley ....(4)

MAYOR OF HELL, THE (1933) Warner Bros. B&W-80min. James Cagney, Madge Evans....................3*

MAYTIME (1937) M-G-M. B&W-132min. Jeanette MacDonald, Nelson Eddy, John Barrymore....................5*

MAYTIME IN MAYFAIR (1949) Realart. B&W-94min. (British). Anna Neagle, Michael Wilding....................(4)

MAZE, THE (1953) Allied Artists. B&W-81min. Richard Carlson, Veronica Hurst ....(4)

McCABE AND MRS. MILLER (1971) Warner Bros. Color-115min. Warren Beatty, Julie Christie....................4½*

McCLOUD: WHO KILLED MISS U.S.A.? (1970) Universal. Color-100min. (Made for TV). Dennis Weaver, Craig Stevens, Julie Newmar....................4½*

McCONNELL STORY, THE (1955) Warner Bros. Color-107min. Alan Ladd, June Allyson, James Whitmore....................4*
British title: TIGER IN THE SKY

McCULLOCHS, THE (1975) American-International. Color-93min. Forrest Tucker, Julie Adams....................5*
Alternate title: WILD McCULLOCHS, THE

Films are rated on a 1 to 10 scale, 10 is highest. **Boldface** ratings followed by an asterisk (*) are for films actually seen and rated by the executive and senior editors. All other ratings are estimates. (See Notes on Entertainment Ratings in the front section.)

McGUIRE, GO HOME! (1965) Continental [Walter Reade]. **Color-101min.** *(British).* Dirk Bogarde, George Chakiris, Susan Strasberg .... (4)
Original title: HIGH BRIGHT SUN, THE

McHALE'S NAVY (1964) Universal. **Color-93min.** Ernest Borgnine, Tim Conway, Joe Flynn.. 3*

McHALE'S NAVY JOINS THE AIR FORCE (1965) Universal. **Color-90min.** Joe Flynn, Tim Conway, Bob Hastings 3*

McKENZIE BREAK, THE (1970) United Artists. **Color-106min.** *(British).* Brian Keith, Helmut Griem 5*

McLINTOCK! (1963) United Artists. **Color-127min.** John Wayne, Maureen O'Hara.. 3*

McMASTERS, THE (1970) Chevron. **Color-90min.** *(British-U.S.).* Brock Peters, Burl Ives, David Carradine, Nancy Kwan...................... (4)
Alternate title: BLOOD CROWD, THE

McQ (1974) Warner Bros. **Color-111min.** John Wayne, Eddie Albert 4*

ME (1968) Altura Films. **Color-83min.** *(French).* Michel Terrazon, Marie-Louise Thierry, René Thierry .... (4)
Original title: ENFANCE NUE, L'
Festival title: NAKED CHILDHOOD

ME AND MY GAL (1932) Fox Film Co. [20th]. **B&W-78min.** Spencer Tracy, Joan Bennett.. (4)
British title: PIER 13

ME AND THE COLONEL (1958) Columbia. **B&W-105min.** Danny Kaye, Curt Jurgens.. 5*

ME, NATALIE (1969) Nat'l General (for Cinema Center). **Color-111min.** Patty Duke, James Farentino .... (5)

MEAL, THE (1975) Ambassador Releasing. **Color-90min.** Dina Merrill, Carl Betz, Susan Logan.. (4)

MEAN DOG BLUES (1978) American-International. **Color-108min.** George Kennedy, Kay Lenz ....

MEAN MACHINE, THE (1974) *see* LONGEST YARD, THE

MEAN STREETS (1973) Warner Bros. **Color-110min.** Harvey Keitel, Robert De Niro... 3*

MEANEST MAN IN THE WORLD, THE (1943) 20th Century-Fox. **B&W-57min.** Jack Benny, Priscilla Lane, Eddie "Rochester" Anderson .... (4)

MECHANIC, THE (1972) United Artists. **Color-100min.** Charles Bronson, Jan-Michael Vincent 5½*

MEDAL FOR BENNY, A (1945) Paramount. **B&W-77min.** J. Carrol Naish, Dorothy Lamour 5*

MEDEA (1970) New Line Cinema. **Color-118min.** *(Italian-French-W. German).* Maria Callas, Massimo Girotti, Giuseppe Gentili .... (4)

MEDICINE BALL CARAVAN (1971) Warner Bros. **Color-89min.** *(U.S.-French, Music Film).* Director: Francois Reichenbach........................ (3)
British title: WE HAVE COME FOR YOUR DAUGHTERS

MEDITERRANEAN HOLIDAY (1962) Continental [Walter Reade]. **Color-158min.** *(German, Travelog).* Director: Hermann Leitner.................... (5)
Original title: FLYING CLIPPER - TRAUMREISE UNTER WEISSEN SEGELN

MEDIUM, THE (1951) Transfilm. **B&W-84min.** *(Italian, English language).* Marie Powers, Anna Maria Alberghetti .... (5)

MEDIUM COOL (1969) Paramount. **Color-110min.** Robert Forster, Verna Bloom .... (5)

MEDUSA AGAINST THE SON OF HERCULES (1963) Avco-Embassy. **Color-95min.** *(Italian-Spanish).* Richard Harrison, Anna Ranalli .... (1)
Original Italian title: PERSEO L'INVINCIBLE *(Perseus the Invincible)*
Original Spanish title: VALLE DE LOS HOMBRES DE PIEDRA, EL *(The Valley of the Stone Men)*
British title: PERSEUS AGAINST THE MONSTERS

MEDUSA TOUCH, THE (1978) Warner Bros. **Color-110min.** *(British).* Richard Burton, Lino Ventura, Lee Remick..................... 4½*

MEET BOSTON BLACKIE (1941) Columbia. **B&W-61min.** Chester Morris, Rochelle Hudson .... (4)

MEET DANNY WILSON (1952) Universal. **B&W-86min.** Frank Sinatra, Shelley Winters 4*

MEET DR. CHRISTIAN (1939) RKO. **B&W-63min.** Jean Hersholt, Robert Baldwin, Dorothy Lovett.. (3)

MEET JOHN DOE (1941) Warner Bros. **B&W-122min.** Gary Cooper, Barbara Stanwyck 6*
British 1950 reissue title: JOHN DOE, DYNAMITE

MEET ME AFTER THE SHOW (1951) 20th Century-Fox. **Color-86min.** Betty Grable, Macdonald Carey, Eddie Albert .... (4)

MEET ME AT THE FAIR (1953) Universal. **Color-87min.** Dan Dailey, Diana Lynn.. (4)

MEET ME IN LAS VEGAS (1956) M-G-M. **Color-112min.** Dan Dailey, Cyd Charisse... 4*
British title: VIVA LAS VEGAS!

MEET JOHN DOE (1941). Anxious reporters are fended off by journalist Barbara Stanwyck, who intends to maintain exclusive rights to personal stories about the bewildered "man of the people," Gary Cooper, whom she's discovered and publicized.

MEET ME IN ST. LOUIS (1944) M-G-M. **Color-113min.** Judy Garland, Margaret O'Brien... 5*

MEET ME TONIGHT (1952) *see* TONIGHT AT 8:30

MEET MR. LUCIFER (1953) J. Arthur Rank. **B&W-83min.** *(British).* Stanley Holloway, Kay Kendall.. (4)

MEET PETER FOSS (1958) **Color-110min.** *(German).* O. W. Fischer, Walter Giller .... (4)

MEET THE GHOSTS (1948) *see* ABBOTT & COSTELLO MEET FRANKENSTEIN

MEET THE NELSONS (1952) *see* HERE COME THE NELSONS

MEET THE PEOPLE (1944) M-G-M. **B&W-100min.** Lucille Ball, Dick Powell, Bert Lahr .... (4)

MEET THE STEWARTS (1942) Columbia. **B&W-73min.** William Holden, Frances Dee.. (4)

MEET WHIPLASH WILLIE (1966) *see* FORTUNE COOKIE, THE

MEETING AT MIDNIGHT (1944) *see* BLACK MAGIC

MEIN KAMPF (1960) Columbia. **B&W-119min.** *(Swedish, Documentary).* Director: Erwin Leiser .... (5)
Original title: DEN BLODIGA TIDEN

MELBA (1953) United Artists. **Color-113min.** *(British).* Patrice Munsel, Robert Morley.. (5)

MELINDA (1972) M-G-M. **Color-109min.** Calvin Lockhart, Rosalind Cash... (3)

MELODY (1971) Levitt-Pickman. **Color-103min.** *(British).* Mark Lester, Jack Wild, Tracy Hyde.. 4½*
Screen title: LOVE, MELODY
U.S. retitling: TO LOVE SOMEBODY
Alternate title: S. W. A. L. K.

MELODY FOR THREE (1941) RKO. **B&W-67min.** Jean Hersholt, Fay Wray .... (3)

MELODY INN (1943) *see* RIDING HIGH

MELODY MAKER (1945) *see* DING DONG WILLIAMS

MELODY OF LIFE (1932) *see* SYMPHONY OF SIX MILLION

MELODY OF YOUTH (1939) *see* THEY SHALL HAVE MUSIC

MELVIN AND HOWARD (1980) Universal. **Color- min.** Paul LeMat, Jason Robards (Jr.), Mary Steenburgen...............................

MELVIN PURVIS, G-MAN (1974) American-International. **Color-74min.** *(Made for TV).* Dale Robertson, Margaret Blye .... (4)

MEMBER OF THE WEDDING, THE (1952) Columbia. **B&W-91min.** Ethel Waters, Julie Harris.. 5*

MEMORIES OF UNDERDEVELOPMENT (1968) Tricontinental Films. **B&W-104min.** *(Cuban).* Sergio Corrieri, Daisy Granados, Eslinda Nunez .... (3)
Original title: MEMORIAS DEL SUBDESAROLLO

MEMORY EXPERT, THE (1935) *see* MAN ON THE FLYING TRAPEZE, THE

MEMORY FOR TWO (1945) *see* I LOVE A BANDLEADER

MEMORY OF JUSTICE, THE (1976) Paramount. B&W-278min. *(U.S.-W. German)*..

MEMORY OF LOVE (1952) Associated British-Pathé [EMI]. B&W-87min. *(U.S.-Swedish).* George Nader, Anita Bjork .... (3)
Alternate title: LONG SEARCH, THE

MEMORY OF US (1974) Cinema Financial of America. Color-93min. Ellen Geer, Jon Cypher, Will Geer .... (4)

MEMPHIS BELLE, THE (1944) Paramount. Color-45min. *(Documentary).* Director: William Wyler...................5½*

MEN, THE (1950) United Artists. B&W-86min. Marlon Brando, Teresa Wright 3½*
Alternate title: BATTLE STRIPE

MEN AGAINST THE ARCTIC (1956) Buena Vista. Color-29min. *(Documentary). Director:* Winston Hibler .... (5)

MEN AGAINST THE SKY (1940) RKO. Color-29min. *(Documentary).* Richard Dix, Wendy Barrie .... (3)

MEN AGAINST THE SUN (1953) Monarch. B&W-75min. *(British).* John Bentley, Zena Marshall .... (4)

MEN AND WOLVES (1956) Columbia. Color-98min. *(Italian-French).* Yves Montand, Silvana Mangano................... (3)
Original Italian title: UOMINI E LUPI
French title: HOMMES ET LOUPS

MEN ARE NOT GODS (1937) United Artists. B&W-82min. *(British).* Rex Harrison, Miriam Hopkins, Gertrude Lawrence .... (4)

MEN ARE SUCH FOOLS (1938) Warner Bros. B&W-70min. Humphrey Bogart, Priscilla Lane 3*

MEN BEHIND BARS (1954) *see* DUFFY OF SAN QUENTIN

MEN IN HER DIARY (1945) Universal. B&W-73min. Jon Hall, Virginia Grey .... (4)

MEN IN HER LIFE, THE (1941) Columbia. B&W-90min. Loretta Young, Conrad Veidt .... (4)

MEN IN WAR (1957) United Artists. B&W-104min. Robert Ryan, Aldo Ray.. 4*

MEN IN WHITE (1934) M-G-M. B&W-80min. Clark Gable, Myrna Loy (4)

MEN OF BOYS TOWN (1941) M-G-M. B&W-106min. Spencer Tracy, Mickey Rooney .... (4)

MEN OF BRAZIL (1960) Color-68min. *(Brazilian).* Damasio Cardoso, Nair Cardoso, Nelson Marcellino de Carvalho .... (3)

MEN OF SHERWOOD FOREST (1954) Astor. Color-77min. *(British).* Don Taylor, Eileen Moore .... (3)

MEN OF THE DEEP (1945) *see* ROUGH, TOUGH AND READY

MEN OF THE DRAGON (1974) Wolper Productions. Color-74min. *(Made for TV).* Jared Martin, Katie Saylor, Robert Ito........... 3*

MEN OF THE FIGHTING LADY (1954) M-G-M. Color-80min. Van Johnson, Walter Pidgeon .... (5)

MEN OF TWO WORLDS (1946) Universal. Color-109min. *(British).* Phyllis Calvert, Eric Portman............................. (4)
Alternate title: WITCH DOCTOR

MEN ON HER MIND (1935) *see* GIRL FROM 10th AVENUE, THE

MEN WHO TREAD ON THE TIGER'S TAIL (1951) Brandon. B&W-60min. *(Japanese).* Denjiro Okochi, Susumu Fujita........... 5*
Original title: TORA NO O O FUMU OTOKOTACHI

MEN WITH WINGS (1938) Paramount. Color-106min. Fred MacMurray, Ray Milland 4*

MEN WITHOUT NAMES (1935) Paramount. B&W-66min. Fred MacMurray, Madge Evans.......................... (4)

MEN WITHOUT SOULS (1940) Columbia. B&W-62min. Barton MacLane, John Litel, Glenn Ford .... (3)

MENACE (1934) Paramount. B&W-58min. Gertrude Michael, Paul Cavanagh .... (4)

MENACE, THE (1960) Warner Bros. B&W-90min. *(French).* Robert Hossein, Elsa Martinelli .... (3)

MENACE IN THE NIGHT (1958) United Artists. B&W-78min. *(British).* Griffith Jones, Lisa Gastoni .... (3)
Original title: FACE IN THE NIGHT

MEPHISTO WALTZ, THE (1971) 20th Century-Fox. Color-115min. Alan Alda, Jacqueline Bisset, Barbara Parkins 4*

MERCENARIES, THE (1968) *see* DARK OF THE SUN

MERCENARY, THE (1968) United Artists. Color-105min. *(Italian-Spanish).* Franco Nero, Tony Musante, Jack Palance .... (3)
Original Italian title: MERCENARIO, IL
Original Spanish title: SALARIO PARA MATAR

MERCILESS TRAP, THE (1964) Commonwealth United TV. B&W-82min. *(Japanese).* Makoto Sato ....(3)

MERMAIDS OF TIBURON, THE (1962) Filmgroup. Color-76min. Diane Webber, George Rowe, Timothy Carey ....(2)
Alternate title: AQUA SEX, THE

MERRILL'S MARAUDERS (1962) Warner Bros. Color-98min. Jeff Chandler, Ty Hardin 4*

MERRILY WE GO TO HELL (1932) Paramount. B&W-78min. Sylvia Sidney, Fredric March .... (4)
British title: MERRILY WE GO TO ----

MERRILY WE LIVE (1938) M-G-M. B&W-90min. Constance Bennett, Brian Aherne, Billie Burke .... (5)

MERRY ANDREW (1958) M-G-M. Color-103min. Danny Kaye, Pier Angeli.. 4*

MERRY-GO-ROUND OF 1938 (1937) Universal. B&W-87min. Bert Lahr, Alice Brady .... (4)

MERRY MONAHANS, THE (1944) Universal. B&W-91min. Donald O'Connor, Peggy Ryan .... (5)

MERRY WIDOW, THE (1925) M-G-M. B&W-111min. *(Silent).* Mae Murray, John Gilbert .... (4)

MERRY WIDOW, THE (1934) M-G-M. B&W-99min. Maurice Chevalier, Jeanette MacDonald 4*
TV title: LADY DANCES, THE

MERRY WIDOW, THE (1952) M-G-M. Color-105min. Lana Turner, Fernando Lamas .... (4)

MERRY WIVES OF RENO (1934) Warner Bros. B&W-64min. Glenda Farrell, Margaret Lindsay .... (4)

MERRY WIVES OF WINDSOR, THE (1965) Sigma III. Color-97min. *(Austrian, English language).* Norman Foster, Colette Boky......... (5)
Original title: LUSIGEN WEIBER VON WINDSOR, DIE

MERTON OF THE MOVIES (1924) Paramount. B&W-85min. *(Silent).* Glenn Hunter, Viola Dana ....

MERTON OF THE MOVIES (1947) M-G-M. B&W-82min. Red Skelton, Virginia O'Brien .... (4)

MESSAGE, THE (1976) *see* MOHAMMAD, MESSENGER OF GOD

MESSAGE FROM SPACE (1978) United Artists. Color-105min. *(Japanese).* Vic Morrow, Mikio Narita, Peggy Lee Brennan, Philip Casnoff.. 3*

MESSAGE TO GARCIA, A (1936) 20th Century-Fox. B&W-77min. John Boles, Barbara Stanwyck 4*

MESSAGE TO MY DAUGHTER (1973) MPC (TV). Color-74min. *(Made for TV).* Bonnie Bedelia, Kitty Winn .... (4)

MESSALINA (1952) *see* AFFAIRS OF MESSALINA

MESSALINA (1959) American-International. Color-84min. *(Italian).* Belinda Lee, Spyros Fokas .... (3)

MESSALINA AGAINST THE SON OF HERCULES (1963) Avco-Embassy. Color-98min. *(Italian).* Richard Harrison, Marilu Tolo .... (3)
Alternate title: EMPRESS MESSALINA MEETS THE SON OF HERCULES

MESSIAH, THE (1975) Color-145min. *(Italian-U.S.).* Pier Maria Rossi, Mita Ungara ....
Original Italian title: MESSIA

MESSIAH OF EVIL (1975) International Cinefilm Corp. Color-89min. Michael Greer, Marianna Hill, Joy Bang 1*

METAMORPHOSES (1978) Sanrio. Color-89min. *(Japanese-U.S., Cartoon).* Director: Takashi........................... 5½*
Alternate title: WINDS OF CHANGE

METAMORPHOSIS (1975) Svensk Filmindustri. B&W-88min. *(Swedish).* Ernst Gunther, Gunn Wallgren........................ (3)
Original title: FORVANDLINGEN

METEOR (1979) American-International. Color-   min. Sean Connery, Natalie Wood, Henry Fonda ....

METEOR MONSTER (1957) *see* TEENAGE MONSTER

METROPOLIS (1926) Paramount. B&W-139min. *(German, Silent).* Brigitte Helm 4*

MEXICAN HAYRIDE (1948) Universal. B&W-77min. Bud Abbott, Lou Costello, Virginia Grey 3*

MEXICAN MANHUNT (1953) Allied Artists. B&W-71min. George Brent, Hillary Brooke .... (3)

MEXICAN SPITFIRE (1940) RKO. B&W-67min. Lupe Velez, Leon Errol.. 4*

MEXICAN SPITFIRE AT SEA (1942) RKO. B&W-72min. Lupe Velez, Leon Errol, Charles (Buddy) Rogers .... (3)

MEXICAN SPITFIRE OUT WEST (1942) RKO. B&W-76min. Lupe Velez, Leon Errol, Donald Woods .... (3)

Films are rated on a 1 to 10 scale, 10 is highest. **Boldface** ratings followed by an asterisk (*) are for films actually seen and rated by the executive and senior editors. All other ratings are estimates. (See Notes on Entertainment Ratings in the front section.)

MEXICAN SPITFIRE SEES A GHOST (1942) RKO. **B&W-69min.** Lupe Velez, Leon Errol, Charles (Buddy) Rogers..............................(3)

MEXICAN SPITFIRE'S BABY (1941) RKO. **B&W-70min.** Lupe Velez, Leon Errol, Charles (Buddy) Rogers ....(3)

MEXICAN SPITFIRE'S BLESSED EVENT (1943) RKO. **B&W-63min.** Lupe Velez, Leon Errol, Walter Reed..............................(3)

MEXICAN SPITFIRE'S ELEPHANT (1942) RKO. **B&W-64min.** Lupe Velez, Leon Errol, Walter Reed ....(3)

MEXICANA (1945) Republic. **B&W-83min.** Constance Moore, Tito Guizar..(3)

MGM'S BIG PARADE OF COMEDY (1964) M-G-M. **B&W-91min.** *(Compilation). Producer:* Robert Youngson 4*
Alternate title: BIG PARADE OF COMEDY, THE

MIAMI EXPOSE (1956) Columbia. **B&W-73min.** Lee J. Cobb, Patricia Medina ....(3)

MIAMI STORY, THE (1954) Columbia. **B&W-75min.** Barry Sullivan, Luther Adler...(3)

MICHAEL AND HELGA (1968) American-International. **Color-87min.** *(German).* Felix Franchy, Ruth Gassmann ....(3)
Original title: HELGA UND MICHAEL

MICHAEL KOHLHAAS (1969) Columbia. **Color-97min.** *(German, English language).* David Warner, Anna Karina ....(4)

MICHAEL SHAYNE, PRIVATE DETECTIVE (1940) 20th Century-Fox. **B&W-77min.** Lloyd Nolan, Marjorie Weaver ....(4)

MICHAEL STROGOFF (1937) *see* SOLDIER AND THE LADY, THE

MICHAEL STROGOFF (1956) Continental [Walter Reade]. **Color-115min.** *(Italian-French-Yugoslavian).* Curt Jurgens, Genevieve Page ....(4)
Alternate title: REVOLT OF THE TARTARS

MICHELANGELO (1940) *see* TITAN, THE

MICHIGAN KID, THE (1947) Universal. **Color-69min.** Jon Hall, Victor McLaglen, Rita Johnson ....(3)

MICKEY (1948) Eagle Lion. **Color-87min.** Lois Butler, Bill Goodwin.......(3)

MICKEY ONE (1965) Columbia. **B&W-93min.** Warren Beatty, Alexandra Stewart 3*

MIDAS RUN (1969) Cinerama Releasing. **Color-106min.** Richard Crenna, Anne Heywood, Fred Astaire.....................................(4)
Alternate title: RUN ON GOLD, A

MIDDLE OF THE NIGHT (1959) Columbia. **B&W-118min.** Fredric March, Kim Novak..(4)

MIDNIGHT (1939) Paramount. **B&W-94min.** John Barrymore, Claudette Colbert..5½*

MIDNIGHT COWBOY (1969) United Artists. **Color-113min.** Dustin Hoffman, Jon Voight 9*

MIDNIGHT EXPRESS (1978) Columbia. **Color-120min.** Brad Davis, Randy Quaid...5½*

MIDNIGHT INTRUDER (1938) Universal. **B&W-68min.** Louis Hayward, Eric Linden...(4)

MIDNIGHT LACE (1960) Universal. **Color-108min.** Doris Day, Rex Harrison 5*

MIDNIGHT MAN, THE (1974) Universal. **Color-117min.** Burt Lancaster, Susan Clark 3*

MIDNIGHT PLEASURES (1975) Cineriz. **Color-112min.** *(Italian).* Claudia Cardinale, Vittorio Gassman, Giancarlo Giannini, Monica Vitti..........(3)
Original title: A MEZZANOTTE VA LA RONDA DEL PIACERE

MIDNIGHT STORY, THE (1957) Universal. **B&W-89min.** Tony Curtis, Marisa Pavan, Gilbert Roland ....(4)
British title: APPOINTMENT WITH A SHADOW

MIDSUMMER NIGHT'S DREAM, A (1935) Warner Bros. **B&W-132min.** James Cagney, Joe E. Brown 3*

MIDSUMMER NIGHT'S DREAM, A (1959) Showcorporation. **Color-74min.** *(Czech, Puppets). Director:* Jiri Trnka ....(5)
Original title: SEN NOCI SVATOJANSKE

MIDSUMMER NIGHT'S DREAM, A (1968) **Color-124min.** *(British).* Diana Rigg, David Warner, Judi Dench 4*

MIDWAY (1976) Universal. **Color-132min.** Charlton Heston, Henry Fonda...5½*
British title: BATTLE OF MIDWAY

MIGHTY BARNUM, THE (1934) United Artists. **B&W-87min.** Wallace Beery, Adolphe Menjou, Virginia Bruce ....(5)

MIGHTY CRUSADERS, THE (1957) Falcon. **Color-87min.** *(Italian).* Francisco Rabal, Sylva Koscina ....(3)
Original title: GERUSALEMME LIBERATA, LA *(Jerusalem Set Free)*

MIGHTY JOE YOUNG (1949) RKO. **B&W-94min.** Terry Moore, Ben Johnson 5½*

MIGHTY JUNGLE, THE (1964) Paramount. **Color-88min.** *(U.S.-Mexican).* Marshall Thompson, David DaLie 2½*

MIGHTY McGURK, THE (1946) M-G-M. **B&W-85min.** Wallace Beery, Edward Arnold, Dean Stockwell 3½*

MIGHTY URSUS (1961) United Artists. **Color-92min.** *(Italian-Spanish).* Ed Fury, Luis Prendes, Moira Orfei ....(2)
Original title: URSUS

MIGHTY WARRIOR, THE (1961) *see* TROJAN HORSE, THE

MIKADO, THE (1939) Universal. **Color-90min.** Kenny Baker, Martyn Green 5*

MIKADO, THE (1967) Warner Bros. **Color-125min.** *(British).* Philip Potter, John Reed 5½*

MIKEY AND NICKY (1976) Paramount. **Color-119min.** Peter Falk, John Cassavetes..(4)

MILDRED PIERCE (1945) Warner Bros. **B&W-113min.** Joan Crawford, Jack Carson, Zachary Scott 5*

MILITARY POLICEMEN (1953) *see* OFF LIMITS

MILKMAID, THE (1955) Vinod International. **B&W-70min.** *(Finnish).* Anneli Sauli, Saulo Haarla, Janno Palo...................(2)

MILKMAN, THE (1950) Universal. **B&W-87min.** Donald O'Connor, Jimmy Durante, Piper Laurie ....(4)

MILKY WAY, THE (1936) Paramount. **B&W-88min.** Harold Lloyd, Adolphe Menjou 4½*

MILKY WAY, THE (1969) United Artists. **Color-105min.** *(French-Italian).* Paul Frankeur, Laurent Terzieff.....................(5)
Original French title: VOIE LACTEE, LA
Original Italian title: VIA LATTEA, LA

MILL OF THE STONE WOMEN (1960) Parade. **Color-94min.** *(Italian-French).* Pierre Brice, Scilla Gabel, Wolfgang Preiss, ...(3)
Original Italian title: MULINO DELLE DONNE DI PIETRA, IL
Original French title: MOULIN DES SUPPLICES
British title: DROPS OF BLOOD
Alternate title: HORROR OF THE STONE WOMEN
Alternate title: HORRIBLE MILL WOMEN, THE

MILL ON THE PO (1949) Lux Film America. **B&W-96min.** *(Italian).* Carla Del Poggio, Jacques Sernas...........................(5)
Original title: MULINO DEL PO, IL

MILLER'S BEAUTIFUL WIFE, THE (1955) Distributors Corp. of America. **Color-95min.** *(Italian).* Vittorio De Sica, Sophia Loren, Marcello Mastroianni ....(5)
Original title: BELLA MUGNAIA, LA
British title: MILLER'S WIFE, THE

MILLERSON CASE, THE (1947) Columbia. **B&W-72min.** Warner Baxter, Nancy Saunders...(3)

MILLHOUSE: A WHITE COMEDY (1971) New Yorker Films. **B&W-92min.** *(Documentary). Director:* Emile de Antonio 4*

MILLIE'S DAUGHTER (1947) Columbia. **B&W-72min.** Gladys George, Ruth Donnelly..(2)

MILLION, LE (1931) Tobis. **B&W-80min.** *(French).* René Lefevre, Annabella 3*

MILLION DOLLAR BABY (1941) Warner Bros. **B&W-100min.** Ronald Reagan, May Robson, Priscilla Lane........................(3)

MILLION DOLLAR DIXIE DELIVERANCE, THE (1978) NBC-TV. **Color-98min.** *(Made for TV).* Brock Peters, Christian Juttner..........................

MILLION DOLLAR DUCK, THE (1971) Buena Vista. **Color-92min.** Dean Jones, Sandy Duncan 4*

MILLION DOLLAR KID (1944) Monogram [Allied Artists]. **B&W-65min.** East Side Kids, Noah Beery ....(4)

MILLION DOLLAR LEGS (1932) Paramount. **B&W-64min.** W. C. Fields, Jack Oakie...3*

MILLION DOLLAR LEGS (1939) Paramount. **B&W-59min.** Betty Grable, John Hartley..(3)

MILLION DOLLAR MANHUNT (1956) Anglo Amalgamated. **B&W-65min.** *(British).* Richard Denning, Carole Mathews....................(2)
Original title: ASSIGNMENT REDHEAD

MILLION DOLLAR MERMAID (1952) M-G-M. **Color-115min.** Esther Williams, Victor Mature ....(4)
British title: ONE-PIECE BATHING SUIT, THE

MILLION DOLLAR PURSUIT (1951) Republic. **B&W-60min.** Penny Edwards, Grant Withers...(3)

MILLION DOLLAR RIP-OFF, THE (1976) NBC-TV. **Color-73min.** *(Made for TV).* Freddie Prinze, Brooke Mills, Allen Garfield ....
Alternate title: MONEY TO BURN

MILLION DOLLAR WEEKEND (1948) Eagle Lion. **Color-72min.** Gene Raymond, Francis Lederer, Stephanie Paull (Osa Massen) ....(3)

Films are rated on a 1 to 10 scale, 10 is highest. **Boldface** ratings followed by an asterisk (*) are for films actually seen and rated by the executive and senior editors. All other ratings are estimates. (See Notes on Entertainment Ratings in the front section.)

MILLION EYES OF SU-MURU, THE (1967) American-International. Color-95min. *(British-U.S.).* Shirley Eaton, George Nader, Frankie Avalon 3*
British title: SUMURU

MILLION POUND NOTE, THE (1954) *see* MAN WITH A MILLION

MILLIONAIRE, THE (1931) Warner Bros. B&W-81min. George Arliss, Evalyn Knapp... (5)

MILLIONAIRE FOR CHRISTY, A (1951) 20th Century-Fox. B&W-91min. Eleanor Parker, Fred MacMurray........................ (3)

MILLIONAIRE PLAYBOY (1937) *see* PARK AVENUE LOGGER

MILLIONAIRE PLAYBOY (1940) RKO. B&W-64min. Joe Penner, Linda Hayes, Richard Lane... (3)
British title: GLAMOUR BOY

MILLIONAIRES IN PRISON (1940) RKO. B&W-64min. Lee Tracy, Linda Hayes .... (4)

MILLIONAIRESS, THE (1960) 20th Century-Fox. Color-90min. *(British).* Sophia Loren, Peter Sellers..................... (4)

MIN AND BILL (1930) M-G-M. B&W-69min. Marie Dressler, Wallace Beery 3*

MIND BENDERS, THE (1963) American-International. B&W-99min. *(British).* Dirk Bogarde, Mary Ure 3½*

MIND OF MR. SOAMES, THE (1970) Columbia. Color-95min. *(British).* Terence Stamp, Robert Vaughn..................... 5*

MIND SNATCHERS, THE (1972) Cinerama Releasing. Color-94min. Christopher Walken, Ralph Meeker, Ronny Cox..... (3)
Original title: HAPPINESS CAGE, THE

MIND YOUR OWN BUSINESS (1937) Paramount. B&W-75min. Charlie Ruggles, Alice Brady.............................. (4)

MINE OWN EXECUTIONER (1947) 20th Century-Fox. B&W-105min. *(British).* Burgess Meredith, Dulcie Gray .... (5)

MINI-SKIRT MOB, THE (1968) American-International. Color-82min. Jeremy Slate, Diane McBain, Sherry Jackson .... (2)

MINISTRY OF FEAR (1944) Paramount. B&W-85min. Ray Milland, Marjorie Reynolds.. 5*

MINIVER STORY, THE (1950) M-G-M. B&W-104min. Greer Garson, Walter Pidgeon... (4)

MINNESOTA CLAY (1965) Harlequin International. Color-95min. *(Italian-Spanish-French).* Cameron Mitchell, Georges Riviere, Ethel Rojo .... (3)
Original French title: HOMME DU MINNESOTA, L' *(The Man from Minnesota)*

MINNIE AND MOSKOWITZ (1972) Universal. Color-114min. Gena Rowlands, Seymour Cassel 2*

MINOTAUR, THE (1961) United Artists. Color-95min. *(Italian).* Bob Mathias, Rosanna Schiaffino, Alberto Lupo ...... (3)
Original title: TESEO CONTRO IL MINOTAURO *(Theseus Against the Minotaur)*
Alternate title: MINOTAUR - THE WILD BEAST OF CRETE, THE
Alternate title: WILD BEAST OF CRETE, THE
British title: WARLORD OF CRETE, THE

MINSTREL MAN (1977) First Artists. Color-100min. *(Made for TV).* Glynn Turman, Ted Ross, Saundra Sharp 5*

MINUTE TO PRAY, A SECOND TO DIE, A (1967) Cinerama Releasing. Color-97min. *(Italian-U.S.).* Alex Cord, Arthur Kennedy, Robert Ryan 4*
Original Italian title: ESCONDIDO
Alternate Italian title: MINUTO PER PREGARE, UN ISTANTE PER MORIRE, UN
Alternate title: DEAD OR ALIVE

MINX, THE (1970) Cambist. Color-84min. Jan Sterling, Robert Rodan (2)

MIRACLE, THE (1950) *see* WAYS OF LOVE

MIRACLE, THE (1959) Warner Bros. Color-121min. Carroll Baker, Roger Moore 4*

MIRACLE CAN HAPPEN, A (1948) *see* ON OUR MERRY WAY

MIRACLE IN MILAN (1951) Joseph Burstyn. B&W-96min. *(Italian).* Francesco Golisano, Paolo Stoppa.................... 4½*
Original title: MIRACOLO A MILANO

MIRACLE IN THE RAIN (1956) Warner Bros. B&W-107min. Jane Wyman, Van Johnson...................................... 3½*

MIRACLE MAN, THE (1919) Paramount-Artcraft. B&W-7reels. *(Silent).* Thomas Meigham, Betty Compson, Lon Chaney .... (4)

MIRACLE OF FATIMA (1952) *see* MIRACLE OF OUR LADY OF FATIMA, THE

MIRACLE OF LIFE, THE (1934) *see* OUR DAILY BREAD

THE MIRACLE WORKER (1962). Partially blind herself, Anne Bancroft is immensely patient and persevering in her dedicated struggle to communicate with Patty Duke, who is playing young Helen Keller, made both deaf and blind by a childhood disease.

MIRACLE OF LOVE, THE (1968) Times Film Corp. B&W-83min. *(German).* Biggi Freyer, Katarina Haertel, Régis Vallée.................... (3)
Original title: OSWALT KOLLE: DAS WUNDER DER LIEBE -- SEXUALITAT IN DER EHE

MIRACLE OF MARCELINO, THE (1955) *see* MARCELINO

MIRACLE OF MORGAN'S CREEK, THE (1944) Paramount. B&W-99min. Eddie Bracken, Betty Hutton 5*

MIRACLE OF OUR LADY OF FATIMA, THE (1952) Warner Bros. Color-102min. Susan Whitney, Sherry Jackson 5*
British title: MIRACLE OF FATIMA, THE

MIRACLE OF THE BELLS, THE (1948) RKO. B&W-120min. Fred MacMurray, (Alida) Valli.................................. 3½*

MIRACLE OF THE HILLS, THE (1959) 20th Century-Fox. B&W-73min. Rex Reason, Nan Leslie................................. (3)

MIRACLE OF THE WHITE STALLIONS, THE (1963) Buena Vista. Color-118min. Robert Taylor, Lilli Palmer............. (4)
British title: FLIGHT OF THE WHITE STALLIONS

MIRACLE ON 34th STREET (1947) 20th Century-Fox. B&W-96min. Maureen O'Hara, John Payne, Edmund Gwenn 6*
British title: BIG HEART, THE

MIRACLE ON 34th STREET (1973) 20th Century-Fox. Color-100min. *(Made for TV).* Sebastian Cabot, Jane Alexander, Suzanne Davidson, David Hartman...

MIRACLE WORKER, THE (1962) United Artists. B&W-106min. Anne Bancroft, Patty Duke.................................. 6*

MIRACLES FOR SALE (1939) M-G-M. B&W-71min. Robert Young, Frank Craven, Florence Rice............................. (3)

MIRACLES STILL HAPPEN (1974) Worldvision. Color-96min. *(U.S.-Italian).* Susan Penhaligon, Paul Muller .... (3)

MIRACULOUS JOURNEY (1948) Film Classics [U.A.]. Color-83min. Rory Calhoun, Jim Bannon, Virginia Grey .... (3)

MIRAGE (1965) Universal. B&W-109min. Gregory Peck, Diane Baker 5½*

MIRAGE (1972) Color-82min. *(Peruvian).* Helena Rojo, Miguel Angel Flores, Orlando Sach......................... (4)

MIRANDA (1948) Eagle Lion. B&W-79min. *(British).* Glynis Johns, Griffith Jones, Margaret Rutherford..................... (4)

MIRROR HAS TWO FACES, THE (1958) Continental [Walter Reade]. B&W-98min. *(French).* Michele Morgan, Bourvil, Yvan Desny .... (4)
Original title: MIROIR A DEUX FACES, LE

MISADVENTURES OF MERLIN JONES, THE (1964) Buena Vista. Color-88min. Tommy Kirk, Annette Funicello............... (4)

MISCHIEF-MAKERS, THE (1957) *see* MISTONS, LES

MISERABLES, LES *see* LES MISERABLES

MISFITS, THE (1961) United Artists. B&W-124min. Clark Gable, Marilyn Monroe 3½*

MISS ANNIE ROONEY (1942) United Artists. B&W-84min. Shirley Temple, William Gargan 4*

MISS GRANT TAKES RICHMOND (1949) Columbia. B&W-87min. Lucille Ball, William Holden 4*
British title: INNOCENCE IS BLISS

MISS JULIE (1950) Trans-Global Pics. B&W-91min. *(Swedish)*. Anita Bjork, Ulf Palme .... (5)
Original title: FROKEN JULIE

MISS PINKERTON (1932) Fine Arts. B&W-66min. Joan Blondell, George Brent .... (3)

MISS ROBIN CRUSOE (1954) 20th Century-Fox. Color-75min. Amanda Blake, Rosalind Hayes, George Nader .... (2)

MISS ROBIN HOOD (1952) Eros Films *(Brit.)*. B&W-78min. *(British)*. Margaret Rutherford, Richard Hearne, James Robertson Justice .... (4)

MISS SADIE THOMPSON (1954) Columbia. Color-91min. Rita Hayworth, José Ferrer 4*

MISS SUSIE SLAGLE'S (1945) Paramount. B&W-88min. Lillian Gish, Veronica Lake .... (4)

MISS TATLOCK'S MILLIONS (1948) Paramount. B&W-101min. John Lund, Wanda Hendrix 5½*

MISSILE BASE AT TANIAK (1953) Republic. B&W-100min. *(Re-edited Serial)*. Bill Henry, Susan Morrow .... (3)
Original title: CANADIAN MOUNTIES VS. ATOMIC INVADERS

MISSILE MONSTERS (1958) Republic. B&W-75min. Walter Reed, Lois Collier, Gregory Gay .... (2)
Original title: FLYING DISC MAN FROM MARS

MISSILE TO THE MOON (1958) Astor. B&W-78min. Richard Travis, Cathy Downs .... (1)

MISSILES FROM HELL (1958) NTA Pictures. B&W-82min. *(British)*. Michael Rennie, Patricia Medina .... (3)

MISSING CORPSE, THE (1945) Producers Rel. Corp. [Eagle Lion]. B&W-62min. J. Edward Bromberg, Isabel Randolph .... (3)

MISSING GUEST, THE (1938) Universal. B&W-68min. William Lundigan, Paul Kelly, Constance Moore .... (3)

MISSING JUROR, THE (1944) Columbia. B&W-65min. Jim Bannon, Janis Carter 4*

MISSION BATANGAS (1968) Manson. Color-100min. Dennis Weaver, Vera Miles, Keith Larsen .... (3)

MISSION FOR A KILLER (1965) *see* O.S.S. 117 - MISSION FOR A KILLER

MISSION MARS (1968) Allied Artists. Color-87min. Darren McGavin, Nick Adams .... (3)

MISSION OF THE SEA HAWK (1962) Independent TV Corp (ITC). B&W-83min. *(British, Telefeature)*. Terence Morgan, Jean Kent .... (3)

MISSION OVER KOREA (1953) Columbia. B&W-85min. John Hodiak, John Derek, Audrey Totter .... (3)
British title: EYES OF THE SKIES

MISSION STARDUST (1968) Times Film Corp. Color-95min. *(Italian-W. German-Spanish)*. Lang Jeffries, Essy Persson .... (2)
Original Italian title: 4... 3... 2... 1... MORTE *(4... 3... 2... 1... Death)*
German title: PERRY RHODAN - SOS AUS DEM WELTALL *(Perry Rhodan - SOS From Space)*
Spanish title: ORBITA MORTAL *(Death Orbit)*

MISSION TO HELL (1964) UCC Films. Color-95min. *(W. German-Italian)*. Paul Hubschmid, Marianne Hold .... (2)
Original German title: DIAMANTENHOELLE AM MEKONG, DIE

MISSION TO MOROCCO (1959) B&W-79min. Lex Barker, Juli Reding, Fernando Rey .... (3)

MISSION TO MOSCOW (1943) Warner Bros. B&W-123min. Walter Huston, Ann Harding 3½*

MISSION TO PARADISE (1965) Allied Artists. Color-87min. Kieron Moore, Alexander Knox, Janette Scott 3*

MISSION TO VENICE (1963) Screen Gems. B&W-88min. *(French)*. Sean Flynn, Madeleine Robinson .... (3)

MISSISSIPPI (1935) Paramount. B&W-73min. Bing Crosby, W. C. Fields 5*

MISSISSIPPI GAMBLER (1942) Universal. B&W-60min. Kent Taylor, Frances Langford .... (3)
Alternate title: DANGER ON THE RIVER

MISSISSIPPI GAMBLER, THE (1953) Universal. Color-98min. Tyrone Power, Piper Laurie 4*

MISSISSIPPI MERMAID, THE (1969) United Artists. Color-123min. *(French-Italian)*. Jean-Paul Belmondo, Catherine Deneuve .... (4)
Original French title: SIRÉNE DU MISSISSIPPI, LA
Original Italian title: MIA DROGO SI CHAMA JULIE, LA

MISSOURI BREAKS, THE (1976) United Artists. Color-125min. Marlon Brando, Jack Nicholson 4*

MISSOURI TRAVELER, THE (1958) Buena Vista. Color-104min. Brandon de Wilde, Gary Merrill, Lee Marvin .... (4)

MR. ACE (1946) United Artists. B&W-84min. George Raft, Sylvia Sidney .... (4)

MR. AND MRS. BO JO JONES (1971) 20th Century-Fox. Color-75min. *(Made for TV)*. Desni Arnaz, Jr., Chris Norris, Dan Dailey 4*

MR. AND MRS. NORTH (1941) M-G-M. B&W-67min. Gracie Allen, William Post, Jr. .... (4)

MR. AND MRS. SMITH (1941) RKO. B&W-95min. Carole Lombard, Robert Montgomery 5*

MR. ARKADIN (1955) Cari. B&W-99min. *(Spanish-Swiss, English language)*. Orson Welles, Robert Arden .... (4)
British title: CONFIDENTIAL REPORT

MR. ASHTON WAS INDISCREET (1947) *see* SENATOR WAS INDISCREET, THE

MR. BELVEDERE GOES TO COLLEGE (1949) 20th Century-Fox. B&W-83min. Clifton Webb, Shirley Temple 4*

MR. BELVEDERE RINGS THE BELL (1951) 20th Century-Fox. B&W-87min. Clifton Webb, Joanne Dru 4*

MR. BILLION (1977) 20th Century-Fox. Color-91min. Terence Hill, Valerie Perrine, Jackie Gleason 4*

MR. BLANDINGS BUILDS HIS DREAM HOUSE (1948) RKO. B&W-94min. Cary Grant, Myrna Loy 4*

MISTER BROWN (1972) Andrieux. Color-85min. Al Stevenson, Judith Elliotte, Tyrone Fulton .... (4)

MISTER BUDDWING (1966) M-G-M. B&W-100min. James Garner, Angela Lansbury .... (4)
British title: WOMAN WITHOUT A FACE

MR. BUG GOES TO TOWN (1941) Paramount. Color-78min. *(Cartoon)*. *Director:* Dave Flescher 4½*
Alternate title: HOPPITY GOES TO TOWN

MR. CORY (1957) Universal. Color-92min. Tony Curtis, Martha Hyer, Charles Bickford 4½*

MR. DEEDS GOES TO TOWN (1936) Columbia. B&W-115min. Gary Cooper, Jean Arthur 6*

MR. DENNING DRIVES NORTH (1951) Carroll Pictures. B&W-93min. *(British)*. John Mills, Phyllis Calvert .... (4)

MR. DISTRICT ATTORNEY (1941) Republic. B&W-69min. Dennis O'Keefe, Peter Lorre, Florence Rice .... (3)

MISTER DISTRICT ATTORNEY (1947) Columbia. B&W-81min. Adolphe Menjou, Dennis O'Keefe, Marguerite Chapman .... (3)

MR. DRAKE'S DUCK (1951) United Artists. B&W-76min. *(British)*. Douglas Fairbanks, Jr., Yolande Donlan .... (4)

MR. DYNAMITE (1941) Universal. B&W-63min. Lloyd Nolan, Irene Hervey, J. Carrol Naish .... (4)

MR. 880 (1950) 20th Century-Fox. B&W-90min. Burt Lancaster, Dorothy McGuire, Edmund Gwenn 5*

MR. EMMANUEL (1944) United Artists. B&W-97min. *(British)*. Felix Aylmer, Greta Gynt 4*

MR. FORBUSH AND THE PENGUINS (1971) *see* CRY OF THE PENGUINS

MR. GRIGGS RETURNS (1946) *see* COCKEYED MIRACLE, THE

MR. HEX (1946) Monogram [Allied Artists]. B&W-63min. The Bowery Boys, Gale Robbins .... (3)
British title: PRIDE OF THE BOWERY, THE

MR. HOBBS TAKES A VACATION (1962) 20th Century-Fox. Color-116min. James Stewart, Maureen O'Hara .... (4)

MR. HOBO (1935) Gaumont-British [Rank]. B&W-87min. *(British)*. George Arliss, Gene Garrard ....
Original title: GUV'NOR, THE

MR. HULOT'S HOLIDAY (1953) G-B-D International. B&W-91min. *(French)*. Jacques Tati, Nathalie Pascaud 3*
Original title: VACANCES DE MONSIEUR HULOT, LES

MR. IMPERIUM (1951) M-G-M. Color-87min. Ezio Pinza, Lana Turner (3)
British title: YOU BELONG TO MY HEART

MR. INSIDE/MR. OUTSIDE (1973) MPC (TV). Color-74min. *(Made for TV)*. Hal Linden, Tony Lo Bianco 4*

MR. JERICHO (1970) Independent TV Corp (ITC). Color-85min. *(British, Made for TV)*. Patrick Macnee, Connie Stevens, Herbert Lom .... (4)

MR. KINGSTREET'S WAR (1973) Gold Key Entertainment. Color-92min. *(Made for TV)*. John Saxon, Tippi Hedren, Rossano Brazzi 4*

Films are rated on a 1 to 10 scale, 10 is highest. **Boldface** ratings followed by an asterisk (*) are for films actually seen and rated by the executive and senior editors. All other ratings are estimates. (See Notes on Entertainment Ratings in the front section.)

MR. KLEIN (1976) Quartet Films. **Color-123min.** *(French-Italian).* Alain Delon, Jeanne Moreau ....(4)

MR. LORD SAYS NO (1952) London Films *(Brit.).* **B&W-76min.** *(British).* Stanley Holloway, Kathleen Harrison.....................(5)
Original title: HAPPY FAMILY, THE

MR. LUCKY (1943) RKO. **B&W-98min.** Cary Grant, Laraine Day 5½*

MR. MAJESTYK (1974) United Artists. **Color-104min.** Charles Bronson, Al Lettieri 4½*

MR. MOSES (1965) United Artists. **Color-113min.** Robert Mitchum, Carroll Baker 3½*

MR. MOTO IN DANGER ISLAND (1939) 20th Century-Fox. **B&W-63min.** Peter Lorre, Jean Hersholt, Amanda Duff ....(3)
British title: MR. MOTO ON DANGER ISLAND

MR. MOTO TAKES A CHANCE (1938) 20th Century-Fox. **B&W-63min.** Peter Lorre, Rochelle Hudson ....(3)

MR. MOTO TAKES A VACATION (1939) 20th Century-Fox. **B&W-61min.** Peter Lorre, Joseph Schildkraut, Lionel Atwill ....(3)

MR. MOTO'S GAMBLE (1938) 20th Century-Fox. **B&W-71min.** Peter Lorre, Keye Luke, Dick Baldwin ....(3)

MR. MOTO'S LAST WARNING (1939) 20th Century-Fox. **B&W-71min.** Peter Lorre, Ricardo Cortez, John Carradine ....(3)

MR. MUGGS RIDES AGAIN (1945) Monogram [Allied Artists]. **B&W-63min.** The East Side Kids, Nancy Brinckman ....(3)

MR. MUSIC (1950) Paramount. **B&W-113min.** Bing Crosby, Nancy Olson..(4)

MR. PEABODY AND THE MERMAID (1948) Universal. **B&W-89min.** William Powell, Ann Blyth ....(4)

MR. PEEK-A-BOO (1951) Eagle Lion. **B&W-74min.** *(French).* Bourvil, Joan Greenwood ....(5)
Original title: PASSE-MURAILLE, LA

MR. PERRIN AND MR. TRAILL (1948) Eagle Lion. **B&W-90min.** *(British).* Marius Goring, David Farrar ....(4)

MR. POTTS GOES TO MOSCOW (1953) Stratford Pictures. **B&W-93min.** *(British).* George Cole, Oscar Homolka ....(5)
Original title: TOP SECRET

MR. QUILP (1975) Avco-Embassy. **Color-117min.** *(British).* Anthony Newley, David Hemmings, David Warner ....(5)

MR. RECKLESS (1948) Paramount. **B&W-66min.** William Eythe, Barbara Britton ....(2)

MR. RICCO (1975) U.A. (for M-G-M). **Color-98min.** Dean Martin, Eugene Roche 4*

MISTER ROBERTS (1955) Warner Bros. **Color-123min.** Henry Fonda, James Cagney...5½*

MR. ROBINSON CRUSOE (1932) United Artists. **B&W-72min.** Douglas Fairbanks, William Farnum, Maria Alba *(Silent).* 4½*

MR. ROCK AND ROLL (1957) Paramount. **B&W-86min.** Alan Freed, Rocky Graziano, Chuck Berry, Little Richard ....(2)

MR. SARDONICUS (1961) Columbia. **B&W-89min.** Guy Rolfe, Ronald Lewis, Audrey Dalton ....(4)

MR. SCOUTMASTER (1953) 20th Century-Fox. **B&W-87min.** Clifton Webb, Edmund Gwenn ....(4)

MR. SKEFFINGTON (1944) Warner Bros. **B&W-127min.** Bette Davis, Claude Rains 4*

MR. SKITCH (1933) Fox Film Co. [20th]. **B&W-70min.** Will Rogers, ZaSu Pitts...(4)

MR. SMITH GOES TO WASHINGTON (1939) Columbia. **B&W-125min.** James Stewart, Jean Arthur 6*

MR. SOFT TOUCH (1949) Columbia. **B&W-93min.** Glenn Ford, Evelyn Keyes 4*
British title: HOUSE OF SETTLEMENT

MR. STEVE (1957) Paramount. **B&W-100min.** *(French).* Jeanne Moreau, Philippe LeMaire ....(4)
Original title: ÉTRANGE MONSIEUR STEVE, L *(The Strange Mister Steve)*

MISTER SUPERVISIBLE (1969) K-Tel. **Color-91min.** *(Spanish-Italian-W. German).* Dean Jones, Ingeborg Schoener, Gastone Moschin ....(3)
Original Spanish title: INVENCIBLE HOMBRE INVISIBLE, EL *(The Invincible Invisible Man)*
Italian title: INAFFERABILE MR. INVISIBLE, L'
German title: MISTER UNSICHTBAR *(Mister Invisible)*
Publicity title: SUPER INVISIBLE MAN
Publicity title: INVINCIBLE MR. INVISIBLE

MR. SYCAMORE (1975) Film Ventures International. **Color-87min.** Jason Robards, Sandy Dennis, Jean Simmons ....(4)

MR. TOPAZE (1961) *see* I LIKE MONEY

MR. UNIVERSE (1951) Eagle Lion. **B&W-79min.** Jack Carson, Janis Paige, Bert Lahr.......................................(3)

MISTER V (1941) *see* PIMPERNEL SMITH

MR. WINKLE GOES TO WAR (1944) Columbia. **B&W-80min.** Edward G. Robinson, Ruth Warrick ....(4)
British title: ARMS AND THE WOMAN

MR. WISE GUY (1942) Monogram [Allied Artists]. **B&W-70min.** The East Side Kids, Billy Gilbert ....(3)

MR. WONG, DETECTIVE (1938) Monogram [Allied Artists]. **B&W-69min.** Boris Karloff, Grant Withers, Maxine Jennings ......(3)

MR. WONG IN CHINATOWN (1939) Monogram [Allied Artists]. **B&W-70min.** Boris Karloff, Marjorie Reynolds..................(3)

MRS. BROWN, YOU'VE GOT A LOVELY DAUGHTER (1968) M-G-M. **Color-95min.** *(British).* Peter Noone, Herman's Hermits, Stanley Holloway ....(3)

MRS. LORING'S SECRET (1946) *see* IMPERFECT LADY, THE

MRS. MIKE (1949) United Artists. **B&W-99min.** Dick Powell, Evelyn Keyes 4*

MRS. MINIVER (1942) M-G-M. **B&W-134min.** Greer Garson, Walter Pidgeon 5½*

MRS. O'MALLEY AND MR. MALONE (1950) M-G-M. **B&W-69min.** Marjorie Main, James Whitmore ....(4)

MRS. PARKINGTON (1944) M-G-M. **B&W-124min.** Greer Garson, Walter Pidgeon 4*

MRS. POLLIFAX - SPY (1971) United Artists. **Color-110min.** Rosalind Russell, Darren McGavin ....(3)

MRS. SUNDANCE (1974) 20th Century-Fox. **Color-75min.** *(Made for TV).* Elizabeth Montgomery, Robert Foxworth 4*

MRS. WIGGS OF THE CABBAGE PATCH (1934) Paramount. **B&W-80min.** Pauline Lord, W. C. Fields.............................3½*

MRS. WIGGS OF THE CABBAGE PATCH (1942) Paramount. **B&W-80min.** Fay Bainter, Hugh Herbert ....(3)

MISTONS, LES (1957) **B&W-26min.** *(French).* Bernadette Lafont, Gérard Blain...4½*
British title: MISCHIEF-MAKERS, THE

MISTRESS, THE (1953) Harrison Pictures. **B&W-106min.** *(Japanese).* Hideko Takamine, Hiroshi Akutagawa, Eijiro Toro ....(4)
Original title: GAN
Alternate title: WILD GEESE

MISTRESS OF THE WORLD (1959) Medallion. **Color-98min.** *(W. German-Italian-French).* Martha Hyer, Carlos Thompson, Micheline Presle .....(3)
Original French title: MYSTERES D'ANGKOR, LES *(The Mysteries of Angkor)*
Original Italian title: MISTERO DEI TREI CONTINENTI, IL *(The Mystery of Three Continents)*
Original German title: HERRIN DER WELT

MISTY (1961) 20th Century-Fox. **Color-92min.** David Ladd, Arthur O'Connell..4½*

MITCHELL (1975) Allied Artists. **Color-97min.** Joe Don Baker, Martin Balsam, John Saxon ....(4)

MITSOU (1956) Zenith International. **Color-92min.** *(French).* Danielle Delorme, Fernand Gravey ....(4)

MIX ME A PERSON (1962) British Lion [EMI]. **B&W-116min.** *(British).* Anne Baxter, Donald Sinden............................(4)

MIXED COMPANY (1974) United Artists. **Color-109min.** Barbara Harris, Joseph Bologna....................................5*

MOB, THE (1951) Columbia. **B&W-87min.** Broderick Crawford, Betty Buehler...3½*
British title: REMEMBER THAT FACE

MOB TOWN (1941) Universal. **B&W-70min.** The Dead End Kids, The Little Tough Guys, Dick Foran...........................(3)

MOBY DICK (1930) Warner Bros. **B&W-116min.** John Barrymore, Joan Bennett...(5)

MOBY DICK (1956) Warner Bros. **Color-116min.** Gregory Peck, Richard Basehart..5½*

MODEL AND THE MARRIAGE BROKER, THE (1952) 20th Century-Fox. **B&W-103min.** Jeanne Crain, Scott Brady, Thelma Ritter.....................4*

MODEL FOR MURDER (1959) Cinema Associates. **B&W-73min.** *(British).* Keith Andes, Hazel Court........................3*

MODEL SHOP (1969) Columbia. **Color-95min.** Anouk Aimee, Gary Lockwood...4*

MODEL WIFE (1941) Universal. **B&W-78min.** Dick Powell, Lee Bowman, Joan Blondell...(4)

Films are rated on a 1 to 10 scale, 10 is highest. **Boldface** ratings followed by an asterisk (*) are for films actually seen and rated by the executive and senior editors. All other ratings are estimates. (See Notes on Entertainment Ratings in the front section.)

MODELS, INC. (1952) Mutual. **B&W-73min.** Howard Duff, Coleen Gray .... (2)
British title: THAT KIND OF GIRL

MODERATO CANTABILE (1960) Royal Films Int'l [Columbia]. **B&W-95min.** *(French-Italian).* Jeanne Moreau, Jean-Paul Belmondo............ (5)
British title: SEVEN DAYS . . . SEVEN NIGHTS

MODERN HERO, A (1940) *see* KNUTE ROCKNE - ALL AMERICAN

MODERN MIRACLE, A (1939) *see* STORY OF ALEXANDER GRAHAM BELL, THE

MODERN TIMES (1936) United Artists. **B&W-85min.** *(Silent).* Charlie Chaplin, Paulette Goddard.. 5½*

MODESTY BLAISE (1966) 20th Century-Fox. **Color-119min.** *(British).* Monica Vitti, Dirk Bogarde, Terence Stamp......................... 2*

MODIGLIANI OF MONTPARNASSE (1958) Continental [Walter Reade]. **B&W-110min.** *(French-Italian).* Gérard Philipe, Lilli Palmer, Anouk Aimée. .... (5)
Original French title: MONTPARNASSE 19
Italian title: MONTPARNASSE
British title: LOVERS OF MONTPARNASSE

MOGAMBO (1953) M-G-M. **Color-115min.** Clark Gable, Ava Gardner, Grace Kelly.. 4*

MOHAMMAD, MESSENGER OF GOD (1976) Irwin Yablans [Compass]. **Color-180min.** *(Lebanese, English version).* Anthony Quinn, Irene Papas, Michael Ansara 5*
Original title: AL-RISALAH
British title: MESSAGE, THE

MOHAWK (1956) 20th Century-Fox. **Color-79min.** Scott Brady, Rita Gam.. 3½*

MOKEY (1942) M-G-M. **B&W-88min.** Donna Reed, Dan Dailey (Jr.), Bobby (Robert) Blake.. (3)

MOLE MEN VS. THE SON OF HERCULES (1961) Avco-Embassy. **Color-98min.** *(Italian).* Mark Forest, Moira Orfei .... (2)
Original title: MACISTE, L'UOMO PIU FORTE DEL MONDO *(Maciste, the Strongest Man in the World)*
Alternate title: MACISTE, THE STRONGEST MAN IN THE WORLD
British title: STRONGEST MAN IN THE WORLD, THE
Publicity title(?): MACISTE AND THE NIGHT QUEEN

MOLE PEOPLE, THE (1956) Universal. **B&W-78min.** John Agar, Cynthia Patrick 3*

MOLLY (1950) Paramount. **B&W-83min.** Gertrude Berg, Philip Loeb..... (4)
Original title: GOLDBERGS, THE

MOLLY AND LAWLESS JOHN (1972) Producers Distributing Corp. **Color-97min.** Vera Miles, Sam Elliott...................................... (4)

MOLLY AND ME (1945) 20th Century-Fox. **B&W-76min.** Gracie Fields, Monty Woolley .... (5)

MOLLY MAGUIRES, THE (1970) Paramount. **Color-123min.** Richard Harris, Samantha Eggar, Sean Connery 5½*

MOM AND DAD (1944) Hygenic Productions. **B&W-111min.** June Carlson, Hardie Albright .... (4)
British title: FAMILY STORY, A

MOMENT BY MOMENT (1978) Universal. **Color-105min.** Lily Tomlin, John Travolta... 3½*

MOMENT OF DANGER (1960) *see* MALAGA

MOMENT OF TRUTH, THE (1952) Arlan Pictures. **B&W-81min.** *(French).* Michele Morgan, Jean Gabin, Daniel Gélin .... (3)
Original title: MINUTE DE VERITE, LA

MODERN TIMES (1936). Chester Conklin wants Charlie Chaplin to pay more attention to his work, but Charlie is steadily going crazy in the mechanized routine of his job.

Films are rated on a 1 to 10 scale, 10 is highest. **Boldface** ratings followed by an asterisk (*) are for films actually seen and rated by the executive and senior editors. All other ratings are estimates. (See Notes on Entertainment Ratings in the front section.)

MOMENT OF TRUTH (1965) Films Around The World. **Color-110min.** *(Italian-Spanish).* Miguel Mateo Miguelin, Pedro Basauri Pedrucho, Linda Christian .... (4)
Original title: MOMENTS DELLA VERITA, IL

MOMENT TO MOMENT (1966) Universal. **Color-108min.** Jean Seberg, Honor Blackman .... (4)

MOMENT'S CARESS, A (1971) Konover Film Dist. **B&W-90min.** *(German).* Angelika Ott, Eva Kinsky, Erik Schuman .... (3)

MON ONCLE (1956) *see* MY UNCLE, MR. HULOT

MON PETIT (1957) *see* MONPTI

MONA KENT (1961) *see* SIN OF MONA KENT, THE

MONDO CANE (1961) Times Film Corp. **Color-105min.** *(Italian, Documentary).* Director: Gualtiero Jacopetti 5½*
Alternate title: DOG'S LIFE, A
Translation title: Dog's World

MONDO PAZZO (1964) Rizzoli Film. **Color-94min.** *(Italian, Documentary).* Director: Gualtiero Jacopetti .... (3)
Original title: MONDO CANE . . . n. 2 *(Mondo Cane # 2)*
Alternate title: CRAZY WORLD
Translation title: Insane World
Alternate title: MONDO INSANITY

MONDO-TEENO (1967) *see* TEENAGE REBELLION

MONEY AND THE WOMAN (1940) Warner Bros. **B&W-65min.** Brenda Marshall, Jeffrey Lynn .... (3)

MONEY BALL (1979) American-International. **Color- min.** ....

MONEY FOR JAM (1943) *see* IT AIN'T HAY

MONEY FROM HOME (1953) Paramount. **Color-100min.** Dean Martin, Jerry Lewis 4*

MONEY, MONEY, MONEY (1972) G.S.F. Productions. **Color-115min.** *(French).* Lino Ventura, Jacques Brel, Charles Denner .... (5)
Original title: AVENTURE C'EST L'AVENTURE, L' *(Adventure Is Adventure)*

MONEY TALKS (1972) United Artists. **Color-81min.** *(Documentary).* Director: Allen Funt .... (4)

MONEY TO BURN (1973) MCA-TV. **Color-73min.** *(Made for TV).* Mildred Natwick, E. G. Marshall, Cleavon Little, David Doyle .... (4)

MONEY TO BURN (1976) *see* MILLION DOLLAR RIP-OFF, THE

MONEY TRAP, THE (1966) M-G-M. **B&W-91min.** Glenn Ford, Rita Hayworth 4*

MONEY, WOMEN AND GUNS (1959) Universal. **Color-80min.** Jock Mahoney, Kim Hunter, Tim Hovey .... (3)

MONEYCHANGERS, THE (1976) Paramount. **Color-322min.** *(Made for TV).* Kirk Douglas, Christopher Plummer 5*

MONGOLS, THE (1961) Colorama Features. **Color-105min.** *(Italian-French).* Jack Palance, Anita Ekberg 3*
Original Italian title: MONGOLI, I
French title: MONGOLS, LES

MONGO'S BACK IN TOWN (1971) Banner Associates. **Color-73min.** *(Made for TV).* Sally Field, Telly Savalas, Joe Don Baker, Martin Sheen .... (5)

MONIKA (1953) Janus Films. **B&W-96min.** *(Swedish).* Harriet Andersson, Lars Ekborg 4*
Original title: SOMMAREN MED MONIKA *(Summer with Monika)*
Alternate title: SUMMER WITH MONICA, A

MONIQUE (1970) Avco-Embassy. **Color-88min.** *(British).* Sibylla Kay, Joan Alcorn .... (3)

MONITORS, THE (1969) Cue. **Color-92min.** Guy Stockwell, Susan Oliver, Shepperd Strudwick 1*

MONK, THE (1969) ABC Films. **Color-75min.** *(Made for TV).* George Maharis, Janet Leigh, Raymond St. Jacques 4*

MONKEY BUSINESS (1931) Paramount. **B&W-77min.** Groucho Marx, Harpo Marx 4*

MONKEY BUSINESS (1952) 20th Century-Fox. **B&W-97min.** Cary Grant, Ginger Rogers 4*

MONKEY HUSTLE, THE (1976) American-International. **Color-90min.** Yaphet Kotto, Rudy Ray Moore 4*

MONKEY IN WINTER (1962) M-G-M. **B&W-104min.** *(French).* Jean Gabin, Jean-Paul Belmondo .... (5)
Original title: SINGE IN HIVER, UN

MONKEY ON MY BACK (1957) United Artists. **B&W-93min.** Cameron Mitchell, Dianne Foster .... (5)

MONKEY WOMAN, THE (1964) *see* APE WOMAN, THE

MONKEYS, GO HOME! (1967) Buena Vista. **Color-101min.** Maurice Chevalier, Dean Jones 5*

MONKEY'S UNCLE, THE (1965) Buena Vista. **Color-87min.** Tommy Kirk, Annette (Funicello) .... (5)

MONOCLE, THE (1964) Four Star. **B&W-97min.** *(French).* Paul Meurisse, Barbara Steele, Marcel Dalio .... (2)
Original title: MONOCLE RIT JAUNE, LE *(The Monocle Gives a Sickly Smile)*

MONOLITH MONSTERS, THE (1957) Universal. **B&W-77min.** Grant Williams, Lola Albright 3*

MONPTI (1957) Bakros International. **Color-97min.** *(German).* Romy Schneider, Horst Buchholz .... (5)
TV title: LOVE FROM PARIS
Alternate title: MON PETIT

MONSIEUR BEAUCAIRE (1924) Paramount. **B&W-132min.** *(Silent).* Rudolph Valentino, Bebe Daniels .... (4)

MONSIEUR BEAUCAIRE (1946) Paramount. **B&W-93min.** Bob Hope, Joan Caulfield 5*

MONSIEUR FABRE (1951) *see* AMAZING MONSIEUR FABRE, THE

MONSIEUR GANGSTER (1963) American-International. **B&W-98min.** *(French).* Lino Ventura, Sabine Sinjen .... (4)
Original title: TONTONS FLINGUEURS, LES
British title: CROOKS IN CLOVER

MONSIEUR ROBINSON CRUSOE (1959) Les Films du Cyclope. **B&W-88min.** *(French).* Darry Cowl, Beatrice Altariba .... (3)

MONSIEUR VERDOUX (1947) United Artists. **B&W-123min.** Charles Chaplin, Martha Raye 6*

MONSIEUR VINCENT (1948) Lopert [U.A.]. **B&W-114min.** *(French).* Pierre Fresnay, Aime Clariond .... (5)

MONSOON (1952) United Artists. **Color-79min.** George Nader, Myron Healey, Ursula Thiess .... (3)

MONSTER, THE (1925) Metro-Goldwyn. **B&W-86min.** *(Silent).* Lon Chaney, Gertrude Olmsted, Hallam Cooley 4½*

MONSTER AND THE GIRL, THE (1941) Paramount. **B&W-63min.** Ellen Drew, Robert Paige, George Zucco 3*

MONSTER DEMOLISHER (1960) Trans-International. **B&W-74min.** *(Mexican, Telefeature).* German Robles, Julio Aleman 1*
Original title: NOSTRADAMUS Y EL DESTRUCTOR DE MONSTRUOS *(Nostradamus and the Destroyer of Monsters)*

MONSTER FROM A PREHISTORIC PLANET (1963) American-International. **Color-85min.** *(Japanese).* Tamio Kawaji, Yoko Yamamoto 1*
Original title: KAIKYAJU GAPPA
Publicity title: GAPPA - TRIPHIBIAN MONSTER

MONSTER FROM GREEN HELL (1957) Distributors Corp. of America. **B&W-71min.** Jim Davis, Robert E. Griffin .... (3)

MONSTER FROM THE SURF (1965) *see* BEACH GIRLS AND THE MONSTER

MONSTER FROM THE UNKNOWN WORLD (1961) *see* ATLAS AGAINST THE CYCLOPS

MONSTER MAKER, THE (1944) Producers Rel. Corp. [Eagle Lion]. **B&W-64min.** J. Carrol Naish, Ralph Morgan .... (3)

MONSTER OF FATE, THE (1914) *see* GOLEM, THE

MONSTER OF PIEDRAS BLANCAS, THE (1958) Vanwick. **B&W-71min.** Les Tremayne, Forrest Lewis, Jeanne Carmen 2*

MONSTER OF TERROR (1965) *see* DIE, MONSTER, DIE!

MONSTER ON THE CAMPUS (1958) Universal. **B&W-76min.** Arthur Franz, Joanna Moore 3*

MONSTER THAT CHALLENGED THE WORLD, THE (1957) United Artists. **B&W-83min.** Tim Holt, Audrey Dalton, Hans Conreid .... (3)

MONSTER ZERO (1970) Maron Films, Ltd. **Color-92min.** *(Japanese).* Godzilla, Ghidrah, Nick Adams, Akira Takarada 1*
Original title: KAIJU DAISENSO
Alternate title: INVASION OF ASTRO-MONSTERS
Alternate title: BATTLE OF THE ASTROS
Alternate title: INVASION OF THE ASTROS

MONSTERS FROM THE MOON (1953) *see* ROBOT MONSTER

MONSTERS INVADE EXPO '70 (1970) *see* GAMERA VS. MONSTER X

MONSTERS OF THE NIGHT (1966) *see* NAVY VS. THE NIGHT MONSTERS, THE

MONSTROSITY (1964) Emerson Films. **B&W-70min.** Frank Gerstle, Erika Peters .... (3)
Alternate title: ATOMIC BRAIN, THE

MONTANA (1950) Warner Bros. **Color-76min.** Errol Flynn, Alexis Smith 4*

MONTANA BELLE (1952) RKO. **Color-81min.** Jane Russell, Scott Brady .... (3)

Films are rated on a 1 to 10 scale, 10 is highest. **Boldface** ratings followed by an asterisk (*) are for films actually seen and rated by the executive and senior editors. All other ratings are estimates. (See Notes on Entertainment Ratings in the front section.)

MONTANA MIKE (1947) see HEAVEN ONLY KNOWS

MONTANA TERRITORY (1952) Columbia. **Color-64min.** Lon McCallister, Wanda Hendrix...(3)

MONTE CARLO (1930) Paramount. **B&W-90min.** Jeanette MacDonald, Jack Buchanan...**4***

MONTE CARLO BABY (1951) Monogram [Allied Artists]. **B&W-79min.** *(French, English language).* Russell Collins, Audrey Hepburn, Cara Williams, John Van Dreelen...(2)

MONTE CARLO OR BUST! (1969) see THOSE DARING YOUNG MEN IN THEIR JAUNTY JALOPIES

MONTE CARLO STORY, THE (1956) United Artists. **Color-99min.** *(U.S.-Italian).* Vittorio de Sica, Marlene Dietrich, Arthur O'Connell.............**4***
Italian title: MONTECARLO

MONTE CRISTO'S REVENGE (1946) see RETURN OF MONTE CRISTO, THE

MONTE WALSH (1970) Nat'l General (for Cinema Center). **Color-98min.** Lee Marvin, Jeanne Moreau..(4)

MONTEREY POP (1967) Leacock-Pennebaker. **Color-80min.** *(Music Film). Director:* Donn Alan Pennebaker.....................................**4***

MONTPARNASSE 19 (1958) see MODIGLIANI OF MONTPARNASSE

MONTY PYTHON AND THE HOLY GRAIL (1975) Cinema 5. **Color-90min.** *(British).* Graham Chapman, John Cleese........................**6***

MONTY'S DOUBLE (1958) see I WAS MONTY'S DOUBLE

MOON AND SIXPENCE, THE (1942) United Artists. **B&W-89min.** George Sanders, Herbert Marshall.....................................**4***

MOON AND THE SLEDGEHAMMER (1971) Impact Films. **Color-65min.** *(British, Documentary). Director:* Philip Trevelyan..............................(4)

MOON IS BLUE, THE (1953) United Artists. **B&W-99min.** William Holden, David Niven, Maggie McNamara..............................**5½***

MOON IS DOWN, THE (1943) 20th Century-Fox. **B&W-90min.** Cedric Hardwicke, Lee J. Cobb...**4***

MOON OF THE WOLF (1972) Filmways. **Color-74min.** *(Made for TV).* David Janssen, Barbara Rush, Bradford Dillman...................**3***

MOON OVER BURMA (1940) Paramount. **B&W-76min.** Dorothy Lamour, Robert Preston, Preston Foster...(2)

MOON OVER HER SHOULDER (1942) 20th Century-Fox. **B&W-68min.** Dan Dailey (Jr.), Lynn Bari, John Sutton...................................(4)

MOON OVER MIAMI (1941) 20th Century-Fox. **Color-91min.** Don Ameche, Robert Cummings, Betty Grable, Carole Landis.................**4½***

MOON PILOT (1962) Buena Vista. **Color-98min.** Tom Tryon, Dany Saval, Brian Keith...**3***

MOON SPINNERS, THE (1964) Buena Vista. **Color-118min.** *(U.S.-British).* Hayley Mills, Eli Wallach...(5)

MOON ZERO TWO (1969) Warner Bros. **Color-100min.** *(British).* James Olson, Catherina von Schell..(3)

MOONCHILD (1974) American Films Ltd. **Color-90min.** Victor Buono, John Carradine, Mark Travis...(4)

MOONFLEET (1955) M-G-M. **Color-89min.** John Whiteley, Stewart Granger...**4***

MOONLIGHT AND CACTUS (1944) Universal. **B&W-60min.** The Andrews Sisters, Eylse Knox...(3)

MOONLIGHT MURDER (1936) M-G-M. **B&W-68min.** Leo Carrillo, Madge Evans, Chester Morris...(3)

MOONLIGHTER, THE (1953) Warner Bros. **B&W-75min.** Barbara Stanwyck, Fred MacMurray...(3)

MOONLIGHTING MISTRESS (1971) Dalia Productions. **Color-88min.** *(German).* Veronique Vendell, Harald Leipnitz, Ruth Maria Kubitscheck...(3)

MOONLIGHTING WIVES (1966) Craddock Films. **Color-86min.** Diane Vivienne, Jan Nash...(3)

MOONRAKER, THE (1958) Associated British-Pathé [EMI]. **Color-82min.** *(British).* George Baker, Sylvia Syms.................................**4***

MOONRAKER (1979) United Artists. **Color-126min.** *(British).* Roger Moore, Michel Lonsdale...**5½***

MOONRISE (1948) Republic. **B&W-90min.** Dane Clark, Gail Russell...**3½***

MOONRUNNERS (1975) United Artists. **Color-110min.** James Mitchum, Kiel Martin, Arthur Hunnicutt..(4)

MOON'S OUR HOME, THE (1936) Paramount. **B&W-80min.** Margaret Sullavan, Henry Fonda...(4)

MOONSHINE COUNTY EXPRESS (1977) New World. **Color-95min.** John Saxon, Susan Howard, William Conrad.................................(4)

MOONSHINE WAR, THE (1970) M-G-M. **Color-101min.** Richard Widmark, Alan Alda, Patrick McGoohan.................................(3)

MOONTIDE (1942) 20th Century-Fox. **B&W-94min.** Jean Gabin, Ida Lupino..**4***

MOONWALK ONE (1972) Francis Thompson, Inc. **Color-96min.** *(Documentary). Director:* Theo Kamecke.....................................(5)

MOONWOLF (1959) Allied Artists. **B&W-74min.** *(W. German-Finnish).* Carl Mohner, Ann Savo...(3)
Original W. German title: . . . UND IMMER RUFT DAS HERZ

MORALIST, THE (1959) Avers Film. **B&W-120min.** *(Italian).* Alberto Sordi, Vittorio De Sica...(3)
Original title: MORALISTA, IL

MORE (1969) Cinema 5. **Color-110min.** *(Luxembourg, English language).* Mimsy Farmer, Klaus Grunberg..(4)

MORE AMERICAN GRAFFITI (1979) Universal. **Color-112min.** Paul Le Mat, Ron Howard, Candy Clark, Charlie Martin Smith..................**7***

MORE DEAD THAN ALIVE (1969) United Artists. **Color-101min.** Clint Walker, Vincent Price, Anne Francis...................................(3)

MORE THAN A MIRACLE (1967) M-G-M. **Color-110min.** *(Italian-French).* Sophia Loren, Omar Sharif...(3)
Alternate title: CINDERELLA - ITALIAN STYLE
Original Italian title: C'ERA UNA VOLTA
Original French title: BELLE ET LE CAVALIER, LA *(The Beauty and the Cavalier)*

MORE THAN A SECRETARY (1936) Columbia. **B&W-77min.** Jean Arthur, George Brent...(4)

MORE THE MERRIER, THE (1943) Columbia. **B&W-104min.** Jean Arthur, Joel McCrea...**5***

MORGAN! (1966) Cinema 5. **B&W-97min.** *(British).* David Warner, Vanessa Redgrave...**7½***
Original title: MORGAN, A SUITABLE CASE FOR TREATMENT
Alternate title: SUITABLE CASE FOR TREATMENT, A

MORGAN THE PIRATE (1960) M-G-M. **Color-93min.** *(Italian-French).* Steve Reeves, Valérie Lagrange, Chelo Alonso..........................**3½***
Original Italian title: MORGAN IL PIRATA
French title: CAPITAINE MORGAN

MORITURI (1965) 20th Century-Fox. **B&W-123min.** Marlon Brando, Yul Brynner...**4½***
Alternate title: SABOTEUR, CODE NAME "MORITURI," THE
Alternate title: SABOTEUR, THE

MORNING AFTER, THE (1974) Wolper Productions. **Color-75min.** *(Made for TV).* Dick Van Dyke, Lynn Carlin.................................**3***

MORNING DEPARTURE (1950) see OPERATION DISASTER

MORNING GLORY (1933) RKO. **B&W-74min.** Katharine Hepburn, Douglas Fairbanks, Jr...**4***

MORO WITCH DOCTOR (1964) 20th Century-Fox. **B&W-61min.** *(U.S.-Philippine).* Jock Mahoney, Margia Dean.................................(2)

MOROCCO (1930) Paramount. **B&W-90min.** Gary Cooper, Marlene Dietrich...**3***

MORGAN! (1966), played by David Warner, is a wacky Marxist who lives in a car outside the home of his rich, estranged wife, and good-natured policeman Bernard Bresslaw gives him a friendly but stern warning.

Films are rated on a 1 to 10 scale, 10 is highest. **Boldface** ratings followed by an asterisk (*) are for films actually seen and rated by the executive and senior editors. All other ratings are estimates. (See Notes on Entertainment Ratings in the front section.)

MOROZHKO (1965) *see* JACK FROST

MORT EN FRAUDE (1957) *see* FUGITIVE IN SAIGON

MORTAL STORM, THE (1940) M-G-M. **B&W-100min.** Margaret Sullavan, James Stewart...5*

MOSCOW NIGHTS (1935) *see* I STAND CONDEMNED

MOSES (1976) Avco-Embassy. **Color-140min.** *(British-Italian, Telefeature).* Burt Lancaster, Ingrid Thulin, Anthony Quayle...........5½*
Original title: MOSES, THE LAWGIVER

MOSES AND AARON (1975) New Yorker Films. **Color-105min.** *(German-Italian-French).* Gunter Reich, Louis Devos ....(4)

MOSQUITO SQUADRON (1970) United Artists. **Color-90min.** *(British).* David McCallum, Suzanne Neve 4*

MOSS ROSE (1947) 20th Century-Fox. **B&W-82min.** Peggy Cummins, Victor Mature ....(5)

MOST DANGEROUS GAME, THE (1932) RKO. **B&W-63min.** Leslie Banks, Joel McCrea, Fay Wray 4*
British title: HOUNDS OF ZAROFF, THE
Alternate title: SKULL ISLAND

MOST DANGEROUS MAN ALIVE (1961) Columbia. **B&W-82min.** Ron Randell, Debra Paget...(2)

MOST DANGEROUS MAN IN THE WORLD, THE (1969) *see* CHAIRMAN, THE

MOST DANGEROUS SIN, THE (1956) *see* CRIME AND PUNISHMENT

MOST UNUSUAL WOMAN, A (1964) *see* APE WOMAN, THE

MOST WANTED MAN (1953) Astor. **B&W-85min.** *(French).* Fernandel, Zsa-Zsa Gabor ....(2)
Original French title: ENNEMI PUBLIC NO. 1, L' *(Public Enemy No. 1)*
Original Italian title: NEMICO PUBBLICO N. 1, IL
Alternate title: MOST WANTED MAN IN THE WORLD, THE

MOST WONDERFUL MOMENT, THE (1957) Ellis Films. **B&W-94min.** *(Italian).* Marcello Mastroianni, Giovanna Ralli ....(4)
Original title: MOMENTO PIU BELLO, IL

MOTHER (1926) Amkino. **B&W-90min.** *(U.S.S.R.).* Vera Baranovskaya, A. P. Khristiakov, Nikolai Batalov...4½*
Original title: MAT

MOTHER AND THE WHORE, THE (1973) New Yorker Films. **B&W-215min.** *(French).* Bernadette Lafont, Jean-Pierre Leaud, Francoise Lebrun ....(4)
Original title: MAMAN ET LA PUTAIN, LA

MOTHER CAREY'S CHICKENS (1938) RKO. **B&W-82min.** Fay Bainter, Ruby Keeler, Anne Shirley ....(4)

MOTHER DIDN'T TELL ME (1950) 20th Century-Fox. **B&W-88min.** Dorothy McGuire, William Lundigan...(4)

MOTHER IS A FRESHMAN (1949) 20th Century-Fox. **Color-81min.** Loretta Young, Van Johnson 4*
British title: MOTHER KNOWS BEST

MOTHER, JUGS & SPEED (1976) 20th Century-Fox. **Color-95min.** Bill Cosby, Raquel Welch, Harvey Keitel......................................4½*

MOTHER KUSTERS GOES TO HEAVEN (1976) New Yorker Films. **Color-108min.** *(German).* Brigitte Mira, Ingrid Caven ....
Original title: MUTTER KUSTERS FAHRT ZUM HIMMER *(Mother Kuster's Trip to Heaven)*

MOTHER RILEY IN DRACULA'S DESIRE (1952) *see* MY SON, THE VAMPIRE

MOTHER RILEY RUNS RIOT (1952) *see* MY SON, THE VAMPIRE

MOTHER - SIR! (1956) *see* NAVY WIFE

MOTHER WORE TIGHTS (1947) 20th Century-Fox. **Color-107min.** Betty Grable, Dan Dailey...4*

MOTHRA (1961) Columbia. **Color-101min.** *(Japanese).* Yumi Ito, Emi Ito..(2)
Original title: MOSURA

MOTORCYCLE GANG (1957) American-International. **B&W-78min.** Anne Neyland, Steve Terrell ....(3)

MOTOWN 9000 (1973) *see* DETROIT 9000

MOULIN ROUGE (1952) United Artists. **Color-123min.** José Ferrer....6½*

MOUNTAIN, THE (1956) Paramount. **Color-105min.** Spencer Tracy, Robert Wagner...4*

MOUNTAIN MAN (1977) *see* GUARDIAN OF THE WILDERNESS

MOUNTAIN MUSIC (1937) Paramount. **B&W-77min.** Bob Burns, Martha Raye ....(3)

MOUNTAIN ROAD, THE (1960) Columbia. **B&W-102min.** James Stewart, Lisa Lu ....

MOURNING BECOMES ELECTRA (1947) RKO. **B&W-173min.** Rosalind Russell, Michael Redgrave...4*

MOUSE AND HIS CHILD, THE (1977) Sanrio. **Color-83min.** *(Japanese-U.S., Cartoon).* Director: Fred Wolf 5*

MOUSE ON THE MOON, THE (1963) Lopert [U.A.]. **Color-85min.** *(British).* Margaret Rutherford, Bernard Cribbins 6*

MOUSE THAT ROARED, THE (1959) Columbia. **Color-83min.** *(British).* Peter Sellers...5½*

MOUSEY (1974) Universal. **Color-74min.** *(U.S.-British, Made for TV).* Kirk Douglas, Jean Seberg, John Vernon ....(4)

MOUTHPIECE, THE (1932) Warner Bros. **B&W-90min.** Warren William, Sidney Fox...(5)

MOVE (1970) 20th Century-Fox. **Color-90min.** Elliott Gould, Paula Prentiss ....(3)

MOVE OVER, DARLING (1963) 20th Century-Fox. **Color-103min.** Doris Day, James Garner..4*

MOVIE CRAZY (1932) Paramount. **B&W-96min.** Harold Lloyd, Constance Cummings..(5)

MOVIE MAKER, THE (1967) MCA-TV. **Color-91min.** *(Made for TV).* Rod Steiger, Robert Culp, Sally Kellerman ....(4)

MOVIE MOVIE (1978) Warner Bros. **Color-105min.** George C. Scott, Trish Van Devere, Red Buttons..6*

MOVIE MURDERER, THE (1970) Universal. **Color-100min.** *(Made for TV).* Arthur Kennedy, Robert Webber, Warren Oates 4*

MOVING TARGET, THE (1966) *see* HARPER

MOVING VIOLATION (1976) 20th Century-Fox. **Color-91min.** Stephen McHattie, Kay Lenz, Eddie Albert..(4)

MOZAMBIQUE (1965) Seven Arts [W.B.]. **Color-98min.** *(British).* Steve Cochran, Hildegard Neff ....(2)

MUDLARK, THE (1950) 20th Century-Fox. **B&W-99min.** Irene Dunne, Alec Guinness, Andrew Ray 5½*

MUG TOWN (1943) Universal. **B&W-60min.** The Dead End Kids, The Little Tough Guys, Grace McDonald ....(4)

MUGGER, THE (1958) United Artists. **B&W-74min.** Kent Smith, Nan Martin ....(3)

MUHAIR (1967) Haven International. **Color-84min.** *(Argentinian).* Isabel Sarli, Armando Bo, Victor Bo, Mario Lozano ....(2)
Original title: MUJER DI MI PADRE, LA *(The Wife of My Father)*

MUMMY, THE (1932) Universal. **B&W-72min.** Boris Karloff, Zita Johann..3*

MUMMY, THE (1959) Universal. **Color-88min.** *(British).* Peter Cushing, Christopher Lee...3*

MUMMY'S CURSE, THE (1944) Universal. **B&W-62min.** Lon Chaney (Jr.), Virginia Christine, Peter Coe...3*

MUMMY'S GHOST, THE (1944) Universal. **B&W-60min.** Lon Chaney (Jr.), John Carradine, Ramsay Ames..3*

MUMMY'S HAND, THE (1940) Universal. **B&W-67min.** Dick Foran, George Zucco, Tom Tyler..3*

MUMMY'S SHROUD, THE (1967) 20th Century-Fox. **Color-84min.** *(British).* André Morell, John Phillips, Elizabeth Sellars ....(2)

MUMMY'S TOMB, THE (1942) Universal. **B&W-61min.** Lon Chaney (Jr.), Turhan Bey, John Hubbard...3*

MUMSY, NANNY, SONNY AND GIRLY (1970) *see* GIRLY

MUNSTER, GO HOME (1966) Universal. **Color-96min.** Fred Gwynne, Yvonne De Carlo..3*

MURDER (1930) British-International. **B&W-92min.** *(British).* Herbert Marshall, Nora Baring ....(4)

MURDER A LA MOD (1968) Aries Documentaries. **B&W-80min.** Margo Norton, Andra Akers, William Finley, Jared Martin ....(4)

MURDER AHOY (1964) M-G-M. **B&W-93min.** *(British).* Margaret Rutherford, Lionel Jeffries ....(4)

MURDER AMONG FRIENDS (1941) 20th Century-Fox. **B&W-67min.** Marjorie Weaver, John Hubbard...(3)

MURDER AT 45 R.P.M. (1960) Gala *(Brit.).* **B&W-98min.** *(French).* Danielle Darrieux, Michel Auclair...(4)
Original title: MEURTRE EN 45 TOURS

MURDER AT MALIBU BEACH (1946) *see* TRAP, THE

MURDER AT THE GALLOP (1963) M-G-M. **B&W-81min.** *(British).* Margaret Rutherford, Robert Morley 3*

MURDER AT THE VANITIES (1934) Paramount. **B&W-70min.** Jack Oakie, Victor McLaglen ....(4)

MURDER BY AGREEMENT (1963) *see* JOURNEY INTO NOWHERE

MURDER BY CONTRACT (1958) Columbia. **B&W-81min.** Vince Edwards, Philip Pine ....(4)

Films are rated on a 1 to 10 scale, 10 is highest. **Boldface** ratings followed by an asterisk (*) are for films actually seen and rated by the executive and senior editors. All other ratings are estimates. (See Notes on Entertainment Ratings in the front section.)

MURDER BY DEATH (1976) Columbia. **Color-94min.** Truman Capote, Alec Guinness.. 6*

MURDER BY DECREE (1979) Avco-Embassy. **Color-120min.** *(Canadian-British).* Christopher Plummer, James Mason 5*

MURDER BY PROXY (1955) *see* BLACKOUT

MURDER CLINIC, THE (1966) Europix-Consolidated. **Color-86min.** *(Italian-French).* William Berger, Francoise Prévost....................(2)
Original Italian title: LAMA NEL CORPO, LA *(The Knife in the Body)*
Original French title: NUITS DE L'ÉPOUVANTE *(The Nights of Terror)*
Alternate title: REVENGE OF THE LIVING DEAD
Publicity title: NIGHT OF TERRORS, THE
Publicity title: MURDER SOCIETY, THE

MURDER CZECH STYLE (1967) Royal Films Int'l [Columbia]. **B&W-90min.** *(Czech).* Rudolf Hrusinsky, Kveta Fialova....................(5)
Original title: VRAZDA PO CESKU
Alternate original title: VRAZDA PO NASEM

MURDER GO ROUND (1970) *see* COP, THE

MURDER, HE SAYS (1945) Paramount. **B&W-91min.** Fred MacMurray, Helen Walker, Marjorie Main.. 3*

MURDER IN GREENWICH VILLAGE (1937) Columbia. **B&W-68min.** Fay Wray, Richard Arlen..(3)

MURDER IN MISSISSIPPI (1965) Tiger Prods. **B&W-84min.** Sheila Britton, Sam Stewart ....(2)

MURDER IN PEYTON PLACE (1977) NBC-TV. **Color-100min.** *(Made for TV).* Ed Nelson, Dorothy Malone, Tim O'Connor ....

MURDER IN REVERSE (1945) Four Continents. **B&W-88min.** *(British).* William Hartnell, Jimmy Hanley ....(5)

MURDER IN THE AIR (1940) Warner Bros. **B&W-55min.** Ronald Reagan, John Litel...(3)

MURDER IN THE BIG HOUSE (1942) Warner Bros. **B&W-59min.** Van Johnson, Faye Emerson ....(3)
TV title: BORN FOR TROUBLE

MURDER IN THE BLUE ROOM (1944) Universal. **B&W-61min.** Grace McDonald, Donald Cook, Anne Gwynne..............................(4)

MURDER IN THE MUSIC HALL (1946) Republic. **B&W-84min.** William Marshall*, Helen Walker ....(4)

MURDER IN THORNTON SQUARE (1944) *see* GASLIGHT

MURDER IN TIMES SQUARE (1943) Columbia. **B&W-65min.** Edmund Lowe, Marguerite Chapman, Sidney Blackmer ....(3)

MURDER, INC. (1951) *see* ENFORCER, THE

MURDER, INC. (1960) 20th Century-Fox. **B&W-103min.** Stuart Whitman, May Britt 4*

MURDER IS MY BEAT (1955) Allied Artists. **B&W-77min.** Paul Langton, Robert Shayne ....(3)

MURDER IS MY BUSINESS (1946) Producers Rel. Corp. [Eagle Lion]. **B&W-64min.** Hugh Beaumont, Cheryl Walker.....................(3)

MURDER MAN (1935) M-G-M. **B&W-70min.** Spencer Tracy, Virginia Bruce ....(4)

MURDER MANSION (1970) Avco-Embassy. **Color-90min.** *(Mexican).* Analia Gade, Evelyn Stewart, Andres Resino 2*

MURDER MOST FOUL (1964) M-G-M. **B&W-90min.** *(British).* Margaret Rutherford, Ron Moody.................................... 4*

MURDER, MY SWEET (1944) RKO. **B&W-95min.** Dick Powell, Claire Trevor... 3*
British title: FAREWELL MY LOVELY

MURDER OF FRED HAMPTON, THE (1971) MGA. **B&W-88min.** *(Documentary). Director:* Mike Gray ....(4)

MURDER ON APPROVAL (1956) RKO. **B&W-90min.** *(British).* Tom Conway, Delphi Lawrence ....(3)
Original title: BARBADOS QUEST

MURDER ON DIAMOND ROW (1937) United Artists. **B&W-77min.** *(British).* Edmund Lowe, Ann Todd.................................(4)
Original title: SQUEAKER, THE

MURDER ON FLIGHT 502 (1975) MPC (TV). **Color-100min.** Robert Stack, Theodore Bikel, Ralph Bellamy, Sonny Bono 4*

MURDER ON MONDAY (1952) Mayer-Kingsley. **B&W-85min.** *(British).* Ralph Richardson, Margaret Leighton ....(5)
Original title: HOME AT SEVEN

MURDER ON THE BRIDGE (1975) *see* END OF THE GAME

MURDER ON THE BRIDLE PATH (1936) RKO. **B&W-66min.** Helen Broderick, James Gleason ....(4)

MURDER ON THE ORIENT EXPRESS (1974) Paramount. **Color-127min.** *(British).* Albert Finney, Martin Balsam 7*

MURDER ONCE REMOVED (1971) MPC (TV). **Color-74min.** *(Made for TV).* John Forsythe, Richard Kiley, Barbara Bain ....(4)

MURDER ON THE ORIENT EXPRESS (1974). Belgian detective Albert Finney (standing center) confronts the host of murder suspects; they are (left to right) Jean-Pierre Cassel, Anthony Perkins, Vanessa Redgrave, Sean Connery, Ingrid Bergman, George Coulouris, Rachel Roberts, Wendy Hiller, Denis Quilley, Michael York, Jacqueline Bisset and Lauren Bacall; railroad official Martin Balsam observes at right.

MURDER OR MERCY (1974) Quinn Martin. **Color-74min.** *(Made for TV).* Melvyn Douglas, Bradford Dillman, Denver Pyle...................5*

MURDER OVER NEW YORK (1940) 20th Century-Fox. **B&W-65min.** Sidney Toler, Marjorie Weaver, Robert Lowery ....(4)
Alternate title: CHARLIE CHAN IN MURDER OVER NEW YORK

MURDER PARTY (1961) Screen Gems. **B&W-79min.** *(German).* Magali Noel, Harry Meyen..(4)

MURDER REPORTED (1957) Columbia. **B&W-58min.** *(British).* Paul Carpenter, Melissa Stribling, Peter Stanwick ....(3)

MURDER RING, THE (1941) *see* ELLERY QUEEN AND THE MURDER RING

MURDER, SHE SAID (1961) M-G-M. **B&W-87min.** *(British-U.S.).* Margaret Rutherford, Arthur Kennedy................................. 4*

MURDER WILL OUT (1952) Kramer Hyams. **B&W-83min.** *(British).* James Robertson Justice, Valerie Hobson ....(5)
Original title: VOICE OF MERRILL, THE

MURDER WITHOUT TEARS (1953) Allied Artists. **B&W-64min.** Craig Stevens, Joyce Holden, Edward Norris ....(3)

MURDERER, THE (1963) *see* ENOUGH ROPE

MURDERER'S ROW (1966) Columbia. **Color-108min.** Dean Martin, Ann-Margret, Karl Malden 4*

MURDERS IN THE RUE MORGUE (1932) Universal. **B&W-75min.** Bela Lugosi, Sidney Fox, Leon Waycroff (Leon Ames) 3*

MURDERS IN THE RUE MORGUE (1971) American-International. **Color-86min.** Jason Robards (Jr.), Herbert Lom, Christine Kaufmann (3)

MURDOCK'S GANG (1973) Don Fedderson Productions. **Color-74min.** *(Made for TV).* Alex Dreier, Janet Leigh, Murray Hamilton, William Daniels ....(4)

MURIEL (1963) Lopert [U.A.]. **Color-115min.** *(French-Italian).* Delphine Seyrig, Jean-Pierre Kérien 1*
Original French title: MURIEL, OU LE TEMPS D'UN RETOUR *(Muriel, or the Time of a Return)*
Original Italian title: MURIEL, IL TEMPO DI UN RITORNO

MURIETA (1965) Warner Bros. **Color-108min.** *(Spanish).* Jeffrey Hunter, Arthur Kennedy, Diana Lorys ....(3)
Original title: JOAQUIN MURRIETA

MURIETTA (1971) *see* DESPERATE MISSION

MURMUR OF THE HEART (1971) Palomar Pictures. **Color-118min.** *(French).* Lea Massari, Benoit Ferreux 5*
Original title: SOUFFLE AU COEUR, LE *(also translates as Heart Murmur, The Murmuring Heart)*
British title: DEAREST LOVE

MURPH THE SURF (1974) *see* LIVE A LITTLE, STEAL A LOT

MURPHY'S WAR (1971) Paramount. **Color-106min.** *(British).* Peter O'Toole, Sian Phillips...(4)

MUSCLE BEACH PARTY (1964) American-International. **Color-94min.** Frankie Avalon, Annette Funicello, Peter Lorre ....(3)

MUSIC BOX KID, THE (1960) United Artists. B&W-74min. Ronald Foster, Luana Patten .... (2)

MUSIC FOR MILLIONS (1944) M-G-M. B&W-120min. Margaret O'Brien, Jimmy Durante, June Allyson, José Iturbi .... (4)

MUSIC IN MANHATTAN (1944) RKO. B&W-80min. Dennis Day, Anne Shirley .... (4)

MUSIC IN MY HEART (1940) Columbia. B&W-70min. Tony Martin, Rita Hayworth .... (4)

MUSIC IN THE AIR (1934) Fox Film Co. [20th]. B&W-85min. Gloria Swanson, John Boles .... (4)

MUSIC IS MAGIC (1935) 20th Century-Fox. B&W-65min. Alice Faye, Ray Walker .... (3)

MUSIC LOVERS, THE (1971) United Artists. Color-122min. (British). Richard Chamberlain, Glenda Jackson 4*

MUSIC MAN, THE (1948) Monogram [Allied Artists]. B&W-68min. Jimmy Dorsey, June Preisser .... (4)

MUSIC MAN, THE (1962) Warner Bros. Color-151min. Robert Preston, Shirley Jones 7½*

MUSKETEERS OF THE SEA (1960) American-International. Color-116min. (Italian). Pier Angeli, Robert Alda, Aldo Ray .... (3)

MUSS 'EM UP (1936) RKO. B&W-68min. Preston Foster, Margaret Callahan .... (4)
British title: HOUSE OF FATE

MUSTANG COUNTRY (1976) Universal. Color-79min. Joel McCrea, Nika Mina, Patrick Wayne .... (4)

MUTATION, THE (1973) Columbia. Color-91min. (U.S.-British). Donald Pleasence, Tom Baker, Michael Dunn .... (3)
Publicity title: MUTATIONS, THE

MUTINEERS, THE (1949) Columbia. B&W-60min. Jon Hall, Adele Jergens, George Reeves .... (3)
Alternate title: PIRATE SHIP

MUTINY (1952) United Artists. Color-77min. Mark Stevens, Angela Lansbury 3½*

MUTINY AT FORT SHARP (1965) Teleworld. Color-91min. (Spanish). Broderick Crawford 3*

MUTINY IN OUTER SPACE (1965) Allied Artists. B&W-85min. William Leslie, Dolores Faith .... (3)
Alternate title: SPACE STATION X-14

MUTINY ON THE BLACKHAWK (1939) Universal. B&W-66min. Constance Moore, Richard Arlen .... (3)

MUTINY ON THE BOUNTY (1935) M-G-M. B&W-132min. Clark Gable, Charles Laughton 6*

MUTINY ON THE BOUNTY (1962) M-G-M. Color-179min. Marlon Brando, Trevor Howard 4½*

MY BABY IS BLACK (1961) U.S. Films. B&W-75min. (French). Gordon Heath, Francoise Giret .... (3)
Original title: LACHES VIVENT D'ESPOIR, LES

MY BEST GIRL (1927) United Artists. B&W-83min. (Silent). Mary Pickford, Charles "Buddy" Rogers .... (4)

MY BILL (1938) Warner Bros. B&W-64min. Kay Francis, Bonita Granville, Dickie Moore .... (4)

MY BLOOD RUNS COLD (1965) Warner Bros. B&W-104min. Troy Donahue, Joey Heatherton, Barry Sullivan .... (3)

MY BLUE HEAVEN (1950) 20th Century-Fox. Color-96min. Betty Grable, Dan Dailey .... (4)

MY BROTHER TALKS TO HORSES (1947) M-G-M. Color-93min. Peter Lawford, Dan Dailey 3*

MY BROTHER, THE OUTLAW (1951) *see* MY OUTLAW BROTHER

MY BROTHER'S KEEPER (1948) Eagle Lion. B&W-96min. (British). Jack Warner, George Cole .... (4)

MY BUDDY (1944) Republic. B&W-69min. Don "Red" Barry, Ruth Terry .... (4)

MY COUSIN RACHEL (1952) 20th Century-Fox. B&W-98min. Olivia de Havilland, Richard Burton 6*

MY DARLING CLEMENTINE (1946) 20th Century-Fox. B&W-97min. Henry Fonda, Linda Darnell 4*

MY DARLING DAUGHTERS' ANNIVERSARY (1973) MCA-TV. Color-74min. (Made for TV). Robert Young, Ruth Hussey, Darleen Carr, Judy Strangis 4*

MY DAUGHTER JOY (1950) *see* OPERATION X

MY DEAR SECRETARY (1948) United Artists. B&W-94min. Laraine Day, Kirk Douglas 4½*

MY DOG BUDDY (1960) Columbia. B&W-77min. London, Travis Lemmond, Ken Curtis .... (4)

MY DREAM IS YOURS (1949) Warner Bros. Color-101min. Doris Day, Jack Carson 4*

MY FAIR LADY (1964) Warner Bros. Color-170min. Rex Harrison, Audrey Hepburn 9*

MY FATHER'S HOUSE (1947) Kline-Levin. B&W-85min. (Palestinian-U.S., English language). Ronnie Cohen, Irene Broza .... (5)

MY FATHER'S HOUSE (1975) Worldvision. Color-100min. (Made for TV). Cliff Robertson, Robert Preston, Eileen Brennan 4*

MY FAVORITE BLONDE (1942) Paramount. B&W-78min. Bob Hope, Madeleine Carroll 4*

MY FAVORITE BRUNETTE (1947) Paramount. B&W-87min. Bob Hope, Dorothy Lamour 4*

MY FAVORITE SPY (1942) RKO. B&W-86min. Kay Kyser, Ellen Drew (4)

MY FAVORITE SPY (1951) Paramount. B&W-93min. Bob Hope 4*

MY FAVORITE WIFE (1940) RKO. B&W-88min. Irene Dunne, Cary Grant 5½*

MY FOOLISH HEART (1949) RKO. B&W-98min. Dana Andrews, Susan Hayward 3*

MY FORBIDDEN PAST (1951) RKO. B&W-81min. Ava Gardner, Robert Mitchum, Melvyn Douglas .... (3)

MY FRIEND FLICKA (1943) 20th Century-Fox. Color-89min. Roddy McDowall, Preston Foster 4*

MY FRIEND IRMA (1949) Paramount. B&W-103min. Marie Wilson, John Lund .... (3)

MY FRIEND IRMA GOES WEST (1950) Paramount. B&W-90min. Marie Wilson, Dean Martin, Jerry Lewis .... (4)

MY FRIENDS (1975) Cineriz. Color-110min. (Italian). Ugo Tognazzi, Philippe Noiret, Gastone Moschin .... (5)
Original title: AMICI MIEI

MY GAL SAL (1942) 20th Century-Fox. Color-103min. Victor Mature, Rita Hayworth 3*

MY GEISHA (1962) Paramount. Color-120min. Shirley MacLaine, Yves Montand 4½*

MY GIRL TISA (1948) United Artists. B&W-95min. Lilli Palmer, Sam Wanamaker 4½*

MY GUN IS QUICK (1957) United Artists. B&W-88min. Robert Bray, Pat Donahue .... (2)

MY HEART BELONGS TO DADDY (1943) Paramount. B&W-75min. Richard Carlson, Martha O'Driscoll .... (3)

MY HEART GOES CRAZY (1946) *see* LONDON TOWN

MY HERO (1948) *see* SOUTHERN YANKEE, A

MY LIFE (1932) *see* ECSTASY

MY LIFE IS YOURS (1941) *see* PEOPLE VS. DR. KILDARE, THE

MY LIFE TO LIVE (1962) Pathé Contemporary. B&W-85min. (French). Anna Karina, Saddy Rebbot .... (4)
Original title: VIVRE SA VIE

MY LIFE WITH CAROLINE (1941) RKO. B&W-81min. Ronald Colman, Anna Lee .... (4)

MY LITTLE CHICKADEE (1940) Universal. B&W-83min. W. C. Fields, Mae West 4*

MY LOVE CAME BACK (1940) Warner Bros. B&W-81min. Olivia de Havilland, Jeffrey Lynn .... (4)

MY LOVE IN JERUSALEM (1971) *see* MARGO

MY LOVER, MY SON (1970) M-G-M. Color-95min. (British-U.S.). Romy Schneider, Donald Houston, Dennis Waterman .... (2)

MY LUCKY STAR (1938) 20th Century-Fox. B&W-84min. Sonja Henie, Cesar Romero .... (4)

MY MAN AND I (1952) M-G-M. B&W-99min. Ricardo Montalban, Shelley Winters, Claire Trevor .... (4)

MY MAN GODFREY (1936) Universal. B&W-95min. William Powell, Carole Lombard 6*

MY MAN GODFREY (1957) Universal. Color-92min. June Allyson, David Niven 4*

MY NAME IS IVAN (1962) Shore International. B&W-95min. (U.S.S.R.). Kolya Burlyayev, Captain Kholin 5*
Original title: DETSTVO IVANA (Ivan's Childhood)
Alternate title: IVAN'S CHILDHOOD
Alternate title: YOUNGEST SPY, THE

MY NAME IS JULIA ROSS (1945) Columbia. B&W-65min. Nina Foch, May Whitty .... (5)

MY NAME IS NOBODY (1974) Titanus. Color-117min. (Italian-French-W. German). Terence Hill, Henry Fonda 5½*
Original Italian title: MIO NOME E NESSUNO, IL

MY NIGHT AT MAUD'S (1969) Pathé Contemporary. **B&W-105min.** *(French).* Jean-Louis Trintignant, Francoise Fabian ....(2)
Original title: MA NUIT CHEZ MAUD
British title: MY NIGHT WITH MAUD

MY OLD MAN'S PLACE (1971) *see* GLORY BOY

MY OUTLAW BROTHER (1951) Eagle Lion. **B&W-82min.** Mickey Rooney, Robert Stack ....(3)
Original title: MY BROTHER, THE OUTLAW

MY OWN TRUE LOVE (1949) Paramount. **B&W-84min.** Phyllis Calvert, Melvyn Douglas ....(3)

MY PAL GUS (1952) 20th Century-Fox. **B&W-83min.** Richard Widmark, George Winslow 3*

MY PAL WOLF (1944) RKO. **B&W-76min.** Sharyn Moffett, Jill Esmond, Una O'Connor ....(4)

MY REPUTATION (1946) Warner Bros. **B&W-96min.** Barbara Stanwyck, George Brent 4*

MY SECRET LIFE (1971) Jack H. Harris. **Color-92min.** *(Canadian).* Jack Woods, Leon Jervis, Lyn Logan ....(3)
Original title: COLUMBUS OF SEX

MY SEVEN LITTLE SINS (1956) Kingsley International. **B&W-98min.** *(French-Italian).* Maurice Chevalier, Paolo Stoppa...........................(3)
Original French title: J'AVAIS SEPT FILLES *(I Have Seven Daughters)*
British title: I HAD SEVEN DAUGHTERS

MY SIDE OF THE MOUNTAIN (1969) Paramount. **Color-100min.** *(U.S.-Canadian).* Teddy Eccles, Theodore Bikel 5*

MY SISTER EILEEN (1942) Columbia. **B&W-96min.** Rosalind Russell, Janet Blair...........................4*

MY SISTER EILEEN (1955) Columbia. **Color-108min.** Janet Leigh, Betty Garrett...........................4*

MY SISTER, MY LOVE (1966) Sigma III. **B&W-97min.** *(Swedish).* Per Oscarsson, Bibi Andersson ....(5)
Original title: SYSKONBADD 1782

MY SIX CONVICTS (1952) Columbia. **B&W-104min.** John Beal, Regis Toomey 4*

MY SIX LOVES (1963) Paramount. **Color-101min.**   Cliff Robertson (4)

MY SON ALONE (1942) *see* AMERICAN EMPIRE

MY SON JOHN (1952) Paramount. **B&W-122min.** Robert Walker, Helen Hayes, Van Heflin ....(3)

MY SON, MY SON (1940) United Artists. **B&W-115min.** Madeleine Carroll, Brian Aherne ....(5)

MY SON, THE HERO (1962) United Artists. **Color-111min.** *(Italian-French).* Giuliano Gemma, Jacqueline Sassard, Pedro Armendariz .....(3)
Original Italian title: ARRIVANOI TITANI *(The Titans Arrive)*
Original French title: TITANS, LES *(The Titans)*

MY SON, THE VAMPIRE (1952) Blue Chip. **B&W-74min.** *(British).* Arthur Lucan, Bela Lugosi, Dora Bryan...........................2*
Original title: OLD MOTHER RILEY MEETS THE VAMPIRE
Alternate title: VAMPIRE OVER LONDON
Alternate title: KING ROBOT
8mm title (1): MOTHER RILEY RUNS RIOT
8mm title (2): MOTHER RILEY IN DRACULA'S DESIRE

MY SWEET CHARLIE (1970) Universal. **Color-97min.** *(Made for TV).* Patty Duke, Al Freeman, Jr...........................5*

MY TEENAGE DAUGHTER (1956) *see* TEENAGE BAD GIRL

MY TWO HUSBANDS (1940) *see* TOO MANY HUSBANDS

MY UNCLE ANTOINE (1971) Nat'l Film Board of Canada. **Color-110min.** *(Canadian).* Jean Duceppe, Olivette Thibault ....(5)
Original title: MON ONCLE ANTOINE

MY UNCLE, MR. HULOT (1956) Continental [Walter Reade]. **Color-116min.** *(French).* Jacques Tati, Jean-Pierre Zola ....(3)
Original title: MON ONCLE *(My Uncle)*

MY WAY (1974) Joseph Brenner. **Color-92min.** *(South African).* Joe Stewardson, Richard Loring...........................(4)

MY WIFE IS A PANTHER (1960) **B&W-85min.** *(French).* Jean Richard, Jean Poiret, Silvana Blasi ....(3)
Original title: MA FEMME EST UNE PANTHERE

MY WIFE'S BEST FRIEND (1952) 20th Century-Fox. **B&W-87min.** Anne Baxter, Macdonald Carey, Catherine McLeod ....(4)

MY WILD IRISH ROSE (1947) Warner Bros. **Color-101min.** Dennis Morgan, Andrea King 4*

MY WORLD DIES SCREAMING (1958) *see* TERROR IN THE HAUNTED HOUSE

MYRA BRECKINRIDGE (1970) 20th Century-Fox. **Color-94min.** Raquel Welch, Mae West, John Huston...........................2*

MYSTERE PICASSO, LE (1956) Lopert [U.A.]. **Color-76min.** *(French, Documentary).* Director: Henri-Georges Clouzot...........................(3)
Alternate title: MYSTERY OF PICASSO, THE

MYSTERIANS, THE (1957) M-G-M. **Color-87min.** *(Japanese).* Takashi Shimura, Kenji Sahara, Yumi Shirakawa 2*
Original title: CHIKYU BOEIGUN *(Earth Defense Forces)*

MYSTERIES FROM BEYOND THE EARTH (1975) CineVue Inc. **Color-105min.** *(Documentary).* 4½*

MYSTERIES OF THE DEEP (1960) Buena Vista. **Color-24min.** *(Documentary).* Producer: Walt Disney 5*

MYSTERIOUS DOCTOR, THE (1943) Warner Bros. **B&W-57min.** John Loder, Eleanor Parker ....(4)

MYSTERIOUS DR. FU MANCHU, THE (1929) Paramount. **B&W-85min.** Warner Oland, Jean Arthur, Neil Hamilton, O. P. Heggie...........................(3)

MYSTERIOUS DR. SATAN (1940) *see* DR. SATAN'S ROBOT

MYSTERIOUS HOUSE OF DR. C., THE (1967) *see* DR. COPPELIUS

MYSTERIOUS INTRUDER, THE (1946) Columbia. **B&W-61min.** Richard Dix, Nina Vale...........................(4)

MYSTERIOUS INVADER, THE (1957) *see* ASTOUNDING SHE MONSTER, THE

MYSTERIOUS ISLAND, THE (1929) M-G-M. **Color-95min.** *(Part-talking).* Lionel Barrymore, Jane Daly, Montagu Love ....(4)

MYSTERIOUS ISLAND (1961) Columbia. **Color-101min.** *(British-U.S.).* Michael Craig, Joan Greenwood 3*

MYSTERIOUS LADY, THE (1928) M-G-M. **B&W-85min.** *(Silent).* Greta Garbo, Conrad Nagel 4*

MYSTERIOUS MAGICIAN, THE (1965) UCC Films. **B&W-95min.** *(German).* Joachim Berger, Heinz Drache ....(3)
Original title: HEXER, DER *(The Wizard)*

MYSTERIOUS MR. MOTO (1938) 20th Century-Fox. **B&W-62min.** Peter Lorre, Harold Huber...........................(3)

MYSTERIOUS MONSTERS, THE (1976) Sunn Classic. **Color-84min.** *(Documentary).* Director: Robert Guenette 4*

MYSTERIOUS SATELLITE (1956) *see* WARNING FROM SPACE

MYSTERY BROADCAST (1943) Republic. **B&W-63min.** Ruth Terry, Frank Albertson...........................(4)

MYSTERY IN MEXICO (1948) RKO. **B&W-66min.** William Lundigan, Jacqueline White ....(4)

MYSTERY OF EDWIN DROOD, THE (1935) Universal. **B&W-86min.** Claude Rains, Valerie Hobson 4*

MYSTERY OF KASPAR HAUSER, THE (1974) Cinema 5. **Color-110min.** *(German).* Bruno S., Brigitte Mira, Hans Musaus...........................(4)
Original title: JEDER FUR SICH UND GOTT GEGEN ALLE
Alternate title: EVERY MAN FOR HIMSELF AND GOD AGAINST ALL
Alternate title: ENIGMA OF KASPAR HAUSER, THE
Alternate title: KASPAR HAUSER

MYSTERY OF MARIE ROGET, THE (1942) Universal. **B&W-91min.** Maria Montez, Patric Knowles...........................(4)
Alternate title: PHANTOM OF PARIS

MYSTERY OF MR. WONG, THE (1939) Monogram [Allied Artists]. **B&W-68min.** Boris Karloff, Dorothy Tree...........................(3)

MYSTERY OF MR. X (1934) M-G-M. **B&W-85min.** Robert Montgomery, Lewis Stone...........................(4)

MYSTERY OF PICASSO, THE (1956) *see* MYSTERE PICASSO, LE

MYSTERY OF THE BLACK JUNGLE (1953) Republic. **B&W-72min.** *(Italian).* Lex Barker, Jane Maxwell, Luigi Tosi ....(2)
Alternate title: BLACK DEVILS OF KALI, THE
Original title: MISTERI DELLA GIUNGLA NERA, I

MYSTERY OF THE WAX MUSEUM, THE (1933) Warner Bros. **Color-72min.** Lionel Atwill, Fay Wray...........................4*
Publicity title: WAX MUSEUM

MYSTERY OF THE WHITE ROOM (1939) Universal. **B&W-57min.** Bruce Cabot, Joan Woodbury ....(3)

MYSTERY OF THUG ISLAND, THE (1964) Columbia. **Color-96min.** *(Italian-W. German).* Guy Madison, Ingeborg Schoner...........................(1)
Original Italian title: MISTERI DELLA GIUNGLA NERA, I *(The Mystery of the Black Jungle)*
Original W. German title: GEHEIMNIS DER LEDERSCHLINGE, DAS

MYSTERY SEA RAIDER (1940) Paramount. **B&W-78min.** Henry Wilcoxon, Carole Landis...........................(3)

MYSTERY SHIP (1941) Columbia. **B&W-65min.** Paul Kelly, Larry Parks...........................(4)

MYSTERY STREET (1950) M-G-M. **B&W-93min.** Ricardo Montalban, Sally Forrest...........................(5)

Films are rated on a 1 to 10 scale, 10 is highest. **Boldface** ratings followed by an asterisk (*) are for films actually seen and rated by the executive and senior editors. All other ratings are estimates. (See Notes on Entertainment Ratings in the front section.)

MYSTERY OF THE WAX MUSEUM (1933). Confined to a wheelchair, wax sculptor Lionel Atwill is tormented by his burned hands, which keep him from practicing his art, and even his assistant Allen Vincent (right) isn't aware of the fiendish plan the older man has concocted for adding new statues to his museum. Matthew Betz works in the background at left

MYSTERY SUBMARINE (1950) Universal. B&W-78min. Macdonald Carey, Marta Toren... 4*

MYSTERY SUBMARINE (1962) Universal. B&W-92min. (British). Edward Judd, James Robertson Justice................................... (3)
Alternate title: DECOY

MYSTIFIERS, THE (1965) see SYMPHONY FOR A MASSACRE

-N-

NABONGA (1944) Producers Rel. Corp. [Eagle Lion]. B&W-75min. Buster Crabbe, Fifi D'Orsay... (3)
Alternate title: GORILLA
British title: JUNGLE WOMAN, THE

NADA (1974) New Line Cinema. Color-110min. (French-Italian). Fabio Testi, Mariangela Melato, Maurice Garrel .... (5)
Publicity title: NADA GANG, THE

NAKED AFRICA (1957) American-International. Color-71min. (Travelog). Director: Ray Phoenix................................ (4)

NAKED ALIBI (1954) Universal. B&W-86min. Sterling Hayden, Gloria Grahame .... (4)

NAKED AMONG THE WOLVES (1963) Lopert [U.A.]. B&W-100min. (East German). Erwin Geschonneck, Fred Delmare .... (5)
Original title: NACKT UNTER WOLFEN

NAKED AND THE DEAD, THE (1958) Warner Bros. Color-131min. Aldo Ray, Cliff Robertson...................................... 4*

NAKED ANGELS (1969) Favorite Films. Color-83min. Michael Greene, Jennifer Gan .... (2)

NAKED APE, THE (1973) Universal. Color-85min. Johnny Crawford, Victoria Principal, Dennis Olivieri .... (4)

NAKED AUTUMN (1961) United Motion Pic. Org. (UMPO). B&W-98min. (French). Simone Signoret, Reginald Kernan .... (5)
Original title: MAUVAIS COUPS, LES (Foul Play)

NAKED BRIGADE, THE (1965) Universal. B&W-99min. (U.S.-Greek). Shirley Eaton, Ken Scott, Mary Chronopoulou..................... (3)
Original Greek title: HE GYMNE TAXIARCHIA

NAKED CITY, THE (1948) Universal. B&W-96min. Barry Fitzgerald, Howard Duff... 5*

NAKED CIVIL SERVANT, THE (1975) Thames Television. Color-90min. (British, Made for TV). John Hurt 6*

NAKED DAWN, THE (1955) Universal. Color-82min. Arthur Kennedy, Betta St. John 3½*

NAKED EARTH (1958) 20th Century-Fox. B&W-96min. (British). Richard Todd, Juliette Greco .... (4)

NAKED EDGE, THE (1961) United Artists. B&W-99min. Gary Cooper, Deborah Kerr... 5*

NAKED EYE, THE (1957) Film Representations. B&W-71min. (Documentary). Director: Louis Clyde Stoumen .... (5)

NAKED GENERAL, THE (1958) Toho. Color-92min. (Japanese). Keiju Kobayashi, Aiko Mimasu.................................. (5)
Original title: HADAKA NO TAISHO

NAKED GUN, THE (1956) Associated Film Dists. B&W-69min. Willard Parker, Mara Corday .... (3)

NAKED HEART, THE (1949) Associated Artists. B&W-96min. (Canadian). Michele Morgan, Kieron Moore .... (2)

NAKED HILLS, THE (1956) Allied Artists. Color-73min. David Wayne, Keenan Wynn .... (3)

NAKED IN THE SUN (1957) Allied Artists. Color-79min. James Craig, Lita Milan .... (4)

NAKED JUNGLE, THE (1954) Paramount. Color-95min. Charlton Heston, Eleanor Parker.. 4*

NAKED KISS, THE (1964) Allied Artists. B&W-93min. Constance Towers, Anthony Eisley.................................... (3)

NAKED LOVERS, THE (1970) see NAKED ZOO, THE

NAKED MAJA, THE (1959) United Artists. Color-111min. Ava Gardner, Anthony Franciosa................................... (3)

NAKED NIGHT, THE (1953) Times Film Corp. B&W-82min. (Swedish). Harriet Andersson, Ake Gronberg................... 3*
Alternate title: SAWDUST AND TINSEL

NAKED PARADISE (1957) American-International. Color-68min. Richard Denning, Beverly Garland............................ (2)
Alternate title: THUNDER OVER HAWAII

NAKED PREY, THE (1966) Paramount. Color-95min. Cornel Wilde, Ken Gampu... 5½*

NAKED RUNNER, THE (1967) Warner Bros. Color-104min. (British). Frank Sinatra, Peter Vaughan 3*

NAKED SPUR, THE (1953) M-G-M. Color-91min. James Stewart, Janet Leigh... 4*

NAKED STREET, THE (1954) United Artists. B&W-84min. Anthony Quinn, Anne Bancroft, Farley Granger .... (4)

NAKED TEMPTATION (1966) see WOMAN AND TEMPTATION

NAKED TRUTH, THE (1957) see YOUR PAST IS SHOWING

NAKED UNDER LEATHER (1968) see GIRL ON A MOTORCYCLE, THE

NAKED YOUTH (1961) see WILD YOUTH

NAKED ZOO, THE (1970) Haven Films. Color-91min. Rita Hayworth, Stephen Oliver .... (2)
Alternate title: NAKED LOVERS, THE
Alternate title: HALLUCINATORS, THE

NAME OF THE GAME IS KILL!, THE (1968) Fanfare. Color-88min. Jack Lord, Susan Strasberg 4*
TV title: FEMALE TRAP, THE

NAMU, THE KILLER WHALE (1966) United Artists. Color-88min. Robert Lansing, John Anderson, Robin Mattson............... 4*

NANA (1934) United Artists. B&W-89min. Anna Sten, Phillips Holmes 4*
British title: LADY OF THE BOULEVARDS

NANA (1955) Times Film Corp. Color-118min. (French-Italian). Martine Carol, Charles Boyer................................. (5)

NANA (1971) Distinction Films. Color-105min. (Swedish-French). Anna Gael, Keve Hjelm, Gillian Hills .... (2)

NANCY DREW AND THE HIDDEN STAIRCASE (1939) Warner Bros. B&W-60min. Bonita Granville, Frankie Thomas, Frank Orth............. (3)

NANCY DREW, DETECTIVE (1938) Warner Bros. B&W-60min. Bonita Granville, Frankie Thomas, James Stephenson 3*

NANCY DREW, REPORTER (1939) Warner Bros. B&W-68min. Bonita Granville, Frankie Thomas, Mary Lee..................... 3*

NANCY DREW, TROUBLE SHOOTER (1939) Warner Bros. B&W-69min. Bonita Granville, Frankie Thomas, Charlotte Wynters......... (3)

NANCY GOES TO RIO (1950) M-G-M. Color-99min. Ann Sothern, Jane Powell, Barry Sullivan.................................. (4)

NANCY STEELE IS MISSING! (1937) 20th Century-Fox. B&W-85min. Victor McLaglen, June Lang, Peter Lorre................ (4)

NANNY, THE (1965) 20th Century-Fox. B&W-93min. (British). Bette Davis, William Dix, Jill Bennett 3*

NANOOK OF THE NORTH (1922) Pathé. B&W-55min. (Silent, Documentary). Director: Robert Flaherty 5*

NAPOLEON AND SAMANTHA (1972) Buena Vista. Color-92min. Johnny Whitaker, Jodie Foster 4*

NAPOLEON II - L'AIGLON (1961) Majestic Pictures. Color-105min. (French). Jean Marais, Bernard Verley .... (3)

Films are rated on a 1 to 10 scale, 10 is highest. **Boldface** ratings followed by an asterisk (*) are for films actually seen and rated by the executive and senior editors. All other ratings are estimates. (See Notes on Entertainment Ratings in the front section.)

NARCO MEN, THE (1968) RAF Industries. **Color-95min.** *(Italian-Spanish).* Tom Tryon, Lorenza Guerrieri .... (3)
Original Italian title: SAPORE DELLA VENDETTA, IL
Spanish title: PERSECUCION HASTA VALENCIA *(Pursuit to Valencia)*

NARROW CORNER, THE (1933) Warner Bros. **B&W-71min.** Douglas Fairbanks, Jr., Patricia Ellis .... (4)

NARROW MARGIN, THE (1952) RKO. **B&W-70min.** Charles McGraw, Marie Windsor .... (3)

NASHVILLE (1975) Paramount. **Color-157min.** Henry Gibson, Ronee Blakely **5***

NASHVILLE REBEL (1966) American-International. **Color-91min.** Waylon Jennings, Gordon Oas-Heim .... (5)

NASTY HABITS (1976) Brut Productions. **Color-98min.** *(British).* Glenda Jackson, Melina Mercouri **4½***

NASTY RABBIT, THE (1964) Fairway International. **Color-85min.** Mischa Terr, Arch Hall, Jr. .... (2)
Alternate title: SPIES-A-GO-GO

NATHALIE (1957) *see* FOXIEST GIRL IN PARIS, THE

NATIONAL BARN DANCE (1944) Paramount. **B&W-76min.** Jean Heather, Charles Quigley .... (3)

NATIONAL HEALTH, OR NURSE NORTON'S AFFAIR, THE (1973) Columbia. **Color-95min.** *(British).* Lynn Redgrave, Eleanor Bron .... (4)

NATIONAL LAMPOON'S ANIMAL HOUSE (1978) Universal. **Color-109min.** John Belushi, Tim Matheson, John Vernon **5½***
Alternate title: ANIMAL HOUSE

NATIONAL VELVET (1944) M-G-M. **Color-125min.** Elizabeth Taylor, Mickey Rooney **7***

NATIVE DRUMS (1955) Walter Reade. **B&W-100min.** *(Italian).* Pedro Armendariz, Kerima .... (1)

NATIVE SON (1951) Classic Pictures. **B&W-95min.** *(Argentine-U.S., English version).* Richard Wright, Jean Wallace .... (3)

NATIVITY, THE (1978) ABC-TV. **Color-98min.** *(Made for TV).* Madeline Stowe, John Shea, Freddie Jones, John Rhys-Davies ....

NATURAL BORN SALESMAN, A (1936) *see* EARTHWORM TRACTORS

NATURE'S HALF ACRE (1952) RKO (for Disney). **Color-32min.** *(Documentary).* Director: James Algar **5***

NATURE'S STRANGEST CREATURES (1959) Buena Vista. **Color-15min.** *(Documentary).* Producer: Walt Disney **5½***

NAUGHTY ARLETTE (1950) Eagle Lion. **B&W-86min.** *(British).* Mai Zetterling, Hugh Williams, Petula Clark **4***
Original title: ROMANTIC AGE, THE

NAUGHTY BUT NICE (1939) Warner Bros. **B&W-90min.** Dick Powell, Gale Page .... (4)

NAUGHTY GIRL (1955) *see* MAM'ZELLE PIGALLE

NAUGHTY MARIETTA (1935) M-G-M. **B&W-106min.** Jeanette MacDonald, Nelson Eddy **5***

NAUGHTY MARTINE (1953) Globe Films, Inc. **B&W-97min.** *(French).* Claude Dauphin, Dany Robin .... (3)

NAUGHTY NINETIES, THE (1945) Universal. **B&W-76min.** Bud Abbott, Lou Costello, Alan Curtis **3***

NAVAJO (1952) Lippert Productions. **B&W-70min.** Francis Kee Teller, John Mitchell **4***

NAVAJO JOE (1966) United Artists. **Color-89min.** *(Italian-Spanish).* Burt Reynolds, Aldo Sambrell, Nicoletta Machiavelli .... (3)
Original Italian title: DOLLARO A TESTA, UN *(A Dollar a Head)*
Original Spanish title: JOE, EL IMPLACABLE *(Joe the Implacable)*

NAVAJO RUN (1964) American-International. **B&W-83min.** Johnny Seven, Virginia Vincent .... (3)

NAVIGATOR, THE (1924) M-G-M. **B&W-80min.** *(Silent).* Buster Keaton, Kathryn McGuire **4***

NAVY BLUE AND GOLD (1937) M-G-M. **B&W-94min.** Robert Young, Lionel Barrymore, James Stewart **4***

NAVY BLUES (1941) Warner Bros. **B&W-108min.** Jack Oakie, Jack Haley **4½***

NAVY BORN (1936) Republic. **B&W-72min.** William Gargan, Claire Dodd .... (3)
Alternate title: MARINERS OF THE SKY

NAVY COMES THROUGH, THE (1942) RKO. **B&W-82min.** Pat O'Brien, George Murphy .... (4)

NAVY HEROES (1955) Distributors Corp. of America. **Color-93min.** *(British).* Kieron Moore, Greta Gynt .... (4)
Original title: BLUE PETER, THE

NAVY STEPS OUT, THE (1941) *see* GIRL, A GUY, AND A GOB, A

NAVY VS. THE NIGHT MONSTERS, THE (1966) Realart. **Color-87min.** Mamie Van Doren, Anthony Eisley **2***
British title: MONSTERS OF THE NIGHT

NAVY WIFE (1956) Allied Artists. **B&W-83min.** Joan Bennett, Shirley Yamaguchi **3***
British title: MOTHER - SIR!

NAZARIN (1959) Altura Films. **B&W-92min.** *(Mexican).* Francisco Rabal, Marga Lopez, Rita Macedo .... (5)

NAZI AGENT (1942) M-G-M. **B&W-82min.** Conrad Veidt, Frank Reicher, Ann Ayars .... (4)

NAZI TERROR AT NIGHT (1958) *see* DEVIL STRIKES AT NIGHT, THE

NEANDERTHAL MAN, THE (1953) United Artists. **B&W-78min.** Robert Shayne, Doris Merrick **3***

NEAPOLITAN CAROUSEL (1954) Lux Film America. **Color-116min.** *(Italian).* Paolo Stoppa, Clelia Matania, Vittoria Barracaracciolo .... (5)
Original title: CAROSELLO NAPOLETANO

NEARLY A NASTY ACCIDENT (1961) Universal. **B&W-86min.** *(British).* Jimmy Edwards, Kenneth Connor .... (3)

'NEATH BROOKLYN BRIDGE (1942) Monogram [Allied Artists]. **B&W-61min.** The East Side Kids, Noah Beery, Jr. .... (3)

NEBRASKAN, THE (1953) Columbia. **Color-68min.** Phil Carey, Roberta Haynes .... (3)

NECROMANCY (1972) Cinerama Releasing. **Color-82min.** Orson Welles, Pamela Franklin **3***

NED KELLY (1970) United Artists. **Color-103min.** *(British).* Mick Jagger, Allen Bickford **4***

NEGATIVES (1968) Continental [Walter Reade]. **Color-90min.** *(British).* Peter McEnery, Diane Cilento **3***

NEIGHBORS (1920) Metro. **B&W-20min.** *(Silent).* Buster Keaton, Virginia Fox, Joe Keaton **4½***

NEITHER THE SEA NOR THE SAND (1974) International Amusement Corp. **Color-92min.** *(British).* Susan Hampshire, Michael Petrovitch .. (4)

NELL GWYN (1926) Paramount. **B&W-103min.** *(British, Silent).* Dorothy Gish, Randle Ayrton ....
Original title: NELL GWYNNE

NELL GWYN (1934) United Artists. **B&W-75min.** *(British).* Anna Neagle, Cedric Hardwicke ....

NELSON AFFAIR, THE (1973) Universal. **Color-115min.** *(British-U.S.).* Glenda Jackson, Peter Finch .... (4)
British title: BEQUEST TO THE NATION

NELSON TOUCH, THE (1943) *see* CORVETTE K-225

NEON CEILING, THE (1971) Universal. **Color-100min.** *(Made for TV).* Gig Young, Lee Grant, Denise Nickerson **5***

NEPTUNE FACTOR -- AN UNDERSEA ODYSSEY, THE (1973) 20th Century-Fox. **Color-98min.** *(Canadian).* Ben Gazzara, Yvette Mimieux **3***
TV title: NEPTUNE DISASTER, THE

NEPTUNE'S DAUGHTER (1949) M-G-M. **Color-93min.** Esther Williams, Red Skelton, Ricardo Montalban **4***

NERO AND THE BURNING OF ROME (1954) Four Star. **B&W-97min.** *(Italian).* Gino Cervi, Steve Barclay .... (3)
Original title: NERONE E MESSALINA

NERO'S MISTRESS (1956) Manhattan Films. **Color-86min.** *(Italian-French).* Alberto Sordi, Brigitte Bardot, Vittorio De Sica, Gloria Swanson .... (1)
Original Italian title: MIO FIGLIO NERONE *(My Son Nero)*
Original French title: WEEK-ENDS DE NÉRON, LES *(The Weekends of Nero)*
British title: NERO'S WEEKEND
Alternate title: NERO'S BIG WEEKEND

NEST OF SPIES (1957) American-International. **B&W-85min.** *(French).* Frank Villard, Genevieve Kervine .... (3)

NET, THE (1953) *see* PROJECT M-7

NETWORK (1976) U.A. (for M-G-M). **Color-121min.** Peter Finch, Faye Dunaway, William Holden **6***

NEVADA (1944) RKO. **B&W-62min.** Robert Mitchum, Nancy Gates .... (4)

NEVADA SMITH (1966) Paramount. **Color-130min.** Steve McQueen, Brian Keith **4½***

NEVADA SMITH (1975) NBC-TV. **Color-74min.** *(Made for TV).* Cliff Potts, Lorne Greene ....

NEVADA, THE (1950) Columbia. **Color-81min.** Randolph Scott, Dorothy Malone .... (3)
British title: MAN FROM NEVADA, THE

NEVER A DULL MOMENT (1950) RKO. **B&W-89min.** Irene Dunne, Fred MacMurray .... (4)

NEVER A DULL MOMENT (1968) Buena Vista. Color-100min. Dick Van Dyke, Edward G. Robinson .... (4)

NEVER BACK LOSERS (1962) Anglo Amalgamated [EMI]. B&W-61min. *(British).* Jack Hedley, Jacqueline Ellis .... (3)

NEVER FEAR (1950) Eagle Lion. B&W-82min. Sally Forrest, Keefe Brasselle .... (4)

NEVER GIVE A SUCKER AN EVEN BREAK (1941) Universal. B&W-71min. W. C. Fields, Gloria Jean 4*
British title: WHAT A MAN

NEVER GIVE AN INCH (1971) *see* SOMETIMES A GREAT NOTION

NEVER LET GO (1960) Continental [Walter Reade]. B&W-90min. *(British).* Richard Todd, Peter Sellers .... (4)

NEVER LET ME GO (1953) M-G-M. B&W-94min. *(British-U.S.).* Clark Gable, Gene Tierney 4*

NEVER LOVE A STRANGER (1958) Allied Artists. B&W-91min. John Drew Barrymore, Lita Milan 3*

NEVER MENTION MURDER (1965) Avco-Embassy. B&W-56min. *(British).* Maxine Audley, Dudley Foster .... (3)

NEVER ON SUNDAY (1960) Lopert [U.A.]. B&W-91min. *(Greek, English language).* Melina Mercouri, Jules Dassin 5½*
Original title: POTE TIN KYRIAKI

NEVER PUT IT IN WRITING (1964) Allied Artists. B&W-93min. *(British).* Pat Boone, Milo O'Shea .... (3)

NEVER SAY DIE (1939) Paramount. B&W-80min. Bob Hope, Martha Raye. 3*

NEVER SAY GOODBYE (1946) Warner Bros. B&W-97min. Errol Flynn, Eleanor Parker 4*

NEVER SAY GOODBYE (1956) Universal. Color-96min. Rock Hudson, Cornell Borchers, George Sanders 3*

NEVER SO FEW (1959) M-G-M. Color-124min. Frank Sinatra, Gina Lollobrigida .... (4)

NEVER STEAL ANYTHING SMALL (1959) Universal. Color-94min. James Cagney, Shirley Jones 4*

NEVER TAKE NO FOR AN ANSWER (1951) Souvaine Selective. B&W-82min. *(British).* Vittorio Manunta, Denis O'Dea .... (5)

NEVER TO LOVE (1940) *see* BILL OF DIVORCEMENT, A

NEVER TOO LATE (1965) Warner Bros. Color-105min. Paul Ford, Maureen O'Sullivan 4*

NEVER TRUST A GAMBLER (1951) Columbia. B&W-79min. Dane Clark, Cathy O'Donnell .... (3)

NEVER WAVE AT A WAC (1953) RKO. B&W-87min. Rosalind Russell, Paul Douglas .... (4)
British title: PRIVATE WORE SKIRTS, THE

NEW ADVENTURES OF DON JUAN, THE (1948) *see* ADVENTURES OF DON JUAN

NEW ADVENTURES OF TARZAN (1935) Burroughs-Tarzan. B&W-75min. Herman Brix (Bruce Bennett), Ula Holt .... (4)
Alternate title: TARZAN AND THE GREEN GODDESS

NEW CENTURIONS, THE (1972) Columbia. Color-103min. George C. Scott, Stacy Keach 5*
British title: PRECINCT 45 - LOS ANGELES POLICE

NEW FACE IN HELL (1968) *see* P. J.

NEW FACES (1954) 20th Century-Fox. Color-99min. Eartha Kitt, Robert Clary .... (5)

NEW FACES OF 1937 (1937) RKO. B&W-100min. Milton Berle, Ann Miller, Harriet Hilliard (Nelson) .... (4)

NEW INTERNS, THE (1964) Columbia. B&W-123min. Michael Callan, Dean Jones 5*

NEW KIND OF LOVE, A (1963) Paramount. Color-110min. Paul Newman, Joanne Woodward 4*

NEW LAND, THE (1973) Warner Bros. Color-161min. *(Swedish).* Max von Sydow, Liv Ullmann 6*
Original title: NYBYGGARNA *(Unto a Good Land)*
Alternate (or working) Swedish title(?): INVANDRARNA
Alternate title: SETTLERS, THE

NEW LEAF, A (1971) Paramount. Color-102min. Walter Matthau, Elaine May 5½*

NEW LIFE STYLE, THE (1968) Dot Distributing. Color-91min. *(German).* Horst Tappert, Renate von Holt .... (2)
Original title: HEISSER SAND AUF SYLT
Alternate title: JUST TO BE LOVED

NEW MEXICO (1948) *see* FOUR FACES WEST

NEW MEXICO (1951) United Artists. Color-76min. Lew Ayres, Marilyn Maxwell .... (4)

NEW MOON (1940) M-G-M. B&W-105min. Jeanette MacDonald, Nelson Eddy .... (4)

NEW ONE-ARMED SWORDSMAN, THE (1972) *see* TRIPLE IRONS

NEW, ORIGINAL WONDER WOMAN, THE (1975) ABC-TV. Color-74min. *(Made for TV).* Lynda Carter, Lyle Waggoner, Stella Stevens, Cloris Leachman

NEW ORLEANS (1947) United Artists. B&W-89min. Arturo De Cordova, Louis Armstrong, Billie Holiday .... (4)

NEW ORLEANS AFTER DARK (1958) Allied Artists. B&W-69min. Stacy Harris, Ellen Moore .... (2)

NEW ORLEANS UNCENSORED (1955) Columbia. B&W-76min. Arthur Franz, Beverly Garland .... (3)
British title: RIOT ON PIER 6

NEW WORLD, A (1958) Azteca. B&W-72min. *(Mexican).* Arturo Arias, Lorena Velasquez .... (3)

NEW YORK CONFIDENTIAL (1955) Warner Bros. B&W-87min. Broderick Crawford, Richard Conte 4*

NEW YORK, NEW YORK (1977) United Artists. Color-153min. Liza Minnelli, Robert De Niro 4½*

NEW YORK TOWN (1941) Paramount. B&W-94min. Fred MacMurray, Mary Martin, Akim Tamiroff 4*

NEWMAN'S LAW (1974) Universal. Color-98min. George Peppard, Roger Robinson, Eugene Roche 3½*

NEWPORT FESTIVAL (1967) *see* FESTIVAL

NEWS HOUNDS (1947) Monogram [Allied Artists]. B&W-68min. The Bowery Boys, Christine McIntyre .... (3)

NEWS IS MADE AT NIGHT (1939) 20th Century-Fox. B&W-73min. Preston Foster, Lynn Bari .... (3)

NEXT! (1970) Maron Films, Ltd. Color-81min. *(Italian-Spanish).* Edwige Fenech, George Hilton, Ivan Rassimov 2*
Original Italian title: STRANO VIZIO DELLA SIGNORA WARDH, LO *(The Strange Weakness of Mrs. Wardh)*
Spanish title: PERVERSA SENORA WARD, LA *(The Perverse Mrs. Ward)*
Alternate title: NEXT VICTIM!, THE

NEXT MAN, THE (1976) Allied Artists. Color-108min. Sean Connery, Cornelia Sharpe 4*

NEXT OF KIN (1942) Universal. B&W-90min. *(British).* Mervyn Johns, David Hutcheson .... (5)

NEXT STOP, GREENWICH VILLAGE (1976) 20th Century-Fox. Color-111min. Lenny Baker, Shelley Winters 6½*

NEXT TIME I MARRY (1938) RKO. B&W-75min. Lucille Ball, James Ellison .... (4)

NEXT TIME WE LOVE (1936) Universal. B&W-87min. Margaret Sullavan, James Stewart 3*
British title: NEXT TIME WE LIVE

NEXT TO NO TIME (1958) Showcorporation. Color-93min. *(British).* Kenneth More, Betsy Drake .... (3)

NEXT VICTIM!, THE (1970) *see* NEXT!

NEXT VOICE YOU HEAR, THE (1950) M-G-M. B&W-82min. James Whitmore, Nancy Davis 4*

NIAGARA (1953) 20th Century-Fox. Color-89min. Marilyn Monroe, Joseph Cotten 4*

NIBELUNGEN, DIE (1923) UFA *(Ger.).* B&W-200min. *(German, Silent).* Paul Richter, Margarete Schoen 4*
Part 1 title: SIEGFRIEDS TOD *(Death of Siegfried)*
Part 1 alternate title: SIEGFRIED
Part 2 title: KRIEMHILDS RACHE *(Kriemhild's Revenge)*

NICE GIRL? (1941) Universal. B&W-95min. Deanna Durbin, Franchot Tone .... (5)

NICE GIRL LIKE ME, A (1969) Avco-Embassy. Color-91min. *(British).* Barbara Ferris, Harry Andrews .... (3)

NICE LITTLE BANK THAT SHOULD BE ROBBED, A (1958) 20th Century-Fox. B&W-87min. Tom Ewell, Mickey Rooney .... (3)
British title: HOW TO ROB A BANK

NICHOLAS AND ALEXANDRA (1971) Columbia. Color-183min. *(British).* Michael Jayston, Janet Suzman 5*

NICHOLAS NICKLEBY (1947) Universal. B&W-105min. *(British).* Derek Bond, Cedric Hardwicke 4*

NICK CARTER - MASTER DETECTIVE (1939) M-G-M. B&W-60min. Walter Pidgeon, Rita Johnson .... (4)

NICKEL RIDE, THE (1974) 20th Century-Fox. Color-106min. Jason Miller, Linda Haynes .... (4)

NICKELODEON (1976) Columbia. Color-121min. Ryan O'Neal, Burt Reynolds 5½*

NIGHT, THE (1961) *see* NOTTE, LA

NICHOLAS AND ALEXANDRA (1971), the last Czar and Czarina of Russia, are played by Michael Jayston and Janet Suzman, who share a tender moment before the war and revolution which will topple the monarchy.

NIGHT AFFAIR (1958) President Films. B&W-92min. (French). Jean Gabin, Danielle Darrieux, Nadja Tiller............................(3)
Original title: DÉSORDRE ET LA NUIT, LE

NIGHT AFTER NIGHT (1932) Paramount. B&W-70min. Constance Cummings, Mae West, George Raft 3*

NIGHT AMBUSH (1957) J. Arthur Rank. B&W-93min. (British). Dirk Bogarde, Marius Goring.............................(5)
Original title: ILL MET BY MOONLIGHT

NIGHT AND DAY (1946) Warner Bros. Color-128min. Cary Grant, Alexis Smith 5*

NIGHT AND FOG (1955) Brown-Hughes Films. B&W-31min. (French, Documentary). Director: Alain Resnais..........5½*
Original title: NUIT ET BROUILLARD

NIGHT AND THE CITY (1950) 20th Century-Fox. B&W-101min. (British). Richard Widmark, Gene Tierney 5*

NIGHT ANGEL, THE (1931) Paramount. B&W-71min. Nancy Carroll, Fredric March.............................(4)

NIGHT AT EARL CARROLL'S, A (1940) Paramount. B&W-63min. Ken Murray, Lillian Cornell ....(3)

NIGHT AT THE OPERA, A (1935) M-G-M. B&W-96min. Groucho Marx, Harpo Marx... 3*

NIGHT BEFORE THE DIVORCE, THE (1942) 20th Century-Fox. B&W-67min. Lynn Bari, Joseph Allen, Jr...........................(2)

NIGHT CALL NURSES (1974) New World. Color-80min. Patti T. Byrne, Alana Collins, Mittie Lawrence ....

NIGHT CALLER, THE (1965) see BLOOD BEAST FROM OUTER SPACE

NIGHT CALLER (1975) Columbia. Color-91min. (French). Jean-Paul Belmondo, Charles Denner, Lea Massari.........................
Original title: PEUR SUR LA VILLE (Fear Over the City)

NIGHT CHASE (1970) Cinema Center 100. Color-100min. (Made for TV). David Janssen, Yaphet Kotto ....(4)

NIGHT CHILD, THE (1975) Film Ventures International. Color-90min. (Italian). Richard Johnson, Joanna Cassidy 3½*

NIGHT CLUB SCANDAL (1937) Paramount. B&W-70min. John Barrymore, Lynne Overman 4*

NIGHT CREATURES (1962) Universal. Color-81min. (British). Peter Cushing, Yvonne Romain ....(3)
Original title: CAPTAIN CLEGG

NIGHT DIGGER, THE (1971) M-G-M. Color-100min. (British). Patricia Neal, Pamela Brown, Nicholas Clay.....................3*
Original title: ROAD BUILDER, THE

NIGHT DRIVE (1976) see NIGHT TERROR

NIGHT EDITOR (1946) Columbia. B&W-68min. William Gargan, Janis Carter.............................(4)
British title: TRESSPASSER, THE

NIGHT ENCOUNTER (1962) see DOUBLE AGENTS, THE

NIGHT EVELYN CAME OUT OF THE GRAVE, THE (1971) Phase 1. Color-99min. (Italian). Anthony Steffen (Antonio De Teffe), Marina Malfatti, Giacomo Rossi-Stuart ....(2)
Original title: NOTTE CHE EVELYN USCA' DELLA TOMBA, LA

NIGHT FIGHTERS, THE (1960) United Artists. B&W-88min. (British). Robert Mitchum, Anne Heywood 4½*
British title: TERRIBLE BEAUTY, A

NIGHT FLIGHT FROM MOSCOW (1973) see SERPENT, THE

NIGHT FREIGHT (1955) Allied Artists. B&W-79min. Forrest Tucker, Barbara Britton.............................(4)

NIGHT FULL OF RAIN (1978) see END OF THE WORLD IN OUR USUAL BED IN A NIGHT FULL OF RAIN

NIGHT GALLERY (1969) Universal. Color-100min. (Made for TV). Joan Crawford, Barry Sullivan, Roddy McDowall, Richard Kiley 5*

NIGHT GAMES (1966) Mondial Films. B&W-104min. (Swedish). Ingrid Thulin, Keve Hjelm......................................(5)
Original title: NATTLEK

NIGHT GAMES (1974) NBC-TV. Color-74min. (Made for TV). Barry Newman, Susan Howard, Stefanie Powers......................

NIGHT GOD SCREAMED, THE (1974) Cinemation. Color-87min. Jeanne Crain, Daniel Spelling, Alex Nicol..............................
British title: SCREAM

NIGHT HAS A THOUSAND EYES (1948) Paramount. B&W-80min. Edward G. Robinson, Gail Russell......................(4)

NIGHT HEAT (1959) see NOTTE BRAVA, LA

NIGHT HEAVEN FELL, THE (1957) Kingsley International. Color-90min. (French-Italian). Brigitte Bardot, Alida Valli ....(3)
Original title: BIJOUTIERS DU CLAIR DE LUNES, LES (The Jewelers of Moonlight)
British title: HEAVEN FELL THAT NIGHT

NIGHT HOLDS TERROR, THE (1955) Columbia. B&W-86min. Jack Kelly, Hildy Parks...(4)

NIGHT IN A HAREM, A (1955) see SON OF SINBAD

NIGHT IN CASABLANCA, A (1946) United Artists. B&W-85min. Groucho Marx, Harpo Marx......................................3½*

NIGHT IN HAVANA (1957) see BIG BOODLE, THE

NIGHT IN NEW ORLEANS, A (1942) Paramount. B&W-75min. Preston Foster, Patricia Morison 4*

NIGHT IN PARADISE, A (1946) Universal. Color-84min. Merle Oberon, Turhan Bey..4½*

NIGHT INTO MORNING (1951) M-G-M. B&W-86min. Ray Milland, Nancy Davis.. 4*

NIGHT IS ENDING, THE (1943) see PARIS AFTER DARK

NIGHT IS MY FUTURE (1947) Avco-Embassy. B&W-87min. (Swedish). Mai Zetterling, Birger Malsten ....(4)
Original title: MUSIK I MORKER (Music in the Dark)

NIGHT IS NOT FOR SLEEP (1958) see NUDE IN A WHITE CAR

NIGHT IS THE PHANTOM (1963) see WHAT!

NIGHT IS YOUNG, THE (1935) M-G-M. B&W-82min. Ramon Novarro, Evelyn Laye.............................(4)

NIGHT KEY (1937) Universal. B&W-67min. Boris Karloff, Jean Rogers (3)

NIGHT MAIL (1936) Brown-Hughes. B&W-23min. (British, Documentary). Director: Basil Wright... 2*

NIGHT MONSTER, THE (1942) Universal. B&W-73min. Ralph Morgan, Irene Hervey, Bela Lugosi.............................. 3*
British title: HOUSE OF MYSTERY

NIGHT MOVES (1975) Warner Bros. Color-99min. Gene Hackman, Jennifer Warren.. 4*

NIGHT MUST FALL (1937) M-G-M. B&W-117min. Robert Montgomery, Rosalind Russell..................................... 5*

NIGHT MUST FALL (1964) M-G-M. B&W-101min. (British-U.S.). Albert Finney, Mona Washbourne 3*

NIGHT MY NUMBER CAME UP, THE (1955) Continental [Walter Reade]. B&W-94min. (British). Michael Redgrave, Michael Hordern .. (5)

NIGHT NURSE (1931) Warner Bros. B&W-72min. Barbara Stanwyck, Joan Blondell.............................(4)

NIGHT OF ADVENTURE, A (1944) RKO. B&W-65min. Tom Conway, Audrey Long......................................(4)

NIGHT OF DARK SHADOWS (1971) M-G-M. Color-97min. David Selby, Lara Parker, Kate Jackson 2*

NIGHT OF FEAR (1964) see EDGE OF FEAR

NIGHT OF JANUARY 16th, THE (1941) Paramount. B&W-79min. Ellen Drew, Robert Preston...................................(3)

NIGHT OF NIGHTS, THE (1939) Paramount. B&W-85min. Pat O'Brien, Olympe Bradna..(3)

NIGHT OF SAN JUAN, THE (1971) RAI-TV. Color-90min. (Italian-Bolivian). ....(4)
Italian title: NOTTE DI SAN JUAN, LA

NIGHT OF TERROR (1972) Paramount. Color-73min. (Made for TV). Donna Mills, Martin Balsam, Chuck Connors 4*

NIGHT OF THE BIG HEAT (1972) *see* ISLAND OF THE BURNING DAMNED

NIGHT OF THE BLIND DEAD, THE (1972) *see* BLIND DEAD, THE

NIGHT OF THE BLOOD BEAST (1958) American-International. B&W-65min. Ed Nelson, Michael Emmet, Angela Greene ....(3)

NIGHT OF THE BLOOD MONSTER (1970) American-International. Color-84min. (Spanish-W. German-Italian). Christopher Lee, Maria Schell, Leo Genn......................................3*
Original Spanish title: PROCESO DE LAS BRUJAS, EL (The Trial of the Witches)
Alternate Spanish title: JUEZ SANGRIENTO, EL (The Bloody Judge)
German title: HEXENTOTER VON BLACKMOOR, DER (The Witch-Killer of Blackmoor)
Italian title: TRONO DI FUOCO, IL (The Throne of Fire)
British title: BLOODY JUDGE, THE

NIGHT OF THE COBRA WOMAN (1972) New World. Color-85min. (U.S.-Philippine). Joy Bang, Marlene Clark, Roger Garrett ....(3)
Publicity title: MOVINI'S VENOM

NIGHT OF THE DEMON (1957) *see* CURSE OF THE DEMON

NIGHT OF THE DEVIL (1974) Hallmark. Color-90min. ....(3)

NIGHT OF THE EAGLE (1962) *see* BURN, WITCH, BURN

NIGHT OF THE FLOWERS (1972) Color-86min. (Italian). Dominique Sanda, Macha Meril, Hiram Keller..(4)

NIGHT OF THE FOLLOWING DAY, THE (1969) Universal. Color-93min. Marlon Brando, Pamela Franklin ....(4)

NIGHT OF THE GENERALS, THE (1967) Columbia. Color-148min. (British-French). Peter O'Toole, Omar Sharif......................4½*
French title: NUIT DES GÉNÉRAUX, LA

NIGHT OF THE GREAT ATTACK, THE (1959) Four Star. Color-91min. (Italian). Agnes Laurent, Fausto Tozzi ....(3)
Original title: NOTTE DEL GRANDE ASSALTO, LA

NIGHT OF THE GRIZZLY, THE (1966) Paramount. Color-102min. Clint Walker, Martha Hyer, Keenan Wynn 4*

NIGHT OF THE HUNTER, THE (1955) United Artists. B&W-90min. Robert Mitchum, Shelley Winters, Billy Chapin 5*

NIGHT OF THE IGUANA, THE (1964) M-G-M. B&W-125min. Richard Burton, Ava Gardner, Deborah Kerr..7*

NIGHT OF THE LEPUS (1972) M-G-M. Color-88min. Stuart Whitman, Janet Leigh..3*

NIGHT OF THE LIVING DEAD (1968) Continental [Walter Reade]. B&W-90min. Duane Jones, Judith O'Dea 3*

NIGHT OF THE QUARTER MOON (1959) M-G-M. B&W-96min. Julie London, John Drew Barrymore, Agnes Moorehead ....(3)
Alternate title: FLESH AND FLAME
Alternate title: COLOR OF HER SKIN, THE

NIGHT OF THE SORCERERS (1970) Avco-Embassy. Color-90min. (Mexican). Jack Taylor, Simon Andrue......................1*

NIGHT PASSAGE (1957) Universal. Color-90min. James Stewart, Audie Murphy..4*

NIGHT PEOPLE (1954) 20th Century-Fox. Color-93min. Gregory Peck, Broderick Crawford..4*

NIGHT PLANE FROM CHUNGKING (1943) Paramount. B&W-68min. Ellen Drew, Robert Preston..(4)

NIGHT PORTER, THE (1974) Avco-Embassy. Color-115min. (Italian, English language). Dirk Bogarde, Charlotte Rampling 4*
Original title: PORTIERE DI NOTTE, IL

NIGHT RIDERS, THE (1939) Republic. B&W-56min. John Wayne, Doreen McKay, Ray "Crash" Corrigan ....(3)

NIGHT RIDERS (1963) Commonwealth United TV. Color-77min. (Mexican). Gaston Santos, Alma Rosa Aguirre..............................(3)

NIGHT RUNNER, THE (1957) Universal. B&W-79min. Ray Danton, Merry Anders..(3)

NIGHT SLAVES (1970) ABC Films. Color-75min. (Made for TV). James Franciscus, Lee Grant, Leslie Nielsen 4*

NIGHT SONG (1947) RKO. B&W-102min. Dana Andrews, Merle Oberon, Ethel Barrymore..(3)

NIGHT STALKER, THE (1971) Worldvision. Color-75min. (Made for TV). Darren McGavin, Caroly Lynley, Simon Oakland, Barry Atwater.......5*

NIGHT STAR - GODDESS OF ELECTRA (1963) *see* WAR OF THE ZOMBIES, THE

NIGHT STRANGLER, THE (1973) Worldvision. Color-74min. (Made for TV). Darren McGavin, Jo Ann Pflug, Simon Oakland, Richard Anderson..5*

NIGHT TERROR (1976) Worldvision. Color-73min. (Made for TV). Valerie Harper, Richard Romanus..(4)
Alternate title: NIGHT DRIVE

NIGHT THAT PANICKED AMERICA, THE (1975) Paramount. Color-100min. (Made for TV). Vic Morrow, Will Geer, Michael Constantine 5½*

NIGHT THE WORLD EXPLODED, THE (1957) Columbia. B&W-94min. Kathryn Grant, William Leslie

NIGHT THEY KILLED RASPUTIN, THE (1960) Brigadier Film Associates. Color-87min. (French-Italian). Edmund Purdom, Gianna Maria Canale ....(3)
Original French title: NUITS DE RASPOUTINE, LES
Original Italian title: ULTIMO ZAR, L' (The Last Czar)
British title: NIGHTS OF RASPUTIN
Alternate title: GIANT MONSTER

NIGHT THEY RAIDED MINSKY'S, THE (1968) United Artists. Color-100min. Jason Robards, Britt Ekland..4½*

NIGHT TIDE (1963) American-International. B&W-84min. Dennis Hopper, Linda Lawson..(4)

NIGHT TO REMEMBER, A (1942) Lopert [U.A.]. B&W-91min. Loretta Young, Brian Aherne..5*

NIGHT TO REMEMBER, A (1958) Lopert [U.A.]. B&W-123min. (British). Kenneth More, Ronald Allen..6½*

NIGHT TRAIN (1940) 20th Century-Fox. B&W-93min. (British). Margaret Lockwood, Rex Harrison..5*
Original title: NIGHT TRAIN TO MUNICH
Alternate title: GESTAPO

NIGHT TRAIN (1959) Curzon. B&W-90min. (Polish). Lucyna Winnicka, Leon Niemczyk, Teresa Szmigielowna..(3)
Original title: POCIAG
Alternate title: BALTIC EXPRESS

NIGHT TRAIN FOR INVERNESS (1959) Paramount. B&W-68min. (British). Norman Wooland, Jane Hylton..(3)

NIGHT TRAIN TO MILAN (1965) Avco-Embassy. B&W-90min. (Italian). Jack Palance, Yvonne Furneaux..(4)
Alternate title: TRAIN TO MILAN

NIGHT TRAIN TO PARIS (1964) 20th Century-Fox. B&W-64min. (British). Leslie Nielsen, Alizia Gur..(2)

NIGHT UNTO NIGHT (1949) Warner Bros. B&W-92min. Ronald Reagan, Viveca Lindfors..(3)

NIGHT VISITOR, THE (1971) UMC Pictures. Color-102min. Max Von Sydow, Trevor Howard, Liv Ullmann..3*

NIGHT WALKER, THE (1965) Universal. B&W-86min. Barbara Stanwyck, Robert Taylor..(4)

NIGHT WATCH, THE (1960) Consort/Orion. B&W-118min. (French). Michel Constantin, Jean Kéraudy..(5)
Original French title: TROU, LE
Original Italian title: BUCO, IL

NIGHT WATCH (1973) Avco-Embassy. Color-105min. (British). Elizabeth Taylor, Laurence Harvey..4½*

NIGHT WE GOT THE BIRD (1962) British Lion [EMI]. B&W-82min. (British). Brian Rix, Dora Bryan..

NIGHT WITHOUT SLEEP (1952) 20th Century-Fox. B&W-77min. Linda Darnell, Gary Merrill..(3)

NIGHT WITHOUT STARS (1951) RKO. B&W-75min. (British). David Farrar, Nadia Gray..(4)

NIGHTCOMERS, THE (1972) Avco-Embassy. Color-95min. (British). Marlon Brando, Stephanie Beacham..5*

NIGHTFALL (1957) Columbia. B&W-78min. Aldo Ray, Anne Bancroft, Brian Keith..(4)

NIGHTHAWKS (1978) Cinegate (Brit.). Color-113min. (British). Ken Robertson, Tony Westrope..

NIGHTMARE (1942) Universal. B&W-81min. Diana Barrymore, Brian Donlevy..(4)

NIGHTMARE (1956) United Artists. B&W-89min. Edward G. Robinson, Kevin McCarthy, Connie Russell..(4)

NIGHTMARE (1964) Universal. B&W-83min. (British). David Knight, Moira Redmond..(4)

NIGHTMARE (1973) Warner Bros. Color-75min. (Made for TV). Richard Crenna, Patty Duke Astin, Vic Morrow 4*

NIGHTMARE ALLEY (1947) 20th Century-Fox. B&W-111min. Tyrone Power, Joan Blondell..4½*

Films are rated on a 1 to 10 scale, 10 is highest. **Boldface** ratings followed by an asterisk (*) are for films actually seen and rated by the executive and senior editors. All other ratings are estimates. (See Notes on Entertainment Ratings in the front section.)

NIGHTMARE CASTLE (1965) Allied Artists. **B&W-90min.** *(Italian).* Barbara Steele, Paul Miller..(3)
Original title: AMANTI D'OLTRETOMBA *(Lovers from Beyond the Tomb)*

NIGHTMARE HONEYMOON (1973) M-G-M. **Color-87min.** Dack Rambo, Rebecca Dianne Smith, Pat Hingle.................(3)
Alternate title: DEADLY HONEYMOON

NIGHTMARE IN BLOOD (1976) Veromega. **Color-90min.** Kerwin Mathews, Jerry Walters......................................(3)

NIGHTMARE IN CHICAGO (1964) MCA-TV. **Color-80min.** *(Made for TV).* Robert Ridgley, Charles McGraw, Ted Knight...............**3***

NIGHTMARE IN THE SUN (1965) Screen Gems. **Color-81min.** Ursula Andress, John Derek, Aldo Ray ....(3)

NIGHTMARE IN WAX (1969) Crown International. **Color-95min.** Cameron Mitchell, Scott Brady, Berry Kroeger...........(2)
Alternate title: CRIMES IN THE WAX MUSEUM

NIGHTS OF CABIRIA (1957) Lopert [U.A.]. **B&W-110min.** *(Italian).* Giulietta Masina, Amedeo Nazzari.......................**4***
Original title: NOTTI DI CABIRIA, LE
British title: CABIRIA

NIGHTS OF LUCRETIA BORGIA, THE (1959) Columbia. **Color-108min.** *(Italian-French).* Belinda Lee, Jacques Sernas.................(3)
Original Italian title: NOTTI DI LUCREZIA BORGIA, LE
British title: NIGHTS OF TEMPTATION

NIGHTS OF RASPUTIN (1960) *see* NIGHT THEY KILLED RASPUTIN, THE

NIGHTWING (1979) Columbia. **Color-105min.** David Warner, Nick Mancuso, Katherine Harrold........................**4½***

NIJINSKY (1980) Paramount. **Color-** min. George de la Pena, Alan Bates, Leslie Browne ....

NIKKI, WILD DOG OF THE NORTH (1961) Buena Vista. **Color-74min.** *(U.S.-Canadian).* Jean Coutu, Emile Genest................(5)

NINA (1976) *see* MATTER OF TIME, A

NINA B. AFFAIR, THE (1959) ABC Films. **B&W-105min.** *(French).* Nadja Tiller, Pierre Brasseur............................(3)
Original title: AFFAIRE NINA B, L'

NINE DAYS A QUEEN (1936) Gaumont-British [Rank]. **B&W-80min.** *(British).* Nova Pilbeam, Cedric Hardwicke..........
Original title: TUDOR ROSE
Alternate title: LADY JANE GRAY

NINE GIRLS (1944) Columbia. **B&W-78min.** Ann Harding, Evelyn Keyes(4)

NINE HOURS TO RAMA (1963) 20th Century-Fox. **Color-125min.** *(British-U.S.).* Horst Buchholz, José Ferrer **4***

NINE LIVES (1958) De Rochemont. **B&W-90min.** *(Norwegian).* Jack Fjeldstad, Henny Moan, Alf Malland ....(5)
Original title: NI LIV

NINE LIVES ARE NOT ENOUGH (1941) Warner Bros. **B&W-63min.** Ronald Reagan, Joan Perry **3***

NINE LIVES OF FRITZ THE CAT, THE (1974) American-International. **Color-76min.** *(Cartoon). Director:* Robert Taylor ....(4)

1984 (1956) Columbia. **B&W-90min.** *(British).* Edmond O'Brien, Jan Sterling..**4***

1941 (1979) Universal. **Color-** min. John Belushi, Toshiro Mifune, Robert Stack, Christopher Lee........................

1900 (1977) 20th Century-Fox. **Color-248min.** *(Italian-U.S.).* Burt Lancaster, Sterling Hayden, Robert De Niro, Dominique Sanda, Gerard Depardieu **3½***
Original Italian title: NOVECENTO

NINETY DEGREES IN THE SHADE (1965) Commonwealth United. **B&W-90min.** *(British-Czech).* Anne Heywood, James Booth **5½***
Original title: 31° IN THE SHADE

99 AND 44/100% DEAD (1974) 20th Century-Fox. **Color-97min.** Richard Harris, Edmond O'Brien ....(3)

99 RIVER STREET (1953) United Artists. **B&W-83min.** John Payne, Evelyn Keyes.....................................**4***

99 WOMEN (1969) Commonwealth United. **Color-86min.** *(Spanish-Italian-W. German).* Maria Schell, Luciana Paluzzi, Mercedes McCambridge, Herbert Lom....................(2)
Original Spanish title: 99 MUJERES
Original Italian title: 99 DONNE
Original West German title: HEISSE TOD, DER
Alternate title: PROSTITUTES IN PRISON

92° IN THE SHADE (1975) United Artists. **Color-88min.** Peter Fonda, Warren Oates, Margot Kidder....................(4)

NINOTCHKA (1939) M-G-M. **B&W-110min.** Greta Garbo, Melvyn Douglas **5***

1984 (1956) is the year an oppressive totalitarian government totally dominates the lives of its citizens, but Outer Party members Edmond O'Brien and Jan Sterling drink with Inner Party member Michael Redgrave to the hoped-for downfall of "Big Brother." Redgrave's servant is Joseph Bull (second from right).

NINTH CIRCLE, THE (1960) Interprogress Trading. **B&W-90min.** Dusica Zegarac, Boris Dvornik ....(5)
Original title: DEVETI KRUG

NIPPON CHINBOTSU (1973) *see* TIDAL WAVE

NITWITS, THE (1935) RKO. **B&W-81min.** Bert Wheeler, Robert Woolsey ....(5)

NO BLADE OF GRASS (1970) M-G-M. **Color-97min.** *(British).* Nigel Davenport, Jean Wallace ....(3)

NO DEPOSIT NO RETURN (1976) Buena Vista. **Color-112min.** David Niven, Darren McGavin, Kim Richards................(4)

NO DOWN PAYMENT (1957) 20th Century-Fox. **B&W-105min.** Joanne Woodward, Sheree North, Tony Randall, Jeffrey Hunter **4***

NO DRUMS, NO BUGLES (1971) Cinerama Releasing. **Color-85min.** Martin Sheen, Davey Davison ....(4)

NO ESCAPE (1943) *see* I ESCAPED FROM THE GESTAPO

NO ESCAPE (1953) United Artists. **B&W-76min.** Lew Ayres, Marjorie Steele...(3)
Alternate title: CITY ON A HUNT

NO ESCAPE (1958) Ellis Films. **B&W-89min.** *(French-Italian).* Raf Vallone, Magali Noel, Charles Vanel.................(3)
Original French title: PIEGE, LE *(The Trap)*
Original Italian title: TRAPPOLA SI CHIUDE, LA
Alternate title: ANY MAN'S WOMAN

NO EXIT (1962) Zenith International. **B&W-85min.** *(U.S.-Argentinian).* Viveca Lindfors, Rita Gam, Morgan Sterne.................(4)
Alternate title: HUIS CLOS
Alternate title: STATELESS

NO FUNNY BUSINESS (1933) Principal. **B&W-76min.** *(British).* Gertrude Lawrence, Laurence Olivier.................(2)
Alternate title: PROFESSIONAL CO-RESPONDENTS

NO GREATER GLORY (1934) Columbia. **B&W-117min.** George Breakston, Jimmy Butler, Frankie Darro.................

NO GREATER LOVE (1932) Columbia. **B&W-70min.** Dickie Moore, Richard Bennett, Beryl Mercer.................
British title: DIVINE LOVE

NO GREATER LOVE (1955) *see* ALFRED NOVEL STORY, THE

NO HANDS ON THE CLOCK (1941) Paramount. **B&W-76min.** Chester Morris, Jean Parker.......................(4)

NO HIGHWAY IN THE SKY (1951) 20th Century-Fox. **B&W-98min.** *(British).* James Stewart, Marlene Dietrich **5***
Original title: NO HIGHWAY

NO HOLDS BARRED (1952) Monogram [Allied Artists]. **B&W-65min.** The Bowery Boys, Marjorie Reynolds.................(3)

NO KIDDING (1960) *see* BEWARE OF CHILDREN

NO KNIFE (1979) Warner Bros. **Color-** min. Gene Wilder, Harrison Ford ....

NO LEAVE, NO LOVE (1946) M-G-M. **B&W-119min.** Van Johnson, Keenan Wynn .... (4)

NO LONGER ALONE (1978) World Wide Pictures. **Color-99min.** Belinda Carroll, Roland Culver, James Fox .... (4)

NO LOVE FOR JOHNNIE (1961) Avco-Embassy. **B&W-110min.** (British). Peter Finch, Stanley Holloway .... (5)

NO MAN IS AN ISLAND (1962) Universal. **Color-114min.** Jeffrey Hunter, Marshall Thompson 4*
British title: ISLAND ESCAPE

NO MAN OF HER OWN (1932) Paramount. **B&W-85min.** Clark Gable, Carole Lombard .... (4)

NO MAN OF HER OWN (1950) Paramount. **B&W-98min.** Barbara Stanwyck, John Lund .... (4)

NO MAN'S LAND (1962) Cinema Video International. **B&W-72min.** Russ Harvey, Kim Lee .... (3)

NO MAN'S WOMAN (1955) Republic. **B&W-96min.** Marie Windsor, Patric Knowles .... (3)

NO MINOR VICES (1948) M-G-M. **B&W-96min.** Dana Andrews, Lilli Palmer, Louis Jourdan .... (3)

NO MORE EXCUSES (1968) Impact Films. **B&W-52min.** Robert Downey, Alan Abel, Lawrence Wolf .... (4)

NO MORE LADIES (1935) M-G-M. **B&W-81min.** Joan Crawford, Robert Montgomery .... (4)

NO, MY DARLING DAUGHTER! (1961) Zenith International. **B&W-85min.** (British). Michael Redgrave, Michael Craig, Juliet Mills .... (3)

NO NAME ON THE BULLET (1959) Universal. **Color-77min.** Audie Murphy, Charles Drake 3*

NO, NO, NANETTE (1940) RKO. **B&W-96min.** Anna Neagle, Richard Carlson .... (4)

NO ONE MAN (1932) Paramount. **B&W-73min.** Carole Lombard, Ricardo Cortez .... (3)

NO ORCHIDS FOR MISS BLANDISH (1948) RKO. **B&W-78min.** (British). Jack La Rue, Linden Travers .... (4)

NO OTHER LOVE (1979) CBS-TV. **Color-97min.** (Made for TV). Richard Thomas, Julie Kavner 5*

NO OTHER WOMAN (1933) RKO. **B&W-61min.** Irene Dunne, Charles Bickford, Gwili Andre ....

NO PLACE FOR A LADY (1943) Columbia. **B&W-67min.** William Gargan, Dick Purcell, Margaret Lindsay .... (3)

NO PLACE FOR JENNIFER (1949) Stratford Pictures. **B&W-90min.** (British). Leo Genn, Rosamund John, Janette Scott .... (3)

NO PLACE LIKE HOMICIDE (1961) Avco-Embassy. **B&W-87min.** (British). Kenneth Connor, Sidney James .... (3)
Original title: WHAT A CARVE-UP!

NO PLACE TO HIDE (1956) Allied Artists. **Color-71min.** David Brian, Marsha Hunt, Hugh Corcoran .... (3)

NO PLACE TO LAND (1958) Republic. **B&W-78min.** John Ireland, Mari Blanchard .... (2)
British title: MAN MAD

NO PLACE TO RUN (1972) Worldvision. **Color-73min.** (Made for TV). Herschel Bernardi, Larry Hagman, Stefanie Powers 4*

NO QUESTIONS ASKED (1951) M-G-M. **B&W-81min.** Barry Sullivan, Arlene Dahl .... (4)

NO RESTING PLACE (1951) Classic Pictures. **B&W-77min.** (British). Michael Gough, Eithne Dunne, Noel Purcell .... (4)

NO RETURN ADDRESS (1961) Teledynamics. **B&W-76min.** Harry Lovejoy, Alicia Hammond .... (3)

NO ROAD BACK (1957) RKO. **B&W-83min.** (British). Skip Homeier, Paul Carpenter .... (3)

NO ROOM FOR THE GROOM (1952) Universal. **B&W-82min.** Tony Curtis, Piper Laurie .... (3)

NO SAD SONGS FOR ME (1950) Columbia. **B&W-89min.** Margaret Sullavan, Wendell Corey .... (5)

NO SAFETY AHEAD (1958) Paramount. **B&W-68min.** (British). James Kennedy, Susan Beaumont .... (3)

NO SLEEP TILL DAWN (1957) *see* BOMBERS B-52

NO SUN IN VENICE (1957) Kingsley International. **Color-97min.** (French-Italian). Francoise Arnoul, Christian Marquand, Robert Hossein .... (4)
Original French title: SAIT-ON JAMAIS?

NO SURVIVORS PLEASE (1963) UCC Films. **B&W-93min.** (German). Maria Perschy, Robert Cunningham .... (3)
Original title: CHEF WUNSCHT KEINE ZEUGEN, DER (*The Chief Wants No Survivors*)

NO TIME FOR COMEDY (1940) Warner Bros. **B&W-93min.** James Stewart, Rosalind Russell 4½*

NO TIME FOR FLOWERS (1953) RKO. **B&W-83min.** Viveca Lindfors, Paul Christian .... (4)

NO TIME FOR LOVE (1943) Paramount. **B&W-83min.** Claudette Colbert, Fred MacMurray .... (5)

NO TIME FOR SERGEANTS (1958) Warner Bros. **B&W-111min.** Andy Griffith, Myron McCormick 4*

NO TIME FOR TEARS (1951) *see* PURPLE HEART DIARY

NO TIME FOR TEARS (1957) Associated British-Pathé [EMI]. **Color-86min.** (British). Anna Neagle, Anthony Quayle .... (5)

NO TIME TO BE YOUNG (1957) Columbia. **B&W-82min.** Robert Vaughn, Roger Smith, Merry Anders .... (3)
British title: TEENAGE DELINQUENTS

NO TIME TO DIE (1958) *see* TANK FORCE

NO TIME TO KILL (1961) Medallion. **B&W-70min.** (Swedish-British-W. German). John Ireland, Ellen Schwiers .... (2)
Original Swedish title: MED MORD I BAGAGET

NO TREES IN THE STREET (1958) Associated British-Pathé [EMI]. **B&W-96min.** (British). Sylvia Syms, Herbert Lom, Stanley Holloway (4)

NO WAY BACK (1955) Fine Arts. **B&W-87min.** (German). Ivan Desny, Ruth Niehaus .... (4)
Original title: WEG OHNE UMKEHR

NO WAY BACK (1976) Atlas Films. **Color-91min.** Fred Williamson, Charles Woolf, Virginia Gregg ....

NO WAY OUT (1950) 20th Century-Fox. **B&W-106min.** Richard Widmark, Linda Darnell 4*

NO WAY OUT (1973) Cinema Shares. **Color-90min.** (Italian-French, English language). Alain Delon, Richard Conte ....
Original title: TONY ARZENTA
Alternate title: BIG GUNS

NO WAY TO TREAT A LADY (1968) Paramount. **Color-108min.** George Segal, Lee Remick, Rod Steiger 5*

NOAH'S ARK (1929) Warner Bros. **B&W-75min.** Dolores Costello, George O'Brien .... (4)

NOB HILL (1945) 20th Century-Fox. **Color-95min.** George Raft, Joan Bennett 3½*

NOBODY LIVES FOREVER (1946) Warner Bros. **B&W-100min.** John Garfield, Geraldine Fitzgerald 4*

NOBODY RUNS FOREVER (1968) *see* HIGH COMMISSIONER, THE

NOBODY WAVED GOODBYE (1964) Cinema 5. **B&W-80min.** (Canadian). Peter Kastner, Julie Biggs 5*

NOBODY'S PERFECT (1968) Universal. **Color-103min.** Doug McClure, Nancy Kwan, James Whitmore 3*

NOCTURNE (1946) RKO. **B&W-88min.** George Raft, Lynn Bari .... (4)

NONE BUT THE BRAVE (1960) *see* FOR THE LOVE OF MIKE

NONE BUT THE BRAVE (1965) Warner Bros. **Color-110min.** (U.S.-Japanese). Frank Sinatra, Tatsuya Mihashi 4*

NONE BUT THE LONELY HEART (1944) RKO. **B&W-113min.** Cary Grant, Ethel Barrymore 3½*

NONE BUT THE LONELY SPY (1964) Four Star. **B&W-90min.** (Italian). Ken Clark, Bella Cortez .... (1)

NONE SHALL ESCAPE (1944) Columbia. **B&W-85min.** Alexander Knox, Marsha Hunt .... (5)

NOOSE HANGS HIGH, THE (1948) Eagle Lion. **B&W-77min.** Bud Abbott, Lou Costello, Leon Errol .... (3)

NOR THE MOON BY NIGHT (1958) *see* ELEPHANT GUN

NORA PRENTISS (1947) Warner Bros. **B&W-111min.** Ann Sheridan, Kent Smith 2*

NORLISS TAPES, THE (1973) MPC (TV). **Color-74min.** (Made for TV). Roy Thinnes, Angie Dickinson, Don Porter 3*

NORMA RAE (1979) 20th Century-Fox. **Color-113min.** Sally Field, Beau Bridges, Ron Leibman 4½*

NORMAN . . . IS THAT YOU? (1976) U.A. (for M-G-M). **Color-91min.** Redd Foxx, Pearl Bailey 5*

NORSEMAN, THE (1978) American-International. **Color-90min.** Lee Majors, Cornel Wilde, Mel Ferrer 3½*

NORTH AVENUE IRREGULARS, THE (1979) Buena Vista. **Color-99min.** Edward Herrmann, Susan Clark, Barbara Harris, Cloris Leachman 4½*

NORTH BY NORTHWEST (1959) M-G-M. **Color-136min.** Cary Grant, Eva Marie Saint 6*

NORTH COUNTRY (1973) American National Enterprises. **Color-105min.** (Documentary). Director: Ron Hayes 4*

NORTH DALLAS FORTY (1979) Paramount. Color-   min. Nick Nolte...

NORTH STAR, THE (1943) RKO. B&W-105min. Dana Andrews, Walter Huston .... (4)
Alternate title: ARMORED ATTACK

NORTH TO ALASKA (1960) 20th Century-Fox. Color-122min. John Wayne, Stewart Granger 5*

NORTH WEST FRONTIER (1959) *see* FLAME OVER INDIA

NORTH WEST MOUNTED POLICE (1940) Paramount. Color-125min. Gary Cooper, Madeleine Carroll 5½*
Alternate title: NORTHWEST MOUNTED POLICE

NORTHERN LIGHTS (1978) B&W-90min. Robert Behling, Susan Lynch 4*

NORTHERN PATROL (1953) Allied Artists. B&W-63min. Kirby Grant, Marian Carr .... (2)

NORTHERN PURSUIT (1943) Warner Bros. B&W-94min. Errol Flynn, Helmut Dantine, Julie Bishop 4*

NORTHWEST OUTPOST (1947) Republic. B&W-91min. Nelson Eddy, Ilona Massey .... (3)
British title: END OF THE RAINBOW

NORTHWEST PASSAGE (1940) M-G-M. Color-126min. Spencer Tracy, Robert Young 5½*

NORTHWEST RANGERS (1942) M-G-M. B&W-64min. James Craig, William Lundigan .... (3)

NORTHWEST STAMPEDE (1948) Eagle Lion. Color-79min. James Craig, Joan Leslie .... (4)

NORWOOD (1970) Paramount. Color-95min. Glen Campbell, Kim Darby, Joe Namath 3½*

NOSFERATU (1922) Film Arts Guild. B&W-65min. (*German, Silent*). Max Schreck, Alexander Granach 3*
Original title: NOSFERATU, EINE SYMPHONIE DES GRAUENS (*Nosferatu, a Symphony of Terror*)
Alternate title: NOSFERATU, THE VAMPIRE
8mm title: TERROR OF DRACULA, THE

NOSFERATU, THE VAMPYRE (1979) 20th Century-Fox. Color-106min. (*W. German-French-U.S.*). Klaus Kinski, Isabelle Adjani, Bruno Ganz..
German title: NOSFERATU -- PHANTOM DER NACHT

NOT A LADIES' MAN (1942) Columbia. B&W-60min. Paul Kelly, Douglas Croft, Fay Wray .... (3)

NOT AS A STRANGER (1955) United Artists. B&W-135min. Olivia de Havilland, Robert Mitchum 5*

NOT FOR EACH OTHER (1940) *see* BILL OF DIVORCEMENT, A

NOT MINE TO LOVE (1967) Noel Meadow. B&W-90min. (*Israeli*). Oded Kotler, Shuy Osherov, Judith Soleh .... (4)
Original title: SHLOSHA YAMIN VE YELED
Alternate title: THREE DAYS AND A CHILD

NOT OF THIS EARTH (1957) Allied Artists. B&W-67min. Paul Birch, Beverly Garland .... (3)

NOT ON YOUR LIFE (1963) Pathé Contemporary. B&W-90min. (*Spanish*). Nino Manfredi, Emma Penella .... (5)
Original title: VERDUGO, EL (*The Executioner*)

NOT SO DUSTY (1956) Eros Films (*Brit.*). B&W-74min. (*British*). Leslie Dwyer, Joy Nichols .... (3)

NOT SO QUIET DAYS (1970) *see* QUIET DAYS IN CLICHY

NOT WANTED (1949) Four Continents. B&W-94min. Sally Forrest, Keefe Brasselle .... (4)

NOT WITH MY WIFE, YOU DON'T! (1966) Warner Bros. Color-118min. Tony Curtis, Virna Lisi, George C. Scott 4*

NOTHING BARRED (1961) *see* TWO-WAY STRETCH

NOTHING BUT A MAN (1965) Cinema 5. B&W-92min. Ivan Dixon, Abbey Lincoln 4*

NOTHING BUT BLONDES (1957) Hal Roach. B&W-92min. (*British*). Mark Miller, Anita Thallaug .... (3)

NOTHING BUT THE BEST (1964) Royal Films Int'l [Columbia]. Color-99min. (*British*). Alan Bates, Denholm Elliott 4*

NOTHING BUT THE NIGHT (1972) Cinema Shares. Color-90min. (*British*). Christopher Lee, Peter Cushing, Georgia Brown .....
Alternate title: RESURRECTION SYNDICATE, THE

NOTHING BUT THE TRUTH (1941) Paramount. B&W-90min. Bob Hope, Paulette Goddard .... (5)

NOTHING BUT TROUBLE (1944) M-G-M. B&W-69min. Stan Laurel, Oliver Hardy, Mary Boland .... (3)

NOTHING BY CHANCE (1975) R. C. Riddell & Associates. Color-93min. (*Documentary*). Director: William H. Barnett ..... (4)

NOTHING SACRED (1937) United Artists. Color-75min. Carole Lombard, Fredric March 5½*

NOTHING TO LOSE (1952) *see* TIME, GENTLEMEN, PLEASE

NOTORIOUS (1946) RKO. B&W-103min. Cary Grant, Ingrid Bergman 5*

NOTORIOUS GENTLEMAN (1945) Universal. B&W-109min. (*British*). Rex Harrison, Lilli Palmer 4*
Original title: RAKE'S PROGRESS, THE

NOTORIOUS LANDLADY, THE (1962) Columbia. B&W-123min. Kim Novak, Jack Lemmon 4½*

NOTORIOUS LONE WOLF, THE (1946) Columbia. B&W-64min. Gerald Mohr, Janis Carter, Eric Blore .... (4)

NOTORIOUS MR. MONKS, THE (1958) Republic. B&W-70min. Vera Ralston, Don Kelly, Paul Fix .... (3)

NOTORIOUS SOPHIE LANG (1934) Paramount. B&W-64min. Gertrude Michael, Paul Cavanagh .... (4)

NOTTE, LA (1961) Lopert [U.A.]. B&W-120min. (*Italian-French*). Jeanne Moreau, Marcello Mastroianni, Monica Vitti ..... (5)
Original French title: NUIT, LA
Alternate title: NIGHT, THE

NOTTE BRAVA, LA (1959) Miller Producion Co. B&W-96min. (*Italian-French*). Elsa Martinelli, Antonella Lualdi, Jean-Claude Brialy .... (2)
Original French title: GARCONS, LES (*The Boys*)
Alternate title: ON ANY STREET
Alternate title: BAD GIRLS DON'T CRY
British title: NIGHT HEAT

NOUS SOMMES TOUS DES ASSASSINS (1952) *see* WE ARE ALL MURDERERS

NOVEL AFFAIR, A (1957) Continental [Walter Reade]. B&W-83min. (*British*). Ralph Richardson, Margaret Leighton ....,(5)
Original title: PASSIONATE STRANGER, THE

NOW AND FOREVER (1934) Paramount. B&W-81min. Gary Cooper, Carole Lombard .... (4)

NOW I'LL TELL (1934) Fox Film Co. [20th]. B&W-87min. Spencer Tracy, Helen Twelvetrees .... (4)
British title: WHEN NEW YORK SLEEPS

NOW IT CAN BE TOLD (1945) *see* HOUSE ON 92nd STREET, THE

NOW, VOYAGER (1942) Warner Bros. B&W-117min. Bette Davis, Paul Henreid 5*

NOW YOU SEE HIM, NOW YOU DON'T (1972) Buena Vista. Color-88min. Kurt Russell, Cesar Romero 5*

NOW YOU SEE IT, NOW YOU DON'T (1968) Universal. Color-100min. (*Made for TV*). Jonathan Winters, Luciana Paluzzi, Steve Allen 4*

NOWHERE TO GO (1958) M-G-M. B&W-87min. (*British*). George Nader, Maggie Smith .... (2)

NOWHERE TO HIDE (1977) NBC-TV. Color-75min. (*Made for TV*). Lee Van Cleef, Tony Musante 3*

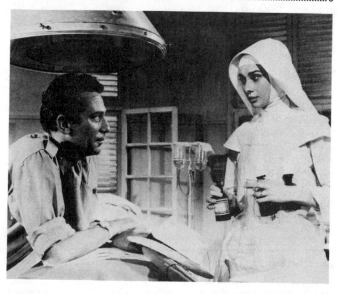

THE NUN'S STORY (1959). Although they have an excellent working relationship at the African clinic, irreligious doctor Peter Finch constantly tries to make nursing nun Audrey Hepburn question her faith.

NUDE IN A WHITE CAR (1958) Trans-Lux Distributing. **B&W-87min.**
(French). Marina Vlady, Robert Hossein, Odile Versois.....................(4)
Original title: TOI LE VENIN *(You Are the Venom)*
British title: NIGHT IS NOT FOR SLEEP
Alternate title: BLONDE IN A WHITE CAR

NUDE IN HIS POCKET (1957) *see* GIRL IN HIS POCKET

NUIT AMERICAINE, LA (1973) *see* DAY FOR NIGHT

NUMBER ONE (1969) United Artists. **Color-105min.** Charlton Heston,
Jessica Walter **3***

NUMBER ONE (1973) D.C.I. **Color-92min.** *(Italian).* Luigi Pistilli, Renzo
Montagnani ....(3)

NUMBER SEVENTEEN (1932) Janus Films. **B&W-83min.** *(British).* Anne
Grey, John Stuart ....(5)

NUMBER SIX (1962) Anglo Amalgamated [EMI]. **B&W-59min.** *(British).*
Ivan Desny, Nadja Regin ....(3)

NUN, THE (1966) Altura Films. **Color-130min.** *(French).* Anna Karina,
Liselotte Pulver, Micheline Presle ....(5)
Original title: RELIGIEUSE, LA
Alternate French title: RELIGIEUSE DE DIDEROT, LA *(The Nun of Diderot)*
Alternate title: SUZANNE SIMONIN, LA RELIGIEUSE DE DIDEROT

NUN AND THE SERGEANT, THE (1962) United Artists. **B&W-73min.**
Robert Webber, Anna Sten ....(3)

NUN OF MONZA, THE (1970) *see* LADY OF MONZA, THE

NUN'S STORY, THE (1959) Warner Bros. **Color-149min.** Audrey
Hepburn, Peter Finch **7***

NUNZIO (1978) Universal. **Color-87min.** David Proval, James Andronica,
Morgana King ....(4)

NURSE EDITH CAVELL (1939) RKO. **B&W-95min.** Anna Neagle, Edna
May Oliver ....(5)

NURSE ON WHEELS (1963) Janus Films. **B&W-86min.** *(British).* Juliet
Mills, Ronald Lewis **4***

NURSE SHERRI (1978) Independent International. **Color-   min.** Jill
Jacobson, Geoffrey Land ....(3)

NURSE'S SECRET, THE (1941) Warner Bros. **B&W-65min.** Lee Patrick,
Julie Bishop, Regis Toomey ....(4)

NUTTY, NAUGHTY CHATEAU (1963) Lopert [U.A.]. **Color-102min.**
(French-Italian). Monica Vitti, Curt Jurgens, Jean-Claude Brialy ......(4)
Original French title: CHATEAU EN SUEDE *(Castle in Sweden)*
Italian title: CASTELLO IN SVEZIA, IL

NUTTY PROFESSOR, THE (1963) Paramount. **Color-107min.** Jerry
Lewis, Stella Stevens..**3½***

NYLON NOOSE, THE (1963) Medallion. **B&W-74min.** *(German).* Richard
Goodman, Laya Raki ....(3)
Original title: NYLONSCHLINGE, DIE

NYOKA AND THE LOST SECRETS OF HIPPOCRATES (1942) Republic.
B&W-100min. *(Re-edited Serial).* Kay Aldridge, Clayton Moore, Lorna
Gray (Adrian Booth) ....(4)
Original title: PERILS OF NYOKA

-O-

08/15 (1954) Times Film Corp. **B&W-110min.** *(German).* Hans Christian
Blech, Eva Ingeborg Scholz ....(4)

O. HENRY'S FULL HOUSE (1952) 20th Century-Fox. **B&W-117min.** Fred
Allen, Charles Laughton, Richard Widmark.................................**5***
British title: FULL HOUSE
Common title error: O'HENRY'S FULL HOUSE

O.K. CONNERY (1967) *see* OPERATION KID BROTHER

O LUCKY MAN! (1973) Warner Bros. **Color-166min.** *(British).* Malcolm
McDowell, Ralph Richardson..**4***

O.S.S. (1946) Paramount. **B&W-107min.** Alan Ladd, Geraldine
Fitzgerald **4½***

OSS 117 - DOUBLE AGENT (1968) UPA. **Color-91min.** *(Italian-French).*
John Saxon, Margaret Lee, Curt Jurgens, Luciana Paluzzi.................**3***
Original Italian title: NIENTE ROSE PER OSS 117 *(No Roses for OSS 117)*
British title: OSS 117 MURDER FOR SALE

OSS 117 - MISSION FOR A KILLER (1965) Avco-Embassy. **Color-84min.**
(French-Italian). Frederick Stafford, Mylene Demongeot..................**3***
Original French title: FURIA A BAHIA POUR OSS 117 *(Fury in Bahia for OSS 117)*
Original Italian title: OSS 117 FURIA A BAHIA
Alternate title: MISSION FOR A KILLER

OASIS (1954) 20th Century-Fox. **Color-84min.** *(W. German-French).*
Michele Morgan, Cornell Borchers, Carl Raddatz..........................(3)
Original title: OASE

OBJECTIVE, BURMA! (1945) Warner Bros. **B&W-142min.** Errol Flynn,
James Brown **4***

OBLIGING YOUNG LADY (1941) RKO. **B&W-80min.** Joan Carroll,
Edmond O'Brien, Ruth Warrick ....(5)

OBLONG BOX, THE (1969) American-International. **Color-91min.**
(British-U.S.). Vincent Price, Christopher Lee, Alister Williamson **3***

OBSESSED (1951) United Artists. **B&W-78min.** *(British).* David Farrar,
Geraldine Fitzgerald ....(3)
Original title: LATE EDWINA BLACK, THE

OBSESSION (1949) *see* HIDDEN ROOM, THE

OBSESSION (1954) Gibe Films. **Color-103min.** *(French-Italian).* Michele
Morgan, Raf Vallone ....(4)

OBSESSION (1964) O.R.P. Company. **Color-104min.** *(Swedish).* Matthias
Henrikson, Maude Adelson, Lars Lind ....(4)
Original title: KUNGSLEDEN
Film Festival title: ROYAL TRACK, THE

OBSESSION (1976) Columbia. **Color-98min.** Cliff Robertson, Genevieve
Bujold **5½***

OCCURRENCE AT OWL CREEK BRIDGE, AN (1962) CBS-TV. **B&W-
27min.** *(French).* Roger Jacquet, Anne Cornaly ....(5)
Original title: RIVIERE DU HIBOU, LA *(Incident at Owl Creek)*

OCEAN'S 11 (1960) Warner Bros. **Color-127min.** Frank Sinatra, Dean
Martin **5½***

OCTA-MAN (1971) Heritage Enterprises. **Color-83min.** Pier Angeli,
Kerwin Mathews **1***
Alternate title: OCTOMAN

OCTAVE OF CLAUDIUS, THE (1922) *see* BLIND BARGAIN, A

OCTOBER (1928) *see* TEN DAYS THAT SHOOK THE WORLD

OCTOBER MAN, THE (1947) Eagle Lion. **B&W-86min.** *(British).* John
Mills, Joan Greenwood **4***
Alternate title: HANGMAN'S NOOSE

OCTOBER MOTH (1959) J. Arthur Rank. **B&W-54min.** *(British).* Lee
Patterson, Lana Morris ....(3)

ODD COUPLE, THE (1968) Paramount. **Color-105min.** Jack Lemmon,
Walter Matthau **6***

ODD JOB, THE (1978) Columbia. **Color-86min.** *(British).* Graham
Chapman, David Jason, Diana Quick ....(4)

ODD MAN OUT (1947) Universal. **B&W-115min.** *(British).* James Mason,
Kathleen Ryan **5***

ODD OBSESSION (1959) Harrison Pictures. **Color-96min.** *(Japanese).*
Machiko Kyo, Ganjiro Nakamura ....(4)
Original title: KAGI

ODDS AGAINST TOMORROW (1959) United Artists. **B&W-95min.**
Harry Belafonte, Robert Ryan..**4***

ODE TO BILLY JOE (1976) Warner Bros. **Color-105min.** Robby Benson,
Glynnis O'Connor **5½***

ODESSA FILE, THE (1974) Columbia. **Color-128min.** *(British-German).*
Jon Voight, Maximillian Schell **5½***

ODETTE (1950) Lopert [U.A.]. **B&W-106min.** *(British).* Anna Neagle,
Trevor Howard ....(5)

ODONGO (1956) Columbia. **Color-85min.** *(British).* Macdonald Carey,
Rhonda Fleming **3***

OEDIPUS REX (1957) Motion Picture Distributors. **Color-87min.**
(Canadian). Douglas Campbell, Eleanor Stuart, Douglas Rain............(5)

OEDIPUS REX (1967) Europix International. **Color-110min.** *(Italian).*
Franco Citti, Silvana Mangano ....(4)
Original title: EDIPO RE

OEDIPUS THE KING (1968) Universal. **Color-97min.** *(British).*
Christopher Plummer, Lilli Palmer, Richard Johnson, Orson Welles ...(4)

OF FLESH AND BLOOD (1963) Times Film Corp. **Color-83min.** *(French-
Italian).* Robert Hossein, Renato Salvatori, Anouk Aimée.................(4)
Original French title: GRANDS CHEMINS, LES *(The Highways)*
Italian title: BARO, IL *(The Cheat)*

OF HUMAN BONDAGE (1934) RKO. **B&W-83min.** Leslie Howard, Bette
Davis **4½***

OF HUMAN BONDAGE (1946) Warner Bros. **B&W-105min.** Eleanor
Parker, Paul Henreid ....(4)

OF HUMAN BONDAGE (1964) M-G-M. **B&W-98min.** *(British-U.S.).*
Laurence Harvey, Kim Novak ....(4)

OF HUMAN HEARTS (1938) M-G-M. **B&W-100min.** Walter Huston,
James Stewart **4½***

OF LIFE AND LOVE (1957) Distributors Corp. of America. **B&W-103min.**
(Italian). Anna Magnani, Aldo Fabrizi......................................(4)

OF LOVE AND DESIRE (1963) 20th Century-Fox. **Color-97min.** Merle
Oberon, Steve Cochran..**3***

OF LOVE AND LUST (1955) Films Around The World. **B&W-103min.** *(Swedish).* Mai Zetterling, Anita Bjork .... (5)
Original title: GIFTAS *(Stories About Marriage)*

OF MEN AND MUSIC (1951) 20th Century-Fox. **B&W-85min.** *(Music Film). Director:* Irving Reis .... (5)

OF MICE AND MEN (1939) United Artists. **B&W-107min.** Lon Chaney, Jr., Betty Field, Burgess Meredith **5½***

OF STARS AND MEN (1961) Brandon. **Color-63min.** *(Cartoon). Director:* John Hubley .... (5)

OFF LIMITS (1953) Paramount. **B&W-89min.** Bob Hope, Mickey Rooney .... (5)
British title: MILITARY POLICEMEN

OFF THE EDGE (1977) Pentacle Films. **Color-77min.** *(Documentary). Director:* Michael Firth .... (4)

OFFENCE, THE (1973) United Artists. **Color-112min.** *(British).* Sean Connery, Trevor Howard .... (4)

OFFICER AND THE LADY, THE (1941) Columbia. **B&W-59min.** Bruce Bennett, Doroth Mackaill .... (4)

OH! CALCUTTA! (1972) Cinemation. **Color-105min.** Bill Macy, Mark Dempsey, Raina Barrett .... (3)

OH DAD, POOR DAD, MAMA'S HUNG YOU IN THE CLOSET AND I'M FEELIN' SO SAD (1967) Paramount. **Color-86min.** Rosalind Russell, Robert Horse, Barbara Harris, Jonathan Winters .... (3)

OH! FOR A MAN! (1957) *see* WILL SUCCESS SPOIL ROCK HUNTER?

"OH, GOD!" (1977) Warner Bros. **Color-97min.** George Burns, John Denver **6***

OH MEN, OH WOMEN (1957) 20th Century-Fox. **Color-90min.** Dan Dailey, Ginger Rogers, David Niven **4***

OH, MR. PORTER (1937) General Film Dists. **B&W-85min.** *(British).* Will Hay, Moore Marriott **3***

OH, SUSANNA (1951) Republic. **Color-90min.** Rod Cameron, Adrian Booth .... (3)

OH! THOSE MOST SECRET AGENTS (1964) Allied Artists. **Color-83min.** *(Italian).* Franco Franchi, Ciccio Ingrassia, Ingrid Schoeller .. (3)
Original title: 002 AGENTI SEGRETISSIMI
Alternate title: 00-2 MOST SECRET AGENTS

OH! WHAT A LOVELY WAR (1969) Paramount. **Color-132min.** *(British).* John Mills, Joe Melia **5***

OH, YOU BEAUTIFUL DOLL (1949) 20th Century-Fox. **Color-93min.** S. Z. "Cuddles" Sakall, June Haver, Mark Stevens .... (4)

O'HARA, UNITED STATES TREASURY (1971) Universal. **Color-98min.** *(Made for TV).* David Janssen, William Conrad, Lana Wood **3½***
Alternate title: OPERATION COBRA

OIL FOR THE LAMPS OF CHINA (1935) Warner Bros. **B&W-110min.** Pat O'Brien, Josephine Hutchinson **4***

OKINAWA (1952) Columbia. **B&W-67min.** Pat O'Brien, Cameron Mitchell .... (3)

OKLAHOMA! (1955) Magna Pictures. **Color-145min.** Gordon MacRae, Shirley Jones **7***

OKLAHOMA ANNIE (1952) Republic. **Color-90min.** Judy Canova, John Russell .... (3)

OKLAHOMA CRUDE (1973) Columbia. **Color-108min.** George C. Scott, Faye Dunaway **4***

OKLAHOMA KID, THE (1939) Warner Bros. **B&W-85min.** James Cagney, Humphrey Bogart .... (5)

OKLAHOMA TERRITORY (1960) United Artists. **B&W-67min.** Bill Williams, Gloria Talbott .... (3)

OKLAHOMA WOMAN, THE (1956) American-International. **B&W-72min.** Richard Denning, Peggie Castle .... (2)

OKLAHOMAN, THE (1957) Allied Artists. **Color-80min.** Joel McCrea, Barbara Hale .... (4)

OLD ACQUAINTANCE (1943) Warner Bros. **B&W-110min.** Bette Davis, Miriam Hopkins **4½***

OLD BOYFRIENDS (1979) Avco-Embassy. **Color-103min.** Talia Shire, Richard Jordan, Keith Carradine, John Belushi **4***

OLD CHISHOLM TRAIL, THE (1943) Universal. **B&W-60min.** Tex Ritter, Johnny Mack Brown .... (4)

OLD DARK HOUSE, THE (1932) Universal. **B&W-74min.** Melvyn Douglas, Charles Laughton **3***

OLD DARK HOUSE, THE (1963) Columbia. **Color-86min.** *(British-U.S.).* Tom Poston, Robert Morley .... (4)

OLD DRACULA (1975) American-International. **Color-89min.** *(British).* David Niven, Teresa Graves **4½***
Original title: VAMPIRA

OLD ENGLISH (1930) Warner Bros. **B&W-88min.** George Arliss, Doris Lloyd .... (5)

OLD-FASHIONED WAY, THE (1934) Paramount. **B&W-66min.** W. C. Fields, Joe Morrison **4***

OLD GUN, THE (1975) Surrogate. **Color-104min.** *(French).* Philippe Noiret, Romy Schneider .... (4)
Original title: VIEUX FUSIL, LE

OLD HUTCH (1936) M-G-M. **B&W-80min.** Wallace Beery, Elizabeth Patterson .... (4)

OLD LOS ANGELES (1948) Republic. **B&W-88min.** Wild Bill Elliott, Andy Devine .... (5)

OLD MAID, THE (1939) Warner Bros. **B&W-95min.** Bette Davis, Miriam Hopkins **4***

OLD MAN AND THE SEA, THE (1958) Warner Bros. **Color-86min.** Spencer Tracy, Felipe Pazos **5***

OLD MAN WHO CRIED WOLF, THE (1970) ABC Films. **Color-75min.** *(Made for TV).* Edward G. Robinson, Martin Balsam **4***

OLD MOTHER RILEY MEETS THE VAMPIRE (1952) *see* MY SON, THE VAMPIRE

OLD SOLDIERS NEVER DIE (1951) *see* FIXED BAYONETS

OLD TESTAMENT, THE (1963) Four Star. **Color-100min.** *(Italian).* John Heston, Susan Paget .... (3)

OLD YELLER (1958) Buena Vista. **Color-83min.** Dorothy McGuire, Fess Parker **5***

OLDEST PROFESSION, THE (1967) VIP Films. **Color-97min.** *(French-Italian-W. German).* Elsa Martinelli, Jeanne Moreau, Raquel Welch, Jean-Pierre Léaud .... (2)
Original French title: PLUS VIEUX MÉTIER DU MONDE, LE
Original Italian title: AMORE ATTRAVERSO I SECOLI, L'
Original W. German title: ALTESTE GEWERBE DER WELT, DAS

OLIVER! (1968) Columbia. **Color-146min.** *(British).* Mark Lester, Ron Moody **7***

OLIVER TWIST (1922) Associated First National. **B&W-103min.** *(Silent).* Jackie Coogan, Lon Chaney, George Siegmann .... (4)

OLIVER TWIST (1948) United Artists. **B&W-105min.** *(British).* John Howard Davies, Alec Guinness **5***

OLIVER'S STORY (1978) Paramount. **Color-92min.** Ryan O'Neal, Candice Bergen **4½***

OLIVIA (1951) *see* PIT OF LONELINESS

OLLY OLLY OXEN FREE (1978) Sanrio. **Color-92min.** Katharine Hepburn, Kevin McKenzie, Dennis Dimster **4½***
Alternate title: GREAT BALLOON ADVENTURE, THE

OLVIDADOS, LOS (1951) Mayer-Kingsley. **B&W-80min.** *(Mexican).* Alfonso Mejia, Roberto Cobo **4***
Alternate title: YOUNG AND THE DAMNED, THE

OLYMPIA (1938) Contemporary. **B&W-220min.** *(German, Documentary). Director:* Leni Riefenstahl **6***

OLIVER! (1968). Shani Wallis reluctantly listens as criminal gang leader Ron Moody reminds her what may happen to her blackguard boyfriend Oliver Reed (right) if she refuses to betray the young title character, Oliver Twist.

Films are rated on a 1 to 10 scale, 10 is highest. **Boldface** ratings followed by an asterisk (*) are for films actually seen and rated by the executive and senior editors. All other ratings are estimates. (See Notes on Entertainment Ratings in the front section.)

OLYMPIC ELK (1952) RKO. **Color-27min.** *(Documentary)*. *Producer:* Walt Disney.. **5***

OLYMPIC VISIONS (1973) *see* VISIONS OF EIGHT

OMAR KHAYYAM (1957) Paramount. **Color-101min.** Cornel Wilde, Debra Paget.. **3½***

OMEGA MAN, THE (1971) Warner Bros. **Color-98min.** Charlton Heston, Anthony Zerbe.. **3***

OMEN, THE (1976) 20th Century-Fox. **Color-111min.** Gregory Peck, Lee Remick... **7***

ON A CLEAR DAY YOU CAN SEE FOREVER (1970) Paramount. **Color-130min.** Barbra Streisand, Yves Montand, Jack Nicholson **4½***

ON AN ISLAND WITH YOU (1948) M-G-M. **Color-107min.** Esther Williams, Peter Lawford .... (4)

ON ANY STREET (1959) *see* NOTTE BRAVA, LA

ON ANY SUNDAY (1971) Cinema 5. **Color-91min.** *(Documentary)*. *Director:* Bruce Brown **6***

ON APPROVAL (1944) English Films. **B&W-80min.** *(British)*. Clive Brook, Beatrice Lillie **4½***

ON BORROWED TIME (1939) M-G-M. **B&W-99min.** Lionel Barrymore, Beulah Bondi.. **5***

ON DANGEROUS GROUND (1952) RKO. **B&W-82min.** Robert Ryan, Ida Lupino.. **3½***

ON DRESS PARADE (1939) Warner Bros. **B&W-62min.** The Dead End Kids, John Litel .... (3)

ON FOOT, ON HORSE, AND ON WHEELS (1957) United Motion Pic. Org. (UMPO). **B&W-90min.** *(French)*. Noel-Noel, Denise Gray............. (3)

ON HER MAJESTY'S SECRET SERVICE (1969) United Artists. **Color-140min.** *(British)*. George Lazenby, Diana Rigg......................... **5***

ON MOONLIGHT BAY (1951) Warner Bros. **Color-98min.** Doris Day, Gordon MacRae **4½***

ON MY WAY TO THE CRUSADES, I MET A GIRL WHO . . . (1969) Warner Bros. **Color-93min.** *(U.S.-Italian, English version)*. Tony Curtis, Monica Vitti .... (3)
Italian title: CINTURA DI CASTIA, LA
British title: CHASTITY BELT, THE

ON OUR MERRY WAY (1948) United Artists. **B&W-107min.** Burgess Meredith, Paulette Goddard, James Stewart, Henry Fonda.................. (4)
Original title: MIRACLE CAN HAPPEN, A

ON STAGE EVERYBODY (1945) Universal. **B&W-65min.** Jack Oakie, Peggy Ryan.. (3)

ON THE AVENUE (1937) 20th Century-Fox. **B&W-89min.** Dick Powell, Madeleine Carroll .... (5)

ON THE BEACH (1959) United Artists. **B&W-133min.** Gregory Peck, Ava Gardner.. **5½***

ON THE BEAT (1962) United Artists. **B&W-105min.** *(British)*. Norman Wisdom, Jennifer Jayne .... (4)

ON THE CARPET (1946) *see* LITTLE GIANT

ON THE DOUBLE (1961) Paramount. **Color-92min.** Danny Kaye........... (4)

ON THE FIDDLE (1961) *see* OPERATION SNAFU

ON THE ISLE OF SAMOA (1950) Columbia. **B&W-65min.** Jon Hall, Susan Cabot .... (2)

ON THE LOOSE (1951) RKO. **B&W-78min.** Joan Evans, Melvyn Douglas, Lynn Bari .... (3)

ON THE RIVIERA (1951) 20th Century-Fox. **Color-89min.** Danny Kaye **5***

ON THE RUN (1963) Anglo Amalgamated [EMI]. **B&W-59min.** *(British)*. Emrys Jones, Sarah Lawson .... (3)

ON THE THRESHOLD OF SPACE (1956) 20th Century-Fox. **Color-98min.** Guy Madison, Virginia Leith **3***

ON THE TOWN (1949) M-G-M. **Color-98min.** Gene Kelly, Frank Sinatra.. **4***

ON THE WATERFRONT (1954) Columbia. **B&W-108min.** Marlon Brando, Eva Marie Saint **6***

ON THE YARD (1978) **Color-103min.** John Heard, Tom Waites ....

ON THEIR OWN (1940) 20th Century-Fox. **B&W-63min.** Spring Byington, Marguerite Chapman .... (3)

ON THIN ICE (1961) Comet Film. **Color-90min.** *(German)*. Tony Sailer, Ina Bauer... (3)
Alternate title: BIG FREEZE, THE

ON TRIAL (1953) New Realm. **B&W-70min.** *(French-Italian)*. Madeleine Robinson, Daniel Gélin, Eleonora Rossi-Drago, Anton Walbrook ...... (3)
Original French title: AFFAIRE MAURIZIUS, L'

ON WINGS OF SONG (1935) *see* LOVE ME FOREVER

ON WITH THE SHOW (1929) Warner Bros. **Color-98min.** Betty Compson, Louise Fazenda... (3)

ON YOUR TOES (1939) Warner Bros. **B&W-94min.** Eddie Albert, Vera Zorina .... (4)

ONCE A THIEF (1965) M-G-M. **B&W-107min.** *(U.S.A.-French)*. Alain Delon, Ann-Margret.. (4)
Foreign title: TUEURS DE SAN FRANCISCO, LES *(The Killers of San Francisco)*

ONCE BEFORE I DIE (1966) Goldstone Film Enterprises. **Color-97min.** *(U.S.-Philippine)*. Ursula Andress, John Derek **3***

ONCE BITTEN (1960) **B&W-90min.** *(French)*. Sascha Distel, Bernadette Lafont .... (3)

ONCE IN A LIFETIME (1932) Universal. **B&W-75min.** Jack Oakie, Sidney Fox.. **3***

ONCE IN PARIS (1978) Atlantic Releasing. **Color-100min.** Wayne Rogers, Gayle Hunnicutt **5½***

ONCE IS NOT ENOUGH (1975) *see* JACQUELINE SUSANN'S ONCE IS NOT ENOUGH

ONCE MORE, MY DARLING (1949) Universal. **B&W-94min.** Lillian Randolph, Robert Montgomery, Ann Blyth **5***

ONCE MORE, WITH FEELING (1960) Columbia. **Color-92min.** Yul Brynner, Kay Kendall **5***

ONCE UPON A DEAD MAN (1971) MCA-TV. **Color-100min.** *(Made for TV)*. Rock Hudson, Susan Saint James, Jack Albertson................... **4***

ONCE UPON A HONEYMOON (1942) RKO. **B&W-117min.** Ginger Rogers, Cary Grant **4***

ONCE UPON A HORSE (1958) Universal. **B&W-85min.** Dan Rowan, Dick Martin, Martha Hyer **3***
Alternate title: HOT HORSE, THE

ONCE UPON A THURSDAY (1942) *see* AFFAIRS OF MARTHA, THE

ONCE UPON A TIME (1944) Columbia. **B&W-89min.** Cary Grant, Janet Blair **4***

ONCE UPON A TIME (1976) G. G. Communications. **Color-83min.** *(W. German-Italian, Cartoon)*. *Director:* Rolf Kauka .... (3)
Original Italian title: MARIA D'ORO UND BELLO BLUE

ONCE UPON A TIME IN THE WEST (1968) Paramount. **Color-165min.** *(Italian-U.S., English language)*. Henry Fonda, Claudia Cardinale, Charles Bronson **4***
Italian title: C'ERA UNA VOLTA IL WEST

ONCE YOU KISS A STRANGER (1969) Warner Bros. **Color-106min.** Paul Burke, Carol Lynley.. **3***

ONE AGAINST SEVEN (1945) *see* COUNTER-ATTACK

ONE AND ONLY, THE (1978) Paramount. **Color-98min.** Henry Winkler, Kim Darby.. **5½***

ONE AND ONLY, GENUINE, ORIGINAL FAMILY BAND, THE (1968) Buena Vista. **Color-110min.** Walter Brennan, Buddy Ebsen **4***

ONE BIG AFFAIR (1952) United Artists. **B&W-80min.** Dennis O'Keefe, Evelyn Keyes.. (3)

ONE BODY TOO MANY (1944) Paramount. **B&W-75min.** Jack Haley, Jean Parker, Bela Lugosi .... (3)

ONE BORN EVERY MINUTE (1967) *see* FLIM-FLAM MAN, THE

ONE CENT (1954) *see* BOOT POLISH

ONE CROWDED NIGHT (1940) RKO. **B&W-68min.** Gale Storm, William Haade .... (3)

ONE DANGEROUS NIGHT (1943) Columbia. **B&W-77min.** Warren William, Marguerite Chapman, Eric Blore .... (4)

ONE DAY BEFORE TOMORROW (1971) *see* HOW TO STEAL AN AIRPLANE

ONE DAY IN THE LIFE OF IVAN DENISOVICH (1971) Cinerama Releasing. **Color-100min.** *(British-Norwegian-U.S.)*. Tom Courtenay, Alfred Burke... **5***

ONE DESIRE (1955) Universal. **Color-94min.** Anne Baxter, Rock Hudson **3½***

ONE EXTRA DAY (1956) *see* EXTRA DAY, THE

ONE-EYED JACKS (1961) Paramount. **Color-141min.** Marlon Brando, Karl Malden **6***

ONE FATAL HOUR (1936) *see* TWO AGAINST THE WORLD

ONE FLEW OVER THE CUCKOO'S NEST (1975) United Artists. **Color-133min.** Jack Nicholson, Louise Fletcher, Will Sampson.................... **6½***

ONE FOOT IN HEAVEN (1941) Warner Bros. **B&W-108min.** Fredric March, Martha Scott.. **5½***

ONE FOOT IN HELL (1960) 20th Century-Fox. **Color-90min.** Alan Ladd, Don Murray **3***

ONE FOR THE BOOK (1948) *see* VOICE OF THE TURTLE

Films are rated on a 1 to 10 scale, 10 is highest. **Boldface** ratings followed by an asterisk (*) are for films actually seen and rated by the executive and senior editors. All other ratings are estimates. (See Notes on Entertainment Ratings in the front section.)

ONE GIRL'S CONFESSION (1953) Columbia. **B&W-74min.** Cleo Moore, Hugo Haas...(2)

ONE GOOD TURN (1954) J. Arthur Rank. **B&W-90min.** *(British).* Joan Rice, Norman Wisdom ....(4)

ONE HEAVENLY NIGHT (1931) United Artists. **B&W-82min.** Evelyn Laye, John Boles...**3***

ONE HORSE TOWN (1936) *see* SMALL TOWN GIRL

ONE HOUR TO DOOMSDAY (1971) *see* CITY BENEATH THE SEA

ONE HOUR WITH YOU (1932) Paramount. **B&W-80min.** Maurice Chevalier, Jeanette MacDonald...**4***

ONE HUNDRED AND ONE DALMATIANS (1961) Buena Vista. **Color-80min.** *(Cartoon). Director:* Wolfgang Reitherman..........................**4***

100 CRIES OF TERROR (1964) K. Gordon Murray. **B&W-96min.** *(Mexican).* Adriana Welter, Joaquin Cordero...............................(3)
Original title: CIEN GRITOS DE TERROR

100 MEN AND A GIRL (1937) Universal. **B&W-84min.** Deanna Durbin, Leopold Stokowski..(5)

100 PER CENT PURE (1934) *see* GIRL FROM MISSOURI, THE

100 RIFLES (1969) 20th Century-Fox. **Color-110min.** Jim Brown, Raquel Welch, Burt Reynolds...(3)

ONE IN A MILLION (1936) 20th Century-Fox. **B&W-95min.** Sonja Henie, Adolphe Menjou...(5)

ONE IS A LONELY NUMBER (1972) M-G-M. **Color-97min.** Trish Van Devere, Monte Markham..**4***

ONE JUMP AHEAD (1955) J. Arthur Rank. **B&W-66min.** *(British).* Paul Carpenter, Diane Hart..(3)

ONE LAST FLING (1949) Warner Bros. **B&W-74min.** Zachary Scott, Alexis Smith ....(3)

ONE LIFE (1958) *see* END OF DESIRE

ONE LITTLE INDIAN (1973) Buena Vista. **Color-90min.** James Garner, Vera Miles, Clay O'Brien...**4½***

ONE MAN MUTINY (1955) *see* COURT MARTIAL OF BILLY MITCHELL, THE

ONE MAN'S WAY (1964) United Artists. **B&W-105min.** Don Murray, Diana Hyland..(5)

ONE MILLION B.C. (1940) United Artists. **B&W-80min.** Victor Mature **3***
Alternate title: CAVE MAN
British title: MAN AND HIS MATE

ONE MILLION YEARS B.C. (1966) 20th Century-Fox. **Color-100min.** *(British).* John Richardson, Raquel Welch...............................**3***

ONE MINUTE TO ZERO (1952) RKO. **B&W-105min.** Ann Blyth, Robert Mitchum..(4)

ONE MORE TIME (1970) United Artists. **Color-93min.** *(British).* Sammy Davis, Jr., Peter Lawford.......................................(3)

ONE MORE TOMORROW (1946) Warner Bros. **B&W-88min.** Ann Sheridan, Dennis Morgan...(3)

ONE MORE TRAIN TO ROB (1971) Universal. **Color-108min.** George Peppard, John Vernon, Diana Muldaur.........................**4½***

ONE MYSTERIOUS NIGHT (1944) Columbia. **B&W-61min.** Chester Morris, Janis Carter..(4)
British title: BEHIND CLOSED DOORS

ONE NIGHT AT DINNER (1969) International Co-Productions. **Color-110min.** *(Italian).* Jean-Louis Trintignant, Tony Musante, Florinda Bolkan, Lino Capolicchio...(3)
Original title: METTI, UNA SERA A CENA *(Imagine, One Evening at Supper)*
Publicity title: LET'S SAY ONE NIGHT FOR DINNER

ONE NIGHT IN LISBON (1941) Paramount. **B&W-97min.** Fred MacMurray, Madeleine Carroll..(4)

ONE NIGHT IN THE TROPICS (1940) Universal. **B&W-82min.** Robert Cummings, Bud Abbott, Lou Costello......................................**4***

ONE NIGHT OF LOVE (1934) Columbia. **B&W-82min.** Grace Moore, Tullio Carminati...**4***

ONE NIGHT STAND (1976) Films La Boetie. **Color-102min.** *(French, English language).* Richard Jordan, Ting Pei ....(4)

ONE NIGHT WITH YOU (1948) Universal. **B&W-92min.** *(British).* Nino Martini, Patricia Roc..(3)

ONE OF OUR AIRCRAFT IS MISSING (1942) United Artists. **B&W-106min.** *(British).* Godfrey Tearle, Eric Portman..................**4½***

ONE OF OUR DINOSAURS IS MISSING (1975) Buena Vista. **Color-93min.** Peter Ustinov, Helen Hayes.......................................(4)

ONE ON ONE (1977) Warner Bros. **Color-98min.** Robby Benson, Annette O'Toole, G. D. Spradlin...**5***

ONE ON TOP OF THE OTHER (1970) GGP Releasing. **Color-104min.** *(Italian-Spanish-French).* Jean Sorel, Marisa Mell, Elsa Martinelli .....(3)
Original Italian title: UNA SULL' ALTRA *(One Over the Other)*
Original Spanish title: HISTORIA PERVERSA, UNA *(A Perverse Story)*

ONE-PIECE BATHING SUIT, THE (1952) *see* MILLION DOLLAR MERMAID

ONE PLUS ONE (1968) *see* SYMPATHY FOR THE DEVIL

ONE POTATO, TWO POTATO (1964) Cinema 5. **B&W-92min.** Barbara Barrie, Bernie Hamilton..**5***

ONE SINGS, THE OTHER DOESN'T (1976) Cinema 5. **Color-105min.** Valérie Mairesse, Thérèse Liotard **4***
Original title: UNE CHANTE L'AUTRE PAS, L'

ONE SPY TOO MANY (1966) M-G-M. **Color-102min.** *(Telefeature).* Robert Vaughn, David McCallum, Rip Torn, Dorothy Provine.............**3½***
Original title: ALEXANDER THE GREATER AFFAIR, THE

ONE STEP TO ETERNITY (1954) Ellis Films. **B&W-94min.** *(French).* Corinne Calvet, Danielle Darrieux, Michel Auclair ....(4)
Original title: BONNES A TUER

ONE SUMMER LOVE (1976) *see* DRAGONFLY

ONE SUMMER OF HAPPINESS (1952) Times Film Corp. **B&W-95min.** *(Swedish).* Folke Sundquist, Ulla Jacobsson **4***
Original title: HON DANSADE EN SOMMAR

ONE SUNDAY AFTERNOON (1948) Warner Bros. **Color-90min.** Dennis Morgan, Janis Paige..**4***

ONE THAT GOT AWAY, THE (1957) J. Arthur Rank. **B&W-111min.** *(British).* Hardy Kruger, Colin Gordon..................................(5)

ONE THIRD OF A NATION (1939) Paramount. **B&W-79min.** Sylvia Sidney, Leif Erikson...(4)

1001 ARABIAN NIGHTS (1959) Columbia. **Color-75min.** *(Cartoon). Director:* Jack Kinney **4***

1,000 CONVICTS AND A WOMAN! (1971) American-International. **Color-94min.** Alexandra Hay, Sandor Eles ....(3)

1,000 PLANE RAID, THE (1969) United Artists. **Color-94min.** Christopher George, Larraine Stephens.................................**4***
Alternate title: THOUSAND PLANE RAID, THE

1000 YEARS FROM NOW (1952) *see* CAPTIVE WOMEN

ONE TOUCH OF VENUS (1948) Universal. **B&W-81min.** Robert Walker, Ava Gardner...**4***

ONE STEP TO HELL (1968) World Entertainment. **Color-94min.** *(U.S.-Italian-Spanish).* Ty Hardin, Pier Angeli, Rossano Brazzi, George Sanders..
Original Italian title: CACCIA AI VIOLENTI
Spanish title: REY DE AFRICA *(King of Africa)*

ONE, TWO, THREE (1961) United Artists. **B&W-108min.** James Cagney, Horst Buchholz...**8***

ONE WAY PASSAGE (1932) Warner Bros. **B&W-69min.** William Powell, Kay Francis...**4***

ONE, TWO, THREE (1961). Bubbly Pamela Tiffin, daughter of a Coca-Cola corporate executive, has married defiant Communist Horst Buchholz, and fiesty James Cagney, the head of Coca-Cola sales for West Berlin, knows her father will be less than overjoyed when he finds out.

ONE WAY STREET (1950) Universal. **B&W-79min.** James Mason, Marta Toren...(4)

ONE WAY TO LOVE (1946) Columbia. **B&W-83min.** Willard Parker, Marguerite Chapman..(4)

ONE WOMAN'S REVENGE (1971) *see* REVENGE!

ONE WOMAN'S STORY (1949) Universal. **B&W-86min.** *(British).* Trevor Howard, Ann Todd, Claude Rains **4***
Original title: PASSIONATE FRIENDS, THE

ONIBABA (1964) Toho. **B&W-100min.** *(Japanese).* Nobuko Otowa, Jitsuko Yoshimura...(5)
Alternate title: HOLE, THE
Alternate title: DEMON, THE
Alternate title(?): DEVIL WOMAN

ONION FIELD, THE (1979) Avco-Embassy. **Color-   min.** John Savage, James Woods..

ONIONHEAD (1958) Warner Bros. **B&W-110min.** Andy Griffith, Felicia Farr, Walter Matthau...(4)

ONLY A WOMAN (1962) Warner Bros. **Color-86min.** *(German).* Maria Schell, Paul Hubschmid..(3)
Original title: ICH BIN AUCH NUR EINE FRAU

ONLY ANGELS HAVE WINGS (1939) Columbia. **B&W-121min.** Cary Grant, Jean Arthur..(5)

ONLY GAME IN TOWN, THE (1970) 20th Century-Fox. **Color-113min.** Elizabeth Taylor, Warren Beatty...**4½***

ONLY ONE DAY LEFT BEFORE TOMORROW (1971) *see* HOW TO STEAL AN AIRPLANE

ONLY ONE NEW YORK (1964) Avco-Embassy. **B&W-72min.** *(French-U.S., Documentary). Director:* Pierre-Dominique Gaisseau...................**4***
French title: NEW-YORK-SUR-MER *(New York-on-the-Sea)*

ONLY THE BEST (1951) *see* I CAN GET IT FOR YOU WHOLESALE

ONLY THE FRENCH CAN (1954) United Motion Pic. Org. (UMPO). **Color-93min.** *(French).* Jean Gabin, Francoise Arnoul ....(5)
Alternate title: FRENCH-CANCAN

ONLY THE VALIANT (1951) Warner Bros. **B&W-105min.** Gregory Peck, Barbara Payton...(4)

ONLY TWO CAN PLAY (1961) Columbia. **B&W-106min.** *(British).* Peter Sellers, Mai Zetterling...**5½***

ONLY WAY OUT IS DEAD, THE (1970) *see* MAN WHO WANTED TO LIVE FOREVER, THE

ONLY WHEN I LARF (1968) Paramount. **Color-104min.** *(British).* Richard Attenborough, David Hemmings, Alexandra Stewart.....................(4)

OPEN CITY (1945) Mayer-Burstyn. **B&W-105min.** *(Italian).* Aldo Fabrizi, Anna Magnani...**4***
Original title: ROMA, CITTA APERTA
Alternate title: CITTA APERTA

OPEN SEASON (1974) Columbia. **Color-103min.** *(Spanish-Swiss, English language).* Peter Fonda, John Philip Law **3***
Original Spanish title: CAZADORES, LOS

OPEN THE DOOR AND SEE ALL THE PEOPLE (1964) Noel Productions and Barney Pitkin Associates. **B&W-82min.** Maybelle Nash ....(4)

OPENED BY MISTAKE (1940) Paramount. **B&W-67min.** Charles Ruggles, Janice Logan, Robert Paige...(3)

OPENING NIGHT (1977) Faces Distribution Corp. **Color-144min.** Gena Rowlands, Ben Gazzara...**2½***

OPERATION ABDUCTION (1957) American-International. **B&W-85min.** *(French).* Frank Villard, Daniele Goedet.............................(3)

OPERATION AMSTERDAM (1959) 20th Century-Fox. **B&W-105min.** *(British).* Peter Finch, Eva Bartok **4***

OPERATION ATLANTIS (1965) American-International. **Color-88min.** *(Italian-Spanish).* John Ericson, Berna Rock ....(3)
Original Italian title: AGENTE S03 OPERAZIONE ATLANTIDE *(Agent S03 Operation Atlantis)*
Original Spanish title: AGENT 003, OPERACION ATLANTIDA

OPERATION BIKINI (1963) American-International. **B&W-84min.** Tab Hunter, Frankie Avalon, Scott Brady...................................(3)

OPERATION BOTTLENECK (1961) United Artists. **B&W-78min.** Ron Foster, Miiko Taka...(3)

OPERATION BULLSHINE (1959) Associated British-Pathé [EMI]. **Color-84min.** *(British).* Donald Sinden, Barbara Murray......................(3)

OPERATION C.I.A. (1965) Allied Artists. **B&W-90min.** Burt Reynolds, Kieu Chinh, Danielle Aubry **3½***

OPERATION CAMEL (1960) American-International. **Color-74min.** *(Danish).* Nora Hayden, Paul Hagen...(2)
Original title: SOLDATERKAMMERATER PA VAGT

OPERATION CAVIAR (1959) American-International. **B&W-85min.** *(W. German-French).* O. W. Fischer, Eva Bartok ....(3)

OPERATION: COBRA (1971) *see* O'HARA: UNITED STATES TREASURY

OPERATION CONSPIRACY (1956) Republic. **B&W-69min.** *(British).* Philip Friend, Mary Mackenzie...(3)
Original title: CLOAK WITHOUT DAGGER

OPERATION CROSS EAGLES (1969) Continental [Walter Reade]. **Color-90min.** *(Yugoslavian-U.S.).* Richard Conte, Rory Calhoun, Aili King....2*
Yugoslavian title: UNAKRSNA VATRA

OPERATION CROSSBOW (1965) M-G-M. **Color-116min.** *(British-Italian).* Sophia Loren, George Peppard............................**5***
Italian title: OPERAZIONE CROSSBOW
Alternate title: CODE NAME: OPERATION CROSSBOW
Alternate title: GREAT SPY MISSION, THE

OPERATION DAMES (1959) American-International. **B&W-74min.** Eve Meyer, Chuck Henderson..(3)
British title: GIRLS IN ACTION

OPERATION DAYBREAK (1976) Warner Bros. **Color-118min.** Timothy Bottoms, Anton Diffring...(4)

OPERATION DELILAH (1966) NTA Pictures. **Color-86min.** *(Spanish-U.S.).* Rory Calhoun, Gia Scala.....................................(3)
Spanish title: OPERACION DALILA

OPERATION DIPLOMAT (1953) Butcher's *(Brit.).* **B&W-70min.** *(British).* Guy Rolfe, Lisa Daniely...(4)

OPERATION DIPLOMATIC PASSPORT (1965) American-International. **B&W-85min.** *(French).* Roger Hanin, Christine Minazzoli ....(3)
Original title: PASSEPORT DIPLOMATIQUE, AGENT K 8

OPERATION DISASTER (1950) Universal. **B&W-102min.** *(British).* John Mills, Richard Attenborough.......................................**4***
Original title: MORNING DEPARTURE

OPERATION EICHMANN (1961) Allied Artists. **B&W-92min.** Werner Klemperer, Ruta Lee, Donald Buka ....(4)

OPERATION GOLD INGOT (1963) American-International. **B&W-85min.** *(French).* Alberto Lionello, Martine Carol...........................(3)

OPERATION HAYLIFT (1950) Lippert Productions. **B&W-75min.** Bill Williams, Ann Rutherford...(4)

OPERATION HEARTBEAT (1969) *see* UMC

OPERATION HONG KONG (1964) Casino Films. **Color-95min.** *(W. German-Italian).* Horst Frank, Maria Perschy............................(2)
Original German title: WEISSE FRACHT FUR HONGKONG
Alternate title(?): SECRET AGENT 007

OPERATION KID BROTHER (1967) United Artists. **Color-104min.** *(Italian).* Neil Connery, Daniela Bianchi, Adolfo Celi..........................(2)
Original title: O.K. CONNERY

OPERATION MAD BALL (1957) Columbia. **B&W-105min.** Jack Lemmon, Kathryn Grant...**4***

OPERATION MANHUNT (1954) United Artists. **B&W-77min.** Harry Townes, Jacques Aubuchon..(3)

OPERATION MERMAID (1963) J. Arthur Rank. **B&W-90min.** *(British).* Keenan Wynn, Mai Zetterling ....(4)
Original title: BAY OF SAINT MICHEL, THE
Alternate title: PATTERN FOR PLUNDER

OPERATION MOONLIGHT (1961) *see* WHISKEY AND SODA

OPERATION PACIFIC (1951) Warner Bros. **B&W-111min.** John Wayne, Patricia Neal..**4***

OPERATION PETTICOAT (1959) Universal. **Color-124min.** Cary Grant, Tony Curtis...**5***

OPERATION PETTICOAT (1977) ABC Films. **Color-100min.** *(Made for TV).* John Astin, Richard Gilliland ....(4)

OPERATION ST. PETER'S (1968) Paramount. **Color-100min.** *(Italian-W. German-French).* Edward G. Robinson, Lando Buzzanca, Jean-Claude Brialy ....(4)
Original Italian title: OPERAZIONE SAN PIETRO
German title: ABENTEUER DES KARDINAL BRAUN, DIE

OPERATION SECRET (1952) Warner Bros. **B&W-108min.** Cornel Wilde, Steve Cochran, Phyllis Thaxter ....(5)

OPERATION SNAFU (1961) American-International. **B&W-97min.** *(British).* Alfred Lynch, Sean Connery **4***
Original title: ON THE FIDDLE
Alternate title: OPERATION WARHEAD

OPERATION SNATCH (1962) Continental [Walter Reade]. **B&W-83min.** *(British).* Terry-Thomas, George Sanders............................(4)

OPERATION STOGIE (1960) Warner Bros. **B&W-75min.** *(British).* John Hewer, Anton Rodgers...(3)

OPERATION THUNDERBOLT (1977) Cinema Shares. **Color-125min.** *(Israeli, English version).* Yehoram Gaon, Assaf Dayan, Klaus Kinski..**5***

OPERATION WARHEAD (1961) *see* OPERATION SNAFU

OPERATION X (1950) Columbia. **B&W-79min.** *(British).* Edward G. Robinson, Peggy Cummins, Richard Greene............................(3)
Original title: MY DAUGHTER JOY

OPERATION "Y" (1966) *see* YPOTRON - FINAL COUNTDOWN

OPHELIA (1962) New Line Cinema. **B&W-100min.** *(French).* Alida Valli, André Jocelyn, Juliette Maynial ....

OPIATE '67 (1963) *see* 15 FROM ROME

OPIUM WAR, THE (197?) Sino-American Corp. **Color-90min.** *(Chinese).* Chao Tan, Kao Chen.
Original title: LIN TSE-HSU

OPPOSITE SEX, THE (1956) M-G-M. **Color-117min.** June Allyson, Joan Collins 4*

OPTIMISTS, THE (1973) Paramount. **Color-110min.** *(British).* Peter Sellers, Donna Mullane, John Chaffey ....(4)
Original title: OPTIMISTS OF NINE ELMS, THE

ORACLE, THE (1953) Mayer-Kingsley. **B&W-84min.** *(British).* Robert Beatty, Mervyn Johns, Virginia McKenna........................(5)
Alternate title: HORSE'S MOUTH, THE

ORCA (1977) Paramount. **Color-92min.** Richard Harris, Charlotte Rampling, Will Sampson 5*
Publicity title: ORCA, THE KILLER WHALE

ORCHESTRA WIVES (1942) 20th Century-Fox. **B&W-98min.** George Montgomery, Ann Rutherford 4½*

ORDERED TO LOVE (1961) Transocean Films. **B&W-82min.** *(German).* Maria Perschy, Joachim Hansen ....(4)
Original title: LEBENSBORN

ORDERS ARE ORDERS (1954) Distributors Corp. of America. **B&W-78min.** *(British).* Brian Reece, Margot Grahame ....(4)

ORDERS TO KILL (1958) United Motion Pic. Org. (UMPO). **B&W-93min.** *(British).* Paul Massie, Eddie Albert 4*

ORDET (1955) Kingsley International. **B&W-126min.** *(Danish).* Morten Borgen, Birgitte Federspiel, Emil Hass Christensen........................(4)
Translation title: The Word

OREGON PASSAGE (1958) Allied Artists. **Color-82min.** John Ericson, Lola Albright ....(3)

OREGON TRAIL, THE (1959) 20th Century-Fox. **Color-86min.** Fred MacMurray, Gloria Talbott 3*

ORGANIZATION, THE (1971) United Artists. **Color-107min.** Sidney Poitier, Barbara McNair 5½*

ORGANIZER, THE (1963) Continental [Walter Reade]. **B&W-126min.** *(Italian-French-Yugoslavian).* Marcello Mastroianni, Renato Salvatori 6*
Original Italian title: COMPAGNI, I *(The Strikers)*
French title: CAMARADES, LES

ORIENTAL DREAMS (1944) *see* KISMET

ORIENTALS, THE (1960) Galatea Productions. **Color-110min.** *(Italian).* Nagwa Fouad, Nick Kendall ....(1)
Alternate title: WOMAN OF THE ORIENT
Alternate title: ORIENTALI

ORLANDO (1961) *see* ROLAND THE MIGHTY

O'ROURKE OF THE ROYAL MOUNTED (1954) *see* SASKATCHEWAN

ORPHAN OF THE RING, THE (1939) *see* KID FROM KOKOMO, THE

ORPHANS OF THE STORM (1921) United Artists. **B&W-133min.** *(Silent).* Lillian Gish, Dorothy Gish 5*

ORPHEUS (1950) Discina International. **B&W-94min.** *(French).* Jean Marais, Maria Casarès 3*
Original title: ORPHÉE

OSCAR, THE (1966) Avco-Embassy. **Color-119min.** Stephen Boyd, Elke Sommer 3*

OSCAR WILDE (1960) Films Around The World. **B&W-96min.** *(British).* Robert Morley, Phyllis Calvert ....(5)

O'SHAUGHNESSY'S BOY (1935) M-G-M. **B&W-88min.** Wallace Beery, Jackie Cooper ....(4)

OSSESSIONE (1942) Brandon. **B&W-135min.** *(Italian).* Clara Calmai, Massimo Girotti 3½*
Translation title: Obsession

OTHELLO (1952) United Artists. **B&W-91min.** *(U.S.-Italian, English language).* Orson Welles, Micheal MacLiammoir, Suzanne Cloutier......(4)

OTHELLO (1955) Universal. **Color-108min.** *(U.S.S.R.).* Sergei Bondarchuk, Andrei Popov, Irina Skobtseva ....(5)

OTHELLO (1965) Warner Bros. **Color-166min.** *(British).* Laurence Olivier, Frank Finlay, Maggie Smith 4*

OTHER, THE (1972) 20th Century-Fox. **Color-100min.** Chris Udvarnoky, Uta Hagen 3*

OTHER HALF OF THE SKY: A CHINA MEMOIR, THE (1975) Shirley MacLaine. **Color-74min.** *(Travelog). Director:* Claudia Weill................(5)

OTHER LOVE, THE (1947) United Artists. **B&W-95min.** Barbara Stanwyck, David Niven 3*

OTHER MAN, THE (1970) Universal. **Color-100min.** *(Made for TV).* Roy Thinnes, Joan Hackett, Tammy Grimes 3*

OTHER SIDE OF HELL, THE (1978) NBC-TV. **Color-98min.** *(Made for TV).* Alan Arkin, Roger E. Mosley 5½*

OTHER SIDE OF MADNESS, THE (1971) Auric Ltd. **B&W-85min.** Brian Klinkett, Debbie Duff ....(3)

OTHER SIDE OF MIDNIGHT, THE (1977) 20th Century-Fox. **Color-165min.** Marie-France Pisier, John Beck, Susan Sarandon........................5

OTHER SIDE OF PARADISE, THE (1976) *see* FOXTROT

OTHER SIDE OF THE MOUNTAIN, THE (1975) Universal. **Color-101min.** Marilyn Hassett, Beau Bridges........................4*
British title: WINDOW TO THE SKY, A

OTHER SIDE OF THE MOUNTAIN - PART II, THE (1978) Universal. **Color-99min.** Marilyn Hassett, Timothy Bottoms 4*

OTHER VOICES (1969) DHS Films. **B&W-100min.** *(Documentary). Director:* David H. Sawyer........................(4)

OTHER WOMAN, THE (1954) 20th Century-Fox. **B&W-81min.** Hugo Haas, Cleo Moore 3*

OTLEY (1969) Columbia. **Color-90min.** *(British).* Tom Courtenay, Romy Schneider 3*

OUR BETTERS (1933) RKO. **B&W-78min.** Constance Bennett, Gilbert Roland........................(4)

OUR BLUSHING BRIDES (1930) M-G-M. **B&W-79min.** Joan Crawford, Anita Page........................(3)

OUR DAILY BREAD (1934) United Artists. **B&W-74min.** Karen Morley, Tom Keene 4*
British title: MIRACLE OF LIFE, THE

OUR DANCING DAUGHTERS (1928) M-G-M. **B&W-85min.** *(Silent).* Joan Crawford, John (Johnny) Mack Brown 4*

OUR GIRL FRIDAY (1954) *see* ADVENTURES OF SADIE, THE

OUR HEARTS WERE GROWING UP (1946) Paramount. **B&W-83min.** Gail Russell, Diana Lynn........................(4)

OUR HEARTS WERE YOUNG AND GAY (1944) Paramount. **B&W-81min.** Gail Russell, Diana Lynn 5*

OUR HOSPITALITY (1923) Metro. **B&W-70min.** *(Silent).* Buster Keaton, Natalie Talmadge........................5*

OUR LEADING CITIZEN (1939) Paramount. **B&W-88min.** Bob Burns, Gene Lockhart ....(4)

OUR LITTLE GIRL (1935) 20th Century-Fox. **B&W-63min.** Shirley Temple, Rosemary Ames........................(4)

OUR MAN FLINT (1966) 20th Century-Fox. **Color-107min.** James Coburn, Lee J. Cobb, Gila Golan........................4½*

OUR MAN IN HAVANA (1959) Columbia. **B&W-111min.** *(British).* Alec Guinness, Noel Coward, Ernie Kovacs........................6*

OUR MAN IN JAMAICA (1965) Paramount. **Color-96min.** *(Foreign).* Larry Pennell, Margarita Scherr........................(3)

OUR MAN IN MARRAKESH (1966) *see* BANG, BANG, YOU'RE DEAD!

OUR MAN IN MARRAKESH (1966) *see* THAT MAN GEORGE

OUR MAN IN THE CARIBBEAN (1962) Transcontinental. **B&W-85min.** *(British).* Carlos Thompson, Clemence Bettany, Diana Rigg................(3)

OUR MISS BROOKS (1956) Warner Bros. **B&W-85min.** Eve Arden, Gale Gordon ....(4)

OUR MOTHER'S HOUSE (1967) M-G-M. **Color-105min.** *(British-U.S.).* Dirk Bogarde, Pamela Franklin 4*

OUR RELATIONS (1936) M-G-M. **B&W-65min.** Stan Laurel, Oliver Hardy........................(4)

OUR TIME (1974) Warner Bros. **Color-90min.** Pamela Sue Martin, Betsy Slade........................5½*
TV title: DEATH OF HER INNOCENCE, THE

OUR TOWN (1940) United Artists. **B&W-90min.** William Holden, Martha Scott 3*

OUR VERY OWN (1950) RKO. **B&W-93min.** Ann Blyth, Farley Granger 3*

OUR VINES HAVE TENDER GRAPES (1945) M-G-M. **B&W-105min.** Edward G. Robinson, Margaret O'Brien 4½*

OUR WIFE (1941) Columbia. **B&W-95min.** Melvyn Douglas, Ruth Hussey........................(4)

OUR WINNING SEASON (1978) American-International. **Color-92min.** Scott Jacoby, Deborah Benson, Dennis Quaid........................4½*

Films are rated on a 1 to 10 scale, 10 is highest. **Boldface** ratings followed by an asterisk (*) are for films actually seen and rated by the executive and senior editors. All other ratings are estimates. (See Notes on Entertainment Ratings in the front section.)

OUT ALL NIGHT (1933) Universal. **B&W-68min.** ZaSu Pitts, Slim Summerville..(4)

OUT OF IT (1970) United Artists. **B&W-97min.** Barry Gordon, Jon Voight, Lada Edmund, Jr. ....(2)

OUT OF SEASON (1975) EMI. **Color-90min.** *(British).* Vanessa Redgrave, Cliff Robertson, Susan George................................(4)

OUT OF SIGHT (1966) Universal. **Color-87min.** Jonathan Daly, Karen Jensen..(2)

OUT OF THE BLUE (1947) Eagle Lion. **B&W-84min.** George Brent, Virginia Mayo ....(4)

OUT OF THE CLOUDS (1954) J. Arthur Rank. **Color-88min.** *(British).* Anthony Steel, Robert Beatty ....(3)

OUT OF THE DARKNESS (1958) *see* TEENAGE CAVEMAN

OUT OF THE DARKNESS (1971) *see* BLACK JESUS

OUT OF THE DARKNESS (1978) Dimension Pictures. **Color-83min.** Donald Pleasence, Nancy Kwan 3½*

OUT OF THE DEPTHS (1945) Columbia. **B&W-61min.** Jim Bannon, Robert Williams...(3)

OUT OF THE FOG (1941) Warner Bros. **B&W-93min.** Ida Lupino, John Garfield 4*

OUT OF THE PAST (1947) RKO. **B&W-97min.** Robert Mitchum, Jane Greer, Kirk Douglas..4*
British title: BUILD MY GALLOWS HIGH

OUT OF THIS WORLD (1945) Paramount. **B&W-96min.** Eddie Bracken, Veronica Lake ....(4)

OUT OF THIS WORLD (1954) Carroll Pictures. **Color-75min.** *(Travelog).* *Director:* Lowell Thomas ....(4)

OUT-OF-TOWNERS, THE (1970) Paramount. **Color-98min.** Jack Lemmon, Sandy Dennis 5½*

OUT ON PROBATION (1959) *see* DADDY-O

OUT WEST WITH THE HARDYS (1938) M-G-M. **B&W-90min.** Lewis Stone, Mickey Rooney ....(4)

OUTBACK (1971) United Artists. **Color-109min.** *(Australian).* Gary Bond, Donald Pleasence, Chips Rafferty.................3½*
Original title: WAKE IN FRIGHT

OUTCAST, THE (1951) *see* MAN IN THE SADDLE, THE

OUTCAST, THE (1954) Republic. **B&W-90min.** John Derek, Joan Evans ....(4)
British title: FORTUNE HUNTER, THE

OUTCAST OF THE ISLANDS (1951) United Artists. **B&W-102min.** *(British).* Ralph Richardson, Trevor Howard 5½*

OUTCASTS OF POKER FLAT, THE (1952) 20th Century-Fox. **B&W-81min.** Anne Baxter, Dale Robertson 3*

OUTCASTS OF THE CITY (1958) Republic. **B&W-61min.** Robert Hutton, Ona Massen ....(3)

OUTCRY, THE (1957) *see* GRIDO, IL

OUTER SPACE CONNECTION, THE (1975) Sunn Classic. **Color-94min.** *(Documentary). Director:* Fred Warshofsky 5*

OUTFIT, THE (1973) M-G-M. **Color-102min.** Robert Duvall, Karen Black, Joe Don Baker 4*
Alternate title: GOOD GUYS ALWAYS WIN, THE

OUTLAW, THE (1943) RKO. **B&W-123min.** Walter Huston, Jack Buetel 3*

OUTLAW BLUES (1977) Warner Bros. **Color-100min.** Peter Fonda, Susan Saint James 5½*

OUTLAW JOSEY WALES, THE (1976) Warner Bros. **Color-135min.** Clint Eastwood, Sondra Locke 6½*

OUTLAW OF RED RIVER (1965) NTA Pictures. **Color-76min.** *(Spanish).* George Montgomery, Elisa Montés, José Nieto 3*
Original title: PROSCRITO DEL RIO COLORADO, EL *(The Outlaw of the Colorado River)*

OUTLAW PLANET (1965) *see* PLANET OF THE VAMPIRES

OUTLAW RIDERS (1971) Ace International. **Color-86min.** Bryan "Sonny" West, Rafael Campos, Lindsay Crosby..........(3)

OUTLAW STALLION, THE (1954) Columbia. **Color-64min.** Phil Carey, Dorothy Patrick, Billy Gray.............................(2)
Alternate title: WHITE STALLION, THE

OUTLAW TERRITORY (1953) Realart. **Color-74min.** Macdonald Carey, Joanne Dru 3*
Alternate title: HANNAH LEE

OUTLAW WOMEN (1952) Lippert Productions. **Color-75min.** Marie Windsor, Richard Rober ....(3)

OUTLAW'S DAUGHTER, THE (1954) 20th Century-Fox. **Color-75min.** Bill Williams, Kelly Ryan 3*

As **THE OUTLAW JOSEY WALES** (1976), Clint Eastwood rides off alone to face a tribe of warring Indians, and Sondra Locke wonders whether she'll ever see him again.

OUTLAWS IS COMING, THE (1965) Columbia. **B&W-89min.** Moe Howard, Larry Fine..3*

OUTLAW'S SON (1957) United Artists. **B&W-89min.** Dane Clark, Lori Nelson ....(3)

OUTPOST IN INDO-CHINA (1964) American-International. **B&W-85min.** *(French).* Jacques Harden, Alain Saury............(3)

OUTPOST IN MALAYA (1952) United Artists. **B&W-88min.** *(British).* Claudette Colbert, Jack Hawkins....................(4)
Original title: PLANTER'S WIFE, THE

OUTPOST IN MOROCCO (1949) United Artists. **B&W-92min.** George Raft, Marie Windsor ....(3)

OUTRAGE (1950) RKO. **B&W-75min.** Mala Powers, Tod Andrews 3*

OUTRAGE, THE (1964) M-G-M. **B&W-97min.** Paul Newman, Laurence Harvey..5*

OUTRAGE (1973) Worldvision. **Color-75min.** *(Made for TV).* Robert Culp, Marlyn Mason 4½*

OUTRAGEOUS! (1977) Cinema 5. **Color-100min.** Craig Russell, Hollis McLaren ....(4)

OUTRIDERS, THE (1950) M-G-M. **Color-93min.** Joel McCrea, Arlene Dahl 4*

OUTSIDE IN (1972) Harold Robbins International. **Color-90min.** Darrell Larson, Heather Menzies, John Bill, Dennis Olivieri ....(3)

OUTSIDE MAN, THE (1973) United Artists. **Color-104min.** *(French-U.S., English language).* Jean-Louis Trintignant, Ann-Margret, Roy Scheider, Angie Dickinson 3*
French title: HOMME EST MORT, UN *(A Man Is Dead)*

OUTSIDE THE LAW (1956) Universal. **B&W-81min.** Ray Danton, Leigh Snowden ....(2)

OUTSIDE THE WALL (1950) Universal. **B&W-80min.** Richard Basehart, Marilyn Maxwell 4*

OUTSIDER, THE (1948) Korda. **B&W-97min.** *(British).* Richard Attenborough, Sheila Sim ....(5)
Original title: GUINEA PIG, THE

OUTSIDER, THE (1962) Universal. **B&W-108min.** Tony Curtis, James Franciscus 3*

OUTSIDER, THE (1967) Universal. **Color-100min.** *(Made for TV).* Darren McGavin, Shirley Knight, Edmond O'Brien ....(4)

OUTWARD BOUND (1930) Warner Bros. **B&W-84min.** Leslie Howard, Douglas Fairbanks, Jr..(5)

OVER-EXPOSED (1956) Columbia. **B&W-80min.** Cleo Moore, Richard Crenna ....(2)

OVER MY DEAD BODY (1942) 20th Century-Fox. **B&W-68min.** Milton Berle, Mary Beth Hughes ....(4)

OVER THE EDGE (1979) Warner Bros. (for Orion). **Color-95min.** Michael Kramer, Pam Ludwig...

OVER-THE-HILL GANG, THE (1969) ABC-TV. Color-74min. *(Made for TV)*. Pat O'Brien, Walter Brennan, Edgar Buchanan.............................3½*

OVER-THE-HILL GANG RIDES AGAIN, THE (1970) ABC-TV. Color-74min. *(Made for TV)*. Walter Brennan, Fred Astaire, Edgar Buchanan..4*

OVER THE MOON (1940) United Artists. Color-78min. *(British)*. Rex Harrison, Merle Oberon..(3)

OVER THE WAVES (1942) *see* THIS TIME FOR KEEPS

OVER THERE 1914-1918 (1963) Pathé Contemporary. B&W-90min. *(French, Documentary)*. Director: Jean Aurel...........................(5)
Original title: 14-18

OVER 21 (1945) Columbia. B&W-102min. Irene Dunne, Alexander Knox..4*

OVERCOAT, THE (1960) Times Film Corp. B&W-78min. *(U.S.S.R.)*. Roland Bykov, Yuri Tolubeyev.................................4*
Original title: SHINEL

OVERLAND PACIFIC (1954) United Artists. Color-73min. Jock Mahoney, Peggie Castle..(4)

OVERLANDERS, THE (1946) Universal. B&W-91min. *(Australian)*. Chips Rafferty, John Nugent Hayward.............................4*

OWD BOB (1938) *see* TO THE VICTOR

OWEN MARSHALL: COUNSELOR AT LAW (1971) MCA-TV. Color-100min. *(Made for TV)*. Arthur Hill, Vera Miles, Joseph Campanella, William Shatner..(4)

OWL AND THE PUSSYCAT, THE (1970) Columbia. Color-96min. Barbra Streisand, George Segal.......................................6*

OX-BOW INCIDENT, THE (1943) 20th Century-Fox. B&W-75min. Henry Fonda, Dana Andrews..5½*
British title: STRANGE INCIDENT, THE

-P-

P. J. (1968) Universal. Color-109min. George Peppard, Raymond Burr ..4*
British title: NEW FACE IN HELL

PACE THAT THRILLS, THE (1952) RKO. B&W-63min. Bill Williams, Carla Belenda.......................................(3)

PACIFIC ADVENTURE (1947) Columbia. B&W-95min. *(Australian)*. Ron Randell, Joy Nichols..(5)

PACIFIC BLACKOUT (1942) Paramount. B&W-76min. Robert Preston, Eva Gabor...(3)

PACIFIC CHALLENGE (1975) Concord Films. Color-83min. *(Documentary)*. Director: Robert Amram..(4)

PACIFIC LINER (1939) RKO. B&W-75min. Victor McLaglen, Chester Morris..(4)

PACIFIC VIBRATIONS (1970) American-International. Color-92min. *(Documentary)*. Director: John Severson..............................3*

PACK, THE (1977) Warner Bros. Color-99min. Joe Don Baker, Hope Alexander-Willis..3½*

PACK UP YOUR TROUBLES (1932) M-G-M. B&W-68min. Stan Laurel, Oliver Hardy...(4)

PACK UP YOUR TROUBLES (1939) 20th Century-Fox. B&W-75min. The Ritz Brothers, Jane Withers.....................................(3)
British title: WE'RE IN THE ARMY NOW

PAD (AND HOW TO USE IT), THE (1966) Universal. Color-86min. Brian Bedford, Julie Sommars..(4)

PADDY (1970) Allied Artists. Color-97min. *(Irish)*. Des Cave, Milo O'Shea, Dearbhla Molloy.....................................3*
Alternate title: GOODBYE TO THE HILL

PAGAN LOVE SONG (1950) M-G-M. Color-76min. Howard Keel, Esther Williams...(4)

PAGANS, THE (1952) Allied Artists. B&W-83min. *(Italian)*. Pierre Cressoy, Helene Remy..(3)
Original title: SACCO DI ROMA, IL *(The Sacking of Rome)*
Alternate title: BARBARIANS, THE

PAGE MISS GLORY (1935) Warner Bros. B&W-90min. Dick Powell, Marion Davies..(4)

PAID (1930) M-G-M. B&W-80min. Joan Crawford, Robert Armstrong...(4)
British title: WITHIN THE LAW

PAID IN FULL (1950) Paramount. B&W-105min. Robert Cummings, Lizabeth Scott..(3)

PAID TO KILL (1954) Lippert Productions. B&W-70min. *(British)*. Dane Clark, Cecile Chevreau.......................................(3)
Original title: FIVE DAYS

PAINT YOUR WAGON (1969) Paramount. Color-166min. Lee Marvin, Clint Eastwood..5½*

PAINTED HILLS, THE (1951) M-G-M. Color-65min. Lassie, Paul Kelly..(3)

PAINTED VEIL, THE (1934) M-G-M. B&W-83min. Greta Garbo, Herbert Marshall..(4)

PAINTING THE CLOUDS WITH SUNSHINE (1951) Warner Bros. Color-87min. Dennis Morgan, Virginia Mayo.................................(3)

PAIR OF BRIEFS, A (1962) J. Arthur Rank. B&W-90min. *(British)*. Michael Craig, Mary Peach...(3)

PAISAN (1946) Mayer-Burstyn. B&W-115min. *(Italian)*. Carmela Sazio, Robert Von Loon...3*
Original title: PAISA

PAJAMA GAME, THE (1957) Warner Bros. Color-101min. Doris Day, John Raitt..5*

PAJAMA PARTY (1964) American-International. Color-85min. Tommy Kirk, Annette Funicello, Buster Keaton...............................2*

PAL JOEY (1957) Columbia. Color-111min. Frank Sinatra, Kim Novak..5½*

PALACES OF A QUEEN (1967) Universal. Color-80min. *(British, Documentary)*. Director: Michael Ingrams..............................(4)

PALE ARROW (1957) *see* PAWNEE

PALEFACE, THE (1948) Paramount. Color-91min. Bob Hope, Jane Russell...4*

PALM BEACH STORY, THE (1942) Paramount. B&W-90min. Claudette Colbert, Joel McCrea...5½*

PALM SPRINGS WEEKEND (1963) Warner Bros. Color-100min. Troy Donahue, Connie Stevens..4*

PALMY DAYS (1931) United Artists. B&W-77min. Eddie Cantor, Charlotte Greenwood..(4)

PALOMINO, THE (1950) Columbia. Color-75min. Jerome Courtland, Beverly Tyler..(4)
British title: HILLS OF THE BRAVE

PALOOKA (1934) United Artists. B&W-86min. Jimmy Durante, Stuart Erwin...5*
Alternate title: JOE PALOOKA
British title: GREAT SCHNOZZLE, THE

PAMELA, PAMELA YOU ARE . . . (1969) Distribpix. B&W-90min. Elaine Edwards, Paul Hardy.......................................(2)

PAN-AMERICANA (1945) RKO. B&W-84min. Phillip Terry, Eve Arden, Robert Benchley..(3)

PAN WOLODYJOWSKI (1968) *see* COLONEL WOLODYJOWSKI

PANACHE (1976) Warner Bros. Color-75min. *(Made for TV)*. René Auberjonois, David Healy......................................5½*

PANAMA HATTIE (1942) M-G-M. B&W-79min. Ann Sothern, Dan Dailey, Jr...(4)

PANAMA LADY (1939) RKO. B&W-65min. Lucille Ball, Allen "Rocky" Lane...(3)

PANAMA SAL (1957) Republic. B&W-70min. Elena Verdugo, Ed Kemmer..(2)

PANCHO VILLA RETURNS (1950) Hispano Continental. B&W-95min. *(Mexican, English language)*. Leo Carrillo, Rodolfo Acosta, Esther Fernandez...3*

PANDEMONIUM (1972) *see* DEMONS

PANDORA AND THE FLYING DUTCHMAN (1951) M-G-M. Color-121min. *(British)*. James Mason, Ava Gardner................................5*

PANDORA'S BOX (1928) Moviegraphs. B&W-85min. *(German, Silent)*. Louise Brooks, Fritz Kortner, Francis Lederer..........................(4)
Original title: BUSCHE DER PANDORA, DIE

PANE, AMORE E FANTASIA (1953) *see* BREAD, LOVE AND DREAMS

PANHANDLE (1948) Monopol. B&W-84min. Rod Cameron, Cathy Downs..(5)

PANIC (1946) Tricolore. B&W-83min. *(French)*. Michel Simon, Viviane Romance...(5)
Original title: PANIQUE

PANIC (1965) Screen Gems. B&W-69min. *(British)*. Janine Gray, Glyn Houston...(3)

PANIC BUTTON (1964) Gorton Associates. B&W-90min. Maurice Chevalier, Eleanor Parker, Jayne Mansfield...........................(4)

PANIC IN NEEDLE PARK, THE (1971) 20th Century-Fox. Color-110min. Al Pacino, Kitty Wynn..3*

PANIC IN THE CITY (1968) Commonwealth United. Color-97min. Howard Duff, Nehemiah Persoff, Linda Cristal..........................(3)

PANIC IN THE PARLOR (1957) Distributors Corp. of America. B&W-80min. *(British)*. Peggy Mount, Shirley Eaton.........................(4)
Original title: SAILOR BEWARE!

PANIC IN THE STREETS (1950) 20th Century-Fox. B&W-83min. Richard Widmark, Paul Douglas..5*

Films are rated on a 1 to 10 scale, 10 is highest. **Boldface** ratings followed by an asterisk (*) are for films actually seen and rated by the executive and senior editors. All other ratings are estimates. (See Notes on Entertainment Ratings in the front section.)

PANIC IN YEAR ZERO! (1962) American-International. **B&W-92min.** Ray Milland, Jean Hagen 4½*
Alternate title: END OF THE WORLD, THE
Common title error: PANIC IN THE YEAR ZERO!

PANTALOONS (1956) United Motion Pic. Org. (UMPO). **Color-93min.** *(French-Spanish).* Fernandel, Carmen Sevilla .... (4)
Original title: DON JUAN

PANTHER GIRL OF THE KONGO (1955) *see* CLAW MONSTERS, THE

PANTHER ISLAND (1949) *see* BOMBA ON PANTHER ISLAND

PANTHER'S MOON (1950) *see* SPY HUNT

PAPA, MAMA, THE MAID AND I (1955) Columbia. **B&W-96min.** *(French).* Fernand Ledoux, Gaby Morlay .... (5)
Original title: PAPA, MAMAN, LA BONNE ET MOI

PAPA'S DELICATE CONDITION (1963) Paramount. **Color-98min.** Jackie Gleason, Glynis Johns, Linda Bruhl 5*

PAPER CHASE, THE (1973) 20th Century-Fox. **Color-111min.** Timothy Bottoms, Lindsay Wagner 7*

PAPER LION (1968) United Artists. **Color-105min.** Alan Alda, Lauren Hutton 5½*

PAPER MAN (1971) 20th Century-Fox. **Color-75min.** *(Made for TV).* Dean Stockwell, Stephanie Powers 4½*

PAPER MOON (1973) Paramount. **B&W-101min.** Ryan O'Neal, Tatum O'Neal 6*

PAPER TIGER (1974) Joseph E. Levine. **Color-104min.** *(British).* David Niven, Ando, Toshiro Mifune .... (5)

PAPILLON (1973) Allied Artists. **Color-150min.** Steve McQueen, Dustin Hoffman 6*

PARACHUTE BATALLION (1941) RKO. **B&W-75min.** Robert Preston, Edmond O'Brien .... (4)

PARACHUTE NURSE (1942) Columbia. **B&W-63min.** William Wright, Kay Harris .... (3)

PARADES (1972) Cinerama Releasing. **Color-95min.** Russ Thacker, Brad Sullivan, David Doyle .... (5)
Alternate title: BREAK LOOSE

PARADINE CASE, THE (1947) Selznick Releasing. **B&W-131min.** Gregory Peck, Anne Todd .... (5)

Steve McQueen is **PAPILLON** (1973), unjustly convicted of a murder he didn't commit and sentenced to life in the notorious Devil's Island penal colony along with counterfeiter Dustin Hoffman.

PARADISE ALLEY (1961) Pathé-America. **B&W-81min.** Hugo Haas, Corinne Griffith, Margaret Hamilton .... (3)

PARADISE ALLEY (1978) Universal. **Color-107min.** Sylvester Stallone, Anne Archer, Joe Spinell 6*

PARADISE FOR THREE (1938) M-G-M. **B&W-75min.** Robert Young, Frank Morgan, Mary Astor .... (3)
British title: ROMANCE FOR THREE

PARADISE -- HAWAIIAN STYLE (1966) Paramount. **Color-91min.** Elvis Presley, Suzanna Leigh .... (4)

PARADISE LAGOON (1957) Columbia. **Color-93min.** *(British).* Kenneth More, Diane Cilento .... (5)
Original title: ADMIRABLE CRICHTON, THE

PARADISIO (1962) VIP Distributors. **B&W-82min.** *(British).* Arthur Howard, Eva Waegner .... (2)

PARALLAX VIEW, THE (1974) Paramount. **Color-102min.** Warren Beatty, Paula Prentiss 4*

PARAMOUNT ON PARADE (1930) Paramount. **B&W-102min.** Clive Brook, Warner Oland .... (4)

PARANOIA (1965) *see* KISS THE OTHER SHEIK

PARANOIA (1968) Commonwealth United. **Color-91min.** *(Italian-French, English language).* Carroll Baker, Lou Castel .... (1)
Original title: ORGASMO *(Orgasm)*

PARANOIAC (1963) Universal. **B&W-80min.** *(British).* Janette Scott, Oliver Reed .... (4)

PARASITE MURDERS, THE (1974) *see* THEY CAME FROM WITHIN

PARATROOP COMMAND (1959) American-International. **B&W-83min.** Richard Bakalyan, Ken Lynch 3*

PARATROOPER, THE (1953) Columbia. **Color-87min.** *(British).* Alan Ladd, Susan Stephen .... (3)
Original title: RED BERET, THE

PARDNERS (1956) Paramount. **Color-90min.** Dean Martin, Jerry Lewis, Lori Nelson 4*

PARDON MON AFFAIRE (1977) First Artists. **Color-105min.** *(French).* Jean Rochefort, Anny Duperery 4*
Original title: ÉLÉPHANT CA TROMPE ÉNORMÉMENT, UN *(An Elephant Can Be Extremely Deceptive)*

PARDON MY BLOOPER (1975) K-Tel. **Color-82min.** John Dale, Danny Street 1½*

PARDON MY FRENCH (1951) United Artists. **B&W-81min.** Paul Henreid, Merle Oberon .... (4)
British title: LADY FROM BOSTON, THE

PARDON MY PAST (1945) Columbia. **B&W-88min.** Fred MacMurray.... 4*

PARDON MY RHYTHM (1944) Universal. **B&W-62min.** Gloria Jean, Patric Knowles, Evelyn Ankers .... (3)

PARDON MY SARONG (1942) Universal. **B&W-84min.** Bud Abbott, Lou Costello 4½*

PARDON MY TRUNK (1952) *see* HELLO, ELEPHANT

PARDON US (1931) M-G-M. **B&W-56min.** Stan Laurel, Oliver Hardy ... (4)
British title: GAOL BIRDS

PARENT TRAP, THE (1961) Buena Vista. **Color-124min.** Hayley Mills, Maureen O'Hara, Brian Keith 5*

PARIAHS OF GLORY (1963) ABC Films. **B&W-100min.** *(French-Spanish-Italian).* Curt Jurgens, Maurice Ronet .... (4)
Original French title: PARIAS DE LA GLOIRE, LES
Spanish title: PARIAS DE LA GLORIA
Italian title: DISPERATI DELLA GLORIA, I

PARIS AFTER DARK (1943) 20th Century-Fox. **B&W-85min.** George Sanders, Brenda Marshall .... (3)
British title: NIGHT IS ENDING, THE

PARIS BLUES (1961) United Artists. **B&W-98min.** Paul Newman, Joanne Woodward 3*

PARIS CALLING (1941) Universal. **B&W-95min.** Elizabeth Bergner, Randolph Scott, Basil Rathbone .... (5)

PARIS DOES STRANGE THINGS (1957) Warner Bros. **Color-86min.** *(French, English version).* Ingrid Bergman, Jean Marais .... (3)
Original title: ELÉNA ET LES HOMMES *(Eléna and the Men)*

PARIS EXPRESS, THE (1953) George Schaefer. **Color-83min.** Claude Rains, Marta Toren, Marius Goring .... (4)
Original title: MAN WHO WATCHED TRAINS GO BY, THE

PARIS FOLLIES OF 1956 (1955) *see* FRESH FROM PARIS

PARIS HOLIDAY (1958) United Artists. **Color-100min.** *(U.S.-French).* Bob Hope, Fernandel .... (4)
French title: A PARIS TOUS LES DEUX

PARIS HONEYMOON (1939) Paramount. **B&W-92min.** Bing Crosby, Shirley Ross .... (4)

PARIS IN SPRING (1935) Paramount. B&W-83min. Tullio Carminati, Mary Ellis .... (4)
British title: PARIS LOVE SONG

PARIS IN THE MONTH OF AUGUST (1966) Trans-Lux Distributing. B&W-97min. *(French).* Charles Aznavour, Susan Hampshire .... (4)
Original title: PARIS AU MOIS D'AOUT
British title: PARIS IN AUGUST

PARIS MODEL (1953) Columbia. B&W-81min. Marilyn Maxwell, Paulette Goddard, Eva Gabor, Barbara Lawrence.................................. 3*

PARIS PICK-UP (1962) Paramount. B&W-90min. *(French-Italian).* Robert Hossein, Léa Massari .... (3)
Original French title: MONTE-CHARGE, LE
Italian title: MORTE SALE IN ASCENSORE, LA

PARIS PLAYBOYS (1954) Allied Artists. B&W-62min. The Bowery Boys, Steven Geray .... (3)

PARIS SECRET (1965) Cinema 5. Color-84min. *(Documentary).* Director: Edouard Logereau .... (3)

PARIS UNDERGROUND (1945) United Artists. B&W-97min. Gracie Fields, Constance Bennett .... (4)
British title: MADAME PIMPERNEL

PARIS UNDERGROUND (1954) see GRISBI

PARIS WHEN IT SIZZLES (1964) Paramount. Color-110min. William Holden, Audrey Hepburn 3*

PARISIENNE, LA (1957) United Artists. Color-87min. *(French-Italian).* Brigitte Bardot, Charles Boyer, Henri Vidal .... (4)

PARK AVENUE LOGGER (1937) RKO. B&W-65min. George O'Brien, Beatrice Roberts .... (4)
Alternate title: TALL TIMBER
British title: MILLIONAIRE PLAYBOY

PARK ROW (1952) United Artists. B&W-83min. Gene Evans, Kay Welch.. (4)

PARNELL (1937) M-G-M. B&W-119min. Clark Gable, Myrna Loy .... (3)

PAROLE, INC. (1948) Eagle Lion. B&W-71min. Michael O'Shea, Evelyn Ankers .... (3)

PARRISH (1961) Warner Bros. Color-137min. Claudette Colbert, Troy Donahue .... (4)

PARSON AND THE OUTLAW, THE (1957) Columbia. Color-71min. Anthony Dexter, Marie Windsor.. 2*

PARSON OF PANAMINT, THE (1941) Paramount. B&W-84min. Phillip Terry, Ellen Drew .... (4)

PART-TIME VIRGINS (1970) see INTERPLAY

PART-TIME WIFE (1961) Warner Bros. B&W-70min. *(British).* Anton Rodgers, Nyree Dawn Porter, Kenneth J. Warren .... (3)

PART 2 SOUNDER (1976) Gamma III. Color-98min. Harold Sylvester, Ebony Wright.. 5*

PART 2 WALKING TALL (1975) American-International. Color-109min. Bo Svenson, Luke Askew.. 4½*
British title: LEGEND OF THE LAWMAN

PARTNER, THE (1963) Anglo Amalgamated [EMI]. B&W-58min. *(British).* Yoko Tani, Guy Doleman... (3)

PARTNER (1968) New Yorker Films. Color-105min. *(Italian).* Pierre Clementi, Tina Aumont, Stefania Sandrelli .... (4)

PARTNERS IN CRIME (1961) Anglo Amalgamated [EMI]. B&W-54min. *(British).* Bernard Lee, John Van Eyssen............................... (3)

PARTNERS IN FORTUNE (1945) see ROCKIN' IN THE ROCKIES

PARTY, THE (1968) United Artists. Color-99min. Peter Sellers, J. Edward McKinley .... (4)

PARTY CRASHERS, THE (1958) Paramount. B&W-78min. Connie Stevens, Robert (Bobby) Driscoll, Mark Damon .... (2)

PARTY GIRL (1958) M-G-M. Color-99min. Robert Taylor, Cyd Charisse, Lee J. Cobb 3½*

PARTY GIRLS FOR THE CANDIDATE (1964) Atlantic Pictures. B&W-84min. Mamie Van Doren, June Wilkinson, Ted Knight .... (2)
Original title: CANDIDATE, THE

PARTY'S OVER, THE (1965) Allied Artists. B&W-94min. *(British).* Oliver Reed, Clifford David, Catherine Woodville .... (3)

PASSAGE, THE (1979) United Artists. Color-98min. *(British).* Anthony Quinn, Malcolm McDowell, James Mason, Patricia Neal 4½*

PASSAGE FROM HONG KONG (1941) Warner Bros. B&W-61min. Keye Luke, Keith Douglas .... (3)

PASSAGE TO MARSEILLE (1944) Warner Bros. B&W-110min. Humphrey Bogart, Claude Rains.. 4*

PASSAGE WEST (1951) Paramount. Color-80min. Dennis O'Keefe, John Payne .... (3)
British title: HIGH VENTURE

PASSAGES FROM "FINNEGAN'S WAKE" (1967) Grove Press. B&W-97min. Martin J. Reilly, Jane Reilly................................. (5)
Alternate title: FINNEGAN'S WAKE
Alternate title: PASSAGES FROM JAMES JOYCE'S "FINNEGAN'S WAKE"

PASSENGER, THE (1963) Altura Films. B&W-60min. *(Polish).* Aleksandra Slaska, Anna Ciepielewska .... (5)
Original title: PASAZERKA

PASSENGER, THE (1975) M-G-M. Color-123min. *(Italian-French-Spanish-U.S.).* Jack Nicholson, Maria Schneider 3*
Original Italian title: PROFESSIONE: REPORTER

PASSING STRANGER, THE (1954) Walter Reade. B&W-67min. *(British).* Diane Cilento, Lee Patterson .... (5)

PASSION (1954) RKO. Color-84min. Cornel Wilde, Yvonne De Carlo.... (3)

PASSION OF ANNA, THE (1969) United Artists. Color-100min. *(Swedish).* Liv Ullmann, Max Von Sydow.......................... 1*
Original title: PASSION, EN
Alternate title: PASSION, A

PASSION OF JOAN OF ARC, THE (1928) M. J. Gourland. B&W-85min. *(French, Silent).* (Marie) Falconetti, Eugene Sylvain, André Berley, Michel Simon .... (3)
Original title: PASSION DE JEANNE D'ARC, LA

PASSION OF SLOW FIRE, THE (1961) Trans-Lux Distributing. B&W-91min. *(French).* Jean Desailly, Alexandra Stewart .... (5)
Original title: MORT DE BELLE, LA *(The Death of Belle)*
Alternate title: END OF BELLE, THE

PASSIONATE FRIENDS, THE (1949) see ONE WOMAN'S STORY

PASSIONATE PLUMBER, THE (1932) M-G-M. B&W-73min. Buster Keaton, Jimmy Durante .... (4)

PASSIONATE SENTRY, THE (1952) Fine Arts. B&W-84min. *(British).* Peggy Cummins, Nigel Patrick, Valerie Hobson .... (4)
Original title: WHO GOES THERE!

PASSIONATE STRANGER, THE (1957) see NOVEL AFFAIR, A

PASSIONATE SUMMER (1955) Kingsley International. B&W-97min. *(French-Italian).* Madeleine Robinson, Raf Vallone .... (4)
Original French title: POSSÉDÉES, LES
Italian title: ISOLA DELLE DONNE SOLE, L'

PASSIONATE SUMMER (1958) J. Arthur Rank. Color-104min. *(British).* Virginia McKenna, Bill Travers.............................. (4)
Alternate title: STORM IN JAMAICA

PASSIONATE THIEF, THE (1960) Avco-Embassy. B&W-95min. *(Italian).* Anna Magnani, Toto, Ben Gazzara................................. 4*
Original title: RISATE DI GIOIA

PASSOVER PLOT, THE (1976) Atlas Films. Color-108min. *(U.S.-Israeli).* Zalman King, Harry Andrews 3½*

PASSPORT FOR A CORPSE (1962) Medallion. Color-84min. *(Italian).* Albert Lupin, Linda Christian .... (3)

PASSPORT TO ADVENTURE (1943) see PASSPORT TO DESTINY

PASSPORT TO ALCATRAZ (1940) Columbia. B&W-60min. Jack Holt, Noah Beery, Jr. .... (3)
British title: ALIEN SABOTAGE

PASSPORT TO CHINA (1960) Columbia. Color-75min. *(British).* Richard Basehart, Lisa Gastoni .... (3)
Original title: VISA TO CANTON

PASSPORT TO DESTINY (1943) RKO. B&W-64min. Elsa Lanchester, Gordon Oliver .... (3)
Alternate title: PASSPORT TO ADVENTURE

PASSPORT TO FAME (1935) see WHOLE TOWN'S TALKING, THE

PASSPORT TO HELL (1965) see AGENT 3S3/PASSPORT TO HELL

PASSPORT TO PIMLICO (1948) Eagle Lion. B&W-72min. *(British).* Stanley Holloway, Betty Warren... 4*

PASSPORT TO SHAME (1958) see ROOM 43

PASSPORT TO TREASON (1956) Astor. B&W-80min. *(British).* Rod Cameron, Lois Maxwell... (3)

PASSWORD IS COURAGE, THE (1962) M-G-M. B&W-116min. *(British).* Dirk Bogarde, Maria Perschy.................................... 5*

PASTOR HALL (1940) United Artists. B&W-97min. *(British).* Wilfrid Lawson, Nova Pilbeam, Seymour Hicks................................ (4)

PAT AND MIKE (1952) M-G-M. B&W-94min. Spencer Tracy, Katharine Hepburn.. 4½*

PAT GARRETT AND BILLY THE KID (1973) M-G-M. Color-106min. James Coburn, Kris Kristofferson.................................... 3*

PATCH OF BLUE, A (1965) M-G-M. B&W-105min. Sidney Poitier, Elizabeth Hartman.. 5½*

Films are rated on a 1 to 10 scale, 10 is highest. **Boldface** ratings followed by an asterisk (*) are for films actually seen and rated by the executive and senior editors. All other ratings are estimates. (See Notes on Entertainment Ratings in the front section.)

A PATCH OF BLUE (1965). Blind illiterate Elizabeth Hartman is forced by her inconsiderate mother to string beads to earn money, but Sidney Poitier takes a sympathetic interest in her and tries to help her improve her situation.

PATH OF HOPE, THE (1951) Lux Film America. **B&W-104min.** *(Italian).* Raf Vallone, Elena Varzi........................**3***
Original title: CAMMINO DELLA SPERANZA, IL *(The Road to Hope)*

PATHER PANCHALI (1956) Harrison Pictures. **B&W-112min.** *(Indian).* Kanu Banerji, Karuna Banerji........................**2***
Translation title: Song of the Road

PATHFINDER, THE (1953) Columbia. **Color-78min.** George Montgomery, Helena Carter........................(3)

PATHFINDER AND THE MOHICAN, THE (1956) Independent TV Corp (ITC). **B&W-90min.** *(Telefeature).* Jon Hart, Lon Chaney (Jr.)..............(3)

PATHS OF GLORY (1957) United Artists. **B&W-86min.** Kirk Douglas, George Macready........................**7½***

PATRICK (1978) Monarch. **Color-106min.** *(Australian).* Susan Penhaligon, Robert Helpmann, Robert Thompson........................**4***

PATRIOT, THE (1928) Paramount. **B&W-113min.** *(Part-talking).* Emil Jannings, Florence Vidor........................(5)

PATSY, THE (1964) Paramount. **Color-101min.** Jerry Lewis, Ina Balin..**4***

PATTERN FOR MURDER (1964) Commonwealth United TV. **B&W-80min.** *(German).* George Mather, Julie Reding........................(2)

PATTERN FOR PLUNDER (1963) *see* OPERATION MERMAID

PATTERNS (1956) United Artists. **B&W-83min.** Van Heflin, Everett Sloane........................**5***
British title: PATTERNS OF POWER

PATTON (1970) 20th Century-Fox. **Color-173min.** George C. Scott, Karl Malden........................**7***
British title: PATTON: LUST FOR GLORY
Publicity title: PATTON: SALUTE TO A REBEL
Publicity title: PATTON: A SALUTE TO A REBEL

PAUL AND MICHELLE (1974) Paramount. **Color-103min.** *(French-British).* Sean Bury, Anicée Alvina, Keir Dullea........................(4)

PAULA (1947) *see* FRAMED

PAULA (1952) Columbia. **B&W-80min.** Loretta Young, Kent Smith.....**3½***
British title: SILENT VOICE, THE

PAWNBROKER, THE (1965) Commonwealth United. **B&W-110min.** Rod Steiger, Geraldine Fitzgerald........................**7***

PAWNEE (1957) Republic. **Color-80min.** George Montgomery, Lola Albright........................(3)
British title: PALE ARROW

PAY-OFF, THE (1959) *see* T-BIRD GANG

PAY OR DIE (1960) Allied Artists. **B&W-110min.** Ernest Borgnine, Zohra Lampert........................**4½***

PAY THE DEVIL (1957) *see* MAN IN THE SHADOW

PAYDAY (1973) Cinerama Releasing. **Color-102min.** Rip Torn, Ahna Capri........................**4½***

PAYING THE PENALTY (1927) *see* UNDERWORLD

PAYMENT DEFERRED (1932) M-G-M. **B&W-75min.** Charles Laughton, Maureen O'Sullivan........................(5)

PAYMENT IN BLOOD (1967) Columbia. **Color-90min.** *(Italian).* Edd Byrnes, Guy Madison........................(1)
Original title: 7 WINCHESTER PER UN MASSACRO *(7 Winchesters for a Massacre)*

PAYMENT ON DEMAND (1951) RKO. **B&W-90min.** Bette Davis, Barry Sullivan........................**4***

PAYROLL (1961) Allied Artists. **B&W-94min.** *(British).* Michael Craig, Francoise Prévost........................(3)

PEACE KILLERS, THE (1971) Transvue Pictures. **Color-88min.** Clint Ritchie, Jess Walton, Paul Prokop........................(2)

PEACEMAKER, THE (1956) United Artists. **B&W-82min.** James Mitchell, Rosemarie Bowe........................(4)

PEACH THIEF, THE (1964) Brandon. **B&W-84min.** Nevena Kokanova, Rade Markovic........................(5)
Original title: KRADETSUT NA PRASKOVI

PEARL, THE (1948) RKO. **B&W-77min.** Pedro Armendariz, Maria Elena Marques........................**5½***

PEARL OF DEATH, THE (1944) Universal. **B&W-69min.** Basil Rathbone, Nigel Bruce........................**4***
Alternate title: SHERLOCK HOLMES AND THE PEARL OF DEATH

PEARL OF THE SOUTH PACIFIC (1955) RKO. **Color-86min.** Virginia Mayo, Dennis Morgan........................**3***

PEASANTS OF THE SECOND FORTRESS, THE (1971) The Other Cinema *(British).* **B&W-143min.** *(Japanese, Documentary).* Director: Shinsuke Ogawa........................(5)

PEAU DOUCE, LA (1964) *see* SOFT SKIN, THE

PECK'S BAD BOY (1921) Associated First National. **B&W-51min.** Jackie Coogan, Wheeler Oakman *(Silent).* ....(4)

PECK'S BAD BOY (1934) Fox Film Co. [20th]. **B&W-70min.** Thomas Meighan, Jackie Cooper........................(4)

PECK'S BAD BOY WITH THE CIRCUS (1938) RKO. **B&W-78min.** Tommy Kelly, Billy Gilbert, Edgar Kennedy........................(3)

PEDESTRIAN, THE (1974) Cinerama Releasing. **Color-90min.** *(W. German-Swiss-U.S.).* Gustav Rudolf Sellner, Peter Hall........................**4***
Original title: FUSSGANGER, DER

PEEPER (1975) 20th Century-Fox. **Color-87min.** Michael Caine, Natalie Wood........................**5***
Original title: FAT CHANCE

PEEPING TOM (1960) Astor. **Color-86min.** *(British).* Karl Boehm, Moira Shearer........................(2)

PEGGY (1950) Universal. **Color-77min.** Diana Lynn, Charles Coburn.....**4***

PEKING EXPRESS (1951) Paramount. **B&W-95min.** Joseph Cotten, Corinne Calvet........................(4)

PEKING MEDALLION, THE (1966) *see* CORRUPT ONES, THE

PENALTY, THE (1920) Goldwyn. **B&W-7reels** *(Silent).* Lon Chaney, Claire Adams........................(4)

PENALTY, THE (1941) M-G-M. **B&W-81min.** Edward Arnold, Lionel Barrymore........................(3)

PENDULUM (1969) Columbia. **Color-106min.** George Peppard, Jean Seberg........................**5***

PENELOPE (1966) M-G-M. **Color-97min.** Natalie Wood, Ian Bannen, Peter Falk........................(3)

PENGUIN POOL MURDER, THE (1932) RKO. **B&W-70min.** Edna May Oliver, James Gleason........................(4)
British title: PENGUIN POOL MYSTERY, THE

PENN OF PENNSYLVANIA (1941) *see* COURAGEOUS MR. PENN

PENNIES FROM HEAVEN (1936) Columbia. **B&W-90min.** Bing Crosby, Madge Evans........................**4***

PENNY PRINCESS (1952) Universal. **Color-94min.** *(British).* Yolande Donlan, Dirk Bogarde........................(4)

PENNY SERENADE (1941) Columbia. **B&W-125min.** Irene Dunne, Cary Grant........................**4***

PENNYWHISTLE BLUES (1951) *see* MAGIC GARDEN, THE

PENROD AND HIS TWIN BROTHER (1938) Warner Bros. **B&W-63min.** Bobby Mauch, Billy Mauch, Spring Byington........................(4)

PENROD AND SAM (1937) Warner Bros. **B&W-64min.** Billy Mauch, Spring Byington........................(4)

PENROD'S DOUBLE TROUBLE (1938) Warner Bros. **B&W-61min.** Billy Mauch, Bobby Mauch, Gene Lockhart........................(4)

PENTHOUSE, THE (1967) Paramount. **Color-100min.** *(British).* Suzy Kendall, Terence Morgan........................(3)

Films are rated on a 1 to 10 scale, 10 is highest. **Boldface** ratings followed by an asterisk (*) are for films actually seen and rated by the executive and senior editors. All other ratings are estimates. (See Notes on Entertainment Ratings in the front section.)

PEOPLE, THE (1971) MPC (TV). **Color-74min.** *(Made for TV).* Kim Darby, Dan O'Herlihy, William Shatner ....(4)

PEOPLE AGAINST O'HARA, THE (1951) M-G-M. **B&W-102min.** Spencer Tracy, Pat O'Brien **4***

PEOPLE ARE FUNNY (1946) Paramount. **B&W-93min.** Jack Haley, Ozzie Nelson, Rudy Vallee, Art Linkletter ....(3)

PEOPLE MEET AND SWEET MUSIC FILLS THE HEART (1967) Trans-Lux Distributing. **B&W-94min.** *(Danish-Swedish).* Harriet Andersson, Preben Neergaard...............(3)
Original Danish title: MENNESKER MODES OG SOD MUSIK OPSTAR I HJERTET
Swedish title: MANNISKOR MOTS OCH LJUV MUSIK UPPSTAR I HJARTAT

PEOPLE NEXT DOOR, THE (1970) Avco-Embassy. **Color-93min.** Eli Wallach, Julie Harris...............(4)

PEOPLE OF THE WIND (1975) Carolyn Films. **Color-127min.** *(Documentary). Director:* Anthony Howard 5½*
Original title: BAKHTIARI MIGRATION, THE

PEOPLE THAT TIME FORGOT, THE (1977) American-International. **Color-90min.** *(U.S.-British).* Patrick Wayne, Sarah Douglas ....(3)

PEOPLE VS. DR. KILDARE, THE (1941) M-G-M. **B&W-78min.** Lew Ayres, Lionel Barrymore ....(3)
British title: MY LIFE IS YOURS

PEOPLE WILL TALK (1935) Paramount. **B&W-67min.** Mary Boland, Charles Ruggles...............(4)

PEOPLE WILL TALK (1951) 20th Century-Fox. **B&W-110min.** Cary Grant, Jeanne Crain **4***

PEOPLETOYS (1974) Cinemation. **Color-90min.** Gene Evans, Sorrell Booke ....(4)
Alternate title: PEOPLE TOYS
Alternate title: HORRIBLE HOUSE ON THE HILL, THE

PEPE (1960) Columbia. **Color-195min.** Cantinflas, Dan Dailey.................**4***

PEPE LE MOKO (1936) Paris Film. **B&W-90min.** *(French).* Jean Gabin, Mirielle Balin.................**2***

PEPOTE (1956) United Motion Pic. Org. (UMPO). **B&W-88min.** *(Spanish-Italian).* Pablito Calvo, Antonio Vico ....(5)

PERCY (1971) M-G-M. **Color-100min.** *(British).* Hywel Bennett, Elke Sommer ....(2)

PERCY'S PROGRESS (1974) *see* IT'S NOT THE SIZE THAT COUNTS!

PERFECT ALIBI, THE (1929) *see* ALIBI

PERFECT COUPLE, A (1979) 20th Century-Fox. **Color-110min.** Tom Dooley, Marta Heflin.................**5***

PERFECT CRIME, THE (1941) *see* ELLERY QUEEN AND THE PERFECT CRIME

PERFECT FRIDAY (1970) Chevron. **Color-94min.** *(British).* Ursula Andress, Stanley Baker 5½*

PERFECT FURLOUGH, THE (1959) Universal. **Color-93min.** Tony Curtis, Janet Leigh **4½***
British title: STRICTLY FOR PLEASURE

PERFECT MARRIAGE, THE (1947) Paramount. **B&W-87min.** Loretta Young, David Niven ....(3)

PERFECT SPECIMEN, THE (1937) First National [W.B.]. **B&W-97min.** Errol Flynn, Joan Blondell...............(5)

PERFECT STRANGERS (1945) *see* VACATION FROM MARRIAGE

PERFECT STRANGERS (1950) Warner Bros. **B&W-88min.** Ginger Rogers, Dennis Morgan ....(4)
British title: TOO DANGEROUS TO LOVE

PERFECT WEEKEND, A (1934) *see* ST. LOUIS KID

PERFECT WOMAN, THE (1949) Eagle Lion. **B&W-87min.** *(British).* Stanley Holloway, Patricia Roc...............(4)

PERFORMANCE (1970) Warner Bros. **Color-106min.** *(British).* Mick Jagger, James Fox 1*

PERIL FROM THE PLANET MONGO (1940) Universal. **B&W-91min.** *(Re-edited Serial).* Larry "Buster" Crabbe, Carol Hughes ....(3)

PERILOUS HOLIDAY (1946) Columbia. **B&W-89min.** Pat O'Brien, Ruth Warrick...............(5)

PERILOUS JOURNEY, A (1953) Republic. **B&W-90min.** Vera Ralston, David Brian, Scott Brady...............(3)

PERILOUS VOYAGE (1969) MCA-TV. **Color-97min.** *(Made for TV).* Michael Parks, William Shatner...............(4)

PERILS OF NYOKA (1942) *see* NYOKA AND THE LOST SECRETS OF HIPPOCRATES

PERILS OF PAULINE (1947) Paramount. **Color-90min.** Betty Hutton, John Lund 5*

PERILS OF PAULINE, THE (1967) Universal. **Color-107min.** Pamela Austin, Pat Boone, Terry-Thomas.................**3***

PERILS OF THE DARKEST JUNGLE (1944) *see* JUNGLE GOLD

PERIOD OF ADJUSTMENT (1962) M-G-M. **B&W-112min.** Tony Franciosa, Jane Fonda **5***

PERMISSION TO KILL (1975) Avco-Embassy. **Color-93min.** *(U.S.-Austrian).* Dirk Bogarde, Ava Gardner, Bekim Fehmiu...............(4)

PERRI (1957) Buena Vista. **Color-74min.** Winston Hibler...............(6)

PERRO, EL (1977) **Color-155min.** *(Spanish).* Jason Miller, Lea Massari ....
Translation title: The Dog

PERRY RHODAN (1968) *see* MISSION STARDUST

PERSECUTION (1974) *see* TERROR OF SHEBA, THE

PERSECUTION AND ASSASSINATION OF JEAN-PAUL MARAT . . . (1967) *see* MARAT/SADE

PERSEUS AGAINST THE MONSTERS (1963) *see* MEDUSA AGAINST THE SON OF HERCULES

PERSONA (1966) Lopert [U.A.]. **B&W-81min.** *(Swedish).* Bibi Andersson, Liv Ullmann **2***

PERSONAL AFFAIR (1953) United Artists. **B&W-83min.** *(British).* Gene Tierney, Leo Genn...............(4)

PERSONAL COLUMN (1947) *see* LURED

PERSONAL MAID (1931) Paramount. **B&W-77min.** Nancy Carroll, Gene Raymond...............(4)

PERSONAL PROPERTY (1937) M-G-M. **B&W-84min.** Jean Harlow, Robert Taylor.................**4½***
British title: MAN IN POSSESSION, THE

PERSONALITY KID (1946) Columbia. **B&W-68min.** Anita Louise, Michael Duane...............(3)

PERSONS UNKNOWN (1958) *see* BIG DEAL ON MADONNA STREET, THE

PERSUADER, THE (1957) Allied Artists. **B&W-72min.** William Talman, James Craig ....(3)

PETE KELLY'S BLUES (1955) Warner Bros. **Color-95min.** Jack Webb, Janet Leigh **4½***

PETE 'N' TILLIE (1972) Universal. **Color-100min.** Walter Matthau, Carol Burnett **6***

PETE SEEGER . . . A SONG AND A STONE (1972) Theatre Exchange Activities. **Color-85min.** *(Documentary). Director:* Robert Elfstrom .....(5)

PETER IBBETSON (1935) Paramount. **B&W-88min.** Gary Cooper, Ann Harding ....(4)

PETER PAN (1953) RKO (for Disney). **Color-77min.** *(Cartoon). Director:* Hamilton Luske.................**6***

PETER RABBIT AND TALES OF BEATRIX POTTER (1971) M-G-M. **Color-90min.** *(British).* Frederick Ashton, Alexander Grant...............(4)
Original title: TALES OF BEATRIX POTTER

PETERSEN (1974) *see* "JOCK" PETERSEN

PETE'S DRAGON (1977) Buena Vista. **Color-134min.** Helen Reddy, Shelley Winters, Mickey Rooney.................**4***

PETEY WHEATSTRAW (1978) Transvue Pictures Corp. **Color-93min.** Rudy Ray Moore, Jimmy Lynch...............

PETIT SOLDAT, LE (1963) West End Films. **B&W-88min.** *(French).* Michel Subor, Anna Karina ....(4)
Translation title: The Little Soldier

PETIT THEATRE DE JEAN RENOIR, LE (1969) *see* LITTLE THEATRE OF JEAN RENOIR, THE

PETRIFIED FOREST, THE (1936) Warner Bros. **B&W-83min.** Leslie Howard, Bette Davis, Humphrey Bogart.................**5***

PETS (1973) IPC. **Color-103min.** Candy Rialson, Ed Bishop, Joan Blackman **2***
British title: SUBMISSION

PETTICOAT FEVER (1936) M-G-M. **B&W-81min.** Robert Montgomery, Myrna Loy ....(4)

PETTY GIRL, THE (1950) Columbia. **B&W-87min.** Robert Cummings, Joan Caulfield **4½***
British title: GIRL OF THE YEAR

PETULIA (1968) Warner Bros. **Color-105min.** *(U.S.-British).* Julie Christie, George C. Scott.................**3***

PEYTON PLACE (1957) 20th Century-Fox. **Color-162min.** Lana Turner, Diane Varsi, Lee Phillips 5½*

PHAEDRA (1962) Lopert [U.A.]. **B&W-115min.** *(Greek-U.S.-French, English language).* Melina Mercouri, Anthony Perkins...............4*

PHANTASM (1979) Avco-Embassy. **Color-90min.** Michael Baldwin, Bill Thornbury.................3½*

Films are rated on a 1 to 10 scale, 10 is highest. **Boldface** ratings followed by an asterisk (*) are for films actually seen and rated by the executive and senior editors. All other ratings are estimates. (See Notes on Entertainment Ratings in the front section.)

PETER PAN (1953). Michael (with teddy bear), John and their older sister Wendy find it's easy to fly with a bit of "pixie dust" from impish fairy Tinker Bell (lower right) as they follow Peter to Never-Never-Land.

PHANTOM BARON, THE (1943) Raymond Rohauer. **B&W-100min.** *(French).* Jean Cocteau, Alain Cuny ....
Original title: BARON FANTOME, LE

PHANTOM FROM SPACE (1953) United Artists. **B&W-72min.** Noreen Nash, James Seay... (3)

PHANTOM HORSE, THE (1956) Harrison Pictures. **Color-90min.** *(Japanese).* Yukhiro Iwatare, Ayako Wakao .... (4)

PHANTOM INDIA (1969) New Yorker Films. **Color-360min.** *(French, Documentary). Director:* Louis Malle .... (5)

PHANTOM LADY (1944) Universal. **B&W-87min.** Ella Raines, Franchot Tone **4***

PHANTOM LOVERS (1960) *see* GHOSTS OF ROME

PHANTOM OF CRESTWOOD, THE (1932) M-G-M. **B&W-77min.** Ricardo Cortez, Anita Louise .... (4)

PHANTOM OF HOLLYWOOD, THE (1974) M-G-M. **Color-74min.** *(Made for TV).* Jack Cassidy, Skye Aubrey, Peter Lawford **4***

PHANTOM OF LIBERTÉ, THE (1974) 20th Century-Fox. **Color-104min.** *(French).* Jean-Claude Brialy, Monica Vitti................ **3***
Original title: FANTOME DE LA LIBERTÉ, LE

PHANTOM OF PARIS (1942) *see* MYSTERY OF MARIE ROGET, THE

PHANTOM OF SOHO, THE (1963) Producers Releasing Org. **B&W-92min.** *(German).* Dieter Borsche, Barbara Rutting............... (2)
Original title: PHANTOM VON SOHO, DAS

PHANTOM OF THE OPERA, THE (1925) Universal. **B&W-94min.** *(Silent).* Lon Chaney, Mary Philbin.......................... **4½***

PHANTOM OF THE OPERA, THE (1943) Universal. **Color-92min.** Claude Rains, Susanna Foster, Nelson Eddy **5***

PHANTOM OF THE OPERA, THE (1962) Universal. **Color-84min.** *(British).* Herbert Lom, Heather Sears................................. **4***

PHANTOM OF THE PARADISE (1974) 20th Century-Fox. **Color-91min.** Paul Williams, William Finley **5***

PHANTOM OF THE RUE MORGUE (1954) Warner Bros. **Color-84min.** Claude Dauphin, Karl Malden............................... **4***

PHANTOM PLANET, THE (1962) American-International. **B&W-82min.** Dean Fredericks, Coleen Gray **2***

PHANTOM PRESIDENT, THE (1932) Paramount. **B&W-80min.** George M. Cohan **4½***

PHANTOM RAIDERS (1940) M-G-M. **B&W-70min.** Walter Pidgeon, Joseph Schildkraut .... (3)

PHANTOM STAGECOACH, THE (1957) Columbia. **B&W-69min.** William Bishop, Kathleen Crowley................................... (3)

PHANTOM SUBMARINE, THE (1940) Columbia. **B&W-71min.** Anita Louise, Bruce Bennett .... (3)

PHANTOM THIEF, THE (1946) Columbia. **B&W-65min.** Chester Morris, Jeff Donnell... (3)

PHANTOM TOLLBOOTH, THE (1970) M-G-M. **Color-90min.** *(Cartoon). Director:* Chuck Jones................................. **5***

PHARAOH'S CURSE, THE (1957) United Artists. **B&W-66min.** Mark Dana, Ziva Rodann .... (3)

PHARAOH'S WOMAN, THE (1960) Universal. **Color-88min.** *(Italian).* John Drew Barrymore, Linda Cristal..................... (3)
Original title: DONNA DEI FARAOINI, LA

PHASE IV (1973) Paramount. **Color-84min.** *(British).* Nigel Davenport, Lynne Frederick **3***

Films are rated on a 1 to 10 scale, 10 is highest. **Boldface** ratings followed by an asterisk (*) are for films actually seen and rated by the executive and senior editors. All other ratings are estimates. (See Notes on Entertainment Ratings in the front section.)

PHENIX CITY STORY, THE (1955) Allied Artists. **B&W-100min.** John McIntire, Richard Kiley 4*
Common title error: PHOENIX CITY STORY, THE

PHFFFT (1954) Columbia. **B&W-91min.** Judy Holliday, Jack Lemmon.... 4*

PHILADELPHIA STORY, THE (1940) M-G-M. **B&W-112min.** Cary Grant, Katharine Hepburn 6*

PHILIP (1969) *see* RUN WILD, RUN FREE

PHILO VANCE RETURNS (1947) Producers Rel. Corp. [Eagle Lion]. **B&W-64min.** William Wright, Terry Austin .... (4)

PHILO VANCE'S GAMBLE (1947) Producers Rel. Corp. [Eagle Lion]. **B&W-62min.** Alan Curtis, Terry Austin .... (4)

PHILO VANCE'S SECRET MISSION (1947) Producers Rel. Corp. [Eagle Lion]. **B&W-58min.** Alan Curtis, Sheila Ryan .... (4)

PHILOSOPHY OF THE BEDROOM (1971) *see* BEYOND LOVE AND EVIL

PHOENIX CITY STORY, THE (1955) *see* PHENIX CITY STORY, THE

PHONE CALL FROM A STRANGER (1952) 20th Century-Fox. **B&W-96min.** Shelley Winters, Gary Merrill 5*

PHONE RINGS EVERY NIGHT, THE (1962) Emery Pictures. **B&W-82min.** *(German).* Elke Sommer .... (3)
Original title: NACHTS GING DAS TELEFON
Alternate title: ADVENTURE IN CAPRI

PHONY AMERICAN, THE (1962) Signal International. **B&W-72min.** *(German).* Christine Kaufmann, Michael Hinz........................ (4)
Original title: TOLLER HECHT AUF KRUMMER TOUR
British title: IT'S A GREAT LIFE

PHOTO FINISH (1957) **B&W-110min.** *(French).* Fernand Gravet, Jean Richard .... (3)

PICASSO SUMMER, THE (1969) Warner Bros. **Color-96min.** Albert Finney, Yvette Mimieux .... (3)

PICCADILLY INCIDENT (1946) M-G-M. **B&W-88min.** *(British).* Anna Neagle, Michael Wilding .... (5)
Alternate title: THEY MET AT MIDNIGHT

PICCADILLY JIM (1936) M-G-M. **B&W-100min.** Robert Montgomery, Madge Evans........................ 4*

PICK A STAR (1937) M-G-M. **B&W-70min.** Patsy Kelly, Jack Haley...... (4)

PICKPOCKET (1959) New Yorker Films. **B&W-75min.** *(French).* Martin La Salle, Marika Green 4*

PICKUP (1951) Columbia. **B&W-78min.** Beverly Michaels, Hugo Haas ..(4)

PICKUP ALLEY (1957) Columbia. **B&W-92min.** *(British).* Victor Mature, Anita Ekberg, Trevor Howard .... (3)
Original title: INTERPOL

PICKUP IN ROME (1960) *see* FROM A ROMAN BALCONY

PICKUP ON 101 (1972) American-International. **Color-93min.** Jack Albertson, Lesley (Ann) Warren, Martin Sheen 4*
British title: ECHOS OF THE ROAD

PICKUP ON SOUTH STREET (1953) 20th Century-Fox. **B&W-80min.** Richard Widmark, Jean Peters 4*

PICKWICK PAPERS (1952) Mayer-Kingsley. **B&W-115min.** *(British).* James Hayter, James Donald 4*

PICNIC (1956) Columbia. **Color-113min.** William Holden, Kim Novak.... 5*

PICNIC ON THE GRASS (1959) Kingsley-Union. **Color-91min.** *(French).* Paul Meurisse, Catherine Rouvel........................ (4)
Original title: DEJEUNER SUR L'HERBE, LE

PICTURA -- ADVENTURE IN ART (1951) Pictura Films. **B&W-82min.** *(U.S.-French-Italian, Documentary).* Director: Luciano Emmer .... (5)

PICTURE MOMMY DEAD (1966) Avco-Embassy. **Color-88min.** Don Ameche, Martha Hyer, Susan Gordon........................ (3)

PICTURE OF DORIAN GRAY, THE (1945) M-G-M. **B&W-110min.** Hurd Hatfield, George Sanders 5½*

PIECE OF PLEASURE, A (1975) Joseph Green. **Color-100min.** *(French).* Paul Gegauff, Danielle Gegauff .... (4)
Original title: PARTIE DI PLAISIR, UNE
Alternate title: PLEASURE PARTY

PIECE OF THE ACTION, A (1977) Warner Bros. **Color-134min.** Sidney Poitier, Bill Cosby, James Earl Jones 5*

PIECES OF DREAMS (1970) United Artists. **Color-100min.** Robert Forster, Lauren Hutton .... (4)

PIED PIPER, THE (1942) 20th Century-Fox. **B&W-87min.** Monty Woolley, Roddy McDowall 5*

PIED PIPER, THE (1972) Paramount. **Color-90min.** *(British-W. German).* Donovan, Donald Pleasence........................ 3*

PIED PIPER OF HAMELIN, THE (1957) NTA Pictures. **Color-87min.** Van Johnson, Claude Rains .... (4)

PIER 5 - HAVANA (1959) United Artists. **B&W-67min.** Cameron Mitchell, Allison Hayes........................ (2)

PIER 13 (1932) *see* ME AND MY GAL

PIER 13 (1940) 20th Century-Fox. **B&W-66min.** Lynn Bari, Lloyd Nolan........................ (3)

PIER 23 (1951) Lippert Productions. **B&W-58min.** Hugh Beaumont, Ann Savage........................ (2)

PIERRE OF THE PLAINS (1942) M-G-M. **B&W-66min.** John Carroll, Ruth Hussey........................ (3)

PIERROT LE FOU (1965) Pathé Contemporary. **Color-110min.** *(French-Italian).* Jean-Paul Belmondo, Anna Karina........................ 3*
Italian title: BADITO DELL 11, IL
Translation title: Pierre the Crazy *or* Crazy Pete

PIGEON, THE (1969) ABC Films. **Color-74min.** *(Made for TV).* Sammy Davis, Jr., Dorothy Malone, Ricardo Montalban .... (3)

PIGEON THAT TOOK ROME, THE (1962) Paramount. **B&W-101min.** Charlton Heston, Elsa Martinelli 4½*

PIGEONS (1971) Plaza Pictures. **Color-87min.** Christopher Jordan, Jill O'Hara........................ (4)
Original title: SIDELONG GLANCES OF A PIGEON KICKER

PIGPEN (1969) New Line Cinema. **Color-93min.** *(Italian-French).* Jean-Pierre Léaud, Pierre Clementi, Ugo Tognazzi .... (4)
Original Italian title: PORCILLE

PIGSKIN PARADE (1936) 20th Century-Fox. **B&W-93min.** Stuart Erwin, Patsy Kelly .... (5)
British title: HARMONY PARADE, THE

PILGRIM, THE (1923) First National [W.B.]. **B&W-45min.** *(Silent).* Charles Chaplin, Edna Purviance, Mack Swain 4½*

PILGRIMAGE (1933) Fox Film Co. [20th]. **B&W-90min.** Henrietta Cranston, Heather Angel 3*

PILLAR OF FIRE, THE (1963) Hoffberg. **B&W-75min.** *(Israeli).* Michael Shillo, Lawrence Montaigne .... (5)

PILLARS OF THE SKY (1956) Universal. **Color-95min.** Jeff Chandler, Dorothy Malone 3*
British title: TOMAHAWK AND THE CROSS, THE

PILLOW OF DEATH (1945) Universal. **B&W-55min.** Lon Chaney (Jr.), Brenda Joyce .... (3)

PILLOW TALK (1959) Universal. **Color-110min.** Rock Hudson, Doris Day 7½*

PILLOW TO POST (1945) United Artists. **B&W-92min.** Ida Lupino, William Prince, Sydney Greenstreet........................ (3)

PILOT NO. 5 (1943) M-G-M. **B&W-70min.** Franchot Tone, Marsha Hunt, Gene Kelly .... (3)

PIMPERNEL SMITH (1941) Anglo-American. **B&W-118min.** *(British).* Leslie Howard, Francis Sullivan........................ 5½*
Alternate title: MISTER V

PIN-UP GIRL (1944) 20th Century-Fox. **Color-83min.** Betty Grable, Martha Raye, Joe E. Brown .... (4)

PINK ANGELS, THE (1971) Crown International. **Color-81min.** John Alderman, Tom Basham .... (3)

PINK FLAMINGOS (1972) Saliva Films. **Color-95min.** Divine, David Lochary, Mink Stole........................ 1*

PINK JUNGLE, THE (1968) Universal. **Color-104min.** James Garner, Eva Renzi, George Kennedy .... (4)

PINK PANTHER, THE (1964) United Artists. **Color-113min.** Peter Sellers, David Niven 5½*

PINK PANTHER STRIKES AGAIN, THE (1976) United Artists. **Color-103min.** *(British).* Peter Sellers, Herbert Lom........................ 4½*

PINK STRING AND SEALING WAX (1946) Eagle Lion. **B&W-95min.** *(British).* Mervyn Johns, Googie Withers .... (4)

PINKY (1949) 20th Century-Fox. **B&W-102min.** Jeanne Crain, Ethel Barrymore 5*

PINOCCHIO (1940) RKO (for Disney). **Color-87min.** *(Cartoon). Director:* Ben Sharpsteen 6½*

PINOCCHIO (1976) CBS-TV. **Color-76min.** *(Made for TV).* Sandy Duncan, Danny Kaye........................

PIONEER WOMAN, THE (1973) Worldvision. **Color-74min.** *(Made for TV).* Joanna Pettet, William Shatner, David Janssen........................ (4)

PIPE DREAMS (1976) Avco-Embassy. **Color-87min.** Gladys Knight, Barry Hankerson 3½*

PIPPI IN THE SOUTH SEAS (1970) G. G. Communications. **Color-85min.** *(Swedish-W. German).* Inger Nilsson, Maria Persson .... (3)
Original Swedish title: PIPPI LANGSTRUMP PA DE SJU HAÉN

PINOCCHIO (1940). Brought to life by the Blue Fairy, wooden puppet Pinocchio meets Jiminy Cricket, who's to be his conscience until Pinocchio can become a real boy.

PIPPI LONGSTOCKING (1969) G. G. Communications. **Color-99min.** *(Swedish-German).* Inger Nilsson, Par Sundberg, Maria Persson .... (3)
Original Swedish title: PIPPI LANGSTRUMP

PIRANHA (1978) New World. **Color-92min.** Bradford Dillman, Heather Menzies, Kevin McCarthy **4***

PIRANHA (1972) Gold Key Entertainment. **Color-96min.** *(Made for TV).* Peter Brown, William Smith, Anha Capri **2***
Publicity title: PIRANHA, PIRANHA

PIRATE, THE (1948) M-G-M. **Color-102min.** Judy Garland, Gene Kelly.. **5***

PIRATE AND THE SLAVE GIRL (1959) Crest. **Color-87min.** *(Italian-French).* Lex Barker, Chelo Alonso......................... (3)
Original Italian title: SCIMITARRA DEL SARACENO, LA *(The Saracen Scimitar)*
Original French title: VENGEANCE DU SARRASIN, LA *(The Revenge of the Saracen)*

PIRATE OF THE BLACK HAWK (1958) Filmgroup. **Color-75min.** *(Italian-French).* Mijanou Bardot, Gérard Landry .... (2)
Original Italian title: PIRATA DELLO SPARVIERO NERO, IL
Original French title: PIRATE DE L'EPERVIER NOIR, LE

PIRATE SHIP (1949) *see* MUTINEERS, THE

PIRATE'S FIANCEÉ, THE (1969) *see* VERY CURIOUS GIRL, A

PIRATES OF BLOOD RIVER, THE (1962) Columbia. **Color-84min.** *(British).* Kerwin Mathews, Glenn Corbett .... (3)

PIRATES OF CAPRI, THE (1949) Four Continents. **B&W-94min.** Louis Hayward, Binnie Barnes .... (4)
Alternate title: CAPTAIN SIROCCO
British title: MASKED PIRATE, THE

PIRATES OF MONTEREY (1947) Universal. **Color-77min.** Maria Montez, Rod Cameron, Gilbert Roland **4***

PIRATES OF THE COAST (1960) Warner Bros. **Color-102min.** *(Italian-French).* Lex Barker, Estella Blain ..... (3)
Original Italian title: PIRATI DELLA COSTA, I

PIRATES OF THE MISSISSIPPI, THE (1963) Rapidfilm. **Color-100min.** *(W. German-Italian-French).* Hanjorg Felmy, Horst Frank .... (3)
Original German title: FLUSSPIRATEN VOM MISSISSIPPI, DIE

PIRATES OF TORTUGA (1961) 20th Century-Fox. **Color-97min.** Ken Scott, Leticia Roman **4***

PIRATES OF TRIPOLI (1955) Columbia. **Color-72min.** Paul Henreid, Patricia Medina .... (3)

PIRATE'S REVENGE (1951) *see* REVENGE OF THE PIRATES

PISTOL FOR RINGO, A (1965) Avco-Embassy. **Color-97min.** *(Italian-Spanish).* Montgomery Wood (Giuliano Gemma), Fernando Sancho, Hally Hammond (Lorella De Luca) .... (3)
Original Italian title: PISTOLA PER RINGO, UNA
Spanish title: PISTOLA PARA RINGO, UNA

PISTOLERO OF RED RIVER, THE (1967) *see* LAST CHALLENGE, THE

PIT AND THE PENDULUM, THE (1961) American-International. **Color-85min.** Vincent Price, Barbara Steele..................... **5***

PIT OF LONELINESS (1951) Arthur Davis Associates. **B&W-84min.** *(French).* Edwige Feuillere, Simone Simon, Claire Olivia .... (4)
Original title: OLIVIA
Alternate title: STRANGE CONDUCT

PIT STOP (1969) Distributors International. **B&W-92min.** Brian Donlevy, Richard Davalos, Ellen McRae.......................... (2)

PITFALL, THE (1948) United Artists. **B&W-84min.** Dick Powell, Lizabeth Scott **4***

PITTSBURGH (1942) Universal. **B&W-98min.** Marlene Dietrich, John Wayne............................. **4***

PIZZA TRIANGLE, THE (1970) Warner Bros. **Color-95min.** *(Italian-Spanish).* Marcello Mastroianni, Monica Vitti, Giancarlo Giannini ..... (4)
Original Italian title: DRAMMA DELLA GELOSIA -- TUTTI I PARTICOLARI IN CRONACA
Alternate title: DRAMA OF JEALOUSY AND OTHER THINGS, A
TV title: JEALOUSY ITALIAN STYLE

PLACE CALLED GLORY, A (1965) Avco-Embassy. **Color-92min.** *(Spanish-W. German).* Les Barker, Pierre Brice, Marianne Koch........................ (3)
Original Spanish title: LUGAR LLAMADO "GLORY," UN
German title: HOLLE VON MANITOBA, DIE

PLACE CALLED TODAY, A (1972) Avco-Embassy. **Color-104min.** J. Herbert Kerr, Jr., Lana Wood, Cheri Caffaro .... (2)

PLACE FOR LOVERS, A (1968) M-G-M. **Color-88min.** *(Italian-French, English language).* Faye Dunaway, Marcello Mastroianni .... (2)
Original Italian title: AMANTI *(Lovers)*
French title: TEMPS DES AMANTS, LE *(The Time of Lovers)*

PLACE IN THE SUN, A (1951) Paramount. **B&W-122min.** Montgomery Clift, Elizabeth Taylor, Shelley Winters **5***

PLACE OF ONE'S OWN, A (1945) Eagle Lion. **B&W-92min.** *(British).* Margaret Lockwood, James Mason .... (4)

PLACE TO GO, A (1964) Walter Reade. **B&W-87min.** *(British).* Rita Tushingham, Mike Sarne .... (3)

PLAGUE OF THE ZOMBIES, THE (1966) 20th Century-Fox. **Color-91min.** *(British).* André Morell, Diane Clare, John Carson .... (3)

PLAINS OF BATTLE (1970) MCA-TV. **Color-96min.** *(Italian).* W. Medor, Lorella De Luca **3***

PLAINSMAN, THE (1936) Paramount. **B&W-113min.** Gary Cooper, Jean Arthur............................. **4½***

PLAINSMAN, THE (1966) Universal. **Color-92min.** Don Murray, Guy Stockwell, Abby Dalton .... (3)

PLAINSMAN AND THE LADY, THE (1946) Republic. **B&W-87min.** William Elliott, Vera Ralston..................... (3)

PLAISIR, LE (1952) Kingsley International. **B&W-96min.** *(French).* Claude Dauphin, Gaby Morlay..................... (5)

PLAN 9 FROM OUTER SPACE (1956) Distributors Corp. of America. **B&W-79min.** Bela Lugosi, Lyle Talbot, Tor Johnson **1***
Alternate title: GRAVE ROBBERS FROM OUTER SPACE

PLANET EARTH (1974) Warner Bros. **Color-75min.** *(Made for TV).* John Saxon, Diana Muldaur, Janet Margolin..................... **3***

PLANET OF BLOOD (1955) *see* QUEEN OF BLOOD

PLANET OF THE APES (1968) 20th Century-Fox. **Color-112min.** Charlton Heston, Roddy McDowell..................... **7½***

PLANET OF THE VAMPIRES (1965) American-International. **Color-86min.** *(Italian-Spanish-U.S.).* Barry Sullivan, Norma Bengell............. **2***
Original Italian title: TERRORE NELLO SPAZIO *(Terror from Space)*
Spanish title: TERROR EN EL ESPACIO
Alternate title: PLANET OF TERROR
Alternate title: DEMON PLANET, THE
Alternate title: OUTLAW PLANET
Alternate title: HAUNTED PLANET

PLANET ON THE PROWL (1965) *see* WAR BETWEEN THE PLANETS

PLANETS AGAINST US (1961) Teleworld. **B&W-83min.** *(Italian-French).* Michel Lemoine, Maria Pia Luzi..................... (2)
Original Italian title: PIANETI CONTRO DI NOI, I
French title: MONSTRE AUX YEUX VERT, LE *(The Monster with Green Eyes)*
British title: HANDS OF A KILLER
Publicity title: MAN WITH THE YELLOW EYES

PLANTER'S WIFE, THE (1952) *see* OUTPOST IN MALAYA

PLATINUM BLONDE (1931) Columbia. **B&W-90min.** Robert Williams, Jean Harlow..................... **4½***

PLATINUM HIGH SCHOOL (1960) M-G-M. **B&W-93min.** Terry Moore, Mickey Rooney, Dan Duryea..................... **3***
British title: RICH, YOUNG AND DEADLY
Alternate title: TROUBLE AT 16

Films are rated on a 1 to 10 scale, 10 is highest. **Boldface** ratings followed by an asterisk (*) are for films actually seen and rated by the executive and senior editors. All other ratings are estimates. (See Notes on Entertainment Ratings in the front section.)

PLAY DIRTY (1968) United Artists. Color-117min. *(British).* Michael Caine, Nigel Davenport, Nigel Green .... (4)

PLAY GIRL (1941) RKO. B&W-75min. Kay Francis, James Ellison .... (4)

PLAY IT AGAIN, SAM (1972) Paramount. Color-86min. Woody Allen, Diane Keaton.................... 6½*

PLAY IT AS IT LAYS (1972) Universal. Color-99min. Tuesday Weld, Anthony Perkins 3*

PLAY IT COOL (1962) Allied Artists. B&W-74min. *(British).* Billy Fury, Michael Anderson, Jr., Dennis Price .... (3)

PLAY MISTY FOR ME (1971) Universal. Color-102min. Clint Eastwood, Jessica Walter 4½*

PLAYBACK (1962) Anglo Amalgamated [EMI]. B&W-63min. *(British).* Margit Saad, Barry Foster.................... (3)

PLAYBOY OF THE WESTERN WORLD, THE (1962) Janus Films. Color-100min. *(Irish).* Siobhan McKenna, Gary Raymond.................... 5*

PLAYERS (1979) Paramount. Color-120min. Dean Paul Martin, Ali MacGraw 5*

PLAYGIRL (1954) Universal. B&W-85min. Shelley Winters, Barry Sullivan .... (4)

PLAYGIRL (1966) *see* THAT WOMAN

PLAYGIRL AFTER DARK (1960) Topaz Films. Color-92min. *(British).* Jayne Mansfield, Leo Genn, Karl Boehm .... (3)
Original title: TOO HOT TO HANDLE

PLAYGIRL AND THE WAR MINISTER, THE (1962) *see* AMOROUS MR. PRAWN, THE

PLAYGROUND, THE (1965) Jerand Pics. B&W-95min. Rees Vaughn, Inger Stratton .... (5)
Alternate title: TAKE ME WHILE I'M WARM

PLAYMATES (1941) RKO. B&W-94min. John Barrymore, Lupe Velez ... (3)

PLAYMATES (1972) Worldvision. Color-74min. *(Made for TV).* Alan Alda, Connie Stevens, Doug McClure, Barbara Feldon 5*

PLAYTHING OF THE DEVIL (1974) Color-90min. *(German).* Marie Forsa, Nadia Henkowa.................... (3)

PLAYTIME (1968) Continental [Walter Reade]. Color-102min. *(French, English version).* Jacques Tati, Barbara Dennek .... (2)

PLAZA SUITE (1971) Paramount. Color-115min. Walter Matthau, Maureen Stapleton, Barbara Harris, Lee Grant 4*

PLEASE BELIEVE ME (1950) M-G-M. B&W-87min. Deborah Kerr, Robert Walker .... (4)

PLEASE DON'T EAT MY MOTHER! (1972) Boxoffice International. Color-98min. René Bond, Buck Kartalian .... (2)
Publicity title: PLEASE NOT MY MOTHER

PLEASE DON'T EAT THE DAISIES (1960) M-G-M. Color-111min. Doris Day, David Niven 5*

PLEASE, MR. BALZAC (1956) Distributors Corp. of America. B&W-99min. *(French).* Brigitte Bardot, Daniel Gelin .... (4)
Original title: EN EFFEUILLANT LA MARGUERITE
British title: MAM'SELLE STRIPTEASE

PLEASE MURDER ME (1956) Distributors Corp. of America. B&W-78min. Angela Lansbury, Raymond Burr.................... (4)

PLEASE TURN OVER (1960) Columbia. B&W-87min. *(British).* Ted Ray, Jean Kent, Julia Lockwood .... (4)

PLEASURE AT HER MAJESTY'S (1976) Amnesty International. Color-100min. *(British, Documentary).* Director: Roger Graef .... (4)

PLEASURE CRUISE (1933) Fox Film Co. [20th]. B&W-72min. Genevieve Tobin, Roland Young .... (4)

PLEASURE GIRL (1961) *see* GIRL WITH A SUITCASE, THE

PLEASURE GIRLS, THE (1965) Times Film Corp. B&W-88min. *(British).* Ian McShane, Francesca Annis, Klaus Kinski .... (3)

PLEASURE OF HIS COMPANY, THE (1961) Paramount. Color-115min. Fred Astaire, Debbie Reynolds 5½*

PLEASURE PARTY (1975) *see* PIECE OF PLEASURE, A

PLEASURE SEEKERS, THE (1965) 20th Century-Fox. Color-107min. Ann-Margret, Carol Lynley.................... 4*

PLOT THICKENS, THE (1935) *see* HERE COMES COOKIE

PLOT THICKENS, THE (1936) RKO. B&W-69min. ZaSu Pitts, Louise Latimer .... (3)
British title: SWINGING PEARL MYSTERY, THE

PLOT TO ASSASSINATE HITLER, THE (1956) Paramount. B&W-90min. *(German).* Maximilian Schell .... (4)
Original title: 20 JULI, DER *(July 20th)*

PLOUGH AND THE STARS, THE (1936) RKO. B&W-78min. Barbara Stanwyck, Preston Foster.................... (4)

PLOW THAT BROKE THE PLAINS, THE (1936) U.S. Government. B&W-25min. *(Documentary). Director:* Pare Lorentz.................... 4*

PLUCK OF THE IRISH (1937) *see* GREAT GUY

PLUNDER OF THE SUN (1953) Warner Bros. B&W-81min. Glenn Ford, Diana Lynn.................... (4)

PLUNDER ROAD (1957) 20th Century-Fox. B&W-71min. Gene Raymond, Wayne Morris.................... 3*

PLUNDERERS, THE (1948) Republic. B&W-87min. Rod Cameron, Forrest Tucker.................... 3*

PLUNDERERS, THE (1960) Allied Artists. B&W-93min. Jeff Chandler, John Saxon 3*

PLUNDERERS OF PAINTED FLATS, THE (1959) Republic. B&W-77min. Skip Homeier, John Carroll, Edmund Lowe .... (3)

PLYMOUTH ADVENTURE (1952) M-G-M. Color-105min. Spencer Tracy, Lloyd Bridges 4½*

POACHER'S DAUGHTER, THE (1958) Showcorporation. B&W-74min. *(Irish).* Julie Harris, Harry Brogan .... (4)

POCKET MONEY (1972) National General. Color-98min. Paul Newman, Lee Marvin 4*

POCKETFUL OF MIRACLES (1961) United Artists. Color-136min. Glenn Ford, Bette Davis .... (5)

POE'S TALES OF TERROR (1962) *see* TALES OF TERROR

POINT, THE (1971) ABC Films. Color-74min. *(Cartoon, Made for TV). Director:* Fred Wolff 5*

POINT BLANK (1967) M-G-M. Color-92min. Lee Marvin, Angie Dickinson 4*

POINT OF ORDER! (1964) Continental [Walter Reade]. B&W-97min. *(Documentary). Director:* Emile De Antonio 5½*

POINT OF TERROR (1971) Crown International. Color-88min. Peter Carpenter, Dyanne Thorne .... (4)

POISON (1951) Gaumont *(French).* B&W-96min. *(French).* Michel Simon, Louis De Funes.................... (4)
Original title: POISON, LA

POISON IVY (1953) Paramount. B&W-90min. *(French).* Eddie Constantine, Dominique Wilms.................... (3)

POLICE DOG STORY, THE (1961) United Artists. B&W-62min. James Brown, Merry Anders, Rocco .... (3)

POLICE NURSE (1963) 20th Century-Fox. B&W-64min. Ken Scott, Merry Anders .... (3)

POLICE STORY (1973) CPT (TV). Color-74min. *(Made for TV).* Vic Morrow, Ed Asner, Chuck Connors.................... 4½*

POLICEMAN, THE (1971) Ephi Ltd. Color-87min. *(Israeli).* Shay K. Ophir, Zaharira Harifai 4*
Original title: HASHOTER AZULAI *(Policeman Azulai)*
Publicity title: COP, THE

POLITICAL ASYLUM (1975) Intercontinental Films. Color-89min. *(Guatemalan, English language).* Rossano Brazzi, Cameron Mitchell ... (3)

POLLY FULTON (1948) *see* B.F.'S DAUGHTER

POLLY OF THE CIRCUS (1932) M-G-M. B&W-72min. Clark Gable, Marion Davies .... (3)

POLLYANNA (1960) Buena Vista. Color-134min. Hayley Mills, Jane Wyman 5*

POLO JOE (1936) Warner Bros. B&W-62min. Joe E. Brown, Carol Hughes.................... (3)

POM POM GIRLS, THE (1976) Crown International. Color-90min. Robert Carradine, Jennifer Ashley.................... (3)

PONTIUS PILATE (1964) U.S. Films. Color-100min. *(Italian-French, English language).* Jean Marais, Jeanne Crain, Basil Rathbone........... (4)
Original Italian title: PONZIO PILATO

PONY EXPRESS (1953) Paramount. Color-101min. Charlton Heston, Rhonda Fleming 4*

PONY EXPRESS RIDER (1976) Doty-Dayton. Color- min. Stewart Petersen, Henry Wilcoxon, Maureen McCormick ....

PONY SOLDIER (1952) 20th Century-Fox. Color-82min. Tyrone Power, Cameron Mitchell.................... 3*
British title: MacDONALD OF THE CANADIAN MOUNTIES

POOKIE (1969) *see* STERILE CUCKOO, THE

POOL OF LONDON (1951) Universal. B&W-85min. *(British).* Susan Shaw, Bonar Colleano .... (5)

POOR BUT BEAUTIFUL (1957) Trans-Lux Distributing. B&W-103min. *(Italian).* Marisa Allasio, Maurizio Arena .... (4)
Original title: POVERI MA BELLI

POOR COW (1967) National General. Color-101min. *(British).* Carol White, Terence Stamp.................... (4)

POOR DEVIL (1972) Paramount. **Color-73min.** *(Made for TV).* Sammy Davis, Jr., Jack Klugman, Christopher Lee..............................4*

POOR LITTLE RICH GIRL, THE (1936) 20th Century-Fox. **B&W-72min.** Shirley Temple, Alice Faye..............................4*

POOR WHITE TRASH (1957) United Artists. **B&W-85min.** Peter Graves, Lita Milan, Timothy Carey ....(2)
Alternate title: BAYOU

POP ALWAYS PAYS (1940) RKO. **B&W-67min.** Leon Errol, Dennis O'Keefe ....(3)

POP GEAR (1965) *see* GO GO MANIA

POPCORN: AN AUDIO/VISUAL ROCK THING (1969) Sherpix. **Color-85min.** *(U.S.-Australian, Music Film). Director:* Peter Clifton.............(2)

POPE JOAN (1972) Columbia. **Color-132min.** Liv Ullmann, Olivia de Havilland ....(3)
Alternate title: DEVIL'S IMPOSTER, THE

POPI (1969) United Artists. **Color-115min.** Alan Arkin, Rita Moreno 5*

POPPY (1936) Paramount. **B&W-75min.** W. C. Fields, Rochelle Hudson 5*

POPPY IS ALSO A FLOWER, THE (1966) Comet Film. **Color-100min.** *(Made for TV).* E. G. Marshall, Trevor Howard, Gilbert Roland 4*
British title: DANGER GROWS WILD

PORGY AND BESS (1959) Columbia. **Color-138min.** Sidney Poitier, Dorothy Dandridge, Sammy Davis, Jr. 5½*

PORK CHOP HILL (1959) United Artists. **B&W-97min.** Gregory Peck, Harry Guardino 4*

PORNOGRAPHY IN DENMARK: A NEW APPROACH (1969) *see* CENSORSHIP IN DENMARK

PORT AFRIQUE (1956) Columbia. **Color-92min.** *(British).* Pier Angeli, Phil Carey..............................3*

PORT OF FORTY THIEVES (1944) Republic. **B&W-58min.** Richard Powers, Stephanie Bachelor ....(4)

PORT OF HELL (1954) Allied Artists. **B&W-80min.** Wayne Morris, Carole Matthews ....(3)

PORT OF NEW YORK (1949) Eagle Lion. **B&W-96min.** Scott Brady, Richard Rober, Yul Brynner..............................(5)

PORT OF REVENGE (1961) **B&W-90min.** *(British).* Dan O'Herlihy, Maurice Teynac ....(3)

PORT OF SEVEN SEAS (1938) M-G-M. **B&W-81min.** Wallace Beery, Maureen O'Sullivan ....(3)

PORT OF SHADOWS (1938) Film Alliance. **B&W-90min.** *(French).* Jean Gabin, Michele Morgan, Michel Simon..............................(4)
Original title: QUAI DE BRUMES

PORT SINISTER (1953) RKO. **B&W-65min.** James Warren, Lynne Roberts..............................(3)
Alternate title: BEAST OF PARADISE ISLE

PORTLAND EXPOSE (1957) Allied Artists. **B&W-72min.** Edward Binns, Carolyn Craig ....(4)

PORTNOY'S COMPLAINT (1972) Warner Bros. **Color-101min.** Richard Benjamin, Karen Black ....(3)

PORTRAIT FROM LIFE (1948) Universal. **B&W-91min.** *(British).* Mai Zetterling, Guy Rolfe 4*
Alternate title: GIRL IN THE PAINTING, THE

PORTRAIT IN BLACK (1960) Universal. **Color-112min.** Lana Turner, Anthony Quinn 4*

PORTRAIT OF A MOBSTER (1961) Warner Bros. **B&W-108min.** Vic Morrow, Leslie Parrish..............................4½*

PORTRAIT OF A SINNER (1959) American-International. **B&W-96min.** *(British).* Nadja Tiller, Tony Britton, William Bendix..............................(4)
Original title: ROUGH AND THE SMOOTH, THE

PORTRAIT OF ALISON (1955) *see* POSTMARK FOR DANGER

PORTRAIT OF AN UNKNOWN WOMAN (1954) Universal. **B&W-86min.** *(German).* Ruth Leuwerik, O. W. Fischer..............................(4)
Original title: BILDNIS EINER UNBEKANNTEN, DAS

PORTRAIT OF CLARE (1951) Stratford Pictures. **B&W-94min.** *(British).* Margaret Johnston, Richard Todd ....(3)

PORTRAIT OF JENNIE (1948) Selznick Releasing. **B&W-86min.** Jennifer Jones, Joseph Cotten 5½*
Alternate title: TIDAL WAVE
British title: JENNIE

PORTRAIT OF THE ARTIST AS A YOUNG MAN, A (1979) Howard Mahler. **Color-98min.** Bosco Hogan, T. P. McKenna ....

POSEIDON ADVENTURE, THE (1972) 20th Century-Fox. **Color-117min.** Gene Hackman, Ernest Borgnine..............................6*

POSSE (1975) Paramount. **Color-92min.** Kirk Douglas, Bruce Dern........6*

POSSE (1975). Ruthless and politically ambitious U.S. marshall Kirk Douglas is held at gunpoint by outlaw Bruce Dern, whom the marshall had hoped to bring to justice to enhance his chances of winning election to the Senate, but the outlaw has far more to lose.

POSSE FROM HELL (1961) Universal. **Color-89min.** Audie Murphy, John Saxon..............................(3)

POSSESSED (1931) M-G-M. **B&W-72min.** Joan Crawford, Clark Gable (4)

POSSESSED (1947) Warner Bros. **B&W-108min.** Joan Crawford, Van Heflin..............................3*

POSSESSED, THE (1977) Warner Bros. **Color-74min.** *(Made for TV).* James Farentino, Joan Hackett , Claudette Nevins, Harrison Ford ...(3)

POSSESSION OF JOEL DELANEY, THE (1972) Paramount. **Color-105min.** Shirley MacLaine, Perry King..............................3*

POSSESSORS, THE (1958) Lopert [U.A.]. **B&W-94min.** *(French).* Jean Gabin, Jean Desailly, Pierre Brasseur ....(5)
Original title: GRANDES FAMILLES, LES *(The Great Families)*

POST OFFICE INVESTIGATOR (1949) Republic. **B&W-59min.** Warren Douglas, Audrey Long ....(3)

POSTMAN ALWAYS RINGS TWICE, THE (1946) M-G-M. **B&W-113min.** Lana Turner, John Garfield..............................4*

POSTMARK FOR DANGER (1956) RKO. **B&W-84min.** *(British).* Terry Moore, Robert Beatty ....(3)
Original title: PORTRAIT OF ALISON

POT BOUILLE (1957) Continental [Walter Reade]. **B&W-115min.** *(French).* Gerard Phillipe, Danielle Darrieux..............................(5)
Alternate title: LOVERS OF PARIS
British title: HOUSE OF LOVERS

POT O' GOLD (1941) United Artists. **B&W-86min.** Paulette Goddard, James Stewart..............................3*
British title: GOLDEN HOUR, THE

POTEMKIN (1925) Amkino. **B&W-70min.** *(U.S.S.R., Silent).* Alexander Antonov, Vladimir Barsky 5*
Original title: BRONENOSETS "POTYOMKIN"
Alternate title: BATTLESHIP POTEMKIN
Alternate title: CRUISER POTEMKIN

POTOP (1974) *see* DELUGE, THE

POTTERS, THE (1927) Paramount. **B&W-74min.** *(Silent).* W. C. Fields, Mary Alden..............................(4)

POUND (1970) United Artists. **Color-92min.** Lawrence Wolf, Stan Gottlieb ....(4)

POVERTY AND NOBILITY (1954) **B&W-83min.** *(Italian).* Toto, Sophia Loren..............................(3)
Original title: MISERIA E NOBILTA

POWDER KEG (1971) Filmways. **Color-93min.** *(Made for TV).* Rod Taylor, Dennis Cole, Fernando Lamas..............................(3)

POWDER RIVER (1953) 20th Century-Fox. **Color-78min.** Rory Calhoun, Corinne Calvet ....(3)

POWDER TOWN (1942) RKO. **B&W-79min.** Victor McLaglen, Edmond O'Brien, June Havoc 4*

POWER, THE (1968) M-G-M. **Color-109min.** George Hamilton, Suzanne Pleshette, Michael Rennie 3*

POWER AND THE GLORY, THE (1933) Fox Film Co. [20th]. B&W-76min. Spencer Tracy, Colleen Moore 4*
British title: POWER AND GLORY

POWER AND THE PRIZE, THE (1956) M-G-M. B&W-98min. Robert Taylor, Elisabeth Mueller, Burl Ives 4*

POWER DIVE (1941) Paramount. B&W-65min. Jean Parker, Richard Arlen.. (3)

POWER OF THE PRESS (1943) Columbia. B&W-64min. Lee Tracy, Guy Kibbee.. (3)

POWER OF THE WHISTLER, THE (1945) Columbia. B&W-66min. Richard Dix, Janis Carter.. (4)

POWER PLAY (1978) Color-109min. (Canadian-British). Peter O'Toole, David Hemmings, Donald Pleasence.................................... 3½*

POWERS GIRL, THE (1943) United Artists. B&W-93min. George Murphy, Anne Shirley, Benny Goodman.................................... (3)
British title: HELLO! BEAUTIFUL

PRACTICALLY YOURS (1944) Paramount. B&W-90min. Claudette Colbert, Fred MacMurray .... (3)

PRAY FOR THE WILDCATS (1974) ABC Entertainment Films. Color-100min. (Made for TV). Andy Griffith, William Shatner, Marjoe Gortner, Angie Dickinson 4*

PREACHERMAN (1971) Preacherman Corp. Color-87min. Amos Huxley, Ilene Kristen .... (4)

PRECINCT 45 - LOS ANGELES POLICE (1972) *see* NEW CENTURIONS, THE

PREHISTORIC WOMEN (1950) United Artists. Color-74min. Laurette Luez, Allan Nixon .... (2)

PREHISTORIC WOMEN (1967) 20th Century-Fox. Color-91min. (British). Martine Beswick, Edina Ronay .... (2)
Original title: SLAVE GIRLS

PRELUDE TO FAME (1950) Universal. B&W-88min. (British). Guy Rolfe, Jeremy Spenser .... (5)

PREMATURE BURIAL, THE (1962) American-International. Color-81min. Ray Milland, Hazel Court... 5*

PREMEDITATED (1960) B&W-90min. (French). Jean-Claude Pascal, Pascale Roberts... (3)

PREMIER MAY (1958) Continental [Walter Reade]. B&W-89min. (French). Yves Montand, Nicole Berger.............................. (4)
Alternate title: MAN TO MAN TALK
Alternate title: MAYDAY IN PARIS
Translation title: The First of May

PREMIERE FOIS, LA (1976) *see* FIRST TIME, THE

PREMONITION, THE (1975) Avco-Embassy. Color-90min. Sharon Farrell, Richard Lynch, Jeff Corey.................................... (3)

PRESCRIPTION: MURDER (1968) Universal. Color-99min. (Made for TV). Peter Falk, Gene Barry, William Windom 4*

PRESENTING LILY MARS (1943) M-G-M. B&W-104min. Judy Garland, Van Heflin 4*

PRESIDENT VANISHES, THE (1935) Paramount. B&W-83min. Arthur Byron, Janet Beecher... 4*
British title: STRANGE CONSPIRACY

PRESIDENT'S ANALYST, THE (1967) Paramount. Color-104min. James Coburn, Godfrey Cambridge................................... 4*

PRESIDENT'S LADY, THE (1953) 20th Century-Fox. B&W-96min. Susan Hayward, Charlton Heston.................................... 5*

PRESIDENT'S PLANE IS MISSING, THE (1971) ABC Circle Films. Color-100min. (Made for TV). Buddy Ebsen, Peter Graves, Rip Torn, Raymond Massey 4*

PRESIDENT'S WOMEN, THE (1975) *see* FOREPLAY

PRESS FOR TIME (1966) J. Arthur Rank. Color-102min. (British). Norman Wisdom, Derek Bond, Angela Browne .... (3)

PRESSURE (1976) British Film Institute. Color-120min. (British). Herbert Norville, Oscar James.. (4)

PRESSURE POINT (1962) United Artists. B&W-91min. Sidney Poitier, Bobby Darin 5½*

PRETENDER, THE (1947) Republic. B&W-69min. Albert Dekker, Catherine Craig 4*

PRETTY BABY (1950) Warner Bros. B&W-92min. Dennis Morgan, Betsy Drake, Zachary Scott.. (4)

PRETTY BABY (1978) Paramount. Color-109min. Susan Sarandon, Keith Carradine, Brooke Shields.. 5*

PRETTY BOY FLOYD (1960) Continental [Walter Reade]. B&W-96min. John Ericson, Barry Newman..................................... (3)

PRETTY BOY FLOYD (1974) *see* STORY OF PRETTY BOY FLOYD, THE

PRETTY MAIDS ALL IN A ROW (1971) M-G-M. Color-92min. Rock Hudson, Angie Dickinson... (3)

PRETTY POISON (1968) 20th Century-Fox. Color-89min. Anthony Perkins, Tuesday Weld 5½*

PRETTY POLLY (1967) *see* MATTER OF INNOCENCE, A

PRICE OF FEAR, THE (1956) Universal. B&W-79min. Merle Oberon, Lex Barker .... (3)

PRICE OF SILENCE, THE (1960) Allied Artists. B&W-75min. (British). Gordon Jackson, June Thorberg............................ (3)

PRIDE AND PREJUDICE (1940) M-G-M. B&W-118min. Greer Garson, Laurence Olivier 4*

PRIDE AND THE PASSION, THE (1957) United Artists. Color-132min. Cary Grant, Frank Sinatra................................... 5*

PRIDE OF KENTUCKY (1949) *see* STORY OF SEABISCUIT, THE

PRIDE OF MARYLAND (1951) Republic. B&W-60min. Frankie Darro, Stanley Clements.. (3)

PRIDE OF ST. LOUIS, THE (1952) 20th Century-Fox. B&W-92min. Dan Dailey, Joanne Dru.. (3)

PRIDE OF THE BLUE GRASS (1954) Allied Artists. Color-71min. Lloyd Bridges, Vera Miles, Stanley Clements................... (3)
British title: PRINCE OF THE BLUE GRASS

PRIDE OF THE BOWERY (1941) Monogram [Allied Artists]. B&W-63min. The East Side Kids, Mary Ainsley..................... (3)
British title: HERE WE GO AGAIN

PRIDE OF THE BOWERY, THE (1946) *see* MR. HEX

PRIDE OF THE MARINES (1945) Warner Bros. B&W-119min. John Garfield, Eleanor Parker.. 4*
British title: FOREVER IN LOVE
Alternate British title: BODY AND SOUL

PRIDE OF THE YANKEES (1942) RKO. B&W-128min. Gary Cooper, Teresa Wright 4*

PRIEST KILLER, THE (1971) MCA-TV. Color-100min. (Made for TV). George Kennedy, Raymond Burr............................ (4)

PRIEST'S WIFE, THE (1970) Warner Bros. Color-106min. (Italian-French). Sophia Loren, Marcello Mastroianni................. 4*
Original Italian title: MOGLIE DEL PRETE, LA

PRIME CUT (1972) Nat'l General (for Cinema Center). Color-91min. Lee Marvin, Gene Hackman 5*

PRIME MINISTER, THE (1941) Warner Bros. B&W-115min. (British). John Gielgud, Diana Wynyard, Fay Compton ....

PRIME OF MISS JEAN BRODIE, THE (1969) 20th Century-Fox. Color-116min. (British-U.S.). Maggie Smith, Robert Stephens, Pamela Franklin 6½*

PRIMROSE PATH, THE (1940) RKO. B&W-93min. Ginger Rogers, Joel McCrea .... (4)

PRINCE AND THE PAUPER, THE (1937) Warner Bros. B&W-120min. Errol Flynn, Bobby Mauch, Billy Mauch.................. 5*

PRINCE AND THE PAUPER, THE (1962) Buena Vista. Color-93min. (Telefeature). Sean Scully, Guy Williams..................... (5)

PRINCE AND THE PAUPER, THE (1977) *see* CROSSED SWORDS

PRINCE AND THE SHOWGIRL, THE (1957) Warner Bros. Color-115min. (U.S.-British). Marilyn Monroe, Laurence Olivier 6*

PRINCE OF FOXES (1949) 20th Century-Fox. Color-107min. Tyrone Power, Orson Welles... 4*

PRINCE OF PIRATES, THE (1953) Columbia. Color-80min. John Derek, Carla Balenda .... (3)

PRINCE OF PLAYERS (1955) 20th Century-Fox. Color-102min. Richard Burton, Maggie McNamara .... (5)

PRINCE OF THIEVES, THE (1948) Columbia. Color-72min. Jon Hall, Adele Jergens .... (3)

PRINCE VALIANT (1954) 20th Century-Fox. Color-100min. Robert Wagner, James Mason...................................... 5*

PRINCE WHO WAS A THIEF, THE (1951) Universal. Color-88min. Tony Curtis, Piper Laurie 5*

PRINCESS, THE (1969) *see* TIME IN THE SUN, A

PRINCESS AND THE PIRATE, THE (1944) RKO. Color-94min. Bob Hope, Virginia Mayo....................................... 5½*

PRINCESS COMES ACROSS, THE (1936) Paramount. B&W-76min. Carole Lombard, Fred MacMurray 4*

PRINCESS OF THE NILE (1954) 20th Century-Fox. Color-71min. Jeffrey Hunter, Debra Paget, Michael Rennie............ (3)

PRINCESS O'ROURKE (1943) Warner Bros. B&W-94min. Olivia de Havilland, Robert Cummings................................... (5)

Films are rated on a 1 to 10 scale, 10 is highest. **Boldface** ratings followed by an asterisk (*) are for films actually seen and rated by the executive and senior editors. All other ratings are estimates. (See Notes on Entertainment Ratings in the front section.)

PRIORITIES ON PARADE (1942) Paramount. **B&W-79min.** Ann Miller, Jerry Colonna .... (2)

PRISON SHIP (1945) Columbia. **B&W-60min.** Nina Foch, Robert Lowery .... (3)

PRISON WARDEN (1949) Columbia. **B&W-62min.** Warner Baxter, Anna Lee .... (3)

PRISONER, THE (1955) Columbia. **B&W-94min.** (British). Alec Guinness, Jack Hawkins 4½*

PRISONER IN THE MIDDLE (1975) World Wide Pictures. **Color-91min.** (U.S.-Israeli). David Janssen, Karin Dor .... (3)

PRISONER OF SECOND AVENUE, THE (1975) Warner Bros. **Color-98min.** Jack Lemmon, Anne Bancroft 5*

PRISONER OF SHARK ISLAND, THE (1936) 20th Century-Fox. **B&W-95min.** Warner Baxter, Gloria Stuart .... (5)

PRISONER OF THE IRON MASK, THE (1962) American-International. **Color-80min.** (Italian-French). Michel Lemoine, Wandisa Guida .... (3)
Original Italian title: VENDETTA DELLA MASCHERA DI FERRO (*Revenge of the Iron Mask*)
French title: VENGEANCE DU MASQUE DE FER, LA

PRISONER OF THE JUNGLE (1958) American-International. **Color-82min.** (French). Georges Marchal, Francoise Rasquin .... (3)

PRISONER OF THE VOLGA (1958) Paramount. **Color-102min.** (Italian-French). John Derek, Elsa Martinelli .... (3)
Original Italian title: BATTELLIERI DEL VOLGA, I (*The Volga Boatmen*)

PRISONER OF WAR (1954) M-G-M. **B&W-80min.** Ronald Reagan, Steve Forrest .... (3)

PRISONER OF ZENDA, THE (1922) Metro. **B&W-140min.** (Silent). Lewis Stone, Alice Terry, Stuart Holmes, Ramon Samaniegos .... (5)

PRISONER OF ZENDA, THE (1937) United Artists. **B&W-101min.** Ronald Colman 5½*

PRISONER OF ZENDA, THE (1952) M-G-M. **Color-101min.** Stewart Granger, James Mason 6*

PRISONER OF ZENDA, THE (1979) Universal. **Color-108min.** Peter Sellers, Lynne Frederick 5*

PRISONERS IN PETTICOATS (1950) Republic. **B&W-62min.** Dorothy Patrick, Robert Rockwell .... (2)

PRISONERS OF THE CASBAH (1953) Columbia. **Color-78min.** Gloria Grahame, Cesar Romero 4*

PRISONNIERE, LA (1968) Avco-Embassy. **Color-104min.** (French-Italian). Laurent Terzieff, Bernard Fresson, Elisabeth Wiener .... (5)
Italian title: PRIGIONIERA, LA
Translation title: The Female Prisoner

PRIVATE AFFAIRS OF BEL AMI, THE (1947) United Artists. **B&W-112min.** George Sanders, Ann Dvorak 4*

PRIVATE ANGELO (1949) Associated British-Pathé [EMI]. **B&W-106min.** (British). Peter Ustinov, Godfrey Tearle .... (5)

PRIVATE BUCKAROO (1942) Universal. **B&W-68min.** The Andrews Sisters, Joe E. Brown .... (3)

PRIVATE DETECTIVE (1939) First National [W.B.]. **B&W-55min.** Jane Wyman, Dick Foran .... (3)

PRIVATE DETECTIVE 62 (1933) Warner Bros. **B&W-67min.** William Powell, Margaret Lindsay .... (4)

PRIVATE DUTY NURSES (1971) New World. **Color-80min.** Kathy Cannon, Joyce Williams .... (3)

PRIVATE EYES (1953) Allied Artists. **B&W-64min.** The Bowery Boys, Joyce Holden .... (3)

PRIVATE FILES OF J. EDGAR HOOVER, THE (1978) American-International. **Color-112min.** Broderick Crawford, Jose Ferrer 4½*

PRIVATE HELL 36 (1954) Filmmakers. **B&W-81min.** Ida Lupino, Howard Duff, Steve Cochran 4*

PRIVATE LIFE OF DR. PAUL JOSEPH GOEBBELS, THE (1944) *see* ENEMY OF WOMEN

PRIVATE LIFE OF DON JUAN, THE (1934) United Artists. **B&W-80min.** (British). Douglas Fairbanks, Merle Oberon .... (3)

PRIVATE LIFE OF HENRY VIII, THE (1933) United Artists. **B&W-97min.** (British). Charles Laughton, Robert Donat 5½*

PRIVATE LIFE OF SHERLOCK HOLMES, THE (1970) United Artists. **Color-125min.** (British-U.S.). Robert Stephens, Colin Blakely 4*

PRIVATE LIVES (1931) M-G-M. **B&W-85min.** Norma Shearer, Reginald Denny .... (5)

PRIVATE LIVES OF ADAM AND EVE, THE (1960) Universal. **B&W-86min.** Mickey Rooney, Mamie Van Doren, Martin Milner 3*

PRIVATE LIVES OF ELIZABETH AND ESSEX, THE (1939) Warner Bros. **Color-106min.** Bette Davis, Errol Flynn 5*
TV title: ELIZABETH THE QUEEN

THE PRIVATE LIFE OF HENRY VIII (1933). The King (played by Charles Laughton) isn't aware that the friendship between his fifth wife, Binnie Barnes, and handsome courtier Robert Donat is more than just platonic.

PRIVATE NAVY OF SERGEANT O'FARRELL, THE (1968) United Artists. **Color-92min.** Bob Hope, Phyllis Diller, Gina Lollobrigida 3*

PRIVATE NUMBER (1936) 20th Century-Fox. **B&W-80min.** Robert Taylor, Loretta Young, Basil Rathbone .... (4)
British title: SECRET INTERLUDE

PRIVATE NURSE (1941) 20th Century-Fox. **B&W-61min.** Brenda Joyce, Ann Todd .... (3)

PRIVATE PARTS (1972) Premier Pictures [MGM]. **Color-87min.** Ayn Ruymen, Lucille Benson, John Ventantonio .... (4)

PRIVATE PROPERTY (1960) Citation. **B&W-79min.** Corey Allen, Warren Oates, Kate Manx .... (3)

PRIVATE WAR OF MAJOR BENSON, THE (1955) Universal. **Color-100min.** Charlton Heston, Julie Adams, Tim Hovey 5*

PRIVATE WORE SKIRTS, THE (1952) *see* NEVER WAVE AT A WAC

PRIVATE WORLDS (1935) Paramount. **B&W-84min.** Claudette Colbert, Charles Boyer .... (4)

PRIVATE'S AFFAIR, A (1959) 20th Century-Fox. **Color-92min.** Sal Mineo, Christine Carrere 3½*

PRIVATE'S PROGRESS (1956) Distributors Corp. of America. **B&W-102min.** (British). Ian Carmichael, Richard Attenborough 4*

PRIVILEGE (1967) Universal. **Color-103min.** (British). Paul Jones, Jean Shrimpton .... (5)

PRIZE, THE (1963) M-G-M. **Color-135min.** Paul Newman, Edward G. Robinson 5½*

PRIZE OF ARMS, A (1961) British Lion [EMI]. **B&W-105min.** (British). Stanley Baker, Helmut Schmidt .... (4)

PRIZE OF GOLD, A (1954) Columbia. **Color-100min.** Richard Widmark, Mai Zetterling 4*

PRIZEFIGHTER AND THE LADY, THE (1933) M-G-M. **B&W-102min.** Myrna Loy, Walter Huston, Max Baer .... (4)
British title: EVERYWOMAN'S MAN

PROBE (1972) *see* SEARCH

PROBLEM GIRLS (1953) Columbia. **B&W-70min.** Helen Walker, Ross Elliott .... (3)

PRODIGAL, THE (1955) M-G-M. **Color-114min.** Edmund Purdom, Lana Turner .... (3)

PRODUCERS, THE (1968) Avco-Embassy. **Color-88min.** Zero Mostel, Gene Wilder 6*

PROFANE COMEDY, THE (1969) see SET THIS TOWN ON FIRE

PROFESSIONAL CO-RESPONDENTS (1934) see NO FUNNY BUSINESS

PROFESSIONAL SOLDIER (1935) 20th Century-Fox. **B&W-75min.** Victor McLaglen, Freddie Bartholomew .... (4)

PROFESSIONAL SWEETHEART (1933) RKO. **B&W-68min.** Ginger Rogers, Norman Foster .... (3)
British title: IMAGINARY SWEETHEART

PROFESSIONALS, THE (1960) American-International. **B&W-61min.** (British). William Lucas, Andrew Faulds .... (3)

PROFESSIONALS, THE (1966) Columbia. **Color-116min.** Burt Lancaster, Lee Marvin 6*

PROFESSOR BEWARE (1938) Paramount. **B&W-87min.** Harold Lloyd, Phyllis Welch .... (4)

PROJECT M-7 (1953) Universal. **B&W-79min.** (British). Phyllis Calvert, James Donald, Herbert Lom .... (4)
Original title: NET, THE

PROJECT X (1968) Paramount. **Color-97min.** Christopher George, Greta Baldwin 2*

PROJECTED MAN, THE (1966) Universal. **Color-77min.** (British). Bryant Halliday, Mary Peach .... (3)

PROJECTIONIST, THE (1971) Maron Films, Ltd. **Color-88min.** Chuck McCann, Ina Balin .... (5)

PROMISE, THE (1979) Universal. **Color-97min.** Kathleen Quinlan, Beatrice Straight 5*

PROMISE AT DAWN (1970) Avco-Embassy. **Color-101min.** (French-U.S.). Melina Mercouri, Assaf Dayan .... (5)
Original French title: PROMESSE DE L'AUBE, LA

PROMISE HER ANYTHING (1966) Paramount. **Color-98min.** (British). Warren Beatty, Leslie Caron 4*

PROMISE OF RED LIPS, THE (1971) see DAUGHTERS OF DARKNESS

PROMISED LAND, THE (1974) Tricontinental Films. **Color-120min.** (Chilean). Nelson Villagra, Marcelo Gaete ...... (4)
Original title: TIERRA PROMETIDA, LA

PROMISED LANDS (1974) New Yorker Films. **Color-87min.** (French, Documentary). Director: Susan Sontag .... (4)

PROMISES IN THE DARK (1979) Warner Bros. Color-   min. Marsha Mason, Ned Beatty ....

PROMISES, PROMISES (1964) NTD, Inc. **B&W-75min.** Jayne Mansfield, Marie McDonald 2*

PROMOTER, THE (1952) Universal. **B&W-88min.** (British). Alec Guinness, Glynis Johns 6½*
Original title: CARD, THE

PROPHECY (1979) Paramount. **Color-102min.** Talia Shire, Robert Foxworth 5*

PROSTITUTES IN PRISON (1969) see 99 WOMEN

PROTECTORS, THE (1971) see COMPANY OF KILLERS

PROUD AND THE BEAUTIFUL, THE (1953) Kingsley International. **B&W-94min.** (French-Mexican). Michele Morgan, Gérard Philipe .... (5)
Original French title: ORGUEILLEUX, LES (The Proud Ones)
British title: PROUD ONES, THE

PROUD AND THE DAMNED, THE (1972) Gold Key Entertainment. **Color-97min.** Chuck Connors, José Greco .... (4)
Alternate title: PROUD, DAMNED AND DEAD

PROUD AND THE PROFANE, THE (1956) Paramount. **B&W-111min.** William Holden, Deborah Kerr 4*

PROUD, DAMNED AND DEAD (1972) see PROUD AND THE DAMNED, THE

PROUD ONES, THE (1953) see PROUD BUT BEAUTIFUL

PROUD ONES, THE (1956) 20th Century-Fox. **Color-94min.** Robert Ryan, Virginia Mayo 4*

PROUD REBEL, THE (1958) Buena Vista. **Color-103min.** Alan Ladd, Olivia de Havilland, David Ladd 5*

PROUD STALLION, THE (1964) Teleworld. **B&W-84min.** (Czech). Jorga Kortbova, Rudolf Prucha .... (4)

PROVIDENCE (1977) Cinema 5. **Color-110min.** (French, English language). John Gielgud, Dirk Bogarde, Ellen Burstyn .... (3)

PROVINCIALE, LA (1953) see WAYWARD WIFE, THE

PROWLER, THE (1951) Universal. **B&W-92min.** Van Heflin , Evelyn Keyes 4*

PROWLERS OF THE EVERGLADES (1954) RKO (for Disney). **Color-32min.** (Documentary). Director: James Algar .... (5)

PRUDENCE AND THE PILL (1968) 20th Century-Fox. **Color-92min.** (British-U.S.). Deborah Kerr, David Niven 3*

PSYCH-OUT (1968) American-International. **Color-101min.** Susan Strasberg, Dean Stockwell, Jack Nicholson 3*

PSYCHE 59 (1964) Columbia. **B&W-94min.** (British). Patricia Neal, Curt Jurgens .... (4)

PSYCHIATRIST: GOD BLESS THE CHILDREN, THE (1970) Universal. **Color-98min.** (Made for TV). Roy Thinnes, Peter Duel ...... (4)
Alternate title: GOD BLESS THE CHILDREN
Alternate title: CHILDREN OF THE LOTUS EATERS

PSYCHIC, THE (1978) Group 1. **Color-89min.** (Italian). Jennifer O'Neill, Gabriel Ferzetti .... (4)

PSYCHIC KILLER (1975) Avco-Embassy. **Color-90min.** Jim Hutton, Paul Burke 3*

PSYCHO (1960) Paramount. **B&W-109min.** Anthony Perkins, Janet Leigh 6*

PSYCHO-CIRCUS (1967) American-International. **Color-65min.** (British). Christopher Lee, Leo Genn .... (3)
Original title: CIRCUS OF FEAR

PSYCHOMANIA (1963) Victoria. **B&W-93min.** Lee Philips, Shepperd Strudwick 2*
Original title: VIOLENT MIDNIGHT

PSYCHOMANIA (1973) see DEATH WHEELERS

PSYCHOPATH, THE (1966) Paramount. **Color-83min.** (British). Patrick Wymark, Margaret Johnston, John Standing 3*

PSYCHOUT FOR MURDER (1969) Times Film Corp. **Color-88min.** (Italian-Argentinian). Adrienne La Russa, Rossano Brazzi ...... (1)
Original Italian title: SALVARE LA FACCIA
U.S. pre-release title: DADDY SAID THE WORLD WAS LOVELY

PSYCOSISSIMO (1961) Ellis Films. **B&W-88min.** (Italian). Ugo Tognazzi, Raimondo Vianello .... (3)
Translation title: "The Most Psycho"

PT 109 (1963) Warner Bros. **Color-140min.** Cliff Robertson, Ty Hardin 4*

PT RAIDERS (1955) see SHIP THAT DIED OF SHAME, THE

PUBLIC AFFAIR, A (1962) Parade. **B&W-75min.** Myron McCormick, Edward Binns 3*

PUBLIC DEB NO. 1 (1940) 20th Century-Fox. **B&W-80min.** George Murphy, Brenda Joyce, Ralph Bellamy .... (3)

PUBLIC ENEMY (1931) Warner Bros. **B&W-83min.** James Cagney, Jean Harlow 3*
British title: ENEMIES OF THE PUBLIC

PUBLIC EYE, THE (1972) Universal. **Color-90min.** Mia Farrow, Topol, Michael Jayston 4*
British title: FOLLOW ME

PUBLIC HERO NUMBER ONE (1935) M-G-M. **B&W-81min.** Chester Morris, Jean Arthur .... (5)

PUBLIC PIGEON NO. 1 (1957) Universal. **Color-79min.** Red Skelton, Vivian Blaine .... (3)

PUEBLO (1973) Dan Goodman. **Color-100min.** (Made for TV). Hal Holbrook, Andrew Duggan, George Grizzard 5½*

PUFNSTUF (1970) Universal. **Color-98min.** Jack Wild, Billie Hayes, Martha Raye, Roberto Gamonet 2*

PULP (1972) United Artists. **Color-96min.** (British). Michael Caine, Mickey Rooney, Lionel Stander, Lizabeth Scott .... (4)

PUMPING IRON (1977) Cinema 5. **Color-85min.** (Documentary). Director: George Butler 4*

PUMPKIN EATER, THE (1964) Royal Films Int'l [Columbia]. **B&W-110min.** (British). Anne Bancroft, Peter Finch 4*

PUNISHMENT BATTALION (1964) Paramount. **B&W-90min.** (German). Werner Peters, George Thomas .... (4)

PUNISHMENT PARK (1971) Sherpix. **Color-89min.** Jim Bohan, Harold Beaulieu, Ronald Gonzalez, Mike Hodel ...... (3)

PUNK ROCK MOVIE, THE (1978) **Color-86min.** (British, Music Film). Director: Don Letts ....

PUPPET ON A CHAIN (1971) Cinerama Releasing. **Color-98min.** (British). Sven-Bertil Taube, Barbara Parkins 4*

PURE HELL OF ST. TRINIANS, THE (1960) Continental [Walter Reade]. **B&W-94min.** (British). Cecil Parker, Joyce Grenfell ...... (4)

PURPLE DEATH FROM OUTER SPACE (1940) Universal. **B&W-87min.** (Re-edited Serial). Buster Crabbe, Anne Gwynne, Charles Middleton . (3)
Original title: FLASH GORDON CONQUERS THE UNIVERSE

PURPLE GANG, THE (1960) Allied Artists. **B&W-85min.** Barry Sullivan, Robert Blake .... (3)

PURPLE HEART, THE (1944) 20th Century-Fox. **B&W-99min.** Dana Andrews, Richard Conte .... (4)

PURPLE HEART DIARY (1951) Columbia. **B&W-73min.** Judd Holdren, Frances Langford .... (3)
British title: NO TIME FOR TEARS

PURPLE HILLS, THE (1961) 20th Century-Fox. **Color-60min.** Gene Nelson, Joanna Barnes... (3)

PURPLE MASK, THE (1955) Universal. **Color-82min.** Tony Curtis, Colleen Miller **5**

PURPLE MONSTER STRIKES, THE (1945) *see* D-DAY ON MARS

PURPLE NOON (1960) Times Film Corp. **Color-115min.** *(French-Italian).* Alain Delon, Marie Laforet **5**
Original French title: PLEIN SOLEIL *(Bright Sun)*
Original Italian title: IN PIENO SOLE
British title: BLAZING SUN

PURPLE PLAIN, THE (1954) United Artists. **Color-100min.** *(British).* Gregory Peck, Win Min Than **4***

PURSUED (1947) Warner Bros. **B&W-101min.** Teresa Wright, Robert Mitchum **4***

PURSUERS, THE (1961) Warner Bros. **B&W-63min.** *(British).* Cyril Shaps, Francis Matthews.................................... (3)

PURSUIT (1935) M-G-M. **B&W-62min.** Chester Morris, Sally Eilers, Scotty Beckett .... (4)

PURSUIT (1972) Lee Rich. **Color-73min.** *(Made for TV).* Ben Gazzara, E. G. Marshall, William Windom, Joseph Wiseman .... (5)
Alternate title: EXPLOSION

PURSUIT ACROSS THE DESERT (1961) Commonwealth United TV. **Color-79min.** *(Spanish).* Pedro Armendariz, Teresa Velasquez .... (3)

PURSUIT AND LOVES OF QUEEN VICTORIA, THE (1958) *see* STORY OF VICKIE, THE

PURSUIT OF HAPPINESS, THE (1934) Paramount. **B&W-72min.** Francis Lederer, Joan Bennett................................... (5)

PURSUIT OF HAPPINESS, THE (1971) Columbia. **Color-93min.** Michael Sarrazin, Barbara Hershey, Arthur Hill......... **4***

PURSUIT OF THE GRAF SPEE (1956) J. Arthur Rank. **Color-106min.** *(British).* Anthony Quayle, John Gregson **4***
Original title: BATTLE OF THE RIVER PLATE, THE
Alternate title: GRAF SPEE

PURSUIT TO ALGIERS (1945) Universal. **B&W-65min.** Basil Rathbone, Nigel Bruce, Marjorie Riordan **4***
Publicity title: SHERLOCK HOLMES IN PURSUIT TO ALGIERS

PUSHER, THE (1960) United Artists. **B&W-81min.** Kathy Carlyle, Felice Orlandi, Douglas F. Rodgers...................... (3)

PUSHOVER (1954) Columbia. **B&W-88min.** Fred MacMurray, Kim Novak **4***

PUSSYCAT, PUSSYCAT, I LOVE YOU (1970) United Artists. **Color-99min.** Ian McShane, Anna Calder-Marshall, Severn Darden................ (2)

PUTNEY SWOPE (1969) Cinema 5. **B&W-84min.** Arnold Johnson, Stanley Gottlieb **3***

PYGMALION (1938). Linguistics expert Leslie Howard begins the almost impossible task of changing guttersnipe flower girl Wendy Hiller into someone who can be accepted in the highest social circles.

PUZZLE OF A DOWNFALL CHILD (1970) Universal. **Color-104min.** Faye Dunaway, Barry Primus................................ **3***

PUZZLE OF THE RED ORCHID, THE (1962) UCC Films. **B&W-94min.** *(German).* Christopher Lee, Marisa Mell, Klaus Kinski .... (3)
Original title: RATSEL DER ROTEN ORCHIDEE, DAS
Alternate title: SECRET OF THE RED ORCHID, THE

PYGMALION (1938) M-G-M. **B&W-85min.** *(British).* Wendy Hiller, Leslie Howard **7***

PYGMIES (1973) Jean-Pierre Hallet Prods. **Color-95min.** *(Documentary).* Director: Jean-Pierre Hallet .... (3)

PYGMY ISLAND (1950) Columbia. **B&W-69min.** Johnny Weissmuller, Ann Savage .... (3)

PYRAMID, THE (1976) Ellman. **Color-90min.** C. W. Brown, Ira Hawkins, Tomi Barrett **1½***

PYRO . . . THE THING WITHOUT A FACE (1964) American-International. **Color-99min.** *(Spanish-U.S.).* Barry Sullivan, Martha Hyer .... (3)
Spanish title: FUEGO *(Fire)*
British title: WHEEL OF FIRE
Publicity title: PYRO -- MAN WITHOUT A FACE

PYX, THE (1973) Cinerama Releasing. **Color-111min.** *(Canadian).* Karen Black, Christopher Plummer .... (3)

-Q-

Q PLANES (1939) *see* CLOUDS OVER EUROPE

QB VII (1974) CPT (TV). **Color-320min.** *(Made for TV).* Ben Gazzara, Anthony Hopkins **6***

QUACKSER FORTUNE HAS A COUSIN IN THE BRONX (1970) UMC Pictures. **Color-90min.** Gene Wilder, Margot Kidder.................... **5½***

QUALITY STREET (1937) RKO. **B&W-84min.** Katharine Hepburn, Franchot Tone.. **5***

QUANTEZ (1957) Universal. **Color-80min.** Fred MacMurray, Dorothy Malone **3***

QUANTRILL'S RAIDERS (1958) Allied Artists. **Color-65min.** Steve Cochran, Diane Brewster, Leo Gordon.................... (3)

QUARANTINED (1970) Paramount. **Color-74min.** *(Made for TV).* John Dehner, Gary Collins, Susan Hayward............. (4)
Alternate title(?): HOUSE ON THE HILL

QUARE FELLOW, THE (1962) Astor. **B&W-85min.** *(Irish-British).* Patrick McGoohan, Sylvia Syms .... (5)

QUARTERBACK, THE (1940) Paramount. **B&W-69min.** Wayne Morris, Virginia Dale... (3)

QUARTET (1948) Eagle Lion. **B&W-120min.** *(British).* Basil Radford, Naunton Wayne **5½***

QUATERMASS AND THE PIT (1967) *see* FIVE MILLION YEARS TO EARTH

QUATERMASS EXPERIMENT, THE (1955) *see* CREEPING UNKNOWN, THE

QUATERMASS II (1957) *see* ENEMY FROM SPACE

QUATERMASS XPERIMENT, THE (1955) *see* CREEPING UNKNOWN, THE

QUATRE CENTS COUPS, LES (1958) *see* 400 BLOWS, THE

QUEBEC (1951) Paramount. **Color-85min.** John Barrymore, Jr., Corinne Calvet .... (3)

QUEEN, THE (1968) Grove Press. **Color-68min.** *(Documentary).* Director: Frank Simon .... (4)

QUEEN BEE (1955) Columbia. **B&W-95min.** Joan Crawford, Barry Sullivan... **3***

QUEEN CHRISTINA (1933) M-G-M. **B&W-97min.** Greta Garbo, John Gilbert... **5½***

QUEEN FOR A DAY (1951) United Artists. **B&W-107min.** Phyllis Avery .... (4)

QUEEN FOR CAESAR, A (1962) Commonwealth United TV. **Color-91min.** *(Italian-French).* Pascale Petit, Gordon Scott, Akim Tamiroff (4)
Original Italian title: REGINA PER CESARE, UNA

QUEEN IS CROWNED, A (1953) J. Arthur Rank. **Color-89min.** *(Documentary). Producer:* Castleton Knight............ **6***

QUEEN OF BABYLON, THE (1956) 20th Century-Fox. **Color-98min.** *(Italian).* Rhonda Fleming, Ricardo Montalban................... **2***

QUEEN OF BLOOD (1966) American-International. **Color-81min.** John Saxon, Basil Rathbone, Florence Marly................. **3***
TV title: PLANET OF BLOOD

QUEEN OF BROADWAY (1942) Producers Rel. Corp. [Eagle Lion]. **B&W-82min.** Rochelle Hudson, Buster Crabbe ....

QUEEN OF BROADWAY (1943) *see* KID DYNAMITE

QUEEN OF BURLESQUE (1946) Producers Rel. Corp. [Eagle Lion]. B&W-70min. Evelyn Ankers, Carleton Young ....(3)

QUEEN OF DESTINY (1938) *see* SIXTY GLORIOUS YEARS

QUEEN OF OUTER SPACE (1958) Allied Artists. Color-80min. Zsa Zsa Gabor, Eric Fleming 2½*

QUEEN OF SHEBA, THE (1921) Fox Film Co. [20th]. B&W-92min. *(Silent).* Betty Blythe, Fritz Leiber ....

QUEEN OF SHEBA, THE (1952) Lippert Productions. B&W-103min. *(Italian).* Leonora Ruffo, Gino Cervi, Gino Leurini ....(3)

QUEEN OF SPADES (1949) Stratford Pictures. B&W-95min. *(British).* Anton Walbrook, Edith Evans 4*

QUEEN OF SPADES (1960) Artkino. Color-105min. *(U.S.S.R.).* Oleg Strizhenov, Yelena Polevitskaya ....(4)
Original title: PIKOVAYA DAMA

QUEEN OF SPIES (1942) *see* JOAN OF OZARK

QUEEN OF THE MOB (1940) Paramount. B&W-61min. Blanche Yurka, Ralph Bellamy ....(3)

QUEEN OF THE NILE (1962) Warner Bros. Color-97min. *(Italian).* Jeanne Crain, Vincent Price, Edmund Purdom ....(3)
Original title: NEFERTITE, REGINA DEL NILO

QUEEN OF THE PIRATES (1960) Columbia. Color-80min. *(Italian-W. German).* Gianna Maria Canale, Massimo Serato ....(2)
Original Italian title: VENERE DEI PIRATI, LA *(The Venus of the Pirates)*
W. German title: VENUS DER PIRATEN

QUEEN OF THE SEAS (1961) American-International. Color-87min. *(Italian).* Lisa Gastoni, Jerome Courtland ....(3)
Original title: AVVENTURE DI MARY READ, LE

QUEEN OF THE STARDUST BALLROOM (1975) Viacom. Color-98min. *(Made for TV).* Maureen Stapleton, Charles Durning 5*

QUEENS, THE (1966) Royal Films Int'l [Columbia]. Color-110min. *(Italian-French).* Monica Vitti, Claudia Cardinale, Raquel Welch, Capucine ....(5)
Original Italian title: FATE, LE *(The Fairies)*
French title: OGRESSES, LES *(The Lady Ogres)*

QUEEN'S DIAMONDS, THE (1974) *see* THREE MUSKETEERS, THE

QUEEN'S GUARDS, THE (1961) 20th Century-Fox. Color-110min. *(British).* Daniel Massey, Raymond Massey ....(3)

QUEIMADA! (1970) *see* BURN!

QUENTIN DURWARD (1955) M-G-M. Color-101min. *(U.S.-British).* Robert Taylor, Kay Kendall..5½*
Alternate title: ADVENTURES OF QUENTIN DURWARD, THE

QUEST FOR LOVE (1971) Viacom. Color-90min. *(British).* Joan Collins, Tom Bell..4*

? (question mark) (1974) *see* F FOR FAKE

QUESTION OF ADULTERY, A (1958) NTA Pictures. B&W-85min. *(British).* Julie London, Anthony Steel ....(4)
Alternate title: CASE OF MRS. LORING, THE

QUESTION 7 (1961) De Rochemont. B&W-107min. *(U.S.-W. German).* Michael Gwynn, Margaret Jahnen, Christian de Bresson..................(4)
W. German title: FRAGE 7

QUESTOR TAPES, THE (1974) MCA-TV. Color-100min. *(Made for TV).* Robert Foxworth, Mike Farrell, John Vernon 3*

QUICK AND THE DEAD, THE (1963) Beckman Films. B&W-92min. Larry D. Mann, Victor French ....(3)

QUICK, BEFORE IT MELTS (1965) M-G-M. Color-98min. George Maharis, Robert Morse..(4)

QUICK GUN, THE (1964) Columbia. Color-87min. Audie Murphy, Merry Anders..3*

QUICK MILLIONS (1931) Fox Film Co. [20th]. B&W-69min. Spencer Tracy, Marguerite Churchill ....(4)

QUICK MILLIONS (1939) 20th Century-Fox. B&W-56min. Spring Byington, Jed Prouty..(3)

QUICKSAND (1950) United Artists. B&W-79min. Mickey Rooney, Jeanne Cagney..(4)

QUIET AMERICAN, THE (1958) United Artists. Color-120min. Audie Murphy, Michael Redgrave..(5)

QUIET DAYS IN CLICHY (1970) Grove Press. B&W-90min. *(Danish, English language).* Paul Valjean, Wayne John Rodda, Ulla Lemvigh-Mueller ....(3)
Original title: STILLE DAGE I CLICHY
Alternate title: NOT SO QUIET DAYS

QUIET MAN, THE (1952) Republic. Color-129min. John Wayne, Maureen O'Hara..7½*

QUIET ONE, THE (1948) Mayer-Burstyn. B&W-67min. *(Documentary).* Director: Sidney Meyers..(5)

QUIET PLACE IN THE COUNTRY, A (1968) United Artists. Color-106min. *(Italian-French).* Franco Nero, Vanessa Redgrave ....(3)
Original Italian title: TRANQUILLO POSTO DI CAMPAGNA, UN
French title: COIN TRANQUILLE A LA CAMPAGNE, UN

QUIET PLEASE, MURDER (1942) 20th Century-Fox. B&W-70min. George Sanders, Gail Patrick ....(4)

QUIET WEDDING (1941) Universal. B&W-80min. *(British).* Margaret Lockwood, Derek Farr ....(3)

QUIET WOMAN, THE (1949) Eros Films *(Brit.).* B&W-69min. *(British).* Derek Bond, Jane Hylton ....(5)

QUILLER MEMORANDUM, THE (1966) 20th Century-Fox. Color-105min. *(British-U.S.).* George Segal, Alec Guinness........................3*

QUINCANNON, FRONTIER SCOUT (1956) United Artists. Color-83min. Tony Martin, Peggie Castle ....(3)
British title: FRONTIER SCOUT

QUINTET (1979) 20th Century-Fox. Color-110min. Paul Newman, Fernando Rey, Vittorio Gassman..2½*

QUO VADIS (1912) B&W-87min. *(Italian).* Amleto Novelli, Gustavo Serna ....(3)

QUO VADIS (1924) B&W-83min. *(Italian-German).* Emil Jannings, Elena Sangro ....(3)

QUO VADIS (1951) M-G-M. Color-171min. Robert Taylor, Deborah Kerr 6½*

-R-

R.C.M.P. AND THE TREASURE OF GHENGHIS KHAN (1948) Republic. B&W-100min. *(Re-edited Serial).* Jim Bannon, Virginia Belmont.........(3)
Original title: DANGERS OF THE CANADIAN MOUNTED

R.P.M. (1970) Columbia. Color-92min. Anthony Quinn, Ann-Margret.... 4*
Publicity title: R.P.M.* (*REVOLUTIONS PER MINUTE)

RA EXPEDITIONS, THE (1971) Interwest Film Corp. Color-105min. *(Documentary).* Director: Lennart Ehrenborg 5½*
Screen title: RA

RABBIT, RUN (1970) Warner Bros. Color-94min. James Caan, Anjanette Comer..(4)

RABBIT TEST (1978) Avco-Embassy. Color-84min. Billy Crystal, Joan Prather, Alex Rocco..5½*

RABBIT TRAP, THE (1959) United Artists. B&W-72min. Ernest Borgnine, David Brian, Kevin Corcoran ....(4)

RABID (1977) New World. Color-91min. *(Canadian).* Marilyn Chambers, Frank Moore, Joe Silver ....(3)

RACE FOR LIFE (1956) *see* IF ALL THE GUYS IN THE WORLD . . .

RACE FOR YOUR LIFE, CHARLIE BROWN (1977) Paramount. Color-75min. *(Cartoon).* Director: Bill Melendez..................5*

RACE STREET (1948) RKO. B&W-79min. George Raft, William Bendix, Marilyn Maxwell ....(3)

QUO VADIS (1951). Roman patricians Alfredo Varelli and Nicholas Hannen indicate that the heroine's life must be spared in the arena, and a slightly surprised Nero, played by Peter Ustinov, realizes he has little choice as Praetorian Guard leader Ralph Truman looks on sullenly.

Films are rated on a 1 to 10 scale, 10 is highest. **Boldface** ratings followed by an asterisk (*) are for films actually seen and rated by the executive and senior editors. All other ratings are estimates. (See Notes on Entertainment Ratings in the front section.)

RACE WITH THE DEVIL (1975) 20th Century-Fox. Color-88min. Peter Fonda, Warren Oates..4*

RACERS, THE (1955) 20th Century-Fox. Color-112min. Kirk Douglas, Bella Darvi, Gilbert Roland..3*
British title: SUCH MEN ARE DANGEROUS

RACHEL AND THE STRANGER (1948) RKO. B&W-93min. Loretta Young, William Holden..(5)

RACHEL, RACHEL (1968) Warner Bros. Color-101min. Joanne Woodward, James Olson..5*

RACING BLOOD (1954) 20th Century-Fox. Color-78min. Bill Williams, Jean Porter, Jimmy Boyd...(3)

RACING FEVER (1965) Allied Artists. Color-90min. Joe Morrison, Charles G. Martin..(2)

RACK, THE (1956) M-G-M. B&W-100min. Paul Newman, Wendell Corey..4*

RACKET, THE (1928) Paramount. B&W-85min. *(Silent).* Thomas Meighan, Marie Prevost..(4)

RACKET, THE (1951) RKO. B&W-88min. Robert Mitchum, Lizabeth Scott..(5)

RACKET BUSTERS (1938) Warner Bros. B&W-71min. George Brent, Humphrey Bogart...4*

RACKET MAN, THE (1944) Columbia. B&W-65min. Tom Neal, Hugh Beaumont...(4)

RADAR MEN FROM THE MOON (1952) *see* RETIK, THE MOON MENACE

RADIO STARS ON PARADE (1945) RKO. B&W-69min. Wally Brown, Alan Carney, Frances Langford.....................................(3)

RAFFERTY AND THE GOLD DUST TWINS (1975) Warner Bros. Color-91min. Alan Arkin, Sally Kellerman, Mackenzie Phillips.....................5*
TV title: RAFFERTY AND THE HIGHWAY HUSTLERS

RAFFLES (1939) United Artists. B&W-72min. David Niven, Olivia de Havilland..(4)

RAGE (1966) Columbia. Color-103min. *(U.S.-Mexican).* Glenn Ford, Stella Stevens..3*
Mexican title: MAL, EL

RAGE (1972) Warner Bros. Color-99min. George C. Scott, Richard Basehart..4*

RAGE AT DAWN (1955) RKO. Color-87min. Randolph Scott, Mala Powers...(4)

RAGE IN HEAVEN (1941) M-G-M. B&W-83min. Robert Montgomery, Ingrid Bergman, George Sanders......................................4*

RAGE OF PARIS, THE (1938) Universal. B&W-75min. Danielle Darrieux, Douglas Fairbanks, Jr...(4)

RAGE OF THE BUCCANEERS (1962) Colorama Features. Color-90min. *(Italian).* Ricardo Montalban, Vincent Price, Giulia Rubini.........(3)
Original title: GORDON IL PIRATA NERO *(Gordon, the Black Pirate)*

RAGE TO LIVE, A (1965) United Artists. B&W-101min. Suzanne Pleshette, Bradford Dillman.......................................3*

RAGGEDY ANN AND ANDY (1977) 20th Century-Fox. Color-84min. *(Cartoon). Director:* Richard Williams..........................(5)

RAGING BULL (1980) United Artists. Color-   min. Robert De Niro......

RAGING MOON, THE (1971) *see* LONG AGO TOMORROW

RAGING TIDE, THE (1951) Universal. B&W-93min. Richard Conte, Shelley Winters...4*

RAGING WATERS (1949) *see* GREEN PROMISE, THE

RAID, THE (1954) 20th Century-Fox. Color-83min. Van Heflin, Anne Bancroft..(5)

RAID ON ENTEBBE (1977) NBC-TV. Color-150min. *(Made for TV).* Charles Bronson, Peter Finch, Yaphet Kotto.....................5½*

RAID ON ROMMEL (1971) Universal. Color-99min. Richard Burton, John Colicos..(4)

RAIDERS, THE (1952) Universal. Color-80min. Richard Conte, Viveca Lindfors..3*
Alternate title: RIDERS OF VENGEANCE

RAIDERS, THE (1964) Universal. Color-75min. Robert Culp, Brian Keith..(3)

RAIDERS FROM BENEATH THE SEA (1965) 20th Century-Fox. B&W-73min. Ken Scott, Merry Anders.................................(2)

RAIDERS OF LEYTE GULF, THE (1963) Hemisphere. B&W-80min. *(Philippine-U.S.).* Jennings Sturgeon, Michael Parsons.........(3)

RAIDERS OF OLD CALIFORNIA (1957) Republic. B&W-72min. Jim Davis, Arleen Whelan...(2)

RAIDERS OF THE SEVEN SEAS (1953) United Artists. Color-88min. John Payne, Donna Reed..(3)

RAIDERS OF THE SPANISH MAIN (1962) B&W-88min. *(British, Telefeature).* Terence Morgan, Jean Kent.........................(3)

RAILROAD MAN, THE (1956) Continental [Walter Reade]. B&W-105min. *(Italian).* Pietro Germi, Luisa Della Noce......................(5)
Original title: FERROVIERE, IL
Alternate title: MAN OF IRON

RAILROADED (1947) Eagle Lion. B&W-71min. John Ireland, Sheila Ryan..(4)

RAILS INTO LARAMIE (1954) Universal. Color-81min. John Payne, Mari Blanchard, Dan Duryea...3*

RAILWAY CHILDREN, THE (1971) Universal. Color-109min. *(British).* Jenny Agutter, Sally Thomsett............................4*

RAIN (1929) B&W-12min. *(Netherlands, Silent, Documentary). Director:* Joris Ivens...2*
Original title: REGEN

RAIN (1932) United Artists. B&W-85min. Joan Crawford, Walter Huston..4½*

RAIN FOR A DUSTY SUMMER (1971) Do'Bar. Color-91min. *(Spanish-U.S.).* Ernest Borgnine, Padre Humberto Almazan...............(3)
Spanish title(?): MIGUEL PRO

RAIN PEOPLE, THE (1969) Warner Bros. Color-102min. Shirley Knight, James Caan..(5)

RAINBOW (1978) NBC-TV. Color-100min. *(Made for TV).* Andrea McArdle, Piper Laurie...

RAINBOW ISLAND (1944) Paramount. Color-97min. Dorothy Lamour, Eddie Bracken...(4)

RAINBOW JACKET, THE (1954) J. Arthur Rank. B&W-99min. *(British).* Kay Walsh, Bill Owen......................................(4)

RAINBOW ON THE RIVER (1936) RKO. B&W-87min. Bobby Breen, May Robson..(4)

RAINBOW 'ROUND MY SHOULDER (1952) Columbia. Color-78min. Frankie Laine, Charlotte Austin, Billy Daniels.................(3)
Alternate title: CASTLE IN THE AIR

RAINMAKER, THE (1956) Paramount. Color-121min. Burt Lancaster, Katharine Hepburn..5½*

RAINS CAME, THE (1939) 20th Century-Fox. B&W-103min. Myrna Loy, Tyrone Power, George Brent....................................(4)

RAINS OF RANCHIPUR, THE (1955) 20th Century-Fox. Color-104min. Lana Turner, Richard Burton..............................4*

RAINTREE COUNTY (1957) M-G-M. Color-185min. Montgomery Clift, Elizabeth Taylor...5½*

RAISE RAVENS (1976) *see* CRIA!

RAISIN IN THE SUN, A (1961) Columbia. B&W-128min. Sidney Poitier, Claudia McNeil...5½*

RAISING A RIOT (1955) Continental [Walter Reade]. Color-91min. *(British).* Kenneth More, Ronald Squire, Mandy Miller.........(4)

RAISING THE WIND (1961) *see* ROOMMATES

RAKE'S PROGRESS, THE (1945) *see* NOTORIOUS GENTLEMAN

RALLY 'ROUND THE FLAG, BOYS! (1958) 20th Century-Fox. Color-106min. Paul Newman, Joanne Woodward......................4*

RAMONA (1936) 20th Century-Fox. Color-90min. Loretta Young, Don Ameche, Kent Taylor...3*

RAMPAGE (1963) Warner Bros. Color-98min. Robert Mitchum, Elsa Martinelli, Sabu...3½*
Alternate title: JUNGLE RAMPAGE

RAMPAGE AT APACHE WELLS (1965) Columbia. Color-91min. *(W. German-Yugoslavian).* Stewart Granger, Pierre Brice...........(3)
Original W. German title: OLPRINZ, ER *(The Oil Prince)*
Yugoslavian title: KRALJ PETROLEJA

RAMPARTS OF CLAY (1970) Cinema 5. Color-87min. *(Algerian-French).* Leila Schenna...(5)
Original French title: REMPARTS D'ARGILE

RAMROD (1947) United Artists. B&W-94min. Joel McCrea, Veronica Lake..(4)

RAMSBOTTOM RIDES AGAIN (1956) British Lion [EMI]. B&W-93min. *(British).* Arthur Askey, Glenn Melvyn.........................(2)

RANCHO DELUXE (1975) United Artists. Color-93min. Jeff Bridges, Sam Waterston..4½*

RANCHO NOTORIOUS (1952) RKO. Color-89min. Marlene Dietrich, Arthur Kennedy...5*

RANDOM HARVEST (1942) M-G-M. B&W-124min. Ronald Colman, Greer Garson...4½*

RANGERS, THE (1975) NBC-TV. Color-74min. *(Made for TV).* James G. Richardson, Colby Chester...............................4*

Films are rated on a 1 to 10 scale, 10 is highest. **Boldface** ratings followed by an asterisk (*) are for films actually seen and rated by the executive and senior editors. All other ratings are estimates. (See Notes on Entertainment Ratings in the front section.)

RANGERS OF FORTUNE (1940) Paramount. **B&W-80min.** Fred MacMurray, Albert Dekker .... (4)

RANGO (1931) Paramount. **B&W-70min.** Ali, Bin .... (4)

RANSOM (1956) M-G-M. **B&W-109min.** Glenn Ford, Donna Reed, Leslie Nielsen 4*

RANSOM (1975) 20th Century-Fox. **Color-97min.** *(British).* Sean Connery, Ian McShane .... (4)
Alternate title: TERRORISTS, THE

RANSOM, THE (1962) *see* HIGH AND LOW

RANSOM FOR A DEAD MAN (1971) Universal. **Color-100min.** *(Made for TV).* Peter Falk, Lee Grant 4*

RAPE, THE (1967) *see* VIOL, LE

RAPE OF THE SABINES (1961) *see* ROMULUS AND THE SABINES

RAPTURE (1965) International Classics [20th]. **B&W-104min.** *(U.S.-French, English language).* Patricia Gozzi, Melvyn Douglas, Dean Stockwell 4*

RARE BOOK MURDER, THE (1938) *see* FAST COMPANY

RARE BREED, THE (1966) Universal. **Color-97min.** James Stewart, Maureen O'Hara 4*

RASCAL (1969) Buena Vista. **Color-85min.** Bill Mumy, Steve Forrest .... (4)

RASCALS (1938) 20th Century-Fox. **B&W-77min.** Jane Withers, Rochelle Hudson .... (3)

RASHOMON (1950) RKO. **B&W-86min.** *(Japanese).* Toshiro Mifune, Masayuki Mori 5*

RASPUTIN (1967) Paramount. **Color-95min.** *(French-Italian).* Gert Frobe, Peter McEnery, Geraldine Chaplin ....
Original title: J'AI TUÉ RASPOUTINE *(I Killed Rasputin)*
British title: I KILLED RASPUTIN

RASPUTIN AND THE EMPRESS (1932) M-G-M. **B&W-133min.** John Barrymore, Ethel Barrymore, Lionel Barrymore .... (5)
British title: RASPUTIN -- THE MAD MONK

RASPUTIN - THE MAD MONK (1966) 20th Century-Fox. **Color-92min.** *(British).* Christopher Lee, Barbara Shelley .... (3)

RAT RACE, THE (1960) Paramount. **Color-105min.** Tony Curtis, Debbie Reynolds 5*

RATIONING (1944) M-G-M. **B&W-93min.** Wallace Beery, Marjorie Main .... (3)

RATON PASS (1951) Warner Bros. **B&W-84min.** Dennis Morgan, Patricia Neal .... (4)
British title: CANYON PASS

RATS ARE COMING! THE WEREWOLVES ARE HERE!, THE (1972) William Mishkin. **Color-92min.** Hope Stansbury, Jacqueline (Jackie) Skarvellis, Noel Collins .... (2)

RATTLE OF A SIMPLE MAN (1964) Continental [Walter Reade]. **B&W-95min.** *(British).* Harry H. Corbett, Diane Cilento 4½*

RATTLERS (1976) Boxoffice International. **Color-82min.** Sam Chew, Elisabeth Chauvet, Dan Priest 3*

RAVAGED (1970) *see* BLOOD ROSE, THE

RAVAGED (1971) *see* JESUS TRIP, THE

RAVAGERS, THE (1965) Hemisphere. **Color-88min.** John Saxon, Fernando Poe, Jr., Bronwyn Fitzsimmons............................. (3)

RAVAGERS (1979) Columbia. **Color-91min.** Richard Harris, Ernest Borgnine 3½*

RAVEN, THE (1935) Universal. **B&W-62min.** Bela Lugosi, Boris Karloff 5*

RAVEN, THE (1963) American-International. **Color-86min.** Boris Karloff, Vincent Price, Peter Lorre 4*

RAVISHING IDIOT, A (1964) *see* AGENT 38-24-36

RAW DEAL (1948) Eagle Lion. **B&W-79min.** Dennis O'Keefe, Claire Trevor 4*

RAW EDGE (1956) Universal. **Color-76min.** Rory Calhoun, Yvonne De Carlo 3*

RAW MEAT (1973) American-International. **Color-87min.** *(British).* Donald Pleasence, Norman Rossington, David Ladd, Sharon Gurney (4)
Original title: DEATH LINE

RAW WEEKEND (1964) Boxoffice International. **B&W-62min.** *(Documentary). Director:* Sidney Niehoff .... (2)

RAW WIND IN EDEN (1958) Universal. **Color-89min.** Esther Williams, Jeff Chandler... 3*

RAWHIDE (1951) 20th Century-Fox. **B&W-86min.** Tyrone Power, Susan Hayward 3*
Alternate title: DESPERATE SIEGE

RAWHIDE TRAIL, THE (1958) Allied Artists. **B&W-67min.** Rex Reason, Nancy Gates .... (3)

RAWHIDE YEARS, THE (1956) Universal. **Color-85min.** Tony Curtis, Colleen Miller 4*

RAYMIE (1960) Allied Artists. **B&W-72min.** David Ladd, Julie Adams..(4)

RAZOR'S EDGE, THE (1946) 20th Century-Fox. **B&W-146min.** Tyrone Power, Gene Tierney 4*

RAZZIA (1958) Kassler Films. **B&W-105min.** *(French).* Jean Gabin, Magali Noel, Marcel Dalio .... (5)
Translation title: Raid

RE: LUCKY LUCIANO (1973) Titanus. **Color-112min.** *(Italian).* Gian Maria Volonte, Rod Steiger, Edmond O'Brien....................... (4)

REACH FOR GLORY (1962) Royal Films Int'l [Columbia]. **B&W-89min.** *(British).* Harry Andrews, Michael Anderson, Jr., Oliver Grimm........ (5)

REACH FOR THE SKY (1956) J. Arthur Rank. **B&W-123min.** *(British).* Kenneth More, Muriel Pavlow .... (5)

REACHING FOR THE MOON (1931) United Artists. **B&W-90min.** Douglas Fairbanks, Bebe Daniels .... (4)

REACHING FOR THE SUN (1941) Paramount. **B&W-90min.** Joel McCrea, Ellen Drew .... (4)

READY FOR THE PEOPLE (1964) Warner Bros. **B&W-54min.** Simon Oakland, Everett Sloane .... (2)

REAL GLORY, THE (1939) United Artists. **B&W-95min.** Gary Cooper, Andrea Leeds 4*

REAL GONE GIRLS, THE (1970) *see* MAN FROM O.R.G.Y., THE

REAL LIFE (1979) Paramount. **Color-99min.** Albert Brooks, Charles Grodin, Frances Lee McCain ....

REAP THE WILD WIND (1942) Paramount. **Color-124min.** John Wayne, Paulette Goddard... 4½*

REAR WINDOW (1954) Paramount. **Color-112min.** James Stewart, Grace Kelly.. 7*

REASON TO LIVE, A REASON TO DIE, A (1974) K-Tel. **Color-92min.** *(Italian-French-W. German-Spanish).* James Coburn, Telly Savalas, Bud Spencer .... (4)
Original Italian title: RAGIONE PER MORIRE, UNA *(A Reason to Die)*

REBECCA (1940) United Artists. **B&W-130min.** Laurence Olivier, Joan Fontaine 6*

REBECCA OF SUNNYBROOK FARM (1938) 20th Century-Fox. **B&W-80min.** Shirley Temple, Randolph Scott........................... 4*

REBEL, THE (1951) *see* BUSHWHACKERS, THE

REBEL, THE (1961) *see* CALL ME GENIUS

REBEL CITY (1953) Allied Artists. **B&W-63min.** Wild Bill Elliott, Marjorie Lord .... (3)

REBEL FLIGHT TO CUBA (1959) Telewide Systems. **B&W-92min.** *(German).* Peter Van Eyck, Linda Christian............................ (3)
Original title: ABSCHIED VON DEN WOLKEN

REBEL GIRLS (1957) Luzo Releasing Co. **B&W-65min.** *(Philippine).* Eddie del Mar... (3)

REBECCA (1940) was the name of Laurence Olivier's deceased first wife, whose continuing influence over him makes his new wife Joan Fontaine anxious to learn more about his real relationship with the dead woman.

REBEL GLADIATORS, THE (1963) Medallion. **Color-98min.** *(Italian).* Dan Vadis, José Greci, Gloria Milland ....(3)
Original title: URSUS GLADIATORE RIBELLE *(Ursus, Rebel Gladiator)*

REBEL IN TOWN (1956) United Artists. **B&W-78min.** John Payne, Ruth Roman ....(3)

REBEL ROUSERS (1970) Four Star-Excelsior. **Color-78min.** Cameron Mitchell, Jack Nicholson, Bruce Dern ....(2)

REBEL SET, THE (1959) Allied Artists. **B&W-72min.** Gregg Palmer, Kathleen Crowley ....(3)

REBEL WITH A CAUSE (1962) *see* LONELINESS OF THE LONG DISTANCE RUNNER, THE

REBEL WITHOUT A CAUSE (1955) Warner Bros. **Color-111min.** James Dean, Natalie Wood **5***

REBELLION (1967) Toho. **B&W-120min.** *(Japanese).* Toshiro Mifune, Takeshi Kato, Yoko Tsukasa ....(5)
Original title: JOI-UCHI
Alternate title: SAMURAI REBELLION

REBELS ON THE LOOSE (1967) Independent TV Corp (ITC). **Color-92min.** *(Italian-Spanish).* Riamondo Vianello, Landro Buzzanca..........**3***
Original Italian title: RINGO E GRINGO CONTRO TUTTI *(Ringo and Gringo Against Everyone)*

RECKLESS (1935) M-G-M. **B&W-96min.** Jean Harlow, William Powell ..(4)

RECKLESS AGE (1944) Universal. **B&W-63min.** Gloria Jean, Marshall Thompson ....(3)

RECKLESS AGE, THE (1958) *see* DRAGSTRIP RIOT

RECKLESS MOMENT, THE (1949) Columbia. **B&W-82min.** James Mason, Joan Bennett ....(5)

RECKONING, THE (1969) Columbia. **Color-108min.** *(British).* Nicol Williamson, Rachel Roberts ....(4)

RECORD CITY (1977) American-International. **Color-88min.** Michael Callan, Larry Storch ....

RECORD OF A LIVING BEING (1955) *see* I LIVE IN FEAR

RED ALERT (1977) Paramount. **Color-100min.** *(Made for TV).* William Devane, Ralph Waite **5***

RED AND THE WHITE, THE (1967) Brandon. **B&W-92min.** *(Hungarian-Soviet).* Jozsef Madaras, Tibo Molnar, Andras Kozak ....(4)
Original Hungarian title: CSILLAGOSOK, KATONAK
Soviet title: ZVYOZDY I SOLDATY

RED BADGE OF COURAGE, THE (1951) M-G-M. **B&W-69min.** Audie Murphy, Bill Mauldin **5***

RED BADGE OF COURAGE, THE (1974) 20th Century-Fox. **Color-74min.** *(Made for TV).* Richard Thomas, Michael Brandon **5***

RED BALL EXPRESS (1952) Universal. **B&W-83min.** Jeff Chandler, Alex Nicol ....(4)

RED BALLOON (1956) Lopert [U.A.]. **Color-35min.** *(French).* Pascal Lamorisse, Sabine Lamorisse ....(5)
Original title: BALLON ROUGE, LE

RED BARON, THE (1971) *see* VON RICHTHOFEN AND BROWN

RED BEARD (1965) Toho. **B&W-185min.** *(Japanese).* Toshiro Mifune, Yuzo Kayama ....
Original title: AKAHIGE

RED BERET, THE (1953) *see* PARATROOPER

RED CANYON (1949) Universal. **Color-82min.** Ann Blyth, Howard Duff ....(4)

RED CIRCLE, THE (1960) UCC Films. **B&W-94min.** *(German).* Renate Ewert, Klaus Wussow ....(3)
Alternate title: CRIMSON CIRCLE, THE

RED CLOAK, THE (1955) Sefo Films International & Allied Artists. **Color-95min.** *(French-Italian).* Patricia Medina, Bruce Cabot, Fausto Tozzi ....(3)
Original Italian title: MANTELLO ROSSO, IL
French title: RÉVOLTÉS, LES
Alternate French title: MANTEAU ROUGE, LE

RED CULOTTES, THE (1963) ABC Films. **B&W-105min.** *(French).* Bourvil, Laurent Terzieff ....(3)

RED DANUBE, THE (1949) M-G-M. **B&W-119min.** Walter Pidgeon, Peter Lawford **4***

RED DESERT (1949) Lippert Productions. **B&W-60min.** Don "Red" Barry, Jack Holt...(4)

RED DESERT (1964) Rizzoli Film. **Color-116min.** *(Italian-French).* Monica Vitti, Richard Harris ....(4)
Original Italian title: DESERTO ROSSO, IL
Original French title: DÉSERT ROUGE, LE

RED DRAGON (1945) Allied Artists. **B&W-64min.** Sidney Toler, Fortunio Bonanova, Benson Fong ....(4)

RED-DRAGON (1965) Woolner Brothers. **Color-89min.** *(W. German-Italian).* Stewart Granger, Rosanna Schiaffino ....(3)
Original W. German title: GEHEIMNIS DER DREI DSCHUNKEN, DAS *(The Mystery of Three Junks)*
Original Italian title: A-009 MISSIONE HONG KONG
U.S. Pre-release title: MISSION TO HONG KONG

RED DUST (1932) M-G-M. **B&W-83min.** Clark Gable, Jean Harlow........**3***

RED GARTERS (1954) Paramount. **Color-91min.** Rosemary Clooney, Jack Carson...**4***

RED HAND, THE (1960) UCC Films. **B&W-98min.** *(W. German-Italian).* Eleanora Rossi-Drago, Paul Hubschmid **3***
Original German title: ROTE HAND, DIE
Italian title: MANO ROSSO, LA

RED HANGMAN, THE (1965) *see* BLOODY PIT OF HORROR

RED HEADED WOMAN (1932) M-G-M. **B&W-74min.** Jean Harlow, Chester Morris...(5)

RED, HOT AND BLUE (1949) Paramount. **B&W-84min.** Betty Hutton, Victor Mature ....(4)

RED HOUSE, THE (1947) United Artists. **B&W-100min.** Edward G. Robinson, Lon McCallister ....(5)

RED INN, THE (1951) Arthur Davis Associates. **B&W-92min.** *(French).* Fernandel, Carette, Francoise Rosay..........................(4)
Original title: AUBERGE ROUGE, L'

RED LIGHT (1949) United Artists. **B&W-83min.** George Raft, Virginia Mayo...(3)

RED LINE 7000 (1965) Paramount. **Color-110min.** James Caan, Laura Devon **3***

RED LION (1969) Toho. **Color-116min.** *(Japanese).* Toshiro Mifune, Etsushi Takahashi ....(4)
Original title: AKAGE

RED MANTLE, THE (1967) *see* HAGBARD AND SIGNE

RED MENACE, THE (1949) Republic. **B&W-87min.** Robert Rockwell, Hanne Axman ....(3)
British title: ENEMY WITHIN, THE

RED MOUNTAIN (1951) Paramount. **Color-84min.** Alan Ladd, Lizabeth Scott 3½*

RED OVER RED (1967) *see* COME SPY WITH ME

RED PLANET MARS (1952) United Artists. **B&W-87min.** Peter Graves, Andrea King ....(3)

RED PONY, THE (1949) Republic. **Color-89min.** Myrna Loy, Robert Mitchum...**4***

RED PONY, THE (1973) NBC-TV. **Color-101min.** *(Made for TV).* Henry Fonda, Maureen O'Hara 3½*

RED RIVER (1948) United Artists. **B&W-125min.** John Wayne, Montgomery Clift **6***

RED SEA ADVENTURE (1952) *see* UNDER THE RED SEA

RED SHEIK, THE (1962) Telewide Systems. **Color-90min.** *(Italian).* Channing Pollock, Luciana Gilli, Mel Welles..................(1)
Original title: SCEICCO ROSSO, LO

RED SHOES, THE (1948) Eagle Lion. **Color-133min.** *(British).* Moira Shearer, Anton Walbrook, Marius Goring 5½*

RED SKIES OF MONTANA (1952) 20th Century-Fox. **Color-89min.** Richard Widmark, Constance Smith...............................(4)

RED SKY AT MORNING (1971) Universal. **Color-113min.** Richard Thomas, Catherine Burns, Desi Arnaz, Jr. **5***
Alternate title: THAT SAME SUMMER

RED SNOW (1952) Columbia. **B&W-75min.** Guy Madison, Ray Mala, Carole Mathews ....(3)

RED STALLION, THE (1947) Eagle Lion. **Color-82min.** Robert Paige, Ted Donaldson ....(3)

RED STALLION IN THE ROCKIES (1949) Eagle Lion. **Color-85min.** Jean Heather, Arthur Franz ....(3)

RED SUN (1971) National General. **Color-112min.** *(French-Italian-Spanish, English version).* Charles Bronson, Toshiro Mifune, Alain Delon **4***
Original French title: SOLEIL ROUGE

RED SUNDOWN (1956) Universal. **Color-81min.** Rory Calhoun, Martha Hyer ....(4)

RED TENT, THE (1969) Paramount. **Color-121min.** *(Italian-Soviet, English version).* Peter Finch, Sean Connery, Claudia Cardinale........**4***
Original Italian title: TENDA ROSSA, LA

RED TOMAHAWK (1967) Paramount. **Color-82min.** Howard Keel, Joan Caulfield, Broderick Crawford.............................(3)

RED TRAIN, THE (1973) Peter Ammann Films. Color-90min. *(Swiss, Documentary)*. Director: Peter Ammann .... (3)
Original title: TRAIN ROUGE, LE

RED, WHITE AND BLACK, THE (1970) Hirschman-Northern. Color-103min. Robert DoQui, Janee Michelle, Lincoln Kilpatrick 3*
Alternate title: SOUL SOLDIER

REDHEAD AND THE COWBOY, THE (1951) Paramount. B&W-82min. Glenn Ford, Rhonda Fleming 3*

REDHEAD FROM MANHATTAN (1943) Columbia. B&W-59min. Lupe Velez, Michael Duane .... (3)

REDHEAD FROM WYOMING, THE (1953) Universal. Color-80min. Maureen O'Hara, Alex Nicol 3*

REDMEN AND THE RENEGADES, THE (1956) Independent TV Corp (ITC). B&W-89min. *(Telefeature)*. John Hart, Lon Chaney (Jr.) .... (3)

REEFER MADNESS (1939) Dwain Esper Productions. B&W-48min. Kenneth Craig, Dorothy Short 3*
Original title: BURNING QUESTION, THE
Alternate title: TELL YOUR CHILDREN
Alternate title: DOPE ADDICT
Alternate title: DOPED YOUTH
Alternate title: LOVE MADNESS

REFLECTION OF FEAR, A (1973) Columbia. Color-90min. *(British)*. Robert Shaw, Sally Kellerman 2½*

REFLECTIONS IN A GOLDEN EYE (1967) Warner Bros. Color-108min. Elizabeth Taylor, Marlon Brando 3*

REFLECTIONS OF MURDER (1974) ABC Circle Films. Color-100min. *(Made for TV)*. Sam Waterston, Joan Hackett, Tuesday Weld 6*

REFORM SCHOOL GIRL (1957) American-International. B&W-71min. Gloria Castillo, Ross Ford .... (2)

REFORMER AND THE REDHEAD, THE (1950) M-G-M. B&W-90min. June Allyson, Dick Powell 4*

REFUGEE, THE (1940) see THREE FACES WEST

REGAL CAVALCADE (1935) Alliance. B&W-104min. *(British)*. Marie Lohr, Hermione Baddeley .... (4)
Original title: ROYAL CAVALCADE

REGLE DE JEU, LE (1938) see RULES OF THE GAME

REIGN OF TERROR (1949) Eagle Lion. B&W-89min. Robert Cummings, Arlene Dahl 4*
Alternate title: BLACK BOOK, THE

REINCARNATION OF PETER PROUD, THE (1975) American-International. Color-104min. Michael Sarrazin, Jennifer O'Neill, Margot Kidder 4½*

REIVERS, THE (1969) Nat'l General (for Cinema Center). Color-107min. Steve McQueen, Sharon Farrell 5½*

RELATIONS (1969) Cambist. Color-91min. *(Danish)*. Gertie Jung, Bjorn Puggaard-Muller, Paul Glargaard .... (2)
Original title: TUMULT
Alternate title: TUMULT - SONJA, AGE 16

RELENTLESS (1948) Columbia. Color-93min. Robert Young, Marguerite Chapman 4*

RELUCTANT ASTRONAUT, THE (1967) Universal. Color-102min. Don Knotts, Arthur O'Connell 3*

RELUCTANT DEBUTANTE, THE (1958) M-G-M. Color-94min. Rex Harrison, Kay Kendall 5*

RELUCTANT DRAGON, THE (1941) RKO (for Disney). Color-73min. *(Part-animated)*. Robert Benchley, Walt Disney .... (5)

RELUCTANT HEROES (1951) Eros Films (Brit.). B&W-81min. *(British)*. Ronald Shiner, Derek Farr .... (3)

RELUCTANT HEROES, THE (1971) Worldvision. Color-73min. *(Made for TV)*. Ken Berry, Cameron Mitchell, Warren Oates, Jim Hutton 5*
Alternate title: EGGHEAD ON HILL 656, THE

RELUCTANT SAINT, THE (1962) Davis-Royal Films International. B&W-105min. *(U.S.-Italian)*. Maximilian Schell, Ricardo Montalban ... (4)
Italian title: CRONACHE DI UN CONVENTO

RELUCTANT SPY, THE (1963) Avco-Embassy. B&W-93min. *(French-Italian)*. Jean Marais, Genevieve Page .... (4)
Original French title: HONORABLE STANISLAS, AGENT SECRET, L'

RELUCTANT WIDOW, THE (1950) Fine Arts. B&W-91min. *(British)*. Jean Kent, Guy Rolfe .... (3)

REMAINS TO BE SEEN (1953) M-G-M. B&W-89min. June Allyson, Van Johnson .... (4)

REMARKABLE ANDREW, THE (1942) Paramount. B&W-80min. William Holden, Brian Donlevy, Ellen Drew .... (4)

REMARKABLE MR. KIPPS, THE (1941) 20th Century-Fox. B&W-82min. *(British)*. Michael Redgrave, Diana Wynyard .... (4)
Original title: KIPPS

REMARKABLE MR. PENNYPACKER, THE (1959) 20th Century-Fox. Color-87min. Clifton Webb, Dorothy McGuire 4*

REMBRANDT (1936) United Artists. B&W-84min. *(British)*. Charles Laughton, Gertrude Lawrence, Elsa Lanchester 5½*

REMEDY FOR RICHES (1940) RKO. B&W-60min. Jean Hersholt, Dorothy Lovett .... (3)

REMEMBER? (1939) M-G-M. B&W-83min. Robert Taylor, Greer Garson, Lew Ayres .... (3)

REMEMBER MY NAME (1978) Lagoon. Color-96min. Geraldine Chaplin, Anthony Perkins, Berry Berenson 4*

REMEMBER PEARL HARBOR (1942) Republic. B&W-76min. Don "Red" Barry, Alan Curtis .... (3)

REMEMBER THAT FACE (1951) see MOB, THE

REMEMBER THE DAY (1941) 20th Century-Fox. B&W-85min. Claudette Colbert, John Payne .... (5)

REMEMBER THE NIGHT (1940) Paramount. B&W-86min. Barbara Stanwyck, Fred MacMurray 5½*

REMEMBER WHEN (1974) Worldvision. Color-96min. *(Made for TV)*. Jack Warden, Nan Martin 4*

RENALDO & CLARA (1978) Circuit Films. Color-232min. Bob Dylan, Sara Dylan 2*

RENDEZVOUS (1935) M-G-M. B&W-91min. William Powell, Rosalind Russell 4*

RENDEZVOUS (1951) see DARLING, HOW COULD YOU?

RENDEZVOUS WITH ANNIE (1946) Republic. B&W-89min. Eddie Albert, Faye Marlowe .... (4)
Alternate title: CORPORAL DOLAN GOES A.W.O.L.

RENEGADE GUNFIGHTER (1966) United Artists. Color-76min. *(Italian-Spanish)*. Warner Baxter, Pier Angeli .... (3)
Original Italian title: PER MILLE DOLLARI AL GIORNO *(For a Thousand Dollars a Day)*
Spanish title: POR MIL DOLARES AL DIA

RENEGADES (1930) Fox Film Co. [20th]. B&W-84min. Warner Baxter, Myrna Loy .... (3)

REPEAT PERFORMANCE (1947) Eagle Lion. B&W-93min. Joan Leslie, Richard Basehart, Louis Hayward .... (4)

REPENT AT LEISURE (1941) RKO. B&W-66min. Kent Taylor, Wendy Barrie .... (3)

REPORT FROM THE ALEUTIANS (1943) Office of War Information. Color-44min. *(Documentary)*. Director: John Huston .... (5)

REPORT ON THE PARTY AND GUESTS, A (1966) Sigma III. B&W-70min. *(Czech)*. Ivan Vyskocil, Jan Klusak .... (4)
Original title: O SLAVNOSTI A HOSTECH

REPORT TO THE COMMISSIONER (1975) United Artists. Color-112min. Michael Moriarty, Yaphet Kotto 5½*
British title: OPERATION UNDERCOVER

REMEMBER THE NIGHT (1940). The trial of attractive jewel thief Barbara Stanwyck has been recessed during the Christmas holidays, so prosecutor Fred MacMurray good naturedly gives her a ride to her mother's home in Indiana, since he happened to be going there to visit his family.

REPRIEVE (1962) *see* CONVICTS FOUR

REPRISAL (1956) Columbia. **Color-74min.** Guy Madison, Felicia Farr, Kathryn Grant ....(4)

REPTILE, THE (1966) 20th Century-Fox. **Color-90min.** *(British).* Noel Willman, Jennifer Daniel, Jacqueline Pearce......................(4)

REPTILICUS (1961) American-International. **Color-81min.** *(U.S.-Danish).* Carl Ottosen, Ann Smyrner...1*

REPULSION (1965) Royal Films Int'l [Columbia]. **B&W-105min.** *(British).* Catherine Deneuve, Ian Hendry 2*

REQUIEM FOR A GUNFIGHTER (1965) Avco-Embassy. **Color-91min.** Rod Cameron, Stephen McNally...3*

REQUIEM FOR A HEAVYWEIGHT (1962) Columbia. **B&W-87min.** Anthony Quinn, Jackie Gleason, Mickey Rooney 6*
British title: BLOOD MONEY

REQUIEM FOR A SECRET AGENT (1965) CPT (TV). **Color-105min.** *(W. German-Italian-Spanish).* Stewart Granger, Daniela Bianchi, Peter Van Eyck ....(3)
Original title: Original German title: CHEF SCHICKT SEINEN BESTEN MANN, DER

REQUIEM FOR A SECRET AGENT (1966) *see* KILLER'S CARNIVAL

RESCUERS, THE (1977) Buena Vista. **Color-76min.** *(Cartoon).* Director: Wolfgang Reitherman 4*

RESERVED FOR LADIES (1932) Paramount. **B&W-93min.** *(British).* Leslie Howard, George Grossmith, Benita Hume..................(4)
Original title: SERVICE FOR LADIES

REST IS SILENCE, THE (1959) Films Around The World. **B&W-106min.** *(German).* Hardy Kruger, Peter Van Eyck..........................(5)
Original title: REST IS SCHWEIGEN, DER

RESTLESS BREED, THE (1957) 20th Century-Fox. **Color-81min.** Scott Brady, Anne Bancroft 3*

RESTLESS YEARS, THE (1958) Universal. **B&W-86min.** John Saxon, Sandra Dee, Teresa Wright ....(4)
British title: WONDERFUL YEARS, THE

RESURRECTION (1927) United Artists. **B&W-122min.** *(Silent).* Rod La Rocque, Dolores Del Rio ....(4)

RESURRECTION (1980) Universal. **Color- min.** Ellen Burstyn, Eva LaGallienne...

RESURRECTION OF EVE (1973) Mitchell Bros. **Color-90min.** Nancy Weich, Mimi Morgan, Marilyn Chambers 1*

RESURRECTION OF ZACHARY WHEELER, THE (1971) Gold Key Entertainment. **Color-100min.** Bradford Dillman, Leslie Nielsen, Angie Dickinson 5*

RESURRECTION SYNDICATE, THE (1972) *see* NOTHING BUT THE NIGHT

RETIK, THE MOON MENACE (1952) Republic. **B&W-100min.** *(Re-edited Serial).* George Wallace*, Aline Towne ....(2)
Original title: RADAR MEN FROM THE MOON

RETREAT, HELL! (1952) Warner Bros. **B&W-95min.** Frank Lovejoy, Richard Carlson ....(5)

RETURN FROM THE ASHES (1965) Warner Bros. **B&W-107min.** *(British-U.S.).* Ingrid Thulin, Maximilian Schell, Samantha Eggar...4½*

RETURN FROM THE PAST (1967) *see* DR. TERROR'S GALLERY OF HORRORS

RETURN FROM THE SEA (1954) Allied Artists. **B&W-80min.** Jan Sterling, Neville Brand...(3)

RETURN FROM WITCH MOUNTAIN (1978) Buena Vista. **Color-93min.** Bette Davis, Christopher Lee, Kim Richards....................4½*

RETURN OF A MAN CALLED HORSE, THE (1976) United Artists. **Color-125min.** Richard Harris, Gale Sondergaard.........................4*

RETURN OF A STRANGER (1961) Warner Bros. **B&W-63min.** *(British).* John Ireland, Susan Stephen.................................(4)

RETURN OF CHARLIE CHAN (1971) *see* CHARLIE CHAN: HAPPINESS IS A WARM CLUE

RETURN OF COUNT YORGA (1971) American-International. **Color-97min.** Robert Quarry, Mariette Hartley, Roger Perry 3*

RETURN OF DR. X, THE (1939) Warner Bros. **B&W-62min.** Humphrey Bogart, Rosemary Lane, Dennis Morgan..............................(3)

RETURN OF DON CAMILLO, THE (1953) Italian Films Export. **B&W-115min.** *(French-Italian).* Fernandel, Gino Cervi......................(4)
Original title: RETOUR DE DON CAMILLO

RETURN OF DRACULA, THE (1958) United Artists. **B&W-77min.** Francis Lederer, Norma Eberhardt ....(3)
Alternate title: CURSE OF DRACULA, THE
British title: FANTASTIC DISAPPEARING MAN, THE

RETURN OF FRANK JAMES, THE (1940) 20th Century-Fox. **Color-92min.** Henry Fonda, Gene Tierney 5*

RETURN OF GIANT MAJIN, THE (1966) American-International. **Color-86min.** *(Japanese).* Kojiro Hongo, Shiho Fujimura.............2*
Original title: DAIMAJIN IKARU
Alternate title: RETURN OF MAJIN, THE

RETURN OF JACK SLADE, THE (1955) Allied Artists. **B&W-79min.** John Ericson, Mari Blanchard ....(3)
British title: TEXAS ROSE

RETURN OF JESSE JAMES, THE (1950) Lippert Productions. **B&W-75min.** John Ireland, Reed Hadley..............................(4)

RETURN OF MONTE CRISTO, THE (1946) Columbia. **B&W-91min.** Louis Hayward, Barbara Britton 4*
British title: MONTE CRISTO'S REVENGE

RETURN OF MR. MOTO, THE (1965) 20th Century-Fox. **B&W-71min.** *(British).* Henry Silva, Terence Longdon ....(2)

RETURN OF OCTOBER, THE (1948) Columbia. **Color-98min.** Glenn Ford, Terry Moore ....(4)
British title: DATE WITH DESTINY

RETURN OF PETER GRIMM, THE (1935) RKO. **B&W-83min.** Lionel Barrymore, Helen Mack..(5)

RETURN OF SABATA (1972) United Artists. **Color-106min.** *(Italian/French/West German, English language).* Lee Van Cleef, Reiner Schone ....(3)
Original title: E'TORNATO SABATA . . . HAI CHIUSO UN' ALTRA VOLTA *(Return of Sabata . . . You Have Done It Again)*

RETURN OF SANDOKAN (1964) *see* SANDOKAN AGAINST THE LEOPARD OF SARAWAK

RETURN OF SOPHIE LANG, THE (1936) Paramount. **B&W-65min.** Ray Milland, Gertrude Michael...(4)

RETURN OF THE APE MAN (1944) Monogram [Allied Artists]. **B&W-60min.** Bela Lugosi, John Carradine, George Zucco ....(3)

RETURN OF THE BAD MEN (1948) RKO. **B&W-90min.** Randolph Scott, Anne Jeffreys, Robert Ryan.......................................4*

RETURN OF THE BOOMERANG (1970) *see* ADAM'S WOMAN

RETURN OF THE CISCO KID, THE (1939) 20th Century-Fox. **B&W-70min.** Warner Baxter, Lynn Bari ....(4)

RETURN OF THE CORSICAN BROTHERS (1953) *see* BANDITS OF CORSICA

RETURN OF THE DRAGON (1972) Bryanston. **Color-90min.** *(Hong Kong).* Bruce Lee, Nora Miao, Chuck Norris ....(2)
British title: WAY OF THE DRAGON
Common title error: REVENGE OF THE DRAGON

RETURN OF THE FLY, THE (1959) 20th Century-Fox. **B&W-80min.** Vincent Price, Brett Halsey 4*

RETURN OF THE FRONTIERSMAN (1950) Warner Bros. **Color-74min.** Gordon MacRae, Rory Calhoun, Julie London ....(3)

RETURN OF THE GUNFIGHTER (1967) M-G-M. **Color-98min.** *(Made for TV).* Robert Taylor, Chad Everett..............................4*

RETURN OF THE PINK PANTHER, THE (1975) United Artists. **Color-115min.** *(British-U.S.).* Peter Sellers, Christopher Plummer 5*

RETURN OF THE SCARLET PIMPERNEL, THE (1937) United Artists. **B&W-81min.** *(British).* Barry K. Barnes, Sophie Stewart, James Mason ....(3)

RETURN OF THE SEVEN (1966) United Artists. **Color-95min.** *(U.S.-Spanish).* Yul Brynner, Robert Fuller ....(3)
Spanish title: REGRESO DE LOS SIETE MAGNIFICOS, EL *(The Return of the Magnificent Seven)*

RETURN OF THE TALL BLOND MAN WITH ONE BLACK SHOE (1975) Lanir Releasing. **Color-78min.** *(French).* Pierre Richard, Mireille Darc, Jean Rochefort 5*
Original title: RETOUR DU GRAND BLOND, LE *(The Return of the Big Blond)*

RETURN OF THE TEXAN (1952) 20th Century-Fox. **B&W-88min.** Dale Robertson, Joanne Dru, Walter Brennan 4*

RETURN OF THE VAMPIRE, THE (1943) Columbia. **B&W-69min.** Bela Lugosi, Frieda Inescort...(3)

RETURN OF THE VIGILANTES, THE (1947) *see* VIGILANTES RETURN, THE

RETURN OF THE WHISTLER, THE (1948) Columbia. **B&W-63min.** Michael Duane, Lenore Aubert.....................................(4)

RETURN OF THE WORLD'S GREATEST DETECTIVE, THE (1976) MCA-TV. **Color-74min.** *(Made for TV).* Larry Hagman, Jenny O'Hara 4*

RETURN TO CAMPUS (1975) Cinepix. **Color-99min.** Earl Keyes, Norma Joseph..(3)

RETURN TO MACON COUNTY (1975) American-International. Color-89min. Nick Nolte, Don Johnson 4½*
British title: HIGHWAY GIRL

RETURN TO PARADISE (1953) United Artists. Color-100min. Gary Cooper, Roberta Haynes .... (4)

RETURN TO PEYTON PLACE (1961) 20th Century-Fox. Color-122min. Carol Lynley, Jeff Chandler 3*

RETURN TO SENDER (1963) Anglo Amalgamated [EMI]. B&W-63min. *(British).* Nigel Davenport, Yvonne Romain .... (3)

RETURN TO TREASURE ISLAND (1954) United Artists. Color-75min. Tab Hunter, Dawn Addams .... (2)

RETURN TO WARBOW (1958) Columbia. Color-66min. Phil Carey, Catherine McLeod, Andrew Duggan .... (3)

RETURNING HOME (1975) ABC-TV. Color-74min. *(Made for TV).* Dabney Coleman, Tom Selleck, James R. Miller .... (3)

REUNION IN FRANCE (1942) M-G-M. B&W-104min. Joan Crawford, John Wayne 3*

REUNION IN RENO (1951) Universal. B&W-79min. Gigi Perreau, Mark Stevens, Peggy Dow 4*

REUNION IN VIENNA (1933) M-G-M. B&W-100min. John Barrymore, Diana Wynyard, Frank Morgan 3½*

REVEILLE WITH BEVERLY (1943) Columbia. B&W-78min. Ann Miller, Larry Parks .... (3)

REVENGE (1971) ABC-TV. Color-72min. *(Made for TV).* Shelley Winters, Carol Rossen, Bradford Dillman 3½*
Alternate title(?): ONE WOMAN'S REVENGE
Alternate title(?): THERE ONCE WAS A WOMAN

REVENGE (1971) *see* INN OF THE FRIGHTENED PEOPLE

REVENGE AT DAYBREAK (1958) B&W-84min. *(French).* Danielle Delorme, Henri Vidal .... (3)

REVENGE IS MY DESTINY (1971) Gold Key Entertainment. Color-95min. *(Made for TV).* Chris Robinson, Elisa Ingram .... (4)

REVENGE IS SWEET (1934) *see* BABES IN TOYLAND

REVENGE OF BLACK EAGLE (1952) Screen Gems. Color-97min. *(Italian).* Rossano Brazzi, Gianna Maria Canale .... (3)
Original title: VENDETTA DI AQUILA NERA, LA

REVENGE OF FRANKENSTEIN, THE (1958) Columbia. Color-91min. *(British).* Peter Cushing, Francis Matthews 5*

REVENGE OF IVANHOE, THE (1964) Trans-America. Color-100min. *(Italian).* Clyde Rogers, Gilda Lousak 3*
Original title: RIVINCITA DI IVANHOE, LA

REVENGE OF MILADY, THE (1975) *see* FOUR MUSKETEERS, THE

REVENGE OF THE BARBARIANS (1960) American-International. Color-104min. *(Italian).* Daniella Rocca, Anthony Steel, Robert Alda .... (3)
Original title: VENDETTA DEI BARBARI, LA

REVENGE OF THE CHEERLEADERS (1976) Monarch. Color-88min. Jerii Woods, Rainbeaux Smith .... (3)

REVENGE OF THE CONQUERED (1960) American-International. Color-84min. *(Italian).* Burt Nelson, Wandisa Guida .... (1)

REVENGE OF THE CREATURE (1955) Universal. B&W-82min. John Agar, Lori Nelson 3*

REVENGE OF THE GLADIATORS (1964) Paramount. Color-100min. *(Italian).* Roger Browne, Scilla Gabel .... (1)
Original title: VENDETTA DI SPARTACUS, LA *(The Revenge of Spartacus)*

REVENGE OF THE LIVING DEAD (1966) *see* MURDER CLINIC, THE

REVENGE OF THE MUSKETEERS (1963) American-International. Color-97min. *(Italian).* Fernando Lamas, Gloria Milland .... (1)
Original title: D'ARTAGNAN CONTRO I TRE MOSCHETTIERI *(D'Artagnan Against the Three Musketeers)*

REVENGE OF THE PINK PANTHER (1978) United Artists. Color-98min. Peter Sellers, Herbert Lom, Dyan Cannon 4½*

REVENGE OF THE PIRATES (1951) Allied Artists. B&W-94min. *(Italian).* Milly Vitale, Jean-Pierre Aumont, Maria Montez .... (3)
Original title: VENDETTA DEL CORSARO, LA
Alternate title: PIRATE'S REVENGE

REVENGE OF THE VAMPIRE (1960) *see* BLACK SUNDAY

REVENGE OF THE ZOMBIES (1943) Monogram [Allied Artists]. B&W-61min. John Carradine, Gale Storm, Mantan Moreland .... (3)
British title: CORPSE VANISHED, THE

REVENGE OF URSUS (1962) Telewide Systems. Color-99min. *(Italian).* Samson Burke .... (1)
Alternate title: VENGEANCE OF URSUS

REVENGERS, THE (1972) National General. Color-106min. *(U.S.-Mexican).* William Holden, Ernest Borgnine, Woody Strode, Susan Hayward .... (3)

REVOLT AT FORT LARAMIE (1957) United Artists. Color-73min. John Dehner, Greg Palmer, Francis Helm .... (4)

REVOLT IN THE BIG HOUSE (1958) Allied Artists. B&W-79min. Gene Evans, Robert Blake, Timothy Carey .... (4)

REVOLT OF MAMIE STOVER, THE (1956) 20th Century-Fox. Color-92min. Jane Russell, Richard Egan 4½*

REVOLT OF THE BARBARIANS (1964) Trans-America. Color-99min. *(Italian).* Roland Caray, Grazia Maria Spina .... (1)

REVOLT OF THE BOYARS (1946) *see* IVAN THE TERRIBLE, PART II

REVOLT OF THE MAMALUKES (1960) Four Star. Color-90min. *(Egyptian).* Omar Sharif .... (3)

REVOLT OF THE MERCENARIES (1962) Warner Bros. Color-102min. *(Italian-Spanish).* Virginia Mayo, Conrado Sanmartin .... (3)
Original Italian title: RIVOLTA DEI MERCENARI, LA
Spanish title: MERCENARIOS, LOS

REVOLT OF THE PRAETORIANS (1964) ABC Films. Color-95min. *(Italian).* Richard Harrison, Moira Orfei .... (1)
Original title: RIVOLTA DEI PRETORIANI, LA

REVOLT OF THE SLAVES, THE (1961) United Artists. Color-102min. *(Italian-Spanish-W. German).* Rhonda Fleming, Lang Jeffries .... (3)
Original Italian title: RIVOLTA DEGLI SCHIAVI, LA
Spanish title: REBELION DE LOS ESCLAVOS, LA
German title: SKLAVEN ROMS, DIE

REVOLT OF THE TARTARS (1956) *see* MICHEAL STROGOFF

REVOLT OF THE ZOMBIES (1936) Academy Pictures. B&W-65min. Dean Jagger, Dorothy Stone .... (3)

REVOLUTION (1968) Lopert [U.A.]. Color-87min. *(Documentary).* Director: Jack O'Connell .... (4)

REVOLUTIONARY, THE (1970) United Artists. Color-100min. John Voight, Jennifer Salt .... (5)

REWARD, THE (1965) 20th Century-Fox. Color-92min. Max Von Sydow, Yvette Mimieux .... (3)

RHAPSODY (1954) M-G-M. Color-115min. Elizabeth Taylor, Vittorio Gassman, John Ericson 5½*

RHAPSODY IN BLUE (1945) Warner Bros. B&W-139min. Robert Alda, Joan Leslie 5½*

RHINO! (1964) M-G-M. Color-91min. Harry Guardino, Shirley Eaton .. 3½*

RHINOCEROS (1974) American Film Theatre. Color-101min. Zero Mostel, Gene Wilder .... (4)

RHODES (1936) Gaumont-British [Rank]. B&W-91min. *(British).* Walter Huston, Oscar Homolka .... (4)
Original title: RHODES OF AFRICA

RHUBARB (1951) Paramount. B&W-95min. Ray Milland, Jan Sterling 4½*

RHYTHM HITS THE ICE (1942) *see* ICE CAPADES REVUE

RHYTHM ON THE RANGE (1936) Paramount. B&W-87min. Bing Crosby, Frances Farmer .... (4)

RHYTHM ON THE RIVER (1940) Paramount. B&W-92min. Bing Crosby, Mary Martin .... (5)

RHYTHM ROMANCE (1939) *see* SOME LIKE IT HOT

RIBALD TALES OF ROBIN HOOD (1969) Entertainment Ventures. Color-83min. Ralph Jenkins, Dee Lockwood .... (2)
Alternate title: ROBIN HOOD

RICE GIRL (1956) Ultra Pictures Corp. Color-85min. *(Italian).* Elsa Martinelli, Folco Lulli, Rik Battaglia .... (4)
Original title: RISAIA, LA *(The Rice Field)*

RICH AND STRANGE (1932) Powers Pictures. B&W-92min. *(British).* Henry Kendall, Joan Barry .... (4)
Alternate title: EAST OF SHANGHAI

RICH ARE ALWAYS WITH US, THE (1932) First National [W.B.]. B&W-73min. George Brent, Ruth Chatterton, Bette Davis .... (4)

RICH, FULL LIFE, THE (1947) *see* CYNTHIA

RICH KIDS (1979) United Artists. Color-   min. Trini Alvarado, Jeremy Levy ....

RICH MAN, POOR GIRL (1938) M-G-M. B&W-65min. Robert Young, Lew Ayres, Ruth Hussey .... (4)

RICH, YOUNG AND DEADLY (1960) *see* PLATINUM HIGH SCHOOL

RICH, YOUNG AND PRETTY (1951) M-G-M. Color-95min. Jane Powell, Danielle Darrieux .... (4)

RICHARD (1972) Aurora City Group. B&W-83min. Richard M. Dixon (James LaRoe), Dan Resin .... (4)

RICHARD PRYOR LIVE IN CONCERT (1979) Special Event Entertainment. **Color-77min.** Richard Pryor **5½***

RICHARD III (1955) Lopert [U.A.]. **Color-158min.** *(British).* Laurence Olivier, John Gielgud **5***

RICHER THAN THE EARTH (1951) *see* WHISTLE AT EATON FALLS, THE

RICHEST GIRL IN THE WORLD, THE (1960) Unifilms. **Color-78min.** *(Danish).* Nina, Frederik .... (3)
Original title: VERDENS RIGESTE

RICOCHET ROMANCE (1954) Universal. **B&W-80min.** Marjorie Main, Chill Wills, Rudy Vallee **3***

RIDDLE OF THE SANDS, THE (1978) J. Arthur Rank. **Color-109min.** *(British).* Michael York, Jenny Agutter, Simon MacCorkindale ....

RIDE A CROOKED MILE (1938) Paramount. **B&W-78min.** Akim Tamiroff, Frances Farmer .... (3)
British title: ESCAPE FROM YESTERDAY

RIDE A CROOKED TRAIL (1958) Universal. **Color-87min.** Audie Murphy, Gia Scala, Walter Matthau **4***

RIDE A VIOLENT MILE (1957) 20th Century-Fox. **B&W-80min.** John Agar, Penny Edwards .... (3)

RIDE A WILD PONY (1975) Buena Vista. **Color-90min.** *(U.S.-Australian).* Robert Bettles, Eva Griffith **4½***

RIDE BACK, THE (1957) United Artists. **Color-79min.** Anthony Quinn, William Conrad **4***

RIDE BEYOND VENGEANCE (1966) Columbia. **Color-100min.** Chuck Connors, Michael Rennie, Kathryn Hays .... (3)

RIDE CLEAR OF DIABLO (1954) Universal. **Color-80min.** Audie Murphy, Dan Duryea................................ **3½***

RIDE 'EM COWBOY (1942) Universal. **B&W-86min.** Bud Abbott, Lou Costello...............................

RIDE IN THE WHIRLWIND (1966) Walter Reade. **Color-82min.** Cameron Mitchell, Jack Nicholson, Millie Perkins .... (5)
Alternate title: RIDE THE WHIRLWIND

RIDE LONESOME (1959) Columbia. **Color-73min.** Randolph Scott, Karen Steele, Pernell Roberts .... (4)

RIDE OUT FOR REVENGE (1957) United Artists. **B&W-79min.** Rory Calhoun, Gloria Grahame....................... (3)

RIDE THE HIGH COUNTRY (1962) M-G-M. **Color-94min.** Joel McCrea, Randolph Scott **5***
British title: GUNS IN THE AFTERNOON

RIDE THE HIGH IRON (1956) Columbia. **B&W-74min.** Don Taylor, Raymond Burr .... (3)

RIDE THE HIGH WIND (1965) Feature Film Corp. **Color-77min.** *(South African).* Darren McGavin, Maria Perschy.............. (3)

RIDE THE MAN DOWN (1953) Republic. **Color-90min.** Brian Donlevy, Rod Cameron .... (4)

RIDE THE HIGH COUNTRY (1962). Joel McCrea and Randolph Scott are former saddle partners turned enemies, but they unite in a common cause after they and Ron Starr have rescued Mariette Hartley from the man she briefly married and his vengeful brothers, who are pursuing them.

RIDE THE PINK HORSE (1947) Universal. **B&W-101min.** Robert Montgomery, Thomas Gomez **5***

RIDE THE WHIRLWIND (1966) *see* RIDE IN THE WHIRLWIND

RIDE THE WILD SURF (1964) Columbia. **Color-101min.** Fabian, Shelley Fabares, Tab Hunter..................... **3½***

RIDE TO HANGMAN'S TREE, THE (1967) Universal. **Color-90min.** Jack Lord, Melodie Johnson, James Farentino .... (3)

RIDE, VAQUERO (1953) M-G-M. **Color-90min.** Robert Taylor, Ava Gardner............................ (4)

RIDER ON A DEAD HORSE (1962) Allied Artists. **B&W-72min.** John Vivyan, Bruce Gordon .... (2)

RIDER ON THE RAIN (1970) Avco-Embassy. **Color-115min.** *(French-Italian, English version).* Marlene Jobert, Charles Bronson **6***
Original title: PASSAGER DE LA PLUIE, LE

RIDERS OF THE PURPLE SAGE (1925) 20th Century-Fox. **B&W-56min.** *(Silent).* Tom Mix, Beatrice Burnham **4***

RIDERS OF VENGEANCE (1952) *see* RAIDERS, THE

RIDERS TO THE STARS (1954) United Artists. **Color-81min.** William Lundigan, Herbert Marshall **3***

RIDING HIGH (1943) Paramount. **Color-88min.** Dorothy Lamour, Dick Powell............................ (4)
British title: MELODY INN

RIDING HIGH (1950) Paramount. **B&W-112min.** Bing Crosby, Collen Gray .... (5)

RIDING SHOTGUN (1954) Warner Bros. **Color-74min.** Randolph Scott, Wayne Morris, Joan Weldon .... (3)

RIFF-RAFF (1959) Ellis Films. **B&W-102min.** *(French-Italian).* Robert Hossein, Marina Vlady.......................... (3)
Original French title: CANAILLES, LES
British title: TAKE ME AS I AM

RIFF RAFF GIRLS (1959) Continental [Walter Reade]. **B&W-97min.** *(French-Italian).* Nadja Tiller, Robert Hossein .... (4)
Original French title: DU RIFIFI CHEZ LES FEMMES *(Rififi Among the Women)*
Italian title: RIFIFI FRA LE DONNE
Alternate title: RIFIFI FOR GIRLS

RIFFRAFF (1935) M-G-M. **B&W-89min.** Jean Harlow, Spencer Tracy...... **4***

RIFFRAFF (1947) RKO. **B&W-80min.** Pat O'Brien, Walter Slezak........... (5)

RIFIFI (1955) United Motion Pic. Org. (UMPO). **B&W-113min.** *(French).* Jean Servais, Carl Mohner **4½***
Original title: DU RIFIFI CHEZ LES HOMMES *(Brawl Among Men)*

RIFIFI FOR GIRLS (1959) *see* RIFF RAFF GIRLS

RIFIFI IN PARIS (1966) *see* UPPER HAND, THE

RIFIFI IN TOKYO (1963) M-G-M. **B&W-89min.** *(French-Italian).* Karl Boehm, Michel Vitold .... (3)
Original title: RIFIFI A TOKYO

RIGHT APPROACH, THE (1961) 20th Century-Fox. **B&W-92min.** Frankie Vaughan, Martha Hyer.................... (3)

RIGHT CROSS (1950) M-G-M. **B&W-90min.** June Allyson, Dick Powell, Ricardo Montalban .... (4)

RIGHT HAND OF THE DEVIL (1963) Cinema Video International. **B&W-72min.** Aram Katcher, Lisa McDonald................. (3)

RIGHT ON! (1970) Leacock-Pennebaker. **Color-78min.** .... (4)

RIGHT TO THE HEART (1942) 20th Century-Fox. **B&W-74min.** Brenda Joyce, Joseph Allen, Jr. .... (3)

RIKISHA MAN, THE (1958) Cory Film Corp. **Color-105min.** *(Japanese).* Toshiro Mifune, Hideko Takamine................... **5***
Original title: MUHOMATSU NO ISSHO *(The Life of Muhomatsu)*

RING, THE (1952) United Artists. **B&W-79min.** Gerald Mohr, Rita Moreno, Lalo Rios **4***

RING-A-DING RHYTHM (1962) Columbia. **B&W-78min.** *(British).* Helen Shapiro, Craig Douglas, Chubby Checker, Acker Bilk .... (3)
Original title: IT'S TRAD, DAD

RING OF BRIGHT WATER (1969) Cinerama Releasing. **Color-107min.** *(British).* Bill Travers, Virginia McKenna **5½***

RING OF FEAR (1954) Warner Bros. **Color-93min.** Clyde Beatty, Pat O'Brien, Mickey Spillane .... (3)

RING OF FIRE (1961) M-G-M. **Color-91min.** David Janssen, Joyce Taylor .... (4)

RING OF PASSION (1978) 20th Century-Fox. **Color-100min.** *(Made for TV).* Bernie Casey, Stephen Macht ....

RING OF TERROR (1962) Ronnie Ashcroft Inc. and Playstar Prods. **B&W-71min.** George Mather, Esther Furst .... (3)

RING OF SPIES (1964) *see* RING OF TREASON

RING OF TREASON (1964) Paramount. **B&W-90min.** *(British).* Bernard Lee, William Sylvester, Margaret Tyzack .... (4)
Original title: RING OF SPIES

RINGER, THE (1979) Columbia. **Color-   min.** Jeff Bridges, Bianca Jagger ....

RINGS AROUND THE WORLD (1966) Columbia. **Color-98min.** *(Documentary). Director:* Gilbert Cates .... (5)

RINGS ON HER FINGERS (1942) 20th Century-Fox. **B&W-85min.** Henry Fonda, Gene Tierney .... (4)

RINGSIDE (1949) Lippert Productions. **B&W-63min.** Don "Red" Barry, Sheila Ryan .... (3)

RINGSIDE MAISIE (1941) M-G-M. **B&W-96min.** Ann Sothern, George Murphy, Robert Sterling .... (3)
British title: CASH AND CARRY

RIO (1939) Universal. **B&W-75min.** Basil Rathbone, Victor McLaglen ... (4)

RIO BRAVO (1959) Warner Bros. **Color-141min.** John Wayne, Dean Martin 3½*

RIO CONCHOS (1964) 20th Century-Fox. **Color-107min.** Richard Boone, Stuart Whitman .... (4)

RIO GRANDE (1950) Republic. **B&W-105min.** John Wayne, Maureen O'Hara 3*

RIO LOBO (1970) Nat'l General (for Cinema Center). **Color-114min.** John Wayne, Jorge Rivero 4*

RIO RITA (1929) RKO. **B&W-135min.** Bebe Daniels, John Boles 3*

RIO RITA (1942) M-G-M. **B&W-91min.** Bud Abbott, Lou Costello, Kathryn Grayson 4*

RIOT (1969) Paramount. **Color-97min.** Jim Brown, Gene Hackman 4*

RIOT IN CELL BLOCK 11 (1954) Allied Artists. **B&W-80min.** Neville Brand, Emile Meyer 4½*

RIOT IN JUVENILE PRISON (1959) United Artists. **B&W-71min.** Jerome Thor, Marcia Henderson .... (3)

RIOT ON PIER 6 (1955) *see* NEW ORLEANS UNCENSORED

RIOT ON SUNSET STRIP (1967) American-International. **Color-85min.** Aldo Ray, Mimsy Farmer, Michael Evans 2*

RIPTIDE (1934) M-G-M. **B&W-90min.** Norma Shearer, Robert Montgomery .... (4)

RISE AND FALL OF LEGS DIAMOND, THE (1960) Warner Bros. **B&W-101min.** Ray Danton, Karen Steele 4*

RISE AND SHINE (1941) 20th Century-Fox. **B&W-93min.** Jack Oakie, George Murphy .... (4)

RISE OF HELGA, THE (1931) *see* SUSAN LENNOX - HER FALL AND RISE

RISE OF LOUIS XIV, THE (1966) Brandon. **Color-100min.** *(French, Made for TV).* Jean-Marie Patte, Raymond Jourdan 3*
Original title: PRISE DE POUVOIR PAR LOUIS XIV, LA

RISING OF THE MOON, THE (1957) Warner Bros. **B&W-81min.** *(Irish).*   Tyrone Power, Noel Purcell 5½*

RISK, THE (1960) Kingsley International. **B&W-81min.** *(British).* Tony Britton, Virginia Maskell .... (4)
Original title: SUSPECT

RISO AMARO (1949) *see* BITTER RICE

RITUAL OF EVIL (1970) Universal. **Color-98min.** *(Made for TV).* Louis Jourdan, Anne Baxter, Diana Hyland 4*

RITUALS (1978) Day and Date International. **Color-94min.** *(Canadian).* Hal Holbrook, Lawrence Dane, Robin Gammell ....

RITZ, THE (1976) Warner Bros. **Color-90min.** *(British).* Jack Weston, Rita Moreno 5*

RIVALRY, THE (1975) NBC-TV. **Color-75min.** *(Made for TV).* Arthur Hill, Charles Durning ....

RIVALS, THE (1963) BBC. **B&W-56min.** *(British).* Jack Gwillim, Erica Rogers .... (3)

RIVALS (1972) Avco-Embassy. **Color-101min.** Joan Hackett, Robert Klein, Scott Jacoby .... (4)

RIVER, THE (1937) U. S. Government. **B&W-30min.** *(Documentary). Director:* Pare Lorentz 4*

RIVER, THE (1951) United Artists. **Color-99min.** *(U.S.-Indian).* Patricia Walters, Thomas E. Breen .... (5)

RIVER AND DEATH, THE (1954) Bauer International. **B&W-90min.** *(Mexican).* Columba Dominguez, Miguel Torruco ....
Original title: RIO Y LA MUERTE, EL

RIVER BEAT (1954) Lippert Productions. **B&W-70min.** *(British).* Phyllis Kirk, John Bentley .... (3)

RIVER CHANGES, THE (1956) Warner Bros. **B&W-91min.** Rosanna Rory, Harold Maresch .... (3)

RIVER GANG (1945) Universal. **B&W-64min.** Gloria Jean, Bill Goodwin .... (4)
British title: FAIRY TALE MURDER

RIVER LADY (1948) Universal. **Color-78min.** Yvonne De Carlo, Dan Duryea 3*

RIVER NIGER, THE (1976) Cine Artists. **Color-105min.** Cicely Tyson, James Earl Jones, Lou Gossett 4*

RIVER OF EVIL (1964) **Color-86min.** *(German).* Barbara Rutting, Harold Leipnitz .... (3)

RIVER OF GOLD (1971) ABC Films. **B&W-74min.** *(Made for TV).* Dack Rambo, Roger Davis, Ray Milland .... (2)

RIVER OF MYSTERY (1969) MCA-TV. **Color-96min.** *(Made for TV).* Vic Morrow, Claude Akins, Edmond O'Brien 3½*

RIVER OF NO RETURN (1954) 20th Century-Fox. **Color-91min.** Robert Mitchum, Marilyn Monroe 4*

RIVER OF THREE JUNKS, THE (1957) Trans-America. **Color-90min.** *(French).* Jean Gaven, Dominique Wilms .... (3)

riverrun (1970) Columbia. **Color-87min.** Louise Ober, John McLiam........ (5)

RIVER'S EDGE, THE (1957) 20th Century-Fox. **Color-87min.** Ray Milland, Anthony Quinn, Debra Paget 3*

RIVER'S END (1940) Warner Bros. **B&W-69min.** Dennis Morgan, Victor Jory .... (3)
Alternate title: DOUBLE IDENTITY

RIVERS OF FIRE AND ICE (1969) *see* AFRICAN SAFARI

ROAD BUILDER, THE (1971) *see* NIGHT DIGGER, THE

ROAD HOUSE (1948) 20th Century-Fox. **B&W-95min.** Ida Lupino, Cornel Wilde 4*

ROAD HOUSE GIRL (1953) *see* WHEEL OF FATE

ROAD HUSTLERS, THE (1968) American-International. **Color-95min.** Jim Davis, Scott Brady, Bruce Yarnell .... (3)

ROAD RACERS (1959) American-International. **B&W-78min.** Joel Lawrence, Marian Collier, Skip Ward .... (3)

ROAD SHOW (1941) United Artists. **B&W-87min.** Carole Landis, Adolphe Menjou .... (4)
Title error: ROADSHOW

ROAD TO BALI, THE (1952) Paramount. **Color-91min.** Bob Hope, Bing Crosby, Dorothy Lamour 4½*

ROAD TO DENVER, THE (1955) Republic. **Color-90min.** John Payne, Mona Freeman 3½*

ROAD TO GLORY, THE (1936) 20th Century-Fox. **B&W-95min.** Fredric March, Warner Baxter, Lionel Barrymore 4*

ROAD TO HONG KONG, THE (1962) United Artists. **B&W-91min.** *(British-U.S.).* Bing Crosby, Bob Hope, Joan Collins 4*

ROAD TO MOROCCO, THE (1942) Paramount. **B&W-83min.** Bing Crosby, Bob Hope, Dorothy Lamour 4*

ROAD TO NASHVILLE (1966) Crown International. **Color-109min.** Doodles Weaver, Richard Arlen, Johnny Cash, Webb Pierce .... (3)

ROAD TO RIO, THE (1947) Paramount. **B&W-100min.** Bing Crosby, Bob Hope, Dorothy Lamour 4*

ROAD TO SALINA (1969) Avco-Embassy. **Color-96min.** *(French-Italian).* Rita Hayworth, Robert Walker (Jr.), Mimsy Farmer .... (3)
Original French title: SUR LA ROUTE DE SALINA *(On the Road to Salina)*

ROAD TO SINGAPORE, THE (1940) Paramount. **Color-84min.** Bing Crosby, Dorothy Lamour, Bob Hope 4*

ROAD TO UTOPIA, THE (1946) Paramount. **B&W-89min.** Bing Crosby, Bob Hope, Dorothy Lamour 4½*

ROAD TO ZANZIBAR, THE (1941) Paramount. **B&W-92min.** Bing Crosby, Bob Hope, Dorothy Lamour 4*

ROADBLOCK (1951) RKO. **B&W-73min.** Charles McGraw, Milburn Stone .... (3)

ROAD SHOW (1941) *see* ROADSHOW

ROAR OF THE CROWD (1953) Allied Artists. **Color-71min.** Howard Duff, Helene Stanley 3*

ROARING TIMBER (1936) *see* COME AND GET IT

ROARING TWENTIES, THE (1939) Warner Bros. **B&W-104min.** James Cagney, Humphrey Bogart, Priscilla Lane 5½*

ROB ROY, THE HIGHLAND ROGUE (1953) RKO (for Disney). **Color-84min.** *(U.S.-British).* Richard Todd, Glynis Johns .... (5)

ROBBER'S ROOST (1955) United Artists. **B&W-82min.** Robert Montgomery, Richard Boone .... (3)

ROBBERY (1967) Avco-Embassy. **Color-114min.** *(British).* Stanley Baker, Joanna Pettet 5*

Films are rated on a 1 to 10 scale, 10 is highest. **Boldface** ratings followed by an asterisk (*) are for films actually seen and rated by the executive and senior editors. All other ratings are estimates. (See Notes on Entertainment Ratings in the front section.)

ROBBERY ROMAN STYLE (1964) Paramount. B&W-93min. *(Italian)*. Claudia Mori, Adriana Celentano ....(3)

ROBBERY UNDER ARMS (1957) J. Arthur Rank. Color-99min. *(British)*. Peter Finch, Maureen Swanson, Ronald Lewis ....(4)

ROBBY (1968) Bluewood Films. Color-91min. Warren Raum, Ryp Siani, John Garces ....(3)

ROBE, THE (1953) 20th Century-Fox. Color-135min. Richard Burton, Jean Simmons, Victor Mature **5***

ROBERTA (1935) RKO. B&W-105min. Irene Dunne, Fred Astaire, Ginger Rogers **5***

ROBIN AND MARIAN (1976) Columbia. Color-106min. Sean Connery, Audrey Hepburn **6***

ROBIN AND THE SEVEN HOODS (1964) Warner Bros. Color-103min. Frank Sinatra, Dean Martin **5***

ROBIN HOOD (1922) United Artists. B&W-142min. *(Silent)*. Douglas Fairbanks, Enid Bennett ....(4)

ROBIN HOOD (1969) *see* RIBALD TALES OF ROBIN HOOD

ROBIN HOOD (1973) Buena Vista. Color-83min. *(Cartoon)*. *Director:* Wolfgang Reitherman **4***

ROBIN HOOD AND THE PIRATES (1963) Avco-Embassy. Color-88min. *(Italian)*. Lex Barker, Jacke Lane ....(3)
Original title: ROBIN HOOD E I PIRATI

ROBIN HOOD OF EL DORADO (1936) M-G-M. B&W-86min. Warner Baxter, Ann Loring, Bruce Cabot ....(4)

ROBINSON CRUSOE (1954) *see* ADVENTURES OF ROBINSON CRUSOE

ROBINSON CRUSOE (1974) NBC-TV. Color-100min. *(British, Made for TV)*. Stanley Baker, Ram John Holder **4***

ROBINSON CRUSOE OF MYSTERY ISLAND (1936) Republic. B&W-100min. *(Re-edited Serial)*. Mala, Mamo Clark ....(3)
Original title: ROBINSON CRUSOE OF CLIPPER ISLAND
British title of the serial: S.O.S. CLIPPER ISLAND

ROBINSON CRUSOE ON MARS (1964) Paramount. Color-110min. Paul Mantee, Vic Lundin **3***

ROBINSON CRUSOELAND (1952) *see* UTOPIA

ROBIN AND MARIAN (1976). Having left her for twenty years of war in Europe, Sean Connery (as Robin Hood) finds Audrey Hepburn (as Maid Marian), now an abbess, more forgiving than he really deserves.

ROBOT MONSTER (1953) Astor. B&W-63min. George Nader, Claudia Barrett ....(1)
TV title: MONSTERS FROM THE MOON

ROBOT VS. THE AZTEC MUMMY, THE (1959) Azteca. B&W-65min. *(Mexican)*. Ramon Gay, Rosita Arenas ....(1)
Original title: ROBOT HUMANO, EL *(The Human Robot)*
Alternate Mexican title: MOMIA AZTECA CONTRA EL ROBOT HUMANO, LA *(The Aztec Mummy vs. the Human Robot)*

ROCAMBOLE (1962) Independent TV Corp (ITC). Color-106min. *(French)*. Channing Pollock, Hedy Vessel ....(4)

ROCCO AND HIS BROTHERS (1960) Astor. B&W-175min. *(Italian-French)*. Alain Delon, Renato Salvatori **4***
Original Italian title: ROCCO I SUOI FRATELLI
French title: ROCCO ET SES FRERES

ROCK-A-BYE BABY (1958) Paramount. Color-103min. Jerry Lewis, Marilyn Maxwell **4***

ROCK ALL NIGHT (1957) American-International. B&W-65min. Dick Miller, Russell Johnson, The Platters ....(3)

ROCK AROUND THE CLOCK (1956) Columbia. B&W-77min. Johnny Johnston, Lisa Gaye ....(3)

ROCK AROUND THE WORLD (1957) American-International. B&W-72min. *(British)*. Tommy Steele, Lisa Daniely ....(3)
Original title: TOMMY STEELE STORY, THE

ROCK ISLAND TRAIL (1950) Republic. B&W-90min. Forrest Tucker, Adele Mara **4***
British title: TRANSCONTINENT EXPRESS

ROCK 'N' ROLL HIGH SCHOOL (1979) New World. Color-92min. Vincent Van Patten, P. J. Soles

ROCK 'N' ROLL REVUE (1956) Studio Films. Color-93min. *(Music Film)*. *Director:* Joseph Kohn ....(3)
Alternate title: ROCK 'N' ROLL JAMBOREE
British title: HARLEM ROCK 'N' ROLL

ROCK, PRETTY BABY (1957) Universal. B&W-89min. Sal Mineo, John Saxon, Luana Patten

ROCK, ROCK, ROCK! (1956) Distributors Corp. of America. B&W-83min. Tuesday Weld, Connie Francis, Chuck Berry ....(3)

ROCKET FROM CALBUCH, THE (1956) Trans-Lux Distributing. B&W-90min. *(Spanish-Italian)*. Edmund Gwenn, Valentina Cortesa ....(4)
Original Spanish title: CALABUCH
Italian title: CALABUIG

ROCKET MAN, THE (1954) 20th Century-Fox. Color-79min. Charles Coburn, George Winslow, John Agar ....(3)

ROCKET SHIP (1936) *see* SPACESHIP TO THE UNKNOWN

ROCKETS GALORE (1958) *see* MAD LITTLE ISLAND

ROCKETSHIP X-M (1950) Lippert Productions. B&W-77min. Lloyd Bridges, Osa Massen **4***

ROCKFORD FILES, THE (1974) MCA-TV. Color-74min. *(Made for TV)*. James Garner, Lindsay Wagner, Joe Santos **4***

ROCKIN' IN THE ROCKIES (1945) Columbia. B&W-63min. Mary Beth Hughes, Jay Kirby ....(3)
British title: PARTNERS IN FORTUNE

ROCKING HORSE WINNER, THE (1949) Universal. B&W-91min. *(British)*. Valerie Hobson, John Howard Davies **5½***

ROCKY (1976) United Artists. Color-119min. Sylvester Stallone, Talia Shire, Burgess Meredith **6½***

ROCKY II (1979) United Artists. Color-119min. Sylvester Stallone, Talia Shire **6½***

ROCKY HORROR PICTURE SHOW, THE (1975) 20th Century-Fox. Color-100min. *(British)*. Tim Curry, Susan Sarandon ....(4)

ROCKY MOUNTAIN (1950) Warner Bros. B&W-83min. Errol Flynn, Patrice Wymore ....(4)

RODAN (1956) Distributors Corp. of America. Color-70min. *(Japanese)*. Kenji Sahara, Yumi Shirakawa, Rodan **2***
Original title: RADON

RODEO (1952) Monogram [Allied Artists]. Color-70min. Jane Nigh, John Archer ....(3)

ROGER TOUHY, GANGSTER (1944) 20th Century-Fox. B&W-65min. Preston Foster, Victor McLaglen ....(4)
British title: LAST GANGSTER, THE

ROGUE COP (1954) M-G-M. B&W-92min. Robert Taylor, Janet Leigh ..**4***

ROGUE RIVER (1950) Eagle Lion. Color-81min. Frank Fenton, Peter Graves **3***

ROGUE SONG, THE (1930) M-G-M. Color-108min. Lawrence Tibbett, Catherine Dale Owen ....(4)

ROGUES' GALLERY (1968) Paramount. Color-82min. Roger Smith, Greta Baldwin, Dennis Morgan, Edgar Bergen **4***

ROGUE'S MARCH (1953) M-G-M. **B&W-84min.** Peter Lawford, Janice Rule .... (3)

ROGUES OF SHERWOOD FOREST (1950) Columbia. **Color-80min.** John Derek, Diana Lynn 4*

ROGUE'S REGIMENT (1948) Universal. **B&W-86min.** Dick Powell, Marta Toren .... (4)

ROLAND THE MIGHTY (1961) ABC Films. **Color-98min.** (Italian). Rick Battaglia, Rosanna Schiaffino .... (3)
Alternate title: ORLANDO

ROLL, FREDDY ROLL (1975) ABC Circle Films. **Color-73min.** Tim Conway, Jan Murray 3*

ROLLER DERBY (1971) see DERBY

ROLLERBALL (1975) United Artists. **Color-129min.** James Caan, John Houseman 5*

ROLLERCOASTER (1977) Universal. **Color-119min.** George Segal, Timothy Bottoms, Richard Widmark 5½*

ROLLING MAN (1972) Aaron Spelling. **Color-73min.** (Made for TV). Dennis Weaver, Don Stroud, Donna Mills .... (4)

ROLLING THUNDER (1977) American-International. **Color-99min.** William Devane, Tommy Lee Jones, Linda Haynes 4*

ROMA (1972) see FELLINI'S ROMA

ROMAN HOLIDAY (1953) Paramount. **B&W-119min.** Gregory Peck, Audrey Hepburn 6*

ROMAN SCANDALS (1933) United Artists. **B&W-93min.** Eddie Cantor, Ruth Etting 4*

ROMAN SPRING OF MRS. STONE, THE (1961) Warner Bros. **Color-104min.** (U.S.-British). Vivien Leigh, Warren Beatty, Lotte Lenya 4*
Alternate title: WIDOW AND THE GIGOLO, THE

ROMANCE (1930) M-G-M. **B&W-78min.** Greta Garbo, Lewis Stone, Gavin Gordon .... (3)

ROMANCE AND RHYTHM (1938) see COWBOY FROM BROOKLYN

ROMANCE AND RHYTHM (1940) Republic. **B&W-86min.** Kenny Baker, Frances Langford .... (4)

ROMANCE AND RICHES (1936) Grand National (American). **B&W-70min.** (British). Cary Grant, Mary Brian .... (4)
Original title: AMAZING QUEST OF ERNEST BLISS, THE
Alternate title: AMAZING QUEST, THE

ROMANCE FOR THREE (1938) see PARADISE FOR THREE

ROMANCE IN PARIS (1937) see KING AND THE CHORUS GIRL, THE

ROMANCE OF A HORSE THIEF (1971) Allied Artists. **Color-101min.** Yul Brynner, Eli Wallach 2*

ROMANCE OF ROSY RIDGE, THE (1947) M-G-M. **B&W-105min.** Van Johnson, Janet Leigh 4*

ROMANCE OF THE RIO GRANDE (1941) 20th Century-Fox. **B&W-73min.** Cesar Romero, Patricia Morison .... (3)

ROMANCE ON THE HIGH SEAS (1948) Warner Bros. **Color-99min.** Jack Carson, Doris Day 5*
British title: IT'S MAGIC

ROMANOFF AND JULIET (1961) Universal. **Color-103min.** Peter Ustinov, Sandra Dee, John Gavin 4*
Alternate title: DIG THAT JULIET

ROMANTIC AGE, THE (1949) see NAUGHTY ARLETTE

ROMANTIC ENGLISHWOMAN, THE (1975) New World. **Color-117min.** (British-French). Glenda Jackson, Michael Caine 3*

ROME ADVENTURE (1962) Warner Bros. **Color-119min.** Suzanne Pleshette, Troy Donahue 4½*

ROME 11 O'CLOCK (1952) Times Film Corp. **B&W-107min.** (Italian). Lucia Bose, Raf Vallone .... (5)
Original title: ROMA, ORE 11

ROME, 1585 (1962) American-International. **Color-85min.** Debra Paget, Daniella Rocca .... (2)

ROMEO AND JULIET (1936) M-G-M. **B&W-127min.** Leslie Howard, Norma Shearer 5½*

ROMEO AND JULIET (1954) United Artists. **Color-140min.** Laurence Harvey, Susan Shentall 5*

ROMEO AND JULIET (1966) Avco-Embassy. **Color-126min.** (British). Margot Fonteyn, Rudolph Nureyev 3*

ROMEO AND JULIET (1968) Paramount. **Color-139min.** (Italian-British-U.S.). Leonard Whiting, Olivia Hussey 7*
Italian title: ROMEO E GIULIETTA

ROMMEL - DESERT FOX (1951) see DESERT FOX, THE

ROMMEL'S TREASURE (1955) Medallion. **Color-85min.** (Italian). Dawn Addams, Paul Christian, Bruce Cabot ..... (4)
Original title: TESORO DI ROMMEL, IL

ROMP OF FANNY HILL (1964) see FANNY HILL: MEMOIRS OF A WOMAN OF PLEASURE

ROMULUS AND THE SABINES (1961) Avco-Embassy. **Color-101min.** (Italian-French). Roger Moore, Mylene Demongeot, Jean Marais ...... (3)
Original Italian title: RATTO DELLE SABINE, IL (The Abduction of the Sabines)
Alternate title: RAPE OF THE SABINES

RONDE, LA (1950) Commercial Pictures. **B&W-100min.** (French). Anton Walbrook, Simone Signoret .... (5)

RONDE, LA (1964) see CIRCLE OF LOVE

ROOF, THE (1956) Trans-Lux Distributing. **B&W-91min.** (Italian). Gabriella Pallotti, Giorgio Listuzzi .... (5)
Original title: TETTO, IL

ROOKIE, THE (1960) 20th Century-Fox. **B&W-86min.** Tommy Noonan, Pete Marshall, Julie Newmar 2*

ROOKIE FIREMAN (1950) Columbia. **B&W-63min.** Bill Williams, Barton MacLane .... (3)

ROOKIES (1941) see BUCK PRIVATES

ROOKIES, THE (1971) Worldvision. **Color-73min.** (Made for TV). Darren McGavin, Robert F. Lyons, Georg Stanford Brown ...... (4)

ROOKIES COME HOME (1947) see BUCK PRIVATES COME HOME

ROOKIES IN BURMA (1943) RKO. **B&W-62min.** Alan Carney, Wally Brown, Joan Barclay .... (3)

ROOM AT THE TOP (1958) Continental [Walter Reade]. **B&W-115min.** (British). Laurence Harvey, Simone Signoret 8*

ROOM FOR ONE MORE (1952) Warner Bros. **B&W-98min.** Cary Grant, Betsy Drake 4*
Alternate title: EASY WAY, THE

ROOM 43 (1958) Cory Film Corp. **B&W-91min.** (British). Odile Versois, Diana Dors, Herbert Lom, Eddie Constantine ...... (3)
Original title: PASSPORT TO SHAME

ROOM SERVICE (1938) RKO. **B&W-78min.** The Marx Brothers, Lucille Ball 3*

ROOM 13 (1964) UCC Films. **B&W-82min.** (German). Jachim Fuchsberger, Karin Dor .... (3)

ROOMMATES (1961) Herts-Lion International. **Color-91min.** (British). James Robertson Justice, Leslie Phillips, Sidney James .... (4)
Original title: RAISING THE WIND

ROOMMATES (1971) Clayton G. Pantages. **Color-97min.** Dan Mason, Harvey Marks, Barbara Press .... (2)

ROONEY (1958) J. Arthur Rank. **B&W-88min.** (British). John Gregson, Muriel Pavlow, Barry Fitzgerald 5*

ROOSEVELT STORY, THE (1947) United Artists. **B&W-80min.** (Documentary). Producer: Martin Levine .... (5)

ROOSTER COGBURN (1975) Universal. **Color-107min.** John Wayne, Katharine Hepburn 5½*
Publicity title: ROOSTER COGBURN AND THE LADY

ROOTS, THE (1954) Harrison Pictures. **B&W-96min.** (Mexican). Beatriz Florez, Juan De La Cruz 4½*

ROOTS OF HEAVEN, THE (1958) 20th Century-Fox. **Color-131min.** Trevor Howard, Juliette Greco 5*

ROPE (1948) Warner Bros. **Color-80min.** (U.S.-British). James Stewart, Farley Granger 6*

ROPE AROUND THE NECK (1964) Commonwealth United TV. **B&W-85min.** (French). Jean Richard, Dany Robin .... (3)

ROPE OF SAND (1949) Paramount. **B&W-104min.** Burt Lancaster, Paul Henreid 4*

ROSE, THE (1979) 20th Century-Fox. **Color-   min.** Bette Midler, Alan Bates, Frederic Forrest ....

ROSE BERND (1957) see SINS OF ROSE BERND, THE

ROSE BOWL STORY, THE (1952) Monogram [Allied Artists]. **Color-73min.** Marshall Thompson, Vera Miles .... (3)

ROSE FOR EVERYONE, A (1967) Royal Films Int'l [Columbia]. **Color-107min.** (Italian). Claudia Cardinale, Nino Manfredi, Akim Tamiroff (3)
Original title: ROSA PER TUTTI, UNA
Alternate title: EVERY MAN'S WOMAN
Alternate title: EVERYMAN'S WOMAN

ROSE-MARIE (1928) M-G-M. **B&W-86min.** (Silent). Joan Crawford, James Murray .... (4)

ROSE MARIE (1936) M-G-M. **B&W-113min.** Jeanette MacDonald, Nelson Eddy 5½*
TV title: INDIAN LOVE CALL

ROSE MARIE (1954) M-G-M. **Color-115min.** Ann Blyth, Howard Keel .. (4)

ROSE OF CIMARRON (1952) 20th Century-Fox. **Color-72min.** Mala Powers, Jack Buetel .... (3)

ROSE OF THE RANCHO (1936) Paramount. **B&W-82min.** Gladys Swarthout, John Boles......(3)

ROSE OF WASHINGTON SQUARE (1939) 20th Century-Fox. **B&W-86min.** Tyrone Power, Alice Faye......(4)

ROSE TATTOO, THE (1955) Paramount. **B&W-117min.** Anna Magnani, Burt Lancaster......**5½***

ROSEANNA McCOY (1949) RKO. **B&W-89min.** Farley Granger, Joan Evans......**3***

ROSEBUD (1975) United Artists. **Color-126min.** Peter O'Toole, Richard Attenborough......**5½***

ROSELAND (1971) Boxoffice International. **Color-90min.** E. Kerrigan Prescott, Victor Alter, Christopher Brooks......(3)

ROSELAND (1977) Cinema Shares. **Color-103min.** Teresa Wright, Lou Jacobi, Geraldine Chaplin......**4***

ROSEMARY (1958) Films Around The World. **B&W-105min.** *(German).* Nadja Tiller, Peter Van Eyck, Mario Adorf......(5)
Original title: MAEDCHEN ROSEMARIE *(The Girl Rosemarie)*

ROSEMARY'S BABY (1968) Paramount. **Color-137min.** Mia Farrow, John Cassavetes......**7***

ROSENKAVALIER, DER (1962) Rank Overseas Film Distribution Ltd. **Color-195min.** *(British).* Elisabeth Schwarzkopf, Otto Edelmann......**3***

ROSES FOR THE PROSECUTOR (1959) American Metropolitan. **B&W-92min.** *(German).* Walter Giller, Martin Held......(5)
Original title: ROSEN FUER DEN STAATSANWALT

ROSIE! (1967) Universal. **Color-98min.** Rosalind Russell, Sandra Dee......**4***

ROSITA (1923) United Artists. **B&W-117min.** *(Silent).* Mary Pickford, Holbrook Binn, George Walsh......(4)

ROTTEN TO THE CORE (1965) Cinema 5. **B&W-88min.** *(British).* Anton Rodgers, Eric Sykes......**5***

ROUÉ, LA (1956) Curzon. **B&W-105min.** *(French).* Jean Servais, Catherine Anouilh......(3)
Alternate title: WHEELS OF FATE

ROUGE ET NOIR (1958) Distributors Corp. of America. **Color-145min.** *(French).* Gerard Philipe, Danielle Darrieux......**5½***
Original title: ROUGE ET LE NOIR, LE *(The Red and the Black)*

ROUGH AND THE SMOOTH, THE (1959) *see* PORTRAIT OF A SINNER

ROUGH COMPANY (1955) *see* VIOLENT MEN, THE

ROUGH NIGHT IN JERICHO (1967) Universal. **Color-104min.** Dean Martin, George Peppard......**4***

ROUGH SHOOT (1953) *see* SHOOT FIRST

ROUGH, TOUGH AND READY (1945) Columbia. **B&W-66min.** Chester Morris, Victor McLaglen......(3)
British title: MEN OF THE DEEP

ROUGHLY SPEAKING (1945) Warner Bros. **B&W-117min.** Rosalind Russell, Jack Carson......**4***

ROUGHSHOD (1949) RKO. **B&W-88min.** Robert Sterling, Gloria Grahame......(4)

ROUND-UP, THE (1941) Paramount. **B&W-90min.** Richard Dix, Patricia Morison......(3)

ROUND UP, THE (1966) Altura Films. **B&W-94min.** *(Hungarian).* Janos Gorbe, Tibor Molnar......(5)
Original title: SZEGENYLEGÉNYEK (NEHÉZÉLETUEK)
Alternate U.S. title: HOPELESS ONES, THE

ROUNDERS, THE (1965) M-G-M. **Color-85min.** Glenn Ford, Henry Fonda......**4***

ROUSTABOUT (1964) Paramount. **Color-101min.** Elvis Presley, Barbara Stanwyck......**4***

ROXIE HART (1942) 20th Century-Fox. **B&W-75min.** Ginger Rogers, Adolphe Menjou......**5½***

ROYAL AFFAIR, A (1950) Discina International. **B&W-98min.** *(French).* Maurice Chevalier, Sophie Desmarets, Annie Ducaux......(4)
Original title: ROI, LE *(The King)*

ROYAL AFFAIRS IN VERSAILLES (1954) Times Film Corp. **Color-144min.** *(French).* Louis Arbessier, Georges Marchal......(4)
Original title: SI VERSAILLES M'ÉTAIT CONTÉ *(If I Were Told About Versailles)*
Alternate title: AFFAIRS IN VERSAILLES
British title: VERSAILLES

ROYAL AFRICAN RIFLES, THE (1953) Allied Artists. **Color-75min.** Louis Hayward, Veronica Hurst......(2)
British title: STORM OVER AFRICA

ROYAL BALLET, THE (1960) Lopert [U.A.]. **Color-131min.** *(British).* Margot Fonteyn, Michael Somes......(4)

ROYAL CAVALCADE (1935) *see* REGAL CAVALCADE

ROXIE HART (1942) is a red-headed dancer, played by Ginger Rogers, on trial for a murder she didn't commit, hoping her confession would bring her the publicity boost her career needs. Her flamboyant lawyer Adolphe Menjou eloquently pleads her case to an all-male jury. Judge is George Lessey.

ROYAL FAMILY OF BROADWAY (1931) Paramount. **B&W-82min.** Fredric March, Mary Brian......(4)

ROYAL FLASH (1975) 20th Century-Fox. **Color-98min.** *(British).* Malcolm McDowell, Alan Bates......**6***

ROYAL FLUSH (1946) *see* TWO GUYS FROM MILWAUKEE

ROYAL HUNT OF THE SUN, THE (1969) Nat'l General (for Cinema Center). **Color-121min.** *(British-U.S.).* Robert Shaw, Christopher Plummer......**4½***

ROYAL JOURNEY (1952) Nat'l Film Board of Canada. **Color-47min.** *(Canadian, Documentary).* Director: David Bairstow......(5)

ROYAL SCANDAL, A (1945) 20th Century-Fox. **B&W-94min.** Tallulah Bankhead, Charles Coburn......**5½***
British title: CZARINA

ROYAL WEDDING (1951) M-G-M. **Color-93min.** Fred Astaire, Jane Powell......**4½***
British title: WEDDING BELLS

RUBY (1977) Dimension Pictures. **Color-84min.** Piper Laurie, Stuart Whitman, Janit Baldwin......**3***

RUBY GENTRY (1953) 20th Century-Fox. **B&W-82min.** Jennifer Jones, Charlton Heston......**5***
Original screen title: RUBY

RUDOLPH AND FROSTY'S CHRISTMAS IN JULY (1979) Avco-Embassy. **Color-102min.** ......

RUE DE PARIS (1959) Lopert [U.A.]. **B&W-90min.** *(French).* Jean Gabin, Claude Brasseur......**4***
Original title: RUE DES PRAIRIES
Alternate title: STREETS OF PARIS

RUFFIANS, THE (1959) Ellis Films. **Color?B&W?-92min.** *(French).* Marina Vlady, Robert Hossein......(3)

RUGGED O'RIORDANS (1949) Universal. **B&W-76min.** *(Australian).* John O'Malley, Thelma Scott, Michael Pate......(5)

RUGGLES OF RED GAP (1935) Paramount. **B&W-90min.** Charles Laughton, Charlie Ruggles......**5***

RULERS OF THE SEA (1939) Paramount. **B&W-96min.** Douglas Fairbanks, Jr., Margaret Lockwood......(4)

RULES OF THE GAME (1938) Janus Films. **B&W-110min.** *(French).* Marcel Dalio, Nora Grégor......**4***
Original title: REGLE DU JEU, LE

RULING CLASS, THE (1972) Avco-Embassy. **Color-154min.** *(British).* Peter O'Toole, Arthur Lowe, Alastair Sim......**5***

RUMBA (1935) Paramount. **B&W-77min.** George Raft, Carole Lombard......(3)

RUMBLE ON THE DOCKS (1956) Columbia. **B&W-82min.** James Darren, Laurie Carroll......(3)

RUN A CROOKED MILE (1969) Universal. **Color-100min.** *(Made for TV).* Louis Jourdan, Mary Tyler Moore, Stanley Holloway......**5***

Films are rated on a 1 to 10 scale, 10 is highest. **Boldface** ratings followed by an asterisk (*) are for films actually seen and rated by the executive and senior editors. All other ratings are estimates. (See Notes on Entertainment Ratings in the front section.)

RUN, ANGEL, RUN! (1969) Fanfare. **Color-95min.** William Smith, Valerie Starrett...2*

RUN, APPALOOSA, RUN (1966) Buena Vista. **Color-48min.** Adle Palacios, Wilbur Plaugher...(5)

RUN FOR COVER (1955) Paramount. **Color-93min.** James Cagney, Viveca Lindfors...4*

RUN FOR THE ROSES (1978) Kodiak Films. **Color-93min.** Vera Miles, Stuart Whitman, Sam Groom...
Alternate title: THOROUGHBREDS, THE

RUN FOR THE SUN (1956) United Artists. **Color-99min.** Richard Widmark, Trevor Howard...4*

RUN FOR YOUR MONEY, A (1949) Universal. **B&W-83min.** *(British).* Donald Houston, Meredith Edwards...........................4*

RUN FOR YOUR WIFE (1965) Allied Artists. **Color-97min.** *(Italian-French).* Ugo Tognazzi, Marina Vlady, Rhonda Fleming.........(3)
Original Italian title: MOGLIE AMERICANA, UNA
French title: MES FEMMES AMÉRICAINES *(My American Wives)*

RUN LIKE A THIEF (1967) Feature Film Corp. **Color-92min.** *(U.S.-Spanish).* Kieron Moore, Ina Balin, Keenan Wynn.......(2)
Spanish title: ROBO DE DIAMENTS

RUN OF THE ARROW (1957) Universal. **Color-86min.** Rod Steiger, Sarita Montiel, Brian Keith..(4)

RUN ON GOLD, A (1969) *see* MIDAS RUN

RUN, PSYCHO, RUN (1966) American-International. **B&W-93min.** *(Italian).* Gary Merrill, Elga Anderson......................3*

RUN SILENT, RUN DEEP (1958) United Artists. **B&W-93min.** Clark Gable, Burt Lancaster..4*

RUN SIMON RUN (1970) ABC Films. **Color-74min.** *(Made for TV).* Burt Reynolds, Inger Stevens.......................................5*

RUN, STRANGER, RUN (1973) *see* HAPPY MOTHER'S DAY . . . LOVE, GEORGE

RUN THE WILD RIVER (1971) Jack Currey. **Color-95min.** *(Documentary).* Director: Jack Currey...................................(5)

RUN WILD, RUN FREE (1969) Columbia. **Color-98min.** *(British).* Mark Lester, John Mills...(5)
Original title: PHILIP

RUNAROUND, THE (1946) Universal. **B&W-86min.** Broderick Crawford, Rod Cameron, Ella Raines....................................(4)

RUNAWAY, THE (1958) **B&W-100min.** *(French).* Pierre Brasseur, Joel Flateau...(3)

RUNAWAY! (1973) MCA-TV. **Color-74min.** *(Made for TV).* Ben Johnson, Martin Milner, Vera Miles....................................4*
British title: RUNAWAY TRAIN, THE

RUNAWAY BUS, THE (1954) Eros Films *(Brit.).* **B&W-78min.** *(British).* Margaret Rutherford, Frankie Howerd.................(3)

RUNAWAY DAUGHTERS (1956) American-International. **B&W-90min.** Marla English, Anna Sten...3*

RUNAWAY TRAIN, THE (1973) *see* RUNAWAY!

RUNNER STUMBLES, THE (1979) **Color-99min.** Dick Van Dyke, Kathleen Quinlan..

RUNNING (1979) Universal. **Color- min.** *(U.S.-Canadian).* Michael Douglas, Susan Anspach...................................

RUNNING FENCE (1978) Maysles Film. **Color-57min.** *(Documentary).* Director: David Maysles..................................

RUNNING MAN, THE (1963) Columbia. **Color-103min.** *(British-U.S.).* Laurence Harvey, Lee Remick...........................5*

RUNNING TARGET (1956) United Artists. **Color-83min.** Arthur Franz, Doris Dowling..(4)

RUNNING WILD (1927) Paramount. **B&W-69min.** *(Silent).* W. C. Fields, Mary Brian...(4)

RUNNING WILD (1955) Universal. **B&W-81min.** William Campbell, Mamie Van Doren..(3)

RUPTURE, LA (1972) New Line Cinema. **Color-125min.** *(French).* Stephane Audran, Jean-Pierre Cassel, Michel Bouquet.....
Translation title: The Breakup

RUSS MEYER'S "UP"! (1976) *see* UP

RUSS MEYER'S VIXEN (1969) Eve Releasing Corp. **Color-71min.** Erica Gavin, Harrison Page..(3)
Publicity title: VIXEN

RUSSIA (1972) Theodore Holcomb. **Color-108min.** *(Travelog).* Director: Theodore Holcomb.......................................(4)

RUSSIAN ADVENTURE (1966) *see* CINERAMA'S RUSSIAN ADVENTURE

RUSSIAN ROULETTE (1975) Avco-Embassy. **Color-93min.** George Segal, Cristina Raines..4½*

RUSSIANS ARE COMING THE RUSSIANS ARE COMING, THE (1966) United Artists. **Color-120min.** Alan Arkin, Carl Reiner.............5*

RUTHLESS (1948) Eagle Lion. **B&W-104min.** Zachary Scott, Diana Lynn...4*

RUTHLESS FOUR, THE (1968) Goldstone Film Enterprises. **Color-96min.** *(Italian-W. German).* Van Heflin, Gilbert Roland, Klaus Kinski..........3*
Original Italian title: ORGUNNO PER SE
W. German title: GOLD VON SAM COOPER, DAS
Prerelease title: SAM COOPER'S GOLD
Prerelease title: EACH MAN FOR HIMSELF

Rx MURDER (1958) 20th Century-Fox. **B&W-85min.** *(British).* Rick Jason, Marius Goring......................................(3)
Original title: FAMILY DOCTOR

RYAN'S DAUGHTER (1970) M-G-M. **Color-192min.** *(British).* Sarah Miles, Robert Mitchum, Christopher Jones...............5½*

-S-

$ (1971) *see* DOLLARS

S.O.S. (1975) Mammoth Films. **Color-84min.** Honeysuckle Divine, Jody Maxwell, Jim Buckley, Al Goldstein...................(2)
Alternate title: SCREW ON THE SCREEN

S.O.S. CLIPPER ISLAND (1936) *see* ROBINSON CRUSOE OF MYSTERY ISLAND

S.O.S. PACIFIC (1959) Universal. **B&W-92min.** *(British).* Eddie Constantine, Pier Angeli.....................................3½*

S. W. A. L. K. (1971) *see* MELODY

SAADIA (1954) M-G-M. **Color-82min.** Cornel Wilde, Rita Gam, Mel Ferrer...(3)

SABAKA (1955) United Artists. **Color-89min.** Boris Karloff, Nino Marcel, Victor Jory..(3)
Alternate title: HINDU, THE

SABATA (1970) United Artists. **Color-106min.** *(Italian).* Lee Van Cleef, William Berger..(3)

SABOTAGE (1936) Gaumont-British [Rank]. **B&W-76min.** *(British).* Sylvia Sidney, Oscar Homolka, John Loder.............3*
Alternate title: WOMAN ALONE, A

SABOTAGE SQUAD (1942) Columbia. **B&W-64min.** Bruce Bennett, Kay Harris...(3)

SABOTEUR (1942) Universal. **B&W-108min.** Robert Cummings, Priscilla Lane...5*

SABOTEUR, CODE NAME - MORITURI, THE (1965) *see* MORITURI

SABRA (1972) *see* DEATH OF A JEW

SABRE AND THE ARROW, THE (1952) *see* LAST OF THE COMANCHES

SABRE JET (1953) United Artists. **Color-96min.** Robert Stack, Coleen Gray..(4)

SABRINA (1954) Paramount. **B&W-113min.** Humphrey Bogart, Audrey Hepburn, William Holden.................................7*
British title: SABRINA FAIR

SABU AND THE MAGIC RING (1957) Allied Artists. **Color-61min.** Sabu, Daria Massey, William Marshall........................(3)

SACCO AND VANZETTI (1971) UMC Pictures. **Color-120min.** *(Italian-French, English language).* Riccardo Cucciolla, Gian Maria Volonte, Cyril Cusack..............4*
Italian title: SACCO E VANZETTI

SACRED KNIVES OF VENGEANCE, THE (1973) Warner Bros. **Color-94min.** *(Hong Kong).* Chin Han, Wang Ping, Tsung Hua...........(2)
British title: KILLER, THE

SAD HORSE, THE (1959) 20th Century-Fox. **Color-78min.** David Ladd, Chill Wills...(3)

SAD SACK, THE (1957) Paramount. **B&W-98min.** Jerry Lewis, David Wayne..(5)

SADDLE THE WIND (1958) M-G-M. **Color-84min.** Robert Taylor, Julie London..4½*

SADDLE TRAMP (1950) Universal. **Color-77min.** Joel McCrea, Wanda Hendrix..4*

SADIE McKEE (1934) M-G-M. **B&W-90min.** Joan Crawford, Gene Raymond...(4)

SADIE THOMPSON (1928) United Artists. **B&W-95min.** *(Silent).* Gloria Swanson, Lionel Barrymore, Raoul Walsh...........(4)

SADKO (1953) *see* MAGIC VOYAGE OF SINBAD

SAFARI (1940) Paramount. **B&W-80min.** Madeleine Carroll, Douglas Fairbanks, Jr...(3)

Films are rated on a 1 to 10 scale, 10 is highest. **Boldface** ratings followed by an asterisk (*) are for films actually seen and rated by the executive and senior editors. All other ratings are estimates. (See Notes on Entertainment Ratings in the front section.)

SAFARI (1956) Columbia. **Color-91min.** *(British).* Victor Mature, Janet Leigh..4*

SAFARI DRUMS (1953) Allied Artists. **B&W-71min.** Johnny Sheffield, Douglas Kennedy, Barbara Bester....................(3)
British title: BOMBA AND THE SAFARI DRUMS

SAFE AT HOME! (1962) Columbia. **B&W-83min.** Bryan Russell, Mickey Mantle, Roger Maris ....(4)

SAFE PLACE, A (1971) Columbia. **Color-94min.** Tuesday Weld, Orson Welles, Jack Nicholson ....(3)

SAFECRACKER, THE (1958) M-G-M. **B&W-96min.** *(British).* Ray Milland, Barry Jones 4*

SAFETY LAST (1923) Pathé Exchange. **B&W-70min.** *(Silent).* Harold Lloyd, Mildred Davis....................................6*

SAGA OF HEMP BROWN, THE (1958) Universal. **Color-80min.** Rory Calhoun, Beverly Garland 3*

SAGA OF THE VIKING WOMEN . . . (1958) *see* VIKING WOMEN AND THE SEA SERPENT, THE

SAHARA (1943) Columbia. **B&W-97min.** Humphrey Bogart, Bruce Bennett..4*

SAIGON (1948) Paramount. **B&W-94min.** Alan Ladd, Veronica Lake 3*

SAIL A CROOKED SHIP (1962) Columbia. **B&W-88min.** Robert Wagner, Ernie Kovacs ....(4)

SAIL INTO DANGER (1957) J. Arthur Rank. **B&W-72min.** *(British).* Dennis O'Keefe, Kathleen Ryan ....(3)

SAILOR BEWARE (1952) Paramount. **B&W-108min.** Dean Martin, Jerry Lewis, Corinne Calvet....................................4*

SAILOR BEWARE! (1956) *see* PANIC IN THE PARLOR

SAILOR FROM GIBRALTAR, THE (1967) Lopert [U.A.]. **B&W-89min.** *(British).* Jeanne Moreau, Ian Bannen ....(3)

SAILOR OF THE KING (1953) 20th Century-Fox. **B&W-83min.** *(British).* Michael Rennie, Jeffrey Hunter, Wendy Hiller 4*
Original title: SINGLE-HANDED

SAILOR TAKES A WIFE, THE (1945) M-G-M. **B&W-91min.** Robert Walker, June Allyson ....(3)

SAILOR WHO FELL FROM GRACE WITH THE SEA, THE (1976) Avco-Embassy. **Color-104min.** *(British).* Kris Kristofferson, Sarah Miles, Jonathan Kahn 5½*

SAILOR'S HOLIDAY (1944) Columbia. **B&W-80min.** Arthur Lake, Jane Lawrence ....(3)

SAILOR'S LADY (1940) 20th Century-Fox. **B&W-66min.** Nancy Kelly, Dana Andrews...(3)

SAILOR'S LUCK (1933) Fox Film Co. [20th]. **B&W-78min.** James Dunn, Sally Eilers..(4)

ST. BENNY THE DIP (1951) United Artists. **B&W-80min.** Dick Haymes, Nina Foch, Roland Young...........................(3)

THE SAILOR WHO FELL FROM GRACE WITH THE SEA (1976) is Kris Kristofferson (right), who explains how a ship's sextant works to young Jonathan Kahn.

SAINT IN LONDON, THE (1939) RKO. **B&W-72min.** George Sanders, Sally Gray ....(4)

SAINT IN NEW YORK, THE (1938) RKO. **B&W-72min.** Louis Hayward, Kay Sutton ....(5)

SAINT IN PALM SPRINGS, THE (1941) RKO. **B&W-66min.** George Sanders, Wendy Barrie ....(4)

ST. IVES (1976) Warner Bros. **Color-93min.** Charles Bronson, John Houseman 3½*

SAINT JACK (1979) New World. **Color-112min.** Ben Gazarra, Denholm Elliot, James Villiers................................

SAINT JOAN (1957) United Artists. **B&W-110min.** Jean Seberg, Richard Widmark 4*

ST. LOUIS BLUES (1958) Paramount. **B&W-93min.** Nat King Cole, Eartha Kitt, Pearl Bailey ....(4)

ST. LOUIS KID (1934) Warner Bros. **B&W-67min.** James Cagney, Patricia Ellis ....(4)
British title: PERFECT WEEKEND, A

ST. MARTIN'S LANE (1938) *see* SIDEWALKS OF LONDON

SAINT MEETS THE TIGER, THE (1941) Republic. **B&W-70min.** *(British).* Hugh Sinclair, Jean Gillie.........................(4)

SAINT STRIKES BACK, THE (1939) RKO. **B&W-64min.** George Sanders, Wendy Barrie ....(4)

SAINT TAKES OVER, THE (1940) RKO. **B&W-69min.** George Sanders, Wendy Barrie ....(4)

ST. VALENTINE'S DAY MASSACRE, THE (1967) 20th Century-Fox. **Color-100min.** Jason Robards, George Segal 4*

SAINTED SISTERS, THE (1948) Paramount. **B&W-89min.** Veronica Lake, Joan Caulfield ....(4)

SAINTLY SINNERS (1962) United Artists. **B&W-78min.** Don Beddoe, Paul Bryar, Stanley Clements...........................(2)

SAINTS AND SINNERS (1949) Lopert [U.A.]. **B&W-85min.** *(British).* Kieron Moore, Christine Norden ....(5)

SAINT'S DOUBLE TROUBLE, THE (1940) RKO. **B&W-68min.** George Sanders, Helene Whitney, Bela Lugosi ....(3)

SAINT'S GIRL FRIDAY, THE (1953) RKO. **B&W-70min.** *(British).* Louis Hayward, Naomi Chance ....(3)
Original title: SAINT'S RETURN, THE

SAINT'S VACATION, THE (1941) RKO. **B&W-78min.** *(British).* Hugh Sinclair, Sally Gray ....(4)

SAKIMA AND THE MASKED MARVEL (1943) Republic. **B&W-100min.** *(Re-edited Serial).* William Forrest, Louise Currie, Tom Steele.............(4)
Original title: MASKED MARVEL, THE

SALADIN AND THE GREAT CRUSADES (1963) New Yorker Films. **Color-125min.** *(Swiss-French).* Ahmed Mazhar, Nadia Lootfi.................(3)

SALAMANDRE, LA (1971) New Yorker Films. **B&W-125min.** *(Swiss).* Bulle Ogier, Jean-Luc Bideau, Jacques Denis....................................3*
Translation title: The Salamander

SALAMBO (1959) *see* LOVES OF SALAMMBO, THE

SALESMAN (1969) Maysles Film. **B&W-90min.** *(Documentary). Director:* Albert Maysles 4*

SALLAH (1964) Palisades International. **B&W-105min.** *(Israeli).* Haym Topol, Geula Noni ....(5)
Original title: SALLAH SHABATI

SALLY AND ST. ANNE (1952) Universal. **B&W-90min.** Ann Blyth, Edmund Gwenn 4*

SALLY, IRENE AND MARY (1925) M-G-M. **B&W-62min.** *(Silent).* Constance Bennett, Joan Crawford, Sally O'Neil ....(4)

SALLY, IRENE AND MARY (1938) 20th Century-Fox. **B&W-72min.** Constance Bennett, Marjorie Weaver, Fred Allen ....(4)

SALLY OF THE SAWDUST (1925) United Artists. **B&W-104min.** *(Silent).* W. C. Fields, Carol Dempster 4*

SALLY'S IRISH ROGUE (1958) British Lion [EMI]. **B&W-74min.** *(British).* Julie Harris, Tim Seely, Harry Brogan ....

SALO, 120 DAYS OF SODOM (1975) Zebra. **Color-117min.** *(Italian).* Paolo Bonacelli, Giorgio Cataldi ....
Original title: SALO O LE CENTIVENT GIRONTE DE SODOMA

SALOME (1923) Allied Producers and Distributors. **B&W-40min.** (Alla) Nazimova, Rose Dione, Mitchell Lewis 3*

SALOME (1953) Columbia. **Color-103min.** Rita Hayworth, Stewart Granger 4*

SALOME, WHERE SHE DANCED (1945) Universal. **B&W-90min.** Rod Cameron, Yvonne De Carlo.....................................(2)

SALON KITTY (1976) *see* MADAM KITTY

SALSA (1976) Fania Records. **Color-80min.** *(Music Film). Director:* Jerry Masucci...(4)
Translation title: Sauce

SALT AND PEPPER (1968) United Artists. **Color-101min.** *(British).* Sammy Davis, Jr., Peter Lawford ....(3)

SALT OF THE EARTH (1954) Independent Productions. **B&W-94min.** Juan Chacon, Rosaura Revueltas.................................**4½***

SALT TO THE DEVIL (1949) Eagle Lion. **B&W-120min.** *(British).* Sam Wanamaker, Lea Padovani, Kathleen Ryan ....(5)
Original title: GIVE US THIS DAY

SALTO (1965) Kanawha Films Ltd. **B&W-104min.** *(Polish).* Zbigniew Cybulski, Gustaw Holoubek ....(5)

SALTY O'ROURKE (1945) Paramount. **B&W-97min.** Alan Ladd, Gail Russell, Stanley Clements....................................**3***

SALUT L'ARTISTE (1973) Exxel. **Color-96min.** *(French).* Marcello Mastroianni, Francoise Fabian, Jean Rochefort......................

SALUTE FOR THREE (1943) Paramount. **B&W-75min.** Macdonald Carey, Betty Rhodes ....(3)

SALUTE TO THE MARINES (1943) M-G-M. **Color-101min.** William Lundigan, Wallace Beery....................................(4)

SALVAGE-1 (1979) ABC-TV. **Color-98min.** *(Made for TV).* Andy Griffith, Richard Jaeckel, Trish Stewart.....................(4)

SALVATION HUNTERS, THE (1925) United Artists. **B&W-79min.** *(Silent).* George K. Arthur, Georgia Hale ....(4)

SALZBURG CONNECTION, THE (1972) 20th Century-Fox. **Color-93min.** Barry Newman, Anna Karina ....(3)

SAM HILL - WHO KILLED THE MYSTERIOUS MR. FOSTER? (1971) Universal. **Color-100min.** *(Made for TV).* Ernest Borgnine, Judy Geeson, Will Geer...**4***
Alternate title: WHO KILLED THE MYSTERIOUS MR. FOSTER?

SAM WHISKEY (1969) United Artists. **Color-96min.** Burt Reynolds, Clint Walker, Angie Dickinson............................**4***

SAMAR (1962) Warner Bros. **Color-89min.** George Montgomery, Gilbert Roland, Ziva Rodann.................................**4***

SAME SKIN, THE (1970) *see* BROTHERLY LOVE

SAME TIME, NEXT YEAR (1978) Universal. **Color-119min.** Ellen Burstyn, Alan Alda..**6***

SAMMY GOING SOUTH (1963) *see* BOY TEN FEET TALL, A

SAMOURAI, LE (1967) *see* GODSON, THE

SAMPO (1959) *see* DAY THE EARTH FROZE, THE

SAMSON (1961) Telewide Systems. **Color-99min.** *(Italian).* Brad Harris, Walter Reeves...(1)
Original title: SANSONE

SAMSON AGAINST THE SHEIK (1960) Telewide Systems. **Color-95min.** *(Italian).* Ed Fury...(1)

SAMSON AND DELILAH (1949) Paramount. **Color-128min.** Victor Mature, Hedy Lamarr **5½***

SAMSON AND THE SEA BEAST (1963) American-International. **Color-84min.** *(Italian).* Kirk Morris, Margaret Lee, Daniele Vargas ....(1)
Original title: SANSONE CONTRO I PIRATI *(Samson Against the Pirates)*

SAMSON AND THE SEVEN CHALLENGES (1964) **Color-91min.** *(Italian).* Alan Steel (Sergio Ciani), Nadir Baltimor ....(1)
Original title: ERCOLE, SANSONE, MACISTE, URSUS: GLI INVINCIBLI *(Hercules, Samson, Maciste, Ursus: the Invincibles)*
Alternate title: SAMSON AND THE MIGHTY CHALLENGE
Alternate title: HERCULES, MACISTE, SAMSON AND URSUS VS. THE UNIVERSE

SAMSON AND THE SEVEN MIRACLES OF THE WORLD (1961) American-International. **Color-80min.** *(Italian-French).* Gordon Scott, Yoko Tani ....(2)
Original Italian title: MACISTE ALLA CORTE DEL GRAN KHAN *(Maciste at the Court of the Great Khan)*
French title: GÉANT A LA COUR DE KUBLAI KHAN, LE *(The Giant at the Court of Kublai Khan)*
Publicity title(?): GOLIATH AND THE GOLDEN CITY

SAMSON AND THE SLAVE QUEEN (1964) American-International. **Color-86min.** *(Italian).* Pierre Brice, Alan Steel (Sergio Ciani) ....(2)
Original title: ZORRO CONTRA MACISTE *(Zorro Against Maciste)*

SAMSON AND THE VAMPIRE WOMAN (1961) Azteca. **B&W-89min.** *(Mexican).* Santo, Lorena Velazquez..................................**1***
Original title: SANTO CONTRA LOS MUJERES VAMPIROS *(Santo vs. the Vampire Women)*
Alternate title: SAMSON VS. THE VAMPIRE WOMEN

SAMSON IN KING SOLOMON'S MINES (1963) *see* MACISTE IN KING SOLOMON'S MINES

SAMSON IN THE WAX MUSEUM (1963) Azteca. **B&W-90min.** *(Mexican).* Santo, Claudio Brook 1*
Original title: SANTO EN EL MUSEO DE CERA *(Santo in the Wax Museum)*

SAMSON VS. THE GIANT KING (1963) Teleworld. **Color-91min.** *(Italian).* Kirk Morris, Massimo Serato...........................(3)
Original title: MACISTE ALLA CORTE DELLO ZAR *(Maciste at the Court of the Czar)*
British title: GIANT OF THE LOST TOMB
Alternate title: ATLAS AGAINST THE CZAR

SAMURAI (Part I) (1954) Fine Arts. **Color-92min.** *(Japanese).* Toshiro Mifune, Kaoru Yachigusa **4***
Original title: MIYAMOTO MUSASHI
Alternate title: LEGEND OF MUSASHI, THE

SAMURAI PIRATE (1964) *see* LOST WORLD OF SINBAD

SAMURAI REBELLION (1967) *see* REBELLION

SAN ANTONE (1953) Republic. **B&W-90min.** Rod Cameron, Arleen Whelan ....(3)

SAN ANTONIO (1945) Warner Bros. **Color-111min.** Errol Flynn, Alexis Smith **5***

SAN DEMETRIO, LONDON (1943) 20th Century-Fox. **B&W-76min.** *(British).* Walter Fitzgerald, Mervyn Johns ....(4)

SAN DIEGO, I LOVE YOU (1944) Universal. **B&W-83min.** Jon Hall, Buster Keaton, Edward Everett Horton ....(5)

SAN FRANCISCO (1936) M-G-M. **B&W-115min.** Clark Gable, Jeanette MacDonald...**5***

SAN FRANCISCO INTERNATIONAL AIRPORT (1970) Universal. **Color-96min.** *(Made for TV).* Pernell Roberts, Van Johnson, Beth Brickell.... **4***

SAN FRANCISCO STORY, THE (1952) Warner Bros. **B&W-80min.** Joel McCrea, Yvonne De Carlo..(3)

SAN PIETRO (1944) *see* BATTLE OF SAN PIETRO

SAN QUENTIN (1937) First National [W.B.]. **B&W-70min.** Pat O'Brien, Humphrey Bogart ....(4)

SAN QUENTIN (1946) RKO. **B&W-66min.** Lawrence Tierney, Barton MacLane ....(4)

SANCTUARY (1961) 20th Century-Fox. **Color-100min.** Lee Remick, Yves Montand **3***

SAND (1949) 20th Century-Fox. **Color-78min.** Mark Stevens, Coleen Gray ....(4)
Alternate title: WILL JAMES' SAND

SAND CASTLE, THE (1961) De Rochemont. **B&W-67min.** Barry Cardwell, Laurie Cardwell..(5)

SAND, LOVE, AND SALT (1957) **B&W-89min.** *(W. German-Italian).* Marcello Mastroianni, Jester Naefe ....(3)
Original German title: HARTE MAENNER HEISSE LIEBE
Alternate German title: SALZ UND BROT
Italian title: RAGAZZA DELLA SALINA, LA *(The Salt Girl)*

SAND PEBBLES, THE (1966) 20th Century-Fox. **Color-191min.** Steve McQueen, Richard Attenborough........................**4***

SANDAKAN NO. 8 (1975) Toho. **Color-121min.** *(Japanese).* Kinuyo Tanaka, Komaki Kurihara, Yoko Takaashi ....(4)
Original title: SANDAKAN HACHIBAN SHOKAN, BOHKYO
Alternate Japanese title(?): BOKYO
Publicity title: BROTHEL NO. 8

SANDCASTLES (1972) MPC (TV). **Color-74min.** *(Made for TV).* Jan-Michael Vincent, Bonnie Bedelia, Mariette Hartley ....(4)

SANDERS (1964) 20th Century-Fox. **Color-83min.** *(British-W. German).* Richard Todd, Marianne Koch ....(4)
Original title: DEATH DRUMS ALONG THE RIVER
German title: TODESTROMMELN AM GROSSEN FLUSS

SANDOKAN AGAINST THE LEOPARD OF SARAWAK (1964) Screen Gems. **Color-88min.** *(Italian-W. German).* Ray Danton, Franca Bettoja, Guy Madison..(3)
Original Italian title: SANDOKAN CONTRO IL LEOPARDO DI SARAWAK
Alternate title: RETURN OF SANDOKAN

SANDOKAN FIGHTS BACK (1964) Screen Gems. **Color-96min.** *(Italian-W. German).* Ray Danton, Franca Bettoja, Guy Madison ....(3)
Original Italian title: SANDOKAN ALLA RICOSSA

SANDOKAN THE GREAT (1964) M-G-M. **Color-110min.** *(Italian-Spanish-French).* Steve Reeves, Genevieve Grad...........................(3)
Original Italian title: SANDOKAN, LA TIGRE DI MOMPRACEM *(Sandokan, the Tiger of Mompracem)*
Spanish title: SANDOKAN
French title: SANDOKAN, LE TIGRE DE BORNÉO *(Sandokan, the Tiger of Borneo)*

SANDPIPER, THE (1965) M-G-M. **Color-116min.** Elizabeth Taylor, Richard Burton **5***

SANDPIT GENERALS, THE (1971) *see* WILD PACK, THE

SANDS OF BEERSHEBA (1965) Commonwealth United. **B&W-90min.** *(Israeli-U.S.).* Diane Baker, David Opatoshu, Tom Bell .... (4)
Israeli title: MORDEI HA'OR

SANDS OF IWO JIMA (1949) Republic. **B&W-110min.** John Wayne, John Agar **4***

SANDS OF THE DESERT (1960) Warner Bros. **Color-92min.** *(British).* Charles Drake, Peter Arne .... (3)

SANDS OF THE KALAHARI (1965) Paramount. **Color-119min.** *(British).* Stuart Whitman, Stanley Baker, Susannah York **5½***

SANDSTONE (1977) Henderson Films. **Color-75min.** *(Documentary).* Director: Jonathan Dana **4***

SANDY GETS HER MAN (1940) Universal. **B&W-74min.** Baby Sandy, Stuart Erwin .... (3)

SANDY IS A LADY (1940) Universal. **B&W-65min.** Baby Sandy, Nan Grey .... (3)

SANGAREE (1953) Paramount. **Color-94min.** Fernando Lamas, Arlene Dahl .... (4)

SANJURO (1962) Toho. **B&W-96min.** *(Japanese).* Toshiro Mifune, Tatsuya Nakadai **4***
Original title: TSUBAKI SANJURO

SANTA CLAUS CONQUERS THE MARTIANS (1964) Avco-Embassy. **Color-81min.** John Call, Vincent Beck, Victor Stiles **3***

SANTA FE (1951) Columbia. **Color-89min.** Randolph Scott, Janis Carter .... (3)

SANTA FE PASSAGE (1955) Republic. **Color-70min.** John Payne, Faith Domergue **3***

SANTA FE TRAIL (1940) Warner Bros. **B&W-110min.** Errol Flynn, Olivia de Havilland **5***

SANTEE (1973) Crown International. **Color-93min.** Glenn Ford, Michael Burns **4***

SANTIAGO (1956) Warner Bros. **Color-93min.** Alan Ladd, Rosanna Podesta **4***
British title: GUN RUNNER, THE

SAPHEAD, THE (1920) Metro. **B&W-70min.** *(Silent).* Buster Keaton, William H. Crane **4***

SAPPHIRE (1959) Universal. **Color-92min.** *(British).* Nigel Patrick, Yvonne Mitchell **5***

SAPPHO, DARLING (1969) Cambist. **Color-100min.** *(Swedish, English language).* Carol Young, Yvonne D'Angers .... (2)

SAPS AT SEA (1940) United Artists. **B&W-57min.** Stan Laurel, Oliver Hardy .... (4)

SARABAND (1948) Eagle Lion. **Color-95min.** *(British).* Stewart Granger, Joan Greenwood **5***
Original title: SARABAND FOR DEAD LOVERS

SARACEN BLADE, THE (1954) Columbia. **Color-76min.** Ricardo Montalban, Betta St. John **4***

SARACENS, THE (1960) American-International. **Color-89min.** *(Italian).* Richard Harrison, Anna Mori Ubaldi .... (3)

SARAGOSSA MANUSCRIPT, THE (1965) Amerpole Enterprises. **B&W-160min.** *(Polish).* Zbigniew Cybulski, Kazimierz Opalinski **2***
Original title: REKOPIS ZNALEZIONY W SARAGOSSIE
Alternate title: ADVENTURES OF A NOBLEMAN
Alternate title: MANUSCRIPT FOUND IN SARAGOSSA

SARAH AND SON (1930) Paramount. **B&W-76min.** Ruth Chatterton, Fredric March .... (3)

SARAH T. - PORTRAIT OF A TEEN-AGE ALCOHOLIC (1975) NBC-TV. **Color-100min.** *(Made for TV).* Linda Blair, Mark Hamill ....

SARATOGA (1937) M-G-M. **B&W-94min.** Clark Gable, Jean Harlow **4***

SARATOGA TRUNK (1945) Warner Bros. **B&W-135min.** Gary Cooper, Ingrid Bergman **4***

SARGE - THE BADGE OR THE CROSS (1971) Universal. **Color-100min.** *(Made for TV).* George Kennedy, Diane Baker, Ricardo Montalban .... (5)
Alternate title: SARGE
Alternate title: BADGE OR THE CROSS, THE

SASKATCHEWAN (1954) Universal. **Color-87min.** Alan Ladd, Shelley Winters **3½***
British title: O'ROURKE OF THE ROYAL MOUNTED

SATAN BUG, THE (1965) United Artists. **Color-114min.** George Maharis, Richard Basehart **4***

SATAN MET A LADY (1936) Warner Bros. **B&W-75min.** Warren William, Bette Davis **3½***

SATAN NEVER SLEEPS (1962) 20th Century-Fox. **Color-126min.** *(U.S.-British).* William Holden, Clifton Webb .... (3)
British title: DEVIL NEVER SLEEPS, THE
Alternate title: FLIGHT FROM TERROR

SATANIC RITES OF DRACULA, THE (1974) Dynamite Entertainment/American International. **Color-88min.** *(British).* Christopher Lee, Peter Cushing **4½***
Alternate title: COUNT DRACULA AND HIS VAMPIRE BRIDE

SATAN'S BLACK WEDDING (1976) Imri Films. **Color-62min.** .... (2)

SATAN'S BREW (1976) New Yorker Films. **Color-110min.** *(German).* Kurt Raab, Margit Carstensen ....
Original title: SATANSBRATEN

SATAN'S CHEERLEADERS (1977) Ellman. **Color-92min.** John Ireland, Yvonne De Carlo .... (3)

SATAN'S SADISTS (1970) Independent International. **Color-86min.** Russ Tamblyn, Scott Brady, Gary Kent .... (2)

SATAN'S SATELLITES (1952) Republic. **B&W-70min.** *(Re-edited Serial).* Judd Holdren, Aline Towne .... (2)
Original title: ZOMBIES OF THE STRATOSPHERE

SATAN'S SCHOOL FOR GIRLS (1973) MPC (TV). **Color-74min.** *(Made for TV).* Roy Thinnes, Kate Jackson, Pamela Franklin **3***

SATAN'S SKIN (1971) *see* BLOOD ON SATAN'S CLAW

SATAN'S TRIANGLE (1975) Worldvision. **Color-74min.** *(Made for TV).* Kim Novak, Doug McClure, Alejandro Ray **3***

SATCHMO THE GREAT (1957) United Artists. **B&W-63min.** *(Documentary).* Producer: Edward R. Murrow .... (5)

SATELLITE IN THE SKY (1956) Warner Bros. **Color-84min.** *(British).* Kieron Moore, Donald Wolfit, Lois Maxwell .... (4)

SATURDAY ISLAND (1952) *see* ISLAND OF DESIRE

SATURDAY MATINEE (1979) United Artists. **Color- min.** Chevy Chase ....

SATURDAY MORNING (1971) Columbia. **Color-88min.** *(Documentary).* Director: Kent Mackenzie .... (5)

SATURDAY NIGHT AND SUNDAY MORNING (1960) Continental [Walter Reade]. **B&W-90min.** *(British).* Albert Finney, Shirley Anne Field **5***

SATURDAY NIGHT AT THE BATHS (1975) Mammoth Films. **Color-86min.** Ellen Sheppard, Robert Aberdeen, Don Scotti .... (4)

SATURDAY NIGHT FEVER (1977) Paramount. **Color-119min.** John Travolta, Karen Gorney **5***

SATURDAY'S CHILDREN (1940) Warner Bros. **B&W-101min.** John Garfield, Anne Shirley, Claude Rains **4***

SATURDAY'S HERO (1951) Columbia. **B&W-111min.** John Derek, Donna Reed **4½***
British title: IDOLS IN THE DUST

SATURDAY'S MILLIONS (1933) Universal. **B&W-72min.** Robert Young, John Mack Brown, Leila Hyams .... (3)

SATYRICON (1970) *see* FELLINI SATYRICON

SAVAGE, THE (1952) Paramount. **Color-95min.** Charlton Heston, Susan Morrow **3***

SAVAGE BEES, THE (1976) NBC-TV. **Color-100min.** Ben Johnson .... (4)

SAVAGE DRUMS (1951) Lippert Productions. **B&W-73min.** Sabu, Lita Baron **3***

SAVAGE EYE, THE (1960) Trans-Lux Distributing. **B&W-68min.** Barbara Baxley, Gary Merrill .... (3)

SAVAGE GRINGO (1965) American-International. **Color-82min.** *(Spanish-Italian).* Ken Clark, Yvonne Bastien, Red Ross (Renato Rossini) .... (3)
Original Spanish title: RINGO DE NEBRASKA *(Ringo from Nebraska)*
Italian title: NEBRASKA IL PISTOLERO *(Nebraska the Gunman)*
Alternate translation: GUNMAN CALLED NEBRASKA, A

SAVAGE GUNS, THE (1962) M-G-M. **Color-84min.** *(Spanish-U.S.).* Richard Basehart, Don Taylor, Alex Nicol **3***
Spanish title: TIERRA BRUTAL *(Brutal Land)*

SAVAGE HORDE (1950) Republic. **B&W-90min.** William Elliott, Adrian Booth .... (4)

SAVAGE HORDES, THE (1961) Eagle. **Color-82min.** *(Italian).* Ettore Manni, Yoko, Akim Tamiroff .... (3)

SAVAGE INNOCENTS, THE (1960) Paramount. **Color-89min.** *(Italian-French-British-U.S., English language).* Anthony Quinn, Yoko Tani ... **4***
Original Italian title: OMBRE BLANCHE *(White Shadows)*
Original French title: DENTS DU DIABLE, LES *(The Teeth of the Devil)*

SAVAGE IS LOOSE, THE (1974) Boasberg-Goldstein Inc. **Color-115min.** George C. Scott, Trish Van Devere, John David Carson, Lee H. Montgomery .... (4)

SATURDAY NIGHT FEVER (1977). In a highly competitive dance contest, Karen Lynn Gorney is the partner of popular John Travolta, king of the dance floor.

SAVAGE MESSIAH (1972) M-G-M. **Color-100min.** *(British).* Dorothy Tutin, Scott Antony, Helen Mirren.. 3*

SAVAGE MUTINY (1953) Columbia. **B&W-73min.** Johnny Weissmuller, Angela Stevens.. (2)

SAVAGE PAMPAS (1966) Comet Film. **Color-97min.** *(Spanish-Argentinian-U.S.).* Robert Taylor, Ron Randell............................ (3)
Spanish title: PAMPA SALVAJE

SAVAGE SAM (1963) Buena Vista. **Color-103min.** Brian Keith, Tommy Kirk, Kevin Corcoran.. (4)

SAVAGE SEVEN, THE (1968) American-International. **Color-97min.** Robert Walker, Jr., Adam Roarke, Joanna Frank............................ (2)

SAVAGE SPLENDOR (1949) RKO. **Color-60min.** *(Travelog).* Director: Armand Denis.. (5)

SAVAGE WILD, THE (1969) American-International. **Color-103min.** *(Documentary).* Director: Gordon Eastman............................ (3)

SAVAGE WILDERNESS (1956) *see* LAST FRONTIER, THE

SAVAGES (1972) Angeliks Productions. **B&W-108min.** Salome Jens, Sam Waterston, Kathleen Widdoes............................ (3)

SAVAGES (1974) ABC-TV. **Color-74min.** *(Made for TV).* Andy Griffith, Sam Bottoms..

SAVE THE CHILDREN (1973) Paramount. **Color-123min.** *(Music Film).* Director: Stan Lathan.. (4)

SAVE THE TIGER (1973) Paramount. **Color-99min.** Jack Lemmon, Jack Gilford.. 4½*

SAWDUST AND TINSEL (1953) *see* NAKED NIGHT, THE

SAXON CHARM, THE (1948) Universal. **B&W-88min.** Robert Montgomery, Susan Hayward............................ 4*

SAY GOODBYE, MAGGIE COLE (1972) Worldvision. **Color-73min.** *(Made for TV).* Susan Hayward, Darren McGavin, Michael Constantine........ (4)

SAY HELLO TO YESTERDAY (1970) Cinerama Releasing. **Color-92min.** *(British).* Jean Simmons, Leonard Whiting............................ 4½*

SAY IT IN FRENCH (1938) Paramount. **B&W-70min.** Ray Milland, Olympe Bradna.. 3½*

SAY ONE FOR ME (1959) 20th Century-Fox. **Color-119min.** Bing Crosby, Debbie Reynolds.. 4*

SAYONARA (1957) Warner Bros. **Color-147min.** Marlon Brando, Miiko Taka.. 6*

SCALAWAG (1973) Paramount. **Color-93min.** *(U.S.-Italian).* Kirk Douglas, Mark Lester.. (4)

SCALPEL (1977) Avco-Embassy. **Color-95min.** Robert Lansing............

SCALPHUNTERS, THE (1968) United Artists. **Color-103min.** Burt Lancaster, Ossie Davis.. 5*

SCALPLOCK (1966) Columbia. **Color-100min.** *(Made for TV).* Dale Robertson, Robert Random, Diana Hyland............................ (3)

SCAMP, THE (1957) *see* STRANGE AFFECTION

SCAMPOLO (1958) Bakros International. **Color-104min.** *(German).* Romy Schneider, Paul Hubschmid............................ (3)
Original title: MADCHEN SCAMPOLO, DAS *(The Girl Scampolo)*

SCANDAL AT SCOURIE (1953) M-G-M. **Color-90min.** Greer Garson, Walter Pidgeon.. (4)

SCANDAL IN PARIS, A (1946) United Artists. **B&W-100min.** George Sanders, Signe Hasso.. (4)
Original title: THIEVES' HOLIDAY

SCANDAL IN SORRENTO (1955) Distributors Corp. of America. **Color-92min.** *(Italian-French).* Sophia Loren, Vittorio De Sica................ (3)
Original Italian title: PANE, AMORE E . . . *(Bread, Love and . . .)*
Alternate title: BREAD, LOVE AND...

SCANDAL, INC. (1956) Republic. **B&W-79min.** Robert Hutton, Patricia Wright.. (3)

SCANDAL SHEET (1952) Columbia. **B&W-82min.** Broderick Crawford, Donna Reed.. 4*

SCANDAL STREET (1931) Paramount. **B&W-77min.** Lew Ayres, Louise Campbell.. (4)
British title: DARK PAGE, THE

SCANDALOUS JOHN (1971) Buena Vista. **Color-114min.** Brian Keith, Alfonso Arau.. (4)

SCAPEGOAT, THE (1959) M-G-M. **B&W-92min.** *(British).* Alec Guinness.. (5)

SCAPEGOAT, THE (1963) Paramount. **Color-94min.** *(Italian-French).* Michele Morgan, Jacques Perrin............................ (3)
Original Italian title: FORNARETTO DI VENEZIA, IL

SCAR, THE (1948) *see* HOLLOW TRIUMPH

SCARAMOUCHE (1923) Metro. **B&W-131min.** *(Silent).* Ramon Novarro, Alice Terry, Lewis Stone............................ (5)

SCARAMOUCHE (1952) M-G-M. **Color-118min.** Stewart Granger, Eleanor Parker, Janet Leigh............................ 6*

SCARECROW (1973) Warner Bros. **Color-112min.** Gene Hackman, Al Pacino.. 3*

SCARECROW IN A GARDEN OF CUCUMBERS (1972) Maron Films, Ltd. **Color-82min.** Holly Woodlawn, Yafa Lerner, Tally Brown......... (2)

SCARECROW OF ROMNEY MARSH, THE (1964) *see* DR. SYN, ALIAS THE SCARECROW

SCARED STIFF (1945) M-G-M. **B&W-115min.** Jack Haley, Ann Savage (4)
Alternate title: TREASURE OF FEAR

SCARED STIFF (1953) Paramount. **B&W-108min.** Dean Martin, Jerry Lewis, Lizabeth Scott.. 4*

SCARED TO DEATH (1947) Screen Guild [Lippert]. **Color-70min.** Bela Lugosi, George Zucco, Joyce Compton............................ 2*

SCARF, THE (1951) United Artists. **B&W-93min.** John Ireland, Mercedes McCambridge.. (4)

SCARFACE (1932) United Artists. **B&W-94min.** Paul Muni, Ann Dvorak.. 5*
Alternate title: SCARFACE, SHAME OF THE NATION

SCARFACE MOB, THE (1962) Cari. **B&W-105min.** *(Telefeature).* Robert Stack, Neville Brand.. 5*

SCARLET ANGEL (1952) Universal. **Color-80min.** Yvonne De Carlo, Rock Hudson.. 4*

SCARLET BARONESS, THE (1959) Casino Films. **B&W-85min.** *(German).* Dawn Addams, Joachim Fuchsberger............................ 3*
Original title: FEUEROETE BARONESSE, DIE

SCARLET BLADE, THE (1963) *see* CRIMSON BLADE, THE

SCARLET BUCCANEER, THE (1976) *see* SWASHBUCKLER

SCARLET CLAW, THE (1944) Universal. **B&W-74min.** Basil Rathbone, Nigel Bruce, Paul Cavanaugh............................ 4*
Publicity title: SHERLOCK HOLMES AND THE SCARLET CLAW

SCARLET CLUE, THE (1945) Monogram [Allied Artists]. **B&W-65min.** Sidney Toler, Benson Fong, Mantan Moreland............................ (4)
Publicity title: CHARLIE CHAN AND THE SCARLET CLUE

SCARLET COAT, THE (1955) M-G-M. **Color-101min.** Cornel Wilde, Michael Wilding, George Sanders............................ (4)

SCARLET DAWN (1932) Warner Bros. B&W-58min. Douglas Fairbanks, Jr., Nancy Carroll .... (4)

SCARLET EMPRESS, THE (1934) Paramount. B&W-110min. Marlene Dietrich, John Lodge, Sam Jaffe .... (4)

SCARLET HOUR, THE (1956) Paramount. B&W-95min. Carol Ohmart, Tom Tryon .... (3)

SCARLET LETTER, THE (1926) M-G-M. B&W-100min. (Silent). Lillian Gish, Lars Hanson, Henry B. Walthall 4½*

SCARLET LETTER, THE (1972) Bauer International. Color-94min. (W. German-Spanish). Senta Berger, Lou Castel, Hans Christian Blech ....
Original German title: SCHARLACHROETE BUCHSTABE, DER
Spanish title: LETRA ESCARLATA, LA

SCARLET PIMPERNEL, THE (1935) United Artists. B&W-95min. (British). Leslie Howard, Merle Oberon 5*

SCARLET SPEAR, THE (1954) United Artists. Color-78min. (British). John Bentley, Martha Hyer .... (2)

SCARLET STREET (1945) Universal. B&W-103min. Edward G. Robinson, Joan Bennett 5*

SCARS OF DRACULA, THE (1970) Levitt-Pickman. Color-96min. (British). Christopher Lee, Dennis Waterman .... (3)

SCAVENGERS, THE (1959) Paramount. B&W-79min. (U.S.-Philippine). Vince Edwards, Carol Ohmart, Vic Diaz .... (4)

SCENE OF THE CRIME (1949) M-G-M. B&W-94min. Van Johnson, Gloria De Haven .... (4)

SCENES FROM A MARRIAGE (1973) Cinema 5. Color-168min. (Swedish, Telefeature). Liv Ullmann, Erland Josephson 3*
Original title: SCENER UR ETT AKTENSKAP

SCENIC ROUTE, THE (1978) New Line Cinema. Color-76min. Randy Danson, Marilyn Jones ....

SCENT OF A WOMAN (1974) 20th Century-Fox. Color-103min. (Italian). Vittorio Gassman, Alessandro Momo 4½*
Original title: PROFUMO DI DONNA

SCHEHERAZADE (1963) Four Star. Color-104min. (French-Italian-Spanish). Anna Karina, Fausto Tozzi .... (3)
Original French title: SHÉHÉRAZADE

SCHEMER, THE (1959) B&W-105min. (French). Michel Auclair, Annie Girardot .... (3)

SCHLOCK (1973) Jack H. Harris. Color-80min. John Landis, Saul Kahan .... (4)

SCHOOL FOR LOVE (1955) NTA Pictures. B&W-76min. (French). Jean Marias, Brigitte Bardot .... (2)
Original title: FUTURES VEDETTES (Future Stars)

SCHOOL FOR SCOUNDRELS (1960) Continental [Walter Reade]. B&W-94min. (British). Ian Carmichael, Terry-Thomas .... (5)

SCHOOL FOR VIOLENCE (1958) see HIGH SCHOOL HELLCATS

SCHWEIK'S YEARS OF INDISCRETION (1964) see TRIALS OF PRIVATE SCHWEIK

SCIPIO AFRICANUS (1937) Telewide Systems. B&W-102min. (Italian). Isa Miranda, Annibale Ninchi .... (3)
Original title: SCIPIO L'AFRICANO
Alternate title: DEFEAT OF HANNIBAL, THE

SCORCHING FURY (1952) B&W-68min. William Leslie, Kay Nelson .... (2)

SCORCHY (1976) American-International. Color-99min. Connie Stevens, Cesare Danova .... (3)

SCORPIO (1973) United Artists. Color-114min. Burt Lancaster, Alain Delon 4*

SCORPIO LETTERS, THE (1967) M-G-M. Color-98min. (Made for TV). Alex Cord, Shirley Eaton 4*

SCOTCH ON THE ROCKS (1953) Kingsley International. B&W-83min. (British). Raymond Huntley, Ronald Squire .... (5)
Original title: LAXDALE HALL

SCOTLAND YARD (1941) 20th Century-Fox. B&W-68min. Nancy Kelly, Edmund Gwenn, John Loder .... (4)

SCOTLAND YARD INSPECTOR (1952) Lippert Productions. B&W-73min. (British). Cesar Romero, Lois Maxwell .... (3)
Original title: LADY IN THE FOG

SCOTLAND YARD INVESTIGATOR (1945) Republic. B&W-68min. C. Aubrey Smith, Erich Von Stroheim .... (3)

SCOTT FREE (1976) MCA-TV. Color-74min. (Made for TV). Michael Brandon, Susan Saint James .... (4)

SCOTT JOPLIN (1977) Universal. Color-96min. Billy Dee Williams, Art Carney, Margaret Avery 4*

SCOTT OF THE ANTARCTIC (1948) Eagle Lion. Color-111min. (British). John Mills, Diana Churchill 4*

SCOUNDREL, THE (1935) Paramount. B&W-68min. Noel Coward, Julie Haydon .... (5)

SCREAM (1974) see NIGHT GOD SCREAMED, THE

SCREAM . . . AND DIE! (1969) see HOUSE THAT VANISHED, THE

SCREAM AND SCREAM AGAIN (1970) American-International. Color-94min. (British-U.S.). Vincent Price, Christopher Lee, Peter Cushing 3*

SCREAM BLACULA SCREAM (1973) American-International. Color-95min. William Marshall, Pam Grier, Don Mitchell .... (3)

SCREAM OF FEAR (1961) Columbia. B&W-81min. (British). Susan Strasberg, Ronald Lewis .... (4)
Original title: TASTE OF FEAR

SCREAM OF THE DEMON LOVER (1970) New World. Color-75min. (Spanish-Italian). Jeffrey Chase (Charles Quiney), Jennifer Hartley (Erna Schurer) .... (2)
Original Spanish title: IVANNA
Publicity title: KILLERS OF THE CASTLE OF BLOOD

SCREAM OF THE WOLF (1974) MPC (TV). Color-74min. (Made for TV). Clint Walker, Peter Graves 3*

SCREAMING EAGLES (1956) Allied Artists. B&W-81min. Tom Tryon, Jan Merlin .... (3)

SCREAMING MIMI (1958) Columbia. B&W-79min. Anita Ekberg, Phil Carey, Gypsy Rose Lee .... (3)

SCREAMING SKULL, THE (1958) American-International. B&W-70min. Alex Nicol, John Hudson, Peggy Webber .... (3)

SCREAMING TIGER, THE (1973) American-International. Color-107min. (Hong Kong). Wang Yu, Chang Chin Chin, Ying Mu 1*

SCREAMING WOMAN, THE (1972) MCA-TV. Color-73min. (Made for TV). Olivia de Havilland, Joseph Cotten, Ed Nelson .... (4)

SCREW ON THE SCREEN (1975) see S.O.S.

SCROOGE (1951) see CHRISTMAS CAROL, A

SCROOGE (1970) Nat'l General (for Cinema Center). Color-118min. (British). Albert Finney, Alec Guinness 6*

SCUDDA HOO! SCUDDA HAY! (1948) 20th Century-Fox. Color-95min. June Haver, Lon McCallister, Walter Brennan 3*
British title: SUMMER LIGHTNING

SEA AROUND US, THE (1953) RKO. Color-61min. (Documentary). Producer: Irwin Allen .... (5)

SEA BEAST, THE (1926) Warner Bros. B&W-137min. (Silent). John Barrymore, Dolores Costello, George O'Hara .... (4)

SEA CHASE, THE (1955) Warner Bros. Color-117min. John Wayne, Lana Turner 4*

SEA DEVILS (1937) RKO. B&W-88min. Victor McLaglen, Preston Foster .... (4)

SEA DEVILS (1953) RKO. Color-91min. Rock Hudson, Yvonne De Carlo .... (3)

SEA FIGHTERS, THE (1964) see TIGER OF THE SEA

SEA GULL, THE (1968) Warner Bros. Color-141min. (British). James Mason, Simone Signoret .... (5)

SEA GYPSIES, THE (1978) Warner Bros. Color-101min. Robert Logan, Mikki Jamison-Olsen 5*
British title: SHIPWRECK!

SEA HAWK, THE (1924) Associated First National. B&W-161min. (Silent). Milton Sills, Enid Bennett, Lloyd Hughes .... (4)

SEA HAWK, THE (1940) Warner Bros. B&W-127min. Errol Flynn, Brenda Marshall 5*

SEA HORNET, THE (1951) Republic. B&W-84min. Rod Cameron, Adele Mara .... (3)

SEA OF GRASS, THE (1947) M-G-M. B&W-131min. Spencer Tracy, Katharine Hepburn 4*

SEA OF LOST SHIPS (1954) Republic. B&W-85min. John Derek, Wanda Hendrix, Walter Brennan .... (3).

SEA OF SAND (1958) see DESERT PATROL

SEA PIRATE, THE (1966) Paramount. Color-83min. (French-Italian-Spanish, English language). Gérard Barray, Antonella Lualdi .... (2)
Original French title: SURCOUF, LE TIGRE DES SEPT MERS (Surcouf, the Tiger of the Seven Seas)
Italian title: SURCOUF L'EROE DEI SETTE MARI (Surcouf the Hero of the Seven Seas)
Spanish title: TIGRE DE LOS SIETE MARES, EL (The Tiger of the Seven Seas)

SEA SHALL NOT HAVE THEM, THE (1954) United Artists. B&W-93min. (British). Michael Redgrave, Dirk Bogarde .... (4)

SEA TIGER (1952) Monogram [Allied Artists]. B&W-75min. John Archer, Marguerite Chapman 3*

Films are rated on a 1 to 10 scale, 10 is highest. **Boldface** ratings followed by an asterisk (*) are for films actually seen and rated by the executive and senior editors. All other ratings are estimates. (See Notes on Entertainment Ratings in the front section.)

SEA WIFE (1957) 20th Century-Fox. Color-82min. *(British)*. Joan Collins, Richard Burton 4*

SEA WOLF, THE (1941) Warner Bros. B&W-100min. Edward G. Robinson, John Garfield 4*

SEAGULLS OVER SORRENTO (1954) *see* CREST OF THE WAVE

SEAL ISLAND (1948) RKO (for Disney). Color-30min. *(Documentary)*. *Director:* James Algar..(5)

SEALED CARGO (1951) RKO. B&W-90min. Dana Andrews, Carla Balenda ....(4)

SEALED LIPS (1933) *see* AFTER TONIGHT

SEALED LIPS (1941) Universal. B&W-62min. William Gargan, June Clyde ....(3)

SEALED VERDICT (1948) Paramount. B&W-83min. Ray Milland, Florence Marly ....(4)

SEANCE ON A WET AFTERNOON (1964) Artixo Prods. B&W-116min. *(British)*. Kim Stanley, Richard Attenborough 5½*

SEARCH, THE (1948) M-G-M. B&W-105min. Montgomery Clift, Aline MacMahon 5*

SEARCH (1972) Warner Bros. Color-97min. *(Made for TV)*. Hugh O'Brian, Elke Sommer, Burgess Meredith, John Gielgud 4½*
Original title: PROBE

SEARCH FOR BRIDEY MURPHY, THE (1956) Paramount. B&W-84min. Louis Hayward, Teresa Wright ....(3)

SEARCH FOR DANGER (1949) Four Continents. B&W-62min. John Calvert, Myrna Dell ....(4)

SEARCH FOR PARADISE (1957) Stanley Warner Cinema Corp. Color-120min. *(Travelog)*. *Director:* Otto Lang 5*

SEARCH FOR THE GODS (1975) Warner Bros. Color-100min. Kurt Russell, Stephen McHattie, Ralph Bellamy, Raymond St. Jacques 3*

SEARCHERS, THE (1956) Warner Bros. Color-119min. John Wayne, Jeffrey Hunter 5½*

SEARCHING WIND, THE (1946) Paramount. B&W-108min. Robert Young, Sylvia Sidney ....(4)

SEASIDE SWINGERS (1965) Avco-Embassy. Color-94min. *(British)*. John Leyton, Ron Moody, Freddie And The Dreamers...................(4)
Original title: EVERY DAY'S A HOLIDAY

SEASON OF PASSION (1959) United Artists. B&W-93min. *(Australian-British-U.S.)*. Ernest Borgnine, John Mills.....................4*
Original title: SUMMER OF THE SEVENTEENTH DOLL

SEATED AT HIS RIGHT (1971) *see* BLACK JESUS

SEBASTIAN (1968) Paramount. Color-100min. *(British)*. Dirk Bogarde, Susannah York ....(4)

2nd BEST SECRET AGENT IN THE WHOLE WIDE WORLD, THE (1965) Avco-Embassy. Color-96min. Tom Adams, Karel Stepanek, Veronica Hurst...3*
Original title: LICENSED TO KILL

SECOND CHANCE (1947) 20th Century-Fox. B&W-62min. Kent Taylor, Louise Currie ....(4)

SECOND CHANCE (1953) RKO. Color-82min. Robert Mitchum, Linda Darnell ....(4)

SECOND CHANCE (1971) MPC (TV). Color-74min. *(Made for TV)*. Brian Keith, Elizabeth Ashley ....(4)

SECOND CHORUS (1940) Paramount. B&W-83min. Fred Astaire, Paulette Goddard, Burgess Meredith 4½*

SECOND COMING OF SUZANNE, THE (1974) Barry Film Co. Color-90min. Sondra Locke, Paul Sand, Richard Dreyfuss ....(3)

SECOND FACE, THE (1950) Eagle Lion. B&W-77min. Ella Raines, Bruce Bennett ....(4)

SECOND FIDDLE (1939) 20th Century-Fox. B&W-86min. Sonja Henie, Tyrone Power ....(4)

SECOND GREATEST SEX, THE (1955) Universal. Color-87min. Jeanne Crain, George Nader..4*

SECOND HONEYMOON (1937) 20th Century-Fox. B&W-79min. Tyrone Power, Loretta Young ....(4)

SECOND POWER, THE (1977) Color-110min. *(Spanish)*. Jon Finch, Juliet Mills, Fernando Rey ....
Original title: SEGUNDO PODER, EL

SECOND TIME AROUND, THE (1961) 20th Century-Fox. Color-99min. Debbie Reynolds, Steve Forrest, Andy Griffith 3½*

SECOND WOMAN, THE (1950) United Artists. B&W-91min. Robert Young, Betsy Drake ....(4)
British title: ELLEN

SECONDS (1966) Paramount. B&W-106min. Rock Hudson, Salome Jens..4*

THE SECRET LIFE OF WALTER MITTY (1947). Habitual daydreamer Danny Kaye is puzzled and concerned when sinister bogus doctor Boris Karloff tries to convince him his recent adventures have merely been another daydream.

SECRET, THE (1955) Modern Sound Pictures. Color-80min. *(British)*. Sam Wanamaker, Mandy Miller, André Morell ....(3)

SECRET, LE (1974) Cinema National. Color-100min. *(French)*. Jean-Louis Trintignant, Marlene Jobert, Philippe Noiret...................

SECRET AGENT, THE (1936) Gaumont-British [Rank]. B&W-86min. *(British)*. John Gielgud, Lilli Palmer, Peter Lorre, Robert Young ......(4)

SECRET AGENT FIREBALL (1965) American-International. Color-89min. *(Italian-French)*. Richard Harrison, Dominique Boschero ....(3)
Original Italian title: SPIE UCCIDONO A BEIRUT, LE *(The Spy Killed in Beirut)*
French title: ESPIONS MEURENT A BEYROUTH, LES *(The Spies Killed in Beirut)*
Alternate title: KILLERS ARE CHALLENGED
British title: SPY KILLERS, THE
TV title: FIREBALL

SECRET AGENT OF JAPAN, THE (1942) 20th Century-Fox. B&W-72min. Lynn Bari, Preston Foster.......................................(3)

SECRET AGENT SUPER DRAGON (1966) United Screen Arts. Color-95min. *(Italian-French-W. German)*. Ray Danton, Marisa Mell ....(2)
Original Italian title: NEW YORK CHIAMA SUPERDRAGO *(New York Calling Superdragon)*
French title: NEW YORK APPELLE SUPER DRAGON
German title: HOLLENJAGD AUF HEISSE WARE
Alternate title: SUPER DRAGON

SECRET AGENTS, THE (1965) *see* DIRTY GAME, THE

SECRET BEYOND THE DOOR (1948) Universal. B&W-98min. Michael Redgrave, Joan Bennett ....(3)

SECRET BRIDE, THE (1934) Warner Bros. B&W-76min. Warren William, Barbara Stanwyck ....(4)
British title: CONCEALMENT

SECRET CEREMONY (1968) Universal. Color-109min. *(British-U.S.)*. Elizabeth Taylor, Mia Farrow, Robert Mitchum 3*

SECRET COMMAND (1944) Columbia. B&W-82min. Pat O'Brien, Carole Landis ....(4)

SECRET CONCLAVE, THE (1952) Italian Films Export. B&W-80min. *(Italian)*. Henry Vidon, Tullio Carminati......................(4)

SECRET DOOR, THE (1964) Allied Artists. Color-72min. *(British)*. Robert Hutton, Sandra Dorne ....(3)

SECRET FILE 1413 (1959) American-International. B&W-85min. *(French)*. Claudine Dupuis, Jean Danet ....(3)

SECRET FILE: HOLLYWOOD (1962) Crown International. B&W-85min. Robert Clarke, Francine York ....(2)
Alternate title: SECRET FILES OF HOLLYWOOD

SECRET FOUR, THE (1952) *see* KANSAS CITY CONFIDENTIAL

SECRET FURY, THE (1950) RKO. B&W-86min. Claudette Colbert, Robert Ryan ....(4)

SECRET GARDEN, THE (1949) M-G-M. B&W-92min. Margaret O'Brien, Dean Stockwell...4*

Films are rated on a 1 to 10 scale, 10 is highest. **Boldface** ratings followed by an asterisk (*) are for films actually seen and rated by the executive and senior editors. All other ratings are estimates. (See Notes on Entertainment Ratings in the front section.)

SECRET HEART, THE (1946) M-G-M. B&W-97min. Claudette Colbert, Walter Pidgeon 3*

SECRET INTERLUDE (1936) see PRIVATE NUMBER

SECRET INTERLUDE (1955) see VIEW FROM POMPEY'S HEAD, THE

SECRET INVASION, THE (1964) United Artists. Color-95min. Stewart Granger, Raf Vallone, Mickey Rooney 4*

SECRET LAND, THE (1948) M-G-M. Color-71min. (Documentary). Producer: Orville O. Dull .... (5)

SECRET LIFE OF AN AMERICAN WIFE, THE (1968) 20th Century-Fox. Color-92min. Walter Matthau, Anne Jackson, Patrick O'Neal 3*

SECRET LIFE OF PLANTS, THE (1978) Paramount. Color-98min. (Documentary). Director: Walon Green.

SECRET LIFE OF WALTER MITTY, THE (1947) RKO. Color-105min. Danny Kaye, Virginia Mayo, Boris Karloff 5½*

SECRET MARK OF D'ARTAGNAN, THE (1962) Medallion. Color-95min. (Italian-French). George Nader, Magali Noel .... (3)
Original Italian title: COLPO SEGRETO DI D'ARTAGNAN, IL
French title: SECRET DE D'ARTAGNAN, LE (The Secret of D'Artagnan)

SECRET MEETING (1959) see MARIE-OCTOBRE

SECRET MISSION (1942) English Films. B&W-82min. (British). Hugh Williams, Clara Lehmann 4*

SECRET NIGHT CALLER, THE (1975) MPC (TV). Color-74min. (Made for TV). Robert Reed, Hope Lange, Michael Constantine 4*

SECRET OF BLOOD ISLAND, THE (1965) Universal. Color-84min. (British). Barbara Shelley, Jack Hedley .... (3)

SECRET OF CONVICT LAKE, THE (1951) 20th Century-Fox. B&W-83min. Glenn Ford, Gene Tierney .... (4)

SECRET OF DEEP HARBOR (1961) United Artists. B&W-70min. Ron Foster, Barry Kelley .... (2)

SECRET OF DR. KILDARE, THE (1939) M-G-M. B&W-84min. Lionel Barrymore, Lew Ayres, Laraine Day .... (3)

SECRET OF DR. MABUSE (1961) Telewide Systems. B&W-90min. (French-W. German-Italian). Peter Van Eyck, Werner Peters, Yvonne Furneaux .... (3)
Original French title: RAYONS MORTELS DU DOCTEUR MABUSE, LES (The Death Ray of Dr. Mabuse)
W. German title: TODESSTRAHLEN DES DOKTOR MABUSE, DIE
Italian title: RAGGI MORTALI DEL DR. MABUSE, I
Publicity title(?): MIRROR DEATH RAY OF DR. MABUSE, THE
Alternate title: DEATHRAY MIRROR OF DR. MABUSE

SECRET OF DORIAN GRAY, THE (1970) see DORIAN GRAY

SECRET OF G.32 (1942) see FLY BY NIGHT

SECRET OF MAYERLING, THE (1949) Commercial Pictures. B&W-90min. (French). Jean Marais, Dominique Blunchar ....
Original title: SECRET DE MAYERLING, LE

SECRET OF MONTE CRISTO, THE (1961) M-G-M. Color-80min. Rory Calhoun, John Gregson, Patricia Bredin .... (3)
Original title: TREASURE OF MONTE CRISTO, THE

SECRET OF MY SUCCESS, THE (1965) M-G-M. Color-112min. (British). James Booth, Shirley Jones, Lionel Jeffries .... (3)

SECRET OF ST. IVES, THE (1949) Columbia. B&W-75min. Richard Ney, Vanessa Brown .... (3)

SECRET OF SANTA VITTORIA, THE (1969) United Artists. Color-139min. Anthony Quinn, Anna Magnani 4*

SECRET OF THE BLACK TRUNK, THE (1962) UCC Films. B&W-96min. (German). Senta Berger, Joachim Hansen .... (3)
Original title: GEHEIMNIS DER SCHWARZEN KOFFER, DAS
Alternate German title(?): SCHLOSS DES SCHRECKENS, DAS (The Castle of the Terrified)

SECRET OF THE BLACK WIDOW, THE (1964) Casino Films. B&W-107min. (W. German-Spanish). O. W. Fischer, Karin Dor 3*
Original W. German title: GEHEIMNIS DER SCHWARZEN WITWE, DAS

SECRET OF THE BLUE ROOM (1933) Universal. B&W-66min. Lionel Atwill, Gloria Stuart .... (3)

SECRET OF THE CHINESE CARNATION, THE (1965) UCC Films. B&W-95min. (W. German-French-Italian). Paul Dahlke, Olly Shoberova, Brad Harris .... (2)
Original W. German title: GEHEIMNIS DER CHINESISCHEN NELKE, DAS

SECRET OF THE INCAS (1954) Paramount. Color-101min. Charlton Heston, Robert Young 4*

SECRET OF THE PURPLE REEF, THE (1960) 20th Century-Fox. Color-80min. Jeff Richard, Margia Dean, Peter Falk 2*

SECRET OF THE RED ORCHID, THE (1962) see PUZZLE OF THE RED ORCHID, THE

SECRET OF THE SPHINX (1964) Independent TV Corp (ITC). Color-95min. (Italian-W. German). Tony Russel, Maria Perschy .... (3)
Original Italian title: SFINGE SORRIDE PRIMA DI MORIRE - STOP - LONDRA, LA (The Sphinx Smiles Before Dying - Stop - London)

SECRET OF THE TELEGIAN, THE (1960) Herts-Lion International. Color-85min. (Japanese). Koji Tsuruta, Yumi Shirakawa .... (3)
Original title: DENSO NINGEN
Publicity title: TELEGIAN, THE

SECRET OF THE WHISTLER, THE (1946) Columbia. B&W-65min. Richard Dix, Leslie Brooks, Mary Currier .... (3)

SECRET OF TREASURE MOUNTAIN, THE (1956) Columbia. B&W-68min. Valerie French, Raymond Burr, William Prince .... (3)

SECRET PARTNER, THE (1961) M-G-M. B&W-92min. (British). Stewart Granger, Haya Harareet .... (4)

SECRET PASSION, THE (1962) see FREUD

SECRET PEOPLE, THE (1952) Lippert Productions. B&W-96min. (British). Valentina Cortesa, Serge Reggiani, Audrey Hepburn .... (4)

SECRET SERVICE IN DARKEST AFRICA (1943) see BARON'S AFRICAN WAR, THE

SECRET SERVICE INVESTIGATOR (1948) Republic. B&W-60min. Lloyd Bridges, Lynne Roberts .... (4)

SECRET SEVEN, THE (1964) M-G-M. Color-92min. (Italian-Spanish). Tony Russell, Helga Liné 2*
Original Italian title: INVINCIBILI SETTE, GLI
Spanish title: INVENCIBLES, LOS

SECRET SIX, THE (1931) M-G-M. B&W-83min. Wallace Beery, Jean Harlow .... (5)

SECRET VENTURE (1955) Republic. B&W-68min. (British). Kent Taylor, Jane Hylton .... (3)

SECRET WAR OF HARRY FRIGG, THE (1968) Universal. Color-110min. Paul Newman, Sylva Koscina 4*

SECRET WAYS, THE (1961) Universal. B&W-112min. Richard Widmark, Sonja Ziemann 3*

SECRET WORLD (1968) 20th Century-Fox. Color-94min. (French, English language). Jacqueline Bisset, Jean-Francois Maurin 3*
Original title: ECHELLE BLANCHE, L' (The White Ladder)
Original title: PROMESSE, LA (The Promise)

SECRETARY, THE (1972) United Film Organization. Color-85min. Josh Gamble, Angela Gale .... (1)

SECRETS (1971) Lone Star Pictures International. Color-92min. Jacqueline Bisset, Per Oscarsson 4½*

SECRETS (1977) ABC-TV. Color-100min. (Made for TV). Susan Blakely, Roy Thinnes ....

SECRETS D'ALCOVE (1954) see BED, THE

SECRETS OF A SECRETARY (1931) Paramount. B&W-71min. Claudette Colbert, Herbert Marshall .... (3)

SECRETS OF AN ACTRESS (1938) Warner Bros. B&W-71min. Kay Francis, George Brent .... (4)

SECRETS OF LIFE (1956) Buena Vista. Color-70min. (Documentary). Director: James Algar .... (5)

SECRETS OF MONTE CARLO (1951) Republic. B&W-60min. Warren Douglas, Lois Hall .... (3)

SECRETS OF SCOTLAND YARD (1944) Republic. B&W-68min. Edgar Barrier, C. Aubrey Smith, Lionel Atwill 3*

SECRETS OF THE REEF (1956) Continental [Walter Reade]. Color-72min. (Documentary). Director: Lloyd Ritter .... (5)

SECRETS OF WOMEN (1952) Janus Films. B&W-114min. (Swedish). Anita Bjork, Maj-Britt Nilsson 3*
Original title: KVINNORS VANTAN (Waiting Women)
British title: WAITING WOMEN

SECURITY RISK (1954) Allied Artists. B&W-69min. John Ireland, Dorothy Malone .... (3)

SEDUCED AND ABANDONED (1964) Continental [Walter Reade]. B&W-118min. (Italian-French). Stefania Sandrelli, Aldo Puglisi 5*
Original Italian title: SEDOTTA E ABBANDONATA
French title: SÉDUITE ET ABANDONNÉE

SEDUCTION OF MIMI, THE (1972) New Line Cinema. Color-89min. (Italian). Giancarlo Giannini, Mariangela Melato 4½*
Original title: MIMI METALLURGICO FERITO NELL' ONORE (Mimi the Metalworker, His Honor Betrayed)

SEE HERE, PRIVATE HARGROVE (1944) M-G-M. B&W-101min. Robert Walker, Donna Reed 4½*

SEE HOW SHE RUNS (1978) NBC-TV. Color-96min. (Made for TV). Joanne Woodward, John Considine, Lissy Newman ....

SEE HOW THEY RUN (1953) see BRIGHT ROAD

Films are rated on a 1 to 10 scale, 10 is highest. **Boldface** ratings followed by an asterisk (*) are for films actually seen and rated by the executive and senior editors. All other ratings are estimates. (See Notes on Entertainment Ratings in the front section.)

SEE HOW THEY RUN (1965) MCA-TV. Color-100min. *(Made for TV).* John Forsythe, Senta Berger, Leslie Nielsen, Pamela Franklin .... (3)
Alternate title(?): WIDOW MAKERS, THE

SEE MY LAWYER (1945) Universal. B&W-67min. Ole Olsen, Chic Johnson, Grace McDonald .... (4)

SEE NO EVIL (1971) Columbia. Color-89min. *(British).* Mia Farrow, Robin Bailey 5*
Original title: BLIND TERROR

SEE THE MAN RUN (1971) MCA-TV. Color-73min. *(Made for TV).* Robert Culp, Angie Dickinson, Eddie Albert .... (4)

SEE YOU IN HELL, DARLING (1966) *see* AMERICAN DREAM, AN

SEEDS OF EVIL, THE (1974) *see* GARDENER, THE

SEEKERS, THE (1954) *see* LAND OF FURY

SEIZURE (1974) American-International. Color-93min. *(Canadian).* Jonathan Frid, Martine Beswick .... (4)

SELLOUT, THE (1952) M-G-M. B&W-83min. Walter Pidgeon, John Hodiak .... (4)

SELLOUT, THE (1976) Venture Distribution. Color-102min. *(British-Italian[-Israeli?]).* Richard Widmark, Oliver Reed, Gayle Hunnicutt (4)

SEMI-TOUGH (1977) United Artists. Color-107min. Burt Reynolds, Kris Kristofferson 5½*

SEMINOLE (1953) Universal. Color-87min. Rock Hudson, Barbara Hale 3*

SEMINOLE UPRISING (1955) Columbia. Color-74min. George Montgomery, Karin Booth .... (3)

SENATOR, THE (1979) Universal. Color-107min. Alan Alda, Barbara Harris ....

SENATOR WAS INDISCREET, THE (1947) Universal. B&W-81min. William Powell, Ella Raines 5*
British title: MR. ASHTON WAS INDISCREET

SEND ME NO FLOWERS (1964) Universal. Color-100min. Rock Hudson, Doris Day 4*

SENECHAL THE MAGNIFICENT (1957) Distributors Corp. of America. B&W-78min. *(French-Italian).* Fernandel, Nadia Gray .... (4)
Original French title: SENECHAL LE MAGNIFIQUE
British title: HIS GREATEST ROLE

SENIOR PROM (1959) Columbia. B&W-82min. Jill Corey, Paul Hampton .... (3)

SENIOR YEAR (1974) MCA-TV. Color-74min. *(Made for TV).* Gary Frank, Glynnis O'Connor 4*

SENSATIONS, THE (1944) United Artists. B&W-86min. Eleanor Powell, Dennis O'Keefe, W. C. Fields .... (4)
Original title: SENSATIONS OF 1945, THE

SENSE OF LOSS, A (1972) Cinema 5. B&W-135min. *(U.S.-Swiss, Documentary).* Director: Marcel Ophuls .... (4)

SENSO (1955) Fleetwood Films. Color-125min. *(Italian).* Alida Valli, Farley Granger .... (4)
TV title: WANTON CONTESSA, THE
Translation title: Sentiment

SENSUAL PARADISE (1972) *see* TOGETHER

SENSUALITA (1953) Italian Films Export. B&W-73min. *(Italian).* Eleanora Rossi-Drago, Amedeo Nazzari, Marcello Mastroianni .... (3)
Alternate title: BAREFOOT SAVAGE, THE
British title: ENTICEMENT

SENTIMENTAL JOURNEY (1946) 20th Century-Fox. B&W-94min. John Payne, Maureen O'Hara, Connie Marshall .... (3)

SENTINEL, THE (1977) Universal. Color-91min. Cristina Raines, Chris Sarandon, Burgess Meredith 4*

SEPARATE BEDS (1963) *see* WHEELER DEALERS, THE

SEPARATE PEACE, A (1972) Paramount. Color-105min. John Heyl, Parker Stevenson 4*

SEPARATE TABLES (1958) United Artists. B&W-98min. Burt Lancaster, Rita Hayworth 5½*

SEPARATION (1968) Continental [Walter Reade]. Color-93min. *(British).* Jane Arden, David De Keyser .... (3)

SEPTEMBER AFFAIR (1951) Paramount. B&W-104min. Joan Fontaine, Joseph Cotten 4*

SEPTEMBER STORM (1960) 20th Century-Fox. Color-90min. Joanne Dru, Mark Stevens 2*

SEPTEMBER 30, 1955 (1977) Universal. Color-101min. Richard Thomas, Susan Tyrrell 5½*
Alternate title: 9/30/55

SERAFINO (1968) Royal Films Int'l [Columbia]. Color-94min. *(Italian-French).* Adriano Celentano, Ottavia Piccolo .... (5)
French title: SERAFINA OU L'AMOUR AUX CHAMPS

SÉRAIL (1976) Caribou. Color-90min. *(French).* Leslie Caron, Corin Redgrave, Marie-France Pisier, Bulle Ogier .... (4)
Original title: SURREAL
Alternate title: SERAGLIO

SERENA (1962) Butcher's *(Brit.).* B&W-62min. *(British).* Patrick Holt, Emrys Jones, Honor Blackman .... (4)

SERENADE (1956) Warner Bros. Color-121min. Mario Lanza, Joan Fontaine, Sarita Montiel .... (4)

SERENGETI SHALL NOT DIE (1959) Allied Artists. Color-84min. *(German, Documentary).* Director: Michael Grzimek.... (5)
Original title: SERENGETI DARF NICHT STERBEN
Alternate title: THEY SHALL NOT DIE

SERGEANT, THE (1968) Warner Bros. Color-108min. Rod Steiger, John Phillip Law 3*

SERGEANT DEADHEAD (1965) American-International. Color-90min. Frankie Avalon, Deborah Walley, Fred Clark .... (3)
Alternate title: SERGEANT DEADHEAD THE ASTRONUT!

SERGEANT MADDEN (1939) M-G-M. B&W-82min. Wallace Beery, Laraine Day................................ (3)

SERGEANT MATLOVICH VS. THE U.S. AIR FORCE (1978) Tomorrow Entertainment. Color-98min. *(Made for TV).* Brad Dourif, Marc Singer .... (5)

SERGEANT MIKE (1944) Columbia. B&W-60min. Larry Parks, Jim Bannon .... (4)

SGT. PEPPER'S LONELY HEARTS CLUB BAND (1978) Universal. Color-111min. Peter Frampton, The Bee Gees............ 4*

SERGEANT RUTLEDGE (1960) Warner Bros. Color-118min. Jeffrey Hunter, Woody Strode 5*
Original title: TRIAL OF SERGEANT RUTLEDGE, THE

SERGEANT RYKER (1968) Universal. Color-86min. *(Telefeature).* Lee Marvin, Bradford Dillman .... (4)
Original title: CASE AGAINST PAUL RYKER, THE

SERGEANT WAS A LADY, THE (1961) Universal. B&W-72min. Martin West, Venetia Stevenson .... (3)

SERGEANT X OF THE FOREIGN LEGION (1960) American-International. B&W-85min. *(French).* Noelle Adam, Christian Marquand .... (3)

SERGEANT YORK (1941) Warner Bros. B&W-134min. Gary Cooper, Walter Brennan 5*

SERGEANTS 3 (1962) United Artists. Color-112min. Frank Sinatra, Dean Martin, Peter Lawford .... (4)

SERPENT, THE (1973) Avco-Embassy. Color-113min. *(French-Italian-W. German).* Yul Brynner, Henry Fonda, Dirk Bogarde, Philippe Noiret 3*
Original French title: SERPENT, LE
TV title: NIGHT FLIGHT FROM MOSCOW

SERPENT OF THE NILE (1953) Columbia. Color-81min. Rhonda Fleming, William Lundigan .... (2)

SERPENT'S EGG, THE (1977) Paramount. Color-120min. *(German).* Liv Ullmann, David Carradine, James Whitmore 4*
West German title: SCHLANGENEI, DAS

SERPICO (1973) Paramount. Color-129min. Al Pacino, John Randolph.. 7*

SERVANT, THE (1963) Commonwealth United. B&W-115min. *(British).* Dirk Bogarde, Sarah Miles, James Fox 5*

SERVICE FOR LADIES (1927) Paramount. B&W-82min. Adolphe Menjou, Kathryn Carver ....

SERVICE FOR LADIES (1932) *see* RESERVED FOR LADIES

SESSION WITH THE COMMITTEE, A (1969) *see* COMMITTEE, THE

SET THIS TOWN ON FIRE (1969) Color-100min. *(Made for TV).* Carl Betz, Chuck Connors .... (4)
Alternate title: PROFANE COMEDY, THE
Alternate title: TO SET THIS TOWN ON FIRE

SET-UP, THE (1949) RKO. B&W-72min. Robert Ryan, Audrey Totter 4½*

SET-UP, THE (1962) Anglo Amalgamated [EMI]. B&W-58min. *(British).* Maurice Denham, John Carson.................... (3)

SETTLERS, THE (1973) *see* NEW LAND, THE

SEVEN ALONE (1975) Doty-Dayton. Color-96min. Aldo Ray, Stewart Petersen ....

SEVEN ANGRY MEN (1955) Allied Artists. B&W-90min. Raymond Massey, Debra Paget 4*

SEVEN BEAUTIES (1976) Cinema 5. Color-115min. *(Italian).* Giancarlo Giannini, Fernado Rey 4½*
Original title: PASQUALINO SETTEBELLEZZE *(Pasqualino Seven-Beauties)*
Publicity title: SEVEN BEAUTIES . . . THAT'S WHAT THEY CALL HIM

THE SEVEN-PER-CENT SOLUTION (1976). At gunpoint, Joel Grey confesses to Nichol Williamson (playing Sherlock Holmes) that he was in on a kidnapping plot.

SEVEN BRIDES FOR SEVEN BROTHERS (1954) M-G-M. Color-102min. Jane Powell, Howard Keel 5½*

SEVEN CAPITAL SINS (1962) Avco-Embassy. B&W-113min. (French-Italian). Dany Saval, Jean-Louis Trintignant, Eddie Constantine, Jean-Pierre Aumont .... (4)
Original French title: SEPT PÉCHÉS CAPITAUX, LES
Italian title: SETTE PECCATI CAPITALI, I

SEVEN CHANCES (1925) Metro-Goldwyn. B&W-57min. (Silent). Buster Keaton, Ruth Dwyer 5½*

SEVEN CITIES OF GOLD (1955) 20th Century-Fox. Color-103min. Richard Egan, Anthony Quinn .... (4)

SEVEN DARING GIRLS (1960) Manson. B&W-76min. (German). Adrian Hoven, Ann Smyrner .... (3)
Original title: INSEL DER AMAZONEN

SEVEN DAYS ASHORE (1944) RKO. B&W-74min. Wally Brown, Alan Carney, Virginia Mayo .... (4)

SEVEN DAYS IN MAY (1964) Paramount. B&W-120min. Burt Lancaster, Kirk Douglas......................... 6*

SEVEN DAYS' LEAVE (1942) RKO. B&W-87min. Victor Mature, Lucille Ball .... (4)

SEVEN DAYS . . . SEVEN NIGHTS (1960) *see* MODERATO CANTIBILE

SEVEN DAYS TO NOON (1950) Mayer-Kingsley. B&W-93min. (British). Barry Jones, Olive Sloane 5*

SEVEN DEADLY SINS (1952) Arlan Pictures. B&W-140min. (French-Italian). Eduardo de Felippo, Isa Miranda .... (5)
Original French title: SEPT PECHES CAPITAUX, LES
Italian title: SETTE PECCATI CAPITALI, I

711 OCEAN DRIVE (1950) Columbia. B&W-102min. Edmond O'Brien, Joanne Dru......................... 4*

7 FACES OF DR. LAO (1964) M-G-M. Color-100min. Tony Randall 4*

SEVEN GOLDEN MEN (1965) Warner Bros. Color-87min. (Italian-French-Spanish, English language). Rossana Podesta, Philippe Leroy (3)
Original Italian title: SETTE UOMINI D'ORO
French title: SEPT HOMMES EN OR
Spanish title: SIETE HOMRES DE ORO

SEVEN GUNS FOR THE MacGREGORS (1966) Columbia. Color-94min. (Italian-Spanish). Robert Woods, Leo Anchoriz......................... (3)
Original Italian title: 7 PISTOLE PER I MacGREGOR
Spanish title: SIETE PISTOLAS PARA LOS MacGREGOR

SEVEN GUNS TO MESA (1958) Allied Artists. B&W-69min. Lola Albright, Charles Quinlivan .... (3)

SEVEN HILLS OF ROME, THE (1958) M-G-M. B&W-107min. (U.S.-Italian). Mario Lanza, Renato Rascel, Marisa Allasio 4*

SEVEN IN DARKNESS (1969) Paramount. Color-74min. (Made for TV). Milton Berle, Dina Merrill, Arthur O'Connell......................... 5*

SEVEN IN THE SUN (1964) Avco-Embassy. B&W-88min. (Italian). Gianna Maria Canale, Frank Latimore......................... (3)

SEVEN KEYS TO BALDPATE (1929) RKO. B&W-75min. Richard Dix, Miriam Seegar......................... (4)

SEVEN KEYS TO BALDPATE (1935) RKO. B&W-80min. Gene Raymond, Margaret Callahan, Eric Blore......................... (4)

SEVEN KEYS TO BALDPATE (1947) RKO. B&W-66min. Phillip Terry, Jacqueline White......................... 4*

SEVEN LITTLE FOYS, THE (1955) Paramount. Color-95min. Bob Hope, Milly Vitale......................... 4*

7 MEN FROM NOW (1956) Warner Bros. Color-78min. Randolph Scott, Gail Russell, Lee Marvin......................... (3)

SEVEN MILES FROM ALCATRAZ (1943) RKO. B&W-62min. James Craig, Bonita Granville......................... (3)

SEVEN MINUTES, THE (1971) 20th Century-Fox. Color-116min. Wayne Maunder, Marianne McAndrew, Yvonne De Carlo......................... 3*

SEVEN NIGHTS IN JAPAN (1976) EMI. Color-104min. (British-French). Michael York, Hidemi Aoki......................... (4)

SEVEN PER-CENT SOLUTION, THE (1976) Universal. Color-113min. Nicol Williamson, Alan Arkin, Robert Duvall......................... 6*

SEVEN SAMURAI, THE (1954) Toho. B&W-160min. (Japanese). Takashi Shimura, Toshiro Mifune......................... 5*
Original title: SHICHININ NO SAMURAI
Alternate title: MAGNIFICENT SEVEN, THE

SEVEN SEAS TO CALAIS (1961) M-G-M. Color-102min. (Italian). Rod Taylor, Keith Michell, Irene Worth......................... (3)
Original title: DOMINATORE DEI SETTE MARI, IL (*The Dominator of the Seven Seas*)

SEVEN SINNERS (1940) Universal. B&W-87min. Marlene Dietrich, John Wayne......................... 5*

SEVEN SLAVES AGAINST THE WORLD (1964) Paramount. Color-96min. (Italian). Roger Browne, Gordon Mitchell, Scilla Gabel............ (2)
Original title: SCHIAVI PIU FORTI DEL MONDO, GLI (*The Strongest Slaves in the World*)
Alternate title: SEVEN SLAVES AGAINST ROME

SEVEN SURPRISES (1964) Quartet International. B&W-77min. (Canadian). .... (4)
Short #1: NAHANNI (*1962*)
Short #2: MERLE, LE (*1958*)
Short #3: CHAIRY TALE, A (*1957*)
Short #4: CARS IN YOUR LIFE, THE (*1960*)
Short #5: CORRAL (*1954*)
Short #6: WRESTLING (*1961*)
Short #7: NEIGHBORS (*1952*)

SEVEN SWEETHEARTS (1942) M-G-M. B&W-98min. Kathryn Grayson, Van Heflin......................... 4*

SEVEN TASKS OF ALI BABA, THE (1963) Medallion. Color-95min. (Italian). Rod Flash, Bella Cortez......................... (3)
Original title: 7 FATICHE DI ALI BABA, LE
Alternate title: ALI BABA AND THE SACRED CROWN

SEVEN THIEVES (1960) 20th Century-Fox. B&W-102min. Edward G. Robinson, Rod Steiger......................... 4½*

SEVEN THUNDERS (1957) *see* BEASTS OF MARSEILLES, THE

SEVEN TIMES SEVEN (1968) Allied Artists. Color-100min. (Italian). Lionel Stander, Terry-Thomas, Adolfo Celi......................... (4)
Original title: 7 VOLTE 7

SEVEN-UPS, THE (1973) 20th Century-Fox. Color-103min. Roy Scheider, Victor Arnold......................... 4*

SEVEN WAVES AWAY (1957) *see* ABANDON SHIP!

SEVEN WAYS FROM SUNDOWN (1960) Universal. Color-87min. Audie Murphy, Barry Sullivan......................... 3*

SEVEN WERE SAVED (1947) Paramount. B&W-73min. Richard Denning, Catherine Craig......................... (3)

SEVEN WOMEN (1966) M-G-M. Color-93min. Anne Bancroft, Sue Lyon, Margaret Leighton......................... (3)

SEVEN WOMEN FROM HELL (1961) 20th Century-Fox. B&W-88min. Patricia Owens, John Kerr......................... (3)

SEVEN WONDERS OF THE WORLD (1956) Stanley Warner Cinema Corp. Color-120min. (Travelog). .... (5)

SEVEN YEAR ITCH, THE (1955) 20th Century-Fox. Color-105min. Marilyn Monroe, Tom Ewell......................... 5½*

SEVENTEEN (1940) Paramount. B&W-78min. Jackie Cooper, Betty Field......................... (4)

SEVENTEEN (1965) *see* ERIC SOYA'S "17"

1776 (1972) Columbia. Color-141min. William Daniels, Howard Da Silva, Ken Howard......................... 6*

Films are rated on a 1 to 10 scale, 10 is highest. **Boldface** ratings followed by an asterisk (*) are for films actually seen and rated by the executive and senior editors. All other ratings are estimates. (See Notes on Entertainment Ratings in the front section.)

7th CAVALRY, THE (1956) Columbia. **Color-75min.** Randolph Scott, Barbara Hale .... (4)

7th COMMANDMENT, THE (1961) Crown International. **B&W-82min.** Jonathan Kidd, Lyn Statten .... (2)

SEVENTH CONTINENT, THE (1967) U-M Prods. **Color-84min.** *(Yugoslavian-Czech).* Iris Vrus, Tomislav Pasaric .... (5)
Original Yugoslavian title: SEDMI KONTINENT
Czech title: SEDMY KONTINENT
Alternate Czech title: SIEDMA PEVNINA

SEVENTH CROSS, THE (1944) M-G-M. **B&W-110min.** Spencer Tracy, Signe Hasso 3*

SEVENTH DAWN, THE (1964) United Artists. **Color-123min.** *(U.S.-British).* William Holden, Susannah York, Capucine 4*

7th HEAVEN (1927) Fox Film Co. [20th]. **B&W-94min.** *(Silent).* Janet Gaynor, Charles Farrell 6*

SEVENTH HEAVEN (1937) 20th Century-Fox. **B&W-102min.** Simone Simon, James Stewart .... (3)

SEVENTH SEAL, THE (1956) Janus Films. **B&W-105min.** *(Swedish).* Max Von Sydow, Bengt Ekerot 5½*
Original title: SJUNDE INSEGLET, DET

SEVENTH SIN, THE (1957) M-G-M. **B&W-94min.** Eleanor Parker, Bill Travers, George Sanders .... (4)

SEVENTH SWORD, THE (1962) Telewide Systems. **Color-96min.** *(Italian).* Brett Halsey .... (3)

SEVENTH VEIL, THE (1945) Universal. **B&W-94min.** *(British).* James Mason, Ann Todd 4*

SEVENTH VICTIM, THE (1943) RKO. **B&W-71min.** Tom Conway, Kim Hunter .... (4)

7th VOYAGE OF SINBAD, THE (1958) Columbia. **Color-89min.** Kerwin Mathews, Kathryn Grant .... (4)

79 A.D. (1961) American-International. **Color-113min.** *(Italian).* Susan Paget, Brad Harris .... (3)

SEVENTY TIMES SEVEN (1962) *see* FEMALE, THE

SEVERED HEAD, A (1971) Columbia. **Color-98min.** *(British).* Lee Remick, Richard Attenborough, Ian Holm .... (3)

SEX AND THE SINGLE GIRL (1964) Warner Bros. **Color-114min.** Tony Curtis, Natalie Wood 4*

SEX AND THE TEENAGER (1972) *see* TO FIND A MAN

SEX IS A WOMAN (1966) *see* DEATH IS A WOMAN

SEX ISN'T SIN (1970) *see* LOVE IN A FOUR-LETTER WORD

SEX KITTENS GO TO COLLEGE (1960) Allied Artists. **B&W-94min.** Mamie Van Doren, Tuesday Weld, Mijanou Bardot .... (2)
TV title: BEAUTY AND THE ROBOT

SEX MADNESS (1929) Public Welfare Pictures. **Color-75min.** *(Italian, English language).* Jack Richardson, Corliss Palmer .... (3)

SEX OF ANGELS, THE (1968) Lopert [U.A.]. **Color-104min.** *(Italian-W. German).* Bernard De Vries, Rosemarie Dexter .... (1)
Original Italian title: SESSO DEGLI ANGELI, IL
German title: GESCHLECHT DER ENGEL, DAS

SEX-SHOP, LE (1973) Peppercorn-Wormser. **Color-92min.** *(French-Italian-W. German).* Juliet Berto, Claude Berri 4½*
Alternate title: SEX SHOP

SEX SYMBOL, THE (1975) CPT (TV). **Color-74min.** Connie Stevens, Don Murray, Shelley Winters 3*

SEX WITH A SMILE (1976) Surrogate. **Color-100min.** *(Italian).* Marty Feldman, Giovanni Lionelli, Sydne Rome, Barbara Bouchet 3*

SEXTETTE (1978) Briggs & Sullivan. **Color-91min.** Mae West, Timothy Dalton, Tony Curtis .... (4)

SHACK OUT ON 101 (1955) Allied Artists. **B&W-80min.** Frank Lovejoy, Terry Moore 3*

SHADOW IN THE SKY (1952) M-G-M. **B&W-78min.** Ralph Meeker, Jean Hagen .... (4)

SHADOW MAN (1953) Lippert Productions. **B&W-75min.** *(British).* Cesar Romero, Kay Kendall .... (4)
Original title: STREET OF SHADOWS

SHADOW OF A DOUBT (1943) Universal. **B&W-108min.** Teresa Wright, Joseph Cotten 5*

SHADOW OF A WOMAN (1946) Warner Bros. **B&W-78min.** Helmut Dantine, Andrea King .... (3)

SHADOW OF BLACKMAIL (1946) *see* WIFE WANTED

SHADOW OF EVIL (1964) Seven Arts [W.B.]. **Color-92min.** *(French-Italian).* Kerwin Mathews, Robert Hossein, Pier Angeli .... (3)
Original French title: BANCO A BANGKOK
Alternate French title: BANCO A BANGKOK POUR OSS 117
Italian title: OSS 117 MINACCIA BANGKOK

SHADOW OF FEAR (1955) United Artists. **B&W-76min.** *(British).* Mona Freeman, Jean Kent, Maxwell Reed .... (4)
Original title: BEFORE I WAKE

SHADOW OF THE CAT (1961) Universal. **B&W-79min.** *(British).* André Morell, Barbara Shelley .... (3)

SHADOW OF THE HAWK (1976) Columbia. **Color-92min.** *(Canadian).* Jan-Michael Vincent, Marilyn Hassett, Chief Dan George 3*

SHADOW OF THE THIN MAN (1941) M-G-M. **B&W-97min.** William Powell, Myrna Loy 4*

SHADOW OF THE WEREWOLF (1970) *see* WEREWOLF VS. THE VAMPIRE WOMAN, THE

SHADOW OF TREASON (1964) Paramount. **B&W-77min.** *(British).* John Bentley, Faten Hamoma .... (2)

SHADOW OF ZORRO, THE (1963) Allied Artists. **Color-84min.** *(Spanish-Italian).* Frank Latimore, Marie Gale (Maria Luz Galicia) ..... (3)
Original Spanish title: CABALGANDO HACIA LA MUERTE *(Riding Toward Death)*

SHADOW ON THE LAND (1968) Screen Gems. **Color-97min.** *(Made for TV).* Jackie Cooper, John Forsythe, Carol Lynley, Gene Hackman 5*

SHADOW ON THE WALL (1950) M-G-M. **B&W-84min.** Gigi Perreau, Ann Sothern .... (5)

SHADOW ON THE WINDOW, THE (1957) Columbia. **B&W-73min.** Phil Carey, Betty Garrett .... (4)

SHADOW OVER ELVERON (1968) Universal. **Color-100min.** *(Made for TV).* James Franciscus, Leslie Nielsen, Shirley Knight .... (4)

SHADOW VS. THE 1,000 EYES OF DR. MABUSE, THE (1960) *see* 1,000 EYES OF DR. MABUSE, THE

SHADOWMAN (1975) New Line Cinema. **Color-90min.** *(French).* Gayle Hunnicutt, Jacques Champreux, Gert Froebe ....
Original title: HOMME SANS VISAGE, L'

SHADOWS (1959) Lion International [British Lion]. **B&W-87min.** Lelia Goldoni, Hugh Hurd .... (4)

SHADOWS GROW LONGER (1961) Times Film Corp. **B&W-91min.** *(Swiss-W. German).* Luise Ullrich, Barbara Rutting .... (3)
Original German title: SCHATTEN WERDEN LAENGER, DIE *(The Shadows Grow Longer)*
Alternate title: DEFIANT DAUGHTERS

SHADOWS IN THE NIGHT (1944) Columbia. **B&W-67min.** Nina Foch, Warner Baxter, George Zucco .... (3)

SHADOWS OF FORGOTTEN ANCESTORS (1964) Artkino. **Color-100min.** *(U.S.S.R.).* Ivan Mikolaychuk, Larisa Kadoch 2*
Original title: TINI ZABUTYKH PREDKIV
Alternate title: SHADOWS OF OUR ANCESTORS
Alternate title: SHADOWS OF OUR FORGOTTEN ANCESTORS

SHADOWS OVER CHINATOWN (1946) Monogram [Allied Artists]. **B&W-64min.** Sidney Toler, Mantan Moreland .... (4)

SHADY LADY (1945) Universal. **B&W-94min.** Charles Coburn, Robert Paige, Ginny Simms .... (3)

SHAFT (1971) M-G-M. **Color-100min.** Richard Roundtree, Moses Gunn .. 4*

SHAFT IN AFRICA (1973) M-G-M. **Color-112min.** Richard Roundtree, Frank Finlay .... (4)

SHAFT'S BIG SCORE (1972) M-G-M. **Color-105min.** Richard Roundtree, Moses Gunn .... (4)

SHAGGY D.A., THE (1976) Buena Vista. **Color-91min.** Dean Jones, Suzanne Pleshette .... (5)

SHAGGY DOG, THE (1959) Buena Vista. **B&W-104min.** Tommy Kirk, Fred MacMurray 5*

SHAKE HANDS WITH THE DEVIL (1959) United Artists. **B&W-100min.** James Cagney, Don Murray 5*

SHAKE, RATTLE AND ROCK! (1956) American-International. **B&W-74min.** Touch (Michael) Connors, Lisa Gaye, Fats Domino 4*

SHAKEDOWN (1950) Universal. **B&W-80min.** Howard Duff, Brian Donlevy .... (4)

SHAKEDOWN, THE (1959) Universal. **B&W-92min.** *(British).* Terence Morgan, Hazel Court, Donald Pleasance .... (3)

SHAKESPEARE WALLAH (1965) Continental [Walter Reade]. **B&W-115min.** *(Indian, English language).* Shashi Kapoor, Felicity Kendal ... 4*

SHAKIEST GUN IN THE WEST, THE (1968) Universal. **Color-101min.** Don Knotts, Barbara Rhoades 3*

SHALAKO (1968) Cinerama Releasing. **Color-113min.** *(British).* Sean Connery, Brigitte Bardot, Stephen Boyd .... (3)

SHALL WE DANCE (1937) RKO. **B&W-116min.** Fred Astaire, Ginger Rogers 5*

SHAME (1962) *see* INTRUDER, THE

SHAME (1968) Lopert [U.A.]. **B&W-103min.** *(Swedish).* Liv Ullmann, Max von Sydow .... (4)
Original title: SKAMMEN

SHAMEFUL (1969) *see* BLACK ON WHITE

SHAMELESS OLD LADY, THE (1965) Continental [Walter Reade]. **B&W-95min.** *(French).* Sylvie, Malka Ribovska 2*
Original title: VIELLE DAME INDIGNE, LA *(The Undignified Old Woman)*
Alternate translation: The Unworthy Old Woman

SHAMPOO (1975) Columbia. **Color-109min.** Warren Beatty, Julie Christie 5½*

SHAMUS (1973) Columbia. **Color-98min.** Burt Reynolds, Dyan Cannon 5*

SHANE (1953) Paramount. **Color-118min.** Alan Ladd, Jean Arthur 5½*

SHANGHAI (1935) Paramount. **B&W-75min.** Charles Boyer, Loretta Young .... (4)

SHANGHAI CHEST, THE (1948) Monogram [Allied Artists]. **B&W-56min.** Roland Winters, Mantan Moreland .... (3)

SHANGHAI COBRA, THE (1945) Monogram [Allied Artists]. **B&W-64min.** Sidney Toler, Benson Fong, Mantan Moreland .... (3)
Publicity title: CHARLIE CHAN IN THE SHANGHAI COBRA

SHANGHAI EXPRESS (1932) Paramount. **B&W-80min.** Marlene Dietrich, Clive Brook 5*

SHANGHAI GESTURE, THE (1941) United Artists. **B&W-106min.** Gene Tierney, Walter Huston .... (3)

SHANGHAI STORY, THE (1954) Republic. **B&W-90min.** Ruth Roman, Edmond O'Brien 3*

SHANKS (1974) Paramount. **Color-93min.** Marcel Marceau 3½*

SHANTY TRAMP (1967) Trans-International. **B&W-72min.** Lee Holland, Bill Rogers .... (3)

SHANTYTOWN HONEYMOON (1972) Lion Dog Enterprises. **Color-85min.** Ashley Brooke, Jim Beck, George Ellis ....

SHARAD OF ATLANTIS, THE (1936) Republic. **B&W-100min.** *(Re-edited Serial).* Ray "Crash" Corrigan, Lois Wilde, Monte Blue .... (3)
Original title: UNDERSEA KINGDOM

SHARE OUT, THE (1962) Schoenfeld Film Distributing. **B&W-61min.** *(British).* Bernard Lee, Alexander Knox .... (4)

SHAMPOO (1975). Julie Christie gets a lot more favors than just hairdos from Beverly Hills hairdresser Warren Beatty, who hopes the financier whose mistress she is will loan him the money he needs to open his own shop.

SHARK! (1968) Excelsior. **Color-92min.** *(U.S.-Mexican).* Burt Reynolds, Barry Sullivan, Arthur Kennedy 3*
Mexican title: UN ARMA DE DOS FILOS

SHARK REEF (1958) *see* SHE-GODS OF SHARK REEF

SHARK RIVER (1953) United Artists. **Color-80min.** Steve Cochran, Carole Matthews .... (3)

SHARKFIGHTERS, THE (1956) United Artists. **Color-73min.** Victor Mature, Karen Steele .... (3)

SHARKS' TREASURE (1975) United Artists. **Color-95min.** Cornel Wilde, Yaphet Kotto 4*

SHATTER (1976) *see* CALL HIM MR. SHATTER

SHE (1935) RKO. **B&W-94min.** Helen Gahagan, Randolph Scott 4*

SHE (1965) M-G-M. **Color-106min.** *(British).* Ursula Andress, John Richardson, Peter Cushing, Christopher Lee .... (4)

SHE AND HE (1963) Brandon. **B&W-110min.** *(Japanese).* Sachiko Hidari, Kikuji Yamashita .... (5)
Original title: KANOJO TO KARE

SHE COULDN'T SAY NO (1940) Warner Bros. **B&W-64min.** Eve Arden, Roger Pryor .... (3)

SHE COULDN'T SAY NO (1953) RKO. **B&W-89min.** Robert Mitchum, Jean Simmons .... (4)
British title: BEAUTIFUL BUT DANGEROUS

SHE CREATURE, THE (1956) American-International. **B&W-77min.** Chester Morris, Marla English, Tom Conway ....

SHE CRIED MURDER! (1973) MCA-TV. **Color-74min.** *(Made for TV).* Telly Savalas, Lynda Day George, Mike Farrell 4*

SHE DEMONS (1958) Astor. **B&W-80min.** Irish McCalla, Tod Griffin .... (2)

SHE DEVIL (1957) 20th Century-Fox. **B&W-77min.** Mari Blanchard, Jack Kelly, Albert Dekker .... (2)

SHE DONE HIM WRONG (1933) Paramount. **B&W-66min.** Mae West, Cary Grant 4*

SHE GETS HER MAN (1945) Universal. **B&W-65min.** Joan Davis, Leon Errol .... (3)

SHE-GODS OF SHARK REEF (1958) American-International. **Color-65min.** Bill Cord, Don Durant, Lisa Montell .... (3)
British title: SHARK REEF

SHE GOT HER MAN (1942) *see* MAISIE GETS HER MAN

SHE LEARNED ABOUT SAILORS (1934) Fox Film Co. [20th]. **B&W-76min.** Alice Faye, Lew Ayres .... (4)

SHE LIVES (1973) Circle Entertainment. **Color-74min.** *(Made for TV).* Desi Arnaz, Jr., Season Hubley .... (4)

SHE LOVES ME NOT (1934) Paramount. **B&W-83min.** Bing Crosby, Miriam Hopkins .... (5)

SHE MARRIED HER BOSS (1935) Columbia. **B&W-85min.** Claudette Colbert, Melvyn Douglas .... (4)

SHE PLAYED WITH FIRE (1957) Columbia. **B&W-95min.** *(British).* Jack Hawkins, Arlene Dahl, Dennis Price 4*
Original title: FORTUNE IS A WOMAN

SHE WAITS (1971) MPC (TV). **Color-74min.** *(Made for TV).* Patty Duke, David McCallum, Lew Ayres 4*

SHE WENT TO THE RACES (1945) M-G-M. **B&W-86min.** Ava Gardner, James Craig .... (3)

SHE-WOLF, THE (1954) *see* LUPA, LA

SHE-WOLF OF LONDON (1946) Universal. **B&W-61min.** June Lockhart, Don Porter 3*
British title: CURSE OF THE ALLENBYS

SHE WORE A YELLOW RIBBON (1949) RKO. **Color-103min.** John Wayne, Joanne Dru 4½*

SHE WOULDN'T SAY YES (1945) Columbia. **B&W-87min.** Rosalind Russell, Lee Bowman .... (4)

SHEEP HAS FIVE LEGS, THE (1954) United Motion Pic. Org. (UMPO). **B&W-95min.** *(French).* Fernandel .... (5)
Original title: MOUTON A CINQ PATTES, LE

SHEEPMAN, THE (1958) M-G-M. **Color-85min.** Glenn Ford, Shirley MacLaine 5*
Alternate title: STRANGER WITH A GUN

SHEIK, THE (1921) Paramount. **B&W-73min.** *(Silent).* Rudolph Valentino, Agnes Ayres, Adolphe Menjou 4*

SHEILA LEVINE IS DEAD AND LIVING IN NEW YORK (1975) Paramount. **Color-113min.** Jeannie Berlin, Roy Scheider 4*

SHELL SHOCK (1964) Parade Releasing Organization. **B&W-84min.** Beach Dickerson, Carl Crow .... (3)

SHELTER OF YOUR ARMS, THE (1973) *see* TURKISH DELIGHT

SHENANDOAH (1965) Universal. Color-105min. James Stewart, Doug McClure............(5)

SHENNANIGANS (1977) see GREAT GEORGIA BANK HOAX, THE

SHEPHERD OF THE HILLS (1941) Paramount. Color-98min. Harry Carey, John Wayne............(4)

SHERIFF, THE (1971) Screen Gems. Color-74min. (Made for TV). Ossie Davis, Ruby Dee............5*

SHERIFF OF FRACTURED JAW, THE (1958) 20th Century-Fox. Color-110min. (British). Kenneth More, Jayne Mansfield............4*

SHERIFF WAS A LADY, THE (1964) Screen Gems. Color-88min. (German). Mamie Van Doren, Ric Battaglia............(2)

SHERIFF'S DAUGHTER, THE (1950) see TICKET TO TOMAHAWK, A

SHERLOCK HOLMES (1922) Goldwyn. B&W-109min. (Silent). John Barrymore, Roland Young, Carol Dempster, Gustav von Seyffertitz...(4)

SHERLOCK HOLMES (1932) 20th Century-Fox. B&W-68min. Clive Brook, Reginald Owen, Ernest Torrence............(5)

SHERLOCK HOLMES (1940) see ADVENTURES OF SHERLOCK HOLMES, THE

SHERLOCK HOLMES AND THE DEADLY NECKLACE (1962) Screen Gems. B&W-84min. (W. German-British). Christopher Lee, Thorley Walters, Senta Berger............(4)
Original German title: SHERLOCK HOLMES UND DAS HALSBAND DES TODES
British title: VALLEY OF FEAR, THE

SHERLOCK HOLMES AND THE PEARL OF DEATH (1944) see PEARL OF DEATH, THE

SHERLOCK HOLMES AND THE SCARLET CLAW (1945) see SCARLET CLAW, THE

SHERLOCK HOLMES AND THE SECRET CODE (1946) see DRESSED TO KILL

SHERLOCK HOLMES AND THE SECRET WEAPON (1942) Universal. B&W-68min. Basil Rathbone, Nigel Bruce............4*

SHERLOCK HOLMES AND THE SPIDER WOMAN (1944) Universal. B&W-62min. Basil Rathbone, Nigel Bruce............4*
British title and U.S. copyright title: SPIDER WOMAN, THE

SHERLOCK HOLMES AND THE VOICE OF TERROR (1942) Universal. B&W-65min. Basil Rathbone, Nigel Bruce............4*

SHERLOCK HOLMES AND THE WOMAN IN GREEN (1945) see WOMAN IN GREEN, THE

SHERLOCK HOLMES FACES DEATH (1943) Universal. B&W-68min. Basil Rathbone, Nigel Bruce............4*

SHERLOCK HOLMES: HOUND OF THE BASKERVILLES (1972) see HOUND OF THE BASKERVILLES

SHERLOCK HOLMES IN NEW YORK (1976) 20th Century-Fox. Color-100min. (Made for TV). Roger Moore, Patrick Macnee, John Huston, Charlotte Rampling............5*

SHERLOCK HOLMES IN PURSUIT TO ALGIERS (1945) see PURSUIT TO ALGIERS

SHERLOCK HOLMES IN TERROR BY NIGHT (1946) see TERROR BY NIGHT

SHERLOCK HOLMES IN WASHINGTON (1943) Universal. B&W-71min. Basil Rathbone, Nigel Bruce, Henry Daniell............4*

SHERLOCK HOLMES' SMARTER BROTHER (1975) see ADVENTURE OF SHERLOCK HOLMES' SMARTER BROTHER, THE

SHERLOCK, JR. (1924) Metro. B&W-51min. (Silent). Buster Keaton, Kathryn McGuire............5½*

SHE'S A SOLDIER TOO (1944) Columbia. B&W-67min. Nina Foch, Beulah Bondi, Lloyd Bridges............(3)

SHE'S A SWEETHEART (1944) Columbia. B&W-69min. Larry Parks, Jane Frazee............(3)

SHE'S BACK ON BROADWAY (1953) Warner Bros. Color-95min. Virginia Mayo, Steve Cochran............(4)

SHE'S MY LOVELY (1942) see GET HEP TO LOVE

SHE'S WORKING HER WAY THRU COLLEGE (1952) Warner Bros. Color-101min. Virginia Mayo, Gene Nelson............(4)

SHIELD FOR MURDER (1954) United Artists. B&W-80min. Edmond O'Brien, John Agar............(4)

SHINBONE ALLEY (1971) Allied Artists. Color-84min. (Cartoon). Director: John D. Wilson............(4)
Alternate title: archy and mehitabel

SHINE ON HARVEST MOON (1944) Warner Bros. B&W-112min. Ann Sheridan, Dennis Morgan............(4)

SHINING, THE (1980) Warner Bros. Color- min. Jack Nicholson, Shelley Duvall............

SHINING HOUR, THE (1938) M-G-M. B&W-80min. Joan Crawford, Robert Young, Melvyn Douglas............(4)

SHINING STAR (1975) see THAT'S THE WAY OF THE WORLD

SHINING VICTORY (1941) Warner Bros. B&W-80min. James Stephenson, Geraldine Fitzgerald............4*

SHIP AHOY (1942) M-G-M. B&W-95min. Eleanor Powell, Red Skelton..(4)

SHIP OF CONDEMNED WOMEN, THE (1953) Globe Pictures & President Films. Color-95min. (Italian). May Britt, Tania Weber, Ettore Manni............(3)
Original title: NAVE DELLE DONNE MALEDETTE, LA

SHIP OF FOOLS (1965) Columbia. B&W-149min. Vivien Leigh, Simone Signoret, Oskar Werner, Lee Marvin............6*

SHIP THAT DIED OF SHAME, THE (1955) Continental [Walter Reade]. B&W-91min. (British). Richard Attenborough, George Baker............(4)
Alternate title: PT RAIDERS

SHIP WAS LOADED, THE (1957) George K. Arthur. B&W-82min. (British). Peggy Cummins, David Tomlinson............(4)
Original title: CARRY ON ADMIRAL

SHIPMATES FOREVER (1935) First National [W.B.]. B&W-109min. Dick Powell, Ruby Keeler............(4)

SHIPS WITH WINGS (1941) United Artists. B&W-102min. (British). John Clements, Leslie Banks............(4)

SHIPWRECK ISLAND (1962) Commonwealth United TV. Color-93min. (Spanish). Pablito Calvo, José Ignacio Corrales............(4)
Original title: DOS ANOS DE VACACIONES (Two Years' Vacation)

SHIPWRECK! (1978) see SEA GYPSIES, THE

SHIRTS/SKINS (1973) M-G-M. Color-74min. (Made for TV). René Auberjonois, Bill Bixby, Leonard Frey............(5)

SHIVERS (1974) see THEY CAME FROM WITHIN

SHOCK (1946) 20th Century-Fox. B&W-70min. Vincent Price, Lynn Bari............(3)

SHOCK CORRIDOR (1963) Allied Artists. B&W-101min. Peter Breck, Constance Towers, Gene Evans............(2)

SHOCK TREATMENT (1964) 20th Century-Fox. B&W-94min. Stuart Whitman, Carol Lynley, Lauren Bacall............(3)

SHOCK TROOPS (1967) United Artists. Color-106min. (French-Italian). Jean-Claude Brialy, Bruno Cremer............(3)
Original French title: HOMME DE TROP, UN

SHOCK WAVES (1977) Joseph Brenner. Color-82min. Peter Cushing, Brooke Adams, John Carradine, Luke Halpin............2*
Original title: DEATH CORPS

SHOCKER (1961) see TOWN WITHOUT PITY

SHOCKING MISS PILGRIM, THE (1947) 20th Century-Fox. Color-85min. Betty Grable, Dick Haymes............(3)

SHOCKPROOF (1949) Columbia. B&W-79min. Cornel Wilde, Patricia Knight............(5)

SHOE SHINE (1946) Lopert [U.A.]. B&W-93min. (Italian). Rinaldo Smordoni, Franco Interlenghi............4*
Original title: SCIUSCIA

SHOES OF THE FISHERMAN, THE (1968) M-G-M. Color-155min. Anthony Quinn, Oskar Werner............4*

SHOOT, THE (1964) Screen Gems. Color-120min. (German). Lex Barker, Ralf Wolter, Marie Versini............(3)

SHOOT (1976) Avco-Embassy. Color-92min. (Canadian-U.S.). Cliff Robertson, Ernest Borgnine............5*

SHOOT FIRST (1953) United Artists. B&W-88min. (British). Joel McCrea, Evelyn Keyes, Herbert Lom............(4)
Original title: ROUGH SHOOT

SHOOT IT: BLACK, SHOOT IT: BLUE (1974) Levitt-Pickman. Color-93min. Michael Moriarty, Eric Laneuville............(3)

SHOOT LOUD, LOUDER . . . I DON'T UNDERSTAND (1966) Avco-Embassy. Color-100min. (Italian). Marcello Mastroianni, Raquel Welch, Eduardo De Filippo............3*
Original title: SPARA FORTE, PIU FORTE . . . NON CAPISCO

SHOOT OUT (1971) Universal. Color-95min. Gregory Peck, Pat Quinn............4½*

SHOOT OUT AT BIG SAG (1962) Parallel. B&W-64min. Walter Brennan, Leif Erickson, Luana Patten, Chris Robinson............(3)
Alternate title: BARB WIRE
Alternate title: RAWHIDE HALO, THE

SHOOT-OUT AT MEDICINE BEND (1957) Warner Bros. B&W-87min. Randolph Scott, James Craig............(3)

SHOOT THE PIANO PLAYER (1960) Astor. **B&W-92min.** *(French).* Charles Aznavour, Marie Du Bois **3***
Original title: TIREZ SUR LE PIANISTE

SHOOTING, THE (1966) Walter Reade. **Color-82min.** Millie Perkins, Jack Nicholson, Will Hutchins...............................(4)

SHOOTING HIGH (1940) 20th Century-Fox. **B&W-65min.** Jane Withers, Gene Autry ....(3)

SHOOTIST, THE (1976) Paramount. **Color-99min.** John Wayne, Lauren Bacall...............................**5***

SHOOTOUT IN A ONE DOG TOWN (1973) Viacom. **Color-74min.** *(Made for TV).* Richard Crenna, Stefanie Powers, Jack Elam.......................**4½***

SHOP AROUND THE CORNER, THE (1940) M-G-M. **B&W-97min.** James Stewart, Margaret Sullavan **5***

SHOP ON MAIN STREET, THE (1965) Prominent Films. **B&W-128min.** *(Czech).* Josef Kroner, Ida Kaminska **5***
Original title: OBCHOD NA KORZE *(The Shop on High Street)*

SHOP SPOILED (1956) Eros Films *(Brit.).* **B&W-67min.** *(British).* Joan Rice, John Gregson...............................(3)

SHOPWORN (1932) Columbia. **B&W-72min.** Barbara Stanwyck, Regis Toomey ....(3)

SHOPWORN ANGEL, THE (1938) M-G-M. **B&W-85min.** Margaret Sullavan, James Stewart, Walter Pidgeon...............................**4***

SHORT CUT TO HELL (1957) Paramount. **B&W-87min.** Robert Ivers, William Bishop ....(4)

SHORT EYES (1977) Film League, Inc. **Color-104min.** Bruce Davison, José Perez ....(4)

SHORT GRASS (1950) Allied Artists. **B&W-82min.** Rod Cameron, Cathy Downs ....(3)

SHORT WALK TO DAYLIGHT (1972) MCA-TV. **Color-73min.** *(Made for TV).* James Brolin, Brooke Bundy, Don Mitchell...............................**4***

SHORTEST DAY, THE (1963) Medallion. **B&W-89min.** *(Italian).* Franco Franchi, Ciccio Ingrassia, Walter Pidgeon, Vittorio De Sica **4***
Original Italian title: GIORNO PIU CORTO COMMEDIA UMARISTICA, IL

SHOT IN THE DARK, A (1941) Warner Bros. **B&W-57min.** William Lundigan, Nan Wynn...............................(4)

SHOT IN THE DARK, A (1964) United Artists. **Color-101min.** Peter Sellers, Elke Sommer **5½***

SHOTGUN (1955) Allied Artists. **Color-81min.** Sterling Hayden, Yvonne De Carlo, Zachary Scott **4***

SHOULDER ARMS (1918) First National [W.B.]. **B&W-40min.** *(Silent).* Charles Chaplin, Albert Austin, Sydney Chaplin...............................**5***

SHOUT, THE (1978) **Color-87min.** *(British).* Alan Bates, Susannah York, John Hurt...............................**3***

SHOUT AT THE DEVIL (1976) American-International. **Color-128min.** *(British).* Lee Marvin, Roger Moore...............................**5***

SHOUT AT THE DEVIL (1976). Adventurer Roger Moore drinks with Lee Marvin, who has successfully conned him into going on an African poaching expedition.

SHOW BOAT (1929) Universal. **B&W-129min.** Laura La Plante, Joseph Schildkraut ....(4)

SHOW BOAT (1936) Universal. **B&W-110min.** Irene Dunne, Allan Jones...............................**6***

SHOW BOAT (1951) M-G-M. **Color-108min.** Kathryn Grayson, Howard Keel, Ava Gardner **5***

SHOW BUSINESS (1944) RKO. **B&W-92min.** Eddie Cantor, Joan Davis ....(4)

SHOW OF SHOWS, THE (1929) Warner Bros. **Color-127min.** Frank Fay, John Barrymore, Beatrice Lillie, Dolores Costello ....(4)

SHOW-OFF, THE (1946) M-G-M. **B&W-83min.** Red Skelton, Marilyn Maxwell...............................(5)

SHOW PEOPLE (1928) M-G-M. **B&W-83min.** *(Silent).* Marion Davies, William Haines, Charles Chaplin, Douglas Fairbanks **4***

SHOW THEM NO MERCY (1935) 20th Century-Fox. **B&W-76min.** Rochelle Hudson, Cesar Romero, Bruce Cabot...............................(4)
British title: TAINTED MONEY

SHOWDOWN (1950) Republic. **B&W-86min.** William Elliott, Walter Brennan **4***

SHOWDOWN (1963) Universal. **B&W-79min.** Audie Murphy, Kathleen Crowley, Charles Drake **3½***

SHOWDOWN (1973) Universal. **Color-99min.** Dean Martin, Rock Hudson...............................**4***

SHOWDOWN AT ABILENE (1956) Universal. **Color-80min.** Jock Mahoney, Martha Hyer...............................**3***

SHOWDOWN AT BOOT HILL (1958) 20th Century-Fox. **B&W-72min.** Charles Bronson, John Carradine **4***

SHRIEK OF THE MUTILATED (1976) American Films Ltd. **Color-92min.** Alan Brock, Jennifer Stock, Michael Harris ....(3)

SHRIKE, THE (1955) Universal. **B&W-88min.** José Ferrer, June Allyson **4½***

SHUT MY BIG MOUTH (1942) Columbia. **B&W-71min.** Joe E. Brown, Adele Mara ....(3)

SHUTTERED ROOM, THE (1967) Warner Bros. **Color-100min.** *(British).* Gig Young, Carol Lynley, Oliver Reed...............................**3***

SICILIAN CLAN, THE (1969) 20th Century-Fox. **Color-121min.** *(French).* Jean Gabin, Alain Delon...............................**5½***
Original title: CLAN DES SICILIENS, LES

SICILIANS, THE (1964) Butcher's *(Brit.).* **B&W-69min.** *(British).* Robert Hutton, Reginald Marsh, Ursula Howells...............................(3)

SIDDHARTHA (1972) Columbia. **Color-95min.** Sashi Kapoor, Simi Garewal...............................**4½***

SIDE SHOW, THE (1927) *see* TWO FLAMING YOUTHS

SIDE STREET (1950) M-G-M. **B&W-83min.** Farley Granger, Cathy O'Donnell ....(4)

SIDECAR RACERS (1975) Universal. **Color-100min.** *(Australian).* Ben Murphy, Wendy Hughes...............................**4***

SIDEKICKS (1974) Warner Bros. **Color-75min.** *(Made for TV).* Lou Gossett, Larry Hagman, Blythe Danner...............................**5***

SIDELONG GLANCES OF A PIGEON KICKER, THE (1971) *see* PIGEONS

SIDEWALKS OF LONDON (1938) Paramount. **B&W-85min.** *(British).* Charles Laughton, Vivien Leigh, Rex Harrison **5***
Original title: ST. MARTIN'S LANE

SIDEWALKS OF NEW YORK (1931) M-G-M. **B&W-70min.** Buster Keaton, Anita Page...............................(3)

SIDEWINDER 1 (1977) Avco-Embassy. **Color-96min.** Michael Parks, Susan Howard, Marjoe Gortner...............................(4)

SIDNEY SHELDON'S BLOODLINE (1979) Paramount. **Color-116min.** Audrey Hepburn, Ben Gazzara...............................**4***

SIEGE AT RED RIVER (1954) 20th Century-Fox. **Color-81min.** Van Johnson, Joanne Dru...............................**4***

SIEGE OF FORT BISMARCK (1963) Paramount. **Color-98min.** *(Japanese).* Makoto Sato, Yosuke Natsuki...............................(3)
Original title: CHINTAO YOSAI BAKUGEKI MEIREI

SIEGE OF PINCHGUT, THE (1959) *see* FOUR DESPERATE MEN

SIEGE OF SIDNEY STREET, THE (1960) Screen Gems. **B&W-93min.** *(British).* Donald Sinden, Nicole Berger, Kieron Moore **3***
Alternate title: SIEGE OF HELL STREET, THE

SIEGE OF SYRACUSE (1960) Paramount. **Color-97min.** *(Italian-French).* Rossano Brazzi, Tina Louise, Sylva Koscina ....(1)
Original Italian title: ASSEDIO DI SIRACUSA, L'
Alternate Italian title: ARCHIMEDE
French title: SIEGE DE SYRACUSE, LE

SIEGE OF THE SAXONS (1963) Columbia. **Color-85min.** *(British).* Ronald Lewis, Janette Scott .... (3)

SIEGFRIED (1923) *see* NIBELUNGEN, DIE

SIERRA (1950) Universal. **Color-83min.** Wanda Hendrix, Audie Murphy .... (4)

SIERRA BARON (1958) 20th Century-Fox. **Color-78min.** Brian Keith, Rick Jason, Rita Gam .... (3)

SIERRA PASSAGE (1951) Monogram [Allied Artists]. **B&W-81min.** Wayne Morris, Lola Albright 3*

SIERRA STRANGER (1957) Columbia. **B&W-74min.** Howard Duff, Gloria McGhee .... (3)

SIGN OF THE CROSS, THE (1932) Paramount. **B&W-124min.** Fredric March, Elissa Landi 4½*

SIGN OF THE GLADIATOR (1958) American-International. **Color-80min.** *(Italian).* Anita Ekberg, Georges Marchal 3*
Original title: NEL SIGNO DI ROMA *(In the Name of Rome)*

SIGN OF THE PAGAN (1954) Universal. **Color-92min.** Jeff Chandler, Jack Palance 3*

SIGN OF THE RAM, THE (1948) Columbia. **B&W-84min.** Susan Peters, Alexander Knox 4*

SIGN OF ZORRO, THE (1960) Buena Vista. **B&W-91min.** *(Telefeature).* Guy Williams, Britt Lomond, Henry Calvin .... (2)

SIGNED, ARSENE LUPIN (1960) **B&W-90min.** *(French-Italian).* Robert Lamoreaux, Alida Valli .... (3)
Original French title: SIGNÉ ARSENE LUPIN
Italian title: RITORNO DI ARSENE LUPIN, IL

SIGNPOST TO MURDER (1965) M-G-M. **B&W-74min.** Joanne Woodward, Stuart Whitman .... (3)

SILENCE, THE (1963) Janus Films. **B&W-95min.** *(Swedish).* Ingrid Thulin, Gunnel Lindblom 3*
Original title: TYSTNADEN

SILENCE (1972) *see* CHINMOKU

SILENCE (1974) Cinema Financial of America. **Color-88min.** Will Geer, Ian Geer Flanders ....
Original title: CRY SILENCE
Alternate title: CRAZY JACK AND THE BOY

SILENCE, THE (1975) Paolmar Pics. Int'l. **Color-74min.** *(Made for TV).* Richard Thomas, Cliff Gorman 5*

SILENCERS, THE (1966) Columbia. **Color-105min.** Dean Martin, Stella Stevens 3*

SILENT BARRIERS (1937) *see* GREAT BARRIER, THE

SILENT CALL, THE (1961) 20th Century-Fox. **B&W-63min.** Gail Russell, Roger Mobley .... (3)

SILENT CRY, THE (1977) **Color-96min.** *(British-W. German-French).* Bobby Gill, Ernst Brightmoer .... (3)

SILENT DEATH (1957) *see* VOODOO ISLAND

SILENT ENEMY, THE (1958) Universal. **B&W-92min.** *(British).* Laurence Harvey, Dawn Addams 5*

SILENT GUN, THE (1971) Paramount. **Color-75min.** *(Made for TV).* Lloyd Bridges, Ed Begley 4*

SILENT INVASION, THE (1961) Warner Bros. **B&W-70min.** *(British).* Eric Flynn, Petra Davies .... (3)

SILENT MOVIE (1976) 20th Century-Fox. **Color-86min.** Mel Brooks, Marty Feldman 5½*

SILENT NIGHT, BLOODY NIGHT (1973) Cannon Releasing. **Color-87min.** Patrick O'Neal, James Patterson, Mary Woronov, John Carradine 3*

SILENT NIGHT, EVIL NIGHT (1975) *see* BLACK CHRISTMAS

SILENT NIGHT, LONELY NIGHT (1969) Universal. **Color-98min.** *(Made for TV).* Lloyd Bridges, Shirley Jones 5½*

SILENT PARTNER (1944) Republic. **B&W-55min.** William Henry, Beverly Loyd .... (4)

SILENT PARTNER, THE (1978) EMC Film Corporation. **Color-103min.** *(Canadian).* Susannah York, Christopher Plummer, Elliott Gould 5½*

SILENT RUNNING (1972) Universal. **Color-90min.** Bruce Dern, Cliff Potts 5*

SILENT STRANGER, THE (1959) *see* STEP DOWN TO TERROR

SILENT VOICE, THE (1932) *see* MAN WHO PLAYED GOD, THE

SILENT VOICE, THE (1952) *see* PAULA

SILENT WITNESS (1932) Fox Film Co. [20th]. **B&W-73min.** Lionel Atwill, Greta Nissen .... (4)

SILENT WITNESS, THE (1978) Independent International. **Color-55min.** *(Documentary). Director:* David W. Wolfe ....

SILENT WORLD, THE (1955) Columbia. **Color-85min.** *(French, Documentary). Director:* Jacques-Yves Cousteau .... (5)

SILK STOCKINGS (1957) M-G-M. **Color-117min.** Fred Astaire, Cyd Charisse 5*

SILKEN AFFAIR, THE (1956) Distributors Corp. of America. **B&W-96min.** *(British).* David Niven, Genevieve Page .... (4)

SILVER BEARS (1977) Columbia. **Color-113min.** Michael Caine, Cybill Shepherd 5½*

SILVER CHALICE, THE (1955) Warner Bros. **Color-144min.** Jack Palance, Paul Newman 4*

SILVER CITY (1948) *see* ALBUQUERQUE

SILVER CITY (1951) Paramount. **Color-90min.** Yvonne DeCarlo, Edmond O'Brien .... (4)
British title: HIGH VERMILION

SILVER DOLLAR (1932) First National [W.B.]. **B&W-84min.** Edward G. Robinson, Bebe Daniels .... (4)

SILVER KEY, THE (1944) *see* GIRL IN THE CASE

SILVER LODE (1954) RKO. **Color-80min.** John Payne, Dan Duryea, Lizabeth Scott .... (3)

SILVER QUEEN (1942) United Artists. **B&W-80min.** Priscilla Lane, George Brent 3*

SILVER RIVER (1948) Warner Bros. **B&W-110min.** Errol Flynn, Ann Sheridan 4*

SILVER STREAK (1976) 20th Century-Fox. **Color-113min.** Gene Wilder, Jill Clayburgh, Patrick McGoohan 6*

SILVER WHIP, THE (1953) 20th Century-Fox. **B&W-73min.** Dale Robertson, Rory Calhoun .... (4)

SIMBA (1955) Lippert Productions. **Color-99min.** *(British).* Dirk Bogarde, Donald Sinden .... (5)

SIMON (1980) Warner Bros. (for Orion). **Color- min.** Alan Arkin, Madeline Kahn ....

SIMON AND LAURA (1955) Universal. **Color-91min.** *(British).* Peter Finch, Kay Kendall .... (5)

SIMON, KING OF THE WITCHES (1971) Fanfare. **Color-89min.** Andrew Prine, Brenda Scott .... (2)

SIMON OF THE DESERT (1965) Altura Films. **B&W-45min.** *(Mexican).* Claudio Brook, Silvia Pinal .... (5)
Original title: SIMEON DEL DESIERTO

SIMON THE SWISS (1971) *see* CROOK, THE

SIN OF ESTHER WATERS, THE (1948) *see* ESTHER WATERS

SIN OF HAROLD DIDDLEBOCK, THE (1947) *see* MAD WEDNESDAY

SIN OF MADELON CLAUDET, THE (1931) M-G-M. **B&W-74min.** Helen Hayes, Lewis Stone .... (4)
British title: LULLABY

SIN OF MONA KENT, THE (1961) Astor. **Color-75min.** Johnny Olson, Sandra Donat .... (2)
Alternate title: MONA KENT

SIN TOWN (1942) Universal. **B&W-75min.** Constance Bennett, Broderick Crawford .... (4)

SINBAD AND THE EYE OF THE TIGER (1977) Columbia. **Color-112min.** *(U.S.-British).* Patrick Wayne, Jane Seymour, Margaret Whiting 4*

SINBAD THE SAILOR (1947) RKO. **Color-117min.** Douglas Fairbanks, Jr., Maureen O'Hara 4½*

SINCE YOU WENT AWAY (1944) United Artists. **B&W-172min.** Claudette Colbert, Jennifer Jones 3*

SINCERELY YOURS (1955) Warner Bros. **Color-115min.** Liberace, Joanne Dru, Dorothy Malone 4*

SINFUL DAVEY (1969) United Artists. **Color-95min.** *(British).* John Hurt, Pamela Franklin .... (4)

SING AND SWING (1963) Universal. **B&W-75min.** *(British).* David Hemmings, Jennifer Moss, Kenny Ball .... (3)
Original title: LIVE IT UP

SING, BABY, SING (1936) 20th Century-Fox. **B&W-87min.** Alice Faye, Adolphe Menjou 3½*

SING BOY SING (1958) 20th Century-Fox. **B&W-90min.** Tommy Sands, Lili Gentle, Edmond O'Brien .... (3)

SING, NEIGHBOR, SING (1944) Republic. **B&W-70min.** Brad Taylor, Ruth Terry .... (3)

SING YOU SINNERS (1938) Paramount. **B&W-88min.** Bing Crosby, Fred MacMurray ....

SING YOUR WAY HOME (1945) RKO. **B&W-72min.** Jack Haley, Anne Jeffreys .... (3)

SING YOUR WORRIES AWAY (1942) RKO. **B&W-71min.** Bert Lahr, June Havoc, Buddy Ebsen .... (4)

Films are rated on a 1 to 10 scale, 10 is highest. **Boldface** ratings followed by an asterisk (*) are for films actually seen and rated by the executive and senior editors. All other ratings are estimates. (See Notes on Entertainment Ratings in the front section.)

SINGAPORE (1947) Universal. **B&W-79min.** Ava Gardner, Fred MacMurray .... (3)

SINGAPORE WOMAN (1941) Warner Bros. **B&W-64min.** Brenda Marshall, David Bruce.. (3)

SINGER NOT THE SONG, THE (1961) Warner Bros. **Color-129min.** *(British).* Dirk Bogarde, John Mills.....................(4)

SINGIN' IN THE RAIN (1952) M-G-M. **Color-103min.** Gene Kelly, Debbie Reynolds, Donald O'Connor **5½***

SINGING FOOL (1928) Warner Bros. **B&W-110min.** Al Jolson, Betty Bronson .... (4)

SINGING GUNS (1950) Republic. **Color-91min.** Vaughn Monroe, Ella Raines, Walter Brennan .... (4)

SINGING IN THE DARK (1956) Budsam Dist. Co. **B&W-84min.** Joey Adams, Al Kelly .... (2)

SINGING NUN, THE (1966) M-G-M. **Color-98min.** Debbie Reynolds, Ricardo Montalban, Greer Garson **4***

SINGLE-HANDED (1953) *see* SAILOR OF THE KING

SINGLE STANDARD, THE (1929) M-G-M. **B&W-73min.** Greta Garbo, Nils Asther .... (4)

SINISTER MAN, THE (1961) Anglo Amalgamated [EMI]. **B&W-61min.** *(British).* John Bentley, Patrick Allen .... (3)

SINK THE BISMARCK! (1960) 20th Century-Fox. **B&W-97min.** *(British).* Kenneth More, Dana Wynter **5***

SINNER, THE (1959) *see* DESERT DESPERADOES

SINNER'S HOLIDAY (1947) *see* CHRISTMAS EVE

SINNERS IN THE SUN (1932) Paramount. **B&W-70min.** Carole Lombard, Chester Morris... (3)

SINNERS OF PARIS (1957) Ellis Films. **B&W-80min.** *(French).* Charles Vanel, Danik Patisson, Michel Piccoli .... (3)
Original title: RAFLES SUR LA VILLE *(Raids on the City)*

SINS OF BABYLON (1963) *see* GOLIATH AND THE SINS OF BABYLON

SINS OF CASANOVA (1954) Times Film Corp. **Color-104min.** *(Italian).* Gabrielle Ferzetti, Corinne Calvet .... (5)
Original title: AVVENTURE DI GIACOMO CASANOVA, L'

SINS OF JEZEBEL (1953) Lippert Productions. **Color-74min.** Paulette Goddard, George Nader .... (2)

SINS OF LOLA MONTES, THE (1955) *see* LOLA MONTES

SINS OF MAN (1936) 20th Century-Fox. **B&W-77min.** Jean Hersholt, Don Ameche .... (4)

SINS OF RACHEL CADE, THE (1961) Warner Bros. **Color-124min.** Angie Dickinson, Peter Finch............................... **4***

SINS OF ROME (1952) RKO. **B&W-90min.** *(Italian).* Ludmilla Tcherina, Massimo Girotti .... (3)
Original title: SPARTACO
Alternate title: SPARTACUS AND THE REBEL GLADIATOR

SITTING PRETTY (1948). Nosy neighbor Richard Haydn takes a snooping interest in supreme jack-of-all-trades Clifton Webb, who's new in town and is understandably contemptuous of the busybody's curiosity.

SINS OF ROSE BERND, THE (1957) President Films. **Color-85min.** *(German).* Maria Schell, Raf Vallone.................(4)
Original title: ROSE BERND

SIREN OF ATLANTIS (1948) United Artists. **B&W-75min.** Maria Montez, Jean-Pierre Aumont, Dennis O'Keefe ....(2)

SIREN OF BAGDAD (1953) Columbia. **Color-77min.** Paul Henreid, Patricia Medina...(3)

SIROCCO (1951) Columbia. **B&W-98min.** Humphrey Bogart, Marta Toren **4***

SIS HOPKINS (1941) Republic. **B&W-98min.** Judy Canova, Bob Crosby (4)

SISTER ANGELE'S SECRET (1956) **B&W-90min.** *(French-Italian).* Raf Vallone, Sophie Desmarets.....................................(3)
Original French title: SECRET DE SOEUR ANGELE, LE
Italian title: SEGRETO DI SUOR ANGELA, IL

SISTER KENNY (1946) RKO. **B&W-116min.** Rosalind Russell, Alexander Knox **5***

SISTERS, THE (1938) Warner Bros. **B&W-98min.** Bette Davis, Errol Flynn **4***

SISTERS (1973) American-International. **Color-92min.** Margot Kidder, Jennifer Salt **4½***
British title: BLOOD SISTERS

SITTING BULL (1954) United Artists. **Color-105min.** *(U.S.-Mexican).* J. Carrol Naish, Dale Robertson .... (4)

SITTING PRETTY (1933) Paramount. **B&W-85min.** Jack Oakie, Jack Haley, Ginger Rogers .... (4)

SITTING PRETTY (1948) 20th Century-Fox. **B&W-84min.** Clifton Webb, Robert Young **7***

SITTING TARGET (1972) M-G-M. **Color-93min.** *(British).* Oliver Reed, Jill St. John, Ian McShane .... (3)

SITUATION HOPELESS - BUT NOT SERIOUS (1965) Paramount. **B&W-97min.** Alec Guinness, Michael Connors, Robert Redford **4***

SIX BLACK HORSES (1962) Universal. **Color-80min.** Audie Murphy, Dan Duryea .... (3)

SIX BRIDGES TO CROSS (1955) Universal. **B&W-96min.** Tony Curtis, Julia (Julie) Adams, George Nader **4***

SIX DAY BIKE RIDER (1934) First National [W.B.]. **B&W-69min.** Joe E. Brown, Maxine Doyle.................................... (4)

SIX DAYS TO ETERNITY (1968) Peppercorn-Wormser. **B&W-88min.** *(Israeli, Documentary). Director:* Yaacov Hameiri .... (5)
Original title: SHESHET HAYAMIM
Alternate title: FOLLOW ME . . .

SIX HOURS TO LIVE (1932) Fox Film Co. [20th]. **B&W-78min.** Warner Baxter, Irene Ware.. (4)

SIX INCHES TALL (1958) *see* ATTACK OF THE PUPPET PEOPLE

SIX LESSONS FROM MADAME LA ZONGA (1941) Universal. **B&W-62min.** Lupe Velez, Leon Errol .... (4)

SIX MILLION DOLLAR MAN, THE (1973) MCA-TV. **Color-74min.** *(Made for TV).* Lee Majors, Darren McGavin .... (3)
Alternate title: CYBORG

SIX OF A KIND (1934) Paramount. **B&W-62min.** Charlie Ruggles, Mary Boland, W. C. Fields.............................. **4***

SIX PACK ANNIE (1975) American-International. **Color-88min.** Lindsay Bloom, Jana Bellan .... (4)

633 SQUADRON (1964) United Artists. **Color-95min.** *(British).* Cliff Robertson, George Chakiris **4***

16 FATHOMS DEEP (1948) Monogram [Allied Artists]. **Color-82min.** Lon Chaney, Jr., Lloyd Bridges................... (4)

SIXTH AND MAIN (1977) National Cinema. **Color-103min.** Leslie Nielsen, Roddy McDowall, Beverly Garland.................**4***

SIXTH COLUMN (1970) *see* LOVE WAR, THE

SIXTY GLORIOUS YEARS (1938) RKO. **Color-90min.** *(British).* Anna Neagle, Anton Walbrook, C. Aubrey Smith............(5)
Alternate title: QUEEN OF DESTINY

SKATEBOARD (1978) Universal. **Color-97min.** Allen Garfield, Kathleen Lloyd, Leif Garrett **3½***

SKEZAG (1970) Cinnamon Prods. **Color-73min.** *(Documentary). Director:* Joel L. Freedman..................................... (4)

SKI BUM, THE (1971) Avco-Embassy. **Color-94min.** Zalman King, Charlotte Rampling... (2)

SKI CHAMP, THE (1962) Comet Film. **Color-90min.** *(German).* Tony Sailer .... (3)

SKI FEVER (1967) Allied Artists. **Color-98min.** *(U.S.-Austrian-Czech).* Martin Milner, Claudia Martin, Dietmar Schonherr...................**3***
Austrian title: LIEBESSPIELE IM SCHNEE

SKI ON THE WILD SIDE (1967) Sigma III. Color-104min. *(Documentary).* Director: Warren Miller .... (5)

SKI PARTY (1965) American-International. Color-90min. Frankie Avalon, Dwayne Hickman 3*

SKI RAIDERS, THE (1972) see SNOW JOB

SKI TROOP ATTACK (1960) Filmgroup. B&W-61min. Michael Forest, Frank Wolff .... (3)

SKIDOO (1968) Paramount. Color-98min. Jackie Gleason, Carol Channing, Groucho Marx .... (3)

SKIN GAME (1971) Warner Bros. Color-102min. James Garner, Lou Gossett, Susan Clark 6*

SKIPALONG ROSENBLOOM (1951) United Artists. B&W-73min. Maxie Rosenbloom, Max Baer .... (4)
TV title: SQUARE SHOOTER, THE

SKIPPER SURPRISED HIS WIFE, THE (1950) M-G-M. B&W-85min. Robert Walker, Joan Leslie .... (3)

SKIPPY (1931) Paramount. B&W-88min. Jackie Cooper, Jackie Searle .. (5)

SKIRTS AHOY! (1952) M-G-M. Color-109min. Esther Williams, Joan Evans .... (4)

SKULL, THE (1965) Paramount. Color-83min. *(British).* Peter Cushing, Christopher Lee 4*

SKULL ISLAND (1932) see MOST DANGEROUS GAME, THE

SKULLDUGGERY (1970) Universal. Color-105min. Burt Reynolds, Susan Clark, Chips Rafferty 3*

SKY ABOVE HEAVEN (1965) Paramount. Color-107min. *(French-Italian).* André Smagghe, Marcel Bozzufi .... (3)
Original French title: CIEL SUR LA TETE, LE *(The Sky Overhead)*
Italian title: CIELO SULLA TESTA, IL

SKY ABOVE, THE MUD BELOW, THE (1961) Avco-Embassy. Color-90min. *(Belgian-French-Dutch, English version, Documentary).* Director: Pierre-Dominique Gaisseau 5½*
Original French title: CIEL ET LA BOUE, LE *(The Sky and the Mud)*

SKY COMMANDO (1953) Columbia. B&W-69min. Dan Duryea, Frances Gifford .... (3)

SKY DRAGON (1949) Monogram [Allied Artists]. B&W-64min. Roland Winters, Mantan Moreland .... (3)

SKY FULL OF MOON (1952) M-G-M. B&W-73min. Carleton Carpenter, Jan Sterling .... (4)

SKY GIANT (1938) RKO. B&W-80min. Richard Dix, Chester Morris ...... (4)

SKY MURDER (1940) M-G-M. B&W-72min. Walter Pidgeon, Kaaren Verne .... (3)

SKY RIDERS (1976) 20th Century-Fox. Color-91min. James Coburn, Susannah York 4½*

SKY TERROR (1972) see SKYJACKED

SKY WEST AND CROOKED (1965) see GYPSY GIRL

SKYDIVERS, THE (1963) Crown International. B&W-75min. Kevin Casey, Marcia Knight .... (3)

SKYJACKED (1972) M-G-M. Color-101min. Charlton Heston, Yvette Mimeiux 5*
TV title: SKY TERROR

SKYLARK (1941) Paramount. B&W-94min. Claudette Colbert, Ray Milland .... (5)

SKY'S THE LIMIT, THE (1943) RKO. B&W-89min. Fred Astaire, Joan Leslie 4*

SKYSCRAPER WILDERNESS (1937) see BIG CITY, THE

SKYWATCH (1960) Continental [Walter Reade]. B&W-90min. Ian Carmichael, Tommy Steele .... (4)
Original title: LIGHT UP THE SKY

SKYWAY TO DEATH (1974) MCA-TV. Color-74min. *(Made for TV).* Bobby Sherman, Stefanie Powers, John Astin, Ross Martin .... (4)

SLADE (1953) see JACK SLADE

SLAMS, THE (1973) M-G-M. Color-91min. Jim Brown, Judy Pace .... (3)

SLANDER (1957) M-G-M. B&W-81min. Van Johnson, Ann Blyth .... (4)

SLAP, THE (1974) Joseph Green. Color-98min. *(French-Italian).* Lino Ventura, Annie Girardot, Isabelle Adjani ....
Original title: GIFLE, LA

SLAP SHOT (1977) Universal. Color-123min. Paul Newman, Strother Martin, Michael Ontkean 5½*

SLATTERY'S HURRICANE (1949) 20th Century-Fox. B&W-83min. Richard Widmark, Linda Darnell 3*

SLAUGHTER (1972) American-International. Color-92min. Jim Brown, Stella Stevens, Rip Torn .... (3)

SLAUGHTER, THE (1976) see SNUFF

SLAUGHTER HOTEL (1971) Hallmark. Color-97min. *(Italian).* Klaus Kinski, John Ely, Margaret Lee .... (3)
Original title: BESTIA UCCIDE A SANGUE FREDDO, LA *(The Beast Kills in Cold Blood)*
British title: COLD BLOODED BEAST
Alternate title: ASYLUM EROTICA

SLAUGHTER HOTEL (1976) see EATEN ALIVE

SLAUGHTER OF THE VAMPIRES (1962) Teleworld. B&W-81min. *(Italian).* Dieter Eppler, Walter Brandi, Graziella Granata 1*
Original title: STRAGE DEI VAMPIRI, LA
Alternate title: CURSE OF THE BLOOD-GHOULS
Publicity title: CURSE OF THE GHOULS

SLAUGHTER ON TENTH AVENUE (1957) Universal. B&W-103min. Richard Egan, Jan Sterling 4*

SLAUGHTER TRAIL (1951) RKO. Color-78min. Brian Donlevy, Gig Young, Virginia Gray .... (3)

SLAUGHTERHOUSE-FIVE (1972) Universal. Color-104min. Michael Sacks, Ron Leibman 4*

SLAUGHTER'S BIG RIP-OFF (1973) American-International. Color-93min. Jim Brown, Ed McMahon .... (3)

SLAVE, THE (1954) Films Around The World. B&W-95min. *(French).* Daniel Gélin, Eleanora Rossi-Drago .... (3)
Original title: ESCLAVE, L'

SLAVE, THE (1962) M-G-M. Color-102min. *(Italian).* Steve Reeves, Jacques Sernas, Claudio Gora 2*
Original title: FIGLIO DI SPARTACUS, IL *(The Son of Spartacus)*
Alternate title: SON OF SPARTACUS

SLAVE GIRL (1947) Universal. Color-80min. Yvonne DeCarlo, George Brent 4*

SLAVE GIRL, THE (1954) see CAPTAIN KIDD AND THE SLAVE GIRL

SLAVE GIRLS (1967) see PREHISTORIC WOMEN

SLAVE GIRLS OF SHEBA (1961) American-International. Color-92min. *(Italian).* Linda Cristal, José Suarez .... (1)

SLAVE OF LOVE, A (1978) Cinema 5. Color-94min. *(U.S.S.R.).* Elena Solovei, Rodion Nakhapetov .... (5)

SLAVE QUEEN OF BABYLON (1962) American-International. Color-101min. *(Italian).* John Ericson, Yvonne Furneaux .... (3)

SLAVE SHIP (1937) 20th Century-Fox. B&W-92min. Warner Baxter, Wallace Beery .... (5)

SLAVE TRADE IN THE WORLD TODAY (1964) Continental [Walter Reade]. Color-87min. *(Italian-French, Documentary).* Director: Roberto Malenotti .... (3)
Original Italian title: SCHIAVE ESISTONO ANCORA, LE *(Slaves Still Exist)*
French title: ESCLAVES EXISTENT TOUJOURS, LES

SLAVES (1969) Continental [Walter Reade]. Color-110min. Stephen Boyd, Dionne Warwick 3*

SLAVES (1973) see SWEET SUZY

SLAVES OF BABYLON (1953) Columbia. Color-82min. Richard Conte, Linda Christian 3*

SLAVES OF THE INVISIBLE MONSTER (1950) Republic. B&W-100min. *(Re-edited Serial).* Richard Webb, Aline Towne .... (2)
Original title: INVISIBLE MONSTER, THE

SLAYRIDE (1972) 20th Century-Fox. Color-100min. *(Made for TV).* Glenn Ford, Leslie Parrish, Edgar Buchanan .... (4)

SLEEP MY LOVE (1948) United Artists. B&W-97min. Claudette Colbert, Robert Cummings 4*

SLEEPER (1973) United Artists. Color-86min. Woody Allen, Diane Keaton 5*

SLEEPERS WEST (1941) 20th Century-Fox. B&W-74min. Lloyd Bridges, Lynn Bari 3*

SLEEPING BEAUTY (1959) Buena Vista. Color-75min. *(Cartoon).* Director: Milt Kahl 6*

SLEEPING CAR MURDER, THE (1965) Seven Arts [W.B.]. B&W-92min. *(French).* Yves Montand, Simone Signoret 4½*
Original title: COMPARTIMENT TUEURS

SLEEPING CAR TO TRIESTE (1948) Eagle Lion. B&W-94min. *(British).* Jean Kent, Albert Lieven 4*

SLEEPING CITY, THE (1950) Universal. B&W-85min. Richard Conte, Coleen Gray .... (4)

SLEEPING DRAGON (1975) Sultan-Emperor Films. Color-104min. *(Philippines).* Raymond Lui, Lotis Key, Eddie Garcia .... (2)

SLEEPING TIGER, THE (1954) Astor. B&W-89min. *(British).* Dirk Bogarde, Alexis Smith .... (5)

SLEEPYTIME GAL (1942) Republic. B&W-82min. Judy Canova, Tom Brown .... (4)

SLEEPING BEAUTY (1959). Princess Aurora is entranced by the hypnotic spell of the evil witch Maleficent, who commands her to touch the deadly spindle of the spinning wheel.

SLENDER THREAD, THE (1965) Paramount. B&W-98min. Sidney Poitier, Anne Bancroft .... (5)

SLEUTH (1972) 20th Century-Fox. Color-138min. *(British).* Laurence Olivier, Michael Caine 7*

SLICE OF LIFE, A (1953) *see* ANATOMY OF LOVE

SLIGHT CASE OF LARCENY, A (1953) M-G-M. B&W-71min. Mickey Rooney, Eddie Bracken .... (4)

SLIGHT CASE OF MURDER, A (1938) Warner Bros. B&W-85min. Edward G. Robinson, Jane Bryan 4*

SLIGHTLY DANGEROUS (1943) M-G-M. B&W-94min. Lana Turner, Robert Young .... (3)

SLIGHTLY FRENCH (1949) Columbia. B&W-81min. Dorothy Lamour, Don Ameche .... (4)

SLIGHTLY HONORABLE (1940) United Artists. B&W-83min. Pat O'Brien, Brod Crawford 4*

SLIGHTLY SCARLET (1956) RKO. Color-99min. Rhonda Fleming, John Payne .... (4)

SLIGHTLY TERRIFIC (1944) Universal. B&W-61min. Leon Errol, Anne Rooney .... (4)

SLIM (1937) Warner Bros. B&W-80min. Pat O'Brien, Henry Fonda....... (4)

SLIM CARTER (1957) Universal. Color-82min. Jock Mahoney, Julie Adams, Tim Hovey 3*

SLIME PEOPLE, THE (1963) Hansen Pictures. B&W-60min. Robert Hutton, Robert Burton, Les Tremayne.. 1*

SLIPPER AND THE ROSE - THE STORY OF CINDERELLA, THE (1976) Universal. Color-146min. *(British).* Gemma Craven, Richard Chamberlain .... (5)

SLIPSTREAM (1974) Pacific Rim Films. Color-92min. *(Canadian).* Luke Askew, Patti Oatman .... (3)

SLITHER (1973) M-G-M. Color-96min. James Caan, Peter Boyle, Sally Kellerman.. 5*

SLOGAN (1969) Royal Films Int'l [Columbia]. Color-90min. *(French).* Serge Gainsbourg, Jane Birkin .... (3)

SLOW DANCING IN THE BIG CITY (1978) United Artists. Color-101min. Paul Sorvino, Anne Ditchburn 5½*

SLUMBER PARTY '57 (1976) Cannon Releasing. Color-89min. Noelle North, Bridget Hollman.. (3)

SMALL BACK ROOM, THE (1948) Snader Prods. B&W-106min. *(British).* David Farrar, Kathleen Byron.. 4*
Alternate title: HOUR OF GLORY

SMALL CHANGE (1976) New World. Color-105min. *(French).* Geory Desmouceaux, Philippe Goldmann 4½*
Original title: ARGENT DE POCHE, L'

SMALL CIRCLE OF FRIENDS, A (1980) United Artists. Color- min. Brad Davis, Karen Allen ....

SMALL TOWN DEB (1941) 20th Century-Fox. B&W-72min. Jane Withers, Jane Darwell.. (3)

SMALL TOWN GIRL (1936) M-G-M. B&W-90min. Janet Gaynor, Robert Taylor.. (5)
Alternate title: ONE HORSE TOWN

SMALL TOWN GIRL (1953) M-G-M. Color-93min. Jane Powell, Farley Granger .... (4)

SMALL TOWN IN TEXAS, A (1976) American-International. Color-95min. Timothy Bottoms, Susan George, Bo Hopkins 4*

SMALL VOICE, THE (1948) British Lion [EMI]. B&W-67min. *(British).* Valerie Hobson, James Donald.. (4)
Alternate title: HIDEOUT, THE

SMALL WORLD OF SAMMY LEE, THE (1963) Seven Arts [W.B.]. B&W-105min. *(British).* Anthony Newley, Julia Foster .... (5)

SMALLEST SHOW ON EARTH, THE (1957) Times Film Corp. B&W-80min. *(British).* Bill Travers, Virginia McKenna.. 4*

SMART ALECKS (1942) Monogram [Allied Artists]. B&W-88min. The East Side Kids, Maxie Rosenbloom .... (3)

SMART GIRLS DON'T TALK (1948) Warner Bros. B&W-81min. Virginia Mayo, Bruce Bennett.. (3)

SMART MONEY (1931) Warner Bros. B&W-90min. Edward G. Robinson, James Cagney.. (4)

SMART WOMAN (1948) Allied Artists. B&W-93min. Brian Aherne, Constance Bennett .... (5)

SMASH-UP ON INTERSTATE 5 (1976) Filmways. Color-100min. *(Made for TV).* Robert Conrad, Buddy Ebsen, Scott Jacoby 2*

SMASH-UP - THE STORY OF A WOMAN (1947) Universal. B&W-103min. Susan Hayward, Lee Bowman.. 4*
British title: WOMAN DESTROYED, A

SMASHING THE CRIME SYNDICATE (1970) *see* HELL'S BLOODY DEVILS

SMASHING THE RACKETS (1938) RKO. B&W-60min. Chester Morris, Frances Mercer, Bruce Cabot.. (4)

SMASHING TIME (1967) Paramount. Color-96min. *(British).* Rita Tushingham, Lynn Redgrave.. (4)

SMIC, SMAC, SMOC (1971) GSF Productions. Color-90min. *(French).* Charles Gerard, Jean Collomb, Amidou .... (5)

SMILE (1975) United Artists. Color-113min. Bruce Dern, Barbara Feldon.. 6*

SMILE JENNY, YOU'RE DEAD (1974) Warner Bros. Color-90min. *(Made for TV).* David Janssen, Jodie Foster, Andrea Marcovicci.. 4*

SMILE ORANGE (1976) Knuts Prods. Ltd. Color-86min. *(Jamaican).* Carl Bradshaw, Glenn Morrison .... (4)

SMILE WHEN YOU SAY "I DO" (1973) Worldvision. Color-74min. *(Documentary, Made for TV). Director:* Allen Funt.. 4*

SMILES OF A SUMMER NIGHT (1956) Janus Films. B&W-108min. *(Swedish).* Eva Dahlbeck, Ulla Jacobsson.. 4*
Original title: SOMMARNATTENS LEENDE

SMILEY (1956) 20th Century-Fox. Color-97min. *(Australian).* Colin Petersen, Ralph Richardson, Chips Rafferty .... (4)

SMILEY GETS A GUN (1958) 20th Century-Fox. Color-89min. *(Australian).* Keith Calvert, Sybil Thorndike, Chips Rafferty .... (3)

SMILIN' THROUGH (1932) M-G-M. B&W-97min. Norma Shearer .... (5)

SMILIN' THROUGH (1941) M-G-M. Color-100min. Jeanette MacDonald .... (4)

SMILING GHOST, THE (1941) Warner Bros. B&W-71min. Wayne Morris, Alexis Smith, Brenda Marshall.. (3)

SMILING LIEUTENANT, THE (1931) Paramount. B&W-102min. Maurice Chevalier, Claudette Colbert.. (4)

SMITH! (1969) Buena Vista. Color-102min. Glenn Ford, Nancy Olson ... (4)

SMITH OF MINNESOTA (1942) Columbia. B&W-66min. Bruce Smith, Arline Judge.. (3)

SMOKE SIGNAL (1955) Universal. Color-88min. Dana Andrews, Piper Laurie.. (3)

SMOKEY AND THE BANDIT (1977) Universal. Color-96min. Burt Reynolds, Sally Field, Jackie Gleason, Jerry Reed 5½*

SMOKY (1946) 20th Century-Fox. Color-87min. Fred MacMurray, Anne Baxter.. 4*

SMOKY (1966) 20th Century-Fox. Color-103min. Fess Parker, Diana Hyland.. 4*

SMOOTH AS SILK (1946) Universal. B&W-65min. Kent Taylor, Virginia Grey .... (5)

SMUGGLERS, THE (1947) Eagle Lion. **Color-87min.** *(British).* Michael Redgrave, Jean Kent ....(4)
Original title: MAN WITHIN, THE

SMUGGLERS, THE (1968) Universal. **Color-100min.** *(Made for TV).* Shirley Booth, David Opatoshu, Carol Lynley ....(3)

SMUGGLER'S COVE (1948) Monogram [Allied Artists]. **B&W-66min.** The Bowery Boys, Martin Kosleck ....(3)

SMUGGLER'S GOLD (1951) Columbia. **B&W-64min.** Cameron Mitchell, Amanda Blake........................(3)

SMUGGLER'S ISLAND (1951) Universal. **Color-75min.** Jeff Chandler, Evelyn Keyes ....(3)

SNAFU (1945) Columbia. **B&W-82min.** Conrad Janis, Robert Benchley (4)
British title: WELCOME HOME

SNAKE PEOPLE, THE (1968) CPT (TV). **Color-90min.** *(Mexican-U.S.).* Boris Karloff, Julissa, Carlos East 1*
Alternate title: MUERTE VIVIENTE, LA *(The Living Death)*
Alternate title: ISLA DE LOS MUERTOS, LA *(The Isle of the Dead)*
Alternate title: ISLE OF THE SNAKE PEOPLE

SNAKE PIT, THE (1948) 20th Century-Fox. **B&W-108min.** Olivia de Havilland, Mark Stevens, Leo Genn 4½*

SNAKE WOMAN, THE (1961) United Artists. **B&W-68min.** *(British).* John McCarthy, Susan Travers......................(2)

SNATCHED (1973) Worldvision. **Color-73min.** *(Made for TV).* Howard Duff, Leslie Nielsen, Sheree North 4*

SNIPER, THE (1952) Columbia. **B&W-87min.** Adolphe Menjou, Arthur Franz 3*

SNIPER'S RIDGE (1961) 20th Century-Fox. **B&W-61min.** Jack Ging, Stanley Clements........................(3)

SNOOP SISTERS, THE (1972) MCA-TV. **Color-96min.** *(Made for TV).* Helen Hayes, Mildred Natwick, Charlie Callas, Art Carney 5*
Alternate title: FEMALE INSTINCT

SNOOPY, COME HOME (1972) Nat'l General (for Cinema Center). **Color-80min.** *(Cartoon). Director:* Bill Melendez................4½*

SNORKEL, THE (1958) Columbia. **B&W-90min.** *(British).* Peter Van Eyck, Mandy Miller........................(4)

SNOUT, THE (1963) *see* UNDERWORLD INFORMERS

SNOW CREATURE, THE (1954) United Artists. **B&W-70min.** Paul Langton, Leslie Denison ....(3)

SNOW JOB (1972) Warner Bros. **Color-90min.** Jean-Claude Killy, Daniele Gaubert, Vittorio De Sica ....(3)
British title: SKI RAIDERS, THE

SNOW QUEEN, THE (1958) Universal. **Color-70min.** *(U.S.S.R., Cartoon).* Sandra Dee, Tommy Kirk, Patty McCormack ....(4)

SNOW WAS BLACK, THE (1954) Continental [Walter Reade]. **B&W-110min.** *(French).* Daniel Gélin, Valentine Tessier ....(5)
Original title: NEIGE ETAIT SALE, LA *(The Snow Was Dirty)*

SNOW WHITE AND THE SEVEN DWARFS (1937) RKO (for Disney). **Color-82min.** *(Cartoon). Director:* David Hand................5½*

SNOW WHITE AND THE THREE STOOGES (1961) 20th Century-Fox. **Color-107min.** Carol Heiss, The Three Stooges 4*
British title: SNOW WHITE AND THE THREE CLOWNS

SNOWBALL (1960) J. Arthur Rank. **B&W-69min.** *(British).* Gordon Jackson, Kenneth Griffith ....(3)

SNOWBALL EXPRESS (1972) Buena Vista. **Color-99min.** Dean Jones, Nancy Olson 4½*

SNOWBEAST (1977) NBC-TV. **Color-96min.** *(Made for TV).* Bo Svenson, Yvette Mimieux, Robert Logan........................

SNOWBOUND (1948) Universal. **B&W-85min.** *(British).* Robert Newton, Dennis Price, Herbert Lom 4*

SNOWFIRE (1958) Allied Artists. **Color-73min.** Molly McGowan, Don Megowan 3*

SNOWS OF KILIMANJARO, THE (1953) 20th Century-Fox. **Color-117min.** Gregory Peck, Susan Hayward, Ava Gardner 3*

SNUFF (1976) Monarch. **Color-82min.** *(Argentinian-U.S.).* ....(1)
Original title: SLAUGHTER, THE

SO BIG (1932) Warner Bros. **B&W-82min.** Barbara Stanwyck, Earl Foxe ....(4)

SO BIG (1953) Warner Bros. **B&W-101min.** Jane Wyman, Sterling Hayden 4*

SO BRIGHT THE FLAME (1952) *see* GIRL IN WHITE, THE

SO CLOSE TO LIFE (1958) *see* BRINK OF LIFE

SO DARK THE NIGHT (1946) Columbia. **B&W-71min.** Steven Geray, Micheline Cheirel........................(5)

SO DEAR TO MY HEART (1948) RKO (for Disney). **Color-84min.** *(Part-animated).* Bobby Driscoll, Burl Ives ....(5)

SO ENDS OUR NIGHT (1941) United Artists. **B&W-117min.** Fredric March, Margaret Sullavan, Glenn Ford............4*

SO EVIL MY LOVE (1948) Paramount. **B&W-109min.** Ray Milland, Ann Todd 4*

SO EVIL SO YOUNG (1960) United Artists. **Color-77min.** *(British).* Jill Ireland, Ellen Pollock ....(3)

SO GOES MY LOVE (1946) Universal. **B&W-88min.** Myrna Loy, Don Ameche ....(4)
British title: GENIUS IN THE FAMILY, A

SO LITTLE TIME (1952) MacDonald. **B&W-88min.** *(British).* John Bailey, Maria Schell 3*

SO LONG AT THE FAIR (1950) Eagle Lion. **B&W-85min.** *(British).* Jean Simmons, Dirk Bogarde 5*

SO LOVELY, SO DEADLY (1957) United Artists. **B&W-67min.** Henry Beckman, Robert Middleton ....(2)

SO PROUDLY WE HAIL! (1943) Paramount. **B&W-126min.** Claudette Colbert, Paulette Goddard 4*

SO RED THE ROSE (1935) Paramount. **B&W-82min.** Margaret Sullavan, Walter Connolly ....

SO THIS IS LOVE (1953) Warner Bros. **Color-101min.** Kathryn Grayson, Merv Griffin ....(4)
British title: GRACE MOORE STORY, THE

SO THIS IS NEW YORK (1948) United Artists. **B&W-79min.** Rudy Vallee, Henry Morgan*................(4)

SO THIS IS PARIS (1926) Warner Bros. **B&W-68min.** *(Silent).* Monte Blue, Patsy Ruth Miller ....

SO THIS IS PARIS (1955) Universal. **Color-96min.** Tony Curtis, Gloria De Haven 4*

SO WELL REMEMBERED (1947) RKO. **B&W-114min.** *(British).* John Mills, Patricia Roc 4*

SO YOU WON'T TALK (1940) Columbia. **B&W-69min.** Joe E. Brown, Frances Robinson ....(3)

SO YOUNG, SO BAD (1950) United Artists. **B&W-91min.** Paul Henreid, Anne Francis 3*

SOCRATES (1969) New Yorker Films. **Color-120min.** *(Italian).* Jean Sylvere, Anne Caprile ....(4)

SODOM AND GOMORRAH (1961) 20th Century-Fox. **Color-154min.** *(Italian-French-U.S., English language).* Stewart Granger, Pier Angeli, Stanley Baker ....(4)
Original Italian title: SODOMA E GOMORRA
French title: SODOME ET GOMORRHE

SODOM AND GOMORRAH - THE LAST SEVEN DAYS (1975) Mitchell Bros. **Color-90min.** Sean Brancato, Deborah Brast............2½*

SOFI (1967) Golden Bear. **B&W-96min.** Tom Troupe ....(4)

SOFIA (1948) Film Classics [U.A.]. **Color-82min.** Gene Raymond, Sigrid Gurie ....(3)

SOFT BEDS -- HARD BATTLES (1973) *see* UNDERCOVERS HERO

SOFT SKIN, THE (1964) Cinema 5. **B&W-120min.** *(French).* Jean Desailly, Francoise Dorleac............(5)
Original title: PEAU DOUCE, LA

SOFT SKIN ON BLACK SILK (1959) Audubon. **B&W-90min.** *(Spanish-French-U.S.).* Agnes Laurent, Armand Mestral, Ira Lewis............(3)
Original Spanish title: MUNDO PARA MI, UN
French title: TENTATIONS

SOHO INCIDENT (1956) *see* SPIN A DARK WEB

SOL MADRID (1968) M-G-M. **Color-90min.** David McCallum, Stella Stevens 4*
British title: HEROIN GANG, THE

SOLARIS (1972) Sci/Fi. **Color-173min.** *(U.S.S.R.).* Natalya Bondarchuk, Donatas Banionis 2*

SOLDIER, THE (1965) M-G-M. **B&W-100min.** *(English language).* Fraser MacIntosh, Rad Markovic 4½*

SOLDIER AND THE LADY, THE (1937) RKO. **B&W-85min.** Anton Walbrook, Margot Grahame 4*
Alternate title: MICHAEL STROGOFF
Alternate title: ADVENTURES OF MICHAEL STROGOFF

SOLDIER BLUE (1970) Avco-Embassy. **Color-112min.** Candice Bergen, Peter Strauss, Donald Pleasence 6*

SOLDIER IN THE RAIN (1963) Allied Artists. **B&W-88min.** Jackie Gleason, Steve McQueen 5*

SOLDIER OF FORTUNE (1955) 20th Century-Fox. **Color-96min.** Clark Gable, Susan Hayward 4*

SOLDIER OF LOVE (1952) *see* FANFAN THE TULIP

SOLDIER WHO DECLARED PEACE, THE (1970) *see* TRIBES

SOLDIERS OF PANCHO VILLA, THE (1959) Color-84min. *(Mexican).* Pedro Armendariz, Dolores Del Rio .... (3)

SOLDIERS THREE (1951) M-G-M. B&W-87min. Stewart Granger, Walter Pidgeon, Robert Newton, Cyril Cusack 4*

SOLE SURVIVOR (1970) Cinema Center 100. Color-100min. *(Made for TV).* Vince Edwards, Richard Basehart, William Shatner 4*

SOLID GOLD CADILLAC, THE (1956) Columbia. B&W-99min. Judy Holliday, Paul Douglas 5½*

SOLITARE MAN (1933) M-G-M. B&W-65min. Herbert Marshall, Mary Boland .... (4)

SOLO FOR SPARROW (1962) Schoenfeld Film Distributing. B&W-56min. *(British).* Anthony Newlands, Glyn Houston .... (3)

SOLOMON AND SHEBA (1959) United Artists. Color-139min. Yul Brynner, Gina Lollobrigida 4½*

SOMBRA, THE SPIDER WOMAN (1947) Republic. B&W-100min. *(Re-edited Serial).* Bruce Edwards, Virginia Lindley .... (3)
Original title: BLACK WIDOW, THE

SOMBRERO (1953) M-G-M. Color-103min. Pier Angeli, Ricardo Montalban, Vittorio Gassman, Cyd Charisse .... (3)

SOME CAME RUNNING (1958) M-G-M. Color-127min. Frank Sinatra, Dean Martin .... (5)

SOME GIRLS DO (1969) United Artists. Color-91min. *(British).* Richard Johnson, Daliah Lavi, James Villiers .... (2)

SOME KIND OF A NUT (1969) United Artists. Color-89min. Dick Van Dyke, Angie Dickinson, Rosemary Forsyth 2*

SOME LIKE IT HOT (1939) Paramount. B&W-64min. Bob Hope, Shirley Ross .... (4)
Alternate title: RHYTHM ROMANCE

SOME LIKE IT HOT (1959) United Artists. B&W-120min. Marilyn Monroe, Tony Curtis, Jack Lemmon 7½*

SOME MAY LIVE (1967) Showcorporation. Color-89min. *(British).* Joseph Cotten, Martha Hyer, Peter Cushing .... (3)
TV title: IN SAIGON: SOME MAY LIVE

SOME OF MY BEST FRIENDS ARE . . . (1971) American-International. Color-109min. Gary Campbell, Carleton Carpenter, Candy Darling .... (4)

SOME PEOPLE (1962) American-International. Color-93min. *(British).* Kenneth More, Ray Brooks, Annika Wills .... (3)

SOMEBODY KILLED HER HUSBAND (1978) Columbia. Color-96min. Farrah Fawcett-Majors, Jeff Bridges 5½*

SOMEBODY LOVES ME (1952) Paramount. Color-97min. Betty Hutton, Ralph Meeker .... (4)

SOMEBODY UP THERE LIKES ME (1956) M-G-M. B&W-113min. Paul Newman, Pier Angeli 5*

SOMEONE BEHIND THE DOOR (1971) GSF Productions. Color-97min. *(French, English language).* Charles Bronson, Anthony Perkins, Jill Ireland 4*
Original title: QUELQU'UN DERRIERE LA PORTE

SOMEONE TO REMEMBER (1943) Republic. B&W-80min. Richard Crane, Mabel Paige .... (5)

something big (1971) Nat'l General (for Cinema Center). Color-108min. Dean Martin, Brian Keith, Honor Blackman .... (3)

SOMETHING EVIL (1972) Color-73min. *(Made for TV).* Sandy Dennis, Darren McGavin, Johnny Whitaker .... (5)

SOMETHING FOR A LONELY MAN (1968) Universal. Color-98min. *(Made for TV).* Dan Blocker, Susan Clark, Warren Oates .... (5)

SOMETHING FOR EVERYONE (1970) Nat'l General (for Cinema Center). Color-110min. Angela Lansbury, Michael York, Jane Carr .. 6½*
British title: BLACK FLOWERS FOR THE BRIDE

SOMETHING FOR THE BIRDS (1952) Metro. B&W-81min. Victor Mature, Patricia Neal .... (4)

SOMETHING FOR THE BOYS (1944) 20th Century-Fox. Color-85min. Vivian Blaine, Perry Como, Phil Silvers, Carmen Miranda .... (4)

SOMETHING IN THE WIND (1947) Universal. B&W-89min. Deanna Durbin, Donald O'Connor .... (4)

SOMETHING MONEY CAN'T BUY (1952) Universal. B&W-82min. *(British).* Anthony Steel, Patricia Roc .... (4)

SOMETHING OF VALUE (1957) M-G-M. B&W-113min. Rock Hudson, Sidney Poitier 4*

SOMETHING TO HIDE (1972) Atlantic Pictures. Color-100min. *(British).* Peter Finch, Linda Hayden, Shelley Winters ....

SOMETHING TO LIVE FOR (1952) Paramount. B&W-89min. Ray Milland, Joan Fontaine .... (4)

SOMETHING FOR EVERYONE (1970). Enigmatic Michael York travels through Bavaria, and Jane Carr notices that her dogs seem to like him; they only feel that way about perverts and murderers, she observes.

SOMETHING TO SHOUT ABOUT (1943) Columbia. B&W-93min. Don Ameche, Janet Blair .... (4)

SOMETHING WILD (1961) United Artists. B&W-112min. Carroll Baker, Ralph Meeker .... (4)

SOMETIME SWEET SUSAN (1974) Variety Films. Color-76min. Shawn Harris, Harry Reems ....

SOMETIMES A GREAT NOTION (1971) Universal. Color-114min. Henry Fonda, Paul Newman 5*
British and TV title: NEVER GIVE AN INCH

SOMEWHERE I'LL FIND YOU (1942) M-G-M. B&W-108min. Clark Gable, Lana Turner .... (4)

SOMEWHERE IN FRANCE (1942) *see* FOREMAN WENT TO FRANCE, THE

SOMEWHERE IN THE NIGHT (1946) 20th Century-Fox. B&W-110min. John Hodiak, Nancy Guild 4*

SON-DAUGHTER, THE (1932) M-G-M. B&W-79min. Helen Hayes, Ramon Novarro .... (4)

SON OF A GUNFIGHTER (1965) M-G-M. Color-92min. *(Spanish-U.S.).* Russ Tamblyn, Kieron Moore, Fernando Rey 3*
Spanish title: HIJO DEL PISTOLERO, EL

SON OF A SAILOR (1933) First National [W.B.]. B&W-73min. Joe E. Brown, Thelma Todd .... (4)

SON OF ALI BABA (1952) Universal. Color-75min. Tony Curtis, Piper Laurie .... (3)

SON OF ATLAS IN THE VALLEY OF THE LIONS, THE (1961) *see* URSUS IN THE VALLEY OF THE LIONS

SON OF BELLE STARR (1953) Allied Artists. Color-70min. Keith Larsen, Dona Drake 3*

SON OF BLOB (1972) *see* BEWARE! THE BLOB

SON OF CAPTAIN BLOOD, THE (1962) Paramount. Color-88min. *(Italian-U.S.-Spanish).* Sean Flynn, Alessandra Parano .... (3)
Italian title: FIGLIO DEL CAPITANO BLOOD, IL
Spanish title: HIJO DEL CAPITAN BLOOD, EL

SON OF DEAR CAROLINE, THE (1954) Color-105min. *(French).* Jean-Claude Pascal, Jacques Dacqmine, Brigitte Bardot .... (3)
Original title: FILS DE CAROLINE CHÉRIE, LE

SON OF DR. JEKYLL, THE (1951) Columbia. B&W-77min. Louis Hayward, Jody Lawrence, Alexander Knox 3½*
Advertising title?: SECOND FACE OF DR. JEKYLL, THE

SON OF DRACULA (1943) Universal. B&W-78min. Lon Chaney, Robert Paige 4*

SON OF DRACULA (1973) Cinemation. Color-90min. *(British).* Harry Nilsson, Ringo Starr, Freddie Jones 2*
Publicity title: YOUNG DRACULA

SON OF FLUBBER (1963) Buena Vista. B&W-100min. Fred MacMurray, Nancy Olson, Keenan Wynn 4½*

Films are rated on a 1 to 10 scale, 10 is highest. **Boldface** ratings followed by an asterisk (*) are for films actually seen and rated by the executive and senior editors. All other ratings are estimates. (See Notes on Entertainment Ratings in the front section.)

SON OF FRANKENSTEIN (1939) Universal. **B&W-95min.** Basil Rathbone, Boris Karloff, Bela Lugosi..................................4*

SON OF FURY - THE STORY OF BENJAMIN BLAKE (1942) 20th Century-Fox. **B&W-98min.** Tyrone Power, Gene Tierney..................5*

SON OF GODZILLA (1968) Walter Reade. **Color-86min.** *(Japanese).* Godzilla, Tadao Takashima, Akira Kubo..................................1*
Original title: GOJIRA NO MUSUKO

SON OF HERCULES IN THE LAND OF DARKNESS, THE (1963) Avco-Embassy. **Color-81min.** *(Italian).* Dan Vadis, Spela Rozin..................(1)

SON OF HERCULES IN THE LAND OF FIRE, THE (1963) Avco-Embassy. **Color-87min.** *(Italian).* Ed Fury, Claudio Mori..................(2)
Original title: URSUS NELLA TERRA DI FUOCO *(Ursus in the Land of Fire)*
Alternate title: URSUS IN THE LAND OF FIRE
Title error: SON OF HERCULES AND FIVE GIANTS

SON OF KONG (1933) RKO. **B&W-70min.** Robert Armstrong, Helen Mack..................................4½*

SON OF LASSIE (1945) M-G-M. **Color-102min.** Peter Lawford, June Lockhart, Lassie..................................4*

SON OF MONTE CRISTO, THE (1940) United Artists. **B&W-102min.** Louis Hayward, Joan Bennett..................................5½*

SON OF PALEFACE (1952) Paramount. **Color-95min.** Bob Hope, Jane Russell..................................4*

SON OF ROBIN HOOD, THE (1958) 20th Century-Fox. **Color-77min.** *(British).* David Hedison, June Laverick..................................3*

SON OF SAMSON (1960) Medallion. **Color-89min.** *(Italian-French-Yugoslavian).* Mark Forest, Chelo Alonso..................(2)
Original Italian title: MACISTE NELLA VALLE DEI RE *(Maciste in the Valley of the Kings)*
French title: GÉANT DE LA VALLÉE DES ROIS, LE *(The Giant of the Valley of the Kings)*

SON OF SINBAD (1955) RKO. **Color-88min.** Dale Robertson, Sally Forrest, Vincent Price..................................(3)
Alternate title: NIGHT IN A HAREM, A

SON OF SPARTACUS (1962) *see* SLAVE, THE

SON OF THE GODS (1930) First National [W.B.]. **B&W-82min.** Richard Barthelmess, Constance Bennett..................................(3)

SON OF THE RED CORSAIR (1960) Medallion. **Color-97min.** *(Italian).* Lex Barker, Sylvia Lopez..................................(3)
Original title: FIGLIO DEL CORSARO ROSSO, IL

SON OF THE SHEIK, THE (1926) United Artists. **B&W-74min.** *(Silent).* Rudolph Valentino..................................4*

SONG AND THE SILENCE, THE (1969) Cloverhouse. **B&W-80min.** Annita Koutsouveli, Harry Rubin..................................(4)

SONG FOR MISS JULIE, A (1945) Republic. **B&W-69min.** Shirley Ross, Barton Hepburn..................................(3)

SONG IS BORN, A (1948) RKO. **Color-113min.** Danny Kaye, Virginia Mayo..................................4½*

SONG OF BERNADETTE, THE (1943) 20th Century-Fox. **B&W-156min.** Jennifer Jones, William Eythe..................................5*

SONG OF INDIA (1949) Columbia. **B&W-77min.** Sabu, Gail Russell, Turhan Bey..................................(3)

SONG OF LOVE (1947) M-G-M. **B&W-119min.** Katharine Hepburn, Paul Henreid, Robert Walker..................................4*

SONG OF MEXICO (1945) Republic. **B&W-59min.** Edgar Barrier, Adele Mara..................................(3)

SONG OF NORWAY (1970) Cinerama Releasing. **Color-150min.** Toralv Maurstad, Florence Henderson..................................5½*

SONG OF RUSSIA (1943) M-G-M. **B&W-107min.** Robert Taylor, Susan Peters..................................(4)

SONG OF SCHEHERAZADE (1947) Universal. **Color-106min.** Yvonne De Carlo, Brian Donlevy..................................(3)

SONG OF SISTER MARIA, THE (1953) Citation. **B&W-81min.** *(Spanish).* Dominique Blanchar, Maria Dulce..................................(4)

SONG OF SONGS (1933) Paramount. **B&W-90min.** Marlene Dietrich, Brian Aherne, Lionel Atwill..................................(5)

SONG OF SURRENDER (1949) Paramount. **B&W-93min.** Macdonald Carey, Wanda Hendrix, Claude Rains..................................(3)

SONG OF THE FIREMEN (1967) *see* FIREMEN'S BALL, THE

SONG OF THE ISLANDS (1942) 20th Century-Fox. **Color-75min.** Betty Grable, Victor Mature, Jack Oakie..................................(3)

SONG OF THE LAND (1953) United Artists. **Color-71min.** *(Documentary).* Director: Henry S. Kesler..................................(4)

SONG OF THE OPEN ROAD (1944) United Artists. **B&W-93min.** Jane Powell, Reginald Denny, W. C. Fields..................................(4)

SONG OF THE SARONG (1945) Universal. **B&W-65min.** William Gargan, Nancy Kelly..................................(3)

SONG OF THE SOUTH (1946) RKO (for Disney). **Color-95min.** *(Part-animated).* James Baskett, Bobby Driscoll..................................5½*

SONG OF THE THIN MAN (1947) M-G-M. **B&W-86min.** William Powell, Myrna Loy..................................(4)

SONG REMAINS THE SAME, THE (1976) Warner Bros. **Color-136min.** *(British, Documentary).* Director: Peter Clifton..................................(4)

SONG TO REMEMBER, A (1945) Columbia. **Color-113min.** Cornel Wilde, Merle Oberon, Paul Muni..................................5*

SONG WITHOUT END (1960) Columbia. **Color-141min.** Dirk Bogarde, Capucine..................................4*

SONNAMBULA, LA (1952) Continental [Walter Reade]. **B&W-79min.** *(Italian).* Gino Sinemberghi, Paola Bertini..................................(3)
Translation title: The Sleepwalker

SONNY & JED (1973) K-Tel. **Color-91min.** *(Italian-Spanish-W. German).* Susan George, Tomas Milian, Telly Savalas..................................(3)
Original Italian title: J. and S. - STORIA CRIMINALE DEL FAR WEST *(J. and S. - A Criminal Story of the Far West)*
Alternate Italian title: BANDA J. & S. CRONACA CRIMINALE DEL FAR WEST, LA *(The J. and S. Gang - Criminal Chronicle of the Far West)*
Spanish title: J. and S. - HISTORIA CRIMINAL DEL FAR WEST

SONS AND LOVERS (1960) 20th Century-Fox. **B&W-100min.** *(U.S.-British).* Dean Stockwell, Trevor Howard, Wendy Hiller..................................6*

SONS O' GUNS (1936) Warner Bros. **B&W-82min.** Joan Blondell, Joe E. Brown..................................(4)

SONS OF ADVENTURE (1948) Republic. **B&W-60min.** Lynne Roberts, Russell Hayden..................................(4)

SONS OF KATIE ELDER, THE (1965) Paramount. **Color-122min.** John Wayne, Dean Martin..................................4*

SONS OF THE DESERT (1933) M-G-M. **B&W-68min.** Stanley Laurel, Oliver Hardy..................................(4)
British title: FRATERNALLY YOURS
Foreign title: SONS OF THE LEGION
Foreign title: CONVENTION CITY

SONS OF THE MUSKETEERS (1952) *see* AT SWORD'S POINT

SOOKY (1931) Paramount. **B&W-85min.** Jackie Cooper, Jackie Coogan (4)

SOPHIE'S PLACE (1969) Warner Bros. **Color-106min.** *(British-U.S.).* Telly Savalas, Edith Evans, Warren Oates..................................4*
British title: CROOKS AND CORONETS

SORCERER (1977) Universal & Paramount. **Color-121min.** Roy Scheider, Bruno Cremer..................................5½*
British title: WAGES OF FEAR, THE

SORCERERS, THE (1967) Allied Artists. **Color-87min.** *(British).* Boris Karloff, Catherine Lacey, Ian Ogilvy..................................4*

SORCERER'S VILLAGE, THE (1958) *see* VOODOO VILLAGE

SORCERESS, THE (1955) Metzger & Woog. **B&W-97min.** *(French).* Marina Vlady, Maurice Ronet..................................(5)
Original title: SORCIERE, LA
Alternate title?: BLONDE WITCH

SORCIERE, LA (1955) *see* SORCERESS, THE

SORORITY GIRL (1957) American-International. **B&W-60min.** Susan Cabot, Dick Miller..................................(3)
British title: BAD ONE, THE

SORRELL AND SON (1928) United Artists. **B&W-100min.** *(Silent).* H. B. Warner, Anna Q. Nilsson, Mickey McBan..................................(4)

SORROW AND THE PITY, THE (1970) Cinema 5. **B&W-265min.** *(French-Swiss-W. German, Documentary).* Director: Marcel Ophuls..................4*
Original French title: CHAGRIN ET LA PITIE, LE

SORROWFUL JONES (1949) Paramount. **B&W-88min.** Bob Hope, Lucille Ball..................................4*

SORRY, WRONG NUMBER (1948) Paramount. **B&W-89min.** Barbara Stanwyck, Burt Lancaster..................................6*

SO'S YOUR OLD MAN (1926) Paramount. **B&W-71min.** *(Silent).* W. C. Fields, Alice Joyce..................................(4)

SOUL OF A MONSTER, THE (1944) Columbia. **B&W-61min.** George Macready, Rose Hobart..................................(2)

SOUL OF NIGGER CHARLEY, THE (1973) Paramount. **Color-110min.** Fred Williamson, D'Urville Martin, Denise Nicholas..................................(3)

SOUL SOLDIER (1970) *see* RED, WHITE AND BLACK, THE

SOUL TO SOUL (1971) Cinerama Releasing. **Color-96min.** *(Music Film).* Director: Denis Sanders..................................(5)

SOULMATES OF SHANGO (1975) *see* LORD SHANGO

SOULS AT SEA (1937) Paramount. **B&W-92min.** Gary Cooper, George Raft..................................(5)

SOUND AND THE FURY, THE (1959) 20th Century-Fox. Color-115min. Yul Brynner, Joanne Woodward 5*

SOUND BARRIER, THE (1952) see BREAKING THE SOUND BARRIER

SOUND OF ANGER, THE (1968) Universal. Color-100min. *(Made for TV).* James Farentino, Burl Ives, Linda Day (George) 4*

SOUND OF FURY, THE (1951) see TRY AND GET ME

SOUND OF MUSIC, THE (1965) 20th Century-Fox. Color-171min. Julie Andrews, Christopher Plummer 6½*

SOUND OF TRUMPETS, THE (1961) Janus Films. B&W-90min. *(Italian).* Sandro Panzeri, Loredana Detto .... (4)
Original title: POSTO, IL

SOUND OFF (1952) Columbia. Color-83min. Mickey Rooney, Anne James .... (4)

SOUNDER (1972) 20th Century-Fox. Color-105min. Cicely Tyson, Paul Winfield 5½*

SOUNDER (1975) ABC-TV. Color-74min. *(Made for TV).* Ebony Wright, Harold Sylvester, Darryl Young ....

SOUNDER, PART 2 (1976) see PART 2 SOUNDER

SOURDOUGH (1977) Film Saturation. Color-94min. Gil Perry, Gene Evans ....

SOUTH OF ALGIERS (1952) see GOLDEN MASK, THE

SOUTH OF PAGO PAGO (1940) United Artists. B&W-98min. Victor McLaglen, Jon Hall 3½*

SOUTH OF ST. LOUIS (1949) Warner Bros. Color-88min. Joel McCrea, Zachary Scott 4*

SOUTH OF SUEZ (1940) Warner Bros. B&W-86min. George Brent, Brenda Marshall .... (3)

SOUTH OF TANA RIVER (1964) Asa Films. Color-88min. *(Danish).* Paul Reichhardt, William Rosenberg .... (3)

SOUTH PACIFIC (1958) Magna Pictures. Color-171min. Rossano Brazzi, Mitzi Gaynor, John Kerr 6*

SOUTH RIDING (1938) United Artists. B&W-91min. *(British).* Ralph Richardson, Edna Best .... (5)

SOUTH SEA SINNER (1950) Universal. B&W-88min. Macdonald Carey, Shelley Winters .... (3)
British title: EAST OF JAVA

SOUTH SEA WOMAN (1953) Warner Bros. B&W-99min. Burt Lancaster, Virginia Mayo .... (4)

SOUTH SEAS ADVENTURE (1958) Stanley Warner Cinema Corp. Color-120min. *(Travelog).* Director: Francis D. Lyon .... (4)

SOUTHERN BLADE (1967) see TIME FOR KILLING, A

SOUTHERN COMFORTS (1971) Boxoffice International. Color-80min. Jacob Oft, Judy Angel, Jack Richesin .... (3)

SOUTHERN STAR, THE (1969) Columbia. Color-104min. *(French-British, English version).* George Segal, Ursula Andress, Orson Welles 5*
French title: ÉTOILE DU SUD, L'

SOUTHERN YANKEE, A (1948) M-G-M. B&W-90min. Red Skelton, Brian Donlevy 5*
British title: MY HERO

SOUTHERNER, THE (1945) United Artists. B&W-91min. Zachary Scott, Betty Field 4½*

SOUTHSIDE 1-1000 (1950) Allied Artists. B&W-73min. Don DeFore, Andrea King .... (3)
British title: FORGERY

SOUTHWEST PASSAGE (1954) United Artists. Color-82min. Rod Cameron, Joanne Dru .... (4)
British title: CAMELS WEST

SOUTHWEST TO SONORA (1966) see APPALOOSA, THE

SOYLENT GREEN (1973) M-G-M. Color-97min. Charlton Heston, Leigh Taylor-Young, Edward G. Robinson 5½*

SPACE CHILDREN, THE (1958) Paramount. B&W-69min. Jackie Coogan, Michel Ray, Adam Williams 2*

SPACE CRUSIER YAMATO (1977) Enterprise Pictures Ltd. Color-107min. *(Japanese, Cartoon).* Director: Yoshinobu Nishizaki 5*

SPACE INVASION OF LAPPLAND (1960) see INVASION OF THE ANIMAL PEOPLE

SPACE MASTER X-7 (1958) 20th Century-Fox. B&W-70min. Bill Williams, Lyn Thomas .... (3)

SPACE MEN (1960) see ASSIGNMENT - OUTER SPACE

SPACE MONSTER (1965) American-International. B&W-80min. Russ Bender, Francine York, James B. Brown 2*

SPACE STATION X-14 (1965) see MUTINY IN OUTER SPACE

SPACEFLIGHT IC-1 (1965) 20th Century-Fox. B&W-65min. *(British).* Bill Williams, Kathleen Breck .... (4)

SPACEMAN AND KING ARTHUR, THE (1979) Buena Vista. Color-min. Jim Dale, Ron Moody ....

SPACESHIP TO THE UNKNOWN (1936) Universal. B&W-97min. *(Re-edited Serial).* Buster Crabbe, Jean Rogers, Charles Middleton .... (3)
Original title: FLASH GORDON
Title of alternate feature condensation: ROCKET SHIP

SPACEWAYS (1953) Lippert Productions. B&W-76min. *(British).* Howard Duff, Eva Bartok .... (2)

SPANISH AFFAIR (1957) Paramount. Color-93min. *(Spanish).* Richard Kiley, Carmen Sevilla .... (4)

SPANISH GARDENER, THE (1956) J. Arthur Rank. Color-97min. *(British).* Dirk Bogarde, Jon Whitely .... (5)

SPANISH MAIN, THE (1945) RKO. Color-100min. Paul Henreid, Maureen O'Hara 4*

SPARE THE ROD (1961) Avco-Embassy. B&W-93min. *(British).* Max Bygraves, Donald Pleasence .... (4)

SPARKLE (1976) Warner Bros. Color-98min. Irene Cara, Philip M. Thomas 3½*

SPARROWS CAN'T SING (1963) Janus Films. B&W-93min. *(British).* James Booth, Barbara Windsor .... (5)

SPARTACUS (1960) Universal. Color-190min. Kirk Douglas, Laurence Olivier 7*

SPARTACUS AND THE REBEL GLADIATOR (1954) see SINS OF ROME

SPARTACUS AND THE TEN GLADIATORS (1964) Four Star. Color-98min. *(Italian-Spanish-French).* John Heston, Dan Vadis, Helga Line .... (1)
Original Italian title: SPARTACUS E I DIECI GLADIATORI
Spanish title: TRIUNFO DE LOS DIEZ GLADIADORES, EL *(The Triumph of the Ten Gladiators)*
French title: SPARTACUS ET LES DIX GLADIATEURS

SPATS TO SPURS (1939) see HENRY GOES ARIZONA

SPAWN OF THE NORTH (1938) Paramount. B&W-110min. George Raft, Henry Fonda 4*

SPEAKING OF MURDER (1957) United Motion Pic. Org. (UMPO). B&W-80min. *(French).* Jean Gabin, Annie Girardot, Lino Ventura .... (4)
Original title: ROUGE EST MIS, LE *(The Red Light Is On)*

SPECIAL AGENT (1935) Warner Bros. B&W-78min. Bette Davis, George Brent .... (4)

SPECIAL DAY, A (1977) Cinema 5. Color-110min. *(Canadian-Italian).* Marcello Mastroianni, Sophia Loren 4*
Original title: GIORNATA PARTICOLARE, UNA

SPECIAL DELIVERY (1955) Columbia. B&W-86min. *(W. German-U.S.).* Joseph Cotten, Eva Bartok .... (3)
West German title: VON HIMMEL GEFALLEN

As **SPARTACUS** (1960), Kirk Douglas (with dagger) angrily suspects treachery on the part of pirate envoy Herbert Lom, who was to have provided the slave army with enough ships to escape the pursuing Romans.

SPECIAL DELIVERY (1976) American-International. Color-98min. Bo Svenson, Cybill Shepherd..(4)

SPECIAL SECTION (1975) Universal. Color-112min. (French-Italian-W. German). Louis Seigner, Michel Lonsdale ....
Original French title: SECTION SPECIALE

SPECTER OF THE ROSE (1946) Republic. B&W-90min. Ivan Kirov, Viola Essen..(5)

SPECTRE, THE (1963) *see* GHOST, THE

SPECTRE (1977) 20th Century-Fox. Color-74min. (Made for TV). Robert Culp, Gig Young, John Hurt ....(4)

SPECTRE OF EDGAR ALLAN POE, THE (1974) Cinerama Releasing. Color-87min. Robert Walker, Cesar Romero, Tom Drake, Mary Grover ....(3)

SPEED CRAZY (1958) Allied Artists. B&W-75min. Brett Halsey, Yvonne Lime ....(2)

SPEEDTRAP (1978) First Artists. Color-98min. Joe Don Baker, Tyne Daly 4½*

SPEEDWAY (1968) M-G-M. Color-95min. Elvis Presley, Nancy Sinatra (3)

SPELL, THE (1977) Worldvision. Color-74min. (Made for TV). Susan Myers, Lee Grant, James Olson 2*

SPELLBOUND (1945) United Artists. B&W-111min. Ingrid Bergman, Gregory Peck..5*

SPENCER'S MOUNTAIN (1963) Warner Bros. Color-119min. Henry Fonda, Maureen O'Hara, James MacArthur 4*

SPIDER, THE (1958) *see* EARTH VS. THE SPIDER

SPIDER AND THE FLY, THE (1949) J. Arthur Rank. B&W-73min. (British). Eric Portman, Nadia Gray 5*

SPIDER-MAN (1977) CBS-TV. Color-74min. (Made for TV). Nicholas Hammond, David White, Thayer David 4*

SPIDER WOMAN, THE (1944) *see* SHERLOCK HOLMES AND THE SPIDER WOMAN

SPIDER WOMAN STRIKES BACK, THE (1946) Universal. B&W-59min. Gale Sondergaard, Brenda Joyce, Rondo Hatton ....(2)

SPIDER'S STRATAGEM, THE (1970) New Yorker Films. Color-97min. (Italian). Giulio Brogi, Alida Valli, Tino Scotti......................(5)
Original title: STRATEGIA DEL RAGNO

SPIDER'S WEB, THE (1960) *see* IT'S HOT IN PARADISE

SPIDER'S WEB, THE (1960) United Artists. Color-89min. (British). Glynis Johns, John Justin ....(3)

SPIES (1928) M-G-M. B&W-90min. (German, Silent). Rudolph Klein-Rogge, Gerda Maurus, Willy Fritsch 2*
Original title: SPIONE (The Spy)
Alternate title: SPY, THE

SPIES A-GO-GO (1964) *see* NASTY RABBIT, THE

SPIKES GANG, THE (1974) United Artists. Color-96min. Lee Marvin, Gary Grimes, Ron Howard ....(4)

SPIN A DARK WEB (1956) Columbia. B&W-76min. (British). Faith Domergue, Lee Patterson ....(3)
Original title: SOHO INCIDENT

SPIN OF A COIN (1961) *see* GEORGE RAFT STORY, THE

SPINOUT (1966) M-G-M. Color-93min. Elvis Presley, Shelley Fabares ..(3)
British title: CALIFORNIA HOLIDAY

SPINSTER (1961) *see* TWO LOVES

SPIRAL ROAD, THE (1962) Universal. Color-145min. Rock Hudson, Burl Ives 4*

SPIRAL STAIRCASE, THE (1946) RKO. B&W-83min. Dorothy McGuire, George Brent..5*

SPIRIT IS WILLING, THE (1967) Paramount. Color-94min. Sid Caesar, Vera Miles...(4)

SPIRIT OF CULVER (1939) Universal. B&W-89min. Jackie Cooper, Freddie Bartholomew ....(4)
British title: MAN'S HERITAGE

SPIRIT OF ST. LOUIS, THE (1957) Warner Bros. Color-138min. James Stewart, Murray Hamilton 4*

SPIRIT OF THE BEEHIVE, THE (1973) Janus Films. Color-95min. (Spanish). Ana Torrent, Fernando Fernan Gomez, Teresa Gimpera....3*
Original title: ESPIRITU DELA COLMENA, EL

SPIRIT OF THE PEOPLE (1940) *see* ABE LINCOLN IN ILLINOIS

SPIRIT OF WEST POINT, THE (1947) Film Classics [U.A.]. B&W-77min. Felix "Doc" Blanchard, Glenn Davis................................(4)

SPIRITISM (1961) Trans-International. B&W-85min. (Mexican). Nora Veyran, José Luis Jiménez ....(1)
Original title: ESPIRITISMO

SPIRITS OF THE DEAD (1968) American-International. Color-117min. (French-Italian). Jane Fonda, Brigitte Bardot, Terence Stamp, Peter Fonda 3*
Original French title: HISTOIRES EXTRAORDINAIRES (Extraordinary Stories)
Italian title: TRE PASSI NEL DELIRIO (Three Steps to Delirium)
British title: TALES OF MYSTERY

SPIRITUALIST, THE (1948) Eagle Lion. B&W-78min. Turhan Bey, Lynn Bari...(3)
Alternate Title(?): AMAZING MR. X, THE

SPITE MARRIAGE (1929) M-G-M. B&W-80min. (Silent). Buster Keaton, Dorothy Sebastian 5*

SPITFIRE (1934) RKO. B&W-88min. Katharine Hepburn, Robert Young...4*

SPITFIRE (1942) RKO. B&W-90min. (British). Leslie Howard, David Niven...(5)
Original title: FIRST OF THE FEW, THE

SPIVS (1953) *see* VITELLONI, I

SPLENDID DAYS, THE (1960) *see* SUMMER TO REMEMBER, A

SPLENDOR (1935) United Artists. B&W-77min. Miriam Hopkins, Joel McCrea...4*

SPLENDOR IN THE GRASS (1961) Warner Bros. Color-124min. Natalie Wood, Warren Beatty 5*

SPLIT, THE (1968) M-G-M. Color-90min. Jim Brown, Diahann Carroll, Gene Hackman...(3)

SPLIT SECOND (1953) RKO. B&W-85min. Stephen McNally, Alexis Smith ....(5)

SPLITFACE (1946) *see* DICK TRACY

SPOILERS, THE (1942) Universal. B&W-87min. Marlene Dietrich, John Wayne, Randolph Scott 4*

SPOILERS, THE (1956) Universal. Color-84min. Anne Baxter, Jeff Chandler, Rory Calhoun 4*

SPOILERS OF THE FOREST (1957) Republic. Color-68min. Rod Cameron, Vera Ralston ....(3)

SPOILERS OF THE NORTH (1947) Republic. B&W-66min. Paul Kelly, Adrian Booth ....(2)

SPOILERS OF THE PLAINS (1951) Republic. B&W-68min. Roy Rogers, Penny Edwards ....(4)

SPOILERS OF THE SEA (1957) Color-91min. (Mexican). Jack Palance, Pedro Armendariz ....(3)

SPOOK BUSTERS (1946) Monogram [Allied Artists]. B&W-68min. The Bowery Boys, Douglass Dumbrille............................(3)

SPOOK CHASERS (1957) Allied Artists. B&W-62min. The Bowery Boys, Robert Shayne ....(3)

SPOOK WHO SAT BY THE DOOR, THE (1973) United Artists. Color-102min. Lawrence Cook, Paula Kelly...........................(4)

SPOOKS RUN WILD (1941) Monogram [Allied Artists]. B&W-69min. The East Side Kids, Bela Lugosi....................................(3)

SPORTING CLUB, THE (1971) Avco-Embassy. Color-105min. Robert Fields, Nicolas Coster, Jack Warden ....(2)

SPREE (1967) United Producers Releasing Organization and Trans American Films. Color-84min. (Music Film). Director: Mitchell Leisen ....(2)

SPRING IN PARK LANE (1948) Eagle Lion. B&W-91min. (British). Anna Neagle, Michael Wilding ....(5)

SPRING MADNESS (1938) M-G-M. B&W-80min. Maureen O'Sullivan, Lew Ayres, Burgess Meredith ....(4)

SPRING PARADE (1940) Universal. B&W-89min. Deanna Durbin, Robert Cummings...(5)

SPRING REUNION (1957) United Artists. B&W-79min. Betty Hutton, Dana Andrews ....(3)

SPRINGFIELD RIFLE (1952) Warner Bros. Color-93min. Gary Cooper, Phyllis Thaxter...4*

SPRINGTIME FOR HENRY (1934) Fox Film Co. [20th]. B&W-73min. Otto Kruger, Nancy Carroll, Heather Angel.........................(4)

SPRINGTIME IN THE ROCKIES (1942) 20th Century-Fox. Color-91min. Betty Grable, John Payne, Carmen Miranda ....(4)

SPUTNIK (1958) Films Around The World. B&W-92min. (French). Noel-Noel, Denise Gray, Mischa Auer...................................(3)
Original title: AU PIED, AU CHEVAL ET PAR SPOUTNIK (By Foot, By Horse and By Sputnik)
Alternate title: DOG, A MOUSE AND A SPUTNIK, A
British title: HOLD TIGHT FOR THE SATELLITE

SPY, THE (1928) *see* SPIES

SPY CHASERS (1955) Allied Artists. **B&W-61min.** The Bowery Boys, Lisa Davis ....(3)

SPY HUNT (1950) Universal. **B&W-75min.** Howard Duff, Marta Toren.. 4*
British title: PANTHER'S MOON

SPY I LOVE, THE (1964) Four Star. **B&W-90min.** *(French).* Dominique Paturel, Virna Lisi, Jacques Bolutin ....(3)

SPY IN BLACK, THE (1939) *see* U-BOAT 29

SPY IN THE SKY (1958) Allied Artists. **B&W-74min.** Steve Brodie, Andrea Domburg, George Coulouris ....(2)

SPY IN YOUR EYE (1965) American-International. **Color-88min.** *(Italian).* Brett Halsey, Pier Angeli, Dana Andrews....................(3)
Original title: BERLINO, APPUNTAMENTO PER LE SPIE *(Berlin, Appointment for the Spies)*

SPY KILLER, THE (1969) ABC Films. **Color-74min.** *(Made for TV).* Robert Horton, Sebastian Cabot, Jill St. John 4*

SPY KILLERS, THE (1965) *see* SECRET AGENT FIREBALL

SPY SHIP (1942) Warner Bros. **B&W-62min.** Craig Stevens, Irene Manning ....(3)

SPY SMASHER RETURNS (1942) Republic. **B&W-100min.** *(Re-edited Serial).* Kane Richmond, Marguerite Chapman ....(4)
Original title: SPY SMASHER

SPY SQUAD (1962) Riviera Productions. **B&W-75min.** Richard (Dick) Miller, Dick O'Neill...(3)
Original title: CAPTURE THAT CAPSULE!

SPY WHO CAME IN FROM THE COLD, THE (1965) Paramount. **B&W-112min.** Richard Burton, Claire Bloom, Oskar Werner.............5½*

SPY WHO LOVED ME, THE (1977) United Artists. **Color-125min.** *(British-U.S.).* Roger Moore, Barbara Bach, Richard Kiel 6*

SPY WITH A COLD NOSE, THE (1966) Avco-Embassy. **Color-93min.** *(British).* Laurence Harvey, Daliah Lavi 5*

SPY WITH MY FACE, THE (1964) M-G-M. **Color-86min.** *(Telefeature).* Robert Vaughn, Senta Berger, David McCallum 3½*
Original title: DOUBLE AFFAIR, THE

S*P*Y*S (1974) 20th Century-Fox. **Color-87min.** *(British-U.S.).* Elliott Gould, Donald Sutherland..4*
British title: SPYS

SQUAD CAR (1960) 20th Century-Fox. **B&W-60min.** Vici Raaf, Paul Bryar ....(1)

SQUARE JUNGLE, THE (1956) Universal. **B&W-86min.** Tony Curtis, Pat Crowley ....(4)

SQUARE OF VIOLENCE (1961) M-G-M. **B&W-98min.** *(Yugoslavian-U.S., English language).* Broderick Crawford, Valentina Cortese, Branko Plesa ....(3)
Yugoslavian title: NASILJE NA TRGU

SQUARE RING, THE (1953) Republic. **B&W-83min.** Kay Kendall, Jack Warner..(3)

SQUARE SHOOTER (1951) *see* SKIPALONG ROSENBLOOM

SQUAW MAN, THE (1914) Famous Players Lasky. **B&W-6reels** *(Silent).* Dustin Farnum, Monroe Salisbury, Winifred Kingston ....(3)

SQUAW MAN, THE (1918) Paramount. **B&W-6reels** *(Silent).* ....(4)

SQUAW MAN, THE (1931) M-G-M. **B&W-106min.** Warner Baxter, Lupe Velez..(4)
British title: WHITE MAN, THE

SQUEAKER, THE (1937) *see* MURDER ON DIAMOND ROW

SQUEAKER, THE (1964) UCC Films. **B&W-93min.** *(German).* Heinz Drache, Barbara Rutting ....(4)
Original title: ZINKER, DER

SQUEEZE, THE (1977) Warner Bros. **Color-106min.** *(British).* Stacy Keach, David Hemmings, Edward Fox, Carol White............(4)

SQUIRM (1976) American-International. **Color-93min.** John Scardino, Patricia Pearey...(3)

SSSSSSS (1973) Universal. **Color-99min.** Strother Martin, Dirk Benedict 4*
Publicity title: SSSSSSSS
British title: SSSSNAKE

STABLEMATES (1938) M-G-M. **B&W-89min.** Wallace Beery, Mickey Rooney 3*

STAGE DOOR (1937) RKO. **B&W-93min.** Katharine Hepburn, Ginger Rogers...5½*

STAGE DOOR CANTEEN (1943) United Artists. **B&W-132min.** Cheryl Walker, William Terry 4½*

STAGE FRIGHT (1950) Warner Bros. **B&W-111min.** Jane Wyman, Marlene Dietrich, Michael Wilding, Richard Todd 5*

STAGE STRUCK (1936) First National [W.B.]. **B&W-86min.** Dick Powell, Joan Blondell, Warren William ....(3)

STAGE STRUCK (1958) Buena Vista. **Color-95min.** Susan Strasberg, Henry Fonda..4*

STAGE TO THUNDER ROCK (1964) Paramount. **Color-82min.** Barry Sullivan, Marilyn Maxwell, Keenan Wynn.........................3*

STAGE TO TUCSON (1951) Columbia. **Color-82min.** Rod Cameron, Wayne Morris..3*

STAGECOACH (1939) United Artists. **B&W-96min.** John Wayne, Claire Trevor..4*

STAGECOACH (1966) 20th Century-Fox. **Color-114min.** Ann-Margret, Alex Cord...4*

STAGECOACH TO DANCERS' ROCK (1962) Universal. **B&W-72min.** Warren Stevens, Martin Landau, Jody Lawrence...................(3)

STAGECOACH TO FURY (1956) 20th Century-Fox. **B&W-76min.** Forrest Tucker, Mari Blanchard 3*

STAIRCASE (1969) 20th Century-Fox. **Color-96min.** Rex Harrison, Richard Burton..(4)

STAIRWAY TO HEAVEN (1946) Universal. **Color-104min.** *(British).* David Niven, Kim Hunter...7*
Original title: MATTER OF LIFE AND DEATH, A

STAKEOUT (1962) Crown International. **B&W-81min.** Bing Russell, Billy Hughes ....(3)

STAKEOUT ON DOPE STREET (1958) Warner Bros. **B&W-83min.** Yale Wexler, Jonathan Haze, Morris Miller ....(3)

STALAG 17 (1953) Paramount. **B&W-120min.** William Holden, Gil Stratton, Jr. 6½*

STALK THE WILD CHILD (1976) Worldvision. **Color-100min.** *(Made for TV).* David Janssen, Trish Van Devere, Joseph Bottoms, Ben Bottoms ....

STALKING MOON, THE (1969) National General. **Color-109min.** Gregory Peck, Eva Marie Saint...4*

STALLION ROAD (1947) Warner Bros. **B&W-97min.** Ronald Reagan, Alexis Smith, Zachary Scott..(4)

STAMBOUL QUEST (1934) M-G-M. **B&W-88min.** Myrna Loy, George Brent...(4)

STAMPEDE (1949) Allied Artists. **B&W-78min.** Rod Cameron, Gale Storm..(4)

STAMPEDED (1957) *see* BIG LAND, THE

STAND AND DELIVER (1941) *see* BOWERY BLITZKREIG

STAND AT APACHE RIVER, THE (1953) Universal. **Color-77min.** Stephen McNally, Hugh O'Brian, Julie Adams..................(3)

STAND BY FOR ACTION (1942) M-G-M. **B&W-109min.** Robert Taylor, Charles Laughton ....(4)
British title: CARGO OF INNOCENTS

STAND-IN (1937) United Artists. **B&W-91min.** Leslie Howard, Humphrey Bogart, Joan Blondell ....(4)

STAND UP AND BE COUNTED (1972) Columbia. **Color-99min.** Jacqueline Bisset, Stella Stevens ....(4)

STAND UP AND CHEER (1934) Fox Film Co. [20th]. **B&W-80min.** Warner Baxter, Madge Evans..(5)

STAND UP AND FIGHT (1939) M-G-M. **B&W-105min.** Wallace Beery, Robert Taylor...(3)

STAND UP VIRGIN SOLDIERS (1977) Warner Bros. **Color-91min.** *(British).* Robin Askwith, Nigel Davenport ....

STANDING ROOM ONLY (1944) Paramount. **B&W-83min.** Paulette Goddard, Fred MacMurray, Edward Arnold ....(4)

STANLEY (1972) Crown International. **Color-106min.** Chris Robinson, Alex Rocco...2*

STANLEY AND LIVINGSTON (1939) 20th Century-Fox. **B&W-101min.** Spencer Tracy, Cedric Hardwicke..............................5½*

STAR! (1968) 20th Century-Fox. **Color-175min.** Julie Andrews, Richard Crenna 4*
Alternate title: THOSE WERE THE HAPPY TIMES
Publicity title: GERTIE WAS A LADY

STAR, THE (1952) 20th Century-Fox. **B&W-89min.** Bette Davis, Sterling Hayden...5*

STAR DUST (1940) 20th Century-Fox. **B&W-85min.** Linda Darnell, John Payne..(4)

STAR IN THE DUST (1956) Universal. **Color-80min.** John Agar, Mamie Van Doren, Richard Boone.......................................3*

STAR IS BORN, A (1937) United Artists. **Color-111min.** Janet Gaynor, Fredric March 5*

STAR IS BORN, A (1976). Remorseful former rock idol Kris Kristofferson is consoled by wife Barbra Streisand after he's made a distressing spectacle of himself at an awards ceremony honoring her.

STAR IS BORN, A (1954) Warner Bros. **Color-154min.** Judy Garland, James Mason 5½*

STAR IS BORN, A (1976) Warner Bros. **Color-140min.** Barbra Streisand, Kris Kristofferson 5*

STAR MAKER, THE (1939) Paramount. **B&W-94min.** Bing Crosby, Louise Campbell .... (4)

STAR OF INDIA (1953) United Artists. **Color-97min.** (British-Italian). Cornel Wilde, Jean Wallace .... (4)

STAR OF MIDNIGHT (1935) RKO. **B&W-90min.** William Powell, Ginger Rogers .... (5)

STAR OF TEXAS, THE (1953) Allied Artists. **B&W-68min.** Wayne Morris, Paul Fix .... (4)

STAR SAID NO, THE (1950) *see* CALLAWAY WENT THATAWAY

STAR SPANGLED GIRL (1971) Paramount. **Color-93min.** Sandy Duncan, Tony Roberts .... (4)

STAR SPANGLED RHYTHM (1942) Paramount. **B&W-99min.** Victor Moore, Betty Hutton, Eddie Bracken .... (5)

STAR TREK - THE MOTION PICTURE (1979) Paramount. **Color-   min.** William Shatner, Leonard Nimoy, DeForrest Kelley ....

STAR WARS (1977) 20th Century-Fox. **Color-121min.** Mark Hamill, Harrison Ford 8*

STAR WITNESS (1931) Warner Bros. **B&W-68min.** Walter Huston, Dickie Moore .... (4)

STARCRASH (1979) New World. **Color-92min.** (Italian). Caroline Munro, Marjoe Gortner, Christopher Plummer 4*

STARDUST (1974) Columbia. **Color-113min.** (British). David Essex, Adam Faith .... (4)

STARFIGHTERS, THE (1963) Parade. **Color-78min.** Robert Dornan, Richard Jordahl 2½*

STARHOPS (1978) First American Films. **Color-82min.** Dorothy Buhrman, Sterling Frazier, Jillian Kesner ....

STARK FEAR (1962) Ellis Films. **B&W-86min.** Beverly Garland, Skip Homeier, Kenneth Tobey .... (3)

STARLIFT (1951) Warner Bros. **B&W-103min.** Jancie Rule, Ron Hagerthy, Doris Day, Ruth Roman .... (3)

STARLIGHT SLAUGHTER (1976) *see* EATEN ALIVE

STARS AND STRIPES FOREVER (1952) 20th Century-Fox. **Color-89min.** Clifton Webb, Debra Paget, Robert Wagner .... (5)
British title: MARCHING ALONG

STARS ARE SINGING, THE (1953) Paramount. **Color-99min.** Rosemary Clooney, Anna Maria Alberghetti, Lauritz Melchior .... (4)

STARS IN MY CROWN (1950) M-G-M. **B&W-89min.** Joel McCrea, Ellen Drew .... (5)

STARS LOOK DOWN (1939) M-G-M. **B&W-110min.** (British). Michael Redgrave, Margaret Lockwood .... (5)

STARS OVER BROADWAY (1935) Warner Bros. **B&W-89min.** Pat O'Brien, James Melton, Jane Froman .... (5)

STARSHIP INVASIONS (1977) Warner Bros. **Color-89min.** (Canadian). Robert Vaughn, Christopher Lee, Tiiu Leek 3*

START CHEERING (1938) Columbia. **B&W-78min.** Charles Starrett, Jimmy Durante, Walter Connolly .... (5)

START THE REVOLUTION WITHOUT ME (1970) Warner Bros. **Color-98min.** Gene Wilder 4*

STARTING OVER (1979) Paramount. **Color-   min.** Burt Reynolds, Candice Bergen ....

STATE DEPARTMENT -- FILE 649 (1948) Four Continents. **Color-87min.** William Lundigan, Virginia Bruce .... (3)
British title: ASSIGNMENT IN CHINA

STATE FAIR (1933) Fox Film Co. [20th]. **B&W-80min.** Will Rogers, Janet Gaynor .... (5)

STATE FAIR (1945) 20th Century-Fox. **Color-100min.** Charles Winninger, Fay Bainter 4*
TV title: IT HAPPENED ONE SUMMER

STATE FAIR (1962) 20th Century-Fox. **Color-118min.** Pat Boone, Bobby Darin 4*

STATE OF SIEGE (1973) Cinema 5. **Color-120min.** (French). Yves Montand, Renato Salvatori 4*
Original title: ETAT DE SIEGE

STATE OF THE UNION (1948) M-G-M. **B&W-124min.** Spencer Tracy, Katharine Hepburn 5½*
British title: WORLD AND HIS WIFE, THE

STATE PENITENTIARY (1950) Columbia. **B&W-66min.** Warner Baxter, Onslow Stevens .... (3)

STATE SECRET (1950) Columbia. **B&W-97min.** (British). Douglas Fairbanks, Jr., Glynis Johns, Jack Hawkins 4*
Alternate title: GREAT MANHUNT, THE

STATELESS (1962) *see* NO EXIT

STATE'S ATTORNEY (1932) RKO. **B&W-73min.** John Barrymore, Helen Twelvetrees .... (4)
British title: CARDIGAN'S LAST CASE

STATION SIX - SAHARA (1963) Allied Artists. **B&W-99min.** (British-W. German). Carroll Baker, Peter Van Eyck, Ian Bannen .... (3)
German title: ENDSTATION 13 SAHARA

STATION WEST (1948) RKO. **B&W-92min.** Dick Powell, Jan Greer ...... (5)

STATUE, THE (1971) Cinerama Releasing. **Color-92min.** David Niven, Virna Lisi, Robert Vaughn .... (2)

STAY AWAY JOE (1968) M-G-M. **Color-101min.** Elvis Presley, Burgess Meredith .... (2)

STAY HUNGRY (1976) United Artists. **Color-102min.** Jeff Bridges, Sally Field, Arnold Schwarzenegger 5*

STEAGLE, THE (1971) Avco-Embassy. **Color-90min.** Richard Benjamin, Chill Wills .... (3)

STEAMBOAT BILL, JR. (1928) United Artists. **B&W-70min.** (Silent). Buster Keaton, Marion Byron 6*

STEAMBOAT 'ROUND THE BEND (1935) 20th Century-Fox. **B&W-96min.** Will Rogers, Anne Shirley .... (4)

STEEL AGAINST THE SKY (1941) Warner Bros. **B&W-68min.** Alexis Smith, Craig Stevens, Lloyd Nolan .... (3)

STEEL ARENA (1973) L-T Films. **Color-98min.** Dusty Russell, Laura Brooks, Bruce Mackey .... (3)

STEEL BAYONET, THE (1957) United Artists. **B&W-84min.** (British). Leo Genn, Kieron Moore .... (3)

STEEL CAGE, THE (1954) United Artists. **B&W-80min.** Paul Kelly, Maureen O'Sullivan .... (3)

STEEL CLAW, THE (1961) Warner Bros. **Color-96min.** George Montgomery, Charito Luna .... (3)

STEEL FIST, THE (1952) Monogram [Allied Artists]. **B&W-73min.** Roddy McDowall, Kristine Miller .... (3)

STEEL HELMET, THE (1951) Lippert Productions. **B&W-84min.** Gene Evans, Robert Hutton .... (4)

STEEL JUNGLE, THE (1956) Warner Bros. **B&W-86min.** Perry Lopez, Beverly Garland .... (3)

STEEL KEY, THE (1953) Eros Films (Brit.). **B&W-69min.** (British). Terence Morgan, Joan Rice .... (4)

STEEL LADY, THE (1953) United Artists. **B&W-84min.** Rod Cameron, Tab Hunter, John Dehner, Anthony Caruso .... (3)
British title: TREASURE OF KALIFA

STEEL TOWN (1952) Universal. **Color-85min.** Ann Sheridan, John Lund, Howard Duff 4½*

STEEL TRAP, THE (1952) 20th Century-Fox. B&W-85min. Joseph Cotten, Teresa Wright ....(5)

STEELYARD BLUES (1973) Warner Bros. Color-92min. Jane Fonda, Donald Sutherland 3*

STEFANIA (1967) Chancellor Films. B&W-92min. *(Greek).* Zoe Laskari, Spiros Focas ....(2)
Original title: STEPHANIA

STELLA (1950) 20th Century-Fox. B&W-83min. Ann Sheridan, Victor Mature ....(4)

STELLA DALLAS (1926) United Artists. B&W-135min. *(Silent).* Ronald Colman, Belle Bennett ....(4)

STELLA DALLAS (1937) United Artists. B&W-111min. Barbara Stanwyck, John Boles 4*

STELLA MARIS (1918) Paramount-Artcraft. B&W-7reels Mary Pickford, Conway Tearle ....(4)

STEP BY STEP (1946) RKO. B&W-62min. Lawrence Tierney, Anne Jeffreys ....(3)

STEP DOWN TO TERROR (1959) Universal. B&W-75min. Colleen Miller, Charles Drake, Rod Taylor ....(3)
British title: SILENT STRANGER, THE

STEP LIVELY (1944) RKO. B&W-88min. Frank Sinatra, George Murphy 4½*

STEP OUT OF LINE, A (1971) Cinema Center 100. Color-100min. *(Made for TV).* Vic Morrow, Peter Falk, Peter Lawford ....(5)

STEPFORD WIVES, THE (1975) Columbia. Color-114min. Katharine Ross, Peter Masterson 5*

STEPMOTHER, THE (1972) Crown International. Color-94min. Alejandro Rey, John Anderson, Katherine Justice 3*

STEPPENWOLF (1974) D/R Films. Color-105min. *(Swiss-U.S., English language).* Max Von Sydow, Dominique Sanda 3*

STEPPIN' IN SOCIETY (1945) Republic. B&W-72min. Edward Everett Horton, Ruth Terry ....(3)

STERILE CUCKOO, THE (1969) Paramount. Color-107min. Liza Minnelli, Wendell Burton 6*
British title: POOKIE

STEVIE (1978) First Artists. Color-102min. Glenda Jackson, Mona Washbourne ....(4)

STEWARDESSES, THE (1969) Sherpix. Color-93min. Christina Hart, Paula Erikson ....(2)
Publicity title: AIRLINE STEWARDESS

STICK UP, THE (1978) Color-101min. *(British).* David Soul, Pamela McMyler ....

STIGMA (1972) Cinerama Releasing. Color-93min. Philip M. Thomas, Harlan Cary Poe, Josie Johnson ....(3)

STILETTO (1969) Avco-Embassy. Color-98min. Alex Cord, Britt Ekland, Patrick O'Neal ....(3)

STING, THE (1973) Universal. Color-127min. Paul Newman, Robert Redford, Robert Shaw 7*

STINGAREE (1934) RKO. B&W-76min. Irene Dunne, Richard Dix ....(4)

STINGRAY (1978) Avco-Embassy. Color-99min. Christopher Mitchum, Sherry Jackson, Les Lannom 4*

STOLEN FACE (1952) Lippert Productions. B&W-71min. *(U.S.-British).* Paul Henreid, Lizabeth Scott 4*

STOLEN HEAVEN (1938) Paramount. B&W-88min. Nancy Carroll, Phillips Holmes ....(4)

STOLEN HOLIDAY (1937) Warner Bros. B&W-80min. Kay Francis, Claude Rains ....(3)

STOLEN HOURS (1963) United Artists. Color-100min. *(U.S.-British).* Susan Hayward, Michael Craig 3½*

STOLEN KISSES (1968) Lopert [U.A.]. Color-90min. *(French).* Jean-Pierre Leaud, Delphine Seyrig 5*
Original title: BAISERS VOLES

STOLEN LIFE, A (1946) Warner Bros. B&W-107min. Bette Davis 4*

STONE KILLER, THE (1973) Columbia. Color-95min. Charles Bronson, Martin Balsam 4*

STONESTREET: WHO KILLED THE CENTERFOLD MODEL? (1976) MCA-TV. Color-74min. *(Made for TV).* Barbara Eden, Joseph Mascolo, Richard Basehart, Joan Hackett ....(4)

STONY ISLAND (1978) Color-97min. Richard Davis, Edward Stoney Robinson ....

STOOGE, THE (1953) Paramount. B&W-100min. Dean Martin, Jerry Lewis, Polly Bergen 4*

STOOGES GO WEST (1951) *see* GOLD RAIDERS

STOOLIE, THE (1972) JaMa Prods. Color-90min. Jackie Mason, Marcia Jean Kurtz 3*

STOP! LOOK! AND LAUGH! (1960) Columbia. B&W-78min. The Three Stooges 3*

STOP ME BEFORE I KILL! (1961) Columbia. B&W-93min. *(British).* Claude Dauphin, Diane Cilento, Ronald Lewis ....(4)
Original title: FULL TREATMENT, THE
Prerelease U.S. title: TREATMENT, THE

STOP THE WORLD - I WANT TO GET OFF (1966) Warner Bros. Color-98min. *(British).* Tony Tanner, Millicent Martin ....(4)

STOP TRAIN 349 (1964) Allied Artists. B&W-95min. *(W. German-French-Italian).* José Ferrer, Sean Flynn, Nicole Courcel ....(3)
Original German title: VERSPATUNG IN MARIENBORN
French title: TRAIN DE BERLIN EST ARRETÉ, LE *(The Berlin Train Is Stopped)*
Italian title: TRENO E FERMO A BERLINO, UN

STOP, YOU'RE KILLING ME (1953) Warner Bros. Color-86min. Broderick Crawford, Claire Trevor 4*

STOPOVER TOKYO (1957) 20th Century-Fox. Color-100min. Edmond O'Brien, Joan Collins, Robert Wagner 4*

STORK CLUB, THE (1945) Paramount. B&W-98min. Betty Hutton, Barry Fitzgerald ....(4)

STORK TALK (1962) Parade. B&W-85min. *(British).* Tony Britton, Anne Heywood ....(3)

STORM, THE (1938) Universal. B&W-85min. Charles Bickford, Barton MacLane ....(4)

STORM AT DAYBREAK (1933) M-G-M. B&W-80min. Kay Francis, Walter Huston ....(4)

STORM BOY (1976) S.A.F.C. *(Australian).* Color-88min. *(Australian).* Greg Rowe, Peter Cummins ....

STORM CENTER (1956) Columbia. B&W-85min. Bette Davis, Brian Keith 3*

STORM FEAR (1956) United Artists. B&W-88min. Cornel Wilde, Jean Wallace, Dan Duryea 4*

STORM IN A TEACUP (1937) United Artists. B&W-87min. *(British).* Rex Harrison, Vivien Leigh 5*

STORM IN JAMAICA (1958) *see* PASSIONATE SUMMER

STORM OF STRANGERS, A (1972) Modern Talking Picture Service. B&W-27min. *(Documentary).* 4½*

STORM OVER AFRICA (1953) *see* ROYAL AFRICAN RIFLES, THE

STORM OVER LISBON (1944) Republic. B&W-86min. Vera Hruba Ralston, Richard Arlen ....(3)

STORM OVER THE NILE (1955) Columbia. Color-107min. *(British).* Anthony Steel, Laurence Harvey 4*

STORM OVER THE PACIFIC, THE (1960) *see* I BOMBED PEARL HARBOR

STORM OVER TIBET (1952) Columbia. B&W-87min. Rex Reason, Diana Douglas ....(4)

STORM RIDER, THE (1957) 20th Century-Fox. B&W-70min. Scott Brady, Mala Powers 2*

STORM WARNING (1951) Warner Bros. B&W-93min. Ginger Rogers, Ronald Reagan ....(5)

STORMY, THE THOROUGHBRED (1954) Buena Vista. Color-45min. M. R. Valdez, George Swinebroad 4*

STORMY WATERS (1939) M-G-M. B&W-77min. *(French).* Jean Gabin, Michele Morgan ....(4)
Original title: REMORQUES

STORMY WEATHER (1943) 20th Century-Fox. B&W-77min. Lena Horne, Bill Robinson 4*

STORY OF A LOVE AFFAIR (1950) New Yorker Films. B&W-102min. *(Italian).* Luca Bose, Massimo Girotti ....
Original title: CRONACA DI UN AMORE

STORY OF A TEENAGER (1976) *see* JIM, THE WORLD'S GREATEST

STORY OF A THREE-DAY PASS, THE (1968) Sigma III. B&W-87min. *(French).* Harry Baird, Nicole Berger ....(5)
Original title: PERMISSION, LA *(The Pass)*

STORY OF A WOMAN (1969) Universal. Color-90min. *(Italian-U.S.).* Bibi Andersson, Robert Stack, James Farentino 3*
Original title: Italian title: STORIA DI UNA DONNA

STORY OF ADELE H., THE (1975) New World. Color-95min. *(French).* Isabelle Adjani, Bruce Robinson 4½*
Original title: HISTOIRE D'ADELE H., L'

Films are rated on a 1 to 10 scale, 10 is highest. **Boldface** ratings followed by an asterisk (*) are for films actually seen and rated by the executive and senior editors. All other ratings are estimates. (See Notes on Entertainment Ratings in the front section.)

STORY OF ALEXANDER GRAHAM BELL, THE (1939) 20th Century-Fox. B&W-97min. Don Ameche, Loretta Young 5*
Publicity title: ALEXANDER GRAHAM BELL
British title: MODERN MIRACLE, THE

STORY OF DAVID, A (1960) American-International. Color-99min. (*British*). Jeff Chandler, Basil Sydney .... (3)
Alternate title: DAVID THE OUTLAW

STORY OF DAVID, THE (1976) CPT (TV). Color-200min. (*Made for TV*). Timothy Bottoms, Keith Michel, Anthony Quayle 5*

STORY OF DINAH EAST, THE (1970) *see* DINAH EAST

STORY OF DR. EHRLICH'S MAGIC BULLET, THE (1940) *see* DR. EHRLICH'S MAGIC BULLET

STORY OF DR. WASSELL, THE (1944) Paramount. Color-140min. Gary Cooper, Laraine Day 4*

STORY OF ESTHER COSTELLO, THE (1957) Columbia. B&W-104min. (*British*). Heather Sears, Joan Crawford, Rossano Brazzi .... (4)

STORY OF G. I. JOE, THE (1945) United Artists. B&W-109min. Burgess Meredith, Robert Mitchum 3*
Alternate title: G. I. JOE

STORY OF GILBERT AND SULLIVAN, THE (1953) *see* GILBERT AND SULLIVAN

STORY OF JACOB AND JOSEPH, THE (1973) CPT (TV). Color-100min. Keith Michell, Tony Lo Bianco, Colleen Dewhurst 4½*

STORY OF JOANNA, THE (1975) Blueberry Hill Films. Color-86min. Terri Hall, Jamie Gillis, Zebedy Colt .... (2)

STORY OF JOSEPH AND HIS BRETHREN, THE (1960) Colorama Features. Color-103min. (*Italian*). Geoffrey Horne, Robert Morley, Belinda Lee .... (3)
Original title: GIUSEPPE VENDUTO DAI FRATELLI (*Joseph Sold By His Brothers*)
Alternate title: JOSEPH AND HIS BRETHREN

STORY OF LENNY BRUCE - DIRTYMOUTH, THE (1970) *see* DIRTYMOUTH

STORY OF LOUIS PASTEUR, THE (1936) Warner Bros. B&W-87min. Paul Muni, Josephine Hutchinson 5*

STORY OF MANDY, THE (1952) *see* CRASH OF SILENCE

STORY OF MANKIND, THE (1957) Warner Bros. Color-100min. Ronald Colman, Vincent Price 4*

STORY OF MOLLY X, THE (1949) Universal. B&W-82min. June Havoc, John Russell .... (4)

STORY OF O, THE (1975) Allied Artists. Color-97min. (*French*). Corinne Clery, Udo Kier 3*
Original title: HISTORIE D'O

STORY OF PRETTY BOY FLOYD, THE (1974) MCA-TV. Color-74min. (*Made for TV*). Martin Sheen, Michael Parks, Kim Darby 3*
Alternate title: PRETTY BOY FLOYD

STORY OF PRIVATE DOOLEY (1962) *see* SURVIVOR, THE

STORY OF ROBIN HOOD, THE (1952) RKO (for Disney). Color-84min. (*U.S.-British*). Richard Todd, Joan Rice, Peter Finch .... (5)
British title: STORY OF ROBIN HOOD AND HIS MERRIE MEN, THE

STORY OF RUTH, THE (1960) 20th Century-Fox. Color-132min. Elana Eden, Stuart Whitman .... (4)

STORY OF SEABISCUIT, THE (1949) Warner Bros. Color-93min. Shirley Temple, Barry Fitzgerald .... (4)
British title: PRIDE OF KENTUCKY

STORY OF THE COUNT OF MONTE CRISTO, THE (1961) Warner Bros. Color-132min. (*French-Italian*). Louis Jourdan, Yvonne Furneaux .... (3)
Original French title: COMTE DE MONTE CRISTO, LE
Italian title: CONTE DI MONTECRISTO, IL
Publicity title: COUNT OF MONTE CRISTO, THE
Publicity title: STORY OF MONTE CRISTO, THE

STORY OF THE GREAT GILBERT AND SULLIVAN, THE (1953) *see* GILBERT AND SULLIVAN

STORY OF THREE LOVES, THE (1953) M-G-M. Color-122min. Moira Shearer, James Mason 4*

STORY OF VERNON AND IRENE CASTLE, THE (1939) RKO. B&W-93min. Fred Astaire, Ginger Rogers 4*

STORY OF VICKIE, THE (1958) Buena Vista. Color-108min. (*Austrian*). Romy Schneider, Adrian Hoven 2*
Original title: MAEDCHENJAHRE EINER KOENIGIN (*Girlhood of a Queen*)
Alternate title: PURSUIT AND LOVES OF QUEEN VICTORIA, THE

STORY OF WILL ROGERS, THE (1952) Warner Bros. Color-109min. Will Rogers, Jr., Jane Wyman 4½*

STORY ON PAGE ONE, THE (1960) 20th Century-Fox. B&W-123min. Rita Hayworth, Anthony Franciosa 4*

STOWAWAY (1936) 20th Century-Fox. B&W-86min. Shirley Temple, Robert Young 4*

STOWAWAY GIRL (1957) Paramount. B&W-87min. (*British*). Trevor Howard, Pedro Armendariz, Elsa Martinelli .... (4)
Original title: MANUELA

STOWAWAY IN THE SKY (1960) Lopert [U.A.]. Color-82min. (*French*). Pascal Lamorisse, André Gille .... (5)
Original title: VOYAGE EN BALLON, LE (*The Voyage in a Balloon*)

STRADA, LA (1954) Trans-Lux Distributing. B&W-115min. (*Italian*). Anthony Quinn, Giulietta Masina, Richard Basehart 4*
Translation title: The Road

STRAIGHT TIME (1978) Warner Bros. Color-114min. Dustin Hoffman, Theresa Russell 5*

STRAIT-JACKET (1964) Columbia. B&W-89min. Joan Crawford, Diane Baker .... (4)

STRANDED (1935) Warner Bros. B&W-76min. George Brent, Kay Francis .... (4)

STRANDED (1967) *see* VALLEY OF MYSTERY

STRANDED IN PARIS (1938) *see* ARTISTS AND MODELS ABROAD

STRANGE ADVENTURE, A (1956) Republic. B&W-70min. Ben Cooper, Marla English .... (3)

STRANGE ADVENTURE OF DAVID GRAY, THE (1932) *see* VAMPYR

STRANGE AFFAIR, THE (1968) Paramount. Color-106min. (*British*). Michael York, Jeremy Kemp, Susan George .... (3)

STRANGE AFFAIR OF UNCLE HARRY, THE (1945) *see* UNCLE HARRY

STRANGE AFFECTION (1957) Joseph Brenner. B&W-84min. (*British*). Richard Attenborough, Colin Petersen .... (4)
Original title: SCAMP, THE

STRANGE ALIBI (1941) Warner Bros. B&W-63min. Arthur Kennedy, Joan Perry .... (3)

STRANGE ALIBI (1946) *see* STRANGE TRIANGLE

STRANGE AWAKENING (1958) Anglo Amalgamated [EMI]. B&W-69min. (*British*). Lex Barker, Carole Mathews .... (2)

STRANGE BARGAIN (1949) RKO. B&W-68min. Martha Scott, Jeffrey Lynn .... (3)

STRANGE BEDFELLOWS (1965) Universal. Color-99min. Rock Hudson, Gina Lollobrigida 4½*

STRANGE CARGO (1940) M-G-M. B&W-105min. Joan Crawford, Clark Gable 5*

STRANGE CASE OF DR. JEKYLL AND MR. HYDE, THE (1968) ABC-TV. Color-136min. (*Made for TV*). Jack Palance, Billie Whitelaw, Oscar Homolka ....
Common title error: DR. JEKYLL AND MR. HYDE

STRANGE CASE OF MADELEINE, THE (1949) *see* MADELEINE

STRANGE CASE OF MURDER, A (1940) *see* ANGEL STREET

STRANGE CONDUCT (1951) *see* PIT OF LONELINESS

STRANGE CARGO (1940). "I said I'd be here, baby," quips convict Clark Gable, having slipped away from the Guiana penal colony where he's a prisoner; café entertainer Joan Crawford hadn't expected him to keep his word so soon.

STRANGE CONFESSION (1944) see IMPOSTOR, THE

STRANGE CONFESSION (1945) Universal. **B&W-62min.** Lon Chaney (Jr.), Brenda Joyce..............(4)

STRANGE CONQUEST (1946) Universal. **B&W-64min.** Jane Wyatt, Lowell Gilmore..............(3)

STRANGE CONSPIRACY (1935) see PRESIDENT VANISHES, THE

STRANGE COUNTESS, THE (1961) Casino Films. **B&W-98min.** *(German).* Joachim Fuchsberger, Brigitte Grothum..............(3)
Original title: SELTSAME GRAEFFIN, DIE

STRANGE DEATH OF ADOLF HITLER, THE (1943) Universal. **B&W-72min.** Gale Sondergaard, Ludwig Donath..............**3***

STRANGE DOOR, THE (1951) Universal. **B&W-81min.** Charles Laughton, Boris Karloff..............**3½***

STRANGE FASCINATION (1952) Columbia. **B&W-80min.** Hugo Haas, Cleo Moore..............(3)

STRANGE HOLIDAY (1946) Producers Rel. Corp. [Eagle Lion]. **B&W-55min.** Claude Rains, Barbara Bates..............(3)
British title: DAY AFTER TOMORROW, THE

STRANGE INCIDENT, THE (1943) see OX-BOW INCIDENT, THE

STRANGE INTERLUDE (1932) M-G-M. **B&W-110min.** Norma Shearer, Clark Gable..............**3***
British title: STRANGE INTERVAL

STRANGE INTRUDER (1956) Allied Artists. **B&W-82min.** Edmund Purdom, Ida Lupino..............**4***

STRANGE INTRUSION (1953) see UNHOLY INTRUDERS, THE

STRANGE JOURNEY (1946) 20th Century-Fox. **B&W-65min.** Paul Kelly, Osa Massen..............(3)

STRANGE LADY IN TOWN (1955) Warner Bros. **Color-112min.** Greer Garson, Dana Andrews..............**4***

STRANGE LOVE OF MARTHA IVERS, THE (1946) Paramount. **B&W-117min.** Barbara Stanwyck, Van Heflin..............**4***

STRANGE MR. GREGORY, THE (1946) Monogram [Allied Artists]. **B&W-64min.** Edmund Lowe, Jean Rogers..............(3)

STRANGE NEW WORLD (1975) Warner Bros. **Color-100min.** John Saxon, Kathleen Miller, James Olson, Martine Beswick..............**3***

STRANGE ONE, THE (1957) Columbia. **B&W-100min.** Ben Gazzara, George Peppard..............**3½***
British title: END AS A MAN

STRANGE ONES, THE (1950) Mayer-Kingsley. **B&W-95min.** *(French).* Nicole Stephane, Edouard Dermithe..............(4)
Original title: ENFANTS TERRIBLES, LES

STRANGE POSSESSION OF MRS. OLIVER, THE (1977) NBC-TV. **Color-74min.** *(Made for TV).* Karen Black, George Hamilton, Robert F. Lyons..............(3)

STRANGE SHADOWS IN AN EMPTY ROOM (1977) American-International. **Color-99min.** *(Canadian).* Stuart Whitman, John Saxon, Tisa Farrow..............
Original title: BLAZING MAGNUMS

STRANGE TRIANGLE (1946) 20th Century-Fox. **B&W-65min.** Preston Foster, Signe Hasso, John Shepperd (Shepperd Strudwick)..............(3)
Alternate title: STRANGE ALIBI

STRANGE VENGEANCE OF ROSALIE, THE (1972) 20th Century-Fox. **Color-107min.** Ken Howard, Bonnie Bedelia..............(2)

STRANGE WOMAN, THE (1946) United Artists. **B&W-100min.** Hedy Lamarr, George Sanders, Louis Hayward..............(4)

STRANGE WORLD (1952) United Artists. **B&W-85min.** Angelica Hauff, Alexander Carlos..............(3)

STRANGE WORLD OF PLANET X, THE (1958) see COSMIC MONSTER, THE

STRANGER, THE (1946) RKO. **B&W-95min.** Orson Welles, Loretta Young, Edward G. Robinson..............**4***

STRANGER, THE (1962) see INTRUDER, THE

STRANGER, THE (1967) Paramount. **Color-104min.** *(Italian-French-Algerian).* Marcello Mastroianni, Anna Karina..............(4)
Original Italian title: STRANIERO, LO
French title: ÉTRANGER, L'

STRANGER, THE (1972) Viacom. **Color-98min.** *(Made for TV).* Glenn Corbett, Cameron Mitchell, Lew Ayres, Sharon Acker..............**4***

STRANGER AND THE GUNFIGHTER, THE (1975) Columbia. **Color-107min.** *(Hong Kong-Italian-Spanish-U.S.).* Lee Van Cleef, Lo Lieh, Patty Shepard..............**4½***
British title: BLOOD MONEY

STRANGER AT MY DOOR (1956) Republic. **B&W-85min.** Macdonald Carey, Patricia Medina..............(4)

STRANGER CAME HOME, THE (1954) see UNHOLY FOUR, THE

STRANGER FROM HONG KONG (1964) American-International. **B&W-85min.** *(French).* Dalila, Chin Sing Long..............(2)

STRANGER IN BETWEEN, THE (1952) Universal. **B&W-84min.** *(British).* Dirk Bogarde, Kay Walsh..............(5)
Original title: HUNTED

STRANGER IN HOLLYWOOD (1968) Emerson Film Enterprises & Roda Productions. **Color-96min.** Sue Bernard, Scott Every..............(3)

STRANGER IN MY ARMS (1959) Universal. **B&W-88min.** June Allyson, Jeff Chandler..............**4***

STRANGER IN THE HOUSE (1967) see COP-OUT

STRANGER IN THE HOUSE (1975) see BLACK CHRISTMAS

STRANGER IN TOWN, A (1943) M-G-M. **B&W-67min.** Frank Morgan, Richard Carlson..............(4)

STRANGER IN TOWN (1957) Astor. **B&W-74min.** *(British).* Alex Nicol, Colin Tapley, Anne Paige..............(3)

STRANGER IN TOWN, A (1966) M-G-M. **Color-86min.** *(Italian-U.S.).* Tony Anthony, Frank Wolff..............(2)
Italian title: DOLLARO TRA I DENTI, UN *(A Dollar in the Teeth)*

STRANGER KNOCKS, A (1959) Trans-Lux Distributing. **B&W-81min.** *(Danish).* Birgitte Federspiel, Preben Lerdorff Rye..............(4)
Original title: FREMMED BANKER PAA, EN

STRANGER ON HORSEBACK (1955) United Artists. **Color-66min.** Joel McCrea, Miroslava..............(4)

STRANGER ON THE PROWL (1953) United Artists. **B&W-87min.** *(Italian-U.S.).* Paul Muni, Joan Lorring..............**3***
Original title: IMBARCO A MEZZANOTTE
U.S. pre-release title: ENCOUNTER

STRANGER ON THE RUN (1967) Universal. **Color-97min.** *(Made for TV).* Henry Fonda, Michael Parks, Anne Baxter, Dan Duryea..............**4***

STRANGER ON THE THIRD FLOOR (1940) RKO. **B&W-64min.** Peter Lorre, John McGuire, Margaret Tallichet..............**4½***

STRANGER RETURNS, THE (1967) M-G-M. **Color-90min.** *(Italian-W. German-U.S.).* Tony Anthony, Dan Vadis, Marco Guglielmi..............(2)
Original Italian title: UOMO, UN CAVALLO, UNA PISTOLA, UN *(A Man, A Horse, A Gun)*

STRANGER WALKED IN, A (1947) see LOVE FROM A STRANGER

STRANGER WHO LOOKS LIKE ME, THE (1974) Worldvision. **Color-74min.** *(Made for TV).* Meredith Baxter, Beau Bridges..............(4)

STRANGER WITH A GUN (1958) see SHEEPMAN, THE

STRANGER WITHIN, THE (1974) Viacom. **Color-74min.** *(Made for TV).* Barbara Eden, George Grizzard..............**3½***

STRANGER WORE A GUN, THE (1953) Columbia. **Color-83min.** Randolph Scott, Claire Trevor..............**3***

STRANGERS (1954) Fine Arts. **B&W-80min.** *(Italian).* Ingrid Bergman, George Sanders..............(3)
Original title: VIAGGIO IN ITALIA *(Journey to Italy)*
Alternate title: JOURNEY TO ITALY
Alternate title: VOYAGE TO ITALY
Alternate title: TRIP IN ITALY, A
Alternate title: LONELY WOMAN, THE

STRANGER'S GUNDOWN, THE (1969) New Line Cinema. **Color-107min.** *(Italian).* Anthony Steffen, Lu Kamante, Rada Rassimov..............(3)
Original title: DJANGO IL BASTARDO *(Django the Bastard)*

STRANGER'S HAND, THE (1954) Distributors Corp. of America. **B&W-85min.** *(British-Italian).* Trevor Howard, Alida Valli..............**4***
Italian title: MANO DELLA STRANGIERO

STRANGERS IN AFRICA (1971) Manson. **Color-95min.** *(Foreign).* Darr Poran, Carrie Rochelle, Alice Marie..............(3)

STRANGERS IN LOVE (1932) Paramount. **B&W-76min.** Fredric March, Kay Francis..............(3)

STRANGERS IN 7A, THE (1972) Viacom. **Color-74min.** *(Made for TV).* Andy Griffith, Ida Lupino, Suzanne Hildur..............**4***

STRANGERS IN THE CITY (1962) Avco-Embassy. **B&W-83min.** Robert Gentile, Camilo Delgado..............(4)

STRANGERS IN THE NIGHT (1944) Republic. **B&W-56min.** William Terry, Virginia Grey..............(4)

STRANGERS MAY KISS (1931) M-G-M. **B&W-85min.** Norma Shearer, Robert Montgomery..............(3)

STRANGERS' MEETING (1957) J. Arthur Rank. **B&W-64min.** *(British).* Peter Arne, Delphi Lawrence..............(3)

STRANGERS ON A TRAIN (1951) Warner Bros. **B&W-101min.** Farley Granger, Robert Walker..............**5***

STRANGER'S RETURN, THE (1933) M-G-M. **B&W-89min.** Lionel Barrymore, Franchot Tone, Miriam Hopkins..............(4)

Films are rated on a 1 to 10 scale, 10 is highest. **Boldface** ratings followed by an asterisk (*) are for films actually seen and rated by the executive and senior editors. All other ratings are estimates. (See Notes on Entertainment Ratings in the front section.)

STRANGERS WHEN WE MEET (1960) Columbia. Color-117min. Kirk Douglas, Kim Novak 4*

STRANGEST CASE, THE (1943) see CRIME DOCTOR'S STRANGEST CASE, THE

STRANGLEHOLD (1962) J. Arthur Rank. B&W-73min. (British). Macdonald Carey, Barbara Shelley .... (4)

STRANGLER, THE (1964) Allied Artists. B&W-89min. Victor Buono, David McLean, Diane Sayer.................... 4*

STRANGLER OF BLACKMOOR CASTLE, THE (1963) Telewide Systems. B&W-89min. (German). Karin Dor, Ingmar Zeisberg .... (3)
Original title: WURGER VON SCHLOSS BLACKMOOR, DER

STRANGLERS OF BOMBAY, THE (1959) Columbia. B&W-80min. (British). Guy Rolfe, Allan Cuthbertson .... (3)

STRANGLER'S WEB (1965) Avco-Embassy. B&W-55min. (British). John Stratton, Pauline Munro, Griffith Jones........ (3)

STRATEGIC AIR COMMAND (1955) Paramount. Color-114min. James Stewart, June Allyson 3*

STRATEGY OF TERROR (1969) Universal. Color-90min. (Telefeature). Hugh O'Brian, Barbara Rush .... (3)
Original title: IN DARKNESS WAITING

STRATFORD ADVENTURE, THE (1954) Continental [Walter Reade]. Color-40min. (Canadian, Documentary). Director: Morten Parker........ (5)

STRATTON STORY, THE (1949) M-G-M. B&W-106min. James Stewart, June Allyson 3*

STRAW DOGS (1971) Cinerama Releasing. Color-113min. (British-U.S.). Dustin Hoffman, Susan George 6½*

STRAWBERRY BLONDE, THE (1941) Warner Bros. B&W-97min. James Cagney, Olivia de Havilland 4*

STRAWBERRY STATEMENT, THE (1970) M-G-M. Color-103min. Bruce Davison, Kim Darby 4*

STRAY DOG (1949) Toho. B&W-122min. (Japanese). Toshiru Mifune, Takashi Shimura, Ko Kimura .... (4)
Original title: NORA INU

STREET ANGEL (1928) Fox Film Co. [20th]. B&W-102min. (Part-talking). Janet Gaynor, Charles Farrell.............. (4)

STREET BANDITS (1951) Republic. B&W-54min. Robert Clarke, Roy Barcroft, Ross Ford .... (2)

STREET CORNER (1953) see BOTH SIDES OF THE LAW

STREET GANGS OF HONG KONG (1974) Cinerama Releasing. Color-100min. (Hong Kong). Wang Chung, Lilli Li, Betty (Pei Ti) .... (2)

STREET OF CHANCE (1930) Paramount. B&W-75min. William Powell, Jean Arthur, Kay Francis................... (4)

STREET OF CHANCE (1942) Paramount. B&W-74min. Burgess Meredith, Claire Trevor......................... (4)

STREET OF DARKNESS (1958) Republic. B&W-60min. Robert Keys, John Close .... (2)

STREET OF MEMORIES (1940) 20th Century-Fox. B&W-70min. Lynne Roberts, Guy Kibbee, John McGuire .... (3)

STREET OF SHADOWS (1953) see SHADOW MAN, THE

STREET OF SHAME (1956) Harrison Pictures. B&W-96min. (Japanese). Machiko Kyo, Toranosuke Ogawa .... (4)

STREET OF SORROW, THE (1925) Brandon. B&W-90min. (German). Greta Garbo, Jaro Furth, Werner Krauss, Asta Nielsen........ 2*
Original title: FREUDLOSE GASSE, DIE (The Joyless Street)
British title: JOYLESS STREET, THE

STREET PEOPLE (1976) American-International. Color-92min. (U.S.-Italian). Roger Moore, Stacy Keach, Ivo Garrani .... (4)

STREET SCENE (1931) United Artists. B&W-80min. Sylvia Sidney, William Collier, Jr. 4½*

STREET WITH NO NAME, THE (1948) 20th Century-Fox. B&W-91min. Mark Stevens, Richard Widmark 5*

STREETCAR NAMED DESIRE, A (1951) Warner Bros. B&W-125min. Vivien Leigh, Marlon Brando.................. 6½*

STREETFIGHTER, THE (1975) New Line Cinema. Color-92min. (Japanese). Sonny (Shin'ichi) Chiba, Gerald Yakamada ...... (2)
Original title: GEKITOTSU SATSUJINKEN
Publicity title: KARATE, THE

STREETFIGHTER, THE (1975) see HARD TIMES

STREETS OF LAREDO (1949) Paramount. Color-92min. William Holden, Macdonald Carey, William Bendix............ 4*

STREETS OF PARIS (1959) see RUE DE PARIS

STREETS OF SAN FRANCISCO (1949) Republic. B&W-60min. Robert Armstrong, Mae Clarke, Wally Cassell .... (3)

STREETS OF SAN FRANCISCO, THE (1972) Warner Bros. Color-98min. (Made for TV). Karl Malden, Michael Douglas, Robert Wagner, Kim Darby .... (4)

STRICTLY CONFIDENTIAL (1934) see BROADWAY BILL

STRICTLY DISHONORABLE (1951) M-G-M. B&W-86min. Ezio Pinza, Janet Leigh .... (4)

STRICTLY FOR PLEASURE (1959) see PERFECT FURLOUGH, THE

STRIKE (1925) Brandon. B&W-82min. (U.S.S.R., Silent). Grigori Alexandrov, Maxim Strauch .... (5)

STRIKE AND HYDE (1980) United Artists. Color- min. Bette Midler ..

STRIKE IT RICH (1948) Allied Artists. B&W-81min. Rod Cameron, Don Castle .... (3)

STRIKE ME DEADLY (1963) see CRAWLING HAND, THE

STRIKE ME PINK (1936) United Artists. B&W-104min. Eddie Cantor, Ethel Merman 4*

STRIKE UP THE BAND (1940) M-G-M. B&W-120min. Mickey Rooney, Judy Garland 4*

STRIP, THE (1951) M-G-M. B&W-85min. Mickey Rooney, Sally Forrest, Louis Armstrong .... (3)

STRIP-TEASE LADY (1943) see LADY OF BURLESQUE

STRIP TEASE MURDER (1963) Paramount. B&W-66min. (British). John Hewer, Ann Lynn .... (3)

STRIPPER, THE (1963) 20th Century-Fox. B&W-95min. Joanne Woodward, Richard Beymer 4*
British title: WOMAN OF SUMMER

STROMBOLI (1950) RKO. B&W-89min. (Italian). Ingrid Bergman, Mario Vitale .... (3)

STRONG MAN, THE (1926) First National [W.B.]. B&W-90min. (Silent). Harry Langdon, Priscilla Bonner......... (5)

STRONGER THAN FEAR (1950) see EDGE OF DOOM

STRONGEST MAN IN THE WORLD, THE (1963) see MOLE MEN AGAINST THE SON OF HERCULES

STRONGEST MAN IN THE WORLD, THE (1975) Buena Vista. Color-92min. Kurt Russell, Joe Flynn, Cesar Romero........ 3*

STRONGHOLD (1952) Lippert Productions. B&W-82min. Zachary Scott, Veronica Lake, Arturo De Cordova .... (2)

STRONGROOM (1962) Union Film Distributors. B&W-80min. (British). Derren Nesbitt, Colin Gordon, Ann Lynn .... (3)

STROSZEK (1977) New Yorker Films. Color-108min. (German). Bruno S., Eva Mattes, Clemens Scheitz........ 4*

STRUGGLE, THE (1931) United Artists. B&W-77min. Hal Skelly, Zita Johann 3*

STUD, THE (1978) Color-90min. (British). Joan Collins, Oliver Tobias, Emma Jacobs .... (4)

STUDENT NURSES, THE (1970) New World. Color-85min. Elaine Giftos, Karen Carlson, Barbara Leigh .... (2)

STUDENT OF PRAGUE, THE (1926) see MAN WHO CHEATED LIFE

STUDENT PRINCE, THE (1954) M-G-M. Color-107min. Ann Blyth, Edmund Purdom 5*

STUDS LONIGAN (1960) United Artists. B&W-103min. Christopher Knight, Frank Gorshin, Venetia Stevenson........ (3)

STUDY IN TERROR, A (1965) Columbia. Color-94min. (British-W. German). John Neville, Donald Houston, John Fraser ...... (3)
German title: SHERLOCK HOLMES GROSSTER FALL

STUNTMAN (1968) Paramount. Color-95min. (Italian-French). Gina Lollobrigida, Robert Vilaro .... (3)
French title: CASCADEUR, LE

STUNTS (1977) New Line Cinema. Color-90min. Robert Forster, Fiona Lewis............................ (4)

SUBJECT WAS ROSES, THE (1968) M-G-M. Color-107min. Patricia Neal, Jack Albertson, Martin Sheen 5½*

SUBMARINE COMMAND (1951) Paramount. B&W-87min. William Holden, Nancy Olson 3*

SUBMARINE D-1 (1937) First National [W.B.]. B&W-54min. Pat O'Brien, George Brent 3*

SUBMARINE PATROL (1938) 20th Century-Fox. B&W-95min. Richard Greene, Nancy Kelly .... (5)

SUBMARINE RAIDER (1942) Columbia. B&W-64min. John Howard, Larry Parks .... (4)

SUBMARINE SEAHAWK (1959) American-International. B&W-83min. John Bentley, Brett Halsey................ (3)

SUBMARINE X-1 (1968) United Artists. B&W-89min. (British). James Caan, Rupert Davies .... (3)

Films are rated on a 1 to 10 scale, 10 is highest. **Boldface** ratings followed by an asterisk (*) are for films actually seen and rated by the executive and senior editors. All other ratings are estimates. (See Notes on Entertainment Ratings in the front section.)

SUBMARINE ZONE (1940) *see* ESCAPE TO GLORY

SUBMERSION OF JAPAN (1973) *see* TIDAL WAVE

SUBMISSION (1973) *see* PETS

SUBMISSION (1975) Joseph Brenner. Color-107min. *(Italian).* Lisa Gastoni, Franco Nero, Raymond Pellegrin ....
Original title: SCANDALO

SUBTERFUGE (1968) Commonwealth United TV. Color-89min. *(British-U.S.).* Gene Barry, Joan Collins, Richard Todd .... (3)

SUBTERRANEANS, THE (1960) M-G-M. Color-89min. Leslie Caron, George Peppard .... (3)

SUBURBAN WIVES (1972) Scotia International *(Brit.).* Color-87min. *(British).* Eva Whishaw, Maggie Wright, Peter May .... (2)

SUBWAY IN THE SKY (1959) United Artists. B&W-85min. *(British).* Van Johnson, Hildegarde Neff .... (3)

SUCCESSFUL CALAMITY, A (1932) Warner Bros. B&W-72min. George Arliss, Mary Astor, Randolph Scott .... (4)

SUCCESSO, IL (1963) Avco-Embassy. B&W-103min. *(Italian-French).* Vittorio Gassman, Anouk Aimée .... (5)
Translation title: The Success

SUCCUBUS (1968) American-International. Color-83min. *(German).* Janine Reynaud, Jack Taylor .... (2)
Original title: NECRONOMICON - GETRAUMTE SUNDEN *(Necronomicon - Dreamed Sins)*

SUCH A GORGEOUS KID LIKE ME (1972) Columbia. Color-98min. *(French).* Bernadette LaFont, Charles Denner .... (5)
Original title: BELLE FILLE COMME MOI, UNE

SUCH GOOD FRIENDS (1971) Paramount. Color-101min. Dyan Cannon, James Coco 4*

SUCH MEN ARE DANGEROUS (1955) *see* RACERS, THE

SUCKER, THE (1965) Royal Films Int'l [Columbia]. Color-112min. *(French-Italian).* Bourvil, Louis De Funes .... (5)
Original title: CORNIAUD, LE *(The Jerk)*

SUDAN (1945) Universal. Color-76min. Maria Montez, Jon Hall, Turhan Bey 4*

SUDDEN DANGER (1955) Allied Artists. B&W-85min. Bill Elliott, Beverly Garland .... (4)

SUDDEN FEAR (1952) RKO. B&W-110min. Joan Crawford, Jack Palance .... (5)

SUDDEN TERROR (1970) National General. Color-95min. *(British).* Mark Lester, Lionel Jeffries, Susan George 4*
Original title: EYEWITNESS

SUDDENLY (1954) United Artists. B&W-77min. Frank Sinatra, Sterling Hayden .... (5)

SUDDENLY IT'S SPRING (1947) Paramount. B&W-87min. Paulette Goddard, Fred MacMurray .... (3)

SUDDENLY, LAST SUMMER (1959) Columbia. B&W-114min. *(British-U.S.).* Elizabeth Taylor, Katharine Hepburn, Montgomery Clift 4½*

SUDDENLY SINGLE (1971) Worldvision. Color-73min. *(Made for TV).* Hal Holbrook, Barbara Rush, Margot Kidder .... (4)

SUEZ (1938) 20th Century-Fox. B&W-104min. Tyrone Power, Loretta Young .... (5)

SUGAR HILL (1974) American-International. Color-90min. Marki Bey, Robert Quarry, Don Pedro Colley 3*
British title: VOODOO GIRL

SUGARFOOT (1951) Warner Bros. Color-80min. Randolph Scott, Raymond Massey, Adele Jergens .... (3)
Alternate title: SWIRL OF GLORY, A

SUGARLAND EXPRESS, THE (1974) Universal. Color-109min. Goldie Hawn, William Atherton, Michael Sacks 5½*

SUICIDE BATTALION (1958) American-International. B&W-79min. Michael Connors, Jewell Lian 2*

SUICIDE CLUB, THE (1936) *see* TROUBLE FOR TWO

SUICIDE COMMANDOS (1968) NTA Pictures. Color-94min. *(Italian-Spanish).* Aldo Ray, Gaetano Cimarossa, Vira Silenti 3*
Italian title: COMMANDO SUICIDA
Spanish title: COMANDO SUICIDA

SUICIDE MISSION (1956) Columbia. B&W-69min. *(British-Norwegian).* Leif Larsen, Michael Aldridge .... (3)

SUICIDE RUN (1970) *see* TOO LATE THE HERO

SUICIDE SQUADRON (1941) RKO. B&W-98min. Anton Walbrook, Sally Gray .... (5)
Original title: DANGEROUS MOONLIGHT

SUITABLE CASE FOR TREATMENT, A (1966) *see* MORGAN!

THE SUGARLAND EXPRESS (1974). Escaped convict William Atherton and wife Goldie Hawn force highway patrolman Michael Sacks to drive them to their destination.

SUITOR, THE (1963) Atlantic Pictures. B&W-83min. *(French).* Pierre Etaix, Laurence Ligneres .... (5)
Original title: SOUPIRANT, LE

SULEIMAN THE CONQUERER (1961) Medallion. Color-99min. *(Italian).* Loris Gizzi, Edmund Purdom, Georgia Moll, Alberto Farnese .... (3)
Original title: SOLIMANO IL CONQUISTATORE

SULLIVANS, THE (1944) 20th Century-Fox. B&W-111min. Anne Baxter, Thomas Mitchell .... (4)
Alternate title: FIGHTING SULLIVANS, THE

SULLIVAN'S EMPIRE (1967) Universal. Color-85min. Martin Milner, Linden Chiles .... (3)

SULLIVAN'S TRAVELS (1941) Paramount. B&W-91min. Joel McCrea, Veronica Lake 6*

SUMMER AND SMOKE (1961) Paramount. Color-118min. Geraldine Page, Laurence Harvey 5*

SUMMER HOLIDAY (1948) M-G-M. Color-92min. Mickey Rooney, Gloria De Haven .... (4)

SUMMER HOLIDAY (1963) American-International. Color-100min. *(British).* Cliff Richard, Lauri Peters .... (4)

SUMMER INTERLUDE (1951) *see* ILLICIT INTERLUDE

SUMMER LIGHTNING (1948) *see* SCUDDA HOO! SCUDDA HAY!

SUMMER LOVE (1958) Universal. B&W-85min. John Saxon, Judy (Judi) Meredith, Rod McKuen .... (3)

SUMMER MADNESS (1955) *see* SUMMERTIME

SUMMER MAGIC (1963) Buena Vista. Color-109min. Hayley Mills, Burl Ives .... (4)

SUMMER MANOEUVRES (1955) *see* GRAND MANEUVER, THE

SUMMER OF '42 (1971) Warner Bros. Color-102min. Jennifer O'Neill, Gary Grimes 6*

SUMMER OF MY GERMAN SOLDIER (1978) NBC-TV. Color-100min. *(Made for TV).* Kristy McNichol, Bruce Davison ....

SUMMER OF SECRETS (1976) Greater Union Film Distributors (Australian). Color-100min. *(Australian).* Arthur Dignam, Rufus Collins, Kate Fitzpatrick ....

SUMMER OF THE SEVENTEENTH DOLL (1960) *see* SEASON OF PASSION

SUMMER PLACE, A (1959) Warner Bros. Color-130min. Richard Egan, Dorothy McGuire, Sandra Dee, Troy Donahue 5*

SUMMER RUN (1974) Lighthouse Prods. Color-96min. Andy Parks, Tina Lund .... (3)

SUMMER SCHOOL TEACHERS (1977) New World. Color-86min. Candice Rialson, Pat Anderson .... (4)

SUMMER SOLDIERS (1972) Roninfilm. Color-107min. *(Japanese).* Keith Sykes, Lee Reisen .... (4)

SUMMER STOCK (1950) M-G-M. Color-109min. Judy Garland, Gene Kelly...4*
British title: IF YOU FEEL LIKE SINGING

SUMMER STORM (1944) United Artists. B&W-106min. George Sanders, Linda Darnell..(4)

SUMMER TALES (1958) *see* LOVE ON THE RIVIERA

SUMMER TO REMEMBER, A (1960) Kingsley International. B&W-80min. (U.S.S.R.). Borya Barkhatov, Sergei Bondarchuk ....(5)
Original Russian title: SERYOZHA *(Serge)*
British title: SPLENDID DAYS, THE

SUMMER WISHES, WINTER DREAMS (1973) Columbia. Color-87min. Joanne Woodward, Martin Balsam 3*

SUMMER WITH MONIKA, A (1953) *see* MONIKA

SUMMER WITHOUT BOYS, A (1973) Warner Bros. Color-74min. *(Made for TV).* Barbara Bain, Kay Lenz, Michael Moriarty 3*

SUMMERSKIN (1961) Angel Productions. B&W-96min. *(Argentinian).* Alfredo Alcon, Graciela Borges ....(4)
Original title: PIEL DE VERANO

SUMMERTIME (1955) United Artists. Color-99min. Katharine Hepburn, Rossano Brazzi 4*
British title: SUMMER MADNESS

SUMMERTIME KILLER, THE (1973) Avco-Embassy. Color-103min. *(Spanish-Italian-French).* Christopher Mitchum, Karl Malden, Olivia Hussey 3*
Original Spanish title: VERANO PARA MATAR, UN
French title: MEURTRES AU SOLEIL

SUMMERTREE (1971) Columbia. Color-88min. Michael Douglas, Jack Warden 4*

SUMURU (1967) *see* MILLION EYES OF SU-MURU, THE

SUN ALSO RISES, THE (1957) 20th Century-Fox. Color-129min. Tyrone Power, Ava Gardner, Errol Flynn 5*

SUN COMES UP, THE (1949) M-G-M. Color-93min. Lassie, Jeanette MacDonald, Claude Jarman, Jr.............................(4)

SUN NEVER SETS, THE (1939) Paramount. B&W-98min. Douglas Fairbanks, Jr., Basil Rathbone 3½*

SUN SETS AT DAWN (1951) United Artists. B&W-71min. Sally Parr, Philip Shawn ....(4)

SUN SHINES BRIGHT, THE (1953) Republic. B&W-92min. Charles Winninger, Arleen Whelan ....(5)

SUN VALLEY SERENADE (1941) 20th Century-Fox. B&W-86min. John Payne, Sonja Henie 4½*

SUNBONNET SUE (1945) Monogram [Allied Artists]. B&W-89min. Gale Storm, Phil Regan ....(3)

SUNDAY BLOODY SUNDAY (1971) United Artists. Color-110min. *(British).* Glenda Jackson, Peter Finch, Murray Head 3*

SUNDAY DINNER FOR A SOLDIER (1944) 20th Century-Fox. B&W-86min. Anne Baxter, John Hodiak 3*

SUNDAY ENCOUNTER (1958) B&W-90min. *(French).* Bourvil, Arletty, Danielle Darrieux ....(3)
Original title: DROLE DE DIMANCHE, UN

SUNDAY IN NEW YORK (1964) M-G-M. Color-105min. Rod Taylor, Jane Fonda 5½*

SUNDAY PUNCH (1942) M-G-M. B&W-75min. William Lundigan, Jean Rogers, Dan Dailey, Jr...............................(3)

SUNDAY WOMAN (1975) 20th Century-Fox. Color-110min. *(Italian-French).* Marcello Mastroianni, Jacqueline Bisset, Jean-Louis Trintignant ....(5)
Original title: DONNA DELLA DOMENICA, LA

SUNDAYS AND CYBELE (1962) Davis-Royal Films International-Columbia. B&W-110min. *(French).* Hardy Kruger, Patricia Gozzi 3*
Original title: DIMANCHES DE VILLE D'AVRAY, LES *(Sundays at Ville D'Avray)*

SUNDERIN, DIE (1951) Cellini Films. B&W-83min. *(German).* Hildegarde Neff, Gustav Froehlich ....(4)
Translation title: The Sinner

SUNDOWN (1941) United Artists. B&W-90min. Gene Tierney, Bruce Cabot, George Sanders ....(4)

SUNDOWNERS, THE (1950) Eagle Lion. Color-83min. Robert Preston, Robert Sterling 4½*
British title: THUNDER IN THE DUST

SUNDOWNERS, THE (1960) Warner Bros. Color-133min. Robert Mitchum, Deborah Kerr....................................6*

SUNFLOWER (1969) Avco-Embassy. Color-101min. *(Italian-French).* Sophia Loren, Marcello Mastroianni........................(4)
Original Italian title: GIRASOLI, I
French title: FLEURS DU SOLEIL, LES

SUNNY (1930) First National [W.B.]. B&W-81min. Marilyn Miller, Lawrence Gray ....(3)

SUNNY (1941) RKO. B&W-98min. Anna Neagle, Ray Bolger.............(4)

SUNNY SIDE OF THE STREET (1951) Columbia. Color-71min. Frankie Laine, Terry Moore....................................(3)

SUNNY SIDE UP (1929) Fox Film Co. [20th]. B&W-115min. Janet Gaynor, Charles Farrell, El Brendel........................(4)

SUNNYSIDE (1979) American-International. Color-100min. Joey Travolta, Stacey Pickren..

SUNRISE - A SONG OF TWO HUMANS (1927) Fox Film Co. [20th]. B&W-97min. *(Silent).* George O'Brien, Janet Gaynor.....................4*
Alternate title: SUNRISE

SUNRISE AT CAMPOBELLO (1960) Warner Bros. Color-143min. Ralph Bellamy, Greer Garson 5*

SUNSCORCHED (1964) Feature Film Corp. Color-78min. *(Spanish-W. German, English language).* Mark Stevens, Mario Adorf, Marianne Koch ....(3)
Original Spanish title: TIERRA DE FUEGO *(Land of Fire)*
German title: VERGELTUNG IN CATANO

SUNSEED (1973) Ram Film. Color-92min. *(Documentary).* Director: Frederick Cohn ....(3)

SUNSET BOULEVARD (1950) Paramount. B&W-110min. Gloria Swanson, William Holden 7*

SUNSET COVE (1978) *see* MALIBU BEACH

SUNSHINE (1973) MCA-TV. Color-121min. *(Made for TV).* Brenda Vaccaro, Cliff DeYoung, Christina Raines ....(4)

SUNSHINE BOYS, THE (1975) U.A. (for M-G-M). Color-111min. Walter Matthau, George Burns 6*

SUNSHINE PATRIOT, THE (1968) Universal. Color-98min. *(Made for TV).* Cliff Robertson, Dina Merrill, Wilfrid Hyde-White ....(5)

SUPER COPS, THE (1974) U.A. (for M-G-M). Color-95min. Ron Leibman, David Selby..4½*

SUPER DICK (1971) *see* CRY UNCLE

SUPER DRAGON (1966) *see* SECRET AGENT SUPER DRAGON

SUPER FLY (1972) Warner Bros. Color-97min. Ron O'Neal, Carl Lee, Sheila Frazier 4*

SUPER FLY T.N.T. (1973) Paramount. Color-87min. Ron O'Neal, Roscoe Lee Browne, Sheila Frazier ....(3)

SUPER GIANT (1964) *see* ATOMIC RULERS OF THE WORLD

SUPER SLEUTH (1937) RKO. B&W-70min. Ann Sothern, Jack Oakie ..(4)

SUPERBEAST (1972) United Artists. Color-93min. Antoinette Bower, Craig Littler, Harry Lauter ....(3)

SUPERDAD (1974) Buena Vista. Color-96min. Bob Crane, Barbara Rush ....(4)

SUPERMAN (1949) Columbia. B&W-88min. *(Re-edited Serial).* Kirk Alyn, Noel Neill ....(4)

SUPERMAN (1978) Warner Bros. Color-143min. *(U.S.-British).* Christopher Reeve, Margot Kidder, Gene Hackman, Marlon Brando 6½*

SUPERNATURAL (1933) Paramount. B&W-60min. Carole Lombard, Randolph Scott ....(4)

SUPPORT YOUR LOCAL GUNFIGHTER (1971) United Artists. Color-92min. James Garner, Susanne Pleshette, Jack Elam 3*

SUPPORT YOUR LOCAL SHERIFF! (1969) United Artists. Color-92min. James Garner, Joan Hackett 5½*

SUPPOSE THEY GAVE A WAR AND NOBODY CAME (1970) Cinerama Releasing. Color-113min. Brian Keith, Tony Curtis ....(4)

SURF PARTY (1964) 20th Century-Fox. B&W-68min. Bobby Vinton, Patricia Morrow, Jackie DeShannon....................................(2)

SURFARI (1967) Don Brown & Canyon Pictures. Color-90min. *(Documentary).* Director: Milton Blair ....(3)
Alternate title: BLUE SURFARI

SURGEON'S KNIFE, THE (1957) Distributors Corp. of America. B&W-75min. *(British).* Donald Houston, Adrienne Corri ....(3)

SURPRISE PACKAGE (1960) Columbia. B&W-100min. Yul Brynner, Mitzi Gaynor..(4)

SURRENDER (1950) Republic. B&W-90min. Vera Ralston, John Carroll, Walter Brennan ....(4)

SURRENDER - HELL! (1959) Allied Artists. B&W-85min. Keith Andes, Susan Cabot ....(3)

SURROGATE, THE (1970) *see* CHALLENGE, THE

SURVIVAL (1965) *see* GUIDE, THE

Films are rated on a 1 to 10 scale, 10 is highest. **Boldface** ratings followed by an asterisk (*) are for films actually seen and rated by the executive and senior editors. All other ratings are estimates. (See Notes on Entertainment Ratings in the front section.)

SURVIVE! (1976) Paramount. **Color-105min.** *(Mexican).* Pablo Ferrel, Hugo Stiglitz 4*
Original title: SUPERVIVIENTES DE LOS ANDES *(Survivors of the Andes)*

SURVIVOR, THE (1962) B&W-83min. *(British).* Gary Wagner 4*
Alternate title: STORY OF PRIVATE POOLEY

SUSAN AND GOD (1940) M-G-M. B&W-115min. Fredric March, Joan Crawford 3½*
British title: GAY MRS. TREXEL, THE

SUSAN LENNOX - HER FALL AND RISE (1931) M-G-M. B&W-75min. Greta Garbo, Clark Gable, Jean Hersholt .... (4)
Alternate title: SUSAN LENNOX
British title: RISE OF HELGA, THE

SUSAN SLADE (1961) Warner Bros. Color-116min. Connie Stevens, Dorothy McGuire 3*

SUSAN SLEPT HERE (1954) RKO. Color-98min. Dick Powell, Debbie Reynolds 4*

SUSANNAH OF THE MOUNTIES (1939) 20th Century-Fox. B&W-78min. Shirley Temple, Randolph Scott .... (4)

SUSPECT, THE (1945) Universal. B&W-85min. Charles Laughton, Ella Raines 5*

SUSPECT (1960) *see* RISK, THE

SUSPENDED ALIBI (1956) J. Arthur Rank. B&W-64min. *(British).* Patrick Holt, Honor Blackman, Valentine Dyall .... (2)
Alternate title: SUSPECTED ALIBI

SUSPENSE (1946) Monogram [Allied Artists]. B&W-101min. Barry Sullivan, Belita .... (4)

SUSPICION (1941) RKO. B&W-99min. Cary Grant, Joan Fontaine 5*

SUSPIRIA (1976) EMI. Color-97min. *(Italian, English version).* Jessica Harper, Stefania Casini 4*

SUTTER'S GOLD (1936) Universal. B&W-94min. Edward Arnold, Lee Tracy .... (5)

SUZY (1936) M-G-M. B&W-99min. Jean Harlow, Franchot Tone, Cary Grant 4*

SVENGALI (1931) Warner Bros. B&W-76min. John Barrymore, Marian Marsh 3½*

SVENGALI (1954) M-G-M. Color-82min. *(British).* Donald Wolfit, Hildegarde Neff .... (4)

SWALLOWS AND AMAZONS (1974) LDS. Color-92min. *(British).* Virginia McKenna, Simon West, Kit Seymour ....

SWAMP DIAMONDS (1955) *see* SWAMP WOMEN

SWAMP FIRE (1946) Paramount. B&W-69min. Buster Crabbe, Johnny Weissmuller .... (3)

SWAMP GIRL (1971) Jack Vaughn Productions. Color-78min. Ferlin Husky, Simone Griffeth, Donna Stanley .... (3)

SWAMP OF THE LOST MONSTER, THE (1965) Trans-International. Color-80min. *(Mexican).* Gaston Santos, Manola Savedra .... (1)
Alternate title: SWAMP OF THE LOST SOULS, THE

SWAMP WATER (1941) 20th Century-Fox. B&W-90min. Dana Andrews, Walter Brennan, Anne Baxter 4*
British title: MAN WHO CAME BACK, THE

SWAMP WOMEN (1955) Woolner Brothers. Color-73min. Michael Connors, Marie Windsor, Beverly Garland .... (3)
Alternate title: SWAMP DIAMONDS
Alternate title: CRUEL SWAMP

SWAN, THE (1956) M-G-M. Color-112min. Grace Kelly, Alec Guinness.. 5*

SWAN LAKE (1957) Columbia. Color-81min. *(U.S.S.R.).* Maya Plisteskaya, Nicolai Fadeyechev .... (5)

SWANEE RIVER (1939) 20th Century-Fox. Color-84min. Don Ameche, Andrea Leeds, Al Jolson .... (4)

SWAPPERS, THE (1970) Trans-America. Color-84min. *(British).* James Donnelly, Larry Taylor, Valerie St. John .... (2)
Alternate title: WIFE SWAPPERS, THE

SWARM, THE (1978) Warner Bros. Color-116min. Michael Caine, Katharine Ross, Richard Widmark 4½*

SWASHBUCKLER (1976) Universal. Color-101min. Robert Shaw, James Earl Jones 5½*
British title: SCARLET BUCCANEER, THE

SWASTIKA (1973) Cinema 5. B&W-105min. *(British, Documentary).* Director: Philippe Mora ....

SWEATER GIRL (1942) Paramount. B&W-77min. Eddie Bracken, June Preisser .... (3)

SWEATER GIRLS (1978) Mirror Releasing. Color-85min. Kate Sarchet, Carol Ann Seflinger 5½*

SWEDEN - HEAVEN AND HELL (1968) Avco-Embassy. **Color-90min.** *(Italian, Documentary).* Director: Luigi Scattini .... (1)
Original title: SVEZIA, INFERNO E PARADISO
Publicity title: SWEDEN - HEAVEN OR HELL

SWEDISH FLY GIRLS (1971) American-International. **Color-100min.** *(U.S.-Danish).* Birte Tove, Clinton Greyn, Daniel Gelin .... (3)
Alternate title: CHRISTA

SWEDISH WEDDING NIGHT (1964) Royal Films Int'l [Columbia]. B&W-95min. *(Swedish).* Jarl Kulle, Christina Schollin, Lars Passgard .... (3)
Original title: BROLLOPSBESVAR

SWEENEY (1977) EMI. Color-98min. *(British).* John Thaw, Dennis Waterman ....

SWEENEY 2 (1978) EMI. Color-108min. *(British).* John Thaw, Dennis Waterman, Denholm Elliott ....

SWEET ADELINE (1935) Warner Bros. B&W-87min. Irene Dunne, Donald Woods .... (4)

SWEET ALOES (1936) *see* GIVE ME YOUR HEART

SWEET AND LOW-DOWN (1944) 20th Century-Fox. B&W-75min. Benny Goodman, James Cardwell, Lynn Bari, Linda Darnell .... (3)

SWEET AND SOUR (1963) Pathé Contemporary. B&W-93min. *(French-Italian).* Guy Bedos, Jean-Pierre Marielle, Sophie Daumier .... (3)
Original French title: DRAGÉES AU POIVRE
Italian title: CONFETTI AL PEPE

SWEET BIRD OF YOUTH (1962) M-G-M. Color-120min. Paul Newman, Geraldine Page 5½*

SWEET BODY OF DEBORAH, THE (1968) Warner Bros. Color-95min. *(Italian-French).* Carroll Baker, Jean Sorel, George Hilton .... (3)
Original Italian title: DOLCE CORPO DI DEBORAH, IL
French title: ADORABLE CORPS DE DEBORAH, L'
Publicity title: SOFT BODY OF DEBORAH, THE
Publicity title: SWEET BODY, THE

SWEET CHARITY (1969) Universal. Color-157min. Shirley MacLaine, Ricardo Montalban 5½*

SWEET CREEK COUNTY WAR, THE (1979) Key International. Color-99min. Richard Egan, Albert Salmi, Tom Jackman .... (3)

SWEET GEORGIA (1972) Boxoffice International. Color-81min. Marsha Jordan, Barbara Mills, Gene Drew, Chuck Lawson .... (4)

SWEET JESUS, PREACHER MAN (1973) M-G-M. Color-103min. Roger E. Mosley, William Smith, Michael Pataki .... (4)

SWEET LIGHT IN A DARK ROOM (1960) Promenade. B&W-93min. *(Czech).* Ivan Mistrik, Dana Smutna .... (5)
Original title: ROMEO, JULIE A TMA

SWEET LOVE, BITTER (1967) Film 2 Associates & Peppercorn-Wormser. B&W-92min. Dick Gregory, Don Murray .... (4)
Alternate title: IT WON'T RUB OFF, BABY!
Alternate title: BLACK LOVE - WHITE LOVE

SWEET NOVEMBER (1968) Warner Bros. Color-114min. Anthony Newley, Sandy Dennis 4*

SWEET CHARITY (1969). A quarrel between movie idol Ricardo Montalban and his girlfriend Barbara Bouchet sets the stage for taxi dancer Shirley MacLaine to spend the evening with him.

SWEET REVENGE (1976) see DANDY, THE ALL AMERICAN GIRL

SWEET RIDE, THE (1968) 20th Century-Fox. Color-110min. Anthony Franciosa, Michael Sarrazin, Jacqueline Bisset......2*

SWEET ROSIE O'GRADY (1943) 20th Century-Fox. Color-74min. Betty Grable, Robert Young......(4)

SWEET SAVIOUR (1971) Trans World Attractions. Color-90min. Troy Donahue, Renay Granville......(2)

SWEET SMELL OF SUCCESS (1957) United Artists. B&W-96min. Burt Lancaster, Tony Curtis......5*

SWEET SUZY (1973) Signal 166, Inc. Color-82min. Anouska Hempel, David Warbeck, Percy Herbert......(3)
Original title: BLACKSNAKE
British title: SLAVES

SWEET, SWEET RACHEL (1971) ABC Films. Color-73min. (Made for TV). Alex Dreier, Stefanie Powers, Chris Robinson......2*

SWEET SWEETBACK'S BAADASSSSS SONG (1971) Cinemation. Color-97min. Melvin Van Peebles, Simon Chuckster......(3)

SWEET TORONTO (1972) Pennebaker Productions. Color-135min. (Music Film). Director: D. A. Pennebaker......(4)
Alternate title: KEEP ON ROCKIN'

SWEETHEART OF SIGMA CHI (1946) Monogram [Allied Artists]. B&W-75min. Phil Regan, Elyse Knox......(3)

SWEETHEART OF THE GODS (1959) Telewide Systems. B&W-107min. (German). Peter Van Eyck, Ruth Leuwerik......(4)

SWEETHEARTS (1938) M-G-M. Color-120min. Jeanette MacDonald, Nelson Eddy......4½*

SWEETHEARTS ON PARADE (1953) Republic. Color-90min. Ray Middleton, Lucille Norman......(3)

SWELL GUY (1947) Universal. B&W-87min. Sonny Tufts, Ann Blyth ...(4)

SWEPT AWAY . . . (1974) Cinema 5. Color-116min. (Italian). Giancarlo Giannini, Mariangela Melato......5½*
Original title: TRAVOLTI DA UN INSOLITO DESTINO NELL'AZZURRO MARE D'AGOSTO
Screen title: SWEPT AWAY . . . BY AN UNUSUAL DESTINY IN THE BLUE SEA OF AUGUST
Publicity title: OVERCOME BY AN UNUSUAL FATE IN A BLUE AUGUST SEA

SWIM TEAM (1979) Color- min. Jenny Newman, Richard Young, Steven Furst......

SWIMMER, THE (1968) Columbia. Color-94min. Burt Lancaster, Janice Rule......5*

SWIMMING POOL, THE (1969) Avco-Embassy. Color-87min. (French-Italian). Alain Delon, Romy Schneider, Maurice Ronet, Jane Birkin..(3)
Original French title: PISCINE, LA
Italian title: PISCINA, LA

SWINDLE, THE (1955) see BIDONE, IL

SWING FEVER (1944) M-G-M. B&W-80min. Kay Kyser, Marilyn Maxwell, Lena Horne......(2)

SWING HIGH, SWING LOW (1937) Paramount. B&W-97min. Carole Lombard, Fred MacMurray......(4)

SWING SHIFT MAISIE (1943) M-G-M. B&W-87min. Ann Sothern, James Craig......(3)
British title: GIRL IN OVERALLS, THE

SWING, TEACHER, SWING (1938) see COLLEGE SWING

SWING TIME (1936) RKO. B&W-103min. Fred Astaire, Ginger Rogers 5*

SWING YOUR LADY (1938) Warner Bros. B&W-79min. Humphrey Bogart, Penny Singleton, Nat Pendleton......3*

SWING YOUR PARTNER (1943) Republic. B&W-72min. Esther Dale, Dale Evans, Roger Clark......(3)

SWINGER, THE (1966) Paramount. Color-81min. Ann-Margret, Tony Franciosa......3*

SWINGERS' PARADISE (1964) American-International. Color-83min. (British). Cliff Richard, Walter Slezak, Susan Hampshire......3*
Original title: WONDERFUL LIFE

SWINGIN' ALONG (1962) 20th Century-Fox. Color-74min. Tommy Noonan, Peter L. Marshall, Barbara Eden......(3)

SWINGIN' MAIDEN, THE (1962) Columbia. Color-98min. (British). Michael Craig, Anne Helm......(3)
Original title: IRON MAIDEN, THE

SWINGIN' ON A RAINBOW (1945) Republic. B&W-72min. June Frazee, Brad Taylor......(4)

SWINGIN' SUMMER, A (1965) United Screen Arts. Color-80min. William Wellman, Jr., Quinn O'Hara, James Stacy, Raquel Welch......(2)

SWINGING PEARL MYSTERY, THE (1936) see PLOT THICKENS, THE

SWINGING SET, THE (1964) see GET YOURSELF A COLLEGE GIRL

SWINGTIME JOHNNY (1944) Universal. B&W-61min. Peter Cookson, Harriet Hilliard, The Andrews Sisters......(3)

SWIRL OF GLORY, A (1951) see SUGARFOOT

SWISS FAMILY ROBINSON (1940) RKO. B&W-93min. Thomas Mitchell, Edna Best......(5)

SWISS FAMILY ROBINSON, THE (1960) Buena Vista. Color-126min. John Mills, Dorothy McGuire......5*

SWISS FAMILY ROBINSON (1975) 20th Century-Fox. Color-74min. (Made for TV). Martin Milner, Pat Delaney, Eric Olsen, Cindy Fisher 4*

SWISS MISS (1938) M-G-M. B&W-72min. Stanley Laurel, Oliver Hardy, Della Lind......3*

SWISS TOUR (1950) see FOUR DAYS' LEAVE

SWITZERLAND (1955) Buena Vista. Color-33min. (Travelog). Director: Ben Sharpsteen......5*

SWORD AND THE CROSS, THE (1956) Valiant. Color-87min. (Italian). Gianna Maria Canale, Jorge Mistral, Marisa Allasio......(2)
Original title: SCHIAVE DE CARTEGENE, LE (The Slaves of Carthage)

SWORD AND THE DRAGON, THE (1956) Valiant. Color-83min. (U.S.S.R.). Boris Andreyev, Andrei Abrikosov, Natalie Medvedeva......(3)
Original title: ILYA MOUROMETZ
British title: EPIC HERO AND THE BEAST, THE

SWORD AND THE ROSE, THE (1953) RKO (for Disney). Color-93min. (British-U.S.). Richard Todd, Glynis Johns......(4)
TV title: WHEN KNIGHTHOOD WAS IN FLOWER

SWORD IN THE DESERT (1949) Universal. B&W-100min. Dana Andrews, Marta Toren......4*

SWORD IN THE STONE, THE (1963) Buena Vista. Color-75min. (Cartoon). Director: Wolfgang Reitherman......(5)

SWORD OF ALI BABA, THE (1965) Universal. Color-81min. Peter Mann, Jocelyn Lane......(3)

SWORD OF DAMASCUS (1963) American-International. Color-93min. (Italian). Tony Russel, Luciana Gilli......(1)
Original title: LADRO DI DAMASCO, IL (The Thief of Damascus)

SWORD OF EL CID, THE (1963) Production Releasing Corp.-Eldorado Pictures. Color-86min. (Spanish-Italian). Roland Carey, Sandro Moretti......(2)
Original Spanish title: HIJAS DEL CID, LAS (The Daughters of the Cid)
Italian title: SPADA DEL CID, LA

SWORD OF GRANADA (1960) Azteca. B&W-80min. (Mexican). Cesar Romero, Katy Jurado......(3)

SWORD OF ISLAM (1962) Color-90min. (Italian). Silvana Pampanini, Abed Elaziz......(1)

SWORD OF LANCELOT (1963) Universal. Color-116min. (British). Cornel Wilde, Jean Wallace, Brian Aherne......4*
Original title: LANCELOT AND GUINEVERE

SWORD OF MONTE CRISTO, THE (1951) 20th Century-Fox. Color-81min. George Montgomery, Paula Corday......3½*

SWORD OF SHERWOOD FOREST (1960) Columbia. Color-80min. (British). Richard Greene, Peter Cushing, Sarah Branch......(4)

SWORD OF THE CONQUEROR (1961) United Artists. Color-95min. (Italian). Jack Palance, Eleanora Rossi-Drago, Guy Madison......(3)
Original title: ROSMUNDA E ALBOINO (Rosamunde and Alboino)

SWORD OF THE EMPIRE (1965) American-International. Color-80min. (Italian). Lang Jeffries, José Greci......(1)
Original title: SPADA PER L'IMPERO, UNA (A Sword for the Empire)

SWORD OF VENGEANCE III (1973) see LIGHTNING SWORDS OF DEATH

SWORD OF VENUS (1953) RKO. B&W-73min. Robert Clarke, Catherine McLeod, Dan O'Herlihy......(2)
British title: ISLAND OF MONTE CRISTO

SWORD WITHOUT A COUNTRY (1960) Avco-Embassy. Color-100min. (Italian). Folco Lulli, Leonora Ruffo......(3)
Original title: SPADE SENZA BANDIERA (Swords Without a Flag)

SWORDSMAN, THE (1948) Columbia. Color-81min. Larry Parks, Ellen Drew......(4)

SWORDSMAN OF SIENA (1962) M-G-M. Color-96min. (Italian-French). Stewart Granger, Sylva Koscina, Christine Kaufmann......(4)
Original Italian title: SPADACCINO DI SIENA, LO
Alternate Italian title: MERCENARIO, IL (The Mercenary)
French title: MERCENAIRE, LE

SWORN ENEMY (1936) M-G-M. B&W-62min. Robert Young, Florence Rice......(4)

SYBIL (1976) NBC-TV. Color-200min. Sally Field, Joanne Woodward....(5)

SYLVIA (1965) Paramount. B&W-115min. Carroll Baker, George Maharis......4*

SYLVIA SCARLETT (1935) RKO. **B&W-97min.** Katharine Hepburn, Cary Grant 5*

SYMPATHY FOR THE DEVIL (1970) New Line Cinema. **Color-110min.** (British). Mick Jagger, The Rolling Stones, Anne Wiazemsky .... (4)
Original title: 1 + 1 (One Plus One)

SYMPHONIE PASTORALE (1946) Films International. **B&W-115min.** (French). Michele Morgan, Pierre Blanchar........................ (5)
Translation title: The Pastoral Symphony

SYMPHONY FOR A MASSACRE (1965) Seven Arts [W.B.]. **B&W-115min.** (French-Italian). Michel Auclair, Claude Dauphin, José Giovanni .... (4)
Original French title: SYMPHONIE POUR UN MASSACRE
Italian title: SINFONIA PER UN MASSACRO
Alternate title: MYSTIFIERS, THE

SYMPHONY OF SIX MILLION (1932) RKO. **B&W-94min.** Ricardo Cortez, Irene Dunne.. 4*
British title: MELODY OF LIFE

SYNANON (1965) Columbia. **B&W-106min.** Edmond O'Brien, Chuck Connors .... (4)
British title: GET OFF MY BACK

SYNCOPATION (1929) RKO. **B&W-85min.** Barbara Bennett, Bobby Watson .... (4)

SYNCOPATION (1942) RKO. **B&W-88min.** Adolphe Menjou, Jackie Cooper .... (3)

SYSTEM, THE (1953) Warner Bros. **B&W-90min.** Frank Lovejoy, Joan Weldon .... (3)

SYSTEM, THE (1964) see GIRL-GETTERS, THE

-T-

T.A.M.I. SHOW, THE (1965) American-International. **B&W-113min.** (Music Film). Director: Steve Binder .... (3)
Alternate title: TEENAGE COMMAND PERFORMANCE
Alternate title: TEENAGE MUSIC INTERNATIONAL
Alternate title: TEENAGE AWARDS MUSIC INTERNATIONAL
Alternate title: T. A. M. I.

T-BIRD GANG (1959) Sparta. **B&W-75min.** Ed Nelson, John Brinkley, Pat George .... (3)
British title: PAY-OFF, THE

T-MEN (1947) Eagle Lion. **B&W-96min.** Dennis O'Keefe, Alfred Ryder 5*

T. R. BASKIN (1971) Paramount. **Color-90min.** Candice Bergen, Peter Boyle 4½*
British title: DATE WITH A LONELY GIRL, A

TABARIN (1958) Mayfair. **Color-110min.** (French). Sylvia Lopez, Michel Piccoli .... (3)

TABOOS OF THE WORLD (1963) American-International. **Color-86min.** (Italian, Documentary). Director: Romolo Marcellini .... (2)
Original title: TABU, I

TABU (1931) Paramount. **B&W-81min.** (Silent). Reri (Anne Chevalier), Matahi 3½*

TAFFY AND THE JUNGLE HUNTER (1965) Allied Artists. **Color-87min.** Jacques Bergerac, Manuel Padilla, Shary Marshall.................... (3)

TAGGART (1965) Universal. **Color-85min.** Tony Young, Dan Duryea .... (3)

TAHITI HONEY (1943) Republic. **B&W-69min.** Simone Simon, Dennis O'Keefe, Lionel Stander.. (4)

TAIL-GUNNER JOE (1977) MCA-TV. **Color-152min.** Peter Boyle, Burgess Meredith 5½*

TAIL SPIN (1939) 20th Century-Fox. **B&W-84min.** Alice Faye, Constance Bennett .... (3)

TAILOR'S MAID, THE (1957) Trans-Lux Distributing. **B&W-92min.** (Italian). Vittorio De Sica, Marcello Mastroianni, Antonella Lualdi .... (5)
Original title: PADRI E FIGLI (Fathers and Sons)
British title: LIKE FATHER, LIKE SON

TAINTED MONEY (1935) see SHOW THEM NO MERCY

TAKE, THE (1974) Columbia. **Color-91min.** Billy Dee Williams, Eddie Albert, Frankie Avalon .... (4)

TAKE A GIANT STEP (1959) United Artists. **B&W-100min.** Johnny Nash, Estelle Hemsley .... (5)

TAKE A GIRL LIKE YOU (1970) Columbia. **Color-96min.** (British). Hayley Mills, Oliver Reed, Noel Harrison .... (3)

TAKE A HARD RIDE (1975) 20th Century-Fox. **Color-103min.** (U.S.-Italian). Jim Brown, Lee Van Cleef.................................... 5*

TAKE A LETTER, DARLING (1942) Paramount. **B&W-93min.** Rosalind Russell, Fred MacMurray.. (5)
British title: GREEN-EYED WOMAN, THE

TAKE ALL OF ME (1978) Group 1. **Color-90min.** (Italian). Richard Johnson, Pamela Vincent, Maria Antonietta Beluzzi .... (3)

TAKE ALL YOU CAN GET (1972) H.K. Film Dist. **B&W-81min.** Fred Dennis, Kim Pope, Lisa Emmet .... (3)

TAKE CARE OF MY LITTLE GIRL (1951) 20th Century-Fox. **Color-93min.** Jeanne Crain, Dale Robertson, Jean Peters .... (4)

TAKE DOWN (1979) Buena Vista. **Color-107min.** Edward Herrmann, Lorenzo Lamas 5*

TAKE HER, SHE'S MINE (1963) 20th Century-Fox. **Color-98min.** James Stewart, Sandra Dee 4*

TAKE IT BIG (1944) Paramount. **B&W-75min.** Jack Haley, Ozzie Nelson, Harriet Hilliard (Nelson) .... (3)

TAKE IT OR LEAVE IT (1944) 20th Century-Fox. **B&W-70min.** Phil Baker, Edward Ryan, Marjorie Massow .... (3)

TAKE ME AS I AM (1959) see RIFF-RAFF

TAKE ME OUT TO THE BALL GAME (1949) M-G-M. **Color-93min.** Gene Kelly, Esther Williams.. 4*
British title: EVERYBODY'S CHEERING

TAKE ME TO TOWN (1953) Universal. **Color-81min.** Ann Sheridan, Sterling Hayden .... (4)

TAKE ME WHILE I'M WARM (1965) see PLAYGROUND, THE

TAKE MY LIFE (1947) Eagle Lion. **B&W-79min.** (British). Hugh Williams, Greta Gynt, Marius Goring .... (5)

TAKE ONE FALSE STEP (1949) Universal. **B&W-94min.** William Powell, Shelley Winters 4*

TAKE THE HIGH GROUND (1953) M-G-M. **Color-101min.** Richard Widmark, Karl Malden, Elaine Stewart.............................. 4*

TAKE THE MONEY AND RUN (1969) Cinerama Releasing. **Color-85min.** Woody Allen, Janet Margolin 5½*

TAKE THE STAGE (1949) see CURTAIN CALL AT CACTUS CREEK

TAKERS, THE (1971) Boxoffice International. **Color-81min.** Fred Bush, Dennis Troy, Susan Apple, Deborah Borroli .... (3)

TAKING OF PELHAM ONE TWO THREE, THE (1974) United Artists. **Color-104min.** Walter Matthau, Robert Shaw................. 5½*

TAKING OFF (1971) Universal. **Color-92min.** Buck Henry, Lynn Carlin 4½*

TALE OF FIVE WOMEN, A (1951) United Artists. **B&W-86min.** (British-U.S.). Bonar Colleano, Barbara Kelly, Gina Lollobrigida, Eva Bartok (4)
Original title: TALE OF FIVE CITIES, A

TALE OF THE COCK (1967) Filmworld. **Color-93min.** Don Murray, Linda Evans, David Brian.. (3)
Alternate title: CHILDISH THINGS

TALE OF TWO CITIES, A (1936) M-G-M. **B&W-121min.** Ronald Colman, Elizabeth Allen 5½*

TALE OF TWO CITIES, A (1958) J. Arthur Rank. **B&W-117min.** (British). Dirk Bogarde, Dorothy Tutin .... (5)

TALES (1969) **Color-70min.** (Documentary). Director: Cassandra Gerstein .... (4)

TALES FROM THE CRYPT (1972) Cinerama Releasing. **Color-92min.** (British). Ralph Richardson, Joan Collins, Peter Cushing, Nigel Patrick 5½*

TALES OF ADVENTURE (1954) Pathé. **B&W-90min.** (Telefeature). Don De Fore, Lon Chaney, Jr.. (3)

TALES OF BEATRIX POTTER (1971) see PETER RABBIT AND TALES OF BEATRIX POTTER

TALES OF HOFFMANN, THE (1951) Lopert [U.A.]. **Color-127min.** (British). Robert Rounseville, Pamela Brown 3*

TALES OF MANHATTAN (1942) 20th Century-Fox. **B&W-126min.** Charles Boyer 4½*

TALES OF MYSTERY (1968) see SPIRITS OF THE DEAD

TALES OF PARIS (1962) Times Film Corp. **B&W-100min.** (French-Italian). Dany Saval, Dany Robin, Francoise Arnoul, Catherine Deneuve .... (5)
Original French title: PARISIENNES, LES
Italian title: PARIGINE, LE
Alternate title: BEDS AND BROADS

TALES OF ROBIN HOOD (1951) Lippert Productions. **B&W-60min.** Robert Clarke, Mary Hatcher .... (3)

TALES OF TERROR (1962) American-International. **Color-90min.** Vincent Price, Maggie Pierce... 4*
Alternate title: POE'S TALES OF TERROR

TALES THAT WITNESS MADNESS (1973) Paramount. **Color-90min.** (British). Jack Hawkins, Donald Pleasence, Peter McEnery, Kim Novak .... (4)

THE TALK OF THE TOWN (1942). Cary Grant plays the unlikely role of a political radical framed for murder, but sympathetic Jean Arthur and distinguished law professor Ronald Colman try to help him prove his innocence.

TALK ABOUT A STRANGER (1952) M-G-M. B&W-65min. George Murphy, Nancy Davis...(2)

TALK OF THE TOWN, THE (1942) Columbia. B&W-118min. Cary Grant, Jean Arthur, Ronald Colman..5½*

TALL BLOND MAN WITH ONE BLACK SHOE, THE (1972) Cinema 5. Color-89min. *(French)*. Pierre Richard, Bernard Blier, Jean Rochefort 5*
Original title: GRAND BLOND AVEC UNE CHAUSSURE NOIRE, LE
British title: FOLLOW THAT GUY WITH THE ONE BLACK SHOE

TALL, DARK AND HANDSOME (1941) 20th Century-Fox. B&W-78min. Cesar Romero, Virginia Gilmore.....................................(4)

TALL HEADLINES (1952) *see* FRIGHTENED BRIDE, THE

TALL IN THE SADDLE (1944) RKO. B&W-87min. John Wayne, Ella Raines...4*

TALL LIE, THE (1952) *see* FOR MEN ONLY

TALL MAN RIDING (1955) Warner Bros. Color-83min. Randolph Scott, Dorothy Malone...3½*

TALL MEN, THE (1955) 20th Century-Fox. Color-122min. Clark Gable, Jane Russell..3*

TALL STORY (1960) Warner Bros. B&W-91min. Anthony Perkins, Jane Fonda...4*

TALL STRANGER, THE (1957) Allied Artists. Color-81min. Joel McCrea, Virginia Mayo..(4)

TALL T, THE (1957) Columbia. Color-78min. Randolph Scott, Richard Boone, Maureen O'Sullivan...4*

TALL TARGET, THE (1951) M-G-M. B&W-78min. Dick Powell, Paula Raymond, Adolphe Menjou...(4)

TALL TEXAN, THE (1953) Lippert Productions. B&W-84min. Lloyd Bridges, Marie Windsor...(4)

TALL TIMBER (1937) *see* PARK AVENUE LOGGER

TALL TROUBLE, THE (1957) *see* HELL CANYON OUTLAWS

TALL WOMEN, THE (1966) Allied Artists. Color-101min. *(Spanish-Italian-Austrian)*. Anne Baxter, Maria Perschy, Gustavo Rojo 2*
Original Spanish title: SIETE MAGNIFICAS, LAS *(The Seven Magnificent Women)*
Italian title: DONNE ALLA FRONTIERA *(Women of the Frontier)*
Austrian title: FRAUEN, DIE DURCH DIE HOLLE GEHEN

TAM LIN (1971) American-International. Color-107min. *(British-U.S.)*. Ava Gardner, Ian McShane...2*
Alternate title: DEVIL'S WIDOW, THE

TAMAHINE (1963) M-G-M. Color-85min. *(British)*. Nancy Kwan, John Fraser, Dennis Price...(4)

TAMANGO (1958) Valiant. Color-98min. *(French)*. Dorothy Dandridge, Curt Jurgens..(4)

TAMARIND SEED, THE (1974) Avco-Embassy. Color-125min. Julie Andrews, Omar Sharif...4*

TAMING, THE (1968) Victoria. B&W-85min. Lindsey Bowen, Liz Stevens, Sharon Church, Sam Stewart...(2)

TAMING OF THE SHREW, THE (1966) Columbia. Color-122min. *(U.S.-Italian)*. Elizabeth Taylor, Richard Burton.............................6*
Italian title: BISBETICA DOMATA, LA

TAMING SUTTON'S GAL (1957) Republic. B&W-71min. John Lupton, Gloria Talbott..(3)

TAMMY AND THE BACHELOR (1957) Universal. Color-89min. Debbie Reynolds, Leslie Nielsen...4*
British title: TAMMY

TAMMY AND THE DOCTOR (1963) Universal. Color-88min. Sandra Dee, Peter Fonda..(4)

TAMMY AND THE MILLIONAIRE (1967) Universal. Color-88min. *(Telefeature)*. Debbie Watson, Frank McGrath, Denver Pyle ....(3)

TAMMY TELL ME TRUE (1961) Universal. Color-97min. Sandra Dee, John Gavin..4*

TAMPICO (1944) 20th Century-Fox. B&W-75min. Edward G. Robinson, Lynn Bari, Victor McLaglen.......................................(3)

TANGANYIKA (1954) Universal. Color-81min. Van Heflin, Ruth Roman, Howard Duff..(3)

TANGIER (1946) Universal. B&W-76min. Maria Montez, Preston Foster, Sabu...4*

TANGIER INCIDENT (1953) Allied Artists. B&W-77min. George Brent, Mari Aldon..(2)

TANK BATTALION (1958) American-International. B&W-80min. Don Kelly, Marjorie Hellen, Edward G. Robinson, Jr. ....(2)
British title: VALLEY OF DEATH, THE

TANK COMMANDOS (1959) American-International. B&W-79min. Robert Barron, Maggie Lawrence, Wally Campo....................4*
British title: TANK COMMANDO

TANK FORCE (1958) Columbia. Color-81min. *(British)*. Victor Mature, Leo Genn, Luciana Paluzzi...(3)
Original title: NO TIME TO DIE

TANKS ARE COMING, THE (1951) Warner Bros. B&W-90min. Steve Cochran, Mari Aldon...(4)

TAP ROOTS (1948) Universal. Color-109min. Van Heflin, Susan Hayward..(4)

TARANTOS, LOS (1963) Sigma III. Color-81min. *(Spanish)*. Carmen Amaya, Sara Lezana, Daniel Martin...................................(5)

TARANTULA (1955) Universal. B&W-80min. John Agar, Leo G. Carroll, Mara Corday..3*

TARAS BULBA (1962) United Artists. Color-122min. Yul Brynner, Tony Curtis...4½*

TARAWA BEACHHEAD (1958) Columbia. B&W-77min. Kerwin Mathews, Julie Adams, Ray Danton...(4)

TARGET EARTH (1954) Allied Artists. B&W-75min. Richard Denning, Virginia Grey...3*

TARGET FOR SCANDAL (1952) *see* WASHINGTON STORY

TARGET FOR TONIGHT (1941) Warner Bros. B&W-48min. *(British, Documentary)*. Director: Harry Watt.............................(4)

TARGET - HONG KONG (1953) Columbia. B&W-66min. Richard Denning, Nancy Gates...(3)

TARGET RISK (1975) MCA-TV. Color-74min. *(Made for TV)*. Bo Svenson, Meredith Baxter...4*

TARGET, SEA OF CHINA (1954) Republic. B&W-100min. *(Re-edited Serial)*. Harry Lauter, Aline Towne, Lyle Talbot.................(2)
Original title: TRADER TOM OF THE CHINA SEAS

TARGET UNKNOWN (1951) Universal. B&W-90min. Mark Stevens, Alex Nicol..(4)

TARGET ZERO (1955) Warner Bros. B&W-92min. Richard Conte, Peggie Castle, Charles Bronson ....(3)

TARGETS (1968) Paramount. Color-90min. Boris Karloff, Tim O'Kelly 4½*

TARNISHED (1950) Republic. B&W-60min. Dorothy Patrick, Arthur Franz...(4)

TARNISHED ANGELS, THE (1958) Universal. B&W-91min. Rock Hudson, Robert Stack, Dorothy Malone................................(4)

TARNISHED HEROES (1961) Warner Bros. B&W-75min. *(British)*. Dermot Walsh, Anton Rogers......................................(3)

TARNISHED LADY (1931) Paramount. B&W-83min. Tallulah Bankhead, Clive Brook...(3)

TARS AND SPARS (1946) Columbia. B&W-86min. Alfred Drake, Janet Blair, Sid Caesar..(4)

TARTAR INVASION (1963) Telewide Systems. **Color-85min.** *(Italian).* Yoko Tani, Akim Tamiroff .... (3)
Alternate title: TARTAR GIRL, THE

TARTARS, THE (1961) M-G-M. **Color-83min.** *(Italian-Yugoslavian).* Victor Mature, Orson Welles 2½*
Original Italian title: TARTARI, I

TARTU (1943) *see* ADVENTURES OF TARTU, THE

TARZAN AND HIS MATE (1934) M-G-M. **B&W-105min.** Johnny Weissmuller, Maureen O'Sullivan 2½*

TARZAN AND THE AMAZONS (1945) RKO. **B&W-76min.** Johnny Weissmuller, Brenda Joyce, Johnny Sheffield, Maria Ouspenskaya 4*

TARZAN AND THE GREAT RIVER (1967) Paramount. **Color-88min.** Mike Henry, Jan Murray 3*

TARZAN AND THE GREEN GODDESS (1938) Principal. **B&W-72min.** Herman Brix (Bruce Bennett), Ula Holt.......................... (4)

TARZAN AND THE HUNTRESS (1947) RKO. **B&W-72min.** Johnny Weissmuller, Brenda Joyce, Johnny Sheffield, Patricia Morison .... (4)

TARZAN AND THE JUNGLE BOY (1968) Paramount. **Color-90min.** *(U.S.-Swiss).* Mike Henry, Rafer Johnson, Steve Bond 3*

TARZAN AND THE JUNGLE GODDESS (1951) *see* TARZAN'S PERIL

TARZAN AND THE JUNGLE QUEEN (1950) *see* TARZAN AND THE SLAVE GIRL

TARZAN AND THE LEOPARD WOMAN (1946) RKO. **B&W-72min.** Johnny Weissmuller, Brenda Joyce, Johnny Sheffield, Acquanetta ...... (4)

TARZAN AND THE LOST SAFARI (1957) M-G-M. **Color-84min.** *(British-U.S.).* Gordon Scott, Yolande Donlan, Wilfrid Hyde-White.................. (3)

TARZAN AND THE MERMAIDS (1948) RKO. **B&W-68min.** Johnny Weissmuller, Brenda Joyce, Linda Christian........................ (4)

TARZAN AND THE SHE-DEVIL (1953) RKO. **B&W-76min.** Lex Barker, Joyce MacKenzie, Monique Van Vooren .... (2)

TARZAN AND THE SLAVE GIRL (1950) RKO. **B&W-74min.** Lex Barker, Vanessa Brown, Denise Darcel.............................. (3)
British title: TARZAN AND THE JUNGLE QUEEN

TARZAN AND THE TRAPPERS (1966) Warner Brothers Television. **B&W-74min.** *(Telefeature).* Gordon Scott, Lesley Bradley, Eve Brent, Ricki Sorenson .... (3)

TARZAN AND THE VALLEY OF GOLD (1966) American-International. **Color-100min.** *(U.S.-Swiss).* Mike Henry, Nancy Kovack, Manuel Padilla, Jr. .... (2)

TARZAN ESCAPES (1936) M-G-M. **B&W-95min.** Johnny Weissmuller, Maureen O'Sullivan, John Buckler .... (4)

TARZAN FINDS A SON (1939) M-G-M. **B&W-90min.** Johnny Weissmuller, Maureen O'Sullivan, Johnny Sheffield .... (4)

TARZAN GOES TO INDIA (1962) M-G-M. **Color-86min.** *(British-U.S.-Swiss).* Jock Mahoney, Jai................................ (4)

TARZAN, KING OF BRUTE FORCE (1963) *see* THOR AND THE AMAZON WOMEN

TARZAN, THE APE MAN (1932) M-G-M. **B&W-99min.** Johnny Weissmuller, Maureen O'Sullivan, Neil Hamilton.................... 3*

TARZAN, THE APE MAN (1959) M-G-M. **Color-82min.** Denny Miller, Cesare Danova.. (3)

TARZAN, THE MAGNIFICENT (1960) Paramount. **Color-88min.** *(British).* Gordon Scott, Jock Mahoney .... (4)

TARZAN TRIUMPHS (1943) RKO. **B&W-78min.** Johnny Weissmuller, Frances Gifford, Johnny Sheffield, Stanley Ridges .... (4)

TARZAN'S DEADLY SILENCE (1970) National General. **Color-82min.** *(Telefeature).* Ron Ely, Manuel Padilla, Jr., Jock Mahoney .... (2)
Original title: DEADLY SILENCE, THE

TARZAN'S DESERT MYSTERY (1943) RKO. **B&W-70min.** Johnny Weissmuller, Nancy Kelly, Johnny Sheffield, Otto Kruger 4*

TARZAN'S FIGHT FOR LIFE (1958) M-G-M. **Color-86min.** Gordon Scott, Eve Brent, Rickie Sorenson, Jill Jarmyn................... (3)

TARZAN'S GREATEST ADVENTURE (1959) Paramount. **Color-88min.** *(British-U.S.).* Gordon Scott, Anthony Quayle, Sara Shane 4*

TARZAN'S HIDDEN JUNGLE (1955) RKO. **B&W-73min.** Gordon Scott, Vera Miles, Peter Van Eyck .... (3)

TARZAN'S JUNGLE REBELLION (1970) National General. **Color-92min.** *(Telefeature).* Ron Ely, Manuel Padilla, Jr., Sam Jaffe .... (2)

TARZAN'S MAGIC FOUNTAIN (1949) RKO. **B&W-73min.** Lex Barker, Brenda Joyce, Albert Dekker .... (4)

TARZAN'S NEW YORK ADVENTURE (1942) M-G-M. **B&W-71min.** Johnny Weissmuller, Maureen O'Sullivan 4*

TARZAN'S PERIL (1951) RKO. **B&W-79min.** Lex Barker, Virginia Huston, Dorothy Dandridge .... (4)
British title: TARZAN AND THE JUNGLE QUEEN

TARZAN'S REVENGE (1938) 20th Century-Fox. **B&W-70min.** Glenn Morris, Eleanor Holm.............................. (4)

TARZAN'S SAVAGE FURY (1952) RKO. **B&W-80min.** Lex Barker, Dorothy Hart, Patric Knowles .... (4)

TARZAN'S SECRET TREASURE (1941) M-G-M. **B&W-81min.** Johnny Weissmuller, Maureen O'Sullivan, Johnny Sheffield, Barry Fitzgerald 3½*

TARZAN'S THREE CHALLENGES (1963) M-G-M. **Color-92min.** *(U.S.-British).* Jock Mahoney, Woody Strode .... (3)

TASK FORCE (1949) Warner Bros. **B&W-116min.** Gary Cooper, Jane Wyatt .... (5)

TASTE OF EVIL, A (1971) Worldvision. **Color-73min.** *(Made for TV).* Barbara Stanwyck, Barbara Parkins, William Windom, Roddy McDowall .... (4)

TASTE OF FEAR (1961) *see* SCREAM OF FEAR

TASTE OF HONEY, A (1961) Continental [Walter Reade]. **B&W-100min.** *(British).* Rita Tushingham, Robert Stephens.................. 6*

TASTE THE BLOOD OF DRACULA (1970) Warner Bros. **Color-95min.** *(British).* Christopher Lee, Geoffrey Keen, Linda Hayden .... (3)

TATTERED DRESS, THE (1957) Universal. **B&W-93min.** Jeff Chandler, Jeanne Crain, Jack Carson........................... 3*

TATTERED WEB, A (1971) MPC (TV). **Color-74min.** *(Made for TV).* Lloyd Bridges, Frank Converse 3*

TATTOOED POLICE HORSE, THE (1964) Buena Vista. **Color-48min.** Sandy Sanders, Shirley Skiles .... (5)

TATTOOED STRANGER, THE (1950) RKO. **B&W-64min.** John Miles, Patricia White .... (4)

TAUR THE MIGHTY (1961) American-International. **Color-89min.** *(Italian).* Joe Robinson, Bella Cortez .... (1)

TAWNY PIPIT, THE (1944) Universal. **B&W-81min.** *(British).* Bernard Miles, Rosamund John .... (5)

TAXI (1932) Warner Bros. **B&W-70min.** James Cagney, Loretta Young (4)

TAXI (1953) 20th Century-Fox. **B&W-77min.** Dan Dailey, Constance Smith .... (4)

TAXI DRIVER (1976) Columbia. **Color-113min.** Robert De Niro, Cybill Shepherd 4½*

TAXI FOR TOBRUK (1961) Seven Arts [W.B.]. **B&W-90min.** *(French-Spanish-W. German).* Hardy Kruger, Charles Aznavour .... (4)
Original French title: TAXI POUR TOBROUK, UN
Spanish title: TAXI PARA TOBROUK, UN
German title: TAXI NACH TOBRUK

TAZA, SON OF COCHISE (1954) Universal. **Color-79min.** Rock Hudson, Barbara Rush... (3)

TAXI DRIVER (1976) is an apt description of Robert De Niro's thankless, lonely job as he sees the big city as a sewer of rotten humanity that has to be flushed clean.

Films are rated on a 1 to 10 scale, 10 is highest. **Boldface** ratings followed by an asterisk (*) are for films actually seen and rated by the executive and senior editors. All other ratings are estimates. (See Notes on Entertainment Ratings in the front section.)

TCHAIKOVSKY (1970) Warner Bros. Color-105min. (U.S.S.R.). Innokenti Smoktunovsky, Antonina Shuranova .... (4)

TEA AND SYMPATHY (1956) M-G-M. Color-122min. Deborah Kerr, John Kerr 5*

TEA FOR TWO (1950) Warner Bros. Color-98min. Doris Day, Gordon MacRae 4½*

TEACHER AND THE MIRACLE, THE (1957) President Films. B&W-88min. (Italian-Spanish). Aldo Fabrizi, Edoardo Nevola, Marco Paoletti .... (4)
Original Italian title: MAESTRO, IL *(The Master)*
Spanish title: MAESTRO, EL

TEACHER'S PET (1958) Paramount. B&W-120min. Clark Gable, Doris Day, Gig Young 6*

TEAHOUSE OF THE AUGUST MOON, THE (1956) M-G-M. Color-123min. Marlon Brando, Glenn Ford 5½*

TEAR GAS SQUAD (1940) Warner Bros. B&W-55min. Dennis Morgan, John Payne, Gloria Dickson .... (3)

TEARS FOR SIMON (1956) Republic. Color-89min. (British). David Farrar, David Knight .... (5)
Original title: LOST

TECKMAN MYSTERY, THE (1954) Associated Artists. B&W-89min. (British). Margaret Leighton, John Justin 3*

TEDDY BEAR, THE (1969) *see* BAMSE

TEEN-AGE CRIME WAVE (1955) Columbia. B&W-77min. Tommy Cook, Sue English .... (3)

TEEN-AGE REBEL (1956) 20th Century-Fox. B&W-94min. Ginger Rogers, Michael Rennie, Betty Lou Keim .... (4)

TEENAGE AWARDS MUSIC INTERNATIONAL (1965) *see* T.A.M.I. SHOW, THE

TEENAGE BAD GIRL (1956) Valiant. B&W-100min. (British). Anna Neagle, Sylvia Sims, Norman Wooland .... (4)
Original title: MY TEENAGE DAUGHTER
Alternate title: BAD GIRL

TEENAGE CAVEMAN (1958) American-International. B&W-65min. Robert Vaughn, Leslie Bradley, Darrah Marshall 4*
British title: OUT OF THE DARKNESS
Working title(?): I WAS A TEENAGE CAVEMAN

TEENAGE COMMAND PERFORMANCE (1965) *see* T.A.M.I. SHOW, THE

TEENAGE DELINQUENTS (1957) *see* NO TIME TO BE YOUNG

TEENAGE DOLL (1957) Allied Artists. B&W-68min. June Kenney, Fay Spain .... (2)
Alternate title: YOUNG REBELS, THE

TEENAGE FRANKENSTEIN (1957) *see* I WAS A TEENAGE FRANKENSTEIN

TEENAGE LOVERS (1960) *see* TOO SOON TO LOVE

TEENAGE MILLIONAIRE (1961) United Artists. B&W-84min. Jimmy Clanton, Rocky Graziano, ZaSu Pitts .... (2)

TEENAGE MONSTER (1957) Howco International. B&W-65min. Anne Gwynne, Gloria Castillo, Gilbert Perkins .... (2)
TV title: METEOR MONSTER

TEENAGE MOTHER (1968) Cinemation. Color-78min. Arlene Sue Farber, Frederick Riccio .... (2)

TEENAGE REBELLION (1967) Trans American. B&W-81min. (British-U.S., Documentary). *Director:* Norman Herman .... (2)
Alternate title: MONDO-TEENO

TEENAGE WOLF PACK (1956) Distributors Corp. of America. B&W-89min. (German). Horst Buccholz, Karen Baal .... (4)
Original title: HALBSTARKEN *(The Half-Strong Ones)*
British title: WOLFPACK

TEENAGE ZOMBIES (1960) Governor. B&W-73min. Don Sullivan, Katherine Victor .... (2)

TEENAGERS FROM OUTER SPACE (1959) Warner Bros. B&W-87min. David Love, Dawn Anderson 2½*
British title: GARGON TERROR, THE

TEENIE TULIP (1969) Cinex. Color-80min. Steve Dickenson, Peggy Simpson .... (2)
Alternate title: DR. LOVE

TELEFON (1977) United Artists. Color-103min. Charles Bronson, Lee Remick 3*

TELEPHONE BOOK, THE (1971) Rosebud Releasing. B&W-89min. Sarah Kennedy, Norman Rose .... (2)

TELL IT TO THE JUDGE (1949) Columbia. B&W-87min. Rosalind Russell, Robert Cummings 4*

TELL ME LIES (1968) Continental [Walter Reade]. Color-118min. (British). Mark Jones, Pauline Munro .... (4)

TELL ME THAT YOU LOVE ME, JUNIE MOON (1970) Paramount. Color-113min. Liza Minnelli, Ken Howard, Robert Moore .... (4)

TELL-TALE HEART, THE (1941) M-G-M. B&W-20min. Joseph Schildkraut, Roman Bohnen .... (4)

TELL-TALE HEART, THE (1962) Brigadier Films. B&W-81min. (British). Laurence Payne, Adrienne Corri .... (4)
Alternate title: HIDDEN ROOM OF 1,000 HORRORS

TELL THEM WILLIE BOY IS HERE (1970) Universal. Color-96min. Robert Redford, Katharine Ross, Robert Blake 3*

TELL YOUR CHILDREN (1939) *see* REEFER MADNESS

TEMBO (1951) RKO. Color-80min. (Documentary). *Director:* Howard Hill .... (4)

TEMPEST (1928) United Artists. B&W-102min. John Barrymore, Camilla Horn .... (5)

TEMPEST (1958) Paramount. Color-125min. (Italian-French-Yugoslavian). Silvana Mangano, Van Heflin, Viveca Lindfors .... (4)

TEMPEST IN THE FLESH (1954) Pacemaker Pictures. B&W-92min. (French). Francoise Arnoul, Raymond Pellegrin, Philippe Lemaire ...... (5)
Original title: RAGE AU CORPS, LA

TEMPLE OF THE WHITE ELEPHANTS (1964) American-International. Color-85min. (Italian). Sean Flynn, Alessandra Panaro, Mimmo Palmara .... (1)
Original title: SANDOK, IL MACISTE DELLA GIUNGLA *(Sandok, the Maciste of the Jungle)*

TEMPTATION (1946) Universal. B&W-92min. Merle Oberon, Paul Lukas .... (3)

TEMPTATION (1959) Cameo International Pictures. B&W-94min. (French). Magali Noel, Dawn Addams, Rossana Podesta, Christian Marquand ....
Original title: ILE DU BOUT DU MONDE, L'

TEMPTER, THE (1974) *see* DEVIL IS A WOMAN, THE

TEMPTRESS, THE (1926) M-G-M. B&W-91min. (Silent). Greta Garbo, Antonio Moreno 3*

10 (1979) Warner Bros. (for Orion). Color- min. Dudley Moore, Julie Andrews ....

TEN CENTS A DANCE (1945) Columbia. B&W-60min. Jimmy Lloyd, Jane Frazee, Robert Scott .... (3)
British title: DANCING LADIES

TEN COMMANDMENTS, THE (1923) Paramount. B&W-110min. (Silent). Theodore Roberts, Richard Dix, Leatrice Joy .... (5)

TEN COMMANDMENTS, THE (1956) Paramount. Color-219min. Charlton Heston, Yul Brynner 6½*

TEN DAYS THAT SHOOK THE WORLD (1928) Amkino. B&W-105min. (U.S.S.R., Silent). Nikandrov, N. Popov 2*
Original title: OKTYABR'
Alternate title: OCTOBER

TEN DAYS TO TULARA (1958) United Artists. B&W-77min. Sterling Hayden, Grace Raynor .... (4)

TEN DAYS' WONDER (1971) Levitt-Pickman. Color-101min. (English language). Orson Welles, Marlene Jobert, Anthony Perkins, Michel Piccoli 4*
Original title: DÉCADE PRODIGIEUSE, LA

TEN FROM YOUR SHOW OF SHOWS (1973) Walter Reade. B&W-92min. (Compilation, Telefeature). *Director:* Bill Hobin 4*

TEN GENTLEMEN FROM WEST POINT (1942) 20th Century-Fox. B&W-102min. George Montgomery, Maureen O'Hara 4*

TEN GLADIATORS, THE (1963) American-International. Color-104min. (Italian). Roger Browne, Susan Paget, Dan Vadis .... (1)
Original title: DIECI GLADIATORI, I

TEN LITTLE INDIANS (1965) Seven Arts [W.B.]. B&W-92min. (British). Hugh O'Brian, Shirley Eaton, Wilfrid Hyde-White 4*

TEN LITTLE INDIANS (1975) Avco-Embassy. Color-105min. (British-French-Spanish-Italian-W. German, English language). Oliver Reed, Richard Attenborough, Elke Sommer 4*
British title: AND THEN THERE WERE NONE

TEN LITTLE NIGGERS (1945) *see* AND THEN THERE WERE NONE

TEN MILLION DOLLAR GRAB, THE (1966) Showcorporation. Color-100min. (Foreign). Dana Andrews, Brad Harris, Elaine DeWitt ....

TEN NORTH FREDERICK (1958) 20th Century-Fox. B&W-102min. Gary Cooper, Diane Varsi 4½*

10 RILLINGTON PLACE (1971) Columbia. Color-111min. (British). Richard Attenborough, Judy Geeson 5*

TEN SECONDS TO HELL (1959) United Artists. B&W-93min. (U.S.-British). Jeff Chandler, Jack Palance .... (4)

TEN TALL MEN (1951) Columbia. Color-97min. Burt Lancaster, Jody Lawrence 5*

Films are rated on a 1 to 10 scale, 10 is highest. **Boldface** ratings followed by an asterisk (*) are for films actually seen and rated by the executive and senior editors. All other ratings are estimates. (See Notes on Entertainment Ratings in the front section.)

10:30 P.M. SUMMER (1966) Lopert [U.A.]. Color-85min. *(U.S.-Spanish)*. Melina Mercouri, Romy Schneider, Peter Finch......................(3)

10,000 BEDROOMS (1957) M-G-M. Color-114min. Dean Martin, Anna Maria Alberghetti 4*

TEN WANTED MEN (1955) Columbia. Color-80min. Randolph Scott, Jocelyn Brando, Richard Boone........................(4)

TEN WHO DARED (1960) Buena Vista. Color-92min. John Beal, Brian Keith ....(4)

TENAFLY (1972) MCA-TV. Color-100min.*(Made for TV)*. James McEachin, Mel Ferrer, Ed Nelson, Lillian Lebman........................(4)

TENANT, THE (1976) CIC. Color-125min. *(French-U.S.)*. Roman Polanski, Isabelle Adjani, Shelley Winters........................3*
French title: LOCATAIRE, LE

TENDER COMRADE (1943) RKO. B&W-102min. Ginger Rogers, Robert Ryan......................(4)

TENDER FLESH (1974) Warner Bros. Color-99min. Laurence Harvey, Joanna Pettet, Stuart Whitman........................(3)
Original title: WELCOME TO ARROW BEACH

TENDER IS THE NIGHT (1962) 20th Century-Fox. Color-146min. Jennifer Jones, Jason Robards, Jr..........................(4)

TENDER MOMENT, THE (1968) Maron Films, Ltd. Color-82min. *(French)*. Renaud Verley, Nathalie Delon, Robert Hossein....................(4)
Original title: LECON PARTICULIERE, LE *(The Private Lesson)*

TENDER SCOUNDREL (1966) Avco-Embassy. Color-94min. *(French-Italian)*. Jean-Paul Belmondo, Nadja Tiller, Robert Morley ....(3)
Original French title: TENDRE VOYOU
Italian title: AVVENTURIERO A TAHITI, UN *(An Adventurer in Tahiti)*

TENDER TRAP, THE (1955) M-G-M. Color-111min. Frank Sinatra, Debbie Reynolds 4*

TENDER WARRIOR, THE (1971) William Thompson International. Color-77min. Charles Lee, David Dalie, Dan Haggerty......................(3)

TENDER YEARS, THE (1948) 20th Century-Fox. B&W-81min. Joe E. Brown, Josephine Hutchinson ....(4)

TENDERFOOT, THE (1932) First National [W.B.]. B&W-70min. Joe E. Brown, Ginger Rogers ....(4)

TENDERLY (1969) *see* GIRL WHO COULDN'T SAY NO, THE

TENDERNESS OF WOLVES, THE (1973) Monument. Color-95min. *(German)*. Kurt Raab, Jeff Roden, Margit Carstensen ....
Original title: ZAERTLICHKEIT DER WOELFE

TENDRESSE ORDINARE (1973) Nat'l Film Board of Canada. B&W-82min. *(Canadian)*. Ester Auger, Jocelyn Berube ....(4)
Translation title: Ordinary Tenderness

TENNESSEE CHAMP (1954) M-G-M. Color-73min. Shelley Winters, Dewey Martin......................(4)

TENNESSEE JOHNSON (1942) M-G-M. B&W-103min. Van Heflin, Ruth Hussey, Lionel Barrymore 4*
British title: MAN ON AMERICA'S CONSCIENCE, THE

TENNESSEE'S PARTNER (1955) RKO. Color-87min. John Payne, Rhonda Fleming, Ronald Reagan ....(4)

TENSION (1949) M-G-M. B&W-95min. Richard Basehart, Audrey Totter 4*

TENSION AT TABLE ROCK (1956) RKO. Color-93min. Richard Egan, Dorothy Malone......................3*

TENTACLES (1977) American-International. Color-102min. *(Italian, English language)*. John Huston, Bo Hopkins, Henry Fonda 3*
Original title: TENTACOLI

TENTH AVENUE ANGEL (1948) M-G-M. B&W-74min. Margaret O'Brien, George Murphy, Angela Lansbury ....(2)

10th VICTIM, THE (1965) Avco-Embassy. Color-92min. *(Italian, English language)*. Marcello Mastroianni, Ursula Andress 4½*
Original Italian title: DECIMA VITTIMA, LA
French title: DIXIEME VICTIME, LA

TEOREMA (1968) Continental [Walter Reade]. Color-93min. *(Italian)*. Terence Stamp, Silvana Mangano ....(4)

TERESA (1951) M-G-M. B&W-102min. Pier Angeli, John Ericson ....(4)

TERM OF TRIAL (1962) Warner Bros. B&W-113min. *(British)*. Laurence Olivier, Simone Signoret 4½*

TERMINAL MAN, THE (1974) Warner Bros. Color-104min. George Segal, Joan Hackett 3*

TERRA TREMA, LA (1948) Fleetwood Films. B&W-162min. *(Italian)*. All non-professional actors 2½*
Translation title: The Earth Will Tremble

TERRIBLE BEAUTY, A (1960) *see* NIGHT FIGHTERS, THE

TERRIBLE PEOPLE, THE (1960) UCC Films. B&W-95min. *(German)*. Joachim Fuchsberger, Karin Dor ....(3)
Original title: BANDE DES SCHRECKENS, DIE *(The Band of Terrors)*
Alternate title: HAND OF THE GALLOWS

TERRIFIED! (1963) Crown International. B&W-81min. Rod Lauren, Steve Drexel, Tracy Olsen, Stephen Roberts 3*

TERROR, THE (1963) American-International. Color-81min. Boris Karloff, Jack Nicholson 3*

TERROR AFTER MIDNIGHT (1962) Warner Bros. TV. B&W-82min. *(German)*. Christine Kaufmann, Martin Held ....(3)
Original title: NEUNZIG MINUTEN NACH MITTERNACHT

TERROR AT BLACK FALLS (1962) Beckman. B&W-76min. Peter Mamakos, House Peters, Jr..............................(2)

TERROR AT MIDNIGHT (1956) Republic. B&W-70min. Scott Brady, Joan Vohs ....(3)
British title: AND SUDDENLY YOU RUN

TERROR BENEATH THE SEA (1966) Teleworld. Color-85min. *(Japanese-U.S.)*. Shinichi Chiba, Peggy Neal, Franz Gruber 1*
Japanese title: KAITEI DAISENSO
Alternate title: WATER CYBORG

TERROR BY NIGHT (1946) Universal. B&W-60min. Basil Rathbone, Nigel Bruce, Alan Mowbray 4*
Alternate title: SHERLOCK HOLMES IN TERROR BY NIGHT

TERROR CASTLE (1965) *see* HORROR CASTLE

TERROR FROM THE YEAR 5000 (1958) American-International. B&W-68min. Ward Costello, Joyce Holden 2*
British title: CAGE OF DOOM

TERROR FROM UNDER THE HOUSE (1971) *see* INN OF THE FRIGHTENED PEOPLE

TERROR HOUSE (1972) *see* FOLKS AT RED WOLF INN, THE

TERROR IN A TEXAS TOWN (1958) United Artists. B&W-80min. Sterling Hayden, Sebastian Cabot, Carol Kelly......................(3)

TERROR IN THE CRYPT (1958) American-International. B&W-84min. *(Spanish-Italian)*. Christopher Lee, Audry Amber (Adriana Ambesi) 3*
Original Spanish title: MALDICION DE LOS KARNSTEIN, LA *(The Curse of the Karnsteins)*
Italian title: CRIPTA E L'INCUBO, LA *(The Crypt and the Nightmare)*
British title: CRYPT OF HORROR

TERROR IN THE HAUNTED HOUSE (1958) Howco International. B&W-80min. Gerald Mohr, Cathy O'Donnell ....(3)
Original title: MY WORLD DIES SCREAMING

TERROR IN THE JUNGLE (1969) Crown International. Color-84min. Jimmy Angle, Robert Burns......................(2)

TERROR IN THE MIDNIGHT SUN (1960) *see* INVASION OF THE ANIMAL PEOPLE

TERROR IN THE SKY (1971) Paramount. Color-74min. *(Made for TV)*. Doug McClure, Roddy McDowall, Keenan Wynn......................4*

TERROR IN THE WAX MUSEUM (1973) Cinerama Releasing. Color-93min. Ray Milland, Mark W. Edwards, Nicole Shelby 3*

TERROR IN THE WOODS (1974) American-International. Color- min. *(Foreign)*. Fabio Testi, Karin Baal ....(3)

TERROR IS A MAN (1959) Valiant. B&W-89min. Francis Lederer, Greta Thyssen ....(3)
Alternate title: GORY CREATURES, THE
Alternate title: BLOOD CREATURE

TERROR OF DR. CHANEY, THE (1975) *see* MANSION OF THE DOOMED

TERROR OF DR. HICHCOCK, THE (1962) *see* HORRIBLE DR. HICHCOCK, THE

TERROR OF DR. MABUSE, THE (1962) *see* TESTAMENT OF DR. MABUSE, THE

TERROR OF DRACULA, THE (1922) *see* NOSFERATU

TERROR OF ROME AGAINST THE SON OF HERCULES (1964) Avco-Embassy. Color-100min. *(Italian-French)*. Mark Forest, Marilu Tolo...(1)
Original Italian title: MACISTE, GLADIATORE DI SPARTA *(Maciste, Gladiator of Sparta)*
French title(?): MACISTE, GLADIATEUR DE SPARTE

TERROR OF SHEBA, THE (1974) Fanfare. Color-92min. *(British)*. Lana Turner, Ralph Bates, Trevor Howard......................(4)
Original title: PERSECUTION

TERROR OF THE BLACK MASK (1963) Avco-Embassy. Color-96min. *(Italian-French)*. Pierre Brice, Helene Chanel......................(3)
Original Italian title: INVINCIBILE CAVALIERE MASCHERATO, L' *(The Invincible Masked Rider)*

TERROR OF THE BLOODHUNTERS (1962) Medallion. B&W-60min. Robert Clarke, Steve Conte, Dorothy Haney ....(2)

Films are rated on a 1 to 10 scale, 10 is highest. **Boldface** ratings followed by an asterisk (*) are for films actually seen and rated by the executive and senior editors. All other ratings are estimates. (See Notes on Entertainment Ratings in the front section.)

TERROR OF THE DEEP (1966) *see* DESTINATION INNER SPACE

TERROR OF THE KIRGHIZ (1964) *see* HERCULES, PRISONER OF EVIL

TERROR OF THE MAD DOCTOR, THE (1962) *see* TESTAMENT OF DR. MABUSE, THE

TERROR OF THE RED MASK (1959) Four Star. **Color-92min.** *(Italian).* Lex Barker, Chelo Alonso .... (3)
Original title: TERRORE DELLA MASCHERA ROSSA, IL

TERROR OF THE STEPPE (1963) Avco-Embassy. **Color-97min.** *(Italian).* Kirk Morris, Moira Orfei, Daniele Vargas.................. (1)
Original title: PREDONI DELLA STEPPA, I *(The Robbers of the Steppes)*

TERROR OF THE TONGS, THE (1961) Columbia. **Color-80min.** *(British).* Christopher Lee, Geoffrey Toone, Yvonne Monlaur **3***

TERROR OF TINY TOWN, THE (1938) Columbia. **B&W-63min.** Billy Curtis, Yvonne Moray, Little Billy (all-midget cast) **2½***

TERROR ON A TRAIN (1953) M-G-M. **B&W-72min.** *(British-U.S.).* Glenn Ford, Anne Vernon.. **4½***
Original title: TIME BOMB

TERROR ON HALF MOON STREET (1969) Sunset International. **Color-87min.** *(German-Austrian).* Horst Tappert, Karin Huebner .... (3)
Original title: MANN MIT DEM GLASAUGE, DER *(The Man With the Glass Eye)*

TERROR ON THE BEACH (1973) 20th Century-Fox. **Color-74min.** *(Made for TV).* Dennis Weaver, Estelle Parsons, Susan Dey **4***

TERROR OUT OF THE SKY (1979) CBS-TV. **Color-98min.** *(Made for TV).* Efrem Zimbalist, Jr., Tovah Feldshuh, Dan Haggerty ....

TERROR STRIKES, THE (1958) *see* WAR OF THE COLOSSAL BEAST

TERRORE NELLO SPAZIO (1965) *see* PLANET OF THE VAMPIRES

TERRORISTS, THE (1975) *see* RANSOM

TERRORNAUTS, THE (1967) Avco-Embassy. **Color-75min.** *(British).* Simon Oates, Zena Marshall .... (2)

TESS OF THE STORM COUNTRY (1960) 20th Century-Fox. **Color-84min.** Diane Baker, Jack Ging .... (4)

TEST PILOT (1938) M-G-M. **B&W-118min.** Clark Gable, Myrna Loy **4½***

TESTAMENT OF DR. MABUSE, THE (1933) Janus Films. **B&W-120min.** *(German).* Rudolf Klein-Rogge, Oskar (Oscar) Beregi **2***
Original title: TESTAMENT DES DOKTOR MABUSE, DAS
British title: CRIMES OF DR. MABUSE

TESTAMENT OF DR. MABUSE, THE (1962) Thunder Pictures. **B&W-88min.** *(German).* Gert Frobe, Helmut Schmid, Wolfgang Preiss .... (4)
Original title: TESTAMENT DES DOKTOR MABUSE, DAS
Alternate title: TERROR OF DR. MABUSE, THE
Alternate title: TERROR OF THE MAD DOCTOR, THE

TEXAN MEETS CALAMITY JANE, THE (1950) Columbia. **Color-71min.** James Ellison, Evelyn Ankers.................................... (2)

TEXANS, THE (1938) Paramount. **B&W-92min.** Joan Bennett, Randolph Scott **3½***

TEXAS (1941) Columbia. **B&W-93min.** Glenn Ford, William Holden....... **4***

TEXAS ACROSS THE RIVER (1966) Universal. **Color-101min.** Dean Martin, Alain Delon, Rosemary Forsyth **3***

TEXAS, BROOKLYN AND HEAVEN (1948) United Artists. **B&W-76min.** Guy Madison, Diana Lynn..................................... (3)
British title: GIRL FROM TEXAS, THE

TEXAS CARNIVAL (1951) M-G-M. **Color-77min.** Esther Williams, Red Skelton .... (4)

TEXAS CHAINSAW MASSACRE, THE (1974) Bryanston. **Color-83min.** Marilyn Burns, Allen Danziger.................................. **1***

TEXAS KID, OUTLAW (1949) *see* KID FROM TEXAS, THE

TEXAS LADY (1955) RKO. **Color-86min.** Claudette Colbert, Barry Sullivan **3***

TEXAS RANGERS, THE (1936) Paramount. **B&W-95min.** Fred MacMurray, Lloyd Nolan, Jean Parker **3***

TEXAS RANGERS, THE (1951) Columbia. **Color-68min.** George Montgomery, Gale Storm.................................... **3***

TEXAS RANGERS RIDE AGAIN (1941) Paramount. **B&W-68min.** John Howard, Ellen Drew .... (3)

TEXAS ROSE (1955) *see* RETURN OF JACK SLADE, THE

TEXAS TO TOKYO (1943) *see* WE'VE NEVER BEEN LICKED

TEXICAN, THE (1966) Columbia. **Color-86min.** *(Spanish-U.S.).* Audie Murphy, Broderick Crawford, Diana Lorys........................ **2***
Original Spanish title: TEXAS KID
Alternate Spanish title: TEJANO, EL

THADDEUS ROSE AND EDDIE (1978) CBS-TV. **Color-100min.** *(Made for TV).* Johnny Cash, Bo Hopkins.................................

THANK GOD IT'S FRIDAY (1978) Columbia. **Color-89min.** Jeff Goldblum, Chick Vennera, Donna Summer **6***

THANK YOU ALL VERY MUCH (1969) Columbia. **Color-106min.** *(British).* Sandy Dennis, Ian McKellen **4***
Original title: TOUCH OF LOVE, A

THANK YOU, JEEVES (1936) 20th Century-Fox. **B&W-68min.** Arthur Treacher, David Niven .... (4)
TV title: THANK YOU, MR. JEEVES

THANK YOU, MR. MOTO (1937) 20th Century-Fox. **B&W-67min.** Peter Lorre, Pauline Frederick, Sidney Blackmer .... (3)

THANK YOUR LUCKY STARS (1943) Warner Bros. **B&W-127min.** Eddie Cantor, Joan Leslie **4***

THANKS A MILLION (1935) 20th Century-Fox. **B&W-87min.** Dick Powell, Fred Allen.. (5)

THANKS FOR EVERYTHING (1938) 20th Century-Fox. **B&W-73min.** Adolphe Menjou, Jack Oakie .... (5)

THANKS FOR THE MEMORY (1938) Paramount. **B&W-75min.** Bob Hope, Shirley Ross.. (4)

THAT BRENNAN GIRL (1946) Republic. **B&W-95min.** Mona Freeman, James Dunn .... (2)

THAT CERTAIN AGE (1938) Universal. **B&W-95min.** Deanna Durbin, Jackie Cooper, Melvyn Douglas.............................. (5)

THAT CERTAIN FEELING (1956) Paramount. **Color-103min.** Bob Hope, Eva Marie Saint **3***

THAT CERTAIN SUMMER (1972) MCA-TV. **Color-74min.** *(Made for TV).* Scott Jacoby, Hal Holbrook.................................. **5***

THAT CERTAIN WOMAN (1937) Warner Bros. **B&W-93min.** Bette Davis, Henry Fonda **3***

THAT COLD DAY IN THE PARK (1969) Commonwealth United. **Color-112min.** *(Canadian-U.S.).* Sandy Dennis, Michael Burns........ **4***

THAT DANGEROUS AGE (1949) *see* IF THIS BE SIN

THAT DARN CAT (1965) Buena Vista. **Color-116min.** Hayley Mills, Dean Jones **5***

THAT FORSYTE WOMAN (1949) M-G-M. **Color-114min.** Errol Flynn, Greer Garson, Walter Pidgeon **4***
British title: FORSYTE SAGA, THE

THAT FUNNY FEELING (1965) Universal. **Color-93min.** Bobby Darin, Sandra Dee, Donald O'Connor .... (4)

THAT GANG OF MINE (1940) Monogram [Allied Artists]. **B&W-62min.** The East Side Kids, Milton Kibbee .... (4)

THAT GIRL FROM PARIS (1936) RKO. **B&W-110min.** Lily Pons, Gene Raymond.. (4)

THAT HAGEN GIRL (1947) Warner Bros. **B&W-83min.** Shirley Temple, Ronald Reagan .... (3)

THAT HAMILTON WOMAN (1941) United Artists. **B&W-128min.** Vivien Leigh, Laurence Olivier **4½***
British title: LADY HAMILTON

THAT JANE FROM MAINE (1959) *see* IT HAPPENED TO JANE

THAT KIND OF GIRL (1952) *see* MODELS, INC.

THAT KIND OF WOMAN (1959) Paramount. **B&W-92min.** Sophia Loren, Tab Hunter **4***

THAT LADY (1955) 20th Century-Fox. **Color-100min.** *(British).* Olivia de Havilland, Gilbert Roland, Paul Scofield **4***

THAT LADY FROM PEKING (1971) NTA Pictures. **Color-93min.** *(Australian).* Nancy Kwan, Carl Betz, Sid Melton .... (3)

THAT LADY IN ERMINE (1948) 20th Century-Fox. **Color-89min.** Betty Grable.. **5½***

THAT LUCKY TOUCH (1975) J. Arthur Rank. **Color-93min.** *(British).* Roger Moore, Susannah York, Shelley Winters.............. (3)

THAT MAD MR. JONES (1948) *see* FULLER BRUSH MAN, THE

THAT MAN BOLT (1973) Universal. **Color-102min.** Fred Williamson, Byron Webster................................... (4)

THAT MAN FROM RIO (1964) Lopert [U.A.]. **Color-114min.** *(French-Italian).* Jean-Paul Belmondo, Francoise Dorleac................ **5½***
French title: HOMME DE RIO, L'
Italian title: UOMO DI RIO, L'

THAT MAN FROM TANGIER (1953) United Artists. **B&W-80min.** Nils Asther, Nancy Coleman .... (3)

Films are rated on a 1 to 10 scale, 10 is highest. **Boldface** ratings followed by an asterisk (*) are for films actually seen and rated by the executive and senior editors. All other ratings are estimates. (See Notes on Entertainment Ratings in the front section.)

THAT MAN FROM RIO (1964) is a fast-paced chase comedy which finds the irrepressible Jean-Paul Belmondo teetering along a plank high above Brasilia as he continues his quest for his kidnapped girlfriend.

THAT MAN GEORGE (1966) Allied Artists. **Color-90min.** *(French-Italian-Spanish, English language).* George Hamilton, Claudine Auger 3*
Original French title: HOMME DE MARRAKECH, L' *(The Man from Marrakesh)*
Italian title: UOMO DI CASABLANCA, L' *(The Man from Casablanca)*
Spanish title: HOMBRE DE MARRAKECH
Alternate title: OUR MAN IN MARRAKESH
Alternate Spanish title: SAQUEADORES DEL DOMINGO, LOS

THAT MAN IN ISTANBUL (1965) Columbia. **Color-117min.** *(French-Italian-Spanish).* Horst Buccholz, Sylva Koscina 3*
Original French title: HOMME D'ISTAMBUL, L'
Italian title: COLPO GROSSO A GALATA BRIDGE *(Big Blow at Galata Bridge)*
Spanish title: ESTAMBUL 65

THAT MIDNIGHT KISS (1949) M-G-M. **Color-96min.** Mario Lanza, Kathryn Grayson, Ethel Barrymore .... (5)

THAT NAUGHTY GIRL (1955) *see* MAM'ZELLE PIGALLE

THAT NIGHT (1957) Universal. **B&W-88min.** John Beal, Augusta Dabney .... (4)

THAT NIGHT IN RIO (1941) 20th Century-Fox. **Color-90min.** Alice Faye, Don Ameche .... (4)

THAT NIGHT WITH YOU (1945) Universal. **B&W-84min.** Franchot Tone, Susanna Foster .... (3)

THAT OBSCURE OBJECT OF DESIRE (1977) First Artists. **Color-100min.** *(French).* Fernando Rey, Carole Bouquet, Angela Molina 5*
Original title: CET OBSCURE OBJET DU DESIR

THAT OTHER WOMAN (1942) 20th Century-Fox. **B&W-75min.** Virgina Gilmore, James Ellison, Dan Duryea .... (3)

THAT RIVIERA TOUCH (1966) Continental [Walter Reade]. **Color-98min.** *(British).* Eric Morecambe, Ernie Wise .... (3)

"THAT ROYLE GIRL" (1926) Paramount. **B&W-114min.** *(Silent).* Carol Dempster, W. C. Fields, James Kirkwood .... (4)
Alternate title: D. W. GRIFFITH'S "THAT ROYLE GIRL"

THAT SAME SUMMER (1971) *see* RED SKY AT MORNING

THAT SPLENDID NOVEMBER (1969) United Artists. **Color-93min.** *(Italian-French).* Gina Lollobrigida, Paolo Turco .... (3)
Original Italian title: BELLISSIMO NOVEMBRE, UN *(A Beautiful November)*

THAT TENNESSEE BEAT (1966) 20th Century-Fox. **Color-84min.** Sharon De Bord, Earl Richards .... (3)

THAT TOUCH OF MINK (1962) Universal. **Color-99min.** Cary Grant, Doris Day 6*

THAT UNCERTAIN FEELING (1941) United Artists. **B&W-84min.** Merle Oberon, Melvyn Douglas .... (5)

THAT WAY WITH WOMEN (1947) Warner Bros. **B&W-84min.** Dane Clark, Martha Vickers, Sydney Greenstreet .... (3)

THAT WOMAN (1966) Globe. **B&W-83min.** *(German).* Eva Renzi, Harald Leipnitz, Paul Hubschmid .... (2)
Original title: PLAYGIRL
Alternate German title: BERLIN IST EINE SÜNDE WELT

THAT WOMAN OPPOSITE (1957) *see* CITY AFTER MIDNIGHT

THAT WONDERFUL URGE (1949) 20th Century-Fox. **B&W-82min.** Tyrone Power, Gene Tierney .... (4)

THAT'LL BE THE DAY (1973) Mayfair Film Group. **Color-90min.** *(British).* David Essex, Ringo Starr 4*

THAT'S ENTERTAINMENT! (1974) U.A. (for M-G-M). **Color-132min.** *(Compilation). Director:* Jack Haley, Jr. 6½*

THAT'S ENTERTAINMENT, PART 2 (1976) U.A. (for M-G-M). **Color-133min.** *(Compilation). Producer:* Saul Chaplin 6*
Foreign title: HOLLYWOOD! HOLLYWOOD!

THAT'S MY BOY (1951) Paramount. **B&W-98min.** Dean Martin, Jerry Lewis 4*

THAT'S MY MAN (1947) Republic. **B&W-104min.** Don Ameche, Catherine McLeod .... (4)
British title: WILL TOMORROW EVER COME?

THAT'S RIGHT, YOU'RE WRONG (1939) RKO. **B&W-88min.** Kay Kyser, Adolphe Menjou, Lucille Ball .... (4)

THAT'S THE SPIRIT (1945) Universal. **B&W-93min.** Jack Oakie, Peggy Ryan, Buster Keaton .... (3)

THAT'S THE WAY OF THE WORLD (1975) United Artists. **Color-99min.** Harvey Keitel, Ed Nelson, Cynthia Bostick .... (4)
Alternate title: SHINING STAR

THEATER OF BLOOD (1973) United Artists. **Color-104min.** Vincent Price, Diana Rigg, Ian Hendry 4½*

THEATRE OF DEATH (1967) *see* BLOOD FIEND

THEIR FIRST TRIP TO TOKYO (1953) *see* TOKYO STORY, THE

THEIR LAST NIGHT (1953) Columbia. **B&W-90min.** *(French).* Jean Gabin, Madeleine Robinson .... (3)
Original title: LEUR DERNIERE NUIT

THEIR SECRET AFFAIR (1957) *see* TOP SECRET AFFAIR

THELMA JORDON (1949) *see* FILE ON THEMLA JORDON, THE

THEM! (1954) Warner Bros. **B&W-94min.** Edmund Gwenn, James Whitmore 3½*

THEN CAME BRONSON (1969) M-G-M. **Color-100min.** *(Made for TV).* Michael Parks, Bonnie Bedelia .... (4)

THEN THERE WERE THREE (1961) Parade. **B&W-74min.** *(U.S.-Italian).* Frank Latimore, Alex Nicol .... (4)
Alternate title: THREE CAME BACK

THEODORA GOES WILD (1936) Columbia. **B&W-98min.** Irene Dunne, Melvyn Douglas 4*

THEODORA, SLAVE EMPRESS (1954) Italian Films Export. **Color-88min.** *(Italian-French).* Gianna-Maria Canale, Georges Marchal, Henri Guisol .... (3)
Original title: THEODORE, IMPERATRICE BYZANTINE *(Theodora, Byzantine Empress)*

THERE GOES BARDER (1955) Paramount. **B&W-90min.** *(French-Italian).* Eddie Constantine, May Britt .... (3)
Original title: CA VA BARDER!
Alternate title: GIVE 'EM HELL

THERE GOES MY GIRL (1937) RKO. **B&W-74min.** Gene Raymond, Ann Sothern .... (5)

THERE GOES MY HEART (1938) United Artists. **B&W-81min.** Fredric March, Virginia Bruce .... (5)

THERE GOES THE GROOM (1937) RKO. **B&W-65min.** Ann Sothern, Burgess Meredith .... (4)

THERE IS ANOTHER SUN (1951) *see* WALL OF DEATH

THERE ONCE WAS A WOMAN (1971) *see* REVENGE!

THERE WAS A CROOKED MAN . . . (1970) Warner Bros. **Color-126min.** Kirk Douglas, Henry Fonda 4½*

THERE WAS A YOUNG LADY (1952) Ellis Films. **B&W-85min.** *(British).* Michael Denison, Dulcie Gray .... (3)

THERE WAS AN OLD COUPLE (1965) Artkino. **B&W-103min.** *(U.S.S.R.).* Anatoly Yabbarov .... (4)
Original title: ZHILIBYLI STARIK SO STARUKHOY *(There Was Once an Old Man and an Old Woman)*
Alternate title: COUPLE, THE

THERE'S A GIRL IN MY SOUP (1970) Columbia. **Color-95min.** *(British).* Peter Sellers, Goldie Hawn 5*

THERE'S ALWAYS A PRICE TAG (1957) J. Arthur Rank. **B&W-103min.** *(French).* Michele Borgan, Daniel Gélin, Peter Van Eyck .... (4)
Original title: RETOUR DE MANIVELLE *(Turn of the Handle)*

Films are rated on a 1 to 10 scale, 10 is highest. **Boldface** ratings followed by an asterisk (*) are for films actually seen and rated by the executive and senior editors. All other ratings are estimates. (See Notes on Entertainment Ratings in the front section.)

THERE'S ALWAYS A THURSDAY (1957) J. Arthur Rank. B&W-62min.
(British). Charles Victor, Marjorie Rhodes .... (3)

THERE'S ALWAYS A WOMAN (1938) Columbia. B&W-82min. Joan
Blondell, Melvyn Douglas .... (5)

THERE'S ALWAYS TOMORROW (1956) Universal. B&W-84min.
Barbara Stanwyck, Fred MacMurray .... (4)

THERE'S ALWAYS VANILLA (1972) Cambist. Color-91min. Ray Laine,
Judith Streiner .... (3)
Alternate title: AFFAIR, THE

THERE'S MAGIC IN MUSIC (1941) Paramount. B&W-80min. Allan
Jones, Susanna Foster .... (3)
Alternate title: HARD-BOILED CANARY, THE

THERE'S NO BUSINESS LIKE SHOW BUSINESS (1954) 20th Century-
Fox. Color-117min. Ethel Merman, Donald O'Connor 4½*

THERE'S THAT WOMAN AGAIN (1938) Columbia. B&W-74min. Melvyn
Douglas, Virginia Bruce .... (4)
British title: WHAT A WOMAN

THERESE AND ISABELLE (1968) Audubon. B&W-118min. (W. German-
U.S.). Essy Persson, Anna Gael .... (3)
W. German title: THERESE UND ISABELL

THERESE ETIENNE (1957) Walter Reade. B&W-95min. (French-Italian).
Francoise Arnoul, James Robertson Justice, Pierre Vaneck .... (3)
Italian title: TERESA ETIENNE

THERESE RAQUIN (1958) *see* ADULTRESS, THE

THESE ARE THE DAMNED (1963) Columbia. B&W-77min. (British).
Macdonald Carey, Shirley Anne Field 2*
Original title: DAMNED, THE

THESE DANGEROUS YEARS (1957) *see* DANGEROUS YOUTH

THESE GLAMOUR GIRLS (1939) M-G-M. B&W-79min. Lew Ayres, Lana
Turner .... (4)

THESE THOUSAND HILLS (1959) 20th Century-Fox. Color-96min. Don
Murray, Richard Egan 4*

THESE THREE (1936) United Artists. B&W-93min. Miriam Hopkins,
Merle Oberon, Joel McCrea 5½*

THESE WILDER YEARS (1956) M-G-M. B&W-91min. James Cagney,
Barbara Stanwyck 4*

THEY ALL DIED LAUGHING (1964) Continental [Walter Reade]. B&W-
94min. (British). Leo McKern, Janet Munro 5½*
Original title: JOLLY BAD FELLOW, A

THEY ALL KISSED THE BRIDE (1942) Columbia. B&W-85min. Joan
Crawford, Melvyn Douglas .... (4)

THEY CALL IT MURDER (1971) 20th Century-Fox. Color-97min. (Made
for TV). Jim Hutton, Jessica Walker, Leslie Nielsen .... (4)
Alternate title: D.A. DRAWS A CIRCLE, THE

THEY CALL IT SIN (1932) First National [W.B.]. B&W-75min. Loretta
Young, George Brent .... (3)
British title: WAY OF LIFE, THE

THEY CALL ME MISTER TIBBS! (1970) United Artists. Color-108min.
Sidney Poitier, Martin Landau, Barbara McNair 4*

THEY CALL ME TRINITY (1970) Avco-Embassy. Color-110min. (Italian).
Terence Hill, Bud Spencer, Farley Granger .... (4)
Original title: LO CHIAMAVANO TRINITA (They Called Him Trinity)

THEY CAME FROM BEYOND SPACE (1967) Avco-Embassy. Color-
85min. (British). Robert Hutton, Jennifer Jayne, Michael Gough........ 2*

THEY CAME FROM WITHIN (1974) Trans-America. Color-88min.
(Canadian). Paul Hampton, Joe Silver, Barbara Steele .... (3)
Original title: PARASITE MURDERS, THE
British title: SHIVERS

THEY CAME TO BLOW UP AMERICA (1943) 20th Century-Fox. B&W-
73min. George Sanders, Anna Sten .... (3)

THEY CAME TO CORDURA (1959) Columbia. Color-123min. Gary
Cooper, Rita Hayworth, Van Heflin .... (4)

THEY CAME TO ROB LAS VEGAS (1968) Warner Bros. Color-129min.
(Spanish-Italian-French-W. German, English version). Gary Lockwood,
Elke Sommer, Jack Palance 3*
Original Spanish title: LAS VEGAS, 500 MILLONES
Italian title: RADIOGRAFIA D'UN COLPO D'ORO
French title: HOMMES DE LAS VEGAS, LES
German title: AN EINEM FREITAG IN LAS VEGAS

THEY CAN'T HANG ME (1955) Lopert [U.A.]. B&W-75min. (British).
Terence Morgan, Yolande Donlon .... (4)

THEY DARE NOT LOVE (1941) Columbia. B&W-76min. George Brent,
Martha Scott, Paul Lukas .... (3)

THEY DIED WITH THEIR BOOTS ON (1942) Warner Bros. B&W-
138min. Errol Flynn, Olivia de Havilland 5½*

THEY DRIVE BY NIGHT (1940) Warner Bros. B&W-93min. George Raft,
Ann Sheridan... 4*
British title: ROAD TO 'FRISCO, THE

THEY FLEW ALONE (1942) *see* WINGS AND THE WOMAN

THEY GAVE HIM A GUN (1937) M-G-M. B&W-94min. Spencer Tracy,
Franchot Tone .... (3)

THEY GOT ME COVERED (1943) RKO. B&W-95min. Bob Hope, Dorothy
Lamour 4*

THEY KNEW WHAT THEY WANTED (1940) RKO. B&W-96min. Carole
Lombard, Charles Laughton 4*

THEY LIVE BY NIGHT (1948) RKO. B&W-95min. Cathy O'Donnell,
Farley Granger 3½*
British title: TWISTED ROAD, THE

THEY LOVE AS THEY PLEASE (1963) *see* GREENWICH VILLAGE
STORY

THEY LOVED LIFE (1956) *see* KANAL

THEY MADE ME A CRIMINAL (1939) Warner Bros. B&W-92min. John
Garfield, Ann Sheridan 4*

THEY MADE ME A CRIMINAL (1947) *see* I BECAME A CRIMINAL

THEY MADE ME A FUGITIVE (1947) *see* I BECAME A CRIMINAL

THEY MADE ME A KILLER (1946) Paramount. B&W-64min. Barbara
Britton, Robert Lowery .... (4)

THEY MET AT MIDNIGHT (1946) *see* PICCADILLY INCIDENT

THEY MET IN ARGENTINA (1941) RKO. B&W-77min. Maureen O'Hara,
Gene Raymond .... (3)

THEY MET IN BOMBAY (1941) M-G-M. B&W-86min. Clark Gable,
Rosalind Russell 4½*

THEY MET IN THE DARK (1943) Hellman. B&W-104min. (British).
James Mason, Joyce Howard...

THEY MIGHT BE GIANTS (1971) Universal. Color-88min. Joanne
Woodward, George C. Scott 3*

THEY ONLY KILL THEIR MASTERS (1972) M-G-M. Color-97min. James
Garner, Katharine Ross 4*

THEY PASSED THIS WAY (1948) *see* FOUR FACES WEST

THEY RODE WEST (1954) Columbia. Color-84min. Robert Francis,
Donna Reed .... (4)

THEY SAVED HITLER'S BRAIN (1964) *see* MADMAN OF MANDORAS

THEY SHALL HAVE MUSIC (1939) United Artists. B&W-101min. Jascha
Heifetz, Gene Reynolds, Walter Brennan, Joel McCrea 4*
British title: MELODY OF YOUTH

THEY SHALL NOT DIE (1959) *see* SERENGETI SHALL NOT DIE

THEY SHOOT HORSES, DON'T THEY? (1969) Cinerama Releasing.
Color-120min. Jane Fonda, Michael Sarrazin 5½*

THEY WERE EXPENDABLE (1945) M-G-M. B&W-135min. Robert
Montgomery, John Wayne... 3*

THEY WERE SISTERS (1945) Universal. B&W-115min. (British). James
Mason, Phyllis Calvert, Dulcie Gray, Anne Crawford 4*

THEY WERE SO YOUNG (1955) Lippert Productions. B&W-80min. (U.S.-
German). Scott Brady, Raymond Burr....................................... 4*

THEY WERE TEN (1960) Schwartz & Sachson. B&W-105min. (Israeli).
Ninette Linar, Oded Teomi .... (5)
Original title: HEM HAYU ASAR

THEY WHO DARE (1953) Allied Artists. Color-100min. (British). Dirk
Bogarde, Denholm Elliott 4*

THEY WON'T BELIEVE ME (1947) RKO. B&W-95min. Robert Young,
Susan Hayward... 4*

THEY WON'T FORGET (1937) Warner Bros. B&W-90min. Claude Rains,
Gloria Dickson.. (5)

THEY'RE COMING TO GET YOU (1973) Independent International.
Color-88min. (Italian-Spanish). Edwige Fenech, George Hilton, Ivan
Rassimov .... (3)
Original Italian title: TUTTI I COLORI DEL BUIO (All the Colors of
Darkness)
Spanish title: TODOS LOS COLORES DE LA OSCURIDAD

THEY'VE KIDNAPPED ANNE BENEDICT (1975) *see* ABDUCTION OF
ST. ANNE, THE

THIEF, THE (1952) United Artists. B&W-85min. Ray Milland, Martin
Gabel.. 3*

THIEF, THE (1971) MPC (TV). Color-74min. (Made for TV). Richard
Crenna, Angie Dickinson .... (4)

THIEF OF BAGDAD, THE (1924) United Artists. B&W-133min. (Silent).
Douglas Fairbanks, Julanne Johnston.. 3*

THIEF OF BAGDAD, THE (1940) United Artists. Color-106min. (British).
Conrad Veidt, Sabu... 5½*

Films are rated on a 1 to 10 scale, 10 is highest. **Boldface** ratings followed by an asterisk (*) are for films
actually seen and rated by the executive and senior editors. All other ratings are estimates. (See Notes on
Entertainment Ratings in the front section.)

THIEF OF BAGHDAD, THE (1961) M-G-M. Color-90min. *(Italian-French)*. Steve Reeves, Georgia Moll..............................(3)
Original Italian title: LADRO DI BAGDAD, IL
French title: VOLEUR DE BAGDAD, LE

THIEF OF BAGHDAD, THE (1978) NBC-TV. Color-98min. *(Made for TV)*. Kabir Bedi, Terence Stamp, Roddy McDowall...............4½*

THIEF OF DAMASCUS (1952) Columbia. Color-78min. Paul Henreid, Jeff Donnell, Lon Chaney (Jr.)...............................4*

THIEF OF PARIS, THE (1967) Lopert [U.A.]. Color-119min. *(French-Italian)*. Jean-Paul Belmondo, Genevieve Bujold...................(5)
Original title: VOLEUR, LE *(The Thief)*

THIEF OF VENICE (1953) 20th Century-Fox. B&W-91min. Maria Montez, Paul Christian..(4)

THIEF WHO CAME TO DINNER, THE (1973) Warner Bros. Color-105min. Ryan O'Neal, Jacqueline Bisset......................6*

THIEVES (1977) Paramount. Color-103min. Marlo Thomas, Charles Grodin...4*

THIEVES FALL OUT (1941) Warner Bros. B&W-72min. Eddie Albert, Joan Leslie..(3)

THIEVES' HIGHWAY (1949) 20th Century-Fox. B&W-94min. Richard Conte, Lee J. Cobb..5*

THIEVES' HOLIDAY (1946) *see* SCANDAL IN PARIS, A

THIEVES LIKE US (1974) United Artists. Color-121min. Keith Carradine, Shelley Duvall..(5)

THIN AIR (1969) *see* INVASION OF THE BODY STEALERS

THIN ICE (1937) 20th Century-Fox. B&W-78min. Sonja Henie, Tyrone Power, Joan Davis..(5)
British title: LOVELY TO LOOK AT

THIN MAN, THE (1934) M-G-M. B&W-93min. William Powell, Myrna Loy..4*

THIN MAN GOES HOME, THE (1944) M-G-M. B&W-100min. William Powell, Myrna Loy.....................................(4)

THIN RED LINE, THE (1964) Allied Artists. B&W-99min. Keir Dullea, Jack Warden..5*

THING FROM ANOTHER WORLD, THE (1951) RKO. B&W-87min. Kenneth Tobey, Margaret Sheridan.................3*
Alternate title: THING, THE

THING THAT COULDN'T DIE, THE (1958) Universal. B&W-69min. William Reynolds, Andra Martin, Robin Hughes.....................2*

THING WITH TWO HEADS, THE (1972) American-International. Color-90min. Ray Milland, Rosey Grier, Don Marshall...........(4)

THINGS OF LIFE, THE (1970) Columbia. Color-90min. *(French-Italian-Swiss)*. Michel Piccoli, Romy Schneider, Léa Massari............(5)
Original French title: CHOSES DE LA VIE, LES

THINGS TO COME (1936) United Artists. B&W-113min. *(British)*. Raymond Massey...5*

THINK FAST, MR. MOTO (1937) 20th Century-Fox. B&W-66min. Peter Lorre, Virginia Field, Thomas Beck........................(3)

THIRD ALIBI, THE (1961) Modern Sound Films. B&W-68min. *(British)*. Laurence Payne, Patricia Dainton, Jane Griffiths...............(3)

THIRD DAY, THE (1965) Warner Bros. Color-119min. George Peppard, Elizabeth Ashley..4*

THIRD FINGER, LEFT HAND (1940) M-G-M. B&W-96min. Myrna Loy, Melvyn Douglas.................................(3)

THIRD GIRL FROM THE LEFT, THE (1973) Warner Bros. Color-73min. *(Made for TV)*. Tony Curtis, Kim Novak.............(4)

THIRD KEY, THE (1956) J. Arthur Rank. B&W-96min. *(British)*. Jack Hawkins, John Stratton.....................................4½*
Original title: LONG ARM, THE

THIRD MAN, THE (1949) Selznick Releasing. B&W-104min. *(British)*. Joseph Cotten, (Alida) Valli..............................5½*

THIRD MAN ON THE MOUNTAIN (1959) Buena Vista. Color-105min. *(U.S.-British)*. James MacArthur, Michael Rennie.............5½*
TV title: BANNER IN THE SKY

THIRD SECRET, THE (1964) 20th Century-Fox. B&W-103min. *(British)*. Stephen Boyd, Jack Hawkins, Richard Attenborough, Pamela Franklin...3*

THIRD SEX, THE (1957) D & F Distribution. B&W-80min. *(German)*. Paula Wessely, Paul Dahlke, Christian Wolff, Ingrid Stenn............(4)
Original title: DRITTE GESCHLECHT, DAS

THIRD VOICE, THE (1960) 20th Century-Fox. B&W-79min. Edmond O'Brien, Julie London..3*

THIRD MAN ON THE MOUNTAIN (1959). Aspiring mountaineer James MacArthur and his admirer Janet Munro share the dangers of an Alpine ascent.

THIRST (1949) Janus Films. B&W-88min. *(Swedish)*. Eva Henning, Birger Malmsten.......................................(3)
Original title: TORST
Alternate title: THREE STRANGE LOVES

THIRSTY DEAD, THE (1974) International Amusement. Color-88min. *(U.S.-Philippine)*. Jennifer Billingsley, John Considine...................

13 FIGHTING MEN (1960) 20th Century-Fox. B&W-69min. Grant Williams, Carole Mathews...(3)

13 FRIGHTENED GIRLS (1963) Columbia. Color-89min. Murray Hamilton, Kathy Dunn...(3)

13 GHOSTS (1960) Columbia. B&W-88min. Donald Woods, Rosemary De Camp...(3)

THIRTEEN HOURS BY AIR (1936) Paramount. B&W-80min. Fred MacMurray, Joan Bennett.............................(3)

13 RUE MADELEINE (1947) 20th Century-Fox. B&W-95min. James Cagney, Annabella..4*

13 STEPS TO DEATH (1960) *see* WHY MUST I DIE?

13 WEST STREET (1962) Columbia. B&W-80min. Alan Ladd, Rod Steiger...(3)

13TH GREEN (1954) Adrian Weiss Productions. B&W-67min. *(British)*. Ronald Howard, Barbara Kelly...............................4*

13TH HOUR, THE (1947) Columbia. B&W-65min. Richard Dix, Karen Morley..(4)

13TH LETTER, THE (1951) 20th Century-Fox. B&W-85min. Charles Boyer, Michael Rennie...4*

-30- (1959) Warner Bros. B&W-96min. Jack Webb, William Conrad.......4*
British title: DEADLINE MIDNIGHT

THIRTY DAY PRINCESS (1934) Paramount. B&W-75min. Sylvia Sidney..(4)

30-FOOT BRIDE OF CANDY ROCK, THE (1959) Columbia. B&W-75min. Lou Costello, Dorothy Provine..................(3)
Alternate title: LOU COSTELLO AND HIS 30-FOOT BRIDE

30 IS A DANGEROUS AGE, CYNTHIA (1968) Columbia. Color-85min. *(British)*. Dudley Moore, Eddie Foy, Jr.................(5)

39 STEPS, THE (1935) Gaumont-British [Rank]. B&W-81min. *(British)*. Robert Donat, Madeleine Carroll.....................5*

39 STEPS, THE (1959) 20th Century-Fox. Color-93min. *(British)*. Kenneth More, Taina Elg..5½*

THIRTY-NINE STEPS, THE (1978) J. Arthur Rank. Color-102min. *(British)*. Robert Powell, David Warner, Karen Dotrice...........(5)

31° IN THE SHADE (1965) *see* NINETY DEGREES IN THE SHADE

THIRTY SECONDS OVER TOKYO (1944) M-G-M. B&W-138min. Van Johnson, Robert Walker..4*

36 HOURS (1965) M-G-M. B&W-115min. James Garner, Eva Marie Saint, Rod Taylor..5½*

Films are rated on a 1 to 10 scale, 10 is highest. **Boldface** ratings followed by an asterisk (*) are for films actually seen and rated by the executive and senior editors. All other ratings are estimates. (See Notes on Entertainment Ratings in the front section.)

30 YEARS OF FUN (1963) 20th Century-Fox. B&W-85min. *(Compilation).* *Producer:* Robert Youngson .... (5)

THIS ABOVE ALL (1942) 20th Century-Fox. B&W-110min. Tyrone Power, Joan Fontaine 4*

THIS ANGRY AGE (1958) Columbia. Color-111min. Anthony Perkins, Silvana Mangano .... (3)

THIS COULD BE THE NIGHT (1957) M-G-M. B&W-103min. Jean Simmons, Paul Douglas, Anthony Franciosa 4*

THIS DAY AND AGE (1933) Paramount. B&W-82min. Charles Bickford, Richard Cromwell .... (4)

THIS EARTH IS MINE (1959) Universal. Color-125min. Rock Hudson, Claude Rains 3*

THIS GUN FOR HIRE (1942) Paramount. B&W-80min. Alan Ladd, Veronica Lake 4*

THIS HAPPY BREED (1944) Universal. Color-110min. *(British).* Robert Newton, Celia Johnson 4*

THIS HAPPY FEELING (1958) Universal. Color-92min. Debbie Reynolds, Curt Jurgens 4*

THIS IS A HIJACK (1973) Fanfare. Color-90min. Adam Roarke, Neville Brand, Lynn Borden .... (3)

THIS IS AMERICA (1977) *see* JABBERWALK

THIS IS CINERAMA (1952) Cinerama. Color-120min. *(Travelog).* 6*

THIS IS KOREA (1951) Republic. Color-80min. *(Documentary). Producer:* John Ford .... (4)

THIS IS MY AFFAIR (1937) 20th Century-Fox. B&W-99min. Robert Taylor, Barbara Stanwyck 4*
British title: HIS AFFAIR

THIS IS MY AFFAIR (1951) *see* I CAN GET IT FOR YOU WHOLESALE

THIS IS MY LOVE (1954) RKO. Color-91min. Linda Darnell, Dan Duryea .... (3)

THIS IS NOT A TEST (1962) Allied Artists. B&W-72min. Seamon Glass, Mary Morlas .... (4)

THIS IS THE ARMY (1943) Warner Bros. Color-115min. George Murphy, Ronald Reagan, Joan Leslie 4½*

THIS IS THE LIFE (1944) Universal. B&W-87min. Susanna Foster, Patric Knowles, Donald O'Connor .... (3)

THIS IS THE NIGHT (1932) Paramount. B&W-78min. Lily Damita, Charlie Ruggles .... (4)

THIS ISLAND EARTH (1955) Universal. Color-87min. Jeff Morrow, Rex Reason, Faith Domergue 4*

THIS LAND IS MINE (1943) RKO. B&W-103min. Charles Laughton, Maureen O'Hara 4½*

THIS LOVE OF OURS (1945) Universal. B&W-90min. Merle Oberon, Charles Korvin 4½*

THIS MAN MUST DIE (1969) Allied Artists. Color-115min. *(French-Italian).* Michel Duchaussoy, Caroline Cellier .... (5)
Original French title: QUE LA BETE MEURE
Italian title: UCCIDERO UN UOMO
British title: KILLER!

THIS MAN REUTER (1940) *see* DISPATCH FROM REUTERS, A

THIS MAN'S NAVY (1945) M-G-M. B&W-100min. Wallace Beery, James Gleason .... (4)

THIS MODERN AGE (1931) M-G-M. B&W-76min. Joan Crawford, Pauline Frederick .... (3)

THIS PROPERTY IS CONDEMNED (1966) Paramount. Color-110min. Natalie Wood, Robert Redford 3*

THIS REBEL AGE (1959) *see* BEAT GENERATION

THIS REBEL BREED (1960) Warner Bros. B&W-90min. Rita Moreno, Mark Damon .... (3)
Alternate title: THREE SHADES OF LOVE

THIS SAVAGE LAND (1969) Universal. Color-97min. *(Telefeature).* Barry Sullivan, Brenda Scott, Kathryn Hays .... (3)

THIS SIDE OF HEAVEN (1934) M-G-M. B&W-76min. Lionel Barrymore, Fay Bainter .... (4)

THIS SIDE OF THE LAW (1950) Warner Bros. B&W-74min. Viveca Lindfors, Kent Smith .... (3)

THIS SPECIAL FRIENDSHIP (1964) Pathé Contemporary. B&W-99min. *(French).* Francis Lacombrade, Didier Haudepin .... (5)
Original title: AMITIES PARTICULIERES, LES *(Special Friendships)*

THIS SPORTING LIFE (1963) Continental [Walter Reade]. B&W-129min. *(British).* Richard Harris, Rachel Roberts 6*

THIS STRANGE PASSION (1952) *see* EL

THIS STUFF'LL KILL YA! (1971) Ultima. Color-100min. Jeffrey Allen, Tim Holt, Terence McCarthy .... (3)

THIS THING CALLED LOVE (1941) Columbia. B&W-98min. Rosalind Russell, Melvyn Douglas .... (5)
British title: MARRIED - BUT SINGLE

THIS TIME FOR KEEPS (1942) M-G-M. B&W-71min. Robert Sterling, Ann Rutherford .... (3)
Alternate title: OVER THE WAVES

THIS TIME FOR KEEPS (1947) M-G-M. Color-105min. Esther Williams, Lauritz Melchior .... (4)

THIS WAS A WOMAN (1948) 20th Century-Fox. B&W-104min. *(British).* Sonia Dresdel, Barbara White, Walter Fitzgerald .... (3)

THIS WOMAN IS DANGEROUS (1952) Warner Bros. B&W-100min. Joan Crawford, Dennis Morgan 4*

THIS WOMAN IS MINE (1941) Universal. B&W-91min. Franchot Tone, Carol Bruce .... (3)

THOMAS CROWN AFFAIR, THE (1968) United Artists. Color-102min. Steve McQueen, Faye Dunaway 5½*

THOMASINE AND BUSHROD (1974) Columbia. Color-93min. Vonetta McGee, Max Julien .... (4)

THOR AND THE AMAZON WOMAN (1963) American-International. Color-95min. *(Italian).* Joe Robinson, Bella Cortez, Susy Anderson ...... (1)
Original title: TARZAN, ROI DE LA FORCE BRUTALE *(Tarzan, King of Brute Force)*
Title following action by Edgar Rice Burroughs, Inc.: THAUR, ROI DE LA FORCE BRUTALE *(Thaur, King of Brute Force)*

THOROUGHBREDS (1944) Republic. B&W-55min. Roger Pryor, Tom Neal .... (3)

THOROUGHBREDS, THE (1978) *see* RUN FOR THE ROSES

THOROUGHBREDS DON'T CRY (1937) M-G-M. B&W-80min. Judy Garland, Mickey Rooney 4*

THOROUGHLY MODERN MILLIE (1967) Universal. Color-138min. Julie Andrews, Mary Tyler Moore 5½*

THOSE CALLOWAYS (1964) Buena Vista. Color-131min. Brian Keith, Vera Miles 5*
Publicity title: THOSE CRAZY CALLOWAYS

THOSE DARING YOUNG MEN IN THEIR JAUNTY JALOPIES (1969) Paramount. Color-122min. *(Italian-French-British, English language).* Tony Curtis, Susan Hampshire 4*
British title: MONTE CARLO OR BUST!

THOSE ENDEARING YOUNG CHARMS (1945) RKO. B&W-81min. Robert Young, Laraine Day .... (3)

THOSE FANTASTIC FLYING FOOLS (1967) American-International. Color-95min. *(British).* Burl Ives, Troy Donahue 3*
Alternate title: BLAST-OFF
Original title: JULES VERNE'S ROCKET TO THE MOON

THOSE MAGNIFICENT MEN IN THEIR FLYING MACHINES (1965) 20th Century-Fox. Color-133min. *(British).* Stuart Whitman, Sarah Miles 6*
Screen title: THOSE MAGNIFICENT MEN IN THEIR FLYING MACHINES; OR HOW I FLEW FROM LONDON TO PARIS IN 25 HOURS AND 11 MINUTES

THOSE REDHEADS FROM SEATTLE (1953) Paramount. Color-90min. Rhonda Fleming, Gene Barry .... (3)

THOSE WERE THE DAYS (1940) Paramount. B&W-76min. William Holden, Bonita Granville .... (4)
British title: GOOD OLD SCHOOL DAYS, THE

THOSE WERE THE HAPPY TIMES (1968) *see* STAR!

THOU SHALT NOT KILL (1961) Gala *(Brit.).* B&W-129min. *(Italian-Yugoslavian-Leichtenstein).* Laurent Terzieff, Horst Frank, Suzanne Flon .... (4)
Original Italian title: NON UCCIDERE
French title: TU NE TUERAS POINT

THOUSAND AND ONE NIGHTS, A (1945) Columbia. Color-93min. Cornel Wilde, Evelyn Keyes .... (5)

THOUSAND AND ONE NIGHTS, A (1974) *see* ARABIAN NIGHTS, THE

THOUSAND CLOWNS, A (1965) United Artists. B&W-118min. Jason Robards, Barry Gordon 6*

1000 EYES OF DR. MABUSE, THE (1960) Ajay Films. B&W-103min. *(W. German-French-Italian).* Dawn Addams, Peter Van Eyck, Gert Frobe, Wolfgang Preiss .... (4)
Original German title: TAUSEND AUGEN DES DOKTOR MABUSE, DIE
French title: DIABOLIQUE DOCTEUR MABUSE, LE *(The Diabolical Dr. Mabuse)*
Italian title: DIABOLICO DR. MABUSE, IL
Alternate title: EYE OF EVIL
Publicity title: SHADOW VS. THE 1,000 EYES OF DR. MABUSE, THE

THOUSAND PLANE RAID, THE (1969) *see* 1,000 PLANE RAID, THE

THOUSANDS CHEER (1943) M-G-M. Color-126min. Kathryn Grayson, Gene Kelly .... (5)

THREAT, THE (1949) RKO. B&W-66min. Michael O'Shea, Virgina Grey .... (5)

THREAT, THE (1960) Warner Bros. B&W-66min. Robert Knapp, Linda Lawson .... (3)

THREE (1965) Impact Films. B&W-79min. *(Yugoslavian)*. Bata Zivojinovic, Ali Raner, Senka Veletanlic-Petrovic .... (4)
Original title: TRI

THREE (1969) United Artists. Color-104min. *(British)*. Charlotte Rampling, Robie Porter, Sam Waterston .... (4)

THREE & ONE-HALF MUSKETEERS (1961) Commonwealth United TV. Color-85min. *(Mexican)*. Tin Tan, Oscar Pulido, Rosita Arena .... (3)

THREE AVENGERS, THE (1964) ABC Films. Color-98min. *(Italian-Tunisian)*. Alan Steel (Sergio Ciani), Mimmo Palmara, Lisa Gastoni (2)
Original title: INVINCIBILI TRE, GLI *(The Invincible Three)*

THREE BAD MEN (1926) Fox Film Co. [20th]. B&W-116min. *(Silent)*. George O'Brien, Olive Borden, J. Farrell MacDonald .... (4)

THREE BAD SISTERS (1956) United Artists. B&W-76min. Marla English, John Bromfield .... (3)

THREE BITES OF THE APPLE (1967) M-G-M. Color-98min. David McCallum, Sylva Koscina .... (3)

THREE BLIND MICE (1938) 20th Century-Fox. B&W-75min. Loretta Young, Joel McCrea .... (4)

THREE BLONDES IN HIS LIFE (1960) Paramount. B&W-86min. Jock Mahoney, Greta Thyssen 3*

THREE BRAVE MEN (1957) 20th Century-Fox. B&W-88min. Ray Milland, Nina Foch, Ernest Borgnine .... (5)

THREE BROADWAY GIRLS (1932) *see* GREEKS HAD A WORD FOR THEM

THREE CABALLEROS, THE (1944) RKO (for Disney). Color-72min. *(Cartoon)*. Director: Norman Ferguson .... (6)

THREE CAME BACK (1961) *see* THEN THERE WERE THREE

THREE CAME HOME (1950) 20th Century-Fox. B&W-106min. Claudette Colbert, Patric Knowles 4½*

THREE CAME TO KILL (1960) United Artists. B&W-71min. Cameron Mitchell, John Lupton, Steve Brodie .... (2)

THREE CASES OF MURDER (1954) Associated Artists. B&W-99min. *(British)*. Alan Badel, Hugh Pryse .... (5)

THREE CHEERS FOR THE IRISH (1940) Warner Bros. B&W-100min. Thomas Mitchell, Priscilla Lane, Dennis Morgan 4*

THREE COINS IN THE FOUNTAIN (1954) 20th Century-Fox. Color-102min. Clifton Webb, Dorothy McGuire 4*

THREE COMRADES (1938) M-G-M. B&W-100min. Robert Taylor, Margaret Sullavan 4*

THREE-CORNERED MOON (1933) Paramount. B&W-77min. Claudette Colbert, Richard Arlen .... (5)

THREE DARING DAUGHTERS (1948) M-G-M. Color-115min. Jeanette MacDonald, José Iturbi 4*
British title: BIRDS AND THE BEES, THE

THREE DAYS AND A CHILD (1967) *see* NOT MINE TO LOVE

THREE DAYS OF THE CONDOR (1975) Paramount. Color-117min. Robert Redford, Faye Dunaway 6*

3 DESPARATE MEN (1951) Lippert Productions. B&W-71min. Preston Foster, Virginia Grey, Jim Davis .... (3)

THREE ETC'S AND THE COLONEL (1960) Emery Pictures. Color-99min. *(Italian-French)*. Anita Ekberg, Vittorio De Sica .... (3)
Original Italian title: TRE ECCETERA DEL COLONELLO, LE *(The Colonel's Three Etceteras)*

THREE FABLES OF LOVE (1963) Janus Films. B&W-76min. *(French-Italian-Spanish)*. Monica Vitti, Leslie Caron, Charles Aznavour ..... (5)
Original French title: QUATRES VÉRITÉS, LES *(The Four Truths)*
Italian title: QUATTRO VERITA, LE
CUATRO VERDADES, LAS

THREE FACES OF EVE, THE (1957) 20th Century-Fox. B&W-91min. Joanne Woodward, David Wayne 4*

THREE FACES WEST (1940) Republic. B&W-79min. John Wayne, Charles Coburn 4*
Original title: REFUGEE, THE

THREE FOR BEDROOM C (1952) Warner Bros. Color-74min. Gloria Swanson, James Warren .... (3)

THREE FOR JAMIE DAWN (1956) Allied Artists. B&W-81min. Laraine Day, Ricardo Montalban .... (3)

THREE FOR THE SHOW (1955) Columbia. Color-93min. Betty Grable, Marge Champion, Gower Champion, Jack Lemmon 4*

THREE FORBIDDEN STORIES (1952) Ellis Films. B&W-109min. *(Italian)*. Eleanora Rossi-Drago, Antonella Lualdi .... (4)
Alternate title: TRE STORIE PROIBITE

THREE GIRLS ABOUT TOWN (1941) Columbia. B&W-73min. Joan Blondell, Janet Blair .... (4)

THREE GODFATHERS (1949) M-G-M. Color-106min. John Wayne, Pedro Armendariz 4*

THREE GUNS FOR TEXAS (1968) Universal. Color-99min. *(Telefeature)*. Neville Brand, Peter Brown, William Smith 3*

THREE GUYS NAMED MIKE (1951) M-G-M. B&W-90min. Jane Wyman, Van Johnson, Howard Keel, Barry Sullivan 4*

THREE HEARTS FOR JULIA (1943) M-G-M. B&W-89min. Ann Sothern, Lee Bowman .... (3)

THREE HOURS TO KILL (1954) Columbia. Color-77min. Dana Andrews, Donna Reed .... (5)

365 NIGHTS IN HOLLYWOOD (1934) Fox Film Co. [20th]. B&W-74min. Alice Faye, James Dunn .... (4)

300 SPARTANS, THE (1962) 20th Century-Fox. Color-114min. Richard Egan, Ralph Richardson 3*

THREE HUSBANDS (1950) United Artists. B&W-78min. Emlyn Williams, Eve Arden .... (5)
Alternate title: LETTER TO THREE HUSBANDS, A

THREE IN THE ATTIC (1968) American-International. Color-91min. Christopher Jones, Yvette Mimieux, Judy Pace, Maggie Thrett ..... (3)

THREE IN THE CELLAR (1970) *see* UP IN THE CELLAR

3 INTO 2 WON'T GO (1969) Universal. Color-93min. *(British)*. Rod Steiger, Claire Bloom, Judy Geeson 4*

THREE IS A FAMILY (1944) United Artists. B&W-81min. Marjorie Reynolds, Fay Bainter .... (4)

THREE LIGHTS, THE (1921) *see* DESTINY

THREE LITTLE GIRLS IN BLUE (1946) 20th Century-Fox. Color-90min. June Haver, Vivian Blaine, Vera-Ellen 4½*

THREE LITTLE SISTERS (1944) Republic. B&W-69min. Mary Lee, Ruth Terry .... (3)

THREE LITTLE WORDS (1950) M-G-M. Color-102min. Fred Astaire, Red Skelton .... (5)

THREE LIVES OF THOMASINA, THE (1963) Buena Vista. Color-97min. *(U.S.-British)*. Patrick McGoohan, Susan Hampshire 5*

THREE LOVES HAS NANCY (1938) M-G-M. B&W-69min. Janet Gaynor, Robert Montgomery, Franchot Tone .... (4)

THREE MEN AND A GIRL (1938) *see* KENTUCKY MOONSHINE

THREE MEN IN A BOAT (1956) Valiant. Color-95min. *(British)*. Laurence Harvey, Martita Hunt, Adrienne Corri .... (4)

THREE MEN IN WHITE (1944) M-G-M. B&W-85min. Lionel Barrymore, Van Johnson, Ava Gardner .... (3)

THREE MEN ON A HORSE (1936) First National [W.B.]. B&W-88min. Joan Blondell, Frank McHugh, Sam Levene 4*

THREE MURDERESSES (1958) 20th Century-Fox. Color-95min. *(French)*. Alain Delon, Mylene Demongeot, Pascale Petit .... (4)
Original title: FAIBLES FEMMES *(Weak Women)*
Alternate title: WOMEN ARE WEAK

THREE MUSKETEERS, THE (1921) United Artists. B&W-110min. *(Silent)*. Douglas Fairbanks, Leon Barry, Eugene Pallette 5*

THREE MUSKETEERS, THE (1935) RKO. B&W-90min. Walter Abel, Paul Lukas 5*

THREE MUSKETEERS, THE (1939) 20th Century-Fox. B&W-73min. Don Ameche, The Ritz Brothers 5*

THREE MUSKETEERS, THE (1948) M-G-M. Color-125min. Gene Kelly, Lana Turner 6*

THREE MUSKETEERS, THE (1953) Alan Enterprises. Color-135min. *(French)*. Georges Marchal, Yvonne Sanson, Bourvil 5½*
Original title: TROIS MOUSQUETAIRES, LES

THREE MUSKETEERS, THE (1961) Prodis (French). Color-100min. *(French)*. Gerard Barry, Mylene Demongeot, Perrette Pradier ....
Original title: TROIS MOUSQUETAIRES, LES

THREE MUSKETEERS, THE (1974) 20th Century-Fox. Color-105min. *(Panamanian, English language)*. Michael York, Oliver Reed 6*
Alternate title: QUEEN'S DIAMONDS, THE

THREE NUTS IN SEARCH OF A BOLT (1964) Harlequin International. B&W-80min. Mamie Van Doren, Tommy Noonan 2*

THREE ON A COUCH (1966) Columbia. Color-109min. Jerry Lewis, Janet Leigh, Mary Ann Mobley 3*

THREE ON A MATCH (1932) First National [W.B.]. B&W-64min. Joan Blondell, Ann Dvorak .... (5)

THE THREE MUSKETEERS (1939). Athos, Porthos and Aramis were never like this! Don Ameche (second from right), as D'Artagnan, has to team up with three buffoonish tavern waiters — The Ritz Brothers — masquerading as the real Three Musketeers. (Left to right, it's Al, Jimmy, Ameche and Harry.)

THREE ON A SPREE (1961) United Artists. B&W-83min. *(British)*. Jack Watling, Carole Lesley .... (3)

THREE ON A WEEK-END (1938) Gaumont-British [Rank]. B&W-86min. *(British)*. John Lodge, Margaret Lockwood ....
Original title: BANK HOLIDAY

THREE OUTLAWS, THE (1956) Associated Film Dists. B&W-74min. Neville Brand, Bruce Bennett, Alan Hale, Jr. .... (3)

THREE PENNY OPERA (1963) Avco-Embassy. Color-83min. *(W. German-French)*. Curd (Curt) Jurgens, June Ritchie, Sammy Davis, Jr. .... (3)
German title: DREIGROSCHENOPER, DIE

THREE RING CIRCUS (1955) Paramount. Color-103min. Dean Martin, Jerry Lewis.. 4*
Publicity title(?): JERRICO THE WONDER CLOWN

THREE SAILORS AND A GIRL (1953) Warner Bros. Color-95min. Jane Powell, Gordon MacRae, Gene Nelson..................... (4)

THREE SCENES WITH INGMAR BERGMAN (1975) Jorn Donner. Color-92min. *(Finnish, Documentary)*. *Director:* Jorn Donner .... (4)
Original title: TRE SCENER MED INGMAR BERGMAN

THREE SECRETS (1950) Warner Bros. B&W-98min. Eleanor Parker, Patricia Neal, Ruth Roman 4*

THREE SHADES OF LOVE (1960) *see* THIS REBEL BREED

THREE SISTERS, THE (1964) Brandon. B&W-112min. *(U.S.S.R.)*. Lyubov Sokolova, Margarita Volodina .... (5)
Original title: TRI SESTRI

THREE SISTERS, THE (1965) Ely Landau. B&W-168min. *(Made for TV)*. Kim Stanley, Geraldine Page, Sandy Dennis, Shelley Winters 4*

THREE SISTERS, THE (1974) American Film Theatre. Color-165min. *(British)*. Jeanne Watts, Joan Plowright, Alan Bates, Laurence Olivier .... (5)

THREE SMART GIRLS (1937) Universal. B&W-86min. Deanna Durbin, Nan Grey, Barbara Read... 4*

THREE SMART GIRLS GROW UP (1939) Universal. B&W-87min. Deanna Durbin, Nan Grey, Helen Parrish .... (4)

THREE SONS O' GUNS (1941) Warner Bros. B&W-64min. Wayne Morris, Irene Rich... (3)

THREE STEPS NORTH (1951) United Artists. B&W-85min. *(U.S.-Italian)*. Lloyd Bridges, Lea Padovani .... (4)
Italian title: TRE PASSI A NORD

THREE STEPS TO THE GALLOWS (1954) *see* WHITE FIRE

THREE STOOGES GO AROUND THE WORLD IN DAZE, THE (1963) Columbia. B&W-94min. Moe Howard, Larry Fine, Joe De Rita.............. 3*

THREE STOOGES IN ORBIT, THE (1962) Columbia. B&W-87min. Moe Howard, Larry Fine, Joe De Rita.................................. (3)

THREE STOOGES MEET HERCULES, THE (1962) Columbia. B&W-89min. Moe Howard, Larry Fine, Joe De Rita........................ (3)

THREE STOPS TO MURDER (1954) Astor. B&W-77min. *(British)*. Tom Conway, Naomi Chance .... (3)

THREE STRANGE LOVES (1949) *see* THIRST

THREE STRANGERS (1946) Warner Bros. B&W-92min. Sydney Greenstreet, Peter Lorre, Geraldine Fitzgerald......................... 4*

THREE STRIPES IN THE SUN (1955) Columbia. B&W-93min. Aldo Ray, Phil Carey .... (4)
British title: GENTLE SERGEANT, THE

THREE SWORDS OF ZORRO, THE (1963) NTA Pictures. Color-88min. *(Spanish-Italian)*. Guy Stockwell, Mikaela, Antonio Prieto .... (3)
Original Spanish title: TRES ESPADAS DEL ZORRO, LAS

3:10 TO YUMA (1957) Columbia. B&W-92min. Glenn Ford, Van Heflin 5½*

THREE THE HARD WAY (1974) Allied Artists. Color-93min. Jim Brown, Fred Williamson, Jim Kelly... 3*

3000 A.D. (1952) *see* CAPTIVE WOMEN

THREE TOUGH GUYS (1974) Paramount. Color-92min. *(U.S.-Italian)*. Lino Ventura, Isaac Hayes, Fred Williamson, Paula Kelly.................. (3)

THREE VIOLENT PEOPLE (1957) Paramount. Color-100min. Charlton Heston, Anne Baxter, Gilbert Roland .... (4)

THREE WARRIORS (1977) Fantasy Films. Color-109min. McKee Red Wing, Charles White Eagle .... (4)

THREE WAX MEN (1924) *see* WAXWORKS

THREE WISE FOOLS (1946) M-G-M. B&W-90min. Margaret O'Brien, Lewis Stone, Lionel Barrymore .... (3)

3 WOMEN (1977) 20th Century-Fox. Color-122min. Shelley Duvall, Sissy Spacek, Janice Rule 4*

THREE WORLDS OF GULLIVER, THE (1960) Columbia. Color-100min. *(U.S.-British-Spanish)*. Kerwin Mathews, June Thorburn .... (5)

THREE YOUNG TEXANS (1954) 20th Century-Fox. Color-78min. Mitzi Gaynor, Jeffrey Hunter, Keefe Brasselle .... (3)

THREEPENNY OPERA, THE (1931) Brandon. B&W-112min. *(German)*. Rudolph Forster, Carola Neher 5*
Original title: DREIGROSHENOPER, DIE

THREE'S A CROWD (1969) Screen Gems. Color-74min. *(Made for TV)*. Larry Hagman, E. J. Peaker, Jessica Walter 4*

THRILL OF A ROMANCE (1945) M-G-M. Color-105min. Esther Williams, Van Johnson .... (3)

THRILL OF BRAZIL, THE (1946) Columbia. B&W-91min. Evelyn Keyes, Allyn Joslyn .... (4)

THRILL OF IT ALL, THE (1963) Universal. Color-108min. Doris Day, James Garner 4*

THRONE OF BLOOD (1957) Brandon. B&W-108min. *(Japanese)*. Toshiro Mifune, Isuzu Yamada 5*
Original Japanese Title: KUMONOSU-JO *(The Castle of the Spider's Web)*

THROUGH A GLASS DARKLY (1960) Janus Films. B&W-91min. *(Swedish)*. Harriet Andersson, Max Von Sydow................... 5*
Original title: SASOM I EN SPEGEL

THROUGH HELL TO GLORY (1958) *see* JET ATTACK

THUMB TRIPPING (1972) Avco-Embassy. Color-94min. Michael Burns, Meg Foster, Bruce Dern ....

THUNDER ACROSS THE PACIFIC (1951) *see* WILD BLUE YONDER, THE

THUNDER AFLOAT (1939) M-G-M. B&W-94min. Wallace Beery, Chester Morris .... (4)

THUNDER ALLEY (1967) American-International. Color-90min. Annette Funicello, Fabian, Diane McBain... (2)

THUNDER AND LIGHTNING (1977) 20th Century-Fox. Color-93min. David Carradine, Kate Jackson, Roger C. Carmel 4½*

THUNDER BAY (1953) Universal. Color-102min. James Stewart, Joanne Dru... 4*

THUNDER BELOW (1932) Paramount. B&W-67min. Tallulah Bankhead, Charles Bickford, Paul Lukas... (4)

THUNDER BIRDS (1942) 20th Century-Fox. Color-78min. Gene Tierney, Preston Foster, John Sutton .... (3)

THUNDER IN CAROLINA (1960) Howco International. Color-92min. Rory Calhoun, Conny Hines .... (3)

THUNDER IN THE DUST (1950) *see* SUNDOWNERS, THE

THUNDER IN THE EAST (1934) *see* BATTLE, THE

THUNDER IN THE EAST (1953) Paramount. B&W-98min. Alan Ladd, Deborah Kerr... 3½*

THUNDER IN THE SUN (1959) Paramount. Color-81min. Susan Hayward, Jeff Chandler 3*

THUNDER IN THE VALLEY (1947) 20th Century-Fox. Color-103min. Lon McCallister, Edmund Gwenn, Peggy Ann Garner................... (4)
British title: BOB, SON OF BATTLE

THUNDER ISLAND (1963) 20th Century-Fox. B&W-65min. Gene Nelson, Fay Spain ....(2)

THUNDER OF DRUMS, A (1961) M-G-M. Color-97min. Richard Boone, George Hamilton ....(4)

THUNDER ON THE HILL (1951) Universal. B&W-84min. Claudette Colbert, Ann Blyth ....(5)
British title: BONAVENTURE

THUNDER OVER ARIZONA (1956) Republic. Color-75min. George Macready, Skip Homeier ....(3)

THUNDER OVER HAWAII (1957) *see* NAKED PARADISE

THUNDER OVER TANGIER (1957) Republic. B&W-66min. *(British).* Robert Hutton, Lisa Gastoni ....(3)
Original title: MAN FROM TANGIER

THUNDER OVER THE PLAINS (1953) Warner Bros. Color-82min. Randolph Scott, Lex Barker, Phyllis Kirk ....(3)

THUNDER PASS (1954) Lippert Productions. B&W-76min. Dane Clark, Dorothy Patrick **3***

THUNDER ROAD (1958) United Artists. B&W-92min. Robert Mitchum, Gene Barry, Jim Mitchum **3***

THUNDER ROCK (1942) English Films. B&W-95min. *(British).* Michael Redgrave, Barbara Mullen ....(5)

THUNDERBALL (1965) United Artists. Color-125min. *(British).* Sean Connery, Claudine Auger **4***

THUNDERBIRDS (1942) *see* THUNDER BIRDS

THUNDERBIRDS (1952) Republic. B&W-98min. John Derek, John Barrymore, Jr. ....(4)

THUNDERBIRDS ARE GO (1966) United Artists. Color-94min. *(British, Puppets). Director:* David Lane ....

THUNDERBIRDS 6 (1968) United Artists. Color-90min. *(British, Puppets). Director:* David Lane ....

THUNDERBOLT (1929) Paramount. B&W-81min. George Bancroft, Fay Wray ....(4)

THUNDERBOLT AND LIGHTFOOT (1974) United Artists. Color-114min. Clint Eastwood, Jeff Bridges, George Kennedy **5***

THUNDERCLOUD (1950) *see* COLT .45

THUNDERCRACK! (1976) Thomas Brothers Film Studio. B&W-150min. Marion Eaton, George Kuchar ....(2)

THUNDERHEAD, SON OF FLICKA (1945) 20th Century-Fox. Color-78min. Roddy McDowall, Preston Foster ....(4)

THUNDERING JETS (1958) 20th Century-Fox. B&W-73min. Rex Reason, Audrey Dalton ....(3)

THUNDERSTORM (1956) Allied Artists. B&W-81min. *(British).* Carlos Thompson, Linda Christian ....(2)

THURSDAY'S GAME (1971) MPC (TV). Color-100min. *(Made for TV).* Bob Newhart, Gene Wilder, Cloris Leachman **5***

THX 1138 (1971) Warner Bros. Color-88min. Robert Duvall, Donald Pleasence **3***

THY NEIGHBOR'S WIFE (1953) 20th Century-Fox. B&W-77min. Hugo Haas, Cleo Moore ....(3)

TIA TULA, LA (1964) United International. B&W-86min. *(Spanish).* Aurora Bautista, Carlos Estrada, Mari Loli Cobos ......(4)
Alternate title: AUNT TULA

TIARA TAHITI (1962) Zenith International. Color-100min. *(British).* James Mason, John Mills ....(4)

. . . tick . . . tick . . . tick . . . (1970) M-G-M. Color-98min. Jim Brown, George Kennedy **3***

TICKET TO TOMAHAWK, A (1950) 20th Century-Fox. Color-90min. Dan Dailey, Anne Baxter ....(4)
Alternate title: SHERIFF'S DAUGHTER, THE

TICKLE ME (1965) Allied Artists. Color-90min. Elvis Presley, Julie Adams **3***

TICKLISH AFFAIR, A (1963) M-G-M. Color-89min. Shirley Jones, Gig Young ....(4)

TIDAL WAVE (1948) *see* PORTRAIT OF JENNIE

TIDAL WAVE (1973) New World. Color-84min. *(Japanese).* Lorne Greene, Keiju Kobayashi, Hiroshi Fujioka, Shogo Shimada **3***
Original title: NIPPON CHINBOTSU *(Japan Sinks)*
Alternate title: SUBMERSION OF JAPAN

TIGER AND THE PUSSYCAT, THE (1967) Avco-Embassy. Color-105min. *(Italian-U.S.).* Vittorio Gassman, Ann-Margret, Eleanor Parker **4***
Italian title: TIGRE, IL

TIGER ATTACKS, THE (1959) Color-100min. *(French).* Lino Ventura, Roger Hanin **4***

TIGER BAY (1959) Continental [Walter Reade]. B&W-105min. *(British).* John Mills, Horst Buchholz, Hayley Mills 5½*

TIGER BY THE TAIL (1955) *see* CROSS UP

TIGER IN THE SKY (1955) *see* McCONNELL STORY, THE

TIGER MAKES OUT, THE (1967) Columbia. Color-94min. Eli Wallach, Anne Jackson **3***

TIGER OF BENGAL (1958) *see* JOURNEY TO THE LOST CITY

TIGER OF THE SEA (1964) American-International. Color-91min. *(Japanese).* Joe Shishido, Hideaki Nitani ....(1)
Alternate title: SEA FIGHTERS, THE

TIGER OF THE SEVEN SEAS (1963) Avco-Embassy. Color-90min. *(Italian-French).* Gianna Maria Canale, Anthony Steel ......(3)
Original Italian title: TIGRE DEI SETTE MARI, LA
French title: TIGRE DES MERS, LE *(The Tiger of the Seas)*

TIGER SHARK (1932) First National [W.B.]. B&W-80min. Edward G. Robinson, Richard Arlen **3***

TIGER WALKS, A (1964) Buena Vista. Color-91min. Brian Keith, Pamela Franklin, Sabu ....(4)

TIGER WOMAN, THE (1944) *see* JUNGLE GOLD

TIGER WOMAN, THE (1945) Republic. B&W-57min. Adele Mara, Kane Richmond ....(4)

TIGHT LITTLE ISLAND (1949) Universal. B&W-81min. *(British).* Basil Radford, Joan Greenwood 5½*
British title: WHISKEY GALORE!

TIGHT SHOES (1941) Universal. B&W-68min. Broderick Crawford, John Howard ....(4)

TIGHT SPOT (1955) Columbia. B&W-97min. Ginger Rogers, Edward G. Robinson **4***

TIJUANA STORY, THE (1957) Columbia. B&W-72min. James Darren, Robert McQueeney ....(2)

TIKO AND THE SHARK (1962) M-G-M. Color-88min. *(French-Italian-U.S.).* Al Kauwe, Denis Pouira, Marlene Among, Diane Samsoi ...**4***
Original French title: TI-KOYO ET SON REQUIN *(Ti-Koyo and His Shark)*
Italian title: TI-KOYO E IL SUO PESCECANE

'TIL WE MEET AGAIN (1940) *alphabetized as* TILL WE MEET AGAIN

TILL THE CLOUDS ROLL BY (1946) M-G-M. Color-137min. Robert Walker, Van Heflin 4½*

TILL THE END OF TIME (1946) RKO. B&W-105min. Guy Madison, Dorothy McGuire **3***

TILL WE MEET AGAIN (1936) Paramount. B&W-87min. Herbert Marshall, Gertrude Michael ....(3)

'TIL WE MEET AGAIN (1940) Warner Bros. B&W-99min. Merle Oberon, George Brent **4***

TILL WE MEET AGAIN (1944) Paramount. B&W-88min. Ray Milland, Barbara Britton **3***

TILLIE AND GUS (1933) Paramount. B&W-58min. W. C. Fields, Alison Skipworth **5***

TILLIE'S PUNCTURED ROMANCE (1914) Crystal Pictures. B&W-50min. *(Silent).* Charles Chaplin, Marie Dressler 1*

TILLIE'S PUNCTURED ROMANCE (1928) Paramount. B&W-64min. *(Silent).* W. C. Fields, Louise Fazenda, Chester Conklin .....(4)
British title: MARIE'S MILLIONS

TILT (1979) Warner Bros. Color-111min. Brooke Shields, Ken Marshall, Charles Durning ....

TIMBER (1942) Universal. B&W-60min. Leo Carrillo, Andy Devine ....(4)

TIMBER QUEEN (1943) Paramount. B&W-66min. Richard Arlen, Mary Beth Hughes ....(3)

TIMBERJACK (1955) Republic. Color-94min. Sterling Hayden, Vera Ralston, David Brian ....(3)

TIMBUKTU (1959) United Artists. B&W-91min. Victor Mature, Yvonne De Carlo **3***

TIME AFTER TIME (1979) Warner Bros. Color- min. Malcolm McDowell, David Warner ....

TIME BOMB (1953) *see* TERROR ON A TRAIN

TIME BOMB (1959) Allied Artists. B&W-92min. *(French-Italian).* Curt Jurgens, Mylene Demongeot ....(4)
Original French title: VENT SE LEVE, LE
Italian title: VENTO SI ALZA, IL

TIME FOR ACTION (1957) *see* TIP ON A DEAD JOCKEY

TIME FOR BURNING, A (1966) Lutheran Film Assoc. B&W-58min. *(Documentary, Made for TV). Director:* William C. Jersey ......(5)

TIME FOR GIVING, A (1969) *see* GENERATION

Films are rated on a 1 to 10 scale, 10 is highest. **Boldface** ratings followed by an asterisk (*) are for films actually seen and rated by the executive and senior editors. All other ratings are estimates. (See Notes on Entertainment Ratings in the front section.)

TIME FOR KILLING, A (1967) Columbia. **Color-88min.** Glenn Ford, George Hamilton **4***
Alternate title: LONG RIDE HOME, THE
Alternate title: SOUTHERN BLADE

TIME FOR LOVE, A (1973) Paramount. **Color-100min.** *(Made for TV).* Jack Cassidy, Bonnie Bedelia .... (4)

TIME GENTLEMEN PLEASE! (1952) Eros Films *(Brit.).* **B&W-83min.** *(British).* Eddie Byrne, Hermione Baddeley .... (4)
Alternate title: NOTHING TO LOSE

TIME IN THE SUN, A (1969) Universal. **B&W-104min.** *(Swedish).* Grynet Molvig, Lars Passgard .... (3)
Original title: PRINSESSAN
Alternate title: PRINCESS, THE

TIME IS MY ENEMY (1954) Republic. **B&W-64min.** *(British).* Dennis Price, Susan Shaw .... (4)

TIME LIMIT (1957) United Artists. **B&W-96min.** Richard Widmark, Richard Basehart **5***

TIME LOCK (1957) *see* TIMELOCK

TIME LOST AND TIME REMEMBERED (1966) Continental [Walter Reade]. **B&W-91min.** *(British).* Sarah Miles, Cyril Cusack **4***
Original title: I WAS HAPPY HERE

TIME MACHINE, THE (1960) M-G-M. **Color-103min.** Rod Taylor, Yvette Mimieux **5½***

TIME MACHINE, THE (1978) NBC-TV. **Color-98min.** *(Made for TV).* John Beck, Priscilla Barnes ....

TIME OF DESIRE, THE (1957) Janus Films. **B&W-86min.** *(Swedish).* Barbro Larsson, Margaretha Lowler .... (4)

TIME OF INDIFFERENCE (1964) Continental [Walter Reade]. **B&W-84min.** *(Italian-French).* Rod Steiger, Claudia Cardinale, Shelley Winters .... (3)
Italian title: INDIFFERENTI, GLI *(The Indifferent Ones)*
French title: DEUX RIVALES, LES *(The Two Rivals)*

TIME OF THEIR LIVES, THE (1946) Universal. **B&W-82min.** Lou Costello, Bud Abbott, Marjorie Reynolds **4½***

TIME OF YOUR LIFE, THE (1948) United Artists. **B&W-109min.** James Cagney, William Bendix .... (5)

TIME OUT FOR LOVE (1961) Zenith International. **B&W-91min.** *(French-Italian).* Jean Seberg, Micheline Presle, Maurice Ronet .... (4)
Original French title: GRANDES PERSONNES, LES *(The Great People)*

TIME OUT FOR RHYTHM (1941) Columbia. **B&W-75min.** Rudy Vallee, Ann Miller, The Three Stooges .... (4)

TIME OUT OF MIND (1947) Universal. **B&W-88min.** Phyllis Calvert, Robert Hutton .... (3)

TIME RUNNING OUT (1950) Warner Bros. **B&W-90min.** *(U.S.-French, English language).* Dane Clark, Simone Signoret, Robert Duke .... (3)
French title: TRAQUE, LE *(The Trap)*
British title: GUNMAN IN THE STREETS

TIME, THE PLACE AND THE GIRL, THE (1946) Warner Bros. **Color-105min.** Dennis Morgan, Jack Carson, Janis Paige .... (4)

TIME TO KILL (1943) 20th Century-Fox. **B&W-61min.** Lloyd Nolan, Heather Angel .... (3)

TIME TO LIVE AND A TIME TO DIE, A (1963) *see* FIRE WITHIN, THE

TIME TO LOVE AND A TIME TO DIE, A (1958) Universal. **Color-133min.** John Gavin, Lilo (Liselotte) Pulver **3***
Publicity title: TIME TO LOVE, A
Publicity title: TIME TO DIE, A

TIME TO REMEMBER (1962) Anglo Amalgamated [EMI]. **B&W-58min.** *(British).* Yvonne Monlaur, Harry H. Corbett .... (3)

TIME TO RUN (1973) World Wide Pictures. **Color-109min.** Ed Nelson, Randall Carver .... (4)

TIME TO SING, A (1968) M-G-M. **Color-91min.** Hank Williams, Jr., Shelley Fabares, Ed Begley .... (3)

TIME TRAVELERS, THE (1964) American-International. **Color-82min.** Preston Foster, Philip Carey **3½***

TIME TRAVELERS (1976) 20th Century-Fox. **Color-74min.** *(Made for TV).* Sam Groom, Tom Hallick, Richard Basehart .... (4)

TIME WITHIN MEMORY (1973) Toho. **Color-118min.** *(Japanese).* Atsuko Kaku, Takahiro Tamura, Hisano Yamaoka .... (5)
Original title: SEIGENKI

TIME WITHOUT PITY (1957) Astor. **B&W-88min.** *(British).* Michael Redgrave, Ann Todd .... (4)

TIMELOCK (1957) Distributors Corp. of America. **B&W-73min.** *(British).* Robert Beatty, Lee Patterson .... (4)
Alternate title: TIME LOCK

TIMES GONE BY (1952) Italian Films Export. **B&W-106min.** *(Italian).* Aldo Fabrizi, Gina Lollobrigida, Vittorio De Sica, Arnoldo Foa .... (5)
Original title: ALTRI TEMPI *(In Olden Days)*

TIMESLIP (1955) *see* ATOMIC MAN, THE

TIMETABLE (1956) United Artists. **B&W-79min.** Mark Stevens, Felicia Farr .... (4)

TIN PAN ALLEY (1940) 20th Century-Fox. **Color-94min.** Alice Faye, Betty Grable .... (5)

TIN STAR, THE (1957) Paramount. **B&W-93min.** Henry Fonda, Anthony Perkins **5***

TINGLER, THE (1959) Columbia. **B&W-80min.** Vincent Price, Philip Coolidge, Judith Evelyn **4½***

TINTORERA (1977) **Color-93min.** *(Mexican).* Susan George, Fiona Lewis, Hugo Stiglitz, Andres Garcia **3½***
Publicity title: TINTORERA, KILLER SHARK

TIP ON A DEAD JOCKEY (1957) M-G-M. **B&W-99min.** Robert Taylor, Dorothy Malone .... (5)
British title: TIME FOR ACTION

'TIS PITY SHE'S A WHORE (1972) International Coproductions. **Color-91min.** *(Italian, English language).* Charlotte Rampling, Oliver Tobias, Fabio Testi .... (4)
Italian title: ADDIO FRATELLO CRUDELE

TITAN, THE (1940) **B&W-70min.** *(Swiss, Documentary).* Director: Richard Lyford .... (5)
Original title: MICHELANGELO
Alternate title: TITAN: STORY OF MICHELANGELO, THE

TITANIC (1943) **B&W-84min.** *(German).* Hans Nielsen, Ernst F. Fuerbringer, Sybille Schmitz ....

TITANIC (1953) 20th Century-Fox. **B&W-98min.** Clifton Webb, Barbara Stanwyck **5***

TITFIELD THUNDERBOLT, THE (1953) Universal. **Color-84min.** *(British).* Stanley Holloway, George Relph **5***

TITICUT FOLLIES, THE (1967) Grove Press. **B&W-87min.** *(Documentary).* Director: Frederick Wiseman .... (5)

TNT JACKSON (1975) New World. **Color-70min.** Jeanne Bell, Stan Shaw .... (4)

TO BE A CROOK (1965) Comet Film. **B&W-93min.** *(French).* Jean-Pierre Kalfon, Amidou Ben Messoud .... (4)
Original title: FILLE ET DES FUSILS, UNE *(A Girl and the Guns)*

TO BE OR NOT TO BE (1942) United Artists. **B&W-99min.** Carole Lombard, Jack Benny **4½***

TO BED . . . OR NOT TO BED (1963) Continental [Walter Reade]. **B&W-103min.** *(Italian).* Alberto Sordi, Bernhard Tarschys .... (5)
Original title: DIAVOLO, IL *(The Devil)*
Alternate Italian title: AMORE IN STOCKHOLM *(Love in Stockholm)*

TO CATCH A SPY (1957) American-International. **B&W-85min.** *(French).* Henri Vidal, Barbara Laage .... (3)

TO CATCH A THIEF (1955) Paramount. **Color-97min.** Cary Grant, Grace Kelly **5½***

THE TIME MACHINE (1960). In the year 802,701, Yvette Mimieux spins a talking ring for time traveler Rod Taylor, who is anxious to learn what's happened to the world after people stopped caring about history.

Films are rated on a 1 to 10 scale, 10 is highest. **Boldface** ratings followed by an asterisk (*) are for films actually seen and rated by the executive and senior editors. All other ratings are estimates. (See Notes on Entertainment Ratings in the front section.)

TO COMMIT A MURDER (1967) Cinerama Releasing. **Color-91min.** (*French-Italian-W. German*). Louis Jourdan, Senta Berger, Edmond O'Brien..(3)
Original French title: PEAU D'ESPION (*Skin of a Spy*)
Italian title: CONGIURA DI SPIE
German title: GRAUSAME JOB, DER

TO DIE IN MADRID (1963) Altura Films. **B&W-85min.** (*French, Documentary*). *Director:* Frédéric Rossif 5*
Original title: MOURIR A MADRID

TO DIE IN PARIS (1968) MCA-TV. **Color-100min.** (*Made for TV*). Louis Jourdan, Kurt Krueger, John Marley.................(4)

TO DIE OF LOVE (1970) M-G-M. **Color-101min.** (*French-Italian*). Annie Girardot, Bruno Pradal ....(5)
Original French title: MOURIR D'AIMER

TO DOROTHY A SON (1954) *see* CASH ON DELIVERY

TO EACH HIS OWN (1946) Paramount. **B&W-122min.** Olivia de Havilland, John Lund 5½*

TO FIND A MAN (1972) Columbia. **Color-93min.** Pamela Sue Martin, Darren O'Connor..5*
Alternate title: BOY NEXT DOOR, THE
Alternate title: SEX AND THE TEENAGER

TO HAVE AND HAVE NOT (1944) Warner Bros. **B&W-100min.** Humphrey Bogart, Lauren Bacall............................5*

TO HAVE AND TO HOLD (1961) Anglo Amalgamated [EMI]. **B&W-71min.** (*British*). Ray Barrett, Katharine Blake ....(3)

TO HELL AND BACK (1955) Universal. **Color-106min.** Audie Murphy, Charles Drake 3*

TO INGRID MY LOVE, LISA (1968) Cannon Releasing. **B&W-76min.** (*Swedish*). Gun Falck, Gunilla Iwansson, Heinz Hopf ....(2)
Original title: KOM I MIN SANG
Alternate title: "YES!" (COUNT THE POSSIBILITIES)
Alternate title: "YES!"

TO KILL A CLOWN (1972) Palomar. **Color-104min.** Alan Alda, Blythe Danner, Heath Lamberts ....(3)

TO KILL A MOCKINGBIRD (1962) Universal. **B&W-129min.** Gregory Peck, Mary Badham 5½*

TO LIVE IN PEACE (1946) Times Film Corp. **B&W-90min.** (*Italian*). Aldo Fabrizi, Gar Moore 4*

TO LOVE (1964) Prominent Films. **B&W-90min.** (*Swedish*). Harriet Andersson, Zbigniew Cybulski........................(4)
Original title: ATT ALSKA

TO LOVE A VAMPIRE (1971) *see* LUST FOR A VAMPIRE

TO LOVE SOMEBODY (1971) *see* MELODY

TO MARY - WITH LOVE (1936) 20th Century-Fox. **B&W-87min.** Warner Baxter, Myrna Loy ....(4)

TO PARIS, WITH LOVE (1955) Continental [Walter Reade]. **Color-78min.** (*British*). Alec Guinness, Odile Versois 4½*

TO PLEASE A LADY (1950) M-G-M. **B&W-91min.** Clark Gable, Barbara Stanwyck ....(4)

TO SAVE HIS LIFE (1971) *see* DEAD MEN TELL NO TALES

TO SET THIS TOWN ON FIRE (1969) *see* SET THIS TOWN ON FIRE

TO SIR, WITH LOVE (1967) Columbia. **Color-105min.** (*British-U.S.*). Sidney Poitier, Christian Roberts, Judy Geeson 6*

TO THE DEVIL A DAUGHTER (1976) EMI. **Color-92min.** (*British-German*). Richard Widmark, Christopher Lee 5*

TO THE ENDS OF THE EARTH (1948) Columbia. **B&W-109min.** Dick Powell, Signe Hasso..4½*

TO THE SHORES OF HELL (1966) Robert Patrick. **Color-82min.** Marshall Thompson, Kiva Lawrence 2*

TO THE SHORES OF TRIPOLI (1942) 20th Century-Fox. **Color-86min.** John Payne, Maureen O'Hara........................(4)

TO THE VICTOR (1938) Gaumont-British [Rank]. **B&W-78min.** (*British*). Will Fyffe, John Loder, Margaret Lockwood...........
Original title: OWD BOB

TO THE VICTOR (1948) Warner Bros. **B&W-100min.** Dennis Morgan ...3*

TO TRAP A SPY (1966) M-G-M. **Color-92min.** (*Telefeature*). Robert Vaughn, Patricia Crowley, Fritz Weaver..................(4)
Original title: VULCAN AFFAIR, THE

TOAST OF NEW ORLEANS, THE (1950) M-G-M. **Color-97min.** Kathryn Grayson, Mario Lanza ....(4)

TOAST OF NEW YORK, THE (1937) RKO. **B&W-109min.** Edward Arnold, Cary Grant..4*

TOAST OF THE LEGION (1931) *see* KISS ME AGAIN

TOBACCO ROAD (1941) 20th Century-Fox. **B&W-84min.** Charley Grapewin, Marjorie Rambeau..................................3*

TOBOR THE GREAT (1954) Republic. **B&W-77min.** Charles Drake, Billy Chapin..3*

TOBRUK (1967) Universal. **Color-110min.** Rock Hudson, George Peppard..5½*

TOBY TYLER (1960) Buena Vista. **Color-96min.** Kevin Corcoran, Henry Calvin..5*

TODAY WE LIVE (1933) M-G-M. **B&W-113min.** Joan Crawford, Gary Cooper ....(3)

TODD KILLINGS, THE (1971) National General. **Color-93min.** Robert F. Lyons, Richard Thomas, Belinda Montgomery.............(3)

TOGETHER (1972) American-International. **Color-72min.** (*Documentary*). Jan Peter Welt, Marilyn Briggs (Chambers), Vic Mohica..................(2)
British title: SENSUAL PARADISE

TOGETHER AGAIN (1944) Columbia. **B&W-93min.** Irene Dunne, Charles Boyer..4*

TOGETHER BROTHERS (1974) 20th Century-Fox. **Color-94min.** Ahmad Nurradin, Anthony Wilson ....(4)

TOGETHER FOR DAYS (1972) Olas Corp. **Color-84min.** Clifton Davis, Lois Chiles ....(3)

TOKE (1973) Esperanza Partners Ltd. **Color-97min.** Carmen Zapata, Ed Faulkner ....(3)

TOKLAT (1971) Sun International. **Color-90min.** Leon Ames, Dick Robinson, Willie ....(4)

TOKOLOSHE (1971) Artists International. **Color-80min.** (*South African*). Saul Pelle, Sidney James ....(3)
Alternate title: TOKOLOSHE THE EVIL SPIRIT

TOKYO AFTER DARK (1959) Paramount. **B&W-80min.** Michi Kobi, Richard Long..(3)

TOKYO FILE 212 (1951) RKO. **B&W-84min.** Richard Peyton, Florence Marly...(4)

TOKYO JOE (1949) Columbia. **B&W-88min.** Humphrey Bogart, Alexander Knox, Florence Marly 4*

TOKYO OLYMPIAD (1965) American-International. **Color-93min.** (*Japanese, Documentary*). *Director:* Kon Ichikawa 5*

TOKYO ROSE (1945) Paramount. **B&W-69min.** Osa Massen, Lotus Long..(3)

TOKYO STORY (1953) New Yorker Films. **B&W-139min.** (*Japanese*). Chishu Ryu, Chiyeko Higashiyama 2*
Original title: TOKYO MONOGATARI
Alternate title: THEIR FIRST TRIP TO TOKYO

TOL'ABLE DAVID (1921) Associated First National. **B&W-95min.** (*Silent*). Richard Barthelmess, Gladys Hulette, Ernest Torrence ....(4)

TOLL GATE, THE (1920) Paramount. **B&W-59min.** William S. Hart, Anna Q. Nilsson ....(4)

TOM (1973) Four Star International. **Color-83min.** Greydon Clark, Tom Johnigarn, Aldo Ray ....(3)

TOM BROWN'S SCHOOL DAYS (1940) RKO. **B&W-81min.** Freddie Bartholomew, Jimmy Lydon, Cedric Hardwicke.................(5)
Alternate title: ADVENTURES AT RUGBY

TOM BROWN'S SCHOOLDAYS (1951) United Artists. **B&W-93min.** (*British*). John Howard Davies, John Charlesworth 5½*

TOM, DICK AND HARRY (1941) RKO. **B&W-86min.** Ginger Rogers, George Murphy, Alan Marshall, Burgess Meredith...........6½*

TOM JONES (1963) United Artists. **Color-128min.** (*British*). Albert Finney, Susannah York....................................8*

TOM SAWYER (1973) United Artists. **Color-100min.** Johnny Whitaker, Jeff East..4*

tom thumb (1958) M-G-M. **Color-95min.** Russ Tamblyn, Alan Young.....4*

TOMA (1973) MCA-TV. **Color-74min.** (*Made for TV*). Tony Musante, Susan Strasberg, Simon Oakland..................................(5)

TOMAHAWK (1951) Universal. **Color-82min.** Van Heflin, Yvonne De Carlo ....(4)
British title: BATTLE OF POWDER RIVER

TOMAHAWK AND THE CROSS, THE (1956) *see* PILLARS OF THE SKY

TOMAHAWK TRAIL, THE (1950) *see* IROQUOIS TRAIL

TOMB OF LIGEIA, THE (1964) American-International. **Color-81min.** (*British-U.S.*). Vincent Price, Elizabeth Shepherd 4*
Alternate title: TOMB OF THE CAT

TOMB OF TORTURE (1963) Trans-Lux Distributing. **B&W-88min.** (*Italian*). Annie Albert, Thony Maky (Adriano Micantoni), Mark Marian (Marco Mariani) ....(3)
Original title: METEMPSYCO

TOMBOY AND THE CHAMP (1961) Universal. **Color-92min.** Candy Moore, Ben Johnson ....(4)

Films are rated on a 1 to 10 scale, 10 is highest. **Boldface** ratings followed by an asterisk (*) are for films actually seen and rated by the executive and senior editors. All other ratings are estimates. (See Notes on Entertainment Ratings in the front section.)

TOM JONES (1963) is the movie's lusty 18th-century hero, played by Albert Finney, who courts Susannah York, the very proper daughter of a wealthy squire.

TOMBSTONE, THE TOWN TOO TOUGH TO DIE (1942) Paramount. B&W-79min. Richard Dix, Kent Taylor, Frances Gifford .... (5)

TOMMY (1975) Columbia. Color-111min. (British). Roger Daltrey, Ann-Margret 4*

TOMMY STEELE STORY, THE (1957) see ROCK AROUND THE WORLD

TOMORROW (1972) Filmgroup. B&W-103min. Robert Duvall, Olga Bellin .... (5)

TOMORROW AT TEN (1963) Governor. B&W-80min. (British). John Gregson, Robert Shaw .... (3)

TOMORROW IS ANOTHER DAY (1951) Warner Bros. B&W-90min. Ruth Roman, Steve Cochran .... (4)

TOMORROW IS FOREVER (1946) RKO. B&W-105min. Claudette Colbert, Orson Welles .... (5)

TOMORROW IS MY TURN (1960) Showcorporation. B&W-117min. (French-Italian-W. German). Charles Aznavour, Nicole Courcel, Georges Riviere .... (5)
Original French title: PASSAGE DU RHIN, LE *(The Crossing of the Rhine)*
Italian title: PASSAGGIO DEL RENO, IL
German title: JENSEITS DES RHEINS

TOMORROW IS TOO LATE (1950) Joseph Burstyn. B&W-90min. (Italian). Vittorio De Sica, Lois Maxwell, Anna Maria Pierangeli (Pier Angeli) .... (5)
Original title: DOMANI E TROPPO TARDI

TOMORROW NEVER COMES (1978) J. Arthur Rank. Color-107min. (British-Canadian). Oliver Reed, Susan George, Stephen McHattie ......

TOMORROW THE WORLD (1944) United Artists. B&W-86min. Fredric March, Skippy (Skip) Homeier, Betty Field .... (5)

TONIGHT AND EVERY NIGHT (1945) Columbia. Color-92min. Rita Hayworth, Lee Bowman 3*

TONIGHT AT 8:30 (1952) Continental [Walter Reade]. Color-81min. (British). Kay Walsh, Stanley Holloway, Valerie Hobson .... (5)
Original title: MEET ME TONIGHT

TONIGHT IS OURS (1933) Paramount. B&W-76min. Claudette Colbert, Fredric March 4*

TONIGHT WE RAID CALAIS (1943) 20th Century-Fox. B&W-70min. John Sutton, Annabella .... (4)

TONIGHT WE SING (1953) 20th Century-Fox. Color-109min. Ezio Pinza, Anne Bancroft, David Wayne 4*

TONIGHT'S THE NIGHT (1954) Allied Artists. Color-87min. (British). David Niven, Yvonne De Carlo, Barry Fitzgerald 4½*
Original title: HAPPY EVER AFTER

TONIO KROGER (1964) Pathé Contemporary. B&W-90min. (W. German-French). Jean-Claude Brialy, Nadja Tiller .... (3)

TONKA (1958) Buena Vista. Color-97min. Sal Mineo, Philip Carey .... (5)
TV title: HORSE CALLED COMANCHE, A

TONY ARZENTA (1973) see NO WAY OUT

TONY DRAWS A HORSE (1950) Fine Arts. B&W-91min. (British). Cecil Parker, Anne Crawford .... (5)

TONY ROME (1967) 20th Century-Fox. Color-109min. Frank Sinatra, Jill St. John 4*

TOO BAD SHE'S BAD (1955) Getz-Kingsley. B&W-96min. (Italian). Sophia Loren, Vittorio De Sica, Marcello Mastroianni .... (4)
Original title: PECCATO CHE SIA UNA CANAGLIA

TOO DANGEROUS TO LOVE (1950) see PERFECT STRANGERS

TOO HOT TO HANDLE (1938) M-G-M. B&W-105min. Clark Gable, Myrna Loy 4*

TOO HOT TO HANDLE (1960) see PLAYGIRL AFTER DARK

TOO LATE BLUES (1962) Paramount. B&W-100min. Bobby Darin, Stella Stevens 4*

TOO LATE FOR TEARS (1949) United Artists. B&W-99min. Dan Duryea, Lizabeth Scott .... (4)

TOO LATE THE HERO (1970) Cinerama Releasing. Color-133min. Michael Caine, Cliff Robertson 4*
TV title: SUICIDE RUN

TOO LATE TO LOVE (1959) Continental [Walter Reade]. B&W-90min. (French[?]-Italian[?]). Michelle Morgan, Henri Vidal .... (4)

TOO MANY CHEFS (1978) see WHO IS KILLING THE GREAT CHEFS OF EUROPE?

TOO MANY CROOKS (1959) Lopert [U.A.]. B&W-87min. (British). Terry-Thomas, Brenda De Banzie .... (4)

TOO MANY GIRLS (1940) RKO. B&W-85min. Lucille Ball, Richard Carlson .... (5)

TOO MANY HUSBANDS (1940) Columbia. B&W-84min. Jean Arthur, Fred MacMurray 5*
British title: MY TWO HUSBANDS

TOO MANY LOVERS (1957) B&W-105min. (French). Jeanmaire, Henri Vidal, Daniel Gélin .... (3)

TOO MANY SUSPECTS (1975) see ELLERY QUEEN

TOO MANY THIEVES (1966) Filmways. Color-95min. (Made for TV). Peter Falk, Britt Ekland, David Carradine .... (4)

TOO MUCH HARMONY (1933) Paramount. B&W-76min. Bing Crosby, Jack Oakie 4*

TOO MUCH, TOO SOON (1958) Warner Bros. B&W-121min. Dorothy Malone, Errol Flynn, Efrem Zimbalist, Jr. 3*

TOO SOON TO LOVE (1960) Universal. B&W-85min. Jennifer West, Richard Evans .... (3)
British title: TEENAGE LOVERS

TOO YOUNG FOR LOVE (1955) Italian Films Export. B&W-88min. (Italian-French). Marina Vlady, Pierre Michel Beck .... (3)
Original Italian title: ETA DELL' AMORE, L'

TOO YOUNG TO KISS (1951) M-G-M. B&W-91min. June Allyson, Van Johnson .... (5)

TOO YOUNG TO KNOW (1945) Warner Bros. B&W-86min. Joan Leslie, Robert Hutton .... (3)

TOO YOUNG TO LOVE (1959) J. Arthur Rank. B&W-88min. (British). Thomas Mitchell, Pauline Hahn .... (3)

TOOLBOX MURDERS, THE (1978) Color-93min. Cameron Mitchell, Pamelyn Ferdin .... (3)

TOP BANANA (1954) United Artists. Color-100min. Phil Silvers, Rose Marie 3*

TOP FLOOR GIRL (1959) Warner Brothers Television. B&W-71min. (British). Kay Callard, Neil Hallett .... (3)

TOP GUN (1955) United Artists. B&W-73min. Sterling Hayden, William Bishop, Karen Booth .... (3)

TOP HAT (1935) RKO. B&W-101min. Fred Astaire, Ginger Rogers 4½*

TOP MAN (1943) Universal. B&W-74min. Donald O'Connor, Susanna Foster, Lillian Gish .... (4)

TOP O' THE MORNING (1949) Paramount. B&W-100min. Bing Crosby, Ann Blyth .... (4)

TOP OF THE FORM (1953) J. Arthur Rank. B&W-75min. (British). Ronald Shiner, Jacqueline Pierreux .... (4)

TOP OF THE HEAP (1972) Fanfare. Color-90min. Christopher St. John, Paula Kelly .... (2)

TOP OF THE WORLD (1955) United Artists. B&W-90min. Dale Robertson, Frank Lovejoy, Evelyn Keyes .... (3)

TOP SECRET (1952) see MR. POTTS GOES TO MOSCOW

TOP SECRET AFFAIR (1957) Warner Bros. B&W-100min. Kirk Douglas, Susan Hayward 4*
British title: THEIR SECRET AFFAIR

Films are rated on a 1 to 10 scale, 10 is highest. **Boldface** ratings followed by an asterisk (*) are for films actually seen and rated by the executive and senior editors. All other ratings are estimates. (See Notes on Entertainment Ratings in the front section.)

TOPAZ (1969) Universal. **Color-125min.** Frederick Stafford, Dany Robin **3***

TOPAZE (1933) RKO. **B&W-78min.** John Barrymore, Myrna Loy............ **6***

TOPEKA (1953) Allied Artists. **B&W-69min.** Wild Bill Elliott, Phyllis Coates .... (4)

TOPKAPI (1964) United Artists. **Color-120min.** Melina Mercouri, Peter Ustinov **6***

TOPPER (1937) M-G-M. **B&W-97min.** Roland Young, Cary Grant, Constance Bennett **4½***

TOPPER RETURNS (1941) United Artists. **B&W-85min.** Roland Young, Joan Blondell, Eddie "Rochester" Anderson **4***

TOPPER TAKES A TRIP (1939) United Artists. **B&W-85min.** Roland Young, Constance Bennett, Billie Burke **5***

TOPS IS THE LIMIT (1936) see ANYTHING GOES

TORA! TORA! TORA! (1970) 20th Century-Fox. **Color-143min.** (U.S.-Japanese). Martin Balsam, So Yamamura **5***

TORCH, THE (1950) Eagle Lion. **B&W-87min.** (U.S.-Mexican, English language). Paulette Goddard, Pedro Armendariz, Gilbert Roland........(3)
Translation of Mexican title: The General and the Senorita
British title: BANDIT GENERAL

TORCH SONG (1953) M-G-M. **Color-90min.** Joan Crawford, Michael Wilding .... (4)

TORMENT (1946) Oxford Films. **B&W-92min.** (Swedish). Stig Jarrel, Alf Kjellin, Mai Zetterling **4***
Original title: HETS
British title: FRENZY

TORMENTED (1960) Allied Artists. **B&W-75min.** Richard Carlson, Juli Reding .... (2)

TORN CURTAIN (1966) Universal. **Color-128min.** Paul Newman, Julie Andrews **4***

TORPEDO ALLEY (1953) Allied Artists. **B&W-84min.** Mark Stevens, Dorothy Malone .... (3)

TORPEDO BAY (1963) American-International. **B&W-95min.** (Italian-French). James Mason, Lilli Palmer, Gabriele Ferzetti .... (4)
Original Italian title: FINCHE DURA LA TEMPESTA
Alternate Italian title: BETA SOM
French title: DÉFI A GIBRALTAR

TORPEDO OF DOOM, THE (1938) Republic. **B&W-100min.** (Re-edited Serial). Lee Powell, Herman Brix (Bruce Bennett)................. **3***
Original title: FIGHTING DEVIL DOGS

TORPEDO RUN (1958) M-G-M. **Color-98min.** Glenn Ford, Ernest Borgnine.. **3***

TORRENT, THE (1926) M-G-M. **B&W-75min.** (Silent). Ricardo Cortez, Greta Garbo .... (4)
Alternate title: IBANEZ' TORRENT

TORRID ZONE (1940) Warner Bros. **B&W-88min.** James Cagney, Ann Sheridan, Pat O'Brien .... (5)

TORSO (1973) Joseph Brenner. **Color-90min.** (Italian). Suzy Kendall, Tina Aumont **3***
Original title: CORPI PRESENTANO TRACCE DI VIOLENZA CARNALE, I (The Body Shows Signs of Bloody Violence)

TORTILLA FLAT (1942) M-G-M. **B&W-105min.** Spencer Tracy, John Garfield, Hedy Lamarr **4***

TORTURE CHAMBER OF DR. SADISM, THE (1969) see BLOOD DEMON

TORTURE GARDEN (1967) Columbia. **Color-92min.** (British). Burgess Meredith, Jack Palance, Peter Cushing **4½***

TOSCA (1957) Casolaro-Giglio & Sol Hurok. **Color-105min.** (Italian). Franca Duval, Franco Corelli.................................. (5)

TOUCH, THE (1971) Cinerama Releasing. **Color-112min.** (Swedish-U.S., English version) Elliott Gould, Bibi Andersson, Max Von Sydow .... (4)
Original title: BERORINGEN

TOUCH AND GO (1955) Universal. **Color-85min.** (British). Jack Hawkins, Margaret Johnson .... (5)
Alternate title: LIGHT TOUGH, THE

TOUCH AND GO (1972) Libra Films. **Color-110min.** (French). Marlene Jobert, Michel Piccoli, Michael York ....
Original title: ROUTE AU SOLEIL, LA

TOUCH OF CLASS, A (1973) Avco-Embassy. **Color-106min.** (British). George Segal, Glenda Jackson **6***

TOUCH OF DEATH (1962) Planet (British). **B&W-58min.** (British). William Lucas, David Sumner, Jan Waters .... (3)

TOUCH OF EVIL (1955) Universal. **B&W-95min.** Charlton Heston, Janet Leigh, Orson Welles **3***

TOUCH OF LARCENY, A (1960) Paramount. **B&W-93min.** (British-U.S.). James Mason, George Sanders .... (5)

A TOUCH OF CLASS (1973). Things are still going smoothly for married businessman George Segal as he and divorcée Glenda Jackson hope to while away a carefree week of infidelity in Malaga, but the real fun is yet to come.

TOUCH OF LOVE, A (1969) see THANK YOU ALL VERY MUCH

TOUCH OF SATAN, THE (1974) Dundee Productions. **Color-87min.** Michael Berry, Emby Mellay **2***
Original title: TOUCH OF MELISSA, A

TOUCH OF THE SUN, A (1956) UCC Films. **B&W-80min.** (British). Frankie Howerd, Ruby Murray, Dennis Price .... (3)

TOUCH OF TREASON, A (1962) Four Star. **B&W-88min.** (French). Roger Hanin, Claude Brasseur .... (3)

TOUCHABLES, THE (1968) 20th Century-Fox. **Color-97min.** (British). Judy Huxtable, Esther Anderson, David Anthony................ (2)

TOUGH GUY (1936) M-G-M. **B&W-77min.** Jackie Cooper, Jean Hersholt, Rin-Tin-Tin, Jr. .... (4)

TOUGHER THEY COME, THE (1950) Columbia. **B&W-69min.** Wayne Morris, Preston Foster .... (2)

TOUGHEST GUN IN TOMBSTONE (1958) United Artists. **B&W-72min.** George Montgomery, Beverly Tyler .... (3)

TOUGHEST MAN ALIVE, THE (1955) Allied Artists. **B&W-72min.** Dane Clark, Lita Milan.. (4)

TOUGHEST MAN IN ARIZONA, THE (1952) Republic. **B&W-90min.** George Montgomery, Beverly Tyler .... (3)

TOURIST TRAP (1979) Compass International. **Color-85min.** Chuck Connors, Jon Van Ness ....

TOURNAMENT TEMPO (1946) see GAY BLADES

TOUT VA BIEN (1972) New Yorker Films. **Color-95min.** (French-Italian). Jane Fonda, Yves Montand, Vittorio Caprioli .... (3)
Translation title: Everything's Fine

TOVARICH (1937) Warner Bros. **B&W-98min.** Claudette Colbert, Charles Boyer.. **5½***

TOWARD THE UNKNOWN (1956) Warner Bros. **Color-115min.** William Holden, Lloyd Nolan **4***
British title: BRINK OF HELL

TOWER OF EVIL (1972) see HORROR ON SNAPE ISLAND

TOWER OF LONDON (1939) Universal. **B&W-92min.** Basil Rathbone, Boris Karloff **4***

TOWER OF LONDON (1962) United Artists. **B&W-79min.** Vincent Price, Michael Pate.. **4***

TOWER OF SCREAMING VIRGINS (1968) Maron Films, Ltd. **Color-90min.** (W. German-Italian-French). Terry Torday, Jean Piat, Uschi Glas..
German title: TURM DER VERBOTENEN LIEBE, DER (The Tower of Forbidden Love)
Publicity title: TOWER OF SIN
Publicity title: SWEETNESS OF SIN, THE

TOWER OF TERROR (1970) see IN THE DEVIL'S GARDEN

TOWERING INFERNO, THE (1974) 20th-Fox/Warner Bros. **Color-165min.** Steve McQueen, Paul Newman **5½***

TOWING (1978) United International. **Color-85min.** Jennifer Ashley, Sue Lyon, Bobby DiCicco...

TOWN CALLED HELL, A (1971) Scotia International *(Brit.)*. **Color-97min.** *(British-Spanish)*. Robert Shaw, Stella Stevens, Martin Landau, Telly Savalas ....(2)
British title: TOWN CALLED BASTARD, A

TOWN LIKE ALICE, A (1956) Lopert [U.A.]. **B&W-117min.** *(British)*. Virginia McKenna, Peter Finch...(5)

TOWN ON TRIAL (1956) Columbia. **B&W-96min.** *(British)*. Charles Coburn, Barbara Bates, John Mills.....................................(4)

TOWN TAMER (1965) Paramount. **Color-89min.** Dana Andrews, Terry Moore, Bruce Cabot ....(3)

TOWN THAT CRIED TERROR, THE (1977) *see* MANIAC

TOWN THAT DREADED SUNDOWN, THE (1977) American-International. **Color-90min.** Ben Johnson, Andrew Prine....................(4)

TOWN WITHOUT PITY (1961) United Artists. **B&W-105min.** *(U.S.-W. German-Swiss)*. Kirk Douglas, Christine Kaufmann 5½*
German title: STADT OHNE MITLEID
Swiss title: VILLE SANS PITIÉ
Alternate title: SHOCKER

TOY, THE (1976) Show Biz Company. **Color-95min.** *(French)*. Jacques Francois, Michel Bouquet, Pierre Richard.............................
Original title: JOUET, LE

TOY BOX, THE (1971) Boxoffice International. **Color-89min.** Ann Myers, Neal Bishope, Evan Steele ....(3)

TOY TIGER (1956) Universal. **Color-88min.** Jeff Chandler, Laraine Day, Tim Hovey 5*

TOY WIFE, THE (1938) M-G-M. **B&W-95min.** Luise Rainer, Robert Young, Melvyn Douglas..(3)
British title: FROU FROU

TOYS ARE NOT FOR CHILDREN (1972) Maron Films, Ltd. **Color-85min.** Marcia Forbes, Evelyn Kingsley, Peter Lightstone ....(3)

TOYS IN THE ATTIC (1963) United Artists. **B&W-90min.** Dean Martin, Geraldine Page, Yvette Mimieux 5½*

TRACK OF THE CAT (1954) Warner Bros. **Color-102min.** Robert Mitchum, Teresa Wright...3*

TRACK OF THE VAMPIRE (1966) *see* BLOOD BATH

TRACK OF THUNDER (1968) United Artists. **Color-83min.** Tom (Tommy) Kirk, Ray Stricklyn ....(2)

TRACK THE MAN DOWN (1953) Republic. **B&W-75min.** *(British)*. Kent Taylor, Renee Houston ....(3)

TRACKDOWN (1976) United Artists. **Color-98min.** Jim Mitchum, Karen Lamm, Erik Estrada 4½*

TRACKERS, THE (1971) Worldvision. **Color-73min.** *(Made for TV)*. Sammy Davis, Jr., Ernest Borgnine, Julia Adams ....(4)

TRACKS (1976) Camera One. **Color-90min.** Dennis Hopper, Taryn Power, Dean Stockwell...(4)

TRADE WINDS (1938) United Artists. **B&W-90min.** Fredric March, Joan Bennett 5*

TRADER HORN (1931) M-G-M. **B&W-123min.** Harry Carey, Duncan Renaldo 3½*

TRADER HORN (1973) M-G-M. **Color-105min.** Rod Taylor, Anne Heywood ....(4)

TRADER HORNEE (1970) Entertainment Ventures. **Color-105min.** Buddy Pantsari, Elisabeth Monica..(2)

TRADER TOM OF THE CHINA SEAS (1954) *see* TARGET: SEA OF CHINA

TRAFFIC (1971) Columbia. **Color-89min.** *(French)*. Jacques Tati, Maria Kimberly...2*

TRAIL OF THE LONESOME PINE (1936) Paramount. **Color-102min.** Henry Fonda, Sylvia Sidney, Fred MacMurray 5*

TRAIL OF THE VIGILANTES (1940) Universal. **B&W-78min.** Franchot Tone, Broderick Crawford 4½*

TRAIL STREET (1947) RKO. **B&W-84min.** Randolph Scott, Robert Ryan ....(3)

TRAIN, THE (1964) United Artists. **B&W-133min.** *(U.S.-French-Italian)*. Burt Lancaster, Paul Scofield......................................6*
French title: TRAIN, LE
Italian title: TRENO, IL

TRAIN OF EVENTS (1949) J. Arthur Rank. **B&W-89min.** *(British)*. Valerie Hobson, John Clements.......................................(4)

TRAIN RIDE TO HOLLYWOOD (1975) Taylor-Laughlin. **Color-85min.** Bloodstone, Michael Payne...(4)

TRAIN ROBBERS, THE (1973) Warner Bros. **Color-92min.** John Wayne, Ann-Margret 3½*

TRAIN ROBBERY CONFIDENTIAL (1962) Times Film Corp. **B&W-105min.** *(Brazilian)*. Eliezer Gomes, Reginaldo Faria 3*
Original title: ASSALTO AO TREM PAGADOR
Alternate Brazilian Title: TIAO MEDONHO
Alternate title: TRAIN ROBBERS, THE

TRAIN TO ALCATRAZ (1948) Republic. **B&W-66min.** Don "Red" Barry, Janet Martin ....(4)

TRAIN TO MILAN (1965) *see* NIGHT TRAIN TO MILAN

TRAITOR, THE (1958) *see* ACCURSED, THE

TRAITOR WITHIN, THE (1942) Republic. **B&W-62min.** Don "Red" Barry, Jean Parker...(4)

TRAITORS, THE (1962) Universal. **B&W-71min.** *(British)*. Patrick Allen, Jacqueline Ellis ....(3)

TRAITOR'S GATE (1964) Columbia. **B&W-80min.** *(British-W. German)*. Albert Levien, Gary Raymond, Margot Trooger ....(4)
German title: VERRATERTOR, DAS

TRAMP, TRAMP, TRAMP (1926) First National [W.B.]. **B&W-65min.** *(Silent)*. Harry Langdon, Joan Crawford 5*

TRAMP, TRAMP, TRAMP (1942) Columbia. **B&W-70min.** Jackie Gleason, Jack Durant...(3)

TRAMPLERS, THE (1966) Avco-Embassy. **Color-105min.** *(Italian)*. Joseph Cotten, Gordon Scott, Ilaria Occhini ....(3)
Original title: UOMINI DAL PASSO PESANTE, GLI

TRANS-EUROP-EXPRESS (1967) Trans-America. **B&W-105min.** *(French)*. Jean-Louis Trintignant, Marie-France Pisier ....(3)

TRANSATLANTIC (1931) Fox Film Co. [20th]. **B&W-78min.** Edmund Lowe, Lois Moran ....(4)

TRANSATLANTIC MERRY-GO-ROUND (1934) United Artists. **B&W-92min.** Jack Benny, Nancy Carroll 4*

TRANSATLANTIC TUNNEL (1935) Gaumont-British [Rank]. **B&W-94min.** *(British)*. Richard Dix, Leslie Banks.......................3½*
Original title: TUNNEL, THE

TRANSCONTINENT EXPRESS (1950) *see* ROCK ISLAND TRAIL

TRANSPLANT (1979) CBS-TV. **Color-97min.** Kevin Dobson, Melinda Dillon ....

TRAP, THE (1946) Monogram [Allied Artists]. **B&W-68min.** Sidney Toler, Mantan Moreland ....(4)
British title: MURDER AT MALIBU BEACH

TRAP, THE (1959) Paramount. **Color-84min.** Richard Widmark, Lee J. Cobb, Tina Louise...4*
British title: BAITED TRAP, THE

TRAP, THE (1966) Continental [Walter Reade]. **Color-106min.** *(Canadian-British)*. Rita Tushingham, Oliver Reed 5½*
French-Canadian title: AVENTURE SAUVAGE, L' *(The Savage Adventure)*

TRAPEZE (1956) United Artists. **Color-105min.** Burt Lancaster, Tony Curtis 5*

TRAPP FAMILY, THE (1958) 20th Century-Fox. **Color-105min.** *(German)*. Ruth Leuwerik, Hans Holt ....(3)

TRAPPED (1949) Eagle Lion. **B&W-78min.** Lloyd Bridges, John Hoyt...(5)

TRAPPED (1973) MCA-TV. **Color-74min.** *(Made for TV)*. James Brolin, Susan Clark, Earl Holliman 3*
Alternate title: DOBERMAN PATROL

TRAPPED BY BOSTON BLACKIE (1948) Columbia. **B&W-67min.** Chester Morris, June Vincent ....(4)

TRAPPED BY FEAR (1960) American-International. **B&W-85min.** *(French-Italian)*. Jean-Paul Belmondo, Sylva Koscina ....(3)
Original French title: DISTRACTIONS, LES
Italian title: DISTRAZIONI, LE

TRAPPED IN TANGIERS (1960) 20th Century-Fox. **B&W-77min.** *(Italian-Spanish)*. Edmund Purdom, Genevieve Page..............(1)
Original Italian title: AGGUATO A TANGERI *(Ambush in Tangiers)*

TRASH (1970) Cinema 5. **Color-103min.** Joe Dallesandro, Holly Woodlawn ....(3)

TRAUMA (1962) Paramount. **B&W-93min.** John Conte, Lynn Bari, Lorrie Richards..3*

TRAVELING EXECUTIONER, THE (1970) M-G-M. **Color-95min.** Stacy Keach, Marianna Hill, Bud Cort ....(3)

TRAVELING SALESWOMAN, THE (1950) Columbia. **B&W-75min.** Joan Davis, Andy Devine ....(3)

TRAVELS WITH MY AUNT (1972) M-G-M. **Color-109min.** Maggie Smith, Alec McCowen 4*

TRAVIATA, LA (1948) *see* LOST ONE, THE

TRAVIATA, LA (1966) Royal Films Int'l [Columbia]. **Color-110min.** *(Italian)*. Anna Moffo, Gino Bechi ....(4)

Films are rated on a 1 to 10 scale, 10 is highest. **Boldface** ratings followed by an asterisk (*) are for films actually seen and rated by the executive and senior editors. All other ratings are estimates. (See Notes on Entertainment Ratings in the front section.)

TRAVIS LOGAN, D.A. (1971) CBS-TV. **Color-100min.** *(Made for TV).* Vic Morrow, Hal Holbrook, Brenda Vaccaro .... **(4)**

TREAD SOFTLY, STRANGER (1958) Bentley Films. **B&W-85min.** *(British).* Diana Dors, George Baker, Terence Morgan .... **(3)**

TREASON (1950) *see* GUILTY OF TREASON

TREASURE ISLAND (1934) M-G-M. **B&W-105min.** Wallace Beery, Jackie Cooper **4½***

TREASURE ISLAND (1949) RKO (for Disney). **Color-96min.** Bobby Driscoll, Robert Newton **5***

TREASURE ISLAND (1972) National General. **Color-94min.** *(British/ French/West German/Spanish).* Orson Welles, Kim Burfield .... **(4)**

TREASURE OF FEAR (1945) *see* SCARED STIFF

TREASURE OF KALIFA (1953) *see* STEEL LADY, THE

TREASURE OF LOST CANYON, THE (1952) Universal. **Color-82min.** Tommy Ivo, William Powell, Julie Adams..................................... **(3)**

TREASURE OF MATECUMBE (1976) Buena Vista. **Color-114min.** Johnny Doran, Billy Attmore, Robert Foxworth, Joan Hackett **5***

TREASURE OF MONTE CRISTO, THE (1961) *see* SECRET OF MONTE CRISTO, THE

TREASURE OF PANCHO VILLA, THE (1955) RKO. **Color-96min.** Rory Calhoun, Shelley Winters, Gilbert Roland **3***

TREASURE OF RUBY HILLS (1955) Allied Artists. **B&W-71min.** Zachary Scott, Carole Mathews .... **(2)**

TREASURE OF SAN GENNARO (1966) Paramount. **Color-102min.** *(Italian-French-W. German).* Nino Manfredi, Senta Berger, Harry Guardino, Toto .... **(3)**
Original Italian title: OPERAZIONE SAN GENNARO *(Operation San Gennaro)*
French title: OPÉRATION SAN GENNARO
German title: UNSER BOSS IST EINE DAME *(Our Boss Is a Dame)*

TREASURE OF SAN TERESA, THE (1959) Continental [Walter Reade]. **B&W-81min.** *(British).* Eddie Constantine, Dawn Addams .... **(3)**
Alternate title: HOT MONEY GIRL

TREASURE OF SILVER LAKE (1962) Columbia. **Color-82min.** *(W. German-French-Yugoslavian).* Lex Barker, Pierre Brice, Gotz George, Herbert Lom .... **(2)**
Original German title: SCHATZ IM SILBERSEE, DER
French title: TRÉSOR DU LAC D'ARGENT, LE
Yugoslavian title: BLAGO U SREBRNOM JEZERU

TREASURE OF THE GOLDEN CONDOR (1953) 20th Century-Fox. **Color-93min.** Cornel Wilde, Constance Smith **5***

TREASURE OF THE SIERRA MADRE, THE (1948) Warner Bros. **B&W-126min.** Humphrey Bogart, Walter Huston....................... **7½***

TREE, THE (1969) Robert Guenette. **B&W-92min.** Jordan Christopher, Eileen Heckart .... **(4)**

TREE GROWS IN BROOKLYN, A (1945) 20th Century-Fox. **B&W-128min.** Dorothy McGuire, Peggy Ann Garner, James Dunn **5½***

TREE GROWS IN BROOKLYN, A (1974) 20th Century-Fox. **Color-74min.** *(Made for TV).* Cliff Robertson, Diane Baker, Nancy Malone, Pamela Ferdin .... **(4)**

TREE OF LIBERTY, THE (1940) *see* HOWARDS OF VIRGINIA, THE

TRENT'S LAST CASE (1952) Republic. **B&W-90min.** *(British).* Michael Wilding, Margaret Lockwood, Orson Welles................................ **(4)**

TRESPASSER, THE (1946) *see* NIGHT EDITOR

TRESPASSER, THE (1947) Republic. **B&W-71min.** Dale Evans, Douglas Fowley .... **(3)**

TRIAL (1955) M-G-M. **B&W-105min.** Glenn Ford, Dorothy McGuire........ **5***

TRIAL, THE (1962) Astor. **B&W-118min.** *(French-Italian-W. German).* Anthony Perkins, Jeanne Moreau **3***
Original French title: PROCES, LE
Italian title: PROCESSO, IL
German title: PROZESS, DER

TRIAL AND ERROR (1962) M-G-M. **B&W-88min.** *(British).* Peter Sellers, Richard Attenborough .... **(4)**
Original title: DOCK BRIEF, THE

TRIAL AT KAMPILI (1963) Paramount. **Color-91min.** *(Japanese).* Minoru Ohki, Elice Richter .... **(3)**

TRIAL OF BILLY JACK, THE (1974) Taylor-Laughlin. **Color-170min.** Tom Laughlin, Delores Taylor... **5½***

TRIAL OF JOAN OF ARC (1962) Pathé Contemporary. **B&W-65min.** *(French).* Florence Carrez, Jean-Claude Fourneau .... **(5)**
Original title: PROCÉS DE JEANNE D'ARC, LE

TRIAL OF LEE HARVEY OSWALD, THE (1964) Falcon International Corp. **B&W-100min.** Charles Mazyrack, Arthur Nations, George Russell ....

THE TREASURE OF THE SIERRA MADRE (1948). Adventurer Tim Holt increasingly fears that his formerly easy-going comrade Humphrey Bogart wants all the gold for himself.

TRIAL OF LEE HARVEY OSWALD, THE (1977) Worldvision. **Color-192min.** *(Made for TV).* John Pleshette, Ben Gazzara, Lorne Greene .....

TRIAL OF SERGEANT RUTLEDGE, THE (1960) *see* SERGEANT RUTLEDGE

TRIAL OF THE CATONSVILLE NINE, THE (1972) Cinema 5. **Color-85min.** Douglass Watson, Davis Roberts, David Spielberg .... **(4)**

TRIAL RUN (1968) Universal. **Color-98min.** *(Made for TV).* James Franciscus, Leslie Nielsen, Diane Baker................................ **(4)**

TRIAL WITHOUT JURY (1950) Republic. **B&W-60min.** Robert Rockwell, Kent Taylor.. **(3)**

TRIALS OF OSCAR WILDE, THE (1960) Kingsley International. **Color-123min.** *(British).* Peter Finch, Yvonne Mitchell **5½***
Alternate title: MAN WITH THE GREEN CARNATION, THE
Alternate title: GREEN CARNATION

TRIALS OF PRIVATE SCHWEIK (1964) Screen Gems. **B&W-83min.** *(German).* Peter Alexander, Rudolf Prack.................................... **(3)**
Alternate title: SCHWEIK'S YEARS OF INDISCRETION

TRIANGLE FACTORY FIRE SCANDAL, THE (1979) NBC-TV. **Color-95min.** *(Made for TV).* Tovah Feldshuh, Stephanie Zimbalist, Janet Margolin ....

TRIBE THAT HIDES FROM MAN, THE (1970) **Color- min.** *(British, Documentary, Made for TV).* Director: Adrian Cowell.......................... **(5)**

TRIBES (1970) 20th Century-Fox. **Color-75min.** *(Made for TV).* Darren McGavin, Jan-Michael Vincent, Earl Holliman **5***
British title: SOLDIER WHO DECLARED PEACE, THE

TRIBUTE TO A BAD MAN (1956) M-G-M. **Color-95min.** James Cagney, Don Dubbins **4½***

TRICK BABY (1972) Universal. **Color-89min.** Kiel Martin, Mel Stewart, Dallas Edward Hayes... **(3)**
TV title: DOUBLE CON, THE

TRILOGY (1968) Allied Artists. **Color-110min.** Mildred Natwick .... **(6)**
Alternate title: TRUMAN CAPOTE'S TRILOGY

TRILOGY OF TERROR (1975) Worldvision. **Color-74min.** *(Made for TV).* Karen Black, John Karlin... **4½***

TRINITY IS STILL MY NAME (1971) Avco-Embassy. **Color-90min.** *(Italian).* Terence Hill, Bud Spencer, Harry Carey, Jr. **4½***
Original title: CONTINUAVANO A CHIAMARLO TRINITA *(They Continued to Call Him Trinity)*

TRIO (1950) Paramount. B&W-91min. (British). James Hayter, Kathleen Harrison..5½*

TRIP, THE (1967) American-International. Color-85min. Peter Fonda, Susan Strasberg, Bruce Dern...(2)

TRIP, THE (1974) see VOYAGE, THE

TRIP TO KILL (1971) see CLAY PIGEON

TRIP TO THE MOON, A (1902) Star. B&W-14min. (French). Georges Méliès...2*
Original title: VOYAGE DANS LA LUNE, LE

TRIPLE CROSS, THE (1951) see JOE PALOOKA IN TRIPLE CROSS

TRIPLE CROSS (1966) Warner Bros. Color-126min. (French-British). Christopher Plummer, Yul Brynner...........................5*
Alternate French title: FANTASTIQUE HISTOIRE VRAIE D'EDDIE CHAPMAN, LA (The Fantastic True Story of Eddie Chapman)

TRIPLE DECEPTION (1956) J. Arthur Rank. Color-85min. (British). Michael Craig, Brenda de Banzie.............................(4)
Original title: HOUSE OF SECRETS

TRIPLE IRONS (1972) National General. Color-115min. (Hong Kong). Li Ching, David Chiang, Ti Lung.........................(2)
Original title: NEW ONE-ARMED SWORDSMAN, THE

TRIPLE PLAY (1970) Screen Gems. Color-100min. (Made for TV). William Windom, Larry Hagman, Rowan & Martin...........5*

TRIPLE TROUBLE (1950) Monogram [Allied Artists]. B&W-66min. The Bowery Boys, Pat Collins.....................................(3)

TRIPOLI (1950) Paramount. Color-95min. Maureen O'Hara, John Payne..4*

TRISTANA (1970) Maron Films, Ltd. Color-95min. (Spanish-French-Italian). Catherine Deneuve, Fernando Rey, Franco Nero.............(5)

TRIUMPH OF HERCULES, THE (1964) see HERCULES VS. THE GIANT WARRIORS

TRIUMPH OF MICHAEL STROGOFF (1964) Screen Gems. Color-118min. (French-Italian). Curt Jurgens, Capucine.................(3)
Original French title: TRIOMPHE DE MICHEL STROGOFF, LE

TRIUMPH OF ROBIN HOOD (1962) Avco-Embassy. Color-92min. (Italian). Don Burnett, Gia Scala, Gerard Philippe..............(3)

TRIUMPH OF THE SON OF HERCULES (1963) Avco-Embassy. Color-87min. (Italian). Kirk Morris, Ljuba Bodine...............(1)
Original title: TRIONFO DI MACISTE, IL (The Triumph of Maciste)

TRIUMPH OF THE TEN GLADIATORS (1964) Four Star. Color-94min. (Italian-Spanish). Dan Vadis, Helga Line, Stanley Kent.....(2)
Original Italian title: TRIONFO DEI DIECI GLADIATORI, IL
Spanish title: TRIUNFO DE LOS DIEZ GLADIADORES, EL

TRIUMPH OF THE WILL (1935) Contemporary. B&W-140min. (German, Documentary). Director: Leni Riefenstahl.................5½*
Original title: TRIUMPH DES WILLENS

TROG (1970) Warner Bros. Color-91min. (British). Joan Crawford, Michael Gough...2*

TROIKA (1969) Emerson. Color-89min. Fredric Hobbs, Nate Thurmond, Richard Faun...(3)

TROIS MOUSQUETAIRES, LES see THREE MUSKETEERS, THE

TROJAN HORSE, THE (1961) Colorama Features. Color-105min. (Italian-French). Steve Reeves, John Drew Barrymore...............(3)
Original Italian title: GUERRA DI TROIA, LA (The Trojan War)
French title: GUERRE DE TROIE, LA
British title: WOODEN HORSE OF TROY, THE
Alternate title: TROJAN WAR, THE
Alternate title: MIGHTY WARRIOR, THE

TROJAN WOMEN, THE (1971) Cinerama Releasing. Color-105min. (U.S.-Greek). Katharine Hepburn, Vanessa Redgrave, Genevieve Bujold, Irene Papas...3*

TROLLENBERG TERROR, THE (1958) see CRAWLING EYE, THE

TROOPER HOOK (1957) United Artists. B&W-81min. Joel McCrea, Barbara Stanwyck..(4)

TROOPSHIP (1937) see FAREWELL AGAIN

TROPIC HOLIDAY (1938) Paramount. B&W-78min. Dorothy Lamour, Ray Milland, Martha Raye..(4)

TROPIC OF CANCER (1970) Paramount. Color-87min. Rip Torn, James Callahan...4*

TROPIC ZONE (1953) Paramount. Color-94min. Ronald Reagan, Rhonda Fleming...(3)

TROPICAL HEAT WAVE (1952) Republic. B&W-74min. Estrelita, Robert Hutton..(3)

TROPICANA (1943) see HEAT'S ON, THE

TROTTIE TRUE (1949) see GAY LADY, THE

TROUBLE ALONG THE WAY (1953) Warner Bros. B&W-110min. John Wayne, Donna Reed..4*

TROUBLE AT 16 (1960) see PLATINUM HIGH SCHOOL

TROUBLE CHASER (1940) see LI'L ABNER

TROUBLE COMES TO TOWN (1972) ABC-TV. Color-73min. (Made for TV). Lloyd Bridges, Hari Rhodes, Thomas Evans, Pat Hingle.............(4)

TROUBLE FOR FATHER (1958) Bill Melleas-Greek Motion Pictures. B&W-100min. (Greek). Basil Logothetidis, Evagelos Protopapas, Dimitris Nikolaidis...(3)
Original title: DELISTAVRO KAI GIOS (Father and Son)

TROUBLE FOR TWO (1936) M-G-M. B&W-75min. Rosalind Russell, Robert Montgomery...(5)
British title: SUICIDE CLUB, THE

TROUBLE IN PARADISE (1932) Paramount. B&W-83min. Miriam Hopkins, Kay Francis...5½*

TROUBLE IN STORE (1953) Republic. B&W-85min. (British). Norman Wisdom, Margaret Rutherford......................................(4)

TROUBLE IN THE GLEN (1953) Republic. Color-90min. (British). Margaret Lockwood, Orson Welles, Forrest Tucker...............(3)

TROUBLE IN THE SKY (1960) Universal. B&W-76min. (British). Michael Craig, Peter Cushing, George Sanders............................4*
Original title: CONE OF SILENCE

TROUBLE MAKERS (1948) Monogram [Allied Artists]. B&W-69min. The Bowery Boys, Lionel Stander, Helen Parrish...............(3)

TROUBLE MAN (1972) 20th Century-Fox. Color-99min. Robert Hooks, Paul Winfield, Paula Kelly......................................(4)

TROUBLE SHOOTER, THE (1955) see MAN WITH THE GUN

TROUBLE WITH ANGELS, THE (1966) Columbia. Color-112min. Rosalind Russell, Hayley Mills...(4)

TROUBLE WITH GIRLS, THE (1969) M-G-M. Color-97min. Elvis Presley, Marilyn Mason..(3)

TROUBLE WITH HARRY, THE (1956) Paramount. Color-99min. Edmund Gwenn, John Forsythe, Shirley MacLaine.................(5)

TROUBLE WITH WOMEN, THE (1947) Paramount. B&W-80min. Ray Milland, Teresa Wright, Brian Donlevy...........................(3)

TROUBLEMAKER, THE (1964) Janus Films. B&W-80min. Tom Aldredge, Joan Darling..(5)

TROUBLES THROUGH BILLETS (1942) see BLONDIE FOR VICTORY

TRUCE, THE (1969) Technique et Exploitation Cinematographique (T.E.C.). Color-85min. (French). Daniel Gélin, Charles Danner, Caroline Car...(4)
Original title: TREVE, LA

TRUCK BUSTERS (1943) Warner Bros. B&W-58min. Richard Travis, Virginia Christine...(3)

TRUCK STOP WOMEN (1974) American-International. Color-82min. Claudia Jennings, Lieux Dressler, John Martino...............(4)

TRUCK TURNER (1974) American-International. Color-91min. Isaac Hayes, Yaphet Kotto...(3)

TRUE CONFESSION (1937) Paramount. B&W-84min. Carole Lombard, Fred MacMurray, John Barrymore.............................(5)

TRUE CONFESSIONS (1980) United Artists. Color- min. ....

TRUE GRIT (1969) Paramount. Color-128min. John Wayne, Kim Darby 6*

TRUE STORY OF JESSE JAMES, THE (1957) 20th Century-Fox. Color-92min. Robert Wagner, Jeffrey Hunter, Hope Lange...............(4)
British title: JAMES BROTHERS, THE

TRUE STORY OF LYNN STUART, THE (1958) Columbia. B&W-78min. Betsy Palmer, Jack Lord, Barry Atwater.........................(3)

TRUE TO LIFE (1943) Paramount. B&W-94min. Mary Martin, Franchot Tone..(5)

TRUE TO THE ARMY (1942) Paramount. B&W-76min. Allan Jones, Ann Miller, Judy Canova...(3)

TRUE TO THE NAVY (1930) Paramount. B&W-71min. Fredric March, Clara Bow..(4)

TRUMAN CAPOTE'S TRILOGY (1968) see TRILOGY

TRUNK, THE (1961) Columbia. B&W-72min. (British). Philip Carey, Julia Arnall, Dermot Walsh..(3)

TRUNK TO CAIRO (1965) American-International. Color-80min. (Israeli-W. German, English language). Audie Murphy, George Sanders, Marianne Koch...(2)
Original Israeli title: MIVTZA KAHIR
German title: EINER SPIELT FALSCH

TRUTH, THE (1960) Kingsley International. **B&W-127min.** *(French-Italian).* Brigitte Bardot, Charles Vanel .... (5)
Original French title: VÉRITÉ, LA
Italian title: VERITA, LA

TRUTH ABOUT MURDER, THE (1946) RKO. **B&W-63min.** Bonita Granville, Morgan Conway .... (3)
British title: LIE DETECTOR, THE

TRUTH ABOUT SPRING, THE (1965) Universal. **Color-102min.** *(British-U.S.).* Hayley Mills, John Mills 4½*

TRUTH ABOUT WOMEN, THE (1958) Continental [Walter Reade]. **Color-98min.** *(British).* Laurence Harvey, Julie Harris, Eva Gabor 4*

TRY AND GET ME (1951) United Artists. **B&W-92min.** Frank Lovejoy, Kathleen Ryan .... (5)
Original and British title: SOUND OF FURY, THE

TRYGON FACTOR, THE (1967) Warner Bros. **Color-87min.** *(British).* Stewart Granger, Susan Hampshire 4*

TUDOR ROSE (1936) *see* NINE DAYS A QUEEN

TUGBOAT ANNIE (1933) M-G-M. **B&W-88min.** Marie Dressler, Wallace Beery 4*

TUGBOAT ANNIE SAILS AGAIN (1940) Warner Bros. **B&W-77min.** Marjorie Rambeau, Jane Wyman, Ronald Reagan .... (3)

TULSA (1949) Eagle Lion. **Color-90min.** Susan Hayward, Robert Preston 4½*

TUMBLEWEED (1953) Universal. **Color-79min.** Audie Murphy, Lori Nelson .... (4)

TUMBLEWEEDS (1925) United Artists. **B&W-81min.** *(Silent).* William S. Hart, Barbara Medford 4*

TUNA CLIPPER (1949) Monogram [Allied Artists]. **B&W-79min.** Roddy McDowall, Elena Verdugo .... (3)

TUNES OF GLORY (1960) Lopert [U.A.]. **Color-107min.** *(British).* Alec Guinness, John Mills 7*

TUNNEL, THE (1935) *see* TRANSATLANTIC TUNNEL

TUNNEL OF LOVE, THE (1958) M-G-M. **B&W-98min.** Doris Day, Richard Widmark 5*

TUNNEL 28 (1962) *see* ESCAPE FROM EAST BERLIN

TUNNELVISION (1976) World Wide Films Corp. **Color-75min.** Larraine Newman 5½*

TURKISH DELIGHT (1973) Cinemation. **Color-102min.** *(Netherlands).* Reuter Hauer, Monique van der Ven 5*
Original title: TURKS FRUIT
Alternate title: SHELTER OF YOUR ARMS, THE

TURN BACK THE CLOCK (1933) M-G-M. **B&W-80min.** Lee Tracy, Mae Clarke .... (4)

TURN OF THE SCREW (1974) John Pearson International. **Color-136min.** *(Made for TV).* Lynn Redgrave, Megs Jenkins, Jasper Jacob (4)

TURN OFF THE MOON (1937) Paramount. **B&W-80min.** Charles Ruggles, Eleanore Whitney .... (4)

TURN ON TO LOVE (1969) Haven International. **B&W-83min.** Sharon Kent, Richard Michaels, Luigi Mastroianni .... (3)

TURN THE KEY SOFTLY (1953) J. Arthur Rank. **B&W-81min.** *(British).* Yvonne Mitchell, Terence Morgan .... (5)

TURN THE OTHER CHEEK (1975) Titanus. **Color-98min.** *(Italian).* Terence Hill, Bud Spencer, Jean-Pierre Aumont .... (3)
Original title: PORGI L'ALTRA GUANCIA

TURNABOUT (1940) United Artists. **B&W-83min.** Carole Landis, John Hubbard, Adolphe Menjou .... (4)

TURNING POINT, THE (1952) Paramount. **B&W-85min.** William Holden, Edmond O'Brien .... (4)

TURNING POINT, THE (1977) 20th Century-Fox. **Color-119min.** Anne Bancroft, Shirley MacLaine 4½*

TUTTLES OF TAHITI, THE (1942) RKO. **B&W-91min.** Charles Laughton, Jon Hall 4*

TUXEDO JUNCTION (1941) Republic. **B&W-71min.** Thurston Hall, Sally Payne .... (3)
British title: GANG MADE GOOD, THE

TWELVE ANGRY MEN (1957) United Artists. **B&W-95min.** Lee J. Cobb, Henry Fonda 7*

TWELVE CHAIRS, THE (1970) UMC Pictures. **Color-94min.** Ron Moody, Frank Langella 6*

12 DESPERATE HOURS (1956) *see* EXTRA DAY, THE

TWELVE HOURS TO KILL (1960) 20th Century-Fox. **B&W-83min.** Nico Minardos, Barbara Eden .... (2)

TWELVE O'CLOCK HIGH (1949) 20th Century-Fox. **B&W-132min.** Gregory Peck, Hugh Marlowe 5½*

THE TWELVE CHAIRS (1970). Con artist Frank Langella has learned that former Russian aristocrat Ron Moody, now a civil servant under the Soviet government, knows the secret about a hidden fortune in jewels, and demands a share of the loot.

12 TO THE MOON (1960) Columbia. **B&W-74min.** Ken Clark, Tom Conway .... (2)

TWENTIETH CENTURY (1934) Columbia. **B&W-91min.** John Barrymore, Carole Lombard 4*

TWENTIETH CENTURY FOXES (1979) United Artists. **Color- min.** Jodie Foster, Scott Baio ....

2076 OLYMPIAD (1977) **Color-90min.** Jerry Zafer, Sandy Martin ....

25th HOUR, THE (1967) M-G-M. **Color-119min.** *(French-Italian-Yugoslavian, English language).* Anthony Quinn, Virna Lisi 4½*
Original French title: 25e HEURE, LA
Italian title: VENTICINQUESIMA ORA, LA

25 YEARS - IMPRESSIONS (1977) EMI. **Color-77min.** *(British, Documentary). Director:* Peter Morley ....

24 HOURS OF A WOMAN'S LIFE (1952) *see* AFFAIR IN MONTE CARLO

24 HOURS TO KILL (1965) Seven Arts [W.B.]. **Color-94min.** *(British).* Lex Barker, Mickey Rooney .... (3)

20 MILLION MILES TO EARTH (1957) Columbia. **B&W-82min.** William Hopper, Joan Taylor 3*

20 MILLION SWEETHEARTS (1934) First National [W.B.]. **B&W-89min.** Pat O'Brien, Dick Powell .... (5)

TWENTY MULE TEAM (1940) M-G-M. **B&W-84min.** Wallace Beery, Leo Carrillo .... (3)

21 DAYS TOGETHER (1939) Columbia. **B&W-72min.** *(British).* Vivien Leigh, Laurence Olivier .... (4)
Original title: FIRST AND THE LAST, THE
British title: TWENTY-ONE DAYS

21 HOURS AT MUNICH (1976) Filmways. **Color-100min.** *(Made for TV).* William Holden, Franco Nero, Shirley Knight, Anthony Quayle 5½*

TWENTY PLUS TWO (1961) Allied Artists. **B&W-102min.** David Janssen, Jeanne Crain .... (3)
Alternate title: IT STARTED IN TOKYO

27th DAY, THE (1957) Columbia. **B&W-75min.** Gene Barry, Valerie French 4*

20,000 EYES (1961) 20th Century-Fox. **B&W-60min.** Gene Nelson, Merry Anders .... (3)

20,000 LEAGUES ACROSS THE LAND (1959) **B&W-90min.** *(French-Soviet).* Jean Gaven, Tatiana Samilova .... (4)

20,000 LEAGUES UNDER THE SEA (1954) Buena Vista. **Color-122min.** James Mason, Kirk Douglas 5*

£20,000 KISS, THE (1963) Anglo Amalgamated [EMI]. **B&W-57min.** *(British).* Dawn Addams, Michael Goodliffe .... (4)

20,000 YEARS IN SING SING (1933) First National [W.B.]. **B&W-81min.** Spencer Tracy, Bette Davis .... (5)

23 PACES TO BAKER STREET (1956) 20th Century-Fox. **Color-103min.** *(British-U.S.).* Van Johnson, Vera Miles 4½*

TWICE BLESSED (1945) M-G-M. B&W-77min. Preston Foster, Gail Patrick, Lee & Lynn Wilde .... (4)

TWICE ROUND THE DAFFODILS (1962) Anglo Amalgamated [EMI]. B&W-89min. (British). Juliet Mills, Donald Houston, Kenneth Williams .... (3)

TWICE-TOLD TALES (1963) United Artists. Color-119min. Vincent Price, Sebastian Cabot, Beverly Garland, Richard Denning 5*

TWILIGHT FOR THE GODS (1958) Universal. Color-120min. Rock Hudson, Cyd Charisse 3*

TWILIGHT OF HONOR (1963) M-G-M. B&W-115min. Richard Chamberlain, Joey Heatherton .... (4)
British title: CHARGE IS MURDER, THE

TWILIGHT OF THE GODS (1969) see DAMNED, THE

TWILIGHT PEOPLE, THE (1972) Dimension Pictures. Color-84min. John Ashley, Pat Woodell, Charles Macaulay .... (2)

TWILIGHT WOMEN (1952) Lippert Productions. B&W-89min. (British). Freda Jackson, Rene Ray, Laurence Harvey .... (3)
Original title: WOMEN OF TWILIGHT
Alternate title: ANOTHER CHANCE

TWILIGHT'S LAST GLEAMING (1977) Allied Artists. Color-146min. Burt Lancaster, Richard Widmark, Charles Durning 5*

TWIN BEDS (1942) United Artists. B&W-85min. Joan Bennett, George Brent .... (3)

TWINKLE AND SHINE (1959) see IT HAPPENED TO JANE

TWINKLE IN GOD'S EYE (1955) Republic. B&W-73min. Mickey Rooney, Coleen Gray .... (3)

TWINKY (1970) see LOLA

TWINS OF EVIL (1971) Universal. Color-85min. (British). Madeleine Collinson, Mary Collinson, Peter Cushing .... (4)

TWIST ALL NIGHT (1961) American-International. B&W-85min. Louis Prima, June Wilkinson .... (2)
British title: YOUNG AND THE COOL, THE

TWIST AROUND THE CLOCK (1961) Columbia. B&W-86min. Chubby Checker, John Cronin, Mary Mitchell .... (3)

TWIST OF FATE (1954) United Artists. B&W-89min. (British). Ginger Rogers, Jacques Bergerac .... (3)
Original title: BEAUTIFUL STRANGER

TWIST OF SAND, A (1968) United Artists. Color-90min. (British). Richard Johnson, Honor Blackman .... (3)

TWISTED BRAIN (1973) see HORROR HIGH

TWISTED NERVE (1968) National General. Color-118min. (British). Hayley Mills, Hywel Bennett .... (4)

TWISTED ROAD, THE (1948) see THEY LIVE BY NIGHT

TWITCH OF THE DEATH NERVE (1971) Hallmark. Color-82min. (Italian). Claudine Auger, Claudio Luigi Pistilli ....
Original title: ANTEFATTO

2 (1968) see I, A WOMAN, PART II

TWO A PENNY (1968) World Wide Pictures. Color-98min. (British). Cliff Richard, Dora Bryan 4*

TWO AGAINST THE WORLD (1936) First National [W.B.]. B&W-64min. Humphrey Bogart, Beverly Roberts .... (3)
British title: CASE OF MRS. PEMBROOK, THE
Alternate title: ONE FATAL HOUR

TWO AND TWO MAKE SIX (1962) Union Films. B&W-89min. (British). George Chakiris, Janette Scott .... (3)
Alternate title: GIRL SWAPPERS, THE
Alternate title(?): CHANGE OF HEART, A

TWO ARABIAN KNIGHTS (1927) United Artists. B&W-90min. (Silent). William Boyd, Mary Astor, Louis Wolheim .... (4)

TWO ARE GUILTY (1962) M-G-M. B&W-131min. (French-Italian). Anthony Perkins, Jean-Claude Brialy, Renato Salvatori 4½*
French title: GLAIVE ET LA BALANCE, LA (The Sword and the Balance)
Italian title: UNO DEI TRE (One Two Three)

TWO CENTS WORTH OF HOPE (1952) Times Film Corp. B&W-107min. (Italian). Maria Fiore, Vincenzo Musolino .... (5)
Original title: DUE SOLDI DI SPERANZA
Alternate title: TWO PENNYWORTH OF HOPE

TWO COLONELS (1963) Comet. B&W-90min. (Italian). Toto, Walter Pidgeon .... (3)
Original title: DUE COLONNELLI, I

TWO DAUGHTERS (1962) Janus Films. B&W-114min. (Indian). Anil Chatterjee, Chandana Bannerjee, Aparna Das Gupta 2*
Original title: TEEN KANYA (Three Daughters)

TWO DOLLAR BETTOR (1951) Realart. B&W-73min. John Litel, Steve Brodie .... (3)
British title: BEGINNER'S LUCK

TWO ENGLISH GIRLS (1971) Janus Films. Color-106min. (French). Kika Markham, Stacey Tendetter, Jean-Pierre Leaud .... (5)
Original title: DEUX ANGLAISES ET LE CONTINENT, LES (Two English Girls on the Continent)
British title: ANNE AND MURIEL

TWO-FACED WOMAN (1941) M-G-M. B&W-94min. Greta Garbo, Melvyn Douglas 4*

TWO FACES OF DR. JEKYLL, THE (1960) see HOUSE OF FRIGHT

TWO FLAGS WEST (1950) 20th Century-Fox. B&W-92min. Joseph Cotten, Linda Darnell 4*

TWO FLAMING YOUTHS (1927) Paramount. B&W-59min. (Silent). W. C. Fields, Chester Conklin, Mary Brian .... (4)
British title: SIDE SHOW, THE

TWO FOR THE MONEY (1971) Worldvision. Color-73min. (Made for TV). Robert Hooks, Stephen Brooks, Walter Brennan, Mercedes McCambridge .... (4)

TWO FOR THE ROAD (1967) 20th Century-Fox. Color-112min. (British-U.S.). Audrey Hepburn, Albert Finney 7½*

TWO FOR THE SEESAW (1962) United Artists. B&W-120min. Robert Mitchum, Shirley MacLaine 5*

TWO FOR TONIGHT (1935) Paramount. B&W-61min. Bing Crosby, Joan Bennett .... (4)

TWO GALS AND A GUY (1951) United Artists. B&W-71min. Janis Paige, Robert Alda .... (3)

TWO GENTLEMEN SHARING (1969) American-International. Color-105min. (British). Robin Phillips, Judy Geeson, Hal Frederick .... (4)

TWO GIRLS AND A SAILOR (1944) M-G-M. B&W-124min. Gloria DeHaven, June Allyson .... (5)

TWO GIRLS ON BROADWAY (1940) M-G-M. B&W-71min. Lana Turner, Joan Blondell, George Murphy .... (4)
British title: CHOOSE YOUR PARTNER

TWO GLADIATORS (1962) ABC Films. Color-97min. (Italian). Richard Harrison, Moira Orfei, Mimmo Palmara .... (3)
Original title: DUE GLADIATORI, I

TWO-GUN CUPID (1941) see BAD MAN, THE

TWO GUN LADY (1956) Associated Film Dists. B&W-75min. Peggie Castle, William Talman 3*

TWO GUNS AND A BADGE (1954) Allied Artists. B&W-69min. Wayne Morris, Morris Ankrum, Beverly Garland .... (3)

TWO GUYS FROM MILWAUKEE (1946) Warner Bros. B&W-90min. Dennis Morgan, Jack Carson, Joan Leslie 4*
British title: ROYAL FLUSH

TWO GUYS FROM TEXAS (1948) Warner Bros. Color-86min. Dennis Morgan, Jack Carson, Dorothy Malone .... (4)
British title: TWO TEXAS KNIGHTS

TWO HEADED SPY, THE (1958) Columbia. B&W-93min. (British-U.S.). Jack Hawkins, Gia Scala .... (5)

TWO HEARTBEATS (1972) Ha'etgar Film Prod. Co. Ltd. Color-90min. (Israeli). Yuda Barkan, Edit Astrok .... (3)

200 MOTELS (1971) United Artists. Color-99min. (British). Frank Zappa, The Mothers Of Invention, Theodore Bikel .... (3)

TWO IN A CROWD (1936) Universal. B&W-85min. Joan Bennett, Joel McCrea .... (3)

TWO IN A TAXI (1941) Columbia. B&W-62min. Anita Louise, Dick Purcell .... (3)

TWO IN THE DARK (1936) RKO. B&W-74min. Walter Abel, Margot Grahame .... (5)

TWO KENNEDYS, THE (1969) B&W-100min. (Italian, Documentary). *Director:* Gianni Bisiach 5*
Original title: DUE KENNEDY, I
Alternate title: TWO KENNEDYS . . . A VIEW FROM EUROPE, THE

TWO-LANE BLACKTOP (1971) Universal. Color-102min. James Taylor, Warren Oates, Laurie Bird 3½*

TWO LITTLE BEARS, THE (1961) 20th Century-Fox. B&W-81min. Eddie Albert, Butch Patrick, Donnie Carter .... (3)

TWO LIVING ONE DEAD (1961) Emerson Films. B&W-92min. (British-Swedish). Virginia McKenna, Bill Travers, Patrick McGoohan .... (4)
Swedish title: TVA LEVANDE OCH EN DOD

TWO LOST WORLDS (1950) Eagle Lion. B&W-61min. James Arness, Laura Elliott .... (3)

TWO LOVES (1961) M-G-M. Color-100min. Shirley MacLaine, Laurence Harvey, Jack Hawkins .... (4)
British title: SPINSTER

TWO-MAN SUBMARINE (1944) Columbia. B&W-62min. Ann Savage, Tom Neal .... (3)

Films are rated on a 1 to 10 scale, 10 is highest. **Boldface** ratings followed by an asterisk (*) are for films actually seen and rated by the executive and senior editors. All other ratings are estimates. (See Notes on Entertainment Ratings in the front section.)

TWO MEN AND A GIRL (1947) *see* HONEYMOON

TWO MEN OF KARAMOJA (1974) *see* WILD AND THE BRAVE, THE

TWO-MINUTE WARNING (1976) Universal. Color-115min. Charlton Heston, John Cassavetes, David Janssen......5*

TWO MRS. CARROLLS, THE (1947) Warner Bros. B&W-99min. Humphrey Bogart, Barbara Stanwyck......4*

TWO MULES FOR SISTER SARA (1970) Universal. Color-114min. (*U.S.-Mexican*). Shirley MacLaine, Clint Eastwood......5½*

TWO NIGHTS WITH CLEOPATRA (1954) Ultra Pictures Corp. Color-80min. (*Italian*). Sophia Loren, Ettore Manni, Alberto Sordi......(3)
Original title: DUE NOTTI CON CLEOPATRA

TWO OF A KIND (1951) Columbia. B&W-75min. Edmond O'Brien, Lizabeth Scott......(4)

TWO OF US, THE (1967) Cinema 5. B&W-86min. (*French*). Michel Simon, Alain Cohen......7*
Original title: VIEL HOMME ET L'ENFANT, LE (*The Old Man and the Child*)
Publicity title: CLAUDE

TWO ON A BENCH (1971) MCA-TV. Color-73min. (*Made for TV*). Patty Duke, Ted Bessell......(4)

TWO ON A GUILLOTINE (1965) Warner Bros. B&W-107min. Connie Stevens......(3)

TWO ORPHANS, THE (1966) Parkside Prods. B&W-97min. (*Italian*). Valeria Ciangotine, Sophia Daress......(3)

TWO PENNYWORTH OF HOPE (1952) *see* TWO CENTS WORTH OF HOPE

TWO PEOPLE (1973) Universal. Color-100min. Peter Fonda, Lindsay Wagner......3*

TWO RODE TOGETHER (1961) Columbia. Color-109min. James Stewart, Richard Widmark......4*

TWO SECONDS (1932) First National [W.B.]. B&W-68min. Edward G. Robinson, Preston Foster......(4)

TWO SISTERS FROM BOSTON (1946) M-G-M. B&W-112min. Kathryn Grayson, June Allyson......4*

TWO SMART PEOPLE (1946) M-G-M. B&W-93min. Lucille Ball, John Hodiak......(3)

TWO TEXAS KNIGHTS (1948) *see* TWO GUYS FROM TEXAS

2001: A SPACE ODYSSEY (1968) M-G-M. Color-141min. (*British-U.S.*). Keir Dullea, Gary Lockwood......7*

TWO THOUSAND WOMEN (1944) Academy-Lux. B&W-97min. (*British*). Phyllis Calvert, Flora Robson......4½*
Alternate title: HOUSE OF 1,000 WOMEN, THE

2000 YEARS LATER (1969) Warner Bros. Color-80min. Terry-Thomas, Edward Everett Horton, John Abbott......(3)

TWO TICKETS TO BROADWAY (1951) RKO. Color-106min. Tony Martin, Janet Leigh......(4)

TWO TICKETS TO LONDON (1943) Universal. B&W-79min. Michele Morgan, Alan Curtis......(3)

TWO TICKETS TO PARIS (1962) Columbia. B&W-78min. Joey Dee, Gary Crosby, Kay Medford, Jeri Lynne Fraser......(2)

TWO-WAY STRETCH (1960) Showcorporation. B&W-87min. (*British*). Peter Sellers, Wilfrid Hyde-White......6*
Alternate title: NOTHING BARRED

TWO WEEKS IN ANOTHER TOWN (1962) M-G-M. Color-107min. Kirk Douglas, Edward G. Robinson......4*

TWO WEEKS IN SEPTEMBER (1967) Paramount. Color-95min. (*French, English version*). Brigitte Bardot, Laurent Terzieff, Jean Rochefort...(3)
French title: A COEUR JOIE (*Heartful of Joy*)

TWO WEEKS WITH LOVE (1950) M-G-M. Color-92min. Jane Powell, Ricardo Montalban......(4)

TWO WIVES AT ONE WEDDING (1960) Warner Bros. B&W-66min. (*British*). Gordon Jackson, Christina Gregg, Lisa Daniely......(3)

TWO WOMEN (1960) Avco-Embassy. B&W-99min. (*Italian-French*). Sophia Loren, Eleanora Brown......5*
Original Italian title: CIOCIARA, LA (*Idiomatic: The Woman from Ciociara*)

TWO WORLDS (1957) B&W-85min. (*German*). Horst Buchholz, Johanna Matz......(3)
Original title: ENDSTATION LIEBE

TWO YANKS IN TRINIDAD (1942) Columbia. B&W-88min. Brian Donlevy, Pat O'Brien......(4)

TWO YEARS BEFORE THE MAST (1946) Paramount. B&W-98min. Brian Donlevy, Alan Ladd......4*

TWONKY, THE (1953) United Artists. B&W-72min. Hans Conried, Gloria Blondell......(2)

TYCOON (1947) RKO. Color-128min. John Wayne, Laraine Day......4*

TYPHOON (1940) Paramount. Color-70min. Dorothy Lamour, Robert Preston......(3)

TYPHOON OVER NAGASAKI (1957) Beverly Pictures. Color-115min. (*French-Japanese*). Jean Marais, Danielle Darrieux, Kishi Keiko......(3)
French title: TYPHON A NAGASAKI (*Typhoon on Nagasaki*)

TYRANT OF CASTILE, THE (1963) Four Star. Color-104min. (*Italian-Spanish*). Mark Damon, Rada Rassimov......(1)
Italian title: SFIDA AL RE DI CASTIGLIA (*Challenge to the King of Castile*)

TYRANT OF LYDIA AGAINST THE SON OF HERCULES (1963) Avco-Embassy. Color-107min. (*Italian*). Gordon Scott, Massimo Serato......(2)

TYRANT OF THE SEA (1950) Columbia. B&W-70min. Rhys Williams, Ron Randell......(3)

-U-

U-BOAT PRISONER (1944) Columbia. B&W-65min. Bruce Bennett, John Abbott......(3)
British title: DANGEROUS MISTS

U-BOAT 29 (1939) Columbia. B&W-82min. (*British*). Conrad Veidt, Valerie Hobson......(4)
Original title: SPY IN BLACK, THE

U-238 AND THE WITCH DOCTOR (1953) Republic. B&W-100min. (*Re-edited Serial*). Clayton Moore, Phyllis Coates......(2)
Original title: JUNGLE DRUMS OF AFRICA, THE

UFO (1956) *see* UNIDENTIFIED FLYING OBJECTS

UFO INCIDENT, THE (1975) MCA-TV. Color-100min. (*Made for TV*). James Earl Jones, Estelle Parsons......5*

UMC (1969) M-G-M. Color-100min. (*Made for TV*). Richard Bradford, James Daly, Edward G. Robinson, Maurice Evans......3*
Alternate title: OPERATION HEARTBEAT
Alternate title: UNIVERSITY MEDICAL CENTER

U.S.S. TEAKETTLE (1951) *see* YOU'RE IN THE NAVY NOW

UGETSU (1953) Harrison Pictures. B&W-96min. (*Japanese*). Machiko Kyo, Mitsuko Mito......4½*
Translation title: Tales After the Rain
Original Japanese title: UGETSU MONOGATARI (*Tales of the Pale and Silvery Moon After the Rain*)

UGLY AMERICAN, THE (1963) Universal. Color-120min. Marlon Brando, Eiji Okada......5*

UGLY DACHSHUND, THE (1966) Buena Vista. Color-93min. Dean Jones, Suzanne Pleshette......5*

UGLY ONES, THE (1966) United Artists. Color-96min. (*Italian-Spanish*). Richard Wyler, Thomas Milian......(1)
Italian title (translation): BOUNTY KILLER, THE
Spanish title: PRECIO DE UN HOMBRE, EL (*The Price of a Man*)

ULTIMATE THRILL, THE (1974) General Cinema. Color- min. Barry Brown, Britt Ekland, Michael Blodgett......

ULTIMATE WARRIOR, THE (1975) Warner Bros. Color-92min. Yul Brynner, Max Von Sydow, Joanna Miles......

ULYSSES (1953) Paramount. Color-104min. (*Italian-French, English language*). Kirk Douglas, Silvana Mangano......4*

ULYSSES (1967) Continental [Walter Reade]. B&W-140min. (*U.S.-British*). Milo O'Shea, Maurice Roeves, Barbara Jefford......4*
Publicity title: JAMES JOYCE'S ULYSSES

ULYSSES AGAINST THE SON OF HERCULES (1961) Avco-Embassy. Color-99min. (*Italian-French*). Georges Marchal, Michael Lane......(3)
Original title: ULISSE CONTRO ERCOLE (*Ulysses Against Hercules*)
British title: ULYSSES AGAINST HERCULES
Publicity title: HERCULES VS. ULYSSES

ULZANA'S RAID (1972) Universal. Color-103min. Burt Lancaster, Bruce Davison......4*

UMBERTO D (1952) Harrison Pictures. B&W-89min. (*Italian*). Carlo Battisti, Maria Pia Casilio......4*

UMBRELLAS OF CHERBOURG, THE (1964) Landau-Unger. Color-90min. (*French-W. German*). Catherine Deneuve, Nino Castelnuovo...6*
Original French title: PARAPLUIES DE CHERBOURG, LES
German title: REGENSCHIRME VON CHERBOURG, DIE

UNCERTAIN GLORY (1944) Warner Bros. B&W-102min. Errol Flynn, Paul Lukas......(3)

UNCHAINED (1955) Warner Bros. B&W-75min. Elroy Hirsch, Barbara Hale......3*

UNCLE, THE (1964) Lenart Productions. B&W-87min. (*British*). Rupert Davies, Brenda Bruce, Robert Duncan......(4)

Films are rated on a 1 to 10 scale, 10 is highest. **Boldface** ratings followed by an asterisk (*) are for films actually seen and rated by the executive and senior editors. All other ratings are estimates. (See Notes on Entertainment Ratings in the front section.)

THE UMBRELLAS OF CHERBOURG (1964). Mechanic Nino Castelnuovo and his sweetheart Catherine Deneuve, the daughter of an umbrella shop keeper, pledge that their love will remain constant throughout the times ahead which will separate them.

UNCLE HARRY (1945) Universal. **B&W-80min.** George Sanders, Geraldine Fitzgerald............................(5)
Original title: STRANGE AFFAIR OF UNCLE HARRY, THE
TV title: ZERO MURDER CASE

UNCLE JOE SHANNON (1978) United Artists. **Color-108min.** Burt Young, Doug McKeon 2½*

UNCLE SILAS (1947) *see* INHERITANCE, THE

UNCLE TOM'S CABIN (1965) Kroger Babb. **Color-118min.** *(W. German-French-Italian-Yugoslavian, English language).* John Kitzmiller, Herbert Lom, Gertraud Mittermayr ....(3)
Original German title: ONKEL TOMS HUTTE
French title: CASE DE L'ONCLE TOM, LA
Italian title: CENTO DOLLARI D'ODIO
Yugoslavian title: CICA TOMINA KOLIBA

UNCLE VANYA (1971) Artkino. **B&W-110min.** *(U.S.S.R.).* Innokenty Smoktunovsky, Sergei Bondarchuk ....(5)
Original title: DIADIA VANYA

UNCLE WAS A VAMPIRE (1959) Avco-Embassy. **Color-95min.** *(Italian).* Renato Rascel, Christopher Lee, Sylva Koscina...................(4)
Original title: TEMPI DURI PER I VAMPIRI *(Hard Times for Vampires)*
Publicity title: HARD TIMES FOR DRACULA
Publicity title: MY UNCLE, THE VAMPIRE

UNCONQUERED, THE (1947) Paramount. **Color-146min.** Gary Cooper, Paulette Goddard 4½*

UNCONVENTIONAL LINDA (1938) *see* HOLIDAY

UNDEAD, THE (1957) American-International. **B&W-75min.** Allison Hayes, Richard Garland, Pamela Duncan ....(3)

UNDEFEATED, THE (1969) 20th Century-Fox. **Color-119min.** John Wayne, Rock Hudson...............................4*

UNDER CAPRICORN (1949) Warner Bros. **Color-117min.** *(British-U.S.).* Ingrid Bergman, Joseph Cotten.......................4*

UNDER-COVER MAN (1932) Paramount. **B&W-70min.** George Raft, Nancy Carroll 4*

UNDER FIRE (1957) 20th Century-Fox. **B&W-78min.** Rex Reason, Steve Brodie...............................(4)

UNDER MILK WOOD (1972) Altura Films. **Color-88min.** *(British).* Richard Burton, Elizabeth Taylor, Peter O'Toole..................(4)

UNDER MY SKIN (1950) 20th Century-Fox. **B&W-86min.** John Garfield, Micheline Prelle (Presle) 3½*

UNDER PRESSURE (1935) 20th Century-Fox. **B&W-70min.** Edmund Lowe, Victor McLaglen...............................4*

UNDER TEN FLAGS (1960) Paramount. **B&W-92min.** *(U.S.-Italian).* Van Heflin, Charles Laughton.......................(4)
Italian title: SOTTO 10 BANDIERE

UNDER THE CLOCK (1945) *see* CLOCK, THE

UNDER THE GUN (1951) Universal. **B&W-83min.** Richard Conte, Audrey Totter 3*

UNDER THE PARIS SKY (1951) Discina International. **B&W-103min.** *(French).* Brigitte Auber, Jean Brochard..................(5)
Original title: SOUS LE CIEL DE PARIS COULE LA SEINE

UNDER THE RED ROBE (1937) 20th Century-Fox. **B&W-82min.** *(British).* Conrad Veidt, Annabella, Raymond Massey.................(4)

UNDER THE RED SEA (1952) RKO. **B&W-67min.** *(German?, Documentary). Director:* Hans Hass ....(4)
Original title: RED SEA ADVENTURE

UNDER THE YUM YUM TREE (1963) Columbia. **Color-110min.** Jack Lemmon, Carol Lynley 4*

UNDER TWO FLAGS (1936) 20th Century-Fox. **B&W-105min.** Ronald Colman, Claudette Colbert.......................(5)

UNDER WESTERN SKIES (1945) Universal. **B&W-83min.** Martha O'Driscoll, Noah Beery ....(2)

UNDERCOVER GIRL (1950) Universal. **B&W-83min.** Alexis Smith, Scott Brady 3*

UNDERCOVER GIRL (1956) *see* ASSIGNMENT REDHEAD

UNDERCOVER MAISIE (1947) M-G-M. **B&W-90min.** Ann Sothern, Barry Nelson ....(3)
British title: UNDERCOVER GIRL

UNDERCOVER MAN, THE (1949) Columbia. **B&W-83min.** Glenn Ford, Nina Foch...............................(5)

UNDERCOVER WOMAN (1946) Republic. **B&W-56min.** Stephanie Batchelor, Robert Livingston 3*

UNDERCOVERS HERO (1973) United Artists. **Color-95min.** *(British).* Peter Sellers 5*
Original title: SOFT BEDS -- HARD BATTLES

UNDERCURRENT (1946) M-G-M. **B&W-116min.** Katharine Hepburn, Robert Taylor 4*

UNDERGROUND (1941) Warner Bros. **B&W-95min.** Jeffrey Lynn, Philip Dorn...............................3*

UNDERGROUND (1970) United Artists. **Color-100min.** Robert Goulet, Daniele Gaubert ....(3)

UNDERGROUND AGENT (1942) Columbia. **B&W-68min.** Bruce Bennett, Leslie Brooks ....(3)

UNDERGROUND COMMANDO (1966) United Screen Arts. **Color-90min.** *(Foreign).* José Vergara, Henry Duval..................(3)

UNDERGROUND MAN, THE (1974) Paramount. **Color-100min.** *(Made for TV).* Peter Graves, Sharon Farrell, Jim Hutton, Jack Klugman..........(4)

UNDERSEA GIRL (1957) Allied Artists. **B&W-75min.** Mara Corday, Pat Conway ....(2)

UNDERSEA KINGDOM (1936) *see* SHARAD OF ATLANTIS

UNDERTOW (1949) Universal. **B&W-71min.** Scott Brady, John Russell...............................3½*

UNDERWATER! (1955) RKO. **Color-99min.** Jane Russell, Richard Egan, Gilbert Roland 4*

UNDERWATER CITY, THE (1962) Columbia. **Color-78min.** William Lundigan, Julie Adams 3*

UNDERWATER WARRIOR (1958) M-G-M. **B&W-90min.** Dan Dailey, Claire Kelly...............................3½*

UNDERWORLD (1927) Paramount Famous Lasky. **B&W-102min.** *(Silent).* George Bancroft, Clive Brook, Evelyn Brent, Larry Semon.................(4)
British title: PAYING THE PENALTY

UNDERWORLD AFTER DARK (1947) *see* BIG TOWN AFTER DARK

UNDERWORLD INFORMERS (1963) Continental [Walter Reade]. **B&W-105min.** *(British).* Nigel Patrick, Margaret Whiting..................(4)
Original title: INFORMERS, THE
Alternate title: SNOUT, THE

UNDERWORLD SCANDAL (1948) *see* BIG TOWN SCANDAL

UNDERWORLD STORY, THE (1950) United Artists. **B&W-90min.** Dan Duryea, Herbert Marshall 4*
Original title: WHIPPED, THE

UNDERWORLD U.S.A. (1961) Columbia. **B&W-98min.** Cliff Robertson, Dolores Dorn ....(4)

UNDYING MONSTER, THE (1942) 20th Century-Fox. **B&W-60min.** James Ellison, Heather Angel, John Howard...................(4)
British title: HAMMOND MYSTERY, THE

UNEARTHLY, THE (1957) Republic. **B&W-73min.** John Carradine, Allison Hayes, Tor Johnson ....(2)

UNEARTHLY STRANGER, THE (1963) American-International. **B&W-68min.** *(British).* John Neville, Gabriella Licudi 4*

UNEASY TERMS (1948) NTA Pictures. **B&W-91min.** *(British).* Michael Rennie, Moira Lister........................

UNEXPECTED UNCLE (1941) RKO. B&W-67min. Charles Coburn, Anne Shirley......(4)

UNFAITHFUL, THE (1947) Warner Bros. B&W-109min. Ann Sheridan, Zachary Scott......4*

UNFAITHFUL WIFE, THE (1969) see FEMME INFIDELE, LA

UNFAITHFULLY YOURS (1948) 20th Century-Fox. B&W-105min. Rex Harrison, Linda Darnell......4*

UNFAITHFULS, THE (1952) Allied Artists. B&W-83min. (Italian). Pierre Cressoy, Gina Lollobrigida, May Britt......(3)
Original title: INFEDELI, LE

UNFINISHED BUSINESS (1941) Universal. B&W-96min. Irene Dunne, Robert Montgomery......(3)

UNFINISHED DANCE, THE (1947) M-G-M. Color-100min. Margaret O'Brien, Cyd Charisse......(4)

UNFINISHED JOURNEY OF ROBERT F. KENNEDY, THE (1969) see JOURNEY OF ROBERT F. KENNEDY, THE

UNFORGIVEN, THE (1960) United Artists. Color-125min. Burt Lancaster, Audrey Hepburn......4*

UNFORGOTTEN CRIME (1942) see AFFAIRS OF JIMMY VALENTINE

UNGUARDED HOUR, THE (1936) M-G-M. B&W-88min. Franchot Tone, Loretta Young......(3)

UNGUARDED MOMENT, THE (1956) Universal. Color-95min. Esther Williams, George Nader, John Saxon......3*

UNHOLY DESIRE (1964) Toho. B&W-150min. (Japanese). Masumi Harukawa, Akira Nishimura, Shigeru Tsuyuguchi......(4)
Original title: AKAI SATSUI

UNHOLY FOUR, THE (1954) Lippert Productions. B&W-80min. (British). Paulette Goddard, William Sylvester......(3)
Original title: STRANGER CAME HOME

UNHOLY GARDEN, THE (1931) United Artists. B&W-85min. Ronald Colman, Fay Wray......(3)

UNHOLY INTRUDERS, THE (1956) Telewide Systems. B&W-80min. (German). Philip Dorn, Olga Tache......(3)
Alternate title: STRANGE INTRUSION

UNHOLY NIGHT, THE (1929) M-G-M. B&W-94min. Ernest Torrence, Claude Fleming, John Miljan......(3)

UNHOLY PARTNERS (1941) M-G-M. B&W-94min. Edward G. Robinson, Edward Arnold......4*

UNHOLY ROLLERS, THE (1972) American-International. Color-88min. Claudia Jennings, Louis Quinn, Betty Anne Rees......(3)

UNHOLY THREE, THE (1925) M-G-M. B&W-86min. (Silent). Lon Chaney, Mae Busch, Victor McLaglen......(4)

UNHOLY THREE, THE (1930) M-G-M. B&W-75min. Lon Chaney, Lila Lee, Elliot Nugent......(3)

UNHOLY WIFE (1957) Universal. Color-94min. Rod Steiger, Diana Dors......(3)

UNIDENTIFIED FLYING OBJECTS (1956) United Artists. B&W-91min. (Documentary). Director: Winston Jones......(3)
Alternate title: U. F. O.

UNINHIBITED, THE (1965) Peppercorn-Wormser. Color-104min. (Spanish-Italian-French). Melina Mercouri, James Mason, Hardy Kruger, Didier Haudepin......(3)
Original Spanish title: PIANOS MECANICOS, LOS (The Player Pianos)
Italian title: AMORI DI UNA CALDA ESTATE
French title: PIANOS MÉCANIQUES, LES

UNINVITED, THE (1944) Paramount. B&W-98min. Ray Milland, Gail Russell......5*

UNION DEPOT (1932) First National [W.B.]. B&W-75min. Joan Blondell, Douglas Fairbanks, Jr.......(5)
British title: GENTLEMAN FOR A DAY

UNION PACIFIC (1939) Paramount. B&W-133min. Barbara Stanwyck, Joel McCrea, Robert Preston......4½*

UNION STATION (1950) Paramount. B&W-80min. William Holden, Nancy Olson......5*

UNIVERSITY MEDICAL CENTER (1969) see UMC

UNKNOWN, THE (1927) M-G-M. B&W-61min. (Silent). Lon Chaney, Joan Crawford......(4)

UNKNOWN GUEST, THE (1943) Monogram [Allied Artists]. B&W-64min. Victor Jory, Pamela Blake......(5)

UNKNOWN ISLAND (1948) Film Classics [U.A.]. Color-76min. Richard Denning, Barton MacLane, Virginia Grey......(3)

UNKNOWN MAN, THE (1951) M-G-M. B&W-86min. Walter Pidgeon, Ann Harding......(4)

UNKNOWN TERROR, THE (1957) 20th Century-Fox. B&W-77min. John Howard, Mala Powers......(3)

UNKNOWN WORLD (1951) Lippert Productions. B&W-63min. Bruce Kellogg, Marilyn Nash......2*

UNMAN, WITTERING AND ZIGO (1971) Paramount. Color-100min. (British). David Hemmings, Carolyn Seymour, Douglas Wilmer......(5)

UNMARRIED WOMAN, AN (1978) 20th Century-Fox. Color-124min. Jill Clayburgh, Alan Bates......5*

UNMASKED (1950) Republic. B&W-60min. Robert Rockwell, Barbara Fuller, Raymond Burr......(3)

UNSEEN, THE (1945) Paramount. B&W-81min. Joel McCrea, Gail Russell......(4)

UNSINKABLE MOLLY BROWN, THE (1964) M-G-M. Color-128min. Debbie Reynolds, Harve Presnell......5*

UNSUSPECTED, THE (1947) Warner Bros. B&W-103min. Claude Rains, Joan Caulfield......(4)

UNTAMED (1940) Paramount. Color-83min. Ray Milland, Patricia Morison......(4)

UNTAMED (1955) 20th Century-Fox. Color-111min. Tyrone Power, Susan Hayward......(4)

UNTAMED BREED, THE (1948) Columbia. Color-79min. Sonny Tufts, Barbara Britton......(3)

UNTAMED FRONTIER (1952) Universal. Color-75min. Joseph Cotten, Shelley Winters......(4)

UNTAMED HEIRESS (1954) Republic. B&W-70min. Judy Canova, Donald Barry......(3)

UNTAMED YOUTH (1957) Warner Bros. B&W-80min. Mamie Van Doren, Lori Nelson......(3)

UNTIL HELL IS FROZEN (1960) D.U.K. (British). B&W-87min. (German). Charles Millot, Gotz George......(3)

UNTIL THEY SAIL (1957) M-G-M. B&W-95min. Jean Simmons, Joan Fontaine, Paul Newman......4*

UNTOUCHED (1956) Excelsior. B&W-85min. (Mexican). Ricardo Montalban, Victor Parra, Ariadna Welter......(4)

UNVANQUISHED, THE (1956) see APARAJITO

UNWED MOTHER (1958) Allied Artists. B&W-74min. Norma Moore, Robert Vaughn......(3)

UNWRITTEN CODE, THE (1944) Columbia. B&W-61min. Ann Savage, Tom Neal......(3)

UP! (1976) Marvin Films. Color-80min. Raven De La Croix, Robert McLane, Janet Wood, Francesca "Kitten" Natividad......(3)
Alternate title: RUSS MEYER'S "UP!"

UP FROM THE BEACH (1965) 20th Century-Fox. B&W-98min. Cliff Robertson, Irina Demick, Marius Goring......4*

UP FROM THE DEPTHS (1979) New World. Color-75min. Sam Bottoms, Susanne Reed......

UP FRONT (1951) Universal. B&W-92min. Tom Ewell, David Wayne...(5)

UP GOES MAISIE (1946) M-G-M. B&W-89min. Ann Sothern, George Murphy......(3)
British title: UP SHE GOES

UP IN ARMS (1944) RKO. Color-106min. Danny Kaye, Constance Dowling......4*

UP IN CENTRAL PARK (1948) Universal. B&W-88min. Deanna Durbin, Dick Haymes, Vincent Price......(3)

UP IN MABEL'S ROOM (1944) United Artists. B&W-76min. Dennis O'Keefe, Marjorie Reynolds......(5)

UP IN SMOKE (1957) Allied Artists. B&W-64min. The Bowery Boys, Byron Foulger......(4)

UP IN SMOKE (1978) Paramount. Color-86min. Cheech Marin, Tommy Chong......4½*

UP IN THE CELLAR (1970) American-International. Color-92min. Wes Stern, Joan Collins, Larry Hagman......(3)
Alternate title: THREE IN THE CELLAR

UP PERISCOPE (1959) Warner Bros. Color-111min. James Garner, Edmond O'Brien......4*

UP SHE GOES (1946) see UP GOES MAISIE

UP THE CREEK (1958) Dominant Pictures. B&W-83min. (British). David Tomlinson, Peter Sellers......5*

UP THE DOWN STAIRCASE (1967) Warner Bros. Color-123min. Sandy Dennis, Patrick Bedford......5*

UP THE JUNCTION (1968) Paramount. Color-119min. (British). Suzy Kendall, Dennis Waterman......

UP THE MacGREGORS (1966) Columbia. **Color-93min.** *(Italian-Spanish).* David Bailey, Agatha Flory (Agata Flori), Leo Anchoriz......................(3)
Original Italian title: SETTE DONNE PER I MacGREGOR *(Seven Women for the MacGregors)*
Spanish title: SIETE MUJERES PARA LOS MacGREGOR

UP THE RIVER (1930) Fox Film Co. [20th]. **B&W-92min.** Spencer Tracy, Humphrey Bogart...4*

UP THE SANDBOX (1972) National General. **Color-97min.** Barbra Streisand, David Selby..4*

UP TO HIS EARS (1965) Lopert [U.A.]. **Color-94min.** *(French-Italian).* Jean-Paul Belmondo, Ursula Andress..(4)
French title: TRIBULATIONS D'UN CHINOIS EN CHINE, LES *(The Troubles of a Chinaman in China)*
Italian title: UOMO DI HONG KONG, L' *(The Man From Hong Kong)*

UP TO HIS NECK (1954) J. Arthur Rank. **B&W-89min.** *(British).* Ronald Shiner, Laya Raki..(3)

UPON THIS ROCK (1971) Levitt-Pickman. **Color-90min.** *(Documentary).* Director: Harry Rosky.

UPPER HAND, THE (1966) Paramount. **Color-86min.** *(French-Italian-W. German).* Jean Gabin, George Raft..(3)
Original French title: DU RIFIFI A PANAME
Italian title: RIFIFI INTERNAZIONALE
British and German title: RIFIFI IN PARIS

UPSTAIRS AND DOWNSTAIRS (1959) 20th Century-Fox. **Color-100min.** *(British).* Michael Craig, Anne Heywood......................................4*

UPTIGHT (1968) Paramount. **Color-104min.** Julian Mayfield, Raymond St. Jacques...(5)

UPTOWN SATURDAY NIGHT (1974) Warner Bros. **Color-104min.** Sidney Poitier, Bill Cosby..5½*

UPTURNED GLASS, THE (1947) Universal. **B&W-86min.** *(British).* James Mason, Rosamund John, Pamela Kellino......................................(3)

URANIUM BOOM (1956) Columbia. **B&W-67min.** Dennis Morgan, William Talman, Patricia Medina...(3)

URANIUM CONSPIRACY, THE (1978) Noah Films. **Color-105min.** *(Israeli).* Siegfried Rauch, Oded Kotler...

URGE TO KILL (1960) Anglo Amalgamated [EMI]. **B&W-58min.** *(British).* Patrick Barr, Howard Bays..(3)

URSUS (1961) *see* MIGHTY URSUS

URSUS IN THE LAND OF FIRE (1963) *see* SON OF HERCULES IN THE LAND OF FIRE

URSUS IN THE VALLEY OF THE LIONS (1961) Golden Era. **Color-82min.** *(Italian).* Ed Fury, Moira Orfei.......................................(3)
Original title: URSUS NELLA VALLE DEI LEONI
Alternate title: VALLEY OF THE LIONS
Alternate title: SON OF ATLAS IN THE VALLEY OF THE LIONS, THE

USERS, THE (1978) ABC-TV. **Color-100min.** *(Made for TV).* Jaclyn Smith, Tony Curtis, George Hamilton...

UPTOWN SATURDAY NIGHT (1974). Bill Cosby (with beard) and Sidney Poitier are in a plush gambling club when it is raided by holdup men, and they later find they've lost a lot more than just some cash.

USUAL UNIDENTIFIED THIEVES, THE (1958) *see* BIG DEAL ON MADONNA STREET, THE

UTAH (1945) Republic. **B&W-78min.** Roy Rogers, Dale Evans................(4)

UTAH BLAINE (1957) Columbia. **B&W-75min.** Rory Calhoun, Susan Cummings...(3)

UTOPIA (1951) Exploitation Pictures. **B&W-82min.** *(French-Italian, English language).* Stan Laurel, Oliver Hardy.....................................(3)
Original French title: ATOLL K
British title: ESCAPADE
Alternate title: ROBINSON CRUSOELAND

-V-

V.I.P.s, THE (1963) M-G-M. **Color-119min.** *(British-U.S.).* Elizabeth Taylor, Richard Burton...5*

VACATION FROM MARRIAGE (1945) M-G-M. **B&W-111min.** *(British).* Robert Donat, Deborah Kerr...4*
Original title: PERFECT STRANGERS

VACATION IN RENO (1946) RKO. **B&W-60min.** Jack Haley, Anne Jeffreys..(3)

VAGABOND KING, THE (1956) Paramount. **Color-88min.** Oreste, Kathryn Grayson..4½*

VALACHI PAPERS, THE (1972) Columbia. **Color-123min.** *(Italian-French, English language).* Charles Bronson, Lino Ventura..............................3*
Original title: JOE VALACHI: I SEGRETI DI COSA NOSTRA *(Joe Valachi: The Secret of the Cosa Nostra)*

VALDEZ IS COMING (1971) United Artists. **Color-90min.** Burt Lancaster, Susan Clark..4*

VALDEZ THE HALFBREED (1973) *see* CHINO

VALENTINO (1951) Columbia. **Color-102min.** Anthony Dexter, Eleanor Parker...3*

VALENTINO (1977) United Artists. **Color-132min.** *(British).* Rudolf Nureyev, Leslie Caron, Michelle Phillips...4½*

VALERIE (1957) United Artists. **B&W-84min.** Sterling Hayden, Anita Ekberg...(3)

VALIANT, THE (1929) Fox Film Co. [20th]. **B&W-62min.** *(Silent).* Brigitte Helm, Paul Wegener, Ivan Petrovich...(4)

VALIANT, THE (1962) United Artists. **B&W-89min.** *(British-Italian).* John Mills, Ettore Manni..(4)
Italian title: AFFONDAMENTO DELLA VALIANT, L'

VALIANT IS THE WORD FOR CARRIE (1936) Paramount. **B&W-112min.** Gladys George, Arline Judge..(4)

VALLEY OF DEATH, THE (1958) *see* TANK BATTALION

VALLEY OF DECISION, THE (1945) M-G-M. **B&W-111min.** Greer Garson, Gregory Peck...4*

VALLEY OF FEAR, THE (1962) *see* SHERLOCK HOLMES AND THE DEADLY NECKLACE

VALLEY OF FURY (1955) *see* CHIEF CRAZY HORSE

VALLEY OF GWANGI, THE (1969) Warner Bros. **Color-95min.** James Franciscus, Gila Golan..3½*

VALLEY OF MYSTERY (1967) Universal. **Color-94min.** *(Telefeature).* Richard Egan, Peter Graves..3*
Original title: STRANDED

VALLEY OF THE DOLLS (1967) 20th Century-Fox. **Color-123min.** Barbara Parkins, Patty Duke...3*

VALLEY OF THE DOOMED (1962) American-International. **Color-83min.** *(German).* Don Megowan, Chelo Alonso, Hildegard Knef....................(3)
Original title: STRADA DEI GIGANTI, LA *(The Road of Giants)*

VALLEY OF THE DRAGONS (1961) Columbia. **B&W-79min.** Cesare Danova, Sean McClory...(3)

VALLEY OF THE EAGLES (1951) Lippert Productions. **B&W-85min.** *(British).* Jack Warner, Nadia Gray...(4)

VALLEY OF THE GIANTS (1938) Warner Bros. **Color-79min.** Wayne Morris, Claire Trevor...(4)

VALLEY OF THE HEADHUNTERS (1953) Columbia. **B&W-67min.** Johnny Weissmuller, Christine Larson...(3)

VALLEY OF THE KINGS (1954) M-G-M. **Color-86min.** Robert Taylor, Eleanor Parker...(4)

VALLEY OF THE LIONS (1961) *see* URSUS IN THE VALLEY OF THE LIONS

VALLEY OF THE REDWOODS (1960) 20th Century-Fox. **B&W-63min.** John Hudson, Lynn Bernay...(3)

VALLEY OF THE SUN (1942) RKO. **B&W-84min.** Lucille Ball, James Craig...(5)

VALLEY OF THE ZOMBIES (1946) Republic. **B&W-56min.** Bob Livingston, Ian Keith...(3)

VALUE FOR MONEY (1955) J. Arthur Rank. **Color-93min.** *(British).* John Gregson, Diana Dors ....(5)

VAMPIRA (1975) *see* OLD DRACULA

VAMPIRE, THE (1957) United Artists. **B&W-74min.** John Beal, Coleen Gray, Kenneth Tobey...3*
TV title: MARK OF THE VAMPIRE, THE

VAMPIRE, THE (1957) K. Gordon Murray Productions. **B&W-84min.** *(Mexican).* German Robles, Abel Salazar, Ariadne Welter 2*
Original title: VAMPIRO, EL

VAMPIRE AND THE BALLERINA, THE (1960) United Artists. **B&W-86min.** *(Italian).* Hélene Remy, Maria Luisa Rolando........................(2)
Original title: AMANTE DEL VAMPIRO, L' *(The Vampire's Lover)*

VAMPIRE BAT, THE (1933) Majestic Pictures. **B&W-63min.** Lionel Atwill, Fay Wray, Melvyn Douglas ....(4)

VAMPIRE BEAST CRAVES BLOOD, THE (1968) Pacemaker Pictures. **Color-81min.** *(British).* Peter Cushing, Robert Flemyng, Wanda Ventham ....(2)
Original title: BLOOD BEAST TERROR, THE

VAMPIRE HOOKERS (1978) Caprican Three. **Color- min.** *(U.S.-Philippine).* John Carradine, Bruce Fairbairn, Karen Stride ....

VAMPIRE LOVERS, THE (1970) American-International. **Color-88min.** *(British).* Ingrid Pitt, Pippa Steel, Peter Cushing.................................(3)

VAMPIRE MEN OF THE LOST PLANET (1970) *see* HORROR OF THE BLOOD MONSTERS

VAMPIRE OVER LONDON (1952) *see* MY SON, THE VAMPIRE

VAMPIRE WOMAN (1973) *see* CRYPT OF THE LIVING DEAD

VAMPIRE'S COFFIN, THE (1957) K. Gordon Murray Productions. **B&W-86min.** *(Mexican).* German Robles, Abel Salazar, Ariadne Welter 1*
Original title: ATAUD DEL VAMPIRO, EL

VAMPIRE'S GHOST, THE (1945) Republic. **B&W-53min.** John Abbott, Peggy Stewart ....(3)

VAMPIRES NIGHT ORGY, THE (1973) International Amusement. **Color-86min.** *(Spanish-Italian).* Jack Taylor, Dianik Zurakowska.................(3)
Original Spanish title: ORGIA NOCTURNA DE LOS VAMPIROS, LA

VAMPYR (1932) **B&W-65min.** *(French-German).* Julian West (Nicholas de Gunzburg), Sybille Schmitz, Henriette Gerard...........................(4)
Original French title: VAMPYR OU L'ETRANGE AVENTURE DE DAVID GRAY *(Vampire or the Strange Adventure of David Gray)*
German title: TRAUM DES ALLAN GRAY, DER *(The Dream of Allan Gray)*
British title: STRANGE ADVENTURE OF DAVID GRAY, THE
Alternate title: ADVENTURES OF DAVID GRAY

VAMPYRES (1974) Cambist. **Color-86min.** *(British).* Marianne Morris, Murray Brown ....(3)
Alternate title: DAUGHTERS OF DRACULA
Publicity title: VAMPYRES, DAUGHTERS OF DRACULA
Publicity title: VAMPYRES . . . MOST UNNATURAL LADIES

VAN, THE (1977) Crown International. **Color-90min.** Stuart Getz, Deborah White..(4)

VAN NUYS BLVD. (1979) Crown International. **Color- min.** Bill Adler, Cynthia Wood...

VANESSA (1977) Intercontinental Films. **Color-91min.** *(German).* Olivia Pascal, Anton Diffring...

VANESSA, HER LOVE STORY (1935) M-G-M. **B&W-74min.** Helen Hayes, Robert Montgomery ....(3)

VANISHED (1970) Universal. **Color-196min.** *(Made for TV).* Richard Widmark, Skye Aubrey, James Farentino, Robert Young....................3*

VANISHING AMERICAN, THE (1955) Republic. **B&W-90min.** Scott Brady, Audrey Totter 3*

VANISHING CORPORAL, THE (1962) *see* ELUSIVE CORPORAL, THE

VANISHING POINT (1971) 20th Century-Fox. **Color-99min.** Barry Newman, Cleavon Little 4½*

VANISHING PRAIRIE, THE (1954) Buena Vista. **Color-71min.** *(Documentary). Director:* James Algar.....................................(6)

VANISHING VIRGINIAN, THE (1942) M-G-M. **B&W-97min.** Frank Morgan, Kathryn Grayson..(3)

VANISHING WILDERNESS, THE (1974) Pacific International Enterprises. **Color-93min.** *(Documentary). Director:* Arthur Dubs.........5*

VANQUISHED, THE (1953) Paramount. **Color-84min.** John Payne, Jan Sterling ....(3)

VARAN, THE UNBELIEVABLE (1958) Crown International. **B&W-70min.** *(Japanese-U.S.).* Myron Healey, Tsuruko Kobayashi 2*
Original title: DAIKAIJU BARAN

VARIETY (1925) Paramount. **B&W-92min.** *(German, Silent).* Emil Jannings, Lya de Putti, Warwick Ward ....(4)
Original title: VARIETEE

VARIETY GIRL (1947) Paramount. **B&W-83min.** Mary Hatcher, Olga San Juan ....(4)

VARIETY LIGHTS (1950) Contemporary. **B&W-93min.** *(Italian).* Peppino De Filippo, Giulietta Masina, Carla Del Poggio.......................(4)
Original title: LUCI DEL VARIETA

VARIETY TIME (1948) RKO. **Color-58min.** *(Compilation).* Jack Paar, Leon Errol, Edgar Kennedy ....(3)

VATICAN AFFAIR, THE (1969) 20th Century-Fox. **Color-94min.** *(Italian).* Walter Pidgeon, Ira Furstenberg, Klaus Kinski ....(3)
Alternate title: AT ANY PRICE

VAULT OF HORROR, THE (1973) Cinerama Releasing. **Color-93min.** *(British-U.S.).* Daniel Massey, Terry-Thomas, Tom Baker 4*

VEIL, THE (1958) Medallion. **B&W-97min.** *(Telefeature).* Boris Karloff......

VEIL, THE (1977) *see* HAUNTS

VEILS OF BAGDAD (1953) Universal. **Color-82min.** Victor Mature, Mari Blanchard..(3)

VELVET HOUSE (1971) *see* CRUCIBLE OF HORROR

VELVET TOUCH, THE (1948) RKO. **B&W-97min.** R. Russell, Leo Genn (4)

VELVET VAMPIRE, THE (1971) New World. **Color-80min.** Michael Blodgett, Sherry Miles, Celeste Yarnall ....(2)

VENDETTA (1950) RKO. **B&W-84min.** Faith Domergue, George Dolenz (3)

VENDETTA (1966) **B&W-80min.** *(Foreign).* Alexander Gavrick, Helen Jovan ....(3)

VENETIAN AFFAIR, THE (1967) M-G-M. **Color-92min.** Robert Vaughn, Elke Sommer ....(3)

VENETIAN ANONYMOUS, THE (1970) *see* ANONYMOUS VENETIAN, THE

VENETIAN BIRD, THE (1952) *see* ASSASSIN, THE

VENGEANCE (1969) *see* BRAIN, THE

VENGEANCE OF FU MANCHU, THE (1967) Warner Bros. **Color-91min.** *(British).* Christopher Lee, Douglas Wilmer ....(2)

VENGEANCE OF SHE, THE (1968) 20th Century-Fox. **Color-101min.** *(British).* John Richardson, Olinka Berova, Edward Judd...................(2)

VENGEANCE OF THE MONSTER, THE (1966) *see* MAJIN

VENGEANCE OF THE THREE MUSKETEERS (1963) Avco-Embassy. **Color-92min.** *(French).* Gerard Barray, Mylene Demongeot.................(3)

VENGEANCE OF URSUS (1962) *see* REVENGE OF URSUS

VENGEANCE VALLEY (1951) M-G-M. **Color-83min.** Burt Lancaster, Robert Walker...4*

VENICE, THE MOON, AND YOU (1958) Gala *(Brit.).* **B&W-100min.** *(Italian).* Alberto Sordi, Marisa Alasio.............................(3)

VENOM (1966) Peppercorn-Wormser. **B&W-96min.** *(Danish).* Soren Stromberg, Sisse Reingaard ....(4)
Original title: GIFT

VENOM (1971) *see* LEGEND OF SPIDER FOREST

VENUS AGAINST THE SON OF HERCULES (1962) Avco-Embassy. **Color-92min.** *(Italian).* Massimo Serato, Roger Browne 2*
Original title: MARTE, DIO DELL GUERRA *(Mars, God of War)*
Publicity title: MARS, GOD OF WAR

VENUS IN FURS (1970) American-International. **Color-86min.** *(British-Italian-W. German).* James Darren, Barbara McNair, Maria Rohm ....(2)
Italian title: PAROXISMUS
Alternate Italian title: PUO UNA MORTA RIVIVERE PER AMORE?
German title: VENUS IN PELTZ

VERA CRUZ (1954) United Artists. **Color-94min.** Gary Cooper, Burt Lancaster...5*

VERBOTEN (1959) Columbia. **B&W-93min.** James Best, Susan Cummings...(3)

VERDICT, THE (1946) Warner Bros. **B&W-86min.** Sydney Greenstreet, Peter Lorre 4*

VERDICT, THE (1964) Avco-Embassy. **B&W-55min.** *(British).* Cec Linder, Zena Marshall, Nigel Davenport ....(3)

VÉRITÉES ET MENSONGES (1974) *see* F FOR FAKE

VERSAILLES (1954) *see* ROYAL AFFAIRS IN VERSAILLES

VERTIGO (1958) Paramount. **Color-120min.** James Stewart, Kim Novak..5*

VERY BIG WITHDRAWAL, A (1979) Avco-Embassy. **Color- min.** Donald Sutherland, Brooke Adams, Paul Mazursky ....

VERY CURIOUS GIRL, A (1969) Regional. **Color-107min.** *(French).* Bernadette Lafont, Georges Géret ....(4)
Original title: FIANCÉE DU PIRATE, LA *(The Pirate's Fiancée)*
Alternate title: PIRATE'S FIANCÉE

Films are rated on a 1 to 10 scale, 10 is highest. **Boldface** ratings followed by an asterisk (*) are for films actually seen and rated by the executive and senior editors. All other ratings are estimates. (See Notes on Entertainment Ratings in the front section.)

VERY EDGE, THE (1963) Teleworld. **B&W-89min.** *(British).* Richard Todd, Anne Heywood.. 4*

VERY HAPPY ALEXANDER (1968) *see* ALEXANDER

VERY HONORABLE GUY, A (1934) First National [W.B.]. **B&W-62min.** Joe E. Brown, Alice White .... (4)

VERY IMPORTANT PERSON (1961) *see* COMING OUT PARTY, A

VERY PRIVATE AFFAIR, A (1962) M-G-M. **Color-95min.** *(French-Italian).* Brigitte Bardot, Marcello Mastroianni.....................................3*
Original French title: VIE PRIVÉE, LA *(The Private Life)*
Italian title: VITA PRIVATA

VERY SPECIAL FAVOR, A (1965) Universal. **Color-104min.** Rock Hudson, Charles Boyer 5*

VERY THOUGHT OF YOU, THE (1944) Warner Bros. **B&W-99min.** Dennis Morgan, Eleanor Parker .... (4)

VERY YOUNG LADY, A (1941) 20th Century-Fox. **B&W-79min.** Jane Withers, Nancy Kelly .... (3)

VESSEL OF WRATH (1938) *see* BEACHCOMBER, THE

VIACCIA, LA (1960) Avco-Embassy. **Color-103min.** *(French-Italian).* Jean-Paul Belmondo, Claudia Cardinale .... (4)
Alternate title: LOVE MAKERS, THE

VICE RAID (1960) United Artists. **B&W-71min.** Mamie Van Doren, Richard Coogan, Brad Dexter .... (2)

VICE SQUAD, THE (1931) Paramount. **B&W-80min.** Paul Lukas, Kay Francis .... (4)

VICE SQUAD (1953) United Artists. **B&W-87min.** Edward G. Robinson, Paulette Goddard.. (5)
British title: GIRL IN ROOM 17, THE

VICIOUS CIRCLE, THE (1957) *see* CIRCLE, THE

VICKI (1953) 20th Century-Fox. **B&W-85min.** Jeanne Crain, Jean Peters, Elliot Reid .... (4)

VICTIM (1961) Pathé-America. **B&W-100min.** *(British).* Dirk Bogarde, Sylvia Syms 5*

VICTIM, THE (1972) MCA-TV. **Color-73min.** *(Made for TV).* Elizabeth Montgomery, George Maharis .... (4)

VICTIM FIVE (1964) *see* CODE 7, VICTIM 5

VICTORIA THE GREAT (1937) RKO. **B&W-112min.** *(British).* Anna Neagle, Anton Walbrook .... (5)

VICTORS, THE (1963) Columbia. **B&W-175min.** *(U.S.-British).* George Hamilton, George Peppard 4*

VICTORY (1940) Paramount. **B&W-78min.** Fredric March, Betty Field.. 4*

VICTORY AT ENTEBBE (1976) ABC-TV. **Color-152min.** *(Made for TV).* Burt Lancaster, Anthony Hopkins, Richard Dreyfuss 5*

VICTORY AT SEA (1954) United Artists. **B&W-97min.** *(Documentary, Telefeature). Producer:* Henry Salomon 5½*

VIE DE CHATEAU, LA (1966) Royal Films Int'l [Columbia]. **B&W-92min.** *(French).* Catherine Deneuve, Philippe Noiret .... (4)
Alternate title: MATTER OF RESISTANCE, A

VIEW FROM POMPEY'S HEAD, THE (1955) 20th Century-Fox. **Color-97min.** Richard Egan, Dana Wynter 4*
British title: SECRET INTERLUDE

VIEW FROM THE BRIDGE, A (1962) Continental [Walter Reade]. **B&W-110min.** *(French-Italian, English language).* Raf Vallone, Jean Sorel .. 5*
French title: VU DU PONT
Italian title: SGUARDO DAL PONTE, UNO

VIEWS OF A CLOWN (1976) *see* CLOWN

VIGIL IN THE NIGHT (1940) RKO. **B&W-96min.** Carole Lombard, Brian Aherne... 4*

VIGILANTE FORCE (1976) United Artists. **Color-89min.** Kris Kristofferson, Jan-Michael Vincent .... (4)

VIGILANTE TERROR (1953) Allied Artists. **B&W-70min.** Wild Bill Elliot, Mary Ellen Kay .... (3)

VIGILANTES RETURN, THE (1947) Universal. **B&W-67min.** Jon Hall, Margaret Lindsay .... (3)
British title: RETURN OF THE VIGILANTES, THE

VIKING QUEEN, THE (1967) 20th Century-Fox. **Color-91min.** *(British).* Don Murray, Carita 2½*

VIKING WOMEN AND THE SEA SERPENT, THE (1958) American-International. **B&W-70min.** Abby Dalton, Susan Cabot, Brad Jackson (3)
Screen title: SAGA OF THE VIKING WOMEN AND THEIR VOYAGE TO THE WATERS OF THE GREAT SEA SERPENT, THE
British title: VIKING WOMEN

VIKINGS, THE (1958) United Artists. **Color-114min.** Kirk Douglas, Tony Curtis 6*

THE VIKINGS (1958). Boistrous Viking leader Ernest Borgnine laughs over the probable fate of Welsh princess Janet Leigh, whom his lusty son Kirk Douglas has brought as a captive.

VILLA! (1958) 20th Century-Fox. **Color-72min.** Brian Keith, Cesar Romero, Rodolfo Hoyos .... (2)

VILLA RIDES (1968) Paramount. **Color-125min.** Yul Brynner, Robert Mitchum 4*

VILLAGE, THE (1953) United Artists. **B&W-83min.** *(Swiss).* John Justin, Eva Dahlbeck .... (5)

VILLAGE OF THE DAMNED, THE (1960) M-G-M. **B&W-78min.** *(British).* George Sanders, Barbara Shelley.................................. 4*

VILLAGE OF THE GIANTS (1965) Avco-Embassy. **Color-80min.** Tommy Kirk, Johnny Crawford, Beau Bridges........................... 3*

VILLAIN (1971) M-G-M. **Color-97min.** *(British).* Richard Burton, Ian McShane .... (4)

VILLAIN, THE (1979) Columbia. **Color- min.** Kirk Douglas, Ann-Margret, Arnold Schwarzenegger ....

VILLAIN STILL PURSUED HER, THE (1940) RKO. **B&W-66min.** Anita Louise, Alan Mowbray, Buster Keaton........................... (4)

VINCENT, FRANCOIS, PAUL AND THE OTHERS (1974) Joseph Green. **Color-113min.** *(French-Italian).* Yves Montand, Michel Piccoli, Stephane Audran 4½*
Original French title: VINCENT, FRANCOIS, PAUL . . . ET LES AUTRES

VINTAGE, THE (1957) M-G-M. **Color-91min.** Pier Angeli, Mel Ferrer, John Kerr .... (3)

VIOL, LE (1967) Freena Films. **Color-90min.** *(Swedish-French).* Bibi Andersson, Bruno Crémer, Frédéric de Pasquale .... (4)
Original Swedish title: OVERGREPPET
Alternate French title: VIOL OU UN AMOUR FOU, LE *(The Rape or a Mad Love)*
Alternate title: RAPE, THE

VIOLATOR, THE (1974) *see* ACT OF VENGEANCE

VIOLENT AND THE DAMNED, THE (1954) A.D.P. Productions. **B&W-60min.** *(Brazilian).* Arturo de Cordova, Tonia Carrero .... (3)
Original title: MAOS SANGRENTAS
Brazilian retitling: ASSASSINOS

VIOLENT CITY (1970) *see* FAMILY, THE

VIOLENT FOUR, THE (1968) Paramount. **Color-98min.** *(Italian).* Gian Maria Volonte, Tomas Milian .... (3)
Original title: BANDITI A MILANO *(Bandits of Milan)*

VIOLENT HOUR, THE (1950) *see* DIAL 1119

VIOLENT JOURNEY, A (1965) *see* FOOL KILLER, THE

VIOLENT MEN, THE (1955) Columbia. **Color-96min.** Glenn Ford, Barbara Stanwyck, Edward G. Robinson.............................. 4*
British title: ROUGH COMPANY

VIOLENT MIDNIGHT (1963) *see* PSYCHOMANIA

VIOLENT MOMENT (1959) Schoenfeld Film Distributing. **B&W-61min.** *(British).* Lyndon Brook, Jane Hylton .... (3)

Films are rated on a 1 to 10 scale, 10 is highest. **Boldface** ratings followed by an asterisk (*) are for films actually seen and rated by the executive and senior editors. All other ratings are estimates. (See Notes on Entertainment Ratings in the front section.)

VIOLENT ONES (1957) B&W-100min. *(French)*. Paul Meurisse, Francoise Fabian .... (5)
Original title: VIOLENTS, LES
British title: COFFIN CAME BY POST, THE

VIOLENT ONES, THE (1967) Feature Film Corp. Color-84min. Fernando Lamas, Aldo Ray, David Carradine .... (2)

VIOLENT PATRIOT, THE (1957) Four Star. Color-94min. *(Italian)*. Vittorio Gassman, Anna Maria Ferrero .... (3)

VIOLENT PLAYGROUND (1958) Lopert [U.A.]. B&W-106min. *(British)*. Stanley Baker, Peter Cushing, Anne Heywood .... (5)

VIOLENT ROAD (1958) Warner Bros. B&W-86min. Brian Keith, Efrem Zimbalist, Jr. .... (4)

VIOLENT SATURDAY (1955) 20th Century-Fox. Color-91min. Victor Mature, Richard Egan 5*

VIOLENT SUMMER (1959) Films Around The World. B&W-99min. *(Italian)*. Eleonora Rossi-Drago, Jean-Louis Trintignant .... (4)
Original title: ESTATE VIOLENTA

VIOLENT SUMMER (1961) S. F. B&W-85min. *(French)*. Martine Carol, Jean Desailly .... (3)
Original title: SOIR SUR LA PLAGE, UN *(A Night on the Beach)*

VIOLETTE (1978) Gaumont-New Yorker. Color-123min. *(French)*. Isabelle Huppert, Stephane Audran .... (5)

VIOLONS DU BAL, LES (1974) Levitt-Pickman. Color-110min. *(French)*. Marie-Jose Nat, Jean-Louis Trintignant, Michel Drach 4*
Translation title: The Violins at the Ball

VIRGIN AND THE GYPSY, THE (1970) Chevron. Color-92min. *(British)*. Joanna Shimkus, Franco Nero 5½*

VIRGIN ISLAND (1958) Films Around The World. Color-84min. *(British)*. John Cassavetes, Virginia Maskell .... (4)

VIRGIN NAMED MARY, A (1975) Euro International. Color-102min. *(Italian)*. Cinzia De Carolis, Turi Ferro .... (4)
Original title: PEPPINO E LA VERGINE MARIA *(Peppino and the Virgin Mary)*
Alternate title: VIRTUE AND MAGIC

VIRGIN QUEEN, THE (1955) 20th Century-Fox. Color-92min. Bette Davis, Richard Todd 5½*

VIRGIN SOLDIERS, THE (1969) Columbia. Color-96min. *(British)*. Lynn Redgrave, Hywel Bennett .... (5)

VIRGIN SPRING, THE (1960) Janus Films. B&W-85min. *(Swedish)*. Max von Sydow, Birgitta Valberg 5½*
Original title: JUNGFRUKALLAN

VIRGIN WITCH, THE (1972) Joseph Brenner. Color-89min. Ann Michelle, Vicky Michelle, Keith Buckley .... (2)

VIRGINIA (1941) Paramount. Color-110min. Madeleine Carroll, Fred MacMurray .... (3)

VIRGINIA CITY (1940) Warner Bros. B&W-121min. Errol Flynn, Miriam Hopkins 4*

VIRGINIA HILL STORY, THE (1974) NBC-TV. Color-74min. *(Made for TV)*. Dyan Cannon, Harvey Keitel, Allen Garfield .... (4)

VIRGINIAN, THE (1929) Paramount. B&W-90min. Gary Cooper, Walter Huston .... (4)

VIRGINIAN, THE (1946) Paramount. Color-90min. Joel McCrea, Brian Donlevy .... (4)

VIRGINS AND THE VAMPIRES (1972) *see* CAGED VIRGINS

VIRIDIANA (1961) Kingsley International. B&W-90min. *(Spanish)*. Silvia Pinal, Francisco Rabal 5*

VIRTUE AND MAGIC (1975) *see* VIRGIN NAMED MARY

VIRTUOUS BIGAMIST, THE (1957) Kingsley International. Color-90min. *(French)*. Fernandel, Giulia Rubini .... (4)
Original title: SOUS LE CIEL DE PROVENCE *(Under the Skies of Provence)*

VIRTUOUS SIN, THE (1930) Paramount. B&W-82min. Walter Huston, Kay Francis .... (4)
British title: CAST IRON

VIRTUOUS TRAMPS, THE (1933) *see* DEVIL'S BROTHER, THE

VISA TO CANTON (1960) *see* PASSPORT TO CHINA

VISCOUNT, THE (1967) Warner Bros. Color-98min. *(French-Italian-Spanish)*. Kerwin Mathews, Edmond O'Brien, Jane Fleming (Silvia Sorente) .... (2)
Original French title: VICOMTE REGLE SES COMPTES, LE
Alternate French title: AVENTURES DU VICOMTE, LES *(The Adventures of the Viscount)*
Italian title: VISCOUNT, FURTO ALLA BANCA MONDIALE, THE
Spanish title: ATRACO AL HAMPA
Alternate Spanish title: AVENTURAS DEL VIZCONDE, LES

VISIONS . . . (1972) Warner Bros. Color-73min. *(Made for TV)*. Monte Markham, Telly Savalas 5*
Alternate title: VISIONS OF DEATH

VISIONS OF EIGHT (1973) Cinema 5. Color-108min. *(Documentary)*. Producer: Stan Margulies 2*
TV title: OLYMPIC VISIONS

VISIT, THE (1964) 20th Century-Fox. B&W-100min. *(U.S.-German-French-Italian)*. Ingrid Bergman, Anthony Quinn 5*
German title: BESUCH, DER
French title: RANCUNE, LA
Italian title: VENDETTA DELLA SIGNORA, LA *(The Revenge of a Woman)*

VISIT TO A CHIEF'S SON (1974) United Artists. Color-92min. Richard Mulligan, John Philip Hogdon, Jesse Kinaru, Johnny Sekka .... (4)

VISIT TO A SMALL PLANET (1960) Paramount. B&W-85min. Jerry Lewis, Joan Blackman 3*

VISITA, LA (1966) Promenade. B&W-115min. *(Italian)*. Sandra Milo, Francois Périer .... (4)

VISITOR, THE (1974) *see* LOVING COUSINS

VISITOR, THE (1979) Color- min. John Huston, Glenn Ford, Shelley Winters ....

VISITORS, THE (1972) United Artists. Color-88min. Patrick McVey, Patricia Joyce, Steve Railsback .... (3)

VITELLONI, I (1953) API Productions. B&W-103min. *(Italian)*. Franco Interlenghi, Franco Fabrizi 4*
Translation title: The Big Calves
Alternate title: WASTRELS, THE
British title: SPIVS
TV title: YOUNG AND THE PASSIONATE, THE

VIVA CISCO KID (1940) 20th Century-Fox. B&W-70min. Cesar Romero, Jean Rogers .... (3)

VIVA ITALIA (1977) Cinema 5. Color-87min. *(Italian)*. Vittorio Gassman, Alberto Sordi, Ugo Tognazzi .... (5)
Original title: NUOVI MOSTRI, I *(The New Monsters)*

VIVA KNIEVEL! (1977) Warner Bros. Color-104min. Evel Knievel, Gene Kelly, Marjoe Gortner, Lauren Hutton 3*

VIVA LAS VEGAS! (1956) *see* MEET ME IN LAS VEGAS

VIVA LAS VEGAS (1964) M-G-M. Color-86min. Elvis Presley, Ann-Margret 4*

VIVA MARIA (1965) United Artists. Color-119min. *(French-Italian)*. Jeanne Moreau, Brigitte Bardot, George Hamilton .... (4)

VIVA MAX! (1969) Commonwealth United. Color-96min. Peter Ustinov, Pamela Tiffin 4*

VIVA REVOLUTION (1956) Columbia. Color-106min. *(Mexican)*. Pedro Armendariz, Maria Felix 4½*

VIVA VILLA! (1934) M-G-M. B&W-115min. Wallace Beery, Fay Wray 5½*

VIVA ZAPATA (1952) 20th Century-Fox. B&W-113min. Marlon Brando, Jean Peters 4*

VIVACIOUS LADY (1938) RKO. B&W-90min. Ginger Rogers, James Stewart 4*

VIVRE SA VIE (1962) *see* MY LIFE TO LIVE

VIXEN (1969) *see* RUSS MEYER'S VIXEN

VIXENS, THE (1969) *see* FRIENDS AND LOVERS

VOGUES OF 1938 (1937) United Artists. Color-108min. Warner Baxter, Joan Bennett .... (3)
TV title: VOGUES
Alternate title: WALTER WANGER'S VOGUES OF 1938

VOICE IN THE MIRROR (1958) Universal. B&W-102min. Richard Egan, Julie London, Walter Matthau 3*

VOICE IN THE NIGHT, A (1941) Columbia. B&W-83min. *(British)*. Clive Brook, Diana Wynyard .... (4)
Original title: FREEDOM RADIO

VOICE IN THE WIND (1944) United Artists. B&W-85min. Francis Lederer, Sigrid Gurie .... (5)

VOICE OF BUGLE ANN, THE (1936) M-G-M. B&W-70min. Lionel Barrymore, Eric Linden, Maureen O'Sullivan .... (4)

VOICE OF MERRILL, THE (1952) *see* MURDER WILL OUT

VOICE OF SILENCE, THE (1953) RKO. B&W-85min. *(Italian-French)*. Aldo Fabrizi, Jean Marais, Daniel Gélin .... (3)
Original Italian title: VOCE DEL SILENZIO, LA

VOICE OF THE TURTLE (1948) Warner Bros. B&W-103min. Eleanor Parker, Ronald Reagan 4½*
Alternate title: ONE FOR THE BOOK

VOICE OF THE WHISTLER (1946) Columbia. B&W-60min. Richard Dix, Lynn Merrick .... (4)

Films are rated on a 1 to 10 scale, 10 is highest. **Boldface** ratings followed by an asterisk (*) are for films actually seen and rated by the executive and senior editors. All other ratings are estimates. (See Notes on Entertainment Ratings in the front section.)

VOICES (1979) U.A. (for M-G-M). Color-106min. Michael Ontkean, Amy Irving, Viveca Lindfors 5½*

VOLCANO (1950) United Artists. B&W-106min. *(Italian-U.S.)*. Anna Magnani, Rossano Brazzi, Geraldine Brooks ....(3)
Original title: VULCANO

VOLCANO (1969) *see* KRAKATOA, EAST OF JAVA

VOLTAIRE (1933) Warner Bros. B&W-72min. George Arliss, Doris Kenyon...(5)

VON RICHTHOFEN AND BROWN (1971) United Artists. Color-97min. John Philip Law, Don Stroud ....(3)
British title: RED BARON, THE

VON RYAN'S EXPRESS (1965) 20th Century-Fox. Color-117min. Frank Sinatra, Trevor Howard 5½*

VOODOO BLACK EXORCIST (1974) Horizon. Color-90min. Aldo Sombrel, Eva Leon ....(3)

VOODOO BLOOD BATH (1971) *see* I EAT YOUR SKIN

VOODOO GIRL (1974) *see* SUGAR HILL

VOODOO HEARTBEAT (1972) Twi National. Color-88min. Ray Molina, Philip Ahn ....(2)

VOODOO ISLAND (1957) United Artists. B&W-76min. Boris Karloff, Murvyn Vye ....(3)
Alternate title: SILENT DEATH

VOODOO MAN (1944) Monogram [Allied Artists]. B&W-62min. Bela Lugosi, George Zucco, John Carradine 3*

VOODOO TIGER (1952) Columbia. B&W-67min. Johnny Weissmuller, Jean Byron ....(3)

VOODOO VILLAGE (1958) Continental [Walter Reade]. Color-70min. *(Documentary). Director:* Hassoldt Davis ....(5)
Original title: SORCERER'S VILLAGE, THE

VOODOO WOMAN (1957) American-International. B&W-77min. Marla English, Tom Conway, Touch (Michael) Connors 3*

VOYAGE, THE (1974) United Artists. Color-102min. *(Italian)*. Sophia Loren, Richard Burton ....(4)
Original title: VIAGGIO, IL
Alternate title: TRIP, THE
Alternate title: JOURNEY, THE

VOYAGE INTO SPACE (1968) American-International. Color-98min. *(Japanese, Telefeature).* Mitsunobo Kaneko, Akio Tito...........................1*
Alternate title: JOHNNY SOKKO AND HIS GIANT ROBOT

VOYAGE OF SILENCE (1967) Lopert [U.A.]. B&W-89min. *(French)*. Marc Pico, Henrique De Sousa ....(5)
Venice Film Festival Title: O SALTO *(The Leap)*
Alternate French title: SAUT, LE

VOYAGE OF THE DAMNED (1976) Avco-Embassy. Color-134min. Oskar Werner, Faye Dunaway, Max Von Sydow 5½*

VOYAGE OF THE YES, THE (1972) Viacom. Color-74min. *(Made for TV)*. Desi Arnaz, Jr., Mike Evans ....(4)

VOYAGE TO A PREHISTORIC PLANET (1965) American-International. Color-80min. Basil Rathbone, Faith Domergue 2*

VOYAGE TO DANGER (1962) Color-87min. *(German)*. John Hansen, Karin Baal ....(3)

VOYAGE TO ITALY (1954) *see* STRANGERS

VOYAGE TO THE BOTTOM OF THE SEA (1961) 20th Century-Fox. Color-105min. Walter Pidgeon, Robert Sterling 4*

VOYAGE TO THE END OF THE UNIVERSE (1963) American-International. Color-81min. *(Czech)*. Dennis Stephans (Zdenek Stepánek), Francis Smolen (Frantisek Smolik) ....(3)
Original title: IKARIE XB 1 *(Icarus XB 1)*

VOYAGE TO THE PLANET OF PREHISTORIC WOMEN (1965) Filmgroup. Color-78min. Mamie Van Doren, Mary Mark 1*

VULCAN AFFAIR, THE (1966) *see* TO TRAP A SPY

VULTURE, THE (1967) Paramount. Color-91min. *(Canadian-British-U.S.)*. Robert Hutton, Akim Tamiroff, Broderick Crawford, Diane Clare 3*

-W-

W (1974) Cinerama Releasing. Color-95min. Twiggy, Michael Witney...(4)

W.C. FIELDS AND ME (1976) Universal. Color-111min. Rod Steiger, Valerie Perrine...........................5½*

W.W. AND THE DIXIE DANCEKINGS (1975) 20th Century-Fox. Color-91min. Burt Reynolds, Conny Van Dyke...........................5½*

WABASH AVENUE (1950) 20th Century-Fox. Color-82min. Betty Grable, Victor Mature ....(5)

WAC FROM WALLA WALLA, THE (1952) Republic. B&W-83min. Judy Canova, Steve Dunne ....(3)
British title: ARMY CAPERS

WACKIEST SHIP IN THE ARMY, THE (1960) Columbia. Color-99min. Jack Lemmon, Ricky Nelson...........................4*

WACO (1966) Paramount. Color-85min. Howard Keel, Jane Russell, Brian Donlevy...........................3*

WAGES OF FEAR, THE (1953) Distributors Corp. of America. B&W-140min. *(French)*. Yves Montand, Charles Vanel...........................5*
Original title: SALAIRE DE LA PEUR, LE

WAGES OF FEAR, THE (1977) *see* SORCERER

WAGONMASTER (1950) RKO. B&W-86min. Ben Johnson, Harry Carey, Jr. 3½*

WAGONS ROLL AT NIGHT, THE (1941) Warner Bros. B&W-84min. Humphrey Bogart, Sylvia Sidney 4*

WAGONS WEST (1952) Monogram [Allied Artists]. Color-73min. Rod Cameron, Peggie Castle ....(4)

WAGONS WESTWARD (1940) Republic. B&W-69min. Chester Morris, Anita Louise ....(3)

WAIKIKI WEDDING (1937) Paramount. B&W-89min. Bing Crosby, Bob Burns 4*

WAIT FOR THE DAWN (1960) *see* ESCAPE BY NIGHT

WAIT 'TIL THE SUN SHINES, NELLIE (1952) 20th Century-Fox. Color-108min. David Wayne, Jean Peters 4*

WAIT UNTIL DARK (1967) Warner Bros. Color-107min. Audrey Hepburn, Alan Arkin 6*

WAITING FOR CAROLINE (1967) Lopert [U.A.]. Color-83min. *(Canadian, Made for TV)*. Alexandra Stewart, Francois Tasse, Robert Howay ....(4)

WAITING FOR FIDEL (1976) Open Circle Cinema. Color-57min. *(Canadian, Documentary). Director:* Michael Rubbo ....(4)

WAITING WOMEN (1952) *see* SECRETS OF WOMEN

WAKE IN FRIGHT (1971) *see* OUTBACK

WAKE ISLAND (1942) Paramount. B&W-78min. Brian Donlevy, Macdonald Carey...........................3*

WAKE ME WHEN IT'S OVER (1960) 20th Century-Fox. Color-126min. Ernie Kovacs, Dick Shawn 3½*

WAKE ME WHEN THE WAR IS OVER (1969) ABC Films. Color-75min. *(Made for TV)*. Ken Barry, Eva Gabor 3*

WAKE OF THE RED WITCH (1948) Republic. B&W-106min. John Wayne, Gail Russell ....(4)

WAKE UP AND DREAM (1946) 20th Century-Fox. Color-92min. John Payne, June Haver ....(3)

WAKE UP AND LIVE (1937) 20th Century-Fox. B&W-91min. Walter Winchell, Ben Bernie, Jack Haley, Alice Faye ....(5)

WALK A CROOKED MILE (1948) Columbia. B&W-91min. Louis Hayward, Dennis O'Keefe, Louise Albritton 3*

WALK A TIGHTROPE (1963) Paramount. B&W-69min. *(British-U.S.)*. Dan Duryea, Patricia Owens, Terence Cooper ....(3)

WAIT UNTIL DARK (1967). Hoodlums Jack Weston and Alan Arkin lurk on the staircase as accomplice Richard Crenna tries to gain the confidence of blind housewife Audrey Hepburn in an attempt to locate a missing doll stuffed with narcotics.

WALK, DON'T RUN (1966) Columbia. **Color-114min.** Cary Grant, Samantha Eggar, Jim Hutton...5*

WALK EAST ON BEACON (1952) Columbia. **B&W-98min.** George Murphy, Finlay Currie ....(4)
British title: CRIME OF THE CENTURY, THE

WALK IN THE SHADOW (1962) Continental [Walter Reade]. **B&W-93min.** *(British).* Michael Craig, Janet Munro, Patrick McGoohan ......(5)
Original title: LIFE FOR RUTH

WALK IN THE SPRING RAIN, A (1970) Columbia. **Color-98min.** Anthony Quinn, Ingrid Bergman ....(3)

WALK IN THE SUN, A (1945) 20th Century-Fox. **B&W-111min.** Dana Andrews, Richard Conte 3*

WALK INTO HELL (1956) Patric Pictures. **Color-93min.** *(Australian-French).* Chips Rafferty, Francoise Christophe 3*
Original Australian title: WALK INTO PARADISE
French title: ODYSSÉE DU CAPITAINE STEVE, L'

WALK LIKE A DRAGON (1960) Paramount. **B&W-95min.** Jack Lord, Nobu McCarthy ....(4)

WALK ON THE WILD SIDE (1962) Columbia. **B&W-114min.** Laurence Harvey, Capucine 4½*

WALK PROUD (1979) Universal. **Color-102min.** Robby Benson, Sarah Holcomb ....

WALK SOFTLY, STRANGER (1950) RKO. **B&W-81min.** Joseph Cotten, (Alida) Valli ....(4)
Original title: WEEP NO MORE

WALK TALL (1960) 20th Century-Fox. **Color-60min.** Willard Parker, Joyce Meadows ....(3)

WALK THE DARK STREETS (1956) Dominant Pictures. **B&W-74min.** Chuck Connors, Don Ross ....(3)

WALK THE PROUD LAND (1956) Universal. **Color-88min.** Audie Murphy, Anne Bancroft 3½*

WALK UP AND DIE (1971) *see* BANYON

WALK WITH LOVE AND DEATH, A (1970) 20th Century-Fox. **Color-90min.** Anjelica Huston, Assaf Dayan ....(4)

WALKABOUT (1971) 20th Century-Fox. **Color-95min.** *(Australian-U.S.).* Jenny Agutter, Lucien John, David Gumpilil 3*

WALKING DEAD, THE (1936) Warner Bros. **B&W-66min.** Boris Karloff, Edmund Gwenn, Ricardo Cortez...............................3*

WALKING DOWN BROADWAY (1933) *see* HELLO, SISTER

WALKING HILLS, THE (1949) Columbia. **B&W-78min.** Randolph Scott, Ella Raines ....(5)

WALKING MY BABY BACK HOME (1953) Universal. **Color-95min.** Donald O'Connor, Janet Leigh ....(3)

WALKING STICK, THE (1970) M-G-M. **Color-101min.** *(British).* David Hemmings, Samantha Eggar ....(5)

WALKING TALL (1973) Cinerama Releasing. **Color-125min.** Joe Don Baker, Elizabeth Hartman 5½*

WALKING TALL, PART 2 (1975) *see* PART 2 WALKING TALL

WALKING TARGET, THE (1960) United Artists. **B&W-74min.** Joan Evans, Ronald Foster ....(3)

WALL IN JERUSALEM, A (1968) Eyr Campus Programs. **B&W-90min.** *(French, Documentary). Director:* Frédéric Rossif...........(5)
Original title: MUR A JERUSALEM, UN

WALL OF DEATH (1951) Realart. **B&W-95min.** *(British).* Maxwell Reed, Susan Shaw, Laurence Harvey ....(3)
Original title: THERE IS ANOTHER SUN

WALL OF FURY (1962) Medallion. **Color-88min.** *(German).* Tony Saller, Richard Goodman ....(3)

WALL OF NOISE (1963) Warner Bros. **B&W-112min.** Suzanne Pleshette, Ty Hardin...4*

WALLFLOWER (1948) Warner Bros. **B&W-77min.** Robert Hutton, Joyce Reynolds ....(5)

WALLS CAME TUMBLING DOWN, THE (1946) Columbia. **B&W-82min.** Lee Bowman, Marguerite Chapman ....(5)

WALLS OF FEAR (1962) American-International. **B&W-85min.** *(French).* Francis Blanche, Moloudji..............................(3)

WALLS OF FIRE (1973) Mentor Productions. **Color-81min.** *(U.S.-Mexican, English language, Documentary). Director:* Herbert Kline 5*

WALLS OF GOLD (1933) Fox Film Co. [20th]. **B&W-74min.** Sally Eilers, Norman Foster ....(3)

WALLS OF HELL, THE (1964) Hemisphere. **B&W-87min.** *(U.S.-Philippine).* Jock Mahoney, Fernando Poe, Jr. ....(3)
Original title: INTRAMUROS

WALLS OF JERICHO, THE (1948) 20th Century-Fox. **B&W-106min.** Kirk Douglas, Cornel Wilde, Anne Baxter ....(3)

WALLS OF MALAPAGA, THE (1949) Films International. **B&W-89min.** *(Italian-French).* Isa Miranda, Jean Gabin, Andrea Checchi ......(5)
Original Italian title: MURA DI MALAPAGA, LA
French title: AU DELA DES GRILLES *(Beyond the Gates)*

WALTER WAGNER'S VOGUES OF 1938 (1938) *see* VOGUES OF 1938

WALTZ OF THE TOREADORS (1962) Continental [Walter Reade]. **Color-105min.** *(British).* Peter Sellers, Dany Robin 4*
Alternate title: AMOROUS GENERAL, THE

WANDA (1970) Bardene International. **Color-101min.** Barbara Loden, Michael Higgins, Frank Jourdano, Valerie Manches.............(5)

WANDA NEVADA (1979) United Artists. **Color-105min.** Peter Fonda, Brooke Shields...

WANDERER, THE (1967) Leacock-Pennebaker. **Color-103min.** *(French).* Brigitte Fossey, Jean Blaise ....(5)
Original title: GRAND MEAULNES, LE

WANDERERS, THE (1979) Warner Bros. (for Orion). **Color- min.** Ken Wahl, Karen Allen ....

WANTED (1948) *see* FOUR FACES WEST

WANTED FOR MURDER (1946) 20th Century-Fox. **B&W-95min.** *(British).* Eric Portman, Dulcie Gray, Derek Farr ....(4)

WANTED: THE SUNDANCE WOMAN (1976) 20th Century-Fox. **Color-100min.** *(Made for TV).* Katharine Ross, Steve Forrest.........(4)

WANTON CONTESSA, THE (1954) *see* SENSO

WAR AGAINST MRS. HADLEY, THE (1942) M-G-M. **B&W-86min.** Van Johnson, Fay Bainter, Edward Arnold ....(3)

WAR AND PEACE (1956) Paramount. **Color-208min.** *(Italian-U.S.).* Audrey Hepburn, Henry Fonda..5½*

WAR AND PEACE (1967) Continental [Walter Reade]. **Color-373min.** *(U.S.S.R.).* Ludmila Savelyeva, Sergei Bondarchuk 6*
Original title: VOINA I MIR

WAR ARROW (1954) Universal. **Color-78min.** Maureen O'Hara, Jeff Chandler...3*

WAR BETWEEN MEN AND WOMEN, THE (1972) Nat'l General (for Cinema Center). **Color-105min.** Jack Lemmon, Barbara Harris............5*

WAR BETWEEN THE PLANETS (1965) Fanfare. **Color-80min.** *(Italian).* Jack Stuart (Giacomo Rossi-Stuart), Amber Collins (Ombretta Colli)..(2)
Original title: MISSIONE PIANETA ERRANTE *(Mission Wandering Planet)*
Alternate title: PLANET ON THE PROWL

WAR DRUMS (1957) United Artists. **Color-75min.** Lex Barker, Joan Taylor, Ben Johnson ....(4)

WAR GAME, THE (1966) Pathé Contemporary. **B&W-47min.** *(British, Documentary, Made for TV). Director:* Peter Watkins 5½*

WAR GODS OF BABYLON (1962) American-International. **Color-82min.** *(Italian).* Howard Duff, Jackie Lane ....(3)

WAR-GODS OF THE DEEP (1965) American-International. **Color-85min.** *(U.S.-British).* Vincent Price, Tab Hunter, Susan Hart 2½*
British title: CITY UNDER THE SEA, THE

WAR HUNT (1962) United Artists. **B&W-81min.** John Saxon, Robert Redford...3*

WAR IS HELL (1963) Allied Artists. **B&W-81min.** Tony Russel, Baynes Barron, Burt Topper ....(3)

WAR IS OVER, THE (1966) *see* GUERRE EST FINIE, LA

WAR ITALIAN STYLE (1966) American-International. **Color-74min.** *(Italian).* Buster Keaton, Franco Franchi, Ciccio Ingrassia ......(2)
Original title: DUE MARINES E UN GENERALE *(Two Marines and a General)*

WAR LORD, THE (1965) Universal. **Color-123min.** Charlton Heston, Rosemary Forsyth 6*

WAR LOVER, THE (1962) Columbia. **B&W-105min.** *(British-U.S.).* Steve McQueen, Robert Wagner 4½*

WAR OF CHILDREN, A (1972) Tomorrow Entertainment. **Color-73min.** *(Made for TV).* Jenny Agutter, Vivian Merchant...........5*

WAR OF THE BUTTONS, THE (1962) Bronston Distributors. **B&W-92min.** *(French).* Martin Lartigue, André Treton, Michel Isella..........(4)
Original title: GUERRE DES BOUTONS, LA

WAR OF THE COLOSSAL BEAST (1958) American-International. **B&W-68min.** Dean Parkin, Sally Fraser, Roger Pace 2½*
British title: TERROR STRIKES, THE

WAR OF THE GARGANTUAS, THE (1966) Maron Films, Ltd. **Color-93min.** *(Japanese-U.S.).* Russ Tamblyn, Kumi Mizuno 1*
Original title: FURANKENSHUTAIN NO KAIJU - SANDA TAI GAILAH
Alternate Japanese title: SANDA TAIL GAILAH

Films are rated on a 1 to 10 scale, 10 is highest. **Boldface** ratings followed by an asterisk (*) are for films actually seen and rated by the executive and senior editors. All other ratings are estimates. (See Notes on Entertainment Ratings in the front section.)

WAR OF THE MONSTERS (1966) American-International. Color-88min. (*Japanese*). Gamera, Kojiro Hongo, Kyoko Enami......................1*
Original title: GAMERA TAI BARUGON (*Gamera vs. Barugon*)

WAR OF THE SATELLITES (1958) Allied Artists. B&W-66min. Susan Cabot, Dick Miller, Richard Devon...................................(2)

WAR OF THE WILDCATS, THE (1943) *see* IN OLD OKLAHOMA

WAR OF THE WORLDS, THE (1953) Paramount. Color-85min. Gene Barry, Ann Robinson,...3*

WAR OF THE ZOMBIES, THE (1963) American-International. Color-85min. (*Italian*). John Drew Barrymore, Susy Andersen, Ettore Manni...(2)
Original title: ROMA CONTRO ROMA (*Rome Against Rome*)
TV title: NIGHT STAR - GODDESS OF ELECTRA

WAR PAINT (1953) United Artists. Color-89min. Robert Stack, Joan Taylor...3*

WAR PARTY (1965) 20th Century-Fox. B&W-72min. Michael T. Mikler, Davey Davison...(2)

WAR SHOCK (1956) *see* WOMAN'S DEVOTION, A

WAR WAGON, THE (1967) Universal. Color-101min. John Wayne, Kirk Douglas...5½*

WARKILL (1967) Universal. Color-100min. (*Philippine-U.S.*). George Montgomery, Tom Drake.......................................(3)

WARLOCK (1959) 20th Century-Fox. Color-121min. Richard Widmark, Henry Fonda, Anthony Quinn.................................5½*

WARLORD OF CRETE, THE (1961) *see* MINOTAUR, THE

WARLORDS OF ATLANTIS (1978) Columbia. Color-96min. (*British*). Doug McClure, Peter Gilmore, Cyd Charisse.................(4)

WARM DECEMBER, A (1973) National General. Color-99min. (*U.S.-British*). Sidney Poitier, Esther Anderson.....................3½*

WARNING FROM SPACE (1956) American-International. Color-87min. (*Japanese*). Toyomi Karita, Keizo Kawasaki............1*
Original title: UCHUJIN TOKYO ARAWARU (*Spacemen Arrive in Tokyo*)
Alternate title: MYSTERIOUS SATELLITE

WARNING SHOT (1967) Paramount. Color-100min. David Janssen, Joan Collins, George Grizzard................................4*

WARNING TO WANTONS (1953) J. Arthur Rank. B&W-98min. (*British*). Anne Vernon, Harold Warrender......................(3)

WARPATH (1951) Paramount. Color-95min. Edmond O'Brien, Polly Bergen...3*

WARRENDALE (1967) Grove Press. B&W-100min. (*Canadian, Documentary, Made for TV*). *Director:* Allan King.............4*

WARRIOR AND THE SLAVE GIRL, THE (1958) Columbia. Color-89min. (*Italian*). Georges Marchal, Mara Cruz, Gianna Maria Canale, Ettore Manni...(3)
Original title: RIVOLTA DEL GLADIATORI, LA (*The Revolt of the Gladiators*)

WARRIOR EMPRESS, THE (1960) Columbia. Color-89min. (*Italian-French*). Kerwin Mathews, Tina Louise...................(2)
Original Italian title: SAFFO, VENERE DI LESBO (*Sapho, Venus of Lesbos*)
French title: SAPHO

WARRIOR WITHIN, THE (1977) Cinevest International. Color-80min. (*Documentary*). *Director:* Burt Rashby.........................

WARRIORS, THE (1955) Allied Artists. Color-85min. Errol Flynn, Joanne Dru...5*
British title: DARK AVENGER, THE

WARRIORS, THE (1979) Paramount. Color-90min. Tom Waites, Michael Beck, James Remar....................................5*

WARRIORS 5 (1962) American-International. B&W-84min. (*Italian-French*). Jack Palance, Giovanna Ralli.....................(3)
French title: DERNIERE ATTAQUE, LA (*The Last Attack*)
Original Italian title: GUERRA CONTINUA, LA (*The War Continues*)

WASHINGTON MELODRAMA (1941) M-G-M. B&W-80min. Frank Morgan, Lee Bowman, Ann Rutherford.........................(3)

WASHINGTON STORY (1952) M-G-M. B&W-81min. Van Johnson, Patricia Neal...(4)
British title: TARGET FOR SCANDAL

WASP WOMAN, THE (1959) Filmgroup. B&W-73min. Susan Cabot, Fred (Anthony) Eisley......................................3*

WASTREL, THE (1961) Medallion. B&W-84min. (*Italian*). Van Heflin, Ellie Lambetti..(3)
Original title: RELITTO, IL

WASTRELS, THE (1953) *see* VITELLONI, I

WATCH IT SAILOR! (1961) Screen Gems. B&W-81min. (*British*). Dennis Price, Marjorie Rhodes.................................(3)

WATCH ON THE RHINE (1943) Warner Bros. B&W-114min. Paul Lukas, Bette Davis...5*

WATCH THE BIRDIE (1951) M-G-M. B&W-70min. Red Skelton, Arlene Dahl...(4)

WATCH YOUR STERN (1960) Magna Pictures. B&W-88min. (*British*). Kenneth Connor, Eric Barker..........................(3)

WATCHED (1974) Penthouse Prods. Color-93min. Stacy Keach, Harris Yulin...(3)

WATER BABIES, THE (1979) Color-93min. (*British*). James Mason, Billie Whitelaw...

WATER BIRDS (1952) RKO (for Disney). Color-31min. (*Documentary*). *Director:* Ben Sharpsteen................................5*

WATER CYBORG (1966) *see* TERROR BENEATH THE SEA

WATERFRONT WOMEN (1950) J. Arthur Rank. B&W-80min. (*British*). Robert Newton, Kathleen Harrison, Richard Burton.........(3)
Original title: WATERFRONT

WATERHOLE #3 (1967) Paramount. Color-95min. James Coburn, Carroll O'Connor, Margaret Blye............................4*

WATERLOO (1971) Paramount. Color-123min. (*Italian-U.S.S.R., English language*). Rod Steiger, Christopher Plummer.........3*
Alternate title: LAST HUNDRED DAYS OF NAPOLEON, THE

WATERLOO BRIDGE (1931) Universal. B&W-81min. Mae Clarke, Kent Douglas...(4)

WATERLOO BRIDGE (1940) M-G-M. B&W-103min. Vivien Leigh, Robert Taylor...4*

WATERLOO ROAD (1944) Eagle Lion. B&W-76min. (*British*). John Mills, Stewart Granger, Alastair Sim...................(4)

WATERMELON MAN (1970) Columbia. Color-97min. Godfrey Cambridge, Estelle Parsons.................................4*

WATERSHIP DOWN (1978) Avco-Embassy. Color-92min. (*British, Cartoon*)...5½*

WATTSTAX (1973) Columbia. Color-102min. (*Music Film*). *Director:* Mel Stuart...2*

WATUSI (1959) M-G-M. Color-85min. George Montgomery, Taina Elg 3½*

WAXWORKS (1924) Viking. B&W-65min. (*German, Silent*). Emil Jannings, Conrad Veidt, Werner Krauss.................(4)
Original title: WACHSFIGURENKABINETT, DAS
Alternate title: THREE WAX MEN

WAY AHEAD, THE (1944) 20th Century-Fox. B&W-106min. (*British*). David Niven, Raymond Huntley............................4*
Alternate title: IMMORTAL BATTALION, THE

WAY DOWN EAST (1920) United Artists. B&W-175min. (*Silent*). Lillian Gish, Richard Barthelmess................................4½*

WAY DOWN EAST (1935) 20th Century-Fox. B&W-84min. Rochelle Hudson, Henry Fonda..(3)

WATERSHIP DOWN (1978). Kehaar, a friendly, whimsical seagull, aids Fiver and the other embattled rabbits in their struggle to establish a new home.

WAY FOR A SAILOR (1930) M-G-M. B&W-83min. John Gilbert, Wallace Beery...(3)

WAY OF A GAUCHO (1952) 20th Century-Fox. Color-91min. Rory Calhoun, Gene Tierney..(3)

WAY OF ALL FLESH, THE (1927) Paramount. B&W-94min. *(Silent).* Emil Jannings, Belle Bennett ....(4)

WAY OF ALL FLESH, THE (1940) Paramount. B&W-86min. Akim Tamiroff, Gladys George ....(3)

WAY OF LIFE, THE (1932) *see* THEY CALL IT SIN

WAY OF THE DRAGON (1972) *see* RETURN OF THE DRAGON

WAY OF THE WIND, THE (1976) R.C. Riddell & Associates. Color-104min. *(Documentary). Director:* Charles Tobias ....(3)

WAY OF YOUTH, THE (1959) B&W-85min. *(French).* Francois Arnoul, Lino Ventura, Alain Delon ....(4)
Original title: CHEMIN DES ESCOLIERS, LE

WAY OUT, THE (1955) RKO. B&W-86min. *(British).* Gene Nelson, Mona Freeman, John Bentley...........................(3)
Original title: DIAL 999

WAY OUT (1967) Premier Presentations. Color-102min. Frank Rodriguez, James Dunleavy...............................(4)

WAY OUT WEST (1936) M-G-M. B&W-65min. Stanley Laurel, Oliver Hardy 4*

WAY TO LOVE, THE (1933) Paramount. B&W-80min. Maurice Chevalier, Ann Dvorak ....(4)

WAY TO THE GOLD, THE (1957) 20th Century-Fox. B&W-94min. Jeffrey Hunter, Sheree North, Walter Brennan..........(3)

WAY TO THE STARS, THE (1945) Two Cities-United Artists. B&W-109min. *(British).* Michael Redgrave, John Mills, Rosamund John 4*
Alternate title: JOHNNY IN THE CLOUDS

WAY . . . WAY OUT (1966) 20th Century-Fox. Color-101min. Jerry Lewis, Connie Stevens 3*

WAY WE LIVE NOW, THE (1970) United Artists. Color-110min. Nicholas Pryor, Joanna Miles..........................(3)

WAY WE WERE, THE (1973) Columbia. Color-118min. Barbra Streisand, Robert Redford 6*

WAY WEST, THE (1967) United Artists. Color-122min. Kirk Douglas, Robert Mitchum..............................(3)

WAYS OF LOVE (1950) Joseph Burstyn. B&W-121min. *(French-Italian).* Sylvia Battaille, Vincent Scotto, Anna Magnani, Federico Fellini ......(5)
Original title of first episode: UNE PARTIE DE CAMPAGNE
Alternate title of first episode: DAY IN THE COUNTRY, A
Original title of second episode: JOFROI
Original title of third episode: MIRACOLO, IL
Alternate title of third episode: MIRACLE, THE

WAYWARD (1932) Paramount. B&W-74min. Nancy Carroll, Richard Arlen ....(4)

WAYWARD BUS, THE (1957) 20th Century-Fox. B&W-89min. Jayne Mansfield, Dan Dailey ....(4)

WAYWARD GIRL, THE (1957) Republic. B&W-71min. Marcia Henderson, Peter Walker ....(2)

WAYWARD GIRL, THE (1959) Compton-Cameo. B&W-91min. *(Norwegian).* Liv Ullmann, Atle Merton ....(4)
Original title: UNG FLUKT

WAYWARD WIFE, THE (1953) Italian Films Export. B&W-92min. *(Italian).* Gina Lollobrigida, Alda Magnani...........(3)
Original title: PROVINCIALE, LA

WE ALL LOVED EACH OTHER SO MUCH (1976) Cinema 5. Color-124min. *(Italian).* Vittorio Gassman, Nino Manfredi, Stefania Sandrelli 5½*
Original title: C'ERAVAMO TANTO AMATI

WE ARE ALL MURDERERS (1952) Kingsley International. B&W-108min. *(French).* Mouloudji, Balpetre ....(5)
Original title: NOUS SOMMES TOUS LES ASSASSINS
British title: ARE WE ALL MURDERERS?

WE ARE IN THE NAVY NOW (1962) *see* WE JOINED THE NAVY

WE ARE NOT ALONE (1939) Warner Bros. B&W-112min. Paul Muni, Jane Bryan ....(5)

WE HAVE COME FOR YOUR DAUGHTERS (1971) *see* MEDICINE BALL CARAVAN

WE JOINED THE NAVY (1962) Associated British-Pathé [EMI]. Color-109min. *(British).* Kenneth More, Lloyd Nolan, Joan O'Brien 4*
TV title: WE ARE IN THE NAVY NOW

WE LIVE AGAIN (1934) United Artists. B&W-82min. Fredric March, Anna Sten..4½*

WE SHALL RETURN (1963) Cari. B&W-92min. Cesar Romero, Tony Ray ....(2)

WE SHALL SEE (1964) Avco-Embassy. B&W-61min. *(British).* Maurice Kaufmann, Faith Brook ....(3)

WE STILL KILL THE OLD WAY (1967) Lopert [U.A.]. Color-92min. *(Italian).* Gian Maria Volonte, Irene Papas ....(5)
Original title: A CIASCUNO IL SUO *(To Each His Own)*

WE, THE WOMEN (1953) Gala-Cameo-Poly *(British).* B&W-102min. *(Italian).* Ingrid Bergman, Alida Valli ....
Original title: SIAMO DONNE

WE WERE DANCING (1942) M-G-M. B&W-94min. Norma Shearer, Lee Bowman, Melvyn Douglas.................(3)

WE WERE STRANGERS (1949) Columbia. B&W-106min. Jennifer Jones, John Garfield 3½*

WE WHO ARE ABOUT TO DIE (1937) RKO. B&W-82min. Preston Foster, Ann Dvorak ....(4)

WE WHO ARE YOUNG (1940) M-G-M. B&W-79min. John Shelton, Lana Turner ....(3)

WE WILL ALL MEET IN PARADISE (1977) First Artists. Color-104min. *(French).* Daniele Delorme, Jean Rochefort...........4½*
Original title: NOUS IRONS TOUS AU PARADIS
British title: PARDON MON AFFAIRE, TOO

WEAK AND THE WICKED, THE (1954) Allied Artists. B&W-81min. *(British).* Glynis Johns, John Gregson ....(4)

WEAKER SEX, THE (1948) Eagle Lion. B&W-84min. *(British).* Ursula Jeans, Cecil Parker ....(3)

WEAPON, THE (1956) Republic. B&W-81min. *(British).* Steve Cochran, Lizabeth Scott, George Colde ....(4)

WEAPONS OF DESTRUCTION (1958) *see* FABULOUS WORLD OF JULES VERNE, THE

WEB, THE (1947) Universal. B&W-87min. Edmond O'Brien, Ella Raines ....(5)

WEB OF EVIDENCE (1959) Allied Artists. B&W-88min. *(British).* Van Johnson, Vera Miles.........................4*
Original title: BEYOND THIS PLACE

WEB OF FEAR (1964) Comet Film. B&W-92min. *(French-Spanish).* Michele Morgan, Dany Saval, Simon Andreu ....(4)
Original French title: CONSTANCE AUX ENFERS *(Constance in Hell)*
Spanish title: BALCON SOBRE EL INFIERNO, UN *(A Balcony Over Hell)*

WEB OF PASSION (1959) *see* LEDA

WEB OF SUSPICION (1959) Paramount. B&W-70min. *(British).* Philip Friend, Susan Beaumont ....(3)

WEDDING, A (1978) 20th Century-Fox. Color-125min. Carol Burnett, Geraldine Chaplin............................6*

WEDDING BELLS (1951) *see* ROYAL WEDDING

WEDDING BREAKFAST, THE (1956) *see* CATERED AFFAIR, THE

WEDDING IN BLOOD (1973) New Line Cinema. Color-98min. *(French).* Michel Piccoli, Stephane Audran, Claude Pieplu...............
Original title: NOCES ROUGES, LES *(Red Wedding Night)*

WEDDING NIGHT, THE (1935) United Artists. B&W-84min. Gary Cooper, Anna Sten 5½*

WEDDING NIGHT (1969) American-International. Color-99min. *(Irish).* Dennis Waterman, Tessa Wyatt.................(3)
Original title: I CAN'T . . . I CAN'T

WEDDING OF LILI MARLENE, THE (1953) Monarch. B&W-87min. *(British).* Lisa Daniely, Hugh McDermott ....(2)

WEDDING PARTY, THE (1969) Ajay Films. B&W-90min. Jill Clayburgh, Charles Pfluger ....(4)

WEDDINGS AND BABIES (1958) Morris Engel. B&W-81min. Viveca Lindfors, John Myhers, Charinda Barile ....(5)

WEDNESDAY'S CHILD (1971) Cinema 5. Color-108min. *(British).* Sandy Ratcliff, Bill Dean, Malcolm Tierney ....(3)
Original title: FAMILY LIFE

WEE GEORDIE (1955) George K. Arthur. Color-100min. *(British).* Bill Travers, Alastair Sim.............................5*
Original title: GEORDIE

WEE WILLIE WINKIE (1937) 20th Century-Fox. B&W-99min. Shirley Temple, Victor McLaglen 4*

WEED (1972) Sherpix. Color-106min. *(Documentary). Director:* Alex de Renzy ....(3)

WEED OF CRIME, THE (1964) Commonwealth United TV. Color-90min. *(Japanese).* Tatsuia Mihashi, Makota Sato ....(3)

WEEK-END IN HAVANA (1941) 20th Century-Fox. Color-80min. Alice Faye, Carmen Miranda, John Payne ....(4)

WEEK-END MARRIAGE (1932) First National [W.B.]. B&W-66min. Loretta Young, George Brent............................(3)
British title: WORKING WIVES

WEEK END WITH FATHER (1951) Universal. **B&W-83min.** Van Heflin, Patricia Neal, Gigi Perreau .... (4)

WEEKEND (1962) Cinema Video International. **B&W-84min.** *(Danish).* Jens Osterholm, Birgit Bruel, Jesper Jensen .... (3)

WEEKEND (1968) Grove Press. **Color-103min.** *(French-Italian).* Mireille Darc, Jean Yanne .... (5)

WEEKEND AT DUNKIRK (1964) 20th Century-Fox. **Color-102min.** *(French-Italian).* Jean-Paul Belmondo, Catherine Spaak 3*
Original French title: WEEKEND A ZUYDCOOTE *(Weekend at Zuydcoote)*
Italian title: WEEK-END A ZUYDCOOTE

WEEKEND AT THE WALDORF (1945) M-G-M. **B&W-130min.** Ginger Rogers, Walter Pidgeon 4½*

WEEKEND BABYSITTER (1970) *see* WEEKEND WITH THE BABYSITTER

WEEKEND FOR THREE (1941) RKO. **B&W-61min.** Dennis O'Keefe, Jane Wyatt, Philip Reed .... (4)

WEEKEND, ITALIAN STYLE (1966) Marvin Films. **Color-90min.** *(Italian-French-Spanish).* Enrico Maria Salerno, Sandra Milo .... (3)
Original Italian title: OMBRELLONE, L'
Spanish title: PARASOL, EL
Alternate title: WEEKEND WIVES

WEEKEND MURDERS (1970) M-G-M. **Color-98min.** *(Italian).* Anna Moffo, Lance Percival .... (3)
Original title: CONCERTO PER PISTOLA SOLISTA *(Concert for a Solo Pistol)*

WEEKEND NUN, THE (1972) Paramount. **Color-78min.** *(Made for TV).* Joanna Pettet, Vic Morrow 4½*

WEEKEND OF TERROR (1970) Paramount. **Color-74min.** *(Made for TV).* Robert Conrad, Lee Majors, Carol Lynley 3*

WEEKEND WITH LULU, A (1961) Columbia. **B&W-91min.** *(British).* Bob Monkhouse, Leslie Philips, Shirley Eaton .... (4)

WEEKEND WITH THE BABYSITTER (1970) Crown International. **Color-93min.** George E. Carey, Susan Romen, Luanne Roberts .... (3)
Alternate title: WEEKEND BABYSITTER

WEEKEND WIVES (1966) *see* WEEKEND, ITALIAN STYLE

WEEP NO MORE (1950) *see* WALK SOFTLY, STRANGER

WEIRD TALES (1964) *see* KWAIDAN

WEIRD WOMAN (1944) Universal. **B&W-64min.** Lon Chaney, Anne Gwynne .... (4)

WEIRD WORLD OF LSD, THE (1967) Americana Enetertainment Association. **B&W-76min.** Terry Tessem, Yolanda Morino .... (2)

WELCOME HOME (1945) *see* SNAFU

WELCOME HOME, JOHNNY BRISTOL (1971) Viacom. **Color-100min.** *(Made for TV).* Martin Landau, Jane Alexander, Brock Peters, Pat O'Brien .... (4)

WELCOME HOME, SOLDIER BOYS (1972) 20th Century-Fox. **Color-91min.** Joe Don Baker, Paul Koslo, Alan Vint, Elliott Street ...... (3)

WELCOME STRANGER (1947) Paramount. **B&W-107min.** Bing Crosby, Joan Caulfield, Barry Fitzgerald 4*

WELCOME TO ARROW BEACH (1974) *see* TENDER FLESH

WELCOME TO BLOOD CITY (1977) EMI. **Color-96min.** *(British-Canadian).* Jack Palance, Keir Dullea .... (4)

WELCOME TO HARD TIMES (1967) M-G-M. **Color-105min.** Henry Fonda, Janice Rule 4*
British title: KILLER ON A HORSE

WELCOME TO L.A. (1977) Lion's Gate Films. **Color-103min.** Keith Carradine, Geraldine Chaplin, Sissy Spacek, Harvey Keitel 2½*

WELCOME TO MY NIGHTMARE (1976) Key Pictures. **Color-85min.** *(British, Music Film).* Director: David Winters .... (4)

WELCOME TO THE CLUB (1971) Columbia. **Color-88min.** *(British).* Brian Foley, Jack Warden .... (2)

WELL, THE (1951) United Artists. **B&W-84min.** Richard Rober, Barry Kelly, Henry (Harry) Morgan 4½*

WE'LL BURY YOU! (1962) Columbia. **B&W-77min.** *(Compilation).* Producer: Jack Leewood .... (4)

WELL-GROOMED BRIDE, THE (1946) Paramount. **B&W-75min.** Olivia de Havilland, Ray Milland .... (3)

WELLDIGGER'S DAUGHTER (1941) Siritzky International. **B&W-123min.** *(French).* Raimu, Fernandel .... (5)
Original title: FILLE DU PUISATIER, LA

WELLINGTON (1934) *see* IRON DUKE, THE

WELLS FARGO (1937) Paramount. **B&W-115min.** Joel McCrea, Frances Dee 4*

WENT THE DAY WELL? (1942) Ealing-United Artists. **B&W-92min.** *(British).* Leslie Banks, Elizabeth Allan .... (4)
Alternate title: 48 HOURS

WE'RE GOING TO BE RICH (1938) 20th Century-Fox. **B&W-78min.** *(British).* Gracie Fields, Brian Donlevy, Victor McLaglen .... (4)

WE'RE IN THE ARMY NOW (1939) *see* PACK UP YOUR TROUBLES

WE'RE NO ANGELS (1955) Paramount. **Color-106min.** Humphrey Bogart, Aldo Ray, Peter Ustinov 4½*

WE'RE NOT DRESSING (1934) Paramount. **B&W-63min.** Bing Crosby, Carole Lombard, George Burns, Gracie Allen 4*

WE'RE NOT MARRIED! (1952) 20th Century-Fox. **B&W-85min.** Victor Moore, Ginger Rogers, Fred Allen 4½*

WEREWOLF, THE (1956) Columbia. **B&W-83min.** Don Megowan, Steven Rich .... (3)

WEREWOLF IN A GIRLS' DORMITORY (1962) M-G-M. **B&W-82min.** *(Italian).* Barbara Lass, Carl Schell, Curt Lowens .... (1)
Original title: LYCANTHROPUS
Alternate title: GHOUL IN SCHOOL, THE

WEREWOLF OF LONDON, THE (1935) Universal. **B&W-75min.** Henry Hull, Valerie Hobson, Warner Oland 4*

WEREWOLF OF WASHINGTON (1973) Diplomat Pictures. **Color-90min.** Dean Stockwell, Biff McGuire .... (4)

WEREWOLF VS. THE VAMPIRE WOMAN, THE (1970) Ellman. **Color-82min.** *(Spanish-W. German).* Paul Naschy, Gaby Fuchs, Barbara Capell .... (2)
Original Spanish title: NOCHE DE WALPURGIS, LA *(Walpurgis Night)*
German title: NACHT DER VAMPIRE *(Night of the Vampire)*
British title: SHADOW OF THE WEREWOLF

WEREWOLVES ON WHEELS (1971) Fanfare. **Color-84min.** Stephen Oliver, D. J. (Donna) Anderson, Severn Darden .... (2)

WEST 11 (1963) Warner Bros. **B&W-93min.** *(British).* Alfred Lynch, Kathleen Breck .... (3)

WEST OF MONTANA (1964) *see* MAIL ORDER BRIDE

WEST OF SHANGHAI (1937) Warner Bros. **B&W-65min.** Boris Karloff, Ricardo Cortez .... (3)

WEST OF SUEZ (1957) *see* FIGHTING WILDCATS

WEST OF THE PECOS (1945) RKO. **B&W-66min.** Robert Mitchum, Barbara Hale .... (4)

WEST OF ZANZIBAR (1928) M-G-M. **B&W-68min.** Lon Chaney, Lionel Barrymore 3*

WEST OF ZANZIBAR (1954) Universal. **Color-94min.** *(British).* Anthony Steel, Sheila Sim .... (3)

WEST POINT OF THE AIR (1935) M-G-M. **B&W-100min.** Robert Young, Maureen O'Sullivan .... (4)

WEST POINT STORY, THE (1950) Warner Bros. **Color-107min.** James Cagney, Virginia Mayo, Doris Day 4*
British title: FINE AND DANDY

WEST POINT WIDOW (1941) Paramount. **B&W-63min.** Anne Shirley, Richard Carlson .... (4)

WEST SIDE KID, THE (1943) Republic. **B&W-58min.** Donald Barry, Dale Evans, Henry Hull .... (4)

WEST SIDE STORY (1961) United Artists. **Color-155min.** Natalie Wood, Richard Beymer 9*

WESTBOUND (1959) Warner Bros. **Color-72min.** Randolph Scott, Virginia Mayo 3½*

WESTERN PACIFIC AGENT (1950) Lippert Productions. **B&W-64min.** Kent Taylor, Sheila Ryan .... (4)

WESTERN UNION (1941) 20th Century-Fox. **Color-94min.** Robert Young, Randolph Scott 4*

WESTERNER, THE (1940) United Artists. **B&W-99min.** Gary Cooper, Walter Brennan 6*

WESTFRONT 1918 (1930) Nero. **B&W- min.** *(German).* Fritz Kampers, Gustav Diessl, Hans Joachim Moebis .... (4)

WESTLAND CASE, THE (1937) Universal. **B&W-63min.** Preston Foster, Carol Hughes .... (4)

WESTWARD HO THE WAGONS! (1957) Buena Vista. **Color-90min.** Fess Parker, Kathleen Crowley .... (5)

WESTWARD PASSAGE (1932) RKO. **B&W-75min.** Laurence Olivier, Ann Harding .... (3)

WESTWARD THE WOMEN (1952) M-G-M. **B&W-118min.** Robert Taylor, Denise Darcel 4*

WESTWORLD (1973) M-G-M. **Color-88min.** Yul Brynner, Richard Benjamin, James Brolin 6*

WET ASPHALT (1958) Screen Gems. **B&W-90min.** *(German).* Horst Buchholz, Gert Frobe, Maria Perschy.................................... (4)
Original title: NASSER ASPHALT

WETBACK HOUND (1957) Buena Vista. **Color-18min.** Marvin Glenn, Warner Glenn, Rex Allen.................................... (5)

WETBACKS (1956) Banner. **B&W-89min.** Lloyd Bridges, Barton MacLane.................................... **3***

WE'VE NEVER BEEN LICKED (1943) Universal. **B&W-103min.** Richard Quine, Noah Beery, Jr., Robert Mitchum .... (3)
British title: TEXAS TO TOKYO

WHAT! (1963) Futuramic Releasing Organization. **Color-90min.** *(Italian-French-British).* Christopher Lee, Daliah Lavi.................................... (3)
Original Italian title: FRUSTA E IL CORPO, LA *(The Whip and the Body)*
French title: CORPS ET LE FOUET, LE *(The Body and the Whip)*
British title: NIGHT IS THE PHANTOM

WHAT? (1972) Avco-Embassy. **Color-112min.** *(Italian-French-West German, English version).* Sydne Rome, Marcello Mastroianni ....(3)
Original Italian title: CHE?
Alternate title: DIARY OF FORBIDDEN DREAMS

WHAT A BLONDE (1945) RKO. **B&W-71min.** Leon Errol, Elaine Riley (3)

WHAT A CARVE UP (1951) *see* NO PLACE LIKE HOMICIDE

WHAT A LIFE (1939) Paramount. **B&W-75min.** Jackie Cooper, Betty Field .... (5)

WHAT A MAN (1941) *see* NEVER GIVE A SUCKER AN EVEN BREAK

WHAT A WAY TO DIE! (1968) *see* BEYOND CONTROL

WHAT A WAY TO GO! (1964) 20th Century-Fox. **Color-111min.** Shirley MacLaine, Dean Martin 4½*

WHAT A WOMAN (1938) *see* THERE'S THAT WOMAN AGAIN

WHAT A WOMAN! (1943) Columbia. **B&W-94min.** Rosalind Russell, Brian Aherne **4***
British title: BEAUTIFUL CHEAT, THE

WHAT A WOMAN! (1945) *see* BEAUTIFUL CHEAT, THE

WHAT A WOMAN! (1955) *see* LUCKY TO BE A WOMAN

WHAT AM I BID? (1967) Emerson Films. **Color-92min.** LeRoy Van Dyke, Kristin Nelson, Stephanie Hill .... (3)

WHAT ARE BEST FRIENDS FOR? (1973) Worldvision. **Color-74min.** *(Made for TV).* Ted Bessell, Lee Grant, Larry Hagman, Barbara Feldon **4***

WHAT BECAME OF JACK AND JILL? (1972) 20th Century-Fox. **Color-93min.** *(British).* Paul Nicholas, Vanessa Howard, Mona Washbourne (3)

WHAT DID YOU DO IN THE WAR, DADDY? (1966) United Artists. **Color-119min.** James Coburn, Dick Shawn **3***

WHAT DO YOU SAY TO A NAKED LADY? (1970) United Artists. **Color-92min.** *(Compilation).* Director: Allen Funt .... (4)

WHAT EVER HAPPENED TO AUNT ALICE? (1969) Cinerama Releasing. **Color-101min.** Geraldine Page, Ruth Gordon 4½*

WHAT EVER HAPPENED TO BABY JANE? (1962) Warner Bros. **B&W-132min.** Bette Davis, Joan Crawford **6***

WHAT EVERY WOMAN KNOWS (1934) M-G-M. **B&W-92min.** Helen Hayes, Brian Aherne .... (5)

WHAT EVERY WOMAN WANTS (1962) United Artists. **B&W-69min.** *(British).* William Fox, Hy Hazell .... (3)

WHAT HAPPENED AT CAMPO GRANDE? (1967) Alan Enterprises. **Color-100min.** *(British).* Eric Morecambe, Ernie Wise, Margit Saad ....(3)
Original title: MAGNIFICENT TWO, THE

WHAT LOLA WANTS (1958) *see* DAMN YANKEES

WHAT NEXT? (1974) Children's Film Foundation. **Color-56min.** *(British).* Peter Robinson, Perry Benson, Lynne White.................................... (4)

WHAT NEXT, CORPORAL HARGROVE? (1945) M-G-M. **B&W-95min.** Robert Walker, Keenan Wynn.................................... (4)

WHAT! NO BEER? (1933) M-G-M. **B&W-66min.** Jimmy Durante, Buster Keaton.................................... (3)

WHAT PRICE GLORY (1927) Fox Film Co. [20th]. **B&W-123min.** *(Silent).* Victor McLaglen, Edmund Lowe **4***

WHAT PRICE GLORY (1952) 20th Century-Fox. **Color-111min.** James Cagney, Dan Dailey .... (4)

WHAT PRICE HOLLYWOOD? (1932) RKO. **B&W-88min.** Constance Bennett, Lowell Sherman **4***

WHAT PRICE MURDER (1958) United Motion Pic. Org. (UMPO). **B&W-190min.** *(French).* Henri Vidal, Mylene Demongeot, Isa Miranda ....(4)
Original title: MANCHE ET LA BELLE, UNE *(colloquial: Beauty Is Only Skin Deep)*

WHAT THE BIRDS KNEW (1955) *see* I LIVE IN FEAR

WHAT'S A NICE GIRL LIKE YOU . . . ? (1971) MCA-TV. **Color-73min.** *(Made for TV).* Brenda Vaccaro, Jack Warden, Vincent Price, Roddy McDowall .... (4)

WHAT'S GOOD FOR THE GOOSE (1969) Nat'l Showmanship Films. **Color-104min.** *(British).* Norman Wisdom, Sally Geeson .... (3)
Publicity title: WHAT'S GOOD FOR THE GANDER

WHAT'S NEW PUSSYCAT? (1965) United Artists. **Color-108min.** *(U.S.-French).* Peter Sellers, Peter O'Toole.................................... **4***

WHAT'S SO BAD ABOUT FEELING GOOD? (1968) Universal. **Color-94min.** George Peppard, Mary Tyler Moore.................................... **3***

WHAT'S THE MATTER WITH HELEN? (1971) United Artists. **Color-101min.** Debbie Reynolds, Shelley Winters **3***

WHAT'S UP, DOC? (1972) Warner Bros. **Color-94min.** Barbra Streisand, Ryan O'Neal **6***

WHAT'S UP FRONT (1964) Fairway International. **Color-83min.** Tommy Holden, Marilyn Manning, Carolyn Walker.................................... (3)
Alternate title: FOURTH FOR MARRIAGE, A

WHAT'S UP TIGER LILY? (1966) American-International. **Color-80min.** Woody Allen, China Lee **4***
Original title: KIZINO KIZI *(Key of Keys)*
Alternate Transliteration: KAGI NO KAGI

WHEEL OF FATE (1953) J. Arthur Rank. **B&W-70min.** *(British).* Patric Doonan, Sandra Dorne .... (3)
Alternate title: ROAD HOUSE GIRL

WHEEL OF FIRE (1964) *see* PYRO

WHEEL OF FORTUNE (1941) *see* MAN BETRAYED, A

WHEELER DEALERS, THE (1963) M-G-M. **Color-106min.** James Garner, Lee Remick **5***
British title: SEPARATE BEDS

WHEELS OF FATE (1956) *see* ROUÉ, LA

WHEN A STRANGER CALLS (1979) Columbia. **Color-   min.** Charles Durning, Carol Kane, Colleen Dewhurst ....

WHEN A WOMAN LOVES (1959) Shochiku. **Color-97min.** *(Japanese).* Ineko Arima, Shin Saburi.................................... (4)
Original title: WAGA AI

WHEN A WOMAN MEDDLES (1957) **B&W-90min.** *(French-Italian-W. German).* Edwige Feuillere, Jean Servais .... (3)
Original French title: QUAND LA FEMME S'EN MELE

WHEN COMEDY WAS KING (1960) 20th Century-Fox. **B&W-81min.** *(Compilation).* Producer: Robert Youngson 4½*

WHEN DINOSAURS RULED THE EARTH (1970) Warner Bros. **Color-100min.** *(British).* Victoria Vetri, Robin Hawdon.................................... **3***

WHEN EIGHT BELLS TOLL (1971) Cinerama Releasing. **Color-94min.** *(British).* Anthony Hopkins, Robert Morley, Nathalie Delon................ **4***

WHEN EVERY DAY WAS THE FOURTH OF JULY (1978) NBC-TV. **Color-100min.** *(Made for TV).* Katy Kurtzman, Dean Jones, Geoffrey Lewis.................................... **5***

WHAT'S UP DOC? (1972). Absent-minded professor Ryan O'Neal realizes he can't go on meeting charming weirdo Barbra Streisand under tables and such.

WHEN GANGLAND STRIKES (1956) Republic. **B&W-70min.** John Hudson, Raymond Greenleaf .... (3)

WHEN HELL BROKE LOOSE (1958) Paramount. **B&W-78min.** Charles Bronson, Violet Rensing .... (3)

WHEN I GROW UP (1951) Eagle Lion. **B&W-80min.** Bobby Driscoll, Charley Grapewin .... (5)

WHEN IN ROME (1952) M-G-M. **B&W-78min.** Van Johnson, Paul Douglas .... (3)

WHEN JOHNNY COMES MARCHING HOME (1943) Universal. **B&W-74min.** Jane Frazee, Allan Jones, Donald O'Connor .... (4)

WHEN KNIGHTHOOD WAS IN FLOWER (1953) *see* SWORD AND THE ROSE, THE

WHEN LADIES MEET (1941) M-G-M. **B&W-108min.** Joan Crawford, Greer Garson **4***

WHEN MICHAEL CALLS (1972) 20th Century-Fox. **Color-73min.** *(Made for TV).* Elizabeth Ashley, Michael Douglas, Ben Gazzara **3½***

WHEN MY BABY SMILES AT ME (1948) 20th Century-Fox. **Color-98min.** Betty Grable, Dan Dailey **4***

WHEN NEW YORK SLEEPS (1934) *see* NOW I'LL TELL

WHEN SEX WAS A KNIGHTLY AFFAIR (1976) *see* AMOROUS ADVENTURES OF DON QUIXOTE AND SANCHO PANZA, THE

WHEN STRANGERS MARRY (1944) Monogram [Allied Artists]. **B&W-67min.** Dean Jagger, Kim Hunter, Robert Mitchum .... (4)
Alternate title: BETRAYED

WHEN THE BOUGH BREAKS (1947) J. Arthur Rank. **B&W-81min.** *(British).* Patricia Roc, Rosamund John, Bill Owen .... (3)

WHEN THE BOYS MEET THE GIRLS (1965) M-G-M. **Color-102min.** Connie Francis, Harve Presnell **3***
Alternate title: GIRL CRAZY

WHEN THE CLOCK STRIKES (1961) United Artists. **B&W-72min.** James Brown, Merry Anders .... (2)
Alternate title(?): CLOCK STRIKES THREE, THE

WHEN THE DALTONS RODE (1940) Universal. **B&W-80min.** Randolph Scott, Broderick Crawford **4***

WHEN THE DEVIL COMMANDS (1941) *see* DEVIL COMMANDS, THE

WHEN THE GIRLS TAKE OVER (1962) Parade. **Color-80min.** Robert Lowery, Marvin Miller, Jackie Coogan .... (2)

WHEN THE LEGENDS DIE (1972) 20th Century-Fox. **Color-106min.** Richard Widmark, Frederic Forrest **4***

WHEN THE REDSKINS RODE (1951) Columbia. **Color-78min.** Jon Hall, Mary Castle .... (2)

WHEN TOMORROW COMES (1939) Universal. **B&W-90min.** Irene Dunne, Charles Boyer **4***

WHEN WILLIE COMES MARCHING HOME (1950) 20th Century-Fox. **B&W-82min.** Dan Dailey, Corinne Calvet .... (5)

WHEN WOMEN HAD TAILS (1970) Film Ventures International. **Color-98min.** *(Italian).* Senta Berger, Giuliano Gemma
Original title: QUANDO LE DONNE AVEVANO LA CODA

WHEN WOMEN LOST THEIR TAILS (1971) Film Ventures International. **Color-95min.** *(Italian-W. German).* Senta Berger, Lando Buzzanca, Frank Wolff .... (3)
Original Italian title: QUANDO LE DONNE PERSERO LA CODA
German title: TOLL TRIEBEN ES DIE ALTEN GERMANEN

WHEN WORLDS COLLIDE (1951) Paramount. **Color-81min.** Richard Derr, Barbara Rush **4***

WHEN YOU COMIN' BACK, RED RYDER (1979) Columbia. **Color-118min.** Marjoe Gortner, Peter Firth **5***

WHEN YOU'RE IN LOVE (1937) Columbia. **B&W-104min.** Grace Moore, Cary Grant .... (4)
British title: FOR YOU ALONE

WHEN YOU'RE SMILING (1950) Columbia. **B&W-75min.** Jerome Courtland, Frankie Laine, Lola Albright .... (3)

WHEN'S YOUR BIRTHDAY? (1937) RKO. **B&W-77min.** Joe E. Brown, Edgar Kennedy, Marian Marsh .... (4)

WHERE ANGELS GO . . . TROUBLE FOLLOWS! (1968) Columbia. **Color-95min.** Rosalind Russell, Stella Stevens .... (4)

WHERE ARE YOUR CHILDREN? (1944) Monogram [Allied Artists]. **B&W-73min.** Jackie Cooper, Patricia Morison .... (3)

WHERE DANGER LIVES (1950) RKO. **B&W-84min.** Robert Mitchum, Faith Domergue, Claude Rains .... (3)

WHERE DO WE GO FROM HERE? (1945) 20th Century-Fox. **Color-77min.** Fred MacMurray, Joan Leslie, June Haver **5***

WHERE DOES IT HURT? (1972) Cinerama Releasing. **Color-90min.** *(British-U.S.).* Peter Sellers, Jo Ann Pflug **5***

WHERE EAGLES DARE (1968) M-G-M. **Color-158min.** *(British).* Richard Burton, Clint Eastwood **5½***

WHERE HAVE ALL THE PEOPLE GONE? (1974) MPC (TV). **Color-74min.** *(Made for TV).* Peter Graves, Verna Bloom, Kathleen Quinlan **4***

WHERE IT'S AT (1969) United Artists. **Color-104min.** David Janssen, Robert Drivas **3***

WHERE LOVE HAS GONE (1964) Paramount. **Color-114min.** Susan Hayward, Bette Davis **3***

WHERE NO VULTURES FLY (1951) *see* IVORY HUNTER

WHERE THE BOYS ARE (1960) M-G-M. **Color-99min.** Dolores Hart, Yvette Mimieux **4***

WHERE THE BULLETS FLY (1966) Avco-Embassy. **Color-90min.** *(British).* Tom Adams, Dawn Addams **3***

WHERE THE HOT WIND BLOWS (1958) Avco-Embassy. **B&W-120min.** *(French-Italian).* Gina Lollobrigida, Yves Montand, Marcello Mastroianni .... (3)
Original French title: LOI, LA *(The Law)*
Original Italian title: LEGGE, LA *(The Law)*
Alternate title: LAW, THE

WHERE THE LILLIES BLOOM (1974) United Artists. **Color-96min.** Julie Gholson, Jan Smithers **5***

WHERE THE RED FERN GROWS (1974) Doty-Dayton. **Color-97min.** Stewart Petersen, James Whitmore **4***

WHERE THE RIVER BENDS (1952) *see* BEND OF THE RIVER

WHERE THE SIDEWALK ENDS (1950) 20th Century-Fox. **B&W-95min.** Dana Andrews, Gene Tierney .... (4)

WHERE THE SPIES ARE (1966) M-G-M. **Color-113min.** *(British-U.S.).* David Niven, Francoise Dorleac **3½***

WHERE THE TRUTH LIES (1962) Paramount. **B&W-83min.** *(French).* Juliette Greco, Jean-Marc Bory .... (2)
Original title: MALEFICES
Prerelease U.S. title: EVIL SPELL

WHERE THERE'S A WILL (1936) Gaumont-British [Rank]. **B&W-81min.** *(British).* Will Hay, Hartley Power .... (4)
Original title: GOOD MORNING, BOYS

WHERE THERE'S A WILL (1955) Eros Films *(Brit.).* **B&W-77min.** *(British).* George Cole, Kathleen Harrison .... (3)

WHERE THERE'S LIFE (1947) Paramount. **B&W-75min.** Bob Hope, Signe Hasso **4***

WHERE WERE YOU WHEN THE LIGHTS WENT OUT? (1968) M-G-M. **Color-94min.** Doris Day, Robert Morse **3½***

WHERE'S CHARLEY? (1952) Warner Bros. **Color-97min.** *(British).* Ray Bolger, Allyn McLerie **4***

WHERE'S JACK? (1969) Paramount. **Color-120min.** *(British).* Tommy Steele, Stanley Baker, Fiona Lewis .... (4)

WHERE'S POPPA? (1970) United Artists. **Color-84min.** George Segal, Ruth Gordon, Trish Van Devere **5½***
Alternate title: GOING APE

WHEREVER SHE GOES (1951) Mayer-Kingsley. **B&W-81min.** *(Australian).* Muriel Steinbeck, Suzanne Parrett .... (5)

WHICH WAY IS UP? (1977) Universal. **Color-95min.** Richard Pryor, Lonette McKee, Margaret Avery **5***

WHICH WAY TO THE FRONT? (1970) Warner Bros. **Color-96min.** Jerry Lewis, Jan Murray **1***
British title: JA, JA, MEIN GENERAL! BUT WHICH WAY TO THE FRONT?

WHIFFS (1975) 20th Century-Fox. **Color-90min.** Elliott Gould, Eddie Albert, Godfrey Cambridge .... (4)
British title: C.A.S.H.

WHILE THE CITY SLEEPS (1956) RKO. **B&W-100min.** Dana Andrews, Ida Lupino, George Sanders .... (5)

WHILE THERE'S WAR THERE'S HOPE (1975) Cineriz. **Color-122min.** *(Italian).* Alberto Sordi, Silvia Monti .... (3)
Original title: FINCHE C'E GUERRA C'E SPERANZA

WHIP HAND, THE (1951) RKO. **B&W-82min.** Elliott Reid, Carla Balenda .... (3)
Original title: MAN HE FOUND, THE

WHIPLASH (1949) Warner Bros. **B&W-91min.** Dane Clark, Alexis Smith .... (4)

WHIPPED, THE (1950) *see* UNDERWORLD STORY, THE

WHIPSAW (1935) M-G-M. **B&W-83min.** Myrna Loy, Spencer Tracy **4***

WHIRLPOOL (1950) 20th Century-Fox. **B&W-97min.** Gene Tierney, Richard Conte .... (5)

WHIRLPOOL (1959) Continental [Walter Reade]. **Color-95min.** *(British).* Juliette Greco, O. W. Fischer .... (3)

WHIRLPOOL (1970) Cinemation. Color-92min. *(Danish).* Karl Lanchbury, Vivian Neves .... (2)

WHISKEY AND SOFA (1961) NTA Pictures. Color-87min. *(German).* Maria Schell, Karl Michael.................... (3)
Original title: ZWEI WHISKY UND EIN SOFA *(Two Whiskies and One Sofa)*
Alternate title: OPERATION MOONLIGHT

WHISKY GALORE! (1949) *see* TIGHT LITTLE ISLAND

WHISPERERS, THE (1967) Lopert [U.A.]. B&W-105min. *(British).* Edith Evans, Eric Portman .... (5)

WHISPERING FOOTSTEPS (1943) Republic. B&W-55min. John Hubbard, Rita Quigley.............................. (5)

WHISPERING GHOSTS (1942) 20th Century-Fox. B&W-75min. Milton Berle, Brenda Joyce, John Carradine .... (3)

WHISPERING SMITH (1949) Paramount. Color-88min. Alan Ladd, Robert Preston, Brenda Marshall........... 3*

WHISPERING SMITH VS. SCOTLAND YARD (1952) RKO. B&W-77min. *(British).* Richard Carlson, Greta Gynt........ (3)
Original title: WHISPERING SMITH HITS LONDON

WHISTLE AT EATON FALLS, THE (1951) Columbia. B&W-96min. Lloyd Bridges, Dorothy Gish .... (4)
British title: RICHER THAN THE EARTH

WHISTLE DOWN THE WIND (1961) Pathé-America. B&W-98min. *(British).* Hayley Mills, Alan Bates 4½*

WHISTLE STOP (1946) United Artists. B&W-85min. Ava Gardner, George Raft, Victor McLaglen .... (3)

WHISTLER, THE (1944) Columbia. B&W-59min. Richard Dix, J. Carrol Naish .... (3)

WHISTLING IN BROOKLYN (1943) M-G-M. B&W-87min. Red Skelton, Ann Rutherford....................... 4½*

WHISTLING IN DIXIE (1942) M-G-M. B&W-74min. Red Skelton, Ann Rutherford........................... 4*

WHISTLING IN THE DARK (1931) M-G-M. B&W-78min. Ernest Truex, Una Merkel............................ (4)

WHISTLING IN THE DARK (1941) M-G-M. B&W-77min. Red Skelton, Ann Rutherford 4*

WHITE ANGEL, THE (1936) First National [W.B.]. B&W-75min. Kay Francis, Ian Hunter .... (4)

WHITE BANNERS (1938) Warner Bros. B&W-88min. Claude Rains, Fay Bainter .... (5)

WHITE BUFFALO, THE (1977) United Artists. Color-97min. Charles Bronson, Will Sampson, Jack Warden ... 4*

WHITE CAPTIVE (1943) *see* WHITE SAVAGE

WHITE CARGO (1942) M-G-M. B&W-90min. Hedy Lamarr, Walter Pidgeon 3*

WHITE CHRISTMAS (1954) Paramount. Color-120min. Bing Crosby, Danny Kaye 4*

WHITE CLIFFS OF DOVER, THE (1944) M-G-M. B&W-126min. Irene Dunne, Alan Marshal.............. 4*

WHITE CORRIDORS (1951) J. Arthur Rank. B&W-85min. *(British).* Googie Withers, Gerald Heinz .... (5)

WHITE CRADLE INN (1947) *see* HIGH FURY

WHITE DAWN, THE (1974) Paramount. Color-109min. Warren Oates, Timothy Bottoms, Lou Gossett...... 4*

WHITE FEATHER (1955) 20th Century-Fox. Color-102min. Robert Wagner, John Lund, Debra Paget...... (4)

WHITE FIRE (1954) Lippert Productions. B&W-82min. *(British).* Scott Brady, Mary Castle .... (3)
Original title: THREE STEPS TO THE GALLOWS

WHITE HEAT (1949) Warner Bros. B&W-114min. James Cagney, Edmond O'Brien 4*

WHITE HUNTRESS (1957) American-International. Color-81min. *(British).* Robert Urquhart, John Bentley, Susan Stephen .... (3)
Original title: GOLDEN IVORY

WHITE LIGHTNING (1953) Allied Artists. B&W-61min. Stanley Clements, Steve Brodie .... (3)

WHITE LIGHTNING (1973) United Artists. Color-100min. Burt Reynolds, Jennifer Billingsley 4½*

WHITE LINE FEVER (1975) Columbia. Color-89min. Jan-Michael Vincent, Kay Lenz, Slim Pickens....... 4*

WHITE MAN, THE (1931) *see* SQUAW MAN, THE

WHITE MANE (1953) William Snyder. Color-39min. *(French).* Alain Emery, Frank Silvera .... (5)
Original title: CRIN BLANC
Alternate French title: CHEVAL SAUVAGE *(Wild Stallion)*

WHITE NIGHTS (1957) United Motion Pic. Org. (UMPO). B&W-105min. *(Italian-French).* Maria Schell, Marcello Mastroianni .... (4)
Original Italian title: NOTTI BIANCHE, LE
French title: NUITS BLANCHES

WHITE ORCHID, THE (1955) United Artists. Color-81min. William Lundigan, Peggie Castle............ (3)

WHITE PARADE, THE (1934) Fox Film Co. [20th]. B&W-83min. Loretta Young, John Boles .... (4)

WHITE ROCK (1977) Color-76min. *(British, Documentary).* Director: Tony Maylam .... (3)

WHITE ROSE, THE (1923) United Artists. B&W-115min. *(Silent).* Mae Marsh, Carol Dempster, Ivor Novello, Neil Hamilton 4*

WHITE SAVAGE (1943) Universal. Color-75min. Maria Montez, Jon Hall, Sabu 4*
British title: WHITE CAPTIVE

WHITE SEARCH, THE (1971) Cinema Horizons. Color-89min. *(Documentary).* Director: Dick Barrymore .... (3)

WHITE SHADOWS IN THE SOUTH SEAS (1929) M-G-M. B&W-89min. *(Part-talking).* Monte Blue, Raquel Torres, Robert Anderson.......... (4)

WHITE SHEIK, THE (1952) Contemporary. B&W-86min. *(Italian).* Alberto Sordi, Leopoldo Trieste, Brunella Bovo, Giulietta Masina...... 4½*
Original title: SCEICCO BIANCO, LO

WHITE SISTER, THE (1924) Metro. B&W-104min. *(Silent).* Lillian Gish, Ronald Colman .... (3)

WHITE SISTER, THE (1933) M-G-M. B&W-101min. Helen Hayes, Clark Gable...................... (4)

WHITE SISTER (1971) Columbia. Color-96min. *(Italian-French-Spanish).* Sophia Loren, Adriano Celentano, Fernando Rey........ (4)
Original Italian title: BIANCO, ROSSO E . . . *(White, Red and . . .)*

WHITE SLAVE SHIP (1962) American-International. Color-92min. *(Italian-French).* Pier Angeli, Edmund Purdom .... (3) .
Original Italian title: AMMUTINAMENTO, L'
French title: RÉVOLTÉES DE L'ALBATROSS, L' *(The Mutineers of the Albatross)*
Prerelease U.S. title: WILD CARGO

WHITE SPIDER, THE (1963) UCC Films. B&W-105min. *(German).* Joachim Fuchsberger, Karin Dor, Horst Frank............ 3*
Original title: WEISSE SPINNE, DIE

WHITE SQUAW, THE (1956) Columbia. B&W-75min. David Brian, May Wynn .... (3)

WHITE STALLION, THE (1954) *see* OUTLAW STALLION, THE

WHITE SUN OF THE DESERT, THE (1970) Color- min. *(U.S.S.R.).* Anatoly Kuznetsov, Pavel Luspekayev .... (3)

WHITE TIE AND TAILS (1946) Universal. B&W-81min. Dan Duryea, Ella Raines, William Bendix .... (4)

WHITE TOWER, THE (1950) RKO. Color-98min. Glenn Ford, (Alida) Valli 5*

WHITE TRAP, THE (1959) Anglo Amalgamated [EMI]. B&W-58min. *(British).* Lee Patterson, Felicity Young......... (3)

WHITE UNICORN, THE (1947) *see* BAD SISTER

WHITE VOICES (1964) Rizzoli Film. Color-93min. *(Italian-French).* Paolo Ferrari, Sandra Milo, Graziella Granata ...... (5)
Original title: Original Italian title: VOCI BIANCHE, LE
Alternate Italian title: CASTRATI, I *(The Castrated Ones)*
French title: SEXE DES ANGES, LE *(The Sex of Angels)*
Alternate title: UNDER COVER ROGUE

WHITE WARRIOR, THE (1959) Warner Bros. Color-86min. *(Italian-Yugoslavian).* Steve Reeves, Georgia Moll .... (3)
Original Italian title: AGI MURAD, IL DIAVOLO BIANCO *(Hadji Murad, the White Devil)*
Yugoslavian title: BELI DJAVO

WHITE WILDERNESS (1958) Buena Vista. Color-72min. *(Documentary).* Director: James Algar.................. (5)

WHITE WITCH DOCTOR (1953) 20th Century-Fox. Color-96min. Susan Hayward, Robert Mitchum......... 3*

WHITE WOMAN (1933) Paramount. B&W-71min. Charles Laughton, Carole Lombard .... (4)

WHITE ZOMBIE (1932) United Artists. B&W-73min. Bela Lugosi, Madge Bellamy.................. 3*

WHITHER GERMANY? (1932) *see* KUHLE WAMPE

WHO? (1974) Allied Artists. Color-91min. *(British).* Elliott Gould, Trevor Howard, Joseph Bova...............

Films are rated on a 1 to 10 scale, 10 is highest. **Boldface** ratings followed by an asterisk (*) are for films actually seen and rated by the executive and senior editors. All other ratings are estimates. (See Notes on Entertainment Ratings in the front section.)

WHO ARE THE DeBOLTS? AND WHERE DID THEY GET 19 KIDS? (1977) Sanrio. Color-72min. (Documentary). Director: John Korty......4*

WHO ARE YOU MR. SORGE? (1960) ABC Films. B&W-135min. (French-Italian-Japanese). Jacques Berthier, Thomas Holtzman.......................(5)
Original French title: QUI ETES-VOUS, MONSIEUR SORGE?

WHO DONE IT? (1942) Universal. B&W-75min. Bud Abbott, Lou Costello, Patric Knowles.......................4*

WHO FEARS THE DEVIL (1972) see LEGEND OF HILLBILLY JOHN, THE

WHO GOES THERE (1952) see PASSIONATE SENTRY, THE

WHO HAS SEEN THE WIND (1977) Astral Films (Canada). Color-106min. (Canadian). Gordon Pinsent, Brian Painchaud, José Ferrer 4½*

WHO IS HARRY KELLERMAN AND WHY IS HE SAYING THOSE TERRIBLE THINGS ABOUT ME? (1971) Nat'l General (for Cinema Center). Color-108min. Dustin Hoffman, Barbara Harris.......................3*

WHO IS HOPE SCHUYLER? (1942) 20th Century-Fox. B&W-57min. Sheila Ryan, Ricardo Cortez.......................(3)

WHO IS KILLING THE GREAT CHEFS OF EUROPE? (1978) Warner Bros. Color-112min. George Segal, Jacqueline Bisset.......................6*
British title: TOO MANY CHEFS

WHO IS THE BLACK DAHLIA? (1975) NBC-TV. Color-96min. (Made for TV). Luci Arnaz, Efrem Zimblast, Jr.......................3*

WHO KILLED GAIL PRESTON? (1938) Columbia. B&W-60min. Don Terry, Rita Hayworth.......................(4)

WHO KILLED MARY WHATS'ERNAME? (1971) Cannon Releasing. Color-90min. Red Buttons, Alice Playten.......................4*

WHO KILLED TEDDY BEAR? (1965) Magna Pictures. B&W-90min. Sal Mineo, Juliet Prowse, Jan Murray.......................4*

WHO KILLED THE MYSTERIOUS MR. FOSTER? (1971) see SAM HILL - WHO KILLED THE MYSTERIOUS MR. FOSTER

WHO SAYS I CAN'T RIDE A RAINBOW! (1971) Transvue Pictures. Color-85min. Jack Klugman, Norma French.......................(3)

WHO SLEW AUNTIE ROO? (1971) American-International. Color-91min. (U.S.-British). Shelley Winters, Mark Lester.......................4*
British title: WHOEVER SLEW AUNTIE ROO?

WHO STOLE THE BODY? (1962) Official Industries. B&W-95min. (French). Francis Blanche, Darry-Cowl, Elke Sommer.......................(3)
Original title: BRICOLEURS, LES
Alternate title: BODY IS MISSING, THE

WHO WAS MADDOX? (1964) Avco-Embassy. B&W-62min. (British). Bernard Lee, Jack Watling, Suzanne Lloyd.......................(3)

WHO WAS THAT LADY? (1960) Columbia. B&W-115min. Tony Curtis, Dean Martin.......................3*

WHOLE TOWN'S TALKING, THE (1935) Columbia. B&W-95min. Edward G. Robinson.......................5*
British title: PASSPORT TO FAME

WHOLE TRUTH, THE (1958) Columbia. B&W-84min. (British). Stewart Granger, Donna Reed, George Sanders.......................(4)

WHOLE TRUTH, THE (1961) see BLIND JUSTICE

WHOLE WORLD IS WATCHING, THE (1969) Universal. Color-97min. (Made for TV). Burl Ives, Joseph Campanella, James Farentino..........4*

WHO'LL STOP THE RAIN (1978) United Artists. Color-125min. Nick Nolte, Tuesday Weld, Michael Moriarty.......................4½*
British title: DOG SOLDIERS

WHOOPEE! (1930) United Artists. Color-94min. Eddie Cantor, Eleanor Hunt.......................(4)

WHO'S AFRAID OF VIRGINIA WOOLF? (1966) Warner Bros. B&W-131min. Elizabeth Taylor, Richard Burton, George Segal, Sandy Dennis.......................8*

WHO'S BEEN SLEEPING IN MY BED? (1963) Paramount. Color-103min. Dean Martin, Elizabeth Montgomery.......................4*

WHO'S GOT THE ACTION? (1962) Paramount. Color-93min. Dean Martin, Lana Turner.......................4*

WHO'S MINDING THE MINT? (1967) Columbia. Color-97min. Jim Hutton, Dorothy Provine.......................4*

WHO'S MINDING THE STORE? (1963) Paramount. Color-90min. Jerry Lewis, Jill St. John, Agnes Moorehead.......................3*

WHO'S THAT KNOCKING AT MY DOOR? (1967) Joseph Brenner. B&W-90min. Zina Bethune, Harvey Keitel.......................(3)
Original title: I CALL FIRST
Alternate title: J.R.

WHY BOTHER TO KNOCK (1961) Seven Arts [W.B.]. Color-88min. (British). Richard Todd, Nicole Maurey, Elke Sommer.......................(3)
Original title: DON'T BOTHER TO KNOCK

WHO'S AFRAID OF VIRGINIA WOOLF? (1966). George Segal hadn't expected Richard Burton to play "get the guests" by repeating a story which seems all too familiar to Sandy Dennis; Elizabeth Taylor watches and listens in amusement.

WHY DOES HERR R. RUN AMOK? (1969) New Yorker Films. Color-88min. (German). Kurt Raab, Lilith Ungerer.......................
Original title: WARUM LAUFT HERR R. AMOK?

WHY MUST I DIE? (1960) American-International. B&W-86min. Terry Moore, Debra Paget.......................3*
British title: 13 STEPS TO DEATH

WICHITA (1955) Allied Artists. Color-81min. Joel McCrea, Vera Miles..(4)

WICKED AS THEY COME (1956) Columbia. B&W-94min. (British). Arlene Dahl, Herbert Marshall.......................(3)

WICKED CITY, THE (1949) United Artists. B&W-80min. (French). Maria Montez, Jean-Pierre Aumont, Lilli Palmer.......................(3)
Original title: HANS LE MARIN (Hans the Seaman)

WICKED DREAMS OF PAULA SCHULTZ, THE (1968) United Artists. Color-113min. Elke Sommer, Bob Crane.......................3*

WICKED GO TO HELL, THE (1956) Fanfare. B&W-74min. (French). Marina Vlady, Henri Vidal, Serge Reggiani.......................(2)
Original title: SALAUDS VONT EN ENFER, LES (Bastards Go to Hell)

WICKED LADY, THE (1945) Universal. B&W-104min. (British). James Mason, Margaret Lockwood.......................(3)

WICKED, WICKED (1973) M-G-M. Color-95min. David Bailey, Scott Brady.......................(3)

WICKED WOMAN (1954) United Artists. B&W-77min. Beverly Michaels, Richard Egan.......................(4)

WICKER MAN, THE (1973) Warner Bros. Color-97min. (British). Christopher Lee, Edward Woodward.......................5*

WIDE BLUE ROAD, THE (1958) Color-100min. (Italian). Yves Montand, Alida Valli.......................(3)
Original title: GRANDE STRADA AZZURRA, LA

WIDE BOY (1952) Realart. B&W-67min. (British). Susan Shaw, Sydney Tafler.......................(3)

WIDE OPEN FACES (1938) Columbia. B&W-67min. Joe E. Brown, Jane Wyman.......................(4)

WIDOW, THE (1955) Distributors Corp. of America. B&W-89min. (Italian-French, English language). Patricia Roc, Massimo Serrato, Akim Tamiroff.......................(3)
Original Italian title: VEDOVA, LA

WIDOW AND THE GIGOLO, THE (1961) see ROMAN SPRING OF MRS. STONE, THE

WIDOW FROM MONTE CARLO, THE (1936) Warner Bros. B&W-60min. Dolores Del Rio, Warren William.......................(3)

WIDOW'S NEST (1977) Navarro Prods. Color-119min. Patricia Neal, Valentina Cortese.......................(3)

WIFE, DOCTOR AND NURSE (1937) 20th Century-Fox. B&W-85min. Loretta Young, Warner Baxter, Virginia Bruce.......................(4)

WIFE, HUSBAND AND FRIEND (1939) 20th Century-Fox. B&W-80min. Loretta Young, Warner Baxter.......................(5)

Films are rated on a 1 to 10 scale, 10 is highest. **Boldface** ratings followed by an asterisk (*) are for films actually seen and rated by the executive and senior editors. All other ratings are estimates. (See Notes on Entertainment Ratings in the front section.)

WIFE OF MONTE CRISTO, THE (1946) Producers Rel. Corp. [Eagle Lion]. B&W-80min. John Loder, Eva Gabor ....(3)

WIFE SWAPPERS, THE (1970) see SWAPPERS, THE

WIFE TAKES A FLYER, THE (1942) Columbia. B&W-86min. Franchot Tone, Joan Bennett ....(3)
British title: YANK IN DUTCH, A

WIFE VERSUS SECRETARY (1936) M-G-M. B&W-88min. Clark Gable, Jean Harlow, Myrna Loy 4*

WIFE WANTED (1946) Monogram [Allied Artists]. B&W-73min. Kay Francis, Peter Cavanaugh ....(3)
British title: SHADOW OF BLACKMAIL

WIFEMISTRESS (1978) Quartet Films. Color-110min. *(Italian).* Marcello Mastroianni, Laura Antonelli 5*
Original title: MOGLIE AMANTE

WILBY CONSPIRACY, THE (1975) United Artists. Color-101min. *(British).* Sidney Poitier, Michael Caine 5½*

WILD AFFAIR, THE (1965) Goldstone Film Enterprises. B&W-88min. *(British).* Nancy Kwan, Terry-Thomas ....(3)

WILD AND THE BRAVE, THE (1974) Tomorrow Entertainment. Color-102min. *(Documentary).* Director: Eugene S. Jones 4*
Original title: TWO MEN OF KARAMOJA

WILD AND THE INNOCENT, THE (1959) Universal. Color-84min. Audie Murphy, Joanne Dru, Gilbert Roland 4*

WILD AND THE WILLING, THE (1962) see YOUNG AND WILLING

WILD AND WONDERFUL (1964) Universal. Color-88min. Tony Curtis, Christine Kaufmann 4*

WILD AND WOOLLY (1917) Artcraft. B&W-65min. *(Silent).* Douglas Fairbanks, Eileen Percy 4*

WILD ANGELS, THE (1966) American-International. Color-90min. Peter Fonda, Nancy Sinatra ....(3)

WILD BILL HICKOK RIDES (1942) Warner Bros. B&W-82min. Bruce Cabot, Constance Bennett..(3)

WILD BEAST OF CRETE, THE (1961) see MINOTAUR, THE

WILD BLUE YONDER, THE (1951) Republic. B&W-98min. Phil Harris, Wendell Corey ....(4)
British title: THUNDER ACROSS THE PACIFIC

WILD BUNCH, THE (1969) Warner Bros. Color-148min. William Holden, Robert Ryan, Ernest Borgnine 5*

WILD CARGO (1934) RKO. B&W-96min. *(Documentary).* Director: Armand Denis ....(5)

WILD CATS ON THE BEACH (1959) American-International. Color-96min. *(Italian-French).* Alberto Sordi, Rita Gam ....(4)
Original Italian title: COSTA AZZURRA
French Title: COTE D'AZURE

WILD CHILD, THE (1970) United Artists. B&W-90min. *(French).* Jean-Pierre Cargol, Francois Truffaut, Jean Daste 5*
Original title: ENFANT SAUVAGE, L'

WILD COMPANY (1930) Fox Film Co. [20th]. B&W-73min. H. B. Warner, Frank Albertson, Sharon Lynn ....(3)

WILD COUNTRY, THE (1971) Buena Vista. Color-100min. Steve Forrest, Vera Miles, Ronny (Ron) Howard 5*

WILD DAKOTAS, THE (1956) Associated Film Dists. B&W-73min. Bill Williams, Jim Davis ....(3)

WILD EYE, THE (1967) American-International. Color-91min. *(Italian).* Philippe Leroy, Delia Boccardo ....(2)
Original title: OCCHIO SELVAGGIO, L' *(The Savage Eye)*

WILD FOR KICKS (1960) Victoria. B&W-91min. *(British).* David Farrar, Noelle Adam, Christopher Lee..(2)
Original title: BEAT GIRL

WILD FRUIT (1954) United Motion Pic. Org. (UMPO). B&W-97min. *(French).* Estella Blain, Michel Reynal..(3)
Original title: FRUITS SAUVAGES, LES

WILD GAME (1972) see JAIL BAIT

WILD GEESE (1953) see MISTRESS, THE

WILD GEESE, THE (1978) Allied Artists. Color-132min. *(British).* Richard Burton, Roger Moore, Richard Harris 5*

WILD GEESE CALLING (1941) 20th Century-Fox. B&W-77min. Henry Fonda, Joan Bennett ....(3)

WILD GOLD (1934) Fox Film Co. [20th]. B&W-75min. John Boles, Claire Trevor..(3)

WILD GUITAR (1962) Fairway International. B&W-87min. Arch Hall, Jr., Nancy Czar, Cash Flagg (Ray Dennis Steckler)..(2)

WILD HARVEST (1947) Paramount. B&W-92min. Alan Ladd, Robert Preston, Dorothy Lamour 3*

WILD HEART, THE (1950) RKO. Color-82min. Jennifer Jones, Hugh Griffith, David Farrar ....(3)
Original title: GONE TO EARTH

WILD HERITAGE (1958) Universal. Color-78min. Will Rogers, Jr., Maureen O'Sullivan, Rod McKuen..(4)

WILD IN THE COUNTRY (1961) 20th Century-Fox. Color-114min. Elvis Presley, Hope Lange, Tuesday Weld..4*

WILD IN THE SKY (1973) American-International. Color-87min. Brandon De Wilde, Keenan Wynn, Dick Gautier ....(4)
Alternate title: BLACK JACK

WILD IN THE STREETS (1968) American-International. Color-97min. Christopher Jones, Hal Holbrook 5*

WILD IS THE WIND (1957) Paramount. B&W-114min. Anna Magnani, Anthony Quinn 5*

WILD JUNGLE CAPTIVE (1945) see JUNGLE CAPTIVE

WILD MAN OF BORNEO, THE (1941) M-G-M. B&W-78min. Frank Morgan, Mary Howard..(3)

WILD McCULLOCHS, THE (1975) see McCULLOCHS, THE

WILD 90 (1968) Supreme Mix Inc. B&W-90min. Norman Mailer, Fuzz Fabar, Mickey Knox ....(2)

WILD NORTH, THE (1952) M-G-M. Color-97min. Stewart Granger, Wendell Corey 3*

WILD ON THE BEACH (1965) 20th Century-Fox. B&W-77min. Frankie Randall, Sherry Jackson, Sonny & Cher..(2)

WILD ONE, THE (1954) Columbia. B&W-79min. Marlon Brando, Mary Murphy..5½*

WILD ORCHIDS (1929) M-G-M. B&W-103min. *(Silent).* Greta Garbo, Lewis Stone, Nils Asther..(4)

WILD PACK, THE (1971) American-International. Color-102min. Kent Lane, Tisha Sterling ....(3)
Original title: SANDPIT GENERALS, THE

WILD PARTY, THE (1929) Paramount. B&W-80min. Clara Bow, Fredric March ....(4)

WILD PARTY, THE (1956) United Artists. B&W-81min. Anthony Quinn, Carol Ohmart ....(3)

WILD PARTY, THE (1975) American-International. Color-100min. James Coco, Raquel Welch 5*

WILD RACERS, THE (1968) American-International. Color-79min. Fabian, Mimsy Farmer..2*

WILD REBELS, THE (1967) Crown International. Color-90min. Steve Alaimo, Willie Pastrano ....(2)

WILD RIDE (1960) Filmgroup. B&W-80min. Jack Nicholson, Georgiana Carter, Robin Bean ....(2)

WILD RIDERS (1971) Crown International. Color-91min. Alex Rocco, Elizabeth Knowles..(3)

WILD RIVER (1960) 20th Century-Fox. Color-107min. Montgomery Clift, Lee Remick 5*
Alternate title: WOMAN AND THE WILD RIVER, THE

WILD ROVERS (1971) M-G-M. Color-109min. William Holden, Ryan O'Neal ....(4)

WILD SEED (1965) Universal. B&W-99min. Michael Parks, Celia Kaye (4)

WILD STALLION (1952) Monogram [Allied Artists]. Color-72min. Ben Cooper, Edgar Buchanan ....(3)

WILD STAMPEDE (1962) Commonwealth United TV. Color-90min. *(Mexican).* Luis Aguilar, Christiane Martel ....(3)

WILD STRAWBERRIES (1958) Janus Films. B&W-90min. *(Swedish).* Victor Sjostrom (Seastrom), Bibi Andersson 6*
Original title: SMULTRONSTALLET

WILD WESTERNERS, THE (1963) Columbia. Color-70min. James Philbrook, Nancy Kovack, Duane Eddy..(3)

WILD WHEELS (1969) Colby Productions. Color-92min. Don Epperson, Robert Dix ....(3)

WILD, WILD PLANET, THE (1966) M-G-M. Color-93min. *(Italian).* Tony Russel, Lisa Gastoni, Massimo Serato ....(1)
Original title: CRIMINALI DELLA GALASSIA, I *(The Criminals of the Galaxy)*

WILD, WILD WINTER (1966) Universal. Color-80min. Gary Clarke, Chris Noel..(3)

WILD, WILD WOMEN, THE (1958) see . . . AND THE WILD, WILD WOMEN

WILD WOMEN (1970) ABC Films. Color-74min. *(Made for TV).* Hugh O'Brian, Anne Francis..3*

WILD YOUTH (1961) Cinema Assoc. **B&W-73min.** Robert Hutton, John Goddard, Carol Ohmart .... (3)
Alternate title: NAKED YOUTH

WILDCAT BUS (1940) RKO. **B&W-63min.** Fay Wray, Charles Lang ...... (3)

WILDERNESS FAMILY, THE (1976) *see* ADVENTURES OF THE WILDERNESS FAMILY, THE

WILL JAMES' SAND (1949) *see* SAND

WILL PENNY (1968) Paramount. **Color-109min.** Charlton Heston, Joan Hackett 4*

WILL SUCCESS SPOIL ROCK HUNTER? (1957) 20th Century-Fox. **Color-94min.** Tony Randall, Jayne Mansfield 4*
British title: OH! FOR A MAN!

WILL TOMORROW EVER COME? (1947) *see* THAT'S MY MAN

WILLARD (1971) Cinerama Releasing. **Color-95min.** Bruce Davison, Ernest Borgnine 4*

WILLIE AND JOE BACK AT THE FRONT (1953) *see* BACK AT THE FRONT

WILLIE AND JOE IN TOKYO (1953) *see* BACK AT THE FRONT

WILLIE AND PHIL (1980) 20th Century-Fox. **Color- min.** Michael Ontkean, Ray Sharkey, Margot Kidder ....

WILLIE DYNAMITE (1973) Universal. **Color-102min.** Roscoe Orman, Diana Sands, Thalmus Rasulala .... (4)

WILLY WONKA AND THE CHOCOLATE FACTORY (1971) Paramount. **Color-100min.** Gene Wilder, Jack Albertson, Peter Ostrum 4½*

WILSON (1944) 20th Century-Fox. **Color-155min.** Alexander Knox, Charles Coburn 5*

WINCHESTER '73 (1950) Universal. **B&W-92min.** James Stewart, Stephen McNally, Dan Duryea 4*

WINCHESTER 73 (1967) Universal. **Color-97min.** *(Made for TV).* Tom Tryon, John Saxon, Dan Duryea .... (4)

WIND, THE (1928) M-G-M. **B&W-75min.** *(Silent).* Lillian Gish, Lars Hanson, Montagu Love .... (4)

WIND ACROSS THE EVERGLADES (1958) Warner Bros. **Color-93min.** Burl Ives, Christopher Plummer 4*

WIND AND THE LION, THE (1975) U.A. (for M-G-M). **Color-119min.** Sean Connery, Candice Bergen 6*

WIND CANNOT READ, THE (1958) 20th Century-Fox. **Color-115min.** *(British).* Dirk Bogarde, Yoko Tani .... (4)

WIND FROM THE EAST (1969) New Line Cinema. **Color-92min.** *(French-Italian-W. German).* Gian Maria Volonte, Anne Wiazemsky .. 1*
Original French title: VENT D'EST, LE
Italian title: VENTO DELL'EST
German title: WIND VON OSTEN
Alternate title: EAST WIND

WINDJAMMER (1958) National Theatres' Presentation. **Color-127min.** *(Travelog).* Director: Louis de Rochemont .... (4)

WINDOM'S WAY (1957) J. Arthur Rank. **Color-108min.** *(British).* Peter Finch, Mary Ure .... (5)

WINDOW, THE (1949) RKO. **B&W-73min.** Bobby Driscoll, Barbara Hale 4*

WINDOW IN LONDON, A (1939) *see* LADY IN DISTRESS

WINDOW TO THE SKY, A (1975) *see* OTHER SIDE OF THE MOUNTAIN, THE

WINDS OF CHANGE (1978) *see* METAMORPHOSES

WINDS OF KITTY HAWK, THE (1978) NBC-TV. **Color-98min.** *(Made for TV).* Michael Moriarty, David Huffman ....

WING AND A PRAYER (1944) 20th Century-Fox. **B&W-97min.** Don Ameche, Dana Andrews 3*

WINGED VICTORY (1944) 20th Century-Fox. **B&W-130min.** Pvt. Lon McCallister, Jeanne Crain 3*

WINGS (1927) Paramount. **B&W-136min.** *(Silent).* Charles "Buddy" Rogers, Richard Arlen 5½*

WINGS AND THE WOMAN (1942) RKO. **B&W-94min.** *(British).* Anna Neagle, Robert Newton .... (5)
Original title: THEY FLEW ALONE

WINGS FOR THE EAGLE (1942) Warner Bros. **B&W-83min.** Ann Sheridan, Dennis Morgan .... (3)

WINGS IN THE DARK (1935) Paramount. **B&W-75min.** Myrna Loy, Cary Grant .... (4)

WINGS OF CHANCE (1961) Universal. **Color-76min.** *(Canadian).* James Brown, Frances Rafferty, Richard Tretter .... (2)

WINGS OF EAGLES, THE (1957) M-G-M. **Color-110min.** John Wayne, Maureen O'Hara 4*

WINGS OF FIRE (1967) Universal. **Color-99min.** *(Made for TV).* Suzanne Pleshette, Lloyd Nolan, James Farentino, Juliet Mills 3*
Alternate title: CLOUDBURST, THE

WINGS OF THE HAWK (1953) Universal. **Color-80min.** Van Heflin, Julie Adams 4*

WINGS OF THE MORNING (1937) 20th Century-Fox. **Color-85min.** *(British).* Annabella, Henry Fonda, Leslie Banks .... (5)

WINGS OF THE NAVY (1939) Warner Bros. **B&W-89min.** George Brent, Olivia de Havilland .... (4)

WINGS OVER HONOLULU (1937) Universal. **B&W-78min.** Ray Milland, Wendy Barrie .... (3)

WINK OF AN EYE (1958) United Artists. **B&W-72min.** Jonathan Kidd, Doris Dowling, Barbara Turner .... (2)

WINNER TAKE ALL (1932) Warner Bros. **B&W-68min.** James Cagney, Marian Nixon .... (4)

WINNER TAKE ALL (1975) NBC-TV. **Color-97min.** *(Made for TV).* Shirley Jones, Laurence Luckinbill, Sam Groom ....

WINNIE THE POOH AND THE HONEY TREE (1965) Buena Vista. **Color-26min.** *(Cartoon). Director:* Wolfgang Reitherman 5*

WINNING (1969) Universal. **Color-123min.** Paul Newman, Joanne Woodward, Robert Wagner 4*

WINNING OF THE WEST (1953) Columbia. **B&W-57min.** Gene Autry, Gail Davis, Smiley Burnette .... (4)

WINNING TEAM, THE (1952) Warner Bros. **B&W-98min.** Ronald Reagan, Doris Day 4*

WINNING WAY, THE (1953) *see* ALL AMERICAN, THE

WINSLOW BOY, THE (1948) Eagle Lion. **B&W-97min.** *(British).* Robert Donat, Margaret Leighton .... (5)

WINTER A GO-GO (1965) Columbia. **Color-88min.** James Stacy, William Wellman, Jr., Beverly Adams .... (2)

WINTER CARNIVAL (1939) United Artists. **B&W-105min.** Ann Sheridan, Richard Carlson .... (4)

WINTER KILL (1974) M-G-M. **Color-100min.** *(Made for TV).* Andy Griffith, Sheree North, John Calvin .... (4)

WINTER KILLS (1979) Avco-Embassy. **Color-97min.** Jeff Bridges, John Huston, Anthony Perkins 4½*

WINTER LIGHT (1963) Janus Films. **B&W-80min.** *(Swedish).* Ingrid Thulin, Gunnar Bjornstrand 4*
Original title: NATTVARDSGASTERNA *(The Communicants)*

WINTER MEETING (1948) Warner Bros. **B&W-104min.** Bette Davis, Jim Davis .... (3)

WINTERHAWK (1976) Howco International. **Color-98min.** Michael Dante, Dawn Wells, Chuck Pierce, Jr. 4*

WINTER'S TALE, THE (1968) Seven Arts [W.B.]. **Color-151min.** *(British).* Laurence Harvey, Jane Asher 4*

WINTERSET (1936) RKO. **B&W-78min.** Burgess Meredith, Margo 3½*

WINTERTIME (1943) 20th Century-Fox. **Color-82min.** Sonja Henie, Cornel Wilde .... (4)

WIRETAPPER (1955) Continental [Walter Reade]. **B&W-80min.** Bill Williams, Georgia Lee .... (2)

WISE GIRL (1937) RKO. **B&W-70min.** Miriam Hopkins, Ray Milland ... (4)

WISHING WELL, THE (1954) Welsh Films. **B&W-78min.** *(British).* Brenda de Banzie, Petula Clark, Donald Houston .... (4)
Original title: HAPPINESS OF 3 WOMEN, THE

WISTFUL WIDOW OF WAGON GAP, THE (1947) Universal. **B&W-78min.** Bud Abbott, Lou Costello, Marjorie Main 3*
British title: WISTFUL WIDOW, THE

WITCH BENEATH THE SEA, THE (1962) *see* MARIZINIA

WITCH DOCTOR (1946) *see* MEN OF TWO WORLDS

WITCH WITHOUT A BROOM, A (1966) Producers Releasing Org. **Color-86min.** *(U.S.-Spanish).* Jeffrey Hunter, Maria Perschy 2*
Spanish title: BRUJA SIN ESCOBA, UNA

WITCHCRAFT (1964) 20th Century-Fox. **B&W-80min.** *(British).* Lon Chaney (Jr.), Yvette Rees, Jack Hedley .... (3)

WITCHCRAFT '70 (1969) Trans-America. **Color-82min.** *(Italian, Documentary). Director:* Luigi Scattini .... (2)
Original title: ANGELI BIANCHI . . . ANGELI NERI *(White Angels . . . Black Angels)*

WITCHES, THE (1966) *see* DEVIL'S OWN, THE

WITCHES, THE (1967) Lopert [U.A.]. **Color-100min.** *(Italian-French).* Silvana Mangano, Alberto Sordi, Toto, Clint Eastwood .... (1)
Original Italian title: STREGHE, LE
French title: SORCIERES, LES

WITCHES OF SALEM, THE (1957) *see* CRUCIBLE, THE

WITCHES: VIOLATED AND TORTURED TO DEATH (1972) *see* MARK OF THE DEVIL, PART II

WITCHFINDER GENERAL (1968) *see* CONQUERER WORM, THE

WITCHING HOUR, THE (1934) Paramount. B&W-66min. Sir Guy Standing, John Halliday, Judith Allen 4*

WITCHMAKER, THE (1969) Excelsior. Color-99min. John Lodge, Thordis Brandt, Anthony Eisley .... (3)

WITCH'S CURSE, THE (1960) Medallion. Color-78min. *(Italian)*. Kirk Morris, Hélene Chanel, Vira Silenti .... (2)
Original title: MACISTE ALL'INFERNO *(Maciste in Hell)*
Common title error: WITCHES CURSE, THE

WITCH'S MIRROR, THE (1960) K. Gordon Murray/Trans-International. B&W-75min. *(Mexican)*. Armand Calvo, Rosita Arenas, Isabela Corona 1*
Original title: ESPEJO DE LA BRUJA, EL

WITH A SONG IN MY HEART (1952) 20th Century-Fox. Color-117min. Susan Hayward, Rory Calhoun 4*

WITH BYRD AT THE SOUTH POLE (1930) Paramount-Publix. B&W-82min. *(Part-talking, Documentary)*. .... (4)

WITH FIRE AND SWORD (1962) *see* INVASION 1700

WITH SIX YOU GET EGGROLL (1968) Nat'l General (for Cinema Center). Color-95min. Doris Day, Brian Keith 4*

WITH THESE HANDS (1950) Classic Pictures. B&W-50min. *(Documentary)*. Sam Levene, Arlene Francis, Joseph Wiseman .... (4)

WITHIN THE LAW (1930) *see* PAID

WITHIN THESE WALLS (1945) 20th Century-Fox. B&W-71min. Thomas Mitchell, Mark Stevens .... (3)

WITHOUT A STITCH (1968) VIP Distributors. Color-96min. *(Danish)*. Anne Grete, Ib Mossin .... (2)
Original title: UDEN EN TRAEVL

WITHOUT APPARENT MOTIVE (1971) 20th Century-Fox. Color-102min. *(French)*. Jean-Louis Trintignant, Dominique Sanda .... (5)
Original title: SANS MOBILE APPARENT

WITHOUT HONOR (1949) United Artists. B&W-69min. Laraine Day, Dane Clark, Franchot Tone .... (3)

WITHOUT LOVE (1945) M-G-M. B&W-111min. Spencer Tracy, Katharine Hepburn 5*

WITHOUT RESERVATIONS (1946) RKO. B&W-107min. Claudette Colbert, John Wayne 4*

WITHOUT WARNING (1952) United Artists. B&W-75min. Adam Williams, Meg Randall, Edward Binns .... (4)

WITNESS, THE (1959) Anglo Amalgamated [EMI]. B&W-58min. *(British)*. Dermot Walsh, Greta Gynt, Martin Stephens .... (3)

WITNESS CHAIR, THE (1936) RKO. B&W-64min. Ann Harding, Walter Abel .... (4)

WITNESS FOR THE PROSECUTION (1957) United Artists. B&W-114min. Tyrone Power, Marlene Dietrich 6½*

WITNESS IN THE CITY (1959) B&W-90min. *(French-Italian)*. Lino Ventura, Sandra Milo .... (4)
Original French title: TÉMOIN DANS LA VILLE, UN

WITNESS IN THE DARK (1959) J. Arthur Rank. B&W-62min. *(British)*. Patricia Dainton, Conrad Phillips .... (3)

WITNESS TO MURDER (1954) United Artists. B&W-83min. Barbara Stanwyck, George Sanders .... (5)

WITNESS VANISHES, THE (1939) Universal. B&W-66min. Edmund Lowe, Wendy Barrie .... (3)

WITNESSES, THE (1961) Altura Films. B&W-82min. *(French, Documentary)*. Director: Frédéric Rossif .... (5)
Original title: TEMPS DU GHETTO, LE *(The Time of the Ghetto)*

WIVES AND LOVERS (1963) Paramount. B&W-103min. Janet Leigh, Van Johnson .... (4)

WIVES NEVER KNOW (1936) Paramount. B&W-75min. Charles Ruggles, Mary Boland, Adolphe Menjou .... (3)

WIVES UNDER SUSPICION (1938) Universal. B&W-75min. Warren William, Gail Patrick .... (4)

WIZ, THE (1978) Universal. Color-133min. Diana Ross, Richard Pryor, Michael Jackson 5*

WIZARD OF BAGHDAD, THE (1960) 20th Century-Fox. Color-92min. Dick Shawn, Diane Baker .... (3)

WIZARD OF GORE, THE (1970) Mayflower Pictures. Color-96min. Ray Sager, Judy Cler .... (1)

WIZARD OF MARS (1964) American General. Color-81min. John Carradine, Roger Gentry, Eve Bernhardt .... (1)

WIZARD OF OZ, THE (1939) M-G-M. Color-101min. Judy Garland, Ray Bolger 6*

WIZARDS (1977) 20th Century-Fox. Color-80min. *(Cartoon)*. Director: Ralph Bakshi 4½*

WOLF DOG (1958) 20th Century-Fox. B&W-61min. *(Canadian)*. Jim Davis, Allison Hayes, Tony Brown .... (2)

WOLF LARSEN (1958) Allied Artists. B&W-83min. Barry Sullivan, Peter Graves, Gita Hall 4*

WOLF MAN, THE (1941) Universal. B&W-71min. Lon Chaney, Jr., Claude Rains, Evelyn Ankers 4*

WOLF OF THE SILA, THE (1950) *see* LURE OF THE SILA

WOLFMAN OF COUNT DRACULA, THE (1968) *see* FRANKENSTEIN'S BLOODY TERROR

WOLFPACK (1956) *see* TEENAGE WOLF PACK

WOLVES OF THE DEEP (1959) American-International. B&W-93min. *(Italian)*. Massimo Girotti, Folco Lulli .... (4)

WOMAN ALONE, A (1936) *see* SABOTAGE

WOMAN AND TEMPTATION (1966) Prentoulis Films. B&W-90min. *(Argentine)*. Isabel Sarli, Armando Bo .... (2)
Original title: TENTACION DESNUDA, LA *(Nude Temptation)*
Alternate title: NAKED TEMPTATION

WOMAN AND THE HUNTER, THE (1957) NTA Pictures. B&W-79min. *(British)*. Ann Sheridan, David Farrar .... (3)

WOMAN AND THE WILD RIVER, THE (1960) *see* WILD RIVER

WOMAN AT HER WINDOW, A (1976) Cinema Shares. Color-110min. *(French)*. Romy Schneider, Victor Lanoux .... (5)
Original title: FEMME A SA FENETRE, UNE

WOMAN BAIT (1958) *see* INSPECTOR MAIGRET

WOMAN BETWEEN, THE (1937) *see* WOMAN I LOVE, THE

WOMAN CALLED MOSES, A (1978) NBC-TV. Color-200min. *(Made for TV)*. Cicely Tyson, Dick Anthony Williams ....

WOMAN CHASES MAN (1937) United Artists. B&W-71min. Miriam Hopkins, Joel McCrea 4*

WOMAN DESTROYED, A (1947) *see* SMASH-UP - THE STORY OF A WOMAN

WOMAN EATER, THE (1957) Columbia. B&W-70min. *(British)*. George Coulouris, Vera Day .... (2)

WOMAN FROM HEADQUARTERS (1950) Republic. B&W-60min. Virginia Huston, Barbara Fuller .... (3)

WOMAN FROM TANGIER, THE (1948) Columbia. B&W-66min. Adele Jergens, Ian MacDonald .... (3)

WOMAN HATER (1948) Universal. B&W-70min. *(British)*. Stewart Granger, Edwige Feuillere, Cyril Ritchard .... (3)

WOMAN HUNT (1962) 20th Century-Fox. B&W-60min. Steve Piccaro, Lisa Lu, Berry Kroeger .... (2)

WITNESS FOR THE PROSECUTION (1957). Charles Laughton is the barrister who attempts to save defendant Tyrone Power, accused of a wealthy woman's murder, from the gallows.

WOMAN HUNTER, THE (1972) Viacom. **Color-74min.** (Made for TV). Barbara Eden, Robert Vaughn, Sydney Chaplin .... (4)

WOMAN I LOVE, THE (1937) RKO. **B&W-85min.** Paul Muni, Miriam Hopkins .... (4)
Alternate title: ESCADRILLE
British title: WOMAN BETWEEN, THE

WOMAN IN A DRESSING GOWN (1957) Warner Bros. **B&W-93min.** (British). Yvonne Mitchell, Sylvia Syms, Anthony Quayle 4*

WOMAN IN GREEN, THE (1945) Universal. **B&W-68min.** Basil Rathbone, Nigel Bruce, Hillary Brooke 4*
Publicity title: SHERLOCK HOLMES AND THE WOMAN IN GREEN

WOMAN IN HIDING (1950) Universal. **B&W-92min.** Ida Lupino, Howard Duff, Stephen McNally 4*

WOMAN IN HIS HOUSE, THE (1932) see ANIMAL KINGDOM, THE

WOMAN IN QUESTION, THE (1950) Columbia. **B&W-88min.** (British). Jean Kent, Dirk Bogarde .... (5)
Alternate title: FIVE ANGLES ON MURDER

WOMAN IN RED (1935) First National [W.B.]. **B&W-68min.** Barbara Stanwyck, Gene Raymond .... (3)

WOMAN IN THE CASE (1945) see ALLOTMENT WIVES

WOMAN IN THE DARK (1952) Republic. **B&W-60min.** Penny Edwards, Ross Elliott .... (2)

WOMAN IN THE DUNES (1964) Pathé Contemporary. **B&W-123min.** (Japanese). Eiji Okada, Kyoko Kishida .... (4)
Original title: SUNO NO ONNA

WOMAN IN THE MOON (1929) UFA (Ger.). **B&W-97min.** (German, Silent). Gerda Marus, Willy Fritsch, Fritz Rasp .... (4)
Original title: FRAU IM MOND, DIE
Alternate title: BY ROCKET TO THE MOON
Alternate title: GIRL IN THE MOON, THE

WOMAN IN THE WINDOW (1944) RKO. **B&W-99min.** Edward G. Robinson, Joan Bennett 5*

WOMAN IN WHITE, THE (1948) Warner Bros. **B&W-109min.** Eleanor Parker, Alexis Smith, Sydney Greenstreet .... (4)

WOMAN IS A WOMAN, A (1964) Pathé Contemporary. **Color-80min.** (French-Italian). Anna Karina, Jean-Claude Brialy, Jean-Paul Belmondo .... (4)
Original French title: FEMME EST UNE FEMME, UNE
Italian title: DONNA E DONNA, LA

WOMAN LIKE SATAN, A (1958) Lopert [U.A.]. **Color-86min.** (French-Italian). Brigitte Bardot, Antonio Vilar .... (2)
Original title: FEMME ET LA PANTIN, LA (The Woman and the Puppet)
Alternate title: FEMALE, THE

WOMAN OBSESSED (1959) 20th Century-Fox. **Color-102min.** Susan Hayward, Stephen Boyd .... (4)

WOMAN OF AFFAIRS, A (1929) M-G-M. **B&W-92min.** (Silent). Greta Garbo, John Gilbert, Lewis Stone .... (4)

WOMAN OF DISTINCTION, A (1950) Columbia. **B&W-85min.** Rosalind Russell, Ray Milland 3½*

WOMAN OF DOLWYN, THE (1949) Lopert [U.A.]. **B&W-95min.** (British). Edith Evans, Emlyn Williams 4*
Original title: LAST DAYS OF DOLWYN, THE
Alternate title: DOLWYN

WOMAN OF PARIS, A (1923) United Artists. **B&W-90min.** (Silent). Edna Purviance, Adolphe Menjou 4½*

WOMAN OF ROME (1954) Distributors Corp. of America. **B&W-92min.** (Italian). Gina Lollobrigida, Daniel Gélin .... (4)
Original title: ROMANA, LA

WOMAN OF STRAW (1964) United Artists. **Color-120min.** (British). Gina Lollobrigida, Sean Connery, Ralph Richardson 4½*

WOMAN OF SUMMER (1963) see STRIPPER, THE

WOMAN OF THE NORTH COUNTRY (1952) Republic. **B&W-90min.** Rod Cameron, Ruth Hussey .... (3)

WOMAN OF THE ORIENT (1960) see ORIENTALS, THE

WOMAN OF THE RIVER (1954) Columbia. **Color-95min.** (Italian). Sophia Loren, Rik Battaglia, Gerard Oury .... (3)
Original title: DONNA DEL FIUME, LA
Publicity title: RIVER GIRL, THE

WOMAN OF THE TOWN, THE (1943) United Artists. **B&W-90min.** Claire Trevor, Albert Dekker 4*

WOMAN OF THE YEAR (1942) M-G-M. **B&W-112min.** Spencer Tracy, Katharine Hepburn 3½*

WOMAN OF THE YEAR (1976) CBS-TV. **Color-98min.** (Made for TV). Joseph Bologna, Renée Taylor .... (4)

WOMAN ON PIER 13, THE (1949) see I MARRIED A COMMUNIST

WOMAN ON THE BEACH, THE (1947) RKO. **B&W-71min.** Joan Bennett, Robert Ryan 4*

WOMAN ON THE RUN (1950) Universal. **B&W-77min.** Ann Sheridan, Dennis O'Keefe .... (5)

WOMAN REBELS, A (1936) RKO. **B&W-88min.** Katharine Hepburn, Herbert Marshall 4½*

WOMAN THEY ALMOST LYNCHED (1953) Republic. **B&W-90min.** Brian Donlevy, Audrey Totter 3*

WOMAN TIMES SEVEN (1967) Avco-Embassy. **Color-100min.** (French-Italian-U.S.). Shirley MacLaine, Peter Sellers, Rossano Brazzi 4*
French title: SEPT FOIS FEMME (Seven Times Woman)
Italian title: SETTE VOLTE DONNA
Alternate title: WOMAN X 7

WOMAN UNDER THE INFLUENCE, A (1974) Faces International Films, Inc. **Color-155min.** Peter Falk, Gena Rowlands 3*

WOMAN WANTED (1935) M-G-M. **B&W-68min.** Maureen O'Sullivan, Joel McCrea .... (4)

WOMAN WHO CAME BACK, THE (1945) Republic. **B&W-68min.** Nancy Kelly, John Loder .... (3)

WOMAN WHO CAME FROM THE SEA (1953) Picturemedia Ltd. **Color-91min.** (Italian, English language). Dawn Addams, Franco Silva 3*

WOMAN WHO CRIED MURDER, THE (1975) see DEATH SCREAM

WOMAN WHO WOULDN'T DIE, THE (1964) Warner Bros. **B&W-84min.** (British-U.S.). Gary Merrill, Jane Merrow 4*
British title: CATACOMBS

WOMAN WITH NO NAME, THE (1950) see HER PANELLED DOOR

WOMAN WITH RED BOOTS, THE (1977) Gamma III. **Color-92min.** (Spanish). Catherine Deneuve, Fernando Rey ....

WOMAN WITHOUT A FACE (1966) see MISTER BUDDWING

WOMAN'S DEVOTION, A (1956) Republic. **Color-88min.** Ralph Meeker, Janice Rule, Paul Henreid .... (3)
British title: WAR SHOCK
Alternate title: BATTLE SHOCK

WOMAN'S FACE, A (1941) M-G-M. **B&W-105min.** Joan Crawford, Melvyn Douglas, Conrad Veidt .... (4)

WOMAN'S SECRET, A (1949) RKO. **B&W-85min.** Maureen O'Hara, Melvyn Douglas 4*

WOMAN'S TEMPTATION, A (1958) Warner Bros. **B&W-60min.** (British). Patricia Driscoll, Robert Ayres .... (3)

WOMAN'S VENGEANCE, A (1948) Universal. **B&W-96min.** Charles Boyer, Ann Blyth .... (5)

WOMAN'S WORLD, A (1954) 20th Century-Fox. **Color-94min.** Clifton Webb, June Allyson 4½*

WOMEN, THE (1939) M-G-M. **B&W-132min.** Norma Shearer, Joan Crawford 4*

WOMEN, THE (1969) see FRIENDS AND LOVERS

WOMEN AND WAR (1961) Parade. **B&W-100min.** (French). Bernard Blier, Lucile Saint-Simon .... (3)
Original title: ARRETEZ LES TAMBOURS
Alternate title: WOMEN IN WAR

WOMEN ARE LIKE THAT (1938) Warner Bros. **B&W-78min.** Kay Francis, Pat O'Brien .... (4)

WOMEN ARE LIKE THAT (1960) D.U.K. (British). **B&W-88min.** (French). Eddie Constantine, Francoise Brion .... (3)
Original title: COMMENT QU'ELLE EST!

WOMEN ARE TALKATIVE (1958) **B&W-90min.** (French). Micheleine Presle, Yves Robert .... (3)
Original title: FEMMES SONT MARRANTES, LES

WOMEN ARE WEAK (1958) see THREE MURDERESSES

WOMEN IN BONDAGE (1944) Monogram [Allied Artists]. **B&W-70min.** Gail Patrick, Nancy Kelly .... (3)

WOMEN IN CAGES (1971) New World. **Color-78min.** Jennifer Gan, Judy Brown .... (2)

WOMEN IN CHAINS (1971) Paramount. **Color-74min.** (Made for TV). Ida Lupino, Lois Nettleton, Jessica Walker 3*

WOMEN IN LIMBO (1972) Universal. **Color-111min.** Kathleen Nolan, Kate Jackson .... (3)
Original title: LIMBO

WOMEN IN LOVE (1969) United Artists. **Color-130min.** (British). Alan Bates, Oliver Reed, Glenda Jackson 3½*

WOMEN IN PARADISE (1959) Telewide Systems. **B&W-81min.** Katy Jurado, Dan O'Herlihy .... (3)

WOMEN IN THE WIND (1939) Warner Bros. **B&W-65min.** Kay Francis, Eddie Foy, Jr., William Gargan .... (4)

Films are rated on a 1 to 10 scale, 10 is highest. **Boldface** ratings followed by an asterisk (*) are for films actually seen and rated by the executive and senior editors. All other ratings are estimates. (See Notes on Entertainment Ratings in the front section.)

WOMEN IN WAR (1961) *see* WOMEN AND WAR

WOMEN MEN MARRY, THE (1937) M-G-M. **B&W-61min.** George Murphy, Claire Dodd .... (3)

WOMEN OF DEVIL'S ISLAND (1961) American-International. **Color-86min.** *(Italian).* Guy Madison, Michelle Mercier .... (2)
Original title: PRIGIONIERE DELL'ISOLA DEL DIAVOLO, LE *(The Condemned Women of Devil's Island)*

WOMEN OF NAZI GERMANY (1962) *see* HITLER

WOMEN OF PITCAIRN ISLAND, THE (1956) 20th Century-Fox. **B&W-72min.** James Craig, Lynn Bari 3*

WOMEN OF THE PREHISTORIC PLANET (1966) Realart. **Color-87min.** Keith Larsen, Wendell Corey, Irene Tsu 1*

WOMEN OF THE WORLD (1963) Avco-Embassy. **Color-107min.** *(Italian, Documentary).* Director: Gualtiero Jacopetti .... (4)
Original title: DONNA NEL MONDO, LA
Alternate Italian title: EVA SCONOSCIUTA

WOMEN OF TWILIGHT (1952) *see* TWILIGHT WOMEN

WOMEN WITHOUT MEN (1956) *see* BLONDE BAIT

WOMEN WITHOUT NAMES (1940) Paramount. **B&W-63min.** Robert Paige, Ellen Drew .... (3)

WOMEN'S PRISON (1955) Columbia. **B&W-80min.** Ida Lupino, Jan Sterling, Howard Duff .... (3)

WON TON TON, THE DOG WHO SAVED HOLLYWOOD (1976) Paramount. **Color-92min.** Bruce Dern, Madeline Kahn 5*

WONDER BAR (1934) First National [W.B.]. **B&W-84min.** Al Jolson, Kay Francis 4*

WONDER MAN (1945) RKO. **Color-98min.** Danny Kaye 5*

WONDER OF IT ALL, THE (1974) Pacific International Enterprises. **Color-95min.** *(Documentary).* Director: Arthur R. Dubs .... (4)

WONDER WOMAN (1974) Warner Bros. **Color-75min.** *(Made for TV).* Cathy Lee Crosby, Ricardo Montalban, Andrew Prine 2*

WONDER WOMEN (1973) General Film Corp. **Color-82min.** Nancy Kwan, Ross Hagen 2*

WONDERFUL COUNTRY, THE (1959) United Artists. **Color-96min.** Robert Mitchum, Julie London 3*

WONDERFUL CROOK, THE (1976) New Yorker Films. **Color-112min.** *(Swiss-French).* Gerard Depardieu, Dominique Labourier, Marlene Jobert .... (5)
Original title: PAS SI MECHANT QUE CA *(Not so crooked as that)*

WONDERFUL LIFE (1964) *see* SWINGERS' PARADISE

WONDERFUL TO BE YOUNG! (1961) Paramount. **Color-92min.** *(British).* Cliff Richard, Robert Morley, Carole Gray .... (3)
Original title: YOUNG ONES, THE

WONDERFUL WORLD OF THE BROTHERS GRIMM, THE (1962) M-G-M. **Color-129min.** Laurence Harvey, Karl Boehm .... (5)

WONDERS OF ALADDIN, THE (1961) M-G-M. **Color-93min.** *(Italian-U.S.).* Donald O'Connor, Noelle Adam .... (3)
Italian title: MERAVIGLIE DI ALADINO, LE

WOODEN HORSE, THE (1950) British Lion [EMI]. **B&W-101min.** *(British).* Leo Genn, David Tomlinson .... (5)

WOODEN HORSE OF TROY, THE (1961) *see* TROJAN HORSE, THE

WOODSTOCK (1970) Warner Bros. **Color-184min.** *(Documentary).* Director: Michael Wadleigh 4*

WORD IS OUT (1978) Mariposa Film Group. **Color-135min.** *(Documentary).* Director: Peter Adair 3½*

WORDS AND MUSIC (1948) M-G-M. **Color-119min.** Tom Drake, Mickey Rooney 4½*

WORK IS A 4-LETTER WORD (1968) Universal. **Color-93min.** *(British).* David Warner, Cilla Black, Zia Mohyeddin .... (4)

WORKING MAN, THE (1933) Warner Bros. **B&W-75min.** George Arliss, Bette Davis .... (4)
Original title: ADOPTED FATHER, THE

WORKING WIVES (1932) *see* WEEK-END MARRIAGE

WORLD AND HIS WIFE, THE (1948) *see* STATE OF THE UNION

WORLD AND THE FLESH, THE (1932) Paramount. **B&W-75min.** George Bancroft, Miriam Hopkins .... (4)

WORLD BY NIGHT (1960) Warner Bros. **Color-103min.** *(Italian, Travelog).* Director: Luigi Vanzi .... (4)
Original title: MONDO DI NOTTE, IL

WORLD CHANGES, THE (1933) First National [W.B.]. **B&W-90min.** Paul Muni, Mary Astor 4*

WORLD FOR RANSOM, THE (1954) Allied Artists. **B&W-82min.** Dan Duryea, Gene Lockhart .... (4)

WORLD IN HIS ARMS, THE (1952) Universal. **Color-104min.** Gregory Peck, Ann Blyth 4½*

WORLD IN MY CORNER (1956) Universal. **B&W-82min.** Audie Murphy, Barbara Rush 4*

WORLD IN MY POCKET (1961) M-G-M. **B&W-93min.** *(W. German-French-Italian).* Rod Steiger, Nadja Tiller, Peter Van Eyck .... (4)
Original German title: AN EINEM FREITAG UM HALB ZWOLF
French title: VENDREDI 13 HEURES
Alternate French title: PAS DE MENTALITÉ
Italian title: MONDO NELLA MIA TASCA, IL

WORLD MOVES ON, THE (1934) Fox Film Co. [20th]. **B&W-90min.** Madeleine Carroll, Franchot Tone .... (4)

WORLD OF ABBOTT AND COSTELLO, THE (1965) Universal. **B&W-75min.** *(Compilation).* Director: Sidney Meyers 4*

WORLD OF APU, THE (1959) Harrison Pictures. **B&W-103min.** *(Indian).* Soumitra Chatterjee, Sarmila Tagore 3*
Original title: APUR SANSAR

WORLD OF HANS CHRISTIAN ANDERSEN, THE (1971) United Artists. **Color-75min.** *(Japanese, Cartoon).* Director: Kimi Yabuki ......
Original title: HANSU KURISHITAN ANDERUSAN NO SEKAI

WORLD OF HENRY ORIENT, THE (1964) United Artists. **Color-106min.** Peter Sellers, Tippy Walker, Merrie Spaeth 6*

WORLD OF SPORT FISHING, THE (1972) Allied Artists. **Color-107min.** Ernest Borgnine, Bing Crosby, Van Heflin .... (4)

WORLD OF SUZIE WONG, THE (1960) Paramount. **Color-129min.** William Holden, Nancy Kwan 4*

WORLD OF THE VAMPIRES, THE (1960) Azteca. **B&W-83min.** *(Mexican).* Mauricio Garces, Silvia Fournier 1*
Original title: MUNDO DE LOS VAMPIROS, EL

WORLD PREMIERE (1941) Paramount. **B&W-70min.** John Barrymore, Frances Farmer .... (4)

WORLD, THE FLESH AND THE DEVIL, THE (1959) M-G-M. **B&W-95min.** Harry Belafonte, Inger Stevens, Mel Ferrer 4½*

WORLD WAS HIS JURY, THE (1958) Columbia. **B&W-82min.** Edmond O'Brien, Mona Freeman .... (3)

WORLD WITHOUT END (1956) Allied Artists. **Color-80min.** Hugh Marlowe, Nancy Gates, Rod Taylor .... (3)

WORLD WITHOUT SUN (1964) Columbia. **Color-93min.** *(French-Italian, Documentary).* Director: Jacques-Yves Cousteau 5*
Original French title: MONDE SANS SOLEIL, LE
Italian title: MONDO SENZA SOLE, IL
Publicity title: JACQUES-YVES COUSTEAU'S WORLD WITHOUT SUN

WORLD'S GREATEST ATHLETE, THE (1973) Buena Vista. **Color-92min.** John Amos, Jan-Michael Vincent .... (4)

WORLD'S GREATEST LOVER, THE (1977) 20th Century-Fox. **Color-89min.** Gene Wilder, Carol Kane 4*

THE WORLD OF HENRY ORIENT (1964). Schoolgirl Merrie Spaeth aids her friend Tippy Walker in constantly following the renowned neurotic concert pianist of the film's title; the latter girl has a crush on him, and he becomes extremely perturbed by their activities.

Films are rated on a 1 to 10 scale, 10 is highest. **Boldface** ratings followed by an asterisk (*) are for films actually seen and rated by the executive and senior editors. All other ratings are estimates. (See Notes on Entertainment Ratings in the front section.)

WORM'S EYE VIEW (1951) Eros Films *(Brit.)*. B&W-77min. *(British)*. Ronald Shiner, Garry Marsh, Diana Dors..................... (4)

WORST WOMAN IN PARIS?, THE (1933) Fox Film Co. [20th]. B&W-78min. Adolphe Menjou, Helen Chandler .... (4)

WOULD-BE GENTLEMAN, THE (1960) Kingsley-Union. Color-95min. *(French)*. Louis Seigner, Jean Meyer..................... (5)
Original title: BOURGEOIS GENTILHOMME, LE *(The Middle-Class Gentleman)*

WR - MYSTERIES OF THE ORGANISM (1971) Cinema 5. Color-80min. *(Yugoslavian-W. German)*. Milena Dravic, Jagoda Kaloper.............. 1*
Yugoslavian title: WR - MISTERIJE ORGANIZMA

WRATH OF GOD, THE (1972) M-G-M. Color-111min. Robert Mitchum, Frank Langella, Rita Hayworth 4*

WRECK OF THE HESPERUS, THE (1948) Columbia. B&W-70min. Willard Parker, Edgar Buchanan, Patricia White .... (3)

WRECK OF THE MARY DEARE, THE (1959) M-G-M. Color-105min. Gary Cooper, Charlton Heston 5*

WRECKING CREW, THE (1968) Columbia. Color-105min. Dean Martin, Elke Sommer, Sharon Tate..................... 3*

WRESTLER, THE (1974) Entertainment Ventures. Color-95min. Edward Asner, Elaine Giftos, Verne Gagne .... (4)
Alternate title: WRESTLER - THE MAIM EVENT, THE

WRESTLING WOMEN VS. THE AZTEC MUMMY, THE (1964) K. Gordon Murray. B&W-88min. *(Mexican)*. Lorena Velazquez, Armando Silvestre 1*
Original title: LUCHADORAS CONTRA LA MOMIA, LAS

WRITTEN ON THE WIND (1956) Universal. Color-99min. Rock Hudson, Lauren Bacall 4*

WRONG ARM OF THE LAW, THE (1963) Continental [Walter Reade]. B&W-91min. *(British)*. Peter Sellers, Lionel Jeffries 5*

WRONG BOX, THE (1966) Columbia. Color-105min. *(British)*. John Mills, Ralph Richardson, Peter Cook 6*

WRONG KIND OF GIRL, THE (1956) *see* BUS STOP

WRONG MAN, THE (1957) Warner Bros. B&W-105min. Henry Fonda, Vera Miles 4*

WRONG NUMBER (1959) Anglo Amalgamated [EMI]. B&W-59min. *(British)*. Peter Reynolds, Lisa Gastoni .... (3)

WUSA (1970) Paramount. Color-116min. Paul Newman, Joanne Woodward..................... 4*

WUTHERING HEIGHTS (1939) United Artists. B&W-103min. Merle Oberon, Laurence Olivier..................... 6*

WUTHERING HEIGHTS (1970) American-International. Color-105min. *(U.S.-British)*. Anna Calder-Marshall, Timothy Dalton 3*

WYOMING (1940) M-G-M. B&W-89min. Wallace Beery, Leo Carrillo..... (3)
British title: BAD MAN OF WYOMING

WYOMING (1947) Republic. B&W-84min. William Elliott, Vera Ralston..................... (4)

WYOMING KID, THE (1947) *see* CHEYENNE

WYOMING MAIL (1950) Universal. Color-87min. Stephen McNally, Alexis Smith .... (4)

WYOMING RENEGADES (1955) Columbia. Color-73min. Phil Carey, Martha Hyer..................... (2)

-X-

X-15 (1961) United Artists. Color-106min. Charles Bronson, Brad Dexter, Mary Tyler Moore 3½*

X FROM OUTER SPACE, THE (1967) American-International. Color-85min. *(Japanese)*. Eiji Okada, Peggy Neal .... (1)
Original title: UCHU DAIKAIJU GUILALA *(Big Space Monster Guilala)*

X-RAY OF A KILLER (1963) American-International. B&W-79min. *(German)*. Marc Johannes, Wolfgang Preiss..................... (3)

'X' - THE MAN WITH THE X-RAY EYES (1963) American-International. Color-80min. Ray Milland, Diana Van Der Vlis 4*
Screen title: X
British title: MAN WITH THE X-RAY EYES, THE

X THE UNKNOWN (1956) Warner Bros. B&W-78min. *(British)*. Dean Jagger, Edward Chapman, Leo McKern 2*

X Y & Z (1972) Columbia. Color-110min. *(British)*. Elizabeth Taylor, Michael Caine, Susannah York 3½*
Original title: ZEE & CO.

-Y-

YAKUZA, THE (1975) Warner Bros. Color-112min. Robert Mitchum, Takakura Ken 4½*

YAMBAO (1956) *see* CRY OF THE BEWITCHED

YANCO (1961) Jerand Films. B&W-85min. *(Mexican)*. Ricardo Acona, Jesus Medina..................... 4*

YANGTSE INCIDENT (1957) *see* BATTLE HELL

YANK AT ETON, A (1942) M-G-M. B&W-88min. Mickey Rooney, Edmund Gwenn..................... (3)

YANK AT OXFORD, A (1938) M-G-M. B&W-105min. *(U.S.-British)*. Robert Taylor, Lionel Barrymore, Maureen O'Sullivan..................... 5½*

YANK IN DUTCH, A (1942) *see* WIFE TAKES A FLYER, THE

YANK IN ERMINE, A (1955) M & A Alexander. Color-84min. *(British)*. Peter Thompson, Noelle Middleton..................... (3)

YANK IN INDO-CHINA, A (1952) Columbia. B&W-67min. John Archer, Jean Willes..................... (3)
British title: HIDDEN SECRET

YANK IN KOREA, A (1951) Columbia. B&W-73min. Lon McCallister, Brett King..................... (3)
British title: LETTER FROM KOREA

YANK IN LONDON, A (1945) 20th Century-Fox. B&W-106min. *(British)*. Anna Neagle, Rex Harrison, Dean Jagger..................... (4)
Original title: I LIVE IN GROSVENOR SQUARE
British title: LETTER FROM KOREA

YANK IN THE R.A.F., A (1941) 20th Century-Fox. B&W-98min. Tyrone Power, Betty Grable..................... 4*

YANK IN VIET-NAM, A (1964) Allied Artists. B&W-80min. Marshall Thompson, Enrique Magalona..................... 3*
Alternate title: YEAR OF THE TIGER, THE

YANK ON THE BURMA ROAD, A (1942) M-G-M. B&W-66min. Barry Nelson, Laraine Day..................... (3)
British title: CHINA CARAVAN

YANKEE AT KING ARTHUR'S COURT, THE (1931) *see* CONNECTICUT YANKEE, A

YANKEE BUCCANEER (1952) Universal. Color-86min. Jeff Chandler, Scott Brady, Suzan Ball..................... (4)

YANKEE DOODLE DANDY (1942) Warner Bros. B&W-126min. James Cagney, Joan Leslie..................... 6*

YANKEE IN KING ARTHUR'S COURT, A (1949) *see* CONNECTICUT YANKEE IN KING ARTHUR'S COURT, A

YANKEE PASHA (1954) Universal. Color-84min. Jeff Chandler, Rhonda Fleming..................... 5*

YANKS (1979) Universal. Color- min. Richard Gere, Vanessa Redgrave, William Devane ....

YAQUI DRUMS (1956) Allied Artists. B&W-71min. Rod Cameron, J. Carrol Naish, Mary Castle..................... (3)

YEAR OF THE CANNIBALS (1971) American-International. Color-95min. *(Italian)*. Britt Ekland, Pierre Clementi ....
Original title: CANNIBALI, I *(The Cannibals)*
Publicity title: CANNIBALS AMONG US, THE

YEAR OF THE TIGER, THE (1964) *see* YANK IN VIET-NAM, A

YEAR OF THE YAHOO (1971) Lewis M. P. Enterprises. Color-90min. Claude King, Ray Sager .... (3)

YEAR 1 (1971) *see* MARRIAGE: YEAR ONE

YEAR ONE (1974) Italnoleggio. Color-123min. *(Italian)*. Luigi Vannucchi, Dominique Darel .... (4)
Original title: ANNO UNO

YEAR 2889 (1968) American-International. Color-80min. *(Made for TV)*. Paul Petersen, Quinn O'Hara, Charla Doherty .... (3)
Alternate title: IN THE YEAR 2889
Publicity title: 2889

YEARLING, THE (1946) M-G-M. Color-126min. Gregory Peck, Jane Wyman 6*

YEARS BETWEEN, THE (1946) Universal. B&W-88min. *(British)*. Michael Redgrave, Valerie Hobson .... (4)

YEARS WITHOUT DAYS (1940) *see* CASTLE ON THE HUDSON

YELLOW BALLOON, THE (1952) Allied Artists. B&W-80min. *(British)*. Andrew Ray, Kathleen Ryan, Kenneth More..................... 4*

YELLOW CAB MAN, THE (1950) M-G-M. B&W-85min. Red Skelton, Gloria De Haven 4*

YELLOW CANARY (1943) RKO. B&W-98min. *(British)*. Anna Neagle, Richard Greene .... (4)

YELLOW CANARY, THE (1963) 20th Century-Fox. B&W-93min. Pat Boone, Barbara Eden, Steve Forrest..................... (3)

YELLOW FIN (1951) Monogram [Allied Artists]. B&W-74min. Wayne Morris, Adrian Booth .... (4)

YELLOW JACK (1938) M-G-M. B&W-83min. Robert Montgomery, Virginia Bruce..................... (5)

YELLOW MOUNTAIN, THE (1954) Universal. **Color-78min.** Lex Barker, Mala Powers, Howard Duff **3***

YELLOW ROLLS-ROYCE, THE (1965) M-G-M. **Color-121min.** *(British).* Rex Harrison, Jeanne Moreau **5***

YELLOW SKY (1948) 20th Century-Fox. **B&W-98min.** Gregory Peck, Anne Baxter **5***

YELLOW SQUADRON (1955) Associated Artists. **B&W-80min.** *(Swedish).* Hasse Ekman, Ann-Marie Byllenspetz .... (3)

YELLOW SUBMARINE (1968) United Artists. **Color-85min.** *(British, Cartoon). Director:* George Dunning **4***

YELLOW TICKET, THE (1931) Fox Film Co. [20th]. **B&W-81min.** Elissa Landi, Laurence Olivier, Lionel Barrymore **4½***
British title: YELLOW PASSPORT, THE

YELLOW TOMAHAWK, THE (1954) United Artists. **B&W-82min.** Rory Calhoun, Peggie Castle **3***

YELLOWNECK (1955) Republic. **Color-83min.** Lin McCarthy, Stephen Courtleigh .... (5)

YELLOWSTONE KELLY (1959) Warner Bros. **Color-91min.** Clint Walker, Edward Byrnes **3***

YES (1964) Hungarofilm. **B&W-75min.** *(Hungarian).* Illoa Beres, Ivan Darvas ....
Original title: IGEN

"YES!" (1968) *see* TO INGRID MY LOVE, LISA

YES, MY DARLING DAUGHTER (1939) Warner Bros. **B&W-86min.** Priscilla Lane, Jeffrey Lynn .... (4)

YES, SIR, THAT'S MY BABY (1949) Universal. **Color-82min.** Donald O'Connor, Charles Coburn .... (4)

YESTERDAY AND TODAY (1953) United Artists. **B&W-57min.** *(Compilation). Director:* Abner J. Greshler .... (4)

YESTERDAY, TODAY AND TOMORROW (1963) Avco-Embassy. **Color-119min.** *(Italian-French).* Sophia Loren, Marcello Mastroianni **5***
Original Italian title: IERI, OGGI E DOMANI
French title: HIER, AUJOURD'HUI ET DEMAIN

YESTERDAY'S CHILD (1977) CBS-TV. **Color-74min.** *(Made for TV).* Shirley Jones, Ross Martin, Claude Akins .... (4)

YESTERDAY'S ENEMY (1959) Columbia. **B&W-95min.** *(British).* Stanley Baker, Guy Rolfe .... (4)

YO YO (1965) Magna Pictures. **B&W-92min.** *(French).* Pierre Etaix, Philippe Dionnet, Claudine Auger .... (4)
Original title: YOYO

YOG - MONSTER FROM SPACE (1970) American-International. **Color-84min.** *(Japanese).* Akira Kubo, Atsuko Takahashi .... (1)
Original title: NANKAI NO DAIKAIJU
Publicity title: SPACE AMOEBA

YOJIMBO (1961) Seneca International. **B&W-110min.** *(Japanese).* Toshiro Mifune, Eijiro Tono, Tatsuya Nakadai **5½***
Translation title: The Bodyguard

YOKEL BOY (1942) Republic. **B&W-69min.** Albert Dekker, Joan Davis (4)
British title: HITTING THE HEADLINES

YOLANDA AND THE THIEF (1945) M-G-M. **Color-108min.** Fred Astaire, Lucille Bremer .... (4)

YOU AND ME (1938) Paramount. **B&W-90min.** Sylvia Sidney, George Raft .... (4)

YOU ARE WHAT YOU EAT (1968) Commonwealth United. **Color-75min.** *(Documentary). Director:* Barry Feinstein .... (3)

YOU BELONG TO ME (1941) Columbia. **B&W-94min.** Henry Fonda, Barbara Stanwyck **4***
British title: GOOD MORNING, DOCTOR

YOU BELONG TO MY HEART (1950) *see* MR. IMPERIUM

YOU CAME ALONG (1945) Paramount. **B&W-103min.** Robert Cummings, Lizabeth Scott **4***

YOU CAN'T BUY EVERYTHING (1934) M-G-M. **B&W-85min.** May Robson, Lewis Stone .... (4)

YOU CAN'T CHEAT AN HONEST MAN (1939) Universal. **B&W-76min.** W. C. Fields, Edgar Bergen **4½***

YOU CAN'T DO THAT TO ME (1944) *see* MAISIE GOES TO RENO

YOU CAN'T GET AWAY WITH MURDER (1939) Warner Bros. **B&W-78min.** Humphrey Bogart, Gale Page **4***

YOU CAN'T GO HOME AGAIN (1979) CBS-TV. **Color-97min.** Chris Sarandon, Lee Grant, Hurd Hatfield .... (4)

YOU CAN'T HAVE EVERYTHING (1937) 20th Century-Fox. **B&W-99min.** Alice Faye, The Ritz Brothers .... (5)

YOU CAN'T RUN AWAY FROM IT (1956) Columbia. **Color-95min.** June Allyson, Jack Lemmon **4***

YOU CAN'T CHEAT AN HONEST MAN (1939). Hillbilly Brentwood is the smallest giant in the world, double-dealing circus owner W.C. Fields unabashedly asserts to an audience, and his twin (?!) brother Elwood is the world's biggest midget.

YOU CAN'T SLEEP HERE (1949) *see* I WAS A MALE WAR BRIDE

YOU CAN'T TAKE IT WITH YOU (1938) Columbia. **B&W-127min.** Jean Arthur, Lionel Barrymore, James Stewart, Edward Arnold **6***

YOU CAN'T TAKE MONEY (1937) *see* INTERNES CAN'T TAKE MONEY

YOU CAN'T WIN 'EM ALL (1970) Columbia. **Color-97min.** *(British).* Tony Curtis, Charles Bronson, Michele Mercier **3***

YOU DON'T NEED PAJAMAS AT ROSIE'S (1969) *see* FIRST TIME, THE

YOU FOR ME (1952) M-G-M. **B&W-71min.** Peter Lawford, Jane Greer (4)

YOU GOTTA STAY HAPPY (1948) Universal. **B&W-100min.** Joan Fontaine, James Stewart **4***

YOU HAVE TO RUN FAST (1961) United Artists. **B&W-71min.** Craig Hill, Elaine Edwards .... (3)
Alternate title(?): MAN MISSING

YOU KNOW WHAT SAILORS ARE (1953) J. Arthur Rank. **Color-89min.** *(British).* Akim Tamiroff, Donald Sinden .... (3)

YOU LIGHT UP MY LIFE (1977) Columbia. **Color-90min.** Didi Conn, Joe Silver, Michael Zaslow **5***

YOU MUST BE JOKING! (1965) Columbia. **B&W-100min.** *(British).* Michael Callan, Lionel Jeffries **4***

YOU NEVER CAN TELL (1951) Paramount. **B&W-78min.** Dick Powell, Peggy Dow, Joyce Holden .... (4)
British title: YOU NEVER KNOW

YOU ONLY LIVE ONCE (1937) United Artists. **B&W-86min.** Sylvia Sidney, Henry Fonda **4***

YOU ONLY LIVE ONCE (1968) Sigma III. **Color-95min.** *(French).* Karen Blanguernon, Leslie Bedos .... (4)
Original title: TU SERAS TERRIBLEMENT GENTILLE

YOU ONLY LIVE TWICE (1967) United Artists. **Color-116min.** *(British).* Sean Connery, Donald Pleasence **4½***

YOU SAID A MOUTHFUL (1932) First National [W.B.]. **B&W-75min.** Joe E. Brown, Ginger Rogers .... (4)

YOU WERE MEANT FOR ME (1948) 20th Century-Fox. **B&W-92min.** Jeanne Crain, Dan Dailey **4***

YOU WERE NEVER LOVLIER (1942) Columbia. **B&W-97min.** Fred Astaire, Rita Hayworth **4***

YOU'LL FIND OUT (1940) RKO. **B&W-97min.** Kay Kyser, Peter Lorre, Boris Karloff, Bela Lugosi **4***

YOU'LL LIKE MY MOTHER (1972) Universal. **Color-93min.** Patty Duke, Rosemary Murphy, Richard Thomas **4½***

YOU'LL NEVER GET RICH (1941) Columbia. **B&W-88min.** Fred Astaire, Rita Hayworth **5***

YOU'LL NEVER SEE ME AGAIN (1973) MCA-TV. **Color-74min.** *(Made for TV).* David Hartman, Joseph Campanella, Jane Wyatt .... (4)

YOUNG AMERICANS (1967) Columbia. **Color-104min.** *(Documentary). Director:* Alex Grasshoff **4***

Films are rated on a 1 to 10 scale, 10 is highest. **Boldface** ratings followed by an asterisk (*) are for films actually seen and rated by the executive and senior editors. All other ratings are estimates. (See Notes on Entertainment Ratings in the front section.)

YOUNG AND DANGEROUS (1957) 20th Century-Fox. B&W-78min. Lilli Gentle, Mark Damon, Connie Stevens 3*

YOUNG AND EAGER (1961) *see* CLAUDELLE INGLISH

YOUNG AND EVIL (1956) *see* CRY OF THE BEWITCHED

YOUNG AND INNOCENT (1937) Gaumont-British [Rank]. B&W-84min. *(British)*. Nova Pilbeam, Derrick de Marney, Percy Marmont 3*
Alternate title: GIRL WAS YOUNG, THE

YOUNG AND THE BRAVE, THE (1963) M-G-M. B&W-84min. Rory Calhoun, William Bendix, Richard Jaeckel .... (3)

YOUNG AND THE COOL, THE (1962) *see* TWIST ALL NIGHT

YOUNG AND THE DAMNED, THE (1951) *see* OLVIDADOS, LOS

YOUNG AND THE PASSIONATE, THE (1953) *see* VITELLONI, I

YOUNG AND WILD (1958) Republic. B&W-69min. Gene Evans, Scott Marlowe, Carolyn Kearney .... (3)

YOUNG AND WILLING (1942) United Artists. B&W-82min. William Holden, Eddie Bracken .... (4)

YOUNG AND WILLING (1962) Universal. B&W-113min. *(British)*. Virginia Maskell, Paul Rogers, Ian McShane .... (3)
Original title: WILD AND THE WILLING, THE
Alternate title: YOUNG AND THE WILLING, THE

YOUNG APHRODITES (1962) Janus Films. B&W-89min. *(Greek)*. Vangelis Joannides, Cleopatra Rota .... (3)
Original title: MIKRES APHRODITES

YOUNG AT HEART (1955) Warner Bros. Color-117min. Doris Day, Frank Sinatra .... (5)

YOUNG BESS (1953) M-G-M. Color-112min. Jean Simmons, Stewart Granger .... (5)

YOUNG BILLY YOUNG (1969) United Artists. Color-88min. Robert Mitchum, Angie Dickinson, Robert Walker, Jr. .... (2)

YOUNG CAPTIVES, THE (1959) Paramount. B&W-61min. Steven Marlo, Tom Selden, Luana Patten .... (4)

YOUNG CARUSO, THE (1951) Italian Films Export. B&W-77min. *(Italian)*. Ermanno Randi, Maurizio di Nardo, Gina Lollobrigida .... (4)
Original title: ENRICO CARUSO, LEGGENDA DI UNA VOCE *(Enrico Caruso, Legend of a Voice)*

YOUNG CASSIDY (1965) M-G-M. Color-110min. Rod Taylor, Maggie Smith 5*

YOUNG COUNTRY, THE (1970) Universal. Color-74min. *(Made for TV)*. Roger Davis, Walter Brennan, Joan Hackett .... (4)

YOUNG COUPLE, A (1969) Trans World Attractions. Color-90min. *(French)*. Anna Gael, Alain Libolt .... (2)
Original title: JEUNE COUPLE, UN

YOUNG CYCLE GIRLS, THE (1979) Peter Perry Pictures. Color-80min. Lorraine Ferris, Daphne Lawrence, Deborah Marcus .... (3)

YOUNG DANIEL BOONE (1950) Monogram [Allied Artists]. Color-71min. David Bruce, Kristine Miller .... (2)

YOUNG DILLINGER (1965) Allied Artists. B&W-102min. Nick Adams, Mary Ann Mobley 3½*

YOUNG DR. KILDARE (1938) M-G-M. B&W-81min. Lew Ayres, Lionel Barrymore .... (5)

YOUNG DOCTORS, THE (1961) United Artists. B&W-100min. Fredric March, Ben Gazzara 5*

YOUNG DON'T CRY, THE (1957) Columbia. B&W-89min. James Whitmore, Sal Mineo .... (3)

YOUNG DRACULA (1973) *see* SON OF DRACULA

YOUNG FRANKENSTEIN (1974) 20th Century-Fox. B&W-98min. Gene Wilder, Peter Boyle, Marty Feldman 6½*

YOUNG GIRLS BEWARE (1957) United Motion Pic. Org. (UMPO). B&W-90min. *(French)*. Robert Hossein, Antonella Lualdi .... (3)
Original title: MEFIEZ-VOUS FILLETTES!

YOUNG GIRLS OF GOOD FAMILIES (1963) Avco-Embassy. B&W-90min. *(French)*. Marie-France Pisier, Ziva Rodann .... (3)

YOUNG GIRLS OF ROCHEFORT, THE (1967) Warner Bros. Color-125min. *(French)*. Catherine Deneuve, Francoise Dorléac .... (4)
Original title: DEMOISELLES DE ROCHEFORT, LES

YOUNG GUNS, THE (1956) Allied Artists. B&W-84min. Russ Tamblyn, Gloria Talbott 3*

YOUNG GUNS OF TEXAS (1963) 20th Century-Fox. Color-78min. James Mitchum, Alana Ladd, Jody McCrea 3*

YOUNG HANNAH, QUEEN OF THE VAMPIRES (1973) *see* CRYPT OF THE LIVING DEAD

YOUNG HELLIONS (1958) *see* HIGH SCHOOL CONFIDENTIAL

YOUNG IDEAS (1943) M-G-M. B&W-77min. Susan Peters, Herbert Marshall .... (3)

YOUNG IN HEART, THE (1938) United Artists. B&W-90min. Douglas Fairbanks, Jr., Janet Gaynor 6*

YOUNG INVADERS, THE (1957) *see* DARBY'S RANGERS

YOUNG JESSE JAMES (1960) 20th Century-Fox. B&W-73min. Ray Stricklyn, Merry Anders .... (3)

YOUNG JOE, THE FORGOTTEN KENNEDY (1977) ABC-TV. Color-100min. *(Made for TV)*. Peter Strauss, Barbara Parkins, Stephen Elliott 4½*

YOUNG KILLERS (1958) *see* HIGH SCHOOL CONFIDENTIAL

YOUNG LAND, THE (1959) Columbia. Color-89min. Pat Wayne, Yvonne Craig, Dennis Hopper .... (3)

YOUNG LAWYERS, THE (1969) Paramount. Color-74min. *(Made for TV)*. Jason Evers, Louise Latham, Michael Parks 4*

YOUNG LIONS, THE (1958) 20th Century-Fox. B&W-167min. Marlon Brando, Montgomery Clift, Dean Martin 5*

YOUNG LOVERS, THE (1949) Filmmakers. B&W-85min. Keefe Brasselle, Sally Forrest .... (5)

YOUNG LOVERS, THE (1954) *see* CHANCE MEETING

YOUNG LOVERS, THE (1964) M-G-M. B&W-110min. Peter Fonda, Sharon Hugueny .... (3)

YOUNG MAN WITH A HORN (1950) Warner Bros. B&W-112min. Kirk Douglas, Lauren Bacall 5*
British title: YOUNG MAN OF MUSIC

YOUNG MAN WITH IDEAS (1952) M-G-M. B&W-84min. Glenn Ford, Ruth Roman .... (4)

YOUNG MR. LINCOLN (1939) 20th Century-Fox. B&W-100min. Henry Fonda, Alice Brady 4*

YOUNG MR. PITT, THE (1942) 20th Century-Fox. B&W-103min. *(British)*. Robert Donat .... (4)

YOUNG ONE, THE (1961) Vitalite. B&W-96min. *(Mexican, English language)*. Zachary Scott, Key Meersman, Bernie Hamilton .... (4)
Original title: JOVEN, LA
British title: ISLAND OF SHAME

YOUNG ONES, THE (1961) *see* WONDERFUL TO BE YOUNG!

YOUNG PEOPLE (1940) 20th Century-Fox. B&W-78min. Shirley Temple, Jack Oakie 4*

YOUNG PHILADELPHIANS, THE (1959) Warner Bros. B&W-136min. Paul Newman, Barbara Rush 5*
British title: CITY JUNGLE, THE

YOUNG RACERS, THE (1963) American-International. Color-82min. Mark Damon, William Campbell, Luana Anders .... (3)

YOUNG RAJAH, THE (1922) Paramount. B&W-103min. *(Silent)*. Rudolph Valentino, Wanda Hawley .... (4)

YOUNG REBEL, THE (1968) American-International. Color-111min. *(Italian-Spanish-French)*. Horst Buchholz, Gina Lollobrigida, Louis Jourdan .... (4)
Original Italian title: AVVENTURE E GLI AMORI DI MIGUEL CERVANTES, LE *(The Adventure and the Loves of Miguel Cervantes)*
Spanish title: CERVANTES
French title: AVENTURES EXTRAORDINAIRES DE CERVANTES, LES *(The Extraordinary Adventures of Cervantes)*
Alternate title: CERVANTES

YOUNG REBELS (1957) *see* TEENAGE DOLL

YOUNG RUNAWAYS, THE (1968) M-G-M. Color-91min. Brooke Bundy, Kevin Coughlin .... (3)

YOUNG SAVAGES, THE (1961) United Artists. B&W-110min. Burt Lancaster, Dina Merrill 5*

YOUNG SCARFACE (1947) *see* BRIGHTON ROCK

YOUNG SINNER, THE (1961) United Screen Arts. B&W-81min. Tom Laughlin, Stefanie Powers, William Wellman, Jr. .... (3)
Original title: LIKE FATHER, LIKE SON

YOUNG SINNERS, THE (1959) *see* HIGH SCHOOL BIG SHOT

YOUNG STRANGER, THE (1957) Universal. B&W-84min. James MacArthur, James Daly 4*

YOUNG SWINGERS, THE (1963) 20th Century-Fox. B&W-71min. Rod Lauren, Molly Bee .... (3)

YOUNG SWINGERS, THE (1971) *see* EXOTIC DREAMS OF CASANOVA, THE

YOUNG, THE EVIL AND THE SAVAGE, THE (1968) American-International. Color-82min. *(Italian)*. Michael Rennie, Mark Damon, Eleonora Brown .... (1)
Original title: SETTE VERGINI PER IL DIAVOLO *(Seven Virgins for the Devil)*
Alternate Italian title(?): NUDE . . . SI MUORE

YOUNG TOM EDISON (1940) M-G-M. **B&W-82min.** Mickey Rooney, Fay Bainter 4½*

YOUNG TORLESS (1966) Kanawha Films Ltd. **B&W-90min.** (W. German-French). Matthieu Carriere, Bernd Tischer .... (5)
Original German title: JUNGE TOERLESS, DER
French title: DÉSSAROIS DE L'ÉLEVE TOERLESS, LES

YOUNG WARRIORS, THE (1967) Universal. **Color-93min.** James Drury, Steve Carlson .... (3)

YOUNG WIDOW (1946) United Artists. **B&W-100min.** Jane Russell, Louis Hayward .... (3)

YOUNG WINSTON (1972) Columbia. **Color-145min.** (British). Simon Ward, Robert Shaw, Anne Bancroft 5*

YOUNG WIVES TALE (1951) Allied Artists. **B&W-79min.** (British). Joan Greenwood, Nigel Patrick .... (4)

YOUNGBLOOD (1978) American-International. **Color-90min.** Bryan O'Dell, Lawrence-Hilton Jacobs 3½*

YOUNGBLOOD HAWKE (1964) Warner Bros. **B&W-137min.** James Franciscus, Suzanne Pleshette 4*

YOUNGER BROTHERS, THE (1949) Warner Bros. **Color-77min.** Wayne Morris, Janis Paige .... (4)

YOUNGEST PROFESSION, THE (1943) M-G-M. **B&W-82min.** Virginia Weidler, Edward Arnold .... (4)

YOUNGEST SPY, THE (1962) *see* MY NAME IS IVAN

YOUR CHEATIN' HEART (THE HANK WILLIAMS STORY) (1965) M-G-M. **B&W-99min.** George Hamilton, Susan Oliver .... (5)

YOUR MONEY OR YOUR LIFE (1966) Gala (Brit.). **Color-91min.** (French). Fernandel, Heinz Ruehmann 4*
Original title: BOURSE ET LA VIE, LA

YOUR MONEY OR YOUR WIFE (1972) MPC (TV). **Color-74min.** (Made for TV). Ted Bessell, Elizabeth Ashley 4*

YOUR PAST IS SHOWING (1957) J. Arthur Rank. **B&W-87min.** (British). Terry-Thomas, Peter Sellers 5*
Original title: NAKED TRUTH, THE

YOUR SHADOW IS MINE (1962) Continental [Walter Reade]. **Color-90min.** (French-Italian). Jill Haworth, Michel Ruhl .... (3)
Original French title: TON OMBRE EST LA MIENNE

YOUR THREE MINUTES ARE UP (1973) Cinerama Releasing. **Color-92min.** Beau Bridges, Ron Leibman, Janet Margolin .... (5)

YOUR TURN, DARLING (1963) Paramount. **B&W-90min.** (French-Italian). Eddie Constantine, Henri Cogan .... (3)
Original French title: A TOI DE FAIRE, MIGNONNE

YOUR WITNESS (1950) *see* EYE WITNESS

YOU'RE A BIG BOY NOW (1967) Seven Arts [W.B.]. **Color-96min.** Peter Kastner, Elizabeth Hartman 3*

YOU'RE A SWEETHEART (1937) Universal. **B&W-96min.** Alice Faye, George Murphy, Ken Murray .... (3)

YOU'RE IN THE ARMY NOW (1941) Warner Bros. **B&W-79min.** Phil Silvers, Jimmy Durante .... (4)

YOU'RE IN THE NAVY NOW (1951) 20th Century-Fox. **B&W-93min.** Gary Cooper, Jane Greer .... (4)
Alternate title: U.S.S. TEAKETTLE

YOU'RE MY EVERYTHING (1949) 20th Century-Fox. **Color-94min.** Dan Dailey, Anne Baxter .... (5)

YOU'RE NEVER TOO YOUNG (1955) Paramount. **Color-102min.** Dean Martin, Jerry Lewis, Diana Lynn 4*

YOU'RE NOT SO TOUGH (1940) Universal. **B&W-71min.** The Dead End Kids, Nan Grey .... (4)

YOU'RE ONLY YOUNG ONCE (1938) M-G-M. **B&W-78min.** Lewis Stone, Mickey Rooney .... (4)

YOU'RE TELLING ME (1934) Paramount. **B&W-66min.** W. C. Fields, Joan Marsh 4*

YOURS, MINE AND OURS (1968) United Artists. **Color-111min.** Lucille Ball, Henry Fonda 5*

YOUTH RUNS WILD (1944) RKO. **B&W-67min.** Kent Smith, Bonita Granville .... (4)

YOUTHQUAKE (1977) World Wide Productions. **Color-90min.** (Documentary). Director: Max B. Miller .... (4)

YOU'VE GOT TO WALK IT LIKE YOU TALK IT OR YOU'LL LOSE THAT BEAT (1971) J.E.R. Pictures. **Color-85min.** Zalman King, Allen Garfield, Suzette Green, Richard Pryor .... (2)

YPOTRON - FINAL COUNTDOWN (1966) H.K. Film Dist. **Color-90min.** (Italian-Spanish). Luis Devill, Gaia Germani, Jesus Puente .... (3)
Italian title: AGENTE LOGAN MISSIONE YPOTRON (Agent Logan's Mission Ypotron)
Spanish title: YPOTRON
British title(?): OPERATION "Y"

YUMA (1971) ABC Films. **Color-74min.** (Made for TV). Clint Walker, Barry Sullivan 3*

-Z-

Z (1969) Cinema 5. **Color-127min.** (French-Algerian). Yves Montand, Irene Papas, Jean-Louis Trintignant 7*

Z. P. G. (1972) Paramount. **Color-95min.** (British-U.S.). Oliver Reed, Geraldine Chaplin, Diane Cilento, Don Gordon .... (2)

ZAAT (1972) Horizon. **Color-100min.** Dave Dickerson, Sanna Ringhaven, Wade Popwell ....
Alternate title: BLOOD WATERS OF DR. Z, THE

ZABRISKIE POINT (1970) M-G-M. **Color-112min.** Mark Frechette, Daria Halprin 1*

ZACHARIAH (1971) Cinerama Releasing. **Color-92min.** John Rubinstein, Pat Quinn, Don Johnson .... (4)

ZAMBA (1949) Eagle Lion. **B&W-75min.** Jon Hall, June Vincent, Beau Bridges .... (3)
British title: ZAMBA THE GORILLA

ZANDY'S BRIDE (1974) Warner Bros. **Color-116min.** Gene Hackman, Liv Ullmann 4*
TV title: FOR BETTER, FOR WORSE

ZANZABUKU (1956) Republic. **Color-64min.** (Documentary). Producer: Lewis Cotlow 4½*

ZANZIBAR (1940) Universal. **B&W-70min.** James Craig, Eduardo Ciannelli, Lola Lane .... (4)

ZAPATA (1971) Azteca. **Color-102min.** (Mexican, English language). Antonio Aguilar, Patricia Azpillaga .... (3)

ZARAK (1956) Columbia. **Color-95min.** (British). Victor Mature, Michael Wilding, Anita Ekberg 4*

ZARDOZ (1974) 20th Century-Fox. **Color-104min.** Sean Connery, Charlotte Rampling 3*

ZATOICHI MEETS YOJIMBO (1970) Biou of Japan. **Color-116min.** (Japanese). Shintaro Katsu, Toshiro Mifune ....
Original title: ZATO-ICHI TO YOJINBO

ZAZIE (1960) Astor. **Color-86min.** (French). Catherine Demongeot, Philippe Noiret .... (4)
Original title: ZAZIE DANS LE MÉTRO (Zazie in the Subway)

ZEBRA IN THE KITCHEN (1965) M-G-M. **Color-92min.** Jay North, Martin Milner .... (4)

ZEE AND CO. (1971) *see* X Y & ZEE

ZENOBIA (1939) United Artists. **B&W-71min.** Oliver Hardy, Harry Langdon, Billie Burke ....
British title: ELEPHANTS NEVER FORGET

ZEPPELIN (1971) Warner Bros. **Color-101min.** (British). Michael York, Elke Sommer 4½*

ZERO FOR CONDUCT (1933) Brandon. **B&W-56min.** (French). Jean D'Asté, Robert Le Flon 3*
Original title: ZÉRO DE CONDUITE

ZERO HOUR (1957) Paramount. **B&W-81min.** Dana Andrews, Linda Darnell .... (4)

ZERO MURDER CASE (1945) *see* UNCLE HARRY

ZIEGFELD FOLLIES (1946) M-G-M. **Color-110min.** William Powell, Fred Astaire 5*

ZIEGFELD GIRL (1941) M-G-M. **B&W-131min.** James Stewart, Judy Garland 4*

ZIEGFELD: THE MAN AND HIS WOMEN (1978) CPT (TV). **Color-145min.** (Made for TV). Paul Shenar, Samantha Eggar 5*

ZIG ZIG (1975) Peppercorn-Wormser. **Color-87min.** (French). Catherine Deneuve, Bernadette Lafont ....

ZIGZAG (1970) M-G-M. **Color-104min.** George Kennedy, Eli Wallach 4*
British title: FALSE WITNESS

ZITA (1968) Regional. **Color-92min.** (French). Joanna Shimkus, Katina Paxinou 3*
Original title: TANTE ZITA (Aunt Zita)

ZOLTAN . . . HOUND OF DRACULA (1977) *see* DRACULA'S DOG

ZOMBIES OF MORA-TAU (1957) Columbia. **B&W-70min.** Gregg Palmer, Allison Hayes .... (3)
British title: DEAD THAT WALK, THE

ZOMBIES OF THE STRATOSPHERE (1952) *see* SATAN'S SATELLITES

Films are rated on a 1 to 10 scale, 10 is highest. **Boldface** ratings followed by an asterisk (*) are for films actually seen and rated by the executive and senior editors. All other ratings are estimates. (See Notes on Entertainment Ratings in the front section.)

ZORBA THE GREEK (1965). Lusty Greek Anthony Quinn demonstrates to Englishman Alan Bates that sometimes the best remedy for one's troubles is to dance them away on the beach.

ZOMBIES ON BROADWAY (1945) RKO. B&W-68min. Wally Brown, Alan Carney, Bela Lugosi .... (3)
British title: LOONIES ON BROADWAY

ZONTAR: THE THING FROM VENUS (1966) American-International. Color-80min. John Agar, Susan Bjurman, Anthony Houston 2*

ZOO IN BUDAPEST (1933) Fox Film Co. [20th]. B&W-85min. Loretta Young, Gene Raymond.. 4*

ZORBA THE GREEK (1965) International Classics [20th]. B&W-142min. *(Greek-U.S., English language).* Anthony Quinn, Alan Bates................ 5*
Greek title: ZORMBA

ZORIKAN THE BARBARIAN (1960) Four Star. Color-92min. *(Italian).* Dan Vadis, Eleonora Bianchi.. (1)

ZORRO (1975) Titanus. Color-125min. *(Italian-French).* Alain Delon, Stanley Baker, Ottavia Piccolo 5*

ZORRO CONTRA MACISTE (1964) *see* SAMSON AND THE SLAVE QUEEN

ZORRO RIDES AGAIN (1937) Republic. B&W-68min. John Carroll, Helen Christian.. 3*

ZORRO, THE AVENGER (1962) Warner Bros. Color-90min. *(Spanish).* Frank Latimore, Maria Luz Galicia, José Marco Davo........................ (3)
Original title: VENGANZA DEL ZORRO, LA *(The Vengeance of Zorro)*

ZOTZ (1962) Columbia. B&W-87min. Tom Poston, Julia Meade.............. (3)

ZULU (1964) Avco-Embassy. Color-138min. *(British).* Stanley Baker, Jack Hawkins 4½*

ZUMA BEACH (1978) NBC-TV. Color-100min. *(Made for TV).*................ (4)

And our book couldn't really be complete without...

John Wayne in his last movie role as **THE SHOOTIST** (1976), in which he played an aging gunfighter with terminal cancer, but was determined to die with his boots on.

SELECTED COMPANIES GUIDE

This is not meant to be a complete listing of all the companies which have ever produced and distributed movies listed in the main section of the book, but hopefully the names and addresses listed here will provide information helpful in determining the rights to about 99% of the films listed. Neither is it meant to be a complete history of all the acquisitions, mergers, name changes and misfortunes of the companies listed here; facts of that nature are one of the most neglected and inadequate areas of film reference literature, and would require the writing of a badly-needed large book (sort of a "Roots" of the movie industry) to cover sufficiently. Most of the films in the book are still owned by the original distributor, and can be easily located by using this guide; for others, we have tried to provide at least a clue as to where to look for films originally distributed by companies seemingly (or actually) no longer in business.

Some of the information on older and inactive companies has been obtained by verbal inquiries with retired persons once associated with those companies. Although our information has been gathered from sources we believe to be reliable and people we presume to be knowledgeable, we offer the user a word of caution: This section is meant to be no more authoritative than what it is called — a "guide," not holy writ — so please be aware that addresses, phone numbers and even names of companies are changing constantly.

This list does not contain all the branch offices of larger companies listed, but generally gives the New York and Los Angeles offices. For larger companies, the 16mm distributor is often given; we sometimes note that these rights are non-theatrical, but we have probably not listed all the cases in which 16mm rights are solely non-theatrical, so 16mm theatrical exhibitors should not assume that all other 16mm distributors can supply films to them. Also, the notation "[16mm films]" next to a company's name means that the company specializes in handling films of that gauge, not that it's the only type of films they have. Some of these companies handle 35mm movies too.

In some cases, brief notes relate important general information about a company's film rights. Although we don't attempt to tell how and why mergers and acquisitions came about, we have listed in brackets [ ] the names of companies to which the main company in the entry is the successor in interest.

For more information about companies listed in this book, see *Distributors* in the NOTES section at the front of the book.

ABC PICTURES INTERNATIONAL
(formerly called "ABC Pictures")
2040 Avenue of the Stars
Los Angeles, CA 90067
213/553-2000
1 Lincoln Plaza
New York, NY 10023
212/581-7777

Films Inc. handles both theatrical and non-theatrical distribution of the ABC Pictures films. ABC acquired all rights, including theatrical, in most of the film properties of Selznick Releasing Organization, and Audio Brandon handles these films non-theatrically.

ABC-TV (American Broadcasting Company)
1330 Avenue of the Americas
New York, NY 10019
212/581-7777
4151 Prospect Avenue
Hollywood, CA 90027
213/663-3311
190 No. State Street
Chicago, IL 60601
312/263-0800

AFT DISTRIBUTING CORP.
(formerly "American Film Theatre")
Their films are distributed theatrically by Ajay Films, and non-theatrically by Paramount Non-Theatrical.
16mm dist: Paramount Non-Theatrical

AJAY FILMS
2743 Long Beach Road
Oceanside, NY 11572
516/776-2425
223 E. Park Avenue
Long Beach, NY 11561
516/431-1090, 431-1095

Has theatrical rights to the American Film Theatre pictures.

ALLIED ARTISTS
(formerly "Monogram")
15 Columbus Circle
New York, NY 10023
212/541-9200
9440 Santa Monica Blvd.
Beverly Hills, CA 90210
213/274-6917
16mm dist: Hurlock Cine World, Inc.

AMERICAN FILM INSTITUTE
John F. Kennedy Center
Washington, DC 20566
202/785-4600

AMERICAN FILM THEATRE
see AFT Distributing Corp.

AMERICAN INTERNATIONAL PICTURES
(formerly "American Releasing Corp.")
Executive Offices:
9033 Wilshire Blvd.
Beverly Hills, CA 90211
213/278-8118
L.A. Distribution:
291 So. La Cienega Blvd.
Beverly Hills, CA 90211
213/652-7573
N.Y. Distribution:
515 Madison Avenue
New York, NY 10022
212/752-4700
16mm dist (non-theatrical): Swank (for films since 1976); Audio Brandon (for films prior to 1976)

AMERICAN RELEASING CORP. see American International Pictures

AMKINO see Artkino Pictures

ANGLO-AMALGAMATED see EMI

ANGLO-EMI see EMI

ARTCLASS PICTURES CORP. see Weiss Global Enterprises

ARTKINO PICTURES
(formerly "Amkino")
410 E. 62nd Street
New York, NY 10021
212/421-4773

American distributor of many Soviet productions. Now associated with Corinth Films.

ASSOCIATED BRITISH-PATHÉ LTD. see EMI

ASSOCIATED FILM DISTRIBUTION CORP.
12711 Ventura Blvd.
Studio City, CA 91604
213/760-1028
888 — 7th Avenue
New York, NY 10019
212/247-3060

Formed in early 1979, this company is owned partly by EMI Films, Ltd. and partly by ITC.

ASTOR
Defunct. Some rights went to Commonwealth United, and then to National Telefilm Associates.

ATLANTIC RELEASING CORP.
8 Newbury Street
Boston, MA 02116
617/266-5400

AUDIO BRANDON FILMS (Macmillan) [16mm films]
34 MacQuesten Parkway South
Mt. Vernon, NY 10550
914/664-5051
toll free: 800/431-1994
in New York: 800/742-1889
8400 Brookfield Avenue
Brookfield, IL 60513
312/485-3925
toll free: 800/323-4881
in Ill.: 800/942-7970
1619 Cherokee Avenue
Los Angeles, CA 90028
213/463-1131
toll free: 800/421-4336
in Calif.: 800/252-9335
3868 Piedmont Avenue
Oakland, CA 94611
415/658-9890
toll free: 800/227-1784
in Calif.: 800/772-3230

In the late 1960s, Audio Film Center (which owned Fleetwood Films) and Brandon Films, both competing 16mm distributors, were taken over by Macmillan and merged to form this company.

AUDIO FILM CENTER
A 16mm distributor whose 35mm branch was Fleetwood films. Became Audio Brandon.

AUDUBON FILMS
850 Seventh Avenue
New York, NY 10019
212/586-4913

AVCO EMBASSY PICTURES CORP.
6601 Romaine Street
Hollywood, CA 90038
213/462-7111
N.Y. distribution:
300 E. 42nd Street
New York, NY 10017
212/949-8900
Avco Embassy TV
3460 Wilshire Blvd.
Los Angeles, CA 90010
213/386-3920
16mm films: Swank

AZTECA FILMS
555 No. La Brea Avenue
Hollywood, CA 90036
213/938-2413
1500 Broadway
New York, NY 10036
212/869-3666
1233 So. Wabash Avenue
Chicago, IL 60605
312/922-6186

Distributor of Mexican films.

BBC (Television Enterprises)
BBC Television Centre
Wood Lane
London W12 7RJ ENGLAND
01-743 8000

55 Bloor Street, West
Toronto, Ontario CANADA
416/925-3891

For U.S. distribution, see Time-Life Films.

BEVERLY PICTURES
321 So. Beverly Drive
Beverly Hills, CA 90212
213/277-8849

Theatrically sub-distributes films in 13 western states for Janus/Kino, Filmways, Toho, Shochiku and others.

BILLY JACK PRODUCTIONS
(formerly "Taylor Laughlin Distribution Co.")
4024 Radford Ave.
Studio City, CA 91604
213/394-0286

BOXOFFICE INTERNATIONAL see Valiant International

BRANDON FILMS see Audio Brandon Films

JOSEPH BRENNER ASSOCIATES
570 Seventh Avenue
New York, NY 10018
212/354-6070

BRITISH LION FILMS LTD.
Foreign distribution arm was Lion International. British Lion merged with EMI in 1976.

BRUT PRODUCTIONS
9200 Sunset Blvd.
Hollywood, CA 90069
213/274-6981

1345 Avenue of the Americas
New York, NY 10019
212/581-3500

Entertainment division of Fabrege, Inc.

BRYANSTON see Swank Motion Pictures

BUDGET FILMS [16mm films]
4590 Santa Monica Blvd.
Los Angeles, CA 90029
213/660-0187, 660-0800

BUENA VISTA DISTRIBUTION CO.
Studio and national distribution:
500 So. Buena Vista Street
Burbank, CA 91521
213/845-3141
L.A. distribution:
350 So. Buena Vista Street
Burbank, CA 91521
213/841-1000

N.Y. distribution:
477 Madison Avenue
New York, NY 10022
212/593-8900

Distributes films of Walt Disney Productions, including Disney films previously distributed by RKO.

CANNON GROUP
(also called "Cannon Releasing")

9911 West Pico Blvd.
Los Angeles, CA 90035
213/553-5978

600 Madison Avenue
New York, NY 10022
212/759-5700

CBS-TV (Columbia Broadcasting System)
51 W. 52nd Street
New York, NY 10019
212/975-4321

7800 Beverly Blvd.
Hollywood, CA 90036
213/852-2345

630 McClurg Court
Chicago, IL 60611
312/944-6000

CIC (Cinema International Corp.)
139 Piccadilly
London W1V 9FH ENGLAND

1 Gulf & Western Plaza
New York, NY 10023
212/333-3777

Handles overseas distribution for Universal, Paramount and MGM.

CINE ARTISTS PICTURES CORP.
2020 Avenue of the Stars
Los Angeles, CA 90067
213/553-4630

CINEMA CENTER FILMS
c/o CBS Studio Center
4024 Radford Avenue
Studio City, CA 91604
213/763-8411

Film properties of Cinema Center once distributed by National General Pictures have now reverted to Cinema Center.

CINEMA 5
595 Madison Ave.
New York, NY 10022
212/421-5555

CINEMA SHARES INTERNATIONAL
450 Park Avenue
New York, NY 10022
212/421-3371

CINEMATION
Defunct. Rights scattered.

CINERAMA RELEASING CORP.
141 So. Robertson Blvd.
Los Angeles, CA 90048
213/278-5271

This company retains exclusive distribution rights in their 3-strip Cinerama process films. For other films, ABC Pictures International handles foreign distribution, and American International Pictures handles domestic distribution. Non-theatrical distribution is by Swank Motion Pictures.

COLUMBIA PICTURES
Studio and executive offices:
One Columbia Plaza
Burbank, CA 91505
213/843-7280 or 843-6000
L.A. distribution:
8671 Wilshire Blvd.
Beverly Hills, CA 90211
213/657-6410
N.Y. distribution:
711 Fifth Avenue
New York, NY 10022
212/751-4400
16mm dist: Swank Motion Pictures

Screen Gems is now called Columbia Pictures Television (or "CPT"); contact Burbank studio.

[Royal Films International]

COMMONWEALTH UNITED
Defunct. Rights status in doubt.

COMPASS INTERNATIONAL PICTURES
(formerly "Irwin Yablans Co.")
9229 Sunset Blvd.
Hollywood, CA 90069
213/273-9125

CONTEMPORARY FILMS
In business from the 1930s as a 16mm distributor of high-class foreign and art films. Acquired distribution rights to De Rochemont films in the 1950s. Became Pathé-Contemporary in the 1960s.

CONTINENTAL see Walter Reade

CORINTH FILMS
410 E. 62nd Street
New York, NY 10021
toll free: 800/221-4720
in N.Y.: 212/421-4770

Handles both 16mm and 35mm films, mostly non-theatrical. Artkino Pictures is now associated with Corinth Films in the same office. Contact Libra Films for theatrical distribution.

CROWN INTERNATIONAL PICTURES
292 South La Cienega Blvd.
Beverly Hills, CA 90211
213/657-6700

LYMAN DAYTON PICTURES

10850 Riverside Drive
No. Hollywood, CA 91602
213/980-7202
[Doty-Dayton]

DE ROCHEMONT

A company of the 1950s. Their distribution rights were acquired by Contemporary Films, but most or all of the principal rights have reverted to the original owners.

DIMENSION PICTURES

9000 Sunset Blvd.
Hollywood, CA 90069
213/278-6844

WALT DISNEY PRODUCTIONS see Buena Vista

DISTRIBPIX

430 W. 54th Street
New York, NY 10019
212/489-8130

DISTRIBUTORS CORPORATION OF AMERICA see Hal Roach Studios

DOTY-DAYTON see Lyman Dayton Pictures

EAGLE LION

Formerly called "Producers Releasing Corp." In 1950, Eagle Lion Classics was formed by merger of Eagle Lion and Film Classics; this company was later absorbed into United Artists. However, NTA now owns many or most of the film properties originally with this company.

EMERY PICTURES, INC.

342 Madison Avenue
New York, NY 10017
212/838-8813

EMI FILMS

1370 Avenue of the Americas
New York, NY 10019
212/757-7470
Head office:
EMI Films, Ltd.
30-31 Golden Square
London W1R 4QX ENGLAND
01-437 9234
U.S. production office:
EMI Films, Inc.
9489 Dayton Way
Beverly Hills, CA 90210
213/278-4770

[Anglo-Amalgamated, Anglo-EMI, Associated British-Pathé Ltd., British Lion Films Ltd., Lion International]

ENTERPRISES PRODUCTIONS, INC.

22548 Pacific Coast Highway
P. O. Box 424
Malibu, CA 90265
213/456-6616

Distributes the films of Jack H. Harris Enterprises.

ENTERTAINMENT VENTURES, INC.

1654 Cordova Street
Los Angeles, CA 90007
213/731-7236

FACES DISTRIBUTION

650 No. Bronson Avenue
Hollywood, CA 90004
213/464-4370

Faces International is also at the same address and phone number. These companies have almost all of the John Cassavetes films.

FAMOUS PLAYERS-LASKY CORP.
see Paramount

FILM CLASSICS see Eagle Lion

FILM POLSKI

6/8 Mazowiecka
00-048 Warsaw POLAND

FILM VENTURES INTERNATIONAL

310 No. San Vincente Blvd.
Los Angeles, CA 90048
213/659-0545

FILMS AROUND THE WORLD

745 Fifth Avenue
New York, NY 10022
212/752-5050

FILMS INC. [16mm films]

733 Greenbay Road
Wilmette, IL 60091
toll free: 800/323-1406
in Ill.: 312/256-6600
5625 Hollywood Blvd.
Hollywood, CA 90028
toll free: 800/421-0612
in Calif.: 213/466-5481
440 Park Avenue South
New York, NY 10016
toll free: 800/223-6244
in N.Y.: 212/889-7910

Handles 16mm films of MGM, 20th Century-Fox, New World, RKO, ABC Pictures International, and some films of Disney (non-theatrical only) and Avco Embassy. Has non-exclusive rights in the non-college non-theatrical market for Paramount's post-1948 features until at least July 31, 1980.

FILMGROUP see New World Pictures

FILMWAYS, INC. (Filmways International)

2049 Century Park East
Los Angeles, CA 90067
213/557-8700
540 Madison Avenue
New York, NY 10022
212/758-5100

Subsidiary is Sigma III.

FIRST ARTISTS

c/o The Burbank Studios
4000 Warner Blvd.
Burbank, CA 91522
213/843-6000, 843-7280

FLEETWOOD FILMS see Audio Film Center

FOUR STAR ENTERTAINMENT (TV)

400 So. Beverly Drive
Beverly Hills, CA 90212
213/277-7444
60 E. 42nd Street
New York, NY 10017
212/867-4489

GAUMONT-BRITISH see Rank Organisation

GENERAL FILM DISTRIBUTORS

In July, 1955 this company became Rank Film Distributors

GOLD KEY ENTERTAINMENT (TV)
(division of Vidtronics Co., Inc.)

855 No. Cahuenga Blvd.
Hollywood, CA 90038
213/466-9741
Tower 53, 159 West 53rd Street
New York, NY 10019
212/486-9116

Primarily a distributor of TV programs and TV movies, but also theatrically distributes features originally distributed by other companies, including RKO and Showcorporation.

GREATEST FIGHTS OF THE CENTURY, INC. see Turn Of The Century Fights, Inc.

JOSEPH GREEN PICTURES

200 W. 58th Street
New York, NY 10019
212/246-9343, 246-9344

GROUP 1 FILMS

9200 Sunset Blvd.
Hollywood, CA 90069
213/550-8767

HALLMARK RELEASING CORP.
(also called "Hallmark Enterprises")

46 Church Street
Boston, MA 02116
617/482-4310

JACK H. HARRIS ENTERPRISES see Enterprises Productions

HEMISPHERE PICTURES see Six Pictures

J. H. HOFFBERG COMPANY

Mainly a distributor of unsubtitled foreign language films to ethnic audiences in the 1940s and 1950s. Owned principal rights to a number of American and British "B" pictures in the 1930s, and some of these have been acquired by Raymond Rohauer.

HURLOCK CINE-WORLD, INC.

13 Arcadia Road
Old Greenwich, CT 08870
203/637-4319

Handles Allied Artists films in 16mm.

ICARUS FILMS

200 Park Avenue South
New York, NY 10003
212/674-3375

In addition to their own films, Icarus now handles the pictures of Impact Films.

IMPACT FILMS see Icarus Films

INDEPENDENT - INTERNATIONAL PICTURES

165 W. 46th Street
New York, NY 10036
212/869-9333

INTERCONTINENTAL RELEASING CORP.

9465 Wilshire Blvd.
Beverly Hills, CA 90212
213/550-8710

INTERNATIONAL CLASSICS see 20th Century-Fox

ITC ENTERTAINMENT INC. (TV)

115 East 57th Street
New York, NY 10022
212/371-6660

IVY FILMS [16mm films]

165 West 46th Street
New York, NY 10036
212/765-3940

RILEY JACKSON FILMS

6353 Homewood Avenue
Hollywood, CA 90028
213/464-4708

Represents successors in interest to rights in films of Parade Pictures, which became inactive in the late 1960s.

JANUS FILMS [16mm films]

745 Fifth Avenue
New York, NY 10022
212/753-7100

Has many classics previously distributed by other companies. Their films in 35mm are handled by Kino International.

KINO INTERNATIONAL

250 West 57th Street
New York, NY 10019
212/586-8720

Handles Janus' films in 35mm.

KODIAK FILMS

11681 San Vincente Blvd.
Los Angeles, CA 90049
213/820-7511

LEACOCK-PENNEBAKER [16mm films]

56 West 45th Street
New York, NY 10036
212/840-2425

LEARNING CORPORATION OF AMERICA [16mm films]

1350 Avenue of the Americas
New York, NY 10019
212/397-9330

Handles non-theatrical distribution of many classic British films.

LEVITT-PICKMAN FILM CORP.

505 Park Avenue
New York, NY 10022
212/832-8842

LIBRA FILMS CORP.

150 E. 58th Street
New York, NY 10022
212/838-7721

Handles theatrical distribution for Corinth and Artkino.

LION INTERNATIONAL see British Lion

LIPPERT PRODUCTIONS

(formerly "Screen Guild")
c/o Robert L. Lippert Theatres
Pier 32
San Francisco, CA 94105
415/546-9200

Films from 1946 thru 1955 are now distributed by Weiss Global Enterprises. Films from 1956 and later are owned and distributed by 20th Century-Fox.

LOEWS, INC. see Metro-Goldwyn-Mayer

LONDON FILM PRODUCTIONS LTD.

130 Jermyn Street, 6th Floor
London SW1Y 4UJ, ENGLAND
01-839 2935

LONE STAR PICTURES INTERNATIONAL

6515 Sunset Blvd.
Hollywood, CA 90028
213/463-3175

LOPERT see United Artists

LORIMAR PRODUCTIONS

c/o M-G-M Studios
10202 W. Washington Blvd.
Culver City, CA 90230
213/836-3000
1345 Avenue of the Americas
New York, NY 10019
212/765-1061

MACMILLAN AUDIO BRANDON see Audio Brandon Films

MAGNA PICTURES CORP.

1700 Broadway
New York, NY 10019
212/765-2800

MANSON INTERNATIONAL

9145 Sunset Blvd.
Hollywood, CA 90069
213/273-8640

QUINN MARTIN PRODUCTIONS (TV)

(also called "QM Productions")
1041 No. Formosa Avenue
Hollywood, CA 90046
213/650-2674

MCA-TV (Universal)

100 Universal City Plaza
Universal City, CA 91608
213/985-4321
445 Park Avenue
New York, NY 10022
212/759-7500

Owns almost all of Paramount's pre-1949 sound films.

McGRAW-HILL/CRM FILMS [16mm films]

(formerly "Contemporary/McGraw-Hill")
110 — 15th Street
Del Mar, CA 92014
714/453-5000

Successor in interest to Pathé-Contemporary, but now handles mostly educational films; rights in most or all of the Pathé-Contemporary films reverted to the principal holders of those rights.

MEDALLION TV ENTERPRISES

8831 Sunset Blvd.
Hollywood, CA 90069
213/652-8100

METRO-GOLDWYN-MAYER (MGM)

(formerly "Loew's, Inc." and "Metro-Goldwyn")
10202 W. Washington Blvd.
Culver City, CA 90230
213/836-3000

16mm dist: Films Inc.

Since 1973, their films have been distributed by United Artists.

[Premier Pictures]

MIDWEST FILMS

600 Madison Avenue
New York, NY 10022
212/355-0282

MIRROR RELEASING
1741 No. Ivar St.
Hollywood, CA 90028
213/463-3181

**WILLIAM MISHKIN MOTION PIC-
TURES**
1501 Broadway
New York, NY 10036
212/398-0133

**MITCHELL BROTHERS FILM
GROUP**
895 O'Farrell Street
San Francisco, CA 94109
415/441-1930

MONARCH RELEASING CORP.
8500 Wilshire Blvd.
Beverly Hills, CA 90211
213/652-9900
1780 Broadway
New York, NY 10019
212/757-3635

MONOGRAM PICTURES see Allied
Artists

MULBERRY SQUARE RELEASING
10300 No. Central Expressway
Dallas, TX 75231
214/369-2430

**NATIONAL FILM BOARD OF
CANADA**
3155 Cote de Liesse Road
Montreal, Quebec H4N 2N4 CANADA
514/333-3333
1251 Avenue of the Americas
New York, NY 10020
212/586-2400
44 Montgomery Street
San Francisco, CA 94104
415/981-1448

NATIONAL GENERAL PICTURES
6310 San Vincente Blvd.
Los Angeles, CA 90048
213/930-2440

In 1973, most of their film properties were
sold to Warner Bros., but the productions of
Cinema Center Films reverted to that company.

NATIONAL TELEFILM ASSOCIATES
(NTA)
12636 Beatrice Street
Los Angeles, CA 90066
213/390-3663
141 E. 56th Street
New York, NY 10022
212/752-4982

16mm dist: contact NTA's legal department

Owns rights to most of the films originally
distributed by Republic. Also owns many of
Paramount's short films and films formerly
owned by Eagle Lion.

**NBC-TV (National Broadcasting
Company)**
3000 W. Alameda Avenue
Burbank, CA 91523
213/849-3911
30 Rockefeller Plaza
New York, NY 10020
212/664-4444
2000 Merchandise Mart
Chicago, IL 60654
312/861-5555

NEW LINE CINEMA
853 Broadway
New York, NY 10003
212/674-7460

NEW WORLD PICTURES
11600 San Vincente Blvd.
Los Angeles, CA 90049
213/820-6733
250 W. 57th Street
New York, NY 10019
212/247-3240
16mm dist: Films Inc.
[Filmgroup]

NEW YORKER FILMS
16 West 61st Street
New York, NY 10023
212/247-6110

OFFICIAL FILMS, INC. (TV)
6 East 45th Street
New York, NY 10017
212/687-8470

ORION PICTURES
4000 Warner Blvd.
Burbank, CA 91522
213/843-6000 or 843-7280

Formed in 1978 by former top executives
of United Artists, this company distributes
theatrically through Warner Bros.

**PACIFIC INTERNATIONAL ENTER-
PRISES**
1133 So. Riverside
Medford, OR 97501
503/779-8880

PARADE PICTURES see Riley Jackson Films

PARAMOUNT
(formerly "Famous Players-Lasky Corp.")
Executive offices and N.Y. distribution:
1 Gulf & Western Plaza
New York, NY 10023
212/333-3710
Classic films dept:
212/333-3750
Studio:
5451 Marathon
Hollywood, CA 90038
213/463-0100

L.A. distribution:
9440 Santa Monica Blvd.
Beverly Hills, CA 90210
213/550-8600
16mm dist: Paramount Non-Theatrical (Films
Inc. has non-exclusive rights in the non-
college non-theatrical market at least
until July 31, 1980)

Rights to almost all of Paramount's pre-
1949 sound features are now owned by MCA
(Universal). Rights to almost all of Paramount's short films (they made very few
after 1951) are now owned by NTA (National
Telefilm Associates) or Raymond Rohauer.

PARAMOUNT NON-THEATRICAL
[16mm films]
5451 Marathon
Hollywood, CA 90038
toll free: 800/421-4432
in Calif.: 213/462-0700

Has Paramount's silent films and post-
1948 sound films, as well as AFT (American
Film Theatre) films, many Charlie Chaplin
films, most Harold Lloyd Films, and BBS
Productions.
[rbc films]

KIT PARKER FILMS [16mm films]
P. O. Box 227
Carmel Valley, CA 93924
408/659-3474

PATHÉ
In the early 1930s, RKO bought Pathé, re-
naming it RKO-Pathé and attempting to run
it as an entity separate from RKO, but within
a few years it was completely absorbed into
RKO. However, some of the sound films of
Pathé were acquired by Columbia Pictures.

PATHÉ-AMERICA see Pathé Contemporary

PATHÉ CINEMA
6 rue Francoeur
75018 Paris FRANCE
(01) 257-1210

PATHÉ-CONTEMPORARY
In the early 1960s, a business arrangement
between Pathé-America (a subsidiary of
Pathé Cinema of Paris) and Contemporary
Films led to the formation of this company,
which theatrically distributed mostly quality
foreign films throughout the rest of the
decade. Acquired by McGraw-Hill in the
early 1970s, and name changed to Con-
temporary/McGraw Hill (now called
"McGraw-Hill/CRM Films") which now distributes mostly educational films and
allowed most or all distribution rights in
Pathé-Contemporary films to revert to
holders of principal rights.

PEPPERCORN-WORMSER
120 East 56th Street
New York, NY 10022
212/758-1820

PREMIER PICTURES see M-G-M

PRO-INTERNATIONAL FILMS
8833 Sunset Blvd.
Los Angeles, CA 90069
213/657-8620

PRODUCERS DISTRIBUTING CORP.
Began 1924; absorbed by Pathé in 1927.

PRODUCERS RELEASING CORP. (PRC)
Originally started as Producers Distributing Corporation (PDC) in 1939 (and apparently having no relation to the 1920s company by the same name), this company came to be called Eagle Lion by the late 1940s; see Eagle Lion.

QM PRODUCTIONS see Quinn Martin Productions

RANK FILM DISTRIBUTORS
(branch of Rank Organisation, formerly "J. Arthur Rank")
127 Wardour Street
London W1V 4AD ENGLAND
01-437 9020

Rank Film Sales
444 Madison Avenue
New York, NY 10022
212/986-9779

[Gaumont-British, General Film Distributors]

rbc films see Paramount Non-theatrical

WALTER READE ORGANIZATION
241 E. 34th Street
New York, NY 10016
212/683-6300

[Continental Distributing]

REPUBLIC PICTURES
322 Vista Del Mar
Redondo Beach, CA 90277
213/373-6312

509 Madison Avenue
New York, NY 10021
212/753-9050

National Telefilm Associates (NTA) now owns virtually all TV rights and some theatrical rights in films previously owned by Republic.

RKO
129 No. Vermont Ave.
Los Angeles, CA 90004
213/383-5525

1440 Broadway
New York, NY 10018
212/764-7108

16mm dist: Films Inc.

No longer produces motion pictures, but still theatrically distributes most of the films they originally owned. TV rights for most pre-1955 RKO films are controlled by Lorimar through United Artists. All Disney Films are now handled by Buena Vista.

HAL ROACH STUDIOS, INC.
4335 Marina City Dr., Suite 142-E
Marina del Rey, CA 90291
213/822-0457

185 Davenport Road
Toronto, Ont. M5R 1J1 CANADA
416/962-9292

[Distributors Corp. of America]

RAYMOND ROHAUER
44 West 62nd Street
New York, NY 10023
212/765-8262

Owns and distributes many films acquired from various sources, including the public domain. Has many of the Buster Keaton films, Paramount shorts, and some of the J. H. Hoffberg films.

ROYAL FILMS INTERNATIONAL see Columbia Pictures

SANRIO DISTRIBUTING
1930 Century Park West
Los Angeles, CA 90067
213/552-0525

Head office:
Sanrio Co., Ltd.
7-22-17 Nishigotanda
Shinagawa-ku
Tokyo, 141 JAPAN
(03) 494-5311

SCHOENFELD FILM DISTRIBUTING
165 West 46th Street
New York, NY 10036
212/765-8977

SCOTIA AMERICAN PRODUCTIONS
600 Madison Avenue
New York, NY 10022
212/758-4775

SCREEN GEMS see Columbia Pictures

SCREEN GUILD see Lippert Productions

SELZNICK RELEASING ORGANIZATION
Defunct. Most film properties, including theatrical rights, were sold to ABC Pictures. GONE WITH THE WIND, of course, went to M-G-M.

SHOCHIKU FILMS OF AMERICA
3860 Crenshaw Blvd.
Los Angeles, CA 90008
213/296-7770

551 — 5th Avenue
New York, NY 10017
212/697-1646

Head office:
Shochiku Company, Ltd.
13-5 Tsukiji
1-Chome Chuo-ku
Tokyo, JAPAN
(03) 542-5551

SHOW CORPORATION OF AMERICA (TV)
(also called "Showcorporation")
79 Victory Street (P.O. Box 1070)
Stamford, CT 06904
203/327-9252

Now functions chiefly as a distributor of TV programs, and no longer distributes films theatrically. Most of the films originally distributed by Showcorporation in the 1960s are now owned by Gold Key Entertainment.

SIGMA III see Filmways, Inc.

SIX PICTURES
715 Park Avenue
New York, NY 10022
212/628-9476

Acquired rights to films of Hemisphere Pictures (now out of business).

SOVEXPORTFILM
Kalashny pereulok 14
103009 Moscow, U.S.S.R.

SPECIAL EVENT ENTERTAINMENT
9200 Sunset Blvd.
Hollywood, CA 90069
213/278-6052

SPECIALTY FILMS
500 Wall Street
Seattle, WA 98121
206/623-5380

SPELLING-GOLDBERG PRODUCTIONS (TV)
c/o 20th Century-Fox
P. O. Box 900
Beverly Hills, CA 90213
213/277-2211

SUNN CLASSIC PICTURES
(formerly "Sun International Pictures")
Executive offices:
556 E. 200 South
Salt Lake City, UT 84102
801/363-2040

L.A. distribution:
1554 Sepulveda Blvd.
Los Angeles, CA 90025
213/478-4034

Also called "Schick Sunn Classic."

SWANK MOTION PICTURES
[16mm films]
201 So. Jefferson Avenue
St. Louis, MO 63103
314/534-6300

6767 Forest Lawn Drive
Los Angeles, CA 90068
213/851-6300

393 Front Street
Hempstead, NY 11550
516/538-6500

Non-theatrical films of Columbia, Warner Bros., Universal, Disney, Avco-Embassy, Cinerama Releasing, National General, American International, and Bryanston. Collect calls accepted for film orders.

TAYLOR-LAUGHLIN DISTRIBU-TION CO. see Billy Jack Productions

TELEDYNAMICS CORPORATION (TV)
202 Mamaroneck Avenue
White Plains, NY 10601
212/994-1152

TELEWIDE SYSTEMS, INC. (TV)
118A East 65th Street
New York, NY 10021
212/628-8600

TIFFANY PRODUCTIONS
(also called "Tiffany-Stahl")
Begain 1922, went defunct 1932. Most (but not all) of their films went into the public domain.

TIME-LIFE TELEVISION [16mm films]
Time & Life Building
New York, NY 10020
212/841-1212
3435 Wilshire Blvd.
Los Angeles, CA 90010
213/385-8151
303 E. Ohio Street
Chicago, IL 60611
312/329-7835

Distributor of entertainment and documentary TV programs. Also has various feature films. Major distributor of BBC productions.

TIMES FILM CORP.
144 West 57th Street
New York, NY 10019
212/757-6980

TOHO CO. LTD.
2049 Century Park East
Los Angeles, CA 90067
213/277-1081
1501 Broadway
New York, NY 10036
212/391-9058
Hibiya Park Building
1-8-1 Yuraku-cho, Chiyoda-ku,
Tokyo, 100 JAPAN
(03) 591-1211

TOPAR FILMS, INC.
116 No. Robertson Blvd.
Los Angeles, CA 90048
213/271-6193

TRANS-LUX CORP.
110 Richards Avenue
Norwalk, CT 06854
203/853-4321

No longer active in film distribution; most film rights have reverted to original owners.

TRANSVUE PICTURES CORP.
14724 Ventura Blvd.
Sherman Oaks, CA 91403
213/990-5600

TURN OF THE CENTURY FIGHTS, INC.
(also called "Greatest Fights of the Century")
9 East 40th Street
New York, NY 10016
212/532-1717

20th CENTURY-FOX
(formerly "Fox Film Co.")
Studio and executive offices:
10201 W. Pico Blvd.
Los Angeles, CA 90064
213/277-2211
L.A. distribution:
9440 Santa Monica Blvd.
Beverly Hills, CA 90210
213/550-1044
N.Y. distribution:
1345 Avenue of the Americas
New York, NY 10019
212/397-8567
16mm dist: Films Inc.
[International Classics]

TWYMAN FILMS [16mm films]
Box 605
Dayton, OH 45401
toll free: 800/543-9594
in Ohio: 513/222-4014

U-M FILM DISTRIBUTORS see Universal-Marion Corp.

UMC PICTURES see Universal-Marion Corp.

UNITED ARTISTS
Executive offices and N.Y. distribution:
729 — 7th Avenue
New York, NY 10019
212/575-3000
Studio:
10202 W. Washington Blvd.
Culver City, CA 90230
213/559-3450
L.A. distribution:
116 No. Robertson Blvd.
Los Angeles, CA 90048
213/657-7000
16mm dist: United Artists 16

Until 1951, UA was a distributor for films of other producers, and rights to virtually all such films have either reverted to the original owners or are in the public domain. UA owns rights to almost all pre-1950 Warner Bros. films, and has distributed MGM's films since 1973.

[Eagle Lion, Film Classics, Producers Releasing Corp., Lopert]

UNITED ARTISTS 16 [16mm films]
729 — 7th Avenue
New York, NY 10019
212/575-4715

Handles non-theatrical films of United Artists films from 1951 to the present, and almost all pre-1950 Warner Bros. films.

UNITED FILM DISTRIBUTION CO.
291 So. La Cienega Blvd.
Beverly Hills, CA 90211
213/657-6210
115 Middle Neck Road
Great Neck, NY 11021
516/466-3300

Division of United Artists Theatres.

UNITED FILMS see V.C.I.

UNIVERSAL-MARION CORP.
(formerly known as "UMC Pictures" and "U-M Film Distributors")
P. O. Box 4369
Jacksonville, FL 32201
904/358-2552

UNIVERSAL PICTURES
445 Park Avenue
New York, NY 10022
212/759-7500
100 Universal City Plaza
Universal City, CA 91608
213/985-4321
16mm dist: Universal 16, Swank Motion Pictures

A division of MCA, Inc. Was known as "Universal-International" from 1946 thru 1963. Owns almost all of Paramount's pre-1949 sound films.

UNIVERSAL 16 [16mm films]
445 Park Avenue
New York, NY 10022
212/759-7500
8901 Beverly Blvd.
Los Angeles, CA 90048
213/550-7461

Non-theatrical films of Universal and for almost all of Paramount's pre-1949 sound films.

VALIANT INTERNATIONAL PICTURES
(formerly called "Boxoffice International")
4774 Melrose Avenue
Hollywood, CA 90029
213/665-5257

V.C.I. (Video Communications Inc.) [16mm films]
(formerly "United Films")
6585 E. Skelly Drive
Tulsa, OK 74145
918/662-6460

VIACOM ENTERPRISES (TV)
1211 Avenue of the Americas
New York, NY 10036
212/575-5175

9720 Wilshire Blvd.
Beverly Hills, CA 90212
213/278-5644

40 Conduit Street
London W1R 9FB ENGLAND
01-930 5084

Branch offices in many other cities and foreign countries.

WARNER BROS.
Studio and executive offices:
4000 Warner Blvd.
Burbank, CA 91522
213/843-6000 or 843-7280

L.A. distribution:
8484 Wilshire Blvd.
Beverly Hills, CA 90211
213/653-9600

N.Y. distribution:
75 Rockefeller Plaza
New York, NY 10019
212/484-8960

16mm dist: Swank Motion Pictures
Almost all of Warner Bros. pre-1950 films are now owned by United Artists. Warner Bros. now owns almost all of the National General Pictures films.
[First National, Seven Arts]

WEISS GLOBAL ENTERPRISES (TV)
333 So. Beverly Drive
Beverly Hills, CA 90212
213/553-5806

TV distributor; also theatrical and non-theatrical films. Owns Lippert's 1946-1955 films.
[Artclass Pictures Corp., Weiss Bros., Stage & Screen]

WOLPER PRODUCTIONS, INC. (TV)
c/o The Burbank Studios
4000 Warner Blvd.
Burbank, CA 91522
213/843-6000, 843-7280

No longer active in TV distribution. Wolper properties from 1970 to the present are now distributed by Warner Bros. TV. Most previous properties have reverted to original owners, and pre-1970 Wolper-owned properties have been sold to various distributors.

WORLD-NORTHAL CORP.
1 Dag Hammarskjold Plaza
New York, NY 10017
212/223-8181

WORLD WIDE FILMS CORP.
15757 Stagg Street
Van Nuys, CA 91406
213/786-1230

WORLD WIDE (Sono Arts)
Defunct. Rights scattered.

WORLD WIDE PICTURES
1201 Hennepin Avenue South
Minneapolis, MN 55403
612/338-3335

2520 W. Olive Avenue
Burbank, CA 91505
213/843-1300

Motion picture arm of the Billy Graham organization.

WORLDVISION ENTERPRISES, INC. (TV)
660 Madison Avenue
New York, NY 10021
212/832-3838

9401 Wilshire Blvd.
Beverly Hills, CA 90212
213/273-7667

625 No. Michigan Avenue
Chicago, IL 60611
312/642-2650

54 Pont Street
London S.W.1 ENGLAND
01-584 5357

IRWIN YABLANS CO. see Compass International Pictures

ASSISTANCE, ANYONE?

The foregoing Selected Companies Guide may well be the most extensive historical record of successors in interest for active and inactive motion picture distributors, but it is still somewhat incomplete. It's understandable that most companies which go out of business are usually disinclined to publicize the circumstances surrounding their demise, but those who acquire the rights to their films make surprisingly little effort to make the fact of their new interests generally known.

If you know of any pertinent facts about these companies that we might have misstated or omitted, please write to us. We'd also like to know about a number of other companies listed below, most of which were not included in this guide for lack of adequate information. It's not essential to send us authoritative documentation (letters, clippings, articles, legal notices, etc.), but it certainly helps.

If you are connected with any of the companies listed and know about (or anticipate) changes we should make, please let us know. Or if your distribution company isn't listed but you think it should be, please tell us.

There are other companies we probably ought to know about, and we're certainly open to suggestions from interested readers, but the ones in which we're currently most interested in gathering more information are the following:

> Atlas Films
> Bryanston
> Chevron Pictures
> Cinemation
> Commonwealth United
> Ellis Films
> English Films
> Europix International
> Fairway International
> Filmmakers
> Majestic Pictures
> Realart
> Tricolore *(French)*
> U.M.P.O. *(French)*
> Zenith International

314

Here are several of the most useful and comprehensive movie and TV reference books available from Hollywood Film Archive. All books are sold on a 30-day moneyback guarantee.

THE VIDEO TAPE/DISC GUIDE: MOVIES AND ENTERTAINMENT

This is an indispensable book for anyone with home video equipment. It lists over 4,000 feature films and entertainment programs which can be purchased or rented for video use. Arranged alphabetically by title, it gives leading actors, story synopsis, genre, year of release, running time, color or black-and-white, video format and name of the company(ies) from which each title can be obtained, with addresses and phone numbers. There is also a category index by genre (musical, sci-fi, western, horror, comedy, adventure, etc.).

Softbound only, 282 pages: $12.95

SCREEN WORLD

Each annual volume of this series lists virtually every feature film (including foreign films) released in the U.S. during the year (the 1980 edition gives the films of 1979), usually about 500-600 movies. Reference information given for each film includes actors (including who played what role), production credits, releasing company, MPAA rating, running time and other vital information. Each book contains about 1,000 photos of movie scenes and actor portraits, and has an alphabetical index of the thousands of actors and production personnel with film credits in the main section.

SCREEN WORLD 1980 (volume 31): $15.95 clothbound
SCREEN WORLD 1979 (volume 30): $15.95 clothbound

There are usually other recent volumes available, so please let us know if you're interested in them.

GADNEY'S GUIDE TO 1,800 INTERNATIONAL CONTESTS, FESTIVALLS & GRANTS

For the first time under one cover, this directory of over 600 pages gives up-to-date information on the multitude of contests, festivals and available grants in virtually every form of communications: film, video, audio, television, radio, poetry, screen and play writing, journalism, advertising and publishing. It gives all the pertinent details for entering each one—addresses, deadlines, requirements, eligibility, fees; and it even evaluates the nature and purpose of various events, with helpful hints on how to win. A gold mine of essential competition information for writers and producers, and an absolutely essential reference for all libraries.

Hardbound, 608 pages: $21.95   Softbound: $15.95

FILM PROGRAMMER'S GUIDE TO 16mm RENTALS

Now in its third edition, it lists 14,000 title entries alphabetically with director, date, country of origin, running time, other pertinent notes, and one or more distributors and rental price information for each film. Over 100 distributors are listed with addresses, phone numbers, and rental policy summaries. Films are cross-referenced by directors in a special supplemental index.

Softbound only, 320 pages: $20.00

THE FILM BUFF'S BIBLE OF MOTION PICTURES (1915-1972)

Now something of a collector's item, this alphabetical listing of 13,000 movie titles was the predecessor of *The Film Buff's Checklist*. There are a few reference items you can get only by buying this book. Particularly if you're interested in ratings, it contains the ratings we assigned to films years ago, and it's the only publication that lists the one- to four-star ratings from Steven Scheuer's *Movies On TV* (through the fifth edition) and Leonard Maltin's *TV Movies* (first edition) side by side, next to ours. It also lists notations for all films nominated for or winning the Academy Award for Best Picture.

Clothbound, 180 pages: $12.95   Softbound: $5.95

Please use the coupon below to order. Sorry, no C.O.D.s, but credit card orders are welcomed.

HOLLYWOOD FILM ARCHIVE
8344 Melrose Avenue, Dept. CK
Hollywood, Calif. 90069 (U.S.A.)

☐ Check or money order enclosed.
Charge my credit card (see below): ☐ Visa
☐ MasterCard   ☐ American Express

PLEASE PRINT OR TYPE

Name _____   Phone (___) _____

_____

Address_____

City _____ Province or State _____ Postal or ZIP code _____

Credit card no._____ Expiration date_____ Sign here x_____

Please send the following books with a 30-day moneyback guarantee:

Quantity	Title	Price Each	Amount

Total for books	$
Shipping charges $1.75 per book*	$
California purchasers add 6% Sales Tax	$
TOTAL AMOUNT ENCLOSED (U.S. Funds)	$

Other Shipping Services:

☐ Special Handling: add $2.00 per order to shipping charges.

☐ Registry: add $6.00 per order.

☐ Foreign Airmail: Add $17.50 per book.

CREDIT CARD HOLDERS CALL TOLL FREE

(in continental U.S.) 800-228-2606,
(in Nebraska call 800-642-8777).
Toll free numbers are for placing credit card orders ONLY.

*If ordering the FILM SUPERLIST or REFERENCE GUIDE TO FANTASTIC FILMS, see next four pages for shipping charges.

Walt Lee's
REFERENCE GUIDE TO
FANTASTIC FILMS

If you purchased the three-volume set back when the price was $27.95 or $29.95, you certainly were fortunate. Most reference works go down in price after they're a few years old, but the fantastic films publications of Walt Lee, who's one of the world's foremost authorities on films of that genre, seem to only increase in value — for example, Lee's *Checklist of Science Fiction, Fantasy and Horror Films,* which originally sold for $2.00 in 1958, increased to $75.00 per copy by the early 1970s.

There are still available a **very limited** number of this truly fantastic reference set, which lists films released through 1974. There are no plans to reprint it. Many people who have a set say they wouldn't part with it for $1,000.00 unless they could be certain of being able to obtain another. When these books go out of print, that amount may turn out to be a bargain.

REFERENCE GUIDE TO
fantastic films

Compiled by Walt Lee

* **20,000 FILMS** * **50 COUNTRIES**
* **75 YEARS** * **MANY RARE PHOTOGRAPHS**

An exhaustive reference of virtually every science fiction, horror and fantasy film ever made (and even those which were planned or started but never completed) from the pre-turn-of-the-century infancy of motion pictures through modern giants like PLANET OF THE APES and 2001: A SPACE ODYSSEY.

A cross-section of reviewers' praise from around the world:

"A monumental reference work . . . a major source for films within its scope." LIBRARY JOURNAL

"If you have any interest in science fiction, this book will prove an indispensable source of basic information." FOCUS (British)

"The virtue lies in Lee's broad interpretation of what constitutes a film's qualifying fantastic content." PERFORMING ARTS

"Mr. Lee's book is so indispensable, so packed with painstakingly collated information, it is worth at least four times the asking price." FILM INDEX (Australian)

VITAL REFERENCE INFORMATION

CAST
PRODUCTION CREDITS
RUNNING TIME IN MINUTES
PRODUCTION AND RELEASE DATA
FANTASTIC CONTENT
SOURCE OF FILM STORY
COUNTRY OF ORIGIN
REFERENCE SOURCES

EXTENSIVE CROSS-REFERENCING

ALTERNATE TITLES
SEQUELS
OTHER VERSIONS
RELATED TITLES

SPECIAL EXCLUSION INDEX

Lists films suggested to be fantastic by titles, casts, ads or reported subject matter, but researched and verified NOT to be fantastic.

Send payment with order to: HOLLYWOOD FILM ARCHIVE, 8344 Melrose Avenue, Hollywood, California 90069

3 VOLUMES!

OVER 700 PAGES

SOFTBOUND
8½" x 11"

3 VOLUME
SET $51.95*

FILM SUPERLIST
20,000 MOTION PICTURES IN
THE U.S. PUBLIC DOMAIN

Whether or not you actually intend to make commercial use of films in the public domain, the *Film Superlist* an indispensable reference to any serious film researcher. The book lists over 57,000 films copyrighted in the U.S. from 1894 thru 1939.

A public domain film is one on which the copyright is no longer in force — this happens when the copyright is not renewed. It can happen when the copyright owner feels that continued protection after the initial 28-year term is not worth the time and expense of filing a renewal application, or copyrights can lapse when the original owner goes out of the movie business and leaves no successor in interest to renew the films. But often enough, a valuable film will lose its copyright protection when the owner simply forgets to renew (this has happened at some of the large studios because of confusion, loss of records, sloppy procedures, or changes in personnel). The law is very precise in requiring that the renewal right be exercised during the 28th year of its term; if the owner fails to do so during that 365-day period, the copyright protection is lost forever, and anyone who can obtain a print of the film can make as many copies as he pleases and exhibit them for profit, rent them, sell them or otherwise exploit them for profit.

People who use the Film Superlist to commercialize public domain films know that the book pays for itself as soon as they've learned about just one good p.d. film (and there are hundreds of worthwhile ones) they hadn't known about. Other movie enthusiasts sometimes hesitate because of the high purchase price, but after they've bought the book they usually can't understand how they ever got along without it. After all, it's undoubtedly the most complete book of American silent films ever published, and it also has virtually all the American movies from the first decade of the sound era. It even gives extensive production credits. And all for less than 1/3¢ per film.

If you're just interested in the movie reference information, and have no need for copyright renewal notations, we can offer you an alternative two-volume set of the same information *except* for copyright renewals at a much lower price.

FILM SUPERLIST 1940-1949 is now available, containing the same types of copyright, credit and renewal information found in the earlier SUPERLIST. As an added bonus, brief story content is given for many of the features of the late 1940s. There is also a less expensive alternative volume of the same information *except* for copyright renewals.

If you need help with motion picture copyright research, Hollywood Film Archive provides such assistance. (At least as far as U.S. copyright status is concerned; other countries have different laws dealing with copyright, so a film which is in the U.S. public domain is not necessarily a p.d. film in all other countries.) You can send requests (with a self-addressed stamped envelope) to:

Copyright Information Department
Hollywood Film Archive
8344 Melrose Avenue
Hollywood, CA 90069

PLEASE NOTE: We have found that FILM SUPERLIST is also quite popular among customs inspectors, especially those who have an opportunity to "acquire" a free copy. Registry is not mandatory, but we cannot be responsible for unregistered copies sent to foreign countries.

FILM SUPERLIST

20,000 MOTION PICTURES IN THE U.S. PUBLIC DOMAIN

by JOHNNY MINUS and WILLIAM STORM HALE

Most film copyrights are not renewed after their initial 28-year term. Anyone may, without obtaining permission, make free public use of those films — commercial or otherwise. FILM SUPERLIST contains listings for all films copyrighted in the U.S. from 1894 thru 1939 — over 57,000 films. Entries include

- Credits for producer, director, screenplay (or story), etc.
- Copyright company, date, and registration number.
- Alternate titles by which the film may be known.
- Renewal date and registration number are shown *if the film's copyright was renewed.*

The copyright owner may exercise the right of renewal only during the 28th year; if that right is not exercised (or even forgotten, as often happens) the film irrecoverably passes into the public domain.

FILM SUPERLIST shows that over 20,000 U.S. film copyrights (many of which originated in Great Britain) were not renewed; there are over 30,000 public domain films from that period if newsreels and serials are counted. Many of these films are famous, popular and historically significant, including

A gold mine of motion picture rights that can profit any collector, exhibitor, society or institution with knowledge of their existence.

Size 9" x 11½"   1456 pages

ABRAHAM LINCOLN (U.A., 1930)	HIS GIRL FRIDAY (Col., 1939)
BEACHCOMBER, THE (Par., 1939)	LITTLE PRINCESS, THE (Fox, 1939)
EVERGREEN (Gaumont-Brit., 1934)	LOVE AFFAIR (RKO, 1939)
FRONT PAGE, THE (U.A., 1931)	MY MAN GODFREY (Univ., 1936)
FAREWELL TO ARMS, A (Par., 1933)	PYGMALION (MGM, 1938)
GENERAL, THE (U.A., 1926)	STAR IS BORN, A (W.B., 1938)
GOLD RUSH, THE (U.A., 1925)	SVENGALI (U.A., 1931)
GULLIVER'S TRAVELS (Par., 1939)	WINTERSET (RKO, 1936)

Film Researchers, Archivists and Librarians use the FILM SUPERLIST for many purposes because of its vast information content on pre-1940 films.

A SPECIAL CROSS-REFERENCE INDEX of over 200 pages alphabetically lists all persons and companies with the films for which they are credited as producer, distributor, author or copyright owner.

- The entry for CHARLES CHAPLIN lists **CITY LIGHTS (1931)** along with the other films he produced.
- The entry for WARNER BROS. gives an alphabetical list of hundreds of films they produced and distributed.
- The entry for WILLIAM SHAKESPEARE shows **TAMING OF THE SHREW (1929)** along with the other films for which he is credited as original author.

Send payment with order to: HOLLYWOOD FILM ARCHIVE, 8344 Melrose Avenue, Hollywood, California 90069

1894-1939 FILM SUPERLIST Clothbound $195.00*
1894-1939 without renewals Clothbound $85.00*
1940-1949 FILM SUPERLIST Clothbound $95.00*
1940-1949 without renewals Clothbound $45.00*

HOLLYWOOD FILM ARCHIVE
8344 Melrose Avenue, Dept. CK
Hollywood, Calif. 90069

I wish to purchase the book(s) indicated below. If I am not completely satisfied, I will exercise my privilege to return the book(s) within 30 days after receipt for a full refund of the purchase price. Payment is enclosed for the following:

_____ FILM SUPERLIST 1894-1939 @ $195.00*

_____ Alternative 1894-1939 volumes without renewal entries @ $85.00*

_____ FILM SUPERLIST 1940-1949 @ $95.00*

_____ Alternative 1940-1949 volume without renewal entries @ $45.00*

plus _____ for shipping and other services

Total amount enclosed $_____ U.S. funds.

Name _____

Address _____

City _____

State or Province _____   Postal or ZIP Code _____

*All purchasers must add shipping charges of $2.50 per book (or set); $3.00 outside U.S. Add 6% Sales Tax to all purchases shipped to California addresses.

OTHER SERVICES: (add amounts shown to purchase and shipping charges)

☐ For registry, add $6.00
FOR FASTER DELIVERY the following options are available:

☐ Special Handling, add $2.00; this speeds delivery to all countries, and it's approximately as fast as first class within U.S.

☐ Airmail to North or Central America, add $22.50.

☐ Airmail to South America or Europe (except U.S.S.R.), add $35.00.

☐ Airmail to Africa, Asia (incl. U.S.S.R.) and elsewhere, add $48.00.

320

INDEX TO ACTORS AND ACTRESSES IN THE PHOTOS

As we go to press, the following films, in production at the time the main text of this book was typeset, have undergone title changes:

AMERICAN GIGOLO is a 1980 release.
BIG RED ONE, THE is a 1980 release.
BON VOYAGE, CHARLIE BROWN (AND DON'T COME BACK!) is a 1980 release.
CAPTAIN AVENGER is a 1980 release titled HERO AT LARGE.
CHILLY SCENES OF WINTER is a 1979 release titled HEAD OVER HEELS.
CORKY is a 1980 release titled WINDOWS.
DAY THE WORLD ENDED, THE is a 1980 release titled WHEN TIME RAN OUT.
DEFIANCE is a 1980 release.
DEVIL CAT (1978) and OUT OF THE DARKNESS (1978) are the same film; it is also
     known as NIGHT CREATURE.
DREAMS DIE FIRST (1979): Production is not scheduled.
EVICTORS, THE (1979): Released by American International (now called Filmways).
FOG, THE is a 1980 release.
GORP is a 1980 release, and the title has no periods or asterisk.
GRAYEAGLE (1977) is 104 minutes.
GREAT SANTINI, THE (1979): Released by Warner Bros. for Orion.
HAMSTER OF HAPPINESS is a 1980 release titled SECOND HAND HEARTS.
HEALTH is a 1980 release.
HEART BEAT is a 1980 release.
HIDE IN PLAIN SIGHT is a 1980 release.
HORN is a 1980 release titled TOM HORN.
HUNTER, THE is a 1980 release.
JUST TELL ME WHAT YOU WANT is a 1980 release.
LADY IN RED, THE (1979): Running time is 93 minutes. Cast is Pamela Sue Martin
     and Robert Conrad. Re-release title is GUNS, SIN AND BATHTUB GIN.
NO KNIFE was released with the title FRISCO KID, THE.
PROMISES IN THE DARK (1979) is 115 minutes; released by Warner Bros. for Orion.
RAGING BULL (1980) is black-and-white, not color.
RINGER, THE is a 1980 release titled AMERICAN SUCCESS COMPANY.
RUNNER STUMBLES, THE (1979): released by 20th Century-Fox.
SATURDAY MATINEE (1979): Production is not scheduled.
SENATOR, THE (1979) was released with the title THE SEDUCTION OF JOE TYNAN.
SEVEN-PER-CENT SOLUTION, THE (1976) photo caption: Actor is Nicol Williamson.
SPACEMAN AND KING ARTHUR, THE (1979) is the British title of the American
     film released with the title UNIDENTIFIED FLYING ODDBALL.
STRIKE AND HYDE (1980): Production is not scheduled.
TRUE CONFESSIONS is a 1981 release starring Robert De Niro, Robert Duvall and
     Charles Durning.
TWENTIETH CENTURY FOXES is a 1980 release titled FOXES.
VERY BIG WITHDRAWAL, A (1979) was released with the title A MAN, A WOMAN
     AND A BANK.

As a service to users of the CHECKLIST, we will provide, without charge, a list of title changes and error corrections each year until a new edition of the CHECKLIST is published. If you haven't received the 1980 corrections list, you can get it and the 1981 list by sending a self-addressed stamped envelope to

Checklist Corrections 1980/81
HOLLYWOOD FILM ARCHIVE
8344 Melrose Avenue
Hollywood, CA 90069 (U.S.A.)

If you've already received the 1980 corrections list, substitute "Checklist Corrections 1981" for the first line shown above. In foreign countries, send us a Universal Postal Union coupon with the envelope instead of stamps.